W9-BBW-672

C. Assessment Strategies

1. Types of assessments	Chapters 14, 15
2. Characteristics of assessments	Chapters 14, 15
3. Scoring assessments	Chapters 14, 15
4. Uses of assessments	Chapters 14, 15
5. Understanding of measurement theory and assessment-related issues	Chapters 14, 15
6. Interpreting and communicating results of assessments	Chapters 14, 15

III. Communication Techniques

A. Basic, Effective Verbal and Nonverbal Communication Techniques — Chapters 5, 12

B. Effect of Cultural and Gender Differences on Communications in the Classroom — Chapters 4, 5

C. Types of Communications and Interactions That Can Stimulate Discussion in Different Ways for Particular Purposes

• Probing for learner understanding	Chapters 4, 10, 13
• Helping students articulate their ideas and thinking processes	Chapters 2, 8, 9, 10
• Promoting risk-taking and problem-solving	Chapters 10, 13
• Facilitating factual recall	Chapters 4, 8, 9, 10
• Encouraging convergent and divergent thinking	Chapters 2, 4, 10, 13
• Stimulating curiosity	Chapters 4, 6
• Helping students to question	Chapters 8, 9, 10
• Promoting a caring community	Chapters 11, 12, 13

IV. Profession and Community

A. The Reflective Practitioner

1. Types of resources available for professional development and learning	Chapters 1, 16
2. Ability to read, understand, and apply articles and books about current research, views, ideas, and debates regarding best teaching practices	Chapters 1, 16
3. Ongoing personal reflection on teaching and learning practices as a basis for making professional decisions	Chapters 1, 16; vignettes in each chapter on revealing and challenging underlying assumptions; pause and reflect features in each chapter

B. The Larger Community

1. Role of the school as a resource to the larger community	Chapter 5
2. Factors in the students' environment outside of school (family circumstances, community environments, health and economic conditions) that may influence students' life and learning	Chapters 3, 5
3. Develop and use active partnerships among teachers, parents/guardians, and leaders in the community to support the educational process	Chapter 5
4. Major laws related to students' rights and teacher responsibilities	Chapter 6

13th
EDITION

Psychology Applied to Teaching

JACK SNOWMAN

Southern Illinois University

RICK McCOWN

Duquesne University

ROBERT BIEHLER

WADSWORTH
CENGAGE Learning™

Australia • Brazil • Japan • Korea • Mexico • Singapore • Spain • United Kingdom • United States

WADSWORTH
CENGAGE Learning

Psychology Applied to Teaching,
Thirteenth Edition
Jack Snowman, Rick McCown, Robert Biehler

Executive Editor, Education: Mark Kerr

Senior Development Editor: Lisa Mafrici

Assistant Editor: Caitlin Cox

Editorial Assistant: Genevieve Allen

Media Editor: Ashley Cronin

Marketing Manager: Kara Kindstrom Parsons

Marketing Assistant: Dimitri Hagnéré

Marketing Communications Manager: Tami Strang

Senior Content Project Manager: Tanya Nigh

Design Director: Rob Hugel

Art Director: Maria Epes

Print Buyer: Linda Hsu

Rights Acquisitions Specialist: Roberta Broyer

Production Service: Graphic World Inc.

Text Designer: Marsha Cohen, Parallelogram

Photo Researcher: Scott Rosen, Bill Smith Group

Text Researcher: Karyn Morrison

Copy Editor: Graphic World Inc.

Cover Designer: Irene Morris

Cover Image: David Roth, Getty Images

Compositor: Graphic World Inc.

© 2012, 2009 Wadsworth, Cengage Learning

ALL RIGHTS RESERVED. No part of this work covered by the copyright herein may be reproduced, transmitted, stored, or used in any form or by any means, graphic, electronic, or mechanical, including but not limited to photocopying, recording, scanning, digitizing, taping, Web distribution, information networks, or information storage and retrieval systems, except as permitted under Section 107 or 108 of the 1976 United States Copyright Act, without the prior written permission of the publisher.

For product information and technology assistance, contact us at
Cengage Learning Customer & Sales Support, 1-800-354-9706.
For permission to use material from this text or product, submit all requests online at **www.cengage.com/permissions.**
Further permissions questions can be e-mailed to
permissionrequest@cengage.com.

Library of Congress Control Number: 2010933811

Student Edition:
ISBN-13: 978-1-111-29811-1
ISBN-10: 1-111-29811-4

Loose-leaf Edition:
ISBN-13: 978-1-111-35612-5
ISBN-10: 1-111-35612-2

Wadsworth
20 Davis Drive
Belmont, CA 94002-3098
USA

Cengage Learning is a leading provider of customized learning solutions with office locations around the globe, including Singapore, the United Kingdom, Australia, Mexico, Brazil, and Japan. Locate your local office at: **www.cengage.com/global.**

Cengage Learning products are represented in Canada by Nelson Education, Ltd.

To learn more about Wadsworth, visit **www.cengage.com/wadsworth.**

Purchase any of our products at your local college store or at our preferred online store **www.CengageBrain.com.**

Printed in Canada
1 2 3 4 5 6 7 14 13 12 11 10

Brief Contents

Preface | xxi

1 Applying Psychology to Teaching | 1

PART I   Developmental Characteristics and Theories | 25

2 Theories of Psychosocial and Cognitive Development | 25

3 Age-Level Characteristics | 72

PART II   Student Differences and Diversity | 110

4 Understanding Student Differences | 110

5 Addressing Cultural and Socioeconomic Diversity | 142

6 Accommodating Student Variability | 181

PART III   Learning and Thinking | 224

7 Behavioral Learning Theory: Operant Conditioning | 224

8 Information-Processing Theory | 249

9 Social Cognitive Theory | 278

10 Constructivist Learning Theory, Problem Solving, and Transfer | 326

PART IV   Creating a Positive Environment for Learning and Teaching | 366

11 Motivation and Perceptions of Self | 366

12 Classroom Management | 403

13 Approaches to Instruction | 439

PART V   Assessing Students' Capabilities | 483

14 Assessment of Classroom Learning | 483

15 Understanding Standardized Assessment | 522

16 Becoming a Better Teacher by Becoming a Reflective Teacher | 559

References | 576

Glossary | 609

Credits | 617

Author Index | 618

Subject Index | 626

Contents

Preface | xxi

CHAPTER 1 **Applying Psychology to Teaching** | 1

What Is Educational Psychology? 2

How Will Learning About Educational Psychology Help You Be a Better Teacher? 2

Teaching Is a Complex Enterprise 3
Research That Informs Teachers 3
Coursework and Competence 5

The Nature and Values of Science 6

Limitations of Unsystematic Observation 6
Strengths of Scientific Observation 7

Complicating Factors in the Study of Behavior and Thought Processes 8

The Limited Focus of Research 8
The Complexity of Teaching and Learning 8
Selection and Interpretation of Data 9
New Findings Mean Revised Ideas 10

Good Teaching Is Partly an Art and Partly a Science 10

The Argument for Teaching as an Art 10
The Argument for Teaching as a Science 12

• CASE IN PRINT
The Joy of Being a Teacher-Artist: One Teacher's Tale 13

The Teacher as Artistic Scholar: Combining the Art and Science of Teaching 15

Reflective Teaching: A Process to Help You Grow from Novice to Expert 15

• VIDEO CASE
Teaching as a Profession: What Defines Effective Teaching? 16

Special Features of This Book 18

Key Points 18
Revealing and Challenging Assumptions 18
Suggestions for Teaching 19
Take a Stand! 19
Case in Print 20
TeachSource Video Cases 20
Emphasis on the Role of Technology in Learning and Instruction 20
Pause and Reflect 20

• VIDEO CASE
An Expanded Definition of Literacy: Meaningful Ways to Use Technology 21

Journal Entries 21
Resources for Further Investigation 21

How This Book Will Help Prepare You to Meet Instructional Standards 21

Praxis II and *Psychology Applied to Teaching* 22
INTASC and *Psychology Applied to Teaching* 22

Summary 23

Resources for Further Investigation 23

PART I **Developmental Characteristics and Theories**

CHAPTER 2 **Theories of Psychosocial and Cognitive Development** | 25

• REVEALING ASSUMPTIONS
What Students Know and *How* Students Know 27

Erikson: Psychosocial Development 28
Basic Principles of Erikson's Theory 28

Epigenetic Principle 28
Psychosocial Crisis 28
Stages of Psychosocial Development 29
Trust Versus Mistrust (Birth to One Year) 29
Autonomy Versus Shame and Doubt (Two to Three Years; Preschool) 29

Initiative Versus Guilt (Four to Five Years; Preschool to Kindergarten) 29

Industry Versus Inferiority (Six to Eleven Years; Elementary to Middle School) 29

Identity Versus Role Confusion (Twelve to Eighteen Years; Middle Through High School) 29

Intimacy Versus Isolation (Young Adulthood) 29

Generativity Versus Stagnation (Middle Age) 30

Integrity Versus Despair (Old Age) 30

Helping Students Develop a Sense of Industry 30

- - - - - - - - - - - - - - - - - - - -

- **TAKE A STAND!**
  Promote Industry; Stamp Out Inferiority 31

Helping Students Formulate an Identity 31

Taking a Psychosocial Moratorium 31

Adolescent Identity Statuses 31

Cultural, Ethnic, and Gender Factors in Identity Status 33

Criticisms of Erikson's Theory 34

- -

- **SUGGESTIONS FOR TEACHING**
  Applying Erikson's Theory of Psychosocial Development 35

Piaget: Cognitive Development 36

Basic Principles of Piaget's Theory 36

Organization 37

Schemes 37

Adaptation 37

Relationships Among Organization, Adaptation, and Schemes 37

Equilibration, Disequilibrium, and Learning 37

Constructing Knowledge 38

Stages of Cognitive Development 38

Sensorimotor Stage (Infants and Toddlers) 39

Preoperational Stage (Preschool and Primary Grades) 40

Concrete Operational Stage (Elementary to Early Middle School) 41

Formal Operational Stage (Middle School, High School, and Beyond) 41

The Role of Social Interaction and Instruction in Cognitive Development 43

How Social Interaction Affects Cognitive Development 43

How Instruction Affects Cognitive Development 44

Criticisms of Piaget's Theory 44

Underestimating Children's Capabilities 44

Overestimating Adolescents' Capabilities 45

Vague Explanations for Cognitive Growth 45

Cultural Differences 45

- -

- **SUGGESTIONS FOR TEACHING**
  Applying Piaget's Theory of Cognitive Development 46

Vygotsky: Cognitive Development 48

How One's Culture Affects Cognitive Development 49

The Importance of Psychological Tools 49

How Social Interaction Affects Cognitive Development 50

How Instruction Affects Cognitive Development 50

Instruction and the Zone of Proximal Development 52

- - - - - - - - - - - - - - -

- **VIDEO CASE**
  Vygotsky's Zone of Proximal Development: Increasing Cognition in an Elementary Literacy Lesson 53

Using Technology to Promote Cognitive Development 54

Technology Applied to Piaget 54

Technology Applied to Vygotsky 55

- - - - - - - - - - - - - - -

- **VIDEO CASE**
  Middle School Reading Instruction: Integrating Technology 56

Piaget, Kohlberg, and Gilligan: Moral Development 56

Piaget's Analysis of the Moral Judgment of the Child 56

Age Changes in Interpretation of Rules 56

Moral Realism Versus Moral Relativism 57

Kohlberg's Description of Moral Development 57

Kohlberg's Use of Moral Dilemmas 57

Kohlberg's Six Stages of Moral Reasoning 58

Criticisms and Evaluations of Kohlberg's Theory 59

The Caring Orientation to Moral Development and Education 60

Gilligan's View of Identity and Moral Development 60

Noddings's Care Theory 61

Does Moral Thinking Lead to Moral Behavior? 63

The Hartshorne and May Studies 63

- - - - - - - - - - - - - - - -

- **CASE IN PRINT**
  Teaching Students to Be Good Characters 64

  Research on Character Education Programs 65

- -

- **SUGGESTIONS FOR TEACHING**
  Encouraging Moral Development 67

- -

- **CHALLENGING ASSUMPTIONS**
  What Students Know and *How* Students Know 69

Summary 69

Resources for Further Investigation 71

CHAPTER 3 — Age-Level Characteristics | 72

- REVEALING ASSUMPTIONS
  Looking Through Lenses 73

Preschool and Kindergarten (Three, Four, and Five Years) 74

Physical Characteristics: Preschool and Kindergarten 74
Social Characteristics: Preschool and Kindergarten 75
Emotional Characteristics: Preschool and Kindergarten 76
Cognitive Characteristics: Preschool and Kindergarten 77

Primary Grades (1, 2, and 3; Six, Seven, and Eight Years) 80

Physical Characteristics: Primary Grades 80
Social Characteristics: Primary Grades 81
Emotional Characteristics: Primary Grades 82
Cognitive Characteristics: Primary Grades 82

Elementary School (Grades 4 and 5; Nine and Ten Years) 84

Physical Characteristics: Elementary Grades 84
Social Characteristics: Elementary Grades 85
Emotional Characteristics: Elementary Grades 86
Cognitive Characteristics: Elementary Grades 88

Middle School (Grades 6, 7, and 8; Eleven, Twelve, and Thirteen Years) 88

Physical Characteristics: Middle School 89
Social Characteristics: Middle School 91

- VIDEO CASE
  Social and Emotional Development: The Influence of Peer Groups 92

Emotional Characteristics: Middle School 92

Cognitive Characteristics: Middle School 94

- TAKE A STAND!
  Meeting the Intellectual Needs of Middle School Students 95

- CASE IN PRINT
  Middle School Anxieties 96

High School (Grades 9, 10, 11, and 12; Fourteen, Fifteen, Sixteen, and Seventeen Years) 97

Physical Characteristics: High School 97
Social Characteristics: High School 100
Emotional Characteristics: High School 100

- VIDEO CASE
  Social and Emotional Development: Understanding Adolescents 103

Cognitive Characteristics: High School 103

Selecting Technologies for Different Age Levels 104

Using Technology to Reduce Egocentrism and Develop Interpersonal Reasoning 104
Effect of Technology on Cognitive Development 105

- CHALLENGING ASSUMPTIONS
  Looking Through Lenses 106

Summary 107

Resources for Further Investigation 108

PART II Student Differences and Diversity

CHAPTER 4 — Understanding Student Differences | 110

- REVEALING ASSUMPTIONS
  Groupthink 111

The Nature and Measurement of Intelligence 112

The Origin of Intelligence Testing 112
What Traditional Intelligence Tests Measure 113
Limitations of Intelligence Tests 114
Contemporary Views of Intelligence 114
  David Wechsler's Global Capacity View 114
  Robert Sternberg's Triarchic View: The Theory of Successful Intelligence 115

  Howard Gardner's Multiple Intelligences Theory 117

- VIDEO CASE
  Multiple Intelligences: Elementary School Instruction 119

Using the New Views of Intelligence to Guide Instruction 120

Sternberg's Triarchic Theory of Successful Intelligence 120
Gardner's Multiple Intelligences Theory 120
Using Technology to Develop Intelligence 121

Learning Styles 123

Reflectivity and Impulsivity 123

Field Dependence and Field Independence 124

Mental Self-Government Styles 125

Using Awareness of Learning Styles to Guide Instruction 126

Using Technology to Accommodate Learning Styles 127

Gender Differences and Gender Bias 128

Gender Differences in Cognition and Achievement 128

Gender Bias 130

How Gender Bias Affects Students 131

Course Selection 131

Career Choice 131

Class Participation 132

• TAKE A STAND!
  Eliminate Gender Bias 133

Working Toward Gender Equity in the Classroom 133

• CASE IN PRINT
  Correcting Gender Bias 134

• VIDEO CASE
  Gender Equity in the Classroom: Girls and Science 135

Gender Differences and Technology: Overcoming the Digital Divide 135

• SUGGESTIONS FOR TEACHING
  Addressing Student Differences 136

• CHALLENGING ASSUMPTIONS
  Groupthink 139

Summary 139

Resources for Further Investigation 140

CHAPTER 5 | Addressing Cultural and Socioeconomic Diversity | 142

• REVEALING ASSUMPTIONS
  Placing Value 143

The Rise of Multiculturalism 144

From Melting Pot to Cultural Pluralism 144

• CASE IN PRINT
  Cultural Diversity and *E Pluribus Unum* (Out of Many, One) 145

The Changing Face of the United States 146

• SUGGESTIONS FOR TEACHING
  Taking Account of Your Students' Cultural Differences 147

Ethnicity and Social Class 148

The Effect of Ethnicity on Learning 148

Verbal Communication Patterns 149

Nonverbal Communication 149

Time Orientation 149

Social Values 149

Instructional Formats and Learning Processes 150

• VIDEO CASE
  Integrating Internet Research: High School Social Studies 151

The Effect of Social Class on Learning 151

Graduation Rates and Achievement Levels 152

Health and Living Conditions 154

Family Environment 154

Students' Motivation, Beliefs, and Attitudes 155

Classroom Environment 157

The Effect of Ethnicity and Social Class on Teachers' Expectations 158

Research on the Effects of Teachers' Expectancies 158

Factors That Help Create Expectancies 159

• SUGGESTIONS FOR TEACHING
  Promoting Classroom Achievement for All Students 160

Multicultural Education Programs 162

Assumptions and Goals 163

Basic Approaches 163

Four Approaches 163

Characteristics of Effective Multicultural Teachers 164

• VIDEO CASE
  Culturally Responsive Teaching: A Multicultural Lesson for Elementary Students 165

Instructional Goals and Methods 165

Instructional Goals 165

Instructional Methods 166

A Rationale for Multicultural Education 168

Bridging the Cultural and SES Gap with Technology 169

• SUGGESTIONS FOR TEACHING
  Promoting Multicultural Understanding and Classroom Achievement 171

Bilingual Education 173

Goals and Approaches 174

Transition Programs 174

Maintenance Programs 174

Two-Way Bilingual Programs 174

• VIDEO CASE

Bilingual Education: An Elementary Two-Way
Immersion Program 176

Research Findings 176

• TAKE A STAND!

Bilingual Education: *Plus les choses
changent, plus elles restent les mêmes* 177

Technology and Bilingual Education 177

• CHALLENGING ASSUMPTIONS

Placing Value 178

Summary 179

Resources for Further Investigation 180

CHAPTER 6 | **Accommodating Student Variability** | 181

• REVEALING ASSUMPTIONS

In Service of Learning 182

Historical Developments 183

The Growth of Public Education and Age-Graded
Classrooms 183

Ability-Grouped Classrooms 183

Special Education 183

Ability Grouping 184

Types of Ability Groups 184

Between-Class Ability Grouping 184

Regrouping 185

Joplin Plan 185

Within-Class Ability Grouping 185

Assumptions Underlying Ability Grouping 185

Evaluations of Ability Grouping 186

To Group or Not to Group? 187

• TAKE A STAND!

Ability Grouping and Tracking: A Practice
That Fails to Deliver What It Promises 188

• VIDEO CASE

Inclusion: Grouping Strategies for Inclusive
Classrooms 188

**The Individuals with Disabilities Education Act
(IDEA) 189**

Major Provisions of IDEA 189

A Free and Appropriate Public Education 189

Preplacement Evaluation 189

Individualized Education Program 190

Least Restrictive Environment 190

The Policy of Inclusion 190

The Debate About Inclusion 191

Response to Intervention 192

What IDEA Means to Regular Classroom Teachers 192

• VIDEO CASE

Foundations: Aligning Instruction with Federal
Legislation 193

*What Kinds of Disabling Conditions Are Included
Under IDEA? 193*

• CASE IN PRINT

Who Swims in the Mainstream? 194

*What Are the Regular Classroom Teacher's Responsibilities
Under IDEA? 195*

Section 504: A Broader View of Disabling Conditions 198

**Students with Intellectual Disability (Formerly
Called Mental Retardation) 198**

Definition of Intellectual Disability 198

Characteristics of Children with
Intellectual Disability 199

• SUGGESTIONS FOR TEACHING

Instructing Students with Intellectual
Disability 200

Students with Learning Disabilities 202

Characteristics of Students
with Learning Disabilities 202

Identifying Students with Learning Disabilities 203

Problems with Basic Psychological Processes 204

Attention-Deficit/Hyperactivity Disorder 205

• SUGGESTIONS FOR TEACHING

Instructing Students with Learning
Disabilities and ADHD 206

Students with Emotional Disturbance 208

Estimates of Emotional Disturbance 208

Definitions of Emotional Disturbance 208

Characteristics of Students with
an Emotional Disturbance 209

- SUGGESTIONS FOR TEACHING
  Instructing Students with Emotional Disturbance 210

Students Who Are Gifted and Talented 212

Identification of Gifted and Talented Students 212
Characteristics of Gifted and Talented Students 213
Instructional Options 214
  Accelerated Instruction 214
  Gifted and Talented Classes and Schools 215
  Enrichment and Differentiated Instruction 215

- VIDEO CASE
  Academic Diversity: Differentiated Instruction 216

- SUGGESTIONS FOR TEACHING
  Instructing Gifted and Talented Students 216

Using Technology to Assist Exceptional Students 217

Technology for Students with Hearing Impairments 218
Technology for Students with Visual Impairments 219
Technology for Students with Orthopedic Impairments 219
Technology for Students with Speech or Language Impairments 219
Technology for Students with Learning Disabilities 219
Technology for Gifted and Talented Students 220

- CHALLENGING ASSUMPTIONS
  In Service of Learning 221

Summary 221

Resources for Further Investigation 223

PART III   Learning and Thinking

CHAPTER 7   Behavioral Learning Theory: Operant Conditioning | 224

- REVEALING ASSUMPTIONS
  Reward Is in the Eye of the Beholder 225

Operant Conditioning 225

Basic Nature and Assumptions 226
Basic Principles of Operant Conditioning 226
  Positive Reinforcement 226
  Negative Reinforcement 227
  Punishment 227
  Time-Out 228
  Extinction 228
  Spontaneous Recovery 228
  Generalization 229
  Discrimination 229
  Shaping 230
  Schedules of Reinforcement 230

Educational Applications of Operant Conditioning Principles 231

Computer-Based Instruction 231
  Does Computer-Based Technology Aid Learning? 231

- VIDEO CASE
  Integrating Technology to Improve Student Learning: A High School Science Simulation 233

Behavior Modification 235
  Shaping 235

  Token Economies 236
  Contingency Contracting 237

- CASE IN PRINT
  Going to School Can Be a Rewarding Experience 238

  Extinction, Time-Out, and Response Cost 239

- VIDEO CASE
  Classroom Management: Handling a Student with Behavior Problems 240

  Punishment 240

- TAKE A STAND!
  Positive Reinforcement Versus Punishment as a Classroom Management Tool 241

  Should You Use Behavior Modification? 241

- SUGGESTIONS FOR TEACHING
  Applying Operant Conditioning in the Classroom 242

- CHALLENGING ASSUMPTIONS
  Reward Is in the Eye of the Beholder 246

Summary 247

Resources for Further Investigation 247

CHAPTER 8 Information-Processing Theory | 249

- REVEALING ASSUMPTIONS
  Information and Meaning 250

The Information-Processing View
of Learning 250

A Model of Information Processing 251

The Sensory Register and Its Control Processes 252
The Sensory Register 252
The Nature of Recognition 253
The Impact of Attention 253
Short-Term Memory and Its Control Processes 254
Short-Term Memory 254
Rehearsal 254

- VIDEO CASE
  Cooperative Learning in the Elementary Grades:
  Jigsaw Model 255

  Organization 255
  Meaningfulness 256
  Visual Imagery Encoding 258
Long-Term Memory 259
  How Information Is Organized in Long-Term Memory 260

- VIDEO CASE
  Using Information-Processing Strategies:
  A Middle-School Science Lesson 261

How Well Do We Remember What We Learn in School? 262

- TAKE A STAND!
  Students Are Learners, Not Just Performers 262

- SUGGESTIONS FOR TEACHING
  Helping Your Students Become Efficient Information
  Processors 263

Metacognition 266

The Nature and Importance of Metacognition 266

- CASE IN PRINT
  Thinking About What We Think About 268

Age Trends in Metacognition 270

Technology as an Information-Processing Tool 271

Technology Tools for Writing 271
Technology Tools for Reading 272
Technology Tools for Science and Math 272
Technology Tools for Art and Music 273
Multimedia, Hypermedia, and Virtual Environments 274
  Hypermedia Tools 274
  Virtual Environments 274

- CHALLENGING ASSUMPTIONS
  Information and Meaning 275

Summary 276

Resources for Further Investigation 276

CHAPTER 9 Social Cognitive Theory | 278

- REVEALING ASSUMPTIONS
  Taking Learning Personally 279

The Triadic Reciprocal Causation Model 280

Self-Control, Self-Regulation, and Self-Efficacy 281

The Role of Self-Efficacy in Self-Regulation 282
Factors That Affect Self-Efficacy 283
Types of Behaviors Affected by Self-Efficacy 284
The Components of a Self-Regulatory System 285
Forethought Phase 286
Performance Phase 287
Self-Reflection Phase 288

- VIDEO CASE
  Performance Assessment: Student Presentations in a
  High School English Class 289

Helping Students Become Self-Regulated
Learners 289

What Is Self-Regulated Learning? 289
How Well Prepared Are Students
  to Be Self-Regulated Learners? 290
The Nature of Learning Tactics
  and Strategies 291
Types of Tactics 292
  Rehearsal 292
  Mnemonic Devices 292
  Self- and Peer-Questioning 295
  Note Taking 295
  Concept Mapping 296
  *Conclusions Regarding
    Learning Tactics 297*

- VIDEO CASE
  Metacognition: Helping Students Become Strategic Learners 297

Supporting Students' Strategy Use 297

- TAKE A STAND!
  Teach Students How to Be Self-Regulated Learners 299

Modeling and Self-Regulated Learning 300
  Observation 300

- CASE IN PRINT
  Wanted: Self-Regulated Learners 301

  Emulation 303
  Self-Control 304
  Self-Regulation 304

- VIDEO CASE
  Modeling: Social Cognitive Theory in a High School Chemistry Lesson 305

Research on Social Cognitive Theory 305

Relationships Among Self-Efficacy,
  Epistemological Beliefs, Self-Regulation
  Processes, and Achievement 305
Effects of Modeling on Self-Efficacy,
  Self-Regulation, and Achievement 307

  Improving Students' Mathematical
    Problem-Solving Skills 307
  Improving Students' Writing Skills 308
Effects of Instruction on Self-Regulated Learning Skills 309

- SUGGESTIONS FOR TEACHING
  Applying Social Cognitive Theory in the Classroom 312

Using Technology to Promote Self-Regulated Learning 318
Modeling 318
Providing Cognitive and Metacognitive
  Feedback 319
Providing Scaffolded Instruction 319
The Effect of Self-Regulated Learning
  Skills on Computer-Based Instruction 320
The Effect of Self-Efficacy on Computer-Based
  Instruction 321
Conclusions About Computer Technology
  and Self-Regulated Learning 322

- CHALLENGING ASSUMPTIONS
  Taking Learning Personally 322

Summary 323

Resources for Further Investigation 324

CHAPTER 10   **Constructivist Learning Theory, Problem Solving, and Transfer** | 326

- REVEALING ASSUMPTIONS
  What's the Problem? 327

Meaningful Learning Within a Constructivist Framework 328

Jerome Bruner and Discovery Learning: An Early
  Constructivist Perspective 328

- VIDEO CASE
  Elementary School Language Arts: Inquiry Learning 329

Constructivism Today 329
  Common Claims That Frame Constructivism 329
  Three Variations on a Constructivist Theme 331
  Conditions That Foster Constructivist Learning 333

- CASE IN PRINT
  Combining Technology and Problems to Construct Knowledge 336

Putting Constructivism in Perspective 338

- VIDEO CASE
  Middle School Science Instruction: Inquiry Learning 338

- SUGGESTIONS FOR TEACHING
  Using a Constructivist Approach to Meaningful Learning 339

The Nature of Problem Solving 343

Three Common Types of Problems 343
Helping Students Become Good Problem Solvers 345
  Step 1: Realize That a Problem Exists 345
  Step 2: Understand the Nature of the Problem 345
  Step 3: Compile Relevant Information 346

- VIDEO CASE
  Constructivist Teaching in Action: A High School Classroom Debate 347

  Step 4: Formulate and Carry Out a Solution 347
  Step 5: Evaluate the Solution 349

- SUGGESTIONS FOR TEACHING
  Teaching Problem-Solving Techniques 350

Transfer of Learning 354

The Nature and Significance
   of Transfer of Learning 355
   The Theory of Identical Elements 355
   Positive, Negative, and Zero Transfer 355
   Specific and General Transfer 355
   Near and Far Transfer 356
Contemporary Views of Specific/Near and General/Far
   Transfer 357
   Low-Road Transfer 357
   High-Road Transfer 357

- TAKE A STAND!
  If You Want Transfer, Then Teach for Transfer 358

   Teaching for Low-Road and High-Road Transfer 358

Technology Tools for Knowledge Construction and Problem Solving 359

Computer-Supported Intentional Learning Environments
   (Knowledge Forum) 359
Quest Atlantis: Gaming and Consequential Engagement 360

- CHALLENGING ASSUMPTIONS
  What's the Problem? 363

Summary 363

Resources for Further Investigation 364

PART IV Creating a Positive Environment for Learning and Teaching

CHAPTER 11 Motivation and Perceptions of Self | 366

- REVEALING ASSUMPTIONS
  Teaching...Learning...Motivation 368

The Behavioral View of Motivation 368

The Effect of Reinforcement 368
Limitations of the Behavioral View 369

The Social Cognitive View of Motivation 370

Power of Persuasive Models 370
The Importance of Self-Efficacy 371
   Choice of Learning Goal 371
   Outcome Expectations 372
   Attributions 372

Other Cognitive Views of Motivation 372

Cognitive Development and the Need
   for Conceptual Organization 373
The Need for Achievement 373
Explanations of Success and Failure:
   Attribution Theory 374
Beliefs About the Nature of Cognitive Ability 374
   Changes in Beliefs About Ability 375
   Types of Beliefs About Ability 375
The Effect of Interest on Intrinsic Motivation 377
   Factors That Influence Personal Interest 377
   Factors That Influence Situational Interest 378

- VIDEO CASE
  Motivating Adolescent Learners: Curriculum Based
  on Real Life 379

   Flow and Engagement 379
Limitations of Cognitive Views 380
   Cognitive Development 380
   Need for Achievement 380
   *Attribution Theory and Beliefs
      About Ability* 380

- CASE IN PRINT
  Taking an Interest in Learning 381

- SUGGESTIONS FOR TEACHING
  Motivating Students to Learn 382

The Humanistic View of Motivation 390

Maslow's Theory of Growth Motivation 390
Implications of Maslow's Theory 391
Limitations of Maslow's Theory 392

The Role of Self-Perceptions in Motivation 393

The Role of Academic Self-Concept
   in Motivation and Learning 394
Motivation and Identity 395

- TAKE A STAND!
  Increase Motivation by Maintaining
  High Self-Worth 395

• SUGGESTIONS FOR TEACHING
Satisfying Deficiency Needs
and Strengthening Self-Perceptions 396

Motivating Students with Technology 398

Extrinsic Versus Intrinsic Motivation 398
Using Technology to Increase
Motivation to Learn 398

• VIDEO CASE
Integrating Internet Research: High School Social
Studies 399

• CHALLENGING ASSUMPTIONS
Teaching…Learning…Motivation 400

Summary 400

Resources for Further Investigation 402

CHAPTER 12 Classroom Management | 403

• REVEALING ASSUMPTIONS
Managing Classrooms and Leading Learning 404

Authoritarian, Permissive, and Authoritative
Approaches to Classroom Management 405

Preventing Problems: Techniques of Classroom
Management 406

Kounin's Observations on Group Management 406
Contemporary Studies of Classroom Management 409

• VIDEO CASE
Elementary Classroom Management: Basic Strategies
409

Managing the Middle, Junior High, and High School
Classroom 410

• VIDEO CASE
Secondary Classroom Management: Basic Strategies
411

Technology Tools for Classroom Management 411
New Classroom Roles for Teachers 412

• SUGGESTIONS FOR TEACHING
Techniques of Classroom Management 412

Techniques for Dealing with Behavior
Problems 415

Influence Techniques 415
Planned Ignoring 416
Signals 416
Proximity and Touch Control 416
Interest Boosting 416
Humor 416
Helping over Hurdles 417
Program Restructuring 417
Antiseptic Bouncing 418
Physical Restraint 418
Direct Appeals 418

Criticism and Encouragement 418
Defining Limits 419
Postsituational Follow-Up 419
Marginal Use of Interpretation 419
I-Messages 419
Problem Ownership 420

• SUGGESTIONS FOR TEACHING
Handling Problem Behavior 420

• VIDEO CASE
Classroom Management: Best Practices 425

Violence in American Schools 425

How Safe Are Our Schools? 425
The Problem of Bullying 426
What Is Bullying? 426
Characteristics of Bullies 427
How Bullying Affects Its Victims 427
How Schools Can Address Bullying 427
Analyzing Reasons for Violence 427
Biological Factors 427
Gender-Related Cultural Influences 428
Academic Skills and Performance 428
Interpersonal Reasoning and Problem-Solving Skills 428
Psychosocial Factors 429
School Environment 429
Reducing School Violence, Bullying,
and Misbehavior 429
Classroom Interventions 429
Schoolwide Programs to Reduce Violence
and Improve Discipline 430

• CASE IN PRINT
Catch 'Em Being Good 431

• TAKE A STAND!
Show Zero Tolerance for Zero Tolerance Policies 433

Using Technology to Keep Students in School 435

- CHALLENGING ASSUMPTIONS
  Managing Classrooms and Leading Learning 436

Summary 437

Resources for Further Investigation 438

CHAPTER 13 Approaches to Instruction | 439

- REVEALING ASSUMPTIONS
  Who Plans for Whom? 440

Devising and Using Objectives 441

Contrasting Objectives with Educational Goals 441
Taxonomies of Objectives 442
  Taxonomy for the Cognitive Domain 442
  Taxonomy for the Affective Domain 443
  Taxonomy for the Psychomotor Domain 444
  Why Use Taxonomies? 444
Ways to State and Use Objectives 444
  Mager's Recommendations for Use of Specific Objectives 444
  Gronlund's Recommendations for Use of General Objectives 446
Aligning Assessment with Objectives and Instruction 447
Evaluations of the Effectiveness of Objectives 447

The Behavioral Approach to Teaching: Direct Instruction 448

The Nature of Direct Instruction 448
The Components of Direct Instruction 449
  Orientation 449
  Presentation 449
  Structured, Guided, and Independent Practice 450
Getting the Most Out of Practice 450
Effectiveness of Direct Instruction 451
Using Technology to Support Behavioral Approaches to Instruction 451

The Cognitive Approach to Teaching: Facilitating Meaningful and Self-Regulated Learning 451

The Nature and Elements of an Information-Processing/Social Cognitive Approach 451
  Communicate Clear Goals and Objectives 452
  Use Attention-Getting Devices 453
  Emphasize Organization and Meaningfulness 453
  Present Information in Learnable Amounts and Over Realistic Time Periods 453

- CASE IN PRINT
  Get Their Attention! Solving the First Challenge of Teaching 454

  Facilitate Encoding of Information into Long-Term Memory 456
The Nature and Elements of a Constructivist Approach 457
  Provide Scaffolded Instruction Within the Zone of Proximal Development 457
  Provide Opportunities for Learning by Discovery 458
  Foster Multiple Viewpoints 458

  Emphasize Relevant Problems and Tasks 458
  Encourage Students to Become More Autonomous Learners 459
The Challenges to Being a Constructivist Teacher 460
Using Technology to Support Cognitive Approaches to Instruction 461
  Helping Students Process Information 461
  Discovery and Exploratory Environments 461
  Guided Learning 462
  Problem- and Project-Based Learning 462
  Situated Learning 463

The Humanistic Approach to Teaching: Student-Centered Instruction 464

Pioneers of the Humanistic Approach 464
  Maslow: Let Children Grow 464
  Rogers: Learner-Centered Education 465
  Combs: The Teacher as Facilitator 465
Teaching from a Humanistic Orientation 465
The Humanistic Model 466
Research on Aspects of Humanistic Education 468

- TAKE A STAND!
  The Perennial Relevance of Humanistic Theory 470

The Social Approach to Teaching: Teaching Students How to Learn from Each Other 471

Types of Classroom Reward Structures 471
  Competitive Structures 471
  Individualistic Structures 471
  Cooperative Structures 472
Elements of Cooperative Learning 472
  Group Heterogeneity 472
  Group Goals/Positive Interdependence 472
  Promotive Interaction 472
  Individual Accountability 473
  Interpersonal Skills 473
  Equal Opportunities for Success 473
  Team Competition 473
Does Cooperative Learning Work? 474
  Effect on Motivation 474
  Effect on Achievement 474
  Effect on Social Interaction 474
Why Does Cooperative Learning Work? 475
  Motivational Effect 475
  Cognitive-Developmental Effect 475
  Cognitive Elaboration Effect 475

- VIDEO CASE
  Cooperative Learning: High School History Lesson 476

Teachers' Use of Cooperative Learning 476
Using Technology to Support Social Approaches to
Instruction 477
Social Constructivist Learning 477
Cooperative and Collaborative Learning 479

• VIDEO CASE
Using Blogs to Enhance Student Learning:
An Interdisciplinary High School Unit 479

• CHALLENGING ASSUMPTIONS
Who Plans for Whom? 480

Summary 480

Resources for Further Investigation 481

PART V Assessing Students' Capabilities

CHAPTER 14 Assessment of Classroom Learning | 483

• REVEALING ASSUMPTIONS
Start at the Finish Line 484

The Role of Assessment in Teaching 485

What Is Assessment? 485
Measurement 486
Evaluation 486
Why Should We Assess Students' Learning? 486
Summative Assessment (Assessment of Learning) 487
Formative Assessment (Assessment for Learning) 487

Ways to Measure Student Learning 489

Written Tests 490
Selected-Response Tests 490
Short-Answer Tests 491
Essay Tests 491
Constructing a Useful Test 491
Performance Assessments 492
What Are Performance Assessments? 492
Types of Performance Assessments 493

• VIDEO CASE
Portfolio Assessment: Elementary Classroom 494
Characteristics of Performance Assessments 494

• VIDEO CASE
Performance Assessment: Student Presentations in a
High School English Class 497

• TAKE A STAND!
Practice Assessment for Learning 498
Some Concerns About Performance Assessment 498

• CASE IN PRINT
How Am I Doing? 499

Ways to Evaluate Student Learning 501

Norm-Referenced Grading 501
The Nature of Norm-Referenced Grading 501
Strengths and Weaknesses of Norm-Referenced Grading 502
Criterion-Referenced Grading 503
The Nature of Criterion-Referenced Grading 503
Strengths and Weaknesses of Criterion-Referenced Grading 503

• VIDEO CASE
Assessment in the Middle Grades: Measurement
of Student Learning 504
A Mastery Approach 505

Improving Your Grading Methods: Assessment
Practices to Avoid 506

Technology for Classroom Assessment 510

Electronic Gradebooks and Grading Programs 510
Technology-Based Performance Assessment 511
Digital Portfolios 511
What Is a Digital Portfolio? 511
The Components and Contents of Digital Portfolios 511
Rubrics for Digital Portfolios and Presentations 512
Performance and Portfolio Assessment Problems 512

• SUGGESTIONS FOR TEACHING
Effective Assessment Techniques 513

• CHALLENGING ASSUMPTIONS
Start at the Finish Line 519

Summary 519

Resources for Further Investigation 520

CHAPTER 15 | Understanding Standardized Assessment | 522

• REVEALING ASSUMPTIONS
The Right Test? 523

Standardized Tests 523

Nature of Standardized Tests 523
Uses of Standardized Tests 524
Criteria for Evaluating Standardized Tests 524

Reliability 524
Validity 526

• VIDEO CASE
Assessment in the Elementary Grades: Formal
and Informal Literacy Assessment 527

Normed Excellence 527
Examinee Appropriateness 527

Types of Standardized Tests 528
Achievement Tests 528
Aptitude Tests 529
Norm-Referenced Tests 529
Criterion-Referenced Tests 529

Interpreting Standardized Test Scores 530
Grade Equivalent Scores 530
Percentile Ranks 530
Standard Scores 531
Stanine Scores 532
Local and National Norms 533

Misconceptions About the Nature and Use of Standardized
Tests 533

**Using Standardized Tests for Accountability
Purposes: High-Stakes Testing 535**

The Push for Accountability in Education 535

• VIDEO CASE
Teacher Accountability: A Student Teacher's
Perspective 535

No Child Left Behind (NCLB) 536
Requirements of NCLB 536
Problems with Implementing NCLB 537

Modifications of NCLB 538
Arguments in Support of High-Stakes Testing Programs 538
Goal Clarity 539
Improved Quality Control 539
Beneficial Effects for Teaching 539
Beneficial Effects for Students 539

Arguments Critical of High-Stakes Testing Programs 539

• VIDEO CASE
Foundations: Aligning Instruction with Federal
Legislation 539

Structural Limitations 539
Misinterpretation and Misuse of Test Results 540
A One-Size-Fits-All Approach to Motivation 541
A One-Size-Fits-All Approach to Standards 541
Undesirable Side Effects 541

Research on the Effects of High-Stakes Testing 542
Effect on Achievement 542

• CASE IN PRINT
Pep Rallies for High-Stakes Tests: Does
Hype Help? 543

Effect on Motivation 545
Effect on Teachers and Teaching 546
Effect on the Curriculum 547
Effect on the Dropout Rate 547
Effect on State Standards and Test Quality 548
Use of Supplemental Education Services 548

Recommendations for Improving High-Stakes Testing 548

• TAKE A STAND!
Healing the Patient: Using the Medical
Model to Guide Educational Accountability 550

Standardized Testing and Technology 550

Using Technology to Prepare Students for Assessments 550
Using Technology to Assess Mastery of Standards 551
Using Technology to Promote Mastery of Standards 552
Computer Adaptive Testing 552

• SUGGESTIONS FOR TEACHING
Using Standardized Tests 553

• CHALLENGING ASSUMPTIONS
The Right Test? 556

Summary 556

Resources for Further Investigation 558

CHAPTER 16 | Becoming a Better Teacher by Becoming a Reflective Teacher | 559

Improving Your Teaching and Reflection Skills to Improve Your Teaching 560

Student Evaluations and Suggestions 561
Peer and Self-Assessment Techniques 562

Classroom Observation Schedules 562

- VIDEO CASE
  Teaching as a Profession: Collaboration with Colleagues 562

  Lesson Study 562
  Self-Recorded Lessons 564
  Guided Reflection Protocol 565
  Developing a Reflective Journal 566
  Using a Portfolio with Your Journal 567

- VIDEO CASE
  Teaching as a Profession: What Defines Effective Teaching? 569

What Makes Reflective Techniques Effective? 569

Using Technology for Reflective Inquiry 570

Digital Portals for Professional Development 570

- CASE IN PRINT
  Highly Qualified Teachers Are Those Who Learn from Teaching 571

- REVEALING AND CHALLENGING ASSUMPTIONS
  Connie's Reflection 573

Summary 575

Resources for Further Investigation 575

References 576

Glossary 609

Credits 617

Author Index 618

Subject Index 626

Preface

Psychology Applied to Teaching has changed dramatically since the first edition was published almost four decades ago. But one thing that has not changed since the first edition, and never will, is this book's main goal, which is reflected in its title. **We remain committed to a practical, reader-oriented approach to educational psychology.**

Consider those who read Psychology Applied to Teaching 40, 20, 10, and even 5 years ago: those groups of readers are very different from each other and from those who will read this 13th edition. The students taught by those who read earlier editions are also very different from the students whom readers of the 13th edition will teach. The contexts in which students live, the ways in which they communicate, the schools in which they learn, and the teachers who guide that learning continue to change as well. In light of such change, it is not surprising that the field of educational psychology continues to offer new findings, new explanations, new methods, and new insights into the process of teaching and learning.

In the new edition of Psychology Applied to Teaching, we have documented the changes in the knowledge base of educational psychology and changes in the contexts of teaching by making decisions. We have made decisions about what to include, what to emphasize, and how to frame emerging ideas. Our goal of providing a practical, reader-oriented approach to educational psychology has been pursued in this edition by framing our decisions within the imperative of educational change. We have tried always to keep in mind that becoming an effective teacher means becoming an effective learner, and that effective learning comes from engaged inquiry. Therefore, in this edition, we have tried to frame our treatment of educational psychology so that the aspiring and developing professionals who read it can see themselves as engaged learners: professionals who inquire continuously to find, and then test, better ways of helping their students succeed.

MAJOR FEATURES OF THIS EDITION

Because of its central role in American society, education is a dynamic enterprise. Tens of thousands of people—including classroom teachers, school administrators, community organizations, accreditation agencies, foundations, state and federal education officials, politicians, educational and psychological researchers, and students themselves—are constantly searching for and trying out new ideas to increase student learning and achievement. Large-scale partnerships are being formed in an effort to advocate for one idea or another. Large-scale funding is being made available to encourage new ideas. Efforts to help students succeed are laudable and there are many of them. But ideas to help students succeed must be tested, and this is where educational and psychological researchers come into play.

Since the previous edition of this text, many new developments have occurred in social, emotional, and cognitive development; learning processes; motivation; classroom assessment and management; standardized testing; bilingual education; inclusion of students with disabilities; and the use of technology to support student learning and achievement. The 13th edition of Psychology Applied to Teaching is extensively revised and updated, incorporating new developments in all its domains.

Noteworthy themes of this edition include:

- **Emphasis on inquiry through assessment.** Research on new designs for teaching and learning–conducted in schools with practicing teachers and administrators–has clarified how assessment can be used in classrooms to inform both student and teacher learning. The role of teacher inquiry and how it is supported through formative assessment practices is addressed in several chapters. Formative assessment's role in reflective teaching is discussed in Chapters 1 and 16. A new definition of formative assessment tied to both student and teacher learning centers a new section in Chapter 14.

- **Advances in social cognitive theory.** Because of the many recent developments in social cognitive research, particularly with respect to self-regulated learning, Chapter 9 now includes extensive coverage of learning strategies and tactics and how students can be taught to create and use them. Research on a program of self-regulation designed to strengthen writing skills shows how the principles of self-regulated learning can be applied in the classroom.

- **Emphasis on critical issues in educational psychology.** All the editions of *Psychology Applied to Teaching* have framed the crucial issues in contemporary education in ways that encourage students to consider the research and make informed judgments. In each chapter's critically acclaimed Take a Stand! feature, we model this behavior for students by stating where we stand on a critical issue and specifying the reasons for that stance.

- **Emphasis on educational technology.** Each chapter contains at least one section, and sometimes several, on how technology can be used to address the main themes and concepts of that chapter. These sections include emerging findings on the impact of Web 2.0 technologies. For example, the reader will find discussions of how such technologies can be used to foster cognitive development, address individual differences, promote greater multicultural understanding, make learning easier for students with disabilities, promote learning and problem solving for all students, increase motivation for learning, help teachers manage their classrooms, and aid in assessment of students. Design research, which is becoming more and more prevalent in educational research, is driving much of the work on technology for learning. Such research appears across chapters, including one large-scale project on a *multi-user virtual environment* (MUVE) called Quest Atlantis.

- **Emphasis on classroom applications.** *Psychology Applied to Teaching* was the first educational psychology textbook to provide numerous specific examples and guidelines for applying psychological concepts and research findings to classroom teaching. We want to ensure that new teachers are prepared for the realities of the classroom. That orientation and emphasis on bridging the gap from preparation to practice to foster teachers' lifelong career success not only continues but is also augmented by Chapter 13, "Approaches to Instruction," which links the writing of instructional objectives with five approaches to instruction that flow from different conceptions of learning.

- **Emphasis on diverse learners.** To help prospective and new teachers understand and cope with the wide range of student diversity they will almost certainly face, we provide extensive treatment of this issue in two chapters: Chapter 4, "Understanding Student Differences," and Chapter 5, "Addressing Cultural and Socioeconomic Diversity." In addition, in Chapter 6, "Accommodating Student Variability," we show how principles of *universal design for learning* (UDL) are being employed via technology. Key ideas on teaching the diversity students (e.g., the emerging work on *critical constructivism* in Chapter 10) appear in other chapters as well.

- **Emphasis on real-life contexts.** To help students negotiate the transition from aspiring to practicing teacher, the Case in Print feature offers news articles about actual classrooms, illustrating the relationship between chapter content and real-life classroom practices. More than half of these articles are new to this edition. Also included in every chapter are references to **TeachSource Video Cases** that students can view on the student website. Each case shows an actual classroom scene in which the teacher describes his or her actions and explains why they were taken. After each Video Case, readers are prompted by questions that help them relate the video to the content of the chapter.

- **Reflective teaching.** Thinking about what one does as a teacher and why has been shown to be an important characteristic of effective teachers. *Psychology Applied to Teaching* tries to foster in students an appreciation of this skill in several ways. First, the concept of reflective teaching, its importance, and the role that a personal journal can play in helping one become a more reflective teacher are introduced in Chapter 1. This theme is picked up again in Chapter 16, in which students learn how to construct a personal journal and how useful this activity is to practicing teachers. Second, Chapters 2 through 15 begin and end with vignettes called "Revealing and Challenging Assumptions" about two fictional teacher education students and one first-year teacher who, reflecting under the guidance of a master teacher, become aware of and challenge common but untenable assumptions they hold about teaching and classroom learning. In Chapter 16, the master teacher draws conclusions and shows how important reflection is in a teaching career. Third, at several locations in Chapters 2 through 15, students encounter a "Pause and Reflect" feature in which they are asked to respond to a question about classroom learning and instruction that is based on that chapter's content. Fourth, the critical role of assessment data in guiding action-oriented reflection is a recurring theme. Fifth, the value of collaborative reflection and feedback from colleagues (e.g., *lesson study* in Chapter 16) is described.

MAJOR CHANGES TO EACH CHAPTER

The following lists highlight some, though not all, of the major changes made to each chapter.

Chapter 1: Applying Psychology to Teaching

- Increased emphasis on the complexity of teaching and the consequent need for teachers to know how to apply various psychological concepts to achieve specific instructional objectives.
- A new discussion of the role of research findings in teaching; specifically, that useful scientific knowledge is specific rather than general and temporary rather than permanent.
- Current research comparing the beliefs of beginning teachers from traditional teacher education programs with those who earned their certification through alternative programs regarding the quality of the preparation and how effective teachers from each group are in the classroom.
- The inclusion of National Board of Professional Teaching Standards to help establish a trajectory for professional learning well into one's teaching career.
- Current research that supports the argument that teaching is as much an art as a science, and the introduction of the concept of the teacher as artistic scholar to reflect the necessity of combining both roles.
- A new Case in Print that illustrates the concept of teacher as artist.
- The role of formative assessment in being a reflective teacher.

Chapter 2: Theories of Psychosocial and Cognitive Development

- New material on identity formation and how life events can affect cycles in one's identity status.

- Current research that updates the 40-year history of research on identity statuses across cultures and how identity status should be understood with regard to other aspects of identity, including ethnic identity.
- Current research on technology use in elementary and secondary schools, the emergent use of Web 2.0 technologies as they relate to cognitive development, and how the classroom is no longer the sole learning environment for students.
- New ideas on how the connections between digital learning environments (such as microworlds) and the role of disequilibrium in schema development and learning.
- Current research on telementoring in the context of Vygotsky's concept scaffolding and a preview of multi-user virtual environments (MUVEs) as constructivist learning environments.
- A new section that updates and emphasizes the caring orientation to moral development and education, including Nel Noddings's care theory.
- Recent research deriving from the classic Hartshorne and May studies, including lying to parents, cheating in the classroom, and how family and classroom conditions are related to such behavior.

Chapter 3: Age-Level Characteristics

- New findings on the contributions that play activities make to the development of preschool through elementary grade children.
- Current research that supports the beneficial effects of recess and similar breaks on the cognitive performance of primary grade children.
- Updates on the effect of early versus late maturation of middle school students.
- New findings on the emotional lives of adolescents.
- Current data on obesity, sexual behavior, after-school employment, substance abuse, depression, and suicide among high school students.
- How social networking websites, collectively referred to as Web 2.0, contribute to the decline of egocentrism and the growth of interpersonal reasoning.

Chapter 4: Understanding Student Differences

- An updated account of the evolution of contemporary views of intelligence, including the evolution of Sternberg's views from his triarchic view of intelligence to the theory of successful intelligence and the WICS model and implications for assessment of cognitive abilities.
- Update on the divide between critics and proponents of MI theory and its continued influence.
- The use of technology to develop practical, creative, and analytical capacities not available in the classroom.
- Current scholarly views on the danger of conflating cultural identity with learning styles.
- Technology as communication and information tools as a "cybergogy" that can engage students who use different approaches to learning.
- Update on the research and implications of the "gender similarities hypothesis."
- New findings indicating that digital learning environments have not lived up to their promise of reducing gender bias and that gender bias must be understood within the context of other social factors.

Chapter 5: Addressing Cultural and Socioeconomic Diversity

- Updated figures on immigration to the United States.
- Instructional techniques preferred by American Indian students.
- Current data on high school graduation rates among students of color.

- New research on the status of the achievement gap between low-SES minority students and middle-SES White students, its likely causes (health and living conditions, family environment, students' motivation, beliefs and attitudes, and classroom environment), and possible solutions.
- New findings on the effect of teacher expectancy on student performance.
- New findings on the beneficial effects of peer tutoring.
- New findings on the effect of various bilingual education programs on the achievement of English Language Learners.

Chapter 6: Accommodating Student Variability

- A new section on "Response to Intervention" and its implications for assessment.
- New figures from the most recent report from the U.S. Department of Education on Students Receiving Special Education Services.
- A new section to emphasize Section 504 in light of The Americans with Disabilities Act Amendments Act of 2008 and what it means for classroom teachers.
- A new account of how "intellectual disability" has replaced the term "mental retardation" and how there is a lag in the usage in the educational community (including the U.S. Department of Education).
- A new emphasis within the discussion of gifted and talented children and youth to emphasize the increased recognition of students who are "twice exceptional."
- Within the section on technology that can assist students who are exceptional, current research on how the principles of "Universal Design for Learning" are being employed with Web 2.0 technologies.

Chapter 7: Behavioral Learning Theory: Operant Conditioning

- New research on the effects of computer-based instruction on achievement.
- New research on the effects of integrated learning systems on achievement.
- Updated figures on the number of states that ban or permit corporal punishment in schools.

Chapter 8: Information-Processing Theory

- New research pointing to the critical role of cognitive load in the design and effectiveness of multimedia learning environments.
- A new section on how virtual environments can provide elaborative, contextualized information to support learning, individually and, in the case of multiuser virtual environments (MUVEs), collaboratively.

Chapter 9: Social Cognitive Theory

- New material on the relationship between epistemological beliefs and self-regulated behavior.
- New material on the relationship between self-regulated learning and how well teachers align course goals, classroom instruction, test content, and test demands.
- New research on the advisability of supplying students with ready-made concept maps versus requiring them to construct their own.
- New section on supporting students' strategy use.
- New research on the relationships among self-efficacy, epistemological beliefs, self-regulation, and achievement.
- Current research on the effectiveness of the self-regulated strategy development (SRSD) program as a way to strengthen students' writing skills.
- Discussion of how to help students develop a strong sense of self-efficacy for self-regulated learning by providing them with timely and effective feedback.

- Revised and updated discussion of the effect of self-regulated learning skills on computer-based instruction.

Chapter 10: Constructivist Learning Theory, Problem Solving, and Transfer

- A new account of the general principles that provide common claims that unite constructivist views of learning and previews variations on the constructivist theme.
- New research on how cultural historical activity theory and, in particular, "activity systems analysis" is being used to investigate efforts to design new kinds of learning environments in and across classrooms and schools.
- A new section on critical constructivism that connects constructivist views of learning to issues of fairness and equity.
- A new Case in Print that describes how technology is gaining traction in schools by using digital learning environments that facilitate problem-based learning.
- New research that has emerged from, among other sources, the MacArthur Foundation's report on learning with new media.
- A new section on learning from digital games, using the design research that underlies "Quest Atlantis"—a virtual world for students and their teachers—as an exemplar.

Chapter 11: Motivation and Perceptions of Self

- New research on how the motivational state of "flow" influences engagement with Web 2.0 technologies.
- A new section on the interaction between motivation and identity.
- New materials on how self-perceptions of skills and competency, on one hand, and values and goals on the other can account for engagement and intrinsic motivation.
- New research that suggests that technology can help first-graders in danger of failing learn to read to develop their literacy capabilities;
- That eighth-graders who are candidates for dropping out of school can be engaged effectively through opportunities to use multimedia to demonstrate their learning;
- That high-school students in Israel who create computer-engineered designs (and, in some cases, create their own computer programs) are able to translate their digital work into working machines.
- New research that shows how e-mail or other messaging systems can connect middle school students from the United States and Iraq and, further, describes how the communication yielded social action.

Chapter 12: Classroom Management

- New section on contemporary studies of classroom management.
- New material on how technology can be used to support a teacher's classroom management efforts.
- Updated suggestions for teaching based on current research.
- Updated statistics on the extent of violence in schools.
- New sections on the nature and extent of bullying, characteristics of bullies, how bullying affects its victims, and what schools can do to reduce and prevent bullying.
- New material on the relationship between violence and interpersonal reasoning skills.

- New material on classroom interventions (Good Behavior Game, Best Foot Forward, Judicious Discipline, Positive Peer Reporting) that reduce violence and other types of misbehavior.
- New Case in Print on how one school uses clear rules and positive incentives to reduce disruptions and misbehavior.

Chapter 13: Approaches to Instruction

- Discussion of a second alternative (Marzano & Kendall) to Bloom's Taxonomy.
- New Case in Print on how a high school science teacher captures and maintains the attention of his students.
- New suggestions for providing scaffolded instruction within a student's zone of proximal development.
- Additional material on the rationale underlying the humanistic model of instruction, its prevalence in classrooms, and the characteristics of teachers who reflect this model.
- New research on the effect of a humanistic classroom environment on student achievement.
- New research on the effect of cooperative learning on student achievement, motivation, and social interaction.
- New material on how social networking websites can support the goal of a social constructivist approach to learning.
- New material on how the use of blogs by students can support the goals of cooperative and collaborative learning.

Chapter 14: Assessment of Classroom Learning

- A new account of assessment and evaluation that reflects the increased emphasis on formative assessment.
- Summative assessment is framed as "assessment *of* learning"; formative assessment is framed as "assessment *for* learning."
- New research conducted in schools and with teachers and administrators documenting the design and development of formative assessment principles is reported and summarized in a new table that illustrates the distinction between "assessment *of* learning" and "assessment *for* learning."
- A new account of the connection between formative assessment and response to intervention (RTI).
- A new section on "Assessment *as* Learning": how assessment provides data that helps teachers learn how to better facilitate student success.
- Current research on how technology broadens opportunities for students to demonstrate learning.
- New online resources for assessment and grading tools.

Chapter 15: Understanding Standardized Assessment

- New discussion of the meaning of accountability in education.
- Updated discussion of the problems involved in implementing No Child Left Behind and modifications to the law made by the Department of Education in recent years.
- Inclusion of additional arguments against high-stakes testing programs.
- New Case in Print that raises the issues of the appropriateness and effectiveness of pep rallies, rewards, and other motivational devices as a way to raise scores on high-stakes tests.

- New research on how well high-stakes testing programs achieve their goal of raising students' test scores and reducing the gap between White students and students of color.
- New research on the effects of high-stakes testing programs on teachers' motivation, how teachers teach, the tendency of teachers to focus their instruction on so-called "bubble kids," the curriculum, the dropout rate, state standards, and test quality.
- New material on using technology to assess mastery of state standards and promote mastery of standards.

Chapter 16: Becoming a Better Teacher by Becoming a Reflective Teacher

- A new opening that builds on a compelling account in *The Atlantic Monthly* of two students from the same neighborhood, but with different teachers, and the impact the teachers have on the students' futures.
- New research and recent arguments for how critical teacher learning is for student success; research that shows that teachers matter.
- A new section on the National Board of Professional Teaching Standards and how they can guide one's professional learning and growth throughout a career in education.
- A new section on "lesson study" as an approach to professional development, including the lesson study cycle and supporting research.
- New research that connects reflective teaching and assessment *as* learning.
- New research that supports a model of reflective teaching as generative change, research that won the 2010 Palmer O. Johnson Award from the American Educational Research Association.
- New information on digital portals that support communities of teacher-learners.
- A new Case in Print that portrays the learning of those who have become National Board Certified Teachers and how the National Board of Professional Teaching Standards are changing teachers and teaching.

Special Features of the Text

The pedagogic features introduced in earlier editions have been improved and augmented to make this 13th edition even more useful and effective.

Suggestions for Teaching A hallmark feature of this text, the Suggestions for Teaching sections provide concrete teaching examples that highlight the application of psychological research in the classroom. This real-world connection helps preservice teachers understand the value of their Educational Psychology course to their development as an educator. Numerous examples of applications at different grade levels are supplied; readers are urged to select applications that will fit their own particular personality, style, and teaching situation and to record their ideas in a Reflective Journal. The Suggestions for Teaching are intended to be read while the book is in use, and also referred to by future teachers and in-service teachers after they have completed coursework. For ease in reference, these suggestions are printed on a colored background and tabbed.

TeachSource Video Case Boxed Features As described later in the preface, this edition includes the integration of award-winning Video Cases to illustrate key topics in the text. Two or more Video Cases are offered for each chapter on the textbook website, and they are correlated to the text with a boxed feature and questions for reflection.

Revealing and Challenging Assumptions In Chapters 8 and 10 we make the point that people use their prior knowledge and experience to help them make sense of a complex and information-filled world. Teaching is a complex world, and those who aspire to teach naturally form assumptions about it. Making and acting on assumptions can be an effective means of dealing with complex matters; it can also lead to problems, especially in those cases in which assumptions are formed on the basis of limited knowledge and experience. The Revealing and Challenging Assumptions features afford aspiring teachers opportunities to confront and reflect on problematic assumptions about teaching and learning. In Chapters 2 through 15, a chapter-opening vignette illustrates, within the context of the chapter's themes, commonly held but unsound assumptions about teaching and learning. Each opening vignette is followed by an opportunity to pause and reflect on how and why the assumption illustrated in the vignette and explicitly cited in the Pause and Reflect feature could be an obstacle to effective teaching and learning. At the end of the chapter, the vignette resumes in order to challenge the problematic assumption in light of the theories, research, and suggestions for teaching in the chapter. The same four characters are included in the vignettes throughout the book.

Take a Stand! In this era of accountability, teachers are frequently criticized and called on to defend their profession and their practices. Although many veteran teachers do this quite confidently and effectively, the novice teacher often feels ill prepared to engage the public. The Take a Stand! feature provides students with brief models of how one can articulate a compelling position on an educational issue. In Chapters 2 through 15, the book's authors draw on their extensive experience and knowledge of the research literature (35 and 32 years respectively) to take a strong but supportable stand on an issue that relates to the chapter content. Further, the feature encourages students to do the same—to articulate and discuss their own opinions on key issues. At the textbook's website this feature is extended with additional resources and pedagogy. This feature became an immediate hit with instructors after its introduction in the 11th edition.

Key Points At the beginning of each chapter, Key Points are listed under major headings. They also appear in the margins of pages opposite sections in which each point is discussed. The Key Points call attention to sections of the text that are considered to be of special significance to teachers and thus serve as instructional objectives.

Case in Print This feature, which uses recent news articles to demonstrate how a basic idea or technique in a chapter is being applied by educators from the primary grades through high school, has proven to be extremely popular with users. Following each article are several open-ended questions designed to encourage the student to think more deeply about the issue in question. The purpose of the Case in Print feature, found in every chapter, is to illustrate to aspiring teachers that the psychological theory and research that their instructors require them to learn does have real-world relevance.

Pause and Reflect Knowing how difficult it is for students to meaningfully grasp the abstract concepts that make up educational psychology and how important it is for them to begin to develop the habit of reflective thinking, this feature was designed to help students make connections between one idea and another and between theory and actual classroom practice. As students read each chapter, they will encounter several Pause and Reflect features that ask them to stop and think about a concept or issue raised in the chapter or to consider how their own experiences relate to what they are reading.

Journal Entries This feature is intended to help students prepare and use a Reflective Journal when they teach. Readers are urged to use the journal entries, which appear in the margins, to prepare a personal set of guidelines for reference before and during the student teaching experience and during the first years of teaching. A guide for setting up and using a Reflective Journal is included in Chapter 16, "Becoming a Better Teacher by Becoming a Reflective Teacher."

 Links to the Education CourseMate Website Because a wealth of material is available on the website that supplements the text, this edition includes marginal icons to suggest points at which the reader may want to refer to the website.

Summary A numbered set of summary statements appears at the end of the chapter. This feature is intended to help students review the main points of a chapter for upcoming examinations or class discussions.

Resources for Further Investigation To conclude the chapter, an annotated bibliography is presented that offers sources of information on the major topics covered in the chapter. Internet addresses for websites that provide additional useful information are also listed. Please note that the websites were active at the time we prepared the text, but we, of course, are not responsible for their continued presence. Readers can access the textbook's website for live, recently updated links.

Glossary A glossary of key terms and concepts is provided at the back of the book as an aid in reviewing for examinations or classroom discussion.

Instructional Components That Accompany the Text

TeachSource Video Cases Available online and organized by topic, each case is a 3- to 5-minute module consisting of video and audio files presenting actual classroom scenarios that depict the complex problems and opportunities teachers face every day. The video and audio clips are accompanied by "artifacts" that provide background information and allow aspiring teachers to experience true classroom dilemmas in their multiple dimensions. A DVD containing all 60 Video Cases is available on request to all textbook adopters.

Instructor's Resource Manual The Instructor's Resource Manual (IRM) has been revised by Rick McCown and his colleagues at Duquesne. The IRM provides an organizing framework that enables instructors to select and access efficiently the learning resources that accompany the text. In addition to facilitating decisions regarding the use of the available resources in the text and on the Education CourseMate website, the IRM provides a quick reference to the Revealing and Challenging Assumptions features, classroom activities, debates, semester projects, a syllabus starter, and formative assessment questions for use during class sessions. The formative assessments in the IRM—contributed by experienced educational psychology instructors—have been found to be effective in engaging aspiring teachers in ways that both check their understanding and help them construct knowledge. The IRM is available entirely online, which we have found aids planning and allows instructors to import easily those organizational tools, guides, activities, and assessments they decide to use.

Test Bank The Test Bank has been thoroughly revised by Jack Snowman. It includes test items consisting of multiple-choice items in alternate forms, short-answer questions, and essay questions. Consistent with this text's long-standing emphasis on mastery, each multiple-choice and short-answer question reflects a Key Point and either the Knowledge, Comprehension, Application, or Analysis level of

Bloom's Taxonomy. Feedback booklets allow instructors to point out misconceptions in students' reasoning.

PowerLecture with ExamView This one-stop digital library and presentation tool includes preassembled Microsoft® PowerPoint® lecture slides. In addition to a full Instructor's Manual and Test Bank, PowerLecture also includes ExamView® testing software with all the test items from the printed Test Bank in electronic format, enabling you to create customized tests in print or online, and all of your media resources in one place including an image library with graphics from the book itself and TeachSource Video Cases.

 Education CourseMate Helping today's instructors and students learn how to use technology meaningfully is a primary strength of this text. As a corollary, a dedicated, interactive website is available; students may go to **CengageBrain.com** to access to the site. This site, updated by Jack Snowman and Rick McCown, brings course concepts to life with interactive learning, study, and exam preparation tools that support the printed textbook. Access an integrated eBook and chapter-specific learning tools including interactive flashcards, tutorial quizzes, concept maps, links related to each chapter, reflective questions, TeachSource Video Cases, and more. We hope that both instructors and students will explore the student website and make full use of it in their classrooms.

The accompanying instructor website offers access to password-protected resources such as an electronic version of the instructor's manual and PowerPoint® slides. Go to **www.cengage.com/login**.

WebTutor on Blackboard and WebCT Jump-start your course with customizable, rich, text-specific content within your Course Management System. Whether you want to Web-enable your class or put an entire course online, WebTutor™ delivers. WebTutor™ offers a wide array of resources including media assets, quizzes, web links, exercises, and more. Visit **webtutor.cengage.com** to learn more.

Acknowledgments

Robert F. Biehler created *Psychology Applied to Teaching* in the late 1960s, establishing the goals the current authors pursue today. We acknowledge the innovative features he brought to educational psychology textbooks and seek to continue that legacy for the foreseeable future.

Authors write books to share what they have learned and, in the case of this book, to facilitate the learning of those who aspire to teach. Unless the book is published, however, learning can neither be shared nor facilitated. We are grateful to our colleagues at Cengage Learning for their efforts to help us share learning. In particular, we express our appreciation to Lisa Mafrici, who worked on *Psychology Applied to Teaching* for many years and who served as the Development Editor of this edition.

In addition to the authors and the publisher, many others have played a significant role in shaping the book. A number of reviewers made constructive suggestions and provided thoughtful reactions at various stages in the development of this edition. Thanks go out to the following individuals for their help:

Joy Brown
University of Mississippi

Judith Costello
Regis College

Gregory Cutler
Bay de Noc Community College

Daniel Fasko
Bowling Green State University

Jeffrey Kaplan
University of Central Florida

Barbara Maestas
Howard Community College

Elizabeth Pearce
Lewis University

Kathy Piechura-Couture
Stetson University

Donna Plummer
Centre College

Donna Seagle
Chattanooga State Technical Community College

Because all teachers—at various points along the way—have been shaped by those who taught them, teachers are living legacies. As it happens, we share a legacy. We were, and continue to be, influenced and inspired by the same teacher. Our teacher brought us both to the study of educational psychology, opened the door, invited us in, and has in the course of his teaching made us part of his academic family: a family that has given us a history, support, a network of colleagues, and friends on whom we can rely. Our teacher is a good man and that helps make him a good teacher. Our teacher's name is Donald J. Cunningham, and we thank him. Our acknowledgment carries also the hope that he is pleased with the legacy he entrusted to us.

The work of writing a book requires spending a lot time inside one's own head, but that time commitment makes demands also on the author's family. For their understanding and their support, Jack thanks his wife, Rickey, and Rick thanks his wife, Nona. In gratitude, we sing: Somewhere, beyond the sea...

1 Applying Psychology to Teaching

 The Education CourseMate website for this text offers many helpful resources. Go to **CengageBrain.com** to preview this chapter's Concept Maps and Chapter Themes.

KEY POINTS

These key points will help you learn the important information in this chapter. To help you study, they also appear in the margins of the pages, next to the text where they are discussed.

What Is Educational Psychology?
- Educational psychologists study how students learn in classrooms

How Will Learning About Educational Psychology Help You Be a Better Teacher?
- Teaching is complex work because it requires a wide range of knowledge and skills
- Research in educational psychology offers many useful ideas for improving classroom instruction
- Teachers who have had professional training are generally more effective

The Nature and Values of Science
- Unsystematic observation may lead to false conclusions
- Grade retention policies are influenced by unsystematic observation

- Scientific methods: sampling, control, objectivity, publication, replication

Complicating Factors in the Study of Behavior and Thought Processes
- Research focuses on a few aspects of a problem
- Complexity of teaching and learning limits uniform outcomes
- Differences of opinion result from selection and interpretation of data
- Accumulated knowledge leads researchers to revise original ideas

Good Teaching Is Partly an Art and Partly a Science
- Teaching as an art: beliefs, emotions, values, flexibility
- Research provides a scientific basis for "artistic" teaching
- Good teachers combine "artistic" and "scientific" characteristics

Reflective Teaching: A Process to Help You Grow from Novice to Expert
- Reflective teachers think about what they do and why
- Reflective teachers have particular attitudes and abilities

As you begin to read this book, you may be asking yourself, "What will this book tell me about teaching that I don't already know? After all, I've been in school for more than 12 years and have observed dozens of teachers." Yet despite your familiarity with education from the student's point of view, you probably have had limited experience with education from the teacher's point of view. Therefore, a major purpose of this book is to help you take the first steps in what will be a long journey to becoming an expert teacher.

Throughout this book, we will describe many different psychological theories, concepts, and principles and illustrate how you might apply them to teaching. The branch of psychology that specializes in understanding how different factors affect the classroom behavior of both teachers and students is **educational psychology**. In the next several sections, we will briefly describe the nature of this field of study and highlight the features of this book that will help you understand psychological principles and apply them in your classroom.

WHAT IS EDUCATIONAL PSYCHOLOGY?

Educational psychologists study how students learn in classrooms

The importance of these topics to classroom learning has been underscored by the American Psychological Association (APA). In November 1997, the APA's Board of Educational Affairs proposed that efforts to improve education be based on a set of fourteen learner-centered psychological principles. These principles, derived from decades of research and practice, highlight the importance of learning processes, motivation, development, social processes, individual differences, and instructional practices in classroom learning. These are the same topics and principles that have long been emphasized by *Psychology Applied to Teaching*. A description of and rationale for each principle can be found on the following APA website: **http://apa.org/ ed/governance/bea/ learner-centered.pdf.**

Most educational psychologists, us included, would define their field as a scientific discipline that is concerned with understanding and improving how students acquire a variety of capabilities through formal instruction in classroom settings. David Berliner (2006), for example, described educational psychology as a scientific discipline that uses psychological concepts and research methods to understand how the various characteristics of students, teachers, learning tasks, and educational settings interact to produce the everyday behaviors common in school settings. This description of educational psychology suggests that you will need to understand your own psychological makeup and such aspects of the learner as physical, social, emotional, and cognitive development; cultural, social, emotional, and intellectual differences; learning and problem-solving processes; self-esteem; motivation; testing; and measurement to formulate effective instructional lessons. In the next section, we'll examine why learning about these topics will be worth your time and effort.

HOW WILL LEARNING ABOUT EDUCATIONAL PSYCHOLOGY HELP YOU BE A BETTER TEACHER?

There's no question that knowledge of psychological concepts and their application to educational settings has the potential to help you be a better teacher. Whether that potential is ever fulfilled depends on how willing you are to maintain an open mind and a positive attitude. We say this because many prospective and practicing teachers have anything but a positive attitude when it comes to using psychological knowledge in the classroom. One teacher, for example, notes that "educational psychology and research are relatively useless because they rarely examine learning in authentic classroom contexts" (Burch, 1993). As you read through the next few paragraphs and the subsequent chapters, you will see that criticisms like this are easily rebutted. We offer a three-pronged argument (teaching is a complex enterprise, research can inform teachers, and professional coursework contributes to competence) to explain how educational psychology can help you be a better teacher, whether you plan to teach in an elementary school, a middle school, or a high school.

The information in this book can help you be a better teacher for three reasons: teaching is a complex activity that requires a broad knowledge base; many instructional practices are supported by research; and teachers who are knowledgeable about that research are better teachers. David Young-Wolff/Photo Edit

[Handwritten margin note, top left: "3 PRONGS of ARG (in our txt):"]

Teaching Is a Complex Enterprise

The first part of our argument is that teaching is not the simple, straightforward enterprise some people imagine it to be; in fact, it ranks in the top quartile on complexity for all occupations (Rowan, 1994), and several analyses include teachers in the same occupational group as accountants, architects, computer programmers, counselors, engineers, and lawyers (Allegreto, Corcoran, & Mishel, 2004; U.S. Department of Labor, 2001). Marilyn Cochran-Smith, for many years the editor of the *Journal of Teacher Education*, has characterized teaching as "unforgivingly complex" (2003). There are many reasons for this complexity. In increasing ways, teachers have daily responsibility for diverse populations of students with varied and sometimes contradictory needs. But perhaps most fundamentally, the complexity of teaching derives from its decision-making nature. Teachers are constantly making decisions—before and after instruction as well as on the spot. If you are to be informed and effective, these decisions should be based on a deep reservoir of knowledge and a wide range of skills.

[Handwritten margin notes, right: "1", "WHAT MAKES IT SO?", "DECISIONS"]

The view that teaching is a complex activity that requires in-depth knowledge in a number of areas has been recognized by the National Board for Professional Teaching Standards (**www.nbpts.org**). This is an independent, nonprofit organization of educators, administrators, and political and business leaders whose mission is to establish clear and measurable standards for what accomplished teachers should know and be able to do and to identify those teachers through a voluntary system of certification. The board's standards are based on the following five propositions (National Board for Professional Teaching Standards, 2003):

[Margin note, left: "Teaching is complex work because it requires a wide range of knowledge and skills"]

1. Teachers are committed to students and their learning.
2. Teachers know the subjects they teach and how to teach those subjects to students.
3. Teachers are responsible for managing and monitoring student learning.
4. Teachers think systematically about their practice and learn from experience.
5. Teachers are members of learning communities.

In general, the standards require teachers to be knowledgeable about learning and development, individual differences, motivation, self-concept, assessment, classroom management, and various approaches to instruction, all of which are covered in this textbook. Although the complexity inherent in teaching makes it a difficult profession to master, making progress toward that goal is also one of teaching's greatest rewards.

To help you prepare to take on such challenges and become an effective teacher, educational psychology offers many useful ideas. It does not, in most cases, provide specific prescriptions about how to handle particular problems; rather, it gives you general principles that you can use in a flexible manner. Fortunately, the research literature contains a wealth of these ideas.

[Handwritten margin note, right: ""LENS" / FRAMES"]

Research That Informs Teachers

The second part of our argument pertains to the potential usefulness of educational psychology research. Contrary to the opinion ventured by the anonymous teacher quoted previously, the research literature contains numerous studies that were conducted under realistic classroom conditions and offer useful ideas for improving instruction. There is consistent classroom-based support for the following instructional practices (Berliner & Casanova, 1996; Marzano, Pickering, & Pollock, 2005; Simonson, Fairbanks, Briesch, Myers, & Sugai, 2008; Walberg, 2006), all discussed in later chapters of this text:

[Margin note, left: "Research in educational psychology offers many useful ideas for improving classroom instruction"]

[Handwritten margin note, right: "STRATEGIES"]

1. Using more advanced students to tutor less advanced students
2. Giving positive reinforcement to students whose performance meets or exceeds the teacher's objectives and giving corrective feedback to students whose performance falls short of the teacher's objectives

3. Communicating to students what is expected of them and why
4. Requiring students to respond to higher-order questions
5. Providing students with cues about the nature of upcoming tasks by giving them introductory information and telling them what constitutes satisfactory performance
6. Teaching students how to monitor and improve their own learning efforts and offering them structured opportunities to practice independent learning activities
7. Knowing the misconceptions that students bring to the classroom that will likely interfere with their learning of a particular subject matter
8. Creating learning situations in which students are expected to organize information in new ways and formulate problems for themselves
9. Accepting responsibility for student outcomes rather than seeing students as solely responsible for what they learn and how they behave
10. Showing students how to work in small, cooperative learning groups

The federal government and other policymaking organizations have acknowledged the importance of applying research on learning and learning-related issues to teaching. As part of the federal No Child Left Behind Act of 2001 (a revision of the earlier Elementary and Secondary Education Act), all schools that receive federal funds to create and maintain programs (such as safe and drug-free schools and Title I) must document how those programs are supported by scientifically based research. The Institute of Education Sciences, a part of the U.S. Department of Education, maintains a What Works Clearinghouse (**http://ies.ed.gov/ncee/wwc**). This website was designed to provide educators with information about how well instructional programs they might be interested in adopting are supported by research. As of this writing, reports on programs for beginning reading, English language learners, early childhood education, elementary school math, middle school math, and dropout prevention were available. Teachers for a New Era, a program funded by the Carnegie Corporation to facilitate the development of exemplary teacher education programs, has as one of its three organizing principles that prospective teachers will develop respect for research-based evidence (Cochran-Smith, 2005). The American Psychological Association created the Applications of Psychological Science to Teaching and Learning Task Force and the Coalition for Psychology in the Schools and Education to help K–12 teachers use research-based practices that enhance classroom learning (American Psychological Association, 2006).

As much as we value the contribution that research can make to your effectiveness as a teacher and hope that you will make consistent use of it in the future, you need to put research in its proper context. For reasons we mention in a later section of this chapter, you should keep in mind that the knowledge produced by science, particularly with respect to classroom learning, is usually qualified and temporary. A few pages ago we described educational psychology as a discipline that studies how characteristics of students, teachers, learning tasks, and educational settings interact to produce the outcomes that will be of interest to you. Consequently, the insights you seek from research should be specific ("For which students will this idea likely work best?" "Under what circumstances?" "With what kinds of tasks?" "For what kinds of outcomes?"), rather than general ("Will my students benefit more from A than B?"). In other words, keep reminding yourself that nothing works for everybody in any and all circumstances. Notice also that we talked about research providing you with insights rather than definitive answers. Our choice of wording here is quite deliberate. Research in any field is a matter of adding to, taking away from, and revising an existing body of knowledge. For all practical purposes, we never get to the point where we say, "This is what we know and it will always be so." Instead, researchers say, "This is what we know for now." That's why we prefer that you treat research findings as providing you with insights or guidelines rather than hard and fast answers.

Coursework and Competence

The third part of our argument that educational psychology can help you be a better teacher concerns the courses you are currently taking, particularly this educational psychology course. Many researchers have asked, "How do the courses teachers take as students relate to how capable they perceive themselves to be as teachers?" One means that researchers have used to determine the answer has been to ask beginning teachers to rate how prepared they feel to handle a variety of classroom tasks.

SKILLS

| Teachers who have had professional training are generally more effective |

Surveys of beginning teachers (e.g., Brouwer & Korthagen, 2005; Maloch, Fine, & Flint, 2002/2003; National Comprehensive Center for Teacher Quality & Public Agenda, 2008a,b; Ruhland & Bremer, 2002; Zientek, 2007) reveal that they are highly satisfied with how well their training has prepared them to deal with certain classroom challenges, but are dissatisfied with their preparation for addressing other challenges. On the plus side, most beginning teachers reported that their training adequately prepared them to teach a specific subject, provide individualized instruction, manage the behavior of students in their classroom, and understand the impact of children's cognitive, social, and emotional development on learning (Maloch, Fine, & Flint, 2003/2003; National Comprehensive Center for Teacher Quality & Public Agenda, 2008a,b; Zientek, 2007). On the negative side, beginning teachers felt their teacher education programs did not do enough to prepare them to deal with children with special needs, children from ethnically and racially diverse backgrounds, assessing learning, and interpreting test results to students and parents (National Comprehensive Center for Teacher Quality & Public Agenda, 2008a,b; Ruhland & Bremer, 2002; Zientek, 2007). This textbook will address all of these issues, including those about which teachers have reported discomfort. Our belief is that this course and this book will be one important means for helping you feel prepared to enter your first classroom.

Despite feeling less than fully prepared to deal with special needs students, ethnically and culturally diverse students, and aspects of classroom assessment, beginning teachers who earned their certification from a standard teacher education program reported higher levels of satisfaction with the quality of their training than did teachers who earned their certification through such alternate means as the

The students of teachers who were trained in teacher education programs and certified by their states score higher on standardized achievement tests than do the students of noncertified teachers. Flash!Light/Stock Boston

Teach for America program, New Teachers Project, and Troops to Teachers program. In one survey, 80 percent of traditionally trained and certified first-year teachers felt they were prepared for their first year of teaching whereas only 50 percent of alternate route teachers felt adequately prepared. Similarly, 74 percent of traditionally trained teachers felt they spent enough time working with classroom teachers during their training whereas only 31 percent of alternate route teachers felt that way (National Comprehensive Center for Teacher Quality & Public Agenda, 2008c).

Although it is reassuring to know that most beginning teachers have a generally favorable opinion of the quality of their preparation programs, we should also ask if the graduates of such programs provide high-quality instruction to their students. There are two lines of evidence that shed some light on this issue.

First are those studies that have examined the effectiveness of certified teachers versus teachers with either nonstandard or no certification. Several studies (see, for example, American Educational Research Association, 2004; Berry, Hoke, & Hirsch, 2004; Darling-Hammond & Youngs, 2002; Darling-Hammond, Holtzman, Gatllin, & Heilig, 2005; Laczko-Kerr & Berliner, 2003;Wayne & Youngs, 2003; and Wilson, Floden, & Ferrini-Mundy, 2002) found that the students of certified teachers scored higher on standardized achievement tests than did the students of teachers with nonstandard certification even though these teachers were judged to have had a good understanding of their subject matter. The second line of evidence has compared how well the scores earned on standardized teacher certification tests, such as the Praxis II, predict teaching competence as compared with the grades those same teachers earned in their teacher preparation program. A recent analysis of this evidence (D'Agostino & Powers, 2009) found that the grades students earned during their coursework and their performance during student teaching were better predictors of how effective they were as teachers than were their scores on a standardized exam.

THE NATURE AND VALUES OF SCIENCE

The primary purpose of this book is to offer suggestions on how psychology (the scientific study of behavior and mental processes) might be applied to teaching. This text is based on the premise that information reported by scientists can be especially useful for those who plan to teach. Some of the reasons for this conviction become apparent when the characteristics of science are examined and compared with the limitations of casual observation.

Limitations of Unsystematic Observation

| Unsystematic observation may lead to false conclusions

Those who make unsystematic observations of human behavior may be easily misled into drawing false conclusions. For instance, they may treat the first plausible explanation that comes to mind as the only possible explanation. Or they may mistakenly apply a generalization about a single episode to superficially similar situations. In the process, they may fail to realize that an individual's reactions in a given situation are due primarily to unrecognized idiosyncratic factors that may never occur again or that the behavior of one person under certain circumstances may not resemble that of other persons in the same circumstances. In short, unsystematic observers are especially prone to noting only evidence that fits their expectations and ignoring evidence that does not.

| Grade retention policies are influenced by unsystematic observation

A clear example of the limitations of unsystematic observation is the practice of retaining children for a second year in a given grade because of poor achievement. Grade retention has long been assumed to be an effective way of dealing with individual differences in learning rate, emotional development, and socialization skills. The percentage of students in grades K–12 in the United States who had ever been retained was 9.8 percent for 2007, with the highest rate (22.9 percent) occurring among students from low-income families (Planty et al., 2009). Retention is an expensive tactic: the average school spent $9,553 per student during the 2005–2006 school year (Planty et al., 2009). To some extent, retention rates are related to the growth of state learning standards and high-stakes testing programs (which we discuss in Chapter 15 on standardized tests); school districts are often required to retain students whose test scores fall below a certain level.

This widespread and expensive use of retention continues even though most research clearly shows that it has negative effects. Retained students are 40 to 50 percent more likely than nonretained students to drop out of school. Moreover, low-achieving children who are promoted learn at least as much, if not more, the following year, have a stronger self-concept, and are better adjusted emotionally than similar children who are retained, even when the retention occurs as early as kindergarten (Duffrin, 2004a; Hong & Raudenbush, 2005; Jimerson, 2001; Jimerson & Kaufman, 2003; Jimerson, Anderson, & Whipple, 2002; Nagaoka & Roderick, 2004; Ramirez & Carpenter, 2009; Rodney, Crafter, Rodney, & Mupier, 1999). Yet grade retention continues to be recommended by some parents, schools, administrators, and teachers because they believe that repeating a grade should be beneficial to a student, and people tend to overgeneralize from the exceptional case in which the outcome was positive (Duffrin, 2004b; Graue & DiPerna, 2000; Owings & Kaplan, 2001; Thomas, 2000). The reason retention does not work is simple: it does not address the causes of students' poor performance. These students typically begin school with more poorly developed academic skills, more serious health problems, and less stable home environments than their peers. In addition, retained students receive the same type of instruction and material the second time around. In short, retention is an attempt by policymakers, administrators, and some teachers to fit a short-term and relatively inexpensive solution to a long-term problem. The best way to minimize, if not avoid, the use of retention is to provide developmentally, cognitively, and culturally appropriate forms of instruction (Darling-Hammond & Falk, 1997). The major goal of this text is to help you know how to provide such instruction as a teacher.

pause & reflect

Imagine that you are a second-grade teacher. Your principal suggests that one of your students who performed poorly this year repeats second grade next year. Given what you know about the research on retention, how would you respond?

Strengths of Scientific Observation

Those who study behavior and mental processes scientifically are more likely to acquire trustworthy information than a casual observer is, and they are likely to apply what they learn more effectively because they follow the scientific procedures of sampling, control, objectivity, publication, and replication. In most cases, researchers study a representative sample of subjects so that individual idiosyncrasies are canceled out. An effort is made to note all plausible hypotheses to explain a given type of behavior, and each hypothesis is tested under controlled conditions. If all factors but one can be held constant in an experiment, the researcher may be able to trace the impact of a given condition by comparing the behaviors of those who have been exposed to it and those who have not.

Scientific methods: sampling, control, objectivity, publication, replication

Scientific observers make special efforts to be objective and guard against being misled by predetermined ideas, wishful thinking, or selected evidence. Observations are made in a carefully prescribed, systematic manner, which makes it possible for different observers to compare reactions.

Complete reports of experiments—including descriptions of subjects, methods, results, and conclusions—are published in professional journals. This dissemination allows other experimenters to replicate a study to discover if they obtain the same results. The existence of reports of thousands of experiments makes it possible to discover what others have done. This knowledge can then serve as a starting point for one's own speculations.

COMPLICATING FACTORS IN THE STUDY OF BEHAVIOR AND THOUGHT PROCESSES

Although the use of scientific methods makes it possible to overcome many of the limitations of unscientific observation, the application of knowledge acquired in a scientific manner to classroom settings is subject to several complicating factors. We want you to be aware of these so that you do not think we are insisting that science can cure all your classroom problems.

The Limited Focus of Research

Human behavior is complex, changes with age, and has many causes. A student may perform poorly on a history exam, for example, for one or more of the following reasons: poorly developed study skills, inattentiveness in class, low interest in the subject, a poorly written text, low motivation to achieve high grades, vaguely worded exam questions, and difficulty with a particular type of exam question (compare-and-contrast essays, for example).

Research focuses on a few aspects of a problem

To understand how these factors affect performance on school-related tasks, research psychologists study at most only a few of them at a time under conditions that may not be entirely realistic. Imagine that a researcher is interested in comparing lectures versus problem-solving exercises in terms of their effect on conceptual understanding. The researcher may recruit subjects who are equivalent in terms of social class, prior knowledge of the topic of the reading passage, and age; randomly assign them to either a teacher who mostly lectures or one who assigns problems to solve; and then examine each group's responses to several types of comprehension items. As a consequence of such focused approaches, most research studies provide specific information about a particular aspect of behavior. More comprehensive knowledge, however, is acquired by combining and interrelating separate studies that have looked at different aspects of a common problem.

The Complexity of Teaching and Learning

David Berliner (2002), a leading educational researcher, considers the scientific study of education to be "the hardest-to-do science of them all" for at least two reasons. First, it is difficult to implement research findings and programs uniformly because schools and classrooms differ from one another along such lines as quality and quantity of personnel, teaching methods, budget, leadership, and community support. Thus, a program or technique may work just as the research says it should in one district or teacher's class, but not in other classes or districts.

Complexity of teaching and learning limits uniform outcomes

Second, the outcomes of schooling that teachers, students, and parents typically value are the result of complex interactions among numerous variables. This is true for both cognitive (thinking) outcomes and affective (emotional) outcomes. Achievement may, for example, be the result of interactions among student characteristics (such as prior knowledge, interests, and socioeconomic levels), teacher characteristics (type of training, ideas about learning, interests, and values, for example), curriculum materials, socioeconomic status of the community, and peer influences. Consequently, students exposed to the same materials and teaching methods are likely to vary in how much and what they learn (Daniel & Poole, 2009; Davis, 2007).

Such differences in student outcomes are largely a result of the fact that ideas are not given from one person to another like so many packages but rather are actively *constructed* by each person (Brooks & Brooks, 2001; Schifter, 1996; Wheatley, 1991). Because different factors come into play for different people and the same factors affect people differently, two people can read the same passage yet construct

Understanding and managing the teaching/ learning process is a challenge for researchers and teachers because it is affected by numerous variables that interact with one another.
© Suzie Fitzhugh

entirely different interpretations of its meaning. This concept, known as *constructivism*, is so fundamental to human behavior and to learning that we will return to it again and again in this text.

Recognizing the complexity of teaching and learning is a good, but hardly sufficient, first step. You will also need a strategy for dealing with such situations. One noteworthy suggestion is to teach adaptively (see, for example, Corno, 2008). Basically, this means forming a small number of groups in which the students are more alike than they are different (for example, those who are motivated and self-confident versus those who are insecure and anxious or those who can work independently versus those who need the support of others), and then using teaching techniques that reduce those differences. To help students who are anxious and less motivated because of poorly developed learning skills become more like their more skilled and assured classmates, you might use a technique that we discuss more fully in Chapter 9 called reciprocal teaching. Other techniques that might be used include scaffolding (discussed in Chapter 2), drawing students' attention to particular aspects of a lesson (discussed in Chapter 8), and modeling (discussed in Chapter 9).

Selection and Interpretation of Data

The amount of scientific information available on behavior and mental processes is so extensive that no individual could examine or interpret all of it. Accordingly, researchers learn to be highly selective in their reading. In addition, conclusions about the meaning of scientific results vary from one researcher to another. As you read this book, you will discover that there are differences of opinion among psychologists regarding certain aspects of development, motivation, and intelligence. Opposing views may be based on equally scientific evidence, but the way in which the evidence is selected and interpreted will vary. The fact that a topic is studied scientifically does not necessarily mean that opinions about interpretations of the data will be unanimous.

Differences of opinion result from selection and interpretation of data

New Findings Mean Revised Ideas

Scientific information is not only voluminous and subject to different interpretations; it is also constantly being revised. A series of experiments may lead to the development of a new concept or pedagogical technique that is highly successful when it is first tried out. Subsequent studies, however, may reveal that the original research was incomplete, or repeated applications of a technique may show that it is less effective once the novelty has worn off. But frequent shifts of emphasis in education also reflect the basic nature of science. A quality of science that sets it apart from other intellectual processes is that the discoveries by one generation of scientists set the stage for far-reaching discoveries by the next. More researchers are studying aspects of psychology and education now than at any previous time in history, and thousands of reports of scientific research are published every month.

> Accumulated knowledge leads researchers to revise original ideas

To repeat what we said earlier, as our knowledge accumulates, it is inevitable that interpretations of how children learn and how we should teach will continue to change. We know more about development, learning, and teaching today than ever before, but because of the nature of some of the factors just discussed and the complexity of human behavior, our answers are tentative and incomplete.

Take, for example, the case of neuroscience research. On the one hand, many educators (see, for example, Jensen, 2008) argue that enough is known about how the brain works under various circumstances to use those findings to create what are called brain-based approaches to education. On the other hand, critics (such as Sternberg, 2008; Varma, McCandless, & Schwartz, 2008; Willingham, 2008; Willis, 2008) argue that, while the results of neuroscience research are promising, those studies were not conducted under realistic classroom conditions nor are the results sufficiently consistent to serve as the basis for instructional tactics or programs. When and if a consensus develops among researchers that brain-based research has something of value to offer teachers (as happened with social cognitive theory, which we discuss at length in Chapter 9), future readers of this book will read about it here. One of our objectives in writing this text is to demonstrate the importance of basing your practices on principles that have solid research support.

pause & reflect

Think of a popular instructional practice. Would you classify it as a fad or as the outgrowth of scientific knowledge? Why? How can you tell the difference?

The science of psychology has much to offer educators, but a scientific approach to teaching does have its limits. Because teaching is a dynamic *decision-making process*, you will be greatly aided by a systematic, objective framework for making your decisions. Research on teaching and learning can give you that framework. But for the reasons just cited, research cannot give you a prescription or a set of rules that specify how you should handle every situation. Often you will have to make on-the-spot, subjective decisions about how to present a lesson, explain a concept, handle mass boredom, or reprimand a student. This contrast between an objective, systematic approach to planning instruction and the need to make immediate (yet appropriate) applications and modifications of those plans calls attention to a question that has been debated for years: Is teaching primarily an art or a science—or a combination of both?

GOOD TEACHING IS PARTLY AN ART AND PARTLY A SCIENCE

The Argument for Teaching as an Art

Some educators have argued that teaching is an art that cannot be practiced or even studied in an objective or scientific manner because of its inherent unpredictability (Eisner, 2002; Flinders, 1989; Hansgen, 1991; Rubin, 1985). Selma Wasserman

Part of the art of teaching is knowing when to introduce an unusual assignment or activity that captures students' interest. © Jim Wileman/Alamy

(1999), who taught public school and college for many years, recounts how her teacher education program prepared her for her first day as a public school teacher:

> Learning the "correct answers" not only had not equipped me for the complex and confusing world of the classroom but, even worse, had led me down the garden path. Implicit in what I had learned was that teaching was merely a matter of stock-piling certain pieces of information about teaching. If I only knew what the answers were, I would be prepared to face the overwhelming and exhausting human dilemmas that make up life in classrooms. Unfortunately, I had been swindled. My training in learning the answers was as useless as yesterday's pizza. I was entering a profession in which there are few, if any, clear-cut answers, a profession riddled with ambiguity and moral dilemmas that would make Solomon weep. Even more of a handicap was that I became desperate in my search for the answers—certain that they were out there, somewhere, if only I could find them. (p. 466)

Wasserman's account suggests that there are no authoritative sources that will provide teachers with fail-safe prescriptions for the myriad problems they will face. Good teaching is as much the result of one's motives, beliefs, values, and emotions as of one's formal knowledge. Teachers who are more internally motivated, for example, are more likely than their more externally motivated colleagues to use teaching practices that promote internal motivation in students (Roth, Assor, Kanat-Maymon, & Kaplan, 2007). Jonathon Kozol, who has written several books about the problems of education and how good teachers can overcome them, points out in his latest book, *Letters to a Young Teacher* (2007), the importance of such beliefs as teaching is one of society's most valuable and rewarding activities, teaching must be done as well as possible every day, there is no such things as an unteachable student, and nothing is more important than having students become excited about and enjoy the process of learning.

When Wasserman states that teaching is not a matter of clear-cut answers, she is urging teachers to be flexible. Flexibility, which can be thought of as a "feel" for doing the right thing at the right time, can take many forms. First, it means being able to choose from among all the techniques and information at your disposal to formulate effective lesson plans that take the diverse needs and interests of all your students into consideration. It means knowing, for example, when to present a formal lesson and when to let students discover things for themselves, when to be demanding and when to make few demands, when and to whom to give direct help, and when and to whom to give indirect help.

Second, flexibility entails the communication of emotions and interest in a variety of ways. David Flinders (1989) describes a teacher who, when talking to students, would lean or step in their direction and maintain eye contact. At various times, she would raise her eyebrows, nod her head, smile, and bring the index finger of her right hand to her lips, indicating serious consideration of the student's comments. In their book *Acting Lessons for Teachers: Using Performance Skills in the Classroom* (2006), Robert Tauber and Cathy Sargent Mester describe the importance for successful teaching of such acting skills as voice animation (variations in pitch, volume, voice quality, and rate), body animation (facial expressions, gestures), and use of classroom space.

pause & reflect

The effective teacher as artist communicates enthusiasm. At some point, however, you may be asked to teach a grade level or subject for which you have little enthusiasm, or you may grow bored teaching the same grade level or subject year after year. How will you fulfill the role of teacher-artist in these situations?

Third, flexibility includes the ability to improvise. When a lesson plan falls flat, the flexible teacher immediately thinks of an alternative presentation that recaptures the students' interest. Expert teachers actually plan improvisation into their lessons. Instead of writing out what they intend to do in great detail, they formulate general mental plans and wait to see how the students react before filling in such details as pacing, timing, and number of examples (Moshavi, 2001; Westerman, 1991). Obviously this type of high-wire act requires a great deal of experience and confidence.

Fourth, flexibility involves the willingness and resourcefulness to work around impediments. Teaching does not always occur under ideal circumstances, and teachers must sometimes cope with inadequate facilities, insufficient materials, interruptions, and other difficulties.

Teacher educator Sharon Feiman-Nemser (2003) underscored the importance of flexibility to the art of teaching by noting what experienced educators said when asked what beginning teachers most needed to learn. One recommended that new teachers focus on helping students understand the essence of each lesson, even if that means going beyond or ignoring guidelines in a teacher's manual. The wisdom of this recommendation has been borne out by research that shows that effective teachers, in addition to being organized and efficient, also know when and how to modify lessons to meet the needs of particular students (Duffy & Kear, 2007). Another noted that because teachers are essentially on stage, they need to develop a performing self that they are comfortable with. A third observation was that new teachers need to learn how to size up situations and think on their feet. In sum, **teaching as an art** involves beliefs, emotions, values, and flexibility. Because these characteristics are intangible, they can be very difficult, if not impossible, to teach. Teachers must find these qualities within themselves. This chapter's Case in Print describes the intrinsic rewards that come from teaching in an environment that fosters the teacher-as-artist role.

| Teaching as an art: beliefs, emotions, values, flexibility

The Argument for Teaching as a Science

The argument for **teaching as a science** is equally persuasive. Although many educational psychologists agree that the science of teaching, as such, does not exist, they contend that it is possible and desirable to have a scientific basis for the art of teaching (e.g., Hiebert, Gallimore, & Stigler, 2002; Kosunen & Mikkola, 2002; Slavin, 2002, 2008). By drawing on established research findings, both prospective and practicing teachers can learn many of the prerequisites that make artistic teaching possible. Also, as Robert Slavin (2008) persuasively argues, working from a scientific basis helps teachers avoid the pitfall of subscribing to the latest fad.

| Research provides a scientific basis for "artistic" teaching

The case for teaching as a science rests on the existence of a usable body of research findings. Research has identified dozens of instructional practices that

Case in Print

The Joy of Being a Teacher-Artist: One Teacher's Tale

Good teaching is as much the result of one's motives, beliefs, values, and emotions as of one's formal knowledge...Jonathan Kozol, who has written several books about the problems of education and how good teachers can overcome them, points out in his latest book, Letters to a Young Teacher *(2007), the importance of such beliefs because teaching is one of society's most valuable and rewarding activities, teaching must be done as well as possible every day, there is no such thing as an unteachable student, and nothing is more important than having students become excited about and enjoy the process of learning. (p. 11)*

Teaching Without a Script

MATTHEW KAY

The New York Times, 9/14/2008

Three weeks ago, when my school asked 20 upperclassmen to help with a summer institute for freshmen, 80 showed up. At the end of August, our technology coordinator asked students to help her configure our laptops. Many kids spent the last free Saturday of summer vacation dragging icons across a screen. The school year at Science Leadership Academy here in Philadelphia has now begun, and our freshmen are noticing that the end of our school day stretches much longer than the end of the teachers' paid instructional time. They are asking the same question that regularly stirs up our visitors. "Why do they stay?" Even as I write this, student laughter is floating up from our café—late on a Friday afternoon. Some have stepped out to get Chinese, and now they are back—to hang out with teachers in the principal's office. Given every opportunity to leave, both our educators and students regularly decide to stay.

All sides of every education debate agree that quality learning happens when knowledgeable, caring teachers use sound pedagogy. While theorists and politicians quibble over the definitions within this definition, most know that once a quality teacher is in an urban classroom, the biggest challenge is keeping them there. What keeps a dynamic, intelligent, young teacher in an urban classroom after they've built up enough experience to skip off to higher paying suburban pastures? How do you encourage them to build 30-year careers where many natives measure success by the ability to escape?

Many say the answer is money. And every election season candidates promise more of it. Whether they want to give it unilaterally, or only to teachers who somehow "merit" it, the theory is that you make the best stay by paying them more. (I treat this debate like so many barber shop disputes over slavery reparations. I don't expect a dime, but should the checks come, I'll be first in line.)

I am a good case study for this issue. I'm one of those young, dynamic teachers, and I want nothing more than to stay in Philadelphia's public schools for the rest of my career. And as my third teaching year begins, I'm wondering what this little downtown academy with big ideas has done to squelch my innate desire to move on. And I wonder why young teachers from all over the country are treating this Philly school like the Mecca of their craft. Why did they come, and why do they seem, like me, to want to stay around for a bit?

It's not money. Great teachers are deft managers, thirsty scholars, and empathetic people—and we would excel in careers that pay a whole lot more if cash was our driving ambition. The reason that the young teachers at S.L.A. are so excited to be here most likely mirrors my own—we are all treated like artists.

I've been a performance poet for the past three years, and though I enjoy the rush and buzz of a packed show, my favorite moments are the dark ones. The times that I spend in "the lab," reading, journaling, and spitting random punch lines to my reflection in the mirror. I give voice to real characters that I have recently been exposed to: an ill, pregnant woman, a Holocaust survivor, a drug runner from our local badlands. These people's scattered experiences are filtered through my brain and turned into something coherent, catchy, and meaningful to a larger audience.

So it is with the inquiry-based learning that we model for the other schools in Philadelphia. Our ninth graders come to us shy about asking questions that are often scattered and incoherent. When encouraged, they open up, and then incessantly offer their ideas. (I illustrate this for all classes on the first full day of every year, when I put a big rubber ball under my shirt and pretend to give laborious birth to it. We name this child "my idea." I pass it around nervously, and when someone drops it, I snatch it up and curl into the fetal position. They laugh. I eventually get over my shock and learn to trust again, slowly passing it, then throwing it around the room for everyone to touch. There are two morals: first, you can't protect your idea forever, and second, our ideas grow when, by dialogue and debate, others are allowed to get their fingerprints on them.)

This is when the S.L.A. teacher-artists go into the "lab." We show 32 young urban voices how to ask probing questions about a text, a formula, or a problem in their communities. We use those questions to flavor each unit plan that we prepare. The end product works much like that call-and-response piece that shouts "Listen!" and quiets all sidebar conversation. The audience owns the words too. The kids are more inspired to pay attention. The artist is more inspired to bring the noise.

I end each year with a speech unit. The kids dream up an injustice, question why it exists, and then seek to change some minds. They read powerful, controversial examples of oratory spanning from Frederick Douglass to Hitler to J.F.K. The idea for it came when, during a "To Kill a Mockingbird" unit two years ago, students got a little excited during a mock jury deliberation. They did such a good job playing the relentlessly racist townspeople of Maycomb that I wondered aloud how such ignorance could be reasoned with. I challenged them to do so. With each child's fingerprint, the idea grew.

Last year, one of my students began her piece with, "I want an Iranian for president. I want a gay person for president. I want a person who has been stopped by the cops so many times because of the color of their skin that it's become a routine." A shyer kid spoke about gun violence. After listing many incidents that had been labeled "wake up calls," she shouted that, "the alarms have been relentless, but our response, again and again, has been to hit the snooze button. But there is no more need for a wake-up call. The need now is for action!" There was no fear.

If I hadn't been allowed to be an artist in the classroom, if my curriculum had been some stranger's standardized script, these girls may not have found their voices. To educate like this, a teacher shouldn't have to break the rules. Experiences like this should be the rule of any curriculum meant to engage this generation. If we want to convince dynamic, young educators to choose the inner city as the place to master their craft—we've got to remember that the best are artists. They like to create. And if they aren't allowed to do so, they will rebel—or they will leave. The chance to be an artist has convinced me to stay—"merit pay" not withstanding.

Questions and Activities

1. The teacher who was the subject of this article is, by any measure, internally motivated, creative, and hardworking. Do you think these are characteristics that artistic teachers are born with or that develop with experience? If you think such characteristics are at least partly learnable and if you think you might be lacking in one or more of these areas, what can you do to become an effective teacher-artist?

2. Regardless of whether you think the characteristics of a teacher-artist are innate or learned, what role does a school's environment play in facilitating this role? Do you believe this teacher would have been as creative and effective in any school?

3. This teacher claims that teachers from all over the country vie for teaching positions at the Science Leadership Academy for reasons other than money. What might those reasons be? Would you take a pay cut to teach at such a school? Why?

improve student achievement. For example, at least twenty-four separate studies have found that giving teachers more instructional time—that is, giving students more time to learn—leads to higher achievement (Walberg, 2006; Wang, Haertel, & Walberg, 1993). (This finding is often used to support proposals for a longer school year.) Other studies have demonstrated the benefits of alerting students to important material through the use of objectives and pretests, engaging students in a task through the use of questions and homework, and providing corrective feedback and reinforcement with written comments, verbal explanations, and praise.

The Teacher as Artistic Scholar: Combining the Art and Science of Teaching

In recent years there have been increasing calls for teaching to be more research-based (the phrase you will see used most often is *evidence-based*) despite the complicating factors we mentioned earlier. But there are critical questions about the evidence we collect and the educational goals and objectives we adopt that must be answered before we fully embrace an evidence-based approach to education.

With respect to the nature of the research evidence, we need answers to at least the following questions: What counts as credible research evidence? How consistent must the evidence be for the claim to be made that a particular practice works? How large does a positive effect have to be before recommending that teachers use a particular practice? Perhaps the most important question for prospective teachers is: To what extent can classroom practices be based on research evidence? Gert Biesta (2007) argues, and we tend to agree, that while research shows us what *has worked* under a particular set of conditions, it cannot tell us what *will work* because the circumstances that surround classroom learning vary from school to school and change over time. Consequently, teachers need to treat research findings as possibilities that they need to validate for a particular group of students at a particular point in time. That is why we chose to title this section "Good Teaching is Partly an Art and Partly a Science." Our choice of wording indicates our belief that good teaching is a skillful blend of artistic and scientific elements. The teacher who attempts to base every action on scientific evidence is likely to come across as rigid and mechanical—perhaps even indecisive (when the scientific evidence is lacking or unclear). The teacher who ignores scientific knowledge about teaching and learning and makes arbitrary decisions runs the risk of using methods that are ineffective.

This analysis of teaching as a science and an art leads us to the conclusion that teachers need to learn how to play the role of artistic scholar in their own classrooms. That is, they need to figure out how to use research findings as ideas and guidelines to design potentially effective classroom practices. While playing this type of role is challenging, you will find yourself becoming better at it by using a valuable source of knowledge available to every teacher: your own classroom experiences. Although the knowledge that teachers gain from teaching actual lessons often lacks the broad generalizability that is characteristic of scientific knowledge, experience-based knowledge does have the following advantages:

- It is linked to a particular task and goal (such as teaching students how to discover the various themes embedded in a reading passage).
- It is sufficiently detailed, concrete, and specific that other teachers can use the same techniques with the same or highly similar material.
- It typically combines knowledge of the task, knowledge of teaching methods, and knowledge of students' characteristics (Hiebert et al., 2002).

pause & reflect

How do good teachers strike a balance between the art and the science of teaching? Are they born with the right personality? Are they the products of good teacher-education programs? If both factors play a role, which is more important?

Good teachers combine "artistic" and "scientific" characteristics

REFLECTIVE TEACHING: A PROCESS TO HELP YOU GROW FROM NOVICE TO EXPERT

Reflective teachers think about what they do and why

The blending of artistic and scientific elements can be seen in discussions of what is called **reflective teaching** (see, for example, Eby, Herrell, & Jordan, 2006; Ellis, 2001; Henderson, 2001; and McEntee et al., 2003). Reflective teachers are constantly

TeachSource **Video Case** ◂◂ ▶ ▸▸

Teaching as a Profession: What Defines Effective Teaching?

Go to the Education CourseMate website to watch the Video Case on Effective Teaching, and then answer the following questions:

1. This section of the chapter explains that teaching is both art and science. How did the teachers in the Video Case combine both artistic and scientific approaches to teaching?

2. Give some specific examples from the Video Case that illustrate how teachers employed the attribute of flexibility that is described in the chapter.

engaged in thoughtful observation and analysis of their actions in the classroom before, during, and after interactions with their students.

Prior to instruction, reflective teachers may think about such things as the types of knowledge and skills students in a democratic society need to learn, the kind of classroom atmosphere and teaching techniques that are most likely to produce this learning, and the kinds of assessments that will provide clear evidence that these goals are being accomplished (a topic that we discuss at some length in the chapters on assessment and testing). Jere Brophy and Janet Alleman (1991) illustrate the importance of thinking about long-range goals by pointing out how the choice of goals affects content coverage and how content coverage affects teachers' choice of classroom activities. If, for example, one goal is for students to acquire problem-solving skills, students would likely be engaged in activities that call for inquiring, reasoning, and decision making. Debates, simulations, and laboratory experiments are just three examples of activities that might be used to meet such a goal. If the goal is for students to memorize facts and information, students will likely be given activities that call for isolated memorization and recall. Worksheets and drill-and-practice exercises are typically used to meet this type of goal. The point here is that effective teachers are reflective: they think about these issues as a basis for drawing up lesson plans.

As they interact with students, reflective teachers are highly aware of how students are responding to what they are doing and are prepared to make minor but significant changes to keep a lesson moving toward its predetermined goal. Consider an elementary school classroom in which some students are having difficulty understanding the relationship between the orbits of the planets around the sun and their position in the night sky. The teacher knows there is a problem: some students have a puzzled expression on their faces, and others cannot describe this phenomenon in their own words. Realizing that some students think in more concrete terms than others, the teacher decides to push the desks to the sides of the room and have the students simulate the planets by walking through their orbits. All in the moment, this teacher engages in thoughtful observation, spontaneous analysis, and flexible, resourceful problem solving.

For events that cannot be handled on the spot, some period of time outside of school should be set aside for reflection. This is the time to assess how well a particular lesson met its objective, wonder why some students rarely participate in class discussions, ponder the pros and cons of grouping students by ability, and formulate plans for dealing with these concerns.

| Reflective teachers have particular attitudes and abilities

To become a reflective teacher, you will need useful information about how well your students are responding to your lessons as well as several critical attitudes and abilities. Gaining insight into the effectiveness of your teaching is best accomplished by constantly monitoring your students' progress through a process known as **formative evaluation** (or **formative assessment,** if you like). As we discuss in Chapter 14, formative evaluation involves a variety of informal and formal assessment techniques. Perhaps the simplest informal technique is to observe how students respond during lessons. Other formative assessments include asking questions during lessons, having students read orally, assigning in-class worksheets and homework, and giving periodic quizzes. The important point to keep in mind is that formative assessment is not done for the purpose of giving students grades. Rather, it is done to provide you with the information you need to reflect on what you are doing and whether any changes need to be made. As for attitudes, three of the most important are an introspective orientation, an open-minded but questioning attitude about educational theories and practices, and the willingness to take responsibility for your decisions and actions. These attitudes need to be combined with the ability to view situations from the perspectives of others (students, parents, principal, other teachers), the ability to find information that allows an alternative explanation of classroom events and produces more effective instructional methods, and the ability to use compelling evidence in support of a decision (Eby et al., 2002; Ross et al., 1993). In short, to become a reflective teacher, you need both the willingness and the ability to question your assumptions about teaching and learning. We hasten to add that although reflection is largely a solitary activity, you should discuss your concerns with colleagues, friends, students, and parents to get different perspectives on the nature of a problem and possible alternative courses of action.

As you can probably see from this brief discussion, the reflection process is likely to work well when teachers have command of a wide range of knowledge about the nature of students, the learning process, and the instructional process. By mastering much of the content of this text, you will be well prepared to make productive use of the time you devote to reflection.

Reflective teaching is a way to become a teacher who never stops learning, which is the hallmark of an expert teacher. Writing is a tool for learning. Thus, writing about your teaching journey—keeping a journal—can help you develop from

Reflective teachers collect information about student performance and then use this information to think about what they do in class, why they do it, and how their methods affect student performance. Ken Whitmore/ Stone/Getty Images

pause & reflect

The reflective teacher sets aside regular blocks of time to think about teaching activities and make new plans. Most teachers complain about having insufficient time to reflect and plan. What would you do to make more time available?

novice to expert (see Ball, 2009; Bennett & Pye, 2000; Good & Whang, 2002; McVarish & Solloway, 2002). Reflective teachers ask questions, consider evidence, and search for ideas that they can use to help their students succeed. We suggest keeping a Reflective Journal. Throughout the text, we make suggestions for the kinds of entries you might consider, and in the final chapter, we describe how you might set up this journal.

SPECIAL FEATURES OF THIS BOOK

This book has several distinctive features that are intended to be used in rather specialized ways: Key Points, Revealing and Challenging Assumptions, Suggestions for Teaching, Take a Stand!, Case in Print, TeachSource Video Cases, Pause and Reflect questions, Journal Entries, and Resources for Further Investigation. At least one section of every chapter is devoted to discussing applications of technology to teaching, and numerous references are made throughout the book to websites related to teaching and learning. In addition, your compilation of a separate component to accompany this book—the Reflective Journal—is recommended. This journal makes use of the text's Journal Entries and the Suggestions for Teaching.

The Education CourseMate website includes additional study aids, such as Thought Questions and Glossary Flashcards for glossary terms.

Key Points

At the beginning of each chapter, you will find a list of *Key Points*. The Key Points also appear within the body of the chapter, printed in the margins. These points have been selected to help you learn and remember sections of each chapter that are of special significance to teachers. (These sections may be stressed on exams, but they were originally selected because they are important, not because they can serve as the basis for test items.) To grasp the nature of the Key Points, turn back to the opening page of this chapter, which lists points stressed under the chapter's major headings. Then flip through the chapter to see how the appearance of the Key Points in the margins calls attention to significant sections of the text.

Revealing and Challenging Assumptions

Teaching is complex. It combines art and science. It demands spur-of-the moment decision making and thoughtful reflection. What we do as teachers affects futures, and so we try to do what we believe is the right thing (Moss, 2000, 2001; Moss & Shank, 2002). As we have seen (in the case of grade retention, for example), what is assumed to be the right decision is not always supported by scientific evidence. Allowing our actions to be governed by beliefs we assume to be true is characteristic of everyone, but it is especially characteristic of aspiring teachers. Aspiring teachers hold beliefs about teaching and learning, and those beliefs tend to be resistant to change (Brookhart & Freeman, 1992). However, there is evidence to suggest that those who aspire to teach can benefit from opportunities to reflect on their assumptions about teaching and learning (Bean & Stevens, 2002; Murphy, Delli, & Edwards, 2004; Stuart & Thurlow, 2000). For these reasons, the opening section of each chapter presents a conversation that reveals assumptions that aspiring teachers often hold. This conversation, followed by an opportunity to *pause and reflect*, is called *Revealing Assumptions*. At the end of each chapter—in a section called *Challenging Assumptions*—the conversation continues but with a shift that challenges the earlier assumptions in light of key concepts in the chapter.

The conversations that reveal and challenge assumptions occur among the same four characters throughout the book. *Don* is an aspiring teacher who anticipates teaching children in either elementary or early childhood classrooms; he wants to bring, in his words, "the joy of reading" to every child he teaches. *Celeste*, also an aspiring teacher, wants to teach science in a middle or high school so that she can be a "role model for young women." *Antonio*, a first-year teacher, is part of an interdisciplinary team in a middle school and is encountering the real world of teaching. *Connie* is a master teacher who, in the course of her long career, has earned certification from the National Board for Professional Teaching Standards, numerous teaching awards, and her doctorate in education. Connie has retired from the classroom and is a university supervisor of field observation experiences (including those of Don and Celeste). She is also a member of Antonio's induction team, a group of expert educators who mentor Antonio in his first year of teaching. These *Revealing Assumptions* and *Challenging Assumptions* offer a glimpse into the thinking of two aspiring teachers, a novice teacher, and a master teacher.

Suggestions for Teaching

In most of the chapters, you will find summaries of research that serve as the basis for related principles or conclusions. These sets of principles or conclusions are the foundation for *Suggestions for Teaching*. Suggestions are usually followed by examples illustrating how they might be applied. In most cases, examples are provided for both elementary and secondary grades because there usually are differences in the way a principle might be applied in dealing with younger and with older students.

There are two reasons why we emphasize concrete suggestions for teaching as well as theory and research. First, many research articles and textbooks provide only vague guidelines for classroom use and no concrete examples. But when new research-based ideas are presented in a concrete and usable form, teachers are much more likely to try them out (Gersten & Brengelman, 1996). Second, many beginning teachers, particularly middle school and high school teachers, criticize their training for overemphasizing theory at the expense of how to deal with the everyday demands of classroom life (National Comprehensive Center for Teacher Quality & Public Agenda, 2008a). But as useful as our suggestions might be, you cannot, as we argued earlier, use them as prescriptions. Every school building and every group of students is different. You have to learn how to adapt the suggestions in this book and any other books that you will read to the particular dynamics of each class. This is the essence of being a reflective teacher.

Take a Stand!

At the textbook's website, Education CourseMate, the Take a Stand! section can help you develop your own positions on major issues.

Earlier in this chapter we discussed why the scientific study of behavior and thought processes in a classroom setting is a complex undertaking. Such factors as the limited focus of research, the complexity of teaching and learning, and the revision of ideas due to new findings make it difficult at times to draw definitive conclusions about why students behave as they do and how teachers might respond. But there are other instances when the evidence is sufficiently deep and consistent, or the logic so compelling, that we feel confident taking a stand on an issue and believe you can as well, be it publicly or privately.

For each of the following chapters, we identify one of these instances with the *Take a Stand!* label, and we state our beliefs succinctly. You may, of course, disagree with our conclusion and decide to take either no stand or a different stand. That's fine, and we commend you for being an independent and critical thinker so long as your decision is based on additional evidence and logical thinking.

At the student website, one section is devoted to the issues highlighted in the Take a Stand! features. Here, you can find additional material related to these important topics. We invite you to take advantage of this resource, because exploring a controversial issue is a good way to both broaden and sharpen your thinking.

Case in Print

This feature in each chapter presents a recent article that either elaborates on an idea or technique described in the chapter or shows how public school educators have applied an idea. The focus is on real-life settings in which you can see the practical effect of ideas you read about in the text.

TeachSource Video Cases

In each chapter you will find one or two (sometimes more) Video Cases. Available at the *Education CourseMate* student website, each "case" is a four- to six-minute module consisting of video and audio files presenting actual classroom scenarios that depict the complex problems and opportunities teachers face every day. The video and audio clips are accompanied by "artifacts" to provide background information and allow you to experience true classroom dilemmas in their multiple dimensions. After each Video Case, you are asked to reflect on questions related to the chapter.

Emphasis on the Role of Technology in Learning and Instruction

Throughout this book, we discuss the role of technology in relation to all the major aspects of learning and instruction. In addition, the *Education CourseMate* website that accompanies this book provides many technology-oriented resources as well as other useful material for developing your skills as a teacher.

When we use the term *technology*, we are referring to devices that extend and amplify people's ability to store, transform, retrieve, and communicate information. Although this broad definition encompasses a wide array of devices (such as calculators, slide and movie projectors, videocassette and audiotape recorders, videodisc players, and computers), our focus will be largely on computers because of their widespread use and potential to transform teaching and learning.

There is no doubt about the computer's ability to help students and teachers analyze, sort, transform, and present information in a variety of formats or about the ability of the Internet to connect students to other individuals and information sources. But we urge you to remember that, as with all other mediums and methods of instruction that we will discuss in subsequent chapters, technology-based instruction is not an all-purpose solution for increasing achievement. Learning and teaching are extremely complex processes and all technologies are subject to limitations.

As you examine the technology resources and ideas mentioned in this book, you should be thinking about the ways in which they might enhance the learning environment of your own classroom. To help you do this, we encourage you to examine the National Educational Technology Standards for students, teachers, and administrators that have been proposed by the International Society for Technology in Education (**www.iste.org**).

Go to the textbook's Education CourseMate website for links to important web pages.

Pause and Reflect

As you have seen several times in this chapter, from time to time we pose a question that invites you to think about issues raised in the text and how you will handle them in your own teaching. You can use these questions either for personal reflection or for discussion with classmates and practicing teachers.

TeachSource Video Case ◀◀ ▶ ▶▶

An Expanded Definition of Literacy: Meaningful Ways to Use Technology

Go to the Education CourseMate website to watch the Video Case, and then answer the following questions:

1. Describe a few specific examples from the Video Case that illustrate meaningful ways to use technology.

2. Can you provide examples of a few different kinds of technologies from the Video Case that match the technology standards on the ISTE website?

Journal Entries

Within the margins of each chapter, you will find numerous instances of the phrase *Journal Entry*. These marginal headings are related to the material just opposite in the text. They are intended to serve as suggested wordings for the headings of pages in a Reflective Journal that we strongly encourage you to keep. In the final chapter, we describe the beneficial effects of reflection and journal writing on teaching, and we describe how you can use the suggested Journal Entries to organize your first Reflective Journal. If you do not have time to begin your journal while taking the course, we hope you will go through the book a second time, after you finish this course, for the purpose of developing a custom-designed journal.

You can find additional Reflective Journal questions at the Education CourseMate website.

Resources for Further Investigation

Despite this book's effort to provide at least partial solutions to the most common difficulties that teachers face, you are bound, sooner or later, to become aware of problems that are not discussed in these pages. You may want additional data on some aspects of teaching, either while you are taking this course or afterward. For this reason, we provide an annotated bibliography at the end of each chapter. *Resources for Further Investigation* lists articles, books, and Internet sources you might consult.

For additional online resources keyed to each chapter, use the textbook's student website, Education CourseMate.

Two important points should be mentioned regarding Internet sources of information. First, all the databases and resources listed or described throughout this book have been checked for accuracy as of the book's publication date. The world of online information, however, is in constant flux: databases are updated, moved, renamed, or deleted from the Internet network every day. If you are unable to find one of the resources mentioned, we recommend that you consult your school's computer support person or your colleagues (because the most current information is often passed by word of mouth), or try to find a similar reputable site by using a search engine.

HOW THIS BOOK WILL HELP PREPARE YOU TO MEET INSTRUCTIONAL STANDARDS

We live in an age of standards and accountability, particularly in education. Just as students, teachers, and administrators are held accountable for students' meeting various learning standards, prospective and beginning teachers are increasingly expected to demonstrate that they have met a set of knowledge standards that are believed to be the foundation of high-quality instruction. Among the standards that govern the preparation and licensing of teachers, two that are particularly prominent are the Praxis II, a standardized test, and a set of ten instructional principles and related standards called the INTASC (Interstate New Teacher Assessment and Support Consortium) standards. In this section, we briefly discuss the content of the Praxis II and the INTASC standards and show you how *Psychology Applied to Teaching* will help prepare you to meet the standards.

Praxis II and *Psychology Applied to Teaching*

As part of recent educational reform efforts, many state boards of education and teacher education programs require that as a condition for licensure, beginning teachers demonstrate that they are knowledgeable about the psychological and educational factors that are likely to affect how well their students will perform in the classroom. A popular instrument used for this purpose is the Praxis II, published by the Educational Testing Service (ETS). The Principles of Learning and Teaching section of the Praxis II assesses a beginning teacher's knowledge of topics that are typically covered in an educational psychology course.

Because *Psychology Applied to Teaching* (PAT) is closely aligned with the Principles of Teaching and Learning section of the Praxis II and emphasizes classroom applications, we believe PAT will help prepare you to do well on this important assessment. On this book's front endpapers, you will find a table that lists the topics and subtopics covered by the Principles of Learning and Teaching test, along with the chapter numbers and pages in PAT where discussions of these topics can be found. Although the publisher of the Praxis II, Educational Testing Service, offers separate sets of principles for grades K–6 and 7–12 (**www.ets.org/Media/Tests/PRAXIS/taag/0522/topics_2.htm** and **www.ets.org/Media/Tests/PRAXIS/taag/0524/topics_1.htm**, respectively), they are largely identical.

To review this chapter's content and help yourself prepare for licensing exams, see the tutorial quizzes and other study aids on the Education CourseMate website.

INTASC and *Psychology Applied to Teaching*

In the early 1990s, the Interstate New Teacher Assessment and Support Consortium (INTASC) published a set of 10 instructional principles and related standards to guide the preparation of beginning teachers. These principles and standards represent the core knowledge, dispositions, and skills that INTASC believes are essential for all beginning teachers, regardless of their specialty or grade level. The INTASC standards are also designed to be compatible with the certification program for highly skilled veteran teachers developed by the National Board for Professional Teaching Standards.

An important part of the philosophy behind the INTASC standards is the belief that well-trained teachers have the knowledge, dispositions, and skills to help all students achieve at acceptable levels. That notion has also been a major part of the philosophy of *Psychology Applied to Teaching*. To help you see how the content of *Psychology Applied to Teaching* corresponds to the INTASC knowledge standards, we have included a correlation table on the book's back endpapers.

Summary

1. Educational psychology is a scientific discipline that seeks to understand and improve how students learn from instruction in classroom settings.

2. Learning about the research findings and principles of educational psychology can help you be a better teacher because (1) teaching is complex work that requires a wide range of knowledge and skills, (2) the research literature contains numerous useful ideas for improving your instruction, and (3) teachers who have had professional training are often more effective than those who have not had such training.

3. Unsystematic observations of students may lead teachers to draw false conclusions because of limited cases, unrecognized or unusual factors, and a tendency to ignore contrary evidence. As an example, although scientific evidence does not support the practice of grade retention, it remains popular among teachers, parents, and educational policymakers, partly because of unsystematic observations about its effectiveness.

4. Scientifically gathered evidence is more trustworthy than casual observation because it involves sampling, control, objectivity, publication, and replication.

5. The scientific study of education is complicated by the limited focus of research, debates about which type of research is most useful, the complexity of teaching and learning, the inability of researchers to keep up with all published research, different interpretations of findings, and the ongoing accumulation of new knowledge.

6. Research on teaching and learning provides a systematic, objective basis for making instructional decisions, but it cannot specify how to handle every classroom situation. Many classroom decisions must be made on the spot. This contrast represents the science and the art of teaching.

7. Those who argue that teaching is an art point to communication of emotions, values and beliefs, and flexibility as qualities that good teachers must possess but are not easily taught. In contrast, other scholars contend that there is a scientific basis for teaching that can be learned.

8. Good teachers strike a balance between the art and the science of teaching.

9. Reflective teachers constantly think about such issues as the goals they are trying to achieve, the types of teaching methods they use and how effective those methods are, and the extent to which their methods and goals are supported by scientific evidence.

Resources for Further Investigation

● The Art and Science of Teaching

Louis J. Rubin examines teaching as art and teaching as theater in *Artistry in Teaching* (1985). Two more recent books elaborate on the concept of acting as theater. One is *Acting Lessons for Teachers: Using Performance Skills in the Classroom* (2nd ed., 2007), by Robert Tauber and Cathy Sargent Mester. Don't overlook that book's Appendix II, which contains testimonials from nineteen award-winning K–12 teachers and college professors about the value of acting skills in the classroom. The other book, *Unscripted Learning: Using Improv Activities Across the K–8 Curriculum*, by Carrie Lobman and Matthew Lundquist, describes how both students and teachers can use improvisational activities to enhance teaching and learning. In Chapter 1 of *Researching the Art of Teaching: Ethnography for Educational Use* (1996), Peter Woods summarizes the various arguments that have been made for teaching as an art, as a science, and as an activity that combines art and science.

To learn about the scientific knowledge base that underlies teaching, you might want to look at *Putting Research to Work in Your School* (1996), by David Berliner and Ursula Casanova. In each of six sections (teaching, instructional strategies, learning, motivation, school and society, and testing), they point out how a research study has shed light on such relevant issues as how to make cross-age tutoring work, teaching memory skills to students, and motivating students through project-based learning. A similar book is *Classroom Instruction That Works: Research-Based Strategies for Increasing Student Achievement* (2005), by Robert Marzano, Debra Pickering, and Jane Pollock. Lastly, take a look at Chapter 6 of *The Scientific Basis of Educational Productivity* (2006), edited by Rena Subotnik and Herbert Walberg. Titled "Improving Educational Productivity: An Assessment of Extant Research," and written by Walberg, the chapter describes nine factors that make major contributions to learning and several instructional tactics that reliably produce gains in achievement.

● Reflective Teaching

Several books explain what it means to be a reflective teacher and describe the benefits that this approach to teaching can produce. The briefest of these books, at seventy-eight pages, is *Reflective Teaching: An Introduction* (1996), by Kenneth M. Zeichner and Daniel P. Liston. Other books you might consult are *Teaching in K-12 Schools: A Reflective Action Approach* (4th ed., 2006), by Judy Eby, Adrienne Herrell, and Michael Jordan; *Reflective Teaching: Evidence-Informed Professional Practice* (3rd ed., 2008), by

Andrew Pollard and Julie Anderson; *Reflective Teaching: Professional Artistry Through Inquiry* (3rd ed., 2001), by James Henderson; and *At the Heart of Teaching: A Guide to Reflective Practice* (2003), edited by Grace Hall McEntee, et al.

● Technology, Teaching, and Learning

As we mentioned earlier in the chapter, computer-based technology has become an integral part of the classroom experience of students and teachers. If you want to strengthen your knowledge of how this technology can be used, we suggest that you examine *Integrating Technology into Teaching: The Teaching and Learning Continuum* (2008), by Arthur Recesso and Chandra Orrill, and *Technology Integration for Meaningful Classroom Use: A Standards-Based Approach* (2010), by Katherine Cennamo, John Ross, and Peggy Ertmer.

2

Theories of Psychosocial and Cognitive Development

The Education CourseMate website for this text offers many helpful resources. Go to **CengageBrain.com** to preview this chapter's Concept Maps and Chapter Themes.

KEY POINTS

These key points will help you learn the important information in this chapter. To help you study, they also appear in the margins of the pages, next to the text where they are discussed.

Erikson: Psychosocial Development

- Erikson's theory encompasses the life span, highlights the role of the person and culture in development
- Personality development based on epigenetic principle
- Personality grows out of successful resolution of psychosocial crises
- 2 to 3 years: autonomy vs. shame and doubt
- 4 to 5 years: initiative vs. guilt
- 6 to 11 years: industry vs. inferiority
- 12 to 18 years: identity vs. role confusion
- Role confusion: uncertainty as to what behaviors others will react to favorably
- Students' sense of industry hampered by unhealthy competition for grades
- Identity: accepting one's body, having goals, getting recognition
- Psychosocial moratorium delays commitment
- Adolescents exhibit a particular process, called an identity status, for establishing an identity
- Individuals in identity diffusion avoid thinking about jobs, roles, values
- Individuals in foreclosure unquestioningly endorse parents' goals and values
- Individuals in moratorium uncertain about identity
- Individuals who have reached identity achievement status have made their own commitments
- Criticisms of Erikson's theory: based largely on personal experience, not applicable to many cultures, gender-biased

Piaget: Cognitive Development

- Organization: tendency to systematize processes
- Adaptation: tendency to adjust to environment
- Scheme: organized pattern of behavior or thought
- Assimilation: new experience is fitted into existing scheme

- Accommodation: scheme is created or revised to fit new experience
- Equilibration: tendency to organize schemes to allow better understanding of experiences
- Sensorimotor stage: schemes reflect sensory and motor experiences
- Preoperational stage: child forms many new schemes but does not think logically
- Perceptual centration, irreversibility, egocentrism: barriers to logical thought
- Egocentrism: assumption that others see things the same way
- Concrete operational stage: child is capable of mentally reversing actions but generalizes only from concrete experiences
- Formal operational stage: child is able to deal with abstractions, form hypotheses, engage in mental manipulations
- Adolescent egocentrism: adolescents preoccupied with their own view of the world and how they appear to others
- Piaget: cognitive development more strongly influenced by peers than by adults
- Instruction can accelerate development of schemes that have begun to form
- Piaget's theory underestimates children's abilities
- Most adolescents are not formal operational thinkers
- Sequence of stages uniform across cultures but rate of development varies

Vygotsky: Cognitive Development

- How we think influenced by current social forces and historical cultural forces
- Psychological tools aid and change thought processes
- Cognitive development strongly influenced by those more intellectually advanced
- Teachers should help students learn how to use psychological tools
- Cognitive development promoted by instruction in zone of proximal development
- Scaffolding techniques support student learning

Using Technology to Promote Cognitive Development

- Virtual learning environments can introduce disequilibrium, promote exploration and visual representations of abstract ideas, and help students construct knowledge
- Technology can act as and provide expert collaborative partners

Piaget, Kohlberg, and Gilligan: Moral Development

- Morality of constraint (moral realism): rules are sacred, consequences determine guilt
- Morality of cooperation (moral relativism): rules are flexible, intent important in determining guilt

- Preconventional morality: avoid punishment, receive benefits in return
- Conventional morality: impress others, respect authority
- Postconventional morality: mutual agreements, consistent principles
- Criticisms of Kohlberg's theory: moral development difficult to accelerate, moral dilemmas not relevant to daily life, relies on macromoral issues, ignores characteristics other than moral reasoning
- Although slight differences do exist, both males and females use both caring and justice orientations to resolve real-life moral dilemmas
- Moral knowledge does not always result in moral behavior

I n the opening chapter, we pointed out that individuals vary in how they perceive and think about the world around them. This commonplace observation implies that you need to be aware of the major ways in which students differ from one another to design potentially effective lessons. What may work well for one part of your class may not work quite so well for another part. The lesson that was a huge success with last year's class may be a disaster with this year's group if you fail to take into account critical differences between the two classes. The five chapters in Part I introduce you to how students may differ from one another in psychosocial development, cognitive development, age, mental ability, thinking style, achievement, ethnic background, and social class. You will also discover how those differences affect classroom learning.

Human development is a complex topic to discuss: in addition to analyzing many different forms of behavior, we must trace the way each type of behavior changes as a child matures. Authors of books on development have adopted different strategies for coping with this challenge. Some have described theories that outline stages in the emergence of particular forms of behavior. Others have summarized significant types of behavior at successive age levels. Still others have examined specific types of behavior, noting age changes for every topic. Each approach has advantages and disadvantages.

Developmental theories call attention to the overall sequence, continuity, and interrelatedness of aspects of development, but they typically account for only limited facets of behavior. Texts organized in terms of age levels make readers aware of varied aspects of children's behavior at a given age but sometimes tend to obscure how particular types of behavior emerge and change. And although texts organized according to types of behavior do not have the limitation of the age-level approach, they may make it difficult for the reader to grasp the overall pattern of behavior at a particular stage of development.

In an effort to profit from the advantages and to minimize the disadvantages of each approach, this chapter and the next present discussions of development that combine all three. This chapter focuses on Erik Erikson's psychosocial stages, Jean Piaget's cognitive stages, and Lev Vygotsky's views on the role of social interaction. It also describes Piaget's ideas about moral development, Lawrence Kohlberg's extension of Piaget's work, and Carol Gilligan's criticism and modification of Kohlberg's theory. The next chapter describes age-level characteristics of students at five levels: preschool, primary school, elementary school, middle school, and high school. Discussion at each age level focuses on four types of behavior: physical, social, emotional, and cognitive. The information in these chapters will help you adapt teaching techniques to the students who are in the age range that you expect to teach, as well as develop expectations of student behavior across age ranges. The patterns of behavior described in these chapters are ones that typical children and adolescents exhibit.

The following three chapters are devoted to individual differences and how to deal with them. Chapter 4, "Understanding Student Differences," discusses the nature of variability and how students vary with respect to gender, mental ability, and cognitive style. Chapter 5, "Addressing Cultural and Socioeconomic Diversity," the characteristics of students from different ethnic and social class backgrounds. And Chapter 6, "Accommodating Student Variability," describes types of students who vary from their classmates to such an extent that they may require special kinds of education.

Teaching Students to Ask Questions Instead of Answering Them

by Matthew H. Bowker

Philosophers, cognitive scientists, anthropologists, and psychologists have argued convincingly that the act of questioning is central to thinking, to storing and communicating knowledge, even to several important types of social interaction.[1] But while scholars of higher education have written extensively on the topic of questioning for more than a century, they have focused on how teachers ask questions and how students answer them, largely neglecting to consider that helping students develop their own questioning skills might be a valuable pedagogical objective in itself. In my teaching, I practice a question-centered pedagogy that is different from the Socratic, critical, and problem-based approaches found in many college courses. I have found that requiring students to create their own questions about course material helps them understand how the answers we have come to accept are connected, contingent, and contextual, how they rely on, imply, and beg additional questions. In this question-centered pedagogy, the questions themselves are the answers.

When Marshall McLuhan wrote that "the problem today isn't that we don't have the answers, but that we don't have the questions," he meant that our capacity to generate answers is often less important than our ability to interrogate the answers we already have, especially as they change, falter, or overlap.[2] The flaw in most Socratic, critical, and problem-based approaches is that the teacher retains control of the inquiry. Students are asked to generate answers in accordance with their roles as naïve interlocutors, while the teacher plays Socrates. When the teacher is the one who constructs the most interesting questions, problems, or critical challenges, students become dependent upon the teacher to catalyze inquiry. On the other hand, a question-centered pedagogy proposes that these question-posing, problem-making functions be carefully handed over to students, so that students engage the course material as independent thinkers.

Teachers may object to this pedagogy, fearing that teaching questions instead of answers somehow impoverishes students. But we should recognize that teaching answers without questions deprives students of crucial learning experiences while inculcating a dangerous ideology. Imagine students of American history who have been taught only answers—perhaps several thousand historical facts. These students of "the pedagogy of the answer" would be incapable of generating interesting hypotheses, inferences, or questions about American history.[3] Not only would they lack practice and confidence in the arts of hypothesizing, inferring, and questioning; worse, they would be likely to see history as little more than a set of facts, a domain where things were what they were and are what they are, much as a favorite saying of contemporary Americans goes: "It is what it is." Learning answers without learning questions produces a kind of ideology in which everything is already settled, in which contingencies appear as necessities, in which social constructs appear as natural inevitabilities, in which everything "is what it is" and nothing more or less.

Convinced that such a state of affairs must be avoided, I have for several years practiced a question-centered approach to teaching whose *primary* objective is to improve students' ability to ask insightful questions about course material. Such an approach does not trivialize answers, but uses answers as stepping-stones from question to question. Nor does a question-centered approach demand that I continually question students; in fact, it is possible to teach a question-centered course without posing any questions to students, as long as the teacher's declarations entice students to

ALEXAND. IIII(

ask progressively better questions. In fact, several studies have shown that students demonstrate greater thought-complexity, initiative, and engagement when teachers do not ask questions but, instead, state propositions or offer non-question alternatives.[4]

To understand more about what a question-centered pedagogy entails, it is necessary to think a bit about what a question really is. The British philosopher R.G. Collingwood's definition of the act of questioning as "essentially a suspension of the activity of asserting" is succinct and to the point.[5] While a question demands that we make certain presuppositions, it

Questions are designed to probe, to find something that is not already there, to discover relationships and possibilities that are not given.

also requires that we cease to assert others. Even to ask a simple question like "What is this?" means that we have refrained, at least momentarily, from asserting, "This is such and such."

An important requisite of asking questions is the ability to abstract from things, to unlock their properties, histories, meanings, causes, correlates, or consequences from the web of givenness that would otherwise make them impenetrable. If I notice a tree, I may admire the tree, or even chop down the tree, without much thought. But if I ask myself why the tree is here, I must imagine the tree not being here, or the tree being over there, or some likely causes of the tree, or some of the scenarios in which those causes were not present. In questioning the tree, I unlock the tree from its place in my experience and open up possibilities of no trees, trees elsewhere, different trees, trees across time, and so on.

All this means that questioning involves speculating about possibilities both real and unreal, given and hypothetical. To question is an immensely creative act because questioning requires that an object be not *just as it is*. If every object were just as it is, then questions would serve no purpose, for the only answer we could give would be to point at the object and say, "But here is your answer." On the contrary, questions are designed to probe, to find something that is *not* already there, to discover relationships and possibilities that are not given.

Therefore, to believe that all students can spontaneously generate great questions is perhaps even more naïve than believing that all students can spontaneously develop great answers. Rather, the difficult and creative work of questioning requires sustained practice and guidance: "Purposeful

inquiry does not happen spontaneously—it must be learned."[6] In the classroom, questioning must be nurtured, questions must keep apace with answers, and both questions and answers must be appropriate to the levels of experience, familiarity, and cognitive functioning of the inquirers. If questions are not taught but merely demanded, if answers are not offered to transition students from question to question, or if the level of question and answer is inappropriate to students, then resistance, frustration, and even hostility to questioning may ensue.

The most basic requirement for a successful question-centered pedagogy is the rediscovery of enjoyment, meaning, and value in questions.

My suspicion is that many of us have had negative experiences with questions, painful experiences of annoyance, frustration, and anxiety. The most basic requirement for a successful question-centered pedagogy, therefore, is the rediscovery of enjoyment, meaning, and value in questions. Of course, this is easier said than done, for most teachers and students have built up defenses against the discomforts of questioning. One common defense is an insistence upon absolute objectivity: "Every question has a certain answer. Either we can find this answer or we can declare the question unknowable and move on." This argument may be proffered by the surprising number of students and teachers who adhere to the "banking concept" of education: the idea that the purpose of education is to store up definitive answers in one's mind as in a bank vault.[7] Indeed, teachers often resist question-centered approaches, claiming they are too nebulous, too uncertain, that students will gain no "real" knowledge at the end of the day.

Likewise, students new to undergraduate research often appear to be uncomfortable asking questions whose answers are not objective, "bankable," and easily located in a textbook or on the Internet. The preliminary research questions students submit to me are often of the following type: "When did steroids become a problem in major league sports?" or "Are more Americans depressed today than in the past?" When I explain that they need to create more analytical, reflective, and open-ended questions, they protest: "How am I supposed to write 20 pages on a question I don't know the answer to?" The underlying problem here is not only a lack of confidence in generating questions and answers, but a belief that questions are nothing more than provocations, test items, or evidence of one's ignorance of "the facts."

A different source of resistance—opinion-oriented relativism—tells us everything is a matter of opinion. What is the point of asking questions, one asks, if every answer is relative? This prejudice looks a bit like the democratic tolerance that institutions of higher education rightly strive to instill. But reducing all ideas to matters of personal opinion is a form of hyper-individualization, a product of cultural narcissism, and even a step toward nihilism. If I am locked in my perspective and you are locked in yours, we can't communicate; a seemingly benign tolerance here becomes a curious mix of radical relativism and fundamentalism.

> *Reducing ideas to matters of personal opinion is a form of hyper-individualization, a product of cultural narcissism, and a step toward nihilism.*

For a question-centered approach to succeed, such resistances to questioning must be overcome. We should start by admitting that questions without definitive answers *can* be frustrating for teachers and students alike. We should also remember that teaching questions does not exclude the teaching of answers. On the contrary, students must have access to a great many answers in order to devise a single educated question. The difference between question-centered and answer-centered approaches is a structural one, a matter of making the questions the milestones of conversation, while tentative answers guide students from question to question. As I inform my students on the first day of class, "We start with answers and end up with questions." This means we begin the semester (and each class day) with some answers we thought we knew, but the discussion prompts students to generate questions that complicate those answers. We leave the classroom with more substantial questions than we had when we started. This notion often elicits laughter from students, but it is the sincere promise of a question-centered pedagogy.

The multiplication and progression of questions in a question-centered approach demands of both student and teacher a real tolerance for ambiguity. To sustain this tolerance requires a delicate touch. Careless questions, pushing students to frustration, or simply repeating "Why?" make questioning into something maddening, even frightening. The teacher-student relationship must be caring, equitable, and responsive. The classroom environment must be free, but not too free; safe, but not too safe. The tone may be playful and creative, but the classroom needs enough regularity that chaos is controlled, so students can think, converse, listen, and question without feeling either lost or crushed.

PRIOR KNOWLEDGE

In several respects, the teacher must create something that resembles what the British psychoanalyst D.W. Winnicott called a "holding environment," a space where students feel secure enough and free enough to question.[8] Winnicott used the term "holding environment" to describe the setting a parent establishes for an infant who, from a state of utter dependence, gradually learns to interact independently with the world. As in the parental holding environment, the teaching environment must begin with a reassurance that the students will not be abandoned, forgotten, or embarrassed by the teacher or other students. From this security arises students'

The teaching environment must reassure students that they will not be abandoned, forgotten, or embarrassed by the teacher or other students.

OPTIMAL ANXIETY...

ability to tolerate the frustrations and anxieties associated with not having all questions answered.

Applying a parental metaphor to the teacher-student relationship might seem paternalistic (or maternalistic), patronizing, or insulting to students, but what is involved is very different from paternalism in the usual sense. The purpose of a holding environment is not, of course, to "hold" students close or to "hold" them to dependence upon the teacher. Quite the opposite. The holding environment "holds" class members and course content together by "holding" anxieties, frustrations, and conflicts in check so that students can creatively explore new and potentially dangerous questions without getting lost or hurt.

MASLOW

The wonderful paradox of "holding" is that, if it is done with respect for students, it represents a kind of liberation whereas both authoritarian environments and "anything goes" environments are types of imprisonment. The teacher who "stays on top of students," who allows little independent questioning, or who "squeezes" work out of students may produce students who have assimilated the material, but not students who have critically learned. Likewise, the teacher who "lets students go" in their questioning, who "drops" them into discussion as in a freefall, without guidance or assistance, is creating chaos. Against this chaos, students will be required to call up their own defenses to protect themselves. Although for different reasons, both the authoritarian classroom and the laissez-faire classroom are likely to make student questioning seem destructive, combative, or pointless.

PRIMING

OUCH

Because teachers of questions must help students avoid becoming lost or hurt, it is crucial that the teacher be comfortable with questioning. If a teacher dreads students' questions, or dreads the idea of being unable to

answer them, then the teacher is likely to shut down the questioning environment in favor of greater security. The absolute knowledge that many teachers aspire to possess, that enlightened state in which every question receives a perfect answer, is actually *not* conducive to teaching questions because it deprives students of the need to explore on their own. Part of the student's freedom in questioning derives from the open space created by the teacher's failure to provide final answers. In this open space, the student may explore a question more independently, trying out and revising successive answers.

If students struggle with this process (and some do), I have found it important to have frequent, frank conversations where I explain that the course is ultimately concerned with a set of problems to which we have several answers, but not *the* answer. I explain that we don't have to figure out the answers alone, and we probably won't figure out *the* answer at all, but we do have to puzzle with the issues by asking smart questions. Such conversations seem to relieve many students' anxieties, but not all, and not completely.

Finally, I have found it extremely important to learn to practice silence in class. This means being comfortable with one or two minutes of silence, if necessary, while the conversation stalls. If the teacher is always ready to comment or ask a provocative question, then students do not have the room (or the need) to take on those responsibilities. Often, after a long silence, students will pose the question that has left them feeling stuck with the material. Sometimes that question is simply, "Who cares?" which I take to be a crucially important question, one I explore as often as possible. Perhaps this simple question reminds us of a final benefit of the question-centered approach: that by posing questions *they* want answered, students learn to invest themselves more fully and to care more deeply about the bodies of knowledge they interrogate. nea

ENDNOTES

Note: In developing my theory and practice of teaching, I have been fortunate to know the example of my teacher and friend, C. Fred Alford.

1.   See Dillon, *The Practice of Questioning.*

2.   Quoted in Berson et al., *Social Studies on the Internet.*

3.   Freire and Faundez. *Learning to Question: A Pedagogy of Liberation.*

4.   Dillon, *The Practice of Questioning.*

5.   Quoted in Somerville, "Collingwood's Logic of Question and Answer."

6.   Baird, "Metacognition, Purposeful Inquiry and Conceptual Change."

7.   Freire, *Pedagogy of the Oppressed.*

8.   Winnicott, *Through Paediatrics to Psycho-Analysis.*

WORKS CITED

Bain, K. *What the Best College Teachers Do*. Cambridge: Harvard University Press, 2004.

Baird, J.R. "Metacognition, Purposeful Inquiry and Conceptual Change." In *The Student Laboratory and the Science Curriculum*, edited by E. Hegarty-Hazel, 183–200. London: Routledge, 1990.

Berson, M.J., B.C. Cruz, J.A. Duplass, and H, Johnston. *Social Studies on the Internet*. 2nd Edition. Englewood Cliffs, N.J.: Prentice Hall.

Dillon, J.T. "The Multidisciplinary Study of Questioning." *Journal of Educational Psychology* 74, no. 2 (1982): 147-165.

Dillon, J.T. *The Practice of Questioning*. London and New York: Routledge, 1990.

Hyman, R. T. *Strategic Questioning*. Englewood Cliffs, N.J.: Prentice-Hall, 1979.

Fitch, J.G. *The Art of Questioning*. Chicago: Flanagan, 1879.

Freire, P. *Pedagogy of the Oppressed*, translated by M.B. Ramos. New York: Continuum, 1970.

Freire, P. and A. Faundez. *Learning to Question: A Pedagogy of Liberation*. New York: Continuum, 1989.

Somerville, J. "Collingwood's Logic of Question and Answer." *Monist* 72, no. 4 (1989): 526-541.

Winnicott, D.W. *Through Paediatrics to Psycho-Analysis*. New York: Basic Books, 1975.

Matthew H. Bowker *is visiting assistant professor of interdisciplinary studies at Medaille College in Buffalo, New York, where he teaches courses in political science, philosophy, critical thinking, and undergraduate research and writing. He holds a Ph.D. and M.A. in political philosophy from the University of Maryland, College Park, and a B.A. in political science from Columbia University. Bowker's current research explores the psychosocial dimensions of absurd literature and philosophy. He welcomes correspondence at mhb34@medaille.edu.*

[Handwritten notes:]

PRELUDE. COLLEGE TEACHER WR RE:
COLLEGE STUDENTS. MY BIAS— YOU WILL
NEVER BE A GOOD TEAM IF ____.
BASED ON COLLEGE EXP SO FAR, EVAL
BOWKER'S ARG.

① SUMMARY 2-3 MAIN POINTS

② ANALYSIS— 3-4 CLEAR CONNECTIONS
TO BIG IDEAS IN THIS COURSE

③ CONCLUSIONS / RECOMM'S — 2-3
MOST IMP THINGS A COLLEGE PROF
WOULD NEED TO DO --BASED UPON
1 & 2. TO IMPLEMENTS THIS
& WHY

EVAL
AGREE?
DISAG? WHY?

WORKS CITED

Bain, K. What the Best College Teachers Do. Cambridge: Harvard University Press, 2004.

Baird, J.R. "Metacognition, Purposeful Inquiry and Conceptual Change." In The Student Laboratory and the Science Curriculum, edited by E. Hegarty-Hazel, 183-200. London: Routledge, 1990.

Berson, M.J., B.C. Cruz, J.A. Duplass, and H. Johnston. Social Studies on the Internet. 2nd Edition. Englewood Cliffs, N.J.: Prentice Hall.

Dillon, J.T. "The Multidisciplinary Study of Questioning." Journal of Educational Psychology 74, no. 2 (1982): 147-165.

Dillon, J.T. The Practice of Questioning. London and New York: Routledge, 1990.

Hyman, R.T. Strategic Questioning. Englewood Cliffs, N.J.: Prentice-Hall, 1979.

Fitch, J.G. The Art of Questioning. Chicago: Flanagan, 1879.

Freire, P. Pedagogy of the Oppressed, translated by M.B. Ramos. New York: Continuum, 1970.

Freire, P. and A. Faundez. Learning to Question: A Pedagogy of Liberation. New York: Continuum, 1989.

Stroyanville, J. "Collingwood's Logic of Question and Answer." Mind 72, no. 4 (1989): 520-541.

Winnicott, D.W. Through Paediatrics to Psycho-Analysis. New York: Basic Books, 1975.

Matthew H. Bowker is a writing assistant professor of interdisciplinary studies at Medaille College in Buffalo, New York, where he teaches courses in political science, philosophy, critical thinking, and undergraduate research and writing. He holds a Ph.D. and M.A. in political philosophy from the University of Maryland, College Park, and a B.A. in political theory from Columbia University. Bowker's current research explores the psychosocial dimensions of absurd literature and philosophy. He welcomes correspondence at mhb34@medaille.edu.

Revealing Assumptions

What Students Know and *How* Students Know

Connie feels at home. She is in a school, and learning happens here. The secretaries in the school office were all very nice to her when she checked in, even though it is late Friday afternoon. As her staccato footsteps echo through the halls of a school that, 10 minutes ago, were filled with kids heading home for the weekend, she thinks back over her 30 years in schools. "My students learned a lot in those 30 years…and so did I." Her steps quicken. Her newest students are waiting in the room just around the corner, and she is looking forward to the learning they will do together.

"Hi, Doc!" say Don and Celeste. Connie is supervising the class-room observations of their undergraduate teacher education program. After so many years teaching in schools, Connie is enjoying her new teaching role as a university supervisor: facilitating the learning of aspiring teachers like Don and Celeste. She is about to ask them about their week when Antonio walks in and flops into a chair, "What a week. Whew, I'm gonna sleep this weekend!" Antonio is 6 weeks into his first teaching job in a middle school. Connie is one of Antonio's mentors for his first year of teaching—his induction year.

Connie allows a little chatting and then says, "Okay, let's find out what we have learned this week. What did you observe, and what did you infer?" Connie has been encouraging her young colleagues to observe carefully and then reflect with equal care on what they have observed. Her goal is for them to become scholars of their teaching.

Antonio speaks up first. "Last week I talked about our interdisciplinary unit. Our seventh graders are trying to identify a real problem and then come up with a solution to that problem. I was leading a discussion on problem identification this week and had them working in small groups. One group suggested that 'the environment' should be the problem. Another group said 'drugs,' and then a kid yelled out, 'Yeah, and sex and rock and roll too.' It just went downhill from there. We never did identify a problem. I don't think they understand what a problem is."

Connie looked at Don and Celeste. "So what do you infer from Antonio's description of what happened in his class?"

"Well," said Celeste, "maybe the students don't care about society's problems, but I think they simply don't know what the problems are. I've observed some high school classes where the students are really unaware of current events."

Don agreed, offering an account of a conversation with some fourth graders: "They didn't know anything. They had just read about the environment, and I was talking to three of them about global warming. They knew nothing about it, so I spent 10 minutes trying to help them understand what global warming is."

Connie paused and said, "Okay, let's stop there for a minute and reflect on what you saw and what you said. First, what did you actually observe, and based on your observations, what have you inferred? Second, is your inference that students know very little about societal problems correct? Third, are you assuming that teaching is simply a matter of focusing on *what* kids know, or is it also important to understand *how* kids come to know?"

pause & reflect

As we observe students in classrooms, it is natural for us to infer: to explain or characterize what we see. Both our observations and our inferences are influenced by what we believe to be true, by the assumptions we make about the nature of teaching and learning. Many people assume that teaching is simply a matter of adding to *what* kids know. Why do teachers need to understand also *how* kids come to know their world and themselves? Are there other assumptions about the nature of teaching and learning revealed in this vignette? How do you conceive of developmental theory, and what assumptions about teaching and learning underlie your conception? How will you test those assumptions?

ERIKSON: PSYCHOSOCIAL DEVELOPMENT

Of all the developmental theories that we could have chosen to discuss, why did we decide to open this chapter with Erik Erikson's theory of psychosocial development? There are several reasons for this choice:

- Erikson described psychological growth from infancy through old age. Thus, one can draw out instructional implications for every level of education from preschool through adult education.
- Erikson's theory portrays people as playing an active role in their own psychological development through their attempts to understand, organize, and integrate their everyday experiences.
- This theory highlights the important role that cultural goals, aspirations, expectations, requirements, and opportunities play in personal growth, a theme discussed in Chapter 4 (Newman & Newman, 2009).

> Erikson's theory encompasses the life span and highlights the role of the person and culture in development

Basic Principles of Erikson's Theory

> Personality development based on epigenetic principle

Epigenetic Principle Erikson based his description of personality development on the **epigenetic principle**, which states that in fetal development, certain organs of the body appear at certain specified times and eventually "combine" to form a child. Erikson hypothesized that just as the parts of the body develop in interrelated ways in a human fetus, so the personality of an individual forms as the ego progresses through a series of interrelated stages. All of these ego stages exist in some form from the very beginning of life, and each has a critical period of development.

> Personality grows out of successful resolution of psychosocial crises

Psychosocial Crisis In Erikson's view, personality development occurs as one successfully resolves a series of turning points, or psychosocial crises. Although the word *crisis* typically refers to an extraordinary event that threatens well-being, Erikson had a more benign meaning in mind. Crises occur when people feel compelled to adjust to the normal guidelines and expectations that society has for them but are not altogether certain that they are prepared to carry out these demands fully. For example, Western societies expect children of elementary and middle school age to develop a basic sense of industry, mostly through success in school. Adolescents are expected to come to terms with such questions as, "Who am I?" and "Where am I going?" (Newman & Newman, 2009).

As you will see in the next section, Erikson described these crises in terms of opposing qualities that individuals typically develop. For each crisis, there is a desirable quality that can emerge and a corresponding unfavorable characteristic. Erikson did not mean to imply that a healthy individual develops only positive qualities. He emphasized that people are best able to adapt to their world when they possess both the positive and negative qualities of a particular stage, provided the positive quality is significantly stronger than the negative quality. In the first stage, for example, it is important that the child learn trust, but a person who never experienced a bit of mistrust would struggle to understand the world. In Erikson's view, difficulties in development and adjustment arise when the negative quality outweighs the positive for any given stage or when the outcome for most stages is negative (Newman & Newman, 2009).

As you read through the following brief descriptions of the stages of psychosocial development, keep in mind that a positive resolution of the issue for each stage depends on how well the issue of the previous stage was resolved. An adolescent who strongly doubts her own capabilities, for example, may have trouble making the commitments required for identity development in adulthood (Fadjukoff, Pulkkinen, & Kokko, 2005; Marcia, 2002, 2007).

Stages of Psychosocial Development

The following designations, age ranges, and essential characteristics of the stages of personality development are proposed by Erikson in *Childhood and Society* (1963).[1]

Trust Versus Mistrust (Birth to One Year) The basic psychosocial attitude for infants to learn is that they can trust their world. The parents' "consistency, continuity, and sameness of experience" in satisfying the infant's basic needs fosters truth. Such an environment will permit children to think of their world as safe and dependable. Conversely, children whose care is inadequate, inconsistent, or negative will approach the world with fear and suspicion.

2 to 3 years: autonomy vs. shame and doubt

Autonomy Versus Shame and Doubt (Two to Three Years; Preschool) Just when children have learned to trust (or mistrust) their parents, they must exert a degree of independence. If toddlers are permitted and encouraged to do what they are capable of doing at their own pace and in their own way—and with judicious supervision by parents and teachers—they will develop a sense of autonomy (willingness and ability to direct one's behavior). But if parents and teachers are impatient and do too many things for young children or shame young children for unacceptable behavior, these children will develop feelings of self-doubt.

4 to 5 years: initiative vs. guilt

Initiative Versus Guilt (Four to Five Years; Preschool to Kindergarten) The ability to participate in many physical activities and to use language sets the stage for initiative, which "adds to autonomy the quality of undertaking, planning, and 'attacking' a task for the sake of being active and on the move." If four- and five-year-olds are given freedom to explore and experiment and if parents and teachers take time to answer questions, tendencies toward initiative will be encouraged. Conversely, if children of this age are restricted and made to feel that their activities and questions have no point or are a nuisance to adults and older siblings, they will feel guilty about acting on their own.

6 to 11 years: industry vs. inferiority

Industry Versus Inferiority (Six to Eleven Years; Elementary to Middle School) A child entering school is at a point in development when behavior is dominated by intellectual curiosity and performance. "He now learns to win recognition by producing things…He develops a sense of industry." If children at this stage are encouraged to make and do things well, helped to persevere, allowed to finish tasks, and praised for trying, industry results. If the children's efforts are unsuccessful or if they are derided or treated as bothersome, feelings of inferiority result. Children who feel inferior may never learn to enjoy intellectual work and take pride in doing at least one kind of thing really well. At worst, they may believe they will never excel at anything.

12 to 18 years: identity vs. role confusion

Role confusion: uncertainty as to what behaviors others will react to favorably

Identity Versus Role Confusion (Twelve to Eighteen Years; Middle Through High School) The goal at this stage is development of the roles and skills that will prepare adolescents to take a meaningful place in adult society. The danger at this stage is **role confusion**: having no clear conception of appropriate types of behavior that others will react to favorably. If adolescents succeed (as reflected by the reactions of others) in integrating roles in different situations to the point of experiencing continuity in their perception of self, identity develops. In common terms, they know who they are. If they are unable to establish a sense of stability in various aspects of their lives, role confusion results.

Intimacy Versus Isolation (Young Adulthood) To experience satisfying development at this stage, the young adult needs to establish close and committed intimate relationships and partnerships with other people. The hallmark of intimacy is the "ethical strength to abide by such commitments, even though they may call for significant sacrifices and compromises." Failure to do so will lead to a sense of isolation.

---

[1] All quotations in "Stages of Psychosocial Development" are drawn from Chapter 7 of *Childhood and Society*.

Generativity Versus Stagnation (Middle Age) "Generativity…is primarily the concern of establishing and guiding the next generation." Erikson's use of the term *generativity* is purposely broad. It refers, of course, to having children and raising them. In addition, it refers to the productive and creative efforts in which adults take part (e.g., teaching) that have a positive effect on younger generations. Those unable or unwilling to "establish" and "guide" the next generation become victims of stagnation and self-absorption.

Integrity Versus Despair (Old Age) Integrity is "the acceptance of one's one and only life cycle as something that had to be and that, by necessity, permitted of no substitutions…Despair expresses the feeling that the time is now short, too short for the attempt to start another life and to try out alternate roads to integrity."

Of Erikson's eight stages, the two you should pay particular attention to are industry versus inferiority and identity versus role confusion, because they are the primary psychosocial issues that students must resolve during their elementary, middle school, and high school years. If you are committed to helping students learn as much as possible, you need to have a basic understanding of these two stages so that your lesson plans and instructional approaches help students achieve a strong sense of industry and identity. The next two sections briefly describe the major factors that contribute to students' sense of industry and their grasp of who they are and what they might become.

Helping Students Develop a Sense of Industry

Between kindergarten and sixth grade, most children are eager to demonstrate that they can learn new skills and successfully accomplish assigned tasks. One factor that has long been known to have a detrimental effect on one's sense of industry is competition for a limited number of rewards. If you have ever taken a class where the teacher graded exams or projects "on a curve," you are familiar with the most common form that such competition takes in schools. What the teacher does is compare each student's score with the score of every other student in that class. The few students who achieve the highest scores receive the top grade, regardless of the actual level of their scores. Then a predetermined number of B's, C's, D's, and F's are awarded. Because the resulting distribution of grades looks something like the outline of a bell, it is often referred to as a "bell-shaped curve" (which explains the origin of the term "grading on the curve").

There are at least two reasons that this practice may damage a student's sense of industry:

1. Grading on the curve limits the top rewards to a relatively small number of students regardless of each student's actual level of performance. If the quality of instruction is good and students learn most of what has been assigned, the range of scores will be relatively small. Consider the impact to your sense of industry if you respond correctly to 85 percent of the questions on an exam but earn only a grade of C. The same problem exists when, for whatever reasons, all students perform poorly. How much pride can you have in a grade of A or B when you know it is based on a low success rate? The senior author of this book endured a college chemistry class in which the top grade on an exam went to a student who answered only 48 percent of the questions correctly.

2. Curve grading also guarantees that some students have to receive failing grades regardless of their actual level of performance. Students who are forced into this unhealthy type of competition (there are acceptable forms of competition, which we describe in Chapter 13) may develop a sense of inadequacy and inferiority that will hamper them for the rest of their school career.

Students' sense of industry hampered by unhealthy competition for grades

pause & reflect

Suppose you were an elementary school teacher. What kinds of things would you do to help your students attain a sense of industry rather than inferiority? How would you help them feel more capable and productive? What would you avoid doing?

Take a Stand!

Promote Industry; Stamp Out Inferiority

For some educators, parents, and educational policymakers, an important purpose of education is to sort children into ability categories by forcing them to compete for a limited number of top grades. We strongly oppose such an approach and urge you to do the same because it promotes a sense of inferiority in most students by interfering with the development of such important characteristics as self-efficacy, self-worth, self-regulated learning skills, and intrinsic motivation. The evidence in support of this stand can be found in most of the subsequent chapters in this book. Instead, emphasize to students and others that a more relevant and useful goal is to help all students develop the attitudes, values, and cognitive skills that lead to high levels of meaningful learning.

What Do You Think?

Do you agree that grading on a curve can promote a sense of inferiority for those who do not earn the top grades? Go to the textbook's website, Education Course-Mate, and select the Take a Stand! section to find out more about this and other controversial issues.

The solution to this problem is to base grades on realistic and attainable standards that are worked out ahead of time and communicated to the students. In Chapter 14 on assessment, we describe how to do this. Also, in Chapter 13, we describe several instructional approaches that will likely have a beneficial impact on students' sense of industry because they all promote learning and a sense of accomplishment. In general, they establish a classroom atmosphere in which students feel accepted for who they are and understand that the teacher is as interested in their success as they are. These goals are accomplished by providing clear expectations as to what students should be able to do after a unit of instruction, designing lessons that are logical and meaningful, and using teaching methods that support effective learning processes.

pause & reflect

American high schools are often criticized for not helping adolescents resolve identity problems. Do you agree? Why? How could schools improve?

Helping Students Formulate an Identity

The most complex of Erikson's stages is identity versus role confusion; he wrote more extensively about this stage than any other. Because this stage is often misunderstood, let's use Erikson's own words to describe the concept of **identity**: "An optimal sense of identity…is experienced merely as a sense of psychosocial well-being. Its most obvious concomitants are a feeling of being at home in one's body, a sense of

> Identity: accepting one's body, having goals, getting recognition

'knowing where one is going' and an inner assuredness of anticipated recognition from those who count" (1968, p. 165). As you may know from your own experience or the experiences of others, the process of identity formation is not always smooth, and it does not always follow the same path. But by being aware of the problems and uncertainties that adolescents may experience as they try to develop a sense of who they are, you can help them positively resolve this major developmental milestone.

Taking a Psychosocial Moratorium One aspect of identity formation that often causes difficulty for adolescents is defining the kind of work they want to do—in other words, choosing a career. For individuals who are unprepared to make a career choice, Erikson suggested the possibility of a **psychosocial moratorium**. This is a period marked

> Psychosocial moratorium delays commitment

by a delay of commitment. Such a postponement occurred in Erikson's own life: after leaving high school, he spent several years wandering around Europe without making any firm decision about the sort of job he would seek. Under ideal circumstances, a psychosocial moratorium should be a period of adventure and exploration, having a positive, or at least neutral, impact on the individual and society.

Adolescent Identity Statuses

Erikson's observations on identity formation have been usefully extended by James Marcia's notion of **identity statuses** (1966, 1980, 2002, 2007). Identity statuses, of

> Adolescents exhibit a particular process, called an identity status, for establishing an identity

which there are four, are styles or processes "for handling the psychosocial task of establishing a sense of identity" (Waterman & Archer, 1990, p. 35). Marcia (1980) developed this idea as a way to test scientifically the validity of Erikson's notions about identity.

Identity, as Erikson defines it, involves acceptance of one's body, knowing where one is going, and recognition from those who count. A high school graduate who is pleased with his or her appearance, has already decided on a college major, and is admired by parents, relatives, and friends is likely to experience a sense of psychosocial well-being. © John Henley/CORBIS

Marcia established the four identity statuses after he had conducted semistructured interviews with a selected sample of male youths. The interviewees were asked their thoughts about a career, their personal value system, their sexual attitudes, and their religious beliefs. Marcia proposed that attainment of a mature identity depends on two variables: crisis and commitment. "Crisis refers to times during adolescence when the individual seems to be actively involved in choosing among alternative occupations and beliefs. Commitment refers to the degree of personal investment the individual expresses in an occupation or belief" (1967, p. 119). Subsequent research has shown that exploring and making commitments to interpersonal relationships also contribute to identity formation (Allison & Schultz, 2001; Marcia, 2001, 2002).

After analyzing interview records with these two criteria in mind, Marcia established four identity statuses, described in Table 2.1, that vary in their degree of crisis and commitment:

- Identity diffusion
- Foreclosure
- Moratorium
- Identity achievement

The moratorium and identity achievement statuses are generally thought to be more developmentally mature than the foreclosure and identity diffusion statuses because individuals exhibiting moratorium and identity achievement have either evaluated alternatives and made a commitment or are actively involved in obtaining and evaluating information in preparation for a commitment (Marcia, 2001, 2007). Support for the hypothesized superiority of the identity achievement status was provided by Anne Wallace-Broscious, Felicisima Serafica, and Samuel Osipow (1994). They found that high school students who had attained the identity achievement status scored higher on measures of career planning and career certainty than did students in the moratorium or diffusion statuses.

As you read the brief descriptions of each identity type in Table 2.1, keep a few points in mind. First, the more mature identity statuses are slow to evolve and are found in a relatively small percentage of individuals. Among one sample of sixth, seventh, and eighth graders, 12 percent were in the moratorium status and 9 percent had reached the identity achievement status (Allison & Schultz, 2001). Among adults, only about 33 percent undergo the exploration and identity construction process that characterizes the achievement status (Marcia, 1999).

Second, an identity status is not a once-and-for-all accomplishment; identity can continue to undergo developmental change in adulthood (Fadjukoff, Pulkkinen, & Kokko, 2005). If an ego-shattering event (loss of a job, divorce) occurs later in life, individuals who have reached identity achievement, for example, may find themselves uncertain about old values and behavior patterns and once again in crisis. But for most

Table 2.1	James Marcia's Identity Statuses		
Identity Status	**Crisis**	**Commitment**	**Characteristics**
Identity diffusion	Not yet experienced. Little serious thought given to occupation, gender roles, values.	Weak. Ideas about occupation, gender roles, values are easily changed as a result of positive and negative feedback.	Not self-directed; disorganized, impulsive, low self-esteem, alienated from parents; avoids getting involved in schoolwork and interpersonal relationships.
Foreclosure	Not experienced. May never suffer doubts about identity issues.	Strong. Has accepted and endorsed the values of his or her parents.	Close-minded, authoritarian, low in anxiety; has difficulty solving problems under stress; feels superior to peers; more dependent on parents and other authority figures for guidance and approval than in other statuses.
Moratorium	Partially experienced. Has given some thought to identity-related questions.	Weak. Has not achieved satisfactory answers.	Anxious, dissatisfied with school; changes major often, daydreams, engages in intense but short-lived relationships; may temporarily reject parental and societal values.
Identity achievement	Fully experienced. Has considered and explored alternative positions regarding occupation, gender roles, values.	Strong. Has made self-chosen commitments to at least some aspects of identity.	Introspective; more planful, rational, and logical in decision making than in other identity statuses; high self-esteem; works effectively under stress; likely to form close interpersonal relationships. Usually the last identity status to emerge.

SOURCES: Cramer (2001); Hoegh & Bourgeois (2002); Kroger (2004); MacKinnon & Marcia (2002); Marcia (1999, 2002, 2007).

Individuals in identity diffusion avoid thinking about jobs, roles, values

Individuals in foreclosure unquestioningly endorse parents' goals and values

Individuals in moratorium are uncertain about identity

Individuals who have reached identity achievement status have made their own commitments

individuals, a new view of oneself is eventually created. This cycling between certainty and doubt as to who one is and where one fits in society may well occur in each of the last three of Erikson's stages and is often referred to as a MAMA (moratorium-achievement-moratorium-achievement) cycle (Marcia, 1999, 2001, 2002).

Finally, after 40 years of research on identity, James Marcia (2007) reminds us that individuals are an amalgam of their experiences; thus, their identities reflect a mixture of identity statuses.

Cultural, Ethnic, and Gender Factors in Identity Status Although the foreclosure status is the historical norm for adolescents in Western societies, things can and do change. For example, individuals in moratorium were more numerous during the 1960s and 1970s than during the 1980s. This was a time of great social and cultural upheaval (opposition to the war in Vietnam, civil rights demonstrations, the women's movement), and many adolescents reacted to the uncertainty produced by these changes by not making a commitment to occupational, sexual, and political values (Scarr, Weinberg, & Levine, 1986; Waterman, 1988). Also, more recent evidence indicates that adolescents are now more likely to be in a moratorium status or an identity achievement status, or in transition between these two statuses, than in the foreclosure status common to earlier generations (Branch & Boothe, 2002; Forbes & Ashton, 1998; Watson & Protinsky, 1991).

Gender differences in identity status are most apparent in the areas of political ideology, family and career priorities, and sexuality. With respect to political beliefs, males are more likely to exhibit a foreclosure process and females a diffusion process. With respect to family and career priorities and sexuality, males are likely to be foreclosed or diffuse, whereas females are likely to express an identity achievement or a moratorium status. These findings indicate that female adolescents are more likely than males to make developmentally advanced decisions in the areas of family and career roles and sexuality. A likely explanation has to do with how the female gender role has and has not changed over the past 20 years. Although most females now work outside the home, they are still expected to have primary responsibility for child rearing (Stier, Lewin-Epstein, Braun, 2001).

A relevant question to ask about Marcia's identity statuses, particularly if you plan to teach in a foreign country or instruct students with different cultural backgrounds, is whether these identity statuses occur only in the United States. The answer appears to be no. Researchers in such diverse countries as Korea, India, Nigeria, Japan, Denmark, Holland, Colombia, and Haiti report finding all four statuses, although the percentage of adolescents and young adults in each status does vary by culture (Portes, Dunham, & Del Castillo, 2000; Scarr et al., 1986).

As you consider how diversity interacts with student identity, it is important not to confuse identity statuses with other aspects of identity. One example is ethnic identity. As the ethnic composition of the United States (in which children of color will eventually outnumber white children) changes, more research is being done on the development of ethnic identity (e.g., French, Seidman, Allen, & Aber, 2006; Ghosh, Michelson, & Anyon, 2007). The work on identity status is one way to understand how identity can shift during the middle and high school years. In other chapters, we will discuss other aspects of background and environment that contribute to an important developmental outcome: one's sense of identity.

Criticisms of Erikson's Theory

Although Erikson's theory has in general been supported by research (Steinberg & Morris, 2001), several aspects have been criticized. For example, while Erikson occasionally carried out research investigations, most of his conclusions were based on personal and subjective interpretations that have been only partly substantiated by controlled investigations of the type that most psychologists value. Consequently, his theory is viewed by many as "a *descriptive* overview of social and emotional development that does not adequately *explain* how and why this development takes place" (Shaffer & Kipp, 2010, p. 46).

Other criticisms focus on Erikson's contention that one's identity is achieved by actively exploring alternatives regarding one's career, ideological beliefs, and interpersonal relationships and then making choices. This is not, in all likelihood, a universal practice. In some societies and cultures, these decisions are, for the most part, made by adults and imposed on adolescents (Marcia, 1999, 2001; Sorell & Montgomery, 2001). There appear to be two basic societal conditions that make it possible for individuals to explore and construct an identity: the willingness to tolerate an extended adolescence that makes a minimal contribution to society, and a certain level of societal wealth. In addition, individuals need to have developed secure attachments to parents and other influential individuals (successful resolution of the trust versus mistrust stage) and a high level of cognitive development (Hoegh & Bourgeois, 2002; Marcia, 1999). The absence of these last two conditions may account for the fact that by adulthood, only about 33 percent of individuals have undergone the exploration and construction processes that characterize the moratorium and achievement statuses.

Some critics, such as Carol Gilligan (1982, 1988), argue that Erikson's stages reflect the personality development of males more accurately than that of females. Gilligan believes that the process and timing of identity formation are different for

Criticisms of Erikson's theory: based largely on personal experience, not applicable to many cultures, gender-biased

each gender. Beginning in about fourth grade (the industry versus inferiority stage), girls are as concerned with the nature of interpersonal relationships as they are with achievement, whereas boys focus mainly on achievement. And during adolescence, many young women seem to work through the crises of identity *and* intimacy simultaneously, whereas most young men follow the sequence that Erikson described: identity versus role confusion, then intimacy versus isolation (Gilligan, 1982; Ochse & Plug, 1986; Sorrell & Montgomery, 2001).

If you keep these reservations in mind, you are likely to discover that Erikson's observations (as well as the identity statuses that Marcia described) clarify important aspects of development. Suggestions for Teaching that draw on Erikson's observations follow. (These suggestions might also serve as the nucleus of a section in your Reflective Journal. Possible Journal Entries are indicated in the margins, and more can be found on the book's website.)

Suggestions for Teaching

Applying Erikson's Theory of Psychosocial Development

1 **Keep in mind that certain types of behaviors and relationships may be of special significance at different age levels.**

2 **With younger preschool children, allow plenty of opportunities for free play and experimentation to encourage the development of autonomy, but provide guidance to reduce the possibility that children will experience doubt. Also avoid shaming children for unacceptable behavior.**

3 **With older preschool children, encourage activities that permit the use of initiative and provide a sense of accomplishment. Avoid making children feel guilty about well-motivated but inconvenient (to you) questions or actions.**

4 **During the elementary and middle school years, help children experience a sense of industry by presenting tasks that they can complete successfully.**

Arrange such tasks so that students will know they have been successful. To limit feelings of inferiority, play down comparisons, and encourage cooperation and self-competition. Also try to help jealous children gain satisfaction from their own behavior. (Specific ways to accomplish these goals are described in several later chapters.)

5 **At the secondary school level, keep in mind the significance of each student's search for a sense of identity.**

The components of identity that Erikson stressed are acceptance of one's appearance, knowledge about where one is going, and recognition from those who count. Role confusion is most frequently caused by failure to formulate clear ideas about gender roles and by indecision about occupational choice.

The American school system, particularly at the high school level, has been described as a place where individual differences are either ignored or discouraged and negative feedback greatly outweighs positive feedback (Johnson, Farkas, & Bers, 1997; Steinberg, 1996; Toch, 2003). Because you are important to your students, you can contribute to their sense of positive identity by recognizing them as individuals and praising them for their accomplishments. If you become aware that particular students lack recognition from peers because of abrasive qualities or ineptness and if you have the time and opportunity, you might also attempt to encourage social skills.

JOURNAL ENTRY
Ways to Apply Erikson's Theory (Preschool and Kindergarten)

JOURNAL ENTRY
Ways to Apply Erikson's Theory (Elementary Grades)

JOURNAL ENTRY
Ways to Apply Erikson's Theory (Secondary Grades)

You might be able to reduce identity problems resulting from indecisiveness about gender roles by having class discussions (for example, in social science courses) centering on changes in attitudes regarding masculinity, femininity, and family responsibilities. You can, for example, encourage boys to become more sensitive to the needs of others and girls to be more achievement oriented. This approach to gender-role development that combines traditional "masculine" and "feminine" behaviors is called **psychological androgyny** (Karniol, Gabay, Ochion, & Harari, 1998; Steinberg, 2008).

Another forum for such discussion is an online bulletin board or class website. Online writing can be conducive to explorations of sensitive issues because it provides a slightly slower, more thoughtful pace and also offers an equal voice to male and female students, even those who feel shy about speaking in class. An online discussion that is carefully moderated by an experienced teacher can both model and explore the territory of psychological androgyny (Woodhill & Samuels, 2004).

Working with your school counselor, you may in some cases be able to help students make decisions about occupational choice by providing them with information (gleaned from classroom performance and standardized test results) about their intellectual capabilities, personality traits, interests, and values. Or you may be able to help students decide whether to apply for admission to college instead of entering the job market after high school graduation.

6 **Remember that the aimlessness of some students may be evidence that they are engaging in a psychosocial moratorium. If possible, encourage such individuals to focus on short-term goals while they continue to search for long-term goals.**

There are many ways to enable students to work toward short-term goals, particularly in your classroom. These will be described in detail in later chapters that deal with approaches to instruction and motivation.

7 **Remain aware that adolescents may exhibit characteristics of different identity status types.**

Some may drift aimlessly; others may be distressed because they realize they lack goals and values. A few high school students may have arrived at self-chosen commitments; others may have accepted the goals and values of their parents.

If you become aware that certain students seem depressed or bothered because they are unable to develop a satisfactory set of personal values, consult your school psychologist or counselor. In addition, you might use the techniques just summarized to help these students experience at least a degree of identity achievement. Perhaps the main value of the identity status concept is that it calls attention to individual differences in the formation of identity. Because students in the foreclosure status will pose few, if any, classroom problems, you must keep in mind that foreclosure is not necessarily desirable for the individual student. Also, those experiencing identity diffusion or moratorium may be so bothered by role confusion that they are unwilling to carry out even simple assignments unless you supply support and incentives.

More ideas for your journal can be found in the Reflective Journal Questions at the textbook's student website, Education CourseMate.

PIAGET: COGNITIVE DEVELOPMENT

Basic Principles of Piaget's Theory

Jean Piaget (1896–1980) earned his doctorate in biology in 1918 and began a program of research that has been called "the master plan" to address the question, "How does knowledge develop?" (Smith, 2002, p. 515). His theory of intellectual development, reflective of his basic interest in biology as well as knowledge, continues to spur research on the problem of how knowledge develops.

Piaget postulated that human beings inherit two basic tendencies: **organization** (the tendency to systematize and combine processes into coherent general systems) and **adaptation** (the tendency to adjust to the environment). For Piaget, these tendencies governed both physiological and mental functioning. Just as the biological process of digestion transforms food into a form that the body can use, so intellectual processes transform experiences into a form that the child can use in dealing with new situations. And just as biological processes must be kept in a state of balance (through homeostasis), intellectual processes seek a balance through the process of equilibration (a form of self-regulation that all individuals use to bring coherence and stability to their conception of the world).

Organization *Organization* refers to the tendency of all individuals to systematize or combine processes into coherent (logically interrelated) systems. When we think of tulips and roses as subcategories of the more general category *flowers*, instead of as two unrelated categories, we are using organization to aid our thinking process. This organizational capacity makes thinking processes efficient and powerful and allows a better fit, or adaptation, of the individual to the environment.

Schemes Children formulate organized patterns of behavior or thought, known as **schemes,** as they interact with their environment, parents, teachers, and age-mates. Schemes can be behavioral (throwing a ball) or cognitive (realizing that there are many different kinds of balls). Whenever a child encounters a new experience that does not easily fit into an existing scheme, adaptation is necessary.

Adaptation The process of creating a good fit or match between one's conception of reality (one's schemes) and the real-life experiences one encounters is called *adaptation*. According to Piaget, adaptation is accomplished by two subprocesses: **assimilation** and **accommodation.** A child may adapt by either interpreting an experience so that it fits an existing scheme (assimilation) or changing an existing scheme to incorporate the experience (accommodation).

Imagine a six-year-old who goes to an aquarium for the first time and calls the minnows "little fish" and the whales "big fish." In both cases, the child is assimilating—attempting to fit a new experience into an existing scheme (in this case, the conception that all creatures that live in the water are fish). When her parents point out that even though whales live in the water, they are mammals, not fish, the six-year-old begins to accommodate—to modify her existing scheme to fit the new experience she has encountered. Gradually (accommodations are made slowly, over repeated experiences), a new scheme forms that contains nonfish creatures that live in the water.

Relationships Among Organization, Adaptation, and Schemes To give you a basic understanding of Piaget's ideas, we have talked about them as distinct elements. But the concepts are all related. In their drive to be organized, individuals try to have a place for everything (accommodation) so they can put everything in its place (assimilation). The product of organization and adaptation is the creation of new schemes that allow individuals to organize at a higher level and adapt more effectively.

Equilibration, Disequilibrium, and Learning Piaget believed that people are driven to organize their schemes to achieve the best possible adaptation to their environment. He called this process **equilibration.** But what motivates people's drive toward equilibration? It is a state of *disequilibrium*, or a perceived discrepancy between an existing scheme and something new. In other words, when people encounter something that is inconsistent with or contradicts what they already know or believe, this experience produces a disequilibrium that they are driven to eliminate (assuming they are sufficiently interested in the new experience to begin with).

Organization: tendency to systematize processes

Adaptation: tendency to adjust to environment

Scheme: organized pattern of behavior or thought

Assimilation: new experience is fitted into existing scheme

Accommodation: scheme is created or revised to fit new experience

Equilibration: tendency to organize schemes to allow better understanding of experiences

Activities that encourage children to create new ideas or schemes through experimentation, questioning, discussion, and discovery often produce meaningful learning because of the inherent drive toward equilibration. © Paul Conklin/Photo Edit

A student may wonder why, for example, tomatoes and cucumbers are referred to as fruits in a science text because she has always referred to them as vegetables and has distinguished fruits from vegetables on the basis of sweetness. This discrepancy may cause the student to read the text carefully or ask the teacher for explanation. Gradually the student reorganizes her thinking about the classification of fruits and vegetables in terms of edible plant roots, stems, leaves, and ovaries so that it is more consistent with the expert view. These processes are two sides of the learning coin: for equilibration to occur, disequilibrium must already have occurred. Disequilibrium can occur spontaneously within an individual through maturation and experience, or it can be stimulated by someone else (such as a teacher).

Constructing Knowledge Meaningful learning, then, occurs when people *create* new ideas, or knowledge (rules and hypotheses that explain things), from existing information (for example, facts, concepts, and procedures). To solve a problem, we have to search our memory for information that can be used to fashion a solution. Using information can mean experimenting, questioning, reflecting, discovering, inventing, and discussing. This process of creating knowledge to solve a problem and eliminate a disequilibrium is referred to by Piagetian psychologists and educators as **constructivism** (Brooks & Brooks, 2001; Elkind, 2005; Haney & McArthur, 2002; Yager, 2000). It is a powerful notion that has motivated a great deal of psychological research that can be applied to teaching and learning (Johnson, 2010). Constructivism will reappear in later chapters and in other forms. (The Pause and Reflect features in each chapter are intended to stimulate constructivist thinking, as is the manner in which we encourage you to set up and use your journal for reflective thinking and teaching.)

Stages of Cognitive Development

Organization and adaptation are what Piaget called *invariant functions*. This means that these thought processes function the same way for infants, children, adolescents, and adults. Schemes, however, are not invariant. They undergo systematic change at particular points in time. As a result, there are real differences between the ways younger children and older children think and between the ways children and adults think. The schemes of infants and toddlers, for example, are sensory and motor in nature. They are often referred to as *habits* or *reflexes*. In early childhood, schemes gradually become more mental in nature; during this period, they are called *concepts* or *categories*. Finally, by late adolescence or early adulthood, schemes are complex and result in what we call *strategic* or *planful* behavior.

On the basis of his studies, Piaget concluded that schemes evolve through four stages. The *rate* at which a particular child proceeds through these stages varies, but Piaget believed the *sequence* is the same in all children.

Piaget's four stages are described in the following sections. To help you grasp the sequence of these stages, Table 2.2 briefly outlines the age ranges to which they generally apply and their distinguishing characteristics.

Although Piaget used this "stage" or stair-step metaphor to describe the pattern of cognitive development, don't be misled into thinking that children jump from one stage to the next. In trying to understand certain concepts or solve certain problems, children may on some occasions use a more advanced kind of thinking but on other occasions revert to an earlier, less sophisticated form. Over time, the more advanced concepts and strategies supplant the less sophisticated ones. Because of this variability in how children think, some developmental psychologists (e.g., Siegler, 1996) prefer to use the metaphor of overlapping waves rather than stages to characterize the nature of cognitive development. But because Piaget spoke in terms of stages, we will as well.

Sensorimotor stage: schemes reflect sensory and motor experiences

Sensorimotor Stage (Infants and Toddlers)

Up to the age of two, children acquire understanding primarily through sensory impressions and motor activities. Therefore, Piaget called this the *sensorimotor stage*. Because infants are unable to move around much on their own during the first months of postnatal existence, they develop schemes primarily by exploring their own bodies and senses. After toddlers learn to walk and manipulate things, however, they get into everything and build up a sizable repertoire of schemes involving external objects and situations.

An important cognitive development milestone, *object permanence*, occurs between the fourth and eighth months. Prior to this point, the phrase "out of sight, out of mind" is literally true. Infants treat objects that leave their field of vision as if they no longer exist. When they drop an object from their hands or when an object at which they are looking is covered, for example, they do not search for it. As object permanence develops, children's intentional search behaviors become increasingly apparent.

Most children under age two are able to use schemes they have mastered to engage in mental as well as physical trial-and-error behavior. By age two, toddlers' schemes have become more mental in nature. You can see this in the way toddlers imitate the behavior of others. They imitate people they have not previously observed, they imitate the behavior of animals, and, most important, they imitate even when the model is no longer present (this is called *deferred imitation*). These types of imitative behaviors show toddlers' increasing ability to think in terms of symbols.

Table 2.2	Piaget's Stages of Cognitive Development	
Stage	**Age Range**	**Characteristics**
Sensorimotor	Birth to two years	Develops schemes primarily through sense and motor activities. Recognizes permanence of objects not seen.
Preoperational	Two to seven years	Gradually acquires ability to conserve and decenter but not capable of operations and unable to mentally reverse actions.
Concrete operational	Seven to eleven years	Capable of operations but solves problems by generalizing from concrete experiences. Not able to manipulate conditions mentally unless they have been experienced.
Formal operational	Eleven years and older	Able to deal with abstractions, form hypotheses, solve problems systematically, engage in mental manipulations.

Preoperational stage: child forms many new schemes but does not think logically

Preoperational Stage (Preschool and Primary Grades) The thinking of preschool and primary grade children (roughly two to seven years old) centers on mastery of symbols (such as words), which permits them to benefit much more from past experiences. Piaget believed that many symbols are derived from mental imitation and involve both visual images and bodily sensations (notice how the schemes of this stage incorporate and build on the schemes of the previous stage). Although the thinking at this stage is much more sophisticated than that of one- and two-year-olds, preschool children are limited in their ability to use their new symbol-oriented schemes. From an adult perspective, their thinking and behavior are illogical.

Perceptual centration, irreversibility, egocentrism: barriers to logical thought

When Piaget used the term *operation*, he meant an action carried out through logical thinking. *Preoperational*, then, means prelogical. The main impediments to logical thinking that preschoolers have to overcome are *perceptual centration, irreversibility*, and *egocentrism*. You can see these impediments at work most clearly when children attempt to solve **conservation problems**—those that test their ability to recognize that certain properties stay the same despite a change in appearance or position.

One of the best-known conservation problems is conservation of continuous quantity. A child is taken to a quiet place by an experimenter, who then pours water (or juice or beans or whatever else) into identical short glasses until the child agrees that each contains an equal amount. Then the water is poured from one of these glasses into a tall, thin glass, and the child is asked, "Is there more water in this glass [the experimenter points to the tall glass] or this one [the short glass]?" Immediately after the child answers, the experimenter asks, "Why do you think so?" If the child's response is evasive or vague, the experimenter continues to probe until the child's underlying thought processes become clear.

In carrying out this experiment (and many others similar to it) with children of different ages, Piaget discovered that children below the age of six or so maintain that there is more water in the tall, thin glass than in the short, squat glass. Although they agree at the beginning of the experiment that the water in the two identical glasses is equal, young children stoutly insist that after the water has been poured, the taller glass contains more. When asked, "Why do you think so?" many preschool children immediately and confidently reply, "Because it's taller." Children over the age of six or so, by contrast, are more likely to reply, "Well, it *looks* as if there's more water in this one because it's taller, but they're really the same."

One reason preoperational stage children have difficulty solving conservation problems (as well as other problems that require logical thinking) is **perceptual centration:** the strong tendency to focus attention on only one characteristic of an object or aspect of a problem or event at a time. The young child focuses only on the height of the water in the two containers and ignores the differences in width and volume. Another way to put this is to say that the child has not yet mastered **decentration**—the ability to think of more than one quality at a time—and is therefore not inclined to contemplate alternatives.

The second impediment to logical thinking is **irreversibility.** This means that young children cannot mentally pour the water from the tall, thin glass back into the short, squat one (thereby proving to themselves that the glasses contain the same amount of water). For the same reason, these youngsters do not understand the logic behind simple mathematical reversals ($4 + 5 = 9$; $9 - 5 = 4$).

Egocentrism: assumption that others see things the same way

The third major impediment is **egocentrism.** When applied to preschool children, egocentric does not mean selfish or conceited. It means that youngsters find it difficult, if not impossible, to take another person's point of view. In their conversations and in experimental situations in which they are asked to describe how something would look if viewed by someone else, preschool children reveal that they often have difficulty seeing things from another person's perspective (Piaget & Inhelder, 1956). They seem to assume that others see things the same way they see them. As a result, attempts to explain the logic behind conservation are usually met with quizzical looks and the insistence (some would mistakenly call it stubbornness) that the tall, thin glass contains more water.

Concrete Operational Stage (Elementary to Early Middle School)

Through formal instruction, informal experiences, social contact, and maturation, children over the age of seven gradually become less influenced by perceptual centration, irreversibility, and egocentrism (DeVries, 1997). Schemes are developing that allow a greater understanding of such logic-based tasks as conservation (matter is neither created nor destroyed but simply changes shape or form or position), class inclusion (the construction of hierarchical relationships among related classes of items), and seriation (the arrangement of items in a particular order).

But operational thinking is limited to objects that are actually present or that children have experienced concretely and directly. For this reason, Piaget described the stage from approximately seven to eleven years as that of *concrete operations*. The nature of the concrete operational stage can be illustrated by the child's mastery of different kinds of conservation.

By the age of seven, most children are able to explain correctly that water poured from a short, squat glass into a tall, thin glass is still the same amount of water. Being able to solve the water-pouring problem, however, does not guarantee that a seven-year-old will be able to solve a similar problem involving two balls of clay. A child who has just explained why a tall glass of water contains the same amount as a short one may inconsistently maintain a few moments later that rolling one of two equally sized balls of clay into an elongated shape causes the rolled one to appear as if it contains more clay.

Children in the primary and early elementary grades tend to react to each situation in terms of concrete experiences. The tendency to solve problems by generalizing from one situation to a similar situation does not occur with any degree of consistency until the end of the elementary school years.

Nevertheless, children in the concrete operational stage are often more capable of learning advanced concepts than most people realize. According to the National Research Council (2000), for example, the fundamental abilities that elementary students (K–4) are expected to acquire include asking questions about objects, conducting simple observations, using simple equipment (such as a magnifying glass) to gather data and extend the senses, and constructing and communicating explanations.

> Concrete operational stage: child is capable of mentally reversing actions but generalizes only from concrete experiences

pause & reflect

From Piaget's point of view, why is it incorrect to think of children as "small adults"?

> Formal operational stage: child is able to deal with abstractions, form hypotheses, engage in mental manipulations

Formal Operational Stage (Middle School, High School, and Beyond)

When children *do* reach the point of being able to generalize and engage in mental trial and error by thinking up hypotheses and testing them in their heads, they are at the stage of *formal operations*, according to Piaget. The term *formal* reflects the ability to respond to the *form* of a problem rather than its content and to *form* hypotheses. For example, the formal operational thinker can read the analogies "5 is to 15 as 1 is to 3" and "penny is to dollar as year is to century" and realize that despite the different content, the form of the two problems is identical (both analogies are based on ratios). In the same way, the formal thinker can understand and use complex language forms: proverbs ("Strike while the iron is hot"), metaphor ("Procrastination is the thief of time"), sarcasm, and satire.

We can see the nature of formal operational thinking and how it differs from concrete operational thinking by looking at a simplified version of Piaget's rod-bending experiment. Adolescents are given a basin filled with water, a set of metal rods of varying lengths, and a set of weights. The rods are attached to the edge of the basin and the weights to the ends of the rods. The subject's task is to figure out how much weight is required to bend a rod just enough to touch the water. Let's say that our hypothetical subject picks out the longest rod in the set (which is 9 inches long), attaches it to the edge of the basin, and puts just enough weight on the end of it to get it to touch the water. This observation is then recorded. Succes-

Students who are within Piaget's formal operational stage of cognitive development are capable of solving problems by systematically using abstract symbols to represent real objects. © Mike Booth/ Alamy

sively shorter rods are selected, and the same procedure is carried out. At some point, the subject comes to the 4-inch rod. This rod does not touch the water even when all of the weights have been attached to it. There are, however, three more rods, all of which are shorter than the last one tested.

This is where the formal and concrete operators part company. The formal operational thinker reasons that if all of the available weights are not sufficient to bend the 4-inch rod enough to touch the water, the same will be true of the remaining rods. In essence, the rest of the experiment is done mentally and symbolically. The concrete operational thinker, however, continues trying out each rod and recording each observation independent of the others. Although both subjects reach the same conclusion, the formal operator does so through a more powerful and efficient process.

But remember that new schemes develop gradually. Although adolescents can sometimes deal with mental abstractions representing concrete objects, most twelve-year-olds solve problems haphazardly, using trial and error. It is not until the end of the high school years that adolescents are likely to approach a problem by forming hypotheses, mentally sorting out solutions, and systematically testing the most promising leads.

Some interpreters of Piaget (e.g., Wadsworth, 2004) note that a significant aspect of formal thought is that it causes the adolescent to concentrate more on possibilities than on realities. This is the ability that Erikson and others (e.g., Kalbaugh & Haviland, 1991) suggest is instrumental in the emergence of the identity crisis. At the point when older adolescents can become aware of all the factors that have to be considered in choosing a career and can imagine what it might be like to be employed, some may feel so threatened and confused that they postpone the final choice. Yet the same capability can also help resolve the identity crisis because adolescents can reason about possibilities in a logical manner. An adolescent girl, for example, may consider working as a pediatrician, teacher, or child psychologist in an underprivileged environment because she has always enjoyed and sought out activities that allowed her to interact with children and has also been concerned with the effects of deprivation on development.

Although mastery of formal thought equips the older adolescent with impressive intellectual skills, it may also lead to a tendency for the burgeoning formal thinker to become preoccupied with abstract and theoretical matters. Barry Wadsworth makes this point in the following way:

> If motivated to do so, and if in possession of the necessary content, adolescents with formal reasoning can reason as logically as adults. The tools for an evaluation of intellectual arguments are formed and fully functional. One of the major affective differences between the thought of the adolescent and that of the adult is that, initially in their use of formal operations, adolescents apply a criterion of pure logic in evaluating reasoning about human events. If it is logical it is good, right, and so on. This is the nature of their egocentrism. Adolescents lack a full appreciation of the way in which the world is ordered. With the capability for generating endless hypotheses, an adolescent believes that what is best is what is logical. He or she does not yet differentiate between the logical world as she thinks it to be and the "real" world. (2004, p. 124)

This inability to differentiate between the world as the adolescent thinks it should be and the world as it actually is was referred to by David Elkind (1968) as **adolescent egocentrism.** This occurs when high school students use their emerging formal operational capabilities to think about themselves and the thinking of others. Because adolescents are preoccupied with themselves and how they appear to others, they assume that peers and adults are equally interested in what they think and do. This is why, in Elkind's view, the typical adolescent is so self-conscious. The major difference between the egocentrism of childhood and that of adolescence is summed up in Elkind's observation: "The child is egocentric in the sense that he is unable to take another person's point of view. The adolescent, on the other hand, takes the other person's point of view to an extreme degree" (1968, p. 153).

Adolescent egocentrism: adolescents preoccupied with their own view of the world and how they appear to others

Elkind believes that adolescent egocentrism also explains why the peer group becomes such a potent force in high school:

> Adolescent egocentrism…accounts, in part, for the power of the peer group during this period. The adolescent is so concerned with the reactions of others toward him, particularly his peers, that he is willing to do many things which are opposed to all of his previous training and to his own best interests. At the same time, this egocentric impression that he is always on stage may help to account for the many and varied adolescent attention-getting maneuvers. (1968, p. 154)

Although the concept of adolescent egocentrism is widely accepted among researchers, ascribing its cause to formal operational thinking gets mixed support. Some studies have found a relationship, while other studies have not (Rycek, Stuhr, & McDermott, 1998; Vartanian, 2000).

The Role of Social Interaction and Instruction in Cognitive Development

How Social Interaction Affects Cognitive Development When it comes to social experiences, Piaget clearly believed that peer interactions do more to spur cognitive development than do interactions with adults. The reason is that children are more likely to discuss, analyze, and debate the merits of another child's view of some issue (such as who should have which toy or what the rules of a game should be) than they are to take serious issue with an adult. The balance of power between children and adults is simply too unequal. Not only are most children quickly taught that adults know more and use superior reasoning, but also the adult always gets to have the last word: argue too long, and it's off to bed with no dessert. But when children interact with one another, the outcome is more dependent on how well each child uses her wits (Light & Littleton, 1999).

Piaget: cognitive development more strongly influenced by peers than by adults

It is the need to understand the ideas of a peer or playmate to formulate responses to those ideas that leads to less egocentrism and the development of new, more complex mental schemes. Put another way, a strongly felt sense of cognitive conflict automatically impels the child to strive for a higher level of equilibrium. Formal instruction by an adult expert simply does not have the same impact regardless of how well designed it might be. That is why parents and teachers are often surprised to find children agreeing on some issue after having rejected an adult's explanation of the very same thing. Thus, educational programs that are patterned after Piaget's ideas usually provide many opportunities for children to interact socially and discover through these interactions basic ideas about how the world works (Crain, 2005; Rogoff, 1990; Tudge & Winterhoff, 1993). In Chapter 13, "Approaches to Instruction," we describe in detail a systematic way to accomplish this goal: cooperative learning. Proof of the feasibility of this approach can be found in several summaries and analyses of the effects of cooperative learning (see, e.g., Johnson & Johnson, 1995; Qin, Johnson, & Johnson, 1995; Slavin, 1995).

How Instruction Affects Cognitive Development   Although Piaget believed that formal instruction by expert adults will not significantly stimulate cognitive development, not all psychologists have been willing to accept this conclusion at face value. Over the past thirty years, dozens of experiments have been conducted to determine whether it is possible to teach preoperational stage children to understand and use concrete operational schemes or to teach students in the concrete operational stage to grasp formal operational reasoning.

The typical conclusion of psychologists who have analyzed and evaluated this body of research ranges from uncertainty to cautious optimism (see, e.g., Case, 1975; Good & Brophy, 1995; Nagy & Griffiths, 1982; Sprinthall, Sprinthall, & Oja, 1998). The uncertainty results from shortcomings in the way some studies were carried out and disagreements about what constitutes evidence of true concrete operational thinking or formal operational thinking.

The cautious optimism comes from the work of Michael Shayer and others (Adey, Shayer, & Yates, 2001; Shayer, 1999) in England. They found that schools that participated in a science instruction program called CASE (Cognitive Acceleration through Science Education), which combined aspects of the cognitive developmental theories of Piaget and Vygotsky, had a much greater percentage of thirteen- and fourteen-year-olds at or above the early formal operational stage than did non-CASE schools. Furthermore, after two years in the program, CASE students scored higher on national tests of mathematics, science, and English than did students in the non-CASE schools. CASE programs have also been implemented to help preoperational stage children acquire concrete operational schemes (Robertson, 2001) and to help teachers accelerate the cognitive development of students with various learning impediments (Simon, 2002).

Instruction can accelerate development of schemes that have begun to form

The safest conclusion that can be drawn from this literature (see, for example, Sigelman & Shaffer, 1991; Sprinthall et al., 1998) is that children who are in the process of developing the schemes that will govern the next stage of cognitive functioning can, with good-quality instruction, be helped to refine those schemes a bit faster than would normally be the case. For example, teachers can teach the principle of conservation by using simple explanations and concrete materials and allowing children to manipulate the materials. This means that teachers should nurture the process of cognitive growth at any particular stage by presenting lessons in a form consistent with but slightly more advanced than the students' existing schemes. The objective here is to help students assimilate and accommodate new and different experiences as efficiently as possible.

Criticisms of Piaget's Theory

Piaget's theory underestimates children's abilities

Underestimating Children's Capabilities   Among the thousands of articles that have been published in response to Piaget's findings are many that offer critiques of his work. Some psychologists argue that Piaget underestimated children's abilities not only because he imposed stringent criteria for inferring the presence of particular cognitive abilities, but also because the tasks he used were often complex and far removed from children's real-life experiences (Case, 1999). The term *preoperational*, for instance, stresses what is absent rather than what is present. Over the past two decades, researchers have focused more on what preoperational children *can* do. The results (summarized by Kamii, 2000; Siegler, 1998) suggest that preschoolers' cognitive abilities are more advanced in some areas than Piaget's work suggests.

| Most adolescents are not formal operational thinkers

Overestimating Adolescents' Capabilities Other evidence suggests that Piaget may have overestimated the formal thinking capabilities of adolescents. Norman Sprinthall and Richard Sprinthall (1987) reported that only 33 percent of a group of high school seniors could apply formal operational reasoning to scientific problem solving. Research summarized by Michael Shayer (1997) indicates that only 20 percent of children exhibit well-developed formal operational thinking by the end of adolescence. According to these studies, formal reasoning seems to be the exception, not the rule, throughout adolescence.

A study of French adolescents (Flieller, 1999) reported similar percentages but also sought to determine if a new pattern had emerged. Of a group of ten- to twelve-year-olds who were tested on formal operational tasks in 1972, only 9 percent were at the beginning of that stage and only 1 percent were mature formal operators. The percentages for a group of ten- to twelve-year-olds tested in 1993 were just slightly higher: 13 percent and 3 percent, respectively. Significantly larger differences were noted, however, between two groups of thirteen- to fifteen-year-olds. Among those tested in 1967, 26 percent were early formal operators and 9 percent were mature formal operators. But among those tested in 1996, 40 percent were early formal operators and 15 percent were mature formal operators. The author of this study suggested that the increase in formal operational thinking among thirteen- to fifteen-year-olds may be attributable in part to teaching practices (such as creating tables to display information and using tree diagrams to clarify grammatical structure) that foster the development of formal operational schemes.

Vague Explanations for Cognitive Growth Piaget's theory has also been criticized for its vagueness in specifying the factors that are responsible for cognitive growth. Why, for example, do children give up conserving responses in favor of nonconserving responses at a particular age?

Robert Siegler (1996) has suggested an explanation: He believes that variability in children's thinking plays an influential role. For example, it is not uncommon to hear children use on successive occasions different forms of a given verb, as in "I *ate* it," "I *eated* it," and "I *ated* it." Similar variability has been found in the use of memory strategies (five-year-old and eight-year-old children do not always rehearse information they want to remember), addition rules, time-telling rules, and block building tasks. Siegler's explanation is that variability gives the child a range of plausible options about how to deal with a particular problem. The child then tries them out in an attempt to see which one produces the best adaptation. Note the use of the qualifying word *plausible*. Most children do not try out any and all possible solutions to a problem. Instead they stick to possibilities that are logically consistent with underlying principles of the problem. Once children have acquired a logical explanation for solving problems, they learn more and persist longer (Siegler & Svetina, 2006).

| Sequence of stages uniform across cultures but rate of development varies

Cultural Differences Key assumptions underlying Piaget's theory, such as adaptation and constructivism, have fueled considerable cross-cultural research (Maynard, 2008). One question that has been raised is whether children from different cultures develop intellectually in the manner Piaget described. The answer at this point is both yes and no. The sequence of stages appears to be universal, but the rate of development may vary from one culture to another (Dasen & Heron, 1981; Hughes & Noppe, 1991; Leadbeater, 1991; Rogoff & Chavajay, 1995).

Although children in Western industrialized societies (such as the United States) usually are not given baby-sitting responsibilities until they are at least ten years old because their high level of egocentrism prevents them from considering the needs of the other child, in Mexican villages Mayan children as young as age five play this role because their culture stresses the development of cooperative behavior (Sameroff & McDonough, 1994).

Research conducted during the 1970s found that individuals living in non-Western cultures who had little formal education did not engage in formal operational thinking. Although these same people used concrete operational schemes when tested with the kinds of tasks Piaget used, they usually did so at a later age than the Swiss children Piaget originally studied. This result was attributed to their lack of schooling, which left them unfamiliar with the language and conventions of formal testing. When concrete operational tasks were conducted with materials that were part of these people's everyday lives (such as asking children from Zambia to reproduce a pattern with strips of wire rather than with paper and pencil), they performed as well as Western children who drew the patterns on paper (Rogoff & Chavajay, 1995).

pause & reflect

Noting that American schoolchildren score lower than many European and Asian children on standardized achievement tests, critics argue that U.S. formal schooling should begin earlier than age five and should focus on basic reading and math skills. In light of research on Piaget's theories, what do you think of this proposal?

Now that you are familiar with Piaget's theory of cognitive development, you can formulate specific classroom applications. You might use the Suggestions for Teaching for the grade level you expect to teach as the basis for a section in your journal.

Suggestions for Teaching

Applying Piaget's Theory of Cognitive Development

GENERAL GUIDELINES

1 **Focus on what children at each stage can do, and avoid what they cannot meaningfully understand.**

This implication must be interpreted carefully, as recent research has shown that children at the preoperational and concrete operational levels can do more than Piaget believed. In general, however, it is safe to say that because preoperational stage children (preschoolers, kindergartners, most first and some second graders) can use language and other symbols to stand for objects, they should be given many opportunities to describe and explain things through the use of speech, artwork, body movement, role play, and musical performance. Although you can introduce the concepts of conservation, seriation, class inclusion, time, space, and number, attempts at mastering them should probably be postponed until children are in the concrete operational stage.

Concrete operational stage children (grades 3–6) can be given opportunities to master such mental processes as ordering, seriating, classifying, reversing, multiplying, dividing, subtracting, and adding by manipulating concrete objects or symbols. Although a few fifth and sixth graders may be capable of dealing with abstractions, most exercises that involve theorizing, hypothesizing, or generalizing should be done with concrete objects or symbols.

Formal operational stage children (grades 7 through high school) can be given activities that require hypothetical-deductive reasoning, reflective thinking, analysis, synthesis, and evaluation.

2 Because individuals differ in their rates of intellectual growth, gear instructional materials and activities to each student's developmental level.

3 Because intellectual growth occurs when individuals attempt to eliminate a disequilibrium, instructional lessons and materials that introduce new concepts should provoke interest and curiosity and be moderately challenging in order to maximize assimilation and accommodation.

4 Although information (facts, concepts, procedures) can be efficiently transmitted from teacher to student through direct instruction, knowledge (rules and hypotheses) is best created by each student through the mental and physical manipulation of information.

Accordingly, lesson plans should include opportunities for activity, manipulation, exploration, discussion, and application of information. Small-group science projects are one example of how to implement this goal.

5 Because students' schemes at any given time are an outgrowth of earlier schemes, point out to them how new ideas relate to their old ideas and extend their understanding. Memorization of information for its own sake should be avoided.

6 Begin lessons with concrete objects or ideas, and gradually shift explanations to a more abstract and general level.

PRESCHOOL, ELEMENTARY, AND MIDDLE SCHOOL GRADES[2]

1 Become thoroughly familiar with Piaget's theory so that you will be aware of how your students organize and synthesize ideas.

You may gain extra insight if you analyze your own thinking, since you are likely to discover that in some situations, you operate at a concrete rather than an abstract level.

2 If possible, assess the level and the type of thinking of each child in your class. Ask individual children to perform some of Piaget's experiments, and spend most of your time listening to each child explain her reactions.

3 Remember that learning through activity and direct experience is essential. Provide plenty of materials and opportunities for children to learn on their own.

4 Arrange situations to permit social interaction, so that children can learn from one another.

Hearing others explain their views is a natural way for students to learn that not everyone sees things the same way. The placement of a few advanced thinkers with less mature thinkers is more likely to facilitate this process than is homogeneous grouping.

JOURNAL ENTRY
Ways to Apply Piaget's Theory (Preschool, Elementary, and Middle Grades)

---

[2]These guidelines are adapted from Elkind (1989); Ginsburg and Opper (1988); Kamii (2000); Singer and Revenson (1996); and Wadsworth (2004).

Suggestions for Teaching

[handwritten margin notes: USE CONTRAST'S core concern s/late cura. 5 conft'l soa]

5 **Plan learning experiences to take into account the level of thinking attained by an individual or group.**

Encourage children to classify things on the basis of a single attribute before you expose them to problems that involve relationships among two or more attributes. Ask many questions, and give your students many opportunities to explain their interpretations of experiences so that you can remain aware of their level of thinking.

6 **Keep in mind the possibility that students may be influenced by egocentric speech and thought.**

Consider the possibility that each child may assume that everyone else has the same conception of a word that he or she has. If confusion becomes apparent or if a child becomes impatient about failure to communicate, request an explanation in different terms. Or ask several children to explain their conception of an object or a situation.

MIDDLE SCHOOL AND SECONDARY GRADES[3]

1 **Become well acquainted with the nature of concrete operational thinking and formal thought so that you can recognize when your students are resorting to either type of thinking or a combination of the two.**

JOURNAL ENTRY
Ways to Apply Piaget's
Theory (Middle School and
Secondary Grades)

2 **To become aware of the type of thinking that individual students use, ask them to explain how they arrived at solutions to problems.**

Do this as part of your classroom curriculum or in response to experimental situations similar to those that Piaget devised.

3 **Teach students how to solve problems more systematically (suggestions for doing this will be provided in later chapters), and provide opportunities for hands-on science experiments.**

4 **Keep in mind that some high school students may be more interested in possibilities than in realities.**

If class discussions become unrealistically theoretical and hypothetical, call attention to facts and practical difficulties. If students are contemptuous of unsuccessful attempts by adults to solve school, local, national, and international problems, point out the complexity of many situations involving conflicts of interest, perhaps by having students develop arguments for both sides.

More ideas for your journal can be found in the Reflective Journal Questions at the textbook's student website, Education CourseMate.

5 **Allow for the possibility that younger adolescents may go through a period of egocentrism that will cause them to act as if they are always on stage and to be extremely concerned about the reactions of peers.**

VYGOTSKY: COGNITIVE DEVELOPMENT

From the time Piaget's work first became known to large numbers of American psychologists in the early 1960s until the 1980s, it was the dominant explanation of cognitive development. Not that Piaget didn't have his critics. As the previous

---

[3]Many of these suggestions are derived from points made in Chapter 2 of *Adolescence* (Steinberg, 2008).

section made clear, many psychologists challenged one aspect or another of his work. But there were no competing explanations of cognitive development. Beginning in the early 1980s, however, the ideas of Russian psychologist Lev Vygotsky began to appear in the psychological literature with increasing frequency. Vygotsky, who died from tuberculosis in 1934, was a contemporary of Piaget who had very different views about the major forces that shape learning and thinking, particularly with respect to the roles of culture, social interaction, and formal instruction (Rowe & Wertsch, 2002).

How One's Culture Affects Cognitive Development

How we think influenced by current social forces and historical cultural forces

Vygotsky's theory of cognitive development is often referred to as a sociocultural theory because it maintains that how we think is a function of both social and cultural forces. If, for example, you were given a list of nouns (such as *plate, box, peach, knife, apple, hoe, cup,* and *potato*) and told to create groupings, you would probably put *plate, knife,* and *cup* in a group labeled "utensils" and *peach, apple,* and *potato* in a group labeled "food." Why? Is there something inherently compelling about those groupings? Not really.

We could just as logically have put *plate, knife,* and *apple* in a group, because we can use the first two to eat the third. But we are more likely to put objects in taxonomic categories than in functional categories because we have been taught by others who organize ideas taxonomically most of the time. And why do we think that way? Because we are the product of a culture that prizes the ability of its members to think at the most abstract levels (which is why Piaget saw formal operations as the most advanced stage of thinking).

Typically, then, parents and schools shape children's thought processes to reflect that which the culture values. So even when individuals are by themselves, what they think and do is the result of cultural values and practices, some of which may stretch back over hundreds or thousands of years, as well as recent social contacts (Cole, 2005; Wertsch & Tulviste, 1996).

Psychological tools aid and change thought processes

The Importance of Psychological Tools Vygotsky believed that the most important things a culture passes on to its members (and their descendants) are what he called *psychological tools.* These are the cognitive devices and procedures with which we communicate and explore the world around us. They both aid and change our mental functioning. Speech, writing, gestures, diagrams, numbers, chemical formulas, musical notation, rules, and memory techniques are some examples of common psychological tools (Gredler & Shields, 2004).

Early explorers, for example, created maps to help them represent where they had been, communicate that knowledge to others, and plan future trips. Today we use the same type of tool to navigate efficiently over long distances or within relatively compact but complex environments (like large cities). Another example is the use of multiplication. If asked to solve the multiplication problem 343×822, you would, in all likelihood, quickly and easily come up with the answer, 281,946, by using the following procedure:

$$
\begin{array}{r}
343 \\
\times 822 \\
\hline
686 \\
686 \\
2744 \\
\hline
281{,}946
\end{array}
$$

But you could have produced the same answer by adding 343 to itself 821 times. Why would you automatically opt for the first procedure? Because the culture in which you operate has, through the medium of formal instruction, provided you with a psychological tool called multiplication as a means of more efficiently and accurately solving certain types of complex mathematical problems (Wertsch, 1998).

Children are introduced to a culture's major psychological tools through social interactions with their parents and later through more formal interactions with classroom teachers. Eventually these social interactions are internalized as cognitive processes that are autonomously invoked. As Vygotsky so elegantly put it, "Through others we become ourselves" (Tudge & Scrimsher, 2003, p. 218).

How Social Interaction Affects Cognitive Development

The difference between Vygotsky's views on the origin and development of cognitive processes and those of other cognitive developmental psychologists is something like the old question, "Which came first: the chicken or the egg?" Influenced by Piaget, many developmental psychologists argue that as children overcome cognitive conflict through the internal processes of assimilation, accommodation, and equilibration, they become more capable of higher-level thinking, and so come to understand better the nature of the world in which they live and their place in it. In other words, cognitive development makes social development possible (see our discussion of Robert Selman's work on the social development of children in the next chapter).

Vygotsky, however, believed that just the opposite was true. He saw social interaction as the primary cause of cognitive development. Unlike Piaget, Vygotsky believed that children gain significantly from the knowledge and conceptual tools handed down to them by those who are more intellectually advanced, whether they are same-age peers, older children, or adults.

Consider, for example, a simple concept like *grandmother*. In the absence of formal instruction, a primary grade child's concept of grandmother is likely to be narrow in scope because it is based on personal experience ("My grandmother is seventy years old, has gray hair, wears glasses, and makes the best apple pie"). But when children are helped to understand the basic nature of the concept with such instructional tools as family tree diagrams, they understand the notion of grandmother (and other types of relatives) on a broader and more general basis. They can then use this concept to compare family structures with friends and, later, to do genealogical research (Tappan, 1998; Tudge & Scrimsher, 2003).

In order for social interactions to produce advances in cognitive development, Vygotsky argued, they have to contain a process called *mediation*. Mediation occurs when a more knowledgeable individual interprets a child's behavior and helps transform it into an internal and symbolic representation that means the same thing to the child as to others (Light & Littleton, 1999; Tudge & Winterhoff, 1993; Wertsch & Tulviste, 1996). Perhaps the following example will help clarify this point: Imagine a child who reaches out to grasp an object that is beyond her reach. A nearby parent thinks the child is pointing at the object and says, "Oh, you want the box of crayons," and retrieves the item for the child. Over time, what began as a grasping action becomes transformed, through the mediation of an adult, into an internalized sign ("I want you to give that object to me") that means the same thing to the child as it does to the adult (Driscoll, 2005). Thus, a child's potential level of mental development can be brought about only by introducing the more advanced thought processes of another person.

How Instruction Affects Cognitive Development

Vygotsky drew a distinction between the type of information that preschool children learn and the type of information that children who attend school learn (or should learn). During early childhood, children acquire what Vygotsky called **spontaneous concepts.** That is, they learn various facts and concepts and rules (such as how to speak one's native language and how to classify objects in one's environment), but they do so for the most part as a by-product of such other activities as engaging in play and communicating with parents and playmates. This kind of

Cognitive development strongly influenced by those more intellectually advanced

Jean Piaget believed that children's schemes develop more quickly when children interact with one another than when they interact with adults. But Lev Vygotsky believed that children learn more from the instructional interactions they have with those who are more intellectually advanced, particularly if the instruction is designed to fall within the child's zone of proximal development. **A,** © Suzie Fitzhugh. **B,** © David Young-Wolff/Photo Edit

Teachers should help students learn how to use psychological tools

knowledge is unsystematic, unconscious, and directed at the child's everyday concrete experiences. Hence, Vygotsky's use of the term *spontaneous.*

Schooling, however, should be directed to the learning of what Vygotsky called **scientific concepts.** Scientific concepts are the psychological tools that allow us to manipulate our environment consciously and systematically. Vygotsky believed that the proper development of a child's mind depends on learning how to use these psychological tools, and this will occur only if classroom instruction is properly designed. This means providing students with explicit and clear verbal definitions as a first step. The basic purpose of instruction, then, is not simply to add one piece of knowledge to another like pennies in a piggy bank but to stimulate and guide cognitive development (Crain, 2005; Rogoff, 1990).

Contemporary psychologists have extended Vygotsky's notions of spontaneous and scientific concepts. They use the term **empirical learning** to refer to the way in which young children acquire spontaneous concepts. The hallmark of empirical learning is that the most observable characteristics of objects and events are noticed and used as a basis for forming general concepts. The main limitation of this approach is that salient characteristics are not necessarily critical or defining characteristics, and it is the latter that form the basis of correct concept formation. For example, in the absence of formal instruction, children come to believe that any utterance that has two or more words is a sentence, that whales are fish, and that bamboo is not a type of grass.

Theoretical learning, on the other hand, involves using psychological tools to learn scientific concepts. As these general tools are used repeatedly with various problems, they are gradually internalized and generalized to a wide variety of settings and problem types. Good-quality instruction, in this view, is aimed at helping children move from the very practical empirical learning to the more general theoretical learning and from using psychological tools overtly, with the aid of an adult, to using these tools mentally, without outside assistance (Karpov & Bransford, 1995; Morra, Gobbo, Marini, & Sheese, 2008).

Here's an example that compares the efficacy of the empirical and theoretical approaches: Two groups of six-year-old children were taught how to write the 22 letters of the Russian alphabet. Group 1 was taught using the empirical approach. The teacher gave the students a model of each letter, showed them how to write each one, and gave a verbal explanation of how to write each letter. The students then copied each letter under the teacher's supervision. When they produced an acceptable copy of a letter, they were taught the next letter. Group 2 was taught using the theoretical approach. First, students were taught to analyze the shape of each letter so they could identify where the direction of the contour of each line changed. Then they were to place dots in those locations outlining the change in contour. Finally, they were to reproduce the pattern of dots on another part of the page and connect the dots with a pencil.

The speed with which the children in each group learned to accurately produce the letters of the alphabet differed by quite a large margin. The average student in the empirical group needed about 170 trials to learn the first letter and about 20 trials to write the last letter. The number of trials taken to learn all 22 letters was about 1,230. The average student in the theoretical group required only about 14 trials to learn how to write the first letter correctly, and from the eighth letter on needed only 1 trial per letter. The number of trials needed to learn all 22 letters for the second group was about 60. Furthermore, these students were able to use the general method they were taught to help them learn to write the letters of the Latin and Arabic alphabets (Karpov & Bransford, 1995; Morra, et al., 2008).

Instruction and the Zone of Proximal Development This discussion of empirical and theoretical learning illustrates Vygotsky's belief that well-designed instruction is like a magnet. If it is aimed slightly ahead of what children know and can do at the present time, it will pull them along, helping them master things they cannot learn on their own. We can illustrate this idea with an experiment that Vygotsky (1986) described. He gave two eight-year-olds of average ability problems that were a bit too difficult for them to solve on their own. (Although Vygotsky did not specify what types of problems they were, imagine that they were math problems.) He then tried to help the children solve the problems by giving them leading questions and hints. He found that one child, with the hints, was able to solve problems designed for twelve-year-olds, whereas the other child, who also received the hints, could reach only a nine-year-old level.

> Cognitive development promoted by instruction in zone of proximal development

Vygotsky referred to the difference between what a child can do on his own and what can be accomplished with some assistance as the **zone of proximal development (ZPD)**. The size of the first eight-year-old's zone was 4 (that is, the eight-year-old could, with help, solve the problem designed for a child 4 years older), whereas the second child has a zone of 1 (he could solve the problem designed for a child 1 year older). According to Vygotsky, students with wider zones are likely to experience greater cognitive development when instruction is pitched just above the lower limit of their ZPD than will students with narrower zones because the former are in a better position to capitalize on the instruction. The ZPD, then, encompasses those abilities, attitudes, and patterns of thinking that are in the process of maturing and can be refined only with assistance (Holzman, 2009; Tappan, 2005; Tudge & Scrimsher, 2003).

> Scaffolding techniques support student learning

Helping students answer difficult questions or solve problems by giving them hints or asking leading questions is an example of a technique called **scaffolding.** Just as construction workers use external scaffolding to support their building efforts, Vygotsky recommended that teachers similarly support learning in its early phases. The purpose of scaffolding is to help students acquire knowledge and skills they would not have learned on their own. As the student demonstrates mastery over the content in question, the learning aids are faded and removed. Scaffolding techniques that are likely to help students traverse their ZPD include prompts, suggestions, checklists, modeling, rewards, feedback, cognitive structuring (using such devices as theories, categories, labels, and rules for helping students organize and understand ideas), and questioning (Gallimore & Tharp, 1990; Ratner, 1991). As students approach the upper limit of their ZPD, their behavior becomes smoother, more internalized, and more automatized. Any assistance offered at this level will likely be perceived as disruptive and irritating.

TeachSource Video Case ◄◄ ▶ ▶▶

Vygotsky's Zone of Proximal Development: Increasing Cognition in an Elementary Literacy Lesson

Go to the Education CourseMate website to watch the Video Case, and then answer the following questions:

1. How does the Video Case illustrate the zone of proximal development as it is explained above? How does the Video Case bring this concept to life?

2. How does the classroom teacher in the Video Case (Dr. Hurley) scaffold instruction for the children? What kinds of hints and leading questions does she give them?

Mark Tappan (1998) has proposed the following four-component model that teachers can use to optimize the effects of their scaffolding efforts and help students move through their ZPD:

1. *Model desired academic behaviors.* Children can imitate many behaviors that they do not have the capability to exhibit independently, and such experiences stimulate them to act this way on their own.

2. *Create a dialogue with the student.* A child's understanding of concepts, procedures, and principles becomes more systematic and organized as a result of the exchange of questions, explanations, and feedback between teacher and child within the child's ZPD. As with modeling, the effectiveness of this dialogue is determined, at least in part, by the extent to which the teacher and student are committed to creating and maintaining a relationship in which each makes an honest effort to satisfy the needs of the other.

3. *Practice.* Practice speeds up the internalizing of thinking skills that students observe and discuss with others (see Schmitz & Winksel, 2008).

4. *Confirmation.* To confirm others is to bring out the best in them by focusing on what they can do with some assistance, and this process helps create a trusting and mutually supportive relationship between teacher and student. For example, you might say to a student, "I know this assignment seems difficult right now and that you have had some problems in the past with similar assignments, but with the help I'm willing to offer, I'm certain you'll do good-quality work."

Vygotsky's notion of producing cognitive development by embedding instruction within a student's ZPD is an attractive one and has many implications for instruction. In Chapter 9, which is about social cognitive theory, for example, we will describe how this notion was used to improve the reading comprehension skills of low-achieving seventh graders.

USING TECHNOLOGY TO PROMOTE COGNITIVE DEVELOPMENT

Piaget and Vygotsky believed that people use physical, mental, and social experiences to construct personal conceptions (schemes) of what the world is like. Engagement with the environment, and with others in the environment, are critical to cognitive development. Although there are numerous opportunities throughout the course of each day to watch what other people do, try out ideas, and interact with others face to face, we are normally limited to the physical and social stimuli that make up our immediate environment. Factors such as distance, time, and cost keep us from wider-ranging interactions. Technology, however, has expanded the range of our experience. This is especially true with the advent of what has been called Web 2.0 technologies, which include interactive information sharing, collaboration, multi-user virtual environments, social networking, blogs, and the like.

The use of technology in both elementary and secondary schools continues to increase (Kulik, 2003a; Pullin, Gitsaki, Baguley, 2010). Although classrooms will likely remain, for some time to come, the primary place where students and teachers gather in person, technology allows students and teachers to engage people and information across time and space. So, the classroom is no longer the only environment for learning. There are now numerous virtual environments that can be accessed through technology.

Technology Applied to Piaget   *SKIP*

Central to Piaget's ideas of cognitive development is cognitive disequilibrium, when a student's understanding of the world does not match her or his experience. Situations that present problems for students to ponder and try to solve drive learning and development because they introduce disequilibrium. Technology gives students access to experiences that contribute to disequilibrium.

> Virtual learning environments can introduce disequilibrium, promote exploration and visual representations of abstract ideas, and help students construct knowledge

Microworlds, for example, are simulated learning environments that provide opportunities for students to think about problems for which there are not obvious solutions or situations that do not immediately "make sense." They also allow researchers to investigate how learners make decisions in contexts that can be more or less controlled (Elliott, Welsh, Nettelbeck, & Mills, 2007; Healy & Hoyles, 2001).

The Conservation of Area and Its Measurement (C.AR.M.E) is a microworld that provides a set of geometric tools to encourage students to create different ways to represent the concept of area measurement. A group of high school students created 11 ways to represent the measurement of area using C.AR.M.E (Kordaki & Potari, 2002). Another microworld, Probability Explorer, allows students to design probability experiments that relate to such real-world activities as weather forecasting; it is intended to help students refine their intuitive understanding of chance (Drier, 2001). As these examples illustrate, microworlds foster cognitive development by encouraging student exploration, student control, and visual representation of abstract ideas. Some microworlds include sensors that are attached to a microcomputer to generate graphs of such physical phenomena as temperature, sound, motion, and electromotive force (Peña & Alessi, 1999; Trumper & Gelbman, 2000, 2002). Because such microworlds, also called **microcomputer-based laboratories,** provide an immediate link between a hands-on, concrete experience and a symbolic representation of that experience (a graph), their use may facilitate the shift from concrete to formal operational thinking (Trumper & Gelbman, 2000).

Opportunities to construct new understandings and conceptions (schemes), come not only from interacting with information and objects in an environment, but from interacting with the people in that environment. Virtual learning allows students to engage environments and collaborate with people not otherwise accessible.

Technological learning environments can provide challenging problems that encourage social construction of knowledge. Jose Luis Pelaez Inc/Blend Images/Jupiter Images

Technology Applied to Vygotsky

Technology can act as and provide expert collaborative partners

As you'll recall, Vygotsky believed that children gain significantly from the knowledge and conceptual tools handed down to them by those who are more intellectually advanced. Roy Pea (1985, 2004) and Gavriel Salomon (1988) were among the first to suggest that technology might play the same role as more capable tutors with such tasks as writing an essay and reading a book. Basically, the software provides prompts and expert guidance during reading and writing tasks. These supports, or scaffolds, are gradually faded as students become more competent at regulating their own behavior. According to some researchers (Cotterall & Cohen, 2003; Donovan & Smolkin, 2002), such support is vital in writing, because young children often lack the cognitive resources and skills to move beyond simple knowledge-telling in their compositions. Salomon, who helped develop both the Reading Partner and Writing Partner software tools, found that they improved children's reading comprehension, essay writing, effort, and awareness of useful self-questioning strategies (Salomon, Globerson, & Guterman, 1989; Zellermayer, Salomon, Globerson, & Givon, 1991). Some studies of the same period did not always report such positive results (Bonk & Reynolds, 1992; Daiute, 1985; Reynolds & Bonk, 1996). However, as educators and researchers have gained experience with technologically based learning environments, Vygotsky's ideas have become better understood in that context and therefore more effectively applied (Alavi & Leidner, 2001; Borthick, Jones, & Wakai, 2003; Roth & Lee, 2007). For example, Yelland and Masters (2007) found that within technological environments, children can support each other's learning, and the scaffolding that occurs in such environments supports learners cognitively, affectively, and technologically. Indeed, within the context of technology-driven learning environments, the technology itself, if it is designed to be supportive of the learner, is sometimes referred to as a scaffold (De Lisi, 2006).

Even so, Vygotsky viewed social interaction as the primary cause of cognitive development. Technology connects people to people and it can do so in a variety of contexts that allow learners to gain knowledge and the psychological tools that help them to grow intellectually. One way in which technology connects people is in **multi-user virtual environments (MUVEs)**. One such MUVE is known as Quest Atlantis, a virtual learning environment that has engaged over 20,000 students from four continents (Barab, Gresalfi, Ingram-Noble, Jameson, Hickey, Akram, & Kizer, 2009;

TeachSource Video Case ◄◄ ▶ ►►

Middle School Reading Instruction: Integrating Technology

Go to the Education CourseMate website to watch the Video Case, and then answer the following questions:

1. How does the online chat room depicted in this Video Case illustrate Piaget's theory of cognitive conflict that is described in the chapter?

2. Describe the way that the online discussion group supports Vygotsky's notion of zone of proximal development (ZPD) and scaffolding.

Gresalfi, Barab, Siyahhan, & Christensen, 2009). The Quest Atlantis project will be examined in more detail in Chapter 10 and we will see how students engage learning activities both online in the virtual environment and offline as well. The point here is that technology can support social interaction of many students in the same virtual environment.

A second way technology connects people is through online mentoring relationships, typically called **telementoring** (Duff, 2000; Murray, 2009; Rea, 2001). The education and technology literature is filled with examples of telementoring in preK–12 education. For instance, international weather projects such as the Kids as Global Scientists project (Mistler-Jackson & Songer, 2000) and the Global Learning and Observations to Benefit the Environment program (Barab & Luehmann, 2003; Finarelli, 1998) involve students in genuine scientific data collection and reporting. The collaborative relationships that students establish with peers and mentors create in students a strong sense of participation in what is called a community of practice. There are also telementoring opportunities for teachers (Whitehouse, McCloskey, Ketelhut, 2010). The website of the International Telementor Program (**http://telementor.org**) provides volunteer mentors from around the world to teachers and students.

PIAGET, KOHLBERG, AND GILLIGAN: MORAL DEVELOPMENT

Piaget's Analysis of the Moral Judgment of the Child

Because he was intrigued by all aspects of children's thinking, Piaget became interested in moral development. He began his study of morality by observing how children played marbles. (He first learned the game himself, so that he would be able to understand the subtleties of the conception.) Piaget discovered that interpretations of rules followed by participants in marble games changed with age.

Age Changes in Interpretation of Rules Four- to seven-year-olds just learning the game seemed to view rules as interesting examples of the social behavior of older children. They did not understand the rules but tried to go along with them. Seven- to ten-year-olds regarded rules as sacred pronouncements handed down by older children or adults. At about the age of eleven or twelve, children began to see rules as agreements reached by mutual consent. Piaget concluded that younger children see rules as absolute and external.

Although children ranging from the age of four to about ten do not question rules, they may frequently break them because they do not understand them completely. After the age of eleven or so, children become increasingly capable of grasping why rules are necessary. At that point, Piaget concluded, they tend to lose interest in adult-imposed regulations and take delight in formulating their own variations of rules to fit a particular situation. Piaget illustrated this point by describing how a group of ten- and eleven-year-old boys prepared for a snowball fight (1965, p. 50). They divided themselves into teams, elected officers, decided on rules to govern the distances from which the snowballs could be thrown, and agreed on a system of punishments for those who violated the rules. Although they spent a substantial amount of playtime engaging in such preliminary discussions, they seemed to thoroughly enjoy their newly discovered ability to make up rules to supplant those that previously had been imposed on them by their elders.

Moral Realism Versus Moral Relativism The way children of different ages responded to rules so intrigued Piaget that he decided to use the interview method to obtain more systematic information about moral development. He made up pairs of stories and asked children of different ages to discuss them. Here is a typical pair of stories:

pause & reflect

Remember our definition of decentration in the earlier discussion of Piaget's theory. How do you think the young child's lack of decentration might affect her moral reasoning?

A: There was a little boy called Julian. His father had gone out and Julian thought it would be fun to play with father's ink-pot. First he played with the pen, and then he made a little blot on the tablecloth.

B: A little boy who was called Augustus once noticed that his father's ink-pot was empty. One day that his father was away he thought of filling the ink-pot so as to help his father, and so that he should find it full when he came home. But while he was opening the ink-bottle he made a big blot on the table cloth. (1965, p. 122)

After reading these stories, Piaget asked, "Are these children equally guilty? Which of the two is naughtier, and why?" As was the case with interpretations of rules, Piaget found that younger children reacted to these stories differently from older children. The younger children maintained that Augustus was guiltier than Julian because he had made a bigger inkblot on the tablecloth. They took no account of the fact that Julian was misbehaving and that Augustus was trying to help his father. Older children, however, were more likely to base their judgment of guilt on the intent of each child. Piaget referred to the moral thinking of children up to the age of ten or so as the **morality of constraint,** but he also called it *moral realism.* The thinking of children of eleven or older Piaget called the **morality of cooperation.** He also occasionally used the term *moral relativism.* Piaget concluded that the two basic types of moral reasoning differ in several ways. We summarize these differences in Table 2.3.

Reflecting on Table 2.3, it is not surprising that Piaget's ideas have led to more recent work that considers how the development of moral thinking informs and is informed by experiences and observations of practices that affect conditions of social justice (Turiel, 2008).

Kohlberg's Description of Moral Development

For an interactive exploration of Kohlberg's moral dilemmas, see the textbook's Education CourseMate website.

Just as James Marcia elaborated Erikson's concept of identity formation, Lawrence Kohlberg elaborated Piaget's ideas on moral thinking. Kohlberg believed that (1) moral reasoning proceeds through fixed stages, and (2) moral development can be accelerated through instruction.

Kohlberg's Use of Moral Dilemmas As a graduate student at the University of Chicago in the 1950s, Lawrence Kohlberg became fascinated by Piaget's studies of moral development. He decided to expand on Piaget's original research by making up stories involving moral dilemmas that would be more appropriate for older children. Here is the story that is most often mentioned in discussions of his work:

In Europe a woman was near death from cancer. One drug might save her, a form of radium that a druggist in the same town had recently discovered. The druggist was charging $2,000, ten times what the drug cost him to make. The sick woman's

Morality of constraint (moral realism): rules are sacred, consequences determine guilt

Morality of cooperation (moral relativism): rules are flexible, intent important in determining guilt

Table 2.3	Morality of Constraint Versus Morality of Cooperation
Morality of Constraint (Typical of Six-Year-Olds)	**Morality of Cooperation (Typical of Twelve-Year-Olds)**
Holds single, absolute moral perspective (behavior is right or wrong).	Is aware of different viewpoints regarding rules.
Believes rules are unchangeable.	Believes rules are flexible.
Determines extent of guilt by amount of damage.	Considers the wrongdoers' intentions when evaluating guilt.
Defines moral wrongness in terms of what is forbidden or punished.	Defines moral wrongness in terms of violation of spirit of cooperation.
(Notice that these first four differences call attention to the tendency for children below the age of ten or so to think of rules as sacred pronouncements handed down by external authority.)	
Believes punishment should stress atonement and does not need to "fit the crime."	Believes punishment should involve either restitution or suffering the same fate as one's victim.
Believes peer aggression should be punished by an external authority.	Believes peer aggression should be punished by retaliatory behavior on the part of the victim.*
Believes children should obey rules because they are established by those in authority.	Believes children should obey rules because of mutual concerns for rights of others.
(Notice how these last three differences call attention to the tendency for children above the age of ten or so to see rules as mutual agreements among equals.)	

*Beyond the age of twelve, adolescents increasingly affirm that reciprocal reactions, or "getting back," should be a response to good behavior, not bad behavior.

SOURCES: Freely adapted from interpretations of Piaget (1932) by Kohlberg (1969) and Lickona (1976).

husband, Heinz, went to everyone he knew to borrow the money, but he could only get together about half of what it cost. He told the druggist that his wife was dying and asked him to sell it cheaper or let him pay later, but the druggist said "No." The husband got desperate and broke into the man's store to steal the drug for his wife. Should the husband have done that? Why? (1969, p. 376)

Kohlberg's Six Stages of Moral Reasoning   After analyzing the responses of ten- to sixteen-year-olds to this and similar moral dilemmas, Kohlberg (1963) eventually developed a description of six stages of moral reasoning. Be forewarned, however, that Kohlberg later revised some of his original stage designations and that descriptions of the stages have also been modified since he first proposed them. In different discussions of his stages, therefore, you may encounter varying descriptions. The outline presented in Table 2.4 is a composite summary of the sequence of moral development as described by Kohlberg, but you should expect to find differences if you read other accounts of his theory.

The scoring system Kohlberg developed to evaluate a response to a moral dilemma is extremely complex. Furthermore, the responses of subjects are lengthy and may feature arguments about a particular decision. To help you understand a bit more about each Kohlberg stage, the following list offers simplified examples of responses to a dilemma such as that faced by Heinz. For maximum clarity, only brief typical responses to the question, "Why shouldn't you steal from a store?" are mentioned.

Table 2.4	Kohlberg's Stages of Moral Reasoning

LEVEL 1: PRECONVENTIONAL MORALITY. (Typical of children up to the age of nine. Called *preconventional* because young children do not really understand the conventions or rules of a society.)

Stage 1: Punishment-obedience orientation. The physical consequences of an action determine goodness or badness. Those in authority have superior power and should be obeyed. Punishment should be avoided by staying out of trouble.

Stage 2: Instrumental relativist orientation. An action is judged to be right if it is instrumental in satisfying one's own needs or involves an even exchange. Obeying rules should bring some sort of benefit in return.

LEVEL 2: CONVENTIONAL MORALITY. (Typical of nine- to twenty-year-olds. Called *conventional* since most nine- to twenty-year-olds conform to the conventions of society because they are the rules of a society.)

Stage 3: Good boy–nice girl orientation. The right action is one that would be carried out by someone whose behavior is likely to please or impress others.

Stage 4: Law-and-order orientation. To maintain the social order, fixed rules must be established and obeyed. It is essential to respect authority.

LEVEL 3: POSTCONVENTIONAL MORALITY. (Usually reached only after the age of twenty and only by a small proportion of adults. Called *postconventional* because the moral principles that underlie the conventions of a society are understood.)

Stage 5: Social contract orientation. Rules needed to maintain the social order should be based not on blind obedience to authority but on mutual agreement. At the same time, the rights of the individual should be protected.

Stage 6: Universal ethical principle orientation. Moral decisions should be made in terms of self-chosen ethical principles. Once principles are chosen, they should be applied in consistent ways.[*]

[*]In an article published in 1978, several years after Kohlberg had originally described the six stages, he described the last stage as an essentially theoretical ideal that is rarely encountered in real life.

SOURCE: Based on descriptions in Kohlberg (1969, 1976, 1978).

Stage 1: punishment-obedience orientation. "You might get caught." (The physical consequences of an action determine goodness or badness.)

Stage 2: instrumental relativist orientation. "You shouldn't steal something from a store, and the store owner shouldn't steal things that belong to you." (Obedience to laws should involve an even exchange.)

Stage 3: good boy–nice girl orientation. "Your parents will be proud of you if you are honest." (The right action is one that will impress others.)

Stage 4: law-and-order orientation. "It's against the law, and if we don't obey laws, our whole society might fall apart." (To maintain the social order, fixed rules must be obeyed.)

Stage 5: social contract orientation. "Under certain circumstances laws may have to be disregarded—if a person's life depends on breaking a law, for instance." (Rules should involve mutual agreements; the rights of the individual should be protected.)

Stage 6: universal ethical principle orientation. "You need to weigh all the factors and then try to make the most appropriate decision in a given situation. Sometimes it would be morally wrong *not* to steal." (Moral decisions should be based on consistent applications of self-chosen ethical principles.)

Preconventional morality: avoid punishment, receive benefits in return

Conventional morality: impress others, respect authority

Postconventional morality: mutual agreements, consistent principles

Criticisms and Evaluations of Kohlberg's Theory Is Kohlberg's contention that moral reasoning proceeds through a fixed universal sequence of stages accurate? Based on analysis of research on moral development, Martin Hoffman (1980) believes that although Kohlberg's sequence of stages may not be true of every individual in every culture, it may provide a useful general description of how moral reasoning develops in American society. Carol Gilligan (1979), whose position we will discuss in detail later, has proposed two somewhat different sequences that reflect differences in male and female socialization.

Paul Vitz (1990) criticizes Kohlberg's use of moral dilemmas on the grounds that they are too far removed from the kinds of everyday social interactions in which children and adolescents engage. He prefers instead the use of narrative stories, both fictional and real accounts of others, because they portray such basic moral values as honesty, compassion, fairness, and hard work in an understandable context. Others (e.g., Rest, Narvaez, Bebeau, & Thoma, 1999) have criticized the fact that Kohlberg relied on the ability of his participants to explain clearly how they solved such hypothetical dilemmas as Heinz's. Individuals not adept at self-reflection or without the vocabulary to express their thoughts clearly either would not be recruited into such studies or would have little to contribute.

Another criticism concerns the type of moral issue that most interested Kohlberg. Kohlberg's theory deals primarily with what are called macromoral issues. These are broad social issues such as civil rights, free speech, the women's movement, and wilderness preservation. The focus is on how the behavior of individuals affects the structure of society and public policy. At this level, a moral person is one who attempts to influence laws and regulations because of a deeply held principle. For some psychologists (e.g., Rest et al., 1999), a limitation of Kohlberg's theory is that it does not adequately address micromoral issues. *Micromoral issues* concern personal interactions in everyday situations, examples of which include courtesy (not interrupting someone before that person has finished speaking), helpfulness (giving up your seat on a crowded bus or train to an elderly person), remembering significant events of friends and family, and being punctual for appointments. For micromoral issues, a moral person is one who is loyal, dedicated, and cares about particular people.

Finally, Kohlberg's work has also been criticized because it places such a strong emphasis on the role of reasoning in moral behavior but says little about the nature of people who behave in moral ways. Studies of adolescents who exhibit high levels of moral commitment and action (such as volunteering to work for social service agencies and community soup kitchens) show that these individuals have a self-concept that distinguishes them from other adolescents. They describe themselves in terms of moral characteristics and goals, have a greater sense of stability, and emphasize the importance of personal beliefs and personal philosophy. Yet these same adolescents did not differ from their peers on measures of moral judgment—their scores ranged from stage 3 to stage 5. It appears that advanced levels of moral reasoning may be only weakly related to moral behavior (Arnold, 2000).

> Criticisms of Kohlberg's theory: moral development difficult to accelerate, moral dilemmas not relevant to daily life, relies on macromoral issues, ignores characteristics other than moral reasoning

pause & reflect

How would you respond to a parent or colleague who argued that students have better things to do in class than discuss ways of resolving moral dilemmas?

The Caring Orientation to Moral Development and Education

Carol Gilligan and Nel Noddings are pioneering educational scholars: they charted a new course in thinking about moral development and moral education. Each, in her own way, asked if our views of how we develop our identity, of how we think and act in moral situations, and of how we see ourselves and our relationships to others are more descriptive of males than females. We look first at Gilligan's objections to Erickson's and Kohlberg's theories and then at Noddings's care theory.

Gilligan's View of Identity and Moral Development Carol Gilligan (1982, 1988) argues that Erikson's view of identity development and Kohlberg's view of moral development more accurately describe what occurs with adolescent males than with adolescent females. In her view, Erikson's and Kohlberg's ideas emphasize separation from parental authority and societal conventions. Instead of remaining loyal to adult authority, individuals as they mature shift their loyalty to abstract principles (for example, self-reliance, independence, justice, and fairness). This process of detachment allows adolescents to assume a more equal status with adults. It's almost as if adolescents are saying, "You have your life, and I have mine; you don't intrude on mine, and I won't intrude on yours."

But, Gilligan argues, many adolescent females have a different primary concern. They care less about separation and independence and more about remaining loyal to others through expressions of caring, understanding, and sharing of experiences. Detachment for these female adolescents is a moral problem rather than a sought after developmental milestone. The problem for them is how to become autonomous while also being caring and connected.

Given this view, Gilligan believes that adolescent females are more likely to resolve Erikson's identity versus role confusion and intimacy versus isolation crises concurrently rather than consecutively. The results of at least one study (Ochse & Plug, 1986) support this view. With respect to Kohlberg's theory, Gilligan argues that because females are socialized to value more highly the qualities of understanding, helping, and cooperation with others than that of preserving individual rights, and because this latter orientation is reflected most strongly in Kohlberg's two conventional stages (stages 3 and 4), females are more likely to be judged to be at a lower level of moral development than males.

Stephen Thoma (1986) has offered a partial answer to Gilligan's criticism. After reviewing more than fifty studies on gender differences in moral development, he drew three conclusions:

1. The effect of gender on scores from the Defining Issues Test (the DIT is a device that uses responses to moral dilemmas to determine level of moral reasoning) was very small. Less than one half of 1 percent of the differences in DIT scores was due to gender differences.
2. Females almost always scored higher. This slight superiority for females appeared in every age group studied (middle school, high school, college, adults).
3. Differences in DIT scores were strongly associated with differences in age and level of education. That is, individuals who were older and had graduated from college were more likely to score at the postconventional level than those who were younger and had less education.

Thoma's findings suggest that females are just as likely as males to use justice and fairness concepts in their reasoning about *hypothetical* moral dilemmas.

But there is one aspect of Gilligan's criticism that cannot be answered by Thoma's analysis. Gilligan argues that when females are faced with their own real-life moral dilemmas (abortion, civil rights, environmental pollution) rather than hypothetical ones, they are more likely to favor a caring-helping-cooperation orientation than a justice-fairness-individual rights orientation.

Noddings's Care Theory The caring orientation advocated by Gilligan in the 1980s arose from her criticism that Erickson's and Kohlberg's theories did not provide the best account of the psychosocial and moral development of female adolescents. In 1984, Nel Noddings, an educational philosopher, published an important book entitled *Caring: A Feminine Approach to Ethics and Moral Education*. The book has remained an important source of ideas in matters of moral education. So much so, that a second edition, with a new preface that explained how some of her thinking had changed since the1980s, was published in 2003. Noddings was careful to point out that her ideas were not descriptive only of females, but rather were framed from a feminine rather than a masculine perspective. She wrote: "The view here is a feminine view. This does not imply that all women will accept it or that men reject it; indeed, there is no reason why men should not embrace it."

(Noddings, 1984/2003, p. 2). (Noddings does consider herself a feminist, but she was not familiar with the term when she wrote the first edition in the early 1980s.)

Noddings provided a different lens through which to view moral development. Rather than using moral reasoning as a starting point, as Kohlberg did, she started with the idea that there is a human desire for goodness, what she called a moral attitude. From that starting point, she developed care theory. Through the last three decades, care theory has come to focus clearly on relationships and how those relationships function. In Noddings view, it is not enough to say that we care—to simply express a concern for someone or some group of people. Care theory focuses on whether a caring relationship exists. Noddings uses an example to illustrate the point: Teachers in a school may claim that they care deeply for students and support their claim by citing the long hours and hard work they spend in service of students and their well-being. But if students genuinely feel as though "nobody cares," then a caring relationship does not exist no matter how hard teachers work or how often they express their concern for students and their desire to help them. In this case, the problem may be neither the teachers nor the students, but the conditions that prevent caring relations to exist and grow. As Noddings says in her preface to the second edition: "Our efforts should be directed to transforming the conditions that make caring difficult or impossible" (p. xiv). Noddings's development of care theory supports Gilligan's criticisms of Erickson and Kohlberg (2008). Together, they have suggested that a "caring orientation" to social and moral development is an alternative to the justice-fairness-individual rights orientation that has emerged from Kohlberg's theory, and one that may lead to more socially just practices and policies.

Perhaps the best approach that educators can take when they involve students in discussions of moral issues is to emphasize the utility of *both* orientations. The recent research on gender differences supports that females use both orientations to think about issues of right and wrong, and so do males. Emphasizing both orientations when classroom discussions focus on matters of right and wrong is one way of acknowledging student diversity. It also makes sense given a more recent review of many studies of gender differences in moral orientation. Jaffee, Hyde, and Shibley (2000) found that females as a group use a caring orientation to a slightly greater extent than the justice orientation. They found also that males as a group tend to use a justice orientation slightly more often. Jaffee, Hyde, and Shibley found small differences between very large groups.

Although slight differences do exist, both males and females use caring and justice orientations to resolve real-life moral dilemmas

Carol Gilligan believes that Erikson's theory of identity development and Kohlberg's theory of moral development do not accurately describe the course of identity formation and moral reasoning in females. She believes that adolescent females place a higher value on caring, understanding, and sharing of experiences than they do on independence, self-reliance, and justice. © Myrleen Ferguson Cate/Photo Edit

Does Moral Thinking Lead to Moral Behavior?

The Hartshorne and May Studies Hugh Hartshorne and Mark May (1929, 1930a, 1930b) observed thousands of children at different age levels reacting in situations that revealed their actual moral behavior. The researchers also asked the children to respond to questions about hypothetical situations to reveal how much they understood about right and wrong behavior. Elementary school children, for example, were allowed to correct their own papers or record their own scores on measures of athletic skill without being aware that accurate measures were being made independently by adult observers. The children were also asked what they thought was the right thing to do in similar situations.

A comparison of the two sets of data made it possible to determine, among other things, whether children practiced what they preached. What Hartshorne and May discovered was that many children who were able to describe right kinds of behavior in hypothetical situations indulged in wrong behavior in real-life situations. Children reacted in specific rather than consistent ways to situations that called for moral judgment. Even a child who was rated as among the most honest in a group would behave in a dishonest way under certain circumstances. A boy who was an excellent student but an indifferent athlete, for example, would not cheat when asked to correct his own paper, but he would inflate scores on sports skills.

Another significant discovery that Hartshorne and May made was that children who went to religious education classes or belonged to such organizations as the Boy Scouts or Girl Scouts were just as dishonest as children who were not exposed to the kind of moral instruction provided by such organizations. Hartshorne and May concluded that one explanation for the ineffectiveness of moral instruction in the 1920s was that too much stress was placed on having children memorize values such as the Ten Commandments or the Boy Scout oath and law. The two researchers suggested that it would be more effective to invite children to discuss real-life moral situations as they occurred.

Recent research shows that Hartshorne and May's basic finding is still valid. Approximately 90 percent of high school students and 70 percent of college students admitted to engaging in academic cheating. At both grade levels, males cheated more often than females. Moreover, cheating was judged to be more or less acceptable depending on the reason. Cheating was deemed more justifiable if it resulted in passing a class and getting a job that would help one's family. It was also seen as more justifiable if it was done to avoid disappointing one's parents, to avoid academic probation, or because the instructor had treated the student unfairly (Jensen, Arnett, Feldman, & Cauffman, 2002). In another study on lying to parents, the same authors found that both high school and college students lied to their parents across a range of real-life issues such as dating, parties, sex, and money (Jensen, Arnett, Feldman, & Cauffman, 2004). Jensen et al. (2004) did find that high school students tended to lie to parents more frequently than college students and attribute the difference to factors related to the development of autonomy. They also found that students from cohesive, rather than controlling, family environments were less likely to report lying to parents and less accepting of lying. As we will see in later chapters, students' perceptions of their teachers can prove critical. In terms of cheating, students who perceive their teacher as less than effective facilitators of learning are more likely to cheat than students who view their instructors as effective teachers (Murdock, Miller, & Kohlhardt, 2004). Research has also shown that students are more likely to cheat when the culture of the classroom emphasizes good grades and high scores on tests (Anderman & Midgley, 2004; Anderman & Murdock, 2007.)

The insights from Piaget, Kohlberg, Gilligan, and Noddings are important for aspiring teachers. But as Hartshorne and May pointed out eight decades ago—and as contemporary researchers are still finding—there are gaps between moral reasoning and moral action or behavior. Mark Tappan (2006) has advocated a "sociocultural" approach to the study of moral development. You'll recall that Vygotsky's views on

> Moral knowledge does not always result in moral behavior

Case in Print

Teaching Students to Be Good Characters

Many parents, educators, and political leaders believe that today's students lack the moral values possessed by previous generations. Concerned adults cite violence in schools and widespread drug abuse, among other problems, as evidence of such a decline. One commonly voiced solution to these problems is for the schools to institute moral education programs (also called character education programs). (p. 65)

Reading, Writing, and Character Education

CAROLYN BOWER
St. Louis Post-Dispatch 11/28/2003

A blue banner over the entrance to Ridgewood Middle School in Arnold reads "Character under construction."

Similar banners appear in the halls and gym. Once a week students take a half-hour to focus on a character education activity. Recently, Justin Schweiss, 12, and Conan Morrison, 14, dusted the lockers. A half dozen other seventh-graders gathered paper from classroom bins to recycle. Some students wrote messages about what they could do to promote peace.

"We don't have too many fights at this school," said Jacob Brydels, 14, an eighth-grade member of the Student Council. "We all get along."

Ridgewood, with about 530 students in grades seven and eight, is often singled out as an example of a school where character education works. Since focusing on character education a little more than three years ago, Ridgewood Principal Tim Crutchley has watched state test scores rise and discipline referrals drop by nearly 70 percent.

Hundreds of schools across the country use character education, defined as any initiative intended to develop student character. Missouri is one of 47 states that have received federal money for character education. Ridgewood is one of 111 school districts in Missouri and Illinois—and one of 38 in the St. Louis region—that take part in CHARACTERplus, a character education program.

Character education can improve academic achievement, behavior and attitudes, according to a study by Marvin Berkowitz and Melinda Bier, both at the University of Missouri at St. Louis. Berkowitz is the Sanford N. McDonnell Endowed Professor in Education at the university and Bier is an affiliate assistant professor.

The study was presented last month at a national forum of the Character Education Partnership, a nonpartisan coalition devoted to improving children's civic virtue and morals. The John Templeton Foundation financed the research.

Berkowitz found effective character education usually includes a number of strategies, requires staff training and needs parent and community involvement.

"We as a society have allowed an erosion of respect," Berkowitz said.

Students who act rudely to each other or cheat on tests reflect what has happened elsewhere in society with high profile scandals such as corporation executives cheating people of their money or celebrities cheating on their wives.

"In families we are not teaching or modeling how to treat other people with respect," Berkowitz said. "In schools we are not standing up to kids and saying, 'Look, this is the norm of civility in society.'"

At Jefferson Elementary School in Belleville, Principal Mark Eichenlaub began a push last year to involve parents and the community in character education.

Jefferson's 343 students in kindergarten through sixth grade have a reputation for strong academic achievement. But Eichenlaub wanted to make sure students, parents and those at the school were on the same page as far as intangible values.

The school adopted one rule for all students: "Be in the right place, at the right time, doing the right thing."

"There is no canned program," Eichenlaub said. "But creating a climate of character has to be the backbone of a school."

At Ridgewood, teachers study books such as Clifton Taulbert's "Eight Habits of the Heart," and talk about nurturing attitudes.

"The staff has to model good behavior, not just talk about it," said Kristen Pelster, assistant principal at Ridgewood. "Kids can't learn respect and responsibility by someone putting those words on paper on a wall. Character education is not a program. It is a way of life."

Questions and Activities

1. Just on the basis of the information provided in the article, what factors might account for the success of the character education program at Ridgewood Middle School? What other factors might have played a role but were not mentioned?

2. Ridgewood Middle School has been identified as "a school where character education works" because state test scores increased and discipline referrals decreased. If you were responsible for designing and evaluating a character education program, would you be satisfied with these two outcomes as a basis for claiming that the program works? If not, what other outcomes would you want to measure? Why?

3. Professor Marvin Berkowitz, a character education researcher mentioned in the article, believes that there has been an erosion of respect in our society and that the reason is at least partly because many parents do not teach or model for their children how to treat other people with respect. Do you believe that people, including children, are unnecessarily rude toward and inconsiderate of others? If so, what other causes might there be besides parents who do a poor job of teaching their children?

4. Kristen Pelster, the assistant principal at Ridgewood Middle School, maintains that the teaching and administrative staff have to model good character and not just talk about it. How might you do that as a teacher?

cognitive development helped to define the sociocultural approach. Tappan's approach takes into account the social culture of a classroom, such as the perceptions of students and an emphasis on grades and test scores in attempting to connect reasoning and behavior in order to understand actions. Tappan's theoretical work may prove very helpful in judging the effectiveness of moral education programs aimed at improving not only students' ability to reason morally but to act in morally responsible ways.

Research on Character Education Programs Many parents, educators, and political leaders believe that today's students lack the moral values possessed by previous generations. Concerned adults cite violence in schools and widespread drug abuse, among other problems, as evidence of such a decline.

One commonly voiced solution to these problems is for the schools to institute moral education programs (also called character education programs). As the Case in Print: "Teaching Students to Be Good Characters" demonstrates, these programs are becoming increasingly popular. After reviewing the research on the effectiveness of character education programs, James Leming (1993) drew the following conclusions:

- Telling students what they should or should not do, through either slogans ("Just say no") or conduct codes, is unlikely to have significant or lasting effects on character.
- Helping students think about how to resolve moral dilemmas in higher-level ways does not automatically result in increases in morally acceptable behavior.
- An individual's social environment plays an important role in the learning and exhibiting of virtuous behavior. When students have clear rules with which to guide their behavior, accept those rules as appropriate and worthwhile, and are rewarded for complying with those rules, they are more likely to exhibit morally acceptable behavior.
- Producing changes in moral behavior requires a commitment to a well-conceived, long-term program.

More recently, Leming (2008) has advocated using a kind of engineering approach to design classroom environments that address what has been learned about effective character education programs. Many social critics recommend that, as part of character education programs, children either read or have read to them stories with a moral theme (sometimes called virtue stories). Being exposed to such stories

The nature of a student's social environment, and the kind of social interactions that are encouraged in that environment, can help students learn and exhibit acceptable behavior.
© JLP/Jose L. Pelaez/Corbis

is supposed to help children develop a strong set of traditional moral values, such as honesty, trustworthiness, responsibility, and loyalty. Darcia Narvaez (2002) points out that such a claim, whether its advocates realize it, rests on five assumptions that are not supported by contemporary research findings on learning: .

Assumption 1: Reading Is a Passive Activity   The picture that emerges from thousands of research studies is that reading comprehension is not passive. Rather, it is the result of considerable cognitive activity. Children attempt to create a coherent, meaningful representation of a text by integrating the information in a text with prior knowledge.

Assumption 2: All Readers Extract the Same Information from a Text   Because of individual differences in prior knowledge, interests, and reading skills, each reader constructs a somewhat unique representation of what a text is about. Furthermore, texts with unfamiliar ideas are likely to be recalled less well and have more distortions than texts with more familiar ideas.

Assumption 3: All Readers Understand the Author's Point   Once again, because of individual differences in prior knowledge, interests, and familiarity with the ideas presented in a text, some readers will "get" an author's point while others will construct something entirely different. (If you have ever argued with someone about the point of a movie or novel, you can appreciate this phenomenon.) Research on summarizing text passages shows that before the age of ten, children can accurately recount much of what they read but have great difficulty synthesizing that information to identify the author's main point.

Assumption 4: Moral Themes Are Readily Accessible to Readers   Because children have different conceptions (moral schemas, or prior moral knowledge) of how to get along with others and why such behavior is important, moral themes in a text are not necessarily accessible. As we noted earlier, people may base moral judgments on a variety of criteria, including personal interests (morally correct behavior is that which benefits me), maintaining norms (morally correct behavior is that which fosters law and order), and ideals (morally correct behavior is that which is consistent with higher-order principles). Older or more intellectually advanced children are more likely to grasp moral themes that reflect maintenance of norms and ideals than are younger or less advanced children. A recent study (Williams et al., 2002), although not done with morality stories, reinforces this point. Second and third graders who were trained to identify and comprehend story themes did better than noninstructed children, but they were unable to apply these themes to real-life situations or to identify and apply themes for which they received no instruction.

Assumption 5: Moral Themes Are Just Another Type of Information Conveyed by a Text Because moral themes vary in their complexity and abstractness, and because children's comprehension of such themes develops through predictable stages, moral themes cannot be treated as the equivalent to fact-based information.

Despite the fact that character education programs have not received strong support in the research literature (probably because many programs are poorly designed and/or implemented), they are popular among parents and educators, and some appear to produce positive effects.

Whether or not your school has a character education program, there are certainly ways you can influence the moral development of your students. The following Suggestions for Teaching section provides several ideas. But before you use any techniques of moral education in your classes, it is wise to check with your principal. In some communities, parents have insisted that they, not teachers, should take the responsibility for moral instruction.

Suggestions for Teaching

Encouraging Moral Development

JOURNAL ENTRY
Ways to Encourage Moral Development

1 **Recognize that younger children respond to moral conflicts differently from older children.**

2 **Try to take the perspective of students, and stimulate their perspective-taking abilities.**

3 **Develop an awareness of moral issues by discussing a variety of real and hypothetical moral dilemmas and by using daily opportunities in the classroom to heighten moral awareness. (Moral education should be an integral part of the curriculum; it should not take place during a "moral education period.")**

Here is a hypothetical moral dilemma that a first-grade teacher presented to her class:

Mark was going to the movies when he met his friend Steven. Although Steven wanted to go to the movie with Mark, he had spent all of his allowance and wouldn't be getting any more until after the movie left town. Both boys were twelve years old but looked much younger. If they lied about their ages, they could both see the movie for the amount of money that Mark had. Mark was unsure if he should lie about his age. Steven said, "It's your money, so it's your decision." What should Mark do?

The responses of the students illustrate both the punishment-obedience orientation (stage 1) and the instrumental relativist orientation (stage 2) of Kohlberg's preconventional level of morality:

More ideas for your journal can be found in the Reflective Journal Questions at the textbook's student website, Education CourseMate.

MS. KITTLE:	*Okay, what do you think Mark should do?*
JOHN:	*Him and Steven should tell them how old they are.*

EMILY:	*They shouldn't lie about their age.*
MS. KITTLE:	*Why do you think they shouldn't lie?*
TINA:	*Because if they did lie, they'd get a spanking.*
JOHN:	*Mark shouldn't lie about his age because it leads to a mess.*
MS. KITTLE:	*What kind of mess?*
JOHN:	*His mother might find out.*
SARA:	*The father too.*
ERIN:	*They'd get punished.*
MS. KITTLE:	*So you all think Mark and Steven shouldn't lie because they might get caught and be punished. What if no one catches them—would it be right to lie then?*
MOST:	*Yes!*
BILLY:	*No, it's not. The manager of the show might catch them.*
MS. KITTLE:	*But what if no one catches them?*
BILLY:	*Then it's all right.*
MS. KITTLE:	*Who thinks it would still be wrong to lie, even if Mark and Steven wouldn't get caught? (Five children raise their hands.)*
TROY:	*They'd still get in a mixed-up mess.*
MS. KITTLE:	*How?*
TROY:	*Somebody might tell somebody that they lied.*
MS. KITTLE:	*He might, that's true. But would it still be wrong even if Steven didn't tell anybody?*
TROY:	*Yes.*
MS. KITTLE:	*Why, Troy?*
TROY:	*I don't know—but it is.*
EMILY:	*It's not nice to lie.*
TROY (IN A RUSH):	*Yeah, and it's not fair to other people, either!*
MS. KITTLE:	*Who wouldn't it be fair to?*
TROY:	*The others in the show. They had to pay full price.*
MS. KITTLE:	*You mean if other twelve-year-old kids had to pay the full price for their tickets, then it's not fair for Mark and Steven to get in cheaper?*
TROY:	*Right.* (Lickona, 1998)

4 **Create a classroom atmosphere that will enhance open discussion. For example, arrange face-to-face groupings, be an accepting model, foster listening and communication skills, and encourage student-to-student interaction.**

Richard Hersh, Diana Paolitto, and Joseph Reimer (1979) offer the following specific suggestions for supervising classroom discussions:

- *Highlight the moral issue to be discussed.* Example: Describe a specific real or hypothetical moral dilemma.

- *Ask "why?" questions.* Example: After asking students what they would do if they were faced with the moral dilemma under discussion, ask them to explain why they would act that way.

- *Complicate the circumstances.* Example: After students have responded to the original dilemma, mention a factor that might complicate matters—for example, the involvement of a best friend in the dilemma.

- *Use personal and naturalistic examples.* Example: Invite students to put themselves in the position of individuals who are confronted by moral dilemmas described in newspapers or depicted on television.

To solidify your understanding of this chapter, see the tutorial quizzes and other study aids on the textbook's Education CourseMate website.

What Students Know and *How* Students Know

Okay," says Don, "so there's a lot of research to suggest that students just plain think differently than teachers."

Challenging Assumptions

"Right," says Celeste. "Assuming that kids in our classes know less than we do may be correct—at least I hope so!—but that assumption alone doesn't get us very far in terms of designing learning experiences for our students. We need to recognize *how* students construct what they know, what kinds of perspectives they use to decide what's important, and even what's right and wrong."

Antonio nods. "So, my students weren't able to connect with my 'problem identification' lesson because they probably did not conceive it the same way I did. And my ideas about what's important are different from theirs. I'm looking at the concept of *problem* from a different developmental perspective, a different set of lenses. Come to think of it, it's not that they simply didn't know what I know, it's more like I didn't connect with the way they construct knowledge and the issues that they are dealing with at that age."

Connie says, "Developmental theory and research give us ways to think about the kinds of issues that influence students' interactions with people and how those interactions help them construct the way they understand their world, including their own sense of identity. It's critical that we recognize that students think differently than we do. We need to understand how they construct knowledge."

Don says, "You know, I've never really thought about teaching as being anything more than just giving students knowledge. But it's more than that. It has to be about helping kids construct their understandings of their world and of themselves. That seems pretty important."

"It is," says Connie. "It is also important that you compare your observations and inferences against relevant theory and research. In fact, it's critical for your development as teachers. We must observe and infer; it's what human beings do. But as educators, we must take the next step and examine our observations and inferences so that we reveal our assumptions and, once revealed, test them against theory and research."

Summary

1. Erikson's theory of psychosocial development is notable because it covers the life span, describes people as playing an active role in their own psychological development as opposed to passively responding to external forces, and emphasizes the role of cultural norms and goals.

2. Erikson's theory describes eight stages, from birth through old age. The stages that deal with the personality development of school-age children are initiative versus guilt (four to five years), industry versus inferiority (six to eleven years), and identity versus role confusion (twelve to eighteen years).

3. Forcing students to compete with one another for grades is likely to have a negative effect on their sense of industry.

4. Individuals with a strong sense of identity are comfortable with their physical selves, have a sense of purpose and direction, and know they will be recognized by others. When faced with making an occupational choice, some adolescents declare a psychosocial moratorium.

5. Erikson's observations about identity were extended by Marcia, who described four identity statuses: identity diffusion, foreclosure, moratorium, and identity achievement.

6. Erikson's theory has been criticized for its heavy reliance on his personal experience, its lack of applicability to other cultures, and its inaccuracies in terms of female personality development.

7. Piaget believed that individuals inherit two basic intellectual tendencies: organization (the tendency

to combine mental processes into more general systems) and adaptation (the tendency to adjust to the environment).

8. Adaptation occurs through the processes of assimilation (fitting an experience into an existing scheme) and accommodation (changing a scheme or creating a new one to incorporate a new experience).

9. A scheme is an organized pattern of behavior or thought that guides what we see, think, and do.

10. Equilibration is the process of trying to organize a system of schemes that allows us to adapt to current environmental conditions. Equilibration is produced by a state of disequilibrium.

11. Piaget concluded on the basis of his studies that schemes evolve through four stages: sensorimotor (birth to two years), preoperational (two to seven years), concrete operational (seven to eleven years), and formal operational (eleven years and older).

12. During the sensorimotor stage, the infant and toddler use senses and motor skills to explore and understand the environment.

13. In the preoperational stage, the child masters symbol systems but cannot manipulate symbols logically.

14. In the concrete operational stage, the child is capable of logical thinking, but only with ideas with which he has had firsthand experience.

15. During the formal operational stage, the individual is capable of hypothetical reasoning, dealing with abstractions, and engaging in mental manipulations. Although some adolescents are capable of formal operational reasoning, adolescent egocentrism restricts its range and power.

16. Piaget believed that social interactions among peers on the same level of development would do more to stimulate cognitive development than social interactions between children and adults because interactions among intellectual equals are more likely to lead to fruitful discussions, analyses, and debates.

17. Systematic instruction may have modest positive effects on the rate of cognitive development as long as the schemes that will govern the next stage have already begun to develop.

18. Piaget's theory has been criticized for underestimating children's abilities, for overestimating the capability of adolescents to engage in formal operational thinking, for vague explanations of how individuals move from stage to stage, and for not addressing cultural differences.

19. Vygotsky believed that cognitive development is shaped by both the interactions children have with others, particularly adults, and historical cultural forces. Parents and teachers help children acquire those psychological tools (such as language skills, concepts, and procedures) that their culture has come to value.

20. For Vygotsky, social interactions between children and more intellectually advanced individuals, such as peers, older siblings, and adults, are primarily responsible for advances in cognitive development, provided those interactions are based on mediation of external behaviors into internal signs.

21. Vygotsky believed that cognitive development is aided by explicitly teaching students how to use cognitive tools to acquire basic concepts and by teaching within a student's zone of proximal development.

22. Technology consistent with Piaget's view of cognitive development helps students explore and construct knowledge, formulate concrete representations of abstract ideas, and understand the ideas of others.

23. Technology consistent with Vygotsky's view of cognitive development provides a virtual environment that plays the role of an expert tutor who gives a high degree of support and structure that is gradually withdrawn (scaffolding). It also allows online mentoring and provides opportunities for students to interact with other students in sophisticated virtual environments.

24. Piaget identified two types of moral reasoning in children: morality of constraint (rules are inflexible and external) and morality of cooperation (rules are flexible and internal).

26. Kohlberg defined six stages in the development of moral reasoning: punishment-obedience, instrumental relativist, good boy–nice girl, law and order, social contract, and universal ethical principle.

26. Structured discussions based on moral dilemmas may have some positive effects on the rate of development of moral reasoning.

27. Kohlberg's theory has been criticized because it is not applicable to other cultures, because its promise that moral development can be accelerated through direct instruction has received only limited support, because Kohlberg's moral dilemmas are not relevant to everyday social settings, because the theory relies too much on macromoral issues, and because it ignores the effect of characteristics other than moral reasoning on moral behavior.

28. Gilligan maintains that Erikson's theory of identity development and Kohlberg's theory of moral development more accurately describe male development than female development.

29. Noddings's care theory emphasizes the critical nature of caring relationships, in which each person feels that she or he is cared for by the other.

30. Character education programs are often based on assumptions that are not supported by research on learning.

Resources for Further Investigation

● Erikson's Description of Development

Erik Erikson's books are of considerable significance for their speculations about development and education. In the first six chapters of *Childhood and Society* (2nd ed., 1963), he describes how studying Native Americans and observing patients in treatment led him to develop the Eight Ages of Man (described in Chapter 7 of the book). In the final chapters of this book, Erikson uses his conception of development to analyze the lives of Hitler and Maxim Gorky (a Russian novelist of the late 1800s and early 1900s). *Identity: Youth and Crisis* (1968) features a revised description of the eight stages of development, with emphasis on identity and role confusion. Erikson comments on many aspects of his work in an interview with Richard Evans, published as *Dialogue with Erik Erikson* (1967). An in-depth look at middle and high school students' sense of identity can be found in *Identity in Adolescence: The Balance Between Self and Other* (2004) by Jane Kroger. Laurence Steinberg provides an overview of Erikson's theory and related research in *Adolescence* (8th ed., 2008).

● Piaget's Theory of Cognitive Development

Jean Piaget has probably exerted more influence on theoretical discussions of development and on educational practices than any other recent psychologist. Of his own books, you might wish to consult *The Language and Thought of the Child* (1952a), *The Origins of Intelligence in Children* (1952b), and *The Psychology of the Child* (1969), the last of which was written in collaboration with Barbel Inhelder. Howard Gruber and Jacques Vonèche have edited *The Essential Piaget: An Interpretive Reference and Guide* (1995), which Piaget describes in the Foreword as "the best and most complete of all anthologies of my work." An inexpensive paperback that provides a biography of Piaget and an analysis of his work is *Piaget's Theory of Intellectual Development* (3rd ed., 1988), by Herbert Ginsburg and Sylvia Opper. Other books about Piaget are *Piaget for Teachers* (1970), by Hans Furth; *Piaget's Theory of Cognitive and Affective Development* (5th ed., 1996), by Barry Wadsworth; *Theories of Developmental Psychology* (5th ed., 2004), by Patricia Miller; and *Piaget's Theory: Prospects and Possibilities* (1992), edited by Harry Beilin and Peter Pufall.

An online source of information and relevant publications for Piaget is the Jean Piaget Society database, located at **www.piaget.org.** It contains information about journals and conferences and is dedicated to "the presentation and discussion of scholarly work on issues related to human knowledge and its development."

● Vygotsky's Theory of Cognitive Development

Comprehensive descriptions and analyses of Lev Vygotsky's ideas about cognitive development can be found in *Vygotsky and Education: Instructional Implications and Applications of Sociohistorical Psychology* (1990), edited by Luis Moll; *Vygotsky's Sociohistorical Psychology and Its Contemporary Application* (1991), by Carl Ratner; and *Lev Vygotsky: Revolutionary Scientist* (1993), by Fred Newman and Lois Holzman. His educational views can be found in *Vygotsky's*

Educational Theory in Cultural Context (2003), edited by Alex Kozulin, Boris Gindis, Vladimir Ageyev, and Suzanne Miller. An overview of the theories of Erikson, Piaget, and Vygotsky can be found in *Theories of Childhood* (2006), by Carol Garhart Mooney.

● Piaget's Description of Moral Development

Piaget describes his observations on moral development in *The Moral Judgment of the Child* (1965). Thomas Lickona summarizes research investigations stimulated by Piaget's conclusions in "Research on Piaget's Theory of Moral Development," in *Moral Development and Behavior: Theory, Research, and Social Issues* (1976), an excellent compilation of articles on all aspects of morality, which Lickona edited.

● Kohlberg's Stages of Moral Development

If you would like to read Kohlberg's own account of the stages of moral development, examine "Moral Stages and Moralization: The Cognitive-Developmental Approach," in *Moral Development and Behavior: Theory, Research, and Social Issues* (1976), edited by Thomas Lickona. Kohlberg discusses changes in his theory in "Revisions in the Theory and Practice of Moral Development," in *New Directions for Child Development: Moral Development* (1978), edited by William Damon. In *Postconventional Moral Thinking: A Neo-Kohlbergian Approach* (1999), James Rest, Darcia Narvaez, Muriel Bebeau, and Stephen Thoma describe an approach to studying postconventional moral thinking that is based on but differs from Kohlberg's theory. Chapter 1 offers a brief (eight pages) overview of their approach, and Chapter 6 provides a concise (ten pages) discussion of why the authors have replaced Kohlberg's use of the stages concept with that of schemas.

● Gilligan's and Noddings's Caring Orientation

If you would like to know more about the basis of Carol Gilligan's critique of Erikson's and Kohlberg's theories and her arguments for a broader view of adolescent development, start with her widely cited book *In a Different Voice: Psychological Theory and Women's Development* (1993). Briefer and more recent analyses of this issue are her chapter in *Mapping the Moral Domain: A Contribution of Women's Thinking to Psychological Theory and Education* (1988), edited by Carol Gilligan, Janie Ward, Jill Taylor, and Betty Bardige; and *Empathy and Moral Development* (2000) by Martin Hoffman. Nel Noddings's classic, with a new preface in the second edition, is *Caring: A Feminine Approach to Ethics and Moral Education* (1984/2003).

● Character Education Programs

The Character Education Partnership (CEP) is a coalition of organizations and individuals dedicated to the implementation of character education programs in schools. Its website (**www.character.org**) contains a discussion of 11 principles that schools can use to design and evaluate their own character education programs (CEP, 2000). Issues of moral reasoning, moral development, and character education are covered in the *Handbook of Moral and Character Education* (2008), edited by Larry Nucci and Darcia Narvaez.

3 Age-Level Characteristics

The Education CourseMate website for this text offers many helpful resources. Go to **CengageBrain.com** to preview this chapter's Concept Maps and Chapter Themes.

KEY POINTS

These key points will help you learn the important information in this chapter. To help you study, they also appear in the margins of the pages, next to the text where they are discussed.

Preschool and Kindergarten (Three, Four, and Five Years)

- Large-muscle control better established than small-muscle control and eye-hand coordination
- Free play provides multiple benefits to young children
- Gender differences in toy preferences and play activities noticeable by kindergarten
- By age four, children have a theory of mind: aware of own mental processes and that others may think differently
- Peer comparisons help four- and five-year-olds more accurately judge their capabilities

Primary Grades (1, 2, and 3; Six, Seven, and Eight Years)

- Primary grade children have difficulty focusing on small print
- Accident rate peaks in third grade because of confidence in physical skills
- Rigid interpretation of rules in primary grades
- To encourage industry, use praise, avoid criticism
- Awareness of cognitive processes begins to emerge

Elementary School (Grades 4 and 5; Nine and Ten Years)

- Boys slightly better at sports-related motor skills; girls better at flexibility, balance, rhythmic motor skills
- Peer group norms for behavior begin to replace adult norms
- Self-image becomes more generalized and stable; is based primarily on comparisons with peers
- Delinquents have few friends, are easily distracted, are not interested in schoolwork, lack basic skills
- Elementary grade students reason logically but concretely

Middle School (Grades 6, 7, and 8; Eleven, Twelve, and Thirteen Years)

- Girls' growth spurt occurs earlier, and so they look older than boys of same age
- Early-maturing boys likely to draw favorable responses
- Late-maturing boys may feel inadequate
- Early-maturing girls may suffer low self-esteem
- Late-maturing girls likely to be popular and carefree
- Average age of puberty: girls, eleven; boys, fourteen
- Discussion of controversial issues may be difficult because of strong desire to conform to peer norms
- Teenagers experience different degrees of emotional turmoil
- Environment of middle schools does not meet needs of adolescents, leading to lower levels of learning
- Self-efficacy beliefs for academic and social tasks become strong influences on behavior

High School (Grades 9, 10, 11, and 12; Fourteen, Fifteen, Sixteen, and Seventeen Years)

- Factors related to initiation of sexual activity vary by gender, race
- Parents influence values, plans; peers influence immediate status
- Girls more likely than boys to experience anxiety about friendships
- Depression most common among females, students of color
- Depression and unstable family situation place adolescents at risk for suicide
- Political thinking becomes more abstract, less authoritarian, more knowledgeable

---

The theories described in the preceding chapter call attention to the course of psychosocial, cognitive, and moral development. Although these types of behavior are important, they represent only a small part of the behavior repertoire of a child or adolescent. This chapter, which is organized by age and grade levels, will present an overview of types of behavior that are not directly related to any particular theory. In selecting points for emphasis, we used one basic criterion: Does this information about development have potential significance for teachers?

To organize the points to be discussed, we have divided the developmental span into five levels, corresponding to common grade groupings in schools:

Preschool and kindergarten. Ages three through five
Primary grades. Grades 1 through 3; ages six through eight
Elementary grades. Grades 4 and 5; ages nine and ten

Middle school. Grades 6 through 8; ages eleven through thirteen

High school. Grades 9 through 12; ages fourteen through seventeen

Because the way grades are grouped varies, you may find yourself teaching in a school system in which the arrangement described in this chapter is not followed. In that case, simply refer to the appropriate age-level designations and, if necessary, concentrate on two levels rather than one.

At each of the five levels, behaviors are discussed under four headings: physical, social, emotional, and cognitive characteristics. Following each characteristic are implications for teachers. To help you establish a general conception of what children are like at each level, brief summaries of the types of behavior stressed by the theorists discussed in the preceding chapter are listed in a table in each section (Tables 3.1, 3.2, 3.3, 3.4, and 3.7).

Revealing Assumptions

Looking Through Lenses

Don is early for today's meeting. He has been sitting quietly, thinking about two different classrooms he observed last Wednesday. As Connie walks into the meeting room, Don looks up and says, "OK, Doc, tell me this: How come second graders can't seem to get enough of a teacher and fourth graders don't even notice the teacher is in the room?"

Connie puts down her bag and settles into the chair across from Don. "That's a good question. Let's start with that one when Celeste and Antonio get here. In the meantime, think about what theory and research might be relevant to your question. Also, think specifically about the observations that have led you to infer that second graders and fourth graders differ in the way they interact with teachers."

Celeste and Antonio are talking about eighth graders as they arrive. Celeste is trying to figure out why one science class she observed went so well and another—the same lesson taught by the same teacher—so poorly.

"Sounds like you two have been reflecting on the 'mysteries of eighth grade.' Let's get back to that, but I asked Don to get us started today with some observations he made." Don describes how second graders sought the teacher's attention, whereas the fourth graders seemed very hesitant to even speak to the teacher. He shares some specific interactions between students and teacher.

"So," says Connie, "what would you infer from Don's observations?" Celeste suggests that maybe the second-grade class experienced more success in their classroom interactions than the fourth graders and, consequently, have developed a sense of industry, whereas the fourth graders felt inferior. Antonio wonders if the difference might be connected to preoperational and concrete operational thinking.

"OK," says Connie, "Celeste is using Erikson to explain the difference and Antonio is applying Piaget's theory. Any other ideas?"

Don sits quietly for a moment and then looks at Connie. "Yeah, a bunch," he says. "It occurred to me that Vygotsky might have something to say about scaffolding, and then I thought about Kohlberg and Gilligan and even Marcia's ideas about

pause & reflect

Is there a "right answer" for each and every classroom situation? Don seems to be assuming that there is. Many people who have not studied teaching and learning make the same assumption. Consequently, they believe teaching is like "following the recipe in a cookbook." Similarly, they consider learning to teach to be a matter of technical training: simply train aspiring teachers to recognize the "right answer" for every possible classroom situation. What are the dangers of assuming that there is one "right answer" and, therefore, one "right theory" for each classroom situation? Why should we seek more than one "right answer" from multiple theories? And why must aspiring teachers be *educated* rather than *trained?*

identity. But each theory would give you a different explanation. How can you tell which theory is the right answer in a particular situation?"

Connie looks up and says, "Is it possible that looking at a situation through the lenses of several theories might give us several right answers? And if so, what should we do with several right answers?"

PRESCHOOL AND KINDERGARTEN (THREE, FOUR, AND FIVE YEARS)

Physical Characteristics: Preschool and Kindergarten

JOURNAL ENTRY
Active Games

1. *Preschool children are extremely active. They have good control of their bodies and enjoy activity for its own sake.* Provide plenty of opportunities for children to run, climb, and jump. Arrange these activities, as much as possible, so that they are under your control. If you follow a policy of complete freedom, you may discover that 30 improvising three- to five-year-olds can be a frightening thing. In your Reflective Journal, you might note some specific games and activities that you could use to achieve semicontrolled play.

JOURNAL ENTRY
Riot-Stopping Signals and Activities

2. *Because of an inclination toward bursts of activity, kindergartners need frequent rest periods. They themselves often don't recognize the need to slow down.* Schedule quiet activities after strenuous ones. Have rest time. Realize that excitement may build up to a riot level if the attention of "catalytic agents" and their followers is not diverted. In your journal, you might list some signals for calling a halt to a melee (for example, playing the opening chords of Beethoven's Fifth Symphony on the piano) or for diverting wild action into more or less controlled activity (marching around the room to a brisk rendition of "Stars and Stripes Forever").

3. *Preschoolers' large muscles are more developed than those that control fingers and hands. Therefore, preschoolers may be quite clumsy at, or physically incapable of, such skills as tying shoes and buttoning coats.* Avoid too many small-motor activities, such as pasting paper chains. Provide big brushes, crayons, and tools. In your journal, you might note other activities or items of king-sized equipment that would be appropriate for the children's level of muscular development.

Large-muscle control better established than small-muscle control and hand-eye coordination

4. *Young children find it difficult to focus their eyes on small objects. Therefore, their eye-hand coordination may be imperfect.* If possible, minimize the necessity for the children to look at small things. (Incomplete eye development is the reason for large print in children's books.) This is also important to keep in mind if you are planning to use computers or software programs; highly graphic programs requiring a simple point-and-click response are most appropriate for very young students.

5. *Although children's bodies are flexible and resilient, the bones that protect the brain are still soft.* Be extremely wary of blows to the head in games or fights between children. If you notice an activity involving such a blow, intervene immediately; warn the class that this is dangerous and explain why.

6. *Gender differences in physical development and motor skill proficiency are usually not noticeable until kindergarten and are fairly small in magnitude.* Differences that do manifest themselves are due in part to biological endowment and in part to differences in socialization (Berk, 2009). Consequently, you may want to encourage all children to participate in tasks that emphasize gross motor skills and tasks that emphasize fine motor skills.

Table 3.1	Applying Theories of Development to the Preschool and Kindergarten Years

Psychosocial development: initiative vs. guilt. Children need opportunities for free play and experimentation, as well as experiences that give them a sense of accomplishment.

Cognitive development: preoperational thought. Children gradually acquire the ability to conserve and decenter but are not capable of operational thinking and are unable to mentally reverse operations.

Moral development: morality of constraint, preconventional. Rules are viewed as unchangeable edicts handed down by those in authority. Punishment-obedience orientation focuses on physical consequences rather than on intentions.

General factors to keep in mind: Children are having their first experiences with school routine and interactions with more than a few peers and are preparing for initial academic experiences in group settings. They need to learn to follow directions and get along with others.

Social Characteristics: Preschool and Kindergarten

1. *Most children have one or two best friends, but these friendships may change rapidly. Preschoolers tend to be quite flexible socially; they are usually willing and able to play with most of the other children in the class. Favorite friends tend to be of the same gender, but many friendships between boys and girls develop.* Young children generally interact with most of the other children in their preschool and kindergarten classes but think of their friends as those with whom they share toys and play the most. These "friendships" can dissolve quickly, however, if one child hits the other, refuses to share a toy, or is not interested in playing (Berk, 2009; Kail, 2010). Whereas some children prefer to play alone or observe their peers, others lack the skills or confidence to join others. In those cases, you might want to provide some assistance.

> Free play provides multiple benefits to young children

2. *Play activities are an important part of young children's development and should be encouraged.* Many adults believe that young children's play activities (meaning they are voluntary and self-organized) are relatively unimportant and so should be either ignored or deemphasized by educators. Nothing could be more wrong. Research clearly shows that children of all ages profit socially, emotionally, and cognitively from engaging in play (Bergen & Fromberg, 2009).

Young children engage in a variety of types of play that have several developmental benefits. © Petr Bonek/ Alamy

The form and types of play that young children exhibit are quite varied. They may, for example, play by themselves with toys that are different from those being used by nearby children, play alongside but not with other children who are playing with the same toys, or play cooperatively with other children in an organized form of play. Common types of play include pretend play (mimicking the behavior of parents, siblings, and peers), exercise play (running, climbing, jumping, and other large-muscle activities), and rough-and-tumble play (mostly wrestling types of activities, as well as pretend fighting) (Bukatko, 2008; Smith, 2005).

3. *Preschool and kindergarten children show definite preferences for gender of play peers and for pair versus group play.* A 3-year study (Fabes, Martin, & Hanish, 2003) of more than 200 preschool children (average age 4.25 years) found the following play preferences:

- Same-sex play occurred more often than mixed-sex play.
- Girls were more likely than boys to play in pairs rather than groups, and boys were more likely than girls to play in groups rather than pairs. When girls did play in groups, they were more likely than boys to play in a group in which they were not the only member of their sex.
- When boys played with each other, whether in pairs or groups, they were more likely than girls who played with each other to engage in active-forceful play. This tendency was less apparent when a boy played in a group that was otherwise made up of all girls. But when a girl played in a group whose other members were boys, her level of active-forceful play tended to increase.

4. *Awareness of gender roles and gender typing is evident.* By the time children enter kindergarten, most of them have developed an awareness of gender differences and of masculine and feminine roles (Wynn & Fletcher, 1987). This awareness of **gender roles** shows up very clearly in the toys and activities that boys and girls prefer. Boys are more likely than girls to play outdoors, to engage in rough-and-tumble play, and to behave aggressively. Boys play with toy vehicles and construction toys, and they engage in action games (such as football). Girls prefer art activities, doll play, and dancing (Carter, 1987). By age six, some children associate job titles that are considered to be gender neutral, such as doctor, librarian, and flight attendant, with either males (in the case of doctors) or females (in the case of librarians and waiters) (Liben, Bigler, & Krogh, 2002). Such strong gender typing in play activities occurs in many cultures, including non-Western ones, and is often reinforced by the way parents behave: they model what their culture has defined as gender-appropriate roles and encourage boys to be active and independent and girls to be more docile (Lancey, 2002). Peers may also reinforce these tendencies. A boy or girl may notice that other children are more willing to play when he or she selects a gender-appropriate toy.

Therefore, if you teach preschool children, you may have to guard against a tendency to respond too soon when little girls ask for help. If they *need* assistance, of course you should supply it; but if preschool girls can carry out tasks on their own, you should urge them to do so. You might also remind yourself that girls often need to be encouraged to become more achievement oriented and boys to become more sensitive to the needs of others.

Emotional Characteristics: Preschool and Kindergarten

1. *Kindergarten children tend to express their emotions freely and openly. Anger outbursts are frequent.* It is probably desirable to let children at this age level express their feelings openly, at least within broad limits, so that they can recognize and face their emotions. In *Between Parent and Child* (1965; Ginott, Ginott, & Goddard, 2003) and *Teacher and Child* (1972), Haim Ginott offers some specific suggestions on how a parent or teacher can help children develop

---

Gender differences in toy preferences and play activities noticeable by kindergarten

JOURNAL ENTRY
Encouraging Girls to Achieve, Boys to Be Sensitive

awareness of their feelings. His books may help you work out your own philosophy and techniques for dealing with emotional outbursts.

Suppose, for example, that a boy who was wildly waving his hand to be called on during share-and-tell time later knocks down a block tower built by a girl who monopolized sharing time with a spellbinding story of a kitten rescued by firefighters. When you go over to break up the incipient fight, the boy angrily pushes you away. In such a situation, Ginott suggests you take the boy to a quiet corner and engage in a dialogue such as this:

You: It looks as if you are unhappy about something, Connor.
Boy: Yes, I am.
You: Are you angry about something that happened this morning?
Boy: Yes.
You: Tell me about it.
Boy: I wanted to tell the class about something at sharing time, and Lily talked for three hours, and you wouldn't let me say anything.
You: And that made you mad at Lily and at me?
Boy: Yes.
You: Well, I can understand why you are disappointed and angry. But Lily had an exciting story to tell, and we didn't have time for anyone else to tell what they had to say. You can be the very first one to share something tomorrow morning. Now how about doing an easel painting? You always do such interesting paintings.

JOURNAL ENTRY
Helping Students
Understand Anger

Ginott suggests that when children are encouraged to analyze their own behavior, they are more likely to become aware of the causes of their feelings. This awareness, in turn, may help them learn to accept and control their feelings and find more acceptable means of expressing them. But because these children are likely to be in Piaget's preoperational stage of intellectual development, bear in mind that this approach may not be successful with all of them. The egocentric orientation of four- to five-year-olds makes it difficult for them to reflect on the thoughts of self or others. Anger outbursts are more likely to occur when children are tired, hungry, or exposed to too much adult interference. If you take such conditions into account and try to alleviate them (by providing a nap or a snack, for example), temper tantrums may be minimized.

JOURNAL ENTRY
Ways to Avoid Playing
Favorites

2. *Jealousy among classmates is likely to be fairly common, as kindergarten children have much affection for the teacher and actively seek approval. When there are 30 individuals competing for the affection and attention of just one teacher, some jealousy is inevitable.* Try to spread your attention around as equitably as possible, and when you praise particular children, do it in a private or casual way. If one child is given lavish public recognition, it is only natural for the other children to feel resentful. Think back to how you felt about teachers' pets during your own school years. If you have observed or can think of other techniques for minimizing jealousy, jot them down in your journal.

Cognitive Characteristics: Preschool and Kindergarten

By age four, children have a theory of mind: aware of own mental processes and that others may think differently

1. *By age four, many children begin to develop a theory of mind.* Children's **theory of mind** concerns the ability of children around the age of four to be aware of the difference between thinking about something and experiencing that same thing; they also begin to understand that it is sometimes possible to predict the thoughts of others. These capacities are critical to understanding such aspects of social life as surprises, secrets, tricks, mistakes, and lies.

By three years of age, most children realize the difference between thinking about something and actually experiencing that same something. But a significant change occurs around age four when children begin to realize that thoughts may be false. In one study described by Janet Astington (1998), a box that children knew normally contained candy was filled instead with pencils. When three-year-olds opened the box and discovered the pencils, they were asked what a friend would think was in the box before it was opened. They replied that the friend would know (just as they now did) that there were pencils inside. When they were asked later what they thought was in the box before it was opened, they replied "pencils" rather than "candy," indicating an inability to recall that their belief had changed. But four-year-olds understood that the friend would be misled by the fact that pencils had replaced the candy. The four-year-olds also remembered that they themselves had expected the box to contain candy. So, beginning at age four, children start to realize that the actions of people are based on how they *think* the world is.

Talking about different viewpoints will help children understand that people have beliefs about the world, that different people believe different things, and that beliefs may change when new information is acquired. Astington (1998) offers the following example of how teachers can foster the development of children's theory of mind:

> In a 1st-grade classroom that I recently observed, the teacher often talked about her own thought processes, saying, for example, "I just learned something new" when she found out that one student had a pet rabbit at home. When she was surprised or made a mistake, she talked about her own wrong beliefs, and at story-time, she had the children talk about the motivations and beliefs of story characters. Her style of talk helped the class focus not just on the thought content, but also on the thinking process—yet the term *theory of mind* was unknown to this teacher. (p. 48)

2. *Kindergartners are quite skillful with language. Most of them like to talk, especially in front of a group.* Providing a sharing time gives children a natural opportunity for talking, but many will need help in becoming good listeners. Some sort of rotation scheme is usually necessary to divide talking opportunities between the gabby and the silent extremes. You might provide activities or experiences for less confident children to talk about, such as a field trip, a book, or a film. In your journal, you might note some comments to use if students start to share the wrong thing (such as a vivid account of a fight between their parents) or if they try to one-up classmates (for example, "Your cat may have had five kittens, but *our* cat had a *hundred* kittens"). For titillating topics, you might say, "There are some things that are private, and it's better not to talk about them to others."

3. *Many preschool and kindergarten children do not accurately assess their competence for particular tasks.* Preschool and kindergarten children typically think of themselves as being much more competent than they actually are, even when their performance lags behind that of their peers. They do not differentiate between effort and ability as factors that affect performance. Although this limitation in self-assessment is influenced, at least in part, by the characteristics of preoperational stage thinking, it can also be the result of classroom environments that are relatively unstructured, that emphasize free play, and that deemphasize peer-peer comparisons. Israeli children who grew up on a kibbutz, a communal form of living in which child rearing occurs as much within a peer group as within one's nuclear family, used peer comparison to construct a sense of their own competence about a year earlier than did urban children who spent most of their time within their own families (Butler, 2005).

Despite this limitation in self-assessed competence, research suggests that under the right conditions even some four-year-olds can draw accurate conclusions about how well or poorly they have completed a task. In one study, children between the ages of four and five were asked to do a simple maze-type task (tracing a winding path between an illustrated child and a house) under one of two conditions: either in the presence of another child's work or in comparison with their own earlier attempt at the same task. About 40 percent of those who had another child's work available were able to use that to accurately

Peer comparisons help four- and five-year-olds more accurately judge their capabilities

assess their own performance. Most of the rest of this group could gauge their own performance by using the goal as a basis for comparison ("I only got halfway to the house"). Children in the second group, however, were unable to use their prior performance on the maze to judge whether their current performance was any better or worse, even when shown both attempts. Self-assessment of competence under this condition does not typically appear until somewhere between seven and eight years of age (Butler, 2005).

JOURNAL ENTRY
Encouraging Competence

4. *Competence is encouraged by interaction, interest, opportunities, urging, limits, admiration, and signs of affection.* Studies of young children rated as highly competent (Burchinal, Peisner-Feinberg, Pianta, & Howes, 2002; Clawson & Robila, 2001; Schweinhart, Weikart, & Hohmann, 2002) show that to encourage preschoolers to make the most of their abilities, adults should

[margin note: BUILDING COMPETENCE]

- Interact with the child often and in a variety of ways.
- Show interest in what the child does and says.
- Provide opportunities for the child to investigate and experience many things.
- Permit and encourage the child to do many things.
- Urge the child to try to achieve mature and skilled types of behavior.
- Establish firm and consistent limits regarding unacceptable forms of behavior, explain the reasons for these as soon as the child is able to understand, listen to complaints if the child feels the restrictions are too confining, and give additional reasons if the limits are still to be maintained as originally stated.
- Show that the child's achievements are admired and appreciated.
- Communicate love in a warm and sincere way.

Diana Baumrind's (1971, 1991a) analysis of four types of child-rearing approaches shows why such techniques contribute to competence in children. Baumrind found that parents of competent children are **authoritative parents.** They have confidence in their abilities as parents and therefore provide a model of competence for their children to imitate. When they establish limits and explain reasons for restrictions, they encourage their children to set standards for themselves and to think about why certain procedures should be followed. And because these parents are warm and affectionate, children value their positive responses as rewards for mature behavior. The children of authoritative parents tend to be self-motivated. They stand up for what they believe, yet are able to work productively with others.

Authoritarian parents, by contrast, make demands and wield power, but their failure to take into account the child's point of view and their lack of warmth lead to resentment and insecurity on the part of the child. Children of authoritarian parents may do as they are told, but they are likely to do so out of compliance or fear, not out of a desire to earn love or approval. They also tend to be other-directed rather than inner-directed.

[margin note: BCX]

Permissive parents, as defined by Baumrind, are disorganized, inconsistent, and lack confidence, and their children are likely to imitate such behavior. Permissive parents make few demands of their children, allow them to make many of their own decisions, do not require them to exhibit mature behavior, and tend to avoid confrontations with their children. As a result, such children are markedly less assertive and intellectually skilled than are children from authoritative homes.

Finally, **rejecting-neglecting parents** do not make demands on their children or respond to their emotional needs. They do not structure the home environment, are not supportive of their children's goals and activities, and may actively reject or neglect their child-rearing responsibilities. Children

pause & reflect

Given the characteristics of preschool and kindergarten children, what classroom atmosphere and instructional tactics would you use to foster learning and enjoyment of school?

of rejecting-neglecting parents are the least socially and intellectually competent of the four types.

You might refer to these observations not only when you plan how to encourage competence but also when you think about the kind of classroom atmosphere you hope to establish.

PRIMARY GRADES (1, 2, AND 3; SIX, SEVEN, AND EIGHT YEARS)

Physical Characteristics: Primary Grades

JOURNAL ENTRY
Building Activity into Class Work

PIAGET

RECESS

"REST"

1. *Primary grade children are still extremely active. Because they are frequently required to participate in sedentary pursuits, energy is often released in the form of nervous habits—for example, pencil chewing, fingernail biting, and general fidgeting.* To minimize fidgeting, avoid situations in which your students must stay glued to their desks for long periods. Have frequent breaks, and try to work activity (such as bringing papers to your desk) into the lessons themselves. When children use computer software that contains sound effects, distribute headphones to ensure that they concentrate on their own work and to minimize distractions between students.

   One of the effects of the current emphasis on preparing students to meet state learning standards is the reduction or elimination of recess time, even for kindergarten and primary grade students. One survey, for example, found that 30 percent of kindergarten classrooms did not have a recess period (Pellegrini & Bohn, 2005). Are educators acting wisely in seeking to reduce the number and length of breaks young children receive to focus more intensively on teaching academic skills? Not according to cognitive development theory and research.

   As we noted in the previous chapter, Piaget believed that children's ability to think beyond their own perspective is greatly facilitated by peer interaction because such interactions involve other points of view that must be comprehended and accommodated. During the school day, these types of interactions occur most frequently during such unstructured activities as recess. A second theoretical perspective, called the *cognitive immaturity hypothesis*, maintains that giving young students unstructured breaks reduces cognitive interference from preceding instruction and increases attention to subsequent instruction. Research findings support the accuracy of these theoretical positions. In one study, the opportunity for kindergarten students to play with peers during recess was a significant predictor of first-grade achievement (Pelligrini & Bohn, 2005). In another study, third graders who were given at least one recess period that was at least 15 minutes long received higher classroom behavior scores from their teacher than did similar peers who were given either no recess or a minimal break (Barros, Silver, & Stein, 2009). Lastly, a review of recent research (Tomporowski, Davis, Miller, & Naglieri, 2008) found exercise to be associated with improvements in children's executive cognitive functions (which we describe at length in Chapters 8–10). These are the kinds of thought processes that are fundamental to self-directed learning, and include the ability to select, organize, and properly use goal-directed actions.

2. *Children still need rest periods; they become fatigued easily as a result of physical and mental exertion.* Schedule quiet activities after strenuous ones (story time after recess, for example) and relaxing activities after periods of mental concentration (art after spelling or math).

3. *Large-muscle control is still superior to fine coordination. Many children, especially boys, have difficulty manipulating a pencil.* Try not to schedule too much writing at one time. If drill periods are too long, skill may deteriorate, and children may develop a negative attitude toward writing or toward school in general.

Primary grade children have difficulty focusing on small print

4. *Many students may have difficulty focusing on small print or objects. Quite a few children may be farsighted because of the shallow shape of the eye.* Try not to require too much reading at one stretch. Be on the alert for children rubbing their eyes or blinking, signs of eye fatigue. When you are preparing class handouts, be sure to print in large letters or use a large-size computer font. Until the lens of the eye can be easily focused, young children have trouble looking back and forth from near to far objects.

Although many children at this age have had extensive exposure to computer games and video games and therefore have begun to develop greater eye-hand coordination with images on screen, it's still appropriate to select software programs that incorporate easy-to-see graphics and easy-to-click buttons to avoid frustration.

Accident rate peaks in third grade because of confidence in physical skills

5. *Children tend to be extreme in their physical activities. They have excellent control of their bodies and develop considerable confidence in their skills. As a result, they often underestimate the danger involved in their more daring exploits. The accident rate is at a peak in the third grade.* You might check on school procedures for handling injuries, but also try to prevent reckless play. During recess, for example, encourage class participation in "wild" but essentially safe games (such as relay races involving stunts) to help the children get devil-may-care tendencies out of their systems. In your journal, you might list other games to use for this purpose.

6. *Bone growth is not yet complete. Therefore, bones and ligaments can't stand heavy pressure.* If you notice students indulging in strenuous tests of strength (punching each other on the arm until one person can't retaliate, for example), you might suggest that they switch to competition involving coordinated skills. During team games, rotate players in especially tiring positions (for example, the pitcher in baseball).

Social Characteristics: Primary Grades

The characteristics noted here are typical of both primary and elementary grade students and underlie the elementary-level characteristics described in the next section.

1. *Children become somewhat more selective in their choice of friends and are likely to have a more or less permanent best friend.* Friendships are typically same-sex relationships marked by mutual understanding, loyalty, cooperation, and sharing. Competition between friends should be discouraged because it can become intense and increase their dissatisfaction with each other. Although friends disagree with each other more often than with nonfriends, their conflicts are shorter, less heated, and less likely to lead to a dissolving of the relationship (Hartup, 1989; Ross & Spielmacher, 2005).

Table 3.2	Applying Theories of Development to the Primary Grade Years

Psychosocial development: industry vs. inferiority. Students need to experience a sense of industry through successful completion of tasks. Try to minimize and correct failures to prevent development of feelings of inferiority.

Cognitive development: transition from preoperational to concrete operational stage. Students gradually acquire the ability to solve problems by generalizing from concrete experiences.

Moral development: morality of constraint, preconventional. Rules are viewed as edicts handed down by authority. Focus is on physical consequences, meaning that obeying rules should bring benefit in return.

General factors to keep in mind: Students are having first experiences with school learning, are eager to learn how to read and write, and are likely to be upset by lack of progress. Initial attitudes toward schooling are being established. Initial roles in a group are being formed, roles that may establish a lasting pattern (for example, leader, follower, loner, athlete, or underachiever).

JOURNAL ENTRY
Enjoyable Team Games

Rigid interpretation of rules
in primary grades

2. *Primary grade children often like organized games in small groups, but they may be overly concerned with rules or get carried away by team spirit.* Keep in mind that, according to Piaget, children at this age practice the morality of constraint: they find it difficult to understand how and why rules should be adjusted to special situations. When you divide a class into teams, you may be amazed at the amount of rivalry that develops (and the noise level generated). One way to reduce both the rivalry and the noise is to promote the idea that games should be fun. Another technique is to rotate team membership frequently. If you know any especially good but not excessively competitive team games, note them in your journal. You might also consult *Cooperative Learning: Theory, Research, and Practice* (2nd ed., 1995), by Robert Slavin, for descriptions of several team learning games that emphasize cooperation.

3. *Quarrels are still frequent. Words are used more often than physical aggression, but many boys (in particular) may indulge in punching, wrestling, and shoving.* Occasional fights are to be expected. If certain children, especially the same pair, seem to be involved in one long battle, you should probably try to effect a truce. But when you can, give children a chance to work out their own solutions to disagreements; social conflict is effective in spurring cognitive growth (Howe, Rinaldi, Jennings, & Petrakos, 2002; Murphy & Eisenberg, 2002; Tudge & Rogoff, 1989).

JOURNAL ENTRY
Handling Feuds and Fights

Although occasional quarrels and minor physical aggression will likely have only temporary effects on students, you should keep an eye out for students who are frequent targets of insults, threats, physical aggression, and exclusion from the peer group. Research has shown that third and fourth graders who were frequently victimized by classmates had lower scores on standardized achievement tests, lower grades, and higher levels of depression than their non-victimized peers both at the time the incidents occurred and a year later (Schwartz, Gorman, Nakamoto, & Toblin, 2005).

Emotional Characteristics: Primary Grades

To encourage industry, use
praise, avoid criticism

1. *Students are sensitive to criticism and ridicule and may have difficulty adjusting to failure.* Young children need frequent praise and recognition. Because they tend to admire or even worship their teachers, they may be crushed by criticism. Provide positive reinforcement as frequently as possible, and reserve your negative reactions for nonacademic misbehavior. Scrupulously avoid sarcasm and ridicule. Remember that this is the stage of industry versus inferiority; if you make a child feel inferior, you may prevent the development of industry.

JOURNAL ENTRY
Spreading Around
Responsibilities

2. *Most primary grade children are eager to please the teacher.* They like to help, enjoy responsibility, and want to do well in their schoolwork. The time-honored technique for satisfying the urge to help is to assign jobs (eraser cleaner, wastebasket emptier, paper distributor, and the like) on a rotating basis. In your journal, you might note other techniques—for example, were there any particular responsibilities you enjoyed as a student?

3. *Children are becoming sensitive to the feelings of others.* Unfortunately, this permits them to hurt others deeply by attacking a sensitive spot without realizing how devastating their attack really is. It sometimes happens that teasing a particular child who has reacted to a gibe becomes a group pastime. Be on the alert for such situations. If you are able to make a private and personal appeal to the ringleaders, you may be able to prevent an escalation of the teasing, which may make a tremendous difference in the way the victim feels about school.

Cognitive Characteristics: Primary Grades

1. *Children understand that there are different ways to know things and that some ways are better than others.* When an observation can be explained with either a

Most primary grade students eagerly strive to obtain "helping" jobs around the classroom. Accordingly, you may wish to arrange a rotating schedule for such jobs. Geoffrey Biddle/Time Life Pictures/Getty Images

possible (that is, a theoretical) explanation or an evidence-based explanation, preschoolers fail to see one as more compelling than the other, but primary grade children usually prefer the explanation based on evidence. This is the beginning of scientific thinking (Kuhn, 2002). In one study described by Deanna Kuhn (1999, 2002), preschoolers viewed a set of pictures depicting two individuals running a race. They were asked to indicate who won the race and to explain what led them to that conclusion. One of the runners was wearing a fancier running shoe, and some of the children said that was the reason he beat his opponent. But because this same individual was also holding a trophy and exhibiting a wide grin in the last picture, some children cited that fact as evidence that the boy won the race. By the time they reach the primary grades, virtually all children understand that a fact-based explanation is superior to a theory-based explanation and so point to the second picture as the reason for their conclusion.

| Awareness of cognitive processes begins to emerge

2. *Primary grade children begin to understand that learning and recall are caused by particular cognitive processes that they can control.* Not until children are about seven or eight years of age do they begin to realize that learning and memory stem from cognitive processes that are under their conscious control. When learning words, for example, younger children may need to be prompted or directed to group the words by category because they do not realize that such a technique aids recall. Likewise, they may not recognize their lack of comprehension when they read difficult or unfamiliar material and may need to be prompted to think about how well they are understanding what they read. By the primary grades, this awareness and monitoring of one's learning processes, called *metacognition*, begins to emerge (Schneider, 2002). We will return to the subject in Chapter 8, "Information-Processing Theory."

JOURNAL ENTRY
Assigning Short and Varied Tasks

3. *Because of continuing neurological development and limited experience with formal learning tasks, primary grade children do not learn as efficiently as older children do.* Therefore, you should assign primary grade children relatively short tasks and switch periodically from cognitively demanding activities to less demanding ones. Providing youngsters with periodic breaks, such as recess, increases their ability to attend to and perform well on subsequent classroom tasks. The nature of the recess activity does not seem to be important. It can be physical activity in a schoolyard or playing games in class (Pelligrini, 2009).

4. *Talking aloud to oneself reaches a peak between the ages of six and seven and then rapidly declines.* Don't be surprised or concerned if you observe students talking to themselves, either when they are by themselves or when they are with classmates. This is a well-documented phenomenon that Vygotsky called private speech. Vygotsky described private speech as a transition between speaking with others and thinking to oneself. Private speech is first noticeable around age three and may constitute anywhere from 20 to 60 percent of a child's utterances between the ages of six and seven. By age eight, however, it all but disappears and is replaced by silent, or inner, speech (Berk, 2009; Bukatko, 2008; Feigenbaum, 2002).

As its name implies, private speech is not intended to communicate a message to someone else, nor does it always take the form of complete sentences. One important purpose of private speech, which may consist of single words or phrases, is to help children clarify their thinking and solve difficult problems, such as those that arise in the course of doing math problems or reading unfamiliar material. For example, a child may count on her fingers out loud while working on a math problem and then say, "The answer's ten." Children who use private speech to help them solve moderately difficult but challenging tasks are more task involved and perform better than classmates who talk to themselves less often (Berk, 2009).

ELEMENTARY SCHOOL (GRADES 4 AND 5; NINE AND TEN YEARS)

Physical Characteristics: Elementary Grades

1. *Both boys and girls become leaner and stronger.* In general, there is a decrease in the growth of fatty tissue and an increase in bone and muscle development. In a year's time, the average child of this age will grow about 2 to 3 inches and gain about 5 to 7 pounds. As a result, the typical child will tend to have a lean and gangly look. Although the average nine-year-old boy is slightly taller and heavier than the average nine-year-old girl, this difference all but disappears a year later. And from age eleven until about fourteen and a half, girls are slightly heavier and taller than boys. Because secondary sex characteristics have not yet appeared, boys and girls can be mistaken for one another. This is particularly likely to happen when girls have close-cropped hair, boys have very long hair, and both genders wear gender-neutral clothing (Berk, 2009; Bukatko, 2008; Hetherington & Parke, 1993).

2. *Obesity can become a problem for some children of this age group.* Because nine- and ten-year-olds have more control over their eating habits than younger children do, there is a greater tendency for them to overeat, particularly junk

Table 3.3	Applying Theories of Development to the Elementary Grade Years

Psychosocial development: industry vs. inferiority. Keep students constructively busy; try to play down comparisons between best and worse learners.

Cognitive development: concrete operational. Except for the most intellectually advanced students, most will need to generalize from concrete experiences.

Moral development: morality of constraint; transition from preconventional to conventional. A shift to viewing rules as mutual agreements is occurring, but "official" rules are obeyed out of respect for authority or out of a desire to impress others.

General factors to keep in mind: Initial enthusiasm for learning may fade as the novelty wears off and as the process of perfecting skills becomes more difficult. Differences in knowledge and skills of fastest and slowest learners become more noticeable. "Automatic" respect for teachers tends to diminish. Peer group influences become strong.

food. When this eating pattern is coupled with a relatively low level of physical activity (mainly because of television watching, computer use, and playing video games) and a genetic predisposition toward obesity, children become mildly to severely overweight. Between 1976 and 1980, 6.5 percent of children from six to eleven years of age were judged to be overweight. By 2004 that percentage increased more than 2½ times to 17.5 percent. Not only do overweight children put themselves at risk for cardiovascular problems and type 2 diabetes later in life, but they also become targets for ridicule and ostracism in the present from peers (Eberstadt, 2003; Kelly & Moag-Stahlberg, 2002; National Center for Health Statistics, 2007).

3. *Although small in magnitude, gender differences in motor skill performance are apparent.* Boys tend to outperform girls on tasks that involve kicking, throwing, catching, running, broad jumping, and batting. Girls surpass boys on tasks that require muscular flexibility, balance, and rhythmic movements. These differences may be due in part to gender-role stereotyping. That is, because of socialization differences, girls are more likely to play hopscotch and jump rope, whereas boys are more likely to play baseball and basketball (Berk, 2009).

> Boys slightly better at sports-related motor skills; girls better at flexibility, balance, rhythmic motor skills

JOURNAL ENTRY
Minimizing Gender Differences in Motor Skill Performance

Both boys and girls attain mastery over large and small muscles; one benefit of this is a relatively orderly classroom. Fourth and fifth graders can sit quietly for extended periods and concentrate on whatever intellectual task is at hand (Hetherington & Parke, 1993). Another benefit is that children enjoy arts and crafts and musical activities.

4. *This is a period of relative calm and predictability in physical development.* Growth in height and weight tends to be consistent and moderate, hormonal imbalances are absent, disease occurs less frequently than at any other period, and bodily coordination is relatively stable (Berk, 2009; Hetherington & Parke, 1993).

Social Characteristics: Elementary Grades

1. *The peer group becomes powerful and begins to replace adults as the major source of behavior standards and recognition of achievement.* During the early school years, parents and teachers set standards of conduct, and most children try to live up to them. But by grades 4 and 5, children are more interested in getting along with one another without adult supervision. Consequently, children come to realize that the rules for behavior within the peer group are not quite the same as the rules for behavior within the family or the classroom. Because children of this age are increasingly concerned with being accepted by their peer group and do not have enough self-assurance to oppose group norms, there is a noticeable increase, by both boys and girls, in gossip about others (Ross & Spielmacher, 2005).

> Peer group norms for behavior begin to replace adult norms

JOURNAL ENTRY
Moderating the Power of Peer Group Norms

2. *Friendships become more selective and gender-based.* Elementary grade children become even more discriminating than primary grade children in the selection of friends and playmates. Most children choose a best friend, usually of the same gender. These relationships, based usually on common ideas, outlooks, and impressions of the world, may last through adolescence. Although children of this age will rarely refuse to interact with members of the opposite sex when directed to do so by parents and teachers, they will avoid the opposite sex when left to their own devices (Ross & Spielmacher, 2005).

3. *Play continues to make numerous contributions to children's development.* In describing some of the characteristics of preschool and kindergarten children earlier in the chapter we noted the importance of play activities to several areas of development. Play is no less important at this age level. The benefits that elementary grade children reap when allowed to play their own games include refining the skills of self-direction and self-control, learning how to join the play activities of others, and fostering the development of such cognitive skills as planning and using symbols (Bergen & Fromberg, 2009). So despite the

Elementary grade boys tend to be better than girls on motor skill tasks that involve large muscle movement, whereas elementary grade girls tend to perform better than boys on motor skill tasks that involve muscular flexibility, balance, and rhythmic movements. **A,** David Grossman/Photo Researchers Inc; **B,** Junebug Clark/Photo Researchers Inc

accountability pressures that are so characteristic of education today (we discuss this at length in Chapter 15), efforts should be made to include opportunities for free play during the school day.

Emotional Characteristics: Elementary Grades

1. *During this period, children develop a more global, integrated, and complex self-image.* Researchers who study self-perceptions (e.g., Harter, 1990, 1999; Marsh & Hattie, 1996) distinguish among the concepts of self-description, self-esteem, and self-concept:

   - A **self-description** is simply the way in which people describe themselves to others. Self-descriptive statements are largely, but not entirely, free of evaluative judgments. Examples of self-descriptions are "I am eleven years old," "I am tall for my age," and "I am an outgoing person."
   - **Self-esteem** (or self-worth, as it is sometimes called) refers to the overall or global evaluation people make of themselves. It is indicated by such statements as "I believe that I am a worthwhile person" and "I am pretty happy with myself."
   - **Self-concept** refers to the evaluative judgments people make of themselves in specific domains, such as academic performance, social interactions, athletic performance, and physical appearance. It is indicated by such statements as "I have a good head for math," "I have a hard time making friends," and "My big nose makes me look ugly."

   Taken together, self-descriptions, self-esteem, and self-concept constitute a person's **self-image** or self-portrait. By middle childhood each of these aspects of self-image is present; children can make an accurate self-description, construct a global evaluation of themselves, and specify their positive and negative attributes in specific domains.

Self-image becomes more generalized and stable; is based primarily on comparisons with peers

JOURNAL ENTRY
Ways to Improve Students' Self-Image

pause & reflect

The primary and elementary years correspond to Erikson's stage of industry versus inferiority. The implication is that educators should encourage a sense of industry and competence in each student. On a scale of 1 to 10, how well do you think schools accomplish this goal? What major factors account for your rating?

Delinquents have few friends, are easily distracted, are not interested in schoolwork, lack basic skills

There are several important facts to keep in mind about the formulation of a child's self-image. First, in elementary grade children self-image is more generalized or integrated than is the case for primary grade children because it is based on information gained over time, tasks, and settings. A child may think of herself as socially adept not just because she is popular at school but because she has always been well liked and gets along well with adults, as well as peers, in a variety of situations. It is this generalized quality that helps make self-portraits relatively stable.

Second, comparison with others is the fundamental basis of a self-image during the elementary grades. This orientation is due in part to the fact that children are not as egocentric as they were a few years earlier and are developing the capability to think in terms of multiple categories. Also, because competition and individualism are highly prized values in many Western cultures, children will naturally compare themselves with one another ("I'm taller than my friend") as well as with broad-based norms ("I'm tall for my age") in an effort to determine who they are. This social comparison process can have detrimental effects on a student's academic self-image when he or she moves from a classroom or school where most classmates are perceived to be less capable to one where most of his or her classmates are perceived to be more able learners, the so-called big-fish-little-pond effect (see, for example, Dai & Rinn, 2008; Seaton, Marsh, & Craven, 2010; Marsh, Seaton, Trautwein, Lüdtke, Hau, O'Mara, & Craven, 2008).

Third, in the elementary grades the self is described for the first time in terms of emotions (pride, shame, worry, anger, happiness) and how well they can be controlled. Fourth, a child's sense of self is influenced by the information and attitudes that are communicated by such significant others as parents, teachers, and friends and by how competent the child feels in areas in which success is important. The implications of this fact will be discussed in many of the remaining chapters of the text.

Because major developmental changes usually do not occur during the elementary grades, a child's self-image will remain fairly stable for a few years if there are no major changes in the child's home or social environment. But as you will see later in this chapter, the developmental changes that typically occur during the middle school and high school grades often produce dramatic changes in the sense of self (Alasker & Olweus, 2002).

2. *Disruptive family relationships, social rejection, and school failure may lead to delinquent behavior.* Gerald Patterson, Barbara DeBaryshe, and Elizabeth Ramsey (1989) marshal a wide array of evidence to support their belief that delinquent behavior is the result of a causal chain of events that originates with dysfunctional parent-child relationships. In their view, poor parent-child relationships lead to behavior problems, which lead to peer rejection and academic failure, which lead to identification with a deviant peer group, which results in delinquent behavior. Parents of such children administer harsh and inconsistent punishment, provide little positive reinforcement, and do little monitoring and supervising of each child's activities.

Because these children have not learned to follow adult rules and regulations but have learned how to satisfy their needs through coercive behavior, they are rejected by their peers, are easily distracted when doing schoolwork, show little interest in the subjects they study, and do not master many of the basic academic skills necessary for subsequent achievement. Attempts at short-circuiting this chain of events stand a greater chance of success if they begin early and are multifaceted. In addition to counseling and parent training, mastery of basic academic skills is important.

Cognitive Characteristics: Elementary Grades

Elementary grade students reason logically but concretely

1. *The elementary grade child can think logically, although such thinking is constrained and inconsistent.* In terms of Piaget's stages, upper elementary grade children are concrete operational stage thinkers. Most will have attained enough mastery of logical schemes that they can understand and solve tasks that involve such processes as class inclusion (understanding the superordinate-subordinate relationships that make up hierarchies), seriation, conservation, and symbolic representation (reading maps, for example), provided that the content of the task refers to real, tangible ideas that the child has either experienced or can imagine. But general and abstract ideas often escape the elementary age child. For example, sarcasm, metaphor, and allegory are usually lost on concrete stage thinkers.

2. *On tasks that call for simple memory skills, elementary grade children often perform about as well as adolescents or adults. But on tasks that require more complex memory skills, their performance is more limited.* When tasks call for recognizing previously learned information, such as vocabulary words or facts about a person or event, or for rehearsing several items for immediate use, elementary grade children can perform about as well as older students. Relatively simple memory processes, such as recognition or rote repetition, approach their maximum levels by this point in cognitive development. But the same is not true for tasks that require such advanced memory processes as elaboration and organization. When asked to sort a set of pictures into categories, for example, elementary grade children create fewer and more idiosyncratic categories (which are generally less effective for later recall of the items in the category) than do older children or adults (Kail, 2010). Also bear in mind that elementary grade children need constant practice on a variety of tasks before they use such memory processes consistently and efficiently (Schneider, 2002).

MIDDLE SCHOOL (GRADES 6, 7, AND 8; ELEVEN, TWELVE, AND THIRTEEN YEARS)

In this section, we use the term *adolescent* for the first time. Although it may strike you as odd to think of eleven- and twelve-year-olds as adolescents, developmental psychologists typically apply this term to individuals as young as ten years of age.

Although elementary grade children understand the logical basis for tasks such as classification, seriation, and conservation, they can solve such tasks only if they are based on concrete objects and ideas. © 2010 Fancy/Jupiter Images Corporation

The reason they do is because adolescence involves a series of transitions (biological, social, emotional, and cognitive, for example) to a more mature life stage, some of which may begin in some individuals as early as ten years of age (Steinberg, 2008). Although a variety of terms are used to denote the initial period of change that marks the adolescent years (ages ten to fourteen), we use two of the more popular: *early adolescence* and *emerging adolescence.*

Physical Characteristics: Middle School

Girls' growth spurt occurs earlier, and so they look older than boys of same age

1. *Physical growth tends to be both rapid and uneven.* During the middle school years, the average child will grow 2 to 4 inches per year and gain 8 to 10 pounds per year. But some parts of the body, particularly the hands and feet, grow faster than others. Consequently, middle school children tend to look gangly and clumsy. Because girls mature more rapidly than boys, their **growth spurt** begins at about age eleven, reaches a peak at about age fourteen, and is generally complete by age fifteen. The growth spurt for boys begins on average at about age thirteen, peaks at about age seventeen, and is generally complete by age eighteen. The result of this timing difference in the growth spurt is that many middle school girls look considerably older than boys of the same age. After the growth spurt, however, the muscles in the average boy's body are larger, as are the heart and lungs (Steinberg, 2008).

Early-maturing boys likely to draw favorable responses

Research on early and later maturation shows that differences in physical maturation are likely to produce specific differences in later behavior (see Table 3.5). Because of their more adult-like appearance, **early-maturing boys** are likely to be more popular with peers, have more positive self-concepts, and have more friends among older peers. But friendships with older adolescents put early-maturing boys at greater risk for delinquency, drug and alcohol abuse, truancy, and increased sexual activity. In addition, recent studies suggest that early-maturing boys may be more susceptible to depression. As adults, early maturers were more likely to be responsible, cooperative, self-controlled, conforming, and conventional. **Late-maturing boys,** by contrast, are likely to have relatively lower self-esteem and stronger feelings of inadequacy. Like their early-maturing counterparts they may also be more susceptible to depression than their on-time peers. But later in adolescence, they show higher levels of intellectual curiosity, exploratory behavior, and social initiative. As adults, late-maturing boys are more impulsive, assertive, insightful, and inventive (DeRose & Brooks-Gunn, 2009; Steinberg, 2008; Steinberg, Vandell, & Bornstein, 2011).

Late-maturing boys may feel inadequate

Early-maturing girls may suffer low self-esteem

Because **early-maturing girls** are taller and heavier than their peers and don't have a thin and "leggy" fashion model look, they are likely to have lower

Table 3.4	Applying Theories of Development to the Middle School Years

Psychosocial development: transition from industry vs. inferiority to identity vs. role confusion. Growing independence leads to initial thoughts about identity. There is greater concern about appearance and gender roles than about occupational choice.

Cognitive development: beginning of formal operational thought for some. There is increasing ability to engage in mental manipulations and test hypotheses.

Moral development: transition to morality of cooperation, conventional level. There is increasing willingness to think of rules as flexible mutual agreements; yet "official" rules are still likely to be obeyed out of respect for authority or out of a desire to impress others.

General factors to keep in mind: A growth spurt and puberty influence many aspects of behavior. An abrupt switch occurs (for sixth graders) from being the oldest, biggest, most sophisticated students in elementary school to being the youngest, smallest, least knowledgeable students in middle school. Acceptance by peers is extremely important. Students who do poor schoolwork begin to feel bitter, resentful, and restless. Awareness grows of a need to make personal value decisions regarding dress, premarital sex, and code of ethics.

Table 3.5	The Impact of Early and Late Maturation	
Maturational Stage	**Characteristics as Adolescents**	**Characteristics as Adults**
Early-maturing boys	Self-confident, high in self-esteem, likely to be chosen as leaders (but leadership tendencies more likely in low-SES boys than in middle-class boys), more likely to socialize with older peers and engage in substance abuse, delinquent behavior	Self-confident, responsible, cooperative, sociable. But also more rigid, moralistic, humorless, and conforming
Late-maturing boys	Energetic, bouncy, given to attention-getting behavior, poor body image, lower self-esteem, lower aspirations for educational achievement, not popular	Impulsive and assertive. But also insightful, perceptive, creatively playful, able to cope with new situations
Early-maturing girls	More likely to date older boys, lower self-esteem, lacking in poise (but middle-class girls more confident than those from low-SES groups), more likely to date, smoke, and drink earlier, greater likelihood of eating disorders and depression	Self-possessed, self-directed, able to cope, emotionally stable, wide range of interests
Late-maturing girls	Confident, outgoing, assured, popular, likely to be chosen as leaders	Likely to experience difficulty adapting to stress, less agreeable, more likely to exhibit fluctuating moods

SOURCES: Hetherington & Parke (1993); Harold, Colarossi, & Mercier (2007); Steinberg (2008); Steinberg, Vandell, & Bornstein (2011); Weichold, Silbereisen, & Schmitt-Rodermund (2003).

Late-maturing girls likely to be popular and carefree

JOURNAL ENTRY
Helping Early and Late Maturers Cope

Average age of puberty: girls, eleven; boys, fourteen

self-esteem and are more likely to suffer from depression, anxiety, eating disorders, and panic attacks. They are more likely to be popular with boys, particularly older boys, and experience more pressure to date and become sexually active than their more normally developing peers. **Late-maturing girls,** whose growth spurt is less abrupt and whose size and appearance more closely reflect the feminine stereotype mentioned, share many of the characteristics (positive self-concept, popularity) of the early-maturing boy. Late-maturing girls are more likely to be seen by peers as attractive, sociable, and expressive.

If late-maturing boys in your classes appear driven to seek attention or inclined to brood about their immaturity, you might try to give them extra opportunities to gain status and self-confidence by succeeding in schoolwork or other nonathletic activities. If you notice that early-maturing girls seem insecure, you might try to bolster their self-esteem by giving them extra attention and by recognizing their achievements.

2. *Pubertal development is evident in practically all girls and in many boys.* From ages eleven through thirteen, most girls develop sparse pubic and underarm hair and exhibit breast enlargement. In boys, the testes and scrotum begin to grow, and lightly pigmented pubic hair appears (McDevitt & Ormrod, 2010).

3. *Concern and curiosity about sex are almost universal, especially among girls.* For girls in the United States puberty can begin as early as age seven or as late as age thirteen. For boys, the onset of puberty can be as early as age nine or as late as age thirteen and a half (Steinberg, Vandell, & Bornstein, 2011). Because sexual maturation involves drastic biological and psychological adjustments, children are concerned and curious. It seems obvious that accurate, unemotional answers to questions about sex are desirable. However, for your own protection, you should find out about the sex education policy at your school. Many school districts have formal programs approved by community representatives and led by designated educators. Informal, spur-of-the-moment class discussions may create more problems than they solve.

Social Characteristics: Middle School

1. *The development of interpersonal reasoning leads to greater understanding of the feelings of others.* Robert L. Selman (1980) has studied the development of **interpersonal reasoning** in children. Interpersonal reasoning is the ability to understand the relationship between motives and behavior among a group of people. The results of Selman's research are summarized in Table 3.6. The stages outlined there reveal that during the elementary school years, children gradually grasp the fact that a person's overt actions or words do not always reflect inner feelings. They also come to comprehend that a person's reaction to a distressing situation can have many facets. Toward the end of the elementary school years and increasingly during adolescence, children become capable of taking a somewhat detached and analytical view of their own behavior, as well as the behavior of others. By mid-adolescence, they can, for example, understand that offering unsolicited academic help to a classmate may embarrass that individual (Hoffman, 2000).

   Selman believes that teachers and therapists might be able to aid children who are not as advanced in role-taking skills as their age-mates by helping them become more sensitive to the feelings of others. If an eight-year-old boy is still functioning at the egocentric level, for example, he may fail to interpret the behavior of classmates properly and become a social isolate. Selman describes how one such boy was encouraged to think continually about the reasons behind his social actions and those of others and acquired sufficient social sensitivity to learn to get along with others.

   Discussion techniques Selman recommends can be introduced in a natural, rather than a formal, way. If you see a boy react with physical or verbal abuse when jostled by a playmate, for example, you might say, "You know, people don't always intentionally bump into others. Unless you are absolutely sure that someone has hurt you on purpose, it can be a lot pleasanter for all concerned if you don't make a big deal out of it."

2. *The desire to conform reaches a peak during the middle school years.* Early adolescents find it reassuring to dress and behave like others, and they are likely to alter their own opinions to coincide with those of a group. When you encourage

JOURNAL ENTRY
Ways to Promote Social
Sensitivity

Discussion of controversial issues may be difficult because of strong desire to conform to peer norms

---

Table 3.6	Stages of Interpersonal Reasoning Described by Selman

Stage 0: egocentric level (about ages four to six). Children do not recognize that other persons may interpret the same social event or course of action differently from the way they do. They do not reflect on the thoughts of self and others. They can label the overtly expressed feelings of others but do not comprehend cause-and-effect relations of social actions.

Stage 1: social information role taking (about ages six to eight). Children are able in limited ways to differentiate between their own interpretations of social interactions and the interpretations of others. But they cannot simultaneously think of their own view and those of others.

Stage 2: self-reflective role taking (about ages eight to ten). Interpersonal relations are interpreted in specific situations whereby each person understands the expectations of the other in that particular context. Children are not yet able to view the two perspectives at once, however.

Stage 3: multiple role taking (about ages ten to twelve). Children become capable of taking a third-person view, which permits them to understand the expectations of themselves and of others in a variety of situations as if they were spectators.

Stage 4: social and conventional system taking (about ages twelve to over fifteen). Each individual involved in a relationship with another understands many of the subtleties of the interactions involved. In addition, a societal perspective begins to develop. That is, actions are judged by how they might influence *all* individuals, not just those who are immediately concerned.

SOURCE: Adapted from discussions in Selman (1980).

student participation in class discussions, you may need to be alert to the tendency for students at these grade levels to be reluctant to voice minority opinions. If you want them to think about controversial issues, it may be preferable to invite them to write their opinions anonymously rather than voice them in front of the class.

TeachSource Video Case ◄◄ ▶ ►►

Social and Emotional Development: The Influence of Peer Groups

Go to the Education CourseMate website to watch the Video Case, and then answer the following questions:

1. Describe how the middle school students in this Video Case illustrate Selman's theory of interpersonal reasoning.

2. How do the students in this Video Case illustrate the "desire to conform"?

pause & reflect

During the middle school years, the peer group becomes the general source for rules of behavior. Why? What advantages and disadvantages does this create?

Because early adolescents are often so concerned with receiving social approval from their peers, they may adapt their explanations of school performance to suit this purpose. This tendency was demonstrated by Jaana Juvonen (2000) in a study of fourth, sixth, and eighth graders. These students were asked to imagine that they had received a low score on an important exam and then to indicate how they would explain their performance to teachers and peers. The results may surprise you. The fourth and sixth graders were willing to explain their poor performance to both teachers and peers as being due to low ability rather than to low effort, whereas the eighth graders were much more likely to offer that explanation to their peers than to their teacher. This seems counterintuitive. Why would adolescents want to portray themselves to their peers as being dumb (to put it crudely)? The answer is that ability is seen by many adolescents as something beyond their control (see our account of Carol Dweck's work along this line in Chapter 11, "Motivation"). They therefore conclude that ascribing poor performance to low ability rather than to low effort will result in expressions of sympathy rather than contempt ("It wasn't Matthew's fault that he got a low grade on the last math exam; he just doesn't have a head for numbers").

Emotional Characteristics: Middle School

1. *The view of early adolescence as a period of "storm and stress" appears to be an exaggeration.* Starting with G. Stanley Hall, who wrote a pioneering two-volume text on adolescence in 1904, some theorists have described adolescence as a period of turmoil. Feelings of confusion, anxiety, and depression; extreme mood swings; and low levels of self-confidence are felt to be typical of this age group. Some of the reasons cited for this turbulence are rapid changes in height, weight, and body proportions; increases in hormone production; the task of identity formation; increased academic responsibilities; and the development of formal operational reasoning (Harold, Colarossi, & Mercier, 2007; Larson & Sheeber, 2009; Susman, 1991).

Since the 1970s, however, a number of psychologists have questioned whether turmoil is universal during the emerging adolescent (and later) years (for example, see Harold, Colarossi, & Mercier, 2007; Larson & Sheeber, 2009;

Teenagers experience different degrees of emotional turmoil

Because of the importance of peer group values, middle school students often dress and behave similarly. © Angela Hampton Picture Library/Alamy

Steinberg & Morris, 2001). Current evidence suggests two things: first, that adolescents experience more intense positive *and* negative emotions than do adults (Larson & Sheeber, 2009), and, second, even though many adolescents experience social and emotional problems from time to time and experiment with risky behavior, most do not develop significant social, emotional, or behavioral difficulties. For example, although most adolescents will have been drunk at least once before high school graduation, relatively few will develop drinking problems or allow alcohol to adversely affect their academic or social lives. Those adolescents who do exhibit a consistent pattern of delinquency, substance abuse, and depression are likely to have exhibited these behaviors as children. In other words, problems displayed *during* adolescence are not necessarily problems *of* adolescence (Steinberg & Morris, 2001).

Although emotional turmoil during adolescence is not universal, some students do find this to be a difficult time and suffer from feelings of anxiety, low self-esteem, and depression. A major contributor to these debilitating emotions is the transition from the elementary to the middle school grades. Among the concerns that some students have as they make this shift are having several teachers who vary in their demands and teaching styles, getting lost in an unfamiliar building, having to make new friends, being picked on by older students, having more assignments that are also more difficult, and getting low grades. One key to being able to cope with these demands is a strong sense of self-esteem and self-efficacy (Jindal-Snape & Miller, 2008). In the next section ("Cognitive Characteristics: Middle School") we describe what teachers can do to promote these self-perceptions by helping students meet academic demands.

2. *As a result of the continued influence of egocentric thought, middle school students are typically self-conscious and self-centered.* Because emerging adolescents are acutely aware of the physical and emotional changes that are taking place within them, they assume that everyone else is just as interested in, and is constantly evaluating, their appearance, feelings, and behavior. Consequently, they are deeply concerned about such matters as what type of clothing to wear for special occasions, with whom they should and should not be seen in public (they should never be seen with their parents at the mall, for example), and how they greet and talk with various people.

Another manifestation of adolescent egocentrism is the assumption that adults do not, indeed cannot, understand the thoughts and feelings of early adolescence. It's as if the early adolescent believes she is experiencing things no one else has ever experienced before. Hence, a teen or preteen will likely say to a parent, "You just don't know what it feels like to be in love" (Wiles, Bondi, & Wiles, 2006).

Cognitive Characteristics: Middle School

1. *Because of the psychological demands of early adolescence, middle school students need a classroom environment that is open, supportive, and intellectually stimulating.* Early adolescence is an unsettling time for students because of changes in their physical development, social roles, cognitive development, and sexuality. As we noted in the previous section, another source of stress is coping with the transition from the elementary grades to a middle school (which often begins in sixth grade) or junior high (which typically begins in seventh grade). Partly because of these personal and environmental stresses, the self-concept, academic motivation, and achievement levels of adolescents decline, sometimes drastically. Are schools at all to blame for these problems? Perhaps they are. Several researchers (e.g., Clements & Seidman, 2002; Juvonen, 2007; Jindal-Snape & Miller, 2008; Roeser & Lau, 2002; Wigfield & Eccles, 2002a) provide persuasive evidence that these negative changes are due in part, perhaps in large part, to the fact that the typical school environment does not meet the needs of developing adolescents.

Their argument is based on an analysis of the psychological needs of early adolescence and the kinds of changes that take place in classroom organization, instruction, and climate as one moves from the last of the elementary grades to the first of the middle school or junior high grades. Although the typical middle school classroom is much improved in meeting students' needs for a sense of community, acceptance, and belonging (our Case in Print for this chapter describes how several schools accomplish this goal), the environment continues to be largely incompatible with students' intellectual needs (Gentry, Gable, & Rizza, 2002; Juvonen, 2007; Midgley, 2001; Midgley, Middleton, Gheen, & Kumar, 2002; Wigfield & Eccles, 2002a). Common problems include these:

> Environment of middle schools does not meet needs of adolescents, leading to lower levels of learning

- Instead of providing students with opportunities to make decisions about such things as classroom rules, seating arrangements, homework assignments, and time spent on various tasks, teachers impose most of the requirements and limit the choices students can make. In one study, most middle school students (grades 6 through 8) characterized their classroom activities as less interesting and enjoyable and as providing fewer opportunities for choice than did students in grades 3 through 5 (Gentry et al., 2002).

- Competition and social comparisons among students are increased as a result of such practices as whole-class instruction, ability grouping, normative grading (also called grading on the curve, a practice we discuss in Chapter 14, "Assessment of Classroom Learning"), and public evaluations of one's work. Small-group instruction is infrequent, and individualized instruction almost never occurs (Brinthaupt, Lipka, & Wallace, 2007). This stressful atmosphere does not go unnoticed by students. Compared with adolescents from 11 other countries, middle school students in the United States were more critical of their school's climate and felt more socially isolated (Juvonen, 2007).

- Many classroom tasks in middle school or junior high involve low-level seatwork, verbatim recall of information, and little opportunity for discussion or group work. In one study of 11 junior high school science classes, the most frequent activity was copying information from the board or textbook onto worksheets. This emphasis on rote learning and recall has unfortunately been intensified in recent years by the growth of statewide learning standards, standardized

Early adolescents are faced with several developmental challenges. Consequently, middle school teachers should make a special effort to establish a supportive classroom atmosphere in which students can meet their social, emotional, and cognitive needs. Elizabeth Crews Photography

Take a Stand!

Meeting the Intellectual Needs of Middle School Students

Research from developmental and cognitive psychologists paints a consistent picture of middle school students. They can handle more abstract and complex tasks and work more independently of the teacher, and they have strong needs for both autonomy and social contact. Consequently, middle school teachers ought to minimize the use of lecture, independent seatwork, and competition for grades. Instead, teachers should design lessons around constructivist learning principles. For example, teachers should create assignments that relate to the issues and experiences adolescents are familiar with and care about, let students work cooperatively in small groups, provide whatever intellectual and emotional support students need to complete assignments, and foster the perception that the purpose of education is personal growth rather than competition for grades. Teachers who fail to provide this kind of environment may be doing more harm than good.

What Do You Think?

Do you agree that middle school teaching practices often leave much to be desired? As you consider this issue, check the additional resources available in the Take a Stand! section of the Education CourseMate website.

testing, and accountability. We say "unfortunately" because this type of testing and these approaches to accountability discourage teachers from using instructional methods that foster meaningful learning.

- Students perceive their relationships with their teachers as being less friendly, supportive, and caring than those in earlier grades.

When middle schools fail to provide students with an intellectually challenging yet emotionally safe classroom environment, one negative consequence is an effect on motivation. Theorists like Carol Dweck describe achievement goals as being either *mastery* or *performance* in nature. Students who subscribe to a mastery goal are primarily interested in understanding ideas and their interrelationships, acquiring new skills, and refining them over time. Students who subscribe to a performance goal are primarily interested in demonstrating their ability to finish first (however that is defined) and avoiding situations in which a relative lack of ability would be apparent. Mastery goals have been associated with positive feelings about one's ability, potential, the subject matter, and school and with the use of effective learning strategies (which we describe in Chapter 9, "Social Cognitive Theory").

The most recent evidence suggests that as students move from the elementary grades to the middle grades, there is a shift in their values and practices that leads to more of an emphasis on performance goals. Some researchers blame this change on teaching practices. For example, middle grade teachers are more inclined to post papers and exams with the highest scores,

Case in Print

Middle School Anxieties

Early adolescence is an unsettling time for students because of changes in their physical development, social roles, cognitive development, and sexuality. Another source of stress is coping with the transition from the elementary grades to a middle school (which often begins in sixth grade) or junior high (which typically begins in seventh grade). Partly because of these personal and environmental stresses, the self-concept, academic motivation, and achievement levels of adolescents decline, sometimes drastically. (p. 94)

Middle Ground

CAROLYN BOWER

St. Louis Post-Dispatch 5/29/2002

Getting lost. Not being able to open the combination lock to your locker. More homework. Less recess. Taunts from eighth-graders.

Those are among the fears some sixth-graders said they had when they first came to middle school from elementary school.

"Last year you got the advantage of being the oldest, but now you are the youngest," said Sara Klarfeld, a sixth-grader at Parkway Northeast Middle School in Creve Coeur. "Now you have to sit in the front of the bus. After a while you get used to it."

Sara and other students in Peggy Flynn's class recently wrote letters that Flynn will share with students entering sixth grade at Parkway Northeast in August. "I asked my students to give the new students advice about what it takes to survive in the sixth grade," Flynn said.

More than 88 percent of public school students nationwide change schools when they enter sixth grade. Some principals say that transition is one of the biggest of a student's school career.

From having one teacher and one classroom in elementary school, many middle-schoolers will change classes and have several teachers. And it's up to the student to find out what work to make up after an absence.

Flynn said teachers in middle school expect a lot of responsibility, independence and time management— things some students have not had to deal with.

"A comparable situation for an adult is changing jobs after working six years in the same place with the same people," said Jack Berckemeyer, assistant executive director of the National Middle School Association based in Columbus, Ohio.

Earlier this year, the middle school association and the National Association of Elementary School Principals issued a paper urging principals, teachers and parents to help ease the transition to middle school. Adults can help new middle school students recover that sense of belonging so common in elementary school, the groups said.

"When students feel more comfortable, they are more likely to perform well," said Nathan Bailey, principal at Ladue Middle School. Like principals in many area middle schools, Bailey meets with fifth-graders in the spring to answer their questions and give them a tour.

Triad Middle School Principal Max Pigg said fifth-graders in that district are invited to visit and to share classrooms with sixth-graders. "It seems to ease the anxiety," Pigg said.

In Parkway, at least one Parkway summer school offers a course in how to survive middle school.

Some of Flynn's students could teach that class.

"Future sixth-graders should never give out the combination to the lock on their locker because people will turn it upside down or take things and put them where you can't find them," Michael Holloran said.

Britt Banaszynski advised future sixth-graders to "get to classes on time, have your books and materials so you don't get in trouble."

"Teachers will say something if your shorts are too short or if you wear pajama pants," Claire Latham wrote to future sixth-graders.

Certain supplies are essential. Mike Caraffa, 12, recommends a calculator, a ruler, and "a focused mind."

Alena Armstrong said: "Let those butterflies out of your stomach and take a deep breath. Wish for the best. Be yourself, and don't try to impress others. It's really not that scary."

Questions and Activities

1. If the middle school years are especially challenging for eleven- to thirteen-year-olds and their parents, then they certainly will be for teachers as well. What characteristics of this age group should you keep uppermost in mind, and what general approaches to instruction should you seek to implement?

2. Peggy Flynn, the sixth-grade teacher mentioned in this article, said that middle school teachers expect students to be more responsible and independent than they were in the elementary grades, yet she suggests that some students may have not had much experience or instruction in these capabilities. What steps can you take, as either an elementary grade or a middle school teacher, to help students learn to be more responsible and independent?

3. To find out for yourself what middle school students are like, arrange to visit several middle school classrooms and then interview some students and teachers.

to grade on a curve, to accord special privileges to high achievers, and to remind students of the importance of getting high grades and producing mistake-free papers. Such an environment tells students that meaningful learning is not necessarily expected and that support of learning will not be provided (Midgley, 2001). Students then are motivated to focus on their scores and grades rather than on what they can learn.

Self-efficacy beliefs for academic and social tasks become strong influences on behavior

2. *Self-efficacy becomes an important influence on intellectual and social behavior.* As we mentioned in point 1 under "Social Characteristics," middle school children become capable of analyzing both their own views of an interpersonal interaction and those of the other person. This newfound analytic ability is also turned inward, resulting in evaluations of one's intellectual and social capabilities. Albert Bandura (1986), a learning theorist whom we will discuss later in the book, coined the term **self-efficacy** to refer to how capable people believe they are at dealing with one type of task or another. Thus a student may have a very strong sense of self-efficacy for math ("I know I can solve most any algebraic equation"), a moderate degree of self-efficacy for certain athletic activities ("I think I play baseball and basketball about as well as most other kids my age"), and a low sense of self-efficacy for interpersonal relationships ("I'm just not good at making friends").

These self-evaluative beliefs influence what activities students choose and for how long they will persist at a given task, particularly when progress becomes difficult. Students with a moderate to strong sense of self-efficacy will persist at a task long enough to obtain the success or corrective feedback that leads to expectations of future success. Students with a low sense of self-efficacy, however, tend to abandon tasks at the first sign of difficulty, thereby establishing a pattern of failure, low expectations of future success, and task avoidance. Because self-efficacy beliefs grow out of personal performance, observation of other people doing the same thing, and verbal persuasion, you can help students develop strong feelings of self-efficacy by following the suggestions we will make in later chapters about modeling and imitation, learning strategies, and effective forms of instruction.

HIGH SCHOOL (GRADES 9, 10, 11, AND 12; FOURTEEN, FIFTEEN, SIXTEEN, AND SEVENTEEN YEARS)

Physical Characteristics: High School

1. *Most students reach physical maturity, and virtually all attain puberty.* Although almost all girls reach their ultimate height, some boys may continue to grow even after graduation from high school. Tremendous variation

exists in height and weight and in rate of maturation. Approximately 16 percent of students are considered to be overweight; 13 percent are obese (Centers for Disease Control and Prevention, 2008). As noted earlier, late-maturing boys seem to have considerable difficulty adjusting to their slower rate of growth. There is still concern about appearance, although it may not be as strong as during the middle school years. Glandular changes leading to acne may be a source of worry and self-consciousness to some students. The most significant glandular change accompanying puberty is arousal of the sex drive.

2. *Many adolescents become sexually active, although the long-term trend is down.* From 2001 through 2007 sexual intercourse among high school students trended up after having declined through the 1990s, as shown in Table 3.8. In 2007, close to two thirds of students reported having engaged in sexual intercourse by the end of grade 12.

Table 3.7	Applying Theories of Development to the High School Years

Psychosocial development: identity vs. role confusion. Concerns arise about gender roles and occupational choice. Different identity statuses become apparent.

Cognitive development: formal operational thought for many students. There is increasing ability to engage in mental manipulations, understand abstractions, and test hypotheses.

Moral development: morality of cooperation, conventional level. There is increasing willingness to think of rules as mutual agreements and to allow for intentions and extenuating circumstances.

General factors to keep in mind: Achievement of sexual maturity has a profound effect on many aspects of behavior. Peer group and reactions of friends are extremely important. There is concern about what will happen after graduation, particularly for students who do not intend to continue their education. Awareness grows of the significance of academic ability and importance of grades for certain career patterns. There is a need to make personal value decisions regarding use of drugs, premarital sex, and code of ethics.

Table 3.8	Trends in Sexual Activity Among High School Students

	Percentage Who Reported Ever Having Sexual Intercourse	
	2001	2007
Gender		
Females	44.5	47.2
Males	49.4	51.2
Grade Levels		
Ninth grade	34.8	33.2
Tenth grade	40.7	43.7
Eleventh grade	51.8	55.4
Twelfth grade	60.5	64.5
Ethnic Groups		
Black	60.8	66.5
Hispanic	48.4	52.0
White	43.2	43.7

SOURCE: Centers for Disease Control and Prevention (2009).

| Factors related to initiation of sexual activity vary by gender, race |

The factors that are significantly related to initiation of sexual activity among high school students vary by gender and race. White males and females with low educational goals and below-average grades are more likely to have sexual intercourse at an earlier age as compared with peers who have higher goals and grades. The factors that were most strongly related to initiation of sexual activity for African American female students were having a mother with 12 or more years of education (presumably, mothers with more education spend less time at home caring for their children), spending less time with one's mother, and being uninvolved in church activities. The factors that predicted onset of sexual activity for African American male students were low grade-point average, living in a one-parent family, limited contact with the father, and lack of participation in family decision making. In addition, the onset of sexual activity is associated with subsequent declines in educational goals and achievement and an increased risk of substance abuse (Hallfors et al., 2002; Ramirez-Valles, Zimmerman, & Juarez, 2002; Schvaneveldt, Miller, Berry, & Lee, 2001).

These findings illustrate the pressing need for sex education during the high school years. In particular, adolescents need to understand the distinction between sex and mature love. A major characteristic of mature love is that "the well-being of the other person is just a little bit more important than the well-being of the self" (Gordon & Gilgun, 1987, p. 180).

pause & reflect

What are the advantages and disadvantages of sex education in school? For help with your answer, visit the websites of the National Campaign to Prevent Teen and Unplanned Pregnancy (**www.thenationalcampaign.org**) and the Sexuality Information and Education Council of the United States (**www.siecus.org**).

3. *Although the birthrate for unmarried adolescents has fallen in recent years, it remains unacceptably high, as is the rate of sexually transmitted diseases.* In 1991, the birthrate for teens of ages fifteen to nineteen was 61.8 births per 1,000. By 2005, that figure had declined to 41.9. Pregnancy rates for teens fifteen to nineteen years old have also declined. In 1990, the pregnancy rate was 117 per 1,000, but it slid to 72.2 per 1,000 in 2004. This decline is attributed to a combination of increased abstinence and contraception (National Center for Health Statistics, 2008). Even so, pregnancy rates and birthrates in the United States are considerably higher than in Canada and many European countries because American teens are less likely than their Canadian and European counterparts to use contraception (Guttmacher Institute, 2006). Among the many factors related to these trends in adolescent sexual behavior, one has clear educational implications: Adolescents who were retained at least once and were behind schedule in their schooling were more likely to have unprotected sex than adolescents who had not been retained (Abma & Sonenstein, 2001).

The relatively high levels of sexual activity and low levels of regular contraception among adolescents are particularly worrisome because they put adolescents at risk for contracting **sexually transmitted diseases (STDs)**. According to the Centers for Disease Control and Prevention (2009), in the United States STDs occur more frequently among adolescents than in any other age group. The rates for syphilis, gonorrhea, and chlamydia among fifteen- to nineteen-year-olds, for example, are 6.0 per 100,000, 977.4 per 100,000, and 3,559.8 per 100,000, respectively.

The worst of the STDs is, of course, HIV/AIDS. HIV stands for human immunodeficiency virus and AIDS stands for acquired immune deficiency syndrome. HIV is the viral cause of AIDS. In 2006, almost 12 adolescents for every 100,000 in the fifteen- to nineteen-year-old age group were diagnosed with HIV/AIDS (Centers for Disease Control and Prevention, 2009).

Because many adolescents are sexually active, there is a strong need for sex education in the schools. Adamsmith/Taxi/Getty Images

Social Characteristics: High School

Parents influence values, plans; peers influence immediate status

1. *Parents and other adults are likely to influence long-range plans; peers are likely to influence immediate status.* When adolescents look for models and advice on such social matters as dress, hairstyle, speech patterns, friendships, and leisure activities, the peer group is likely to have the greatest influence (as a visit to any high school will reveal). Peer values can also influence academic performance. When the issues are which courses to take in school and what different careers are like, teachers, guidance counselors, and parents are likely to have more influence over decision making than peers. For questions about values, ethics, and future plans, the views of parents are usually sought (Steinberg, Vandell, & Bornstein, 2011).

   Not surprisingly, most conflicts between parents and their adolescent children are about such peer-influenced issues as personal appearance, friends, dating, hours, and eating habits (Hill, 1987). This general pattern may be modified, however, by type of parenting style. The adolescent children of parents who have an authoritarian style (see Diana Baumrind's work on parenting styles in the section on the cognitive characteristics of preschool and kindergarten children) have a stronger tendency than other adolescents to make decisions that are consistent with peer group advice. The adolescent children of parents who have an authoritative style, on the other hand, are more likely to make decisions that are consistent with parental advice (Steinberg & Morris, 2001). Perhaps this is why the influence of parents appears to be greatest when there are mutual affection and respect between parent and child (Baumrind, 1991b; Hill, 1987).

Girls more likely than boys to experience anxiety about friendships

2. *Girls seem to experience greater anxiety about friendships than boys do.* Factors that cause girls to become concerned about the reactions of others were summarized in the preceding chapter. Adolescent girls tend to seek intimacy in friendships. Boys, in contrast, often stress skills and interests when they form friendships, and their tendencies to be competitive and self-reliant may work against the formation of close relationships with male companions. Because adolescent girls often wish to form an intimate relationship with another girl, they are more likely than boys to experience anxiety, jealousy, and conflicts regarding friendships with same-sex peers. You should not be surprised, therefore, if secondary school girls are much more preoccupied with positive and negative aspects of friendships than boys are (Hardy, Bukowski, & Sippola, 2002; Pleydon & Schner, 2001; Steinberg, Vandell, & Bornstein, 2011).

3. *Many high school students are employed after school.* For any number of reasons, a fair percentage of high school students have part-time jobs during the school year. In 2007, 21 percent of sixteen- to seventeen-year-olds and 26 percent of eighteen- to nineteen-year-olds worked after school. These percentages have been trending lower, however, from their 2000 peak of 31 percent and 30 percent, respectively (Morisi, 2008).

   The pros and cons of after-school employment have been vigorously debated. On the positive side, it is thought to enhance self-discipline, a sense of responsibility, self-confidence, and attitudes toward work. On the negative side, part-time employment leaves less time for homework, participation in extracurricular activities, and development of friendships; it may also lead to increased stress, lower grades, and lower career aspirations. Most experts agree that students who work more than 20 hours per week are likely to have lower grades than students who work less or not at all (Steinberg, Vandell, & Bornstein, 2011).

Emotional Characteristics: High School

1. *Many psychiatric disorders either appear or become prominent during adolescence. Included among these are eating disorders, substance abuse, schizophrenia, depression, and suicide.* Eating disorders are much more common in females than in

males. *Anorexia nervosa* is an eating disorder characterized by a preoccupation with body weight and food, behavior directed toward losing weight, peculiar patterns of handling food, weight loss, intense fear of gaining weight, and a distorted perception of one's body. This disorder occurs predominantly in females (more than 90 percent of the cases) and usually appears between the ages of fourteen and seventeen (American Psychiatric Association, 2000).

Bulimia nervosa is a disorder in which binge eating (uncontrolled rapid eating of large quantities of food over a short period of time), followed by self-induced vomiting, is the predominant behavior. Binges are typically followed by feelings of guilt, depression, self-disgust, and fasting. As with anorexia, more than 90 percent of individuals with bulimia are female (American Psychiatric Association, 2000).

Adolescents who engage in *substance abuse* (tobacco, alcohol, and illegal drugs) not only jeopardize their physical and emotional health but also increase their risk of doing poorly in school or of dropping out of school. A 2007 survey of high school students (Centers for Disease Control and Prevention, 2008) found that:

- Twenty percent reported smoking on one or more of the 30 days before the survey, and about 8 percent reported smoking on 20 or more of the previous 30 days.
- Almost 45 percent of high school students reported drinking in the previous 30 days. Twenty-four percent of female students and 27.8 percent of male students engaged in episodic heavy drinking (commonly known as binge drinking).
- Thirty-eight percent had used marijuana at least once during their lifetimes, and 19.7 percent had used marijuana one or more times in the preceding 30 days.
- A little more than 7 percent reported using some form of cocaine at least once during their lifetimes, and 4.33 percent reported using cocaine in the preceding 30 days.
- About 4.5 percent of students reported using methamphetamine at least once during their lifetimes.

Schizophrenia, a thinking disorder characterized by illogical and unrealistic thinking, delusions, and hallucinations, is relatively rare among adolescents, affecting less than 0.25 percent of all thirteen- to nineteen-year-olds. Yet it is the most frequently occurring psychotic disorder, and the number of cases diagnosed between the ages of twelve and eighteen is steadily increasing. Early symptoms include odd, unpredictable behavior; difficulty communicating with others; social withdrawal; and rejection by peers (Beiser, Erickson, Fleming, & Iacono, 1993; Conger & Galambos, 1997; Gilberg, 2001).

2. *The most common type of emotional disorder during adolescence is depression.* The most common forms of **depression,** from least to most serious, are *depressed mood, depressive syndrome,* and *clinical depression.* Depressed mood is primarily characterized by feelings of sadness or unhappiness, although emotions such as anxiety, fear, guilt, anger, and contempt are frequently present, as well (Peterson et al., 1993). In 2007, 35.8 percent of high school females and 21.2 percent of high school males reported feeling so sad and hopeless almost every day for two or more weeks in a row that they stopped engaging in some usual activities. The percentages of White, Black, and Latino students who gave this response were 26.2, 29.2, and 36.3, respectively (Centers for Disease Control and Prevention, 2008). As you can see from these data, more girls than boys report having emotional responses indicative of depression, as do students of color, particularly those of Latino origin. In the case of female adolescents, increases in sex hormones, specifically testosterone and estradiol, have been linked to depression (Angold, Worthman, & Costello, 2003).

Common symptoms of depression include feelings of worthlessness and lack of control over one's life, crying spells, and suicidal thoughts, threats, and attempts. Additional symptoms include moodiness, social isolation, fatigue,

| Depression most common among females, students of color

hypochondria, and difficulty in concentrating (Cicchetti &Toth, 1998; Peterson et al., 1993). Depression in adolescents precedes substance abuse (MacKay et al., 2000). High school students who experience such symptoms typically try to ward off their depression through restless activity or flight to or from others. They may also engage in problem behavior or delinquent acts carried out in ways that make it clear they are appealing for help. (A depressed fifteen-year-old boy may carry out an act of vandalism, for instance, at a time when a school authority or police officer is sure to observe the incident.)

Although many techniques exist for changing a negative self-concept to a positive view of self, one effective approach to minimizing depression is to help as many of your students as possible to experience success as they learn. Techniques to accomplish that goal will be discussed in subsequent chapters of this book.

3. *If depression becomes severe, suicide may be contemplated.* In 2007, 14.5 percent of high school students had seriously considered attempting suicide during the previous 12 months, 11.3 percent had made a suicide plan, and 6.9 percent had made one or more attempts. Many more females than males considered attempting suicide (18.7 percent versus 10.3 percent, respectively) and made one or more attempts (9.3 percent versus 4.6 percent). The only good news in these statistics is that they are lower than they were in 2005.

Latino teens are more likely than White or Black teens to consider a suicide attempt (15.9 percent, 14 percent, and 13.2 percent, respectively) and to make a suicide attempt (10.2 percent, 5.6 percent, and 7.7 percent, respectively) (Centers for Disease Control and Prevention, 2008). As of 2005, the death rate from suicide in the fifteen- to twenty-four-year-old age group was highest for American Indian/Alaskan Native males (32.7 per 100,000) and females (10.1 per 100,000) and lowest for Asian or Pacific Islander males (7.2 per 100,000) and Black females (21.7 per 100,000) (National Center for Health Statistics, 2007).

The single most important signal of a youth at risk for suicide is depression. Along with the common symptoms noted earlier under point 2, other signs of depression and potential suicide include poor appetite, weight loss, changes in sleeping patterns, difficulty in concentrating, academic problems, poor self-concept, withdrawing from friends and/or social activities, giving away prized

JOURNAL ENTRY
Helping Students
Overcome Depression

Depression and unstable family situation place adolescents at risk for suicide

Many high school students, girls in particular, experience periods of depression, loneliness, and anxiety. Because severe depression often precedes a suicide attempt, teachers should refer students they believe to be depressed to the school counselor. © Richard Hutchings/Photo Edit

possessions, lack of interest in personal appearance, and feelings of loneliness. These symptoms take on added significance when accompanied by a family history of suicide or parents who commit abuse or use drugs and alcohol excessively. The factors that usually trigger a suicide include a shameful or humiliating experience, such as perceived failure at school or rejection by a romantic partner or parent (Fisher, 2006; Perkins & Hartless, 2002; Sofronoff, Dalgliesh, & Kosky, 2005).

TeachSource Video Case ◀◀ ▶ ▶▶

Social and Emotional Development: Understanding Adolescents

Go to the Education CourseMate website to watch the Video Case, and then answer the following questions:

1. The preceding material describes signs of adolescent students who might be "at risk." Based on your observations of the students in this Video Case, would you consider any of the students in this video to be at risk? Are there observable factors/characteristics that you can detect?

2. How does this Video Case illustrate the powerful influence of peer groups in adolescents' lives?

If you notice that a student in one of your classes seems extremely depressed, take the trouble to ask if there is anything you can do to provide support and seek the advice of the school counselor. To encourage students to discuss their concerns with you, suggest that they read books written for adolescents that address suicide in a direct and forthright manner (Fisher, 2006). Your interest and sympathy may prevent a suicide attempt. Also, be aware that recent prevention efforts include school-based programs. These programs, which are run by a mental health professional or an educator (or both), are typically directed at high school students, their parents, and their teachers. They usually include a review of suicide statistics, a list of warning signs, a list of community mental health resources and how to contact them, and a discussion of how to refer a student or peer to counseling.

Cognitive Characteristics: High School

1. *High school students become increasingly capable of engaging in formal thought, but they may not use this capability.* These students are more likely than younger students to grasp relationships, mentally plan a course of action before proceeding, and test hypotheses systematically. Without supervision and guidance, however, they may not use such capabilities consistently (Harold, Colarossi, & Mercier, 2007). Accordingly, you might take advantage of opportunities to show students at these grade levels how they can function as formal thinkers. Call attention to relationships and to ways that previously acquired knowledge can be applied to new situations. Provide specific instruction in techniques of problem solving. (Ways you might do this will be discussed in Chapter 10, "Constructivist Learning Theory, Problem Solving, and Transfer.") Although some students may ignore your advice, others will probably take it more seriously. Despite the constant attempts of adolescents to appear totally self-sufficient and independent, they still view parents and teachers as knowledgeable authority figures when it comes to school achievement (Amiram, Bar-Tal, Alona, & Peleg, 1990; Harold, Colarossi, & Mercier, 2007).

Political thinking becomes more abstract, less authoritarian, more knowledgeable

2. *Between the ages of twelve and sixteen, political thinking becomes more abstract, liberal, and knowledgeable.* Joseph Adelson (1972, 1986) used an interview approach to obtain information about the development of political thought during the adolescent years. At the start of the interviews, the participants were requested to imagine that 1,000 people had ventured to an island in the Pacific for the purpose of establishing a new society. The respondents were then asked to explain how these people might establish a political order; devise a legal system; establish a balance among rights, responsibilities, personal liberty, and the common good; and deal with other problems of public policy.

The analysis of the interview responses showed no significant gender differences in the understanding of political concepts and no significant differences attributable to intelligence and social class, although brighter students were better able to deal with abstract ideas and upper-class students were less likely to be authoritarian. The most striking and consistent finding was the degree to which the political thinking of the adolescent changed in the years between ages twelve and sixteen. Adelson concluded that the most significant changes were (1) an increase in the ability to deal with such abstractions as freedom of speech, equal justice under law, and the concept of community; (2) a decline in authoritarian views; (3) an increase in the ability to imagine the consequences of current actions; and (4) an increase in political knowledge.

Increased ability to deal with abstractions is a function of the shift from concrete to formal operational thought. When thirteen-year-olds were asked, "What is the purpose of laws?" a typical answer was, "So people don't steal or kill" (Adelson, 1972, p. 108). A fifteen- or sixteen-year-old, by contrast, was more likely to say, "To ensure safety and enforce the government" (p. 108).

When considering punishment for crimes, younger children (Piaget's moral realists) hold the conviction that laws are immutable and that punishment should be stern. But by age fourteen and fifteen, the adolescents whom Adelson interviewed were more likely to consider circumstances and individual rights and to recommend rehabilitation rather than punishment.

If you will be teaching courses in social studies, you may find this information useful in lesson planning. It may also help you understand why students may respond to discussions of political or other abstract matters in different ways.

SELECTING TECHNOLOGIES FOR DIFFERENT AGE LEVELS

As this chapter and the preceding one indicate, your teaching approaches will be influenced by the developmental level of your students. Your incorporation of educational technology will be no different. For kindergarten and primary grade teachers, tools to enhance student literacy are likely to be a priority. Elementary, middle school, and high school teachers will be more interested in tools that promote thinking, problem solving, and communication.

Using Technology to Reduce Egocentrism and Develop Interpersonal Reasoning

As we pointed out in the preceding chapter, primary to elementary grade children are limited by egocentrism in their ability to think logically. Egocentrism, as you may recall, is the inability to understand the world from any perspective but your own. According to Jean Piaget, who first proposed the concept, the main factor that contributes to the decline of egocentrism is exposure to different points of view through social interaction. Because these interactions do not have to be face-to-face, it is quite possible that sharing experiences and points of view by computer may produce the same result.

For quick links to featured websites, use the Education CourseMate website.

One way to accomplish these exchanges is through Kidlink (**www.kidlink.org/ kidspace/index.php**), a nonprofit organization that helps teachers and students arrange electronic exchanges with students from around the world. The goal of Kidlink is to help children understand themselves, identify and define life goals, and collaborate with peers. Joyce Burtch, a middle school teacher, has described how she created a program through Kidlink for her students, including three students with moderate neurological and physical impairments (Burtch, 1999).

A project with implications for egocentrism reduction occurred between fifth-grade students in Italy and Greece. Each group of students wrote the beginning of a fairy tale that contained a moral issue and posted it to a website. The fifth graders from the other country downloaded the partially written story, discussed it in class, wrote an ending, and then posted the completed story to the website. The group that started the story then downloaded it, discussed it among themselves, wrote a final draft, and posted a summary of their discussion on the website. The comments made by the students reflected a strong effort to come to grips with the perspective of the other group (Ligorio, Talamo, & Pontecorvo, 2005).

For schools that do not have the luxury of arranging real-time videoconferences, written asynchronous exchanges via e-mail have proven useful for accomplishing the same goal. One advantage of e-mail exchanges is that children who are outgoing and fluent speakers are less likely to discourage others from participating. In a test of this idea, fifth and sixth graders from two schools in the Netherlands worked on a biology project for several weeks, both among themselves and with students from the other school, by periodically exchanging e-mails about various aspects of the project. The researchers found that over the course of the study, the students became more reflective and aware of the different views of their peers (De Vries, Van der Meij, Boersma, & Pieters, 2005).

In recent years new options for encouraging the decline of egocentrism and the growth of interpersonal reasoning have emerged. Referred to collectively as **Web 2.0,** these options include such tools as blogs, podcasts, and videos, and such social networking websites as Facebook, Twitter, Flickr, YouTube, and LinkedIn (see, for example, Bull, Hammond, & Ferster, 2008; Rosen & Nelson, 2008). These tools and websites allow individuals who share a common interest to work together to create, discuss, and modify a particular product, such as fiction or nonfiction stories, without having to purchase expensive software (Alexander & Levine, 2008; Berson, 2009; Nebel, Jamison, & Bennett, 2009). The website ePals (**www.epals.com**) provides a general lesson plan for a digital storytelling class-room project in which students create, share, and reflect on their stories. Podcasts from students in a New Zealand school about their life there are available at **www.ptengland.school.nz.** As we pointed out earlier, these types of activities require students to consider points of view different from their own and to think about how best to interact with their online peers to assure the success of the project.

Effect of Technology on Cognitive Development

One of the advantages of educational technology is that it can be readily used to support the development of such higher-level cognitive skills as inquiry, critical thinking, and problem solving. For example, **adventure learning** programs allow students to interact electronically with experts and explorers around the world. Students from various schools might get together for virtual field trips to places such as the Statue of Liberty for insights on immigration policies or the Civil War battlefield at Gettysburg for demonstrations of military tactics (Siegel & Kirkley, 1998). They also might communicate electronically with explorers traversing the Arctic tundra or the Amazon rain forest. While on virtual field trips, students are electronically transported to the actual site to view historical reenactments, listen to experts, ask questions, and electronically correspond with peers across the nation.

To review this chapter, try the tutorial quizzes and other study aids on the textbook's website, Education Course-Mate.

Adventure-learning explorations can be incorporated into the **problem-based learning (PBL)** approach, a technique that promotes formal operational thought by emphasizing real-world problem solving. We discuss PBL in Chapter 13, "Approaches to Instruction." Two adventure-learning websites that you might want to take a look at are the Global Online Adventure Learning Site at **www.goals.com/index.htm** and ThinkQuest's Ocean Adventure site at **http://library.thinkquest.org/18828**.

Challenging Assumptions

Looking Through Lenses

"OK," says Don, "so theories of development tend to focus on certain aspects of behavior and thought, but not on everything at once. If we really want to understand how kids change and why they behave as they do, we need to take into account not just how they reason or how they interact with others or how they develop physically or emotionally, but how all of those come together to influence what happens in classrooms."

Connie nods. "Looking at students through the lens of well-established theory can certainly provide insights. But behavior is complex, and so are the ways in which students develop. When a student comes into our classroom, she or he is not simply, for example, 'a concrete operational thinker with feelings of inferiority who reasons conventionally.' A student is all those things and more. Students bring myriad experiences with them into our classrooms. They bring their academic capabilities, their emotional insecurities, their social status in the class, their family relationships, their physical appearance. No one theory explains everything, but that does not mean that a theory is useless to us. Theories grow from research, and when research supports a theory, there is good reason to use that theory as a way to understand our students and as a basis for testing ways to facilitate their learning."

Connie continues, "Let's go back, for a minute, to Celeste and Antonio's conversation about eighth graders. Celeste, you saw a lesson work well in one class but not in another. Did that ever happen to you, Antonio?"

"Absolutely," says Antonio. "I have a group of kids who do very well in my class. But then I teach the same lesson to another group and they just don't get it. I used to think that it was just that I had a 'bad group' of students or that they just wouldn't try because they didn't like me."

"Do you have any other thoughts now?" asks Connie.

"Yeah, I do," Antonio says. "It seems to me that there might be a lot of reasons why a group of students—who are going through a ton of changes and who are very focused on what other kids think—might not be focused on a lesson that I'm teaching."

"And what are you going to do with those explanations?" Connie asks.

"Test them until I have found ways to help each student in each class."

Connie smiles. "That's what effective teachers do."

Summary

1. Preschool and kindergarten children are quite active and enjoy physical activity. Their incomplete muscle and motor development limits what they can accomplish on tasks that require fine motor skills, eye-hand coordination, and visual focusing.

2. The social behavior of preschool and kindergarten children is marked by rapidly changing friendships and play groups, a variety of types of play, short quarrels, and a growing awareness of gender roles.

3. Kindergartners openly display their emotions. Anger and jealousy are common.

4. By age four, children are skilled language users and are aware of their own mental activity and the fact that others may think about the world differently. Although they are not particularly adept at judging how well they perform various tasks, they can be helped to overcome this limitation by being given opportunities to compare their performances with those of more accomplished peers.

5. An authoritative approach by parents and teachers is more likely to produce competent preschoolers than are authoritarian, permissive, or rejecting-neglecting approaches.

6. Primary grade children exhibit many of the same physical characteristics as preschool and kindergarten children (high activity level, incomplete muscle and motor development, frequent periods of fatigue). Most accidents occur among third graders because they overestimate their physical skills and underestimate the dangers in their activities.

7. Primary grade children's friendships are typically same sex and are made on a more selective basis than among younger children. Quarrels among peers typically involve verbal arguments, although boys may engage in punching, wrestling, and shoving.

8. Primary grade students are becoming more emotionally sensitive. As a result, they are more easily hurt by criticism, respond strongly to praise, and are more likely to hurt another child's feelings during a quarrel.

9. Primary grade children recognize that fact-based explanations are superior to theory-based explanations and are beginning to realize that their cognitive processes are under their control. They learn best when tasks are relatively short and when less cognitively demanding tasks occasionally follow more cognitively demanding tasks.

10. Elementary grade boys and girls become leaner and stronger and tend to have a gangly look. But some run the risk of becoming overweight because of poor eating habits and lack of exercise. Boys usually outperform girls on such sports-related motor skills as kicking, throwing, catching, running, and jumping, whereas girls often surpass boys on such play-related motor skills as flexibility, balance, and rhythm.

11. The peer group becomes a strong influence on the norms that govern the behavior of elementary grade children. Friendships in the elementary grades become even more selective and gender based than they were in the primary grades.

12. A child's self-image (the combination of self-descriptions, self-concept, and self-esteem) becomes more stable and generalized during the elementary grades. As a result of the decline of egocentric thought and the competitive nature of American society, self-image is based primarily on comparisons with peers.

13. Delinquency occurs more frequently among elementary grade children than at earlier ages and is associated with dysfunctional parent-child relationships and academic failure.

14. The thinking of elementary grade children, although more logical, can be wildly inconsistent and is constrained by the limitations of Piaget's concrete operational stage.

15. Although most children grow rapidly during the middle school years, girls grow more quickly and begin puberty earlier than boys. Early versus late maturation in boys and girls may affect subsequent personality development.

16. The social behavior of middle school children is increasingly influenced by peer group norms and the development of interpersonal reasoning. Children are now capable of understanding why they behave as they do toward others and vice versa. Because the peer group is the primary source for rules of acceptable behavior, conformity and concern about what peers think reach a peak during the middle school years.

17. Although anxiety, worry, and concern about self-esteem, physical appearance, academic success, and acceptance by peers are prominent emotions among many adolescents, some cope with these emotions better than others.

18. Although middle schools are doing a better job of meeting the social and emotional needs of early adolescents than they did in the past, the intellectual needs of these youngsters are still largely unmet.

19. Self-efficacy beliefs, or how competent one feels at carrying out a particular task, begin to stabilize

during the middle school years and influence the willingness of students to take on and persist at various academic and social tasks.

20. Physical development during the high school years is marked by physical maturity for most students and by puberty for virtually all. Sexual activity increases.

21. The long-range goals, beliefs, and values of adolescents are likely to be influenced by parents, whereas immediate status is likely to be influenced by peers. Many teens have part-time, after-school employment.

22. Eating disorders, substance abuse, schizophrenia, depression, and suicide are prominent emotional disorders among adolescents. Depression is the most common emotional disorder during

adolescence. Depression coupled with an unstable family situation places adolescents at risk for suicide.

23. Cognitively, high school students become increasingly capable of formal operational thought, although they may function at the concrete operational level a good deal of the time. The influence of formal operational reasoning can be seen in political thinking, which becomes more abstract and knowledgeable.

24. Technology tools can help primary to elementary grade children cope with the barriers to logical thinking created by egocentrism, and can support the development of such higher-level cognitive skills as inquiry, critical thinking, and problem solving among older children.

Resources for Further Investigation

● How Children Develop

Helen Bee and Denise Boyd describe how children develop physically, socially, emotionally, and cognitively in *The Developing Child* (12th ed., 2009). Robert V. Kail does the same in *Children and Their Development* (5th ed., 2010).

● Children's Play Behavior

In *Children, Play, and Development* (1999), Fergus Hughes discusses the history of play in the Western world; different theories of play; cultural differences in play behaviors; patterns of play among toddlers, preschoolers, school-age children, and adolescents; gender differences in play; and the play behaviors of children with disabilities. Anthony Pellegrini provides a comprehensive discussion of the nature of children's play and its effects in *The Role of Play in Human Development* (2009). Chapter 12 is about the role of play in education, including the place of recess.

● Cognitive Development

A basic but comprehensive treatment of cognitive development can be found in *Cognitive Development* (2002), by John Flavell, Patricia Miller, and Scott Miller, and *Children's Thinking: Cognitive Development and Individual Differences* (2005), by David Bjorklund. Specialized treatments of cognitive development in infancy, early childhood, and childhood, as well as atypical cognitive development and models of development, appear in the *Blackwell Handbook of Childhood Cognitive Development* (2002), edited by Usha Goswami.

   If you are interested in using technology, particularly those applications that are considered to be part of the Web 2.0 era, to promote the social and cognitive development of your students, you may want to take a look at the following two books: *Blogs, Wikis, Podcasts, and Other Powerful Web Tools for Classrooms* (2009, 2nd ed.), by Will Richardson, and *Making the Most of the Web in Your Classroom* (2008), by Timothy Green, Abbie Brown, and LeAnne Robinson.

● Teaching the Middle School Grades

Different instructional strategies for teaching middle and high school students (e.g., lecture and direct instruction, questioning, cooperative learning, classroom discussion and debate) are described by Bruce Larson and Timothy Keiper in *Instructional Strategies for Middle and High School* (2007). Jon Wiles, Joseph Bondi, and Michele Tillier Wiles discuss such aspects of teaching at the middle school level as the rationale behind middle schools, the nature of preadolescent learners, the middle school curriculum, and instructional materials and technologies in *The Essential Middle School* (2006).

   Several foundations and organizations are committed to helping educators make education in the middle grades more consistent with what is known about the characteristics of early adolescence. For example, the website of the National Forum to Accelerate Middle-Grades Reform (**www.mgforum.org**) contains a Schools to Watch page (click on Improving Schools) that specifies a set of criteria that middle schools must meet if they are to be judged as having an exemplary program. The page also describes award-winning schools that were judged to have met those criteria.

   The website of MiddleWeb (**www.middleweb.com**) includes the latest news and updates on middle school reform, as well as a resources page with links to such topics as teaching secrets: taming classroom chaos, teacher-to-teacher lesson resources, using Twitter for professional growth, motivating students to accept challenging tasks, and connecting with parents.

● Characteristics of Adolescence

For a good overall treatment of the major developmental changes that occur during adolescence—biological, cognitive, moral reasoning, self-concept and self-esteem, identity, gender role socialization, sexuality, vocational choice—consult the eighth edition of *Adolescence* (2008), by Laurence Steinberg.

If you expect to be teaching adolescents, you should read *Understanding Youth: Adolescent Development for Educators* (2006), by Michael Nakkula and Eric Toshalis, and/or *Smooth Sailing or Stormy Waters: Family Transitions Through Adolescence and Their Implications for Practice and Policy* (2007), by Rena Harold, Lisa Colarossi, and Lucy Mercier. The former book discusses identity development, risk taking, and school-to-career transitions, among other topics. The latter book contains interesting quotes from parents and teenagers about the topics covered by each chapter.

4 Understanding Student Differences

The Education CourseMate website for this text offers many helpful resources. Go to **CengageBrain.com** to preview this chapter's Concept Maps and Chapter Themes.

KEY POINTS

These key points will help you learn the important information in this chapter. To help you study, they also appear in the margins of the pages, next to the text where they are discussed.

The Nature and Measurement of Intelligence

- Intelligence test scores most closely related to school success, not job success, marital happiness, or life happiness
- IQ scores can change with experience, training
- Intelligence involves more than what intelligence tests measure
- Triarchic view: part of intelligence is ability to achieve personal goals
- Multiple intelligences theory: intelligence composed of eight distinct forms of intelligence
- Individuals with a high level of a particular intelligence may use it in different ways
- Factors other than high levels of a particular intelligence influence interests, college major, career choice

Using the New Views of Intelligence to Guide Instruction

- Triarchic view suggests that instruction and assessment should emphasize all types of ability
- Various technology tools may strengthen different intelligences

Learning Styles

- Learning styles are preferences for dealing with intellectual tasks in a particular way
- Impulsive students prefer quick action; reflective students prefer to collect and analyze information before acting

- Field-independent students prefer their own structure; field-dependent students prefer to work within existing structure
- Legislative style prefers to create and plan; executive style prefers to follow explicit rules; judicial style prefers to evaluate and judge
- Teachers should use various instructional methods to engage all styles of learning at one time or another
- Teachers should use various test formats to expand students' repertoire of learning styles and measure accurately what students have learned

Gender Differences and Gender Bias

- Evidence that boys score higher on tests of visual-spatial ability and math reasoning and that girls score higher on tests of memory and language skills is being called into question
- Gender bias: responding differently to male and female students without having sound educational reasons for doing so
- Gender bias can affect course selection, career choice, and class participation of male and female students
- Academic success, encouragement, models influence women to choose careers in science, math
- Loss of voice: students suppress true beliefs about various topics in the presence of parents, teachers, and classmates of opposite sex
- Females and males have equal access to computers, but differences in anxiety still exist

Sit back for a few minutes, and think about some of your friends and classmates from elementary and high school. Make a list of their physical characteristics (height, weight, visual acuity, and athletic skill, for example), social characteristics (outgoing, reserved, cooperative, sensitive to the needs of others, assertive), emotional characteristics (self-assured, optimistic, pessimistic, egotistical), and intellectual characteristics (methodical, creative, impulsive, good with numbers, terrible at organizing ideas). Now analyze your descriptions in terms of similarities and differences. In all likelihood, they point to many ways in which your friends and classmates have been alike but to even more ways in which they have differed from one another. Indeed, although human beings share many important characteristics, they also differ from one another in significant ways (and we tend to notice the differences more readily than the similarities).

Now imagine yourself a few years from now, when your job as a teacher is to help every student learn as much as possible despite all the ways in which students differ from one another. By fourth grade, for example, the range of achievement in some classes is greater than four grade levels. Some children's reading or math skills may be at the second-grade level, whereas other children may be functioning at the sixth-grade level. By sixth grade, about a third of all children will be working one grade level or more below the average student in class (Biemiller, 1993). In one study of a group of first graders from a suburban school district, the number of words correctly read from a list of 100 words ranged from none to 100. By the middle grades, the least capable students will have read about 100,000 words, the average student will have read about 1 million words, and the most capable students will have read between 10 million and 50 million words (Roller, 2002).

The variability among any group of students is one reason that teaching is both interesting and challenging. Richard Snow, who has written extensively about individual differences in education, has summarized this challenge as follows:

> At the outset of instruction in any topic, students of any age and in any culture will differ from one another in various intellectual and psychomotor abilities and skills, in both general and specialized prior knowledge, in interests and motives, and in personal styles of thought and work during learning. These differences, in turn, appear directly related to differences in the students' learning progress. (1986, p. 1029)

Although it usually will be essential for you to plan lessons, assignments, and teaching techniques by taking into account typical characteristics, you will also have to expect and make allowances for differences among students. The practice of using different learning materials, instructional tactics, and learning activities with students who vary along such dimensions as intelligence, learning style, gender, ethnicity, and social class is commonly referred to as *differentiated instruction* (see, e.g., Benjamin, 2005; Tomlinson, Brimijoin, & Narvaez, 2008). The aim is for all students to meet the same goals.

Over the next two chapters, we examine five broad characteristics that distinguish one group of students from another and have a demonstrated effect on learning. In this chapter, we focus on differences in mental ability (usually referred to as *intelligence*), learning styles, and gender. In the next chapter, we explore two related characteristics that are becoming more important every year: cultural and socioeconomic background. Teachers and researchers have demonstrated a strong interest in all five characteristics in recent years, and much has been written about them.

Revealing Assumptions

Groupthink

In preparation for their weekly meetings, Connie always reads the journals of her developing teachers. Antonio, in his first year of teaching, will use his journal to create a teaching portfolio that will be part of his evaluation at the end of this, his induction year. Celeste and Don will also use their journals to create portfolios that will be used to evaluate them prior to student teaching. Because her young charges are at different stages in their development as teachers, their classroom observations and their inferences based on those observations sometimes differ. Sometimes they are quite similar, and Connie is contemplating one such similarity. In one way or another, all

pause & reflect

The finding Connie mentioned is only one of several findings reviewed—and then contradicted—in a study comparing beliefs of students, aspiring teachers, and practicing teachers (Murphy, Delli, & Edwards, 2004). Many people fail to distinguish a research finding from a sound conclusion. They also assume that research-based descriptions of groups apply to individuals. Given the nature of educational research, we often encounter findings that compare one group with another group. Why is it important to keep in mind that group characteristics do not define the individual within a group? In addition to the one finding Connie mentioned, what do you think might be some other findings in this article?

three have expressed concerns about the "problem of group differences" in classrooms. Connie decides to address this concern at their next meeting.

At the Friday meeting, Connie opens the discussion as follows: "I ran across a rather depressing research finding the other day. It said that students can't tell the difference between master teachers and aspiring teachers. So, from the point of view of the students, one teacher is just as good or as bad as any other teacher. If that's the case, then it doesn't make much sense for us to be meeting or for you to be keeping journals, or going through induction, or even trying to earn a degree. A teacher is a teacher is a teacher, I guess."

"Wait a minute," says Antonio. "That's not true. That can't be true."

"That's what the research finding said," Connie replies.

Celeste and Don throw in their objections, tripping over each other's comments: "No way. I've had really great teachers and some really lousy teachers." "I've *seen* good teachers teach and I *know* I have a lot to learn from them." "Listen, I had a teacher who changed my life. I'm not kidding; she absolutely changed my life. I mean I'd be in jail right now if it wasn't for her."

Connie says, "Hey, don't shoot the messenger. I'm just telling you about a research finding I read, and the finding is that students see no difference between master teachers and aspiring teachers."

"Well, that research can't be right, that's all," Antonio says. "It doesn't make sense. How can you say that all teachers are the same just because they are all teachers?"

THE NATURE AND MEASUREMENT OF INTELLIGENCE

The Origin of Intelligence Testing

The form and content of contemporary intelligence tests owe much to the pioneering work of French psychologist Alfred Binet. In 1904, Binet was appointed to a commission of experts charged by the minister of public instruction for the Paris school system with figuring out an accurate and objective way of distinguishing between children who could profit from normal classroom instruction and those who required special education. Because the point of this project was to predict degree of future academic success, Binet created a set of questions and tasks that reflected the same cognitive processes as those demanded by everyday classroom activities. Thus Binet's first scale measured such processes as memory, attention, comprehension, discrimination, and reasoning.

In 1916, Lewis Terman of Stanford University published an extensive revision of Binet's test. This revision, which came to be known as the Stanford-Binet, proved to be extremely popular. One reason for its popularity was that Terman, following the 1912 suggestion of a German psychologist named William Stern, expressed a child's level of performance as a global figure called an intelligence quotient (IQ). Stern's original formula divided a child's mental age, which was determined by performance on the test, by the child's chronological age and multiplied the resulting figure by 100 to eliminate fractional values (Seagoe, 1975).

We have provided this abbreviated history lesson to illustrate two important points:

1. The form and function of contemporary intelligence tests have been directly influenced by the task Binet was given a century ago. Intelligence test items are still selected on the basis of their relationship to school success (Furnham, Monsen, & Ahmetoglu, 2009). Thus predictions about job success, marital bliss, happiness in life, or anything else made on the basis of an IQ score are attempts to make the test do something for which it was not designed. As some psychologists have pointed out, this type of test might better have been called a test of scholastic aptitude or school ability rather than a test of intelligence.

2. Stern and Terman's use of the IQ as a quantitative summary of a child's performance was not endorsed by Binet, who worried that educators would use a summary score as an excuse to ignore or get rid of uninterested or troublesome students. Binet's intent was "to identify in order to help and improve, not to label in order to limit" (Gould, 1981, p. 152).

Individually administered intelligence tests (such as the one shown here) are usually given to determine eligibility for a special class. They were designed to predict, and are moderately good predictors of, academic performance. © Ray Stott/The Image Works

Intelligence test scores most closely related to school success, not job success, marital happiness, or life happiness

Later in this section, we will see that Binet's concern was well placed. First, however, we will turn to a more detailed consideration of what intelligence tests do and do not measure.

What Traditional Intelligence Tests Measure

In 1904, British psychologist Charles Spearman noticed that children given a battery of intellectual tests (such as the memory, reasoning, and comprehension tests that Binet and Terman used) showed a strong tendency to rank consistently from test to test: children who scored high (or average or below average) on memory tests tended to score high (or average or below average) on reasoning and comprehension tests. Our use of the words *tendency* and *tended* indicates, of course, that the rankings were not identical. Some children scored well on some tests but performed more poorly on others.

Spearman explained this pattern by saying that intelligence is made up of two types of factors: a general factor (abbreviated as *g*) that affects performance on all intellectual tests and a set of specific factors (abbreviated as *s*) that affects performance on only specific intellectual tests. Spearman ascribed to the *g* factor the tendency for score rankings to remain constant over tests. That the rankings varied somewhat from test to test, he said, resulted from individual differences in specific factors. Not surprisingly, Spearman's explanation is called the *two-factor theory of intelligence*.

When you examine such contemporary intelligence tests as the Stanford-Binet Intelligence Scales–Fifth Edition (SB-5; Roid, 2003), the Wechsler Intelligence Scale for Children–IV (Wechsler, 2003), and the Wechsler Adult Intelligence Scale–III (Psychological Corporation, 2002; Wechsler, 1997), you will notice that the items in the various subtests differ greatly from one another. They may involve performing mental arithmetic, explaining the meanings of words, reproducing a pictured geometric design with blocks, or selecting from a larger set three pictures that share a common characteristic and form a group. These varied items are included because, despite their apparent differences, they relate strongly to one another and to performance in the classroom. In other words, intelligence tests still reflect Binet's original goal and Spearman's two-factor theory. In practice, the examiner can combine the scores from each subtest into a global index (the IQ score), offer a prediction about the tested individual's degree of academic success for the next year or so, and make some judgments about specific strengths and weaknesses.

Limitations of Intelligence Tests

So where does all this leave us in terms of trying to decide what traditional intelligence tests do and do not measure? Four points seem to be in order:

1. The appraisal of intelligence is limited by the fact that it cannot be measured directly. Our efforts are confined to measuring the overt manifestations (responses to test items) of what is ultimately based on brain function and experience.

2. The intelligence we test is a sample of intellectual capabilities that relate to classroom achievement better than they relate to anything else. That is why, as stated earlier, many psychologists prefer the terms *test of scholastic aptitude* or *test of school ability*.

3. Because current research demonstrates that the cognitive abilities measured by intelligence tests can be improved with systematic instruction (Sternberg, 2002a, 2002b, 2003; Sternberg, Jarvin, & Grigorenko, 2009), intelligence test scores should not be viewed as absolute measures of ability. Many people—parents, especially—fail to grasp this fact. An IQ score is not a once-and-for-all judgment of how bright a child is. It is merely an estimate of how successful a child is in handling certain kinds of problems at a particular time on a particular test as compared with other children of the same age.

4. Because IQ tests are designed to predict academic success, anything that enhances classroom performance (such as a wider range of factual information or more effective learning skills) will likely have a positive effect on intelligence test performance. This means that IQ scores are not necessarily permanent. Research on the stability of IQ scores shows that, although they do not change significantly for most people, they can change dramatically for given individuals and that changes are most likely to occur among individuals who were first tested as preschoolers (Weinert & Hany, 2003). This last point is often used to support early intervention programs such as Head Start and Follow-Through.

Because traditional theories of intelligence and their associated IQ tests view intelligence as being composed of a relatively small set of cognitive skills that relate best to academic success (Canivez, 2008), and because the results of such tests are used primarily to place students in special programs, contemporary theorists have proposed broader conceptions of intelligence that have more useful implications for classroom instruction.

> **IQ scores can change with experience, training**

> **pause & reflect**
>
> Imagine that a colleague tells you about one of her students, who has a C+ average and received an IQ score of 92 (low average) on a recent test. Your colleague says that because the student is working up to his ability level, he should not be encouraged to set higher goals because that would only lead to frustration. Your colleague then asks for your opinion. How do you respond?

Contemporary Views of Intelligence

David Wechsler's Global Capacity View As David Wechsler (1975) persuasively points out, intelligence is not simply the sum of one's tested abilities. Wechsler defines **intelligence** as the global capacity of the individual to act purposefully, think rationally, and deal effectively with the environment. Given this definition, which many psychologists endorse, an IQ score reflects just one facet of a person's global capacity: the ability to act purposefully, rationally, and effectively on academic tasks in a *classroom* environment. However, people display intelligent behavior in other settings (at work, home, and play, for example), and other characteristics contribute to intelligent behavior (such as persistence, realistic goal setting, the productive use of corrective feedback, creativity, and moral and aesthetic values). A true assessment of intelligence would take into account behavior related to these other settings and characteristics.

> **Intelligence involves more than what intelligence tests measure**

In fact, more recent research (Perkins, Tishman, Ritchhart, Donis, & Andrade, 2000) has shown that in everyday settings, intelligent behavior is related to the ability to recognize occasions that call for various capabilities and the motivation to actually use those capabilities. For example, in a situation that has the potential to become confrontational and hostile, intelligence might involve being open-minded and using a sense of humor. If this sounds to you like a description of the well-known concept of wisdom, Robert Sternberg, a leading intelligence theorist and researcher whose work we describe in the next section, would agree. He defines wisdom as the use of one's abilities for the benefit of oneself and others by either adapting to one's environment, shaping it to better suit one's needs, or selecting a more compatible environment in which to function (Keane & Shaughnessy, 2002; Sternberg et al., 2009).

Assessment of intelligence in everyday settings would be highly subjective and would take a great deal of time. That is one reason that current intelligence tests assess only a small sample of cognitive abilities. But if recent formulations of intelligence by Robert Sternberg and Howard Gardner become widely accepted, future intelligence tests may be broader in scope than those in use today. Even before such tests are devised, these theories serve a useful purpose by reminding us that intelligence is multifaceted and can be expressed in many ways.

Robert Sternberg's Triarchic View: The Theory of Successful Intelligence

Like David Wechsler, Robert Sternberg (2002a, 2002b, 2003) believes that most of the research evidence supports the view that intelligence has many facets, or dimensions, and that traditional mental ability tests measure just a few of these facets. Sternberg's **triarchic theory of intelligence** (which in later versions is called *the theory of successful intelligence*) has, as its name suggests, three main parts (see Figure 4.1):

Triarchic view: part of intelligence is ability to achieve personal goals

- *Practical ability* involves applying knowledge to everyday situations, using knowledge and tools, and seeking relevance.
- *Creative ability* involves inventing, discovering, imagining, and supposing.
- *Analytical ability* involves breaking ideas and products into their component parts, making judgments, evaluating, comparing and contrasting, and critiquing.

Figure 4.1 The Three Components of Sternberg's Triarchic View of Successful Intelligence

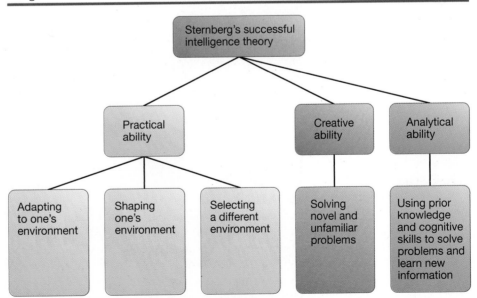

SOURCE: Adapted from Sternberg (1985, 2003); Stemler, Sternberg, Grigorenko, Jarvin, & Sharpes (2009).

Because these abilities need information on which to operate, memory ability underlies each of them (Grigorenko, Jarvin, & Sternberg, 2002).

Sternberg's work is a break with tradition in two respects. First, it includes an aspect of intelligence that has been—and still is—largely overlooked: how people use practical intelligence to adapt to their environment. Second, Sternberg believes that each of these abilities can be improved through instruction and that students learn best when all three are called into play.

In describing the nature of practical intelligence, Sternberg argues that part of what makes an individual intelligent is the ability to achieve personal goals (for example, graduating from high school or college with honors, working for a particular company in a particular capacity, or having a successful marriage). One way to accomplish personal goals is to understand and adapt to the values that govern behavior in a particular setting. For example, if most teachers in a particular school (or executives in a particular company) place a high value on conformity and cooperation, the person who persistently challenges authority, suggests new ideas without being asked, or operates without consulting others will, in all likelihood, receive fewer rewards than those who are more willing to conform and cooperate. According to Sternberg's theory, this person would be less intelligent.

Where a mismatch exists and the individual cannot adapt to the values of the majority, the intelligent person explores ways to make the values of others more consistent with his or her own values and skills. An enterprising student may try to convince her or his teacher, for example, that short-answer questions are better measures of achievement than essay questions or that effort and classroom participation should count just as much toward a grade as test scores. Finally, where all attempts at adapting or attempting to change the views of others fail, the intelligent person seeks out a setting in which his or her behaviors are more consistent with those of others. For instance, many gifted and talented students will seek out private alternative schools where their particular abilities are more highly prized.

Sternberg's basic point is that intelligence should be viewed as a broad characteristic of people that is evidenced not only by how well they answer a particular set of test questions but also by how well they function in different settings. The individual with average test scores who succeeds in getting people to do what

Robert Sternberg's theory maintains that intelligence is composed of practical ability, creative ability, and analytical ability. © Will Hart/Photo Edit

she or he wants is, in this view, at least as intelligent as the person who scores at the 99th percentile of a science test.

Elena Grigorenko, Linda Jarvin, and Robert Sternberg (2002) conducted three experiments to test the educational applicability of the triarchic theory. In each study, instructional lessons and materials were designed to improve the analytical, creative, and practical thinking skills of middle and high school students, as well as their vocabulary and reading comprehension skills. As an example of an analytical task, students read a story about a pioneer family and then drew a family tree diagram to show how the characters were related and a timeline to show when key events occurred. As an example of a creative task, students looked for examples in another story of how the author appealed to the human senses and then tried to describe what one would hear, see, and smell in such settings as a park, a pizza restaurant, and a zoo. As an example of a practical task, after reading a story about a family's Christmas celebration, students discussed all the steps involved in preparing a meal for a large group of people and how you might solve such problems as overcooking the main course.

The first study was done with two sets of inner-city fifth graders in each of two consecutive years. For each group, the study lasted about 5 months. Half the students in each set were exposed to triarchically based instruction and half were exposed to instruction that emphasized the learning and recall of factual information. Using stories from their basal reader, students in the experimental (triarchic) group completed classroom and homework tasks that emphasized the use of analytical, creative, and practical abilities. Students in the control group completed tasks that emphasized recall. As predicted, the experimental students significantly outscored the control students on tests of vocabulary and reading comprehension skills that tapped analytical, creative, and practical thinking skills, as well as on a standardized reading test.

The second study investigated the effect of a 6-week triarchic reading program on high-achieving, low-socioeconomic-status (SES), inner-city sixth graders. As in the first study, the triarchic and control groups read passages both in class and at home and answered questions that emphasized analytical, creative, and practical thinking skills. On the posttest, the triarchic group outscored the control group on analytical, creative, and practical measures.

The third study investigated the effect of a 6-week triarchic program on inner-city high school students' analytical, creative, and practical vocabulary and comprehension skills. Unlike the second study, which was a stand-alone reading program, the triarchic instruction in this study was integrated into students' English, social sciences, French, physical sciences, history, and art classes. Although students in the triarchic group scored higher on the vocabulary and comprehension skills posttest, their scores and those of the control group were not significantly different. Despite this one disappointing result, the research to date indicates that triarchically based instruction produces significant gains in students' vocabulary and reading comprehension skills, as well as their analytical, creative, and practical thinking skills (Sternberg & Grigorenko, 2004). As we will see later in the chapter, more recent work supports these conclusions and points to promising advances in assessments of cognitive abilities (Stemler, Sternberg, Grigorenko, Jarvin, & Sharpes, 2009; Sternberg et al., 2009).

Howard Gardner's Multiple Intelligences Theory Howard Gardner's conception of intelligence, like Sternberg's, is broader than traditional conceptions. It is different from Sternberg's, however, in that it describes eight separate types of intelligence. Accordingly, Gardner's work is referred to as the **theory of multiple intelligences** (or *MI theory*). The intelligences that Gardner describes are *logical-mathematical, linguistic, musical, spatial, bodily-kinesthetic, interpersonal* (understanding of others), *intrapersonal* (understanding of self), and *naturalist* (the ability to notice the characteristics that distinguish one plant, mineral, or animal from another and to create useful classification schemes called *taxonomies*) (Gardner, 1999). Table 4.1 describes each of these intelligences and provides examples of the kind of person who best represents each one.

Multiple intelligences theory: intelligence composed of eight distinct forms of intelligence

Table 4.1	Gardner's Eight Intelligences	
Intelligence	Core Components	End States
Logical-mathematical	Sensitivity to, and capacity to discern, logical or numerical patterns; ability to handle long chains of reasoning	Scientist Mathematician
Linguistic	Sensitivity to the sounds, rhythms, and meanings of words; sensitivity to the different functions of language	Poet Journalist
Musical	Abilities to produce and appreciate rhythm, pitch, and timbre; appreciation of the forms of musical expression	Violinist Composer
Spatial	Capacities to perceive the visual-spatial world accurately and to perform transformations on one's initial perceptions	Sculptor Navigator
Bodily-kinesthetic	Abilities to control one's body movements and handle objects skillfully	Dancer Athlete
Interpersonal	Capacities to discern and respond appropriately to the moods, temperaments, motivations, and desires of other people	Therapist Salesperson
Intrapersonal	Access to one's own feelings and the ability to discriminate among them and draw on them to guide behavior; knowledge of one's own strengths, weaknesses, desires, and intelligences	Person with detailed, accurate self-knowledge
Naturalist	Ability to recognize and classify the numerous plants and animals of one's environment and their relationships on a logical, justifiable basis; talent of caring for, taming, and interacting with various living creatures	Botanist Entomologist

SOURCE: Armstrong, 2009; Gardner (1999); Gardner & Hatch (1989).

Because these intelligences are presumed to be independent of one another, an individual would likely exhibit different levels of skill in each of these domains. One student, for example, may show evidence of becoming an outstanding trial lawyer, novelist, or journalist because his or her linguistic intelligence produces a facility for vividly describing, explaining, or persuading. Another student may be able to manipulate aspects of sound (such as pitch, rhythm, and timbre) to produce musical experiences that people find highly pleasing. And the student who is adept at understanding her or his own and others' feelings and how those feelings relate to behavior would be exhibiting high intrapersonal and interpersonal intelligence. Like Sternberg's work, Gardner's theory cautions us against focusing on the results of IQ tests to the exclusion of other worthwhile behaviors.

Gardner's MI theory has become extremely popular among educators. As usually happens with such ideas, they are often misinterpreted. A number of misconceptions have arisen:

> Individuals with a high level of a particular intelligence may use it in different ways

1. *Misconception: A person who has a strength in a particular intelligence will excel on all tasks within that domain.* Not so. A student with a high level of linguistic intelligence may be quite good at writing insightful essays on various topics but be unable to produce a good poem. Another student may excel at the kind of direct, fact-oriented style of writing that characterizes good newspaper reporting but be limited in her ability to write a long, highly analytical essay.

> Factors other than high levels of a particular intelligence influence interests, college major, career choice

Instead of focusing on how much intelligence students have, we need to attend to the different ways in which students make the most of their intelligences. For example, Thomas Hatch (1997), an associate of Gardner, describes how three children, all of whom were judged to have a high level of interpersonal intelligence, used that ability in different ways. One child was very adept at organizing the classroom activities of his classmates. The second was able to resolve conflicts among his classmates far better than anybody else in that class. The third child shunned leadership and was sometimes excluded from group activities but excelled at forming friendships among his peers. He was so good at this that he was able to make friends with one of the least popular students in class.

2. *Misconception: Ability is destiny.* If a child exhibits a high level of linguistic intelligence, she will not necessarily choose to major in English or journalism or seek a job as a writer. Not only do intelligences change over time in how they are used, but decisions about a college major and career are influenced by many other factors. The student who wrote such interesting stories as a child may grow up to be a college professor who excels at writing journal articles and textbooks or a noted politician or a successful business leader (Hatch, 1997).

TeachSource **Video Case** ◀◀ ▶ ▶▶

Multiple Intelligences: Elementary School Instruction

Go to the Education CourseMate website to watch the Video Case, and then answer the following questions:

1. Which of Gardner's eight intelligences, as described in Table 4.1, are depicted in this Video Case? How do specific students within the Video Case illustrate these intelligences?

2. How does the teacher in this Video Case use MI theory to teach traditional academic skills and subject matter? Do you think his approach is effective? Why or why not?

Contemporary theories typically view intelligence as being composed of several types of capabilities. Howard Gardner's theory of multiple intelligences, for example, describes several different ways of expressing intelligent behavior. A, © David Young-Wolff/Photo Edit B, © Suzie Fitzhugh

3. *Misconception: Every child should be taught every subject in eight different ways to develop all of the intelligences.* MI theory does not indicate or even suggest that such a step is necessary for learning to occur. In fact, it may be counterproductive if students are turned off by lessons that appear forced and contrived. And as a practical matter, there simply isn't enough time in the day to teach every lesson eight ways (Gardner, 1999; Hatch, 1997).

Although critics have argued that MI theory lacks the research support to substantiate its claims, proponents have defended it tirelessly (Gardner & Moran, 2006; Waterhouse, 2006).

Regardless of the research evidence, MI theory has nevertheless influenced the preparation and professional development of teachers as well as curricula and instructional practice around the world (Chen, Moran, & Gardner, 2009). Educators have used MI theory in a variety of ways to help students understand that they could be smart in different ways and that, in varying degrees, they possessed all eight intelligences.

pause & reflect

Assuming that Robert Sternberg and Howard Gardner are correct in thinking that people can be intelligent in ways other than the traditional analytical, linguistic, and logical-mathematical modes, why do you think schools have been so reluctant to address other abilities?

USING THE NEW VIEWS OF INTELLIGENCE TO GUIDE INSTRUCTION

The various theories of intelligence that were formulated during the first half of the twentieth century are of limited value to educators because they do not allow teachers to match instructional approaches and learning assessments to abilities. For example, because traditional intelligence tests, such as the Stanford-Binet or the Wechsler Intelligence Scale for Children–IV, are designed to rank students according to how they score rather than to assess how they think, their basic educational use is to determine eligibility for programs for the gifted and talented, learning disabled, and mentally disabled. What sets the theories of Sternberg and Gardner apart is their belief in a broad view of intelligence that can inform instructional practice and improve student performance (Armstrong, 2009; Chen et al., 2009; Sternberg et al., 2009). As we have shown, the preliminary evidence suggests that these beliefs have merit. What follows are a few illustrations of how you can use Sternberg's and Gardner's ideas in your classroom.

Sternberg's Triarchic Theory of Successful Intelligence

Triarchic view suggests that instruction and assessment should emphasize all types of ability

Based on his triarchic view of successful intelligence, Sternberg proposes a teaching and assessment model (Stemler et al., 2009; Sternberg, 1996, 1997a). He suggests that for any grade level and for any subject, teaching and testing can be designed to emphasize the three abilities in his triarchic theory—analytical, creative, and practical—as well as memory. To take into account individual differences, instruction and testing should involve all four abilities. At some point, each student has an opportunity to excel because the task and related test match the student's ability. Table 4.2 shows how language arts, mathematics, social studies, and science can be taught so as to emphasize all four of these abilities. Notice that Sternberg does not suggest that *all* instruction and assessment match a student's dominant ability. Some attempts need to be made to strengthen abilities that are relatively weak.

As was mentioned earlier and as can be seen from the research we have reviewed, Sternberg's triarchic theory of intelligence has become known more recently as a theory of "successful intelligence." Using the framework of successful intelligence—sometimes called the WICS model (referring to wisdom, intelligence, creativity, and success)—Sternberg and his colleagues have addressed how teachers can successfully interact with other teachers, with parents, and with principals and other administrators (Stemler, Elliott, Grigorenko, & Sternberg, 2006; Sternberg et al., 2009). Their framework suggests future research designed to describe more clearly the nature of effective teaching and successful schools. Sternberg's ideas are likely to be around for a while and to remain influential. You are likely to encounter his ideas not only as you prepare to teach your own students but also as you engage in continuing professional development as a practicing teacher.

Gardner's Multiple Intelligences Theory

Gardner's general recommendation for applying MI theory in the classroom is essentially the same as Sternberg's. He believes that teachers should use MI theory as a framework for devising alternative ways to teach subject matter (Chen et al., 2009).

MI theory should lead to increased transfer of learning to out-of-school settings. Because MI theory helps students mentally represent ideas in multiple ways, students are likely to develop a better understanding of the topic and be able to use that knowledge in everyday life. For the same reason, MI theory also suggests that learning in out-of-school settings should lead to increased transfer of learning in school subjects. For example, musical experiences—both listening to music and taking music lessons—have been shown to have a positive relationship with scores on a variety of cognitive measures, including IQ tests (Schellenberg, 2006a). Listening to music that one enjoys enhances performance on a variety of cognitive performance measures for both adults and children. For preschool-age children, listening to music enhances creativity (Schellenberg, 2006b). Taking music lessons is positively related to academic ability, even when other factors, such as family income, parental education, and participation in activities other than music, are taken into account (Schellenberg, 2006a).

Because MI theory stresses different ways of learning and expressing one's understanding, it fits well with the current emphasis on performance assessment (described in Chapter 14, "Assessment of Classroom Learning"). For example, instead of using just multiple-choice questions to measure linguistic competence, teachers can ask students to play the role of newspaper editor and write an editorial in response to a current issue.

As we mentioned earlier, it is a mistake to think that every lesson has to be designed to involve all eight intelligences. But with a little thought, many lessons can be designed to include two or three. For example, a high school algebra teacher combined kinesthetic and logical-mathematical abilities to teach a lesson on graphing. Instead of using in-class paper-and-pencil exercises, this teacher took the students outside to the school's courtyard. Using the large cement pavement squares as a grid and the grooves between the squares as X and Y coordinates, she had the students stand at various junctures and plot their own locations. Similarly, as part of a primary grade lesson on birds and their nesting habits, students designed and built birdhouses and then noted whether the birds used them, thereby using spatial, bodily-kinesthetic, and logical-mathematical abilities (Armstrong, 2009; Campbell, 1997).

Using Technology to Develop Intelligence

Because contemporary theories view intelligence as being made up of modifiable cognitive skills, you shouldn't be overly surprised that there are technology implications for the development of intelligence. In fact, technology education can support

Table 4.2	Teaching Different Subjects from a Triarchic Perspective			
	Memory	Analysis	Creativity	Practicality
Language arts	Remember the name of Tom Sawyer's aunt.	Compare the personality of Tom Sawyer with that of Huckleberry Finn.	Write a very short story with Tom Sawyer as a character.	Describe how you could use Tom Sawyer's power of persuasion.
Mathematics	Remember the mathematical formula Distance = Rate × Time.	Solve a mathematical word problem using the $D = R \times T$ formula.	Create your own mathematical word problem using the $D = R \times T$ formula.	Show how to use the $D = R \times T$ formula to estimate driving time from one city to another.
Social studies	Remember a list of factors that led up to the U.S. Civil War.	Compare, contrast, and evaluate the arguments of those who supported slavery versus the arguments of those who opposed it.	Write a page of a journal from the viewpoint of either a Confederate or a Union soldier.	Discuss the applicability of the lessons of the Civil War to countries today.
Science	Name the main types of bacteria.	Analyze the means the immune system uses to fight bacterial infections.	Suggest ways to cope with the increasing immunity bacteria are showing to antibiotic drugs.	Suggest three steps that individuals might take to reduce the chances of bacterial infection.

SOURCE: Adapted from Sternberg (1997a) and Sternberg et al. (2009).

higher-level thinking such as metaphorical and analogical thinking; it provides students opportunities to "think outside the box" and, by doing so, to develop their cognitive capabilities (Lewis, 2005). Robert Sternberg (1997c) expressed that sentiment when he said, "Technology can enable people to better develop their intelligence—no question about it" (p. 13). Technological environments provide opportunities for students to engage their practical, creative, and analytical abilities in ways not always available in traditional classroom environments (Sternberg, Grigorenko, & Zhang, 2008). The following study (Howard, McGee, Shin, & Shia, 2001) provides one example of how technology was used to facilitate certain aspects of intelligence from a triarchic perspective.

Ninth-grade students were administered the Sternberg Triarchic Abilities Test and classified as being relatively stronger either in analytical, creative, or practical thinking. They then learned how to conduct and communicate the results of scientific research by working in groups of three with a computer simulation program called Astronomy Village (modeled after the famous Kitt Peak Observatory in Arizona). To assess both their understanding of the content and their problem-solving ability, students were given scenarios and related questions to answer such as the following:

Scenario: You are a member of a research team that has been asked to calculate the distance to a particular star. A famous astronomer has suggested that the star is relatively close to Earth (within 25 light years).

Content comprehension question: Put an X in the boxes next to the five concepts that are most important to finding the distance to that star.

Problem-solving question: You have been asked to meet with the press to discuss how the team will proceed with this research. Assume that the people who will be reading your explanation have little or no knowledge of astronomy. Write your explanation so that it is easy enough for anyone to understand. Make sure you provide specific details of the procedures you will follow to measure the distance. You may want to use drawings to illustrate your thinking.

As expected, students who had relatively strong analytical or practical abilities scored significantly higher on the content comprehension questions than did students who were relatively strong in creative ability. The explanation given by the authors was that analytically oriented students did well because this is the type of question they are most used to seeing in school and have the most success answering. Students high in practical ability did well because the simulation appealed to their preference for real-life tasks. But a different pattern emerged for the problem-solving items. Students who had relatively strong creative or practical ability scored significantly higher on these items than did students who were relatively strong in analytical ability. Presumably, the unfamiliarity of the astronomy problems provided students high in creative ability an opportunity to use this form of thinking. Because students with high practical ability did well on both types of questions, simulation types of computer programs appear to be a particularly good match for them.

Like Robert Sternberg, Howard Gardner believes that technology has a role to play in fostering the development of intelligence (or, from his perspective, intelligences). For example, he notes that computer programs allow students who cannot read music or play an instrument to create musical compositions and that interactive virtual environments can engage several intelligences (Gee, 2007; Weiss, 2000). In later chapters, especially in Chapter 8, "Information-Processing Theory," and in Chapter 10, "Constructivist Learning Theory, Problem Solving, and Transfer," we will examine virtual learning environments, including multiple-user virtual environments (MUVEs) in more detail.

| Various technology tools may strengthen different intelligences

For many educators, technology holds great promise in addressing the MI theory promoted by Gardner (McKenzie, 2002). For instance, web-based conferencing might promote students' interpersonal intelligence. Programs that make it easy to do concept mapping, flowcharts, photo editing, and three-dimensional imaging are closely tied to visual-spatial intelligence (Lach, Little, & Nazzaro, 2003; McKenzie,

2002). Idea generation and prewriting software tools, such as Sunbuddy Writer, Imagination Express, and Inspiration, can assist verbal intelligence (Quenneville, 2001). Computer programming with tools such as LEGO/LOGO can help students' problem-solving and logical-mathematical intelligence (Doppelt, 2009; Gillespie & Beisser, 2001; Suomala & Alajaaski, 2002). Other software addresses musical intelligence (for instance, by enabling students to see musical scores as the notes are played) and bodily-kinesthetic intelligence (by offering a visual breakdown of an athletic skill such as a tennis swing). Clearly, there are technology tools for all the aspects of intelligence that Sternberg and Gardner described.

As a teacher, these tools allow you a great deal of flexibility. With the many options that digital applications offer, you can let students choose ways of learning that match their own strongest abilities, or you can have students use software that helps them improve in areas in which they are weak.

LEARNING STYLES

Whether one conceives of intelligence as having one major component or several, psychologists agree that it is an *ability*. Typically, it is better to have more of an ability than less of it. In recent years, psychologists have also studied how students use their abilities, and this line of research has led to the concept of a *learning style*. Unlike abilities, styles are value neutral—that is, all styles are adaptive under the right circumstances.

| Learning styles are preferences for dealing with intellectual tasks in a particular way

A **learning style** can be defined as a consistent preference over time and subject matter for perceiving, thinking about, and organizing information in a particular way (Sternberg & Grigorenko, 2001; Zhang & Sternberg, 2006, 2009). Some students, for example, prefer to think about the nature of a task, collect relevant information, and formulate a detailed plan before taking any action, whereas others prefer to run with the first idea they have and see where it leads. Some students prefer to work on several aspects of a task simultaneously, whereas others prefer to work on one aspect at a time in a logical sequence.

Notice that styles are referred to as *preferences*. They are not fixed modes of behavior that we are locked into. When the situation warrants, we can, at least temporarily, adopt different styles, although some people are better than others at switching styles.

In the psychological literature on styles, a distinction is drawn between cognitive styles and learning styles. Because learning style is considered to be the more inclusive concept and because the implications for instruction are the same, we will use the term *learning style*. Among the many learning style dimensions that have been investigated, we will examine three. Two of these (reflectivity-impulsivity and field dependence–field independence) were formulated more than 40 years ago and have a long history of research. The third (mental self-government) is more recent in origin and contains some original elements but also includes styles that have been the subject of much research.

Reflectivity and Impulsivity

One of the first learning style dimensions to be investigated was reflectivity-impulsivity. During the early 1960s, Jerome Kagan (1964a, 1964b) found that some students seem to be characteristically **impulsive,** whereas others are characteristically **reflective.** Impulsive students are said to have a fast conceptual tempo (Zhang & Sternberg, 2009). When faced with a task for which there is no ready solution or a question for which the answer is uncertain, the impulsive student responds more quickly than students who are more reflective. In problem-solving situations, the impulsive student collects less information, does so less systematically, and gives less thought to various solutions than do more reflective students. Reflective students, in contrast, prefer to spend more time

| Impulsive students prefer quick action; reflective students prefer to collect and analyze information before acting

During the elementary years it becomes apparent that students approach tasks in different ways. This preference for doing things in a particular way is often referred to as a cognitive style. Some students, for example, are impulsive thinkers who tend to react quickly when asked a question; other students are reflective thinkers who prefer to mull over things before answering. **A,** Laura Drukis/Stock Boston; **B,** © ERIKA STONE

collecting information (which means searching one's memory as well as external sources) and analyzing its relevance to the solution before offering a response (Morgan, 1997).

Kagan discovered that when tests of reading and inductive reasoning were administered in the first and second grades, impulsive students made more errors than reflective students did. He also found that impulsiveness is a general trait; it appears early in a person's life and is consistently revealed in a great variety of situations.

Field Dependence and Field Independence

Another very popular learning style dimension, known as field dependence–field independence, was proposed by Herbert Witkin (Witkin, Moore, Goodenough, & Cox, 1977) and refers to the extent to which a person's perception and thinking about a particular piece of information are influenced by the surrounding context. For example, when some individuals are shown a set of simple geometric figures and asked to locate each one (by outlining it with a pencil) within a larger and more complex display of intersecting lines, those with a field-dependent style take significantly longer to respond and identify fewer of the figures than individuals with a field-independent style. The former are labeled **field dependent** because their perception is strongly influenced by the prevailing field. The latter are called **field independent** because they are more successful in isolating target information despite the fact that it is embedded within a larger and more complex context.

When we talk about individuals who have a field-dependent style and compare them with individuals who have a field-independent style, we do not mean to imply that there are two distinctly different types of individuals. That is like saying that people are either tall or short. Just as people's heights range over a measured span, students can vary in the extent to which they are field dependent or field independent. In fact, relatively few individuals exhibit a pure field-dependent or field-independent style (Morgan, 1997; Zhang & Sternberg, 2009).

In school, the notes that field-dependent students take are more likely to reflect the structure and sequence of ideas as presented by the teacher or textbook author, whereas the notes of field-independent students are more likely to reflect their own ideas about structure and sequence. When reading, field-independent students are more likely than field-dependent students to analyze the structure of the story. The significance of this difference in approach is clearly seen with materials and tasks that are poorly structured. Field-independent students usually perform better in these situations because of their willingness to create a more meaningful structure.

The positive effect of field independence on achievement is particularly noticeable in the sciences because of their emphasis on analyzing objects and ideas into their component parts, reorganizing ideas into new configurations, and identifying potential new uses of that information. Biology students, for example, need to be able to identify tissues, organs, and systems that are difficult to see at first glance because they are embedded in the surrounding tissue of an organism.

Field-independent students prefer their own structure; field-dependent students prefer to work within existing structure

In social situations, field-dependent people, in comparison with field-independent people, spend more time looking directly at the faces of others; are more aware of prevailing attitudes, values, and behaviors; prefer to be in the company of other people; and are generally thought of as more tactful, considerate, socially outgoing, and affectionate than field-independent individuals (Fehrenbach, 1994; Morgan, 1997; Witkin et al., 1977). Not surprisingly, in one study kindergarten children gave field-dependent teachers higher ratings than field-independent teachers. They also preferred teachers whose styles matched their own (Saracho, 2001).

Mental Self-Government Styles

Robert Sternberg (1994), whose ideas on intelligence we discussed earlier in this chapter, has proposed an interesting learning style theory that is roughly modeled on the different functions and forms of civil government. Sternberg's **styles of mental self-government** theory has attracted considerable research (Black & McCoach, 2008; Nielsen, Kreiner, & Styles, 2007; Zhang, 2005). Although research to test the theory continues, it is viewed as a useful approach to understanding learning styles in a variety of settings. In Sternberg's theory, thirteen mental self-government styles fall into one of five categories: functions, forms, levels, scope, and leaning. Within these categories, there are legislative, executive, and judicial functions; monarchic, hierarchic, oligarchic, and anarchic forms; global and local levels; internal and external scopes; and liberal and conservative leanings. Most individuals have a preference for one style within each category.

Legislative style prefers to create and plan; executive style prefers to follow explicit rules; judicial style prefers to evaluate and judge

In Table 4.3 we briefly describe the main characteristics of each style and suggest an instructional activity consistent with it. If you are wondering how to identify these styles, Sternberg offers a simple solution: Teachers can simply note the type of instruction that various students prefer and the test types on which they perform best.

Evidence that these styles can apply to various cultures comes from Hong Kong, where instructional methods tend to emphasize rote learning and to be more regimented than is the case in many U.S. schools. High school students in Hong Kong who expressed a preference for the legislative, liberal, and judicial styles tended to have lower grades than did students who preferred the conservative and executive styles (Zhang & Sternberg, 2001).

Table 4.3	Matching Instructional Activities to Sternberg's Mental Self-Government Styles

Styles	Characteristics	Instructional Activities
Legislative	Prefers to formulate rules and plans, imagine possibilities, and create ideas and products.	Require students to design science projects, write stories, imagine how historical figures might have done things differently, organize work groups.
Executive	Prefers to follow rules and guidelines.	Present well-organized lectures, require students to prepare book reports, work out answers to problems.
Judicial	Prefers to compare things and make evaluations about quality, worth, effectiveness.	Require students to compare literary characters, critique an article, evaluate effectiveness of a program.
Monarchic	Prefers to work on one task at a time or to use a particular approach to tasks.	Assign one project, reading assignment, or homework assignment at a time. Allow ample time to complete all aspects of the assignment before assigning another.
Hierarchic	Prefers to have several tasks to work on, deciding which one to do first, second, and so on, and for how long.	Assign several tasks that vary in length, difficulty, and point value and are due at various times over several weeks.
Oligarchic	Prefers to have several tasks to work on, all of which are treated equally.	Assign several tasks that are equivalent in length, difficulty, and point value.
Anarchic	Prefers an unstructured, random approach to learning that is devoid of rules, procedures, or guidelines.	Assign tasks and problems that require nonconventional thinking and methods, self-directed form of study.
Global	Prefers to have an overall view of a task before beginning work.	Require students to scan a reading assignment to identify major topics, create an outline before writing, formulate a plan before beginning a complex task.
Local	Prefers to identify and work on the details of a particular part of a task before moving to another part.	Present a detailed outline or overview of a lecture or project. Require students to identify and interrelate particular details of each part of a reading assignment.
Internal	Prefers to work alone.	Require seatwork, projects, and assignments that do not depend on others for completion.
External	Prefers to work with others.	Assign group projects or reports, encourage study groups, create discussion groups.
Liberal	Prefers to work out own solution to problems.	Assign projects for which students must work out solution procedures. For example, identify and report on proposed legislation that concerns the environment.
Conservative	Prefers to do things according to established procedures.	Assign homework or projects that specify the steps, procedures, or rules for accomplishing the task.

SOURCE: Adapted from Sternberg (1994) and Zhang (2005).

Using Awareness of Learning Styles to Guide Instruction

Teachers should use various instructional methods to engage all styles of learning at one time or another

Because the typical classroom contains two dozen or more students who collectively exhibit several styles, teachers must be flexible and learn to use a variety of teaching and assessment methods so that, at some point, every student's style is addressed (recall our discussion of the teacher-as-artist earlier in the book). An impulsive boy, for example, may disrupt a class discussion by blurting out the first thing that pops into his head, thereby upstaging the reflective types, who are still in the process of formulating more searching answers. To minimize this possibility, you may want to have an informal rotation scheme for recitation or sometimes require that everyone sit and think about a question for two or three minutes before answering. To give the impulsive style its place in the sun, you might schedule speed drills or question-and-answer sessions covering previously learned basic material.

To motivate students with a legislative style, for example, have them describe what might have happened if a famous historical figure had acted differently than

pause & reflect

Analyze yourself in terms of the learning styles discussed in this chapter. Recall classroom situations that made you comfortable because they fit your style(s) and classroom situations in which you were uncomfortable because of a mismatch of style. Now imagine the students who will fill your classroom. Should you even try to design your lessons and assessments so that they match the styles of most students at least some of the time? If so, how will you do that?

| Teachers should use various test formats to expand students' repertoire of learning styles and measure accurately what students have learned

he or she did. For example, how might World War II have ended if President Harry Truman had decided *not* to drop the atomic bomb on Japan? To motivate students with a judicial style, have them compare and contrast the literary characters Tom Sawyer (from Mark Twain's novel of the same name) and Holden Caulfield (from J. D. Salinger's novel *The Catcher in the Rye*). As implied in these examples, a consideration of the diversity of intellectual styles has implications not only for designing instructional activities, but also—as we will see in Chapter 14— for designing assessments (Sternberg et al., 2008).

Using a variety of instructional techniques and assessments makes sense for several reasons. As we will see in the next section—and in the next two chapters—students bring different experiences and perspectives to the classroom. Student diversity calls for a diversity in learning experiences and in opportunities to demonstrate what has been learned. Having made that general point, however, it is important not to stereotype groups of students as having a single learning style. Students may be male or female and members of a particular cultural group, but each student can and does learn in a number of ways that can change over time and situations (Compton-Lilly, 2009; Gutièrrez & Rogoff, 2003; Pacheco & Gutièrrez, 2009). Another reason for using various teaching techniques and testing formats is that it may stimulate students to expand their own repertoire of learning styles (Sternberg, 1994; Zhang & Sternberg, 2009). Finally, recent research suggests that, although students display learning style preferences, they can learn through a variety of instructional tasks (Krätzig & Arbuthnot, 2006). Table 4.3 can serve as a guide for varying your instructional tasks and, consequently, expanding your students' repertoires.

Using Technology to Accommodate Learning Styles

Just as technology can be used to strengthen different forms of intelligence, it can also be used to accommodate learning styles. Consider a recent study in which elementary students who used a web-based virtual science laboratory—one that integrated both information and communication in their science lessons—earned higher grades than students who engaged the lessons through traditional classroom instruction (Sun, Lin, & Yu, 2008). Although the students who used the web-based virtual lab exhibited different learning styles, there were no differences across learning styles. This finding allowed the authors to conclude that the web-based virtual lab accommodated the diversity of learning styles.

Aside from specific programs, such as a web-based virtual science lab, the range of technological tools that have become available in the Web 2.0 world can be used at all grade levels to address the varied learning styles that students bring to the classroom. Indeed, Minjuan Wang and Myunghee Kang (2006) have coined the term "cybergogy" to refer to ways in which information and communication technologies can be used to engage learners that vary in terms of not only their learning styles, but their cultural backgrounds as well. Amy Benjamin is a veteran teacher who has written a number of books that focus on differentiating instruction in middle and high school classrooms (see Resources for Further Investigation at the end of the chapter). She argues that technology not only is an effective tool for accommodating student differences but also offers a unique opportunity for collaboration among novice and veteran teachers. Speaking to veteran teachers, she writes, "Our young colleagues, like our students, are used to e-communications and e-learning…We know about classroom management, they know about technology… As never before, novices and veteran teachers have much to offer each other" (2005, p. 5). As you encounter veteran teachers and learn how they accommodate student differences, consider that technology enables learners to engage information in different ways, and consider how you might collaborate with your veteran colleagues in the service of student learning.

GENDER DIFFERENCES AND GENDER BIAS

At the beginning of this chapter, we asked you to think about the ways in which friends and classmates over the past 12 or so years may have differed from one another. In all likelihood, you thought about how those people differed cognitively, socially, and emotionally. And with good reason. As we have seen so far in this chapter and in preceding ones, students' academic performance is strongly influenced by their cognitive, social, and emotional characteristics. But there is another major characteristic you may have ignored: gender. Although it may not be obvious, there are noticeable differences in the achievement patterns of males and females and in how they are taught. As Myra Sadker and David Sadker (1994) point out, "Sitting in the same classroom, reading the same textbook, listening to the same teacher, boys and girls receive very different educations" (p. 1). Just how different is the subject of the next few sections.

Gender Differences in Cognition and Achievement

A large body of research shows that there are reliable gender differences in cognitive functioning and achievement. On some tests, boys outscore girls, and on other tests girls have the upper hand (Halpern & LaMay, 2000; Royer, Tronsky, Chan, Jackson, & Marchant, 1999; Wigfield, Battle, Keller, & Eccles, 2002). Although these differences are statistically significant (meaning they are probably not due to chance), they tend to be modest in size—about 10 to 15 percentile ranks. As research on gender differences has continued, it appears that the differences that were found in earlier studies may be due to factors that go beyond cognitive abilities (Spelke, 2005).

Generally, research on gender differences has found that males tend to outscore females on the following tests:

- *Visual-spatial ability.* This category includes tests of spatial perception, mental rotation, spatial visualization, and generation and maintenance of a spatial image. A substantial body of research exists indicating that male superiority in visual-spatial ability appears during the preschool years and persists throughout the life span. More recent research suggests that the male advantage in spatial tasks is true only for children from middle- and high-SES groups. When males and females from low-SES groups are compared, no difference exists (Levine, Vasilyeva, Lourenco, Newcombe, & Huttenlocher, 2005).

- *Mathematical reasoning.* This difference, thought to be related to males' superior visual-spatial skill, may have more to do with social influences on academic and career choices than with cognitive abilities. When such influences are taken into account, more recent analyses of gender differences do not always show that males are superior to females (Halpern, Wai, & Saw, 2005).

- *College entrance.* Tests such as the SAT Reasoning Test (which includes mathematical reasoning) are designed to predict grade-point average after the freshman year of college. The overall superiority of males in this category may be related to differences in mathematical experiences, which may give them increased opportunity to develop mathematical reasoning.

Research shows that females tend to outscore males on the following tests:

- *Memory.* This is a broad category that includes memory for words from word lists, working memory (the number of pieces of information that one is aware of and that are available for immediate use), name-face associations, first-last name associations, memory for spatial locations, and episodic

Evidence that boys score higher on tests of visual-spatial ability and math reasoning and that girls score higher on tests of memory and language skills is being called into question

memory (memories for the events in one's own life). This difference appears to persist throughout the life span.

- *Language use.* This is another broad category that encompasses tests of spelling, reading comprehension, writing, onset of speech, and rate of vocabulary growth. Gender differences in language use appear anywhere between one and five years of age and grow larger over time. For example, the average difference in the size of males' and females' vocabulary at sixteen, twenty, and twenty-four months of age is 13, 51, and 115 words, respectively. On tests of reading comprehension, the gender gap also grows larger over time. By the senior year of high school, girls outscore boys by almost 10 percentile ranks. The superior scores that girls get on tests of writing are due in large part to the fact that their essays are better organized, more grammatically correct, and more logical. It is worth noting that although these writing skills would strike most people as being reflective of intelligence, they are not part of standardized tests of intelligence.

Just as gender differences appear on tests of cognitive skills, the same differences appear in academic performance. A 1999 study of mathematics achievement among eighth graders in 38 countries concluded that most of the participating countries, including the United States, were making progress toward gender equity in mathematics education, but the study found a few notable differences between the genders (Mullis et al., 2001). Among the major findings were the following:

- In most countries, the mathematics achievement differences between boys and girls were statistically nonsignificant. Boys significantly outscored girls in only four countries: Israel, the Czech Republic, Iran, and Tunisia.
- There was, however, a modest overall significant difference in favor of boys.
- A slightly higher percentage of boys had scores above the median (the midpoint of a distribution) and above the 75th percentile.

Although gender differences have been found and documented in the research literature over many years, recent research that takes into account a number of social and cultural factors is calling many of the "well-established" findings into question. Even so, gender differences have been and continue to be found.

Why do gender differences in cognition and achievement exist? No one knows for sure, although hormonal differences, differences in brain structure, differences in cognitive processes, and socialization differences are all thought to play a role. Despite increased awareness of how society reinforces gender-role stereotyping and measures taken to ensure greater gender equity, girls and boys continue to receive different messages about what is considered to be appropriate behavior. Are gender differences the result of social pressures to participate in some activities and not others, or are socialization patterns the result of biological differences, or do both factors play a role? We simply do not know yet.

In addition to gender differences on tests of cognitive skills and in academic performance, students' emotional reactions to grades show gender differences. A study of more than 900 fourth-, fifth-, and sixth-grade children (Pomerantz, 2002) showed that the girls on average received higher grades than the boys in language arts, social studies, science, and mathematics. But, somewhat unexpectedly, girls expressed greater worry about academic performance, higher levels of general anxiety, and higher levels of depression. The girls' perceived self-competence was lower than that of the boys for social studies, science, and math.

To put this picture in stark terms, girls achieve higher grades than boys but don't seem to be able to enjoy the fruits of their labors as much. One possibility is that girls are more concerned than boys with pleasing teachers and parents. Thus failure or lower-than-expected achievement is interpreted as disappointing those on whom they depend for approval. Another possibility is that girls are more likely than boys to use academic performance as an indicator of their abilities, spurring them to higher levels of learning, as well as higher levels of internal distress because of the possibility of failure. Boys may be better able to maintain higher levels of self-confidence by denying the link between performance and ability.

A more recent study by Angela Duckworth and Martin Seligman (2006) offers an alternative, but related, explanation for the existence of gender differences in cognition and achievement. They note that throughout the school-age years, girls earn higher grades than boys in all major subjects, even though girls do not perform better than boys on achievement or IQ tests. In a study of eighth graders in an urban magnet school, Duckworth and Seligman found that, as a group, females demonstrated more self-discipline than their male counterparts. In this study, eighth-grade girls earned higher grade-point averages (GPAs) than boys but did only slightly better on an achievement test and less well on an IQ test. After extensive analyses, Duckworth and Seligman (2006) concluded that part of the reason girls had higher GPAs was their greater self-discipline. The more researchers learn about gender differences, the more a number of factors beyond cognitive and perceptual abilities seem either to account for those differences or to suggest that such differences are less significant than once thought.

Although you should be aware of the gender differences we have mentioned and should take steps to try to reduce them, you should also keep the following points in mind. First, there are many tasks for which differences do not exist. In fact, a recent review of research on gender differences, supported by the National Science Foundation, advanced the "gender similarities hypothesis" over the hypothesis of "gender differences" (Hyde, 2005; see also Marsh, Martin, & Cheng, 2008). Second, some differences do not appear until later in development. For example, boys and girls have similar scores on tests of mathematical problem solving until adolescence, when boys begin to pull ahead. Third, what is true in general is not true of all individuals. Some boys score higher than most girls on tests of language use, and some girls score higher than most boys on tests of mathematical reasoning (Halpern et al., 2005; Wigfield et al., 2002). Finally, as Robert Sternberg and Howard Gardner have argued, virtually all cognitive skills can be improved to some degree with the aid of well-designed instruction.

Gender Bias

If you asked your class a question and some students answered without waiting to be called on, how do you think you would react? Do you think you would react differently to male students than to female students? Do not be so sure that you would not. Studies have found that teachers are more willing to listen to and accept the spontaneous answers of male students than female students. Female students are often reminded that they are to raise their hands and be recognized by the teacher before answering. Boys also receive more extensive feedback than do girls, but they are punished more severely than girls for the same infraction. These consistent differences in responses to male and female students when there is no sound educational reason for them are the essence of **gender bias.**

Gender bias: responding differently to male and female students without having sound educational reasons for doing so

Why do some teachers react differently to males and females? Probably because they are operating from traditional gender-role stereotypes: they expect boys to be more impulsive and unruly and girls to be more orderly and obedient (American Association of University Women, 1999; Corbett, Hill, & St. Rose, 2008.)

Exposure to gender bias apparently begins early in a child's school life. Most preschool programs stress the importance of following directions and rules (impulse control) and contain many activities that facilitate small-muscle development and language skills. Because girls are typically better than boys in these areas before they go to preschool, the typical preschool experience does not help girls acquire new academically related skills and attitudes. For example, preschool-age girls are usually not as competent as boys at large-motor activities (such as jumping, climbing, throwing, and digging) or investigatory activities (such as turning over rocks or pieces of wood to see what is under them). Lest you think that climbing, digging, and investigating one's environment are trivial behaviors, bear in mind that they are critical to the work of scientists who do field research (for example, botanists, geologists, anthropologists, and oceanographers), occupations in which women are significantly underrepresented. As technology became more available in classrooms, many hoped that digital environments would reduce gender bias, but recent research suggests that biases have simply taken on a new form within technologically mediated learning. Moreover, there is evidence that some of the bias-reducing practices that were introduced in classrooms in recent years have been reversed within technologically mediated learning environments (Plumm, 2008).

Gender bias is not a simple problem and understanding it requires placing gender within the context of other social influences such as race, family structures, and socioeconomic class (Corbett, Hill, & St. Rose, 2008). Nevertheless, gender bias has been shown to affect students in a variety of ways.

How Gender Bias Affects Students

Gender bias can affect course selection, career choice, and class participation of male and female students

Gender bias can affect students in at least three ways: the courses they choose to take, the careers they consider, and the extent to which they participate in class activities and discussions.

Course Selection There are modest but noticeable differences in the percentage of high school boys and girls who take math and science courses. In 1998, a larger percentage of girls than boys took algebra II (63.7 versus 59.8 percent) and trigonometry (9.7 versus 8.2 percent). Although there was no difference in the percentages of boys and girls who took geometry and precalculus, slightly more boys than girls took calculus (11.2 versus 10.6 percent). The pattern for science courses was similar. A larger percentage of girls than boys took biology (94.1 versus 91.4 percent), advanced placement or honors biology (18 versus 14.5 percent), and chemistry (63.5 versus 57.1 percent), whereas more boys than girls took physics (31.7 versus 26.2 percent) and engineering (7.1 versus 6.5 percent) (Bae, Choy, Geddes, Sable, & Snyder, 2000).

Career Choice As you may be aware because of numerous stories in the media, relatively few girls choose careers in science or mathematics. Wigfield and colleagues (2002) found that a much smaller percentage of women than men held positions in such math-and science-oriented professions as chemistry and biological science (about 31 percent), engineering (about 18 percent), computer systems analysis (about 27 percent), and drafting/surveying/ mapping (about 17 percent). On the other hand, a much greater percentage of women than men were found in such nonmath and nonscience fields as educational administration (63 percent), educational and vocational counseling (69 percent), social work (68 percent), and public relations (68 percent).

pause & reflect

Can you recall any instances of gender bias from teachers or friends? If so, do you think it had any effect on your choice of career?

Several factors are thought to influence the choice male and female students make to pursue a career in science or engineering. One is familiarity with and interest in the tools of science. In one study of middle school science classes in which instructors who were committed to increasing girls' active participation emphasized hands-on experiences, gender differences were still noted. Boys spent more time than girls manipulating the equipment, thereby forcing girls to participate in more passive ways (Jovanovic & King, 1998).

A second factor is perceived self-efficacy (how confident one feels in being able to meet the demands of a task). In the middle school science classes just mentioned (Jovanovic & King, 1998), even though end-of-year science grades were equal for girls and boys, only girls showed a significant decrease in their perception of their science ability over the school year. A 1996 survey found that although fourth-grade boys and girls were equally confident about their math abilities, by twelfth grade only 47 percent of girls were confident about their math skills, as compared with 59 percent of the boys (Bae et al., 2000).

A third factor is the competence-related beliefs and expectations communicated by parents and teachers. Girls who believe they have the ability to succeed in male-dominated fields were encouraged to adopt these beliefs by parents and teachers (Wigfield et al., 2002). This chapter's Case in Print describes the findings of a report from the National Academy of Sciences and how those findings account for the gender bias we observe in scientific career fields.

Supporting evidence that factors such as self-efficacy influence career choice comes from a recent study of 15 women with established careers in math, science, or technology. Because there have always been women who have successfully carved out careers in math or science, Amy Zeldin and Frank Pajares (2000) wanted to know what sets them apart from equally qualified women who choose other fields. Zeldin and Pajares found that these 15 women had very high levels of self-efficacy for math and science that could be traced to three sources: (1) early and consistent academic success, (2) encouragement to pursue math and science careers from such influential others as parents and teachers, and (3) the availability of respected models (both male and female) whom they could observe and model themselves after. All three sources working in concert appear necessary to persuade women to consider a career in math, science, or technology.

Class Participation As we pointed out earlier, many children tend to adopt the gender role that society portrays as the more appropriate and acceptable. Through the influence of parenting practices, advertising, peer norms, textbooks, and teaching practices, girls are reinforced for being polite, helpful, obedient, nonassertive, quiet, and aware of and responsive to the needs of others. Although views of girls' academic abilities are changing (Corbett, Hill, & St. Rose, 2008), boys, to a greater extent than girls, are reinforced for being assertive, independent, aggressive, competitive, intellectually curious, and achievement oriented. The degree to which girls feel comfortable expressing themselves and their views is known as "level of voice." According to Carol Gilligan and others, adolescent girls learn to suppress their true personalities and beliefs. Instead of saying what they really think about a topic, they

Academic success, encouragement, models influence women to choose careers in science, math

Women who choose a career in math or science are likely to be those who do well in science classes, are encouraged to pursue math or science careers by parents or teachers, and have respected models available to emulate. © Michael Newman/Photo Edit

Loss of voice: students suppress true beliefs about various topics in the presence of parents, teachers, and classmates of opposite sex

say either that they have no opinion or what they think others want to hear. Gilligan refers to this behavior as **loss of voice** (Harter, Waters, & Whitesell, 1997).

To measure the extent of loss of voice in different contexts, Susan Harter, Patricia Waters, and Nancy Whitesell gave questionnaires to several hundred students of both genders in grades 6 through 12. The questionnaire items asked students to rate how honestly they voiced their ideas when they were in the presence of teachers, male classmates, female classmates, parents, and close friends. Their main findings were as follows:

- Males and females are most likely to speak their minds when they are with close friends and classmates of the same gender and are less likely to do so when they are in the presence of members of the opposite gender, parents, and teachers.
- Loss of voice did not increase between grades 6 and 12.
- Equal numbers of males and females reported suppressing their true thoughts in certain circumstances.
- Girls who strongly identified with the stereotypical female gender role were more likely than androgynous females (those who exhibit behaviors that are characteristic of both gender roles) to suppress their true thoughts when interacting with their teachers and male classmates. This difference between feminine and androgynous females disappeared with close friends and parents.
- Androgynous males and females who said they were frequently encouraged and supported by teachers for expressing their views were most likely to speak their minds in classroom and other settings.

These findings have major implications for the way in which teachers address female students, particularly those who have adopted a strong feminine gender role, and for the use of constructivist approaches to teaching (discussed in detail in Chapter 13, "Approaches to Instruction"). Because constructivism relies heavily on free and open discussion to produce its effects, teachers need to monitor carefully the verbal exchanges that occur among students and to intervene when necessary to ensure that all students feel that their opinions are getting a fair and respectful hearing.

Take a Stand!

Eliminate Gender Bias

Gender bias, or treating male students differently from female students when such differences are neither warranted nor desirable, should have no place in any teacher's classroom. Because such biases are typically based on stereotypes and prejudices (the type of nonsystematic data we criticized in Chapter 1, "Applying Psychology to Teaching"), they are likely to have the negative impact on students' attitudes toward school, motivation for learning, classroom participation, course selection, and career choice that researchers have documented.

One way to avoid this undesirable practice is to think about the normally unconscious assumptions you make about the capabilities, motives, and interests of males and females, perhaps because of your own socialization. And when students, colleagues, or parents make broad-based, stereotypical statements such as "Girls aren't interested in technology" or "Boys don't like to display their emotions," respond by saying, "Oh, which girl [or boy]?" to get across the point that any given individual can deviate from whatever average trends might exist.

What Do You Think?

Do you think that all teachers need to take specific steps to combat gender stereotypes? Look into the additional resources on this issue at the Take a Stand! section at the textbook's Education CourseMate website.

Working Toward Gender Equity in the Classroom

Although much of the literature on gender bias highlights the classroom obstacles that make it difficult for girls to take full advantage of their talents, gender equity is about producing an educational experience that will be equally meaningful for students of both genders. Several authors (Bailey, 1996; Jobe, 2002/2003; Taylor & Lorimer, 2002/2003) suggest the following techniques to benefit both genders:

1. Use work arrangements and reward systems that will encourage all students to value a thorough understanding of a subject or task and that emphasize group success as well as individual accomplishment. In Chapter 13, "Approaches to Instruction," we will describe how a technique called cooperative learning does just this.

Case in Print

Correcting Gender Bias

Gender bias can affect students in at least three ways: the courses they choose to take, the careers they consider, and the extent to which they participate in class activities and discussions... As you may be aware because of numerous stories in the media, relatively few girls choose careers in science or mathematics...Several factors are thought to influence the choice male and female students make to pursue a career in science or engineering. (p. 131)

Gender Still Hinders Women Scientists

WASHINGTON POST 9/18/2006
The Associated Press

Gender bias—not any biological difference between the sexes—stifles the careers of female scientists at the nation's universities, says a new report that calls for wide-ranging steps to level the playing field.

The study is the latest since Harvard University's president ignited controversy last year by suggesting that innate gender differences may partly explain why fewer women than men reach top university science jobs. The comment eventually cost him his job.

Four times more men than women who hold doctorates in science and engineering have full-time faculty positions, the National Academy of Sciences reported Monday. Minority women are virtually absent from leading tenured positions.

Female scientists typically are paid less, promoted more slowly and receive less funding than male colleagues, discrepancies not explained by productivity, the scientific significance of their work or other performance measures, the report found.

"It is not lack of talent but unintentional biases and outmoded institutional structures that are hindering the access and advancement of women," the report said. "Neither our academic institutions nor our nation can afford such underuse of precious human capital in science and engineering."

University of Miami President Donna Shalala, chairwoman of the committee that wrote the report and a former Health and Human Services secretary, said today's bias is more subtle than she faced in the late 1960s. Shalala switched universities after a boss told her women scientists would never gain tenure because they were "a bad investment"—they might want time off to have babies.

The report calls on:

- The government to enforce existing anti-discrimination laws.
- University leaders to publicize the gender makeup of student enrollments and faculty ranks each year, and counteract bias in hiring and promotion.
- Funders of scientific research to allow grant money for dependent care, so scientists can attend work-related conferences or perform after-hours research.

Questions and Activities

1. This article shows how stereotyping operates—how group characteristics are assumed to be the same for every person belonging to a group. What are the effects of stereotyping cited in this article? How might those same effects operate in a classroom? Have you ever experienced stereotyping? As a teacher, how will you avoid the pitfalls of stereotyping?

2. The National Academy of Sciences report cited in the article makes recommendations to reduce gender bias. How might those recommendations be translated into actions that might be taken to reduce gender bias in classrooms?

3. Keeping in mind that research documents that some gender differences exist while supporting the gender similarities hypothesis, what ideas can you come up with to ensure that girls think of themselves as equal in ability to boys in math and science?

4. In view of the facts that there are so few female scientists in universities and that a large percentage of education majors are female, what should be done to ensure that future teachers do not help perpetuate the gender bias described in the article?

2. Emphasize concrete, hands-on science, math, and technology activities.

3. Incorporate math, science, and technology concepts into such other subjects as music, history, art, and social studies.

4. Talk about the practical, everyday applications of math and science. Although girls seem more interested in science when they understand how such knowledge transfers to everyday life, so do many boys. Nobody suffers when the curriculum is made more meaningful and relevant.

5. Emphasize materials that highlight the accomplishments and characteristics of women (such as Hillary Rodham Clinton, Linda Darling-Hammond, and Sonia Sotomayor) and women's groups.

6. From the titles listed on the website **www.guysread.com,** create a reading list that appeals to boys.

As you consider ways to work toward gender equity in your classroom, note that gender is only one source of the diversity that students bring to the classroom. To illustrate, a recent recommendation for working toward gender equity in social studies emphasizes the need to include not only more materials that address the experiences of women and girls, but the experiences of females by race, ethnicity, social class, and sexual orientation (Hahn, Bernard Powers, Crocco, & Woyshner, 2007). In the next chapter, we explore other sources of diversity. Diversity can be a strength in the classroom; it supplies the learning environment with different perspectives and experiences that can enrich discussions and lead to new questions. To be a strength, however, diverse voices must be welcomed and included in the discourse of learning.

TeachSource | **Video Case** ◀◀ ▶ ▶▶

Gender Equity in the Classroom: Girls and Science

Go to the Education CourseMate website to watch the Video Case, and then answer the following questions:

1. How does the Girls and Science program depicted in this Video Case try to address the problem of gender bias?

2. Describe some of the strategies used by the group leaders to promote gender equity and student interest in the material. Are these strategies effective?

Gender Differences and Technology: Overcoming the Digital Divide

In the 1980s, when desktop computers first started appearing in classrooms, surveys showed that females were less likely than males to use a computer at both school and home. That difference disappeared by the turn of the twenty-first century. A 2001 national survey of children and adolescents between the ages of five and seventeen found that about 80 percent of males and females reported using a computer at school and about 65 percent of both sexes reported using a computer at home (DeBell & Chapman, 2003).

Although there is no overall difference between males and females in computer use, gender differences still exist. In a comparison of males and females of college age, females were shown to experience more computer anxiety than males. This was the case even though females perceived themselves to be as capable or "fluent" in using the computer for communication and accessing the web (Bunz, 2009).

Females and males have equal access to computers, but differences in anxiety still exist

The greater anxiety that females experience in the use of computers is thought to be related to the continuing phenomenon of underrepresentation of women in technological fields such as engineering (Bunz, 2009; Kusku, Ozbilgin, & Ozkale, 2007). Among the steps that can be taken to continue to reduce the gender gap is to use *telementoring* to put female students in touch with women professionals, especially in occupations in which women are underrepresented (Murray, 2009; Whitehouse, McCloskey, & Ketelhut, 2010).

The Suggestions for Teaching that follow will help you better respond to differences in intelligence, learning styles, and gender.

Suggestions for Teaching

Addressing Student Differences

1 **Design lessons and test items that call for memory, analytical, creative, and practical abilities.**

Robert Sternberg (1997a; Sternberg et al., 2008) has pointed out that many teachers tend to emphasize memory and analytical abilities, which is fine for students—male or female—who are good at memorizing facts or breaking things down into their component parts and explaining how the parts relate to each other. But students whose abilities are in the creative or practical areas may appear to be less capable than they really are. You can get a better idea of each student's strengths and weaknesses and how well students have learned the subject matter you just taught by using a variety of instructional cues and test items.

To emphasize students' memory abilities when you teach and test, use prompts such as:

"Who said . . . ?"
"Summarize the ideas of . . ."
"Who did . . . ?"
"When did . . . ?"
"How did . . . ?"
"Describe . . ."

To emphasize students' analytical abilities, use prompts such as:

"Why in your judgment . . . ?"
"Explain why . . ."
"Explain what caused . . ."
"Critique . . ."

To emphasize creative abilities, use prompts such as:

"Imagine . . ."
"Design . . ."
"Suppose that . . ."
"What would happen if . . . ?"

To emphasize practical thinking, ask students to:

"Show how you can use . . ."
"Implement . . ."
"Demonstrate how in the real world . . ."

JOURNAL ENTRY
Encouraging the
Development of Multiple
Intelligences

2 Design lessons that emphasize different intelligences.

As Howard Gardner and others point out, most of the tasks that we ask students to master reflect the linguistic and logical-mathematical forms of intelligence. But there are other ways that students can come to know things and demonstrate what they have learned. Potentially, lesson plans for any subject can be designed that incorporate each of Gardner's eight intelligences. Here are a few examples suggested by Thomas Armstrong (1994, 2009) and David Lazear (2003).

ELEMENTARY GRADES: PUNCTUATION MARKS

Bodily-kinesthetic: Students use their bodies to mimic the shape of various punctuation marks.

Musical: Students make up different sounds or songs for each punctuation mark.

Interpersonal: In small groups of four to six, students teach and test one another on proper punctuation usage.

MIDDLE SCHOOL GRADES: AMERICAN HISTORY

Linguistic: Students debate the pros and cons of key historical decisions (such as Abraham Lincoln's decision to use military force to prevent the Confederate states from seceding from the Union, the Supreme Court decision in *Plessy v. Ferguson* that allowed separate facilities for Blacks and Whites, or President Harry Truman's decision to drop the atomic bomb on Japan).

Musical: Students learn about and sing some of the songs that were popular at a particular point in the country's history.

Spatial: Students draw murals that tell the story of a historical period.

HIGH SCHOOL GRADES: BOYLE'S LAW (PHYSICS)

Logical-mathematical: Students solve problems that require the use of Boyle's law: for a fixed mass and temperature of gas, the pressure is inversely proportional to the volume, or $P \times V = K$.

Bodily-kinesthetic: Students breathe air into their mouths, move it to one side of their mouths (so that one cheek is puffed out), indicate whether the pressure goes up or down, distribute it to both sides of their mouths, and indicate again whether the pressure goes up or down.

Intrapersonal: Students describe times in their lives when they felt they were either under a lot of psychological pressure or little pressure and whether they felt as if they had either a lot of or a little psychological space.

JOURNAL ENTRY
Allowing for Differences in
Cognitive Style

3 Recognize that different styles of learning call for different methods of instruction.

Robert Sternberg's work on styles of mental self-government calls for the same approach to instruction and testing as does his work on intellectual abilities: use a variety of instructional methods and testing formats. Not only will you have a more accurate picture of what students know, but you will also be helping them learn how to shift styles to adapt to changing conditions. For example, students with a judicial style have a preference for "why" questions (for example, Why did the United States go to war with Iraq in 2003?), whereas students with a legislative style have a preference for "suppose" or "what if" questions (for example, If you were President George W. Bush, would you have gone to war with Iraq?). Table 4.3 indicates which of Sternberg's learning styles are most compatible with particular methods of instruction.

JOURNAL ENTRY
Taking Steps to Eliminate
Gender Bias

4 **Help students become aware of the existence of gender bias.**

The following techniques have all been used by teachers to demonstrate that males often receive preferential treatment in our society in somewhat subtle ways (Bailey, 1996; Rop, 1998; Rutledge, 1997):

- Have students count how often in the space of a month male and female athletes are mentioned in the sports section of the local paper, and have the students create a graph depicting the difference.
- Have students survey similar-aged friends and classmates about the size of their allowance and report the results by gender.
- Have students review several textbooks and record how often men and women are mentioned.
- Have students keep a record of who participates in class discussions, how often they speak, for how long, and how they respond to comments made by male versus female classmates.

JOURNAL ENTRY
Encouraging Girls to Excel
in Math and Science

5 **Encourage girls to consider pursuing a career in science.**

Anna Kasov, the high school chemistry teacher we mentioned earlier, offers the following suggestions to teachers interested in encouraging adolescent girls to consider a career in science:

- Invite female scientists to class to talk about science as a career, or arrange for an electronic exchange through e-mail.
- Have students read articles written by female scientists, contact the authors with questions about the articles, and report the findings to the class.
- Contact recent female graduates who are majoring in science in college, and ask them to talk to the class about their experiences.

More ideas for your journal can be found in the Reflective Journal Questions at the textbook's student website, Education CourseMate.

6 **Recognize that you will not be able to address the various abilities and cognitive styles of all of your students all of the time.**

Although this chapter has described three major ways in which students differ from one another and explained why it is important to gear instruction to these differences (the goal of differentiated instruction), we do not want you to get the impression that you should strive to accommodate the unique needs of each student every minute of the day. When you have 25 or more students in a class, such a goal is nearly impossible. But that does not mean you should make no attempt to get to know and work with students as individuals, either. You might, for example, adopt the practice of Lori Tukey (2002), a sixth-grade teacher. She allowed students themselves to provide basic instruction on various aspects of writing. Each student listed aspects of writing, such as spelling, punctuation, and organization, that he or she wanted to improve. Then those who were proficient at one or more of these aspects were identified as "experts" to whom other students could go for help. This tactic gave the teacher enough extra time to work individually with each student twice a month.

To review this chapter, try the tutorial quizzes and other study aids on the textbook's website, Education CourseMate.

Challenging Assumptions

Groupthink

Celeste says, "So that research you mentioned that says students can't tell the difference between master teachers and education majors was just a finding, not a conclusion."

"Yes, that's right," says Connie. "It was the outcome of a much earlier research study that Professor Murphy and her colleagues reviewed before conducting their own separate study. Professor Murphy and her colleagues were really interested in learning what students and teachers believe good teaching to be. But you make an important point, Celeste. Research may yield findings, but those findings have to be placed in context to be meaningful."

"So why didn't you tell us about the context when you first mentioned it?" asks Don. "All three of us practically went berserk on you."

"Practically?" They laugh, and then Connie continues. "Remember your reactions to the suggestion that all teachers were the same? That one teacher was just like any other teacher?"

"Sure do," says Antonio, "and I didn't like it one bit. It wasn't respectful of the great teachers I have known or to some great teachers I work with. And it wasn't respectful of me or my own talents, even though I'm still learning."

"You're learning," says Connie. "Don't forget how you felt when you were treated not as an individual, but as a member of some demographic group. And don't forget your students can feel exactly the same way."

Summary

1. The extent to which students differ from one another can be substantial, even in the primary grades. By fourth grade, the range of achievement can vary by four or more grade levels.

2. The first practical test of intelligence was devised by Alfred Binet to identify students who would be best served in a special education program.

3. Because they were designed to predict academic success, intelligence tests predict that outcome better than they predict other outcomes, such as job success, marital happiness, or life satisfaction.

4. Traditional intelligence tests seem to measure a general intellectual factor and a factor specific to the particular test being taken.

5. Traditional intelligence tests measure a relatively small sample of cognitive skills that can change over time as additional knowledge and skills are acquired.

6. Intelligence, broadly defined, is the global capacity of the individual to act purposefully, think rationally, and deal effectively with the environment.

7. Sternberg's triarchic theory of successful intelligence is composed of analytical, creative, and practical abilities. The practical component, which includes the ability to adapt to one's environment to achieve personal goals, has been ignored by traditional theories.

8. Research has shown that students learn more when learning tasks require them to use all three of Sternberg's types of abilities: analytical, creative, and practical.

9. Gardner's multiple intelligences (MI) theory holds that each person has eight distinct intelligences, and that some are better developed than others.

10. Several misconceptions exist about Gardner's multiple intelligences theory. Individuals who have a high level of a particular intelligence should not be expected to excel on all tasks involving that intelligence or to choose a career that calls for that intelligence. Also, it is not necessary, and may be counterproductive, to try to teach every subject in eight different ways.

11. Sternberg's triarchic view implies that instruction and testing should be designed to involve memory, analytical, creative, and practical abilities.

12. To accommodate the different profiles of intelligences that exist in a typical classroom, Gardner recommends that teachers use MI theory as a framework for devising alternative ways of teaching subject matter.

13. Digital tools can strengthen the different aspects of intelligence that Sternberg and Gardner described.

14. A learning style is a consistent preference students have for perceiving, thinking about, and organizing information.

15. When faced with a question or a problem for which the answer is uncertain, students with an impulsive learning style spend less time than classmates with a reflective style collecting and analyzing information before making a response.

16. Students with a strong field-dependent learning style prefer to work in situations in which the procedures are clear and well defined because they take their cues for acceptable behavior from the context in which they work. Students with a strong field-independent style prefer to work in situations in which they can impose their own structure and procedures on a task. Most students exhibit both field-dependent and field-independent behaviors to some degree, depending on the nature of the task.

17. Sternberg has proposed a theory of mental self-government that is modeled after the structure and functions of civil government and contains 13 learning styles.

18. Boys in high or middle socioeconomic groups tend to outscore girls on tests of visual-spatial ability. In general, boys outscore girls on tests of mathematical reasoning, whereas girls tend to outscore boys on tests of memory and language skills.

19. International comparisons of mathematics achievement among eighth graders reveal that, overall, boys score significantly higher than girls, but that girls and boys score at about the same level in many countries.

20. Late elementary grade and middle school girls tend to receive higher grades than boys in language arts, social studies, science, and math. Girls in these grades also show higher levels of self-discipline and experience higher levels of worry and depression over their academic performance.

21. Gender bias is the consistent differential response (both positive and negative) to male and female students when there is no sound educational reason for doing so.

22. The likely source of gender bias, which is communicated by both teachers and students, is a belief in traditional gender-role stereotypes.

23. The persistent exposure of students to gender bias is thought to play a role, particularly for females, in the courses that students select in high school, the career choices they make, and the extent to which they participate in class discussions.

24. Females who choose careers in science or mathematics have a high level of self-efficacy for science and math that was the result of early and consistent academic success, encouragement to pursue a career in science or math from significant others, and the availability of respected models in the math and science areas.

25. Both adolescent males and females have a tendency not to express their true beliefs and opinions when in the company of teachers, parents, and members of the opposite sex. This phenomenon is called *loss of voice*.

26. Among children between the ages of five and seventeen, the same percentage of males and females use computers at school and at home. Females do experience more anxiety about using computers, which may be related to career choice.

Resources for Further Investigation

● The New Views of Intelligence

In *Teaching for Wisdom, Intelligence, Creativity, and Success* (2009), Robert Sternberg, Linda Jarvin, and Elena Grigorenko provide an overiew of the WICS model and teaching examples and suggestions for fostering student learning. In *Multiple Intelligences and Portfolios* (2002), Evangeline Stefanakis describes how to teach and assess children through portfolios from a multiple intelligences perspective. Each chapter contains anecdotes from teachers about how they used MI theory to help them individualize their instruction, create student portfolios, and assess student progress.

Contemporary Intellectual Assessment (2005), edited by Dawn Flanagan and Patti Harrison, provides a comprehensive survey of the theory and research on the measurement of intellectual abilities, including substantial sections on Gardner's theory of multiple intelligences and Sternberg's triarchic theory.

● Learning Styles and Classroom Instruction

In her book, *Teaching for Thinking Today* (2009), Selma Wasserman offers innovative classroom strategies that can help students who learn and think differently to think well. In *Thinking Styles* (1997b), Robert J. Sternberg provides a very readable and detailed description of his theory of mental self-government styles, the factors that affect their development, and how teachers can use this knowledge to improve the classroom performance of students. The first chapter contains an interesting account of how Sternberg did poorly in his first psychology course and temporarily abandoned psychology as a college major because of a mismatch between his thinking style and that of his instructor. Li-fang Zhang has joined Sternberg in researching styles of learning and thinking. In their book, *The Nature of Intellectual Styles* (2006), Zhang and Sternberg offer updated views on instructional practice, including the assessment of learners.

● The Impact of Gender Bias on Students

The research literature on sex differences in cognition is very complex and can easily be misinterpreted. A useful aid to reading this literature is the chapter "Causes, Correlates, and Caveats: Understanding the Development of Sex Differences in Cognition" by Diane Halpern and Simay Ikier in *Biology, Society, and Behavior: The Development of Sex Differences in Cognition* (2002), edited by Anne McGillicuddy-De Lisi and Richard De Lisi.

The issue of gender bias in education is taken up in a different way by Frances Maher and Janie Victoria Ward in *Gender and Teaching* (2002). Part I contains four case histories about different aspects of gender bias (such as sexism in the classroom and the effect of teacher expectations), Part II summarizes the arguments made by public figures from different parts of the political spectrum, and Part III provides suggestions and resources for further reflection.

Two books offer perspectives on the changing landscape of gender bias and equity. The first is *The Psychological Development of Girls and Women: Rethinking Change in Time* (2003) by Sheila Greene. The second is *Future Girl: Young Women in the 21st Century* (2004) by Anita Harris. Annette Hatcher Parkerson reviewed both books in the August 2004 issue of the *Educational Researcher*.

Susan Klein is the general editor of the *Handbook for Achieving Gender Equity Through Education* (2007). The handbook addresses the facts and assumptions that underlie issues of gender equity, and provides chapters on gender equity strategies in the content areas as well as chapters on gender equity for diverse populations (e.g., Olga Welch and her colleagues have written a chapter on gender equity for African Americans).

● Differentiated Instruction

You will find helpful ideas in the work of Carol Ann Tomlinson and Amy Benjamin. Tomlinson, with colleagues Kay Brimijoin and Lane Narvaez (2008), studied an elementary school and a high school. The result was *The Differentiated School: Making Revolutionary Changes in Teaching and Learning*. Amy Benjamin has written two books that span grade levels: *Differentiated Instruction: A Guide for Elementary School Teachers* (2003) and *Differentiated Instruction: A Guide for Middle and High School Teachers* (2005). The author of both books is a veteran English teacher who has taught at all levels. In Chapter 1 of her 2005 book, she explains what differentiated instruction is and is not by discussing seven myths about the concept. In Chapters 4-9 she describes how to practice differentiated instruction for a variety of subjects. Chapter 10 contains 14 case studies that illustrate how differentiated instruction can be used at the high school level. Amy Benjamin also provides guidance in the inventive use of technology in *Differentiated Instruction Using Technology: A Guide for Middle and High School Teachers* (2005). Robert Sternberg and Li-fang Zhang (2005) offer a theory of "thinking styles" as the foundation for differentiating instruction in their article "Styles of Thinking as a Basis of Differentiated Instruction."

5 Addressing Cultural and Socioeconomic Diversity

 The Education CourseMate website for this text offers many helpful resources. Go to **CengageBrain.com** to preview this chapter's Concept Maps and Chapter Themes.

KEY POINTS

These key points will help you learn the important information in this chapter. To help you study, they also appear in the margins of the pages, next to the text where they are discussed.

The Rise of Multiculturalism

- Cultural pluralism assumes that societies should maintain different cultures, that every culture within a society should be respected, that individuals have the right to participate in society without giving up cultural identity
- U.S. becoming more culturally diverse because of changes in immigration, birthrates
- Ethnocentrism: belief that one's own culture is superior to other cultures

Ethnicity and Social Class

- Culture: how a group of people perceives, believes, thinks, behaves
- Ethnic group members differ in verbal and nonverbal communication patterns
- Ethnic group members may hold different values
- Ethnic group members may favor different learning arrangements and processes
- Poverty rates higher for ethnic families of color than for Whites
- Children of color often score lower on tests, drop out of school sooner
- Achievement gap between low-SES minority students and White students due to living conditions, family environment, characteristics of the student, and classroom environment
- Low-SES children more likely to live in stressful environment that interferes with studying

- Classroom atmosphere, teachers' approaches connected with achievement levels of low-SES students
- Teacher expectancy effect: students behave in ways that are consistent with expectations that teachers communicate
- Strong effect of teacher expectancy on achievement, participation
- Teacher expectancies influenced by social class, ethnic background, achievement, attractiveness, gender

Multicultural Education Programs

- Multicultural programs aim to promote respect for diversity, reduction of ethnocentrism and stereotypes, improved learning
- Multicultural education can be approached in different ways
- Peer tutoring improves achievement
- Cooperative learning: students work together in small groups
- Cooperative learning fosters better understanding among ethnically diverse students
- Mastery learning: most students can master the curriculum
- Multicultural understanding can be promoted by electronically linking students from different cultural backgrounds

Bilingual Education

- Transition programs focus on rapid shift to English proficiency
- Maintenance programs focus on maintaining native-language competence
- Two-way bilingual education programs feature instruction in both languages
- Bilingual education programs produce moderate learning gains

reviously in this text, we pointed out that if your instructional plans are to be effective, they have to take into account what your students are like. In previous chapters, we described students in terms of their age-related differences in psychosocial, cognitive, and moral development, and we discussed how students typically are similar to and different from one another in terms of physical, social, and cognitive characteristics. In this chapter, we will turn to two other important ways in which students differ: cultural background and language. In the next chapter, we will discuss still another dimension of diversity: the concepts of ability and disability.

Culture is a term that describes how a group of people perceives the world; formulates beliefs; evaluates objects, ideas, and experiences; and behaves. It can be thought of as a blueprint that guides the ways in which individuals within a group do such important things as communicate with others (both verbally and nonverbally), handle time and space, express emotions, and approach work and play. The concept of culture typically includes ethnic group but can also encompass religious beliefs and socioeconomic status (Banks, 2009; Gollnick & Chinn, 2009).

Different groups of people vary in their beliefs, attitudes, values, and behavior patterns because of differences in cultural norms. (By *norms,* we mean the perceptions, beliefs, and behaviors that characterize most members of a group.) Students who were raised with mainstream American values, for example, find acceptable the practice of working individually and competing with others for academic rewards. Many Native American and Mexican American children, in contrast, have been taught to deemphasize competition and individual accomplishment in favor of cooperation and group solidarity (Sadker, Sadker, & Zittleman, 2008).

To provide the appropriate classroom and school conditions that will help your students from different cultural backgrounds master a common curriculum, you must come to understand and take into account your students' differing cultural backgrounds. A culturally aware teacher will emphasize the ways in which American society has been enriched by the contributions of many different ethnic groups (and place special emphasis on those ethnic groups to which the students belong) and will not schedule a major exam or field trip for a day when certain students are likely to be out of school in observance of a religious holiday.

The approach to teaching and learning that we will describe in this chapter, one that seeks to foster an understanding of and mutual respect for the values, beliefs, and practices of different cultural groups, is typically referred to as **multicultural education** (although the terms *culturally responsive schooling* and *culturally relevant education* are also used). Because culturally diverse children often come to school with different language backgrounds, another related issue is bilingual education, described at the end of this chapter.

Revealing Assumptions

Placing Value

Connie is reading Celeste's journal. Celeste, describing a tenth-grade biology class, wrote: "I was very excited about the upcoming lab on water quality. After observing for two weeks, the lab was going to be my first opportunity to see the students 'in action.' The teacher spent a week preparing the students for the lab—it was their first of the year—and most of the students were looking forward to testing water samples to determine their source. Although the lab was going to be done in groups— 'lab teams' they were called—the students knew that each person had to complete a separate lab report and that the report was going to be a major part of each student's grade for the unit. So, although the students were excited about the lab, they were nervous about the evaluation." Connie thinks for a moment about tomorrow's meeting and continues reading.

According to Celeste's account, the lab did not go very well. The students did not work as teams; rather, they worked in parallel. Everyone did everything for herself or himself: there was no division of labor. Celeste described one group in particular. A student mentioned that she really liked working in cooperative teams. She suggested that they each perform the prescribed tests but then compare their results and include each other's observations in each individual report. "It would be cool," she said. "Each report would be based on four observations instead of just one." Another student gave her a funny look and said, "We can't do that! Each report is being evaluated. That would be cheating." Connie writes a note— "values in evaluation"—and then moves on to Don's journal.

pause & reflect

To know whether students have learned what we want them to learn, we must evaluate their learning. We try to make our evaluations relevant and appropriate so that they will be fair and objective. In other words, we tend to assume that evaluation of learning is value-free. But our judgments of relevance and appropriateness are based on what we consider valuable, on what we value. We often forget that evaluation is, quite literally, the placement of value (McCown & Hopson, 2006; Schreiber & McCown, 2006). Do people from different cultures value the same things? What values were reflected in the way the lab reports were to be graded? Why might some students think cooperation was a good idea and others view it as cheating? What is your interpretation of Connie's note that there are "values in evaluation"?

THE RISE OF MULTICULTURALISM

From Melting Pot to Cultural Pluralism

More than most other countries, the United States is made up of numerous ethnic groups with widely diverse histories, cultural backgrounds, and values. In addition to the hundreds of thousands of Blacks who were brought to the United States as slaves, the United States was peopled by many waves of immigrants, mostly from Europe but also from Asia and Latin America. Throughout the eighteenth and nineteenth centuries, the United States needed large numbers of people to settle its western frontier, build its railroads, harvest its natural resources, and work in its growing factories. As Table 5.1 indicates, approximately 33 million people immigrated to the United States between 1820 and 1920.

Throughout this period, the basic view of American society toward immigrants was that they should divest themselves of their old customs, views, allegiances, and rivalries as soon as possible and adopt English as their primary language, along with mainstream American ideals, values, and customs. This assimilation of diverse ethnic groups into one national mainstream was known as the **melting pot** phenomenon, a term and viewpoint popularized in a 1909 play by Israel Zangwill, *The Melting Pot*. The main institution responsible for bringing about this assimilation was the public school (Ornstein, Levine, & Gutek, 2011).

The notion of America as a great melting pot was generally accepted until the social unrest of the late 1960s and early 1970s. As an outgrowth of urban riots and the civil rights movement, minority ethnic groups argued not only for bilingual education programs in public schools but also for ethnic studies. Since the early 1970s, factors such as discrimination, the desire to maintain culturally specific ideas and practices, and continued immigration from different parts of the world have served to maintain, if not accelerate, this trend toward cultural diversity—or **cultural pluralism**, to use the preferred term. Cultural pluralism rests on three beliefs: (1) that a society should strive to maintain the different cultures that reside within it; (2) that each culture within a society should be respected by others; and (3) that individuals within a society have the right to participate in all aspects of that society without having to give up their cultural identity (Sleeter & Grant, 2009). Our Case in Print for this chapter illustrates how all of these beliefs can be realized.

> Cultural pluralism assumes that societies should maintain different cultures, that every culture within a society should be respected, and that individuals have the right to participate in society without giving up cultural identity

Table 5.1	Number of Immigrants to the United States, by Decade		
Years	Number	Years	Number
1820–1829	128,502	1910–1919	6,347,380
1830–1839	538,318	1920–1929	4,295,510
1840–1849	1,427,337	1930–1939	699,375
1850–1859	2,814,554	1940–1949	856,608
1860–1869	2,018,261	1950–1959	2,499,268
1870–1879	2,742,137	1960–1969	3,213,749
1880–1889	5,248,568	1970–1979	4,248,203
1890–1899	3,694,294	1980–1989	6,244,379
1900–1909	8,202,388	1990–1999	9,775,398
		2000-2007	8,061,486
		Total	73,118,778

SOURCE: U.S. Department of Homeland Security (2008).

Case in Print

Cultural Diversity and *E Pluribus Unum* (Out of Many, One)

Since the early 1970s, factors such as discrimination, the desire to maintain culturally specific ideas and practices, and continued immigration from different parts of the world have served to maintain, if not accelerate, this trend toward cultural diversity—or cultural pluralism, to use the preferred term. Cultural pluralism rests on three beliefs: (1) that a society should strive to maintain the different cultures that reside within it; (2) that each culture within a society should be respected by others; and (3) that individuals within a society have the right to participate in all aspects of that society without having to give up their cultural identity (p. 144).

Melting Pot Seems to Be Working Fine at This School

THERESA TIGHE

St. Louis Post-Dispatch, 10/20/06

This year students at Affton High School selected Selma Delic, a Bosnian refugee, to be senior class president and also homecoming queen.

Some people in the district say those honors mean that the tension that once existed between Bosnian and native-born Affton students has dissipated.

In the late 90s, Bosnian refugees began settling in the Affton area and sending their children to its schools. About 20 percent of the students in the district spoke a language other than English first. The majority of them are Bosnian.

Teri Blackburn, who teaches English as a second language at the school, said Selma's election couldn't have happened 10 to 12 years ago.

She said, "Native speakers were overwhelmed by people speaking a foreign language. People thought they were being talked about. There were cliques. They didn't sit together. If an argument were started by either side, neither side wanted to back down because of their differences."

Blackburn said the school didn't have any real trouble such as fights, which some districts experienced with the influx of Bosnian students. But she said it took four years before the two groups started to mingle.

Teachers at the high school say the tension there eased because of the passage of time. The youngsters have become accustomed to one another. The Bosnians speak better English. Bosnians and Affton natives began to know one another by working together on class projects and in school activities.

Dzenita Horic, 20, lived through the change. A Bosnian, she began attending Affton district schools in the eighth grade. She said, "It was Bosnian kids on one side and American kids on another."

Horic said that by the time she graduated from Affton High, "we were all mixed together. I think we all grew up and realized we are all in the same boat. I think curiosity for each other's lifestyle helped."

She said it had irritated her that the other students didn't initially want to know about the Bosnian culture.

Horic said religion wasn't the reason for the division; rather, it helped break down the walls. She said other students would ask her about things such as the fast in Ramadan. She said she wanted to know what the Affton natives did after school and on Saturdays and about their values.

The success of Affton High's soccer team two years ago also helped. Five of the eleven starters were Bosnian, and the team won its district and went to the state finals. There was a little initial friction, but the players learned that wins weren't possible without team cooperation. The school cheered for the Affton High team, not the Bosnian or the American team.

Phil Beermann, the school's athletic director, said that when the Bosnians arrived in the school district, the players tended to play with their own nationalities. He said, "I really felt like we needed two soccer balls. It wasn't malicious. It was just that they were working with players of the same culture."

Admir Gledovic, an Affton graduate who played on that team, says Bosnians love soccer. He says that for Bosnian players, soccer is a link to their homeland and helps them build relationships with Americans.

The principal of Affton High, Jeff Morris, said, "Now it's just Affton High School. If we have trouble between kids, it's not because of ethnic differences."

Selma and her friends drew a blank when asked about ethnic divisions.

Selma said, "I never was picked on. It's not really like that."

Carl Stafford—a senior, a football player and an African-American at the school—said, "Bosnians hang with Bosnians, and blacks with blacks, and white with white. But they don't only hang with each other."

Selma is a hardworking young woman with a winning smile and engaging manner. She divides the school into those who take part in school activities and those who don't. Her goal for the year is to unite them.

She said, "I want to make sure that everyone helps with class activities and goes to the dances."

Questions and Activities

1. Teri Blackburn, the English-as-a-second-language teacher at Affton High School, noted that for the first 4 years the Bosnian and native Affton students were suspicious of each other and remained in separate cliques. Based on what you read in Chapters 2 and 3, what characteristics of adolescence may also have contributed to this type of behavior?

2. After approximately 4 years, tension between the two groups eased, they began working together on class projects, and friendships formed. According to the teachers, this was due largely to the passage of time and the Bosnian students becoming more fluent in English. Can you think of things the teachers might have done to help bring this goal about sooner? Here's a hint: a Bosnian student said she thought curiosity about each other's lifestyles helped.

3. A Bosnian student who attended Affton High School commented that because Bosnians love to play soccer, that sport was a link to their homeland and culture and helped them build relationships with the American students who also played soccer. How might you help students from different cultures that do not have a particular sport in common accomplish the same goal?

The Changing Face of the United States

Given recent changes in birthrates and immigration patterns and population projections for the next 30 to 50 years, one could argue that the decline of the melting pot philosophy and the rise of cultural pluralism and multicultural education will only accelerate in the years ahead. Consider the following statistics.

Between 1998 and 2007, 85 percent of legal immigrants to the United States came from non-European countries. Most of these immigrants came from Asia (principally China, the Philippine Islands, and India) and the Americas (principally Mexico and South America) and settled in the major cities of California, New York, Florida, and Texas. In the 10-year period from 1990 through 1999, about 9.7 million legal immigrants arrived in the United States, an all-time U.S. immigration record for a decade. The first decade of the twenty-first century may well top that figure, as slightly more than 8 million individuals legally entered the United States from 2000 through 2007 (U.S. Office of Homeland Security, 2008). Adding to the change produced by immigration itself is the fact that immigrant mothers have a higher average birthrate than native-born mothers. As of 2006, native-born women averaged 52 births per 1,000, whereas foreign-born women averaged 70.8 per 1,000 (U.S. Census Bureau, 2008a).

These immigration and birthrate patterns are expected to have a significant effect over the next two decades on the makeup of the school-age population (see Figure 5.1).

According to Census Bureau projections, the populations of Latino and Asian American schoolchildren will increase rapidly, raising their combined percentage of the school-age population to about 34 percent. The percentage of Black school-age

U.S. becoming more culturally diverse because of changes in immigration, birthrates

Figure 5.1 Projected Change in Percentage of School-Age Children for Four Ethnic Groups Between 2010 and 2025

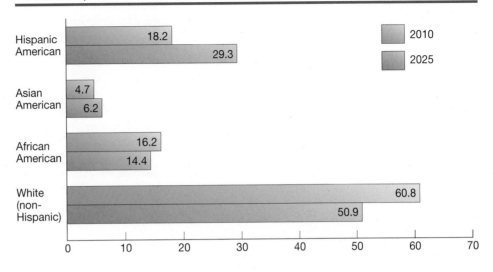

Percentage of children from 5 through 18 years of age

SOURCE: U.S. Census Bureau (2008b).

*Because of rounding errors, percentages for each year do not add up to exactly 100 percent.

children is expected to decrease to about 14 percent. The proportion of White non-Hispanic schoolchildren will fall from just over 60 percent to just under 51 percent. As these figures make clear, not only is the United States rapidly on its way to becoming an even more ethnically diverse nation than ever before, but certain areas of the country (for example, southern California, Texas, southern Florida, and New York) already have very large minority populations.

Much of the rest of this chapter will focus on characteristics of certain groups of students. But for you and your students to benefit from your knowledge of cultural diversity, you must view it in the proper perspective. The perspective we encourage you to adopt has three aspects, which are described in the following Suggestions for Teaching.

Suggestions for Teaching

Taking Account of Your Students' Cultural Differences

1 **Recognize that differences are not necessarily deficits.**

Ethnocentrism: belief that one's own culture is superior to other cultures

JOURNAL ENTRY
Minimizing Ethnocentric Tendencies

Students who subscribe to different value systems and exhibit different communication patterns, time orientations, learning modes, motives, and aspirations should not be viewed as incapable (García, 2002). Looking on ethnic and social class differences as deficits usually stems from an attitude called *ethnocentrism*. This is the tendency of people to think of their own culture as superior to the culture of other groups. You may be able to moderate your ethnocentric tendencies and motivate your students to learn by consciously using instructional tactics that are congruent with the different cultural backgrounds of your students.

2 Recognize that the groups we and others describe with a general label are frequently made up of subgroups with somewhat different characteristics.

These subgroups, in fact, may use different labels to refer to themselves. Among Native Americans, for example, Navajos differ from the Hopi in physical appearance, dress, and hairstyle. Individuals who are called Hispanic may trace their ancestry to one of a dozen or more countries and often refer to themselves as either Chicano, Latino, Mexicano, of Mexican descent, or of Spanish descent (Okagaki, 2006; P. Schmidt, 2003). One teacher, despite 18 years' experience, found herself ill prepared to teach children on a Chippewa-Cree reservation partly because she knew relatively little about the history, culture, and community in which she taught (Starnes, 2006). Learn as much as you can about the subgroups your students come from, and keep these specific qualities in mind as you teach.

3 Above all, remember that each student is a unique person. Although descriptions of various ethnic groups and subgroups may accurately portray some general tendencies of a large group of people, they may apply only partly or not at all to given individuals.

pause & reflect

How can you use the concept of constructivism (discussed in Chapter 2) to help students overcome any ethnocentrism they may have and understand the beliefs and practices of other cultures?

Rather than thinking of culture as a set of perceptions, thoughts, beliefs, and actions that are inherent in all individuals who nominally belong to a culture (perhaps because of surname or country of origin), you will be far better served in working with students and their parents if you take the time to understand the extent to which individuals participate in the practices of their cultural communities. For example, some Latino students may prefer cooperative learning arrangements because such behavior is the norm at home and in their community, whereas others may prefer to work independently because that behavior is more typical for them (Gutiérrez & Rogoff, 2003). And although many Latino students earn lower grades and test scores than their White peers, there are also many who do not fit this pattern. Researchers have found that Latino students who spoke English at home, who came from two-parent families, who spent more time on homework than their peers, and who had parents who supervised their homework not only significantly outscored their Latino peers who did not share these characteristics but also scored at the same level as White students who shared the same characteristics (Ramirez & Carpenter, 2005).

ETHNICITY AND SOCIAL CLASS

Culture: how a group of people perceives, believes, thinks, behaves

As we pointed out in the opening paragraphs of this chapter, **culture** refers to the ways in which a group of people perceives, thinks about, and interacts with the world. It provides a set of norms that guide what we say and how we say it, what we feel, and what we do in various situations. Two significant factors that most readily distinguish one culture from another are ethnicity and social class.

The Effect of Ethnicity on Learning

An **ethnic group** is a collection of people who identify with one another on the basis of one or more of the following characteristics: country from which one's ancestors came, race, religion, language, values, political interests, economic interests, and behavior patterns (Banks, 2009; Gollnick & Chinn, 2009). Viewed separately, the ethnic groups in the United States, particularly those of color, are numerical minorities; collectively, however, they constitute a considerable portion of American society (Banks, 2009). Most Americans identify with some ethnic group (Blacks, Chinese Americans, Latinos, German Americans, Irish Americans, and Italian Americans, to name but a few). As a teacher, you need to know how your students' ethnicity can affect student-teacher relationships.

Christine Bennett (2007) identifies five aspects of ethnicity that are potential sources of student-student and student-teacher misunderstanding: verbal communication patterns, nonverbal communication, time orientation, social values, and instructional formats and learning processes.

Verbal Communication Patterns Problems with verbal communication can occur in a number of ways. First, classroom discussions may not go as planned if teachers have students who do not understand—or feel overly confined by—the mainstream convention of "you take a turn and then somebody else takes a turn." For example, in Latino families in which there are several siblings and the parenting style is authoritarian, children may be reluctant to enter into a teacher-led discussion in class. Because teachers, like parents, are viewed as authority figures, many children consider it disrespectful to offer their opinions. They are there to learn what the teacher tells them. But as with their siblings at home, they may be quite active in small-group discussions composed entirely of peers (García, 2002).

Second, because of differences in cultural experiences, some students may be reluctant to speak or perform in public, whereas others may prefer exchanges that resemble a free-for-all shouting match. Some American Indian children, for example, prefer to work on ideas and skills in private. A public performance is given only after an acceptable degree of mastery is attained (Bennett, 2007; Morrison, 2009). This practice is not as unique to American Indian culture as it might seem at first glance. Music lessons and practices are typically done in private, and public performances are not given until a piece or program is mastered.

Ethnic group members differ in verbal and nonverbal communication patterns

Nonverbal Communication A form of nonverbal communication that mainstream American culture highly values is direct eye contact. Most people are taught to look directly at the person to whom they are speaking, because this behavior is believed to signify honesty on the part of the speaker and interest on the part of the listener. Among certain American Indian, Latino, and Asian cultures, however, averting one's eyes is a sign of deference to and respect for the other person, whereas looking at someone directly while being corrected is a sign of defiance. Thus an Asian American, Latino, or American Indian student who looks down or away when being questioned or corrected about something is not necessarily trying to hide guilt or ignorance or to communicate lack of interest (Bennett, 2007; Castagno & Brayboy, 2008; Pewewardy, 2002).

Time Orientation Mainstream American culture is very time oriented, and people who know how to organize their time and work efficiently are praised and rewarded. We teach our children to value such statements as "Time is money" and "Never put off until tomorrow what you can do today." Nowhere else is this time orientation more evident than in our schools. Classes begin and end at a specified time regardless of whether one is interested in starting a project, pursuing a discussion, or finishing an experiment. But for students whose ethnic cultures are not so time bound (Latinos and American Indians, for example), such a rigid approach to learning may be upsetting. Indeed, it may also be upsetting to some students who reflect the mainstream culture (Bennett, 2007; Pewewardy, 2002).

Social Values Two values that lie at the heart of mainstream American society are competition ("Competition brings out the best in people") and rugged

Ethnic group members may hold
different values

individualism ("People's accomplishments should reflect their own efforts"). Because schools tend to reflect mainstream beliefs, many classroom activities are competitive and done on one's own for one's personal benefit. However, students from some ethnic groups, such as Mexican Americans, are more likely to have been taught to value cooperative relationships and family loyalty. These students may thus prefer group projects; they may also respond more positively to praise that emphasizes family pride rather than individual glory (Bennett, 2007).

Instructional Formats and Learning Processes Finally, ethnic groups may differ in terms of the instructional formats and learning processes they prefer. The dominant instructional format, especially at the middle school and high school levels, is one in which all students work from the same text, workbook, and worksheets. Rows of chairs face the front of the room, and the teacher governs exchanges with students by talking, asking questions, and listening to answers (Sleeter & Grant, 2009). Although we don't advocate totally abandoning this format, we do believe that it should be supplemented by other formats such as role-play, peer tutoring, and small-group activities, all of which encourage interpersonal interactions and the use of several sensory modalities. For example, native Hawaiian children's achievement improved when teachers switched from whole-class instruction and independent seatwork to small-group learning centers, because the latter approach was more similar to the children's out-of-school social structure (Okagaki, 2001). Black students also seem to favor learning tasks that allow for interpersonal interaction, multiple activities, and the use of multiple sensory modalities (such as combining body movement with sound) (Sleeter & Grant, 2009). One way of teaching math to students with these preferences might be to engage them with problems that involve buying, trading, or borrowing.

Aspects of American Indian culture also call for flexibility in instructional formats and processes. Because longer periods of silence between speakers are more customary in Navajo than in Anglo-American culture, teachers need to wait longer for students to answer questions (Okagaki, 2001). Furthermore, because Navajo students are taught by their culture to treat serious learning as private, they may not fully participate in such traditionally Western activities as question-and-answer sessions, tests, debates, and contests (Morrison, 2009; Okagaki, 2001; Soldier, 1997). Bobby Ann Starnes, who taught on a Chippewa-Cree reservation in northern Montana, found that her students learned best when she used such instructional techniques and approaches as collaborative learning arrangements, open-ended questioning, inductive reasoning, whole-to-part sequencing of lessons, emphasis on visual learning strategies, and emphasizing students' cultural identity (Starnes, 2006). Other instructional techniques that have proven to be successful when teaching American Indian students include teaching at a slower and more measured pace, incorporating tribal histories and stories into the curriculum, including Native tribes' knowledge of animal behavior and plant use into science lessons, and inviting community elders to teach lessons (Castagno & Brayboy, 2008).

Ethnic group members may favor
different learning arrangements
and processes

With respect to learning processes, some researchers have found that many American Indians prefer, and learn more when they are prompted to use, visual imagery and drawing as a supplement to written and spoken forms of instruction (Castagno & Brayboy, 2008; Marley & Levin, 2006; Marley, Levin, & Glenberg, 2007). Additional evidence that the cultural backgrounds of students influence the learning process they use comes from the work of Nola Purdie and John Hattie (1996). They sought to determine whether there was any truth to the common perception that Japanese students tend to be literal learners who emphasize memorizing at the expense of their own views and interpretations. People who believe this description attribute it to the emphasis in Japanese culture on subordination of individual viewpoints to the group's perceptions and goals.

Purdie and Hattie found that the Japanese students they interviewed chose memorizing as their preferred learning process, whereas a similar group of Australian

Students from different ethnic groups often prefer different instructional formats and learning processes. Black students, for example, may favor cooperative learning over lecture/recitation, whereas American Indian students may dislike debates and contests. © Bob Daemmrich/ Photo Edit

students gave it a very low preference rating (18th out of 24 options). A group of Japanese students who had been living in Australia for almost 3 years at the time of the study fell in between these two extremes. These differences in learning processes may be related to differences in attitudes toward learning. Western students place a higher value on working independently, competing with others, and completing tasks efficiently (and Australian students can be considered Western in these respects). Japanese students, by contrast, place a higher value on working cooperatively with others, complying with authority, and being thorough in their approach to tasks (Li, 2002).

These findings suggest that although cultural background does influence choice of learning activity, the effects of culture seem to diminish as one becomes more accustomed to and comfortable with the values and practices of another culture.

TeachSource Video Case ◀◀ ▶ ▶▶

Integrating Internet Research: High School Social Studies

Go to the Education CourseMate website to watch the Video Case, and then answer the following questions:

1. Why is the computer-based assignment on the civil rights movement that is portrayed in this video clip likely to help high school students, especially those from minority groups, learn more about the topic than if they simply read about it or listened to their teacher lecture?

2. Elizabeth Sweeney, the teacher in this clip, says that as a relatively new teacher she was hesitant to use the computer lab because it meant allowing the task to become more student-centered and less teacher-directed. Do you think you will feel the same as a novice teacher? How did Ms. Sweeney get over her reluctance? Do you agree with her explanation?

The Effect of Social Class on Learning

The social class from which a student comes plays an influential role in behavior. **Social class** is an indicator of an individual's or a family's relative standing in society. It is determined by such factors as annual income, occupation, amount of education, place of residence, types of organizations to which family members belong, manner of dress, and material possessions. The first three factors are used by the federal government to determine the closely related concept of **socioeconomic status (SES)**.

Keep in mind as you read the next several pages that although we often mention the impact of social class on Black, Latino, and American Indian students, the effects are often the same for low-SES Whites (see, for example, Evans & English, 2002; Wiggan, 2007).

> Poverty rates higher for ethnic families of color than for Whites

Because of the severe and long-lasting historic pattern of discrimination experienced by ethnic groups of color in the United States, many members of these groups have fewer years of education, less prestigious occupations, and lower incomes than the average White person (Wiggan, 2007). In 2008, 18.5 percent of American children under age eighteen lived in families with incomes below the poverty level. Although most such children are White (meaning of European ancestry), Figure 5.2 shows that the poverty rates among Black, American Indian, and Hispanic American families are usually about three times higher than those for White children (DeNavas-Walt, Proctor, & Smith, 2009; U.S. Census Bureau, 2009).

Graduation Rates and Achievement Levels How do such differences in social class influence learning and performance in school? One major effect is that significantly fewer Black, Latino, and American Indian adolescents graduate from high school than do Whites, thereby shortening their years of education and earning potential. Because researchers do not always use the same sets of data to determine the percentage of Black students who graduate from high school (some use data from the Census Bureau whereas others use data published by the National Center for Educational Statistics), you can often find large

pause & reflect

What steps might you take to reduce or eliminate the sense of alienation that causes many students of color to drop out of school?

Figure 5.2 Percentage of Families Within Ethnic Groups Living Below Poverty Level in 2008

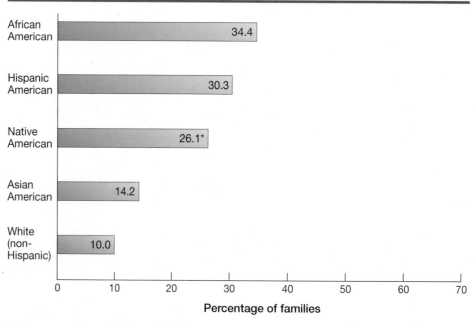

*The average from 2004 and 2005.

SOURCES: DeNavas-Walt, Proctor, & Smith (2009); U.S. Census Bureau (2009).

differences in this statistic. Some researchers (such as Swanson, 2004) claim that almost half of all Black and Latino students do not receive a high school diploma; others (such as Mishel & Roy, 2007) claim that the figure is approximately 25 percent, and that half of the remaining 25 percent eventually obtain a GED. Investigations into the reasons that minority students fail to complete school have found that social class factors, economic factors, school environment factors, and individual factors may all play a role. Compared with White students who graduate, minority students have lower levels of motivation, lower self-esteem, and weaker academic skills; they are also more impulsive. In addition, students who do not graduate nearly always report a sense of alienation from school because of low teacher expectations (more on this later in the chapter), expressions of racial or ethnic group prejudice from teachers and students, and unfair discrimination. Students of any racial or ethnic group, whether White, Black, or Hispanic, who are required to repeat grades (recall our discussion of this topic earlier in the text) are among the most likely to drop out of school and not graduate (Menzer & Hampel, 2009; Ramirez & Carpenter, 2009).

> Children of color often score lower on tests, drop out of school sooner

During their time in school, many students of color achieve at significantly lower levels than do White students. Compared with White high school sophomores and seniors, Black, Latino, and American Indian students score lower on standardized tests of vocabulary, reading, writing, mathematics, and science (Reardon, 2008; Reardon & Galindo, 2009). This achievement gap has been found even among Black students who are members of relatively affluent middle-SES families (Ogbu, 2003; Rothstein, 2004). These differences appear during the preschool years and continue to grow during the primary and elementary grades. Between first and third grade the gap in math achievement has been estimated to grow by 10 percent and the gap in reading by 40 percent. The gap continues to grow in subsequent grades, but at a slower rate (Reardon, 2008; Reardon & Galindo, 2009). Over the past 15 or so years, progress in narrowing the achievement gap (as measured by the National Assessment of Educational Progress test results) has been inconsistent. From 1992 until 2007, the gap between fourth-grade White and Black students' reading scores narrowed, but no progress was made among eighth graders. The gap in reading scores between White and Hispanic students was unchanged for both grades (Lee, Grigg, & Donahue, 2007). For math, the White-Black gap narrowed between 1990 and 2007 for fourth graders, but then no further progress was made between 2007 and 2009. Among eighth graders, the White-Black gap was unchanged between 1990 and 2009. The gap between White and Hispanic students was unchanged for both grades between 1990 and 2009 (National Center for Education Statistics, 2009). Obviously, much remains to be learned about why these gaps exist and what can be done to consistently work toward their elimination.

> Achievement gap between low-SES minority students and White students due to living conditions, family environment, characteristics of the student, and classroom environment

The long-standing achievement gap between low-SES (and some middle-SES) students of color and their White classmates is perhaps the most researched and discussed effect of social class on learning (e.g., Bell, 2002/2003; Denbo, 2002; Gardner, 2007; Ladson-Billings, 2002; Lee & Bowen, 2006; Nieto, 2002/2003; Ogbu, 2003; Rothstein, 2004; Singham, 2003; Sirin, 2005; Wiggan, 2007). The exact reasons for the gap relate to a number of interweaving factors, including living conditions, family environment, characteristics of the student, and classroom environment. To cite just one example, kindergarten children whose parents had recently emigrated from Mexico or Central America had lower scores on tests of reading and math skills than did students whose parents recently emigrated from Cuba or South America (Reardon & Galindo, 2009). This example illustrates a couple of points we have made several times throughout the book. First, most problems have several contributing causes that interact with one another. Second, to assume that all members of a particular group are alike and can be taught in the same way is to engage in stereotyping. Keep in mind that not all Asian Americans are high achievers and not all students of color have a negative attitude toward education and low levels of motivation.

Health and Living Conditions Many low-SES Americans do not receive satisfactory health care (Stinson, 2003). For example, there is a greater incidence of premature births, birth defects, and infant mortality among low-SES children as compared with middle-SES children (Umar, 2003). Because poor children do not receive medical or dental care regularly, accurate statistics on general health are difficult to compile. It seems reasonable to assume, however, that the same inadequate nutrition and health care that leads to elevated infant mortality rates probably also leads to higher rates of illness in later years.

Another health-related factor in the development and intellectual performance of low-SES children is lead poisoning. Because many of these children live in homes that were painted prior to the discontinuation of lead-based paint, their ingestion of paint dust and chips leads to elevated levels of lead in the blood. Exposure to lead, even in small amounts, is associated with low standardized test scores, attention deficits, and disruptive behavior in children. Almost 37 percent of Black children and 17 percent of Mexican American children between the ages of one and five have lead levels in their blood that are associated with cognitive impairments and behavioral problems. These impairments need not be permanent, however: medication can reduce the level of lead in the blood, leading to an improvement in the children's academic performance (Jackson, 1999).

Furthermore, many low-SES students, especially those in urban areas, live in relatively small, and sometimes overcrowded, apartments. Adequate study space is often nonexistent, and parental supervision is spotty or absent. Their neighborhoods tend to be characterized by high levels of street crime and low levels of cohesion. That is, people often do not get along, are unwilling to help their neighbors, and do not watch over each other's property when they are away. Such adverse living conditions are associated with lower aspirations for attending college (Stewart, Stewart, & Simons, 2007). An additional burden for approximately 25 percent of Black and Latino primary grade children is changing schools due to a change in residence by the family. The challenge of new peers, instructional methods, and curricula may exacerbate whatever learning problems these students already have (Evans, 2005).

Family Environment Considerable research has shown that various aspects of family life, including those discussed in the following paragraphs, affect a child's cognitive development and school achievement (see, for example, Barton & Coley, 2007; Raudenbush, 2009). Low-SES students are more likely than middle-SES students to grow up in one-parent families. About 54 percent of Black students live with one parent versus approximately 19 percent of White students, with the father

Low-SES children more likely to live in stressful environment that interferes with studying

On average, ethnic minority and low-SES students do not perform as well as other groups in school because of such factors as poor health care, an unstable family environment, low motivation, negative attitudes toward school, and negative classroom environments. © Catherine Karnow/CORBIS

usually being the missing parent (Planty et al., 2008). Like many other risk factors, the effect of a one-parent family on the academic performance of a child is not straightforward. It depends on such factors as the duration and cause of the absent parent's separation, the age and sex of the child, and the type of interactions the child has with the remaining parent. But although one-parent families may not negatively affect a child's performance in school, two-parent families are likely to be more effective because both parents have the potential to exert a positive influence (Barton & Coley, 2007).

Some studies show that parents' support for their children's schooling varies by social class and ethnic group. For example, White and Asian American adolescents are more likely than Latino or Black adolescents to get support for academic achievement from parents as well as friends (Castagno & Brayboy, 2008; Lee & Bowen, 2006; Okagaki, 2001, 2006).

Moreover, compared with the parents of low-SES children, the parents of middle-SES children in the United States expose their children to a wider variety of experiences. They tend to buy their children more books and educational toys and games, to take them on more trips that expand their knowledge of the world, to read to them more, and to talk to them more. Because low-SES parents speak about 600 words per hour to their children, whereas middle- and upper-middle-SES parents speak about 2,100 words per hour to their children, many Black and Latino children start school with a vocabulary of about 5,000 words, whereas the average White student has a vocabulary of about 20,000 words (Hart & Risley, 1995). These experiences accumulate and make school learning more familiar and easy than it would otherwise be. A child who has not had such experiences is likely to be at a disadvantage when placed in competitive academic situations (Barton & Coley, 2007; Raudenbush, 2009). Furthermore, there has been increasing concern about the development of a technological underclass of children whose families cannot afford to provide access to computers and online services at home. In 2004, 66 percent of children whose average family income was under $35,000 per year had Internet access at home, whereas 84 percent of children whose average family income was over $50,000 had such access (Henry J. Kaiser Family Foundation, 2004).

Overall, the interactions that occur between low-SES parents and their children tend to lack the characteristic of mediation (a concept we introduced earlier in the book in connection with Vygotsky's theory of cognitive development). When mediation occurs, someone who is more intellectually advanced than the learner presents, explains, and interprets stimuli in a way that produces a more meaningful understanding than the learner could have obtained working alone.

To illustrate this process, imagine a child walking alone through a hands-on science museum looking at the various exhibits, occasionally pushing the buttons of interactive displays, and listening to some of the prerecorded messages. What the child learns from this experience is likely to be a haphazard collection of isolated fragments of information that are not meaningful. Now imagine another child of the same age looking at and interacting with the same exhibits but accompanied by a parent or older sibling who wants this to be a meaningful learning experience. The parent or sibling points out specific aspects of the displays, names them, describes their purpose, and explains how they work. This child is more likely than the first child to construct a set of cohesive, interrelated, and meaningful knowledge structures (Ben-Hur, 1998).

Students' Motivation, Beliefs, and Attitudes Many low-SES students (as well as some middle-SES students) may not be strongly motivated to do well in school because of one or more of several variables. One is lower levels of a characteristic called *need for achievement*. A need for achievement (which is discussed more fully in Chapter 11, "Motivation") is a drive to accomplish tasks and is thought to be one of the main reasons that people vary in their willingness to invest time and energy in the achievement of a goal. Research suggests that low-SES

Black students score lower than comparable groups of White students on tests of need for achievement, but this racial difference is considerably smaller among middle-SES samples (Cooper & Dorr, 1995).

Other studies have found that some ethnic minority students, especially males, tend to develop beliefs and attitudes that inhibit strong academic performance:

- Black and Latino adolescents are more likely than Asian American or White adolescents to believe that they can get a good job without first getting a good education. Asian American, White, and Latino adolescents who are doing well in school, on the other hand, see getting a good education as a prerequisite to getting a good job (Ogbu, 2003; Okagaki, 2001).
- Black and Hispanic girls in the second, fourth, and seventh grades were much more likely to admire, respect, and want to be like high-achieving female classmates than average- or low-achieving classmates. Although Black and Hispanic second- and fourth-grade boys responded similarly, the seventh-grade boys included many more low achievers on their list of admired and respected peers (Taylor & Graham, 2007). Data from other studies indicate that although Black males recognize the importance of working hard, many of them adopt an indifferent attitude toward high levels of school achievement.
- Personal experiences with racial discrimination (or even the suspicion that one has been discriminated against) have been linked to decreased perceptions of mastery, mistrust of teachers and school rules, and negative attitudes toward school (Graham & Hudley, 2005; Taylor & Graham, 2007).

This decline in achievement-related values and attitudes on the part of minority male adolescents, which is sometimes referred to as an aversion to "acting White," has been corroborated by the observations of teachers, who made such comments as "They can do the work but they just don't seem to care" and "In the peer culture, one risks rejection by exerting effort in school" (Graham & Taylor, 2002). In addition, research finds that Black students with a B+ or higher grade-point average (GPA) and Latino students with a C+ or higher GPA were less popular with their peers than were Black and Latino students with lower grades (Fryer & Torelli, 2005). This inability to establish what might be called an academic identity appears to be related to a sense that one is not part of the larger school community, that school does not meet one's needs, that one is incapable of meeting academic demands, and that schoolwork is not part of who one wants to be (Fryer & Torelli, 2005; Jackson, 2003; Okagaki, 2006).

The frustration that is created by peers who do not share one's academic values was described by a Black female student who was attending a student conference of the Minority Student Achievement Network:

> I'm a member from Amherst, Massachusetts, and it is predominantly White…I'm able to get along with the White kids, but it's the Black kids that I find I have a hard time relating to…In class, they're always thinking, "There goes that girl, trying to be smart, trying to 'act White.'" It seems like I can't relate to them, and I'm Black myself. How is that supposed to make me feel? I'm trying to fit in both worlds, and it's like I have no place. (Ash, 2000, p. 6)

The relationship of low self-esteem to low achievement is dramatic but not always simple. In one study (van Laar, 2000), many Black high school and college students scored as high on measures of self-esteem as did Whites even though the Black students had lower levels of achievement. This seeming paradox results from minority students' belief that because of discrimination, they will not have available to them the same opportunities for employment and career advancement that are available to White students. Being able to blame the environment rather than oneself allows one to maintain a healthy sense of self-esteem. This perception may also play a role in minorities' lower need for achievement, the characteristic we discussed at the beginning of this section.

Classroom Environment Although teachers cannot work magical changes in a student's social class, health, family, or peer group, they can, as the following study illustrates, do a great deal to encourage learning among students of all social classes. First-grade children who were judged to be at risk for academic failure, either because their mothers had below-average levels of education or because they demonstrated such maladaptive classroom behaviors as aggression, defiance, lack of sustained attention, and poor ability to follow instructions, scored at about the same level on a standardized achievement test as their not-at-risk peers when they experienced high levels of emotional and instructional support from their teachers. By contrast, at-risk children whose teachers were judged to provide lower levels of emotional and instructional support scored significantly below their not-at-risk peers (Hamre & Pianta, 2005). Sadly, it is often the case that less capable teachers are assigned to schools that have the highest percentages of low-income and ethnic minority students (Gardner, 2007).

> Classroom atmosphere, teachers' approaches connected with achievement levels of low-SES students

Other studies have found high levels of achievement among low-SES students to be associated with the following attitudes and approaches among teachers (Burris & Welner, 2005; Denbo, 2002; Gardner, 2007; Hamre & Pianta, 2005; Mathis, 2005; Pogrow, 2009):

- Awareness of child's needs, moods, interests, and capabilities
- Classroom atmosphere characterized by pleasant conversations, spontaneous laughter, and exclamations of excitement
- Teachers' high but realistic expectations for their students
- Mastery goals (an approach discussed later in this chapter and in Chapter 12, "Classroom Management")
- Never accepting low-quality work
- The use of scaffolded instruction (as discussed in Chapter 2, "Theories of Psychosocial and Cognitive Development")
- Teaching thinking skills (discussed more fully in Chapter 9, "Social Cognitive Theory")
- Aligning instruction with standards (discussed more fully in Chapter 13, "Approaches to Instruction")
- Using formative evaluation (discussed more fully in Chapter 14, "Assessment of Classroom Learning")
- Eliminating ability grouping (in the elementary and middle school grades) and tracking (in the high school grades) systems and using heterogeneously grouped classes supplemented by extra support classes and after-school help. One New York high school that did this increased its graduation rate for Black/Latino and White students from 32 percent and 88 percent, respectively, to 82 percent and 97 percent (Burris & Welner, 2005). We discuss ability grouping and tracking more fully in Chapter 6, "Accommodating Student Variability."

A general suggestion for putting many of the previous suggestions into practice is to create a classroom environment and set of instructional processes that are similar to those found in such favorite extracurricular activities as athletics. Following the example of good athletic coaches, you should strive to make your classroom one where students respect and support one another, where students recognize that making mistakes is an inevitable part of learning, where each student's strengths are used to contribute to a larger group goal, where students receive constant feedback about their progress, and where students with more advanced knowledge and skills serve as models for and actively tutor classmates whose skills are not as well developed (Nasir, 2008).

Teachers' expectations for their students are so important that we devote the next section to this subject.

The Effect of Ethnicity and Social Class on Teachers' Expectations

So far we have described how students' ethnic and social class backgrounds influence their approach to and success with various learning tasks. Now we would like to tell you how those and other characteristics often affect (consciously and unconsciously) the expectations that teachers have for student performance and how those expectations affect the quantity and quality of work that students exhibit. This phenomenon has been extensively studied since it was first proposed in 1968 and is typically referred to as the **teacher expectancy effect**. By becoming aware of the major factors that influence teachers' perceptions of and actions toward students, you may be able to reduce subjectivity to a minimum, particularly with students whose cultural backgrounds are very different from your own.

The teacher expectancy effect basically works as follows:

1. On the basis of such characteristics as race, SES, ethnic background, dress, speech pattern, and test scores, teachers form expectancies about how various students will perform in class.
2. They subtly communicate those expectancies to the students in a variety of ways.
3. Students come to behave in a way that is consistent with what the teacher expects.

> Teacher expectancy effect: students behave in ways that are consistent with expectations that teachers communicate

pause & reflect

How have your experiences with members of ethnic or racial minority groups been similar to or different from what you have heard and read about those groups? Which source (personal experience or ideas derived from others) most affects your expectations for minority students?

> Strong effect of teacher expectancy on achievement, participation

Research on the Effects of Teachers' Expectancies Given the obvious implications of the teacher expectancy effect for shaping student behavior, researchers have been investigating its validity and limits for the last 40 years (see Spitz, 1999, for an excellent summary and analysis of the original and subsequent research, and Rosenthal, 2002, for the views of the senior author of the original study).

Research that has investigated the effect of teacher expectancy on classroom achievement and participation has generally found sizable positive *and* negative effects (Benner & Mistry, 2007; Chen & Bargh, 1997; Good & Nicholls, 2001; Jussim, Eccles, & Madon, 1996). For example, a study of several hundred low-income students between the ages of nine and sixteen (Benner & Mistry, 2007) found that both mothers' and teachers' expectations were positively related to students' expectations and students' perceptions of their own ability, and that students' expectations and ability perceptions were positively related to achievement. This study also found that low expectations by both mother and teacher had a negative impact on student achievement. In addition, it appears that teacher expectations are more likely to maintain already existing tendencies than to alter well-established behaviors drastically. For example, primary grade teachers react differently to students in the fast-track reading group than to students in the slow-track group. When working with the more proficient readers, teachers tend to smile, lean toward the students, and establish eye contact more often, and they tend to give criticism in friendlier, gentler tones than they use in the slow-track group. They often overlook the oral reading errors of proficient readers, and when they give corrections, they do so at the end of the sentence or other meaningful unit rather than in the middle of such units. And they ask comprehension questions more often than factual questions as a means of monitoring students' attention to the reading selection.

In contrast, teachers correct less proficient readers more often and in places that interrupt meaningful processing of the text, give these students less time to decode difficult words or to correct themselves, and ask low-level factual questions as a way of checking on students' attention. Teachers' body posture is often characterized by frowning, pursing the lips, shaking the head, pointing a finger, and sitting erect. Offering unsolicited help and giving enthusiastic praise to Black students may lead at least some of those students to infer that they have lower levels of academic ability. In sum, through a variety of subtle ways, teachers communicate to students that they expect them to perform well or poorly and then create a situation that is consistent with the expectation. As a result, initial differences between good and poor readers either remain or widen over the course of the school career (Graham & Hudley, 2005; Wuthrick, 1990).

Factors That Help Create Expectancies In addition to documenting the existence of teacher expectancy effects and the conditions under which they occur, researchers have sought to identify the factors that might create high or low teacher expectations. Here are some important factors taken from analyses by Thomas Good and Sharon Nicholls (2001), Vonnie McLoyd (1998), Sonia Nieto (2008), Harriet Tenenbaum and Martin Ruck (2007), and Yong Zhao and Wei Qiu (2009):

Teacher expectancies influenced by social class, ethnic background, achievement, attractiveness, gender

- Middle-SES students are expected to receive higher grades than low-SES students, even when their IQ scores and achievement test scores are similar.
- Teachers have the highest achievement expectations for Asian American students, and more positive expectations for White students than for minority (meaning Black and Latino) students.
- Teachers direct more neutral and positive statements (such as questions and encouragement) to White students than to minority students, but they criticize all students equally often.
- Minority students are more likely than White students to be referred for disciplinary action or for special education placement.
- Teachers tend to perceive children from poor homes as less mature, less capable of following directions, and less capable of working independently than children from more advantaged homes.
- Teachers who think of intelligence as a fixed and stable capacity are more likely to formulate negative and positive expectations of students than are teachers who think of intelligence as a collection of skills that can be shaped.
- Teachers are more influenced by negative information about students (for example, low test scores) than they are by neutral or positive information.
- High-achieving students receive more praise than low-achieving ones.
- Attractive children are often perceived by teachers to be brighter, more capable, and more social than unattractive children.
- Teachers tend to approve of girls' behavior more frequently than they approve of boys' behavior.

It is important to bear in mind that these factors (plus others such as ethnic background, knowledge of siblings, and impressions of parents) usually operate in concert to produce an expectancy. The following Suggestions for Teaching will give you some ideas for combating the damaging effects of teacher expectancies, as well as other problems often faced by low-SES and minority students.

Suggestions for Teaching

Promoting Classroom Achievement for All Students

1 **Use every possible means for motivating educationally disadvantaged students to do well in school.**

Good suggestions for teaching educationally disadvantaged students come not only from those who teach them, but also from the students themselves. You may notice some overlap in the two following lists, but that only serves to strengthen the validity of the suggestions.

David Gardner (2007), who taught for 33 years in schools that had high concentrations of low-income and ethnic minority students, was able to motivate his students and raise their achievement levels by doing the following:

- Setting high standards for students because he was convinced they were capable of meeting them.
- Telling students every day, both explicitly and implicitly, that he believed they were capable of high levels of achievement.
- Telling students that he would not accept poor-quality work and would return it to them to be redone.
- Avoiding helping students figure out how to meet the demands of a task when he was convinced they were capable of figuring it out for themselves.
- Telling students that failure was inevitable yet acceptable because that's how we learn.
- Making learning fun by using games and manipulables.

According to the responses of almost 400 low-income, inner-city middle school and high school students, good teachers do the following:

- Push students to learn by such actions as not accepting excuses for missed or late work, constantly checking homework, giving rewards, and keeping parents informed.
- Maintain an orderly and well-run classroom in which disruptions are kept to a minimum. (You will find more detailed information on how to create such an environment in Chapter 12, "Classroom Management.")
- Make themselves always available to provide a student with help in whatever form the student prefers. Some students, for example, want help after school, some during class, some individually, some by working with peers, and some through whole-class question-and-answer sessions. Some students may ask for help only if they are sure that no one besides the teacher knows they are receiving it.
- Strive to have all students understand the material by not rushing through lessons and by offering explanations in a clear step-by-step fashion and in various ways.
- Use a variety of instructional tactics, such as group work, lecture, textbook reading, worksheets, whole-class instruction, and hands-on activities.
- Make an effort to understand students' behavior by trying to understand the personalities and after-school lives of students (Corbett & Wilson, 2002).

We need to add a last word about homework as a way to promote achievement. The amount of homework assigned to students over the past 15 years has increased, largely because of the need for increasing numbers of students to achieve state-mandated standards and comply with the provisions of the No Child Left Behind Act of 2001. Educators believed that increasing the amount of homework assigned to students would lead to higher grades and test scores. Does it? Not surprisingly, the main conclusion to be drawn from the research literature (see, for example,

Cooper, 2001; Cooper, Robinson, & Patall, 2006; Marzano & Pickering, 2007; and Muhlenbruck, Cooper, Nye, & Lindsay, 2000) is that it depends on the student's grade level and how the homework is structured. Compared with peers who did no homework, there was a small benefit for late primary and elementary grade students and only a modest benefit for middle school students. The greatest benefit occurred among high school students. The benefits experienced by late primary and elementary grade students occurred only when the homework was sufficiently easy that they could successfully complete all or most of it. As one former K–12 teacher pointed out (Jackson, 2007), there is still much to be learned about how such variables as students' skill levels, level of parental involvement, and attitudes of parents and siblings toward school affect the benefits of doing homework, so keep an eye out for updates to this topic.

JOURNAL ENTRY
Using Productive
Techniques of Teaching

2 **Use a variety of instructional techniques to help educationally disadvantaged students master both basic and higher-order knowledge and skills.**

Research from the 1970s (Brophy & Evertson, 1976) found that the classroom and standardized test performances of educationally disadvantaged students improves when teachers follow these seven guidelines:

- Eliminate distractions and maximize the amount of time students actually spend working on a task.
- Establish high expectations and a classroom climate that supports achievement.
- Break tasks down into small, easy-to-manage pieces, and arrange the pieces in a logical sequence.
- Have students work on specific exercises in small groups.
- Ask direct questions that have direct answers.
- Provide frequent opportunities for practice and review.
- Provide timely corrective feedback.

Designing classroom instruction along these guidelines has both benefits and costs. The benefits are that students spend more time on-task, success tends to be more consistent, and more students reach a higher level of mastery of content knowledge and skills. The main cost is the lack of transfer that usually occurs when knowledge and skills are learned as isolated segments in a nonmeaningful context. A second cost is that students have few opportunities to interact with one another.

If teachers combine the seven guidelines just mentioned with current learning theory and research (Gordon, Rogers, Comfort, Gavula, & McGee, 2001; Knapp & Shields, 1990; Knapp, Shields, & Turnbull, 1995; Means & Knapp, 1991; as well as later chapters of this book), they may be able to raise the basic skill level of educationally disadvantaged students *and* improve their ability to transfer what they have learned to meaningful and realistic contexts. To accomplish this two-pronged goal, a teacher should also do the following:

- Provide opportunities for students to apply ideas and skills to real-life or realistic situations to make the lesson more meaningful. For example, after collecting and analyzing information, students might write letters to the mayor or city council requesting more streetlights for increased safety at night or improvements to basketball courts and baseball fields.

- Allow students the opportunity to discuss among themselves the meaning of ideas and their potential applications. In making a request of a government official, students should be encouraged to discuss which arguments are likely to be most effective and how they would respond should the official turn their proposal down.

- Embed basic skills instruction within the context of complex and realistic tasks. Letter-writing campaigns, for example, can be used to practice such basic English skills as vocabulary acquisition, spelling, punctuation, and grammar.

- Point out how classroom tasks relate to students' out-of-school experiences. One example is to draw attention to the basic similarities between poetry and rap music.

- Model for and explain to students the various thinking processes that are activated and used when one engages in a complex task. As you will see when you read Chapter 9, "Social Cognitive Theory," effective learners approach tasks strategically, which is to say they analyze the task, formulate a plan for dealing with it, use a variety of specific learning skills, and monitor their progress. These are fundamental learning processes that are almost never made explicit to students.

- Gradually ease students into the process of dealing with complex and realistic tasks. There is no question that the approach described in this list carries with it more risk of failure than was the case for the structured, small-scale approach of the 1970s. But much of this risk can be minimized by *scaffolding,* which we described in Chapter 2. As you may recall, in scaffolding, the teacher initially provides a considerable amount of support through explanations, demonstrations, and prompts of various types. As students demonstrate their ability to carry out more of a task independently, the scaffolding is withdrawn.

3 **Be alert to the potential dangers of the teacher expectancy effect. Concentrate on individuals while guarding against the impact of stereotyping.**

Myrna Gantner (1997), an eighth-grade teacher in an inner-city middle school near the Mexican border, learned the following lessons about treating her Latino students as individuals:

- Treat Latino students the same as you would treat any other student. When teachers believe that inner-city Latino students are less capable than other students, they tend to give them less time and attention. Students quickly notice these differences and may respond with lower-quality work and more disruptive behavior.

- Don't prejudge students. If you believe that most Latino children use drugs, belong to gangs, or have limited academic ability, students will eventually become aware of your prejudice and act accordingly. Gantner's students said they were most appreciative of teachers who were interested in them as individuals, had high expectations for them, and showed them how to achieve their goals.

- Don't ridicule or make fun of students' limited English proficiency. The best way to acquire proficiency in a second language is to use it frequently. Students will be less inclined to do so if they think teachers and other students will laugh at their mistakes.

JOURNAL ENTRY
Ways to Minimize
Subjectivity

4 **Remember that in addition to being a skilled teacher, you are also a human being who may at times react subjectively to students.**

Try to control the influence of such factors as name, ethnic background, gender, physical characteristics, knowledge of siblings or parents, grades, and test scores. If you think you can be honest with yourself, you might attempt to describe your prejudices so that you will be in a position to guard against them. (Do you tend to be annoyed when you read descriptions of the exploits of members of a particular religious or ethnic group, for example?) Try to think of a student independently of his or her siblings and parents.

MULTICULTURAL EDUCATION PROGRAMS

The concept of multicultural education has been around for some time. Many of the elements that constitute contemporary programs were devised 70 to 80 years ago as part of a then-current emphasis on international education (Gollnick & Chinn, 2009). In this section, we will give you some idea of what it might be like to teach today from a multicultural perspective by describing the basic goals, assumptions, approaches, and characteristics of modern programs.

Assumptions and Goals

The various arguments in favor of multicultural education that are made by its proponents (for example, Banks, 2008, 2009; Bennett, 2007; Castagno & Brayboy, 2008; García, 2002; Gollnick & Chinn, 2009; Singer, 1994) stem from several assumptions. These assumptions and the goals that flow from them appear in Table 5.2.

Basic Approaches

Four Approaches James Banks (2009), a noted authority on multicultural education, describes four approaches to multicultural education. Most multicultural programs, particularly those in the primary grades, adopt what he calls the *contributions approach*. In this approach, ethnic historical figures whose values and behaviors are consistent with American mainstream culture (for example, Booker T. Washington, Sacajawea) are studied, whereas individuals who have challenged the dominant view (such as W. E. B. Du Bois, Geronimo) are ignored.

A second approach, which incorporates the first, is called the *ethnic additive approach*. Here, an instructional unit composed of concepts, themes, points of view, and individual accomplishments is simply added to the curriculum. The perspective from which an ethnic group's contributions are viewed, however, tends to be that of the mainstream.

In a third approach, which Banks calls the *transformative approach*, the assumption is that there is no one valid way of understanding people, events, concepts, and themes. Rather, there are multiple views, and each has something of value to offer. For example, the view of the early pioneers who settled the American West could be summed up by such phrases as "How the West Was Won" and "The Westward

> Multicultural education can be approached in different ways

Table 5.2	Common Assumptions and Goals of Multicultural Education Programs
Assumptions of Multicultural Education	**Goals of Multicultural Education**
U.S. culture has been formed by the contributions of different cultural groups	Promote understanding of the origins and lack of validity of ethnic stereotypes (e.g., Blacks are violent, Jews are stingy, Asian Americans excel at math and science, Latinos are hot tempered)
Individuals must have self-esteem and group esteem to work productively with people from other cultures	Teachers should give all students a sense of being valued and accepted by expressing positive attitudes, using appropriate instructional methods, and formulating fair disciplinary policies and practices
Learning about the achievements of one's cultural group will raise self and group esteem	Promote self-acceptance and respect for other cultures by studying the impact ethnic groups have had on American society
American society benefits from positive interactions among members of different cultural groups	Reduce ethnocentrism and increase positive relationships among members of different ethnic groups by understanding the viewpoints and products of these groups
Academic performance is enhanced when teachers incorporate various cultural values and experiences into instructional lessons	Help students master basic reading, writing, and computation skills by embedding them in a personally meaningful (i.e., ethnically related) context

pause & reflect

Think about the four approaches to multicultural education described in this section. What advantages and disadvantages do you see for each approach? Which approach would you use? Why?

Multicultural programs aim to promote respect for diversity, reduction of ethnocentrism and stereotypes, improved learning

Movement." But the Native American tribes who had lived there for thousands of years may well have referred to the same event as "How the West Was Taken" or "The Westward Plague." You may recognize that the transformative approach is based on the principle of constructivism (discussed in earlier chapters). Because this approach requires the concrete operational schemes described in Chapter 2, it is typically introduced at the middle school level.

Finally, there is the *decision-making and social action approach*. It incorporates all of the components of the previous approaches and adds the requirement that students make decisions and take actions concerning a concept, issue, or problem being studied.

Characteristics of Effective Multicultural Teachers

Although Banks's ideas about how to structure multicultural education programs are well conceived, they require the efforts of effective teachers for their potential benefits to be realized. Several researchers (e.g., Castagno & Brayboy, 2008; Garcia, 2002) have identified specific characteristics that contribute to the success some teachers have in teaching students from culturally diverse backgrounds. Briefly stated, the effective multicultural teacher does the following:

1. Provides students with clear objectives.
2. Continuously communicates high expectations to the student.
3. Monitors student progress and provides immediate feedback.
4. Has several years of experience in teaching culturally diverse students.
5. Can clearly explain why she or he uses specific instructional techniques (such as the ones described in the next section).
6. Strives to embed instruction in a meaningful context. For example, a topic from one subject, such as controlling crop-damaging insects with insecticide, could be extended to other subjects (examining the effects of insecticide on human health, graphing crop yields sprayed with various types and amounts of insecticides).

For children to understand and appreciate different cultural values and experiences, those values and experiences have to be integrated into the curriculum and rewarded by the teacher. © Robert Holmes/Alamy

Advocates of multicultural education believe that ethnic minority students learn more effectively when some of their learning materials and assignments contain ethnically related content. © Li-Hua Lan/Syracuse Newspapers/The Image Works

7. Provides opportunities for active learning through small-group work and hands-on activities. One teacher, for example, created writing workshops in which students wrote, revised, edited, and published their products for others to read.

8. Exhibits a high level of dedication. Effective multicultural teachers are among the first to arrive at school and among the last to leave, work on weekends, buy supplies with their own money, and are constantly looking for opportunities to improve their instructional practices.

9. Enhances students' self-esteem by having classroom materials and practices reflect students' cultural and linguistic backgrounds.

10. Has a strong affinity for students. Effective multicultural teachers describe their culturally diverse students in such terms as "I love these children like my own" and "We are a family here."

TeachSource Video Case ◄◄ ▶ ►►

Culturally Responsive Teaching: A Multicultural Lesson for Elementary Students

Go to the Education CourseMate website to watch the Video Case, and then answer the following questions:

1. Does the "Coming to America" lesson shown in this Video Case meet any of the goals listed in Table 5.2? If so, which ones?

2. Do you find Mrs. Hurley to be an effective multicultural teacher? How does she meet the criteria listed?

Instructional Goals and Methods

Instructional Goals Teachers whose classes have a high percentage of children from ethnic minority and low-SES backgrounds often assume that they need to emphasize mastery of basic skills (such as computation, spelling, grammar, and word decoding) because minority and low-SES students are often deficient in those skills. Although this approach does improve children's performance on tests of basic skills, some educators argue that it does so at the expense of learning higher-level skills and that it is possible for students from poverty backgrounds to acquire both basic and higher-level skills.

Michael Knapp, Patrick Shields, and Brenda Turnbull (1995) conducted a study to investigate this issue. They examined teaching practices in almost 140 first-through sixth-grade classrooms in 15 elementary schools that served large numbers of children from low-SES families to determine whether the assumption that low-SES children can acquire both basic and higher-level skills is true. Over a 2-year period, these authors studied classrooms in which the learning of basic skills was paramount, as well as classrooms that emphasized higher-level and more meaning-ful outcomes. Teachers in the first group made extensive use of drill and practice, tasks that were limited in their demands, and tasks that could be completed quickly. Teachers in the second group used classroom discussions to let students work out the reasons behind mathematical procedures or explore alternative solutions to math problems, required students to read longer passages and gave them opportuni-ties to discuss what they had read, taught them reading comprehension strategies, and gave them more extended writing assignments.

Knapp and his colleagues found that children whose instruction emphasized conceptual understanding and problem solving performed better on mathematics, reading comprehension, and writing test items that measured advanced skills than their counterparts whose instruction focused on mastery of basic skills. And their performance on basic skill items was either no worse or better than that of students whose teachers emphasized the learning of basic skills.

Instructional Methods The three instructional tactics that are recommended most often by proponents of multicultural education are peer tutoring, cooperative learning, and mastery learning. Although each of these techniques can be used with any group of students and for almost any purpose, they are so well suited to the goals of multicultural education that the phrase "culturally responsive teaching" has been used to describe them (Wlodkowski & Ginsberg, 1995).

Peer Tutoring   As its name implies, **peer tutoring** involves the teaching of one student by another. The students may be similar in age or separated by one or more years. (The latter arrangement is usually referred to as *cross-age tutoring.*) The theoretical basis of peer tutoring comes from Jean Piaget's notions about cognitive development. Recall from our discussion of Piaget earlier in the book that cognitive growth depends on the presence of a disequilibrating stimulus that the learner is motivated to eliminate. When children with different cognitive schemes (because of differences in age, knowledge, or cultural background) are forced to interact with each other, cognitive conflict results. Growth occurs when children try to resolve this conflict by comparing and contrasting each other's views. As this theoretical analysis suggests, both the student doing the tutoring and the one receiving the tutoring should benefit from the interaction. In the next two paragraphs we'll briefly summarize the research on the cognitive benefits of tutoring for both parties.

Researchers have consistently found that peer tutoring (also referred to as peer-assisted learning) aids achievement for a wide range of students and subject matters. On average, students who received peer tutoring scored at the 63rd percentile on a measure of achievement, whereas students who did not receive peer tutoring scored at the 50th percentile. The strongest effects were obtained for younger students (grades 1–3), urban students, ethnic minority students, and low-SES students (Rohrbeck, Ginsburg-Block, Fantuzzo, & Miller, 2003). Peer tutoring also has posi-tive effects on nonachievement outcomes. An analysis of 36 studies by the same researchers (Ginsburg-Block, Rohrbeck, & Fantuzzo, 2006) found positive effects for social outcomes (such as ability to make friends and cooperativeness) and self-concept for the same groups.

Students who provide the tutoring also reap substantial learning benefits, but only if they are trained and periodically reminded to provide what are called

Peer tutoring improves achievement

knowledge-building explanations and questions. Instead of merely telling the other student the answer, summarizing facts, or describing procedures, the tutor should, like any good teacher, also provide new examples, discuss underlying concepts, connect ideas, and pose questions that require integration and application (Roscoe & Chi, 2007).

Cooperative Learning   Closely related to peer tutoring is cooperative learning. The general idea behind **cooperative learning** is that by working in small, heterogeneous groups (of four or five students total) and by helping one another master the various aspects of a particular task, students will be more motivated to learn, will learn more than if they had to work independently, and will forge stronger interpersonal relationships than they would by working alone.

David Johnson and Roger Johnson (1998, 2009), who have been researching the effects of cooperative learning for over 25 years, make a basic observation about the relevance of cooperative learning to the goals of multicultural education programs: students cannot learn everything they need to know about cultural diversity from reading books and articles. A deeper understanding of the nature and value of diversity is gained by learning how to work cooperatively with individuals from different cultural backgrounds.

Robert Slavin (1995), a leading exponent of cooperative learning, reports that cooperative learning produced significantly higher levels of achievement than did noncooperative arrangements in 63 of 99 studies (64 percent). The results for the student team learning programs have been the most consistently positive. Of particular relevance to this chapter are the findings that students who cooperate in learning are more likely to list peers from different ethnic groups as friends and are better able to take the perspective of a classmate than are students who do not work in cooperative groups.

Cooperative learning is a generally effective instructional tactic that is likely to be particularly useful with Latino, Black, and American Indian students. These cultures value a communal orientation that emphasizes cooperation and sharing. Thus these students may be more prepared than other individuals to work productively as part of a group by carrying out their own responsibilities, as well as helping others do the same (Bennett, 2007; Castagno & Brayboy, 2008; Nieto, 2008). One study found that small groups of Black fifth-grade students who were told that they had to help one another learn a reading passage recalled more of the text than did similar students who worked either in pairs or individually (Dill & Boykin, 2000). We will have more to say about cooperative learning and its effects on learning in Chapter 11.

Mastery Learning   The third frequently recommended instructional tactic, **mastery learning,** is an approach to teaching and learning that assumes that most students can master the curriculum if the following conditions are established: that students (1) have sufficient aptitude to learn a particular task, (2) have sufficient ability to understand instruction, (3) are willing to persevere until they attain a certain level of mastery, (4) are allowed whatever time is necessary to attain mastery, and (5) are provided with good-quality instruction.

Mastery learning proponents assume that all of these conditions can be created if they are not already present. Aptitude, for example, is seen as being partly determined by how well prerequisite knowledge and skills have been learned. And perseverance can be strengthened by the deft use of creative teaching methods and various forms of reward for successful performance. The basic mastery learning approach is to specify clearly what is to be learned, organize the content into a sequence of relatively short units, use a variety of instructional methods and materials, allow students to progress through the material at their own rate, monitor student progress to identify budding problems and provide corrective feedback, and allow students to relearn and retest on each unit until mastery is attained (Block, Efthim, & Burns, 1989; Gentile & Lalley, 2003).

Cooperative learning: students work together in small groups

Cooperative learning fosters better understanding among ethnically diverse students

Mastery learning: most students can master the curriculum

Like the research on peer tutoring and cooperative learning, the research on mastery learning has generally been positive. On the basis of a comprehensive review of this literature, Chen-Lin Kulik, James Kulik, and Robert Bangert-Drowns (1990) conclude that mastery learning programs produce moderately strong effects on achievement. The average student in a mastery learning class scored at the 70th percentile on a classroom examination, whereas the average student in a conventional class scored at the 50th percentile. The positive effect of mastery learning was slightly more pronounced for lower-ability students. As compared with students in conventional classes, those in mastery classes had more positive feelings about the subjects they studied and the way in which they were taught.

A Rationale for Multicultural Education

Some people seem to believe that multicultural education programs represent a rejection of basic American values and that this opposition to traditional values is the only rationale behind such programs. We feel this belief is mistaken on both counts. We see multicultural programs as being consistent with basic American values (such as tolerance of differences and equality of opportunity) and consider them to be justified in several ways.

1. *Multicultural programs foster teaching practices that are effective in general as well as for members of a particular group.* For example, expressing an interest in a student through occasional touching and smiling and allowing the child to tutor a younger student are practices likely to benefit most students, not just those of Latino origin.

2. *All students may profit from understanding different cultural values.* For example, the respect for elders that characterizes American Indian and Asian American cultures is likely to become increasingly desirable as the percentage of elderly Americans increases over the years. Similarly, learning the American Indian value of living in harmony with nature may come to be essential as we run out of natural resources and attempt to alleviate environmental pollution (Triandis, 1986).

3. *The United States is becoming an increasingly multicultural society, and students thus need to understand and know how to work with people of cultures different from their own.*

4. *Multicultural education programs expose students to the idea that "truth" is very much in the eye of the beholder.* From a European perspective, Christopher Columbus did indeed discover a new world. But from the perspective of the Arawak Indians who were native to the Caribbean, Columbus invaded territories that they had occupied for thousands of years. Similarly, one can describe the history of the United States as one in which continual progress toward democratic ideals has been made or as one in which progress has been interrupted by conflict, struggle, violence, and exclusion (Banks, 2009).

5. *Multicultural programs can encourage student motivation and learning.* These programs demonstrate respect for a child's culture and teach about the contributions that the student's group has made to American society. Proponents argue that these features both personalize education and make it more meaningful. Conversely, when children perceive disrespect for their cultural background, the result can be disastrous. Consider the following comment by a Mexican American student who realized for the first time that his teachers viewed him as both different and inferior:

> One recreation period, when we were playing our usual game of soccer, I took time out to search for a rest room. I spotted a building on the north side of the playground and ran for it. As I was about to enter, a teacher blew her whistle very loudly, freezing me on the spot. She approached me and demanded to know where I was going, who I was, and what I was doing on that side of the playground. I was dumbfounded

and afraid to respond, so she took me by the ear and escorted me back across the playground to the south side. Her parting remark was a stern admonition not to cross the line and to stay with all the other Mexicans.

At that very moment I stopped, turned, and looked at the school as if for the first time. I saw a white line painted across the playground. On one side were the white children playing; on my side were the Mexicans. Then I looked at the building, which was divided in half. The office was in the center, with two wings spreading north and south—one wing for whites and the other for Mexicans. I was overwhelmed with emotions that I could not understand. I was hurt, disappointed, and frustrated. But more than anything else, I was profoundly angry. (Mendoza, 1994, p. 294)

6. *The rationale for multicultural education that we have provided has been reinforced by numerous studies that document the disappointing academic performance of a significant number of minority-group students.* As we mentioned earlier, Black, Latino, and American Indian students tend to score lower than White students on standardized tests of vocabulary, reading, writing, mathematics, and science (Ornstein, Levine, & Gutek, 2011), and these differences appear as early as the fourth grade. Although such problems are not easy to solve, the inclusion of ethnically related content and activities in the curriculum helps make classroom assignments more meaningful and encourages minority students to master reading, writing, computational, and reasoning skills (Castagno & Brayboy, 2008).

Bridging the Cultural and SES Gap with Technology

As we stated earlier, a basic purpose of multicultural education is to give students the opportunity to learn about the characteristics of people from different cultures and to try to understand how those individuals view the world. For schools that draw from an ethnically, racially, and socioeconomically diverse population, acquiring firsthand experience with the history, beliefs, and practices of different cultures is not likely to be a major problem. But schools that draw from more homogeneous populations have traditionally been limited to such resources as books, magazines, and videotapes. This limitation on multicultural education is being surmounted, however, by the ability of technology to bring the world to the student, and in a very real sense.

Telecommunication projects allow students from different places and varied backgrounds to interact with one another, sharing ideas and experiences and learning new points of view. These exchanges can lead to a greater respect for diversity (Kontos & Mizell, 1997; Salmon & Akaran, 2001). Michaele Salmon and Susan Akaran (2001), for example, describe an e-mail exchange program between kindergarten students from New Jersey and first-grade Eskimo children from Alaska that produced greater respect for and understanding of each other's culture. For those teachers interested in providing their students with more in-depth knowledge about Alaskan Native culture and related approaches to instruction, a wealth of ideas and resources are available at the Alaska Native Knowledge Network (**www.ankn.uaf.edu**).

The 4Directions Project is another significant example. Developed by a consortium of 19 American Indian schools in 10 states and 11 public and private universities and organizations, the project allows isolated far-flung members of American Indian schools to share local customs and values with other American Indian tribes around the country. The students display their projects and achievements and participate in virtual communities through Internet teleconferencing. Although the 4Directions website (**http://4directions.org**) was created to facilitate communication among American Indian communities, the project welcomes other schools to participate in the project or use its resources (Allen et al., 1999). The Resources page contains several features, including culturally relevant lesson plans for eight subject areas and a virtual tour of the National Museum of the American Indian.

Earlier in this chapter, we indicated that many students from low-SES homes are considered to be at risk for educational failure because of adverse conditions

For quick links to relevant websites, go to the web links section of the textbook's website, Education CourseMate.

Multicultural understanding can be promoted by electronically linking students from different cultural backgrounds

Computer-based technology helps students learn more about other cultures and social classes by providing access to various reference sources and individuals from almost anywhere in the world. © Ian Shaw/Alamy

surrounding their physical, social, emotional, and cognitive development. Technology may be an effective tool in combating this problem, as it has demonstrated its effectiveness at raising the achievement levels of at-risk, low-SES students. In one study (Cole & Hilliard, 2006), a group of low-SES third-grade students from an inner-city school who were two or more grade levels behind in reading were given 8 weeks of reading instruction using a web-based program called *Reading Upgrade*. This program uses music and video within an interactive environment to maintain student attention to and interest in lessons that focus on decoding, phonemic awareness, fluency, and comprehension. The *Reading Upgrade* group significantly outscored a similar group of students who received conventional reading instruction without the aid of computers; they gained the equivalent of one grade level on measures of decoding, fluency, and comprehension in just 8 weeks.

In another study (Page, 2002), half of the third- and fifth-grade low-SES students in five schools worked in technology-enriched classrooms while the other students worked on the same lessons without the aid of technology. For a unit on the planets and constellations within the Milky Way galaxy, for example, students in the technology-enriched classrooms would gather information for a report from science software or the World Wide Web and then prepare a slide show presentation using PowerPoint. For other lessons they might have videoconferences with same-grade students from other schools. Although there were no differences between the two groups on a standardized test of reading, students in the technology-enriched classes did score higher than their peers who did not use technology on a standardized test of mathematical skills and a test of self-esteem. In addition, there was considerably more student-to-student interaction and less teacher-to-student interaction in the technology-enriched classes.

In previous editions of this book we pointed out that schools with high levels of poor students did not provide the same access to the Internet as did schools that enrolled larger numbers of students from more wealthy families. That particular gap appears to have been virtually erased. In 2005, the ratio of students per Internet-connected computer for students in low- and high-poverty schools was 3.8 and 4.0, respectively. Somewhat larger gaps continue to exist, however, for city versus rural schools and larger versus smaller schools (Wells & Lewis, 2006). Thus, as we have also noted in past editions, insufficient technology resources may hinder the efforts to bridge the cultural and SES gap that we have described in this section.

Now that you are familiar with the nature and goals of multicultural education programs and some of the instructional tools that are available to you, the following Suggestions for Teaching should help you get started.

Suggestions for Teaching

Promoting Multicultural Understanding and Classroom Achievement

1 Use culturally relevant teaching methods.

To fulfill the goals of multicultural education, teachers should practice what is referred to as either culturally relevant pedagogy (Ladson-Billings, 2002) or culturally responsive pedagogy (Nieto, 2002/2003). This approach to instruction is based on two premises. First, all students, regardless of their ethnic, racial, and social class backgrounds, have assets they can use to aid their learning. Second, teachers need to be aware of and meet students' academic needs in any number of ways. In other words, simply adopting a multicultural basal reader is not culturally responsive pedagogy. In addition to adopting multicultural reading material, you should do everything possible to help all students learn to read. For example, successful teachers of Latino students in Arizona and California have high expectations for students, make their expectations clear, never accept low-quality work, scaffold students' learning, and use Spanish for instruction or allow students to speak Spanish among themselves when working in pairs or groups (Rolón, 2002/2003).

Gloria Ladson-Billings (2002), who has written extensively about working with minority and at-risk students, provides several examples of culturally relevant or responsive teaching. A second-grade teacher allowed her students to bring in lyrics from rap songs that both she and the students deemed to be inoffensive. The students performed the songs, and the teacher and students discussed the literal and figurative meanings of the words and such aspects of poetry as rhyme scheme, alliteration, and onomatopoeia. The students acquired an understanding of poetry that exceeded both the state's and school district's learning standards. Another teacher invited the parents of her students to conduct "seminars" in class for 2 to 4 days, 1 to 2 hours at a time. One parent who was famous for the quality of her sweet potato pie taught the students how to make one. In addition, the students were required to complete such related projects as a written report on George Washington Carver's research on the sweet potato, a marketing plan for selling pies, and a statement of the kind of education and experience one needed to become a cook or chef. Similar seminars were done by a carpenter, a former professional basketball player, a licensed practical nurse, and a church musician, all of whom were parents or relatives of the students.

JOURNAL ENTRY
Ways to Promote Awareness of Contributions of Ethnic Minorities

2 Help make students aware of the contributions that specific ethnic groups have made to the development of the United States and the rest of the world.

As we noted earlier, James Banks (2009) has identified four approaches to multicultural education, the first of which is the contributions approach. This approach emphasizes the contributions that prominent individuals of various ethnic groups have made to the United States, as well as each group's major holidays, celebrations, and customs. One suggestion for implementing this approach is to invite family members of students (and other local residents) of different ethnic backgrounds to the classroom. Ask them to describe the values subscribed to by members of their group and explain how those values have contributed to life in the United States and the rest of the world.

3 **Use instructional techniques and classroom activities that are consistent with the value system of students who share a particular cultural background and that encourage students to learn from and about one another's cultures.**

Students from Latino cultures place a high value on the concept of collectivism, or the interdependence of family members. From an early age, children are taught to think first about fostering the success of any group to which they belong by seeking to work cooperatively with others (Rothstein-Fisch, Greenfield, & Trumbull, 1999). To capitalize on this value, consider doing some or all of the following:

- Assign two or three children rather than just one to a classroom task, such as cleaning up after an art period, and allow them to help one another if necessary.

- Increase the use of choral reading with students whose English proficiency is limited so they can practice their decoding and pronunciation skills without being the center of attention.

- After distributing a homework assignment, allow students to discuss the questions but not to write down the answers. Those who are more proficient in English and have better-developed intellectual skills can help their less skilled classmates better understand the task. One third-grade teacher who used this technique was surprised to find that every student completed the assignment.

Bear in mind, however, that students whose families have recently immigrated to the United States may not be familiar or comfortable with such student-centered techniques. In some cultures, for example, students are taught not to speak unless asked a direct question by the teacher, not to volunteer answers without being asked (so as not to appear boastful or conceited), and never to question what the teacher says, even when they know it to be wrong. These students will need time to become used to such practices as working with other students and asking the teacher for additional explanations (Miller & Endo, 2004).

4 **At the secondary level, involve students in activities that explore cultural differences in perceptions, beliefs, and values.**

A well-conceived multicultural education program cannot, and should not, avoid or minimize the issue of cultural conflict. There are at least two reasons for helping students examine this issue. One is that conflict has been a constant and salient aspect of relationships among cultural groups. Another is that cultural conflicts often produce changes that benefit all members of a society (a prime example is the civil rights movement of the 1960s, with its boycotts, marches, and demonstrations).

Cultural conflicts arise from differences in perceptions, beliefs, and values. American culture, for example, places great value on self-reliance. Americans generally respect and praise individuals who, through their own initiative, persistence, and ingenuity, achieve substantial personal goals, and they tend to look down on individuals who are dependent on others for their welfare. Consequently, American parents who are financially dependent on their children, even though the children may be prosperous enough to support them, would probably feel ashamed enough to hide the fact. The same situation in China would likely elicit a different reaction because of different values about self-reliance and family responsibilities. Chinese parents who are unable to provide for themselves in their old age but have children successful enough to support them might well brag about it to others (Appleton, 1983).

One technique for exploring cultural conflict is to have students search through newspapers and news magazines for articles that describe clashes. Ask them to identify the source of the conflict and how it might be positively resolved. Another technique is to involve students in games that simulate group conflict. Class members can,

JOURNAL ENTRY
Ways to Help Students
Explore Conflicts Between
Cultures

for example, play the role of state legislators who represent the interests of diverse ethnic groups and who have been lobbied to change the school funding formula so that poorer school districts receive more money (Appleton, 1983). The use of both simulations and the discussion of newspaper articles will probably work best at the high school level because adolescents are better able than younger students to understand the abstract concepts involved in these activities.

5 **Involve students, especially at the secondary level, in community service activities.**

Service-learning programs, found in many school systems, serve several purposes. First, they afford students the opportunity to broaden the knowledge they acquire in school by working to solve real problems in a community setting. Second, they help students develop a sense of civic and social responsibility. Third, they help students become more knowledgeable about career options. And fourth, they provide a useful and needed service to the community (Billig, 2000). To cite one example, Natalie Russell (2007), who teaches English as a second language to high school students, describes how she uses service-learning projects, such as the creation of a Spanish/English phrasebook that was distributed free to community members, as a way to help students feel more connected to their community and to make their English lessons more meaningful and immediately useful. More detailed information about service-learning programs and organizations can be found on the website of the Corporation for National and Community Service (**www.learnandserve.org**).

6 **Make every effort to contact and work with the parents of ethnic minority students.**

More ideas for your journal can be found in the Reflective Journal Questions at the textbook's student website, Education CourseMate.

To help students and their parents make a successful transition to a new country and school system, educators and multicultural education scholars (e.g., Castagno & Brayboy, 2008; Little Soldier, 1997) suggest trying the following:

- During the first week of the school year, hold parent-teacher-child conferences. Be willing to hold these meetings in the parents' home and during the evening hours if necessary.
- Recruit bilingual parent volunteers to help teachers and staff members talk with parents and students.
- In discussing classroom tasks and student performance with parents, avoid technical terminology and acronyms. Not only does this result in fewer misunderstandings, but it also lessens the sense of inferiority that some parents feel.
- Participate in the cultural events hosted by your students' community.
- Recruit community members to help your students with culture-specific projects that you would like the students to carry out.

BILINGUAL EDUCATION

As we mentioned earlier, the 1990s set a U.S. record for the number of immigrants during a decade. Slightly more than 9.7 million legal immigrants arrived in the United States from 1990 through 1999. Not surprisingly, many of the school-age children of these families have either limited or no English proficiency. For 2006, 2.8 million K–12 students spoke a language other than English (most often Spanish) at home and spoke English with difficulty (Planty et al., 2008).

To address the needs of these students, the federal government provides financial support for the establishment of bilingual education programs. Because language is viewed as an important part of a group's culture, many school districts integrate bilingual education with multicultural education. In this section, we will examine the nature and effectiveness of bilingual education programs.

Before we consider different approaches to bilingual education, there are three general points we would like you to keep in mind.

1. Bilingual programs have become an emotionally charged and politicized topic (Macedo, 2000; Pérez, 2004; Porter, 2000; Thompson, DiCerbo, Mahoney, & MacSwan, 2002). Educators, parents, and legislators have strong opinions regarding the amount of time and resources that should be devoted to helping students master native-language skills and whether such programs should include cultural awareness goals. Some people favor moving students into all-English classes as quickly as possible, whereas others believe that students should have a firm grasp of their native language *and* English before attempting to make the transition to regular classes. Although research on this issue is helpful because it informs us about what *is*, such research cannot tell us what we should do about what we know.

2. Some language-minority students may suffer from problems that bilingual education alone cannot solve, such as the multiple difficulties associated with low SES.

3. No one approach to bilingual education is likely to be equally effective for all language-minority students. What works well for some low-SES Puerto Rican children may not work well for middle-SES Cuban children, and vice versa.

Goals and Approaches

Most bilingual education programs have a common long-term goal, but they differ in their approach to that goal. The goal is to help minority-language students acquire as efficiently as possible the English skills they will need to succeed in school and society. The approaches to that goal usually fall into one of three categories: *transition, maintenance,* or *two-way bilingual.*

Transition programs focus on rapid shift to English proficiency

Transition Programs Programs that take a transition approach teach students wholly (in the case of non-English-proficient students) or partly (in the case of limited-English-proficient students) in their native language so as not to impede their academic progress, but only until they can function adequately in English. At that point, they are placed in regular classes, in which all of the instruction is in English. To make the transition time as brief as possible, some programs add an English-as-a-second-language (ESL) component. ESL programs typically involve pulling students out of their regular classes and providing them with full-time intensive instruction in English (Gersten, 1999; Mora, Wink, & Wink, 2001; Thomas & Collier, 1999).

Maintenance programs focus on maintaining native-language competence

Maintenance Programs Programs that take a maintenance approach try to maintain or improve students' native-language skills. Instruction in the students' native language continues for a significant time before transition to English. Supporters of maintenance programs point to the results of psychological and linguistic studies that suggest that a strong native-language foundation supports the subsequent learning of both English and subject-matter knowledge. In addition, many proponents of multicultural education favor a maintenance approach because they see language as an important part of a group's cultural heritage (Mora et al., 2001; Robledo & Cortez, 2002).

Two-way bilingual education programs feature instruction in both languages

Two-Way Bilingual Programs Some bilingual education scholars (e.g., Calderón & Minaya-Rowe, 2003; Pérez, 2004; Thomas & Collier, 1997/1998, 1999) are critical of both transitional and maintenance bilingual education programs because they are remedial in nature and because students who participate in such programs tend to be perceived as inferior in some respect. These educators favor what is

Some bilingual education programs emphasize using the student's native language competence to help the student learn English as quickly as possible. Other programs emphasize the maintenance or improvement of both the student's native language and English. Bob Daemmrich/Stock Boston

generally known as **two-way bilingual (TWB) education** (although the terms *bilingual immersion, two-way immersion,* and *dual language* are also used). In a TWB program, subject-matter instruction is provided in two languages to all students. This approach is typically used when English is the primary language of about half the students in a school and the other language (usually Spanish) is the primary language of the other half of the students.

TWB programs are used in 346 schools in 27 states in the United States (Center for Applied Linguistics, 2009). Although most of these programs are English-Spanish, other programs include Korean, French, Cantonese, Navajo, Japanese, Arabic, Portuguese, Russian, and Mandarin Chinese as the minority language. TWB programs differ from traditional transition and ESL programs in that they begin as early as kindergarten and continue throughout the elementary school years to maintain facility in the student's native language while building facility in the nonnative language.

Canada and Miami, Florida, have two of the oldest and largest TWB programs. Canada has always had a large French-speaking population, mostly in the province of Québec. Because many parents wanted their children to be proficient in both English and French, Canadian schools in the 1960s began a K–12 program. In kindergarten and first grade, 90 percent of the instruction is in French and the remaining 10 percent is in English. From grade 2 through grade 5, the proportion gradually shifts to 50/50. By grade 6, most students can work equally well on any subject matter in either language.

The impetus for a TWB program in the Miami area was the large number of residents who emigrated from Cuba. As with all other two-way programs, students whose primary language is Spanish *and* students whose primary language is English participate in the program together. Unlike the Canadian model, which has a strong immersion component in the early grades (80 to 90 percent of the instruction is in French), teachers in Miami's program teach in Spanish for half the day and in English for the other half of the day at all grade levels.

TWB programs typically include the following features:

- At least 6 years of bilingual instruction
- High-quality instruction in both languages
- Separation of the two languages for instruction (for example, by time of day, day of the week, or even by week)

- Use of the minority language for teaching and classroom discussion at least 50 percent of the time
- A roughly balanced percentage of students for whom each language is primary
- Use of peer tutoring

Despite the growth and success of TWB programs, as well as data showing that it takes most English language learners 7 to 10 years to become sufficiently fluent in English to compete academically with their peers (Lewis-Moreno, 2007), some states have eliminated all bilingual education programs. In 1998, Californians voted to eliminate their state's bilingual education program and provide instead a 1-year English-immersion program, in which language-minority students are taught only in English. In 2000, voters in Arizona approved a similar proposition (Thompson et al., 2002). An English-immersion program was approved in Massachusetts in 2002 but was later amended to allow TWB programs to continue to operate (Saltzman, 2003).

TeachSource Video Case ◀◀ ▶ ▶▶

Bilingual Education: An Elementary Two-Way Immersion Program

Go to the Education CourseMate website to watch the Video Case, and then answer the following questions:

1. The two teachers in this Video Case work together closely to teach students in two different languages. In your opinion, what are the pros and cons of this approach to bilingual education?

2. What are some of the specific challenges that teachers in a two-way program (such as the one depicted in the Video Case) might face?

Research Findings

Much of the research on bilingual education has addressed one or the other of the following questions: Do English-language learners (ELLs) become proficient in English more quickly in bilingual programs or in English-only immersion programs? Do English-language learners score higher on subject-matter tests in bilingual programs or immersion programs? Before we get into a brief summary of this research, a word of caution. As with all of the other topics we cover in this book, the research on bilingual education is complex and evolving. What follows is, to use a photography metaphor, a snapshot of what we currently know. Nevertheless, the weight of the evidence to date seems to support the following conclusions:

| Bilingual education programs produce moderate learning gains

- Despite heated arguments about whether immersion programs or transition programs (the most common form of bilingual instruction) help ELLs acquire English proficiency more quickly, the answer, at least for now, seems to be that it may not matter very much. In one large-scale study (Tong, Lara-Alecio, Irby, Mathes, & Kwok, 2008), about 800 kindergarten Spanish-speaking ELLs were randomly assigned to one of four types of programs: regular transition, enhanced transition, regular immersion, enhanced immersion. The main difference between the regular and enhanced versions of the transition and immersion programs was additional daily English instruction activities. After 2 years, students in the two enhanced groups were equally proficient in English, and both groups were more proficient than students in the traditional transition group.

Take a Stand!

Bilingual Education: *Plus les choses changent, plus elles restent les mêmes*

The preceding French phrase translates to "The more things change, the more they remain the same." So it is with the current dispute over the goals and methods of bilingual education. In the early part of the twentieth century, prior to World War I, bilingual public schools were common, particularly in areas with large numbers of German immigrants. After the war, however, public financing of bilingual schools was abruptly withdrawn, partly as a reaction against Germany (which lost the war and was seen as the aggressor) and partly because of increasing nationalism and isolationism. American society strongly endorsed a one country/one culture policy and stressed once again the idea of America as a melting pot. As a result, English-immersion programs for immigrant students became the norm.

But during and after World War II, as now, American students' deficiencies in foreign-language fluency became noticeable and a source of concern. This situation contributed to the first Bilingual Education Act in 1965, which emphasized the maintenance of one's native language, as well as mastery of English.

As a future educator whose decisions will rest partly on scientific evidence, we suggest that you ignore as much as possible both the pro and con arguments about bilingual education that appear to be based on biases and political beliefs. Focus instead on what the research has to say. Our reading of the current research leads us to conclude that bilingual education, particularly in the form of two-way bilingual programs, benefits both limited-English-proficient and native English-speaking students. Given the ease with which technology allows students from different countries to communicate and work collaboratively, as well as the trend toward international commerce, programs that increase students' bilingual fluency should be encouraged and strongly supported.

What Do You Think?

Have you ever taken part in bilingual education? What is your position on expanding its use in U.S. schools? For more material on this subject, go to the Take a Stand! section of the textbook's Education CourseMate website.

- In comparison with immersion (English-only) programs, participation in bilingual education programs produces small to moderate gains in reading, language skills, mathematics, and total achievement when measured by tests in English. When measured by tests administered in the student's native language, participation in bilingual education leads to significantly better performance on tests of listening comprehension, reading, writing, total language, mathematics, social studies, and attitudes toward school and self. Thus, increasing the amount of time devoted to instruction in English (as is done in immersion programs) does not necessarily lead to higher levels of achievement (Cummins, 1999; Slavin & Cheung, 2005; Willig, 1985). Early analysis of California's immersion program indicates that although ELL students improved their scores on the Stanford-9 (a standardized achievement test), the scores of non-ELL students increased by a similar amount. Consequently, the achievement gap between ELL and non-ELL students remained unchanged (Thompson et al., 2002).

- ESL programs appear to have positive effects on reading comprehension skills and grade-point average. ESL students recognize cognate vocabulary (related words) fairly well (although there is a wide range of proficiency for this outcome), demonstrate the ability to monitor their comprehension, and use prior knowledge to help them understand and remember what they read (Fitzgerald, 1995). Also, Mexican American students who had more years of ESL/bilingual education than their peers had higher grades (Padilla & Gonzalez, 2001).

- Students who participate in TWB programs score at or above grade level on subject-matter tests and score higher on reading and mathematics tests than ELL students who are taught only in English (Pérez, 2004; Slavin & Cheung, 2005).

TECHNOLOGY AND BILINGUAL EDUCATION

Multimedia, hypermedia, e-mail, and other technologies are enhancing opportunities for bilingual students and ELL students to more efficiently acquire English language skills and other subject matter. Former ESL teacher Jan Lacina describes, for example, how Internet chat sessions, discussion boards, and computer programs can be used to help students refine their language skills. Chat rooms and discussion boards have the advantage of letting students review and possibly revise what they have written before sending it off and may be particularly beneficial for students who are shy or are anxious about mispronunciations (Lacina, 2004/2005). A computer program that may be worth investigating is the Reading Assistant from Scientific Learning (**www.scilearn.com/products/reading-assistant**). Students read aloud into a headset microphone, and the program provides audio and visual help for words the student mispronounces or has trouble pronouncing.

There are also numerous Web resources that support bilingual instruction. One site that serves both teachers and students is **www.eslcafe.com.** A menu called "Stuff for Students" contains the following pages: Help Center (a discussion forum), Hint-of-the Day, Idioms, Phrasal Verbs, Pronunciation Power, Quizzes, Slang, and Student Forums. The website Science Fair Assistant (**www.iteachilearn.com/teach/tech/science.htm**), written in both English and Spanish, is designed to help children in grades K–8 find experiments and ideas for a science project. Finally, a number of publications describe how to use websites in creating lessons to improve ELL students' listening, oral proficiency, reading comprehension, and writing skills (e.g., Feyten et al., 2002).

To review this chapter, see the tutorial quizzes and other study aids on the textbook's Education CourseMate website.

Challenging Assumptions

Placing Value

"Your journals were intriguing," Connie says to her young colleagues. "I learned quite a lot from reading them, and I will certainly be discussing them with each of you individually. For now, though, I want to focus on the lab that Celeste observed."

Connie asks Celeste to recount her observations for Antonio and Don. Connie then says, "Keeping in mind that students were placed in groups for the lab session, why do you think the groups were not particularly effective?"

Antonio clearly has something to say. He looks at the ceiling as he speaks: "As Celeste was describing the lab team, I started to wonder if maybe there were kids in that class who grew up in families that valued group accomplishment more than individual rewards. I grew up in that kind of family. I remember once, when I was in second grade, a new kid joined our class. He was born here and talked like everybody else, but his parents had come here as refugees. I thought he was Chinese, but he was Hmong. We were supposed to write a story. The new kid had a very hard time and when the teacher asked him why, he said, 'Stories are something we tell together, not something we make by ourselves.' The teacher tried to be very nice about it, but she told him that he needed to write a story so that she would know he could do it and so that he would not be the only kid without a story in his folder for Parent's Night. I started to feel sad and even angry because a lot of what my own family said was important was not what my school said was important." Antonio looks out the window.

After a moment, Don says, "You know, I have been working really hard to find materials to make my lessons more multicultural. But what you just said, Antonio, makes me think it's not just the materials we choose to use in our classrooms, it's what we decide our students should do—and how they should do it—that makes students feel more or less included."

"The life lessons our students bring to us," says Connie, "are critical to what they will learn from us. They bring their values to us. How we evaluate—how we place value on our students' work—is a measure of respect for the values they bring into our classrooms. We must recognize that evaluation is, inevitably, the placement of value."

Summary

1. Culture refers to the perceptions, emotions, beliefs, ideas, experiences, and behavior patterns that a group of people have in common.

2. Beginning in the 1960s, the notion of the United States as a cultural melting pot became less popular, and the concept of cultural diversity, or cultural pluralism, increased in popularity. As the latter became more widely accepted, calls were made for the establishment of multicultural education programs in American public schools.

3. The concept of cultural pluralism is based on three beliefs: (a) societies should strive to maintain different cultures, (b) each culture within a society should be respected by others, and (c) individuals within a society have the right to participate in all aspects of that society without having to give up their cultural identity.

4. Because of immigration patterns and high birthrates in some ethnic groups, the United States is becoming an increasingly diverse country.

5. Two important factors that distinguish one culture from another are ethnicity and social class.

6. People of the same ethnic group typically share many of the following characteristics: ancestral country of origin, race, religion, values, political interests, economic interests, and behavior patterns.

7. Ethnic differences in communication patterns and preferences, time orientation, values, and instructional format and learning process preferences can lead to misunderstandings among students and between students and teachers.

8. Social class indicates an individual's or a family's relative position in society in terms of such factors as income, occupation, level of education, place of residence, and material possessions. Socioeconomic status (SES) is a somewhat narrower concept that focuses on the first three of these factors.

9. Low-SES students, especially those from minority groups, tend to achieve at significantly lower levels than White, middle-SES children for a variety of reasons. They are more likely than middle-SES students to grow up in one-parent households in which the father is the missing parent. Often, too, they receive irregular health care, live in urban areas in small apartments that lack adequate study space, are not exposed to a wide variety of experiences, have low career and academic aspirations, and face classroom environments that are less than fully supportive.

10. The teacher expectancy effect occurs when teachers communicate a particular expectation about how a student will perform and the student's behavior changes so as to be consistent with that expectation.

11. Research has demonstrated that teacher expectancy strongly affects classroom achievement and participation in both positive and negative ways.

12. Factors that seem to play a strong role in producing a teacher expectancy effect are a student's social class, ethnic background, gender, achievement, and attractiveness and teachers' conception of the nature of intelligence.

13. Multicultural education programs assume that minority students will learn more and have a stronger self-concept if teachers understand, accept, and reward the thinking and behavior patterns characteristic of the students' culture.

14. Effective multicultural teachers use such proven instructional techniques as providing clear objectives, communicating high expectations, monitoring progress, providing immediate feedback, and making lessons meaningful. In addition, they have experience in teaching culturally diverse classes, exhibit a high level of dedication, and have a strong affinity for their students.

15. Peer tutoring, cooperative learning, and mastery learning are three generally effective instructional tactics that are particularly well suited to multicultural education programs.

16. Calls for multicultural education were stimulated by changing immigration and birthrate patterns, low levels of school achievement by many ethnic minority children, and students' need to work productively with members of other cultures.

17. For students who live in culturally homogeneous communities, an increased understanding of the characteristics of students from different cultural backgrounds and the problems they face can be gained by using such technological tools as videoconferencing and electronic communities.

18. Most bilingual education programs reflect a transition goal, a maintenance goal, or a two-way bilingual goal. Transition programs teach students in their native language only until they speak and understand English well enough to be placed in a regular classroom. Maintenance programs try to maintain or improve students' native language skills. Two-way programs provide subject matter instruction in both the majority and minority languages in roughly equal proportions to all students, and they are growing in popularity.

19. A few states have eliminated their bilingual education programs in favor of 1-year English immersion programs.

20. Teachers can use such technology tools as Internet discussion boards, e-mail exchanges, computer programs, and websites to help ELL students refine their English skills.

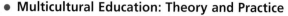

Resources for Further Investigation

● Multicultural Education: Theory and Practice

James Banks offers a detailed discussion of multicultural education in *Teaching Strategies for Ethnic Studies* (8th ed., 2009). Part 1 discusses goals for multicultural programs, key concepts, and planning a multicultural curriculum. Parts 2 through 5 provide background information about 10 ethnic groups and strategies for teaching about each group. The book concludes with such useful appendixes as a list of visual media on U.S. ethnic groups, a list of Internet resources for teaching about ethnic and cultural diversity, and a chronology of key events concerning ethnic groups in U.S. history.

Another practical book is *Comprehensive Multicultural Education: Theory and Practice* (6th ed., 2007), by Christine Bennett. Part 1 of this book (Chapters 1 to 3) presents the case for multicultural education. Part 2 (Chapters 4 and 5) describes assimilation and pluralism among eight culturally diverse groups. Part 3 (Chapters 6, 7, and 8) describes culturally based individual differences and societal inequities that affect teaching and learning. Part 4 (Chapter 9) presents a model for multicultural curriculum development, six instructional goals, and twenty-six lesson plans that address one or another of the six goals. The lessons include statements of goals and objectives, a description of the instructional sequence, a list of needed materials, and a means for evaluating how well the objectives were met.

Paul Gorski outlines how teachers can use the Internet to help them meet their multicultural goals and provides a wealth of online resources in *Multicultural Education and the Internet: Intersections and Integrations* (2nd ed., 2005). Among the many websites mentioned throughout the book is his own, the Multicultural Pavilion (**www.edchange.org/ multicultural**). Some of the features of this site are a teacher's corner, a research room, awareness activities, an index of related websites, and a multicultural awareness quiz.

Another phrase for what we have called culturally relevant pedagogy is "culturally proficient instruction." In the book *Culturally Proficient Instruction* (2nd ed., 2006), Kikanza Nuri Robins, Randall B. Lindsey, Delores B. Lindsey, and Raymond D. Terrell discuss the elements of this method and provide readers with an opportunity to reflect on and record their answers to a set of directions or questions that relate to this approach to teaching. On page 37, for example, the authors pose the following questions and provide space for the reader to write in a response: "Why do you seek to become a culturally proficient instructor? What

do you think that is?" On page 86 they ask the questions, "Have you heard colleagues or other learners excuse the low academic performance of learners in a nondominant group by pointing to the one person who is an outstanding example in that group? How did you react in this situation?"

A large number of multicultural resources are available on the Internet. Several good starting points include:

National Association for Multicultural Education: **www.nameorg.org**

Center for Multicultural Education: **education.washington.edu/cme/index.html**

● Bilingual Education

Judith Lessow-Hurley offers a readable introduction to bilingual education in *The Foundations of Dual Language Instruction* (5th ed., 2009). The use of technology to teach ELLs is discussed in *Teaching English Language Learners Through Technology* (2009), by Tony Erben, Ruth Ban, and Martha Castañeda. Part 3 of this book describes how to use a variety of technology tools (such as listservs, discussion boards, instant messaging, and blogs) and provides sample lessons. Don't overlook the large Resources section at the end of the book.

Avoiding the mistake of treating all ELLs the same is the theme of *Differentiated Literacy Instruction for English Language Learners* (2009), by Alice Quiocho and Sharon Ulanoff. They describe how to tailor the curriculum and instructional processes to the needs of each ELL in your classroom.

For those interested in English-immersion programs or who teach in states in which immersion programs are mandated (such as Arizona and California), *Structured English Immersion: A Step-by-Step Guide for K–6 Teachers and Administrators* (2003), by Johanna Haver, is a useful resource. Ms. Haver, a retired teacher with 32 years of classroom experience, discusses the characteristics of structured English-immersion (SEI) programs and provides concrete examples of SEI teaching methods for K–6 teachers and administrators.

An excellent resource for information on bilingual education is the website of the Center for Applied Linguistics (**www.cal.org/topics/ell**). It provides, for example, a directory of two-way bilingual programs and a set of online articles about two-way programs.

6 Accommodating Student Variability

The Education CourseMate website for this text offers many helpful resources. Go to **CengageBrain.com** to preview this chapter's Concept Maps and Chapter Themes.

KEY POINTS

These key points will help you learn the important information in this chapter. To help you study, they also appear in the margins of the pages, next to the text where they are discussed.

Ability Grouping

- Ability grouping assumes intelligence is inherited, reflected in IQ, and unchangeable and that instruction will be superior
- No research support for between-class ability grouping
- Joplin Plan and within-class ability grouping for math and science produce moderate increases in learning
- Between-class ability grouping negatively influences teaching goals and methods
- Joplin Plan and within-class ability grouping may allow more focused instruction

The Individuals with Disabilities Education Act (IDEA)

- Before placement, student must be given complete, valid, and appropriate evaluation
- IEP must include objectives, services to be provided, criteria for determining achievement
- Students with disabilities must be educated in least restrictive environment
- Mainstreaming: policy of placing students with disabilities in regular classes
- Inclusion policy aims to keep students with disabilities in regular classrooms for entire day
- Students with learning disabilities, speech impairments, intellectual disability, or emotional disturbance most likely to be served under IDEA
- Multidisciplinary assessment team determines whether student needs special services
- Classroom teacher, parents, and several specialists prepare IEP

Students with Intellectual Disability (formerly called Mental Retardation)

- Students with intellectual disability may frustrate easily, lack confidence and self-esteem
- Students with intellectual disability tend to oversimplify, have difficulty generalizing

- Give students with intellectual disability short assignments that can be completed quickly

Students with Learning Disabilities

- Learning disabilities: disorders in basic processes that lead to learning problems not due to other causes
- Students with learning disabilities have problems with perception, attention, memory, metacognition
- Symptoms of ADHD include inattention, hyperactivity, and impulsivity
- Help students with learning disabilities to reduce distractions, attend to important information

Students with Emotional Disturbance

- Emotional disturbance: poor relationships, inappropriate behavior, depression, fears
- Term *behavior disorder* focuses on behavior that needs to be changed, objective assessment
- Students with behavior disorders tend to be either aggressive or withdrawn
- Foster interpersonal contact among withdrawn students
- Use techniques to forestall aggressive or antisocial behavior

Students Who Are Gifted and Talented

- Gifted and talented students show high performance in one or more areas
- Students of color are underrepresented in gifted classes because of overreliance on test scores
- Gifted and talented students differ from their nongifted peers intellectually and emotionally
- Separate classes for gifted and talented students aid achievement but may lower academic self-concept of some students

Using Technology to Assist Exceptional Students

- Universal design for learning (UDL) treats diversity as a strength in learning environments
- Federal legislation has led to the development of various assistive technologies

---

Prior to the twentieth century, few educators had to deal with the challenge of teaching extremely diverse groups of students. Most communities were fairly small, and students in a given school tended to come from similar backgrounds. Many children, especially those of low socioeconomic status (SES), attended school irregularly or not at all. In 1900, for example, only 8.5 percent of eligible students attended high school (Boyer, 1983), and these students were almost entirely from the upper and middle classes (Gutek, 1992). In addition, children with mental, emotional, or physical disabilities were sent to special schools, educated at home, or not educated at all. In comparison with today's schools, earlier student populations were considerably less diverse.

In the preceding chapter, you read about the varieties of cultural and socioeconomic diversity among today's students. This chapter focuses on another dimension of diversity: the twin (but often somewhat fuzzy) concepts of ability and disability. Before explaining how educators attempt to meet the needs of diverse students, we take a brief look at historical developments that helped shape current educational practices.

Revealing Assumptions

In Service of Learning

The Friday meeting becomes lively as soon as Connie asks Don about the lesson on Wednesday. At last Friday's meeting, Don had been very excited that he was going to get a chance to teach a language arts lesson to the second-grade class he had been observing. Celeste and Antonio had given Don lots of feedback on his ideas. As he left the meeting, he had turned to Connie and, with a salute and a big smile, said, "This lesson plan is going to work!"

That was last week; things are different this week. Clearly, the lesson had not gone well. "So, tell us what happened," says Connie.

"Well," says Don, "it started okay, I guess. I passed out the materials and read the 'story-starter.'" His colleagues nod, remembering how confident Don had been last week as he explained that the story-starter would help the students draw characters and actions that, in turn, would help them write about what might happen next. "I was maybe 2 minutes into the lesson," Don continues, "when a little girl—she has a learning disability or something—asked, 'Why are we doing this?' and I thought, 'Uh-oh, here we go.' I had seen her in my observations; she was always disrupting class with her questions. Anyway, I stayed calm and explained again what we were going to do. She smiled and said, 'Oh, okay.' So I read the story-starter again and was just about to get them going on the illustrations, when she asked another question and then another and another. She just kept asking questions and I couldn't get through my lesson plan at all. I only had 25 minutes for the whole lesson and I bet I spent 15 minutes on her. I spent my time answering questions rather than teaching. I think that little girl should be in a special class. I mean, she is a sweet little kid, but she was such a distraction."

Celeste sympathizes. "I know how frustrating it is when one or two kids keep distracting you from getting through a lesson plan you have slaved over for a week."

Connie is quiet for a moment and then says, "Don, I'm wondering: Whose needs focused your thinking on Wednesday? Was your teaching in service of student learning or were you trying to accomplish something else?"

pause & reflect

If we attend carefully to Don's language, he seems to be assuming that teaching means doing what he planned; anything that disrupts his plan disrupts his "teaching." As we learned in our discussion of Piaget's theory in Chapter 2, accommodation requires change. In this chapter we again consider accommodation, but this time in the context of the variety of needs that learners bring with them into the classroom. Don's assumption about the nature of teaching and learning influences his interpretation of what constitutes disruption. How might his assumptions affect his ability to accommodate students who bring special learning needs to his classroom? What does it mean to "accommodate student variability"? Do you think Don was, as Connie put it, "teaching in service of student learning?"

HISTORICAL DEVELOPMENTS

The Growth of Public Education and Age-Graded Classrooms

By 1920, public education in the United States was no longer a small-scale and optional enterprise, largely because of three developments. First, by 1918, all states had passed compulsory attendance laws. Second, child labor laws had been enacted by many states, as well as by Congress in 1916, to eliminate the hiring of children and adolescents in mines and factories. Third, large numbers of immigrant children arrived in the United States from 1901 through 1920. The result was a vast increase in the number and diversity of children attending elementary and high school.

Educators initially dealt with this growth in student variability by forming age-graded classrooms. Introduced in Quincy, Massachusetts, schools in the mid-1800s, these classrooms grouped all students of a particular age together each year to master a certain portion of the school's curriculum (Gutek, 1992). The main assumptions behind this approach were that teachers could be more effective in helping students learn and that students would have more positive attitudes toward themselves and school when classrooms were more homogeneous than heterogeneous (Oakes, 2005; Peltier, 1991). Regardless of whether these assumptions were well founded (an issue we will address shortly), they were (and still are) so widely held by educators that two additional approaches to creating even more homogeneous groups were eventually implemented: ability grouping and special class placement.

Ability-Grouped Classrooms

Ability grouping involved the use of standardized mental ability or achievement tests to create groups of students who were considered very similar to each other in learning ability. In elementary and middle schools, students typically were (and frequently still are) placed in low-, average-, or high-ability groups. At the high school level, students were placed into different tracks that were geared toward such different post-high school goals as college, secretarial work, and vocational school.

Ability grouping was another means for school authorities to deal with the large influx of immigrant students. Because many of these children were not fluent in English and had had limited amounts of education in their native countries, they scored low on standardized tests when compared with American test norms. In addition, many of these children came from poor homes and were in poor health. At the time, their assignment to a low-ability group seemed both logical and appropriate (Wheelock, 1994).

In the next major part of this chapter, we will look at current applications of ability grouping, which now takes several forms and is still used to reduce the normal range of variability in cognitive ability and achievement found in the typical classroom.

Special Education

For children whose abilities and disabilities fell within the normal range, age grading and ability testing were seen as workable approaches to creating more homogeneous classes. However, compulsory attendance laws also brought to school many children with mild to severe mental and physical disabilities. These students were deemed incapable of profiting from any type of normal classroom instruction and so were assigned to special schools. Unfortunately, as Alfred Binet feared, the labeling of a student as "mentally retarded" or "physically disabled" often resulted in a vastly inferior education. Early in the twentieth century, special schools served as convenient dumping grounds for all kinds of children who could not adapt to the regular classroom (Vallecorsa, deBettencourt, & Zigmond, 2000).

In the latter two-thirds of this chapter, we will detail the varied types and degrees of special class placement for children whose intellectual, social, emotional, or physical development falls outside (above as well as below) the range of normal variation. In discussing this approach, we pay particular attention to Public Law (PL) 101-476, the Individuals with Disabilities Education Act (IDEA), which was enacted to counter past excesses of special class placement and to encourage the placement of children with disabilities in regular classes.

ABILITY GROUPING

Ability grouping is a widespread practice (Dornbusch & Kaufman, 2001; Lleras & Rangel, 2009). In the elementary grades, virtually all teachers form separate groups within their classrooms for instruction in reading, and many do so for mathematics as well. At the middle school level, approximately two-thirds to three-fourths of schools assign students to different self-contained classes in one or more subjects on the basis of standardized test scores. This proportion rises to about 85 percent at the high school level, where students are assigned to different classes (e.g., honors, college preparatory, basic) on a subject-by-subject basis (Dornbusch & Kaufman, 2001). At the middle and high school levels, the term *tracking* rather than *ability grouping* is typically used. In this section, we will describe the most common ways in which teachers group students by ability, examine the assumptions that provide the rationale for this practice, summarize research findings on the effectiveness of ability grouping, and look at alternative courses of action.

Types of Ability Groups

Four approaches to ability grouping are popular among educators today: between-class ability grouping, regrouping, the Joplin Plan, and within-class grouping. You may be able to recall a few classes in which one or another of these techniques was used. If not, you will no doubt encounter at least one of them during your first year of teaching.

Between-Class Ability Grouping   The goal of **between-class ability grouping** is for each class to be made up of students who are homogeneous in standardized intelligence or achievement test scores. Three levels of classes are usually formed:

In ability grouping, students are selected and placed in homogeneous groups with other students who are considered to have very similar learning abilities.
© Myrleen Ferguson Cate/ Photo Edit

high, average, and low. Students in one ability group typically have little or no contact with students in other ability groups during the school day. Although each group covers the same subjects, a higher group does so in greater depth and breadth than lower groups. At the high school level, as we mentioned, this approach is often called *tracking*.

Regrouping The groups formed under a **regrouping** plan are more flexible in assignments and narrower in scope than between-class groups. Students of the same age, ability, and grade but from different classrooms come together for instruction in a specific subject, usually reading or mathematics. If a student begins to outperform the other members of the group significantly, a change of group assignment is easier because it involves just that particular subject.

Regrouping has two major disadvantages, however. First, it requires a certain degree of planning and cooperation among the teachers involved. They must agree, for example, to schedule reading and arithmetic during the same periods. Second, many teachers are uncomfortable working with children whom they see only once a day for an hour or so.

Joplin Plan Although regrouping (as described in the previous section) combines students from different classes, the students are all in the same grade level. The **Joplin Plan,** in contrast, combines students across grade levels. For example, all third, fourth, and fifth graders whose grade-equivalent scores in reading are 4.6 (fourth grade, sixth month) would come together for reading instruction. The same would be done for mathematics. The Joplin Plan has the same advantages and disadvantages as simple regrouping, and it is the basis for a successful reading program called Success for All (Kulik, 2003b; Slavin, Madden, Chambers, & Haxby, 2009).

Within-Class Ability Grouping The most popular form of ability grouping, occurring in almost all elementary school classes, **within-class ability grouping** involves the division of a single class of students into two or three groups for reading and math instruction. Like regrouping and the Joplin Plan, within-class ability grouping has the advantages of being flexible in terms of group assignments and being restricted to one or two subjects. One disadvantage of this approach is that the teacher needs to be skilled at keeping the other students in the class productively occupied while working with a particular group. Other disadvantages will be seen as we examine the research later in this section.

pause & reflect

You probably experienced ability grouping in one form or another at the elementary and secondary levels. Think about whether it might have been between-class grouping, regrouping, the Joplin Plan, or within-class grouping. Could you tell which group you were in? Did you have feelings about being in that group?

Assumptions Underlying Ability Grouping

Ability grouping assumes intelligence is inherited, reflected by IQ, and unchangeable and that instruction will be superior

When ability grouping was initiated early in the twentieth century, much less was known about the various factors that affect classroom learning. Consequently, educators simply assumed certain things to be true. One of those assumptions was that intelligence, which affects the capacity to learn, was a fixed, inherited trait and that little could be done to change the learning capacity of individuals. A second assumption was that intelligence was adequately reflected by an intelligence quotient (IQ) score. A third assumption was that all students would learn best when grouped with those of similar ability (Hong & Hong, 2009; Ornstein, Levine, & Gutek, 2011). Although many educators still believe these assumptions are true, the research evidence summarized here and elsewhere in this book casts doubt on their validity.

Evaluations of Ability Grouping

Because ability grouping occurs in virtually all school districts, its effects have been intensively studied (Abrami, Lou, Chambers, Poulsen, & Spence, 2000; Applebee, Langer, Nystrand, & Gamoran, 2003; Callahan, 2005; Kulik, 2003b; Lleras & Rangel, 2009; Lou, Abrami, & Spence, 2000; Robinson, 2008; Yonezawa, Wells, & Serna, 2002). The main findings of these analyses are as follows:

No research support for between-class ability grouping

1. There is little to no support for between-class ability grouping. Students assigned to low-ability classes generally performed worse than comparable students in heterogeneous classes. Students assigned to average-ability classes performed at about the same level as their nongrouped peers. High-ability students sometimes performed slightly better in homogeneous classes than in heterogeneous classes. A report by the Carnegie Corporation on educating adolescents (Jackson & Davis, 2000) noted: "Instruction in tracked classes thus falls short on measures of both equity and excellence. Tracking affects students unequally, both by grouping students of color and economically disadvantaged students in lower tracks and by providing unequal educational opportunities to students. Instruction in lower-track classes is typically far from excellent, often depending on rote memorization and recall, isolated facts, worksheets, and a slow pace" (p. 66). A study conducted in California of high school students learning English as a second language supports the Carnegie report. The academic track in which the high school students were placed was a better predictor of a variety of academic performances—including grades and scores on standardized achievement tests—than was the students' proficiency in English. Lower-track placement meant also that students took fewer classes that would qualify them for college admission (Callahan, 2005; see also Robinson, 2008).

2. Research on the effect of regrouping for reading or mathematics is inconclusive. Some of the relatively few studies that have been done on this form of ability grouping suggest that it can be effective if the instructional pace and level of the text match the student's actual achievement level rather than the student's nominal grade level. In other words, a fifth grader who scores at the fourth-grade level on a reading test should be reading out of a fourth-grade reading book.

Joplin Plan and within-class ability grouping for math and science produce moderate increases in learning

3. The Joplin Plan yields moderately positive effects compared with instruction in heterogeneous classes.

4. Within-class ability grouping in mathematics and science in grades 1 through 12 has produced modestly positive results (about 8 percentile ranks) compared with whole-class instruction and an even smaller positive effect (about 4 percentile ranks) when compared with mixed-ability groups. Average-achieving students benefit most from being placed in homogeneous-ability groups, whereas low-achieving students benefit most from being placed in mixed-ability groups. Because within-class ability grouping for reading is an almost universal practice at every grade level, researchers have not had the opportunity to compare its effectiveness with whole-class reading instruction. Nevertheless, it would be reasonable to expect much the same results for reading as were found for mathematics and science (see Saleh, Lazonder, & De Jong, 2005).

   Research also shows that some within-class grouping practices are more effective than others. The largest positive effects were found in classrooms that had the following two conditions: (1) students were assigned to groups not only on the basis of ability but also on the basis of other factors that contributed to group cohesiveness and (2) cooperative learning techniques were used that included the features of positive interdependence and individual accountability (Abrami et al., 2000; Lou et al., 2000). (See Chapter 13, "Approaches to Instruction," for a discussion of these and other features of cooperative learning.)

5. Students in homogeneously grouped classes scored the same as students in heterogeneously grouped classes on measures of self-esteem.

6. Students in high-ability classes had more positive attitudes about school and higher educational aspirations than did students in low-ability classrooms (Ireson & Hallam, 2009).

7. Between-class ability grouping affected the quality of instruction received by students in several ways:

Between-class ability grouping negatively influences teaching goals and methods

   a. The best teachers were often assigned to teach the highest tracks, whereas the least experienced or weakest teachers were assigned to teach the lowest tracks.

   b. Teachers of high-ability classes stressed critical thinking, self-direction, creativity, and active participation, whereas teachers of low-ability classes stressed working quietly, following rules, and getting along with classmates. This effect was particularly noticeable in math and science.

   c. Teachers of low-ability groups covered less material and simpler material than did teachers of high-ability groups.

   d. Teachers of low-ability students expected and demanded less of them than did teachers of high-ability students.

Despite the evidence against between-class ability grouping, students of color and low-SES students are frequently assigned to the lowest tracks, where they fall further behind White, middle-SES students (Lleras & Rangel, 2009). This situation has prompted accusations of discrimination, and some districts have responded by adopting policies that specifically allow low-track students to enroll in honors courses. However, this technique (sometimes called a "freedom of choice program") does not necessarily increase the participation of students of color in higher-level courses. An examination of this practice in four middle schools and six high schools indicates that it is largely ineffective in encouraging students of color and low-SES students to enroll in honors classes (Yonezawa et al., 2002). The major reasons for the failure of freedom of choice programs are as follows:

   a. In some of the schools studied, low-track students (who were mostly low-income and students of color) were not always informed that they could request honors classes.

   b. In some cases, the requests of low-track students were delayed by such tactics as not being able to get an appointment with a counselor. In fact, some counselors tried to dissuade students from taking an honors or high-track class.

   c. Only after requesting a high-track class did students learn that they needed to have taken prerequisite courses or had to have a minimum grade-point average. In one case, a counselor administered an abbreviated reading comprehension test before allowing students to enroll in advanced courses.

   d. Because of their previous academic placement and history, low-track students felt they did not have the ability or confidence to succeed in advanced classes. They had, in essence, come to identify themselves as "low-track" or "slow" (see Hong & Hong, 2009).

   e. Some students were uninterested in advanced classes because that action would have separated them from their friends and a familiar culture. Others believed that they simply would not be accepted by the other (mostly White, middle-SES) students.

To Group or Not to Group?

The findings just summarized suggest three courses of action. The first course is to discontinue the use of full-day, between-class ability groups or tracks. Despite the fact that most middle and high schools continue to use this form of ability grouping, students do not learn more or have more positive feelings about themselves and

Take a Stand!

Ability Grouping and Tracking: A Practice That Fails to Deliver What It Promises

At the beginning of this book, we stated that an advantage of using scientific methods to study education was that it helped us avoid drawing false conclusions about an idea or practice because of subjective and unsystematic thinking. When people substitute personal values and experience for systematic research findings, educational decisions that are detrimental to students are usually the result. So it is with between-class ability grouping and rigid tracking systems at the middle school and high school levels. Many educators fervently believe that teachers are more effective and students learn more when classrooms are more homogeneous in ability than heterogeneous. But almost all of the research conducted on ability grouping and tracking over the past several decades refutes these beliefs. Consequently, this is a practice that should rarely, if ever, be used. Among other detriments, it destroys the motivation of students and stunts their intellectual growth.

We believe that teachers should speak out forcefully against between-class ability grouping and in favor of the effective instructional practices that can be used with all students, especially cooperative learning and peer tutoring. When the opportunity arises, let your colleagues know that the assumptions they carry about the benefits of ability grouping are not supported by the scientific literature.

What Do You Think?

Do you share the authors' opposition to ability grouping and tracking? Do you think such practices aided or hindered your own educational progress? Explore this subject further at the Take a Stand! section at the textbook's student website, Education CourseMate.

Joplin Plan and within-class ability grouping may allow more focused instruction

school. This is a case in which even widely held beliefs must be modified or eliminated when the weight of evidence goes against them.

The second course of action is to use only those forms of ability grouping that produce positive results: within-class grouping and the Joplin Plan, especially for reading and mathematics. It is unclear why these forms of ability grouping work. It is assumed (Tieso, 2003) that the increase in group homogeneity allows for more appropriate and potent forms of instruction (for example, greater effort by the teacher to bring lower-achieving groups up to the level of higher-achieving groups). If this assumption is correct, within-class ability grouping and the Joplin Plan must be carried out in such a way that homogeneous groups are guaranteed to result. The best way to achieve similarity in cognitive ability among students is to group them on the basis of past classroom performance, standardized achievement test scores, or both. The least desirable (but most frequently used) approach is to base the assignments solely on IQ scores.

The third course of action is to dispense with all forms of ability grouping, a practice called *detracking*. Detracking practices vary widely. When implemented well, however, detracking has been shown to support learning of all students in heterogeneous classrooms (Burris, Wiley, Welner, & Murphy, 2008; Rubin, 2006; Watanabe, 2008).

In keeping with the concept of differentiated instruction mentioned earlier in the book (Tomlinson, Brimijoin, & Narvaez, 2008), teachers can use a variety of organizational and instructional techniques that will allow them to cope with a heterogeneous class, or they can use these same techniques in conjunction with the Joplin Plan or within-class grouping. As you encounter the variety of instructional techniques in the remaining chapters, keep in mind how each technique can be become one more tool for addressing the diverse learning needs of a heterogeneous group of learners.

TeachSource Video Case ◄◄ ► ►►

Inclusion: Grouping Strategies for Inclusive Classrooms

Go to the Education CourseMate website to watch the Video Case, and then answer the following questions:

1. In the Video Case, we see a class that groups students in a heterogeneous fashion. Discuss the pros and cons of this grouping strategy.

2. Describe some of the strategies that the teachers in the Video Case use to ensure that all students participate in their various learning groups.

THE INDIVIDUALS WITH DISABILITIES EDUCATION ACT (IDEA)

Many of the criticisms and arguments marshaled against ability grouping have come to be applied as well to special classes for students with disabilities. In addition, the elimination of racially segregated schools by the U.S. Supreme Court in the case of *Brown v. Board of Education* (1954) established a precedent for providing students with disabilities with an equal opportunity for a free and appropriate education (Ornstein, Levine, & Gutek, 2011). As a result, influential members of Congress were persuaded in the early 1970s that it was time for the federal government to take steps to correct the perceived inequities and deficiencies in our educational system. The result was a landmark piece of legislation, Public Law 94-142, the Education for All Handicapped Children Act of 1975. This law was revised and expanded in 1986 as the Handicapped Children's Protection Act (PL 99-457) and again in 1990 as the Individuals with Disabilities Education Act (IDEA, PL 101-476). IDEA was amended in 1997 to broaden and clarify a number of its provisions ("Individuals with Disabilities," 1997; Ysseldyke, Algozzine, & Thurlow, 2000). It was amended again in 2004 to enhance parental involvement resulting from the No Child Left Behind Act of 2001 (Dardig, 2005), and to provide a method of identifying students with disabilities called "Response to Intervention" or RTI (Fuchs & Fuchs, 2006, 2009). The most recent regulations governing the implementation of IDEA were issued in 2006. (The U.S. Department of Education statistics reported later in the chapter come from its 2006 annual report to Congress on the implementation of IDEA.)

Major Provisions of IDEA

A Free and Appropriate Public Education
The basic purpose of IDEA is to ensure that all individuals from birth through age twenty-one who have an identifiable disability, regardless of how severe, receive at public expense supervised special education and related services that meet their unique educational needs. These services can be delivered in a classroom, at home, in a hospital, or in a specialized institution and may include physical education and vocational education, as well as instruction in the typical academic subjects ("Individuals with Disabilities," 1997).

Preplacement Evaluation

> Before placement, student must be given complete, valid, and appropriate evaluation

Before a child with a disability can be placed in a program that provides special education services, "a full and individual evaluation of the child's educational needs" must be conducted. Such an evaluation must conform to the following rules:

1. Tests must be administered in the child's native language.
2. A test must be valid for the specific purpose for which it is used.
3. Tests must be administered by trained individuals according to the instructions provided by the test publisher.
4. Tests administered to students who have impaired sensory, manual, or speaking skills must reflect aptitude or achievement rather than the impairment.
5. No single procedure (such as an IQ test) can be the sole basis for determining an appropriate educational program. Data should be collected from such non-test sources as observations by other professionals (such as the classroom teacher), medical records, and parental interviews.
6. Evaluations must be made by a multidisciplinary team that contains at least one teacher or other specialist with knowledge in the area of the suspected disability.
7. The child must be assessed in all areas related to the suspected disability ("Individuals with Disabilities," 1997).

When you deal with students whose first language is not English, it is important to realize that standardized tests are designed to reflect cultural experiences common to the United States and that English words and phrases may not mean quite the same thing when translated. Therefore, these tests may not be measuring what they were developed to measure. In other words, they may not be valid. The results of such assessments should therefore be interpreted very cautiously (Kubiszyn & Borich, 2010; Robinson, 2008).

Individualized Education Program Every child who is identified as having a disability and who receives special education services must have an **individualized education program (IEP)** prepared. The IEP is a written statement that describes the educational program that has been designed to meet the child's unique needs. The IEP must include the following elements:

(margin note: IEP must include objectives, services to be provided, criteria for determining achievement)

1. A statement of the child's existing levels of educational performance
2. A statement of annual goals, including short-term instructional objectives
3. A statement of the specific special education and related services to be provided to the child and the extent to which the child will be able to participate in regular educational programs
4. The projected dates for initiation of services and the anticipated duration of the services
5. Appropriate objective criteria and evaluation procedures and schedules for determining, on at least an annual basis, whether short-term objectives are being achieved ("Individuals with Disabilities," 1997)

The IEP is to be planned by a multidisciplinary team composed of the student's classroom teacher in collaboration with a person qualified in special education, one or both of the student's parents, the student (when appropriate), and other individuals at the discretion of the parents or school. (An example of an IEP is depicted later in this chapter in Figure 6.1.)

Least Restrictive Environment According to the 1994 Code of Federal Regulations that governs the implementation of IDEA, educational services must be provided to children with disabilities in the **least restrictive environment** that their disability will allow. A school district must identify a continuum of increasingly restrictive placements (instruction in regular classes, special classes, home instruction, instruction in hospitals and institutions) and, on the basis of the multidisciplinary team's evaluation, select the least restrictive setting that will best meet the student's special educational needs. This provision was often referred to as **mainstreaming** because the goal of the law was to have as many children with disabilities as possible, regardless of the severity of the disability, enter the mainstream of education by attending regular classes with nondisabled students. In recent years, mainstreaming has frequently evolved into *inclusion*, a practice we discuss later in this chapter. The practice becomes controversial when mainstreaming is applied unequally to different ethnic groups, a controversy that mirrors the "achievement gap" and that continues in schools today (Blanchett, Klingner, & Harry, 2009). The controversy is addressed in the Case in Print later in the chapter.

(margin note: Students with disabilities must be educated in least restrictive environment)

(margin note: Mainstreaming: policy of placing students with disabilities in regular classes)

The Policy of Inclusion

Although IDEA calls for children with disabilities to be placed in the least restrictive environment, the law clearly allows for more restrictive placements than those of the regular classroom "when the nature or severity of the disability is such that education in regular classes with the use of supplementary aids and services cannot be achieved satisfactorily" ("Individuals with Disabilities," 1997, p. 61). Nevertheless, there has been a movement in recent years to eliminate this option. Known as **inclusion** or **full inclusion**, this extension of the mainstreaming provision has become one of the most controversial outgrowths of IDEA.

The least restrictive environment provision of IDEA has led to mainstreaming—the policy that children with disabilities should attend regular classes to the maximum extent possible. Some special education proponents argue that full-time regular classroom placement should be the only option for such students.
© Bob Daemmrich/Photo Edit

Inclusion policy aims to keep students with disabilities in regular classrooms for entire day

As most proponents use the term, *inclusion* means keeping special education students in regular classrooms and bringing support services to the children rather than the other way around. *Full inclusion* refers to the practice of eliminating all pullout programs *and* special education teachers and of providing regular classroom teachers with training in teaching special-needs students so that they can teach these students in the regular classroom (Kirk, Gallagher, Coleman, & Anastasiow, 2009; Smith & Tyler, 2010).

The Debate About Inclusion Because of the challenges presented by inclusion, teachers often question the practice. Proponents of inclusion and full inclusion often raise four arguments to support their position:

1. Research suggests that special-needs students who are segregated from regular students perform more poorly academically and socially than comparable students who are mainstreamed (Kavale, 2002).

2. Given the substantial body of evidence demonstrating the propensity of children to observe and imitate more competent children (see, for example, Schunk, 1987), it can be assumed that students with disabilities will learn more by interacting with nondisabled students than by attending homogeneous classes (see Kleinert, Browder, & Towles-Reeves, 2009; Sapon-Shevin, 1996, 2003).

3. The Supreme Court in *Brown v. Board of Education* declared the doctrine of separate but equal to be unconstitutional. Therefore, pullout programs are a violation of the civil rights of children with special needs because these programs segregate them from their nondisabled peers in programs that are assumed to be separate but equal (Kavale, 2002; Mock & Kauffman, 2002; Skrtic, Sailor, & Gee, 1996).

4. Disproportionate numbers of minority students are placed in special education (Artiles, Klingner, & Tate, 2006; Harry & Klingner, 2006). As one example, according to the National Research Council (2002), Black students are disproportionately placed in special education categories, such as "intellectual disabilities" and "learning disabilities" (these and other types of special needs are described later in this chapter). Black students who are placed in special education

achieve at lower levels and are less likely to leave special education placements than their White counterparts (U.S. Department of Education, 2004). The gap in special education not only mirrors the "achievement gap" discussed in Chapter 5 but also results in Black students with special needs being separated from the curriculum that nondisabled peers experience (Blanchett, 2006). This harkens back to the violations of segregation addressed in *Brown v. Board of Education* (see Oakes, 2005) and can also contribute to a lack of tolerance among groups (Sapon-Shevin, 2003).

The opponents of inclusion often cite cases of special-needs students disrupting the normal flow of instruction or of teachers being inadequately prepared to assist learners with special needs (Kavale, 2002; Mock & Kauffman, 2002).

Response to Intervention When the original Individuals with Disabilities Education Act (IDEA) was updated in 2004 to the Individuals with Disabilities Education Improvement Act (called IDEA, 2004), an important change occurred. Prior to IDEA, 2004, school professionals were encouraged to identify children with learning disabilities on the basis of the discrepancy between a student's IQ and her or his achievement. Those whose achievement levels were considerably lower than one would predict on the basis of IQ were identified as having a learning problem. IDEA, 2004 introduced an additional method of identifying students with learning problems: **"Response to Intervention"** or RTI (Bocala, Mello, Reedy, & Lacireno-Paquet, 2009; Fuchs & Fuchs, 2006, 2009; Jackson, Pretti-Frontczak, Harjusola-Webb, Grisham-Brown, & Romani, 2009; Stepanek & Peixotto, 2009).

RTI was introduced as a way to determine how much students benefit from—or are responsive to—the instructional interventions they experience in the classroom. Students who respond to instruction are successful learners. Those who have difficulties with the instruction they encounter, especially in the early grades, have learning problems, placing them at-risk. The idea is to discover problems early because if they go unchecked, the child's difficulties can multiply from grade to grade to the point of dropping out of school. Thus, one of the purposes of RTI was to assess students early, to discover learning problems that students may be having, and to provide support through appropriate, research-based instructional interventions (Fletcher & Vaughn, 2009). A second purpose was to help teachers document each instructional intervention with a student and how well that student responded to each intervention; this documentation would help teachers assess how effective their instructional practices were in advancing student learning (Daly, Martens, Barnett, Witt, & Olson, 2007).

As we will see in later chapters, RTI has evolved as a means of collecting data on student learning and using those data to address learning difficulties that all students will, from time to time, experience. If we think about RTI in the context of the dynamic interactions that constitute teaching and learning, it suggests a teach-test-teach pattern (Fuchs et al., 2007) and moves the purpose of assessment beyond simply the identification of students who may be at-risk to helping all students in all classrooms (Griffiths, VanDerHeyden, Skokut, & Lilles, 2009; VanDerHeyden, Witt, & Gilbertson, 2007). As mentioned, we will revisit RTI again in other chapters. For now, we return to IDEA and the disabling conditions that are addressed in it.

What IDEA Means to Regular Classroom Teachers

By the time you begin your teaching career, the original legislation governing the delivery of educational services to the disabled, PL 94-142, will have been in effect for more than 30 years. Each state was required to have established laws and policies for implementing the various provisions by 1978. The first guiding principle to follow, therefore, is *find out what the local ground rules are.* You will probably be told during orientation meetings about the ways IDEA is being put into effect in your state and local school district. But if such a presentation is not given or is incomplete, it would be wise to ask about guidelines you should follow. Your second guiding principle, then, should be *when in doubt, ask*. With these two caveats in mind, consider some questions you may be asking yourself about the impact of IDEA as you approach your first teaching job.

TeachSource Video Case ◄◄ ▶ ▶▶

Foundations: Aligning Instruction with Federal Legislation

Go to the Education CourseMate website to watch the Video Case, and then answer the following questions:

1. After reading about the inclusion debate and listening to the school professionals in this Video Case, discuss your thoughts and position on this important educational issue.

2. Based on both the teacher interviews in this Video Case and the material you just read about the regular classroom teacher's responsibilities under IDEA, which of these responsibilities do you think are most important? Explain your answer.

What Kinds of Disabling Conditions Are Included Under IDEA?

According to the U.S. Department of Education (2009b), during the 2004–2005 academic year, 5.72 million children and youths from ages six through seventeen (11.6 percent of the total number of individuals in this age group) received special education services under IDEA.

For individuals between the ages of three and twenty, IDEA recognizes twelve categories of disability. A thirteenth category, developmental delay, applies only to children from ages three through nine and is optional for state programs. The first twelve categories described in the legislation are listed as follows in alphabetical order, with brief definitions of each type:

Autism. Significant difficulty in verbal and nonverbal communication and social interaction that adversely affects educational performance.

Deaf-blindness. Impairments of both hearing and vision, the combination of which causes severe communication, developmental, and educational problems. The combination of these impairments is such that a child's educational and physical needs cannot be adequately met by programs designed for only deaf children or only blind children.

Hearing impairment. Permanent or fluctuating difficulty in understanding speech that adversely affects educational performance.

Mental retardation. Significant subaverage general intellectual functioning accompanied by deficits in adaptive behavior (how well a person functions in social environments).

Multiple disabilities. Two or more impairments (such as mental retardation–blindness and mental retardation–orthopedic, but not deaf-blindness) that cause such severe educational problems that a child's needs cannot be adequately met by programs designed solely for one of the impairments.

Orthopedic impairments. Impairment in a child's ability to use arms, legs, hands, or feet that significantly affects that child's educational performance.

Other health impairments. Conditions such as asthma, hemophilia, sickle cell anemia, epilepsy, heart disease, and diabetes that so limit the strength, vitality, or alertness of a child that educational performance is significantly affected.

Case in Print

Who Swims in the Mainstream?

A school district must identify a continuum of increasingly restrictive placements. This provision is often referred to as mainstreaming *because the goal of the law is to have as many children with disabilities as possible, regardless of the severity of the disability, enter the mainstream of education by attending regular classes with non-disabled students. In recent years, mainstreaming has frequently evolved into inclusion. The practice becomes controversial when mainstreaming is applied unequally to different ethnic groups. The controversy mirrors the "achievement gap" and that continues in schools today* (Blanchett, Klingner, & Harry, 2009). *(p. 190)*

Study Finds Special Ed Disparities

LINDA PERLSTEIN
Washington Post, 12/18/2003

African American and Hispanic students in special education were far more likely than white and Asian students in recent years to be educated in special classrooms instead of integrated into the general population, according to a study of special education in Montgomery County Public Schools.

The study also found that students who live in poverty were almost 2½ times more likely than higher-income students to be labeled emotionally disturbed, and African Americans were almost three times more likely than whites to be identified as mentally retarded, a ratio that lowers only slightly when controlling for income.

The report was prepared by Margaret J. McLaughlin and Sandra Embler of the University of Maryland School of Education under the auspices of the county's Continuous Improvement Team. The Board of Education had directed the team to come up with a set of indicators for measuring the status of special education in the county. The report was completed in the summer but presented to the board last week as part of an update on special education services.

"Most of it was anticipated, but to get anything done you have to have a baseline for improvement," said Ricki Sabia, a co-chairman of the Continuous Improvement Team. "The whole point of the report was to bring up these issues, and the next step is to drill down what to do about it."

Black students received an average of 16.8 hours of special education services in total weekly compared with 14.8 for Hispanics and 12.4 hours for whites. Low-income students received 16.3 hours weekly, compared with 12 hours for the rest of the population.

For students with and without disabilities, a gap in academic performance exists by race and by income. Brian Bartels, Montgomery County's director of special education, said this correlation may partially explain why black, Hispanic and low-income disabled students are receiving more intensive services in less integrated environments, not just in Montgomery County but elsewhere in the state as well.

Educators may recommend more intensive services—not necessarily in separate settings—because of the greater instructional needs of students with lower achievement levels, Bartels said.

Attendance rates for special education students were, depending on school level, from 1 percentage point to 3 percentage points lower than rates for students in regular programs. Disparity in absences was greatest in high schools. Students with emotional disabilities and low-income students were most likely to have many absences.

Bartels said depression and behavioral problems may be keeping some emotionally disturbed students home, though he also said the attendance rate may have been skewed by a small number of students with very large numbers of absences.

Regardless of income, Asian American students were less likely than those in any other racial or ethnic group to receive special education services. They were, however, more likely to receive assistance in speech and language.

Thirteen percent of students with disabilities received no scores on the Comprehensive Test of Basic Skills. The CTBS is not used to comply with the federal No Child Left Behind Act, but test participation is a concern because the law requires that 95 percent of students in any group, including special education, take standardized tests.

Of the students who took the test, 70 percent received extra time to complete it, and more than 50 percent of sixth-graders and 25 percent of second-graders used a calculator—both permitted accommodations.

In surveys, special education teachers said parents do not support them in discipline or instruction or recognize their accomplishments, while parents and special education teachers felt that teachers in regular classrooms have low expectations for disabled students.

Questions and Activities

1. The study of special education placements in the Montgomery County (Maryland) school system that is described in this article replicates the findings of other, more recent, studies: compared with White, middle-SES students, a larger percentage of ethnic minority, racial minority, and low-income students are placed in special education classes. What factors, one of which was mentioned in the article, might account for this difference?

2. Assuming for the moment that all of these students met IDEA guidelines for receiving special education services, how likely is it that a special education class is the most appropriate placement (that is, the least restrictive environment) for all or most of these students? Why or why not?

3. The last paragraph of the article indicates that special education teachers, regular education teachers, and parents of students with disabilities are not in agreement about how to handle students with disabilities. Form your own opinion by talking to individuals from these three groups about their views on special education class placement versus mainstreaming. If there are differences, try to identify their basis.

Emotional disturbance. Personal and social problems exhibited in an extreme degree over a period of time that adversely affect a child's ability to learn and get along with others (prior to the 1997 amendments to IDEA, this category was called "serious emotional disturbance").

Specific learning disability. A disorder in one or more of the basic psychological processes involved in understanding or using language that leads to learning problems not traceable to physical disabilities, mental retardation, emotional disturbance, or cultural-economic disadvantage.

Speech or language impairment. A communication disorder such as stuttering, impaired articulation, or a language or voice impairment that adversely affects educational performance.

Traumatic brain injury. A brain injury due to an accident that causes cognitive or psychosocial impairments that adversely affect educational performance.

Visual impairment including blindness. A visual impairment so severe that even with corrective lenses a child's educational performance is adversely affected.

Students with learning disabilities, speech impairments, mental retardation, or emotional disturbance most likely to be served under IDEA

The percentages of each type of student who received special educational services during the 2004–2005 school year are indicated in Table 6.1. As you can see, the children with disabilities who most commonly received services (90 percent of the total) were those classified as having a specific learning disability, a speech or language impairment, mental retardation, or an emotional disturbance.

What Are the Regular Classroom Teacher's Responsibilities Under IDEA? Regular classroom teachers may be involved in activities required directly or indirectly by IDEA in four possible ways: referral, assessment, preparation of the IEP, and implementation and evaluation of the IEP.

Referral Most referrals for assessment and possible special instruction are made by a child's teacher or his or her parents because they are the ones most familiar with the quality of the child's daily work and progress as compared with other children.

Table 6.1	Students Receiving Special Education Services, 2004–2005	
Disabling Condition	Percentage of Total School Enrollment[a]	Percentage of Students with Disabilities Served[b]
Specific learning disabilities	5.42	46.4
Speech or language impairments	2.32	18.8
Mental retardation	1.00	9.3
Other health impairments	1.00	8.4
Emotional disturbance	0.93	7.9
Autism	0.32	2.7
Multiple disabilities	0.23	2.2
Hearing impairments	0.14	1.2
Orthopedic impairments	0.12	1.1
Visual impairments	0.05	0.4
Traumatic brain injury	0.04	0.4
Deaf-blindness	0.00	0.0
Total	**11.57**	**98.8[c]**

[a]Percentages are based on children with disabilities ages 6–17 as a percentage of total school enrollment for kindergarten through 12th grade.

[b]Percentages are based on children with a disability ages 6–21 as a percentage of the total number of students receiving special education.

[c]Percentage does not add to 100 percent because of rounding.

SOURCE: U.S. Department of Education (2009a, 2009b).

Assessment The initial assessment procedures, which must be approved by the child's parents, are usually carried out by school psychologists who are certified to administer tests. If the initial conclusions of the school psychologist support the teacher's or parents' perception that the student needs special services, the

The decision as to whether a child qualifies for special education services under IDEA is made largely on the basis of information supplied by the multidisciplinary assessment team. Classroom teachers typically contribute information about the child's academic and social behavior. Suzie Fitzhugh

> Multidisciplinary assessment team determines whether student needs special services

multidisciplinary assessment team required under IDEA will be formed. Because the 1997 and 2004 amendments of IDEA require that classroom teachers be part of the multidisciplinary assessment team and potentially use RTI, you should be prepared to provide such information as the child's responsiveness to instructional interventions, the quality of the child's homework and test scores, ability to understand and use language, ability to perform various motor functions, alertness at different times of the day, and interpersonal relationships with classmates (Fuchs & Fuchs, 2006, 2009; Kubiszyn & Borich, 2010).

> Classroom teacher, parents, several specialists prepare IEP

Preparation of the IEP At least some, if not all, of the members of the assessment team work with the teacher (and the parents) in preparing the IEP. The necessary components of an IEP were described earlier, and they are illustrated in Figure 6.1.

Implementation and Evaluation of the IEP Depending on the nature and severity of the disability, the student may spend part or all of the school day in a regular classroom or be placed in a separate class or school. If the student stays in a regular classroom, the teacher will be expected to put into practice the various instructional techniques listed in the IEP. Because the IEP is planned by a multidisciplinary team, you will be given direction and support in providing regular class instruction for students who have a disabling condition as defined under IDEA. The classroom teacher may also be expected to determine whether the listed objectives are being met and to furnish evidence of attainment. Various techniques

Figure 6.1 Example of an Individualized Education Program (IEP)

INDIVIDUAL EDUCATIONAL PLAN 11/2008
DATE

STUDENT: Last Name First Middle
5.3 8 - 4 - 98
School of Attendance Home School Grade Level Birthdate/Age

School Address School Telephone Number

Child Study Team Members

Name	Homeroom (Title)	Case Manager	L D Teacher
Name	Facilitator (Title)	Name	Parents (Title)
Name	Speech (Title)	Name	Title
		Name	Title

Summary of Assessment results

IDENTIFIED STUDENT NEEDS: Reading from last half of DISTAR II - present performance level

LONG TERM GOALS: To improve reading achievement level by at least one year's gain. To improve math achievement to grade level. To improve language skills by one year's gain.

SHORT TERM GOALS: Master Level 4 vocabulary and reading skills. Master math skills in basic curriculum. Master spelling words from Level 3 list. Complete units 1-9 from Level 3 curriculum.

MAINSTREAM MODIFICATIONS:

White Copy—Cumulative Folder
Pink Copy—Special Teacher
Goldenrod Copy—Case Manager
Yellow Copy—Parent

Description of Services to Be Provided

Type of Service	Teacher	Starting Date	Amt. of time per day	OBJECTIVES AND CRITERIA FOR ATTAINMENT
SLD level III	LD Teacher	11 - 11 - 96	2 1/2 hrs	Reading: will know all vocabulary through the "Honeycomb" level. Will master skills as presented through Distar II Will know 1 2 3 second - symbols presented in "Sound Way to Reading." Math: will pass all tests at Basic 4 level. Spelling: 5 words each week from level 3 lists Language: will complete Units 1 - 9 of the 4th grade language program. Will also complete supplemental units from "Language Step by Step."

Mainstream Classes	Teacher	Amt. of time per day	OBJECTIVES AND CRITERIA FOR ATTAINMENT
		3 1/2 hrs	Out of seat behavior: Sit attentively and listen during mainstream class discussions. A simple management plan will be implemented if he does not meet this expectation. Mainstream modifications of Social Studies: will keep a folder in which he expresses through drawing the topics his class will cover. Modified district Social Studies curriculum. No formal testing will be made.

The following equipment and other changes in personnel, transportation, curriculum methods, and educational services will be provided: Distar II Reading Program, Spelling Level 3, "Sound Way to Reading" Program, Vocabulary tapes

Substantiation of least restrictive alternatives: The planning team has determined academic needs are best met with direct SLD support in reading, math, language, and spelling

ANTICIPATED LENGTH OF PLAN 1 yr. The next periodic review will be held: May 2009
DATE/TIME/PLACE

☐ I approve this program placement and the above IEP
☐ I do not approve this placement and/or the IEP
☐ I request a conciliation conference

PARENT/GUARDIAN

Form 2011 Principal or Designee

of instruction, as well as approaches to evaluation that stress student mastery of individualized assignments, will be discussed in several of the chapters that follow.

Section 504: A Broader View of Disabling Conditions   The civil rights movement of the 1960s led to the Vocational Rehabilitation Act of 1973. Section 504 of that act prevents discrimination against people with disabilities who participate in any federally funded program, which includes public schools. The Americans with Disabilities Act Amendments Act of 2008 (ADAAA), which became effective on January 1, 2009, broadens the interpretation of disability as it is applied in Section 504. The ADAAA addresses the possibility that some students in your class who are not covered by IDEA may have a condition that, if not addressed, could limit their access to and participation in learning opportunities. In such cases, under ADAAA, the school must provide a plan to overcome the limitation. For example, a student with diabetes may need accommodations to monitor and control her blood sugar levels. A 504 plan for the student with diabetes may include a "private space" in the school or classroom for testing. Most 504 plans cover students with health or medical challenges or those with attention-deficit/hyperactivity disorder who are not already covered by IDEA.

Regardless of whether a disability is covered legally through IDEA or through ADAAA changes to Section 504, the types of students you will sometimes be expected to teach in your classroom will vary. Some will be special education students who are included in your classroom for part of the school day. Others, although different from many students in some noticeable respect, will not qualify for special education services under IDEA. The remainder of this chapter will describe students from both categories and techniques for teaching them. Students with intellectual disability, learning disabilities, and emotional disturbance often require special forms of instruction, and we will focus on these categories. In addition, though not mentioned in IDEA or Section 504, students who are gifted and talented require special forms of instruction, as we will also discuss.

pause & reflect

Many teachers say that although they agree with the philosophy behind IDEA, they feel that their training has not adequately prepared them to meet the needs of students with disabling conditions. Would you say the same about your teacher education program? Why? What might you do to prepare yourself better?

STUDENTS WITH INTELLECTUAL DISABILITY (FORMERLY CALLED MENTAL RETARDATION)

Definition of Intellectual Disability

On January 1, 2007, the American Association on Mental Retardation (AAMR) became the American Association on Intellectual and Developmental Disabilities (AAIDD) and in 2009, the premier research journal of the 130-year-old organization changed from the *American Journal on Mental Retardation* to the *American Journal on Intellectual and Developmental Disabilities*. The name changes were made to reflect the scope of the work that is done by researchers and the organization, to better advocate for political and social change, and to find a more socially acceptable way of addressing people with an intellectual disability. AAIDD defines **intellectual disability** as "...a disability characterized by significant limitations both in intellectual functioning and in adaptive behavior, which covers many everyday social and practical skills. This disability originates before the age of 18" (American Association on Intellectual and Developmental Disabilities, 2009).

Although we will use the term *intellectual disability* from this point on in the chapter, you will recall earlier references to "mental retardation" as one of the disabling conditions included under IDEA and in Table 6.1. Our reason for using the old term is that the language of IDEA still refers to it. Indeed, the percentages and the disabling conditions reported in Table 6.1 are taken directly from the annual report on IDEA submitted by the U.S. Department of Education to Congress in 2009. It will undoubtedly take some time for the term "mental retardation" to disappear from educational discourse and so we expect that educators will have to live with both terms for some period to come. Nevertheless, the name change is not purely "cosmetic." The term "intellectual disability" differs from "mental retardation" in important, albeit subtle, ways.

Older notions of mental retardation used IQ score as the key criterion. An individual whose score is two or more standard deviations below the mean (a score of 70 to 75 or below) on a standardized test of intelligence is considered to have a significant limitation in intellectual functioning. (If you're not sure what a standard deviation is, take a look now at Chapter 15, "Understanding Standardized Assessment," in which we discuss this statistical concept.)

The new definition of intellectual disability is documented in the 11th edition of the AAIDD Definition Manual entitled *Intellectual Disability: Definition, Classification, and Systems of Supports* (Schalock et al., 2010). The book, seven years in the writing, is authored by 18 experts[1] and focuses on both intellectual functioning and adaptive behavior in three areas: conceptual skills, social skills, and practical, everyday living skills. Thus, understanding intellectual disability is not simply interpreting a number on a test, but interpreting how well one develops adaptive behaviors that allow one to live successfully within her or his environment. Perhaps this new view reminds you of Sternberg's triarchic theory of intelligence, also known as the theory of successful intelligence. Sternberg's idea that intelligence manifests itself in a variety of ways in a variety of contexts is consistent with the effort to replace the idea of mental retardation with the concept of intellectual disability. That concept includes a multifaceted evaluation and ties that evaluation to a system for planning and providing supports that helps the student with intellectual disability participate successfully in daily life.

Characteristics of Children with Intellectual Disability

Students with intellectual disability may frustrate easily, lack confidence and self-esteem

Students who have below-average IQ scores follow the same general developmental pattern as their peers with higher IQ scores, but they differ in the rate and degree of development. Accordingly, students with low IQ scores may possess social and practical skills typical of students with average IQ scores who are younger than they are. One general characteristic of such students, therefore, is that they often appear immature compared with their age-mates. Immature students are likely to experience frustration frequently when they find they are unable to do things their classmates can do, and many students with intellectual disability tend to have a low tolerance for frustration and a tendency toward low self-esteem, low confidence, and low motivation. These feelings, in conjunction with the cognitive deficits outlined in the next paragraph, sometimes make it difficult for the child with intellectual disability to make friends and get along with peers of average ability.

Students with intellectual disability tend to oversimplify, have difficulty generalizing

The cognitive characteristics of children with intellectual disability include a tendency to oversimplify concepts, limited ability to generalize, smaller memory capacity, shorter attention span, the inclination to concentrate on only one aspect of a learning situation and to ignore other relevant features, the inability to formulate learning strategies that fit particular situations, and delayed language development. These children also show a limited amount of *metacognition*, that is, knowledge about how one learns and the factors that affect learning. (This concept will be discussed more fully in Chapter 8, "Information-Processing Theory.")

---

[1]Schalock, R., Borthwick-Duffy, S., Bradley, V., Buntinx, W., Coulter, D., Craig, E., Gomez, S., Lachapelle, Y., Luckasson, R., Reeve, A., Shogren, K., Snell, M., Spreat, S., Tassé, M., Thompson, J., Verdugo-Alonso, M., Wehmeyer, M., & Yeager, M. (2010).

Several of these cognitive deficits often operate in concert to produce or contribute to the learning problems of students with intellectual disability. Consider, for example, the problem of generalization (also known as transfer). This refers to the ability of a learner to take something that has been learned in one context, such as paper-and-pencil arithmetic skills, and use it to deal with a similar but different task, such as knowing whether one has received the correct change after making a purchase at a store. Students with mild intellectual disability may not spontaneously exhibit transfer because (1) their metacognitive deficits limit their tendency to look for signs of similarity between two tasks, (2) their relatively short attention span prevents them from noticing similarities, and (3) their limited memory capacity and skills lessen their ability to recall relevant knowledge.

These characteristics can be understood more completely if they are related to Jean Piaget's description of cognitive development. Middle and high school students with intellectual disability may never move beyond the level of concrete operations. They may be able to deal with concrete situations but find it difficult to grasp abstractions, generalize from one situation to another, or state and test hypotheses. Younger children with intellectual disability tend to classify things in terms of a single feature.

The following Suggestions for Teaching take into account the characteristics just described, as well as points made by Michael Hardman, Clifford Drew, and M. Winston Egan (2011); William L. Heward (2009); Nancy Hunt and Kathleen Marshall (2006); Samuel Kirk, James Gallagher, Mary Ruth Coleman, and Nicholas Anastasiow (2009); and Deborah Deutsch Smith and Naomi Chowdhuri Tyler (2010).

Suggestions for Teaching

Instructing Students with Intellectual Disability

JOURNAL ENTRY
Helping Students with
Intellectual Disability Deal
with Frustration

1 **As much as possible, try to avoid placing students with intellectual disability in situations that are likely to lead to their frustration. When, despite your efforts, such students indicate that they are close to their limit of frustration tolerance, encourage them to engage in relaxing change-of-pace pursuits or in physical activities.**

Because children with intellectual disability are more likely to experience frustration than their more capable peers, try to minimize the frequency of such experiences in the classroom. Probably the most effective way to do this is to give students with intellectual disability individual assignments so that they are not placed in situations in which their work is compared with that of others. No matter how hard you try, however, you will not be able to eliminate frustrating experiences, partly because you will have to schedule some all-class activities and partly because even individual assignments may be difficult for a child with intellectual disability to handle. If you notice that such a student appears to be getting more and more bothered by an inability to complete a task, you might try to divert attention to a less demanding form of activity or allow the student to take a short break by sharpening pencils or going for a drink of water.

2 **Do everything possible to encourage a sense of self-esteem.**

Children with intellectual disability are prone to devalue themselves because they are aware that they are less capable than their classmates at doing many things. One way to combat this tendency toward self-devaluation is to make a point of showing that you have positive feelings about less capable students. You might, for example, say something like, "I'm so glad you're here today. You make the classroom a nicer place to be in." If you indicate that you have positive feelings about an individual, that person is likely to acquire similar feelings about herself.

As you saw in the preceding chapter, many teachers, usually inadvertently, tend to communicate low expectations to some of their students. To avoid committing the same error, you might do one or more of the following: make it clear that you will allow plenty of time for all students to come up with an answer to a question, repeat the question and give a clue before asking a different question, remind yourself to give frequent personal attention to students with intellectual disability, or try to convey to these students the expectation that they *can* learn. Perhaps the best overall strategy to use in building self-esteem is to help children with intellectual disability successfully complete learning tasks. Suggestions 3 through 5 offer ideas you might use.

3 **Present learning tasks that contain a small number of elements, at least some of them familiar to students, and that can be completed in a short period of time.**

Because students with intellectual disability tend to oversimplify concepts, try to provide learning tasks that contain only a few elements, at least some of which they have previously learned. For example, you might ask middle or secondary school social studies students with intellectual disability to prepare a report on the work of a single police officer, as opposed to preparing an analysis of law enforcement agencies (which might be an appropriate topic for the most capable student in the class).

Also, because students with intellectual disability tend to have a short attention span, short assignments are preferable to long ones.

4 **Try to arrange what is to be learned into a series of small steps, each of which leads to immediate feedback.**

Again because of their short attention span, students with intellectual disability may become distracted or discouraged if they are asked to concentrate on demanding tasks that lead to a delayed payoff. Therefore, it is better to give a series of short activities that produce immediate feedback than to use any sort of contract approach or the equivalent, in which the student is expected to engage in self-directed effort leading to a remote goal.

Students who lack confidence, tend to think of one thing at a time, are unable to generalize, and have a short memory and attention span usually respond quite positively to programmed instruction and certain forms of computer-assisted instruction (described more completely in Chapter 7, "Behavioral Learning Theory: Operant Conditioning"). Some computer programs offer a systematic step-by-step procedure that emphasizes only one specific idea per step or frame. They also offer immediate feedback. These characteristics closely fit the needs of children with intellectual disability. You might look for computer programs in the subject or subjects you teach or develop your own materials, perhaps in the form of a workbook of some kind.

5 **Teach simple techniques for improving memory, and consistently point out how use of these techniques leads to more accurate recall.**

In Chapter 9, "Social Cognitive Theory," we describe a set of memory aids called *mnemonic devices*. Used for thousands of years by scholars and teachers in different countries, most are fairly simple devices that help a learner organize information,

JOURNAL ENTRY
Combating the Tendency to Communicate Low Expectations

JOURNAL ENTRY
Giving Students with Intellectual Disability Simple Assignments

Give students with intellectual disability short assignments that can be completed quickly

encode it meaningfully, and generate cues that allow it to be retrieved from memory when needed. The simplest mnemonic devices are rhymes, first-letter mnemonics (also known as acronyms), and sentence mnemonics. For example, a first-letter mnemonic or acronym for the Great Lakes is *HOMES:* Huron, Ontario, Michigan, Erie, Superior.

6 **Devise and use record-keeping techniques that make it clear that students have completed assignments successfully and are making progress.**

JOURNAL ENTRY
Giving Students with
Intellectual Disability Proof
of Progress

Students who are experiencing difficulties in learning are especially in need of tangible proof of progress. When, for instance, they correctly fill in blanks in a programmed workbook and discover that their answers are correct, they are encouraged to go on to the next question. You might use the same basic approach in more general ways by having students with intellectual disability keep their own records showing their progress. (This technique might be used with all students in a class.) For example, you could make individual charts for primary grade students. As they successfully complete assignments, have them color in marked-off sections, stick on gold stars or the equivalent, or trace the movement of animal figures, rockets, or something else toward a destination.

STUDENTS WITH LEARNING DISABILITIES

By far the greatest number of students who qualify for special education under IDEA are those classified as having **learning disabilities.** According to U.S. Department of Education (2009a) figures, the number of students identified as learning disabled increased from approximately 800,000 in 1976–1977 to more than 2.5 million in 2004–2005. In the 1976–1977 school year, students with learning disabilities accounted for about 24 percent of the disabled population. By the 2004–2005 school year, that estimate had grown to nearly 50 percent. Especially because so many students are now classified as learning disabled, it is important to define and explore the characteristics of students with learning disabilities.

Characteristics of Students with Learning Disabilities

According to IDEA, an individual who has a specific learning disability can be described as follows:

Learning disabilities: disorders in
basic processes that lead to
learning problems not due to
other causes

1. The individual has a *disorder in one or more of the basic psychological processes.* These processes refer to intrinsic prerequisite abilities such as memory, auditory perception, and visual perception.
2. The individual has *difficulty in learning,* specifically in the areas of speaking, listening, writing, reading (word recognition skills and comprehension), spelling, and mathematics (calculation and reasoning).
3. The problem is *not due primarily to other causes,* such as visual or hearing impairments, motor disabilities, mental retardation, emotional disturbance, or economic, environmental, or cultural disadvantage.

In addition to problems with cognitive processing and learning, many students with a learning disability (as well as students with intellectual disability and students with emotional disturbance) have more poorly developed social skills than their nondisabled peers. Such students are more likely to ignore the teacher's directions, cheat, use profane language, disturb other students, disrupt group activities, and start fights. Consequently, they are often rejected by the rest of the class, which contributes to lowered self-esteem and poor academic performance (Gresham & MacMillan, 1997; Toth & King, 2010).

Some people dismiss the notion of learning disability as a fiction because, they say, everyone at one time or another has misread numbers, letters, and words; confused pronunciations of words and letters; and suffered embarrassing lapses of attention and memory. But students with learning disabilities really are different from others—mostly in degree rather than in kind. Although the individual without a disability may occasionally exhibit lapses in basic information processing, the individual with a learning disability does so consistently and with little hope of self-correction. The important point to keep in mind is that you need to know what a student with a learning disability (as well as a low-achieving student without a learning disability) can and cannot do so that you can effectively remediate those weaknesses (Lerner & Johns, 2009; Spear-Swerling & Sternberg, 1998).

Identifying Students with Learning Disabilities

The major criterion used by most school districts to identify children with learning disabilities is at least an average score on a standardized test of intelligence and a significantly below average score (one standard deviation or more) on a standardized achievement test. In other words, districts typically look for a discrepancy between achievement and IQ scores.

Because about 80 percent of children with learning disabilities have difficulty with reading (Meyer, 2000), a considerable amount of research has been done to determine whether a discrepancy between IQ and reading comprehension scores is a valid indicator of a learning disability. One approach to this problem has been to compare children who exhibit the discrepancy we just described with children whose IQ and reading scores are both below average. Researchers often refer to students in the first group as IQ-discrepant and students in the second group as IQ-consistent. Two analyses of almost four dozen studies that have examined this issue (Meyer, 2000; Steubing et al., 2002) conclude that IQ-consistent students are indistinguishable from IQ-discrepant students in terms of reading skills (such as phonological awareness and word naming) and behavior (such as social skills and fine motor skills).

This research casts doubt on the usefulness of the discrepancy criterion. Learning disabilities certainly exist, but educators may need to develop a more sophisticated means of identifying them.

Students with a learning disability learn more slowly than other students because of difficulties in perception, attention, and memory.
© Mike Goldwater/Alamy

Problems with Basic Psychological Processes

The fundamental problem that underlies a learning disability is, as the law states, "a disorder in one or more basic psychological processes." Although this phrase is somewhat vague, it generally refers to problems with how students receive information, process it, and express what they have learned. Specifically, many students with learning disabilities have deficits in perception, attention, memory encoding and storage, and metacognition.

Some students with learning disabilities have great difficulty perceiving the difference between certain sounds (*f* and *v*, *m* and *n*, for example) or letters (*m* and *n*, or *b*, *p*, and *d*, for example). As a result, words that begin with one letter (such as *v*ase) are sometimes perceived and pronounced as if they begin with another letter (as in *f*ase). As you can no doubt appreciate from this simple example, this type of deficit makes learning to read and reading with comprehension long and frustrating for some students.

Many students with learning disabilities also have difficulty with attention and impulse control: focusing on a task, noticing important cues and ideas, and staying with the task until it is completed. The source of the distraction may be objects and activities in the classroom, or it may be unrelated thoughts. In either case, the student misses much of what the teacher says or what is on a page of text or misinterprets directions.

Because so many students with learning disabilities have problems with perception and attention, they also have problems with accurate recall of information. Accurate recall is heavily dependent on what is stored in memory in the first place and where information is stored in memory (Hunt & Marshall, 2006), so students who encode partial, incorrect, or unimportant information have memory problems.

Like students with intellectual disability, many students with learning disabilities have a deficit in metacognitive skills (Hunt & Marshall, 2006). As a result, their learning activities are chaotic, like those of young children. For example, they may begin a task before they have thought through all of the steps.

Students with learning disabilities tend to be characterized as passive and disorganized: passive in the sense that they take few active steps to attend to relevant information, store it effectively in memory, and retrieve it when needed; and disorganized in the sense that their learning activities are often unplanned and subject to whatever happens to capture their attention at the moment.

Given these problems with basic processes, researchers have studied ways to help students structure the way they learn. For example, one approach to improving the reading skills of students with learning disabilities that shows some promise is teaching students how to use reading comprehension strategies (Gersten, Fuchs, Williams, & Baker, 2001). One such program that was tested on middle school students with reading disabilities (Bryant et al., 2000) contained the following components:

1. *Word identification:* Students used a first-letter mnemonic to help them recall the seven steps involved in decoding multisyllabic words.
2. *Partner reading:* To improve reading fluency (reading whole words in text accurately and at an appropriate speed), pairs of students modeled fluent reading for one another and helped each other decode unfamiliar words.
3. *Collaborative strategic reading:* This technique is aimed at improving reading comprehension and combines two proven instructional techniques—reciprocal teaching and cooperative learning (we discuss both techniques in detail in later chapters). Students first learn how to use the four comprehension-aiding techniques that are part of reciprocal teaching: (a) previewing a reading passage to help students make predictions about what they will read and already know about the topic, (b) monitoring reading to identify and fix comprehension failures, (c) identifying main ideas, and (d) asking questions and reviewing. Students then apply the techniques by working either in pairs or small cooperative groups.

> Students with learning disabilities have problems with perception, attention, memory, metacognition

Compared with pretest scores, students using these reading comprehension strategies achieved higher posttest scores on word identification, reading fluency, and reading comprehension tests. The differences for word identification and reading fluency were statistically significant (meaning they were not likely due to chance).

Attention-Deficit/Hyperactivity Disorder

Many children who have a learning disability are also diagnosed as having **attention-deficit/hyperactivity disorder (ADHD)**. Estimates of the extent to which these two conditions co-occur range from 25 to 40 percent (Lerner, 2003; Lerner & Johns, 2009). Approximately 3.3 percent of six- to eleven-year-old children have ADHD alone, with boys outnumbering girls by at least three to one (Bowman, 2002). In addition, some studies have found that as many as 30 percent of children with ADHD exhibit aggressive behaviors (such as fighting, stealing, lying, and vandalism) that are consistent with the psychiatric diagnosis of conduct disorder (Connor, 2002). The co-occurrence of ADHD and conduct disorder (called *comorbidity*) is seen more frequently among children from urban homes than middle-SES suburban homes and is associated with significant social, behavioral, and academic problems (Bloomquist & Schnell, 2002).

Symptoms of ADHD include inattention, hyperactivity, and impulsivity

The American Psychiatric Association recognizes three types of children with ADHD: (1) children who are predominantly inattentive, (2) children who are predominantly hyperactive and impulsive, and (3) children who exhibit a combination of all three behaviors. For a student to be judged as having ADHD, the symptoms have to appear before the age of seven; they have to be displayed in several settings, such as at home, at school, and at play; and they have to persist over time (American Psychiatric Association, 2000). Although ADHD is not mentioned in IDEA as a separate disability category, services for children with ADHD can be funded under the "specific learning disabilities" category, the "emotionally disturbed" category, or the "other health impaired" category of IDEA (Lerner, 2003).

In general, the treatments for ADHD fall into one of the following three categories (Lerner, 2003; Purdie, Hattie, & Carroll, 2002):

1. *Prescribed stimulant medication:* The most popular class of drugs prescribed for children with ADHD is psychostimulants. The psychostimulants that are prescribed most often are Ritalin, Dexedrine, Cylert, and Adderall. The effect of these medications is highly specific. Some children do better on one drug, others on another, and still others do not respond to any of them.

2. *School-based psychological/educational programs:* These programs typically involve behavior management, cognitive behavioral therapy, or classroom environment restructuring. Behavior management programs (which we describe in more detail in Chapter 7, "Behavioral Learning Theory: Operant Conditioning") involve the systematic use of reinforcement and punishment to increase the frequency of desired behaviors and decrease the frequency of undesired behaviors. Cognitive behavior therapy programs involve teaching students to remind themselves to use effective learning skills, monitor their progress, and reinforce themselves. Classroom environment restructuring programs use such techniques as reducing classroom noise, assigning students permanent seats, seating students with ADHD at the front of the class, and providing frequent breaks between tasks.

3. *Multimodal programs:* Multimodal programs involve combinations of one or more of the preceding treatments, typically stimulant medications and cognitive behavioral programs.

An analysis of 74 research studies (Purdie et al., 2002) found, not surprisingly, that an overall best treatment for ADHD does not exist. Rather, different treatments had stronger effects depending on the outcome that was being examined. For example, stimulant medications were more effective than other treatments in minimizing impulsivity, hyperactivity, and attentional deficits; multimodal programs were most effective in reducing classmates' dislike and fostering more effective prosocial skills and positive peer interactions; and school-based programs were most effective in aiding the growth of cognitive skills.

The following Suggestions for Teaching will give you some ideas about how to help students with learning disabilities and ADHD improve their learning skills and feel better about themselves.

Suggestions for Teaching

Instructing Students with Learning Disabilities and ADHD

1 **Structure learning tasks to help students with learning disabilities and ADHD compensate for weaknesses in psychological processes.**

JOURNAL ENTRY
Helping Students with
Learning Disabilities
Improve Basic Learning
Processes

Because of their weaknesses in basic psychological processes, students with learning disabilities and ADHD are often distractible, impulsive, forgetful, disorganized, poor at comprehension, and unaware of the factors that affect learning. Research findings indicate that the most effective instructional approach in such cases is one that combines direct instruction with strategy instruction (both methods are described in Chapter 13, "Approaches to Instruction"). This combined approach has produced substantial improvements in reading comprehension, vocabulary, word recognition, memory, writing, cognitive processing, and self-concept (Lerner & Johns, 2009; Rotter, 2009; Swanson & Hoskyn, 1998).

The following examples are consistent with an instructional approach that is based on both direct instruction and strategy instruction.

EXAMPLES

- For students who have difficulty distinguishing between similar-looking or -sounding stimuli (such as letters, words, or phrases), point out and highlight their distinguishing characteristics. For example, highlight the circular part of the letters *b, p,* and *d* and place a directional arrow at the end of the straight segment to emphasize that they have the same shape but differ in their spatial orientation. Or highlight the letters *t* and *r* in the words *though, thought,* and *through* to emphasize that they differ from each other by the absence or presence of one letter.

- For students who are easily distracted, instruct them to place only the materials being used on top of the desk or within sight.

- For students who seem unable to attend to important stimuli such as significant sections of a text page, show them how to underline or outline in an effort to distinguish between important and unimportant material. Or suggest that they use a ruler or pointing device under each line as they read so that they can evaluate one sentence at a time. To help them attend to important parts of directions, highlight or write keywords and phrases in all capitals. For especially important tasks, you might want to ask students to paraphrase or repeat directions verbatim.

- For students who have a short attention span, give brief assignments, and divide complex material into smaller segments. After each short lesson segment, provide both immediate positive feedback and tangible evidence of progress. (Many sets of published materials prepared for use with students with learning disabilities are designed in this way.)

Suggestions for Teaching

Help students with learning disabilities to reduce distractions, attend to important information

- To improve students' memory for and comprehension of information, teach memorization skills and how to relate new information to existing knowledge schemes to improve long-term storage and retrieval. Also, make frequent use of simple, concrete analogies and examples to explain and illustrate complex, abstract ideas. (We will describe several techniques for enhancing memory and comprehension in Chapter 9, "Social Cognitive Theory.")

- To improve organization, suggest that students use a notebook to keep a record of homework assignments, a checklist of materials needed for class, and a list of books and materials they need to take home for studying and homework.

- To improve general awareness of the learning process, emphasize the importance of thinking about the factors that could affect one's performance on a particular task, of forming a plan before actually starting to work, and of monitoring the effectiveness of learning activities.

- Consider the variety of learning environments available through multimedia software programs. Some students with learning disabilities may respond better to a combination of visual and auditory information, whereas others may learn best in a hands-on setting. Multimedia programs provide options to address these different styles and also allow the student to control the direction and pace of learning. Examples of such programs can be found on the Special Needs page of the website of the Educational Software Directory (**www.educational-software-directory.net**).

2 **Capitalize on the resources in your classroom to help students with learning disabilities and ADHD improve academically, socially, and emotionally.**

Although you and the resource teacher will be the main sources of instruction and support for mainstreamed students, recognize that other sources of classroom support are almost always available. The other students in your class, for example, can supplement your instructional efforts. As we pointed out in the previous chapter, peer tutoring typically produces gains in achievement and improvements in interpersonal relationships and attitudes toward subject matter. These effects have been documented for students with learning disabilities as well as for low-achieving students without learning disabilities (Fuchs, Fuchs, Mathes, & Simmons, 1997). And do not overlook the benefits of having students with learning disabilities play the role of tutor. Giving students with disabilities the opportunity to tutor either a low-achieving classmate in a subject that is not affected by the student's disability or a younger student in a lower grade can produce a noticeable increase in self-esteem.

Another way to make use of the other students in your class is through cooperative learning. This technique was described in the last chapter and is explored in more detail in Chapter 13, "Approaches to Instruction." Like peer tutoring, which it incorporates, cooperative learning also produces gains in achievement, interpersonal relationships, and self-esteem.

Finally, make use of the various ways in which information can be presented to students and in which students can respond. In addition to text material and lecturing, you can use films, computer-based presentations, picture charts, diagrams, and demonstrations. In addition to having students demonstrate what they have learned through paper-and-pencil tests and other written products, you can have them make oral presentations, produce pictorial products, create an actual product, or give a performance. Hands-on activities are particularly useful for students with ADHD.

More ideas for your journal can be found in the Reflective Journal Questions at the textbook's student website, Education CourseMate.

STUDENTS WITH EMOTIONAL DISTURBANCE

Estimates of Emotional Disturbance

In the 2009 report to Congress on the implementation of IDEA, the U.S. Department of Education noted that 453,795 students between the ages of six and seventeen were classified as emotionally disturbed in the 2004–2005 school year. This figure accounted for 8 percent of all schoolchildren with disabilities and slightly less than 1 percent of the general school-age population. Not everyone agrees that these figures accurately reflect the scope of the problem. Other scholars believe that 3 to 5 percent of all school-age children qualify for special education services under IDEA's emotional disturbance criteria (Heward, 2009).

Definitions of Emotional Disturbance

Emotional disturbance: poor relationships, inappropriate behavior, depression, fears

Two reasons that estimates of **emotional disturbance** vary are the lack of clear descriptions of such forms of behavior and different interpretations of the descriptions that do exist. Children with *emotional disturbance* are defined in IDEA in this way:

(I) The term means a condition exhibiting one or more of the following characteristics over a long period of time and to a marked degree that adversely affects a child's educational performance:
  (A) An inability to learn that cannot be explained by intellectual, sensory, or health factors;
  (B) An inability to build or maintain satisfactory interpersonal relationships with peers and teachers;
  (C) Inappropriate types of behavior or feelings under normal circumstances;
  (D) A general pervasive mood of unhappiness or depression; or
  (E) A tendency to develop physical symptoms or fears associated with personal or school problems.
(II) The term includes schizophrenia. The term does not apply to children who are socially maladjusted, unless it is determined that they have a serious emotional disturbance. (Office of the Federal Register, 1994, pp. 13–14)

Several special education scholars (Kirk et al., 2009; Heward, 2009; Smith & Tyler, 2010) point out the difficulties caused by vague terminology in distinguishing between students who have emotional disturbance and students who do not. The phrase *a long period of time*, for example, is not defined in the law (although many special education experts use 6 months as a rough rule of thumb). Indicators such as *satisfactory interpersonal relationships*, *a general pervasive mood*, and *inappropriate types of behavior or feelings under normal circumstances* are difficult to measure objectively and can often be observed in nondisturbed individuals. Because long-term observation of behavior is often critical in making a correct diagnosis of emotional disturbance, you can aid the multidisciplinary assessment team in this task by keeping a behavioral log of a child you suspect may have this disorder.

Term *behavior disorder* focuses on behavior that needs to be changed, objective assessment

That many educators and psychologists use such terms as *emotionally disturbed*, *socially maladjusted*, and *behavior disordered* synonymously makes matters even more confusing. The term **behavior disorder** has many adherents and has been adopted by several states for two basic reasons. One reason is that it calls attention to the actual behavior that is disordered and needs to be changed. The second reason is that behaviors can be directly and objectively assessed. Although there are subtle differences between the terms *emotionally disturbed* and *behavior disorder*, they are essentially interchangeable, and you can probably assume that those who use them are referring to children who share similar characteristics. Because of the nature of bureaucracies, however, it may be necessary for anyone hoping to obtain special assistance for a child with what many contemporary psychologists would call a behavior disorder to refer to that child as *emotionally disturbed*, as that is the label used in IDEA.

Characteristics of Students with an Emotional Disturbance

The most frequently used classification system of emotional disturbance (or behavior disorder) involves two basic patterns: externalizing and internalizing (Heward, 2009; Wicks-Nelson & Israel, 2003).

Students with behavior disorders tend to be either aggressive or withdrawn

- *Externalizing* students are often aggressive, uncooperative, restless, and negativistic. They tend to lie and steal, defy teachers, and be hostile to authority figures. Sometimes they are cruel and malicious.
- *Internalizing* students, by contrast, are typically shy, timid, anxious, and fearful. They are often depressed and lack self-confidence.

Teachers tend to be more aware of students who display aggressive disorders because their behavior often stimulates or forces reactions. The withdrawn student, however, may be more likely to develop serious emotional problems such as depression and may even be at risk of suicide during the adolescent years. The following Suggestions for Teaching will help you teach both the withdrawn student and the aggressive student.

Students who have an emotional disturbance tend to be either aggressive or withdrawn. Because aggressive students disrupt classroom routines, teachers need to focus on classroom design features and employ behavior management techniques to reduce the probability of such behaviors. Frank Siteman/ Stock Boston

Suggestions for Teaching

Instructing Students with Emotional Disturbance

1 **Design the classroom environment and formulate lesson plans to encourage social interaction and cooperation.**[2]

Foster interpersonal contact among withdrawn students

Students whose emotional disturbance manifests itself as social withdrawal may stay away from others on purpose (perhaps because they find social contacts threatening), or they may find that others stay away from them (perhaps because they have poorly developed social skills). Regardless of the cause, the classroom environment and your instructional activities can be designed to foster appropriate interpersonal contact.

JOURNAL ENTRY
Activities and Materials That Encourage Cooperation

EXAMPLES

- Preschool and elementary school teachers can use toys and materials, as well as organized games and sports, that encourage cooperative play and have a reduced focus on individual performance. Activities might include dress-up games or puppet plays; games might include soccer, variations of It (such as tag), and kickball or softball modified such that everyone on the team gets a turn to kick or bat before the team plays in the field.

- Elementary and middle school teachers can use one or more of several team-oriented learning activities. *Cooperative Learning* (1995) by Robert Slavin provides details on using such activities as student teams—achievement divisions, jigsaw, and team-accelerated instruction (see also Slavin, Lake, & Groff, 2009).

2 **Prompt and reinforce appropriate social interactions.**

Prompting and positive reinforcement are basic learning principles that will be discussed in Chapter 7, "Behavioral Learning Theory: Operant Conditioning." Essentially, a prompt is a stimulus that draws out a desired response, and positive reinforcement involves giving the student a positive reinforcer (something the student wants) immediately after a desired behavior. The aim is to get the student to behave that way again. Typical reinforcers are verbal praise, stickers, and small prizes.

EXAMPLE

- You can set up a cooperative task or activity: "Marc, I would like you to help Carol and Raquel paint the scenery for next week's play. You can paint the trees and flowers, Carol will paint the grass, and Raquel will do the people." After several minutes, say something like, "That's good work. I am really pleased at how well the three of you are working together." Similar comments can be made at intervals as the interaction continues.

3 **Train other students to initiate social interaction.**

In all likelihood, you will have too many classroom responsibilities to spend a great deal of time working directly with a withdrawn child. It may be possible, however, using the steps that follow, to train other students to initiate contact with withdrawn students.

---

[2]Most of these suggestions are derived from points made in Chapters 7, 8, and 9 of *Strategies for Addressing Behavior Problems in the Classroom* (6th ed., 2010), by Mary Margaret Kerr and C. Michael Nelson.

EXAMPLE

- First, choose a student as a helper who interacts freely and well, can follow your instructions, and can concentrate on the training task for at least 10 minutes. Second, explain that the goal is to get the withdrawn child to work or play with the helping student but that the helper should expect rejection, particularly at first. Role-play the actions of a withdrawn child so that the helper understands what you mean by rejection. Emphasize the importance of making periodic attempts at interaction. Third, instruct the helper to suggest games or activities that appeal to the withdrawn student. Fourth, reinforce the helper's attempts to interact with the withdrawn child.

JOURNAL ENTRY
Getting Students to
Initiate Interaction with a
Withdrawn Child

④ **Design the classroom environment to reduce the probability of disruptive behavior.**

Use techniques to forestall
aggressive or antisocial behavior

The best way to deal with aggressive or antisocial behavior is to nip it in the bud. This strategy has at least three related benefits. One benefit of fewer disruptions is that you can better accomplish what you had planned for the day. A second benefit is that you are likely to be in a more positive frame of mind than if you spend half the day acting as a referee. A third benefit is that because of fewer disruptions and a more positive attitude, you may be less inclined to resort to permissible or even impermissible forms of physical punishment (which often produces undesirable side effects).

EXAMPLES

- With student input, formulate rules for classroom behavior and penalties for infractions of rules. Remind all students of the penalties, particularly when a disruptive incident seems about to occur, and consistently apply the penalties when the rules are broken.

- Place valued objects and materials out of reach when they are not needed or in use.

- Minimize the aggressive student's frustration with learning by using some of the same techniques you would use for a child with intellectual disability: break tasks down into small, easy-to-manage pieces; provide clear directions; and reinforce correct responses.

⑤ **Reinforce appropriate behavior, and, if necessary, punish inappropriate behavior.**

In suggestion 2, we described the use of positive reinforcement to encourage desired behavior. Reinforcement has the dual effect of teaching the aggressive student which behavior is appropriate and reducing the frequency of inappropriate behavior as it is replaced by desired behavior. Disruptive behavior will still occur, however. Three effective techniques for suppressing it while reinforcing desired behaviors are contingency contracts, token economies and fines, and time-out. Each of these techniques will be described in Chapter 7.

⑥ **Use group contingency-management techniques.**

You may want to reward the entire class when the aggressive student behaves appropriately for a certain period of time. Such rewards, which may be free time, special classroom events, or certain privileges, should make the aggressive student the hero and foster better peer relationships.

STUDENTS WHO ARE GIFTED AND TALENTED

Students who learn at a significantly faster rate than their peers or who possess superior talent in one or more areas also need to be taught in special ways if they are to make the most of their abilities. Unlike students with intellectual disability, learning disabilities, and emotional disturbance, however, students with superior capabilities are not covered by IDEA. Instead, the federal government provides technical assistance to states and local school districts for establishing programs for superior students. Although most states have such programs, some experts in special education (Colangelo & Davis, 2003b; Gallagher, 2003) feel that school systems are not given the resources they need to meet the needs of all gifted and talented students adequately. The Suggestions for Teaching that follow a bit later reflect this situation. All of the suggestions are inexpensive to implement and require few additional personnel.

A definition of the term **gifted and talented** was part of a bill passed by Congress in 1988:

> The term *gifted and talented children and youth* means children and youth who give evidence of high performance capability in areas such as intellectual, creative, artistic, or leadership capacity, or in specific academic fields, and who require services or activities not ordinarily provided by the school in order to fully develop such capabilities.

Identification of Gifted and Talented Students

Eligibility for gifted and talented programs has traditionally been based on standardized test scores, particularly IQ tests. It was not uncommon in years past for students to have to achieve an IQ score of at least 130 to be admitted to such programs. But criticisms about the narrow range of skills covered by such tests (and their heavy reliance on multiple-choice items) have led most states to deemphasize or eliminate the use of traditional intelligence tests and a numerical cutoff score for identification (Reid, Romanoff, & Algozzine, 2000; Renzulli, 2002).

Evidence that alternative assessments can do a better job of identifying gifted and talented children does exist. In one study (Reid et al., 2000), 434 second-grade students who were recommended for a gifted education program were tested with both traditional and nontraditional measures. The traditional assessment was a nonverbal test of analogical reasoning. The nontraditional assessment, which combined aspects of both Gardner's and Sternberg's theories of intelligence, was a set of linguistic, logical-mathematical, and spatial problem-solving tasks that called for analytical, synthetic, and practical thinking. For example, students were given a bag of small items, each of which had to be used as the basis of a 5-minute story. For another task, students were given a set of colored cardboard pieces and told to make a variety of objects, such as an animal, a building, something that moves, and whatever they wanted. On the basis of analogical reasoning scores, about 17 percent of the sample would have been recommended for placement in the gifted program. That percentage rose to 40 percent when scores from the problem-solving assessment were used. Another interesting statistic was that almost 70 percent of the students recommended on the basis of their problem-solving performances would not have been recommended on the basis of their analogical reasoning scores.

Joseph Renzulli (2002), a leading researcher of giftedness and gifted education, believes that the concept of giftedness should be expanded beyond the dimensions examined in the study we just described to include students who can channel their assets into constructive social actions that benefit others. As an example, he describes Melanie, a fifth-grade girl, who befriended Tony, a visually impaired first-grade boy who was ignored by most other students and teased by a few others. Melanie persuaded some of the school's most popular students to sit with Tony in the lunchroom, and she recruited other students to create and illustrate large-print

Gifted and talented students show high performance in one or more areas

books on topics of interest to Tony. Over the course of several months, Tony was accepted by many of the school's students, and his attitude toward school markedly improved. According to Howard Gardner's multiple intelligences theory, Melanie's gift likely stems from an above-average interpersonal (and possibly intrapersonal) intelligence. In the adult world, two examples of this type of person are Mother Teresa and Martin Luther King Jr.—and, as Renzulli points out, no one really cares what their test scores or grade-point averages were.

Broadening the definition and instruments used to assess giftedness is necessary given the diversity of students who are identified as gifted and talented (Harris, Plucker, Rapp, & Martínez, 2009; Reis & Renzulli, 2009). Students from many minority cultures are underrepresented in programs for the gifted and talented. In fact, there is a general ignorance of characteristics that are more highly valued by a minority culture than by the majority culture. Some American Indian tribes, for example, deemphasize the concept of giftedness because it runs counter to their belief that the welfare and cohesion of the group are more important than celebrating and nurturing the talents of any individual. The members of other tribes may place as much value on a child's knowledge of tribal traditions, storytelling ability, and artistic ability as they do on problem-solving ability and scientific reasoning (Callahan & McIntire, 1994). A child's giftedness may therefore be evident only when examined from the perspective of a particular culture. The same can be said of identifying giftedness in students whose first language is something other than English (Harris et al., 2009).

> Students of color are underrepresented in gifted classes because of overreliance on test scores

Characteristics of Gifted and Talented Students

In one sense, gifted and talented students are like any other group of students. Some are healthy and well-coordinated, whereas others are not. Some are extremely popular and well-liked, but others are not. Some are well-adjusted; others are not (Kirk et al., 2009). Some formulate strong identities (Marcia's identity achievement status) and are successful later in life, whereas others are not (Zuo & Cramond, 2001). But as a group, gifted and talented students are often noticeably different (Hardman et al., 2011). Here are some of the main characteristics that many gifted and talented students share:

- They excel on tasks that involve language, abstract logical thinking, and mathematics.
- They are faster at encoding information and retrieving it from memory.
- They are highly aware of how they learn and the various conditions that affect their learning. As a result, they excel at transferring previously learned information and skills to new problems and settings.
- They exhibit such high levels of motivation and task persistence that the phrase "rage to master" is sometimes used to describe their behavior. Their motivation to learn is partly due to high levels of self-efficacy and appropriate attributions. That is, they believe they have the capability to master those tasks and subject matters they choose to tackle and that their success is the result of both high ability and hard work.
- They tend to be more solitary and introverted than average children.
- They tend to have very intense emotional lives. They react with intense feelings, such as joy, regret, or sorrow, to a story, a piece of music, or a social encounter. They also tend to be emotionally sensitive and sometimes surpass adults in their ability to notice and identify with the feelings of others.

> Gifted and talented students differ from their nongifted peers intellectually and emotionally

Researchers who favor broadening the traditional definition of giftedness add other characteristics to the mix. Joseph Renzulli (2002), for example, believes that people like Melanie (the student who befriended an unpopular boy) possess characteristics such as optimism, courage, passion, energy, sensitivity to others, and a sense of vision—characteristics that are often found in people who achieve positions of leadership (see also Sternberg, 2005). In a longitudinal study, Wai, Lubinski, and Benbow (2005) found that students who were identified at age thirteen as intellectually precocious tended to be recognized for their creativity and achievements twenty years later. Furthermore, when the preferences of the youth were taken into account, the nature and quality of accomplishments were well predicted.

A final point about the characteristics of gifted and talented students is that some of them are challenged with learning disabilities, attention disorders, or autism spectrum disorders—such as Asperger syndrome—which means they have difficulty with social relations. Such students are identified as **twice exceptional:** they are exceptional because they are gifted and talented and they are exceptional because they are challenged in some intellectual, social, physical, or emotional way (e.g., Assouline, Nicpon, & Doobay, 2009). If you find yourself working with twice exceptional students, you may need to combine the following instructional options with Suggestions for Teaching from earlier sections.

Instructional Options

Gifted and talented students constantly challenge a teacher's skill, ingenuity, and classroom resources. While trying to instruct the class as a whole, the teacher is faced with the need to provide more and more interesting and challenging materials and ideas to gifted students. In this section, we will examine three possible ways to engage these students.

Accelerated Instruction Accelerated instruction is often suggested as one way to meet the academic needs of gifted and talented students. For many people, the phrase *accelerated instruction* means allowing the student to skip one or more grades,

Because gifted and talented students understand and integrate abstract ideas more quickly than do their nongifted classmates, they are capable of successfully completing tasks that older students routinely carry out. Bob Daemmrich/The Image Works

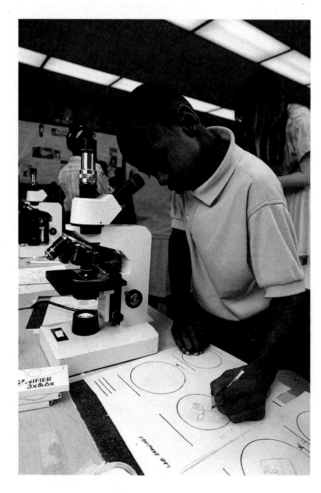

which, although not as common as in years past, does occasionally occur. But there are at least three other ways of accomplishing the same goal: (1) the curriculum can be compressed, allowing gifted and talented students to complete the work for more than one grade during the regular school year; (2) the school year can be extended by the use of summer sessions; and (3) students can take college courses while still in high school.

Whatever the form of accelerated instruction, this is always a hotly debated topic, with pros and cons on each side. Two often quoted advantages for giving gifted students the opportunity to work on complex tasks are that it keeps them from becoming bored with school and that it produces more positive attitudes toward learning. On the negative side, two frequent arguments are that a gifted student may have trouble with the social and emotional demands of acceleration and that acceleration produces an undesirable sense of elitism among gifted students. Research evidence supports the presumed academic benefits of acceleration and fails to confirm the predicted negative social and emotional outcomes (Gallagher, 2003; Kulik, 2003b). As with all other informed educational decisions, the unique needs of the individual and the situation must be considered before the best course of action can be determined.

Gifted and Talented Classes and Schools Some public school districts offer separate classes for gifted and talented students as either an alternative to accelerated instruction or as something that follows accelerated instruction. In addition, so-called magnet schools are composed of students whose average level of ability is higher than that found in a typical elementary, middle, or high school. Finally, many states sponsor high-ability high schools, particularly in mathematics and science.

Recent findings suggest that such placements do not produce uniformly positive results and should be made only after the characteristics of the student and the program have been carefully considered. In terms of achievement, the typical gifted student can expect to score moderately higher (at about the 63rd percentile) on tests than comparable students who remain in heterogeneous classes (Kulik & Kulik, 1991). But the effects of separate class or school placement on measures of academic self-concept have been inconsistent; some researchers find them to be higher than those of students who remain in heterogeneous classes, whereas other researchers have found either no differences or declines (Hoge & Renzulli, 1993; Kulik & Kulik, 1991; Seaton, Marsh, & Craven, 2010).

> Separate classes for gifted and talented students aid achievement but may lower academic self-concept of some students

Enrichment and Differentiated Instruction Because of the potential negative effects of grade skipping, the limited availability of special classes and schools, and the fact that such classes and schools are not good options for some gifted and talented students, teachers may find themselves with one or two gifted and talented students in a regular classroom. A solution for meeting the special needs of these students (as well as those with disabilities) is a practice often referred to as *differentiated instruction*, a technique we have mentioned earlier. Basically, this means using different learning materials, instructional methods, assignments, and tests to accommodate differences in students' abilities, learning styles, prior knowledge, and cultural background (Benjamin, 2005; Gregory, 2003; Gregory & Kuzmich, 2005; Tomlinson et al., 2008).

One scheme for delivering differentiated instruction to gifted and talented learners has been developed by Joseph Renzulli and Sally Reis (Reis & Renzulli, 1985; Renzulli, Gentry, & Reis, 2003; Renzulli & Reis, 1985). Based on their view that giftedness is a combination of above-average cognitive ability, creativity, and task commitment, Renzulli and Reis describe three levels of curriculum enrichment for gifted and talented learners:

Type I enrichment: Exploratory activities that are designed to expose students to topics, events, books, people, and places not ordinarily covered in the regular curriculum. The basic purpose of these activities is to stimulate new interests. Among the many suggestions Renzulli and Reis offer are having students view and write reports on films and videos (such as *The Eagle Has Landed: The Flight of Apollo 11*) and having local residents make presentations on their occupations or hobbies.

Type II enrichment: Instructional methods and materials aimed at the development of such thinking and feeling processes as thinking creatively, classifying and analyzing data, solving problems, appreciating, and valuing.

Type III enrichment: Activities in which students investigate and collect data about a real topic or problem. For example, a student may decide to document the history of her school, focusing on such issues as changes in size, instructional materials and methods, and curriculum.

Numerous sites on the Internet are devoted to long-distance education, enrichment, and tutoring. The website of the Talent Identification Program at Duke University contains information about online teaching and learning opportunities and various telementoring programs (**www.tip.duke.edu**). The following Suggestions for Teaching provide further ideas for working with gifted and talented students.

pause & reflect

Relatively little money is spent on programs for the gifted and talented compared with the amounts made available for the disabled. Defenders of this arrangement sometimes argue that because gifted students have a built-in advantage, we should invest most of our resources in services for those with disabilities. Do you agree or disagree? Why?

TeachSource Video Case ◄◄ ▶ ►►

Academic Diversity: Differentiated Instruction

Go to the Education CourseMate website to watch the Video Case, and then answer the following questions:

1. What did the teacher in this Video Case do to make the lesson work for all of her students? Describe some of the strategies and tools that she used.

2. Based on reading the chapter and watching the Video Case, what do you think would be most challenging for a classroom teacher about "doing" differentiated instruction?

Suggestions for Teaching

Instructing Gifted and Talented Students

1 Consult with gifted and talented students regarding individual study projects, perhaps involving a learning contract.

JOURNAL ENTRY
Individual Study for Students Who Are Gifted and Talented

One of the most effective ways to deal with gifted students is to assign individual study projects. These may involve a contract approach, in which you consult with students on an individual basis and agree on a personal assignment that is to be completed by a certain date.

Such assignments should probably be related to some part of the curriculum. If you are studying Mexico, for example, a gifted student could devote free time to a special report on some aspect of Mexican life that intrigues him. In making these assignments, you should remember that even very bright students may not be able to absorb, organize, and apply abstract concepts until they become formal thinkers. Thus, until early middle school years, it may be preferable to keep these assignments brief rather than comprehensive.

To provide another variation of the individual study project, you could ask the gifted student to act as a research specialist and report on questions that puzzle the class. Still another individual study project is the creation of an open-ended, personal yearbook. Any time a gifted student finishes the assigned work, she might be allowed to write stories or do drawings for such a journal.

When possible, unobtrusive projects are preferable. Perhaps you can recall a teacher who rewarded the fast workers by letting them work on a mural (or the equivalent) covering the side board. If you were an average student, you can probably attest that the sight of the class "brains" having the time of their lives was not conducive to diligent effort on the part of the have-nots sweating away at their workbooks. Reward assignments should probably be restricted to individual work on unostentatious projects.

2 **Encourage supplementary reading and writing.**

Encourage students to spend extra time reading and writing. A logical method of combining both skills is the preparation of book reports. It is perhaps less threatening to call them book *reviews* and emphasize that you are interested in personal reaction, not a précis or an abstract. Some specialists in the education of the gifted have suggested that such students be urged to read biographies and autobiographies. The line of reasoning here is that potential leaders might be inspired to emulate the exploits of a famous person. Even if such inspiration does not result, you could recommend life stories simply because they are usually interesting.

Other possibilities for writing are e-mail exchanges with other students, siblings at college, or friends in different areas. Or a student may write a review of a website that she has discovered. If the appropriate software and support are available, students could be encouraged to create home pages or websites for themselves, either on a topic mutually selected with the teacher or on their personal interests (the latter would be much like a yearbook entry).

3 **Have gifted students act as tutors.**

Depending on the grade, subject, and personalities of those involved, gifted students might be asked to act occasionally as tutors, lab assistants, or the equivalent. Some bright students will welcome such opportunities and are capable of providing instruction in such a way that their peers do not feel self-conscious or humiliated. Others may resent being asked to spend school time helping classmates or may lack skills in interpersonal relationships. If you do decide to ask a gifted student to function as a tutor, it would be wise to proceed tentatively and cautiously.

JOURNAL ENTRY
Providing Gifted and Talented Students with Opportunities for Additional Reading and Writing

USING TECHNOLOGY TO ASSIST EXCEPTIONAL STUDENTS

There is perhaps no other area in education today in which technology is making as significant an impact as in the field of special education, and this is largely due to the notion of universal design for learning (UDL) and the use of assistive technology (Hitchcock & Stahl, 2003; Scott, McGuire, & Shaw, 2003).

Universal design for learning (UDL): treats diversity as a strength in learning environments

Universal design for learning is an approach that seeks to eliminate the barriers to learning for all students no matter what challenges they bring with them to school. According to the Center for Applied Special Technology (CAST; 2008), UDL is guided by three principles: (1) providing multiple means of representing what is to be learned, (2) providing multiple means of action and expression (the "how" of learning), and (3) providing multiple means of engagement (the "why" of learning). The underlying assumption of UDL is that students represent a continuum of differences rather than falling into one of two categories: normal versus disabled. Furthermore, UDL assumes that this diversity is the norm rather than the exception and that the norm of diversity, if embraced in schools and classrooms, strengthens the learning environment (Grabinger, Aplin, Ponnappa-Brenner, 2008; Meo, 2008).

Federal legislation has led to the development of various assistive technologies

Although UDL has application for face-to-face learning environments such as classrooms, it has also been used to enable the addition "of Web 2.0 tools into the mix for teaching and learning" (Grabinger et al., 2008, p. 68). Following CAST's principles of UDL, Scott Grabinger and his colleagues have identified Web 2.0 tools that can provide access and support for learners with problems in attention and memory, language, executive functions, problem solving, and social functioning. We will encounter these cognitive processes in Part III, "Learning and Thinking." We now turn to the role that assistive technology can play to support learners.

Mandated by IDEA for any need related to the learning or development of a child with a disability, **assistive technology** is defined in IDEA as "any item, piece of equipment, or product system, whether acquired commercially off the shelf, modified, or customized, that is used to increase, maintain, or improve functional capabilities of a child with a disability" ("Individuals with Disabilities," 1997, Section 602[1]).

Assistive technology tools may range from less expensive low-tech equipment such as adapted spoons, joysticks, taped stories, adaptive switches, head-pointing devices, captioned programming, and communication boards (message display devices that contain vocabulary choices from which the child can select an answer) to commercially developed high-tech devices such as screen magnifiers, speech synthesizers and digitizers, voice-recognition devices, touch screens, alternative computer keyboards, word prediction programs, and special reading software (Maanum, 2009).

Technology for Students with Hearing Impairments

For links to the websites mentioned in this section, plus other important web resources, go to the textbook's website, Education CourseMate.

Hearing-impaired students can be assisted with technology tools in a number of ways, including closed captioning, audio amplification, and cochlear implants. Closed captioning (presenting spoken words as text on a screen) occurs most often in connection with television programs. But this technology can also be used in classrooms to help hearing-impaired students follow a teacher's lectures or explanations. There are several systems that allow 120–225 words per minute to be typed by an aide (using a stenographic keyboard) and sent to a student's computer monitor. Another way to accomplish the same goal is through audio amplification. With some of these systems, the teacher wears a small microphone and transmitter whose signal is amplified and sent to a student who wears a lightweight receiver (Camp & Stark, 2006; Compton, Tucker, & Flynn, 2009). A third option for students with severe to profound hearing loss is a cochlear implant. This system involves several external components (microphone, speech processor, transmitter, power pack) and a surgically implanted receiver-stimulator. Cochlear implants can also be combined with audio amplification systems (Moore & Teagle, 2002). The website for Gallaudet University, a well-known school for the deaf in Washington, D.C., includes a page that describes its Technology Access Program (**http://tap.gallaudet.edu**).

As helpful as the preceding devices are, one thing they are not is a magic bullet. They cannot, for example, overcome students' lack of learning skills. A group of mainstreamed high school hearing-impaired students who were given class notes from a speech-to-text support service simply read them (which is what most non–hearing-impaired students would do) rather than using them in conjunction with other study methods (Elliott, Foster, & Stinson, 2002).

Technology for Students with Visual Impairments

Closed captioning and audio amplification are popular among deaf students; speech synthesizers and magnification devices offer similar liberating assistance to those who are visually impaired. With speech synthesis, the user can select a word, sentence, or chunk of information from any written or scanned text and hear it pronounced by a speech synthesizer. For example, the Kurzweil Reader scans printed material and converts it into high-quality speech. The Braille 'n Speak is a note-taking system that also relies on speech synthesis. As students type on a seven-key keyboard, their input is converted into standard text that can either be read aloud or stored in the system's memory. In addition to devices that magnify the content of computer screens, head-mounted magnifiers allow students to see over various distances (Duhaney & Duhaney, 2000; Griffin, Williams, Davis, & Engleman, 2002; Gold & Lowe, 2009).

Software programs called screen readers (such as Job Access with Speech, Window-Eyes, and WinVision) allow individuals with visual impairments to have the contents of a screen read to them by a speech synthesis program. The websites of the National Federation of the Blind (**www.nfb.org**) and the American Printing House for the Blind (**www.aph.org**) describe screen readers and other software and hardware devices that are available for individuals with visual impairments.

Technology for Students with Orthopedic Impairments

For students who have physical limitations, pointing devices that are held in the mouth, attached to the head, or voice activated may provide the needed device control. Students with more limited fields of motion but acceptable fine motor skill may also benefit from condensed or mini keyboards that position the keys more closely together and require less strength to use. For students with less fine motor control, touch-sensitive expanded keyboards offer more space between keys and are often programmed to accept overlay plastic sheets for different applications or user needs (Duhaney & Duhaney, 2000). Free programs (called freeware) and inexpensive ones (called shareware) for helping individuals with physical and other disabilities use computers more effectively can be found at the Virtual Assistive Technology Center website (**http://vatc.freeservers.com**).

Technology for Students with Speech or Language Impairments

Technology can also help individuals with communication impairments. Research has shown positive effects of computer training in vocabulary, early grammar skills, and social communication among toddlers with Down syndrome as well as young children with severe language and behavioral disabilities (Westwood, 2009). In a small pilot study, the researchers later discovered that parent volunteers briefly trained in using this software can be more effective than a professional speech pathologist. Computer programs designed to help students with speech or language impairments acquire language and communication skills can be found on the websites of Apple Computer (**www.apple.com/education/accessibility/disabilities/language**) and the International Society for Augmentative and Alternative Communication (**www.isaac-online.org**).

Technology for Students with Learning Disabilities

As we saw earlier in this chapter, learning disabled (LD) students typically have problems with reading, writing, and mathematics. But research has shown that the severity of these troubles can be reduced by using software programs designed for students with learning problems (Westwood, 2009). For instance, in one study, LD students who responded to the demands of a computerized study guide (read a passage as many times as possible within a 15-minute period, respond silently to study guide questions at least twice, and then take a 15-item multiple-choice test) achieved higher scores than LD students who were not exposed to the program. In another study, a videodisc program helped LD students achieve higher scores on a test of math fractions. In a third study, students who worked on a hypermedia study guide for social studies scored higher on factual and inferential questions than students who experienced a lecture covering the same material (Maccini, Gagnon, & Hughes, 2002). Finally, software that allowed for a synchronized visual and auditory presentation of text helped college students with ADHD to read for longer time periods with less stress and fatigue (Hecker, Burns, Elkind, Elkind, & Katz, 2002).

In the area of writing, there are many tools for students with learning disabilities that can help them—and other students—with basic sentence generation, transcription, and revision. Spelling, style, and grammar checkers can help raise student focus from mechanical demands and surface-level concerns to higher-level text cohesion and integration issues. Word prediction software can help students write more coherent and meaningful sentences by offering a choice of several words based on what the student has already written (Duhaney & Duhaney, 2000). Something as simple as an e-pal program (an electronic version of a pen pal) can improve certain aspects of LD students' writing. In one study (Stanford & Siders, 2001), sixth, seventh, and eighth graders with learning disabilities did one of three writing tasks: exchanged e-mails with college students, exchanged written letters with college students, or wrote to an imaginary pen pal. At the end of 8 weeks, students in the e-pal group wrote longer and more complex letters than students in the other two groups. However, technology by itself does not improve the writing of LD students. Instead, sound instructional practices such as peer tutoring on the word-processed text raise the quality and number of student revisions and overall quality of their writing (MacArthur, 1994). Additional information about resources and teaching strategies for students with learning disabilities can be found on this book's student website, Education CourseMate.

Technology for Gifted and Talented Students

Gifted students can also benefit from advances in instructional technology, such as distance education. Stanford University, for instance, has been experimenting with providing year-round accelerated instruction in mathematics, physics, English, and computer science to gifted high school students through the Education Program for Gifted Youth (EPGY) (Ravaglia, Alper, Rozenfeld, & Suppes, 1998; Ravaglia, Sommer, Sanders, Oas, & DeLeone, 1999). In addition to digitized lectures and online quizzes, students in EPGY can contact the instructors using e-mail, telephone project staff, attend discussion sessions at Stanford, and try out various physics experiments at home. Given all these supports, it is not surprising that students have done exceedingly well in this program (Tock & Suppes, 2002). The website for EPGY—which contains recent evaluation reports on the program—can be found at **http://epgy.stanford.edu.**

An online enrichment activity that can be used for any student, including the gifted and talented, is a web quest (Ridgeway, Peters, & Tracy, 2002). This is an inquiry-oriented activity in which most or all of the information that students need is drawn from the Internet. An excellent source of web quests is the Web-Quest Page of San Diego State University (**http://webquest.org**). Here you will find dozens of activities arranged by grade level and by subject matter within each grade level.

To review this chapter, try the tutorial quizzes and other study aids on the textbook's Education CourseMate website.

In Service of Learning

Don thinks about Connie's phrase, "teaching in service of learning," and says, "Looking back on how I approached that lesson, I realize that I was so focused on my instruction that I really didn't think that much about my students' learning. I think the only time I thought about student learning at all was when I decided what I wanted them to do in the class. I mean, I really did think about designing a lesson that would help students predict elements in a story. But once that lesson was planned, I was so focused on executing my plan that I did not think of much else. I mean, the little girl who asked the questions was a disruption to me, but only because I was thinking of my instruction rather than her learning."

Challenging Assumptions

"I think that's an important insight," says Celeste, "but still, wouldn't it have been easier for the other kids to learn if that little girl did not need to ask so many questions?"

Antonio, thinking of his first class of middle school students, responds, "I used to think that way. But I am learning that a lesson plan is just that, a plan. My plan can guide me, but so can my students. Those questions that seemed so disruptive to me at first became clues about what my students needed. Think about it: even if you present a lesson exactly as you planned it and with no disruptions, that does not mean that your students have learned exactly what you thought they should learn. You have to know what your students need to help them learn. And the more you know about the different kinds of needs kids have, the more confident you become."

Connie nods. "At the beginning of a teaching career, we worry about how well we are going to teach and so we focus our energies on what we are going to do. But as we gain experience, our focus shifts to our students and the needs they bring to the learning opportunities we provide. If special education means we take into account the needs of the learner in designing our instruction, then all education should be special."

Summary

1. Three early attempts at dealing with student variability were age-graded classrooms, ability grouping, and special class placement. Age-graded classrooms grouped students who were roughly the same age. Ability grouping sorted nondisabled students into separate classes according to mental ability test scores. Special class placement was used to separate nondisabled students from those with mental and physical disabilities.

2. Virtually all elementary schools and most middle and high schools use some form of ability grouping. At the middle and high school levels, the term *tracking* is commonly used.

3. The four currently popular approaches to ability grouping are between-class ability grouping, regrouping, the Joplin Plan, and within-class ability grouping. Within-class ability grouping is most frequently used in the elementary grades, whereas between-class ability grouping is most frequently used in the high school grades.

4. Ability grouping is based on the assumptions that intelligence is genetically determined, is reflected by an IQ score, is unchangeable, and that instruction is more effective with homogeneous groups of students.

5. There is no research support for between-class ability grouping and limited support for regrouping. Moderately positive results have been found for the Joplin Plan and within-class ability grouping.

6. Students in low-ability groups often receive lower-quality instruction.

7. Allowing low-track students to take honors classes does not in itself result in more students moving into higher tracks.

8. In the light of research findings on ability grouping, educators may choose to discontinue the

use of between-class ability grouping, use only within-class grouping and the Joplin Plan, or discontinue all forms of ability grouping.

9. The Education for All Handicapped Children Act (Public Law 94-142) was enacted in 1975 to ensure that students with disabling conditions receive the same free and appropriate education as nondisabled students. Since then, the law has been revised and expanded, and it is now known as the Individuals with Disabilities Education Act (IDEA).

10. Major provisions of IDEA include the right to a free and appropriate public education, an appropriate and valid preplacement evaluation, the development of an individualized education program (IEP), the education of students with disabilities in the least restrictive environment (also known as mainstreaming), and procedural safeguards.

11. In some school districts, mainstreaming has been extended to the point at which students with disabilities are taught only in regular classrooms by regular and special education teachers. This practice is known as inclusion, or full inclusion.

12. The evidence on inclusion, although somewhat limited and inconsistent, indicates that the practice produces at least moderate benefits for some students with disabilities but has little beneficial effect on others.

13. Inclusion is likely to work best for students with disabilities for whom the regular classroom is an appropriate setting and in classrooms in which the teacher uses instructional methods that are proven to be effective with a wide variety of learners.

14. The regular classroom teacher's responsibilities under IDEA may include participation in referral, assessment, preparation of the IEP, and implementation of the IEP.

15. Children with mild intellectual disability score two or more standard deviations below the mean on a standardized test of intelligence and are likely to be mainstreamed for some part of the school day and week. They are likely to have a low tolerance for frustration, lack confidence and self-esteem, oversimplify matters, and have difficulty generalizing from one situation to another.

16. Students with learning disabilities account for more than half of all students with disabilities.

They have a disorder in one or more of such basic psychological processes as perception, attention, memory, and metacognition, which leads to learning problems not attributable to other causes.

17. Using a discrepancy between a student's IQ score (average or above) and standardized achievement test score (one or more standard deviations below the mean) as a primary indicator of a learning disability does not appear to be useful.

18. Anywhere from 25 to 40 percent of children with a learning disability also have attention-deficit/hyperactivity disorder (ADHD). Children with ADHD may be inattentive, hyperactive, and impulsive, or all three, over an extended period of time and in such different settings as home, school, and at play.

19. Students with ADHD may be treated with stimulant medication, psychological/educational programs, or a combination of the two.

20. The actual number of schoolchildren with serious emotional disturbance is unknown because of vague definitions of emotional disturbance and differences in interpretation of definitions, but it is estimated to be 3 to 5 percent of all school-age children.

21. Most classifications of disturbed behavior focus on aggressive behavior or withdrawn behavior.

22. Students who are gifted and talented excel in performing tasks that require intellectual, creative, artistic, or leadership ability.

23. Minorities are underrepresented in gifted and talented classes because standardized test scores are emphasized at the expense of other indexes.

24. The academic needs of students who are gifted and talented are usually met through accelerated instruction, placement in classes or schools for the gifted and talented, or classroom enrichment activities. Special classes and schools typically produce moderate achievement benefits but can also produce declines in academic self-concept.

25. A variety of adaptive technologies exist to help students with special needs. These include closed captioning, speech synthesis, voice recognition, screen magnifiers, special keyboards, writing tools, and distance education.

Resources for Further Investigation

● Ability Grouping

Additional discussions of ability grouping and alternatives to it can be found in a number of books and journal articles. For a comprehensive treatment of this topic, look at *Keeping Track* (2nd ed., 2005) by Jeannie Oakes. The first edition of the book was acclaimed as one of the "Books of the Century" by the South Carolina Museum of Education when it was published 20 years ago. The new edition discusses "tracking wars" of the past two decades.

● Texts on the Education of Exceptional Children

The following books provide general coverage of the education of exceptional children: *Exceptional Children and Youth* (4th ed., 2006), by Nancy Hunt and Kathleen Marshall, and *Educating Exceptional Children* (12th ed., 2009), by Samuel Kirk, James Gallagher, Mary Ruth Coleman, and Nicholas Anastasiow. A book that emphasizes both general and specific teaching techniques for students with learning problems is *Teaching Students with Learning Problems* (7th ed., 2005), by Cecil D. Mercer and Ann R. Mercer. Part 1, "Foundations of Teaching," describes the general teaching skills that all teachers of students with special needs should possess. Part 2, "Teaching Academic Skills," describes assessment and teaching techniques for improving language skills, reading, spelling, writing, mathematics, and study skills.

● Mainstreaming and Inclusion

In *Effective Teaching Strategies That Accommodate Diverse Learners* (3rd ed., 2007), Edward Kameenui and Douglas Carnine illustrate how various subjects (such as reading, writing, mathematics, science, social studies) can be effectively taught to groups of students who vary in cultural background, social class, and learning ability. Each chapter on teaching a particular subject matter is organized around six instructional principles whose effectiveness has been supported by research: Big Ideas, Conspicuous Strategies, Mediated Scaffolding, Primed Background Knowledge, Strategic Integration, and Judicious Review. *Successful Inclusive Teaching: Proven Ways to Detect and Correct Special Needs* (4th ed., 2003), edited by Joyce S. Choate, is a comprehensive treatment of how to accommodate special-needs students in the regular classroom. Part 1 covers the legal issues surrounding mainstreaming and inclusion, the characteristics of students with special needs, and basic principles of inclusive instruction. Part 2 describes how to use those basic principles to teach reading comprehension, language skills, writing, arithmetic, mathematical problem solving, science, and social studies. Part 3 covers classroom management.

Edlaw, a national legal organization and publisher, supports a website that follows developments in IDEA and legal requirements for educators and administrators of special education programs. It can be found at **www.edlaw.org.**

● Teaching Students with Intellectual Disability

Specialized techniques for teaching students with intellectual disability can be found in *Education of Students with Intellectual Disability: Research and Practice* (2009), by Phil Foreman, and *Mental Retardation: An Introduction to Intellectual Disability* (7th ed., 2006), by Mary Beirne-Smith, James Patton, and Shannon Kim.

● Teaching Students with Learning Disabilities

The following books provide information about the nature of learning disabilities and how to teach students with learning disabilities: *Learning Disabilities and Related Mild Disabilities: Characteristics, Teaching Strategies, and New Directions* (11th ed., 2009), by Janet Lerner and Beverly Johns; *Learning Disabilities: Characteristics, Identification, and Teaching Strategies* (5th ed., 2004), by William Bender; and *Differentiating Instruction for Students with Learning Disabilities* (2002), also by William Bender.

● Teaching Students with Emotional and Behavior Disorders

Information on the nature of behavior disorders and on how the regular classroom teacher can deal with such students can be found in *Characteristics of Emotional and Behavioral Disorders of Children and Youth* (8th ed., 2005), by James M. Kauffman; *Teaching Students with Behavior Disorders: Techniques and Activities for Classroom Instruction* (2nd ed., 2000), by Patricia Gallagher; and *Strategies for Addressing Behavior Problems in the Classroom* (6th ed., 2010), by Mary Margaret Kerr and C. Michael Nelson.

● Teaching Gifted and Talented Learners

These books describe various techniques to use in instructing gifted and talented learners: *Handbook of Gifted Education* (3rd ed., 2003a), edited by Nicholas Colangelo and Gary Davis; *Conceptions of Giftedness* (2nd ed., 2005), edited by Robert J. Sternberg and Janet E. Davison; and *Designing and Developing Programs for Gifted Students* (2003), edited by Joan Smutny.

You should also visit the websites of the National Association for Gifted Children (**www.nagc.org**), the National Research Center on the Gifted and Talented (**www.gifted.uconn.edu/nrcgt.html**), and *2e: The Twice-Exceptional Newsletter* (**http://www.2enewsletter.com/welcome%20page.htm**).

7

Behavioral Learning Theory: Operant Conditioning

The Education CourseMate website for this text offers many helpful resources. Go to **CengageBrain.com** to preview this chapter's Concept Maps and Chapter Themes.

KEY POINTS

These key points will help you learn the important information in this chapter. To help you study, they also appear in the margins of the pages, next to the text where they are discussed.

Operant Conditioning

- Operant conditioning: voluntary response strengthened or weakened by consequences that follow
- Positive reinforcement: strengthen a target behavior by presenting a positive reinforcer after the behavior occurs
- Negative reinforcement: strengthen a target behavior by removing an aversive stimulus after the behavior occurs
- Punishment: weaken a target behavior by presenting an aversive stimulus after the behavior occurs
- Time-out: weaken a target behavior by temporarily removing a positive reinforcer after the behavior occurs
- Extinction: weaken a target behavior by ignoring it
- Spontaneous recovery: extinguished behaviors may reappear spontaneously
- Generalization: responding in similar ways to similar stimuli
- Discrimination: responding in different ways to similar stimuli
- Complex behaviors are shaped by reinforcing closer approximations to terminal behavior
- Fixed interval schedules: reinforce after regular time intervals
- Variable interval schedules: reinforce after random time intervals

- Fixed ratio schedules: reinforce after a set number of responses
- Variable ratio schedules: reinforce after a different number of responses each time

Educational Applications of Operant Conditioning Principles

- Skinner's approach to instruction: clear goals, logical sequencing of material, self-pacing
- Types of computer-based instruction (CBI) programs include drill and practice, simulations, tutorials
- Tutorial and simulation programs produce higher achievement than conventional instruction
- Integrated learning system (ILS): comprehensive, self-paced learning system
- CBI no substitute for high-quality teaching
- Behavior modification: shape behavior by ignoring undesirable responses, reinforcing desirable responses
- Premack principle: required work first, then chosen reward
- Token economy is a flexible reinforcement system
- Contingency contracting: reinforcement supplied after student completes mutually agreed-on assignment
- Time-out works best with disruptive, aggressive children
- Research unclear about strength of negative effects of corporal punishment

N

ow that you are familiar with how students develop from preschool through high school, with some of the major ways in which students differ from one another, and with the main ways in which schools try to address student variability, it is time to examine what is perhaps the most fundamental and important aspect of schooling: the learning process. Because the primary reason that we have schools is to help children acquire the knowledge

and skills that adults consider necessary for successful functioning in society, the instructional and curricular decisions that teachers make should be based on an understanding of how people learn. But as with most of the other topics in this text, learning is a complex phenomenon that has been studied from different perspectives.

This chapter is devoted to what is generally called behavioral learning theory. More precisely, the chapter describes a theory called operant conditioning and some of its implications. Operant conditioning focuses on the environmental factors that influence the types of behaviors people exhibit and the extent to which they are likely to exhibit those behaviors in the future. As you will see, this theory underlies many computer-based instructional applications. Subsequent chapters will examine the roles that other people and our own thought processes play in learning.

Revealing Assumptions

Reward Is in the Eye of the Beholder

Antonio has described a reward system that he and his interdisciplinary team have been trying to use to motivate their middle school students. The reward system seems reasonable, but Antonio and his team are not satisfied with the results. Celeste, sharing observations of an advanced placement physics class and a general earth science class, suggests, "The kids in the AP class don't need rewards, but the general science kids sure do." Connie asks Don if he has seen rewards being used in the third-grade class he observed this past week.

"Yeah, I did," says Don. "The teacher has a system they call 'Daily Points.' The kids earn points for doing work, daily classroom chores, being organized—stuff like that. The points are put on a chart each day and at the end of the week, students can 'cash in' their points for pencils, pens, note cards, stickers. They can also buy time to play computer games—educational ones, of course. Some of the kids are really into it, but some aren't."

Connie wonders aloud whether teachers and students always see eye-to-eye on rewards. "I remember a particular day in my sixth-grade class when I was a student teacher. I had given a pop quiz the day before. I thought: if students see one of their peers rewarded for good performance, they will all try harder. So, before I returned the quizzes I made a big speech about homework and how the quiz had shown me who was really putting in effort and who wasn't. Then I said, 'and it is obvious to me that the hardest working student in the class is . . . tah-dah' . . . and I named the kid as I handed him his quiz. I actually said 'tah-dah.' I thought I was rewarding the young man; instead, I messed up his life at school for a month. His friends gave him endless grief about it. I still feel bad about that mistake, but what I learned was that reward is in the eye of the beholder."

pause & reflect

We all like to be rewarded for our accomplishments; it's human nature (and, as we will learn, one of the reasons that positive reinforcement works). However, we often assume that others perceive rewards in the same way we do. There is a tendency to predict that what we ourselves perceive to be rewarding will also be rewarding (and, therefore, motivating) for others. Did you ever have the experience of being singled out by a teacher for an accomplishment only to suffer at the hands of your peers? What was your response to that situation? How did your behavior change? Can you think how a teacher might avoid making the mistake Connie made when she was a student teacher?

OPERANT CONDITIONING

In 1913, with the publication of an article titled "Psychology as the Behaviorist Views It," the influential American psychologist John Watson argued that psychology would quickly lose credibility as a science if it focused on internal mental and emotional states that could not be directly observed or accurately measured. The solution was to study what could be directly observed and objectively and accurately measured: the external stimuli that people experienced and what people did in response—in a word, behavior.

From that point until the late 1960s, behavioral theories of one sort or another dominated the psychology of learning. Although they are considerably less popular today, they still offer many useful ideas for classroom teachers.

Basic Nature and Assumptions

Behavioral learning theories culminated in the work of B. F. Skinner. Skinner put together a theory that not only successfully combines many different ideas but also serves as the basis for a variety of applications to human behavior. Skinner's theory, **operant conditioning,** takes as its starting point the fact that many of the voluntary responses of animals and humans are strengthened when they are reinforced (followed by a desirable consequence) and weakened when they are either ignored or punished. In this way, organisms learn new behaviors and when to exhibit them and "unlearn" existing behaviors. The term *operant conditioning* refers to the fact that organisms learn to "operate" on their environment (make a particular response) to obtain or avoid a particular consequence. Some psychologists use the term *instrumental* because the behavior is instrumental in bringing about the consequence.

> **Operant conditioning: voluntary response strengthened or weakened by consequences that follow**

Most of the experiments on which the principles of operant conditioning are based involved an ingenious apparatus that Skinner invented, which is appropriately referred to as a *Skinner box*. This is a small enclosure that contains only a bar (or lever) and a small tray. Outside the box is a hopper holding a supply of food pellets that are dropped into the tray when the bar is pressed under certain conditions.

A hungry rat is placed in the box, and when in the course of exploring its new environment the rat approaches and then presses the bar, it is rewarded with a food pellet. The rat then presses the bar more frequently than it did before being rewarded. If food pellets are supplied under some conditions when the bar is pushed down—for example, when a tone is sounded—but not under others, the rat learns to discriminate one situation from the other, and the rate of bar pressing drops noticeably when the tone is not sounded. If a tone is sounded that is very close in frequency to the original tone, the rat generalizes (treats the two tones as equivalent) and presses the bar at the same rate for both. But if the food pellets are not given after the rat presses the bar, that behavior stops, or is extinguished.

Basic Principles of Operant Conditioning

To repeat the basic idea behind operant conditioning: all behaviors are accompanied by certain consequences, and these consequences strongly influence (some might say determine) whether these behaviors are repeated and at what level of intensity. In general, the consequences that follow behavior are either pleasant and desirable or unpleasant and aversive. Depending on conditions that we will discuss shortly, these consequences either increase (strengthen) or decrease (weaken) the likelihood that the preceding behavior will recur under the same or similar circumstances.

pause & reflect

Operant conditioning holds that we learn to respond or not respond to certain stimuli because our responses are followed by desirable or aversive consequences. How many of your own behaviors can you explain in this fashion? Why, for example, are you reading this book and pondering these questions?

When consequences strengthen a preceding behavior, *reinforcement* has taken place. When consequences weaken a preceding behavior, *punishment* and *extinction* have occurred. There are two forms of reinforcement and two forms of punishment. This section describes both forms of reinforcement, both forms of punishment, extinction, and several related principles that can be applied to aspects of human learning.

Positive Reinforcement Although the term *positive reinforcement* may be unfamiliar to you, the idea behind it probably is not. If you can recall spending more time studying for a certain subject because of a compliment from the teacher or a high grade on an examination, you have experienced positive reinforcement. Specifically, **positive reinforcement** involves strengthening a target behavior—that is, increasing and maintaining the probability that a particular behavior will be repeated—by presenting a stimulus (called a *positive reinforcer*) immediately after

> **Positive reinforcement: strengthen a target behavior by presenting a positive reinforcer after the behavior occurs.**

the behavior has occurred. Praise, recognition, and the opportunity for free play are positive reinforcers for many (but not all) students.

The term *positive* as Skinner used it refers to the act of presenting a stimulus (think of positive as *adding* here); it does not refer to the pleasant nature of the stimulus itself. You will understand better why this distinction is very important as we consider the other form of reinforcement.

Negative Reinforcement   People frequently have difficulty understanding the concept of negative reinforcement, most often confusing it with punishment, so we will examine it carefully here. The goal of **negative reinforcement** is the same as that of positive reinforcement: to *increase* the strength of a particular behavior. The method, however, is different. Instead of supplying a desirable stimulus, *one removes an unpleasant and aversive stimulus* whenever a target behavior is exhibited. As you study this definition, pay special attention to the removing action. Just as positive refers to adding, negative refers to the act of *removing* a stimulus. By removing something unwanted, you encourage the student to learn new behaviors.

In everyday life, negative reinforcement occurs quite frequently. A child picks up his clothes or toys to stop his parents' nagging. A driver uses a seat belt to stop the annoying buzzer sound. Later in the chapter, we will describe how educators use negative reinforcement. We will also discuss its desirability relative to positive reinforcement.

Punishment   There are three procedures that reduce the likelihood that a particular behavior will be repeated. The first is **punishment,** also known as Type I punishment or presentation punishment. Punishment is defined by operant psychologists as the presentation of an aversive stimulus (such as scolding, paddling, ridiculing, or making a student write 500 times "I will not chew gum in class") that reduces the frequency of a target behavior. From an operant perspective, you can claim to have punished someone else only if the target behavior is actually reduced in frequency. (Note that whether these methods of punishment do achieve their

> Negative reinforcement: strengthen a target behavior by removing an aversive stimulus after the behavior occurs

> Punishment: weaken a target behavior by presenting an aversive stimulus after the behavior occurs

Students are likely to be motivated to learn if they are positively reinforced for completing a project or task. Awards and praise from the teacher and one's peers are strong positive reinforcers for many students. Yellow Dog Productions/Getty Images

goal and are effective and whether they are ethical are other issues—ones that we will discuss later in this chapter.)

Many people confuse negative reinforcement with punishment. Both involve the use of an aversive stimulus, but the effects of each are opposite. Remember that negative reinforcement strengthens a target behavior, whereas punishment weakens or eliminates a behavior.

Time-Out   The second procedure that decreases the frequency of or eliminates a target behavior is another form of punishment, **time-out.** But instead of presenting an aversive stimulus, time-out *temporarily removes the opportunity to receive positive reinforcement.* (Time-out is sometimes called Type II punishment or removal punishment.) For instance, a student who frequently disrupts classroom routine to get attention may be sent to sit in an empty room for 5 minutes. Removal from a reinforcing environment (as well as the angry tone of voice and facial expression that normally accompany the order to leave the classroom) is usually looked on as an aversive consequence by the individual being removed. An athlete who is suspended from competition is another example of this form of punishment.

Extinction   A third consequence that weakens undesired behavior is extinction. **Extinction** occurs when a previously reinforced behavior decreases in frequency, and eventually ceases altogether, because reinforcement is withheld. Examples of extinction include a mother's ignoring a whining child or a teacher's ignoring a student who spontaneously answers a question without waiting to be called on. Both extinction and time-out are most effective when combined with other consequences, such as positive reinforcement. To help yourself define and remember the distinguishing characteristics of positive reinforcement, negative reinforcement, punishment, and extinction, study Figure 7.1.

Spontaneous Recovery   When used alone, extinction is sometimes a slow and difficult means of decreasing the frequency of undesired behavior because extinguished behaviors occasionally reappear without having been reinforced, an occurrence known as **spontaneous recovery.** Under normal circumstances, however, the time between spontaneous recoveries lengthens, and the intensity of the recurring behavior becomes progressively weaker. If the behavior undergoing

---

Margin notes:

Time-out: weaken a target behavior by temporarily removing a positive reinforcer after the behavior occurs

Extinction: weaken a target behavior by ignoring it

Spontaneous recovery: extinguished behaviors may reappear spontaneously

---

The time-out procedure recommended by behavior modification enthusiasts involves weakening an undesirable form of behavior (such as shoving on the playground) by temporarily removing positive reinforcement (by having the misbehaving student remain in a corner of the classroom for 5 minutes while the rest of the class continues to enjoy another activity).
© Stock Connection Blue/ Alamy

Figure 7.1 Conditions That Define Reinforcement, Punishment, and Extinction

TYPE OF STIMULUS	ACTION	EFFECT ON BEHAVIOR	CONCEPT
Desirable	Present	Strengthen	Positive Reinforcement
Aversive	Remove	Strengthen	Negative Reinforcement
Aversive	Present	Weaken	Type I Punishment
Desirable	Remove	Weaken	Type II Punishment (also called time-out)
Desirable	Withhold	Weaken	Extinction

extinction is not terribly disruptive and if the teacher (or parent, counselor, or supervisor) is willing to persevere, these episodes can sometimes be tolerated on the way to more complete extinction.

Generalization   When an individual learns to make a particular response to a particular stimulus and then makes the same or a similar response in a slightly different situation, **generalization** has occurred. For example, students who were positively reinforced for using effective study skills in history go on to use those same skills in chemistry, social studies, algebra, and other subjects. Or, to use a less encouraging illustration, students ignore or question a teacher's every request and direction because they have been reinforced for responding that way to their parents at home. The less similar the new stimulus is to the original, however, the less similar the response is likely to be.

Discrimination   When inappropriate generalizations occur, as in the preceding example, they can be essentially extinguished through discrimination training. In **discrimination** individuals learn to notice the unique aspects of seemingly similar situations (for example, that teachers are not parents, although both are adults) and to respond differently to each situation. Teachers can encourage this process by reinforcing only the desired behaviors (for instance, attention, obedience, and cooperation) and withholding reinforcement following undesired behaviors (such as inattention or disobedience).

Generalization: responding in similar ways to similar stimuli

Discrimination: responding in different ways to similar stimuli

Shaping   Up to now, we have not distinguished relatively simple learned behaviors from more complex ones. A bit of reflection, however, should enable you to realize that many of the behaviors human beings learn (such as playing a sport or writing a term paper) are complex and are acquired gradually. The principle of **shaping** best explains how complex responses are learned.

In shaping, actions that move progressively closer to the desired *terminal behavior* (to use Skinner's term) are reinforced. Actions that do not represent closer approximations of the terminal behavior are ignored. The key to success is to take one step at a time. The movements must be gradual enough so that the person or animal becomes aware that each step in the sequence is essential. This process is typically called *reinforcing successive approximations to the terminal behavior.*

> Complex behaviors are shaped by reinforcing closer approximations to terminal behavior

Schedules of Reinforcement   If you have been reading this section on basic principles carefully, you may have begun to wonder whether the use of operant conditioning principles, particularly positive reinforcement, requires you as the teacher to be present every time a desired response happens. If so, you might have some justifiable reservations about the practicality of this theory. The answer is yes, up to a point, but after that, no. As we have pointed out, when you are trying to get a new behavior established, especially if it is a complex behavior that requires shaping, learning proceeds best when every desired response is positively reinforced and every undesired response is ignored. This is known as a *continuous reinforcement* schedule.

Once the behavior has been learned, however, positive reinforcement can be employed on a noncontinuous, or intermittent, basis to perpetuate that behavior. There are four basic *intermittent reinforcement* schedules: fixed interval (FI), variable interval (VI), fixed ratio (FR), and variable ratio (VR). Each schedule produces a different pattern of behavior.

Fixed Interval Schedule   In this schedule, a learner is reinforced for the first desired response that occurs after a predetermined amount of time has elapsed (for example, 5 minutes, 1 hour, or 7 days). Once the response has occurred and been reinforced, the next interval begins. Any desired behaviors that are made during an interval are ignored. The reinforced behavior occurs at a lower level during the early part of the interval and gradually rises as the time for reinforcement draws closer. Once the reinforcer is delivered, the frequency of the relevant behavior declines, then gradually rises toward the end of the next interval.

> Fixed interval schedules: reinforce after regular time intervals

FI schedules of reinforcement occur in education when teachers schedule exams or projects at regular intervals. The grade or score is considered to be a reinforcer. As you are certainly aware, it is not unusual to see little studying or progress occur during the early part of the interval. However, several days before an exam or due date, the pace quickens considerably.

Variable Interval Schedule   If you would like to see a more consistent pattern of behavior, you might consider using a variable interval schedule. With a VI schedule, the length of time between reinforcements is essentially random but averages out to a predetermined interval. Thus four successive reinforcements may occur at the following intervals: 1 week, 4 weeks, 2 weeks, 5 weeks. The average interval is 3 weeks. Teachers who give surprise quizzes or call on students to answer oral questions on the average of once every third day are invoking a variable interval schedule.

> Variable interval schedules: reinforce after random time intervals

Fixed Ratio Schedule   Within this schedule, reinforcement is provided whenever a predetermined number of responses are made. A rat in a Skinner box may be reinforced with a food pellet whenever it presses a lever 50 times. A factory worker may earn $20 each time he assembles five electronic circuit boards. A teacher may reinforce a student with praise for every 10 arithmetic problems correctly completed. FR schedules tend to produce high response rates because the faster the

> Fixed ratio schedules: reinforce after a set number of responses

learner responds, the sooner the reinforcement is delivered. However, a relatively brief period of no or few responses occurs immediately after the reinforcer is delivered.

Variable ratio schedules: reinforce after a different number of responses each time

Variable Ratio Schedule Like a variable interval schedule, this schedule tends to eliminate irregularities in response rate, thereby producing a more consistent rate. This is accomplished through reinforcement after a different number of responses from one time to the next according to a predetermined average. If you decided to use a VR 15 schedule, you might reinforce a desired behavior after 12, 7, 23, and 18 occurrences, respectively (that is, after the 12th, 19th, 42nd, and 60th desired behaviors). Because the occurrence of reinforcement is so unpredictable, learners tend to respond fairly rapidly for long periods of time. If you need proof, just watch people play the slot machines in gambling casinos.

EDUCATIONAL APPLICATIONS OF OPERANT CONDITIONING PRINCIPLES

In the late 1940s, when Skinner's daughter was in elementary school, he observed a number of instructional weaknesses that concerned him. These included the excessive use of aversive consequences to shape behavior (students studying to avoid a low grade or embarrassment in the classroom), an overly long interval between students taking tests or handing in homework and getting corrective feedback, and poorly organized lessons and workbooks that did not lead to specific goals. Skinner became convinced that if the principles of operant conditioning were systematically applied to education, all such weaknesses could be reduced or eliminated.

How well do you understand reinforcement? Try this chapter's Netlab at the textbook's website, Education CourseMate.

That belief, which he then reiterated consistently until his death in 1990 (see, for example, Skinner, 1984), is based on four prescriptions that come straight from his laboratory research on operant conditioning:

Skinner's approach to instruction: clear goals, logical sequencing of materials, self-pacing

1. Be clear about what is to be taught.
2. Teach first things first.
3. Allow students to learn at their own rate.
4. Program the subject matter.

This straightforward formulation became the basis for two educational applications: an approach to teaching that we now call computer-based instruction and a set of procedures for helping students learn appropriate classroom behaviors referred to as behavior modification. The next few sections will describe the nature of these applications and assess the extent to which they improve classroom learning.

Computer-Based Instruction

Does Computer-Based Technology Aid Learning? When desktop computers and the instructional programs that were created for them were introduced into public schools in the early 1980s, many educators and psychologists believed that students would learn significantly more through this medium than through traditional teacher-led, text-based instruction. This approach to instruction has been referred to mostly as **computer-based instruction (CBI)**, although the term **technology-enhanced instruction** is being used with increasing frequency.

Types of CBI programs include drill and practice, tutorials, simulations and games

Instructional programs designed for computers generally fall into one of the categories described in Table 7.1. The research that has been done on the effectiveness of these varieties of CBI paints an interesting picture.

Research on the Effects of CBI Computer-based instruction is such a widely researched topic that several authors from time to time have attempted to summarize what has been learned about one aspect or another of this matter. In the typical

Table 7.1	Major Types of CBI Programs	
Type of Program	**Purpose**	**Main Features***
Drill and practice	Practice knowledge and skills learned earlier to produce fast and accurate responses	• Presents many problems, questions, and exercises. • Checks answers and provides feedback. • Provides cues when student is not sure of correct responses. • Keeps track of errors. • Adjusts difficulty level of problems and questions to the proficiency level of the student.
Tutorial	Teach new information (e.g., facts, definitions, concepts) and skills	• New material presented in linear or branching format. • Linear programs require all students to begin with first frame and work through subsequent frames in given sequence. Incorrect responses minimized by brief answers, small steps, and frequent prompts. • Branching programs allow students to respond to different sets of frames depending on correctness of responses. For incorrect responses, program provides supplementary material that attempts to reteach. • Dialogue programs mimic teacher-student interactions by presenting material, evaluating responses, and adjusting subsequent instruction by presenting either more difficult or easier material.
Problem-solving programs: Simulations and games	Teach new information and skills and provide an opportunity to apply what was learned in a meaningful context that would otherwise be unavailable because of cost, physical danger, and time constraints	• Student uses newly learned and existing information to solve a realistic problem. • Settings may be realistic (e.g., piloting a plane), historical/adventure (e.g., guiding a wagon train across the Oregon Trail), or imaginary (e.g., colonizing a new world). • Students practice creating and testing hypotheses on effects of different variables on achieving a goal.

* Not all programs contain all of the listed features.

SOURCE: Grabe & Grabe (2007).

experiment, one group of students receives instruction either partly or entirely via computer while an equivalent group receives either conventional instruction (a text assignment supplemented by classroom lecture and discussion) or an alternative form of CBI. Here is a brief summary of the main findings from several of these analyses:

Tutorial and simulation programs produce higher achievement than conventional instruction

1. Studies conducted during the 1970s and 1980s on the effect of tutorial programs showed a positive average effect of 0.36 of a standard deviation. This meant that the typical student who learned from a computer-based tutorial scored 14 percentile ranks higher on an achievement test than the typical conventionally taught student. For studies on tutorial programs conducted during the 1990s, the effect was even stronger. CBI-taught students scored 22 percentile ranks higher than their conventionally taught peers (Kulik, 2003a).

2. The average effect of simulation programs on achievement for studies conducted during the 1990s was a positive average effect of 0.32 of a standard deviation. Students who worked on simulation programs scored 13 percentile ranks higher than their conventionally taught peers (Kulik, 2003a).

3. An analysis of 52 studies published between 1983 and 2003 also found a moderate positive effect for CBI. Students who received CBI outscored those who received traditional instruction by an average of 21 percentile ranks, or a little more than a half of a standard deviation (Liao, 2007).

4. Students whose beginning reading skills (e.g., phonological awareness, word reading, text reading, reading/listening) were supported by CBI outscored students whose instruction was not computer-based on reading tests by about 10 percentile ranks (Blok, Oostdam, Otter, & Overmaat, 2002). Interestingly, the findings of this review were about the same as those from reviews conducted 10 to 15 years earlier. Despite the introduction of more sophisticated computer programs in recent years (providing verbal feedback, for example), their effect on the learning of beginning reading skills has remained fairly constant.

5. An analysis of 78 studies that were published between 1998 and 2007 reported some of the strongest positive effects to date. On average, students given CBI scored at the 83rd percentile on achievement tests and their non-CBI counterparts scored at the 50th percentile (Camnalbur & Erdogan, 2008).

6. An analysis of data collected from tens of thousands of students in 31 countries found that performance in school was positively related to the use of a computer at home for accessing the Internet, to the availability of educational software at home, and to moderate computer use at school. Both low and high levels of use at school were associated with lower levels of achievement (Bielefeldt, 2005).

TeachSource **Video Case** ◄◄ ▶ ►►

Integrating Technology to Improve Student Learning: A High School Science Simulation

Go to the Education CourseMate website to watch the Video Case, and then answer the following questions:

1. Is Mr. Bateman's biology lesson and use of technology in class a good example of Skinner's approach to instruction?

2. According to current educational research, computer-based simulation programs like the one depicted in this Video Case greatly improve student achievement in science. Using the Video Case and the text's discussion of behavioral theory, explain why this might be true.

Computer-based instruction has been shown to produce moderate increases in learning, particularly with tutorial and simulation programs. Tim Platt/ Iconica/Getty Images

Integrated Learning Systems In recent years, some software packages have combined tutorial programs based on operant conditioning principles with programs that keep track over time of student performance and provide feedback to both the student and the teacher. These packages are called **integrated learning systems (ILS)** (Kulik, 2003a; Mazyck, 2002; O'Byrne, Securro, Jones, & Cadle, 2006). Technology experts estimate that ILS may be used by as many as 25 percent of all school districts and, because of their high cost ($60,000 and up), account for about 50 percent of all technology-related expenditures by schools (Brush, Armstrong, Barbrow, & Ulintz, 1999; Kulik, 2003a; Mazyck, 2002).

| ILS: comprehensive, self-paced learning system

Such systems present information in a more sequenced and comprehensive fashion than traditional CBI programs. Integrated learning systems can, in fact, cover the content for entire K–8 mathematics, reading, language arts, and science curricula. Some systems include an English-language curriculum to address the needs of schools with high levels of limited-English-proficient students. Integrated learning systems allow students to go through tutorials at their own pace; they also administer tests, track student progress across grade levels, and present students with appropriate remediation or enrichment activities.

A review of 16 studies published since 1990 resulted in a mixed conclusion (Kulik, 2003a). The 7 studies that examined the effect of an ILS on mathematics achievement alone produced a positive average effect of 0.40 of a standard deviation. This means that the typical ILS-taught student scored 16 percentile ranks higher on a math test than did the typical conventionally taught student. The remaining 9 studies examined the effect of an ILS on both mathematics achievement and reading comprehension. For these studies, the effect on math was positive but quite small, just 0.17 of a standard deviation, and the effect for reading was almost zero (meaning that ILS-taught and conventionally taught students scored about the same on a reading test). Why the difference in the two groups of studies? One possible, if not likely, reason is that ILS that covered both subjects tried to do so in less time than would have been allotted for either subject alone (Kulik, 2003a).

A study conducted in two middle schools sought to answer a more focused question: Does an ILS have the same effect on low-achieving students as on high-achieving students? The answer, in brief, is no. After students scoring in the lowest quartile on a state-mandated test worked with an ILS, they performed better than their conventionally taught peers on tests of reading/language arts, social studies, and science (but not mathematics). For high-achieving students, on the other hand, there were no differences between ILS and non-ILS students on any of the four measures (O'Byrne, Securro, Jones, & Cadle, 2006). Low-achieving first-grade students have also shown significant gains in beginning reading skills as a result of ILS instruction (Cassady & Smith, 2005).

| CBI no substitute for high-quality teaching

Evaluation of Computer-Based Instruction How can we sum up the varieties of CBI or technology-enhanced instruction that have evolved from operant conditioning principles? Overall, the research findings suggest that CBI is not the equivalent of a wonder drug, but, when properly designed and used, it can effectively supplement a teacher's attempts to present, explain, apply, and reinforce knowledge and skills. Simulation programs seem to be particularly useful for helping students understand scientific concepts and procedures.

These findings also reaffirm what we suggested in the opening chapter about good teaching being partly an art and partly a science. Whenever you as a teacher apply any psychological principle in your classroom, you will need to ask yourself: For whom is this instructional technique likely to be beneficial? With what

pause & reflect

Many educators feel that operant conditioning presents a cold, dehumanizing picture of human learning and ignores the role of such factors as free will, motives, and creativity. Do you feel that way while reading this chapter? Do you think positive attributes of operant conditioning balance out possible negative aspects?

materials? For what outcome? In other words, as effective as computer-based instruction may be in certain circumstances, it should never be looked upon as a substitute for high-quality instruction. Talented teachers will always be needed to create a positive classroom environment, monitor student progress, and orchestrate the sequence and pace of instructional events.

Behavior Modification

Behavior modification: shape behavior by ignoring undesirable responses, reinforcing desirable responses

Although applied in many ways, the term **behavior modification** basically refers to the use of operant conditioning techniques to (as the phrase indicates) modify behavior. Because those who use such techniques attempt to manage behavior by making rewards contingent on certain actions, the term *contingency management* is also sometimes used.

After Skinner and his followers had perfected techniques of operant conditioning in modifying the behavior of animals, they concluded that similar techniques could be used with humans. In this section we will briefly discuss several techniques that teachers may use to strengthen or weaken specific behaviors. Techniques applied in education to strengthen behaviors include shaping, token economies, and contingency contracts. Techniques that aim to weaken behaviors include extinction and punishment.

Shaping   You may want to take a few minutes now to review our earlier explanation of shaping. Most attempts at shaping important classroom behaviors should include at least the following steps (Alberto & Troutman, 2009; Miltenberger, 2008):

1. Select the target behavior.
2. Obtain reliable baseline data (that is, determine how often the target behavior occurs in the normal course of events).
3. Select potential reinforcers.
4. Reinforce successive approximations of the target behavior each time they occur.
5. Reinforce the newly established target behavior each time it occurs.
6. Reinforce the target behavior on a variable reinforcement schedule.

To illustrate how shaping might be used, imagine that you are a third-grade teacher (or a middle or high school teacher) with a chronic problem: one of your students rarely completes more than a small percentage of the arithmetic (or algebra) problems on the worksheets you distribute in class, even though you know the student possesses the necessary skills. To begin, you decide that a reasonable goal would be for the student to complete at least 85 percent of the problems on a given worksheet. Next, you review the student's work for the past several weeks and determine that, on average, he completed only 25 percent of the problems per worksheet. Your next step is to select positive reinforcers that you know or suspect will work.

Reinforcers come in a variety of forms. Most elementary school teachers typically use such things as stickers, verbal praise, smiles, and classroom privileges (for example, feeding the gerbil, cleaning the erasers). Middle school and high school teachers can use letter or numerical grades, material incentives (such as board games and computer games, as long as school policy and your financial resources allow it), and privately given verbal praise.

With certain reservations, public forms of recognition can also be used. The reservations include the following:

- Because many adolescents are acutely self-conscious, any public display of student work or presentation of awards should be made to several students at the same time to avoid possible embarrassment (Emmer & Evertson, 2009).

- Awards should be made without letter grades.
- Awards should be given with an awareness that public displays of recognition are not appropriate or comfortable for all cultures.

One popular shaping technique that has stood the test of time involves having students list favorite activities on a card. Then they are told that they will be able to indulge in one of those activities for a stated period of time after they have completed a set of instructional objectives. This technique is sometimes called the **Premack principle** after psychologist David Premack (1959), who first proposed it. It is also called *Grandma's rule* because it is a variation of a technique that grandmothers have used for hundreds of years ("Finish your peas, and you can have dessert").

| Premack principle: required work first, then chosen reward |

Once you have decided on a sequence of objectives and a method of reinforcement, you are ready to shape the target behavior. For example, you can start by reinforcing the student for completing five problems (25 percent) each day for several consecutive days. Then you reinforce the student for completing five problems and starting a sixth (a fixed ratio schedule). Then you reinforce the student for six completed problems, and so on. Once the student consistently completes at least 85 percent of the problems, you provide reinforcement after every fifth worksheet on the average (a variable ratio schedule).

Although you control the classroom environment while students are in school, this accounts for only about half of their waking hours. Accordingly, parents might supplement your efforts at shaping behavior. The first step in a home-based reinforcement program is obtaining the parents' and student's formal agreement to participate. Then you typically send home a brief note or form on a regular basis (daily, weekly) indicating whether the student exhibited the desired behaviors. For example, in response to the items "Was prepared for class" and "Handed in homework," you would circle "yes" or "no." In response to a homework grade or test grade, you would circle the appropriate letter or percentage-correct designation. The parents are then responsible for providing the appropriate reinforcement or punishment (temporary loss of a privilege, for example). Home-based reinforcement programs are readily learned by parents and are effective in reducing undesired behaviors (e.g., Benoit, Edwards, Olmi, Wilczynski, & Mandal, 2001; Mackay, McLaughlin, Weber, & Derby, 2001). Overall, this procedure has been successful in both reducing disruptive classroom behavior and increasing academic performance (longer time on tasks and higher test scores, for example). Some studies suggest that it may not be necessary to target both areas because improved academic performance often results in decreased disruptiveness (Kelley & Carper, 1988).

Token Economies A second technique used to strengthen behavior in the classroom, the **token economy,** was introduced first with people who had been hospitalized for emotional disturbances and then with students in special education classes. A token is something that has little or no inherent value but that can be used to "purchase" things that do have inherent value. In society, money is our most ubiquitous token. Its value lies not in what it is made of but in what it can purchase—a car, a house, or a college education. By the same token (if you will excuse the pun), students can accumulate check marks, gold stars, or happy faces and "cash them in" at some later date for any one of several reinforcers. Such instructional activities as doing math worksheets, working at the computer, engaging in leisure reading, and playing academic games have proven to be effective reinforcers in token economies (Higgins, Williams, & McLaughlin, 2001). Token economies have even been proven effective in getting college students to increase their degree of in-class participation (Boniecki & Moore, 2003).

| Token economy is a flexible reinforcement system |

One reason for the development of the token economy approach was the limited flexibility of more commonly used reinforcers. Candies and cookies, for instance, tend to lose their reinforcing value fairly quickly when supplied continually. It is not always convenient to award free time or the opportunity to engage in a highly preferred activity immediately after a desired response. And social rewards may or may not be sufficiently reinforcing for some individuals. Tokens, however, can always be given immediately after a desirable behavior, can be awarded according to one of the four schedules mentioned earlier, and can be redeemed for items or activities that have high reinforcing value.

Our Case in Print for this chapter illustrates how several school systems are trying to modify students' attendance and studying behaviors with attractive positive reinforcers.

Token economies—especially when combined with classroom rules, appropriate delivery of reinforcers, and response cost (a concept we describe a bit later in the chapter)—are effective in reducing such disruptive classroom behaviors as talking out of turn, being out of one's seat, fighting, and being off-task. Reductions of 50 percent or more in such behaviors are not uncommon. Token economies are also effective in improving academic performance in a variety of subject areas (Higgins et al., 2001; Kehle, Bray, Theodore, Jenson, & Clark, 2000; Naughton & McLaughlin, 1995). Token economies have been used successfully with individual students, groups of students, entire classrooms, and even entire schools.

Contingency Contracting A third technique teachers use to strengthen behavior is **contingency contracting.** A contingency contract is simply a more formal method of specifying desirable behaviors and consequent reinforcement. The contract, which can be written or verbal, is an agreement worked out by two people (teacher and student, parent and child, counselor and client) in which one person (student, child, client) agrees to behave in a mutually acceptable way and the other person (teacher, parent, counselor) agrees to provide a mutually acceptable form of reinforcement. For example, a student may contract to sit quietly and work on a social studies assignment for 30 minutes. When the student is done, the teacher may reinforce the child with 10 minutes of free time, a token, or a small toy.

> Contingency contracting: reinforcement supplied after student completes mutually agreed-on assignment

One useful method for positively reinforcing desired behavior is a token economy—supplying students with objects that have no inherent value but that can be accumulated and redeemed for more meaningful reinforcers. Jim Pickerell/Stock Boston

Case in Print

Going to School Can Be a Rewarding Experience

Although applied in many ways, the term **behavior modification** *basically refers to the use of operant conditioning techniques to (as the phrase indicates) modify behavior. Because those who use such techniques attempt to manage behavior by making rewards contingent on certain actions, the term* **contingency management** *is also sometimes used. (p. 235)*

Attendance Prize: Schools Offer Kids Big Rewards Just to Get Them to Show Up

MEAD GRUVER
The Associated Press, 12/01/2006

CASPER, Wyo.—Sixteen-year-old Kaytie Christopherson was getting ready to do her homework on a Friday when she got a call that made a big improvement in her life: She had won a brand-new pickup truck for near-perfect school attendance.

The truck was a $28,000 Chevrolet Colorado crew cab, in red, that included an MP3 player.

"I take it everywhere," the high school junior said. "I pay attention to where I park it, though."

Public schools commonly reward excellent attendance with movie tickets, gas vouchers and iPods. But some diligent students like Kaytie are now hitting the ultimate teenage jackpot for going to school: They have won cars or trucks.

School districts in Hartford, Conn., Pueblo, Colo., South Lake Tahoe, Calif., and Wickenburg and Yuma, Ariz., are also giving away vehicles this school year.

In most cases the car or truck is donated by a local dealership, and the prizes typically are awarded through drawings open only to students with good attendance.

So does bribing students with the possibility of winning a car or truck actually get them to think twice about staying home from school? Some educators think so, and say their giveaways have boosted attendance. But the evidence is not clear-cut.

Kaytie—who has a 4.0 average at Natrona County High, Dick Cheney's alma mater—won her truck last spring, in the school system's first such drawing. But she said that wasn't what motivated her to keep up her attendance; she just didn't want to fall behind.

District attendance officer Gary Somerville said he hopes to raise attendance and also reduce the district's 29 percent dropout rate, which he blames in part on Wyoming's booming gas-and-oil industry.

"These kids can go out and earn $15, $16, $17 an hour swinging a hammer. It's kind of hard to keep them in school past their 16th birthday," he said.

Hartford has been holding a drawing—for either a car or $10,000—for the past six years. Five of those times the winning family chose the money.

"I can't tell you that it's increased attendance," district spokesman Terry D'Italia said. "But what it has done over the years is just kept a focus on it and kept it at the top of kids' minds."

Jack Stafford, associate principal at South Tahoe High School, said changing times call for such incentives. "My mom had the three-B rule: There'd better be blood, bone or barf, or I was going to school," Stafford said. But "that's not the case now."

Districts have a lot to gain and little to lose by holding car drawings. The vehicles are usually free. And in Wyoming, even a one-student increase in average daily enrollment means another $12,000 in state funding for the year.

Questions and Activities

1. Assume that you are an expert on operant conditioning and behavior modification techniques and have been asked to defend a school board's decision to award a $28,000 vehicle to the high school student with the best yearly attendance record. What are the strongest arguments that you think you could make? Now assume that you have been asked to criticize the very same practice. Again, what would be your strongest arguments?

2. Gary Somerville, the district attendance officer quoted in this article, expressed the hope that the prospect of winning an expensive truck would discourage students from dropping out of school to take jobs that pay $15 an hour or more working for Wyoming's oil

and gas industry. If you wanted to argue that Mr. Somerville is overlooking more important variables that influence both attendance and dropping out of school, what points would you make?

3. Make a judgment as to how successful you think this positive reinforcement program is likely to be, particularly over the long term, by evaluating how closely it meets accepted guidelines for shaping behavior through positive reinforcement.

4. Jack Stafford, an associate principal at a California high school, claimed that changing times call for larger and more attractive reinforcers to strengthen school attendance. Using your own high school experience as a guide, do you agree or disagree with this assessment? Interview at least six of your peers for their reactions.

Contracts can be drawn up with all members of a class individually, with selected individual class members, or with the class as a whole. As with most other contracts, provisions can be made for renegotiating the terms. Moreover, the technique is flexible enough to incorporate the techniques of token economies and shaping. It is possible, for example, to draw up a contract that provides tokens for successive approximations to some target behavior (Bushrod, Williams, & McLaughlin, 1995).

Extinction, Time-Out, and Response Cost   The primary goal of behavior modification is to strengthen desired behaviors. Toward that end, techniques such as shaping, token economies, and contingency contracts are likely to be very useful. There will be times, however, when you have to weaken or eliminate undesired behaviors because they interfere with instruction and learning. For these occasions, you might consider some form of extinction. Research has demonstrated that extinction is effective in reducing the frequency of many types of problem behaviors (Miltenberger, 2008).

The most straightforward approach is to ignore the undesired response. If a student bids for your attention by clowning around, for instance, you may discourage repetition of that sort of behavior by ignoring it. It is possible, however, that classmates will not ignore the behavior but laugh at it. Such response-strengthening reactions from classmates will likely counteract your lack of reinforcement. Accordingly, you need to observe what happens when you try to extinguish behavior by not responding. Another complication that you should consider before trying extinction is that a student's behavior may progress from being mildly annoying to so disruptive that it interferes with your ability to teach. If you are then forced to attend to the disruptive student, you will, in all likelihood, have reinforced that disruptive behavior (Obenchain & Taylor, 2005).

If other students are reinforcing a youngster's undesired behavior or if a behavior becomes disruptive, you may want to apply the time-out procedure. Suppose a physically active third-grade boy seems unable to keep himself from shoving classmates during recess. If verbal requests, reminders, or warnings fail to limit shoving, the boy can be required to take a 5-minute time-out period immediately after he shoves a classmate. He must sit alone in the classroom for that period of time while the rest of the class remains out on the playground. Time-out is an effective means of reducing or eliminating undesired behaviors, particularly those that are aggressive or disruptive, for both regular and mainstreamed children (Alberto & Troutman, 2009; Miltenberger, 2008). The rules for the procedure should be clearly explained, and after being sentenced to time-out (which should last no more than 5 minutes), a child should be given reinforcement for agreeable, helpful behavior—for example, "Thank you for collecting all the playground balls so nicely, Tommy."

| Time-out works best with disruptive, aggressive children

Another technique, **response cost**, is similar to time-out in that it involves the removal of a stimulus. It is often used with a token economy. With this procedure, a certain amount of positive reinforcement (for example, 5 percent of previously earned tokens) is withdrawn every time a child makes an undesired response. Anyone who has been caught exceeding the speed limit and been fined at least $50 can probably attest to the power of response cost as a modifier of behavior. As with extinction and time-out, research confirms that response cost helps reduce a variety of problem behaviors (such as getting off-task, not following directions, and engaging in disruptive behavior) for a wide range of children (Miltenberger, 2008).

TeachSource Video Case ◀◀ ▶ ▶▶

Classroom Management: Handling a Student with Behavior Problems

Go to the Education CourseMate website to watch the Video Case, and then answer the following questions:

1. Which basic principles of operant conditioning did Mrs. Henry use when trying to help the troubled student in the Video Case? Explain your answer.

2. Give some examples of positive reinforcement that the teachers could use with this student (to decrease his negative behavior).

Punishment   Punishment is one of the most common behavior modification techniques, particularly when it takes the form of corporal punishment. It is also one of the most controversial. One factor that makes this issue controversial is that many parents believe in corporal punishment and spank their children, whereas lobbying groups (such as End Physical Punishment of Children and the National Coalition to Abolish Corporal Punishment in Schools) work to persuade state and federal officials to pass laws that outlaw the practice, partly on the basis of moral grounds and partly because there is no scientific evidence that corporal punishment helps children develop more effective social and self-control skills (Dupper & Dingus, 2008; Gershoff, 2002).

A second factor is that researchers have different views about what the existing research means. For example, Elizabeth Gershoff (2002) analyzed 88 studies conducted over the past 60 years and concluded that corporal punishment was strongly associated with such negative behaviors and experiences as low internalization of moral rules, aggression, delinquent and antisocial behavior, low-quality parent-child relationships, and being the recipient of physical abuse. The definition of corporal punishment used by Gershoff was "the use of physical force with the intention of causing a child to experience pain but not injury for the purposes of correction or control of the child's behavior" (p. 540).

Gershoff's conclusions were challenged by Diana Baumrind, Robert Larzelere, and Philip Cowan (2002) on several grounds, one of which concerned the definition Gershoff chose to work from. These researchers argued that Gershoff's findings were due in part to the fact that the definition she used allowed her to include studies whose forms of punishment were more severe than most parents administer. Baumrind et al. advocated limiting the analysis to studies in which the form of corporal punishment used was the more common mild to moderate spanking. They defined spanking as a "subset of the broader category of corporal punishment that

pause & reflect

Skinner argued that society too frequently uses aversive means (particularly punishment) to shape desired behavior rather than the more effective positive reinforcement. As you think about how your behavior has been shaped, would you agree or disagree? Why do you think we use punishment so frequently?

Take a Stand!

Positive Reinforcement Versus Punishment as a Classroom Management Tool

Common sense suggests that when one pedagogical technique is shown to be largely effective for achieving a particular objective and a second technique is shown to be largely ineffective, the former would be used by at least a sizable minority of teachers while the latter would be ignored by most. Well, common sense does not always prevail, particularly in the case of using positive reinforcement and punishment as classroom management tools. As we've documented on these pages, few teachers use positive reinforcement in their classrooms despite its demonstrated effectiveness in promoting desired behaviors. Various forms of punishment, which have numerous disadvantages, are more popular.

One reason for this contrary state of affairs undoubtedly has to do with the decline in popularity of operant conditioning theory in educational psychology textbooks and courses. It is not unusual these days for students in teacher education programs to have learned little or nothing about operant conditioning principles and their classroom applications. As a result, many teachers fall into what is called the negative reinforcement trap. Here's how it works: A student's misbehavior instinctively elicits a punishing

response from a teacher because punishment can be administered quickly and easily and often produces a rapid (albeit temporary) suppression of the undesired behavior. Let's say the teacher sends the offending student to the principal's office. Having obtained at least temporary relief, the teacher is now more inclined to send the next misbehaving student to the office. Now let's examine this situation from the student's perspective. Some students may misbehave because they find the work boring or, even worse, threatening because of a fear of failure. Sending such a student out of the room removes the student from a punishing environment. This is a form of negative reinforcement, which increases the likelihood that the student will engage in subsequent misbehavior.

The best way to deal with this problem is to avoid it in the first place by using a combination of effective teaching methods and positive reinforcement, an approach that is referred to in the literature as positive behavior support (see Gettinger & Stoiber, 2006; Marquis et al., 2000). In our Suggestions for Teaching section, we discuss several ways in which positive reinforcement can be used appropriately and effectively.

What Do You Think?

Have you seen the type of situation described here during your own schooling? What do you think about it? For more on this topic, go to the Take a Stand! section of the textbook's Education CourseMate website.

is a) physically non-injurious; b) intended to modify behavior; and c) administered with an opened hand to the extremities or buttocks" (p. 581). A reanalysis of those studies examined by Gershoff that were more consistent with this narrower definition produced a considerably weaker (but still positive) relationship between spanking and aggressive behavior. For this reason, as well as limitations in many of the studies, Baumrind and colleagues concluded that a blanket condemnation of spanking cannot be made on the basis of the existing research (although it may be made on other bases).

A final word of caution before leaving this topic. As Elizabeth Gershoff pointed out, the studies she reviewed were correlational in nature. That is, researchers simply sought to determine whether a relationship exists between corporal punishment and aggressive behaviors exhibited by children. Consequently, one cannot draw the conclusion from this research that spanking children *causes* them to be more aggressive. It is just as plausible, until additional research proves otherwise, that children who are inherently more aggressive than others cause their parents and other adults to administer more corporal punishment. Another possibility is that a third variable, such as inconsistent discipline, is responsible for both increased use of corporal punishment and aggressive behavior in children.

The use of corporal punishment in schools is currently banned in 29 states and Washington, D.C., by either state law or state department of education regulation. Ohio falls somewhere between those states that ban punishment and those that permit

| Research unclear about strength of negative effects of corporal punishment

it. Ohio state law allows corporal punishment in schools only when districts follow state procedures. Nevertheless, any parent may prohibit school authorities from punishing their children. The remaining 20 states either explicitly permit schools to punish students physically or are silent on the matter. In states that allow corporal punishment, local school districts may regulate, but not prohibit, its use. Where states have not addressed the issue, local districts may regulate the use of corporal punishment or ban it altogether (Center for Effective Discipline, 2009a). The use of corporal punishment in schools has consistently fallen over the past 27 years. In 1976, approximately 3.5 percent of schoolchildren received some form of corporal punishment. By 2004 the percentage had fallen to 0.46 (Center for Effective Discipline, 2009b).

Should You Use Behavior Modification? This may seem a strange question to ask given the number of pages we have just spent covering behavior modification methods. Obviously, we feel that the results of decades of research on these techniques justify their use by teachers. Nevertheless, there are criticisms of behavior modification that are not adequately addressed by research findings and that you should carefully consider.

One criticism is that many students, including those in the primary grades, will eventually catch on to the fact that they get reinforced only when they do what the teacher wants them to do. Some may resent this and misbehave out of spite. Others may weigh the amount of effort required to earn a favorable comment or a privilege and decide the reinforcer is not worth the trouble. Still others may develop a "What's in it for me?" attitude. That is, some students may come to think of learning as something they do only to earn an immediate reinforcer. The potential danger of using behavior modification over an extended period of time is that learning may come to an abrupt halt when no one is around to supply reinforcement (Kohn, 1993). (This point will be addressed in the chapter on social cognitive theory.)

A second major criticism is that behavior modification methods, because of their potential power, may lend themselves to inappropriate or even unethical uses. For example, teachers may shape students to be quiet and obedient because it makes their job easier, even though such behaviors do not always produce optimum conditions for learning.

In response to these criticisms, Skinner and other behavioral scientists (see Chance, 1993; Flora, 2004; Maag, 2001, for example) argue that if we do not systematically use what we know about the effects of stimuli and consequences on behavior, we will leave things to chance. In an uncontrolled situation, some fortunate individuals will have a favorable chain of experiences that will equip them with desirable attitudes and skills, but others will suffer an unfortunate series of experiences that will lead to difficulties and disappointment. In a controlled situation, it may be possible to arrange experiences so that almost everyone acquires desirable traits and abilities. What behavioral psychologists seem to be saying is that educators could be accused of being unethical for not making use of an effective learning tool. The challenge, of course, is to use it wisely. The following Suggestions for Teaching will give you additional ideas for putting operant conditioning principles into practice.

Suggestions for Teaching

Applying Operant Conditioning in the Classroom

JOURNAL ENTRY
Checking on Causes
of Behavior

1 Remain aware that behavior is the result of particular conditions.

Unlike the controlled environment of a Skinner box, many causes of behavior in a real-life classroom may not be observable or traceable. You might as well accept the fact, therefore, that quite often you are going to be a haphazard shaper of behavior. Nevertheless, there will be times when you and your students may benefit if you say to yourself, "Now, there have to be some causes for that behavior. Can I figure out what they are and do something about changing things for the better? Am I doing something that is leading to types of behavior that are making life difficult for some or all of us in the room?" When you are engaging in such speculations, keep in mind that reinforcement strengthens behavior. Check to see whether you are inadvertently rewarding students for misbehavior (by calling attention to them, for example, or by failing to reinforce those who engage in desirable forms of behavior).

EXAMPLES

• If you become aware that it takes a long time for your students to settle down at the beginning of a period and that you are reacting by addressing critical remarks specifically to those who dawdle the longest, ignore the dawdlers and respond positively to those who are ready to get to work.

- Let's say that you have given students 30 minutes to finish an assignment. To your dismay, few of them get to work until almost the end of the period, and you find that you have to do a lot of nagging. When you later analyze why this happened, you conclude that you actually encouraged the time-killing behavior because of the way you set up the lesson. The next time you give a similar assignment, tell the students that as soon as they complete it, they can have class time to work on homework and that you will be available to give help or advice to those who want it.

2 Use reinforcement, and use it appropriately to strengthen behaviors you want to encourage.

Why would we remind you to do something as obvious as reinforce behaviors you want students to acquire and exhibit in the future? Wouldn't you do that almost automatically? Well, we certainly hope so, but statistics suggest otherwise. A large team of researchers headed by John Goodlad (1984) observed the classroom behavior of 1,350 teachers and 17,163 students in 38 schools from seven sections of the country. What they found may surprise you. Teachers' praise of student work occurred about 2 percent of the observed time in the primary grades and about 1 percent of the time in high school.

Once you have resolved to reinforce desired behavior systematically, you need to be sure that you do it appropriately. Although reinforcement is a simple principle that can be readily understood at an intuitive level, it has to be used in the right way to produce desired results. Paul Chance (1992) offers seven guidelines for the effective use of positive reinforcement:

JOURNAL ENTRY
Ways to Supply
Reinforcement

- Use the weakest reward available to strengthen a behavior. In other words, do not use material rewards when you know that praise will be just as effective a reinforcer. Save the material rewards for that special behavior for which praise or other reinforcers may not be effective.

- When possible, avoid using rewards as incentives. What Chance means is not to get into the habit of automatically telling the student that if she does what you want, you will provide a specific reward. Instead, sometimes ask the student to do something (like work quietly or help another student), and then provide the reinforcer.

- Reward at a high rate in the early stages of learning, and reduce the frequency of rewards as learning progresses.

- Reward only the behavior you want repeated. Although you may not realize it, students are often very sensitive to what is and is not being reinforced. If you decide that one way to encourage students to be more creative in their writing is to tell them not to worry about spelling and grammar errors, then do not be surprised to see many misspelled words and poorly constructed sentences. Or if you decide to reward only the three highest scorers on a test, reasoning that competition brings out the best in people, be prepared to deal with the fact that competition also brings out some of the worst in people (like cheating and refusing to help others).

- Remember that what is an effective reinforcer for one student may not be for another. For some students, comments such as "Very interesting point," "That's right," or "That was a big help" will strengthen the target behavior. But for others, something less overt, such as smiling encouragingly, may be just right.

- Set standards so that success is a realistic possibility for each student. You may have students whose English proficiency is limited or who have disabilities related to learning and intellectual functioning. One way to deal with such diversity is to reward students for making steady progress from whatever their baseline level of performance was at the beginning of the term.

- An often-mentioned goal of teachers is to have students become intrinsically motivated or to take personal pride and satisfaction in simply doing something well. You can use natural instructional opportunities to point this out—for example, explore with students how satisfying it is to write a clear and interesting story as they are writing.

Suggestions for Teaching

One of the basic principles of instruction derived from operant conditioning experiments is that teachers should provide elementary grade students with immediate reinforcement for correct responses. © Peter Hvizdak/The Image Works

3 **Take advantage of knowledge about the impact of different reinforcement schedules to encourage persistent and permanent learning.**

a. When students first attempt a new kind of learning, supply frequent reinforcement. Then supply rewards less often.

When students first try a new skill or type of learning, praise almost any genuine attempt, even though it may be inept. As they become more skillful, reserve your praise for especially good performances. Avoid a set pattern of commenting on student work. Make favorable remarks at unpredictable intervals.

b. If you want to encourage periodic spurts of activity, use a fixed interval schedule of reinforcement.

Occasionally, you will want to encourage students to engage in spurts of activity, as steady output might be too demanding or fatiguing. In such cases, supply reinforcement at specified periods of time. For example, when students are engaging in strenuous or concentrated activity, circulate and provide praise and encouragement by following a set pattern that will bring you in contact with each student at predictable intervals.

4 **Give students opportunities to make overt responses, and provide prompt feedback.**

a. Require students to make frequent, overt, and relevant responses.

The tendency of teachers is to talk, and for large chunks of time. Those who advocate a programmed approach to teaching recommend that teachers limit the amount of information and explanation they give to students and substitute opportunities for students to respond overtly. In addition, the responses should be directly related to the objectives. If your objectives emphasize the application of concepts and principles, then most of the responses students are asked to make should be about applications. The reason for this suggestion is that the delivery of corrective feedback and other forms of positive reinforcement can be increased when students make frequent responses, thereby accelerating the process of shaping.

EXAMPLES

- Instead of lecturing for 20 to 30 minutes at a time about the development of science and technology in the twentieth century, present information in smaller chunks, perhaps 8 to 10 minutes at a time, and then ask students to describe how an everyday product or service grew out of a particular scientific principle.
- Periodically ask students to summarize the main points of the material you presented over the past several minutes.

JOURNAL ENTRY
Ways to Supply Immediate Feedback

b. Provide feedback so that correct responses will be reinforced and students will become aware of and correct errors.

Research clearly shows that students who study material about a topic, answer a set of questions about that material, and are then told whether their responses are correct and why score significantly higher on a subsequent test of that material than do students who receive no feedback. The difference was about three fourths of a standard deviation, meaning that the average student who received no feedback scored at the 50th percentile, whereas the average student who received feedback scored at the 77th percentile. Here are a couple of examples of how you can provide timely and useful feedback to students (Bangert-Drowns, Kulik, Kulik, & Morgan, 1991).

EXAMPLES

- Immediately after students read a chapter in a text, give them an informal quiz on the key points you listed. Then have them pair off, exchange quizzes, and correct and discuss them.
- As soon as you complete a lecture or demonstration, ask individual students to volunteer to read to the rest of the class what they wrote about the points they were told to look for. Indicate whether the answer is correct; if it is incorrect or incomplete, ask (in a relaxed and nonthreatening way) for additional comments. Direct students to amend and revise their notes as they listen to the responses.

5 **When students must struggle to concentrate on material that is not intrinsically interesting, use special forms of reinforcement to motivate them to persevere.**

JOURNAL ENTRY
Ways to Encourage Perseverance

For a variety of reasons, some students may have an extraordinarily difficult time concentrating on almost anything. And, as we all know, to master almost any skill or subject, we have to engage in a certain amount of tedious effort. Accordingly, you may sometimes find it essential to use techniques of behavior modification to help students stick to a task. If and when that time comes, you might follow these procedures:

a. Select, with student assistance, a variety of reinforcers.

A behavior modification approach to motivation appears to work most successfully when students are aware of and eager to earn a payoff. Because students react differently to rewards and because any reward is likely to lose effectiveness if used to excess, it is desirable to list several kinds of rewards and permit students to choose. Some behavior modification enthusiasts (for example, Alberto & Troutman, 2009) even recommend that you make up a *reinforcement preference list* for each student. If you allow your students to prepare individual reinforcement menus themselves, they should be instructed to list school activities they really enjoy doing. It would be wise, however, to stress that the students' lists must be approved by you so that they will not conflict with school regulations or interfere with the rights of others. A student's reward menu might include activities such as reading a book of one's choice, working on an art or craft project, or viewing a videotape or DVD in another room.

Suggestions for Teaching

More ideas for your journal can be found in the Reflective Journal Questions at the textbook's website, Education CourseMate.

To review this chapter, try the tutorial quizzes and other study aids on the textbook's Education CourseMate website.

b. Establish, in consultation with individual students, an initial contract of work to be performed to earn a particular reward.

Once you have established a list of payoffs, you might consult with students (on an individual basis, if possible) to establish a certain amount of work that must be completed for students to obtain a reward selected from the menu. (Refer to Chapter 13 on instructional approaches for Robert Mager's suggestions for preparing specific objectives.) To ensure that students will earn the reward, the first contract should not be too demanding. For example, it might be something as simple as, "Successfully spell at least seven out of ten words on a list of previously misspelled words" or "Correctly answer at least six out of ten questions about the content of a textbook chapter."

c. Once the initial reward is earned, establish a series of short contracts leading to frequent, immediate rewards.

The results of many operant conditioning experiments suggest that the frequency of reinforcement is of greater significance than the amount of reinforcement. Therefore, having students work on brief contracts that lead to frequent payoffs immediately after the task is completed is preferable to having them work toward a delayed, king-sized reward.

Challenging Assumptions

Reward Is in the Eye of the Beholder

"So," says Celeste, "we can't assume that a desirable stimulus for one student will be desirable for all."

"Right," says Don, "and even if a kid's behavior does—from our point of view—'improve,' we can't be sure that it will work the same way in all situations. So, if we can never be sure what will and will not be a positive reinforcer, how does behavioral learning theory help us figure out what to do in our classrooms?"

"Good question," says Connie. She turns to Antonio. "What do you think?"

"I think it's really critical to know your students," says Antonio, "to know what works for each of them and to know that what works one day may not work the next. I mean, every day, every lesson, is an experiment. Going into the lesson, you have an idea of what might work, so you conduct your experiment and watch your kids' behavior to see if the experiment worked."

Celeste picks up on Antonio's mention of the scientific method: "So, you develop a hypothesis: if we do X in this lesson, then Y—some learning—should occur. You test your hypothesis by teaching the lesson. You collect data (you observe student behavior in the environment) to determine whether your hypothesis is supported or not." She continues, "Now, it is at this point—when you analyze your data and draw conclusions—that operant principles can be most helpful: they help you figure out what happened."

"I see where you're going," says Don. "You can't know whether some change you make in a student's environment is reinforcement or punishment until you see the effect on the student's behavior. You have to observe behavior to see whether it is strengthened or weakened." The three of them are nodding together, and they go on to analyze additional examples for 40 minutes.

The meeting finally draws to a close. On her way home, Connie smiles as she thinks, "These meetings present very desirable stimulation. I think I'll come back next week."

Summary

1. Operant conditioning is a theory of learning devised by B. F. Skinner. It focuses on how voluntary behaviors are strengthened (made more likely to occur in the future) or weakened by the consequences that follow them.

2. Operant conditioning assumes that human behavior is a natural phenomenon that can be explained by a set of general laws, that the best way to understand complex behaviors is to analyze and study the components that make them up, that the results of animal learning studies are potentially useful in understanding human learning, and that learning is the ability to exhibit a new behavior pattern.

3. Basic learning principles that derive from Skinner's work are positive reinforcement, negative reinforcement, punishment (Type I, or presentation punishment), time-out (Type II, or removal punishment), extinction, spontaneous recovery, generalization, and discrimination.

4. Positive reinforcement and negative reinforcement strengthen behaviors. Punishment, time-out, and extinction weaken target behaviors.

5. Complex behaviors can be learned by the reinforcement of successive approximations to the terminal (final) behavior and by the ignoring of nonapproximate behaviors, a process called shaping.

6. Once a new behavior is well established, it can be maintained at that level by the supplying of reinforcement on an intermittent schedule. The four basic schedules are fixed interval, variable interval, fixed ratio, and variable ratio.

7. Of the three main ways in which computers are used in schools—using the computer as a tutor (meaning the use of drill-and-practice, tutorial, and simulation programs), using the computer as a learning and problem-solving tool, and learning how to program computers—the first is most closely allied with the principles of operant conditioning.

8. In general, computer-based instruction (CBI) has had a moderate positive effect on learning. In particular, simulation programs have had a positive effect on science achievement.

9. Integrated learning systems (ILS) present an entire curriculum on computer, keep track of student performance, and provide feedback to the student and teacher. Research on the effectiveness of such systems is mixed.

10. Another application of operant conditioning principles is behavior modification. The goal of behavior modification is for the teacher to help students learn desirable behaviors by ignoring or punishing undesired behaviors and reinforcing desired ones. Techniques for achieving this goal include shaping, token economies, contingency contracts, extinction, and punishment.

11. Researchers disagree about the strength of the negative effects of corporal punishment, partly because of differences in how corporal punishment is defined.

Resources for Further Investigation

● Basic Principles of Operant Conditioning

In Chapters 6 through 10 of *Learning and Behavior* (6th ed., 2006), James E. Mazur describes all of the basic principles covered in this chapter, as well as numerous others. Stephen Ray Flora provides a spirited defense of reinforcement in *The Power of Reinforcement* (2004). Part I of Flora's book contains eight chapters that deal with what he believes are myths and misrepresentations of reinforcement (for example, that reinforcement is bribery and destroys creativity).

● B. F. Skinner

In three highly readable volumes—*Particulars of My Life* (1976), *The Shaping of a Behaviorist* (1979), and *A Matter of Consequences* (1983)—B. F. Skinner describes his interests, aspirations, triumphs, and failures; the people and events that led him into psychology; and the forces that led him to devise operant conditioning. *The Technology of Teaching* (1968) is Skinner's most concise and application-oriented discussion of operant conditioning techniques related to pedagogy.

A highly readable summary and critical analysis of Skinner's brand of operant conditioning can be found in Robert Nye's *The Legacy of B. F. Skinner* (1992). According to Nye, "Two major thoughts accompanied the writing of this book: a growing sense of the importance of Skinner's work and the awareness that his ideas are often misjudged" (p. ix).

In *Walden Two* (1948), Skinner describes his conception of a utopia based on the application of science to human behavior. To get the full impact of the novel and of Skinner's ideas, you should read the entire book. However, if you cannot read the whole book at this time, Chapters 12 through 17, which describe the approach to child rearing and education at Walden Two, may be of special interest to you as a future teacher.

● Behavior Modification

If the possibilities of behavior modification seem attractive, you may wish to examine the following: *Classroom Management for Elementary Teachers* (8th ed., 2009), by Carolyn Evertson and

Edmund Emmer; *Classroom Management for Middle and High School Teachers* (8th ed., 2009), by Edmund Emmer and Carolyn Evertson; *Behavior Modification: What It Is and How to Do It* (8th ed., 2007), by Garry Martin and Joseph Pear; and *Applied Behavior Analysis for Teachers* (8th ed., 2009), by Paul A. Alberto and Anne C. Troutman. Chapters 7 ("Arranging Consequences That Increase Behavior"), 8 ("Arranging Consequences That Decrease Behavior"), and 11 ("Teaching Students to Manage Their Own Behavior") of the Alberto and Troutman book should be particularly useful.

● Software Programs to Explore

The following are a few software programs whose excellence is generally recognized. They cover the range of drills, tutorials, simulations, and games:

- Operation: Frog (Scholastic): allows students to simulate the dissection of a frog, complete with full graphics and video. Students can also "rebuild" the frog to practice locating its organs.

- My Reading Coach (MindPlay Educational Software): contains lessons on phonemic awareness, grammar, and reading comprehension.

- Oregon Trail (The Learning Company): enables students to experience the journey from Independence, Missouri, to Oregon as the pioneers did in 1865. Students are responsible for stocking a wagon, avoiding obstacles on the trail, making decisions about how to cross rivers and catch food, and so forth.

- Great Solar System Rescue (Scholastic): a simulation in which groups of students role-play scientific experts who must collaborate with one another to find and rescue probes lost in the solar system.

- Where in the World Is Carmen Sandiego? (The Learning Company): requires students to interpret clues, put new or known facts (such as the location of cities) to use, and problem-solve creatively.

8 Information-Processing Theory

 The Education CourseMate website for this text offers many helpful resources. Go to **CengageBrain.com** to preview this chapter's Concept Maps and Chapter Themes.

KEY POINTS

These key points will help you learn the important information in this chapter. To help you study, they also appear in the margins of the pages, next to the text where they are discussed.

The Information-Processing View of Learning

● Information processing: how humans attend to, recognize, transform, store, retrieve information

A Model of Information Processing

● Sensory register: stimuli held briefly for possible processing
● Recognition: noting key features and relating them to stored information
● Attention: focusing on a portion of currently available information
● Information in long-term memory influences what we attend to
● Short-term memory: about seven bits of information held for about 20 seconds
● Maintenance rehearsal: hold information for immediate use
● Elaborative rehearsal: use stored information to aid learning
● Organizing material reduces number of chunks, provides recall cues
● Meaningful learning occurs when organized material is associated with stored knowledge

● Long-term memory: permanent storehouse of unlimited capacity
● Information in long-term memory organized as schemata
● Students remember much of what they learn in school, especially if mastery and active learning are emphasized

Suggestions for Teaching

● Unpredictable changes in environment usually command attention
● Attention span can be increased with practice
● Distributed practice: short study periods at frequent intervals
● Serial position effect: tendency to remember items at beginning and end of a long list
● Concrete analogies can make abstract information meaningful

Metacognition

● Metacognition: our own knowledge of how we think
● Insight into one's learning processes improves with age

Technology as an Information-Processing Tool

● Virtual environments provide rich content and context that can support collaborative learning

---

In Chapter 7, "Behavioral Learning Theory: Operant Conditioning," we noted that operant conditioning emphasizes the role of external factors in learning. Behavioral psychologists focus on the nature of a stimulus to which a student is exposed, the response that the student makes, and the consequences that follow the response. They see no reason to speculate about what takes place in the student's mind before and after the response. The extensive Suggestions for Teaching presented in Chapter 7 serve as evidence that conclusions and principles based on analyses of external stimuli, observable responses, and observable consequences can be of considerable value to teachers.

But cognitive psychologists, meaning those who study how the mind works and influences behavior, are convinced that it is possible to study nonobservable behavior, such as thought processes, in a scientific manner. Some cognitive psychologists focus on how people use what they know to solve different kinds of problems in different settings; their work will be discussed in Chapter 10, "Constructivist Learning Theory, Problem Solving, and Transfer." Many cognitive psychologists are especially interested in an area of study known as **information-processing theory**, which seeks to understand how people acquire new information, how they store information and recall it from memory, and how what they already know guides and determines what and how they will learn.

Information-processing theory became a popular approach to the study of learning because it provided psychologists with a framework for investigating the role of a variable that behaviorism had ignored: the nature of the learner. Instead of being viewed as relatively passive organisms that respond in fairly predictable ways to environmental stimuli, learners were now seen as highly active interpreters and manipulators of environmental stimuli. The basic principles of information-processing theory were established in the 1960s and refined over the next two decades (and you will notice that in many of the citations in this chapter). Thus, almost 50 years ago the stage was set for psychology to study learning from a broader and more complicated perspective—namely, as an *interaction* between the learner and the environment.

Revealing Assumptions

Information and Meaning

Celeste says, "Poetry has always been hard for me. I can never quite 'hear' the phrases in the same way others can, and I have never been able to memorize more than a couple of lines."

"It's hard for a lot of people, including my middle schoolers," says Antonio. Describing a unit his interdisciplinary team had taught, he says, "We were going to read 'The Rime of the Ancient Mariner' and then study the text to see what we could learn about the social customs of the period, geography, navigation, climate, how language evolves, and even technology. Besides being very long—it has seven parts—the language of the poem is unusual, with changes of voice and perspective. I had the bright idea that we would learn the poem through a dramatic choral reading. So that's what we did. We practiced reciting each part in unison and then went through the whole thing five or six times. Actually, the choral reading turned out quite well. We even recorded it with transitional music, and it sounded great. The real problem was taking the next step: they couldn't apply what they had read so well to anything. They knew the poem, but they didn't have a clue what it meant."

Connie says, "I'm guessing that the team made some sort of adjustment that helped the students, right?" Antonio nodded, "Yes, we did. And in the end, they surprised me with what they learned."

pause & reflect

Too often, information and meaning are assumed to be equivalent measures of student learning. We assume that if a student can remember, he or she has learned. Although it is true that students need to remember information to construct meaning, acquiring information does not lead automatically to meaningful learning. Perhaps you once memorized a piece of information—say, a formula—so that you could write it in the margin the moment you were handed the test. Perhaps you even used the memorized formula to answer several test items. Do you still remember the formula? Even if you remember the formula, could you—at this moment—explain its significance? Antonio's idea to learn the poem and then apply what was learned seems, intuitively, to be a good idea. How did he confuse information and meaning? What changes might he have made in the unit to bring about positive outcomes in the end?

THE INFORMATION-PROCESSING VIEW OF LEARNING

Information processing: how humans attend to, recognize, transform, store, retrieve information

Information-processing theory rests on a set of assumptions of which three are worth noting.

1. **Information is processed in steps, or stages.** The major steps typically are attending to a stimulus, recognizing it, transforming it into some type of mental representation, comparing it with information already stored in memory, assigning meaning to it, and acting on it in some fashion (Linnel, 2007; Searleman & Herrmann, 1994). At an early processing stage, human beings *encode* information (represent

it in thought) in somewhat superficial ways (as when they represent visual and auditory stimuli as true-to-life pictures and sounds) and at later stages in more meaningful ways (as when they grasp the gist of an idea or its relationship to other ideas).

2. There are limits on how much information can be processed at each stage. Although the absolute amount of information human beings can learn appears to be limitless, it must be acquired gradually.

3. The human information-processing system is interactive. Information already stored in memory influences and is influenced by perception and attention. We see what our prior experiences direct us to see, and, in turn, what we see affects what we know.

Thus, according to the information-processing view, learning results from an interaction between an environmental stimulus (the *information* that is to be learned) and a learner (the one who *processes*, or transforms, the information). What an information-processing psychologist wants to know, for instance, is what goes on in a student's mind as a teacher demonstrates how to calculate the area of a triangle or as the student reads 20 pages of a social studies text. In the sense that contemporary information processing emphasizes the use of existing knowledge schemes to interpret new information and build new knowledge structures, it can be considered a *constructivist* view of learning (Winne, 2001). (See Chapter 10 for a full description of this view.)

A careful reading of this chapter is important because the information-processing decisions you make affect when you learn, how much you learn, how well you learn—indeed, whether you learn at all. To give you an appreciation of the information-processing approach to learning and how it can help teachers and students do their jobs, the next section will describe several basic cognitive processes and their role in how people store and retrieve information. Later in the chapter we will describe research on selected learning tactics and discuss the nature of strategic learning.

A MODEL OF INFORMATION PROCESSING

Information-processing psychologists assume that people process new information in stages, that there are limits on how much information can be processed at each stage, and that previously learned information affects how and what people currently learn. Consequently, many psychologists think of information as being held in and transferred among three memory stores: a sensory register, a short-term store, and a long-term store. Each store varies as to the processes required to move information into and out of it, how much information it can hold, and for how long it can hold information. A symbolic representation of these memory stores and their associated processes appears in Figure 8.1. Called a *multi-store* model, it is based on the work of several theorists (for example, Atkinson & Shiffrin, 1968; Norman & Rumelhart, 1970).

Note that our use of the term *memory stores* is not meant to suggest specific locations in the brain where information is held; it is simply a metaphorical device for classifying different memory phenomena. Nevertheless, studies of neurological functioning using techniques such as positron emission tomography (PET) and functional magnetic resonance imaging (fMRI) scans (e.g., Haier, 2001; Ivanoff, Branning, & Marois, 2009; Owen, McMillan, Laird, & Bullmore, 2005) suggest that different types of tasks do activate different parts of the brain. For example, verbal memory tasks are correlated with heightened activity in the thalamus. Another interesting finding is that as people become more proficient at a task, activity decreases in the cortex, suggesting that the brain becomes

pause & reflect

Can you think of any personal experiences that illustrate one or more of the three memory stores? Have you recently, for instance, retrieved a long-dormant memory because of a chance encounter with an associated word, sound, or smell?

more efficient at processing information. But as interesting as findings such as these are, research that translates neurological functioning during learning and memory tasks into educational materials and practices is lacking, and educators should be highly skeptical of "brain-based" methods (Jorgenson, 2003).

Shortly after the introduction of multi-store models, information-processing theorists divided themselves into two groups. In one camp are those who believe that a multi-store model is the best way to explain a variety of memory phenomena. In the other camp are those who favor a theoretically leaner, single-memory system. Although this debate has yet to be firmly resolved, the multi-store model is seen as having enough validity that it can be productively used to organize and present much of what is known about how humans store, process, and retrieve information from memory (Searleman & Herrmann, 1994; Wickens, Lee, Liu, & Gordon-Becker, 2004; Winne, 2001).

As shown in Figure 8.1, *control processes* govern both the manner in which information is encoded and its flow between memory stores. These processes include *recognition, attention, maintenance rehearsal, elaborative rehearsal* (also called *elaborative encoding*), and retrieval. Each control process is associated primarily with a particular memory store.

The control processes are an important aspect of the information-processing system for two reasons. First, they determine the quantity and quality of information that the learner stores in and retrieves from memory. Second, it is the learner who decides whether, when, and how to employ them. That the control processes are under our direct, conscious control will take on added importance when we discuss educational applications a bit later. Before we get to applications, however, we need to make you more familiar with the three memory stores and the control processes specifically associated with each of them.

The Sensory Register and Its Control Processes

The Sensory Register   A description of how human learners process information typically begins with environmental stimuli. Our sense receptors are constantly stimulated by visual, auditory, tactile, olfactory, and gustatory stimuli. These

Figure 8.1 A Model of Information Processing

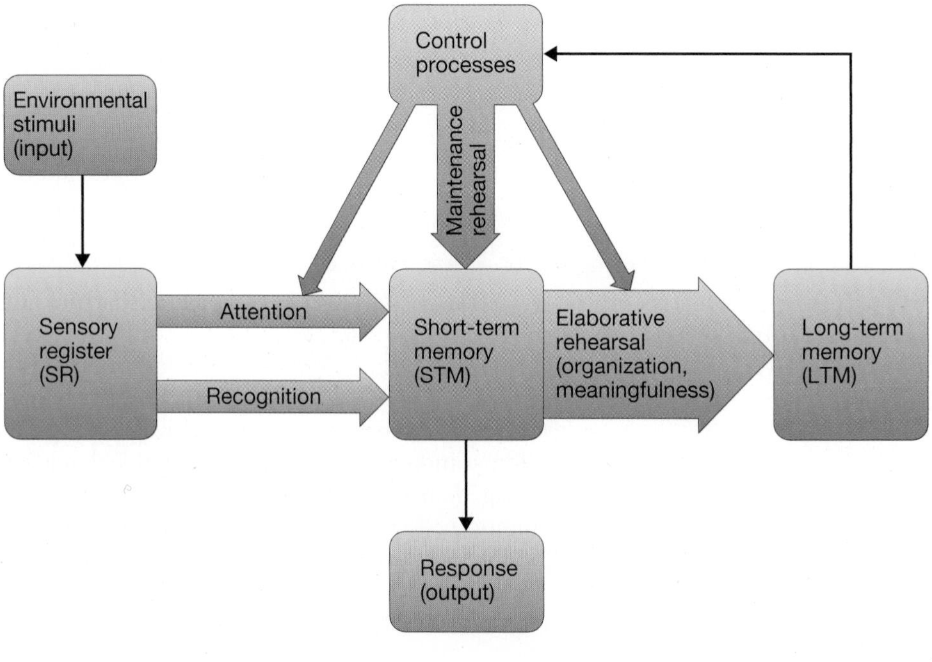

Sensory register: stimuli held briefly for possible processing

experiences are initially recorded in the **sensory register (SR)**, the first memory store. It is called the sensory register because the information it stores is thought to be encoded in the same form in which it is originally perceived—that is, as raw sensory data.

The purpose of the SR is to hold information just long enough (about 1 to 3 seconds) for us to decide whether we want to attend to it further. Information not selectively attended to and recognized decays or disappears from the system. At the moment you are reading these words, for example, you are being exposed to the appearance of letters printed on paper, sounds in the place where you are reading, and many other stimuli. The sensory register might be compared to an unending series of instant-camera snapshots or videotape segments, each lasting from 1 to 3 seconds before fading away. If you recognize and attend to one of the snapshots, it will be "processed" and transferred to short-term memory.

Recognition: noting key features and relating them to stored information

The Nature of Recognition The process of **recognition** involves noting key features of a stimulus and relating them to already stored information. This process is interactive in that it depends partly on information extracted from the stimulus itself and partly on information stored in long-term memory. The ability to recognize a dog, for example, involves noticing those physical features of the animal that give it "dogness" (for example, height, length, number of feet, type of coat) and combining the results of that analysis with relevant information from long-term memory (such as that dogs are household pets, are walked on a leash by their owners, and are used to guard property).

To the degree that an object's defining features are ambiguous (as when one observes an unfamiliar breed of dog from a great distance) or that a learner lacks relevant prior knowledge (as many young children do), recognition and more meaningful processing will suffer. Recognition of words and sentences during reading, for example, can be aided by such factors as clear printing, knowledge of spelling patterns, knowledge of letter sounds, and the frequency with which words appear in natural language. The important point to remember is that recognition and meaningful processing of information are most effective when we make use of all available sources of information (Driscoll, 2005; Leacock & Nesbitt, 2007).

One implication of this information-processing view is that elementary school students need more structured learning tasks than middle school or high school students. Because of their limited store of knowledge in long-term memory and narrow ability to relate what they do know logically to the task at hand, younger students should be provided with clear, complete, explicit directions and learning materials (Doyle, 1983; Palmer & Wehmeyer, 2003).

The Impact of Attention The environment usually provides us with more information than we can deal with at one time. From the multitude of sights, sounds, smells, and other stimuli impinging on us at a given moment, we notice and record in the sensory register only a fraction. At this point, yet another reduction typically occurs. We may process only one third of the already-selected information recorded in the SR. We continually focus on one thing at the expense of something else. This selective focusing on a portion of the information currently stored in the sensory register is what we call attention.

Attention: focusing on a portion of currently available information

Information in long-term memory influences what we attend to

As with any other human characteristic, there are individual differences in attention. Some people can concentrate on a task while they are surrounded by a variety of sights and sounds. Others need to isolate themselves in a private study area. Still others have difficulty attending under any conditions. What explains these differences? Again, information from long-term memory plays an influential role. According to one of the pioneers of cognitive psychology, Ulric Neisser, "Perceivers pick up only what they have schemata for, and willy-nilly ignore the rest" (1976, p. 79). In other words, we choose what we will see (or hear) by using our prior knowledge and experiences (i.e., schemata) to anticipate the nature of incoming information.

Students daydream, doodle, and write letters rather than listen to a lecture because they anticipate hearing little of value.

Moreover, these anticipatory schemata are likely to have long-lasting effects. If someone asked you now to read a book about English grammar, you might recall having been bored by diagramming sentences and memorizing grammatical rules in elementary school. If that was the case, you might not read the grammar text very carefully. A basic challenge for teachers is to convince students that a learning task will be useful, enjoyable, informative, and meaningful. Later in this chapter, we will present some ideas as to how this might be accomplished.

Short-Term Memory and Its Control Processes

Short-Term Memory Once information has been attended to, it is transferred to **short-term memory (STM)**, the second memory store. Short-term memory can hold about seven unrelated bits of information for approximately 20 seconds. Although this brief time span may seem surprising, it can be easily demonstrated. Imagine that you look up and dial an unfamiliar phone number and receive a busy signal. If you are then distracted by something or someone else for 15 to 20 seconds, chances are you will forget the number. Short-term memory is often referred to as *working memory* because it holds information we are currently aware of at any given moment and is the place where various encoding, organizational, and retrieval processes occur.

> Short-term memory: about seven bits of information held for about 20 seconds

Working memory is increasingly being viewed as a critical component in our information-processing system (Thorn & Page, 2009). In fact, as multimedia resources for learning have become more common, researchers have paid close attention to the capacity of working memory. Understanding its limits, researchers have investigated how to present information in ways that minimize the *cognitive load* on working memory to maximize comprehension and understanding. Such applied research contributes to what is known as cognitive load theory (CLT) and has yielded principles for the design of multimedia learning (Leacock & Nesbitt, 2007; Mayer & Moreno, 2003; Reed, 2006). In general, the principles help designers of multimedia environments (1) to identify what is critical, i.e., what must be presented to achieve the learning objective; (2) to consider context that will help learners understand the information that is critical; and (3) to eliminate extraneous material that increases cognitive load without contributing to the attainment of the learning objective.

Rehearsal A severe limitation of short-term memory is how quickly information disappears or is forgotten in the absence of further processing. This problem can be dealt with through *rehearsal*. Most people think of rehearsal as repeating something over and over either in silence or out loud. The usual purpose for such behavior is to memorize information for later use, although occasionally we simply want to hold material in short-term memory for immediate use (for example, to redial a phone number after getting a busy signal). Rehearsal can serve both purposes, but not in the same way. Accordingly, cognitive psychologists have found it necessary and useful to distinguish two types of rehearsal: maintenance and elaborative.

Maintenance rehearsal (also called *rote rehearsal* or *repetition*) has a mechanical quality. Its only purpose is to use mental and verbal repetition to hold information in short-term memory for some immediate purpose. Although this is a useful and often-used capability (as in the telephone example), it has no effect on long-term memory storage.

> Maintenance rehearsal: hold information for immediate use

Elaborative rehearsal (also called *elaborative encoding*) consciously relates new information to knowledge already stored in long-term memory. Elaboration occurs when we use information stored in long-term memory to add details to new information, clarify the meaning of a new idea, make inferences, construct visual images, and create analogies (Dunlosky & Bjork, 2008). In these ways, we facilitate both the transfer of information to long-term memory and its maintenance in short-term

> Elaborative rehearsal: use stored information to aid learning

memory. For example, if you wanted to learn the lines for a part in a play, you might try to relate the dialogue and behavior of your character to similar personal experiences you remember. As you strive to memorize the lines and actions, your mental "elaborations" will help you store your part in long-term memory so that you can retrieve it later.

Elaborative rehearsal, whereby information from long-term memory is used in learning new information, is the rule rather than the exception. Mature learners don't often employ maintenance rehearsal by itself. The decision to use one or the other, however, depends on the demands you expect the environment to make on you. If you need to remember things for future use, use elaborative rehearsal; if you want to keep something in consciousness just for the moment, use rote rehearsal.

It is important for you to keep in mind that younger children may not use rehearsal processes in the same way as more mature learners. Kindergarten students rarely engage in spontaneous rehearsal. By the age of seven, however, children typically use simple rehearsal strategies. When presented with a list of items, the average seven-year-old rehearses each word by itself several times. From the age of ten, rehearsal becomes more like that of an adult. Several items may be grouped together and rehearsed as a set.

So far, we have explained the effect of elaborative rehearsal in terms of relating new information to information already stored in long-term memory. That's fine as a very general explanation. But to be more precise, we need to point out that elaborative rehearsal is based on *organization* (as in the preceding example, in which several items were grouped together on some basis and rehearsed as a set) and *meaningfulness* (as in the earlier example, in which lines in a play were related to similar personal experiences).

TeachSource Video Case ⏪ ▶ ⏩

Cooperative Learning in the Elementary Grades: Jigsaw Model

Go to the Education CourseMate website to watch the Video Case, and then answer the following questions:

1. How do the students in this Video Case demonstrate the information-processing concepts of attention and elaborative rehearsal?

2. What are some ways that students in this Video Case demonstrate how their prior knowledge (information in long-term memory) influences their preparation in expert groups, their peer teaching to their home groups, and their assessments?

Organization Quite often the information we want to learn is complex and interrelated. We can simplify the task by organizing multiple pieces of information into a few "clumps," or "chunks," of information, particularly when each part of a chunk helps us remember other parts (Cowan, 2005). The value of organizing material was illustrated by a classic experiment (Bower, Clark, Lesgold, & Winzenz, 1969) in which two groups of participants were asked to learn 112 words in four successive lists but under different conditions. One group was given each of the four lists for four trials in the hierarchical or "blocked" arrangement displayed in Figure 8.2. The other group was given the same lists and the same hierarchical tree arrangement, but the words from each list were randomly arranged over the four levels of the hierarchy.

Figure 8.2 Hierarchical Arrangement of Words Produces Superior Recall

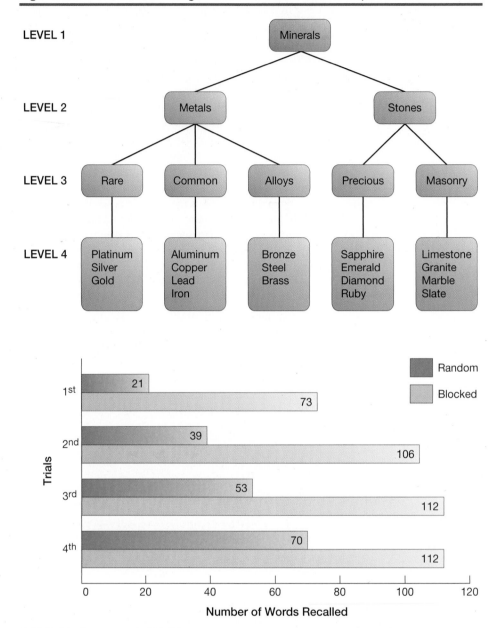

SOURCE: Bower et al. (1969).

Organizing material reduces number of chunks, provides recall cues

As you can see, through the first three trials, the first group recalled more than twice as many words as the second and achieved perfect recall scores for the last two trials. The organized material was much easier to learn not only because there were fewer chunks to memorize but also because each item in a group served as a cue for the other items. When you decide to store pertinent material from this chapter in your long-term memory in preparation for an exam, you will find the job much easier if you organize what you are studying. To learn the various parts of the information-processing model under discussion, for instance, you might group the ideas being described under the various headings used in this chapter.

Meaningful learning occurs when organized material is associated with stored knowledge

Meaningfulness The meaningfulness of new information that one is about to learn has been characterized as "potentially the most powerful variable for explaining the learning of complex verbal discourse" (Johnson, 1975, pp. 425–426). According to David Ausubel (Ausubel, Novak, & Hanesian, 1978), **meaningful learning**

To help students encode information, teach them how to group objects and ideas according to some shared feature. © Michael Newman/Photo Edit

occurs when a learner encounters clear, logically organized material and consciously tries to relate the new material to ideas and experiences stored in long-term memory. To understand learning theory principles, for example, you might imagine yourself using them to teach a lesson to a group of students. Or you might modify a previously constructed flowchart on the basis of new information. The basic idea behind meaningful learning is that the learner actively attempts to associate new ideas to existing ones (Driscoll, 2005; Thorn & Page, 2009). As another example, many of the Pause & Reflect questions in this book are designed to foster meaningful encoding by getting you to relate text information to relevant prior experience.

Lev Vygotsky, the Russian psychologist we mentioned in Chapter 2 on stage theories of development, emphasized the role of teachers, parents, siblings, and other kinds of expert tutors in meaningful learning. Vygotsky pointed out that some of what we learn about the world in which we live comes from direct, unfiltered contact with stimuli. Touch a hot stove, and you get burned. Insult or ridicule a friend, and you are likely to have one fewer friend at the end of the day. The limitation of this kind of learning, which Vygotsky called *direct* learning, is that one is likely to miss the general lesson or principle that underlies the event. Consequently, Vygotsky favored *mediated* learning. A mediator is an individual, usually older, more knowledgeable, and skilled, who selects stimuli to attend to, directs attention to certain aspects of the chosen stimulus, and explains why things are the way they are and why things are done in a certain way. Thus parents explain to their children why it is not acceptable to hit or tease playmates, and teachers explain to students why it is necessary for them to learn how to use the concepts and rules of English grammar, plane geometry, and the like (Kozulin & Presseisen, 1995).

From a Vygotskian perspective, the main goal of instruction is to provide learners with the psychological tools they will need to engage in *self*-mediation. If individuals are to function effectively once they leave school, they have to learn how to look beyond the immediate situation and see how they can use new knowledge and skills in future situations. Psychologists refer to this process as transfer of learning; we will discuss it at length in Chapter 10 on constructivism and problem solving.

This brief description of meaningfulness and its role in learning contains a strong implication for teaching in culturally diverse classrooms. You can foster meaningful learning for students from other cultures by pointing out similarities between ideas presented in class and students' culture-specific knowledge. For example, you might

According to Russian psychologist Lev Vygotsky, meaningful learning is most likely to occur when a more knowledgeable and skilled individual explains to a less knowledgeable individual why things are the way they are, as when one points out the reasons behind various rules and procedures, the causes of different events, and the motives for people's behaviors. Jim Cummins/ Taxi/Getty Images

point out that September 16 has the same significance to people of Mexican origin as July 4 has to U.S. citizens because the former date commemorates Mexico's revolution against and independence from Spain.

Visual Imagery Encoding As you will see in the Case in Print, generating mental images of objects, ideas, and actions is a particularly powerful form of elaborative encoding. Like pictures, images can be said to be worth a thousand words because they contain a wealth of information in a compact, organized, and meaningful format. Consider Benjamin Banneker, who has been called the first Black intellectual. Banneker was a self-taught mathematician, astronomer, and surveyor (Cothran, 2006). He predicted a solar eclipse in 1789, published tides tables, and was appointed by President George Washington to the commission that established the boundaries of Washington, D.C. His accomplishments suggest that mental imagery was critical to his thinking. Other notable individuals, such as Albert Einstein (physics), Michael Faraday (physics), James D. Watson (biochemistry), and Joan Didion (literature), have described how mental imagery played a significant role in their thinking and problem-solving efforts (Shepard, 1978).

Research has consistently shown that directing students to generate visual images as they read lists of words or sentences, several paragraphs of text, or lengthy text passages produces higher levels of comprehension and recall as compared with students who are not so instructed. Also, text passages that contain many concrete words and phrases are more easily understood and more accurately recalled than passages that contain more abstract than concrete ideas (Clark & Paivio, 1991). In one study (Sadoski, Goetz, & Rodriguez, 2000), the beneficial effect of concreteness was obtained for several passage types (such as expository text, persuasive text, stories, and narratives). The more concrete the passage was, the more it was rated comprehensible by students, and students who read concrete passages recalled 1.7 times as much information as students who read abstract passages. As we will see in the next chapter, concreteness and visual imagery are an integral part of several effective study skills.

The theory that these findings support is Allan Paivio's dual coding theory (Clark & Paivio, 1991; Meilinger, Knauff, & Butlthoff, 2008; Sadoski & Paivio, 2007).

According to the **dual coding theory,** concrete material (such as pictures of familiar objects) and concrete words (such as *horse, bottle, water*) are remembered better than abstract words (such as *deduction, justice, theory*) because the former can be encoded in two ways—as images and as verbal labels—whereas abstract words are encoded only verbally. This makes retrieval easier because a twice-coded item provides more potential retrieval cues than information that exists in only one form.

Before you go on to read about long-term memory, look at Table 8.1, which summarizes some important points about the control processes of short-term memory and the implications for teachers. Later in the chapter, our Suggestions for Teaching section will help you put these ideas into practice.

Long-Term Memory

Long-term memory: permanent storehouse of unlimited capacity

We have already referred in a general way to the third memory store, **long-term memory (LTM),** which is perhaps the most interesting of all. On the basis of neurological, experimental, and clinical evidence, most cognitive psychologists think that the storage capacity of LTM is unlimited and that it contains a permanent record of everything an individual has learned, although some doubt exists about the latter point (see, for example, Rogers, Pak, & Fisk, 2007; Schunk, 2004).

The neurological evidence comes from the work of Wilder Penfield (1969), a Canadian neurosurgeon who operated on more than 1,000 patients who experienced epileptic seizures. To determine the source of the seizures, Penfield electrically stimulated various parts of the brain's surface. During this procedure, many patients reported vivid images of long-dormant events from their past. It was as if a neurological videotape had been turned on.

The experimental evidence, although less dramatic, is just as interesting, and it too has its origins in the early days of information-processing theory. In a typical memory study (such as Tulving & Pearlstone, 1966), participants receive

Table 8.1	Implications for Instruction: How Findings About the Control Processes of Short-Term Memory Should Influence Your Teaching
Research Finding	**Implications**
Recognition involves relating a stimulus to information from long-term memory.	Compared with older students, elementary school students have less knowledge stored in long-term memory, and therefore they need structured learning tasks in which one step leads clearly to the next.
Attention is influenced by previous experience stored in long-term memory—we notice what we expect to be important.	Teachers should develop techniques for capturing students' attention and convincing them that the information being presented will be important to them.
Rehearsal prevents the quick disappearance of information from short-term memory. Most children do not begin to rehearse on their own until about age seven.	All children, especially younger ones, can benefit from being taught rehearsal techniques.
Organization of material into chunks makes it much easier to remember.	Teachers can aid students by presenting material in logical chunks and by showing students how to organize information on their own.
Meaningful learning occurs when the learner relates new information to prior ideas and experiences.	Teachers should mediate learning by relating new information to students' cultural knowledge and by helping students to learn techniques of self-mediation.
Visual imagery is easier to recall than abstractions.	Teachers should help students develop learning skills that incorporate visual imagery and other memory-aiding techniques.

a list of nouns to learn. After giving participants ample opportunity to recall as many of the words as possible, researchers provide retrieval cues—for instance, category labels such as "clothing," "food," or "animals." In many cases cued participants quickly recall additional items. Experiments on how well people recognize previously seen pictures have produced some startling findings. Thirty-six hours after viewing more than 2,500 pictures, a group of college students correctly identified an average of about 2,250, or 90 percent (Standing, Conezio, & Haber, 1970). In fact, it has been estimated that if 1 million pictures could be shown, recognition memory would still be 90 percent or better (Standing, 1973). Finally, psychiatrists and psychotherapists have reported many case histories of individuals who have been helped to recall seemingly forgotten events through hypnosis and other techniques (Erdelyi & Goldberg, 1979; Oakley & Halligan, 2009).

Information in long-term memory organized as schemata

How Information Is Organized in Long-Term Memory As you have seen, long-term memory plays an influential role throughout the information-processing system. The interests, attitudes, skills, and knowledge of the world that reside there influence what we perceive, how we interpret our perceptions, and whether we process information for short-term or long-term storage. In most instances, retrieval of information from long-term memory is extremely rapid and accurate, like finding a book in a well-run library. Accordingly, we can conclude that information in long-term memory must be organized. The nature of this organization is a key area in the study of memory. The insights it provides help to illuminate the encoding and retrieval processes associated with long-term memory.

Many cognitive psychologists believe that our store of knowledge in long-term memory is organized in terms of **schemata** (which is plural for *schema* and is related in meaning to Jean Piaget's *scheme*). A schema is typically defined as an abstract structure of information. It is abstract because it summarizes information about many different cases or examples of something, and it is structured because it represents how its own informational components are interrelated. Schemata give us expectations about objects and events (dogs bark, birds fly, students listen to their teachers and study industriously). When our schemata are well formed and a

Because people interpret new information and experiences on the basis of existing memory schemes, and because no two people's schemes are identical, each person is likely to represent the same idea or experience in a unique fashion. © Jeff Greenberg/Photo Edit

specific event is consistent with our expectation, comprehension occurs. When schemata are poorly structured or absent, learning is slow and uncertain (Bruning, Schraw, Norby, & Ronning, 2004; Lewandowsky & Thomas 2009; Moreno, 2006; Schunk, 2004). The following example should make this notion of schemata more understandable.

For almost everyone raised in the United States, the word *classroom* typically calls to mind a scene that includes certain people (teacher, students), objects (desks, chalkboard, books, pencils), rules (attend to the teacher's instructions, stay in the classroom unless given permission to leave), and events (reading, listening, writing, talking, drawing). This is a generalized representation, and some classrooms may contain fewer or more of these characteristics. However, as long as students and teachers share the same basic classroom schema, each will generally know what to expect and how to behave in any classroom. It is when people do not possess an appropriate schema that comprehension, memory, and behavior problems arise.

This notion was first investigated during the early 1930s by Sir Frederick Bartlett (1932), an English psychologist. In one experiment, Bartlett had participants read and recall a brief story, titled "The War of the Ghosts," that was based on North American Indian folklore. Because Bartlett's participants had little knowledge of American Indian culture, they had difficulty accurately recalling the story; they omitted certain details and distorted others. The distortions were particularly interesting because they reflected an attempt to interpret the story in terms of the logic and beliefs of Western culture. Similar studies, conducted more recently with other kinds of reading materials, have reported similar results (Derry, 1996; Griffiths, Steyvers, & Tenenbaum, 2007). The conclusion that Bartlett and other researchers have drawn is that remembering is not simply a matter of retrieving a true-to-life record of information. People often remember their *interpretations* or *constructions* of something read, seen, or heard (Lampinen & Odegard, 2006). In addition, when they experience crucial gaps in memory, they tend to fill in these blanks with logical reconstructions of what they think must have been. People then report these reconstructions as memories of actual events (Derry, 1996).

These experiments vividly demonstrate the interactive nature of memory. What we know influences what we perceive and how we interpret and store those perceptions. And because our memories of specific events or experiences are assembled, constructed, and sometimes reassembled by the brain over time, accurate and complete recall of information we once stored is not always possible. As a teacher, then, you should pay deliberate attention to how your students use their background knowledge, helping them to use it as accurately and completely as possible to process new information.

TeachSource Video Case ◄◄ ▶ ►►

Using Information-Processing Strategies: A Middle-School Science Lesson

Go to the Education CourseMate website to watch the Video Case, and then answer the following questions:

1. What kinds of encoding strategies does Mr. Beucler facilitate in his lesson?
2. How does the efficient processing of information contribute to critical thinking?

Take a Stand!

Students Are Learners, Not Just Performers

Visit a school in the last 2 months of winter and you will see teachers preparing their students to perform as well as they possibly can on the state exams in April and May. Ask teachers why they are so focused on the state exams, and they will tell you that the administration has made student performance on the state exams a top priority. Ask the administrators why student performance on the state exams deserves so much time and energy, and they will tell you that poor student performance on the exams can decrease property values in the community, can mean the replacement—at considerable expense—of an entire curriculum, can even cost teachers and administrators their jobs. As you will see in Chapter 15, "Understanding Standardized Assessment," a lot is riding on students' performance on the state exams. And so teachers guide students through the material they expect to be on the tests; teachers go over and over it in an effort to ensure that every student gets every possible test item correct. The teachers lead the students through seemingly endless drill and practice. (Some teachers—and some students—call it "drill and kill.") The teachers work very hard, the students work very hard, and the administrators feel the pressure and keep the pressure on.

Days and weeks of drill and practice, focused on rote learning that serves only to make students perform better on a test, go against what research tells us about effective learning. By focusing on discrete information or skills, students have few opportunities to draw on their prior knowledge, to learn in authentic settings, to explore and investigate so as to understand new information in meaningful contexts. Research shows us that prior knowledge is critical for student learning. Drilling students to perform can kill learning. We believe educational professionals must be held accountable, but they should be held accountable for student learning, not just test performance. If we are content simply to focus on performance, then let's continue to devote each winter to test preparation. But if we value our students as learners instead of performers, then the time has come to end the winter of our discontent. And we should do it now.

What Do You Think?

Does the authors' position accord with your own experience? That is, did you feel as if you were learning material solely for the purpose of answering questions correctly on a state-mandated test and not for any future meaningful use? If so, how can you prepare your students for these exams and still make the learning experience relevant to their lives? Explore this issue further at the Take a Stand! section of the textbook's Education CourseMate website.

How Well Do We Remember What We Learn in School? Conventional wisdom (which is often wrong, by the way) holds that much of the information that we learn in school is forgotten soon after a unit of instruction or course has ended. You may have felt the same way yourself on more than one occasion. But is this belief true? To answer this question, George Semb and John Ellis (1994) reviewed the results of 56 research articles published between 1930 and 1993. Their main findings are very consistent with the information-processing principles that you have read about and should at least partially reassure you that you haven't been wasting your time all these years:

- More than seven out of ten studies reported less than a 20 percent loss of what was learned when measured with a recognition task. Half of the studies reported less than a 20 percent loss of what was learned when measured with free recall.
- Subject matter that had a higher-than-average level of unfamiliar facts and associations (such as zoology, anatomy, and medical terminology) and for which students would have little relevant prior knowledge (such as electricity, mechanics, and linguistics) was associated with increased levels of forgetting.
- Most of the forgetting of information occurred within 4 weeks after the end of a unit of instruction. Additional declines in recall occurred more slowly.
- Less forgetting occurred among students who learned the material to a high level either by being required to achieve a high score on an exam before moving on to the next unit of instruction, by having to teach it to less knowledgeable students, or by taking advanced courses.
- Less forgetting occurred in classes in which students were more actively involved in learning (as in a geography field trip on which students had to observe, sketch, record, and answer questions).

The instructional implications that flow from these findings include an emphasis on mastery learning, peer tutoring, frequent testing with corrective feedback, and forms of instruction that actively involve students in learning. In addition, the Suggestions for Teaching that begin on page 263 point out several ways in which you can help your students improve their information processing.

Students remember much of what they learn in school, especially if mastery and active learning are emphasized

Suggestions for Teaching

Helping Your Students Become Efficient Information Processors

1 **Develop and use a variety of techniques to attract and hold attention, and give your students opportunities to practice and refine their skills in maintaining attention.**

a. Be aware of what will capture your students' attention.

JOURNAL ENTRY
Techniques for Capturing
Attention

Unpredictable changes in
environment usually command
attention

The ability to capture your students' attention is affected by characteristics of the information itself and the learners' related past experiences. Learners are more likely to attend to things they expect to find interesting or meaningful. It is also true that human beings are sensitive to abrupt, sudden changes in their environment. Thus anything that stands out, breaks a rhythm, or is unpredictable is almost certain to command students' attention.

EXAMPLES

- Print key words or ideas in extra-large letters on the board.
- Use colored chalk to emphasize important points written on the board.
- When you come to a particularly important part of a lesson, say, "Now really concentrate on this. It's especially important." Then present the idea with intensity and emphasis.
- Start off a lesson with unexpected remarks, such as, "Imagine that you have just inherited a million dollars and . . ."

b. To maintain attention, emphasize the possible utility of learning new ideas.

JOURNAL ENTRY
Techniques for
Maintaining Attention

Although it is possible to overdo attempts at making the curriculum relevant, it never hurts to think of possible ways of relating school learning to the present and future lives of students. When students realize that the basic purpose of school is to help them adapt to their environment, they are more likely to pay close attention to what you are trying to do.

EXAMPLE

- Teach basic skills—such as arithmetic computation, arithmetic reasoning, spelling, writing, and reading—as part of class projects that relate to students' natural interests (for example, keeping records of money for newspaper deliveries; measuring rainfall, temperature, and wind speed; writing letters to local television stations to express opinions on or request information about television shows).

c. Teach students how to increase their span of attention.

Attention span can be increased
with practice

Remember that paying attention is a skill that many students have not had an opportunity to refine. Give your students plenty of opportunities to practice and improve their ability to maintain attention.

EXAMPLES

JOURNAL ENTRY
Techniques for Increasing
Attention Span

- Institute games that depend on maintaining attention, such as playing Simon Says, keeping track of an object hidden under one of several boxes (the old shell game), or determining whether two pictures are identical or different. At first, positively reinforce students for all correct responses. Then reinforce only for improvements in performance. Remind students that their success is a direct result of how well they pay attention.
- Read a short magazine or newspaper story and ask students to report who, what, where, when, and why.

2 Point out and encourage students to recognize that certain bits of information are important and can be related to what they already know.

Attention is one control process for the sensory register; the other is recognition. Sometimes the two processes can be used together to induce students to focus on important parts of material to be learned. Sometimes you can urge your students to recognize key features or familiar relationships on their own.

EXAMPLES

- Say: "This math problem is very similar to one you solved last week. Does anyone recognize something familiar about this problem?"
- Say: "In this chapter, the same basic point is made in several different ways. As you read, try to recognize and write down as many variations on that basic theme as you can."
- Give students opportunities to express ideas in their own words and relate new knowledge to previous learning.
- Have students practice grouping numbers, letters, or classroom items according to some shared feature, such as odd numbers, multiples of five, letters with circles, or things made of wood.

JOURNAL ENTRY
Ways to Use Chunking to Facilitate Learning

3 Use appropriate rehearsal techniques, including an emphasis on meaning and chunking.

The power of chunking information into meaningful units was demonstrated in a study conducted with a single college student of average memory ability and intelligence (Ericsson, Chase, & Faloon, 1980). Over 20 months, he was able to improve his memory for digits from 7 to almost 80. Being a track and field buff, he categorized 3- and 4-digit groups as running times for imaginary races. Thus 3,492 became "3 minutes and 49.2 seconds, near world record time." Number groups that could not be encoded as running times were encoded as ages. These two chunking techniques accounted for almost 90 percent of his associations.

The main purpose of chunking is to enhance learning by breaking tasks into small, easy-to-manage pieces. To a large degree, students who are ten and older can learn to do this for themselves if you show them how chunking works. In addition, you can help by not requiring students to learn more than they can reasonably handle at one time. If you have a list of 50 spelling words to be learned, it is far better to present 10 words a day, 5 days in a row, during short study periods than to give all 50 at once. This method of presentation is called **distributed practice** (Cepeda et al., 2009). A description of the positive effect of distributed practice on classroom learning and an explanation of why educators do not make greater use of it have been offered by Frank Dempster (1988).

Distributed practice: short study periods at frequent intervals

In distributed practice, it is usually necessary to divide the material into small parts, which seems to be the best way for students to learn and retain unrelated material (for example, spelling words). This approach makes use of the **serial position effect**, which is people's tendency to learn and remember the words at the beginning and end of a long list more easily than those in the middle. By using short lists, you in effect eliminate the hard-to-memorize middle ground.

Serial position effect: tendency to remember items at beginning and end of a long list

Distributed practice may not be desirable for all learning tasks. If you ask students to learn roles in a play, short rehearsals might not be effective because students may have a difficult time grasping the entire plot. If you allow enough rehearsal time to run through a whole act, your students will be able to relate one speech to another and comprehend the overall structure of the play. When students learn by way of a few rather long study periods, spaced infrequently, psychologists call it **massed practice.**

You might also tell your students about the relative merits of distributed versus massed practice. Robert Bjork (1979) has pointed out that most students not only are unaware of the benefits of distributed study periods but also go to considerable lengths to block or mass the study time devoted to a particular subject, even when that tactic is a hindrance rather than a help.

JOURNAL ENTRY
Organizing Information
into Related Categories

4 Organize what you ask your students to learn, and urge older students to organize material on their own.

At least some items in most sets of information that you ask your students to learn will be related to other items, and you will find it desirable to call attention to interrelationships. The Bower et al. (1969) experiment described earlier in which one group of students was given a randomly arranged set of items to learn and another group was presented the same items in logically ordered groups illustrates the value of organization. By placing related items in groups, you reduce the number of chunks to be learned and also make it possible for students to benefit from cues supplied by the interrelationships between items in any given set. And by placing items in logical order, you help students grasp how information at the beginning of a chapter or lesson makes it easier to learn information that is presented later.

EXAMPLES

- If students are to learn how to identify trees, birds, rocks, or the equivalent, group items that are related (for example, deciduous trees and evergreen trees). Call attention to distinctive features and organizational schemes that have been developed.

- Print an outline of a chapter on the board, or give students a duplicated outline, and have them record notes under the various headings. Whenever you give a lecture or demonstration, print an outline on the board. Call attention to the sequence of topics, and demonstrate how various points emerge from or are related to other points.

JOURNAL ENTRY
Ways to Present
Information Concretely

Concrete analogies can make
abstract information meaningful

5 Make what students learn more meaningful by presenting information in concrete, visual terms.

To avoid blank stares and puzzled expressions from students when you explain an idea in abstract terms, try using representations that can more easily be visualized. Concrete analogies, for example, offer one effective way to add meaning to material. Consider someone who has no knowledge of basic physics but is trying to understand a passage about the flow of electricity through metal. For this person, statements about crystalline lattice arrays, free-floating electrons, and the effects of impurities will mean very little. However, such abstract ideas can be explained in more familiar terms. You might compare the molecular structure of a metal bar to a Tinker Toy arrangement, for example, or liken the effect of impurities to placing a book in the middle of a row of falling dominoes. Such analogies increase recall and comprehension (Royer & Cable, 1975, 1976).

You should also consider using what are called graphical displays. These are visual-symbolic spatial representations of objects, concepts, and their relationships. Examples of graphical displays include diagrams, matrices, graphs, concept maps, and charts.

According to Allan Paivio's dual coding theory (discussed earlier), the use of graphical displays leads to higher levels of learning because the displays increase the concreteness of information, thereby allowing the information to be encoded in memory in both a visual and a language format. Evidence from both cognitive and neuroscience research supports the idea that information can be stored in long-term memory in both visual and linguistic forms. Another theory, called the visual argument hypothesis, holds that graphical representations aid learning because the spatial arrangement of the items that make up the display allows for a visual form of chunking, thereby decreasing the demands on working memory. Support for the visual argument hypothesis comes from research that shows that students who are given graphic organizers are better able to integrate information and draw inferences about relationships than are students who are given plain text (Vekiri, 2002).

EXAMPLES

- When you explain or demonstrate, express complex and abstract ideas in several different ways. Be sure to provide plenty of examples.

- Use illustrations, diagrams, and concept maps.

- Make sure the type of visual display used is consistent with the goal of a lesson. For example, when the goal is to understand a cause-and-effect relationship, diagrams that show relationships among objects or concepts should be used, but when the goal is to learn about changes over time, as in plant or animal growth, animation would be a better choice than a static display.

METACOGNITION

The discussion up to this point has focused on a general explanation of how people attend to, encode, store, and retrieve information. In a word, we have described some of the major aspects of thinking. During the past few decades, researchers have inquired into how much knowledge individuals have about their own thought processes and what significance this knowledge has for learning. The term that was coined to refer to how much we know of our own thought processes is *metacognition*. As we will see, metacognition plays a very important role in learning.

The Nature and Importance of Metacognition

The notion of metacognition was proposed by developmental psychologist John Flavell (1976) to explain why children of different ages deal with learning tasks in different ways. For example, when seven-year-olds are taught how to remember pairs of nouns using both a less effective technique (simply repeating the words) and a more effective technique (imagining the members of each pair doing something together), most of these children will use the less effective technique when given a new set of pairs to learn. Most ten-year-olds, however, will opt to use the more effective method (Kail, 1990). The explanation for this finding is that the seven-year-old has not had enough learning experiences to recognize that some problem-solving methods are better than others. To the younger child, one means is as good as another. This lack of metacognitive knowledge makes true strategic learning impossible for young children.

One way to grasp the essence of metacognition is to contrast it with cognition. The term *cognition* is used to describe the ways in which information is processed—that is, the ways it is attended to, recognized, encoded, stored in memory for various lengths of time, retrieved from storage, and used for one purpose or another. **Metacognition** refers to our knowledge about those operations and how they might best be used to achieve a learning goal (Van Overschelde, 2008). As Flavell put it:

> Metacognition: our own knowledge of how we think

> I am engaging in metacognition . . . if I notice that I am having more trouble learning A than B; if it strikes me that I should double-check C before accepting it as a fact; if it occurs to me that I had better scrutinize each and every alternative in any multiple-choice type task situation before deciding which is the best one; if I become aware that I am not sure what the experimenter really wants me to do; if I sense that I had better make a note of D because I may forget it; if I think to ask someone about E to see if I have it right. Such examples could be multiplied endlessly. (1976, p. 232)

Metacognition refers to the knowledge we have about how we learn. It is a key component of our ability to regulate our learning processes. © VStock/Alamy

Metacognition is obviously a very broad concept. It covers everything an individual can know that relates to how information is processed (Van Overschelde, 2008). To get a better grasp of this concept, you may want to use the three-part classification scheme that Flavell (1987) proposed:

- *Knowledge-of-person variables:* for example, knowing that you are good at learning verbal material but poor at learning mathematical material, or knowing that information not rehearsed or encoded is quickly forgotten.
- *Knowledge-of-task variables:* for instance, knowing that passages with long sentences and unfamiliar words are usually harder to understand than passages that are more simply written.
- *Knowledge-of-strategy variables:* for example, knowing that one should skim through a text passage before reading it to determine its length and difficulty level.

Lev Vygotsky believed that children acquire metacognitive knowledge and skills most effectively through direct instruction, imitation, and social collaboration in the following ways:

1. Children are told by more experienced and knowledgeable individuals what is true and what is false, what is right and what is wrong, how various things should and should not be done, and why. ("Jason, don't touch that stove. It's hot and will give you a painful burn if you touch it.")
2. As opportunities arise, children use this knowledge to regulate their own behavior (saying out loud, "Hot stove. Don't touch.") as well as the behavior of others. If you have ever seen young children play "house" or "school" and faithfully mimic the dictates of their parents or teacher, then you have seen this process at work.
3. Children regulate their own behavior through the use of inner speech. ("Hot stove. Don't touch" is said to oneself, not said aloud.)

Vygotsky's analysis strongly suggests that providing children with opportunities to regulate their own and others' behavior, as in peer tutoring, is an excellent way to help them increase their metacognitive knowledge and skills and to improve the quality of their learning. In Chapter 9, we will describe one such program, reciprocal teaching. Programs such as reciprocal teaching have produced high levels of learning, motivation, and transfer (Karpov & Haywood, 1998; Kim, Baylor, & PALS Group, 2006; Spörera, Brunstein, & Kieschke, 2009).

Case in Print

Thinking About What We Think About

One way to grasp the essence of metacognition is to contrast it with cognition. The term cognition is used to describe the ways in which information is processed—that is, the ways it is attended to, recognized, encoded, stored in memory for various lengths of time, retrieved from storage, and used for one purpose or another. Metacognition refers to our knowledge about those operations and how they might best be used to achieve a learning goal. (p. 266)

This Is Harder than We Thought: Using Our Imagination Can Be Pleasant and Produce Great Things; It's Just Not That Easy to Do

ANDREW CHUNG
Toronto Star 4/23/2006

What would life be like without imagination?

For one thing, we probably couldn't answer that question, for such an effort requires . . . imagination.

Imagination can propel us to dream and give us a sense of the sublime when all around us is the mundane. By definition, it gives us images in our heads even when none of those images is before our many senses.

Through the imagination, we can go anywhere, be anyone, do anything, for good or for bad. And we can imagine these things for reasons all together fanciful, as in a kind of escape to unreality, or purposeful, as in trying to come up with an answer to a "What if?" question.

Without imagination, we would be something akin to routinized drones that have had frontal lobotomies, unable to come up with a higher-level thought.

The trouble is, for a great number of us, our existence is something kind of close to that. Rarely do we actually use our imaginations to mind-sketch anything more than what is already in our daily lives.

Instead, we are a highly pragmatic lot. Wake up to the alarm. Think about the shower. Get in the shower. Think about breakfast. Eat breakfast. Think about commuting. Board the train. Think about work. Work.

When was the last time you thought about a never before-heard-of way of solving outbreaks of famine in Africa?

What about a sure-fire cure for absent-mindedness? Or a better transit system for Toronto?

These kinds of problems require conscious thought. They require imagination.

"It's only a small percentage of our lives that we spend consciously considering things," says Steve Joordens, a cognitive psychologist and professor at the University of Toronto at Scarborough.

"We may go through 80 percent of our life without much conscious thought of what we are thinking or doing."

Partly, this is not something we can control.

"Imagination is something we consciously do," Joordens says. "I can sit down with you and say, 'Let's generate ideas for Toronto,' and by talking about things, we can control it a little bit. But, especially if we are alone, our minds would wander. Holding our conscious thoughts on one thing turns out to be very difficult."

That's because exercising our imaginations while doing daily tasks is "effortful and easily disruptable," Joordens says. "In order to get to the creative thing, you have to expend an effort. A lot of people don't tend to make those efforts."

Those who do, however, are getting a big payoff. Exercising your imagination and being creative can make you happy or even lead to success.

For instance, sports psychologists regularly guide elite athletes, such as downhill skiers and swimmers, through a process called visualization.

The athletes imagine the race in which they are about to compete, their body movements, the course terrain, even physically moving according to what they're picturing. Research shows this can improve race results.

For ordinary folks, imagination can at least be a refreshing change from the everyday.

Joordens, for instance, learned to play the guitar a few years ago. Now he's in a band that has gone from doing cover songs to originals. Imagining an exciting new riff can keep him up all night.

"I think it can be energizing," he says.

The reverse of this is that depressed people tend to imagine certain events in life, such as another person's reaction, as worse than they actually are.

Likewise, if you're forced to use your imagination to come up with something brilliant under duress, the pleasure might turn to fatigue. "We can try and turn the receiver on and hope something comes in and starts transmitting," Joordens says. "But if it doesn't, it can be quite annoying."

Any writer who has suffered writer's block knows what that's like.

Through the ages, books have been able to capture readers' imaginations because authors have used theirs.

This has most often been simply by transporting the reader to another earthbound time and place. But some authors have transcended imaginable real life, coming up with worlds that were, in their time, nearly beyond comprehension. Think of H. G. Wells' landscapes and alien species, and J. R. R. Tolkien's Middle-earth in *Lord of the Rings*.

One celebrated book in this regard is William Gibson's *Neuromancer*, which in 1984 allowed readers to "jack in" to a kind of cyber-matrix alongside the book's hero, long before the Internet became part of daily life.

Romantic poets like Samuel Taylor Coleridge thought imagination was of primary importance to poets—it made them nearly godlike.

And many of the greatest advances in science, like the theory of relativity, were the product of an abundance of imagination. Scientists such as Albert Einstein were considered to be avant-garde.

"A lot of people would argue that imagination leads to innovation," Joordens says. "Had the Wright brothers not thought that maybe it was possible, then we quite simply wouldn't have developed airplanes. That's the cost. If there's no imagination, then you're left with the world you have."

Even at a year and a half, a baby can solve problems not just through trial-and-error but also by imagining outcomes.

And in an era when math and basic science are emphasized, some education experts have been pleading with teachers to get their students to use their imaginations more.

It's a debate that has been going on for centuries. In the Enlightenment, for instance, as a counterpoint to John Locke's empiricism, other philosophers believed ideas came from the imagination.

While it may be good to use our imaginations, it can also be a problem, especially when it comes to memories, or more specifically, false memories. Psychologists have done hundreds of experiments to show that imagination can alter memory.

For example, researchers have shown that simply telling a person a story can affect that person's recollection as to whether the event described in the story actually happened or not.

Still, why don't we use our imaginations more? Sure, there's the effort it requires, but Joordens says it could also be explained by famed psychologist Abraham Maslow's hierarchy of needs.

Our needs range from the most basic, such as food and shelter, to those required for growth, such as love and self-esteem, to the most esoteric—self-actualization. It is at this highest level where the imagination can run free, Joordens says.

Many, if not most, of us are stuck trying to get there.

"To get to that level, to think outside the box, to not worry about mundane things, maybe you have to have a lot of those bottom levels in place," the psychologist says.

"If someone is still worried about paying the bills, that might be their primary motivator. So spending an hour a day talking fanciful thoughts may be a luxury."

There is a solution to this dilemma, however.

Just imagine yourself with lots of money, and go from there.

Questions and Activities

1. Because we have to attend to so much information that is presented in our immediate environment, we find it difficult at times to "step back and think." As the Case in Print indicates, the busy lives we lead keep us bombarded with "things to do" and reminders of "places to be" and "people to see." Imagination, as it is described in the Case in Print, not only can be used as a brief respite from a busy day but also can allow us to elaborate on ideas in creative ways. How might you encourage the development of metacognitive skills through the use of imagination in your classroom?

2. The Case in Print suggests that imagining is something that we do consciously and that it requires effort. One reason is that our working memory (also called short-term memory) is of limited capacity. If our working memory is taken up with the vast amount of stimulation that exists in our immediate environment, how can we provide students with an opportunity to imagine, to retrieve or activate schemata from long-term memory, and to construct unique thoughts in working memory?

3. How does the Case in Print demonstrate visual imagery encoding? Is there a distinction to be made between visual imagery and imagination?

Recent research indicates significant differences in what younger and older children know about metacognition. What follows is a discussion of some of these differences.

Age Trends in Metacognition

Two reviews of research on metacognition (Duell, 1986; Kail, 1990) examined how students of different ages use memorization techniques and how well they understand what they are doing. Following are some of the key conclusions of the reviews:

- In terms of diagnosing task difficulty, most six-year-olds know that more familiar items are easier to remember than less familiar items and that a small set of items is easier to recall than a large set of items. What six-year-olds do not yet realize is that the amount of information they can recall immediately after they study it is limited.

- Similar findings have been obtained for reading tasks. Most second graders know that interest, familiarity, and story length influence comprehension and recall. However, they are relatively unaware of the effect of how ideas are sequenced, the introductory and summary qualities of first and last paragraphs, and the relationship between reading goals and tactics. Sixth graders, by contrast, are much more aware of the effects of these variables on comprehension and recall.

- Most young children know very little about the role their own capabilities play in learning. For example, not until about nine years of age do most children realize that their recall right after they study something is limited. Consequently, children through the third grade usually overestimate how much they can store in and retrieve from short-term memory.

- There are clear developmental differences in how well students understand the need to tailor learning tactics to task demands. For example, four- and six-year-old children in one study cited by Robert Kail (1990) did not alter how much time they spent studying a set of pictures when they were told that a recognition test would follow either 3 minutes later, 1 day later, or 1 week later. Eight-year-olds did use that information to allocate less or more study time to the task.

- In terms of monitoring the progress of learning, most children younger than seven or eight are not very proficient at determining when they know something well enough to pass a memory test. Also, most first graders typically don't know what they don't know. When given multiple opportunities to study and recall a lengthy set of pictures, six-year-olds chose to study pictures they had previously seen and recalled, as well as ones they hadn't. Third graders, by contrast, focused on previously unseen pictures.

Insight into one's learning processes improves with age

The general conclusion that emerges from these findings is that the youngest school-age children have only limited knowledge of how their cognitive processes work and when to use them. Consequently, primary grade children do not systematically analyze learning tasks, formulate plans for learning, use appropriate techniques of enhancing memory and comprehension, or monitor their progress because they do not (some would say cannot) understand the benefits of doing these things. But as children develop and gain more experience with increasingly complex academic tasks, they experience growth in executive functions, or control processes (see Figure 8.1). Through such growth, they acquire a greater awareness of metacognitive knowledge and its relationship to classroom learning (Azevedo, 2009; Swanson, 2006). In this process, teachers can assist their students and guide them toward maximum use of their metacognitive knowledge.

With some effort and planning, a teacher can make logically organized and relevant lessons. However, this is only half the battle, because students must then attend to the information, encode it into long-term memory, and retrieve it when needed. Helping students to use the attention, encoding, and retrieval processes discussed in the previous sections is not always easy. The sad fact is that most children and adults are inefficient learners (Bond, Miller, & Kennon, 1987; Brown, Campione, & Day, 1981; Graham & Perin, 2007; Peverly, Brobst, Graham, & Shaw, 2003; Winne & Jamieson-Noel, 2002, 2003). Their attempts at encoding rarely go beyond rote rehearsal (for example, rereading a textbook chapter), simple organizational schemes (outlining), and various cueing devices (underlining or highlighting), and they have a poor sense of how well prepared they are to take a test.

In the next chapter, we address learning strategies and tactics that can help overcome information-processing difficulties. Before considering how we can help students become strategic learners, we suggest ways in which you can encourage your students to develop their metacognitive skills.

Our major suggestion is that you encourage your students to develop their metacognitive skills and knowledge by thinking about the various conditions that affect how they learn and remember. The very youngest students (through third grade) should be told periodically that such cognitive behaviors as describing, recalling, guessing, and understanding mean different things, produce different results, and vary in how well they fit a task's demands. For older elementary school and middle school students, explain the learning process, and focus on the circumstances in which different learning tactics are likely to be useful. Then have students keep a diary or log in which they note when they use learning tactics, which ones, and with what success. Look for cases in which good performance corresponds to frequent reported use of tactics and positively reinforce those individuals. Encourage greater use of tactics among students whose performance and reported use of them are below average.

Although this same technique can be used with high school and college students, they should also be made aware of the other elements that make up strategic learning. Discuss the meaning of and necessity for analyzing a learning task, developing a learning plan, using appropriate tactics, monitoring the effectiveness of the plan, and implementing whatever corrective measures might be called for.

Next we examine several ways in which you can use computer-based technology to improve your students' information-processing skills for a variety of learning tasks.

TECHNOLOGY AS AN INFORMATION-PROCESSING TOOL

Although computer-based technology may have had its roots in behavioral learning theory, as you saw in the chapter on that subject, current technology is more likely to reflect an information-processing perspective. The technological tools described in this section influence how we access, filter, represent, and evaluate knowledge. As matters of cognitive load and the difficulty of creating learning strategies have been clarified, technology has been called on to help overcome these constraints and reduce the cognitive-processing burden of complex tasks. For instance, technology can help a learner grasp an idea for a musical composition, see the structure of her writing plans, watch chemical molecules react, or provide complex environments, complete with problems that need solutions.

In this section, we will examine technological tools that help students process and represent information, so that they can acquire important knowledge and skills from different subject areas, and provide multiple representations of knowledge to regulate their own thinking. We consider technology tools for writing, reading, science and math, and art and music, as well as multimedia and hypermedia tools.

Technology Tools for Writing

Because of its flexibility, technology can be used in a variety of ways to make writing less threatening and to increase both the quantity and quality of students' writing. In classrooms where computers are networked, teachers can use a technique called

Electronic Read Around. Sitting at separate computers, each student writes on a topic the teacher gives. Each student then clicks on an icon representing another student's computer, reads what that student wrote, and provides feedback in a different font at the end of the document. This process is repeated until each student has read and commented on every other student's text. Students then use the comments to revise and edit their own pieces (Strassman & D'Amore, 2002).

One of the most important parts of the writing process is the prewriting phase. This is the point at which authors generate, evaluate, and organize their ideas. For novice writers, which most students are, the prospect of having to do this entirely on one's own can be quite anxiety provoking. For many students it is comforting to have a friend available as a sounding board. This can be easily accomplished through the use of online synchronous chats (basically, instant messaging). A student can share ideas in real time with one or more classmates on the topic they are writing about. Not only does this give students additional opportunities to write, but the chat writing doesn't have to follow the same grammatical conventions as formal writing assignments (Strassman & D'Amore, 2002).

The Internet is yet another technology resource teachers can use to make writing more attractive to students. One approach that shows promise is the use of weblogs (commonly referred to as blogs; see discussions in previous chapters, especially the Resources for Further Investigation in Chapter 3). A blog can take the form of a personal journal in which the writer makes periodic entries for others to read, or they can be like bulletin boards in which the online audience responds both to what the author has written and to the comments of others (Weiler, 2003). To learn more about blogs and how to start one, visit the Education World website (**www.educationworld.com**). Two other websites that provide opportunities for collaborative writing projects are Classroom 2.0 (**www.classroom20.com**)—a social network for those interested in Web 2.0 technologies in education—and the Kidlink Project (**www.kidlink.org/KIDPROJ**).

For quick links to websites mentioned here, go to the textbook's Education Course-Mate website.

Technology Tools for Reading

As with writing, the use of electronic support systems to increase students' reading skills has increased around the world (Lai, Chang, & Ye, 2006; Llabo, 2002). In comparison with primary grade students who read a print version of a story, students who listened to a story from a CD-ROM storybook significantly increased their sight word vocabulary, reading level, and ability to retell the story accurately and completely (Matthew, 1996; McKenna, Cowart, & Watkins, 1997). When third graders had to read a CD story themselves but were able to use such other features as clicking on words and illustrations to obtain pronunciations and definitions, their retelling scores did not differ from those of children who read a print version, but they did score significantly higher on comprehension questions (Doty, Popplewell, & Byers, 2001).

The American Library Association provides access and evaluations of online resources that encourage learning. One online resource for educators is the Young Adult Library Services Association (YALSA), which holds monthly online chats including "Using Web 2.0 tools to encourage reading" (**http://connect.ala.org/yalsa**). This and other chats are archived on the site for access anytime.

Technology Tools for Science and Math

In mathematics and science, Marcia Linn (1992) and other prominent researchers have argued that students should spend less time manually calculating and plotting data and more time using technology to summarize and interpret data, look for trends, and predict relationships. To help teachers put this philosophy into practice, Linn and others created the Web-based Inquiry Science Environment (WISE) Project (**wise.berkeley.edu**). Based largely on constructivist learning principles and

Web 2.0 technologies can enable children from different cultures to share experiences in shared virtual environments. **A,** Eye Ubiquitous/Alamy; **B,** photolibrary.com

15 years of classroom research (Slotta & Linn, 2009), the WISE website contains a variety of science projects that teachers can adapt to local curricula and to state and national standards. The overarching goal of the WISE learning environment is to help students make connections among science ideas rather than learn by rote isolated facts whose relevance is not understood and that are soon forgotten. For each project, students have to locate relevant information on the Web, record and organize their findings in an electronic notebook, and participate in online discussions to refine their procedures and conclusions. The Houses in the Desert project, for example, requires pairs of middle school students to design a desert house that will be comfortable to live in. Using resources available on the Web, students have to, among other things, analyze the suitability of various materials for walls, roofs, and windows and perform a heat-flow analysis. The WISE site also allows students to compare climate data in a desert with climate data from their own community (Linn & Slotta, 2000).

Math teachers can also use the Web to help students understand the connections among math topics and to other disciplines. For example, data from the website of the National Center for Health Statistics (**www.cdc.gov/nchs**) on the number of births in the United States for various time periods can be used to teach such concepts as absolute and relative yearly increases and decreases. These same data can also be used to analyze the relationship between birthrates and other societal trends, such as immigration patterns. Connections between oscillating functions in math and the tides, planetary movements, and average monthly temperatures can be made with data from the websites of the National Oceanic and Atmospheric Administration (**www.noaa.gov**) and the National Geophysical Data Center (**www. ngdc.noaa.gov**). These relationships can be made more concrete, and hence more meaningful, by using graphing tools and spreadsheets to create graphic representations (Alagic & Palenz, 2006; Drier, Dawson, & Garofalo, 1999).

Technology Tools for Art and Music

As you may be aware, computer tools are also being used in the fine and performing arts. Art education, for instance, benefits from electronic tools such as the draw and paint modules that quickly erase or alter ideas. Students can use these tools to mimic the branching, spiraling, and exploding structures of nature (as seen, for example, in trees, vines, and flowers) (Lach et al., 2003), and they can create abstract patterns by repeating, changing the horizontal and vertical orientation, and changing the alignment of a basic pattern (Yoerg, 2002). With these tools, students can also draw objects in two-point perspective (Patterson, 2002) and create stylized portraits by using shadows, contour lines, stippling, and cross-hatching (Mathes, 2002).

For the music classroom, there are tools such as digital oscilloscopes that help students understand relationships between pitch and wavelength. In addition, CD technology can be used to present graphical representations of notes as they are played, sections of which can be saved and compared with other verses of the same song or with other songs, thereby helping students understand themes and patterns in music. Moreover, computer tools such as a musical instrument digital interface (MIDI) and formal instrumental music tuition (FIMT) allow students to compose at the keyboard, play a musical instrument and record it on a computer, and play one part of a multi-instrument piece while the program plays the other instruments (Peters, 2001; Reninger, 2000; Seddon & O'Neill, 2006). Students can explore concepts of pitch, duration, sound combination, repetition, and melody and engage in the process of musical thinking.

Multimedia, Hypermedia, and Virtual Environments

As mentioned in previous chapters, multimedia encyclopedias, databases, and libraries provide students with a wide variety of information resources. Multimedia tools offer multiple views (text, photographs, digitized video, animation, sound) on difficult concepts that can enrich student understanding of the topic. The use of multimedia tools is related to such information-processing concepts as meaningful learning, the dual coding of information, the use of visual imagery, and elaborative rehearsal (Leacock & Nesbitt, 2007; Mayer & Moreno, 2002; 2003; Reed, 2006). Like the mind, multimedia tools provide more than one way to retrieve or visit information; the richer or more dense the network or web of connections, the more likely one will comprehend the meaning.

Hypermedia Tools   Hypermedia technology exists when multimedia information can be nonsequentially accessed, examined, and constructed by users, thereby enabling them to move from one information resource to another while controlling which options to take (Grabe & Grabe, 2007). There are clear advantages to hypermedia, such as the richness of the network of ideas, the compact storage of information, the rapid nonlinear access to information, the flexible use of information, and learner control over the system. Not surprisingly, it has been suggested that hypermedia tools radically alter the way people read, write, compute, and perhaps even think (Keengwe, Onchwari, Wachira, 2008; Yang, 2001).

Virtual Environments   By combining multimedia and hypermedia capabilities, researchers and designers have developed rich, complex virtual environments in which multiple learners can engage in individual or collaborative learning experiences. (We mentioned these environments, called multi-user virtual environments, or MUVEs, in Chapter 2.) One such environment is Quest Atlantis (**http://atlantis. crlt.indiana.edu**), which has been well-researched and documented by Sasha Barab and his colleagues at Indiana University (Barab et al., 2009; Barab, Scott et al., 2009; Thomas, Barab, & Tuzun, 2009) and continues to attract much attention from researchers, teachers, parents, and organizations such as the National Science Foundation, the MacArthur Foundation, and NASA. We will revisit Quest Atlantis in Chapter 10, "Constructivist Learning Theory, Problem Solving, and Transfer," but it is mentioned here as an example of how information across a variety of content areas can be engaged by students.

> Virtual environments provide rich content and context that can support collaborative learning

The virtual world of Quest Atlantis includes various kinds of learning experiences for students: quests, missions, and units. Quests are tasks that are tied to particular areas of the curriculum to ensure that students acquire content knowledge. Missions combine a number of tasks and other learning opportunities that are integrated through general problem-solving exercises and driven by a narrative or "storyline." Units provide teachers with lesson plans that combine virtual and face-to-face learning activities. For example, the Taiga Water Quality Unit in Quest

To review this chapter, try the tutorial quizzes and other study aids on the textbook's Education CourseMate website.

Atlantis challenges students to address an ecological situation that has resulted in dead and dying fish in Taiga Park. Students acquire information by navigating through the park to collect data and evidence to make a recommendation about how to solve the problem. After deciding what action to take, students then travel 20 years into the future to see the consequences of their decisions.

Engaging curricular content in math, science, and social studies within the context of the virtual world of Quest Atlantis provides students with elaborate information-processing opportunities and helps them develop their metacognitive capability by thinking about their thinking.

Challenging Assumptions

Information and Meaning

"So," Connie says to Don and Celeste, "Why were Antonio's students having trouble making sense of 'The Rime of the Ancient Mariner'? And what do you think his team did to turn it around?"

Celeste says, "I think Antonio had the right idea at the beginning—he knew the poem was going to be hard to understand, so he tried to help the students process the information. But reading it aloud didn't help them understand it."

"Right," Don adds. "It's a matter of finding a way for the students themselves to take the information and make something meaningful out of it. And I think I know what Antonio's team did. I think they gave them illustrations of the poem!"

"Not exactly," says Antonio, "although illustrations were used."

"I think you gave them a 'simplified version,' you know, maybe an annotation," says Celeste.

"Not exactly," says Antonio, "although a simplified version was used."

Don and Celeste look at Connie. She says, "I'm not quite sure what Antonio's team did, but whatever they did it certainly helped their students, first, to make sense of the poem, and second, to apply their understanding. In some way or another, the team helped the students to process the poem in elaborative ways that connected to what they already knew, to their prior knowledge."

"You're all on the right track," says Antonio. "We needed to find a way for our students to not simply recite the poem but to construct meaning from the words, the phrases, the voice, the structure. There is a lot of meaning in the poem, but the students needed to construct that meaning for themselves. And so, we divided them into teams and asked each team to produce *A Teaching Guide to 'The Rime of the Ancient Mariner.'* The guide could be in any form they chose. The only requirement was that their guide was to be used to help next year's students understand the poem and how the poem relates to people in today's world."

Antonio chuckles as he continues. "They went nuts—in a good way. They started doing research on the Internet, they produced maps, they recorded interviews with each other, they wrote comprehension questions, they 'translated' the poem into a rap song. The new assignment to teach others gave them a reason to reread the poem for meaning and to bring in stuff they already knew. Just today, one group suggested that we combine the work of all the groups into a web page to see if other teachers might want to use it."

"Information is important for learners; they need to know things," says Connie. "But once students have a reason to make meaning from information, they process it in some very elaborate ways. Antonio, your students will remember 'The Rime of the Ancient Mariner' because they made meaning from the information."

Summary

1. Information-processing theory attempts to explain how individuals acquire, store, recall, and use information.

2. A popular model of information processing is composed of three memory stores and a set of control processes that determine the flow of information from one memory store to another. The memory stores are the sensory register, short-term memory, and long-term memory. The control processes are recognition, attention, maintenance rehearsal, elaborative rehearsal, and retrieval.

3. The sensory register holds information in its original form for 1 to 3 seconds, during which time we may recognize and attend to it further.

4. Recognition involves noticing key features of a stimulus and integrating those features with relevant information from long-term memory.

5. Attention is a selective focusing on a portion of the information in the sensory register. Information from long-term memory influences what we focus on.

6. Short-term memory holds about seven bits of information for about 20 seconds (in the absence of rehearsal). It is often called working memory because it is where various encoding, organizational, and retrieval processes occur. Working memory appears to be strongly related to proficiency of learning.

7. Information can be held in short-term memory indefinitely through the use of maintenance rehearsal, which is rote repetition of information.

8. Information is transferred from short-term memory to long-term memory by the linking of the new information to related information in long-term memory. This process is called elaborative rehearsal.

9. Elaborative rehearsal is based partly on organization. This involves grouping together, or chunking, items of information that share some important characteristic.

10. Elaborative rehearsal is also based on meaningfulness. Meaningful learning occurs when new information that is clearly written and logically organized is consciously related to information the learner currently has stored in long-term memory.

11. Long-term memory is thought by some psychologists to be an unlimited storehouse of information from which nothing is ever lost.

12. Many psychologists believe the information in long-term memory is organized in the form of schemata. A schema is a generalized abstract structure of information. When schemata are absent or crudely formed, learning and recall problems occur.

13. Contrary to popular belief, students remember much of the information they learn in school, especially if it was well learned to start with and if it was learned in a meaningful fashion.

14. Metacognition refers to any knowledge an individual has about how humans think and how those processes can be used to achieve learning goals.

15. Metacognition increases gradually with experience. This helps explain why junior high and high school students are more flexible and effective learners than primary grade students.

16. Contemporary computer-based technology supports information processing by helping students to organize and mentally represent ideas, write more clearly, better comprehend text, interpret scientific and mathematical data, understand musical patterns, and solve problems.

Resources for Further Investigation

• The Nature of Information-Processing Theory

For more on information-processing theory and how it relates to teaching and learning, read *The Handbook of Applied Cognition* (2nd ed., 2007), edited by Frank Durso and his associates—especially Chapters 1-5, which focus on the memory and control processes, and Chapter 21, which addresses instruction. Other sources include Chapter 4 of *Learning Theories: An Educational Perspective* (5th ed., 2008), by Dale Schunk, and Chapters 2-5 of *Cognitive Psychology and Instruction* (4th ed., 2004), by Roger Bruning, Gregory Schraw, Monica Norby, and Royce Ronning.

• Memory Structures and Processes

Norman Spear and David Riccio describe various aspects of memory structures and processes in *Memory: Phenomena and Principles* (1994). As the title suggests, Alan Searleman and Douglas Herrmann cover the same ground, plus such additional topics as the role of social factors in memory, individual differences in memory, and changes in memory ability, in *Memory from a Broader Perspective* (1994). Alan Baddeley provides a basic account of memory phenomena, including a chapter on improving your memory, in *Essentials of Human Memory* (1999).

Metacognition

If you would like to know more about the nature of meta-cognition and its role in learning, the *Handbook of Metamemory and Memory* (2008), edited by John Dunlosky and Robert Bjork, provides numerous chapters of interest. Another recent collection is the *Handbook of Metacognition in Education* (2009), edited by Douglas Hacker, John Dunlosky, and Arthur Graesser; Robert Sternberg—whose theories we encountered in Chapter 4, "Understanding Student Differences"—has written a forward that provides a useful roadmap for educators.

Individual Differences in Memory

One of the most striking accounts of supernormal memory is provided by Alexander Luria in *The Mind of a Mnemonist: A Little Book About a Vast Memory* (1968). Luria describes his experiments and experiences over a period of almost 30 years with the man he refers to as S, who could recall nonsense material he had not seen for 15 years. Charles Thompson, Thaddeus Cowan, and Jerome Frieman describe in *Memory Search by a Memorist* (1993) a series of studies done with Rajan Mahadevan, who earned a place in the *Guinness Book of World Records* by memorizing the first 31,811 digits of pi. Additional articles about people with unusually proficient memory capability can be found in *Memory Observed: Remembering in Natural Contexts* (2nd ed., 2000), edited by Ulric Neisser and Ira Hyman, Jr.

Robert Kail describes memory differences among normal children, as well as differences between normal and intellectually disabled children, in *The Development of Memory in Children* (1990). Also briefly discussed is the phenomenon of idiot savants—individuals who are below average on all measures of ability except one, in which they far surpass almost all other individuals—and the reliability of children's eyewitness testimony. Leon Miller describes musical savants, individuals with intellectual disability who can perfectly reproduce musical passages on an instrument after one hearing, in *Musical Savants: Exceptional Skill in the Mentally Retarded* (1989).

9 Social Cognitive Theory

 The Education CourseMate website for this text offers many helpful resources. Go to **CengageBrain.com** to preview this chapter's Concept Maps and Chapter Themes.

KEY POINTS

These key points will help you learn the important information in this chapter. To help you study, they also appear in the margins of the pages, next to the text where they are discussed.

The Triadic Reciprocal Causation Model

- Triadic reciprocal causation model: behavior is the result of interactions among personal characteristics, behavior, environmental factors

Self-Control, Self-Regulation, and Self-Efficacy

- Self-control: controlling one's behaviors in a particular setting in the absence of reinforcement or punishment
- Self-regulation: consistently using self-control skills in new situations
- Self-regulation is important because students are expected to become increasingly independent learners as they progress through school
- Self-efficacy: how capable one feels to handle particular kinds of tasks
- Self-efficacy beliefs influence use of self-regulating skills
- Self-efficacy influenced by past performance, verbal persuasion, emotions, observing models
- Self-efficacy influences goals and activities, cognitive processes, perseverance, emotions
- Self-regulated learners set goals, create plans to achieve those goals
- Self-regulated learners focus on task, process information meaningfully, self-monitor
- Self-regulated learners evaluate their performance, make appropriate attributions for success and failure, reinforce themselves

Helping Students Become Self-Regulated Learners

- Self-regulated learning: thoughts, feelings, and actions purposely generated and controlled to maximize a learning outcome

- Strategy: plan to achieve a long-term goal
- Tactic: specific technique that helps achieve immediate objective
- Rote rehearsal not a very effective memory tactic
- Acronym: word made from first letters of items to be learned
- Acrostic: sentence made up of words derived from first letters of items to be learned
- Loci method: visualize items to be learned stored in specific locations
- Keyword method: visually link pronunciation of foreign word to English translation
- Mnemonic devices meaningfully organize information, provide retrieval cues
- Self-questioning improves comprehension, knowledge integration
- Taking notes and reviewing notes aid retention and comprehension
- A strategic learner is a mindful learner
- Self-regulation skills learned best in a four-level process: observation, emulation, self-control, self-regulation
- People learn to inhibit or make responses by observing others

Research on Social Cognitive Theory

- Self-efficacy, epistemological beliefs, self-regulation related to each other and to achievement
- Observing a peer model improves students' self-efficacy for math problem solving ability and math problem-solving ability
- Observing a peer model improves the quality of students' writing more than simply practicing writing
- Reciprocal teaching: students learn comprehension skills by demonstrating them to peers

Using Technology to Promote Self-Regulated Learning

- Computer programs that include models can improve students' problem-solving skills
- Computer programs that let students control access to information work best with those who have some self-regulatory skills

---

In the last two chapters, we examined two very different descriptions of how learning occurs. Operant conditioning focuses exclusively on the role of observable, external events on learning new behaviors and strengthening or weakening existing ones. According to this theory, people are exposed to stimuli, they make some sort of response, and the reinforcing or punishing consequences that do or do not follow influence the probability that those responses will be made again. Consequently, operant conditioning requires that people make observable responses for others to conclude that learning has occurred. The strength of operant conditioning is the insight it provides about how environmental consequences affect learning. Its main weakness is that it offers no insights into what people do with that information.

Information-processing theory, on the other hand, focuses almost exclusively on the role of internal processes in learning. In this view, people are exposed to stimuli, and whether and how they attend to, encode, store, and retrieve that information influences what they know and can do. But information-processing theory has very little to say about how the social setting in which behavior occurs influences what people learn.

This chapter will examine a third approach that shares common ground with operant conditioning and information-processing theory but goes beyond both. Known initially as *social learning theory* and more recently as **social cognitive theory,** this explanation of learning was based on the premise that neither spontaneous behavior nor reinforcement was necessary for learning to occur. New behaviors could also be learned by observing and imitating a model. The current version of social cognitive theory incorporates elements of both operant conditioning and information processing, and it emphasizes how behavioral and personal factors interact with the social setting in which behavior occurs.

Albert Bandura (1986, 1997, 2001, 2002) is generally considered to be the driving force behind social cognitive theory. His goal is to explain how learning results from interactions among three factors: (1) personal characteristics, such as the various cognitive processes covered in the chapter on information processing, as well as self-perceptions and emotional states; (2) behavioral patterns; and (3) the social environment, such as interactions with others. Bandura calls the process of interaction among these three elements **triadic reciprocal causation.** This impressive-sounding mouthful is not as difficult to understand as it sounds. *Triadic* simply means having three elements, and *reciprocal* indicates that the elements influence one another. The entire term means that one's internal processes, behavior, and social environment (the "triadic" part of the term) can affect one another (the "reciprocal" part) to produce learning (the "causation" part). To simplify our writing and your reading, we will refer to Bandura's triadic reciprocal causation model as the *triadic model.*

Bandura and others (e.g., Pajares, 2009; Schunk, 1998, 2001; Zimmerman, 2000) are particularly interested in using social cognitive theory to describe how people become *self-controlled and self-regulated* learners. Consequently, we'll begin our exploration of social cognitive theory by taking a more detailed look at the triadic model. Then we'll explain the meaning of and differences between self-control and self-regulation.

Revealing Assumptions

Taking Learning Personally

Connie leans back in her chair and looks again at the three questions she has culled from her young colleagues' journals. Don had asked: *Why don't parents prepare their children for school?* Antonio had written: *How can I get my students to study harder?* Celeste's reflection included the question: *Will the students in the class be ready for college?*

Connie begins the Friday afternoon meeting by writing the questions on the board. She sits down with the others and says, "These questions from your journals are very important for us to consider today. And our first consideration is, where did they come from? Celeste, you questioned students' readiness for college. Why?"

"Well, it just seemed to me that the students in that class weren't learning very well. I mean, they would do the work in class and read enough to get good grades on the quizzes, but I just didn't have the sense that they were reaching their potential. Whatever was covered in class was always followed by the question 'Is this going to be on the test?'"

Connie nods. "OK. Thanks, Celeste. That's helpful." She turns to Antonio. "Where did your question come from, Antonio? Why do you need to make your students study harder?"

pause & reflect

The questions from the journals of Don, Antonio, and Celeste suggest that they, like most people, recognize that effective learners take responsibility for their own learning. However, most people also believe that—somehow—students arrive at school having automatically acquired the ability to take that responsibility. In other words, they assume that students fail to be responsible for their own learning not because they are unable but because they are unwilling. Their failure is viewed as an issue of motivation rather than of learning. Don, Antonio, and Celeste are concerned about student motivation, but Connie asks them to consider student learning as well. Why should teachers, regardless of the content they teach, help their students to learn how to take responsibility? How would learning to be responsible influence students' motivation and help them become better learners? How will you teach your students how to learn?

Antonio says, "My students never go 'above and beyond,' either. Once they know exactly what they have to do for a grade, they just do it and then they're done. It's like pulling teeth to get them to go beyond what's on the test, to really think. If they would just study harder, they would become better students overall."

Don chimes in, "Yeah, kids don't come to school ready to learn. Maybe that's why the teacher I observed had to spend so much time getting the kids ready for the state tests."

Connie says, "You seem worried that students don't take responsibility for their own learning. Is that right?" They all nod. "So, how are you going to teach them to take that responsibility?"

THE TRIADIC RECIPROCAL CAUSATION MODEL

The triadic model holds that a person's behavior is always the result of interactions among personal characteristics, behavioral patterns, and environmental factors. Bandura and others describe these three elements as follows:

- *Personal characteristics* include mental and emotional factors (such as goals and anxiety), metacognitive knowledge (understanding how one's own cognitive processes affect learning), and *self-efficacy* (beliefs about one's ability to successfully carry out particular tasks). Self-efficacy is a concept we introduced in Chapter 3 on age-level characteristics, and we will discuss it in detail in a later section of this chapter. To cite just one example of the role of personal characteristics in learning, students who have higher levels of reading ability, relevant prior knowledge, and interest, learn more from text passages than do students who have low levels of these same characteristics (Fox, 2009).

- *Behavioral patterns* include self-observation (such as using personal journals to note how various factors influence learning, motivation, and self-efficacy); self-evaluation; making changes in behavior to overcome or reduce perceptions of low self-efficacy, anxiety, and ineffective learning strategies; and creating productive study environments.

> Triadic reciprocal causation model: behavior is the result of interactions among personal characteristics, behavior, environmental factors

- *Environmental factors* refer to an individual's social and physical environment. They include such things as the nature of a task, reinforcing and punishing consequences, explanations and modeling of various skills by others, and verbal persuasion from others to exhibit particular behaviors.

As shown in Figure 9.1, Bandura portrays these relationships in a triangular arrangement with bidirectional arrows (Bandura, 1997; Zimmerman, 1990).

To grasp the interactive nature of the triadic model, consider the following two examples. The components of the model are represented by the letter *P* for personal characteristic, *B* for behavioral pattern, or *E* for environmental factor. In each example, notice how the elements influence one another.

1. A student's high self-efficacy for mathematical problem solving (P) leads the student to work on mathematical problems (B) rather than painting a picture. High self-efficacy also makes the student likely to persist in the face of difficulty (B). At the same time, the act of successfully working on mathematical tasks (B) raises the student's self-efficacy for solving mathematical problems (P).

Figure 9.1 The Triadic Reciprocal Causation Model

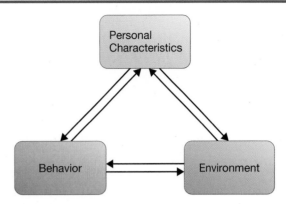

SOURCE: Bandura (1997).

2. A teacher introduces a new science topic by describing the theory and research that contributed to the current state of knowledge in this area (B). But when students show signs of confusion or boredom (E), thereby making the teacher uncomfortable and dissatisfied (P), the teacher tries a different approach (B).

Bear in mind, however, that things do not operate as simply as Figure 9.1 suggests. As the activity and setting change, the strength of certain P-B-E connections can be expected to change. If, for example, you happen to be in a setting, such as school, in which rules and regulations place limits on behavior, the behavioral aspect of the model is likely to have less impact than if you are allowed more freedom of expression. Also, some relationships may be stronger than others at particular points in time (Pajares, 2009; Schunk, 1998).

Social cognitive theory assumes that people, and not environmental forces, are the predominant cause of their own behavior (recall that operant conditioning assumes that one's choices and actions are strongly influenced, if not determined, by environmental stimuli and consequences). Bandura uses the term **personal agency** to refer to the potential control we have over our own behavior, and he believes that our capacity for personal agency grows out of our skills of self-control and self-regulation (Martin, 2004).

SELF-CONTROL, SELF-REGULATION, AND SELF-EFFICACY

Self-control: controlling one's behaviors in a particular setting in the absence of reinforcement or punishment

Self-control (also referred to as self-discipline) is the ability to control one's actions in the absence of external reinforcement or punishment. In other words, self-control involves behaving in ways that lead to the accomplishment of desirable goals and suppressing behaviors that are detrimental when no one is looking. A student who has been taught by the teacher to start a new task after finishing a seatwork assignment and who does that when the teacher is not present is exhibiting self-control. Although self-control is generally thought of as a good thing, the argument has been made that too much can stifle creativity and flexibility (Kohn, 2008).

Self-regulation: consistently using self-control skills in new situations

Self-regulation involves the consistent and appropriate application of self-control skills to new situations. It is the product of interactions among the three components that make up Bandura's triadic model: personal characteristics, behavioral patterns, and environmental factors. Self-regulating individuals set their own performance standards, evaluate the quality of their performance, and reinforce themselves when their performance meets or exceeds their internal standards (Zimmerman, 1990, 2000; Zimmerman & Kitsantas, 2005). A teacher who modifies a particular day's lesson plan to capitalize on students' interest in a major news story, monitors students' reaction to the new lesson, compares her students' and her own performance against an internal standard, and rewards herself if she feels that standard has been met is illustrating the essence of self-regulation.

Self-regulation is a critically important capability for students to acquire for at least three reasons:

Self-regulation is important because students are expected to become increasingly independent learners as they progress through school

1. As students get older, and especially when they get into the middle and high school grades, they are expected to assume greater responsibility for their learning than was the case in earlier grades; thus, they receive less prompting and guidance from teachers and parents.

2. As students move through the primary, elementary, middle school, and high school grades, they have to learn and be tested over increasingly larger amounts of more complex material. With less parental and teacher supervision, the temptation to put off studying or to do it superficially increases. Unfortunately, the damaging long-term consequences of poorly regulated academic behavior (low grades and diminished opportunities for higher education and employment) are not immediately apparent.

3. Because of the rapid pace of change in today's world, individuals increasingly need to be self-directed, autonomous learners not just during their school years but over their lifetimes (Zimmerman, 1990, 2002).

pause & reflect

Should the development of self-regulated learning skills be left to parents and out-of-school experiences, or should this be a primary goal of our education system? If the latter, when should it begin?

Although the skills of self-control and self-regulation are important to academic success, some students are more successful than others in acquiring and using these skills. The characteristic that is most strongly related to and best explains differences in self-regulation is perceived self-efficacy, a concept we mentioned several times earlier in this chapter. In the next section, we further describe self-efficacy and its relationship to self-regulation.

The Role of Self-Efficacy in Self-Regulation

Self-efficacy: how capable one feels to handle particular kinds of tasks

Unlike self-esteem, which we described in an earlier chapter as the overall, or global, evaluation that people make of themselves, **self-efficacy** refers to how capable or prepared we believe we are to handle particular kinds of tasks (Bandura, 1997, 2001, 2002). For example, a student may have a high level of self-efficacy for mathematical reasoning—a feeling that she can master any math task she might encounter in a particular course—but have a low level of self-efficacy for critical analysis of English literature.

Self-efficacy beliefs occupy a central role in social cognitive theory because of their widespread and significant effects. They help influence whether people think optimistically or pessimistically, act in ways that are beneficial or detrimental to achieving goals, approach or avoid tasks, engage tasks with a high or low level of motivation, persevere for a short or lengthy period of time when tasks are difficult, and are motivated or demoralized by failure. These beliefs are often called the single most important factor that affects the strength of a person's sense of agency.

Bandura argues that self-efficacy is more influential than expected rewards or punishments or actual skills because it is based on a belief that one can or cannot produce the behaviors that are required to bring about a particular outcome. Students with the same level of mathematical skill may, for example, have different attitudes about mathematics and perform differently on tests of mathematical problem solving because of differences in their self-efficacy beliefs (Bandura, 2001; Pajares, 2009).

Self-efficacy beliefs influence use of self-regulating skills

Students who believe they are capable of successfully performing a task are more likely than students with low levels of self-efficacy to use such self-regulating skills as concentrating on the task, creating strategies, using appropriate tactics, managing time effectively, monitoring their own performance, and making whatever adjustments are necessary to improve their future learning efforts. By contrast, students who do not believe they have the cognitive skills to cope with the demands of a particular subject are unlikely to do much serious reading or thinking about the subject or to spend much time preparing for tests. Such students are often referred to as lazy, inattentive, lacking initiative, and dependent on others. They often find themselves in a vicious circle as their avoidance of challenging tasks and dependence on others reduces their chances of developing self-regulation skills and a strong sense of self-efficacy (Bandura, 1997; Pajares, 2009).

Self-efficacy can be affected by one or more of several factors and, in turn, can affect one or more of several important self-regulatory behaviors (see Figure 9.2).

Factors That Affect Self-Efficacy   Four factors that affect self-efficacy are shown on the "Antecedents" side of Figure 9.2.

> Self-efficacy influenced by past performance, verbal persuasion, emotions, observing models

1. *Performance accomplishments.* One obvious way in which we develop a sense of what we can and cannot do in various areas is by thinking about how well we have performed in the past on a given task or a set of closely related tasks. If, for example, my friends are always reluctant to have me on their team for neighborhood baseball games, and if I strike out or ground out far more often than I hit safely, I will probably conclude that I just do not have whatever skills it takes to be a competitive baseball player. Conversely, if my personal history of performance in school includes mostly grades of A and consistent rank among the top 10 students, my sense of academic self-efficacy is likely to be quite high.
2. *Verbal persuasion.* A second source of influence mentioned by Bandura—verbal persuasion—is also fairly obvious. We frequently try to convince a child, student, relative, spouse, friend, or coworker that he or she has the ability to perform some task at an acceptable level. Perhaps you can recall feeling somewhat more confident about handling some task (such as college classes) after having several family members and friends express their confidence in your ability.

Figure 9.2 Antecedents and Effects of Self-Efficacy

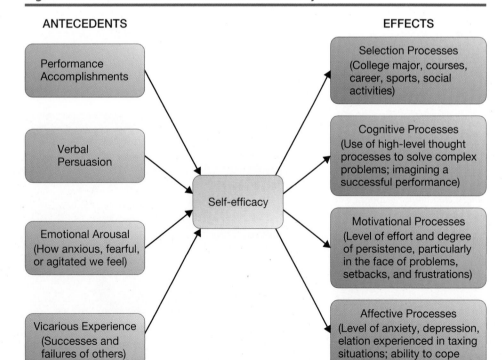

3. *Emotional arousal.* A third source of influence is more subtle. It is the emotions we feel as we prepare to engage in a task. Individuals with low self-efficacy for science may become anxious, fearful, or restless prior to attending chemistry class or to taking an exam in physics. Those with high self-efficacy may feel assured, comfortable, and eager to display what they have learned. Some individuals are acutely aware of these emotional states, and their emotions become a cause as well as a result of their high or low self-efficacy.

4. *Vicarious experience.* Finally, our sense of self-efficacy may be influenced by observing the successes and failures of individuals with whom we identify. This is what Bandura refers to as vicarious experience. If I take note of the fact that a sibling or neighborhood friend who is like me in many respects but is a year older has successfully adjusted to high school, I may feel more optimistic about my own adjustment the following year. We will have more to say a bit later in this chapter about the role of observing and imitating a model.

Of these four self-efficacy factors, personal accomplishment is the most important because it carries the greatest weight. As important as it is to feel calm and be free of crippling fear or anxiety; to have parents, peers, and teachers express their confidence in us; and to have successful models to observe, actual failures are likely to override these other influences. In other words, our feelings, the comments of others, and the actions of models need to be confirmed by our own performance if they are to be effective contributors to self-efficacy.

pause & reflect

On the basis of your own experience, do you agree that personal experience is the most important factor affecting self-efficacy? What steps can you take to raise the probability that your students will experience more successes than failures?

Types of Behaviors Affected by Self-Efficacy Bandura has identified four types of behaviors that are at least partly influenced by an individual's level of self-efficacy. These are shown on the "Effects" side of Figure 9.2.

| Self-efficacy influences goals and activities, cognitive processes, perseverance, emotions

1. *Selection processes.* By the term *selection processes*, we mean the way the person goes about selecting goals and activities. Individuals with a strong sense of self-efficacy, particularly if it extends over several areas, are more likely than others to consider a variety of goals and participate in a variety of activities. They may, for example, think about a wide range of career options, explore several majors while in college, take a variety of courses, participate in different sporting activities, engage in different types of social activities, and have a wide circle of friends.

A person's self-efficacy for a particular task is influenced primarily by past performance but also by encouragement from others, emotional reactions, and observing others.
© Paul Barton/CORBIS

2. *Cognitive processes.* Individuals with high self-efficacy, compared with their peers who are low in self-efficacy, tend to use higher-level thought processes (such as analysis, synthesis, and evaluation) to solve complex problems. Thus, in preparing a classroom report or a paper, students with low self-efficacy may do little more than repeat a set of facts found in various sources; often this behavior stems from their belief that they are not capable of more. In contrast, students with high self-efficacy often discuss similarities and differences, inconsistencies and contradictions, and make evaluations about the validity and usefulness of the information they have found. Another cognitive difference is that people high in self-efficacy are more likely to visualize themselves being successful at some challenging task, whereas individuals low in self-efficacy are more likely to imagine disaster. This leads to differences in the next category of behaviors—motivation.

3. *Motivational processes.* Those who rate their capabilities as higher than average can be expected to work harder and longer to achieve a goal than those who feel less capable. This difference should be particularly noticeable when individuals experience frustrations (poor-quality instruction, for example) and setbacks (such as a serious illness).

4. *Affective processes.* Finally, when faced with a challenging task, the individual with high self-efficacy is more likely to experience excitement, curiosity, and an eagerness to get started rather than the sense of anxiety, depression, and impending disaster that many individuals with low self-efficacy feel.

Before leaving this discussion of self-efficacy, we would like to make one last point about its role in self-regulated behavior. As important as self-efficacy is, you should realize that other factors play a role as well. In addition to feeling capable of successfully completing a particular task, students also need to possess basic knowledge and skills, anticipate that their efforts will be appropriately rewarded, and value the knowledge, skill, or activity that they have been asked to learn or complete (Pajares, 2009).

As we noted earlier, students (as well as adults) vary in how extensively and how well they regulate their thoughts, feelings, and behavior as they pursue goals. To help students with poorly developed self-regulation skills become better learners, you need to know what a well-formed self-regulatory system includes. In the next section we describe a system of self-regulatory processes that has been proposed by Barry Zimmerman (2000, 2002), a leading social cognitive theorist and researcher.

The Components of a Self-Regulatory System

Self-regulatory processes and their related beliefs can be grouped into one of three categories, each of which, ideally, comes into play at different points in time in the course of pursuing a goal (see Figure 9.3). Notice how we qualified the first sentence of this paragraph by saying that the various categories of self-regulatory processes *ideally* come into play at different points during the process. Keep in mind that learners can, for example, cycle back to the forethought phase from the performance phase before going on to the self-reflection phase, begin a task without doing a task analysis, or make self-judgments and self-reactions at any point in the process (Muis, 2007).

The first category of a self-regulatory system's components includes the *forethought* processes and self-beliefs that occur prior to beginning a task. Next are the *performance* processes that are activated during the course of a task. Third are the *self-reflection* processes that occur after a response or series of responses have been made. Because self-reflection influences subsequent forethought processes, this system is cyclical in nature. Consequently, Zimmerman (2000, 2002; Zimmerman & Kitsantas, 2005) refers to these three processes as occurring in phases.

Figure 9.3 Phases and Categories of the Self-Regulation Cycle

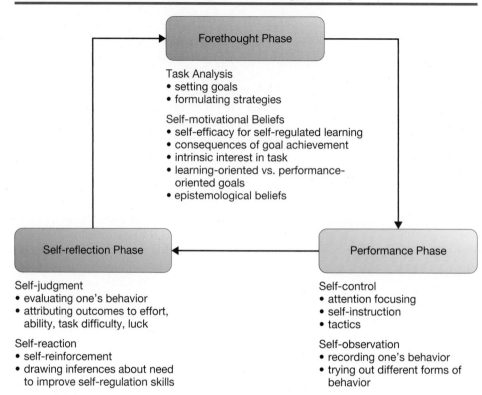

SOURCES: Zimmerman (2000, 2008); Zimmerman & Kitsantas (2005).

As you know from earlier chapters, children acquire their cognitive skills gradually. So in addition to describing the main self-regulatory processes that come into play at each phase, we will also note the developmental limitations you can expect to see if you teach primary grade children.

Forethought Phase   The forethought phase is subdivided into the categories of task analysis and self-motivational beliefs. Task analysis includes the self-regulatory processes of *goal setting* and *strategic planning*. When setting goals, self-regulated learners do not just specify one or more long-term goals, especially those that take time to achieve. Instead, for each long-term goal, they establish a series of near-term subgoals that are achievable and provide evidence of progress. For example, to accomplish the long-term goal of achieving a grade of A in physics, a self-regulating student will set subgoals that pertain to number of hours spent per week studying, working sample problems at the end of the textbook chapter, doing homework as accurately as possible, and seeking help when problems arise. As we point out later in this chapter, planning is a necessary self-regulatory skill because the circumstances under which one learns are constantly changing. Thus self-regulated learners constantly assess themselves and the nature and demands of a learning task so they can select those methods that are most likely to lead to goal attainment.

As we also point out later, possessing these skills is of little value if one isn't motivated to use them. This is why the self-motivational beliefs category is part of this phase. Included here are self-efficacy beliefs, outcome expectations, intrinsic interest, goal orientation, and epistemological beliefs. In the context of this discussion, self-efficacy pertains to how capable people believe themselves to be about using self-regulatory processes. Outcome expectations refer to what one believes will be the consequences of achieving a goal (such as praise, prestige, increased responsibility). Intrinsic interest can maintain motivation for self-regulated learning in situations in which external rewards are either unavailable or unattractive. Goal orientations (which we discuss in Chapter 11, "Motivation") can be learning oriented or performance oriented. Individuals who have a learning orientation are interested in learning primarily for its internal rewards (better understanding of the world in which one lives, increased competence) and are more apt to be motivated to use self-regulation processes than are performance-oriented individuals whose goal is to achieve a higher score or grade than others.

Epistemological beliefs refer to what we believe about the nature of knowledge and how we come to know things. There are several types of epistemological beliefs and they range, particularly when you compare children and adolescents with adults, from naïve and absolute to mature and relative. We can believe, for example, that knowledge is certain (there is a correct, clear-cut answer for every question or problem that, once known, does not change) or that it evolves as scholars conduct further inquiries. We can believe that the acquisition of knowledge occurs either quickly or gradually. We can believe that authority figures are the sole source of all knowledge or that knowledge is also acquired through personal observation, experimentation, and reasoning. Lastly, we can believe that knowledge is composed of mostly unrelated pieces or that it is organized, like schemas, into integrated and interrelated bodies.

The significance of epistemological beliefs is that they have been shown to affect all aspects of self-regulated learning. For example, students who believe that knowledge is a collection of mostly unrelated facts are more likely to use rote rehearsal tactics than are students who believe that knowledge is best thought of as interrelated bodies of information whose structure is likely to change over time. In the course of doing a research project, students who believe that knowledge is certain and unchanging may see nothing wrong with consulting out-of-date reference materials. Students who believe that learning either occurs quickly or not at all are less likely to persevere with difficult tasks or to try a different approach when their first approach fails than are students who believe that learning occurs gradually and with effort (Muis, 2007).

Developmental Limitations In the forethought phase, young children are likely to be more limited than older children in their ability to do the following:

- Attend to a model, such as a teacher, for long periods of time
- Distinguish relevant model behaviors and verbalizations from less relevant ones
- Encode a model's behavior as generalized verbal guidelines
- Formulate and maintain well-defined long-term goals (Schunk, 2001)

Performance Phase This phase contains several self-regulatory processes, and again they divide into two categories: the self-control category and the self-observation category. Self-control processes help learners focus on the task and meaningfully process the information they are trying to learn. *Attention focusing*, for example, involves ignoring distractions, executing a task at a slower than normal pace, and not thinking about prior mistakes or failed efforts. *Self-instruction* involves describing to oneself, either silently or out loud, how to carry out the steps of a task or process. *Tactics* (or *task strategies*) include the many memory-directed and comprehension-directed techniques that we discuss later in this chapter.

Self-observation processes, also known as self-monitoring, increase awareness of one's performance and the conditions that affect it, and have been shown to be a key component of self-regulated learning (Greene & Azevedo, 2009). These processes include *self-recording* and *self-experimentation*. Two frequently used methods of self-recording are written journals and logbooks. When done consistently, self-recording can reveal desirable and undesirable behavioral patterns that correspond to particular environmental conditions, such as putting off homework or studying for an exam in favor of socializing with friends. The results of self-recording can lead

Self-regulated learners set goals, create plans to achieve those goals

Self-regulated learners focus on task, process information meaningfully, self-monitor

learners to self-experimentation, or trying out different forms of behavior. For instance, a student might change the time and place of study or the techniques that are used to see whether these changes produce better results.

Developmental Limitations   For the performance phase, you can expect primary grade children to be limited in their ability to do the following:

- Ignore both external and internal distractions (such as self-doubts and thoughts of prior difficulties)
- Perform the steps of a task more slowly and deliberately to avoid making mistakes
- Provide themselves with verbal reminders of the steps needed to carry out a task
- Select appropriate tactics for a particular task (Schunk, 2001)

Self-Reflection Phase   As with the first two phases, this phase of the self-regulatory system is composed of two categories, self-judgment and self-reaction, each of which involves two self-regulatory processes.

The first of the self-judgment processes is *self-evaluation*. Whenever we label our performance as good or bad, acceptable or unacceptable, satisfactory or unsatisfactory, we are engaging in self-evaluation. There are basically four ways in which students can make these self-evaluative judgments:

1. *Students can adopt what is called a mastery criterion.* This system uses a graded scale that was created by someone with extensive knowledge about the range of performances for that skill or topic; the scale ranges from novice to expert. By using a mastery criterion, learners know where they stand with respect to an absolute standard of performance and whether they are making progress with additional study and practice.
2. *Students can compare their current performance against their own previous performance.*
3. *Students can use a normative standard.* This involves comparing one's performance against the performances of others, such as classmates, rather than some external standard. In fact, evidence suggests that students prefer to compare themselves with similar peers (same gender, age, and race, for example) who perform better than they do (Dijkstra, Kuyper, van der Werf, Buunk, & van der Zee, 2008).
4. *Students can use a collaborative standard.* This method applies to situations in which an individual is part of a group effort. The student would make a positive self-evaluation if he or she had fulfilled those responsibilities identified as necessary for the group to succeed in its endeavor.

Causal attributions, which we also cover in Chapter 11 in the section titled "Attribution Theory," are the second self-judgment process. They involve ascribing a major cause to a behavior. A student's successes and failures can be attributed to effort, ability, task difficulty, and luck, among other factors. Students who attribute their successes to effort and ability and their failures to insufficient effort are more likely to engage in self-regulated learning behaviors than are students who attribute success to good luck or easy tasks and failure to bad luck or low ability.

The self-reaction category is composed of *self-satisfaction* and *adaptive inferences*. Self-satisfaction is the positive feeling we get when we know we have done a job well and achieved whatever goal we established at the outset. Think of it as **self-reinforcement**, which is the label used for it in Figure 9.3. Adaptive inferences are the conclusions that learners draw about the need to improve their self-regulatory skills. Learners can, however, make defensive rather than adaptive inferences. These individuals see no need to improve their self-regulatory skills because they have little interest in the task at hand or feel incapable of developing the skills necessary to successfully carry out the task. Consequently, they resort to such maladaptive

> Self-regulated learners evaluate their performance, make appropriate attributions for success and failure, reinforce themselves

behaviors as helplessness, procrastination, task avoidance, apathy, and disengagement in an effort to protect themselves from the aversive effects of anticipated failure. Teachers can, however, affect the direction of students' adaptive inferences. Students who view their teachers as being emotionally and instructionally supportive are more likely to engage in help-seeking and are less likely to conceal their learning problems than are students who view their teachers as hostile and coercive (Marchand & Skinner, 2007).

Developmental Limitations For the self-reflection phase, expect primary grade children to be limited in their ability to do the following:

- Compare themselves to peers as a basis for judging their own capabilities. Young children's beliefs about their capabilities are more likely to be influenced by teacher feedback than by comparisons to peers' performance. For older students, the reverse is true.
- Make appropriate attributions for their successes and failures. In the primary grades the concepts of effort and ability are not clearly distinguished, and so effort is viewed as the primary cause of success and failure. Older students, however, are more likely to ascribe success primarily to ability and failure primarily to insufficient ability.
- Accurately assess the level of their own capabilities. Primary grade children are likely to overestimate what they can do if they have learned only some aspects of a skill or if they use incorrect learning or problem-solving skills that accidentally produce an acceptable outcome. Conversely, young children can underestimate their competence when they are uncertain about the correctness of their responses (Schunk, 2001).

TeachSource Video Case ◄◄ ▶ ▶▶

Performance Assessment: Student Presentations in a High School English Class

Go to the Education CourseMate website and watch the Video Case, and then answer the following questions:

1. How do the class presentations in this Video Case allow students to practice their self-regulation skills?

2. Explain how the peer assessment component of this literature lesson illustrates the self-reflection phase of Zimmerman's model.

Now that we've laid out the basic structure of social cognitive theory and described its major focus (self-regulated behavior), we can turn our attention to how the concepts of self-regulation apply to classroom learning.

HELPING STUDENTS BECOME SELF-REGULATED LEARNERS

What Is Self-Regulated Learning?

Self-regulated learning: thoughts, feelings, and actions purposely generated and controlled to maximize a learning outcome

As we have suggested in the preceding sections, the concept of self-regulation can be directly applied to learning academic material in and out of classrooms. **Self-regulated learning** (which is also referred to as intentional learning; see, for example, Sinatra & Pintrich, 2003) refers to any thoughts, feelings, or actions that are purposely generated and controlled by a student to maximize learning of knowledge and skills for a given task and set of conditions. Self-regulated learning involves, among other things, knowing under what circumstances to use particular learning techniques and why they work (part of the metacognition concept we introduced in the previous chapter), analyzing the characteristics of learning tasks, using various techniques for learning new information, using various techniques for remaining calm and confident, estimating how much time it will take to complete a task, monitoring one's progress, knowing when and from whom to seek help, and feeling a sense of pride and satisfaction about accomplishing one's learning goals (Paris & Paris, 2001; Pressley & Hilden, 2006; Schunk, 2001; Zimmerman & Kitsantas, 2005).

Not surprisingly, self-regulated learners are also referred to as *self-directed, autonomous,* or *strategic* learners. An example of a self-regulating student is one who does the following:

- Prepares for an upcoming exam by studying for 2 hours each night for several nights instead of trying to cram all the studying into one or two nights (thereby applying the principle of distributed practice, discussed in Chapter 8, "Information-Processing Theory")
- Uses memory-directed tactics, such as mnemonic devices, to accurately store and recall information for test items that will demand verbatim recall
- Uses comprehension-directed tactics, such as concept maps and self-questioning, to deal with test items that will require comprehension, analysis, and synthesis of information
- Creates self-tests to monitor the effectiveness of study efforts and takes some time off from studying if the results of a self-test are satisfactory

How Well Prepared Are Students to Be Self-Regulated Learners?

We would like to be able to report that most students possess the self-regulated learning skills just listed, but, unfortunately, we cannot. Although evidence exists that students are more likely to use effective learning skills as they get older (Greene & Azevedo, 2009; Schneider, Knopf, & Stefanek, 2002) and that some students behave strategically by using different learning skills for different tasks (Hadwin, Winne, Stockley, Nesbit, & Woszczyna, 2001), many do not do so either systematically or consistently. Their attempts at encoding rarely go beyond rote rehearsal (for example, rereading a textbook chapter), simple organizational schemes (outlining), and various cuing devices (underlining or highlighting), and they have a poor sense of how well prepared they are to take a test (Bond, Miller, & Kennon, 1987; Callender & McDaniel, 2009; Karpicke, Butler, & Roediger, 2009; Kornell & Bjork, 2007; McDaniel, Howard, & Einstein, 2009; Peverly, Brobst, Graham, & Shaw, 2003; Winne & Jamieson-Noel, 2002, 2003). Because of its complexity, you can expect expertise in self-regulated learning (SRL) to develop gradually over many years. Based on research on the development of related skills, researchers estimate that students will need at least several years of systematic strategy instruction to become highly proficient self-regulated learners (Harris, Alexander, & Graham, 2008; Pressley & Hilden, 2006; Winne & Stockley, 1998).

This chapter's Case in Print pinpoints the fact that many students still seem to lack SRL skills when they reach college. One reason for this state of affairs is that students are rarely taught how to make the most of their cognitive capabilities. In one study, 69 kindergarten through sixth-grade teachers instructed students about how to effectively use learning strategies only 9.5 percent of the time they were observed. Rationales for strategy use were given less than 1 percent of the time, and 10 percent of the teachers gave no strategy instructions at all. Moreover, the older

Students who are self-regulated learners tend to achieve at high levels by using appropriate cognitive and metacognitive skills for particular tasks in the right way and at the right time.
© Michael Newman/Photo Edit

the students were, the less likely they were to receive strategy instruction (Moely et al., 1992). A similar study of 11 middle school teachers 8 years later produced the same findings. Teaching behaviors that reflected strategy instruction occurred only 9 percent of the time (Hamman, Berthelot, Saia, & Crowley, 2000).

Another reason that students have difficulty using SRL skills is that teachers sometimes make it difficult for students to formulate and use effective strategies by not aligning course goals, classroom instruction, test content, and test demands. That is, teachers may tell students that their goal is for students to understand concepts, integrate ideas, and apply what they have learned to other tasks and subjects, but then emphasize the memorization and recall of facts both in class and on tests. Under these circumstances, students are likely to be unsure as to which type of demand should govern how they study, so they settle on a "middle-of-the-road" approach that does justice to neither (Broekkamp & Van Hout-Wolters, 2007).

Findings such as these are surprising, not to mention disappointing, as it is widely recognized that the amount of independent learning expected of students increases consistently from elementary school through high school and into college. The rest of this chapter will try to convince you that it need not be this way, at least for your students. In the next section, we describe two cognitive skills that students will need to learn how to use if they are to become proficient self-regulated learners: strategies and tactics.

pause & reflect

Many teachers have said that they would like to teach their students more about the nature and use of learning processes but that they don't have time because of the amount of subject material they must cover. What can you do to avoid this pitfall?

The Nature of Learning Tactics and Strategies

Strategy: plan to achieve a long-term goal

Tactic: specific technique that helps achieve immediate objective

A **learning strategy** is a general *plan* that a learner formulates for achieving a somewhat distant academic goal (such as getting an A on the next exam). Like all other strategies, it specifies what will be done to achieve the goal, where it will be done, and when it will be done. A **learning tactic** is a specific *technique* (such as a memory aid or a form of note taking) that a learner uses to accomplish an immediate objective (such as to understand the concepts in a textbook chapter and how they relate to one another).

As you can see, tactics have an integral connection to strategies. They are the learning tools that move you closer to your goal. Thus they have to be chosen so as to be consistent with the goals of a strategy. If you had to recall verbatim the

Preamble to the U.S. Constitution, for example, would you use a learning tactic that would help you understand the gist of each stanza or one that would allow accurate and complete recall? It is surprising how often students fail to consider this point. Because understanding the different types and roles of tactics will help you better understand the process of strategy formulation, we will discuss tactics first.

Types of Tactics

Most learning tactics can be placed in one of two categories based on the tactic's primary purpose:

- *Memory-directed tactics*, which contain techniques that help produce accurate storage and retrieval of information
- *Comprehension-directed tactics*, which contain techniques that aid in understanding the meaning of ideas and their interrelationships (Levin, 1982)

Because of space limitations, we cannot discuss all the tactics in each category. Instead, we have chosen to briefly discuss a few that are either very popular with students or have been shown to be reasonably effective. The first two, *rehearsal* and *mnemonic devices*, are memory-directed tactics. Both can take several forms and are used by students of almost every age. The last three, *self-questioning*, *note taking*, and **concept mapping,** are comprehension-directed tactics and are used frequently by students from the upper elementary grades through college.

Rehearsal   The simplest form of rehearsal—rote rehearsal—is one of the earliest tactics to appear during childhood, and almost everyone uses it on occasion. It is not a particularly effective tactic for long-term storage and recall because it does not produce distinct encoding or good retrieval cues (although, as discussed earlier, it is a useful tactic for purposes of short-term memory). The consensus among researchers is that most five- and six-year-olds do not spontaneously rehearse but can be prompted to do so. Seven-year-olds sometimes use the simplest form of rehearsal. By eight years of age, youngsters start to rehearse several items together as a set instead of rehearsing single pieces of information one at a time. A slightly more advanced version, *cumulative rehearsal*, involves rehearsing a small set of items for several repetitions, dropping the item at the top of the list and adding a new one, giving the set several repetitions, dropping the item at the head of the set and adding a new one, rehearsing the set, and so on (Pressley & Hilden, 2006; Schlagmüller & Schneider, 2002). Even among college students (yes, reader, this means you), rehearsal, in the form of rereading sections of text, is a very popular tactic (Callender & McDaniel, 2009).

By early adolescence, rehearsal reflects the learner's growing awareness of the organizational properties of information. When given a list of randomly arranged words from familiar categories, thirteen-year-olds will group items by category to form rehearsal sets. This version of rehearsal is likely to be the most effective because of the implicit association between the category members and the more general category label. If at the time of recall the learner is given the category label or can generate it spontaneously, the probability of accurate recall of the category members increases significantly.

Mnemonic Devices   A **mnemonic device** is a memory-directed tactic that helps a learner transform or organize information to enhance its retrievability. Such devices can be used to learn and remember individual items of information (a name, a fact, a date), sets of information (a list of names, a list of vocabulary definitions, a sequence of events), and ideas expressed in text. These devices range from simple, easy-to-learn techniques to somewhat complex systems that require a fair amount of practice. Because they incorporate visual and verbal forms of elaborative encoding, their effectiveness is due to the same factors that make imagery and category clustering successful: organization and meaningfulness.

Margin notes:

Rote rehearsal not a very effective memory tactic

Acronym: word made from first letters of items to be learned

Acrostic: sentence made up of words derived from first letters of items to be learned

Loci method: visualize items to be learned stored in specific locations

Keyword method: visually link pronunciation of foreign word to English translation

Mnemonic devices meaningfully organize information, provide retrieval cues

Although mnemonic devices have been described and practiced for more than 2,000 years, they were rarely made the object of scientific study until the 1960s (see Yates, 1966, for a detailed discussion of the history of mnemonics). Since that time, mnemonics have been frequently and intensively studied by researchers, and several reviews of mnemonics research have been done (for example, Bellezza, 1981; Carney & Levin, 2002; Levin, 1993; Snowman, 1986). Table 9.1 provides descriptions, examples, and uses of five mnemonic devices: rhymes, acronyms, acrostics, the loci method, and the keyword method.

Why Mnemonic Devices Are Effective Mnemonic devices work so well because they enhance the encodability and retrievability of information. First, they provide a context (such as acronyms, sentences, mental walks) in which apparently unrelated items can be organized. Second, the meaningfulness of material to be learned is enhanced through associations with more familiar meaningful information (for example, memory pegs or loci). Third, they provide distinctive retrieval cues that must be encoded with the material to be learned. Fourth, they force the learner to be an active participant in the learning process (Morris, 1977).

An example of these mnemonic benefits can be seen in a study conducted with college students (Rummel, Levin, & Woodward, 2003). You may find this study particularly relevant because the students used a variation of the keyword mnemonic to learn about a topic you covered in a previous chapter—theories of intelligence. Students assigned to the mnemonic condition were asked to read a 1,800-word passage that discussed the contributions of five psychologists to the measurement of intelligence and seven psychologists to the development of theories of intelligence. After each paragraph they encountered a mnemonic illustration that linked the theorist's surname to his major contribution. For example, after the paragraph about Charles Spearman, students saw a drawing of a man holding a "primary" hunting spear along with several specialized spears on the ground to represent Spearman's theory that intelligence is composed of one general and several specialized factors. Students assigned to the non-mnemonic condition encountered a summary sentence after each paragraph instead of an illustration. After reading the passage, all students were asked to write two short essays in which they compared and contrasted the work of each theorist and summarized the major aspects of each theory. They then took a three-column matching test in which they had to match each theorist's name with that person's major contribution and other information about that person's work. A second matching test was taken 1 week later. On the essay test, the two groups had equivalent scores on structural coherence and correct chronological sequence, but the mnemonic students scored considerably higher on correctly associating each theorist's name with his major accomplishment. On the matching test, the mnemonic group outscored the non-mnemonic group by a wide margin for matching names and major facts on both the immediate test and the delayed test.

Why You Should Teach Students How to Use Mnemonic Devices Despite the demonstrated effectiveness of mnemonic devices, many people argue against teaching them to students. They think that students should learn the skills of critical thinking and problem solving rather than ways to recall isolated bits of verbatim information reliably. When factual information is needed, one can always turn to a reference source. Although we agree with the importance of teaching students to be critical thinkers and problem solvers, we think this view is shortsighted for three reasons.

- It is very time-consuming to be constantly looking things up in reference books.
- The critique of mnemonic training ignores the fact that effective problem solving depends on ready access to a well-organized and meaningful knowledge base. Indeed, people who are judged to be expert in a particular field have an impressive array of factual material at their fingertips.

Table 9.1	Five Types of Mnemonic Devices

Mnemonic	Description	Example	Uses
Rhyme	The items of information that one wants to recall are embedded in a rhyme that may range from one to several lines. A rhyme for recalling the names of the first 40 U.S. presidents, for example, contains 14 lines.	• Thirty days hath September, April, June, and November • Fiddlededum, fiddlededee, a ring around the moon is $\pi \times d$. If a hole in your sock you want repaired, use the formula π r squared (to recall the formulas for circumference and area).	Recalling specific items of factual information
Acronym	The first letter from each to-be-remembered item is used to make a word. Often called the first-letter mnemonic.	• HOMES (for the names of the Great Lakes—Huron, Ontario, Michigan, Erie, Superior)	Recalling a short set of items, particularly abstract items, in random or serial order
Acrostic	The first letter from each to-be-remembered item is used to create a series of words that forms a sentence. The first letter of each word in the sentence corresponds to the first letters of the to-be-remembered items.	• Kindly Place Cover Over Fresh Green Spring Vegetables (for the taxonomic classification of plants and animals—Kingdom, Phylum, Class, Order, Family, Genus, Species, and Variety) • A Rat In The House May Eat The Ice Cream (to recall the spelling of the word *arithmetic*)	Recalling items, particularly abstract ones, in random or serial order
Method of loci	Generate visual images of and memorize a set of well-known locations that form a natural series (such as the furniture in and the architectural features of the rooms of one's house). Second, generate images of the to-be-learned items (objects, events, or ideas), and place each in a separate location. Third, mentally walk through each location, retrieve each image from where it was placed, and decode into a written or spoken message. *Loci* (pronounced *low-sigh*) is the plural of *locus*, which means "place."	• To recall the four stages of Piaget's theory: For sensorimotor stage, picture a car engine with eyes, ears, nose, and a mouth. Place this image in your first location (fireplace mantel). For preoperational stage, picture Piaget dressed in a surgical gown scrubbing up before an operation. Place this image in your second location (bookshelf). For concrete-operational stage, picture Piaget as a surgeon cutting open a piece of concrete. Place this image in your third location (chair). For formal-operational stage, picture Piaget as an operating room surgeon dressed in a tuxedo. Place this image in your fourth location (sofa).	Can be used by children, college students, and elderly people to recall lists of discrete items or ideas from text passages. Works equally well for free recall and serial recall, abstract and concrete items.
Keyword	Created to aid the learning of foreign language vocabulary but is applicable to any task in which one piece of information has to be associated with another. First, isolate some part of the foreign word that, when spoken, sounds like a meaningful English word. This is the keyword. Then create a visual image of the keyword. Finally, form a compound visual image between the keyword and the translation of the foreign word.	• Spanish word *pato* (pronounced *pot-o*) means "duck" in English. Keyword is *pot*. Imagine a duck with a pot over its head or a duck simmering in a pot. • English psychologist Charles Spearman proposed that intelligence was composed of two factors—*g* and *s*. Keyword is "spear." Imagine a spear being thrown at a gas (for *g* and *s*) can.	For kindergarten through fourth grade, works best when children are given keywords and pictures. Can be used to recall cities and their products, states and their capitals, medical definitions, and famous people's accomplishments.

SOURCES: Atkinson (1975); Atkinson & Raugh (1975); Bellezza (1981); Carney, Levin, & Levin (1994); Raugh & Atkinson (1975); Yates (1966).

- Critics of mnemonics education focus only on the "little idea" that mnemonic usage aids verbatim recall of bits of information. The "big idea" is that students come to realize that the ability to learn and remember large amounts of information is an acquired capability. Too often students (and adults) assume that an effective memory is innate and requires high intelligence. Once they realize that learning is a skill, students may be more inclined to learn how to use other tactics and how to formulate broad-based strategies.

Self- and Peer-Questioning   Because students are expected to demonstrate much of what they know by answering written test questions, self-questioning can be a valuable learning tactic. The key to using questions profitably is to recognize that different types of questions make different cognitive demands. Some questions require little more than verbatim recall or recognition of simple facts and details. If an exam is designed to stress factual recall, then it may be helpful for a student to generate such questions while studying. Other questions, however, assess comprehension, application, or synthesis of main ideas or other high-level information.

To ensure that students fully understood how to write comprehension-aiding questions, Alison King (1992b) created a set of question stems (see Table 9.2) that were intended to help students identify main ideas and think about how those ideas related to each other and to what the student already knew. When high school and college students used these question stems, they scored significantly better on tests of recall and comprehension of lecture material than did students who simply reviewed the same material. King (1994, 1998) also demonstrated that pairs of fourth- and fifth-grade students who were taught how to ask each other high-level questions and respond with elaborated explanations outperformed untrained students on tests that measured both comprehension and the ability to integrate text information with prior knowledge.

Self-questioning improves comprehension, knowledge integration

Self-questioning is a highly recommended learning tactic because it has a two-pronged beneficial effect:

- It helps students to understand better what they read. To answer the kinds of question stems King suggested, students have to engage in such higher-level thinking processes as translating ideas into their own words ("What is the meaning of . . .?" "Explain why . . ."), looking for similarities and differences ("What is the difference between . . . and . . .?" "How are . . . and . . . similar?"), thinking about how ideas relate to one another ("Compare . . . and . . . with regard to . . .") and to previously learned information ("How does . . . tie in with what we learned before?"), and evaluating the quality of ideas ("What are the strengths and weaknesses of . . .?").
- It helps students to monitor their comprehension. If too many questions cannot be answered or if the answers appear to be too superficial, this provides clear evidence that the student has not achieved an adequate understanding of the passage.

Studies that have examined the effect of responding to question stems report very strong effects. The average student who responded to question stems while reading a passage scored at the 87th percentile on a subsequent teacher-made test, whereas the average student who did not answer questions scored only at the 50th percentile. Differences of this magnitude do not appear in research studies very often and, in this case, argue strongly for providing students with question stems and teaching them how to construct their own questions and answers (Rosenshine, Meister, & Chapman, 1996). Discussion of the conditions that underlie effective self-questioning instruction can be found in articles by Bernice Wong (1985), Zemira Mevarech and Ziva Susak (1993), and Alison King (2002).

Taking notes and reviewing notes aid retention and comprehension

Note Taking   As a learning tactic, note taking comes with good news and bad. The good news is that note taking can benefit a student in two ways. First, the process of taking notes while listening to a lecture or reading a text leads to better

Table 9.2	Self-Questioning Stems

What is a new example of . . .?

How would you use . . . to . . .?

What would happen if . . .?

What are the strengths and weaknesses of . . .?

What do we already know about . . .?

How does . . . tie in with what we learned before?

Explain why . . .

Explain how . . .

How does . . . affect . . .?

What is the meaning of . . .?

Why is . . . important?

What is the difference between . . . and . . .?

How are . . . and . . . similar?

What is the best . . ., and why?

What are some possible solutions to the problem of . . .?

Compare . . . and . . . with regard to . . .

How does . . . cause . . .?

What do you think causes . . .?

SOURCE: From King, A. (1992b). "Facilitating Elaborative Learning Through Guided Student-Generated Questioning," *Educational Psychologist, 27*(1), 111–126. Reprinted by permission of Lawrence Erlbaum Associates, Inc.

retention and comprehension of the noted information than just listening or reading does. For example, Andrew Katayama and Daniel Robinson (2000) found that college students who were given a set of partially completed notes for a text passage and told to fill in the blank spaces scored higher on a test of application than students who were given a complete set of notes. Second, the process of reviewing notes produces additional chances to recall and comprehend the noted material. The bad news is that we know very little about the specific conditions that make note taking an effective tactic.

This uncertainty as to what constitutes a good set of notes probably explains the results Alison King (1992a) obtained in a comparison of self-questioning, summarizing, and note taking. One group of students was given a set of question stems, shown how to generate good questions with them, and allowed to practice. A second group was given a set of rules for creating a good summary (identify a main idea or subtopic and related ideas, and link them together in one sentence), shown how to use them to create good summaries, and allowed to practice. A third group, however, was told simply to take notes as group members normally would in class. Both the self-questioning and summarizing groups scored significantly higher on both an immediate and a 1-week-delayed retention test.

Concept Mapping This is a technique that helps students identify, visually organize, and represent the relationships among a set of ideas. We mention concept maps again and provide an example in Chapter 13, "Approaches to Instruction." Considerable research documents the positive effect of concept mapping on students' recall and comprehension when compared with just reading text. These benefits are stronger for students with low verbal ability or low prior knowledge, and for middle school students as compared to high school students (Nesbit &

Adesope, 2006; Novak, 2009; O'Donnell, Dansereau, & Hall, 2002; Romance & Vitale, 1999). But should you provide students with ready-made concept maps or let them construct their own? The answer to that question is that it depends, at least in part, on two factors. First, students who have no familiarity with concept mapping will probably learn more when they are provided with concept maps. Second, if you intend to test students simply for their ability to store and retrieve the information they read, it probably won't make much of a difference. But if you intend to test them for their ability to transfer what they have learned to similar but new contexts, you should probably give them concept maps that you have created (Stull & Mayer, 2007).

Conclusions Regarding Learning Tactics   On the basis of this brief review, we draw two conclusions. One is that students need to be systematically taught how to use learning tactics to make connections among ideas contained in text and lecture, as well as between new and previously learned information. No one expects students to teach themselves to read, write, and compute. So why should they be expected to teach themselves how to use a variety of learning tactics?

The second conclusion is that learning tactics should not be taught as isolated techniques, particularly to high school students. If tactics are taught that way, most students probably will not keep using them for very long or recognize that as the situation changes, so should the tactic. Therefore, as we implied earlier, students should be taught how to use tactics as part of a broader learning strategy.

TeachSource Video Case ◄◄ ▶ ►►

Metacognition: Helping Students Become Strategic Learners

Go to the Education CourseMate website and watch the Video Case, and then answer the following questions:

1. To help her students better understand the newspaper article she has assigned them to read, the teacher in this video, Julie Craven, has them write in the margins whatever questions and reactions come to mind as they read. Explain how such a tactic might improve students' comprehension.

2. Earlier in this chapter we noted that expertise in self-regulated learning develops gradually. Ms. Craven makes the same observation, as do her students. This slow progress may cause some students to give up on becoming self-regulated learners. How might you keep students motivated while they gradually acquire and refine their self-regulation skills?

3. There are several benefits to becoming a strategic learner, one of which has to do with self-efficacy. Can you identify where in the video this benefit is mentioned?

Supporting Students' Strategy Use

As noted earlier, a learning strategy is a plan for accomplishing a learning goal that takes into account various internal and external conditions. As such, it is the product of the forethought phase of the self-regulation cycle outlined in Figure 9.3. The pertinent internal and external conditions may include the knowledge and skills that the teacher wants students to acquire, the amount of time allotted to learn certain amounts of material, the types of tests students take, the type of information teachers give students about test content, and the students' goals, motives, and level of self-regulated learning skills (see Broekkamp & Van Hout-Wolters, 2007, for a detailed discussion of these and other conditions).

With the teacher's help, students can learn how to formulate strategic learning plans by identifying and analyzing the important aspects of a task. Then they can tailor these plans to their own strengths and weaknesses as learners.
© ACE STOCK LIMITED/ Alamy

A strategic learner is a mindful learner

To help your students create good-quality strategies, you should use the three-phase self-regulation model as a guide for teaching those self-regulation skills. But you should also remind yourself and your students of the following four points. The first is that learning conditions constantly change. Subject matters contain different types of information and structures, teachers use different instructional methods and have different styles, exams differ in the kinds of demands they make, and the interests, motives, and capabilities of students change over time. Accordingly, strategies must be *formulated* or constructed anew as one moves from task to task rather than *selected* from a bank of previously formulated strategies. The true strategist, in other words, exhibits a characteristic that is referred to as *mindfulness* (Alexander, Graham, & Harris, 1998). A mindful learner is aware of the need to be strategic, attends to the various elements that make up a learning task, and thinks about how to use the learning skills he possesses to greatest effect. For example, a mindful learner would be aware that the age-old read-recite-review study technique produces higher levels of free recall than either taking notes or reading a passage twice, but she would also know that for multiple-choice or short-answer tests, there is no appreciable difference among these three tactics (McDaniel, Howard, & Einstein, 2009).

The second point you and your students should know about good-quality learning strategies is that because this is a new skill that will take some time to master, you will need to provide students with what is called metacognitive feedback. If you expect students to continue to create strategies and use various tactics for different types of tasks, you will need to explain why they work, the circumstances under

Take a Stand!

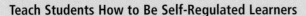

Teach Students How to Be Self-Regulated Learners

A perennial complaint among educators is that many students lack the skills and knowledge to function as self-regulated learners. This is a strange complaint because everyone from politicians to parents endorses the goals of self-directed learning and lifelong learning. Like motherhood and apple pie, they are easy goals to endorse because nobody could be against them. But when it comes to putting one's resources where one's rhetoric is, much of this support disappears like the morning mist. The following reasons account for a large part of this inconsistency:

1. Many people (including teachers, parents, and students) believe that self-regulation is a natural process that students will figure out and master if they just work at it long and hard enough. This leads to the ubiquitous but mostly useless advice to "study harder."

2. School is thought of as a place where students acquire bodies of information about various subject matters and the so-called basic skills of reading, writing, and computing. There is simply not enough room in the curriculum to teach students how to be self-directed learners.

3. Teachers and administrators are held accountable for how well students score on state-mandated tests. Consequently, school curricula and classroom instruction emphasize those skills and bodies of knowledge that relate most directly to state learning standards and test items, and SRL skills are either ignored or take a back seat.

If this situation is to change, everyone involved in education needs to realize that there is nothing more basic than learning how to be a self-regulated learner. These skills allow students to become proficient at reading, writing, and computing and to direct their learning long after they finish school. Consequently, SRL skills should be as much a part of the curriculum as the three Rs.

The place to start is the individual classroom. At the very least, you should teach students that a relationship exists between the cognitive processes they use and the outcomes they observe, how and when to use various learning tactics, how to determine whether learning is proceeding as planned, and what to do if it is not.

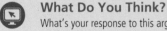

What Do You Think?

What's your response to this argument? Is SRL so "basic" that teachers ought to teach it? At the Education CourseMate website, you can find out more about this important issue.

which they work best, and point out how much more they learn when they use these strategies and tactics (Pressley & Hilden, 2006).

The third point follows from the second and concerns both your motivation and that of your students. Becoming a self-regulated or strategic learner requires concentrated effort over an extended period of time. Consequently, you may be inclined to believe that such a goal is beyond the reach of most elementary, middle school, and possibly even high school students. In the next section we will summarize research that we hope convinces you that even elementary school youngsters can be trained to use a variety of self-regulation skills in context-appropriate ways. We hope you will use this evidence to remind your students that with persistence and effort they can indeed become effective self-regulated learners.

Finally, because strategic learners tailor their learning processes to the perceived demands of a task, teachers need to clearly convey to students such critical information as what tasks or parts of tasks (such as certain parts of a reading assignment) are sufficiently important that they will test students on them and what form the tests will take. Students, in turn, need to accurately perceive those demands (Beishuizen & Stoutjesdijk, 1999). A study conducted in the Netherlands (Broekkamp, van Hout-Wolters, Rijlaarsdam, & van den Bergh, 2002) shows that this process occurs less frequently than one would desire. The study examined how 22 history teachers and their 11th-grade students rated the importance of sections of an 8,000-word textbook passage on U.S. presidents. In brief, here is what the researchers found:

1. There was only limited agreement among teachers about which sections of the text students should focus on in preparation for a test.
2. There was only limited agreement among students, as well as between students and their teacher, as to which sections of the text were most important.

In other words, teachers had only limited success in communicating to students what parts of the passage were more important than others, and students were as apt to focus on the less important parts as the more important ones.

These findings suggest that teachers should provide students with clear and comprehensive information about the relative importance of various parts of a reading passage, instruct students in how to identify the important parts of a reading passage, and avoid dwelling on or overemphasizing aspects of a reading assignment that they have no intention of testing students on.

Modeling and Self-Regulated Learning

What little students know about the nature and use of self-regulatory skills has usually been acquired through direct instruction (by teachers, parents, and peers) and trial-and-error learning. But there is another way to strengthen self-efficacy beliefs and learn how to use self-regulatory skills: observing and imitating the behavior of a skilled model. This form of learning is often referred to as **observational learning** or **modeling.**

The notion that learning occurs by watching and imitating the behavior of others has been acknowledged and valued for thousands of years. Social cognitive theory, with its belief that the student's environment interacts with personal characteristics and behavior, has stressed the role of observational learning in schools.

Observational learning can play an especially strong role in the acquisition of self-regulatory skills. Specifically, evidence suggests that these skills are learned most efficiently and effectively when they are acquired according to the following four-level model: observation, emulation, self-control, and self-regulation (Zimmerman, 2000, 2002; Zimmerman & Kitsantas, 2002, 2005). In the description that follows, note how the high levels of support and guidance (or *scaffolding*, to use the constructivist terminology) that are present for the observation and emulation levels are reduced at the self-control level and eliminated at the self-regulation level. Table 9.3 summarizes the cognitive and behavioral requirements of the learner and the source of the learner's motivation for each level.

Observation   At the observation level, learners pick up the major features of a skill or strategy, as well as performance standards, motivational beliefs, and values, by watching and listening as a model exhibits the skill and explains the reasons for his behavior: for example, a model who persists at trying to solve a problem and expresses the belief that he is capable of solving the problem. What would motivate a student to observe and then try to emulate a model's behavior? At least four factors do so:

Self-regulation skills learned best in a four-level process: observation, emulation, self-control, self-regulation

Table 9.3	A Social Cognitive Model of Self-Regulated Skill Learning	
Level	Main Requirement of the Learner	Source of Motivation
Observation	Attend to actions and verbalizations of the model and discriminate relevant from irrelevant behaviors	Vicarious: note rewards received by the model and anticipate receiving similar rewards for exhibiting similar behavior
Emulation	Exhibit the general form of the modeled behavior	Direct: feedback from the model and/or others
Self-control	Learn to exhibit the modeled behavior automatically through self-directed practice (focus on the underlying rule or process that produces the behavior and compare the behavior with personal standards)	Self-satisfaction from matching the standards and behavior of the model
Self-regulation	Learn to adapt the behavior to changes in internal and external conditions (such as the reactions of others)	Self-efficacy beliefs; degree of intrinsic interest in the skill

SOURCES: Zimmerman (2000, 2002); Zimmerman & Kitsantas (2002).

Case in Print

Wanted: Self-Regulated Learners

Self-regulated learning...refers to any thoughts, feelings, or actions that are purposely generated and controlled by a student to maximize learning of knowledge and skills for a given task and set of conditions . . . Because of its complexity, you can expect expertise in self-regulated learning (SRL) to develop gradually over many years. One estimate, based on research on the development of related skills, is that most students will need about 85 percent of the approximately 12,000 hours they spend in school through 12th grade to become highly proficient in SRL. (p. 289–290)

Students Unprepared for Rigors of College

FREDREKA SCHOUTEN

Gannett News Service, 10/30/2003

High school graduates in Nevada with at least a B average can win $10,000 college scholarships—enough to guarantee them free rides at any public university in the state.

But that ride has proved rough for many. Nearly one-third of the kids who get the scholarships, created to keep the state's most promising students in Nevada, have to take remedial classes when they start college.

They are not alone. Around the country, students, even those with stellar high school records, have discovered they don't have all the skills to survive in college. In Georgia, for instance, four out of 10 students who earn the popular Hope Scholarships to the state's university system lose the scholarship after they earn about 30 credits—roughly one year's worth of work—because they can't keep their grades up.

Student performance on college-admissions tests also point to possible grade inflation. Fifteen years ago, students with A averages accounted for 28 percent of SAT test takers, said Wayne Camara, who oversees research for the College Board.

Today, a whopping 42 percent of college-bound seniors have A averages, but they score no better on the college admissions tests than did "A" students a decade earlier.

Some education experts say the trend is a clear sign that high school teachers are handing out high grades for weak work. But many argue the real culprit is the typical high school course load. Students just aren't taking the rigorous math, science and writing classes in high school that they need to succeed in college and the workplace.

Only one in three 18-year-olds is even minimally prepared for college, according to a recent report by the Manhattan Institute, a New York–based think tank. The picture was even bleaker for minority students. Only 20 percent of blacks in the class of 2001 were college-ready.

Lack of Preparation

Researchers defined minimum preparation as having a regular high school diploma—instead of merely passing the General Educational Development test—the GED—and taking at least four years of English, three years of math, and two years each of social studies, science and a foreign language in high school. They also counted students who performed at least at the basic level on a national reading test.

The preparation gap is particularly acute for graduates of inner-city and rural high schools, said Gary Henry, a Georgia State University professor who studies the Hope Scholarships.

Schools in those areas "can't hire really qualified math and science teachers so the course gets lowered to the level that the teacher is capable of teaching," he said.

"The students have no way of knowing whether the algebra class was decent. All they know is that they passed it."

Ivrekia Stanley thought her prospects were bright when she graduated from Forest Park High School in suburban Atlanta in 1999. Her 3.6 grade-point average earned her a Hope Scholarship and a ticket to college. But when she entered Georgia Perimeter College, a two-year community college, she had to take remedial classes in reading and math.

"You get very discouraged. You don't want to tell anybody you're in these classes," Stanley recalled. She said she kept telling herself, "I have a Hope Scholarship. I'm smarter than this."

But she said the classes taught her some lessons she hadn't learned in high school, like stopping to look up unfamiliar words in the dictionary and quickly determining the main point of a written passage.

This fall, the 22-year-old transferred to Georgia State, where she majors in criminal justice. She has a 3.8 grade-point average and has retained the Hope Scholarship.

40% Lose Scholarships

About 40 percent of Hope Scholars who entered Georgia schools as freshmen in fall 2000 failed to maintain the minimum 3.0 GPA in their first 30 credit hours of college work and lost the scholarships.

Statistics like those from Georgia have inspired officials in Nevada to set up strong mentoring programs to help their Millennium Scholarship recipients and students from the state's rural areas stay in school, said Barbara King, who oversees tutoring programs at the Reno campus of the University of Nevada.

King runs an Internet listserv for the students where she posts reminders about finding tutors and deadlines for dropping classes. She also tries to improve their study habits.

"I tell them to pay attention to repetition during lectures," King said. "The second time a professor says something, underline it. The third time, put a 'T' for 'test' next to it. It probably will be on the test."

Other King tips: Set aside two to three hours of study for every hour spent in class, keep that time commitment in mind when considering taking on a part time job, and read the review questions at the end of a chapter first.

She advises students to try and answer those questions before tackling the reading assignment, because that will help pinpoint important material.

"We're not just assuming that because students got a 3.0 in high school that they come in here knowing what to do," King said.

Class Choice Important

Researchers say that when it comes to college success, what students study in high school is as important as their study skills.

Those who continue studying math for a fourth year in high school—taking classes such as trigonometry and calculus that are harder than second-year algebra—double their chances of earning a bachelor's degree, said Clifford Adelman, a U.S. Department of Education researcher who has examined thousands of high school and college transcripts.

His advice to parents: "Encourage your kids to be challenged in (high) school, and worry less about grades." Before granting merit-based scholarships like Hope, more states now demand that students demonstrate they passed rigorous classes in high school.

Under the Texas Grant program, which pays college tuition for financially needy students, eligible students must take the state's basic college-prep curriculum. That includes four years of English and three years of math, along with three years of science classes.

Starting with the high school freshman class of 2004, all Texas public high schools automatically will enroll students in the college-prep curriculum unless their parents or guardians formally object.

Questions and Activities

1. This article notes that many high school students in Nevada have to take remedial classes during their first year of college, and 40 percent of students in Georgia with state scholarships lose them after the first year of college because of low grades. Two explanations that were offered for students' difficulty in coping with the academic demands of college are grade inflation in high school and students' avoidance of rigorous math, science, and writing courses. A third, and more likely, explanation for students' lack of preparedness for college is poorly developed self-regulation skills. Explain why this factor, and not grade inflation or course selection, is likely to be the primary cause of so many students' academic difficulties in college.

2. One student quoted in the article, Ivrekia Stanley, said that despite her 3.6 grade-point average in high school, she had to take remedial math and reading courses at a community college, where she learned such valuable skills as looking up unfamiliar words in a dictionary and figuring out the main point of a passage. Do you think these basic SRL skills were not learned in high school because they weren't taught or because Ms. Stanley simply didn't learn them at the time? Try using your own high school experience and those of your friends to justify your answer.

3. The first sentence of the last section of the article states, "Researchers say that when it comes to college success, what students study in high school is as important as their study skills." The reporter backs up this claim with the finding by Clifford Adelman, a U.S. Department of Education researcher, that students who take 4 years of math in high school, and who take advanced math classes during their senior year, are twice as likely to graduate from college. Given what we said earlier in the book about how several plausible causal explanations can be generated from correlational data, come up with another explanation of the finding cited by Mr. Adelman.

1. Students are more likely to closely attend to a model and retain what has been observed if they are unfamiliar with the task at hand or if they feel incapable of carrying out the task.

2. Students attend to models they admire, respect, and perceive as having knowledge, skills, and attributes that they themselves would like to have. The popular conception, by the way, that older children and adolescents look primarily to sports or music stars rather than family members as models is not supported by research. In response to the question "What persons are your personal model?" about 46 percent of a large sample (over 1,000) of European children and adolescents listed either their mother or father, and 31 percent listed a relative. Music and sports stars were named by only 15 percent and 12 percent of respondents, respectively (Bucher, 1997).

3. Students attend to models whose behavior they judge to be acceptable and appropriate. Thus students will often model a peer's behavior.

4. Students are more likely to imitate a model's behavior if they see that the model is reinforced for exhibiting the behavior and anticipate that they will be similarly reinforced (Schunk, 2001). This type of reinforcement is referred to as **vicarious reinforcement.** A middle school student, for example, who observes an admired classmate being praised by the teacher for promptly completing an assignment may strive to work quickly and diligently on the next assignment in anticipation of receiving similar praise.

Emulation   At the emulation level, learners reproduce the general form of the model's behavior. Because learners rarely copy the exact behaviors of a model, the term *emulation* is used here instead of the word *imitation*. The learner's response can be refined by the model's use of guidance, feedback, and direct reinforcement (such as praise from the model). Social cognitive theorists identify four types of emulation effects that result from observing models: inhibition, disinhibition, facilitation, and true observational learning.

Inhibition occurs when we learn not to do something that we already know how to do because a model we are observing refrains from behaving in that way, is punished for behaving in that way, or does something different from what we intended to do. Consider the following example: A ten-year-old is taken to her first symphony concert by her parents. After the first movement of Beethoven's Fifth Symphony, she is about to applaud but notices that her parents are sitting quietly with their hands in their laps. She does the same.

Disinhibition occurs when we learn to exhibit a behavior that is usually disapproved of by most people because a model does the same without being punished. For example, a student attends his school's final football game of the season. As time expires, thousands of students run onto the field and begin tearing up pieces of turf to take home as a souvenir. Noticing that the police do nothing, the student joins in.

An early, and now classic, experiment on disinhibition was conducted by Bandura in the early 1960s (Bandura, Ross, & Ross, 1961). A child was seated at a table and encouraged to play with a toy. The model sat at a nearby table and either played quietly with Tinkertoys for 10 minutes or played with the Tinkertoys for a minute and then played aggressively with an inflatable clown "Bobo" doll for several minutes, punching, kicking, and sitting on it and hitting it with a hammer. In a subsequent unstructured play situation, children who did not observe a model, as well as those who observed a nonaggressive model, displayed little aggression. By contrast, children exposed to the aggressive model behaved with considerably more aggression toward the Bobo doll and other toys.

> People learn to inhibit or make responses by observing others

pause & reflect

Can you recall a teacher you admired so much that you emulated some aspect of her behavior (either then or later)? How might you have the same effect on your students?

Social cognitive theory holds that one way students acquire self-regulated learning skills is by observing and imitating the behavior of admired models, such as teachers, siblings, and peers. Copyright © Stephen McBrady/Photo Edit

Facilitation occurs whenever we are prompted to do something that we do not ordinarily do because of insufficient motivation rather than social disapproval. For example, a college student attends a lecture on reforming the American education system. Impressed by the lecturer's enthusiasm and ideas, the student vigorously applauds at the end of the presentation. As several members of the audience stand and applaud, the student stands as well.

The last of the four types of emulation effects, *true observational learning*, occurs when we learn a new behavioral pattern by watching and imitating the performance of someone else. A teenage girl learning how to hit a topspin forehand in tennis by watching her instructor do the same is an example of true observational learning.

Self-Control   The self-control level of observational learning is marked by the learner's being able to exhibit the modeled behavior in the absence of the model. Self-control is achieved through self-directed practice. The learner focuses on the underlying rule or process that produces the behavior and compares the behavior with personal standards. At this level, the learner's motivation comes from a sense of self-satisfaction at matching the standards and behavior of the model.

Self-Regulation   The self-regulation level is attained when learners can adapt the modeled behavior to changes in internal and external conditions (such as a low level of interest in a topic or negative reactions of others). The motivation for self-regulated behavior comes from one's perceived self-efficacy and degree of intrinsic interest in the modeled behavior.

Before leaving this description of SRL and examining some of the relevant research, we would like you to keep the following point in mind: self-regulation is possible only in an environment that allows students the opportunity to make choices. Teachers who specify in great detail what students will do, when they will do it, where they will do it, and how they will do it will see very little development and use of SRL processes (Schunk, 2004).

TeachSource | **Video Case** ◀◀ ▶ ▶▶

Modeling: Social Cognitive Theory in a High School Chemistry Lesson

Go to the Education CourseMate website and watch the Video Case, and then answer the following questions:

1. Do you find this teacher's use of modeling/observational learning to be effective? Explain why or why not.

2. Based on the character and the Video Case, give some ideas of subject areas or lessons in which modeling/observational learning would work especially well.

RESEARCH ON SOCIAL COGNITIVE THEORY

Although social cognitive theory offers a compelling explanation of learning, its value to teachers and others depends on the extent to which its concepts and their proposed relationships are supported by research findings. The research that we summarize in this section falls into three broad categories: (1) correlational studies that have examined how self-efficacy, epistemological beliefs, and self-regulation relate to each other and to achievement, (2) experimental studies that have examined the effect of modeling on self-efficacy, self-regulation, and achievement, and (3) experimental studies that have examined the effect of instruction on self-regulated learning skills.

Relationships Among Self-Efficacy, Epistemological Beliefs, Self-Regulation Processes, and Achievement

Self-efficacy, epistemological beliefs, self-regulation related to each other and to achievement

Social cognitive theory holds that self-efficacy, epistemological beliefs, and self-regulation processes should be positively related to each other and that both should be positively related to achievement. A number of studies, including the following, support these relationships.

- For eighth-grade students in Sweden, scores on an instrument that measured self-efficacy, as well as self-control and academic self-concept, were strongly and positively related to these same students' self-reported use of goal-oriented strategies (Swalander & Taube, 2007).
- Boys often report having a stronger sense of self-efficacy and lower anxiety than girls for math and science, whereas girls often report having a stronger sense of self-efficacy and less anxiety than boys for writing tasks (Usher & Pajares, 2008a).
- Tenth-grade students who were assigned to complete either a well-structured assignment or an ill-structured assignment (we define and illustrate these concepts in the next chapter) filled out a self-efficacy questionnaire at six points during the course of the assignment that assessed both their self-efficacy for learning (for example, "I'm confident I'm learning the basic ideas in this project"

and "I know which mental techniques would best meet the needs of this project") and self-efficacy for performance (such as, "I expect to do well on this project" and "I believe I will receive an excellent grade on this project"). The well-structured task required students to choose a form of cancer and write a report about it that included its causes, symptoms, and treatments; an assessment of their risk for that form of cancer; and a list of behaviors that would likely reduce their risk for that form of cancer. Students who were assigned to the ill-structured task were required to role-play members of a task force who were asked by the government how to best combat cancer and to explain their conclusions in a written report. This exercise was designed to stimulate critical thinking about how government should fund treatment versus preventative measures.

Consistent with the prediction from social cognitive theory that the nature of a task affects students' perception of the task's difficulty and their self-efficacy, students' self-efficacy for learning and their task performance were higher for the well-structured task than for the ill-structured task. The researchers also found that at the outset of the task, regardless of whether it was well-structured or ill-structured, self-efficacy for performance was significantly higher than self-efficacy for learning, but the difference disappeared by the end of the task (Lodewyk & Winne, 2005).

- The more high school students believe that learning occurs quickly or not at all, the more likely they are to have a lower grade-point average than students who believe that learning occurs gradually (Schommer-Aikins, Duell, & Hutter, 2005).
- High school students who believed that knowledge was certain were more likely to have lower grades than students who believed that knowledge could be ambiguous and subject to change, even when intelligence and family background were similar (Trautwein & Lüdtke, 2007).
- Middle school students combine the epistemological beliefs of quick learning ("If I cannot understand something quickly, it usually means I will never understand it") and fixed learning ("Some people are just born smart, others are born dumb," "Students who are average in school will remain average for the rest of their lives") into a more global belief in quick/fixed learning. Those who had more naïve beliefs about quick/fixed learning were less likely than classmates with more advanced beliefs about quick/fixed learning to believe that mathematics was useful to them and were less successful at solving mathematical problems (Schommer-Aikins, Duell, & Hutter, 2005).
- High school students who had more advanced beliefs about fixed/quick ability to learn had higher grades and higher scores on an ill-structured task (a concept we discuss in the next chapter) than did students whose beliefs about fixed and quick ability to learn were more naïve. Furthermore, and this will come as no surprise given the gender differences we discussed in Chapter 4, girls had significantly more sophisticated beliefs about fixed/quick ability to learn and about certain knowledge than did boys (Lodewyk, 2007).

While the research summarized above notes that self-efficacy, self-regulation, and epistemological beliefs affect how K–12 students learn, we want you to keep in mind that these variables also affect how you learn. Students in a teacher education program who believed that learning occurred quickly or not at all were less likely to focus on learning how to master a task and improve one's competence (a mastery goal orientation) and were more likely to focus on getting as high a grade as possible while not revealing any academic weaknesses (a performance-avoidance goal orientation) than their peers who believed that learning occurs gradually (Bråten & Strømsø, 2004). We more fully discuss goal orientations, including the two mentioned here, in Chapter 11.

Effects of Modeling on Self-Efficacy, Self-Regulation, and Achievement

In social cognitive theory, modeling is seen as an effective means of enhancing self-efficacy, teaching students how to use self-regulation skills, and increasing achievement, particularly when the observer is similar to the model or when the observer strongly identifies with the model (Schunk & Zimmerman, 1997; Usher & Pajares, 2008a). Support for the theory has come from a number of studies, particularly ones that focus on skills in mathematics and writing.

Improving Students' Mathematical Problem-Solving Skills Mathematical problem-solving ability is a difficult skill for many students to master, and it has a prominent place in the curriculum (it is one of the three Rs). For these reasons, it has often been studied by social cognitive researchers who are interested in the effects of modeling. The research we describe in this section is just a sample of what has appeared in the literature in the past several years.

Effect of Peer Models Early support for social cognitive theory came from studies like these two: In one, when children watched same-sex peers solve arithmetic problems they scored higher on a test of similar problems and rated themselves higher on a self-efficacy for mathematical problem solving scale than did children who either watched an adult model or who worked solely from written instructions (Schunk & Hanson, 1985). Further proof was provided by a study of middle school students with below-average math achievement scores. These students first watched a teacher solve fractions problems. Then they watched a peer attempt to solve similar problems under the supervision of the teacher. Some of the observing students watched a peer who first made mistakes but overcame them and then performed flawlessly, while other students watched a model solve all the problems without making any mistakes. Because the observing students were low math achievers, it was expected that they would identify more strongly with the model that learned to solve these fractions problems gradually. And that's exactly what the researchers found. Children who observed what was called a coping model reported significantly higher levels of self-efficacy for learning to solve fractions problems and solved significantly more problems correctly than did children who observed a mastery model (Schunk, Hanson, & Cox, 1987).

Observing a peer model improves students' self-efficacy for math problem solving and math problem-solving ability

Effect of Self-Modeling A further study (Schunk & Hanson, 1989) took the similarity hypothesis to its logical conclusion by having students use themselves as their model. Children in grades 4, 5, and 6 whose arithmetic achievement was below the 35th percentile were assigned to either a peer-model, self-model, peer-model + self-model, or no-model condition. Children in the first and third groups watched a videotape in which each of six fractions skills was modeled by a teacher and then by three same-sex peers under the supervision of the teacher. The teacher demonstrated how to do a problem and then asked a student-peer model to do a similar one. The model verbalized the procedure and was then told by the teacher that the solution was correct.

Students in all four groups were then given written instructions for 6 days on how to solve different types of fractions problems (with an adult present to answer questions) and were videotaped working out similar problems at a chalkboard. After days 4, 5, and 6, children in the self-model and peer-model + self-model conditions watched the videotape of their performance from the previous day (thereby serving as their own model). Although there were no differences among the three modeling conditions, students in all three scored significantly higher than the students in the no-model condition on measures of self-efficacy for solving fractions problems and numbers of fractions problems solved correctly.

Improving Students' Writing Skills   Writing skills are also frequently used by researchers to investigate the effects of modeling. Writing is particularly important in the middle school years because writing tasks are more complex than in earlier years and play a larger role in classroom performance. Students who feel poorly prepared to carry out writing tasks tend to be more anxious about them and to spend less time on them (Klassen, 2002). As with the studies we summarized on mathematical problem solving, the research summarized next is just a sample.

Modeling for Strategy Development   As we noted earlier in the chapter, self-regulation skills make significant contributions to achievement, especially when students reach the middle school grades, and modeling can be an effective way to help students acquire these skills. A recent study (Harris, Graham, & Mason, 2006) investigated the feasibility of providing self-regulated strategy instruction in the primary grades. Second-grade students who had scored significantly below average on a writing test were assigned to one of three groups: self-regulated strategy development (SRSD), self-regulated strategy development plus peer support (SRSD + PS), and comparison. In five steps, pairs of students in the two SRSD groups were taught a general planning strategy for writing stories and persuasive essays. The strategy involved picking an idea to write about, organizing one's thoughts, and writing the story or essay. To help the students remember these three elements, they were taught the mnemonic POW. They were also taught specific techniques to help them organize their story and generate persuasive essay ideas. For example, to help them write good stories, they were taught to ask themselves such questions as: Who are the main characters? When does the story take place? What do the main characters want to do? How does the story end? Students assigned to the comparison condition received their normal writing instruction from their classroom teacher.

Students in the two SRSD conditions significantly outscored their peers in the comparison condition in a number of ways. On a posttest administered at the end of the instructional sequence, they spent more time planning their stories and essays, and they wrote essays that were longer, more complete, and of a higher quality. These advantages carried over to the classroom, where the two SRSD groups continued to produce not only better-quality persuasive essays than the comparison students but also better-quality narrative and information papers as well (for which they had received no specific training). Furthermore, students in the SRSD + PS condition wrote persuasive papers for their classroom teacher that were higher in quality than those produced by students in the SRSD-only condition.

A study published the following year (Glaser & Brunstein, 2007) replicated the findings reported by Harris, Graham, & Mason (2006) and also demonstrated that fourth-grade students who were taught both a writing strategy and the SRSD strategy produced stories that were of better quality both immediately after instruction and 5 weeks later than either a group that was taught just the writing strategy or a group that was given traditional writing instruction. The writing strategy + SRSD group also outscored the other two groups on a test that required them to write down as much of an orally presented story as they could recall.

Two researchers (Graham & Perin, 2007) corroborated the positive effects reported by both of the above studies by analyzing the results of more than 100 studies on writing instruction. They found that the average effect size for SRSD instruction on the quality of students' writing was 1.14 standard deviations (which equates to a score at the 87th percentile) whereas the average effect size for all other types of instruction was 0.62 (which equates to a score at the 73rd percentile). This, as you can readily appreciate, is a rather large difference. As an aside, for those who maintain that the best way to improve the quality of students' writing is to adopt a strict back-to-basics approach, the results of this review offer little support. In no study did the explicit teaching of grammar (such as parts of speech and sentence construction) produce better-quality writing than the type of instruction with which it was being compared.

Observing Weak and Strong Models In another test of the model-observer similarity principle (Braaksma, Rijlaarsdam, & van den Bergh, 2002), eighth-grade students in a Dutch school who were classified as having either low, medium, or high verbal ability observed a weak peer model and a strong peer model write an argumentative passage.

Argumentative passages contain an opinion (such as "It is better to live in a city than in a village"), one or more supporting arguments (for example, a city offers more choices for shopping and going to school, cities are more conducive to personal growth, and there are more job opportunities in a city), one or more subordinate arguments (for example, cities are more conducive to personal growth because there is a wider range of people to meet and there are more cultural events to attend), and connective words such as *because* and *and* that logically relate the supporting arguments to the opinion and the subordinate arguments to each other and to the supporting argument.

In the study, the weak models omitted critical aspects of an argumentative passage and produced passages that were less coherent than those produced by the strong models. Both weak and strong models verbalized their thought processes: planning what to write and then checking to make sure that it was complete and made sense. One group of students was asked to identify the model who performed less well and to explain why this was the less competent model. A second group was asked to identify which model performed better and to explain why this was the more competent model.

Students with low verbal ability who were asked to identify and evaluate the weak model received higher scores on the argumentative passages they wrote than did students with low verbal ability who either were asked to identify and evaluate the strong model or who just practiced writing argumentative passages. Students with high verbal ability who wrote argumentative passages after identifying and evaluating the strong model or who merely practiced writing argumentative passages received higher scores than did their peers with high verbal ability who identified and evaluated the weak model. Both groups, in other words, seemed to respond better to models they perceived as similar to themselves.

Modeling Versus Practice Most people have come to believe, partly because of their own experience and partly because of supporting research, that practice makes perfect. But one study (Couzijn, 1999) provides support for the contention of social cognitive theory that observing a model can be more effective than rote practice in helping students acquire new skills.

A group of ninth-grade students worked through a four-part self-instructional course on argumentative writing. After each part, they participated in one of the following four exercises: (1) working individually on writing exercises, (2) watching a videotape of two students of the same age who were doing writing exercises and thinking aloud while they wrote, (3) watching a peer doing writing exercises while the peer thought aloud and then watching another peer verbally analyze the writer's passage, or (4) writing an argumentative passage and then observing a peer analyze the passage while thinking aloud. All students were then asked to write argumentative passages (e.g., "Do you think students should give grades to their teachers?") that were scored for putting the issue in context, text structure, argumentation structure, and presentation of argument (e.g., use of paragraphing, markers, and connectors).

As expected, students in groups (2), (3), and (4)—all the students exposed to modeling of one sort or another—produced better-quality argumentative passages than did students who simply practiced their writing.

Observing a peer model improves the quality of students' writing more than simply practicing writing

Effects of Instruction on Self-Regulated Learning Skills

Research clearly shows that training students to use various tactics and strategies is a worthwhile use of the teacher's time. In one study, students who were trained to use a single mnemonic technique outperformed untrained students by a wide

pause & reflect

A major problem in training students to use learning strategies and tactics is getting the youngsters to spend the time and effort required. Suppose some students expressed a lack of interest, saying their own methods were just as effective (although you knew they were not). How would you convince these students otherwise?

Reciprocal teaching: students learn comprehension skills by demonstrating them to peers

margin on subsequent tests of memory (68th percentile versus 50th percentile, respectively). The effect was particularly noticeable among primary grade and low-achieving students. A similar advantage was found for students who had been taught to use a variety of tactics and were tested for memory and low-level comprehension (75th percentile versus the control group's 50th percentile). Although the weakest effect was found in studies in which students were taught a general strategy rather than specific tactics, these students nevertheless performed significantly better than students who were left to their own devices (70th percentile versus 50th percentile, respectively) (Hattie, Biggs, & Purdie, 1996).

A particularly effective strategy-training program is the *reciprocal teaching* (RT) program of Annemarie Palincsar and Ann Brown (1984). As the title of this program indicates, students learn certain comprehension skills by demonstrating them to each other. Palincsar and Brown trained a small group of seventh graders whose reading comprehension scores were at least 2 years below grade level to use the techniques of summarizing, self-questioning, clarifying, and predicting to improve their reading comprehension. They chose these four methods because students can use them to improve *and* monitor comprehension.

During the early training sessions, the teacher explained and demonstrated the four methods while reading various passages. The students were then given gradually increasing responsibility for demonstrating these techniques to their peers, with the teacher supplying prompts and corrective feedback as needed. Eventually, each student was expected to offer a good summary of a passage, to pose questions about important ideas, to clarify ambiguous words or phrases, and to predict upcoming events, all to be done with little or no intervention by the teacher. (This approach to strategy instruction is based on Vygotsky's zone of proximal development concept that we mentioned previously in the book.)

Palincsar and Brown found that the RT program produced two general beneficial effects. First, the quality of students' summaries, questions, clarifications, and predictions improved. Early in the program, students produced overly detailed summaries and many unclear questions. But in later sessions, concise summaries and questions dealing explicitly with main ideas were the rule. For example, questions on main ideas increased from 54 percent to 70 percent. In addition, the questions were increasingly stated in paraphrase form rather than as verbatim statements. Second, the RT-trained students, who had begun the sessions well below grade level, scored as high as a group of average readers on tests of comprehension (about 75 percent correct for both groups) and much better than a group taught how to locate information that might show up in a test question (75 percent correct versus 45 percent correct).

Subsequent research on the effectiveness of RT under both controlled and realistic conditions has continued to produce positive findings across a broad age spectrum (fourth grade through college). On average, students using RT have scored at the 62nd percentile on standardized reading comprehension tests (compared with the 50th percentile for the average control student) and at the 81st percentile on reading comprehension tests that were created by the experimenters (Alfassi, 1998; Carter, 1997; Kim, Baylor, & PALS Group, 2006; Rosenshine & Meister, 1994a).

In a comparison of strategies designed to improve reading comprehension (Mason, 2004), half of a sample of fifth-grade students with poor reading comprehension skills were taught how to *think before reading, while reading, and after* reading (TWA for short). Students were taught to think prior to reading about the author's purpose in writing the story, what relevant information they already possessed about the subject, and what they wanted to learn from the passage. While they were reading, they were asked to think about reading at an optimal speed, making connections between prior knowledge and the information in the passage, and rereading parts of the passage they felt they did not understand. After reading, they were asked to think about the main idea and create a summary of the passage and what they learned from the passage. Consistent with social cognitive theory, the elements of this technique were taught through a combination of modeling, direct instruction, and guided practice. The remaining students were taught a questioning technique called *reciprocal questioning* (parts of which were incorporated into Palinscar and Brown's reciprocal teaching strategy). The heart of reciprocal questioning, or RQ, is the following five-step procedure: (1) the teacher and students silently read a passage; (2) the teacher closes his or her book; (3) the students ask the teacher questions, which the teacher answers; (4) the students close their books; and (5) the teacher asks the students questions, which the students answer. As with the TWA strategy, RQ was taught using modeling, direct instruction, and guided practice.

Students who were taught the TWA strategy outscored their peers who were taught RQ on ability to orally and accurately state the main idea of the 15 passages they had read, to summarize a given paragraph of each passage, and to retell what they had read. The oral retellings of the students using TWA were of a higher quality and contained more information and main idea units than the retellings of the students who used RQ. Strangely, this advantage did not carry over to parallel written tests of reading comprehension.

An excellent example of how social cognitive theory (as well as such related theories as cognitive development and motivation) has been thoroughly integrated into a school curriculum is the Benchmark School in Media, Pennsylvania (Pressley, Gaskins, Solic, & Collins, 2006). Benchmark is a private school that serves students between the ages of six and twelve who have experienced several years of academic failure largely because of such self-regulatory deficits as poor attention, poor listening, working too fast, poor frustration tolerance, organizational difficulties, and lack of willingness to expend effort. To overcome these problems, Benchmark teachers use a variety of techniques derived from social cognitive and other theories, including modeling of cognitive processes, teaching reading comprehension techniques, encouraging the use of background knowledge, teaching note-taking skills, teaching students how to analyze and break down large tasks into smaller, easier-to-manage parts, teaching reflection and monitoring techniques, and consistently using positive reinforcement.

As a result of these and other characteristics of the school, Benchmark students at the end of the 2003–2004 school year scored on average at the 77th percentile on the reading section of a standardized achievement test, whereas they had scored at the 34th percentile 2 years earlier. In addition, almost all students graduate from high school (or earn their GEDs) and attend college.

Despite these positive findings, we need to remind you that applying them in your classroom will be as much an art as a science (you might want to go back to Chapter 1 to review this distinction) because there is much about the nature of self-regulated learning that remains to be clarified. For example, little is known at present about how long students continue to create and implement learning strategies once formal instruction ends, whether students use SRL skills across a variety of subject areas, and why some students quickly acquire SRL skills and use them effectively whereas other students do not (Harris, Alexander, & Graham, 2008).

Now that you are familiar with social cognitive theory and research, it is time to examine several Suggestions for Teaching derived from these principles and research findings.

Suggestions for Teaching

Applying Social Cognitive Theory in the Classroom

1 **Include the development of self-regulated learning skills in your objectives and lesson plans.**

The research that we summarized clearly shows that SRL skills make a significant contribution to students' achievement. But this same research also suggests that students should not be given responsibility for their own learning without adequate preparation (Greene & Azevedo, 2007). Consequently, the development of students' SRL skills should be included in your instructional objectives and lesson plans. You can help students become more effective self-regulated learners by incorporating the following elements into your classroom instruction (Ley & Young, 2001; Randi & Corno, 2000; Schunk, 2001).

    a. Emphasize the importance of SRL skills to learning and when they should be used.

In all likelihood, you will want students to attain some degree of proficiency in goal setting, planning, use of tactics and strategies, monitoring of one's actions and progress, self-evaluation, and self-reinforcement. When teaching planning skills, for example, point out that students who are good planners know the conditions under which they learn best and choose or arrange environments that eliminate or decrease distractions. To raise students' awareness of the value of a good learning environment, you can have them keep a log of how much time they spend studying in various places and at various times, what internal and external distractions they experience, and how they deal with those distractions. On the basis of this information, they can draw conclusions about when and under what circumstances they best learn. To help students choose or create a hospitable learning environment, you can prepare and distribute a checklist of desirable features. Likely features of a good learning environment would include relative quiet, good lighting and ventilation,

Teachers can help students acquire and refine self-regulated learning skills by providing direct instruction in such skills as goal setting, planning, using learning tactics, monitoring, and self-evaluation. Copyright © Michael Newman/Photo Edit

and comfortable furniture; it would be best to not include other people, a television set, and alternative reading material such as comic books or magazines.

Self-regulated learners commonly use many types of memory and comprehension tactics. You can help students appreciate the value of these skills by using such techniques as mnemonic devices, outlines, concept maps, previews, graphs, flowcharts, and tables as you teach and by explaining how they are used and the ways in which they aid learning. To increase the probability that students will use such techniques themselves, teach them how to make outlines before they write essays, and show them how to create concept maps, graphs, flowcharts, and tables after they have read a section of text.

Lastly, continually remind students that self-regulated behavior is the product of self-motivational beliefs as well as various cognitive skills. The success of any instruction you will provide on SRL skills will greatly depend on students' beliefs about their self-efficacy and the basic nature of their learning ability. As we discuss in more detail in Chapter 11, many students believe that they have inherited a certain capacity to learn that cannot be changed. Such students are much less likely to engage in SRL behaviors after a failure or two (Molden & Dweck, 2006).

b. Model SRL skills, including the standards you use to evaluate your performance and reinforce yourself.

You can enhance the learning of SRL skills by having students observe and imitate what you and other skilled learners do. As noted, when you demonstrate a skill or process, you should first explain what you are going to do. Then take time to describe why you are going to do it and how you will evaluate the quality of your performance. Then demonstrate the behavior, evaluate your performance, and, if you feel your behavior has met your standards, verbally administer some self-praise. The importance of modeling thought processes that are normally hidden from observation was noted by Margaret Metzger (1998), a high school English teacher. To help students better understand the process of literary interpretation and criticism, she recommended a procedure in which she led some students through a discussion of a story while other students observed and took notes on the process.

c. Provide guided practice and corrective feedback for the SRL skills you want students to learn.

As we noted earlier in this chapter, self-observation or self-monitoring is an important SRL skill that plays a role at several points in the learning process. Self-regulating students are very proficient at monitoring their progress in meeting goals, the effectiveness of their learning strategies and tactics, and the quality of their achievements. They do this by comparing their performance both to internal standards and external feedback. Once you have explained and demonstrated self-monitoring, give students structured opportunities to practice this skill and provide feedback.

To familiarize students with the process of self-monitoring, you can require them to keep a log or journal in which they (a) state goals, (b) note how they prepare for and address the demands of projects, homework, and other tasks, and (c) assess the extent to which they have achieved one or more goals. Students could record, for example, how much time they spent on a task, the types of tactics they used, the number of problems they worked, and the extent to which they felt they understood the material.

External feedback should be constructive regardless of whether the basic message contains good news or bad news. On one hand, when you point out mistakes or omissions students have made on assignments and tests, focus on the cognitive processes students may have misused or omitted and provide suggestions for correcting such problems in the future. On the other hand, when the quality of a student's work has improved over time, point that out and relate it to one or more cognitive processes.

JOURNAL ENTRY
Helping Students Practice and Refine Self-Regulated Learning Skills

JOURNAL ENTRY
Ways to Teach Memory
Tactics

2 **Teach students how to use both memory and comprehension tactics and to take notes.**

    a. Teach students how to use various forms of rehearsal and mnemonic devices.

We have at least two reasons for recommending the teaching of rehearsal. One is that maintenance rehearsal is a useful tactic for keeping a relatively small amount of information active in short-term memory. The other is that maintenance rehearsal is one of a few tactics that young children can learn to use. If you do decide to teach rehearsal, we have two suggestions. First, remind young children that rehearsal is something that learners consciously decide to do when they want to remember things. Second, remind students to rehearse no more than seven items (or chunks) at a time.

    Upper elementary grade students (fourth, fifth, and sixth graders) can be taught advanced forms of maintenance rehearsal, such as cumulative rehearsal, and forms of elaborative rehearsal, such as rehearsing sets of items that form homogeneous categories. As with younger students, provide several opportunities each week to practice these skills.

    As you prepare class presentations or encounter bits of information that students seem to have difficulty learning, ask yourself if a mnemonic device would be useful. You might write up a list of the devices discussed earlier and refer to it often. Part of the value of mnemonic devices is that they make learning easier. They are also fun to make up and use. Moreover, rhymes, acronyms, and acrostics can be constructed rather quickly. You might consider setting aside about 30 minutes two or three times a week to teach mnemonics. First, explain how rhyme, acronym, and acrostic mnemonics work and then provide examples of each (see Table 9.1). Once students understand how the mnemonic is supposed to work, have them construct mnemonics to learn various facts and concepts. You might offer a prize for the most ingenious mnemonic.

JOURNAL ENTRY
Ways to Teach
Comprehension Tactics

    b. Teach students how to formulate comprehension questions.

We concluded earlier that self-questioning could be an effective comprehension tactic if students were trained to write good comprehension questions and given opportunities to practice the technique. We suggest you try the following instructional sequence:

1. Discuss the purpose of student-generated questions.
2. Point out the differences between knowledge-level questions and different types of comprehension-level questions (such as analysis, synthesis, and evaluation). An excellent discussion of these types can be found in the *Taxonomy of Educational Objectives, Handbook I: Cognitive Domain* (Bloom, Englehart, Furst, Hill, & Krathwohl, 1956).
3. Explain and illustrate the kinds of responses that should be given to different types of comprehension-level questions.
4. Provide students with a sample paragraph and a set of high-level question stems. Have students formulate questions and responses either individually or in pairs.
5. Provide corrective feedback.
6. Give students short passages from which to practice.
7. Provide corrective feedback (Hattie & Timperley, 2007; King, 1994).

JOURNAL ENTRY
Teaching Students How to
Take Notes

    c. Teach students how to take notes.

Despite the limitations of research on note taking mentioned earlier, these suggestions should lead to more effective note taking:

• Provide students with clear, detailed objectives for every reading assignment. The objectives should indicate what parts of the assignment to focus on and how that material should be processed (whether memorized verbatim, reorganized and paraphrased, or integrated with earlier reading assignments).

- Inform students that note taking is an effective comprehension tactic when used appropriately. Think, for example, about a reading passage that is long and for which test items will demand analysis and synthesis of broad concepts (as in "Compare and contrast the economic, social, and political causes of World War I with those of World War II"). Tell students to concentrate on identifying main ideas and supporting details, to paraphrase this information, and to record similarities and differences.

- Provide students with practice and corrective feedback in answering questions that are similar to those on the criterion test (meaning the test that assesses how well the students met the teacher's objectives).

JOURNAL ENTRY
Providing a Foundation for
Self-Regulated Learning
Skills in the Primary Grades

❸ Establish the foundation for self-regulated learning in kindergarten and the primary grades.

As we noted earlier, becoming a proficient self-regulated learner requires thousands of hours of instruction and experience spread over many years. Consequently, the foundation for SRL should be established in kindergarten and the primary grades. Observations of teachers in kindergarten through third grade (Perry, VandeKamp, Mercer, & Nordby, 2002) provide some insight as to how this might be accomplished. In general, teachers whose classrooms were rated as high-SRL classrooms emphasized student choice of activities, support in meeting academic challenges (a technique we referred to earlier in the book as scaffolding), and evaluation of oneself and classmates in a nonthreatening, mastery-oriented environment. Here are some specific examples of how SRL-oriented instruction was carried out.

EXAMPLES

- Prior to an oral reading of the story *The Three Little Pigs*, students were allowed to decide whether to track the text with their fingers or their eyes.

- When a student had trouble decoding a word during an oral story reading, the teacher asked the other children in the group to suggest a solution. They then tried each suggestion to see which one worked.

- Students were asked to create an alternative story ending for *The Three Little Pigs*. To help them meet this challenge, the teacher allowed students to share their ideas with a classmate and, later, with the teacher. The teacher recorded each child's idea on chart paper so everyone in class could see everyone else's ideas.

Research findings demonstrate that note taking in one form or another is an effective tactic for improving comprehension of text and lecture material. Consequently, students should be taught the basic principles that support effective note taking.
Rhoda Sidney/Stock Boston

- Kindergarten and first-grade children who had trouble writing out their ideas for a writing assignment were encouraged to start with drawings as a way to plan and organize their ideas.
- In preparation for student/parent–teacher conferences, students were asked to select samples of their work to share with parents and reflect on what they could do now that they could not do earlier in the school year.
- To help second-grade students choose and carry out a research topic, the teacher asked them to answer three questions: Am I interested in this topic? Can I find books about this topic? Can I read the books by myself, or will I need help from a friend or an adult?

4   When teaching SRL skills, bear in mind the developmental limitations of younger students.

If basic instruction in SRL skills is to begin as early as kindergarten, teachers need to acknowledge that, because young children are more limited cognitively than older children, they will require more support and guidance. Dale Schunk (2001) suggests that teachers of primary and early elementary grade children do the following:

- Keep demonstrations and explanations of various skills and behaviors relatively short.
- As you or someone else models a skill, point out which aspects of the model's behaviors are more important than others.
- Set a series of short-term goals, each of which can be accomplished after a limited amount of instruction.
- Design your lessons to minimize interruptions and distractions and periodically tell students that you believe they are capable learners.
- Periodically remind students to carry out a task more slowly and think about the skills needed to complete the task.
- Provide verbal feedback about children's capabilities (e.g., "You're good at reading").
- Help students make appropriate attributions for success and failure by reminding them that effort is the primary cause of success and insufficient effort is the primary cause of failure. If you mention that ability also plays a role in performance, emphasize that ability is a set of learnable skills and not a fixed cognitive capacity.
- Provide students with clear guidelines for determining the appropriateness of their behavior and point out when they have and have not satisfied those guidelines.

JOURNAL ENTRY
Ways to Help Students
Develop Self-Efficacy for
Self-Regulated Learning

5   Embed instruction in SRL in interesting and challenging classroom tasks.

Researchers (see, for example, Greene & Azevedo, 2007; Randi & Corno, 2000) suggest that if teachers want to teach their students SRL skills, they should embed their instruction in classroom tasks that are meaningful and that both illustrate and require students to use those skills. One such task, which Judy Randi and Lynn Corno (2000) describe in detail, is to analyze a story about a hero who has to undertake a dangerous journey and rely on personal resources to accomplish a goal. This is often called a journey tale. Two well-known examples from Greek literature are the *Odyssey* and *Jason and the Argonauts*. The students are then asked to draw parallels between the self-regulatory skills used by the story's hero and their own journeys as learners. For instance, just as Odysseus created a plan to escape from the Cyclops's cave, students should first think about the steps they will need to take to accomplish a goal.

6   Help students develop a sense of self-efficacy for SRL with timely and effective feedback.

When you think of feedback, you probably think of teachers giving students information about how well they performed on a recent task or exam. This type of feedback is certainly beneficial; it has been shown to have strong positive effects on achievement. But it does have a limitation: it frequently does not carry over to other tasks. That drawback can be reduced to some extent by also giving students feedback about the quality of the learning processes they used and how much closer they now are to achieving their learning goals. You might, for example, comment on how closely a student followed your directions, constructed a concept map that identified the interrelationships among a set of concepts from a reading assignment, or reviewed her work in an effort to identify mistakes. Evidence suggests that this type of feedback leads to a deeper understanding of the task and more transfer to other learning tasks. The increased use of self-regulatory skills on other tasks is likely due to a strengthening of students' self-efficacy and their attributing successful performances to effort and ability (Hattie & Timperley, 2007; Pajares, 2009; Schunk & Miller, 2002; Usher, 2009).

More Ideas for your journal can be found in the Reflective Journal Questions at the textbook's student website, Education CourseMate.

7 **Use effective strategy training programs such as reciprocal teaching, but be prepared to make adaptations to fit your particular circumstances.**

As an instructional tool, RT has at least two positive characteristics: it is defined by a set of clear components and procedures, and it has been demonstrated to improve reading comprehension in numerous studies. But as a 3-year study of 17 elementary grade teachers demonstrated, you may encounter some obstacles to implementing a textbook version of RT that will cause you to make some modifications in how you use it (Hacker & Tenent, 2002).

In the study, only 3 teachers implemented RT as it is described in the literature. The remaining 14 teachers felt compelled to implement a modified form of the technique because of the problems they encountered. Here are the main obstacles encountered by many of the teachers and their solutions:

1. *Strategy use problems:* Students' use of the four comprehension techniques of RT was infrequent or of low quality. For example, most of the questions posed by students were superficial and fact-oriented, predictions were not logical, and clarifying comments were rarely made. *Solutions:* Many teachers spent a great deal of time teaching students (through explicit instruction and modeling) how to formulate high-quality questions and tried to stimulate use of clarifying by having students identify words and sentences they did not understand.

2. *Dialogue problems:* Discussions among the students of the proper use of the four reading skills and the content of the reading passages were both limited and of low quality, largely due to their limited cooperative learning skills, but also because some students were shy about speaking in front of peers. *Solutions:* Using whole-class instruction and modeling, teachers taught students how to be good listeners, to take turns talking, to reach a consensus about the details and meaning of a passage, and to give constructive feedback to one another.

3. *Scaffolding problems:* Because of the previously mentioned problems with strategy use and dialogue, some teachers continued to provide a high level of support to students long beyond the point suggested by the literature on reciprocal teaching. The amount and duration of scaffolding were related to the age and reading ability of the students. Younger students and those with weaker reading skills required more scaffolding. *Solutions:* Teachers provided additional scaffolding through whole-class instruction; reading partnerships; modeling; allowing students more time to learn the elements of RT; writing predictions, clarifications, and summaries; and direct instruction of group skills.

This study points to an interesting conclusion and lesson. The conclusion is that RT may well require more training, practice, and time than the literature suggests. The lesson, which echoes a basic theme of the first chapter of this book, is that even when a solid scientific basis exists for a particular technique, an effective implementation often requires those improvisational skills referred to as the art of teaching.

USING TECHNOLOGY TO PROMOTE SELF-REGULATED LEARNING

As we noted earlier, teaching students to become proficient self-regulated learners will require thousands of hours of instruction spread over many years. With the many instructional responsibilities teachers have, you stand a better chance of contributing to this goal if you can use technology to supplement and reinforce your efforts. The studies we summarize in this section suggest that, with certain qualifications, this is a real possibility.

Modeling

Modeling, as we saw earlier in this chapter, is an effective way to help students acquire important SRL skills. It can also strengthen students' self-efficacy for computer-based learning (Moos & Azevedo, 2009). But what if a teacher does not have sufficient time to perform this function or cannot always supply the modeling just when students need it? Might not a computer-based video model serve as an effective substitute? This was the driving question behind a study conducted with sixth-grade students (Pedersen & Liu, 2002).

The students, divided into three groups, worked on a computer-based hypermedia problem-solving simulation over the course of fifteen 45-minute class periods. Called *Alien Rescue*, the simulation had students play the role of scientists on an international space station whose mission was to rescue alien life forms. They encountered a ship that contained six species of aliens, survivors of a distant solar system that was destroyed by the explosion of a nearby star. The life-support system of the alien ship had been damaged, and its members were in suspended animation. The students' task was to figure out which planets or moons of our solar system might serve as suitable homes for each of the alien species by using existing databases and a simulation within the program that let them design and launch probes. They recorded their notes and solutions in an online notebook.

The students were assigned to one of three conditions:

- In the modeling condition, students watched video segments of an expert scientist solving the same problem for one of the alien species. At four points in the program the model explained what he was trying to accomplish and how he used various tools, such as the online notebook and the probe design room. He also modeled such cognitive processes as self-questioning, making connections, identifying missing information, forming hypotheses, and taking notes in a list format.
- In the direct instruction condition, students received the same information, but without modeling. The scientist explained the function of various tools and provided tips about how to work effectively (e.g., "If I were building a probe, I would use my mission statement to help me decide what to include on my probe").
- In the help condition, the scientist explained the function of various tools but provided no advice or modeling on how to use them.

Although the students in each group worked at their own computers, they were encouraged to share information with classmates and ask one another for help.

The students in the modeling condition significantly outscored those in the direct instruction and help conditions on several measures. They were more apt to take notes in list format, to separate their notes into sections by topic, and to consult their notes. They designed fewer probes, but this was expected because they spent more time thinking about and designing probes that were consistent with their mission statements. The modeling group also attained significantly higher scores than the other two groups for the quality of their problem solutions.

Computer programs that include models can improve students' problem-solving skills

Subsequent research (e.g., Pedersen & Liu, 2002, 2003; Wouters, Paas, & van Merriënboer, 2009) has shown that watching a computer-based model, even an animated one, produces better learning and transfer of problem solving skills than if no model is available.

Providing Cognitive and Metacognitive Feedback

As you undoubtedly know from your own experience, although we do mention it in later chapters, efficient and effective learning of new skills requires timely feedback. Because teachers may not always be in a position to offer feedback precisely when it is needed, computer programs have been created to fill this need. One such program, *Summary Street*, was designed to help students improve their ability to summarize text by giving them many opportunities to summarize different types of text, by providing feedback, and by having them revise their summaries (with more feedback) as often as necessary until they meet the standards built into the program. Eighth-grade students who worked with *Summary Street* for 4 weeks showed greater improvement both in the amount of relevant information contained in their summaries and in the quality of their summaries than did a comparable group of students who summarized the same passages but did not receive feedback. Furthermore, low- and medium-performing students made the largest improvements (Franzke, Kintsch, Caccamise, Johnson, & Dooley, 2005).

As we noted earlier in the chapter, self-regulated learners monitor their thinking as they work through a task to ensure a high level of learning. Teachers and parents often help students develop and strengthen this skill by reminding them to think about key operations, such as appropriately defining the problem or issue at hand and recalling relevant prior knowledge. This type of support is often referred to as *metacognitive feedback*. The type of feedback students more commonly receive, called *results feedback*, takes the form of such cautionary and positive statements as "Try again," "Check once more," and "Very good, wonderful job!"

One study (Kramarski & Zeichner, 2001) compared computer-provided instruction and metacognitive feedback with computer-provided instruction and results feedback on 11th graders' mathematical problem solving. As students in the metacognitive feedback group worked through the program, the computer would prompt them to think about the nature of the problem, the relevance of prior knowledge, and the use of appropriate problem-solving techniques by posing such questions as "What is the problem all about?" "What are the similarities and differences between the problem at hand and problems you have solved in the past?" and "What tactics or principles are appropriate for solving this problem and why?" Students in the results feedback group received comments such as "Think about it, you made a mistake," "Try again," "Check it once more," "Very good," and "Wonderful job!"

On a 27-item test that required students to explain their reasoning behind their solutions to each problem, students who received metacognitive feedback significantly outscored students who received results feedback. The explanations of the metacognitive-feedback group were of a significantly higher quality (they included both algebraic formulas and verbal arguments) than the explanations of the results-feedback group.

Providing Scaffolded Instruction

Earlier in the book we described Vygotsky's theory of cognitive development and his recommendation that teachers use various instructional aids, called scaffolds, to help students acquire the knowledge and self-regulatory skills that they would probably not otherwise acquire. But as busy as most classrooms are, it is not always possible for teachers to maximize the use of scaffolded instruction. Many advocates of computer-based instruction believe that computer programs that have various types of scaffolds built into them can accomplish what some teachers cannot. A study designed to assess that belief (Brush & Saye, 2001) examined the extent to which 11th-grade students used the features of a hypermedia database called Decision Point! that contained both information about the civil rights movement in the United States during the 1960s and several types of scaffolds designed to encourage students to make optimal use of the database.

Each student was assigned to a four-person group. The students in each group were told to assume that they were civil rights leaders in 1968 shortly after the assassination of Martin Luther King Jr. They were asked to develop a solution to the following problem: What strategies should be used to continue pursuing the goal of the civil rights movement? Using the Decision Point! database, each group was assigned to gather relevant information on particular aspects of the civil rights movement (e.g., the legal system, desegregation, voting rights, the Student Non-Violent Coordinating Committee, and the rejection of integration).

The Decision Point! database contained four types of scaffolds. The first was a set of interactive essays. Each essay provided an overview of a historical event, such as the March on Washington to secure voting rights for all Blacks, with hyperlinks to related documents within the database. If you have seen online encyclopedias in which certain names, places, events, and concepts of an essay are highlighted and linked to related documents, you can visualize how these interactive essays worked. The second scaffold was a set of recommended documents for each event. The program suggested that students first examine 8 to 10 recommended documents for an event before exploring any other information sources. The third scaffold was a student guide that provided categories that might be used by a professional historian to organize and synthesize information about an event (such as groups involved in the event, goals of each group, and strategies used by each group). The final scaffold was a journal in which students could note the effectiveness of their daily information-gathering strategies, the problems they had encountered, and the progress they had made toward completing the task. The purpose of the journal was to help students monitor their efforts.

Of the four scaffolds designed into the database, the interactive essays were used the most. Each group examined at least one of the essays, and two of the four groups read the essays for each event they were assigned. A third group examined all but one of the essays. The hyperlinks, however, were used much less frequently. Only 39 percent of the total number of documents available were accessed. Although students ignored most of the available documents, the ones they did examine were usually those recommended by the program. Consequently, this was felt to be a somewhat effective scaffold. Only two groups used the student guide scaffold to summarize their analyses for each event they were assigned to research. Moreover, the students' responses to this scaffold were judged to be inadequate. Most contained just a single phrase or sentence for each category. The student journals were used least of all. No group completed a journal for each day of data collection, and the entries were brief and superficial.

The results of this study provide limited support for embedding self-regulatory scaffolds in computerized databases. Students are most likely to use those scaffolds that they perceive to be most relevant to the successful completion of a task and ignore those that appear less relevant or require more time to complete than they have available. As the next set of studies indicates, it is also possible that students declined to use most of the scaffolds in the Decision Point! program because they lacked other self-regulatory qualities such as persistence and self-efficacy.

The Effect of Self-Regulated Learning Skills on Computer-Based Instruction

From the earliest days of computer-based instruction, the designers of instructional programs have disagreed over the issue of how much control to give students. Some programs offer students no choices; the program provides the same material to all students in the same sequence, under the same conditions, and at the same rate. Other programs allow students to choose which material they will examine, for how long, and in what sequence. Although the learner control option has been strongly promoted by many designers because of its potential to increase student interest, motivation, and achievement, research findings have been inconclusive (Moos & Azevedo, 2009).

An analysis of studies that have examined learner control in hypermedia programs (Scheiter & Gerjets, 2007) concluded that the complexity of such programs and the freedom to choose how to investigate the programs' many facets overwhelm many students and negate the programs' potential benefits. Students may, for example, become disoriented. If you've ever clicked on several levels of links starting from the home page of a website and then realized that you couldn't recall how you got to the page you were viewing or how to get back to where you started, you can appreciate how easy it is to become disoriented in hyperspace. Another problem is distraction. Hypermedia programs and websites have so much information embedded in them that it is easy to forget what your main goal is and to become distracted investigating those related but somewhat beside-the-point links.

For students to be able to avoid these potential problems and experience the benefits that hypermedia programs can offer, you will have to take steps to ensure that they have a reasonable amount of prior knowledge about the subject being studied, are interested in the subject, and have well developed SRL skills. The Suggestions for Teaching that we offered earlier in this chapter as well as those in Chapter 11 ("Motivation") should help you formulate some concrete ideas about how to accomplish these goals.

> Computer programs that let students control access to information work best with those who have some self-regulatory skills

The Effect of Self-Efficacy on Computer-Based Instruction

Use of the World Wide Web as an information-gathering and problem-solving resource is becoming increasingly popular in schools. But social cognitive theory suggests that successful use of the Web for this purpose will require high levels of self-efficacy and self-regulation because of the large number of independent decisions students must make. Because self-efficacy is task-specific, the following types of self-efficacy will play a role in web-based instruction (WBI): self-efficacy for learning the subject matter, self-efficacy for using the Web, and, because WBI requires learners to locate and analyze information with little or no teacher guidance, self-efficacy for self-regulated learning. The effect of these forms of self-efficacy on achievement and Web use was investigated among high school sophomores in Korea (Joo, Bong, & Choi, 2000).

Before the study began, students were given measures of self-efficacy for SRL, academic self-efficacy, Internet self-efficacy, and cognitive strategy use. The students were then given worksheets for three topics (common diseases of the organs in our body, smoking and health, drugs and prevention) that contained questions to be answered and blank tables to be completed. Each worksheet listed the addresses of websites that were likely to contain useful information. The students were responsible for locating whatever information the site contained that would help them fill out the worksheet. In addition, they could use commercial search engines to identify other sites that contained relevant information. Following the third session, students took two tests: a written exam of multiple-choice and short-answer questions that covered the three topics, and a performance test in which students had to access two websites and locate information pertaining to given questions.

Several gender differences were found that are consistent with the research findings we described in Chapter 4, "Understanding Student Differences." Female students scored significantly higher than male students on the self-efficacy for SRL and cognitive strategy use measures. The fact that the females also significantly outscored the males on the written exam suggests that higher levels of self-efficacy for SRL and greater use of SRL skills account for the finding that females typically earn higher grades than males. Consistent with research findings reported earlier in this chapter, self-efficacy for SRL was highly correlated with academic self-efficacy and strategy use. Finally, previous experience with computers and self-efficacy for SRL were both related significantly to self-efficacy for Internet use, which in turn was related significantly to performance on the Web search test.

Conclusions About Computer Technology and Self-Regulated Learning

The studies we have summarized, and many others, indicate that computer-based instructional programs can play a productive role in the development and support of students' SRL skills. They can provide students with concrete examples of self-regulation skills and explanations of how those skills relate to achieving a goal. They can support and strengthen the skill of self-monitoring by reminding students at critical points to think about the nature of the problem being solved, similar problems encountered in the past, and appropriate problem-solving tactics. They can also provide a variety of scaffolds.

In short, technology can do for SRL many of the things that teachers do, giving teachers more time to work individually with students who need additional help. But (and to repeat a point we made earlier in the book), the use of technology to promote SRL has its limits. Without teacher guidance and oversight, some students will profit from such open-ended tools as simulations, databases, the Internet, and the various social networking tools that are part of what is called Web 2.0, whereas others will likely feel overwhelmed and confused. If you use these tools to promote SRL and other goals, one of the first things you will need to do is determine students' current levels of SRL ability and self-efficacy.

To review this chapter, see the tutorial quizzes and other study aids on the textbook's Education CourseMate website.

Challenging Assumptions

Taking Learning Personally

Celeste says, "I've been thinking about how to teach students to be better learners. I guess I had always thought that school was where students encountered stuff to learn and that by encountering stuff, they just naturally learned how to learn. I'm thinking differently now."

Antonio says, "So am I. I think of myself as a 'model for learning' rather than just the 'content provider.' And it is making a difference. One of the things I have noticed recently is that my students become very interested when I share some of my own difficulties as a learner and show them how I have coped with those difficulties. I have also tried to bring in other models to show students that learning a new skill is not easy. We were working on writing, and our team brought in a local writer who really inspired the kids. Instead of just reading a published piece, she passed out six different drafts and showed the kids the problems with each one. Then she described how she solved the problems, including all the false starts she made and all of the efforts she threw away. She talked about how hard it was to write, but how rewarding it was to solve each problem and work through to an end product. She was terrific! And since then, the kids are taking more responsibility for revising and editing their own work. We have 'workshop days' now, and they are great. Kids are talking to each other about what they are trying to write, talking to me and to the other teachers in the team. It's really a lot of fun."

"Learning *is* fun," says Connie. "Learning to become more capable, learning to persist when something is difficult, learning that problems are opportunities to gain skill and confidence, learning to take responsibility for yourself . . ."

Don says to Connie, "You're right, Doc." He leans back from the table. "Learning to help students become better learners makes me feel a lot more confident about becoming a teacher. And you know what? That's the kind of learning that really *is* fun, and I want my students to feel exactly the same way."

Summary

1. Social cognitive theory was created by Albert Bandura to explain how an individual's personal characteristics, behavioral patterns, and environment interact to produce learning, a process Bandura called triadic reciprocal causation.

2. Personal characteristics include such things as metacognitive knowledge, self-efficacy beliefs, goals, and anxiety. Behavioral patterns include self-observation, self-evaluation, and changes made to overcome perceptions of low self-efficacy and improve learning strategies. The social environment includes the types of tasks on which people work, the reinforcing and punishing consequences they receive for exhibiting various behaviors, and the explanations and modeling skills they get from others.

3. Social cognitive theory emphasizes that, through the use of self-control and self-regulation skills, people are the cause of and have control over their behavior, a process that Bandura calls personal agency.

4. Self-control is controlling one's actions in the absence of reinforcement or punishment. Self-regulation is the consistent and appropriate application of self-control skills to new situations.

5. It is important for students to acquire self-regulation skills for at least three reasons. First, as students progress through school, they are expected to assume more responsibility for their learning and so receive less prompting and guidance from teachers and parents. Second, as they move from grade to grade, the amount and complexity of material they have to learn and be tested on increases. Third, when they leave school, they will have to cope with a world that changes at a rapid rate.

6. Individual differences in self-regulation are strongly related to the personal characteristic of self-efficacy. Self-efficacy is a belief about how capable or prepared individuals feel they are to meet the demands of particular types of tasks.

7. A person's level of self-efficacy is affected by past accomplishments, by the persuasive comments of others, by emotional states such as anxiety or well-being, and by observing the accomplishments of similar others with whom we identify.

8. Self-efficacy affects a person's choice of goals and activities, the cognitive processes one uses to meet the demands of various tasks, the amount and persistence of effort expended to accomplish a goal, especially in the face of obstacles, and the emotions one experiences while working on a task, such as excitement, curiosity, anxiety, and dread.

9. Self-regulation is, under ideal circumstances, a cyclical process that moves through three phases. These phases and some of their associated self-regulatory processes are: forethought (goal setting, planning, self-efficacy for self-regulated learning, beliefs about consequences of achieving a goal, intrinsic interest, and learning-oriented versus performance-oriented goals), performance (attention focusing, self-instruction, learning tactics, recording one's behavior, trying out different forms of behavior), and self-reflection (evaluating one's behavior, making constructive attributions for success and failure, self-reinforcement, and drawing inferences about improving self-regulation skills).

10. Self-regulated learning occurs when a person purposely generates and controls thoughts, feelings, and actions to achieve a learning goal. Because of their complexity, self-regulation skills develop throughout one's school career.

11. Most students do not use strategic learning skills either systematically or consistently.

12. Most teachers provide little or no direct instruction to students in the formulation and use of strategies and tactics and make strategy formulation difficult by not aligning course goals, instruction, test content, and test demands.

13. A learning strategy is a general plan that specifies the resources one will use, when they will be used, and how one will use them to achieve a learning goal.

14. A learning tactic is a specific technique one uses to help accomplish an immediate task-related objective.

15. Learning tactics can be classified as memory directed or comprehension directed. The former are used when accurate storage and retrieval of information are important. The latter are used when comprehension of ideas is important.

16. Two types of memory-directed tactics are rehearsal and mnemonic devices. Because most forms of rehearsal involve little or no encoding of information, they are not very effective memory tactics. Because mnemonic devices organize information and provide built-in retrieval cues, they are effective memory tactics.

17. Popular mnemonic devices include rhymes, acronyms, acrostics, the loci method, and the keyword method.

18. Effective comprehension tactics are self-questioning, peer questioning, note taking, and concept mapping.

19. Teachers can support students' strategy use by using the three-phase self-regulation model as a guide for teaching self-regulation skills, by reminding students that strategies have to be constructed to fit a particular learning task, and by making sure they clearly tell students what it is they want students to learn.

20. Self-regulation skills are best learned according to the following four-step model: (1) observe a model who exhibits a skill and verbalizes performance standards and motivational beliefs, (2) emulate, or reproduce, the general form of the model's behavior, (3) exhibit the modeled behavior under similar conditions but without the model present, and (4) adapt the modeled behavior to different tasks, settings, and conditions. In general terms, models exhibit inhibited behaviors, disinhibited behaviors, facilitated behaviors, and new behaviors.

21. Correlational studies show that, as expected, self-efficacy, epistemological beliefs, and self-regulation processes are strongly related to each other and strongly related to achievement.

22. Modeling has been shown to be an effective means of helping students acquire the SRL skills and self-efficacy beliefs that contribute both to mathematical problem solving ability and to writing ability.

23. Learning strategy training, particularly in the form of reciprocal teaching, raises the reading comprehension scores of both average and below-average readers.

24. Technology is a useful tool for helping students acquire SRL skills. It can provide them with models they would not otherwise get to see, with metacognitive feedback, and with scaffolded instruction. Students who already possessed some self-regulation skills and exhibited self-efficacy for SRL reaped the greatest advantages from technologies.

Resources for Further Investigation

• Social Cognitive Theory

Albert Bandura's recent thoughts about social cognitive theory can be found in the first chapter ("Social Cognitive Theory: An Agentic Perspective") of volume 52 of the *Annual Review of Psychology* (2001).

• Self-Regulated Learning

The *Handbook of Self-Regulation* (2000), edited by Monique Boekaerts, Paul Pintrich, and Moshe Zeidner, contains numerous chapters on various aspects of self-regulation. The chapter by Barry Zimmerman, "Attaining Self-Regulation: A Social Cognitive Perspective," provides a detailed treatment of his cyclical model of self-regulation.

Another excellent resource is *Self-Regulated Learning and Academic Achievement: Theoretical Perspectives* (2001), edited by Barry Zimmerman and Dale Schunk. Barry Zimmerman describes different theoretical approaches to the issue of SRL and academic achievement in his chapter, "Theories of Self-Regulated Learning and Academic Achievement: An Overview and Analysis." Mary McCaslin and Daniel Hickey describe SRL from a Vygotskyian perspective in their chapter, "Self-Regulated Learning and Academic Achievement: A Vygotskyian View."

Self-regulated learning is also referred to as self-directed learning. In *The Self-Directed Learning Handbook: Challenging Adolescent Students to Excel* (2002), Maurice Gibbons describes how middle and high school teachers can create a self-directed learning program that ranges from trying out a few ideas to implementing a complete program. The end of the book contains a set of resources, labeled A–J, to help teachers design and implement a self-directed learning program. Arthur Costa and Bena Kallick (2004) discuss various aspects of self-directed learning, including how to use classroom assessment data to help students improve their learning skills, in *Assessment Strategies for Self-Directed Learning*.

• Self-Efficacy

Dale Schunk and Frank Pajares are coauthors of "The Development of Academic Self-Efficacy," a chapter in *The Development of Achievement Motivation* (2002), edited by Allan Wigfield and Jacquelynne Eccles. They discuss factors that affect the development of self-efficacy, gender and ethnic differences in self-efficacy, self-efficacy for learning and achievement, and research on self-efficacy.

Helping teachers enhance the self-efficacy and achievement of mainstreamed students with special learning needs (those with learning disabilities, mild mental retardation, and behavior disorders) is the goal of *Self-Efficacy: Raising the Bar for Students with Learning Needs* (2nd ed., 2005), by Joanne Eisenberger, Marcia Conti-D'Antonio, and Robert Bertrando. All three authors have worked in the public school system for 26 to 36 years. Their book describes how to teach for self-efficacy and provides in two appendices a set of strategies and forms to supplement the instructional approach they describe.

● Learning Tactics and Strategies

In Chapter 12 of the *Handbook of Educational Psychology* (2006), edited by Patricia Alexander and Philip Winne, Michael Pressley and Karen Harris provide an excellent overview of cognitive strategy instruction research from its beginnings in the 1960s to the present. The title of their chapter is "Cognitive Strategies Instruction: From Basic Research to Classroom Instruction."

If you would like some ideas about how to help students become strategic learners, consult *Teaching How to Learn* (2009), by Kenneth Kiewra. Part I is titled SOAR Strategies, an acronym taken from four chapters that describe how to teach students to attend to, or select, relevant information from a lesson; organize information; associate new information to what they already know; and regulate their learning skills.

Two books describe the characteristics of and benefits from creating various kinds of visual tools, such as graphic organizers, concept maps, spider maps, thinking maps, flowcharts, and classification grids. The first is *Visual Tools for Transforming Information Into Knowledge* (2nd ed., 2009), by David Hyerle. The second is James Bellanca's *A Guide to Graphic Organizers* (2nd ed., 2007).

10 Constructivist Learning Theory, Problem Solving, and Transfer

The Education CourseMate website for this text offers many helpful resources. Go to **CengageBrain.com** to preview this chapter's Concept Maps and Chapter Themes.

KEY POINTS

These key points will help you learn the important information in this chapter. To help you study, they also appear in the margins of the pages, next to the text where they are discussed.

Meaningful Learning Within a Constructivist Framework

- Constructivism: creating a personal interpretation of external ideas and experiences
- Bruner: discover how ideas relate to each other and to existing knowledge
- Construction of ideas strongly influenced by student's prior knowledge
- In addition to prior knowledge, construction of ideas is aided by multiple perspectives, self-regulation, and authentic tasks
- Cognitive constructivism emphasizes role of cognitive processes in meaningful learning
- Social constructivism emphasizes role of culture and social interaction in meaningful learning
- Critical constructivism emphasizes role of cultural myths and how they influence learning environments
- Constructivist-oriented teaching encourages creating new views; uses scaffolding, realistic tasks, and class discussion

The Nature of Problem Solving

- Well-structured problems: clearly stated, known solution procedures; known evaluation standards
- Ill-structured problems: vaguely stated, unclear solution procedures; vague evaluation standards
- Issues: ill-structured problems that arouse strong feelings
- Problem finding depends on curiosity, dissatisfaction with status quo
- Problem framing depends on knowledge of subject matter, familiarity with problem types
- Inert knowledge due to learning isolated facts under limited conditions
- Studying worked examples is an effective solution strategy
- Solve simpler version of problem first; then transfer process to harder problem

- Break complex problems into manageable parts
- Work backward when goal is clear but beginning state is not
- Backward fading: a procedure that helps students develop problem-solving capability by reasoning from the solution back to first steps
- Solve a similar problem and then apply the same method
- Create an external representation of the problem
- Evaluate solutions to well-structured problems by estimating or checking

Suggestions for Teaching

- Comprehension of subject matter critical to problem solving

Transfer of Learning

- Early view of transfer based on degree of similarity between two tasks
- Positive transfer: previous learning makes later learning easier
- Negative transfer: previous learning interferes with later learning
- Specific transfer: due to specific similarities between two tasks
- General transfer: due to use of same cognitive strategies
- Near transfer: previously learned knowledge and skills used relatively soon on highly similar task
- Far transfer: previously learned knowledge and skills used much later on dissimilar tasks and under different conditions
- Low-road transfer: previously learned skill automatically applied to similar current task
- High-road transfer: formulate rule from one task and apply to related task
- Low-road and high-road transfer produced by varied practice at applying skills, rules, memory retrieval cues

Technology Tools for Knowledge Construction and Problem Solving

- Technology tools are available to help students construct knowledge, become better problem solvers

---

When you begin to teach, you may devote a substantial amount of class time to having students learn information discovered by others. But the acquisition of a storehouse of facts, concepts, and principles is only part of what constitutes an appropriate education. Students must also learn how to *find, evaluate,* and *use* what they need to know to accomplish whatever goals they set for themselves. In other words, students need to learn how to be effective problem solvers.

One justification for teaching problem-solving skills in *addition* to ensuring mastery of factual information is that life in technologically oriented countries is marked by high-speed change. New products, services, and social conventions are rapidly introduced and integrated into our lifestyles. Computers, cellular telephones, portable music players—once requiring separate devices and now in a single PDA that fits in your hand—anticancer drugs, and in vitro fertilization, to name just a few examples, are relatively recent innovations that significantly affect the lives of many people.

But change, particularly rapid change, can be a mixed blessing. Although new products and services can make life more convenient, efficient, and enjoyable, they can also make it more complicated and problematic. The green revolution promises new jobs, but requires major changes in how companies earn profits and employees earn livings. Advances in medical care promise healthier and longer lives, but they introduce a host of moral, ethical, legal, and economic problems.

The educational implication that flows from these observations is clear: if we are to benefit from our ability to produce rapid and sometimes dramatic change, our schools need to invest more time, money, and effort in teaching students how to be effective problem solvers. As Lauren Resnick, a past president of the American Educational Research Association, argued,

> We need to identify and closely examine the aspects of education that are most likely to produce ability to adapt in the face of transitions and breakdowns. . . . school should focus its efforts on preparing people to be good adaptive learners, so that they can perform effectively when situations are unpredictable and task demands change. (1987, p. 18)

Resnick's argument, which echoes many others, is not without some justification. A survey by the American Management Association (Greenberg, Canzoneri, & Joe, 2000) found that 38 percent of job applicants lacked sufficient skills for the positions they sought. Rather than blaming "a 'dumbing down' of the incoming workforce," the authors attributed the problem to "the higher skills required in today's workplace" (p. 2).

Good problem solvers share two general characteristics: a well-organized, meaningful fund of knowledge and a systematic set of problem-solving skills. Historically, cognitive learning theories have been particularly useful sources of ideas for imparting both. In this chapter, then, we will examine the issue of meaningful learning from the perspective of a cognitive theory that we introduced previously in the book: constructivism. We will then go on to describe the nature of the problem-solving process and what you can do to help your students become better problem solvers. After describing the circumstances under which learned capabilities are applied to new tasks, a process known as transfer of learning, we conclude the chapter by considering how technology can contribute to knowledge construction and problem-solving.

Revealing Assumptions

What's the Problem?

Celeste brings the lesson to a close. Then, as the bell rings and the students file out, she approaches Connie, who has observed the lesson. Celeste is clearly upset. "I just cannot believe it! I cannot believe that those students ever got into the physics class. They don't know the math they need. They don't know basic concepts. They don't even seem to know the scientific method very well. I don't know who they had for science and math before, but whoever it was, they sure missed the boat."

"The students or their teachers?"

"They boat missed the both!" She chuckles, takes a deep breath, and sits down next to Connie. "I mean they *both* missed the *boat*." Connie smiles. Celeste says, "Sorry about that. But that was a very simple problem that I gave them today and they just couldn't get their heads around it. They had trouble even getting started."

"OK, let's reflect on that," says Connie. "You made some observations while you were teaching the lesson. You also made a few inferences . . . and you seemed to feel

pause & reflect

Clearly, problem solving is a critical skill for students at all grade levels. When students have difficulties with problems, we often infer that they don't know how to solve the problem. In other words, we assume that problem solving is simply a matter of finding solutions. Not all problems are listed at the end of the chapter in the textbook, however. In many cases, the difficulty students experience with problems is not in "finding the solution" but in "finding the problem" in the first place. What was your experience, as a learner, when math problems in a text were assigned as homework? What about problems that were not as well defined or well structured? How might you help your students engage in both problem finding and problem solving?

pretty strongly about those inferences. I observed that the students had difficulty working with the scenario you gave them and I am not so sure about your inferences." Connie pauses to make sure that Celeste has understood.

"I suppose there could be another explanation for why they didn't do well with the problem," says Celeste. "I'm sure there are prerequisites for them to get into the class. And I know from my own observations early in the year that there are very good students in this class. But if they had the right knowledge, then why couldn't they solve the problem?"

"Maybe they didn't understand that there was a problem to solve," says Connie. "To be honest, I wasn't sure why you presented the scenario; perhaps your students thought you were presenting an example and that's why they asked questions about concepts that they thought might be relevant. They were trying, but they just didn't know how to engage." After a pause, Connie continues. "Perhaps they were unable to solve the problem you had in mind because they were unable to identify a problem in the scenario. Before a problem can be solved, it must first be understood as a problem."

MEANINGFUL LEARNING WITHIN A CONSTRUCTIVIST FRAMEWORK

Constructivism: creating a personal interpretation of external ideas and experiences

Constructivism, as you may recall, holds that meaningful learning occurs when people actively try to make sense of the world—when they construct an interpretation of how and why things are—by filtering new ideas and experiences through existing knowledge structures (referred to in previous chapters as schemes). For example, an individual who lives in a country that provides, for little or no cost, such social services as medical care, counseling, education, job placement and training, and several weeks of paid vacation a year is likely to have constructed a rather different view of the role of government in people's lives from that of someone who lives in a country with a more market-oriented economy. To put it another way, meaningful learning is the active creation of knowledge structures (such as concepts, rules, hypotheses, and associations) from personal experience. In this section, we'll take a brief look at an early constructivist-oriented approach to learning, examine the nature of the constructivist model, and then put it all in perspective by considering the limits, as well as the advantages, of the constructivist viewpoint.

Jerome Bruner and Discovery Learning: An Early Constructivist Perspective

Constructivist explanations of learning are not new. Over the past 75 years, they have been promoted by such notable scholars as John Dewey, Jean Piaget, Lev Vygotsky, and Jerome Bruner. One of Bruner's contributions from the 1960s was the concept of **discovery learning.**

Bruner: discover how ideas relate to each other and to existing knowledge

Bruner argued that too much school learning takes the form of step-by-step study of verbal or numerical statements or formulas that students can reproduce on cue but are unable to use outside the classroom. When students are presented with such highly structured materials as worksheets and other types of drill-and-practice exercises, Bruner argues, they become too dependent on other people. Furthermore, they are likely to think of learning as something done only to earn a reward.

Instead of using techniques that feature preselected and prearranged materials, Bruner believes teachers should confront children with problems and help them seek solutions either independently or by engaging in group discussion. True learning, says Bruner, involves "figuring out how to use what you already know in order to go beyond what you already think" (1983, p. 183). Like Piaget, Bruner argues that conceptions that children arrive at on their own are usually more meaningful than those proposed by others and that students do not need to be rewarded when they seek to make sense of things that puzzle them.

Bruner does not suggest that students should discover every fact or principle or formula they may need to know. Discovery is simply too inefficient a process to be used that widely, and learning from others can be as meaningful as personal discovery (Mayer, 2004, 2009). Rather, Bruner argues that certain types of outcomes—understanding the ways in which ideas connect with one another, the possibility of solving problems on our own, and how what we already know is relevant to what we are trying to learn—are the essence of education and can best be achieved through personal discovery.

TeachSource Video Case ◄◄ ▶ ►►

Elementary School Language Arts: Inquiry Learning

Go to the Education CourseMate website and watch the Video Case, and then answer the following questions:

1. How does this Video Case illustrate the concepts of constructivism and discovery learning?

2. How does the classroom teacher in this Video Case encourage students to construct their own knowledge? What strategies and instructional approaches does she use?

Constructivism Today

Constructivism is an umbrella term. It covers several views of learning that share common claims (Rikers, van Gog, & Paas, 2008; Tobias & Duffy, 2009). After a brief examination of the claims that unite the various views of learning under the classification of constructivism, we will describe three variations of constructivist learning theory and look at the conditions that foster constructivist learning.

| Construction of ideas strongly influenced by student's prior knowledge

Common Claims That Frame Constructivism Four key ideas provide a constructivist frame through which we can view learning and learners: prior knowledge, multiple perspectives, self-regulation, and authentic learning (Loyens, Rikers, & Schmidt, 2007). We will briefly describe the claim that captures each idea.

1. *Meaningful learning is the active creation of knowledge structures from personal experience.* Constructivists view the learner as an active agent in the construction of knowledge (Cunningham, 1992; Gijbels, van de Watering, Dochy, & van den Bossche, 2006; Loyens, Rikers, & Schmidt, 2008). Each learner builds a personal view of the world by using existing knowledge, interests, attitudes, goals, and the like to select and interpret the information she encounters (Koohang, Riley, Smith, & Schreurs, 2009; Mayer, 2008). This assumption highlights the importance of what educational psychologists call prior

knowledge—the previously learned knowledge and skill that students bring to the classroom (Ozuru, Dempsey, & McNamara, 2009).

The knowledge that learners bring with them to a learning task has long been suspected of having a powerful effect on subsequent performance. In 1978, David Ausubel wrote on the flyleaf of his textbook, *Educational Psychology: A Cognitive View*, "If I had to reduce all of educational psychology to just one principle, I would say this: the most important single factor influencing learning is what the learner already knows. Ascertain this and teach him [or her] accordingly" (Ausubel, Novak, & Hanesian, 1978).

2. *Social interaction and the negotiation of understanding with others can help learners construct knowledge.* One person's knowledge can never be identical to another person's because knowledge is the result of a personal interpretation of experience, which is influenced by such factors as the learner's age, gender, race, ethnic background, and knowledge base. By interacting with others, learners have the opportunity to gain a perspective different from their own. Thus, the additions to, deletions from, or modifications of individuals' knowledge structures result from the sharing of multiple perspectives. Systematic, open-minded discussions and debates are instrumental in helping individuals create personal views (Azevedo, 2009; Paavola, Lipponen, & Hakkarainen, 2004).

Engaging with others helps learners develop their own views, but does not guarantee that those views will match the views of others. There are many instances in which people cannot reconcile their views and so agree to disagree. For example, in January 2002, President George W. Bush signed into law the reauthorization of the Elementary and Secondary Education Act, more popularly known as No Child Left Behind (NCLB). Although everyone agrees on what the law requires (e.g., all children in grades 3 through 8 scoring at the proficient level or above on tests of math and reading/language arts by 2014, with negative consequences for schools and districts that fail to show progress toward these goals), there is sharp disagreement about the true purpose of this legislation and its likely effects on students and teachers (Schwartz, Lindgren, & Lewis, 2009). Some see it as an effective means of school reform, whereas others see it as an attempt to undercut the autonomy and efficacy of public education (see Nichols & Berliner, 2007). In matters such as these, truth is where it always is for the constructivist: in the mind of the beholder.

3. *Self-regulation by learners is a key to successful learning.* Self-regulated learning, as you will recall from the previous chapter, occurs when a person generates and controls thoughts, feelings, and actions in an effort to achieve a learning goal. If you reflect on the discussions of self-regulated learning in the previous chapter—and keep in mind the first two claims above—this third claim of constructivists should come as no surprise. Constructivists view learners not as passive recipients of new information, but as active agents who use their prior knowledge and experiences to engage their environments (including other people) to enhance their existing knowledge structures (Piaget's concept of assimilation) and to build new knowledge structures (e.g., accommodation). Self-regulation skills allow learners to take charge: to function as the agents of their own learning rather than objects of instruction.

Research is a form of learning that requires highly developed self-regulation skills. Scholars use their prior knowledge to decide what questions need to be asked next and how to go about answering those questions. As we have seen in previous chapters, scholars form and reform their positions on aspects of theory or research as a result of years of discussion and debate with colleagues who bring multiple perspectives and experiences to the issues at hand. The debate between the Piagetians and the Vygotskians (discussed in Chapter 2 on stage theories of development) is a good example of how constructivist learning works.

4. *Authentic problems provide realistic contexts that contribute to the construction and transfer of knowledge.* When students encounter problems that are realistic, they are able to use what they already know about the problem situation (Driscoll, 2005). For example, imagine that a middle school class in Juneau, Alaska, needs to learn how to use mathematical formulae to make predictions. They need to understand what variables are, how some variables can be used or combined to predict other variables, and what to do with the values of predictor variables to make their predictions. One way to approach the task would be to memorize the formulae, plug in values that are provided on a test or in a problem workbook, generate their predictions, and find out if their predictions match the "correct answers." Another way to approach the task would be to pose the question: "What might happen to the economy of Juneau as the nearby Mendenhall Glacier (which is a major tourist attraction near Juneau) shrinks?" Such a question provides rich opportunities for students to identify and work with variables related to the glacier's ecology and the town's tourism industry: number of tourist visits to the glacier, jobs supported by tourism, hotel bookings, cruise ship fees, customers at restaurants and shops, and tax dollars. Students' research questions might include: How do we find out that information? How do the variables influence the economy? How do we measure that influence?

In addition to allowing students to engage their prior knowledge, authentic tasks often provide opportunities for learners to work collaboratively, thus providing opportunities for social interaction and the negotiation of meaning through multiple perspectives (Kordaki, 2009).

Taken together, the constructivist claims above provide a frame for understanding meaningful learning as the construction of knowledge. When we look through the constructivist frame, our view is directed toward the key concepts of prior knowledge, multiple perspectives, self-regulation, and authentic learning. As mentioned earlier, however, constructivist theory has several variations. We can think of those variations as lenses that can be placed in the frame. The frame keeps our attention directed toward the common constructivist claims and the key concepts they represent. But each lens changes slightly how we focus among the key concepts. One lens, for example, brings prior knowledge into relief, another places the multiple perspectives of social interaction in the foreground. Each lens represents a variation on the constructivist theme. We look briefly through the three lenses: cognitive, social, and critical constructivism.

Three Variations on a Constructivist Theme   One view of meaningful learning that we have described, Jean Piaget's, holds that it is the natural result of an intrinsic drive to resolve inconsistencies and contradictions—that is, always to have a view of the world that makes sense in the light of what we currently know. One variation of constructivism, **cognitive constructivism,** is an outgrowth of Piaget's ideas because it focuses on the cognitive processes that take place within individuals. In other words, an individual's conception of the truth of some matter (for example, that both birds and airplanes can fly because they use the same aeronautical principles) is based on her ability, with guidance, to assimilate information effectively into existing schemes and develop new schemes and operations (the process Piaget called *accommodation*) in response to novel or discrepant ideas (Fosnot & Perry, 2005; Windschitl, 2002).

The constructivist variation known as **social constructivism** holds that meaningful learning occurs when people are explicitly taught how to use the psychological tools of their culture (such as language, mathematics, and approaches to problem solving) and are then given the opportunity to use these tools in authentic, real-life activities to create a common, or shared, understanding of some phenomenon (Burton, Lee, Younie, 2009; McInerney, 2005). Students are encouraged to engage in open-ended discussion with peers and teachers about such things as the meaning

---

Margin notes:

In addition to prior knowledge, construction of ideas is aided by multiple perspectives, self-regulation, and authentic tasks

Cognitive constructivism: emphasizes role of cognitive processes in meaningful learning

Social constructivism: emphasizes role of culture and social interaction in meaningful learning

Most constructivist theories take one of three forms: cognitive constructivism, social constructivism, or critical constructivism. The first emphasizes the effect of one's cognitive processes on meaningful learning, whereas the latter two emphasize the effect of other people's arguments and cultural points of view on meaningful learning.
A, © David R. Frazier Photolibrary, Inc./Alamy; B, Will & Deni McIntyre/ Photo Researchers

of terms and procedures, the relationships among ideas, and the applicability of knowledge to specific contexts. This process is often referred to by social constructivists as *negotiating meaning*. This view has its roots in the writings of such individuals as the psychologist Lev Vygotsky and the educational philosopher John Dewey (Cole & Gajdamaschko, 2007; Postholm, 2008; Windschitl, 2002).

Social constructivism has also given rise to an increasing focus by researchers on how culture and history influence people's thoughts and actions as they engage with others and with their environment. A framework that guides this focus is called cultural-historical activity theory or "CHAT" for short (Cole, 1996; Roth & Lee, 2007; Saka, Southerland, Brooks, 2009; Yamagata-Lynch & Haudenschild, 2008, 2009). CHAT provides a way of analyzing and understanding activity in complex, real-life situations. For example, Lisa Yamagata-Lynch (2007) used "activity systems analysis" (see Engeström, 1999) to investigate an effort to integrate technology in a school district in hopes that increased use of technology would enhance student learning. The analysis of the activities of individual teachers, teacher groups, technology staff in the school and the district, and the activities in a professional development program allowed Yamagata-Lynch to observe how the activities of various individuals and groups interacted. By using activity systems analysis, she was able to identify obstacles to attaining the goal of technology integration and the tensions that were created as people in various roles worked toward the goal (some tensions can contribute positively to attaining the goal).

The CHAT framework—and especially activity systems analysis—provides a way to examine the activities of one person or group in relation to other persons and groups and to do so while considering the context in which all are in pursuit of a goal. As such, CHAT is a promising framework, especially in light of the push to create a new partnership that builds the research and development capacity within the education profession (Bryk, Bender Sebring, Allensworth, Luppescu, & Easton, 2010; Bryk & Gomez, 2008). As teachers, administrators, curriculum developers, community agencies, and researchers come together in new ways to design new learning tools and environments to help students succeed (Bryk & Gomez, 2008), it will be critical to analyze the activities of the individuals and groups who seek to design more effective learning environments for students. As you enter the teaching profession in this time of change, you can expect to engage with other educational professionals in developing and testing new learning environments designed to help students construct knowledge.

Cultural-historical activity theory evolved from the social constructivism of Vygotsky. As CHAT has evolved, the importance of culture and one's history within a culture have been brought into clearer focus by the third lens through which we can view the constructivist view of meaningful learning.

The third variation on the constructivist theme is referred to as **critical constructivism** (Fok & Watkins, 2009; Jean-Marie, Normore, & Brooks, 2009; Stears, 2009). The label "critical" was applied to constructivism as some researchers began to

Critical constructivism: emphasizes role of cultural myths and how they influence learning environments

incorporate a critical theory perspective to study how learners constructed knowledge. According to philosopher James Bohman, "a theory is critical to the extent that it seeks human emancipation . . ." He goes on to say that ". . . a critical theory provides the descriptive and normative bases for social inquiry aimed at decreasing domination and increasing freedom in all their forms" (Bohman, 2009, para. 1). Thus, critical constructivists seek (1) to understand why learners from some cultural and/or social groups more easily construct knowledge in school environments than others and (2) to liberate the learning of learners who experience difficulty in school environments so that all students can successfully construct knowledge (Harrington & Enochs, 2009).

As we discussed in Chapter 5, "Addressing Cultural and Socioeconomic Diversity," two important factors that distinguish one culture from another are ethnicity and social class. We learned also that cultural differences can mean differences in communication patterns that lead to misunderstandings among students and between students and teachers. Finally, we learned that teacher expectations can influence how students perform in school. Critical constructivism focuses on the social aspects of learning environments that teachers create in their classrooms, whether those environments perpetuate cultural myths (for example, "children from lower socioeconomic groups do not have sufficient prior knowledge to construct knowledge"), and how learners' cultural backgrounds influence how they interact with others and with the content they are being asked to learn (Goodman, 2008; Loyens & Gijbels, 2008; Taylor, 1996).

Although the cognitive, social, and critical constructivist perspectives emphasize different aspects of learning, they are not incompatible. The cognitive approach does not deny the value of learning in group activities nor the influence of one's cultural background, the social approach does not deny the value of working independently of others, and the critical approach acknowledges that cognitive processing and social negotiation are key to constructing knowledge. As one constructivist observed, "learning is an act of both individual interpretation and negotiation with other individuals" (Windschitl, 2002, p. 142). As we learned in Chapter 5, individual interpretation and negotiation with others are influenced by the cultural perspectives. Consider, for example, musicians in an orchestra. They practice both in a group and by themselves because some things are best learned in isolation (e.g., aspects of technique, such as breathing, fingering, or bowing) and others are best learned as part of the orchestra (e.g., discussing—from the perspective of their own cultural experiences—how various techniques best express the composer's intent). All three variations on the constructivist theme assume that "learning is an active process that is student-centered in the sense that, *with the teacher's help*, learners select and transform information, construct hypotheses, and make decisions" (Chrenka, 2001, p. 694; italics added).

Conditions That Foster Constructivist Learning   The fostering conditions that constructivists typically mention include a cognitive apprenticeship between student and teacher, a use of realistic problems and conditions, and an emphasis on multiple perspectives.

Cognitive Apprenticeship   The first condition, that of a cognitive apprenticeship, was illustrated in Chapter 9 on social cognitive theory when we described the reciprocal teaching program of Annemarie Palincsar and Ann Brown (1984). Its main feature is that the teacher models a cognitive process that students are to learn and then gradually turns responsibility for executing the process over to students as they become more skilled (Seezink, Poell, & Kirschner, 2009). As you may recall from our earlier discussions—in Chapter 2, for example—providing such environmental supports as modeling, hints, leading questions, and suggestions and then gradually removing them as the learner demonstrates increased competence is called *scaffolding*. Cognitive apprenticeships also occur in less formal circumstances, as when a child joins an existing peer group (such as a play group), at first mostly watches what the other children do, and then gradually, with little explicit direction from the others, participates in one or more aspects of the task.

Situated Learning In the second condition, often called **situated learning** (or situated cognition), students are given learning tasks set in realistic contexts. A realistic context is one in which students must solve a meaningful problem by using a variety of skills and information. The rationale for this condition is twofold:

1. Learning is more likely to be meaningful (related to previously learned knowledge and skills) when it is embedded in a realistic context (Duffy & Cunningham, 1996; Hung, 2002).

2. Traditional forms of classroom learning and instruction, which are largely decontextualized in the sense that what students learn is relevant only to taking tests and performing other classroom tasks, leads to a condition that has been referred to as **inert knowledge** (Gentner, Loewenstein, Thompson, & Forbus, 2009). That is, students fail to use what they learned earlier (such as mathematical procedures) to solve either real-life problems (such as calculating the square footage of the walls of a room to determine how many rolls of wallpaper to buy) or other school-related problems because they don't see any relationship between the two (Perkins, 1999). But as we point out later in this chapter when we discuss transfer of learning, some have argued that too strong an emphasis on situated cognition can make it difficult for students to see how to apply prior knowledge (Bereiter, 1997; Cooper & Harries, 2005).

As an example of situated learning, the game of baseball can be used as a vehicle for middle school or high school students to apply aspects of science, mathematics, and sociology. Students could be asked to use their knowledge of physics to explain how pitchers are able to make the ball curve left or right or drop down as it approaches home plate. They could be asked to use their mathematical skills to figure out how far home runs travel. They could also be asked to read about the Negro Leagues and Jackie Robinson and discuss why it took until the late 1940s for major league baseball to begin integration.

A more formal way of implementing situated learning is to use problem-based learning (PBL) (Hung, 2002; Jeong & Hmelo-Silver, 2010). Unlike a traditional approach to instruction in which students first learn a body of knowledge and then use that knowledge to solve problems, PBL presents students with complex, authentic problems (such as creating a water management plan for the desert southwest) and requires them to identify and locate the information they need to solve the problem. In other words, students decide what they need to know to solve the problem (Angeli, 2002; Soderberg & Price, 2003). In Chapter 13, "Approaches to Instruction," we describe how PBL can be used with computer-based technology. In the Resources for Further Investigation section of this chapter, we describe a website that provides information about PBL, directions for designing PBL units, and model problems. The Case in Print provides an account of how technology is being combined with problem-based learning, a topic we will return to again in the technology section at the end of the chapter.

Multiple Perspectives The third condition that fosters constructivism is students' viewing ideas and problems from multiple perspectives. The rationale, again, is twofold: most of life's problems are multifaceted, and the knowledge base of experts is a network of interrelated ideas. The complex process of becoming an effective teacher is a good example of the need for multiple perspectives, including the perspectives of other teachers (Chan & Pang, 2006). As we mentioned at the beginning of the book, being an effective teacher requires the mastery of many skills and disciplines so that classroom problems can be analyzed and attacked from several perspectives.

The following section provides an example of a constructivist-oriented teaching lesson, and Table 10.1 notes the major characteristics of a constructivist classroom.

An Example of Constructivist Teaching A fifth-grade teacher wanted his students to understand that the mathematical concept of pi expresses the relationship between the circumference of a circle and its diameter. On the first day of school he gave students writing tablets divided into three columns. He told them that over the next 3 weeks they were to identify circular objects of all sizes outside of school and measure how many inches each one was across its center and around its perimeter (he purposely avoided using the terms diameter and circumference at this point). The first measurement was to be recorded in the first column of the tablet and the second measurement in the second column. Over the next 3 weeks the students measured all manner of round things (such as coins, tires, and dishes), all the time wondering why they were doing this project and what the teacher's explanation would be. When the class met on the day of the project's deadline, the students were both surprised and disappointed that the teacher did not offer an explanation. Instead, he had the students look over their two columns of numbers and said, "Now tell me what you can see that is interesting about these two sets of numbers."

Gradually, the students noticed that the measurements of the circumference were always larger than the measurements of the diameter. He then asked, "How much bigger are the numbers in the second column, the distance around the circle, in relation to the numbers in the first column, the distance across the circle?" Once again, students wondered when the teacher would simply tell them the answer. But with a bit of coaxing, students began to guess, until one girl realized that the answer to the question could be gained by dividing the larger number by the smaller one. The students did so, recorded their answers in the third column of their tablet, and were astounded to realize that the answer was always the same (3.14) regardless of the size of the circles.

Table 10.1 Characteristics of a Constructivist Classroom

- Teaching and learning start from a student's current understanding of a subject. Therefore, the teacher needs to determine what students currently know and what relevant experiences they have had with key topics.

- Teachers help students create realistic learning experiences that will lead students to elaborate on and restructure current knowledge. Teachers believe that meaningful learning involves discovering, questioning, analyzing, synthesizing, and evaluating information.

- Students frequently engage in complex, meaningful, problem-based activities whose content and goals are negotiated with the teacher.

- Students have frequent opportunities to debate and discuss substantive issues.

- A primary goal of instruction is for students to learn to think for themselves. Consequently, teachers use a variety of indirect teaching methods, such as modeling the thinking processes they want students to use; providing prompts, probes, and suggestions; providing heuristics (a topic discussed later in this chapter); and using technology to organize and represent information.

- Students engage in such high-level cognitive processes as explaining ideas, interpreting texts, predicting phenomena, and constructing arguments based on evidence.

- In addition to assessing student learning with written exams, teachers also require students to write research reports, make oral presentations, build models, and engage in problem-solving activities.

- Student progress (and the effectiveness of the learning environment) is assessed continually rather than just at the end of a unit and the end of a semester.

- Subject-matter disciplines and their knowledge bases are seen as continually undergoing revision.

SOURCES: Gabler, Schroeder, & Curtis (2003); Loyens & Gijbels (2008); Windschitl (2002).

Case in Print

Combining Technology and Problems to Construct Knowledge

The fostering conditions that constructivists typically mention include a cognitive apprenticeship between student and teacher, a use of realistic problems and conditions, and an emphasis on multiple perspectives.... In the second condition, often called situated learning (or situated cognition), students are given learning tasks set in realistic contexts... A more formal way of implementing situated learning is to use problem-based learning (PBL) (Hung, 2002; Jeong & Hmelo-Silver, 2010). Unlike a traditional approach to instruction in which students first learn a body of knowledge and then use that knowledge to solve problems, PBL presents students with complex, authentic problems (such as creating a water management plan for the desert southwest) and requires them to identify and locate the information they need to solve the problem. (p. 333–334)

At School, Technology Starts to Turn a Corner

STEVE LOHR

The New York Times (nytimes.com) 8/17/2008

Count me a technological optimist, but I have always thought that the people who advocate putting computers in classrooms as a way to transform education were well intentioned but wide of the mark. It's not the problem, and it's not the answer.

Yet as a new school year begins, the time may have come to reconsider how large a role technology can play in changing education. There are promising examples, both in the United States and abroad, and they share some characteristics. The ratio of computers to pupils is one to one. Technology isn't off in a computer lab. Computing is an integral tool in all disciplines, always at the ready.

Web-based education software has matured in the last few years, so that students, teachers and families can be linked through networks. Until recently, computing in the classroom amounted to students doing Internet searches, sending e-mail and mastering word processing, presentation programs and spreadsheets. That's useful stuff, to be sure, but not something that alters how schools work.

The new Web education networks can open the door to broader changes. Parents become more engaged because they can monitor their children's attendance, punctuality, homework and performance, and can get tips for helping them at home. Teachers can share methods, lesson plans and online curriculum materials.

In the classroom, the emphasis can shift to project-based learning, a real break with the textbook-and-lecture model of education. In a high school class, a project might begin with a hypothetical letter from the White House that says oil prices are spiking, the economy is faltering and the president's poll numbers are falling. The assignment would be to devise a new energy policy in two weeks. The shared Web space for the project, for example, would include the White House letter, the sources the students must consult, their work plan and timetable, assignments for each student, the assessment criteria for their grades and, eventually, the paper the team delivers. Oral presentations would be required.

The project-based approach, some educators say, encourages active learning and produces better performance in class and on standardized tests.

The educational bottom line, it seems, is that while computer technology has matured and become more affordable, the most significant development has been a deeper understanding of how to use the technology.

"Unless you change how you teach and how kids work, new technology is not really going to make a difference," said Bob Pearlman, a former teacher who is the director of strategic planning for the New Technology Foundation, a nonprofit organization.

The foundation, based in Napa, Calif., has developed a model for project-based teaching and is at the forefront of the drive for technology-enabled reform of education. Forty-two schools in nine states are trying the foundation's model, and their numbers are growing rapidly.

Behind the efforts, of course, are concerns that K-12 public schools are falling short in preparing students for the twin challenges of globalization and technological change. Worries about the nation's future competitiveness led to the creation in 2002 of the Partnership for 21st Century Skills, a coalition whose members include the Department of Education and technology companies like Apple, Cisco Systems, Dell and Microsoft.

The government-industry partnership identifies a set of skills that mirror those that the New Technology Foundation model is meant to nurture. Those skills include collaboration, systems thinking, self-direction and communication, both online and in person.

State officials in Indiana took a look at the foundation's model and offered travel grants for local teachers and administrators to visit its schools in California. Sally Nichols, an English teacher, came away impressed and signed up for the new project-based teaching program at her school, Decatur Central High School in Indianapolis.

Last year, Ms. Nichols and another teacher taught a biology and literature class for freshmen. (Cross-disciplinary courses are common in the New Technology model.) Typically, half of freshmen fail biology, but under the project-based model the failure rate was cut in half.

"There's a lot of ownership by the kids in their work instead of teachers lecturing and being the givers of all knowledge," Ms. Nichols explained. "The classes are just much more alive. They don't sleep in class."

In Indiana, the number of schools using the foundation model will increase to six this year, and an additional dozen communities have signed up for the next year, said David Shane, a member of the state board of education. "It's caught fire in Indiana, and we've got to have this kind of education to prepare our young people for the future in a global economy that is immersed in technology."

The extra cost for schools that have adopted the New Technology model is about $1,000 per student a year, once a school is set up, says Mr. Pearlman of the foundation. After the first three years, the extra cost should decline considerably, he said.

In England, where the government has promoted technology in schools for a decade, the experiment with technology-driven change in education is further along.

Five years ago, the government gave computers to students at two schools in high-crime neighborhoods in Birmingham. For the students, a Web-based portal is the virtual doorway for assignments, school social activities, online mentoring, discussion groups and e-mail. Even students who are suspended from school for a few days beg not to lose their access to the portal, says Sir Mark Grundy, 49, the executive principal of Shireland Collegiate Academy and the George Salter Collegiate Academy. Today, the schools are among the top in the nation in yearly improvements in students' performance in reading and math tests.

Sir Mark says he is convinced that advances in computing, combined with improved understanding of how to tailor the technology to different students, can help transform education.

"This is the best Trojan horse for causing change in schools that I have ever seen," he said.

Questions and Activities

1. What principles of constructivist learning theory are reflected in the instructional activities described in this story?

2. What other problem-based projects can you think of that could take advantage of technology? Describe the problem, what you would have students do, and what you would hope they accomplish.

In a much more meaningful way than would have occurred had the students simply memorized the fact that pi is the ratio of the circumference of a circle to its diameter, the students learned, as one put it, "No matter how big a circle is, the distance around it is always a little more than three times the distance across it." They also learned that discovering ideas is fun and that mathematics has a basis in the real world (Funk, 2003).

Constructivist-oriented teaching encourages creating new views; uses scaffolding, realistic tasks, and class discussion

The essence of a constructivist-oriented lesson is to provide students with realistic problems that cannot be solved with their current level of understanding and, by allowing them to interact mainly among themselves, to work out new understandings. It's important to emphasize the social nature of this approach. The experiences and ideas of others become springboards for further experimentation and discussion.

Putting Constructivism in Perspective

Although constructivism has much to offer teachers, like any other theory, it does have its limitations, and there may be problems with its implementation (Kirschner, Sweller, & Clark, 2006; Mayer, 2009). Here are a few of constructivism's drawbacks you should keep in mind:

- Because of constructivism's emphasis on guiding rather than telling, accepting different perspectives on issues and solutions to problems, modifying previous conceptions in the light of new information, and creating an atmosphere that encourages active participation, it is almost impossible to create highly detailed lesson plans. Much of what teachers do depends on how students respond. Teaching from this perspective will place a premium on your teacher-as-artist abilities.

- Teaching from a constructivist perspective is more time-consuming and places higher demands on learners as compared with a typical lecture format (Perkins, 1999; Schwartz, Lindgren, & Lewis, 2009).

- Constructivism is not the only orientation to learning and teaching that you will ever need (nor is any other theory, for that matter). You need to know which theory or approach best fits which purposes and circumstances. Sometimes memorization of factual information is essential, and sometimes an instructional objective can be accomplished more efficiently (and just as effectively) with a clear and well-organized lecture (Mayer, 2009; Schwartz, Lindgren, & Lewis, 2009).

pause & reflect

Can you recall a class in which the instructor used constructivist techniques? What did the instructor do? How did you react? Was the learning outcome more meaningful than for other classes?

The extent to which teachers engage in constructivist teaching practices is determined in large part by how completely they accept its underlying principles (e.g., knowledge is temporary, knowledge is the result of discussions among students and between students and the teacher, students have input into the curriculum, learning is grounded in real-life tasks and settings to make it relevant to students' lives). Teachers who believe that they, and not the students, should decide what gets learned and how and that their primary responsibility is to prepare students for high-stakes tests are less likely to use a constructivist approach (Haney & McArthur, 2002; Nichols & Berliner, 2007).

TeachSource **Video Case** ⏪ ▶ ⏩

Middle School Science Instruction: Inquiry Learning

Go to the Education CourseMate website and watch the Video Case, and then answer the following questions:

1. Does Robert Cho's science class meet the criteria for a constructivist classroom?

2. Based on this Video Case and the discussion on constructivism in this section of the text, why do you think that teaching using a constructivist approach is more time-consuming for teachers (as opposed to other teaching methods)? Cite some possible reasons.

Assuming you do accept some constructivist principles and that you acknowledge that there is a beneficial role for instructional support within constructivist classrooms (Hardy, Jonen, Möller, & Stern, 2006), there are many techniques you can use to foster meaningful learning within a constructivist framework. Several computer-based approaches are described at the end of this chapter. One technique that does not rely on computer technology, but that is particularly well suited to developing, comparing, and understanding different points of view, is the classroom discussion (Brookfield & Preskill, 2005; Fok & Watkins, 2009). Because this format also allows students to deal with realistic problems that are often complex and ambiguous and to exercise cognitive skills taught by the teacher, it is an excellent general-purpose method for helping students construct a meaningful knowledge base. It is also an effective way to improve the quality of students' writing. A study of discussion-based approaches to literature instruction in middle and high school classrooms (involving almost 1,000 students) found that higher levels of discussion-based instruction about reading assignments were associated with more abstract and elaborated reports, analyses, and essays based on the readings (Applebee, Langer, Nystrand, & Gamoran, 2003).

Let's turn our attention to some specific Suggestions for Teaching that describe how to use discussion and other techniques to emphasize meaningful learning in your classroom.

Suggestions for Teaching

Using a Constructivist Approach to Meaningful Learning

JOURNAL ENTRY
Ways to Arrange for
Discovery to Take Place

1 **Arrange the learning situation so that students are exposed to different perspectives on a problem or an issue.**

This is the crux of the discovery approach and the constructivist view of learning. The basic idea is to *arrange* the elements of a learning task and *guide* student actions so that students discover, or construct, a personally meaningful conception of a problem or issue (as opposed to someone else's conception). In some cases, you may present a topic that is a matter of opinion or that all students are sure to know something about. In other cases, you might structure the discussion by exposing all participants to the same background information.

  a. Ask students to discuss familiar topics or those that are matters of opinion.

EXAMPLES

- "What are some of the techniques that advertising agencies use in television commercials to persuade us to buy certain products?"
- "What do you think is the best book you ever read, and why do you think so?"

  b. Provide necessary background information by asking all students to read all or part of a book, take notes on a lecture, view a film, conduct library research, or conduct research on the Internet.

EXAMPLES

- After the class has read *Great Expectations,* ask, "What do you think Dickens was trying to convey when he wrote this novel? Was he just trying to tell a good story, or was he also trying to get us to think about certain kinds of relationships between people?"
- "After I explain some of the principles of electrical currents, I'm going to ask you to suggest rules for connecting batteries in series and in parallel. Then we'll see how well your rules work."

JOURNAL ENTRY
Questions That Are Likely
to Stimulate Productive
Classroom Discussion

2 **Structure discussions by posing a specific question, presenting a provocative topic-related issue, or asking students to choose topics or subtopics.**

It is important to structure a discovery session by giving students something reasonably specific to discuss; otherwise, they may simply engage in a disorganized and desultory bull session. You might supply direction in the following ways:

a. In some cases, encourage students to arrive at conclusions already reached by others.

Thousands of books provide detailed answers to such questions as, "What is human about human beings? How did they get that way? How can they be made more so?" But constructivists believe that answers mean more when they are constructed by the individual, not supplied ready-made by others. As you look over lesson plans, therefore, you might try to put together some questions for students to answer by engaging in discussion rather than by reading or listening to what others have already discovered. In searching for such topics, you might take into account the techniques that Bruner described. Here is a list of those techniques, together with an example of each one. Keep in mind that students often acquire a deeper understanding of ideas and issues when they have had appropriate previous experience:

JOURNAL ENTRY
Similar Applications You
Could Use

- *Emphasize contrast.* In an elementary school social studies unit on cultural diversity, say, "When you watch this film on Mexico, look for customs and ways of living that differ from ours. Then we'll talk about what these differences are and why they may have developed."

- *Stimulate informed guessing.* In a middle school unit on natural science, you might say, "Suppose we wanted to figure out some kind of system to classify trees so that we could later find information about particular types. What would be the best way to do it?" After students have developed a classification scheme, show them schemes that specialists have developed.

- *Encourage participation.* In a high school political science class, illustrate the jury system by staging a mock trial. (Note that the use of a simulation satisfies the constructivist criterion of realistic tasks and contexts.)

- *Stimulate awareness.* In a high school English class, ask the students to discuss how the author developed the plot.

b. In other cases, present a controversial topic for which there is no single answer.

Discussions might center on provocative issues about which there are differences of opinion. One caution here is to avoid topics (such as premarital sex or legalized abortion) that parents may not want discussed in school, either because they are convinced it is their prerogative to discuss them with their children or because they feel that students may be pressured to endorse your opinion because you assign grades. You should not avoid controversy, but neither should you go out of your way to agitate students and their parents.

Another caution is to avoid selecting issues that provoke more than they instruct. You may be tempted to present a highly controversial topic and then congratulate yourself at the end of the period if most students engaged in heated discussion. But if they simply argued enthusiastically about something that had nothing to do with the subject you are assigned to teach, you cannot honestly claim to have arranged an instructive exchange of ideas.

EXAMPLES

- In a middle school science class, ask students to list arguments for and against attempting to alter the genetic code of human beings.

- In a high school political science class, ask students to list arguments for and against democratic forms of government.

JOURNAL ENTRY
Ways to Supervise
Discussion Sessions

3 **If time is limited and if only one topic is to be covered, ask students to form a circle and have an all-class discussion.**

You may sometimes wish to have the entire class discuss a topic. Such discussions are most likely to be successful if all students have eye contact with one another. The simplest way to achieve this is to have students sit in a circle. Next, invite responses to the question you have posed. As students make remarks, serve more as a moderator than as a leader. Try to keep the discussion on the topic, but avoid directing it toward a specific predetermined end result. If one or more students tend to dominate the discussion, say something like, "Kim and Carlos have given us their ideas. Now I'd like to hear from the rest of you." If an aggressive student attacks or belittles something that a classmate says, respond with something like, "It's good to *believe* in a point of view, but let's be friendly as we listen to other opinions. This is supposed to be a discussion, not an argument or a debate."

Factors that lead to successful or unsuccessful discussions are often idiosyncratic, but there are certain procedures you might follow to increase the likelihood of success.

a. Ask questions that stimulate students to apply, analyze, synthesize, and evaluate.

When you first structure a discussion session, but also while it is under way, take care to ask questions likely to elicit different points of view. If you ask students to supply information (for example, "When did Charles Dickens write *Great Expectations*?"), the first correct response will lead to closure. You may end up asking a series of questions leading to brief answers—the equivalent of a fill-in exam. When you seek to encourage students to construct personally meaningful interpretations of the issues or to develop skills as deductive thinkers, it is preferable to ask questions that are likely to tap higher levels of thinking.

EXAMPLES

- "You just learned how to calculate the area of a circle. Think of as many different ways as you can of how you might be able to use that bit of knowledge if you were a do-it-yourself homeowner." (Application)

- "Last month we read a novel by Dickens; this month we read a play by Shakespeare. What are some similarities in the way each author developed the plot of his story?" (Synthesis)

b. Allow sufficient time for initial responses, and then probe for further information (if appropriate).

Recent research has found that many teachers fail to allow enough time for students to respond to questions. Quite often, instructors wait only 1 second before repeating the question, calling on another student, or answering the question themselves. When teachers wait at least 3 seconds after asking a question, students are more likely to participate; their responses increase in frequency, length, and complexity; and their achievement improves. There are changes in teacher behavior as well. As a function of waiting longer, teachers ask more complex questions and have higher expectations for the quality of students' responses (Orlich, Harder, Callahan, Trevisan, & Brown, 2010).

One possible explanation for improved student recitation when teachers wait longer for a response is that reflective thinkers have an opportunity to figure out what they want to say. But even impulsive thinkers probably welcome a few more seconds of thinking time. It seems logical to expect that snap answers will be more superficial than answers supplied after even a few seconds of reflection.

In addition to giving students ample time to make an initial response, you should encourage them to pursue an idea. If it seems appropriate, probe for further information or clarification of a point by asking students who give brief or incomplete answers to explain how or why they arrived at a conclusion or to supply additional comments.

EXAMPLE

- "Well, Keesha, I'm sure a gardener might sometimes need to figure the area of a circle, but can you give a more specific example? If you can't think of one right away, put up your hand as soon as you can describe a specific situation in which it would help to know the area of a circular patch of lawn or soil."

  c. When selecting students to speak in class, use techniques likely to sustain steady but nonthreatening attention. At the same time, guard against the temptation to call primarily on bright, articulate, assertive students.

The way you moderate student contributions may not only determine how successful the discussion will be but may also influence how students feel about themselves and each other. Jacob Kounin (1970) points out that when a teacher first names a student and then asks a question, the rest of the class may tend to turn its attention to other things. The same tendency to tune out may occur if a teacher follows a set pattern of calling on students (for example, by going around a circle). To keep all the students on their toes, you might ask questions first and then, in an unpredictable sequence, call on those who volunteer to speak, frequently switching from one part of the room to another. Guard against the temptation to call primarily on students you expect to give good or provocative answers. Repeatedly ignoring students who may be a bit inarticulate or unimaginative may cause them and their classmates to conclude that you think they are incompetent. These students may then lose interest in and totally ignore what is taking place.

JOURNAL ENTRY
Techniques for Satisfying
Constructivist Principles
and State Learning
Standards

4 **Use guided experiences to satisfy both constructivist principles and state learning standards.**

Because constructivism is strongly student-centered and emphasizes high-level outcomes, it is sometimes perceived as being incompatible with the need for teachers to prepare students for high-stakes tests that are based on state learning standards. But through the use of guided experiences, teachers can do both. The trick is to embed standards in learning experiences that students care about. Geoffrey Caine, Renate Nummela Caine, and Carol McClintic (2002) describe how this was done for eighth-grade classes studying the U.S. Civil War.

To satisfy state learning standards, students needed to learn such things as the nature of slavery, the causes of the war, important dates and the sequence of events, major battles, and significant individuals who affected the course of the war. The first step was to teach students how to listen to one another and express disagreements in a nonjudgmental way.

An introductory event was then used to spark students' interest in the topic. They were read a story about a woman who disguised herself as a man, enlisted in the Union Army, and worked as a coal handler on a canal boat. They were then shown a short segment from the motion picture *Gettysburg* in which Confederate soldiers marched directly into cannon and rifle fire. The last part of the introduction involved telling students that over 400 women disguised themselves as men and participated in the war and that the 51,000 soldiers who were killed during the 3-day battle of Gettysburg exceeded the number of U.S. soldiers who were killed during the entire Vietnam War. When invited to raise questions, the students wanted to know such things as why women fought in the war, how it was that nobody knew they were women, why the North and South went to war, and why soldiers would walk into enemy gunfire.

The students were assigned to groups based on the similarity of the questions they raised and were told to seek answers from library resources, the Internet, and interviews with war veterans. The teachers used the subsequent reports each group made to the class and the discussions that followed to ensure that such standards-related issues as the different groups involved in the war and the nature of slavery were introduced and discussed.

JOURNAL ENTRY
Techniques for Arranging
Small-Group Discussions

5 **If abundant time is available and if a controversial or subdivided topic is to be discussed, divide the class into groups of about five.**

A major limitation of any kind of discussion is that only one person can talk at a time. You can reduce this difficulty by dividing the class into smaller groups before asking them to exchange ideas. A group of about five seems to work best. If only two or three students are interacting with one another, the exchange of ideas may be limited. If there are more than five, not all members will be able to contribute at frequent intervals.

Raymond Brown and Peter Renshaw (2000) describe an approach to small-group classroom discussion based on the following five principles derived from Vygotsky's sociocultural theory of cognitive development:

1. Students should present their ideas with sufficient clarity that other students can distinguish relevant from irrelevant ideas.
2. Relevant ideas can be rejected by others only if their validity can be questioned on the basis of past experience or logical reasoning.
3. Ideas that contradict one another or that belong to mutually exclusive points of view must be resolved through group argument.
4. All members understand and agree that the group will strive to reach a consensus on an issue by each member actively contributing to arguments that lead to a solution.
5. The group will present its arguments to the other members of the class.

THE NATURE OF PROBLEM SOLVING

As with most of the other topics covered in this book, an extensive amount of theorizing and research on problem solving has been conducted over the years. We will focus our discussion on the types of problems that students are typically required to deal with, the cognitive processes that play a central role in problem solving, and various approaches to teaching problem solving in the classroom.

Let's begin by asking what we mean by the terms *problem* and *problem solving*. Most, if not all, psychologists would agree that "a problem is said to exist when one has a goal and has not yet identified a means for reaching that goal" (Gagné, Yekovich, & Yekovich, 1993, p. 211). **Problem solving,** then, is the identification and application of knowledge and skills that result in goal attainment (Kruse, 2009; Martinez, 1998). Although this definition encompasses a wide range of problem types, we will focus on three types that students frequently encounter both in and out of school.

Three Common Types of Problems

Well-structured problems: clearly stated, known solution procedures; known evaluation standards

In the first category are the well-structured problems of mathematics and science—the type of problems that students from kindergarten through middle school are typically required to solve. **Well-structured problems** are clearly formulated, can be solved by recall and application of a specific procedure (called an *algorithm*), and

Well-structured problems have a clear structure, can be solved by using a standard procedure, and produce solutions that can be evaluated against an agreed-on standard. They are the type of problem that students are asked to solve most frequently. © Bob Daemmrich/Photo Edit

result in a solution that can be evaluated against a well-known, agreed-on standard (Kapur & Kinzer, 2009)—for example:

$$5 + 8 =$$
$$732 - 485 =$$
$$8 + 3x = 40 - 5x$$

What constitutes a problem to be solved varies with the age and experience of the learner and the nature of the problem itself (Martinez, 1998). The second of the mathematical examples is likely to be a genuine problem for some first or second graders who are used to seeing subtraction exercises arrayed vertically (minuend on top, subtrahend beneath, horizontal line under the subtrahend). Fifth graders, however, who have had experience with arithmetic assignments in a variety of formats, would be able to retrieve and use the correct algorithm automatically. Because the fifth graders know the means to reach their goal, they do not face a problem-solving task according to our definition, but just a type of exercise or practice.

In the second category are the ill-structured problems often encountered in everyday life and in disciplines such as economics or psychology. **Ill-structured problems** are more complex, provide few cues pointing to solution procedures, and have less definite criteria for determining when the problem has been solved (Choi & Lee, 2009; Kapur & Kinzer, 2007). Examples of ill-structured problems are how to identify and reward good teachers, how to improve access to public buildings and facilities for persons with physical disabilities, and how to increase voter turnout for elections.

> Ill-structured problems: vaguely stated, unclear solution procedures; vague evaluation standards

The third category includes problems that are also ill structured but that differ from the examples just mentioned in two respects. First, these problems tend to divide people into opposing camps because of the emotions they arouse. Second, the primary goal, at least initially, is not to determine a course of action but to identify the most reasonable position. These problems are often referred to as **issues** (Ruggiero, 2009; Troyer & Youngreen). Examples of issues are capital punishment, gun control, and nondenominational prayer in classrooms. High school students typically have more opportunities than younger students to deal with ill-structured problems and issues of the type cited above. That does not mean, however, that younger students have no opportunities to deal with ill-structured problems or issues. Consider self-regulated learning, discussed in the preceding chapter. Goal

> Issues: ill-structured problems that arouse strong feelings

orientation plays a role in the development of self-regulated learning and self-efficacy. Performance goals provide clear, easily specified outcomes; they are similar to well-structured problems. Learning goals, however, are more similar to ill-structured problems or issues. Suppose you have young students who desire to become politicians or firefighters. They will see value in establishing goals that will help them learn the knowledge and skills they need to become politicians or firefighters. Generating personally valued goals (Miller & Brickman, 2004) can be opportunities for younger students to solve ill-structured problems.

Helping Students Become Good Problem Solvers

Despite the differences that exist among well-structured problems, ill-structured problems, and issues, recent theory and research suggest that good problem solvers employ the same general approach when solving one or another of these problem types (Bransford & Stein, 1993; Gagné et al., 1993; Matthew & Sternberg, 2009; Pretz, Naples, & Sternberg, 2003; Ruggiero, 2009). This approach consists of five steps or processes:

1. Realize that a problem exists.
2. Understand the nature of the problem.
3. Compile relevant information.
4. Formulate and carry out a solution.
5. Evaluate the solution.

Well-structured problems may call only for the implementation of steps 2, 4, and 5, but the other two problem types require all five steps. We will discuss each of these steps in the next few pages, along with some specific techniques that you can use to help your students become good problem solvers.

Step 1: Realize That a Problem Exists   Most people assume that if a problem is worth solving, they won't have to seek it out; it will make itself known. Like most other assumptions, this one is only partly true. Well-structured problems are often thrust on us by teachers, in the form of in-class exercises or homework, or by supervisors at work. Ill-structured problems and issues, however, often remain hidden from most people. It is a characteristic of good problem solvers that they are more sensitive to the existence of problems than most of their peers (Kruse, 2009; Pretz et al., 2003).

The keys to problem recognition, or *problem finding* as it is sometimes called, are curiosity and dissatisfaction. You need to question why a rule, procedure, or product is the way it is or to feel frustrated or irritated because something does not work as well as it might. The organization known as Mothers Against Drunk Driving, for example, was begun by a woman who, because her daughter had been killed in a traffic accident by a drunk driver, was dissatisfied with current, ineffective laws. This organization has been instrumental in getting state legislatures to pass laws against drunk driving that mandate more severe penalties.

Problem finding depends on curiosity, dissatisfaction with status quo

Problem finding does not come readily to most people, possibly because schools emphasize solving well-structured problems and possibly because most people have a natural tendency to assume that things work as well as they can. Like any other cognitive process, however, problem recognition can improve with instruction and practice. Students can be sensitized in a number of ways to the absence or flaws and shortcomings of products, procedures, rules, or whatever else. We will make some specific suggestions about improving problem recognition and the other problem-solving processes a bit later in Suggestions for Teaching: Teaching Problem-Solving Techniques.

Step 2: Understand the Nature of the Problem   The second step in the problem-solving process is perhaps the most critical. The problem solver has to construct an *optimal* representation, or understanding, of the nature of a problem or issue. The preceding sentence stresses the word *optimal* for two reasons. First, most problems can be expressed in a number of ways. Written problems, for example, can be recast as pictures, equations, graphs, charts, or diagrams. Second, because the way we represent the problem determines the amount and type of solution-relevant information we recall from long-term memory, some representations are better than others. For obvious reasons, problem-solving researchers often refer to this process as **problem representation** or **problem framing** (Derry et al., 2005; Giaccardi, 2005; Miller, Fagley, & Casella, 2009).

To achieve an optimal understanding of a problem, an individual needs two things: a high degree of knowledge of the subject matter (facts, concepts, and principles) on which the problem is based and familiarity with that particular type of problem. This background will allow the person to recognize important elements (words, phrases, and numbers) in the problem statement and patterns of relationships among the problem elements. This recognition will activate one or more solution-relevant schemes from long-term memory. It is this level of knowledge of subject matter and problem types that distinguishes the high-quality problem representations of the expert problem solver from the low-quality representations of the novice. Experts typically represent problems in terms of one or more basic patterns or underlying principles, whereas novices focus on limited or superficial surface features of problems.

To give you a clearer idea of the nature and power of an optimal problem representation, consider the following situation. When novices are given a set of physics problems to solve, they sort them into categories on the basis of some noticeable feature. For example, they group together all problems that involve the use of an inclined plane or all the ones that involve the use of pulleys. Then novices search their memories for previously learned information. The drawback to this approach is that although two or three problems may involve the use of an inclined plane, their solutions may depend on the application of different laws of physics. Experts, in contrast, draw on their extensive and well-organized knowledge base to represent groups of problems according to a common underlying principle, such as conservation of energy or Newton's third law (Pretz et al., 2003; Stemler et al., 2009; Sternberg, 2009).

An important aspect of the problem-solving process is the ability to activate relevant schemes (organized collections of facts, concepts, principles, and procedures) from long-term memory when they are needed. The more relevant and powerful the activated scheme is, the more likely it is that an effective problem solution will be achieved. But as many observers of education have pointed out, acquiring this ability is often easier said than done. John Bransford argues that standard educational practices produce knowledge that is *inert*. As mentioned earlier in the chapter, inert knowledge can be accessed only under conditions that closely mimic the original learning context (Bransford, Sherwood, Vye, & Rieser, 1986). Richard Feynman, a Nobel Prize–winning physicist, made the same observation in describing how his classmates at the Massachusetts Institute of Technology failed to recognize the application of a previously learned mathematical formula: "They didn't put two and two together. They didn't even know what they 'knew.' I don't know what's the matter with people: they don't learn by understanding; they learn by some other way—by rote, or something. Their knowledge is so fragile!" (1985, p. 36). To overcome this limitation of inert and fragile knowledge, teachers need to present subject matter in a highly organized fashion, and students need to learn more about the various conditions under which their knowledge applies.

Step 3: Compile Relevant Information

For well-structured problems that are relatively simple and familiar (such as arithmetic drill problems), this step in the problem-solving process occurs simultaneously with problem representation. In the process of defining a problem, we very quickly and easily recall from long-term memory all the information needed to achieve a solution. As problems and issues

---

Problem framing depends on knowledge of subject matter, familiarity with problem types

Inert knowledge due to learning isolated facts under limited conditions

become more complex, however, we run into two difficulties: the amount of information relevant to the solution becomes too great to keep track of mentally, and there is an increasing chance that we may not possess all the relevant information. As a result, we are forced to compile what we know in the form of lists, tables, pictures, graphs and diagrams, and so on, and to seek additional information from other sources.

The key to using oneself as an information source is the ability to accurately retrieve from long-term memory information that will aid in the solution of the problem. We need to think back over what we have learned in other somewhat similar situations, make a list of some other form of representation of those ideas, and make a judgment as to how helpful that knowledge might be. Techniques for ensuring accurate and reliable recall were discussed in Chapter 8 on information-processing theory.

In addition to relying on our own knowledge and experience to solve problems, we can draw on the knowledge and experience of friends, colleagues, and experts. The main purpose of soliciting the views of others about solutions to problems and positions on issues is to identify the reasons and evidence those people offer in support of their positions. This skill of asking questions and analyzing responses is quite useful in debates and classroom discussions of controversial issues.

TeachSource | **Video Case** ◄◄ ▶ ►►

Constructivist Teaching in Action: A High School Classroom Debate

Go to the Education CourseMate website and watch the Video Case, and then answer the following questions:

1. Why is the classroom debate an excellent example of constructivism in action? Do you find the classroom debate format to be an example of social constructivism or cognitive constructivism?

2. How does the classroom teacher in this Video Case arrange the elements of this lesson and guide students so that their constructivist learning experience is effective? Please cite specific examples.

Want to test your own problem-solving process? See the Netlabs at the textbook's Education CourseMate website.

Studying worked examples is an effective solution strategy

Step 4: Formulate and Carry Out a Solution When you think that you understand the nature of a problem or issue and possess sufficient relevant information, you are ready to attempt a solution. The first step is to consider which of several alternative approaches is likely to be most effective. The literature on problem solving mentions quite a few solution strategies. Because these solution strategies are very general in nature—they can apply to different kinds of problems in different content areas and offer only a general approach to solving a problem—they are referred to as *heuristics* (Martinez, 1998). We will discuss seven **heuristics** that we think are particularly useful.

- *Study worked examples.* This approach may strike you as so obvious that it hardly merits attention, but it is worth mentioning for two reasons. First, obvious solution strategies are the ones that are most often overlooked. Second, it is a very effective solution strategy (Renkl, Hilbert, & Schworm, 2009). The beneficial effect is thought to be due to the learners' acquisition of a general problem schema. To get the most out of this heuristic, use multiple examples and different formats for each problem type and encourage learners to explain to themselves the problem-solving strategy illustrated by the examples (Atkinson, Derry, Renkl, & Wortham, 2000; Kalyuga, 2009).

Solve simpler version of problem first; then transfer process to harder problem

- *Work on a simpler version of the problem.* This is another common and very effective approach. Geometry offers a particularly clear example of working on a simpler problem. If you are having difficulty solving a problem of solid geometry (which involves three dimensions), work out a similar problem in plane geometry (two dimensions) and then apply the solution to the three-dimensional example (Nickerson, 1994; Polya, 1957). Architects and engineers employ this approach when they construct scaled-down models of bridges, buildings, experimental aircraft, and the like. Scientists do the same thing by creating laboratory simulations of real-world phenomena.

Break complex problems into manageable parts

- *Break the problem into parts.* The key to this approach is to make sure you break the problem into manageable parts. Whether you can do this will depend largely on how much subject-matter knowledge you have. The more you know about the domain from which the problem comes, the easier it is to know how to break a problem into logical, easy-to-handle parts.

  At least two benefits result from breaking a problem into parts: (1) it reduces the amount of information you have to keep in short-term memory to a manageable level, and (2) the method used to solve one part of the problem can often be used to solve another part (Hilbert & Renkl, 2009). Bransford and Stein (1993) use the following example to illustrate how this approach works.

  Problem: What day follows the day before yesterday if two days from now will be Sunday?

  1. What is today if two days from now will be Sunday? (Friday)
  2. If today is Friday, what is the day before yesterday? (Wednesday)
  3. What day follows Wednesday? (Thursday)

Work backward when goal is clear but beginning state is not

- *Work backward.* This is a particularly good solution strategy to use whenever the goal is clear but the beginning state is not. Bransford and Stein (1993) offer the following example. Suppose you arranged to meet someone at a restaurant across town at noon. When should you leave your office to be sure of arriving on time? By working backward from your destination and arrival time (it takes about 10 minutes to find a parking spot and walk to the restaurant; it takes about 30 minutes to drive to the area where you would park; it takes about 5 minutes to walk from your office to your car), you would more quickly and

To figure out the solution to a problem, good problem solvers often work first on a simpler version of the problem. Good problem solvers also make use of external representations.
© Susie Fitzhugh

easily determine when to leave your office (about 11:15) than if you had worked the problem forward.

| Backward fading: a procedure that helps students develop problem-solving capability by reasoning from the solution back to first steps

- *Backward fading.* Students vary in how much they know about the subject matter on which the problems are based, and students with more prior knowledge do better on problem-solving tests when they are given problem-solving instruction and practice than when they are given worked examples to study (Atkinson et al., 2000; Paas & van Gog, 2009). For these reasons, a good procedure to use with all students is something called *backward fading*. Backward fading is basically a combination of studying worked examples, working backward, and practicing solving problems. First, a completely worked-out example (such as one that requires three steps to complete) is provided. Then a similar problem is presented with only the first two steps worked out. The last step has to be completed by the learner. A third problem provides the solution to the first step and requires the learner to determine the solution for steps two and three. Finally, the fourth problem requires the learner to solve all three steps. Compared with peers who saw ordinary worked examples and practiced solving problems, a group of college students who were exposed to the backward fading procedure scored significantly better on problems that were both similar to and different from the practice problems (Atkinson, Renkle, & Merrill, 2003).

| Solve a similar problem and then apply the same method

- *Solve an analogous problem.* If you are having difficulty solving a problem, possibly because your knowledge of the subject matter is incomplete, it may be useful to think of a similar problem about a subject in which you are more knowledgeable (Hoffman & Schraw, 2009). Solve the analogous problem, and then use the same method to solve the first problem. In essence, this is a way of making the unfamiliar familiar.

    Although solving analogous problems is a very powerful solution strategy, it can be difficult to employ, especially for novices. In our previous discussion of understanding the problem, we made the point that novices represent problems on the basis of superficial features, whereas experts operate from knowledge of underlying concepts and principles. The same is true of analogies. Most of us know that DNA is somehow related to the image of a "twisted ladder" called the *double helix*, but there is much more to mapping the human genome than visualizing a twisted ladder. Novices are more likely than experts to use superficial analogies (Gick, 1986). Analogous problems are discussed in the upcoming Suggestions for Teaching and in the Resources for Further Investigation at the end of the chapter.

| Create an external representation of the problem

- *Create an external representation of the problem.* This heuristic is doubly useful because it also aids in problem framing. Many problems can be represented as pictures, equations, graphs, flowcharts, and the like (Mueller, 2009). The figures in the next Suggestions for Teaching section illustrate how a pictorial or symbolic form of representation can help one both understand and solve the problem (Martinez, 1998).

Step 5: Evaluate the Solution The last step in the problem-solving process is to evaluate the adequacy of the solution. For relatively simple, well-structured problems in which the emphasis is on producing a correct response, two levels of evaluation are available:

| Evaluate solutions to well-structured problems by estimating or checking

- The problem solver can ask whether, given the problem statement, the answer makes sense. For example, if the problem reads $75 \times 5 = ?$ and the response is 80, a little voice inside the problem solver's head should say that the answer cannot possibly be right. This signal should prompt a reevaluation of the way the problem was represented and the solution procedure that was used (for example, "I misread the times sign as a plus sign and added when I should have multiplied").
- The problem solver can use an alternative algorithm to check the accuracy of the solution. This is necessary because an error in carrying out an algorithm can produce an incorrect response that is still in the ballpark. For example, a

common error in multiple-column subtraction problems is to subtract a smaller digit from a larger one regardless of whether the small number is in the minuend (top row) or the subtrahend (bottom row) (Mayer, 1987), as in

$$\begin{array}{r} 522 \\ -418 \\ \hline 116 \end{array}$$

Because this answer is off by only 12 units, it "looks right." The flaw can be discovered, however, by adding the answer to the subtrahend to produce the minuend.

The evaluation of solutions to ill-structured problems is likely to be more complicated and time-consuming for at least two reasons. First, the evaluation should occur both before and after the solution is implemented. Although many flaws and omissions can be identified and corrected beforehand, some will slip through. There is much to be learned by observing the effects of our solutions. Second, because these ill-structured problems are complex, often involving a dozen or more variables, some sort of systematic framework should guide the evaluation. Vincent Ruggiero suggests a four-step procedure (1988, pp. 44–46):

1. Ask and answer a set of basic questions. Imagine, for example, that you have proposed a classroom incentive system (a token economy, perhaps) to enhance student motivation. You might ask such questions as, How will this program be implemented? By whom? When? Where? With what materials? How will the materials be obtained?

2. Identify imperfections and complications. Is this idea, for example, safe, convenient, efficient, economical, and compatible with existing policies and practices?

3. Anticipate possible negative reactions from other people. For instance, might parents or the school principal object?

4. Devise improvements.

The next section contains guidelines and examples that will help you improve the problem-solving skills of your students.

pause & reflect

Critics of American education argue that students are poor problem solvers because they receive little systematic instruction in problem-solving processes. How would you rate the instruction you received in problem solving? In terms of the five steps discussed on the preceding pages, which ones were you taught? What can you do to ensure that your students become good problem solvers?

Suggestions for Teaching

Teaching Problem-Solving Techniques

1 Teach students how to identify problems.

Because the notion of finding problems is likely to strike students as an unusual activity, you may want to introduce this skill in gradual steps. One way to start is to have students list different ways in which problems can be identified. Typical responses are to scan newspaper and magazine articles, observe customer and employee behavior in a store, watch traffic patterns in a local area, and interview local residents, including, for instance, teachers, business owners, police, clergy, or government officials. A next step is to have students carry out these suggested activities to gain an understanding of the status quo and to find out how people identify problems. They may learn, for example, that a principal periodically has lunch with a teacher to learn of conditions that decrease the teacher's effectiveness.

2 **Teach students how to represent problems.**

Problem representation involves transforming the words that express a problem into an internal representation of those words. To do this, students must understand the concepts embedded in the problem statement and the relationships among those concepts. Consequently, the ability to construct a good representation of a problem is based on a command of the subject matter surrounding the problem and familiarity with the particular type of problem.

| Comprehension of subject matter critical to problem solving

As the work of Jerome Bruner and David Ausubel indicates, students need to acquire a genuine understanding of many of the associations, discriminations, concepts, and rules of a discipline before they can effectively solve problems in that subject-matter area. Too often, students are taught to state principles on cue, but they reveal by further responses that they do not understand what they are saying. The recommendations we make in this book about presenting information in an organized fashion and in meaningful contexts will go a long way toward helping students understand the subject matter on which problems are based; see the specific suggestions in Chapters 8 and 13.

The classic illustration of what can occur when information is not learned meaningfully was given over a century ago by William James in his *Talks to Teachers:*

> A friend of mine, visiting a school, was asked to examine a young class in geography. Glancing at the book, she said: "Suppose you should dig a hole in the ground, hundreds of feet deep, how should you find it at the bottom—warmer or colder than on top?" None of the class replying, the teacher said: "I'm sure they know, but I think you don't ask the question quite rightly. Let me try." So, taking the book, she asked: "In what condition is the interior of the globe?" and received the immediate answer from half the class at once: "The interior of the globe is in a condition of igneous fusion." (1899, p. 150)

If these students had genuinely understood concepts and principles regarding the composition of the earth (such as the relationship between igneous fusion and heat), instead of having simply memorized meaningless phrases, they would have been able to answer the original question.

Once you are satisfied that students meaningfully understand the elements of a problem, you can demonstrate methods to represent those elements and how they interrelate. One frequent recommendation is to use visual forms of problem representation (concept maps, Venn diagrams, flowcharts, and drawings, for example). Visual representations of ideas foster comprehension because of their concreteness. The following two examples illustrate how a Venn diagram (a set of intersecting circles) and a flow diagram can represent a particular type of problem.

EXAMPLE PROBLEM

The government wants to contact all druggists, all gun store owners, and all parents in a town without contacting anyone twice. Based on the following statistics, how many people must be contacted?

Druggists	10
Gun store owners	5
Parents	3,000
Druggists who own gun stores	0
Druggists who are parents	7
Gun store owners who are parents	3

Suggestions for Teaching

Solution Using Venn Diagram

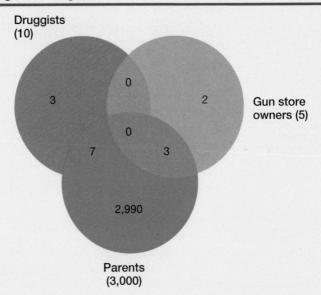

As the Venn diagram illustrates, the total number of people who must be contacted is 2,990 + 7 + 3 + 3 + 2 = 3,005 (adapted from Whimbey & Lochhead, 1999, p. 104).[1]

EXAMPLE PROBLEM

Sally loaned $7.00 to Betty. But Sally borrowed $15.00 from Estella and $32.00 from Joan. Moreover, Joan owes $3.00 to Estella and $7.00 to Betty. One day the women got together at Betty's house to straighten out their accounts. Which woman left with $18.00 more than she came with?

Solution Using Flow Diagram

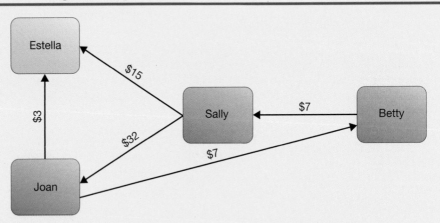

Verbal reasoning problems that describe transactions can take the form of a flow diagram, as shown here. From the diagram, it is clear that Estella left with $18.00 more than she came with (adapted from Whimbey & Lochhead, 1999, p. 128).

---

[1]Excerpts and diagrams in this section are from "Solution Using Venn Diagram," adapted from A. Whimbey and J. Lochhead, *Problem Solving and Comprehension*, Sixth Edition (Mahwah, NJ: Lawrence Erlbaum Associates, Inc., Publishers), pp. 104, 128. © 1999 reprinted by permission.

3 Teach students how to compile relevant information.

Good problem solvers start with themselves when compiling information to solve a problem or evidence to support a position on an issue. They recognize the importance of recalling earlier-learned information (metacognitive knowledge) and are adept at doing so (cognitive skill). Poor problem solvers, by contrast, lack metacognitive knowledge, cognitive skills, or both. If their deficiency is metacognitive, they make little or no effort to recall solution-relevant memories, even when the information was recently learned, because they do not understand the importance of searching long-term memory for potentially useful knowledge. Even if a student poor in problem solving recognizes the value of searching long-term memory for relevant information, he may still be handicapped because of inadequate encoding and retrieval skills.

To minimize any metacognitive deficiency, make sure your instruction in problem-solving methods emphasizes the importance of retrieving and using previously learned knowledge. To minimize retrieval problems, make sure you recall and implement the Suggestions for Teaching section that we offered in Chapter 8.

If a student does not possess all the relevant information needed to work out a solution or analyze an issue, you will have to guide her toward individuals and sources that can help. In referring students to individuals, select people who are judged to be reasonably knowledgeable about the subject, are careful thinkers, and are willing to share their ideas (Ruggiero, 1988, 2009). As an example, consider the issue of whether certain books (such as the novels *Catcher in the Rye* by J. D. Salinger, *I Know Why the Caged Bird Sings* by Maya Angelou, *Native Son* by Richard Wright, and *Tom Sawyer* by Mark Twain) should be banned from a school's reading list. In interviewing a knowledgeable person, students might ask questions such as the following because they allow some insight into the individual's reasoning process and the evidence used to support his position:

- What general effects do you think characters in novels who rebel against adult authority have on a reader's behavior?
- Are certain groups of people, such as middle and high school students, likely to be influenced by the motives and actions of such characters? Why do you think so?
- Does a ban on a certain book violate the author's right to free speech?
- Does a book ban violate the principle of academic freedom? Why?
- Is it the proper role of a school board to prevent or discourage students from exposure to certain ideas during school hours?

If a reasonably informed person is not available, recognized authorities can often be interviewed by phone. If a student chooses this tactic, Ruggiero suggests calling or writing in advance for an appointment, preparing questions in advance, and asking permission to tape-record the interview.

Obviously, in addition to or in lieu of personal interviews, students can find substantial information in a good library. For example, you can steer them toward books by recognized authorities, research findings, court cases, and interviews with prominent individuals in periodicals. Although the Internet potentially contains a vast amount of information on any topic, warn students about using material gathered there indiscriminately. As with any other medium, there are more and less reliable sources, and only material from reputable sources should be gathered. One additional benefit is that an extra layer of problem-solving activity is introduced when students must decide how to gather and evaluate online information.

4 Teach several methods for formulating problem solutions.

Previously, we mentioned seven methods for formulating a problem solution: study worked examples, work on a simpler version of the problem, break the problem into

More ideas for your journal can be found in the Reflective Journal Questions at the textbook's student website, Education CourseMate.

parts, work backward, use backward fading, solve an analogous problem, and create an external representation of the problem. At the end of the chapter, under Resources for Further Investigation, we recommend several recently published books on problem solving that, taken together, provide numerous examples of each method. We encourage you to check out one or more of those references and other sources as demonstrations of worked problems and as opportunities for you to practice your own problem-solving skills so that you will be well prepared to teach each of these seven methods.

5   **Teach students the skills of evaluation.**

Solutions to well-structured problems are usually evaluated through the application of an estimating or checking routine. Such procedures can be found in any good mathematics text. The evaluation of solutions to ill-structured problems and analyses of issues, however, is more complex and is less frequently taught. Ruggiero (1988, 2009) discusses the following 10 habits and skills as contributing to the ability to evaluate complex solutions and positions:

- Being open-minded about opposing points of view.
- Selecting proper criteria of evaluation. Violations of this skill abound. A current example is the use of standardized achievement test scores to evaluate the quality of classroom instruction.
- Understanding the essence of an argument. To foster this skill, Ruggiero recommends that students be taught how to write a *précis,* which is a concise summary of an oral argument or a reading passage.
- Evaluating the reliability of sources.
- Properly interpreting factual data (for example, recognizing that an increase in a state's income tax rate from 4 to 6 percent is an increase not of 2 percent but of 50 percent).
- Testing the credibility of hypotheses. On the basis of existing data, hypotheses can range from highly improbable to highly probable.
- Making important distinctions (for instance, between preference and judgment, emotion and content, appearance and reality).
- Recognizing unstated assumptions (for example, that because two events occur close together in time, one causes the other; that what is clear to us will be clear to others; that if the majority believes something, it must be true).
- Evaluating the validity and truthfulness of one's arguments (by, for example, checking that conclusions logically follow from premises and that conclusions have not been influenced by such reasoning flaws as either-or thinking, overgeneralizing, or oversimplifying).
- Recognizing when evidence is insufficient.

All of these 10 skills can be modeled and taught in your classroom.

TRANSFER OF LEARNING

Throughout this chapter and preceding ones, we have indicated that classroom instruction should be arranged in such a way that students independently apply the knowledge and problem-solving skills they learn in school to similar but new situations. This capability is the main goal of problem-solving instruction and is typically valued very highly by educators (Craig, Chi, & VanLehn, 2009; De Corte, 2003). Referred to as **transfer of learning,** it is the essence of being an autonomous learner and problem solver, both in and out of school (Pugh & Bergin, 2005). In this section, we will examine the nature of transfer and discuss ways in which you can help bring it about.

The Nature and Significance of Transfer of Learning

The Theory of Identical Elements During the early 1900s, it was common practice for high schools and colleges to require that students take such subjects as Latin, Greek, and geometry. Because they were considered difficult topics to learn, mastery of them was expected to improve a student's ability to memorize, think, and reason. These enhanced abilities were then expected to facilitate the learning of less difficult subjects. The rationale behind this practice was that the human mind, much like any muscle in the body, could be exercised and made stronger. A strong mind, then, would learn things that a weak mind would not. This practice, known as the *doctrine of formal discipline*, constituted an early (and incorrect) explanation of transfer (Barnett & Ceci, 2002; Haag & Stern, 2003).

In 1901, Edward Thorndike and Robert Woodworth proposed an alternative explanation of how transfer occurs. They argued that the degree to which knowledge and skills acquired in learning one task can help someone learn another task depends on how similar the two tasks are (if we assume that the learner recognizes the similarities). The greater the degree of similarity is between the tasks' stimulus and response elements (as in riding a bicycle and riding a motorcycle), the greater the amount of transfer will be. This idea became known as the **theory of identical elements** (Wohldmann, Healy, & Bourne, 2008).

Early view of transfer based on degree of similarity between two tasks

Positive, Negative, and Zero Transfer In time, however, other psychologists (among them Ellis, 1965; Osgood, 1949) identified different types of transfer and the conditions under which each type prevailed. A useful distinction was made among positive transfer, negative transfer, and zero transfer (Osman, 2008).

The discussion up to this point has been alluding to **positive transfer,** defined as a situation in which prior learning aids subsequent learning. According to Thorndike's analysis, positive transfer occurs when a new learning task calls for essentially the same response that was made to a similar, earlier-learned task. The accomplished accordion player, for instance, probably will become a proficient pianist faster than someone who knows how to play the drums or someone who plays no musical instrument at all, all other things being equal. Similarly, the native English speaker who is also fluent in French is likely to have an easier time learning Spanish than is someone who speaks no foreign language.

Positive transfer: previous learning makes later learning easier

Negative transfer is defined as a situation in which prior learning interferes with subsequent learning. It occurs when two tasks are highly similar but require different responses. A tennis player learning how to play racquetball, for example, may encounter problems at first because of a tendency to swing the racquetball racket as if it were a tennis racket. Primary grade children often experience negative transfer when they encounter words that are spelled alike but pronounced differently (as in "I will *read* this story now since I *read* that story last week").

Negative transfer: previous learning interferes with later learning

Zero transfer is defined as a situation in which prior learning has no effect on new learning. It can be expected when two tasks have different stimuli and different responses. Learning to conjugate Latin verbs, for example, is not likely to have any effect on learning how to find the area of a rectangle.

Specific and General Transfer The preceding description of positive transfer, although useful, is somewhat limiting because it is unclear whether transfer from one task to another is due to specific similarities or to more general similarities (Cornoldi, 2010). Psychologists decide whether transfer is due to specific or general factors by setting up learning tasks such as the following for three different but equivalent groups of learners.

	Initial Task	Transfer Task
Group 1	Learn French	Learn Spanish
Group 2	Learn Chinese	Learn Spanish
Group 3	Learn Spanish	

If on a Spanish test, group 1 scores higher than group 2, the difference is attributed to **specific transfer** of similarities between French and Spanish (such as vocabulary, verb conjugations, and sentence structure). If groups 1 and 2 score the same but both outscore group 3, the difference is attributed to nonspecific transfer, or **general transfer,** of similarities between the two tasks because Chinese shares no apparent specific characteristics with French or Spanish, both Romance languages. In this case, it is possible that learners use cognitive strategies—such as imagery, verbal elaboration, and mnemonic devices—when learning a foreign language and that these transfer to the learning of other foreign languages. Such nonspecific transfer effects have also been demonstrated for other classroom tasks, such as problem solving and learning from text (Cornoldi, 2010; Royer, 1979).

Support for specific transfer, as well as for the identical elements theory, comes from a study of college students in Germany who had taken either French or Latin as their second foreign language when they were in seventh grade. At the time of the study, these students were enrolled in an intensive beginners' course in Spanish. On a written test that required the students to translate a passage into Spanish, those who had taken French several years earlier made significantly fewer grammar and vocabulary errors than did students who had taken Latin (Haag & Stern, 2003).

Near and Far Transfer Another common distinction, similar to the specific/general distinction, is based on the perceived similarity of the original learning task to the transfer task. **Near transfer** refers to situations in which the knowledge domains are highly similar, the settings in which the original learning and transfer tasks occur are basically the same, and the elapsed time between the two tasks is relatively short. **Far transfer** occurs when the knowledge domains and settings are judged to be dissimilar and the time between the original learning and transfer tasks is relatively long (Rosen, 2009). Thus using math skills one acquired over the past several weeks to solve the problems at the end of the current chapter in a textbook is an example of near transfer. Using those same skills several years later to determine which of several investment options is most likely to produce the highest rate of return is an example of far transfer.

You may have noticed our use of such imprecise and subjective terms as "highly similar," "basically the same," "relatively long," and "judged to be dissimilar." This is

Marginal notes:

Specific transfer: due to specific similarities between two tasks

General transfer: due to use of same cognitive strategies

Near transfer: previously learned knowledge and skills used relatively soon on highly similar task

Far transfer: previously learned knowledge and skills used much later on dissimilar tasks and under different conditions

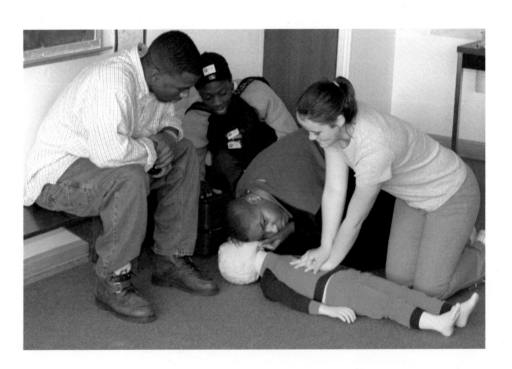

If teachers want students to apply what they learn in the classroom in other settings in the future, they should create tasks and conditions that are similar to those that students will encounter later.
© Steve Skjold/Alamy

done for a good reason. At present, there is no way to precisely measure the similarity between a learning task and a transfer task. The best we can do is identify the major dimensions that two tasks share (such as subject matter, physical setting, time between two tasks, and the conditions under which each is performed) and subjectively decide that the two dimensions are sufficiently similar or dissimilar to warrant the label *near transfer* or *far transfer*. Sometimes this approach produces a high degree of agreement, but at other times one person's far transfer is another person's near transfer (Barnett & Ceci, 2002).

Contemporary Views of Specific/Near and General/Far Transfer

Gavriel Salomon and David Perkins (1989) combine aspects of specific and near transfer and general and far transfer under the labels *low-road transfer* and *high-road transfer*, respectively.

Low-Road Transfer **Low-road transfer** refers to a situation in which a previously learned skill or idea is almost automatically retrieved from memory and applied to a highly similar current task. For example, a student who has mastered the skill of two-column addition and correctly completes three-column and four-column addition problems with no prompting or instruction is exhibiting low-road transfer. Another example is a student who learns how to tune up car engines in an auto shop class and then almost effortlessly and automatically carries out the same task as an employee of an auto repair business. As you may have suspected, low-road transfer is basically a contemporary version of Thorndike and Woodworth's identical elements theory (King, Bellocchi, & Ritchie, 2008).

| | Low-road transfer: previously learned skill automatically applied to similar current task |

Two conditions need to be present for low-road transfer to occur:

1. Students have to be given ample opportunities to practice using the target skill.
2. Practice has to occur with different materials and in different settings. The more varied the practice is, the greater is the range of tasks to which the skill can be applied.

If, for example, you want students to be good note takers, give them instruction and ample practice at taking notes from their biology, health, and English textbooks. Once they become accomplished note takers in these subjects, they will likely apply this skill to other subjects in an almost automatic fashion.

In essence, what we are describing is the behavioral principle of generalization. Because the transfer task is similar in one or more respects to the practice task and tends to occur in similar settings, low-road transfer is similar to specific and near transfer.

High-Road Transfer **High-road transfer** refers to the ways people transfer prior knowledge and skills over longer time periods to new situations that look rather different from the original task. High-road transfer involves the conscious, controlled, somewhat effortful formulation of an "abstraction" (that is, a rule, a schema, a strategy, or an analogy) that allows a connection to be made between two tasks (King, Bellocchi, & Ritchie, 2008). For example, an individual who learns to set aside a certain number of hours every day to complete homework assignments and study for upcoming exams formulates the principle that the most efficient way to accomplish a task is to break it down into small pieces and work at each piece according to a set schedule. As an adult, the individual uses this principle to deal successfully with complex tasks at work and at home.

As another example, imagine a student who, after much observation and thought, has finally developed a good sense of what school is and how one is supposed to behave there. This student has developed a school schema. Such a schema would probably be made up of actors (teachers and students), objects (desks, books, computers), and events (reading, listening, writing, talking, drawing). Because this is

Take a Stand!

If You Want Transfer, Then Teach for Transfer

From the elementary grades through graduate school, you will find teachers who believe that it is perfectly acceptable to provide students with basic explanations and examples of concepts and procedures during classroom instruction and then test them on their ability to answer more advanced questions or solve more difficult problems. Their intuitively appealing rationale is that if the students are paying attention in class, carefully reading the textbook, and diligently doing the assigned homework, they will be able to make the jump from the simpler, lower-level classroom examples to the more difficult and advanced test items.

We hope you have learned from the discussion of transfer in this chapter that nothing could be further from the truth. Students have to be exposed to the same types of concepts, problems, and procedures during instruction that they will be held accountable for on an exam, and they may even have to be prompted on the exam to use the knowledge they were taught. In other words, if you want transfer, then teach for transfer. Give your students opportunities to use what they learn in new situations. If you expect transfer to occur spontaneously, like so many other teachers, you will be disappointed most of the time.

What Do You Think?

What are your own experiences with teachers who expect transfer to occur automatically? To investigate this subject further, see the Take a Stand! section of the textbook's student website, Education CourseMate.

For help in remembering the key terms introduced in this chapter, you may want to use the interactive flashcards at the Education CourseMate website.

an idealized abstraction, actual classrooms may contain fewer or greater numbers of these characteristics in varying proportions. Even so, with this schema, a student could walk into any instructional setting (another school classroom, a training seminar, or a press briefing, for example) and readily understand what was going on, why it was going on, and how one should behave. Of course, with repeated applications of schemata, rules, strategies, and the like, the behaviors become less conscious and more automatic. What was once a reflection of high-road transfer becomes low-road transfer.

Researchers (e.g., Bereiter, 1997; Lim, Reiser, Olina, 2009; Salomon & Perkins, 1989) refer to this deliberate, conscious, effortful formulating of a general principle or schema that can be applied to a variety of different-looking but fundamentally similar tasks as *mindful abstraction*. The *mindful* part of the phrase indicates that the abstraction must be thought about and fully understood for high-road transfer to occur. That is, people must be aware of what they are doing and why they are doing it. This is essentially training in metacognition. Recall our earlier discussion in this chapter of inert knowledge and Richard Feynman's observations of how his classmates at the Massachusetts Institute of Technology failed to recognize the application of a previously learned mathematical formula because it was initially learned for use only in that course. Carl Bereiter (1997) argues that when learning is too strongly situated in a particular context, as in the case of Feynman's MIT classmates, high-road transfer is impeded.

Teaching for Low-Road and High-Road Transfer   As we noted at the beginning of this section, transfer of previously learned knowledge and skill to new tasks and settings is a goal that is high on almost every teacher's list. Yet one study of classroom activity found that only 7 percent of tasks required students to use information they had learned previously (Bennett, Desforges, Cockburn, & Wilkinson, 1984). Perhaps most teachers feel they simply don't know how to teach for transfer. That need not be your fate. The following guidelines (based on Cox, 1997; De Corte, 2003; Lim, Reiser, Olina, 2009; Salomon & Perkins, 1989) should produce greater levels of both low-road and high-road transfer:

1. Provide students with multiple opportunities for varied practice to help them develop a rich web of interrelated concepts.
2. Give students opportunities to solve problems that are similar to those they will eventually have to solve, and establish conditions similar to those they will eventually face.
3. Teach students how to formulate, for a variety of tasks, general rules, strategies, or schemes that they can use in the future with a variety of similar problems.
4. Give students cues that will allow them to retrieve from memory earlier-learned information that can be used to make current learning easier.
5. Teach students to focus on the beneficial effects of creating and using rules and strategies to solve particular kinds of problems.

> Low-road and high-road transfer produced by varied practice at applying skills, rules, memory retrieval cues

TECHNOLOGY TOOLS FOR KNOWLEDGE CONSTRUCTION AND PROBLEM SOLVING

Previously in the book, we noted that one use of computers in schools is as a learning and problem-solving tool. This use of computer-based technology supports a constructivist approach to learning and is often called learning *with* computers (Jonassen, Howland, Moore, Marra, & Crismond, 2008; Rosen, 2009). Students learn with computers when computers support knowledge construction, exploration, learning by doing, learning by conversing, and learning by reflecting.

The term *mindtools* refers to computer applications that lend themselves to these types of activities. Mindtools include databases, semantic networks (concept mapping programs), spreadsheets, expert systems (artificial intelligence), microworlds, search engines, visualization tools, hypermedia, and computer conferencing (Jonassen et al., 2008). Rather than using computer programs just to present and represent information more efficiently, which is what drill and tutorial programs do, mindtools allow learners to construct, share, and revise knowledge in more open-ended environments. In effect, learners become producers, designers, and "authors of knowledge" (Moos & Azevedo, 2009).

A basic principle of constructivism is that meaningful learning involves learning by doing, as opposed to learning just by reading and/or listening. Because actual hands-on experience is not always feasible, computer-based simulation programs can be used as the next best thing. But learning by doing, particularly in the context of computer simulations, seems to work best when accompanied by careful and appropriate scaffolding (Mayer, Mautone, & Prothero, 2002). We examine two highly researched online learning environments that provide different forms of scaffolding. The first is Computer-Supported Intentional Learning Environments, which has evolved into Knowledge Forum. The second is a game-based learning environment called Quest Atlantis.

> Technology tools are available to help students construct knowledge, become better problem solvers

Computer-Supported Intentional Learning Environments (Knowledge Forum)

Marlene Scardamalia and Carl Bereiter (1996, p. 10) ask us to "imagine a network of networks—people from schools, universities, cultural institutions, service organizations, businesses—simultaneously building knowledge within their primary groups while advancing the knowledge of others. We might call such a community network a knowledge-building society." Since the 1980s these researchers have developed and tested aspects of such a network with the Computer-Supported Intentional Learning Environments (CSILE) project (Scardamalia & Bereiter, 1991).

The CSILE project is built around the concept of intentional learning (Scardamalia & Bereiter, 1991). In an intentional learning environment, students learn how to set goals, generate and interrelate new ideas, link new knowledge to old, negotiate meaning with peers, and relate what they learned to other tasks. The product of these activities, like the product of any scientific inquiry, is then made available to other students (Watkins, 2005).

The CSILE project allows students to create informational links, or "notes," in several ways (for example, text notes, drawings, graphs, pictures, timelines, and maps). CSILE also contains designated "cooperation" icons that encourage students to reflect on how their work links to others, as well as idea browsing and linking tools for marking notes that involve or intend cooperation. Using this database system, students comment on the work of others, read responses to their hypotheses, or search for information posted by their peers under a particular topic title. For instance, a search for the word *whales* would call up all the work of students who assigned that word as a keyword in their CSILE contributions. In such a decentralized, free-flowing environment, no longer must the teacher initiate all discussion and coordinate turn taking (Hewitt, 2002; Scardamalia & Bereiter, 1991, 1996). Jim Hewitt (2002) describes how a sixth-grade teacher used CSILE to gradually transform his instructional approach from being teacher directed and task centered to being collaborative and knowledge centered.

Studies show that students who use CSILE perform better on standardized language and reading tests, ask deeper questions, are more elaborate and coherent in their commentaries, demonstrate more mature beliefs about learning, and engage in discussions that are more committed to scientific progress (Scardamalia & Bereiter, 1996).

A version of CSILE for the Web, called Knowledge Forum, is also available. The goal of Knowledge Forum is to have students mimic the collaborative knowledge-building process that characterizes the work of expert learners. Consequently, students must label their contribution to a communal database topic prior to posting it by using such labels as *My Theory, I Need to Understand, New Information, This Theory Cannot Explain, A Better Theory,* and *Putting Our Knowledge Together.* So, if in the course of helping to build a knowledge base about human vision, a student wrote, "I need to understand why we have two eyes instead of one or three," another member of this community could post a New Information note that discussed the relationship between binocular vision and depth perception. The resulting knowledge base would then be subject to modifications and additions from others. A recent 3-year study of fourth-graders suggests that the Knowledge Forum supports the development of collective responsibility for learning and effective participation in a "knowledge-creating culture" (Zhang, Scardamalia, Reeve, & Messina, 2009). You can obtain more information about Knowledge Forum at **www.knowledgeforum.com.**

Use the web links section of this textbook's Education CourseMate website for convenient links to sites mentioned in this section.

Quest Atlantis: Gaming and Consequential Engagement

The first decade of the twenty-first century may well be remembered as the decade of what we call—at the time we are writing this—"new media." We may not call it "new media" for long, however, because *newer* media are being created all the time. Our terminology has a hard time keeping up with the technology. But one thing is certain, the first decade of the twenty-first century was when we began to see serious, extensive scholarship, research, and development on how new media influence learning and socialization. In November 2008, the MacArthur Foundation issued an influential report called *Living and Learning with New Media: Summary of Findings from the Digital Youth Project.* Among the report's conclusions is the following: "New media forms have altered how youth socialize and learn, and this raises a new set of issues that educators, parents, and policymakers should consider" (p. 2).

Among the issues raised by new media is gaming. Many educators worry that online games are a bad influence on today's youth. They worry that those who spend hours and hours in difficult, often frustrating, effort to gain access to a game's "next level" are wasting time that could be better spent reading books. Others worry that the content of online games sends negative social messages steeped in violence and sexual exploitation. But there are voices emerging from the worry that suggest that games provide effective learning environments (Barab & Dede, 2007). James Paul Gee (2007) published a collection of essays titled *Good Video Games and Good Learning.* Steven Johnson (2006) wrote a best-seller arguing that popular culture—including gaming and other new media—enhances rather than diminishes intellectual development. His book is called *Everything Bad Is Good for You.*

Among the increasing number of online gaming environments is one that we have mentioned in previous chapters and that deserves mention again in the context of constructivist learning theory and problem solving: Quest Atlantis (QA) (see Barab et al., 2009; Barab et al., 2009; Gresalfi, Barab, Siyahhan, & Christensen, 2009).

Sasha Barab, a founder of the QA project, and QA colleagues describe some key design features of QA as follows:

> Quest Atlantis is chiefly a virtual world housed on a central Internet server, accessible from school or home to children with online access, password permission, and the client software. As a multi-user virtual environment, Quest Atlantis immerses children in educational tasks in an adventure to save a fictional Atlantis from impending disaster. Participating as "Questers," children engage in the virtual environment and respond to associated inquiry-based challenges called Quests, and through these challenges, they help the Atlantian Council restore the lost wisdom of their civilization, one much like our own. The story line, associated structures, and governing policies constitute what is referred to in the commercial gaming sector as the metagame. Specifically, the Quest Atlantis metagame consists of several key elements:
>
> - A shared mythological context that establishes and supports program activities.
> - A set of online spaces in which children, mentors, and the Atlantian Council can interact with each other.
> - A well-defined advancement system centered on pedagogically valid activities that encourage academic and social learning.
> - Regalia and rewards associated with advancement and wisdom.
> - An individual homepage for each child, showing their advancement and serving as a portfolio of their work.
>
> Through this metacontext, the primary function of which is both structural (providing a cohesive framework) and motivational (providing an engaging context to stimulate participation and learning), Quests and member behaviors are targeted and instilled with meaning. However, in contrast to traditional role-playing games, one's game identity and activity depend on the child exiting the virtual environment to respond to Quests in the physical world. In this way, Quest Atlantis is not simply a "computer game" but incorporates "real-world" activities as well. (Barab, Dodge, Thomas, Jackson, & Tuzun, 2007, pp. 268–269)

Although the design of QA takes advantage of what has been learned from other online games, it also incorporates other features that are consistent with constructivist learning, in all of its variations. Looking through a cognitive lens, video and online games engage users. They spend many hours—often long stretches of time—in problem-solving mode: cognitively processing information and testing hypotheses to achieve a goal. QA's constructivist features can also be viewed through social and critical constructivist lenses.

Unlike most video and online games, QA forms a community through both its virtual space and through face-to-face interaction at Quest Atlantis Centers. For students to participate, they must be part of a particular QA Center such as a school, a museum, or an after-school program. Students and their teachers are registered formally as participants online and have access to materials that are used for "real world" learning activities in which they engage offline. The learning environments of "Questers" include collaboration with "virtual" others online and with teachers and students in their local QA Center.

One of the criticisms of commercial video and online games is that they advocate violence and other antisocial behavior. QA was designed to help learners develop an awareness of seven dimensions that, taken together, address constructivism in its social and critical forms (see Barab, et al., 2007). The seven dimensions, which are part of QA's "Project Mission," follow:

- Compassionate Wisdom: "Be Kind"
- Creative Expression: "I Create"
- Environmental Awareness: "Think Globally, Act Locally"
- Personal Agency: "I Have Voice"
- Healthy Communities: "Live, Love, Grow"
- Social Responsibility: "We Can Make a Difference"
- Diversity Affirmation: "Everyone Matters"

Constructivist learning requires that students be engaged actively in creating their own understanding of concepts and procedures and in developing their own problem-solving skills. As educational practice continues to evolve via the design and development of technological innovations, researchers are asking an essentially constructivist question: What are the features of an effective instructional design to support collaborative, creative learning? (Hong & Sullivan, 2009). Quest Atlantis— which has been well researched throughout its design and development—provides one answer to the question: **consequential engagement.**

As we have seen in the overview of QA above (and in descriptions from previous chapters), QA offers learners ways to engage actively in their learning. From a design standpoint, QA has sought to engage students at three levels: procedural, conceptual, and consequential. Procedural engagement refers to using procedures accurately, but using procedures does not necessarily mean that students understand why the procedures are important. (Have you ever memorized a formula for a test without really understanding why the formula was developed in the first place?) Conceptual engagement means more than rote use of a procedure; when learners are conceptually engaged, they understand why the procedure works, under what conditions it works, and why it has value.

Consequential engagement occurs when learners choose certain tools (a procedure or concept, for example) to understand and solve problems *and* when learners evaluate the effectiveness of the tools they have chosen. QA invites students to "inhabit roles and assume identities as they adopt conceptually-relevant intentions in a virtual world in which they make choices" (Gresalfi et al., 2009, p. 24). Having made choices of what to do, how to do it, and what tools to use, learners influence the situation in which they are learning. Building on an example from Gresalfi and her colleagues, suppose that you compared and contrasted Piaget's stages of cognitive development with Vygotsky's notion of scaffolding and decided to use heterogeneous grouping for a particular lesson. You've made the decision to use heterogeneous grouping; now what happens with that decision? If you are writing or answering a test question, you engage the procedure and the concepts to justify the decision in writing. But suppose you could implement your decision in a real or virtual classroom environment. Implementing your decision allows you to change the learning environment; you also have the opportunity to observe the effects of your decision within the real or virtual environment. Did the heterogeneous grouping work? What were the consequences of your decision?

Designing learning experiences that enhance consequential engagement contributes significantly to the active participation of learners in the construction of their own knowledge. QA is designed for "engaged participation" that affords learners procedural, conceptual, and—most critically— consequential engagement in contextually and conceptually rich learning environments. It has emerged as an exemplar of game-based curricula that are likely to influence the learning environments you will experience in your teaching career. Research on QA has shown significant learning gains on assessments that are oriented toward established standards and that are entirely independent of the QA curriculum. Perhaps even more important, both teachers and students who have participated in QA report "transformative personal experiences" that have led to increased motivation to pursue the curricular issues raised in QA outside of school. You can learn more about Quest Atlantis at **http://atlantis.crlt.indiana.edu.** See "Resources for Further Investigation" at the end of the chapter for information on how to apply for a guest account.

pause & reflect

This chapter argues that if teachers want transfer, they should teach for transfer. Go to the Quest Atlantis website and investigate overview materials, including the available videos. Do you think the "student quests" are likely to produce transfer? Why?

For help in reviewing this chapter, try the tutorial quizzes and other study aids on the textbook's Education CourseMate website.

Challenging Assumptions

What's the Problem?

At her next observation of Celeste's physics class, Connie notes that Celeste guides her students through the five-step approach designed to help students become good problem solvers. In particular, Connie notes that the students are very interested in the first step: problem finding. As the class ended, Celeste joins Connie to debrief the lesson.

"That went much better," says Celeste. "It was really fun and I think the students got a lot out of it."

"I think so, too," says Connie. "It's important for us to understand that learning is not something we can *give* our students; it is something they must do for themselves. They have to construct their own understandings and develop their own skills for those understandings and skills to be useful to them. They need to become self-regulated learners. But it is also important for us to realize that construction is not *invention*. There is plenty of research to suggest that constructing understanding and developing skill are tasks better done with others. And the teacher is a very critical construction supervisor."

"That makes sense," says Celeste. "I think one of the reasons the students were so interested in problem finding today was that they were so confused by the last class."

"Good point." says Connie. "Perhaps their earlier confusion provided the impetus for their engagement today. Curiosity and dissatisfaction—what Piaget called *disequilibrium*—does not have to be a bad thing in the classroom: it can lead to problems! And problems, once found, are opportunities for learning."

Summary

1. The constructivist view of learning holds that meaningful learning occurs when people use existing knowledge schemes and the viewpoints of others to interpret the world around them.

2. During the 1960s, Jerome Bruner proposed a constructivist view of learning that relied on giving students realistic problems for which they had to discover appropriate solutions. Contemporary approaches to discovery learning frequently use computer simulation programs to help students grasp basic concepts and skills.

3. The major aspects of constructivism are that meaningful learning occurs when people actively construct personal knowledge structures, that only part of a teacher's understanding of some concept or issue can be transferred to students through direct instruction, that the knowledge structures of different people have much in common, and that the formation and changing of knowledge structures come mainly from peer interaction.

4. A cognitive constructivist view, such as that of Piaget, focuses on how individuals' cognitive processes influence the view of the world they construct.

5. A social constructivist view, such as that of Vygotsky, focuses on how social processes influence the view of reality that students construct.

6. A critical constructivist view focuses on cultural myths and how they affect interactions in the learning environment.

7. Three conditions that support constructivism are a cognitive apprenticeship between teacher and student, the use of realistic learning tasks (situated learning), and exposure to multiple perspectives.

8. The situated learning condition can be met by using a problem-based approach to learning.

9. The classroom discussion is an instructional technique that teachers can use to support a constructivist view of meaningful learning, for it allows students to share different perspectives of realistic problems.

10. A problem exists when a learner has a goal but no means of reaching the goal. Problem solving involves identifying and using knowledge and skills that result in achieving one's goal.

11. The types of problems that students most often come into contact with are well-structured problems, ill-structured problems, and issues. Well-structured problems are clearly stated and

can be solved by applying previously learned procedures, and their solutions can be accurately evaluated. Ill-structured problems are often vaguely stated, they cannot always be solved by applying previously learned procedures, and their solutions cannot always be evaluated against clear and widely accepted criteria. Issues are like ill-structured problems, but with two differences: they arouse strong emotions that tend to divide people into opposing camps, and they require that one determine the most reasonable position to take before working out a solution.

12. A general problem-solving model is composed of five steps: realize that a problem exists, understand the nature of the problem, compile relevant information, formulate and carry out a solution, and evaluate the solution.

13. Understanding the nature of a problem, also known as problem representation or problem framing, requires a high level of knowledge about the subject matter surrounding the problem and familiarity with the particular type of problem.

14. A problem solver can compile relevant information by searching long-term memory, retrieving solution-relevant information, and representing that information as lists, tables, pictures, graphs, diagrams, and so on. In addition, friends, colleagues, and experts can be tapped for information.

15. A problem solver can formulate solutions by studying worked examples, working on a simpler version of the problem, breaking the problem into parts, working backward, backward fading, solving an analogous problem, or creating an external representation of the problem.

16. A problem solver can evaluate solutions for well-structured problems by estimating or checking. To evaluate solutions for ill-structured problems, the problem solver can answer a set of basic questions that deal with who, what, where, when, why, and how; identify imperfections and complications; anticipate possible negative reactions; and devise improvements.

17. Transfer of learning occurs when students apply knowledge and skills learned at one point in time and in a particular context to similar but different problems and tasks at a later point in time.

18. Positive transfer occurs when a new learning task is similar to a previously learned task and calls for a similar response. Negative transfer occurs when a new learning task is similar to a previously learned task but calls for a different response. Zero transfer occurs when previously learned information or skills are so dissimilar to new information or skills that they have no effect on how quickly the latter will be learned.

19. Positive transfer that is due to identifiable similarities between an earlier-learned task and a current one is referred to as specific transfer. Positive transfer that is due to the formulation, use, and carryover of cognitive strategies from one task to another is referred to as general transfer.

20. Near transfer occurs when the knowledge and skills that are acquired for a particular task are used relatively soon after for a highly similar task. Far transfer occurs when the knowledge and skills that are acquired for a particular task are used much later for another task that is dissimilar in appearance and represents a different knowledge domain.

21. A current view of specific transfer is called low-road transfer. This kind of transfer is produced by giving students many opportunities to practice a skill in different settings and with different materials.

22. A current view of general transfer is called high-road transfer. This kind of transfer is produced by teaching students how to formulate a general rule, strategy, or schema that can be used in the future with a variety of problems that are fundamentally similar to the original.

23. Students' knowledge construction and problem-solving skills can be improved by well-constructed digital games that engage students by helping them see the consequences of their decisions.

Resources for Further Investigation

● Constructivism

Bruce Marlow and Marilyn Page discuss the nature of constructivism and how to create a constructivist classroom in the second edition of *Creating and Sustaining the Constructivist Classroom* (2005). In a section of the preface titled "How This Book Is Different from Others," they discuss how the book synthesizes the theory and research with the practical issues that face both novice and experienced teachers in creating and sustaining a constructivist classroom.

Jerry Willis has edited *Constructivist Instructional Design: Foundations, Models, and Examples* (2009). The book includes discussions of constructivist theory and how it can be used to design instructional environments, including digital environments. Additionally, the book compares and contrasts different design models using examples to illustrate how theory can inform practice.

In the ninth edition of *Dynamic Social Studies for Constructivist Classrooms: Inspiring Tomorrow's Social Scientists*, George Maxim (2010) provides illustrations of constructivist principles in the social studies classroom. Chapter 3 of the book addresses standards that cross several content areas.

● Problem-Solving Processes

In *Problem Solving in Mathematics* (2009), Alfred Posamentier and Stephen Krulik discuss problem-solving strategies for elementary school math students. The book shows how to integrate the problem-solving strategies into existing math curricula.

In *The Art of Thinking* (9th ed., 2009), Vincent Ruggiero describes a four-part model for helping students become better thinkers and problem solvers. The chapters that describe each part ("Be Aware," "Be Creative," "Be Critical," "Communicate Your Ideas") are clearly written and contain a wealth of suggestions for classroom use.

In *Meaningful Learning with Technology* (3rd ed., 2008), David Jonassen, Jane Howland, Rose Marra, and David Crismond describe how technology can be used from a constructivist perspective to foster meaningful learning and problem solving. Included are chapters on learning from the Internet; use of such video-based technologies as television, camcorders, and videodiscs; learning with hypermedia; and virtual realities.

Teacher Tap is a professional development website that links teachers to resources regarding the use of technology in teaching and learning. (The site advises to "Start slow and let it flow!") The "technology-enhanced learning" resources page includes links that address project-, problem-, and inquiry-based learning (**http://eduscapes.com/tap/topic43.htm**).

● Transfer of Learning

Steve Trautman, in *Teach What You Know* (2007), discusses how to enhance the transfer of learning by using peer tutors. An examination of transfer from a variety of disciplinary perspectives is available in *Transfer of Learning from a Modern Multidisciplinary Perspective* (2005), edited by Jose Mestre.

● Technology Tools

As indicated earlier in the chapter, Quest Atlantis is a password-protected online environment. For those interested in exploring the metagame, Quest Atlantis, you can apply for a guest account at **http://atlantis.crlt.indiana.edu.** Details of the Digital Media and Learning Project of the MacArthur Foundation can be found in the book by Mizuko Ito and her colleagues, *Hanging Out, Messing Around, and Geeking Out: Kids Living and Learning with New Media* (2010).

Motivation and Perceptions of Self

The Education CourseMate website for this text offers many helpful resources. Go to **CengageBrain.com** to preview this chapter's Concept Maps and Chapter Themes.

KEY POINTS

These key points will help you learn the important information in this chapter. To help you study, they also appear in the margins of the pages, next to the text where they are discussed.

The Behavioral View of Motivation

- Behavioral view of motivation: reinforce desired behavior
- Extrinsic motivation: occurs when learner does something to earn external rewards
- Intrinsic motivation: occurs when learner does something to experience inherently satisfying results
- Excessive use of external rewards may lead to temporary behavior change, materialistic attitudes, decreased intrinsic motivation
- Intrinsic motivation enhanced when reward provides positive feedback, is available to all who qualify
- Intrinsic motivation undermined by forcing students to compete for limited supply of rewards
- Give rewards sparingly, especially on tasks of natural interest

The Social Cognitive View of Motivation

- Social cognitive view of motivation: observe and imitate admired models; raise self-efficacy
- Self-efficacy affects choice of goals, expectations of success, attributions for success and failure

Other Cognitive Views of Motivation

- Cognitive development view of motivation: strive for equilibration; master the environment
- Need for achievement revealed by desire to attain goals that require skilled performance
- High-need achievers prefer moderately challenging tasks
- Low-need achievers prefer very easy or very hard tasks
- Unsuccessful students attribute success to luck, easy tasks; failure, to lack of ability
- Successful students attribute success to effort, ability; failure, to lack of effort
- Students with incremental beliefs tend to have mastery goals and are motivated to learn meaningfully, improve skills

- Students with entity beliefs tend to have performance goals and are motivated to get high grades, avoid failure
- Personal interest marked by intrinsic desire to learn that persists over time; situational interest is context dependent and short term
 Flow experienced as intense engagement or absorbed concentration
- Often difficult to arouse cognitive disequilibrium
- Need for achievement difficult to assess on basis of short-term observations
- Faulty attributions difficult to change

The Humanistic View of Motivation

- People are motivated to satisfy deficiency needs only when those needs are unmet
- Self-actualization depends on satisfaction of lower needs, belief in certain values
- When deficiency needs not satisfied, person likely to make bad choices
- Encourage growth choices by enhancing attractions, minimizing dangers
- Teachers may be able to satisfy some deficiency needs but not others

The Role of Self-Perceptions in Motivation

- Self-esteem is global judgment we make of self; self-concept is judgment we make of self in specific domains; self-efficacy is belief in our ability to carry out a specific action
- Academic self-concept and achievement can positively affect each other
- Design instruction to improve both academic self-concept and achievement

Motivating Students with Technology

- Technology can be used to support both extrinsic and intrinsic motivation
- Technology increases intrinsic motivation by making learning more interesting and meaningful

Teaching is very much like putting together a puzzle. You first have to identify the pieces and then figure out how to construct them into a meaningful whole. This book is designed to help you identify the relevant pieces that make up the effective teaching puzzle and give you some ideas for using them in a coordinated fashion. In Part I, for example, you learned the importance of understanding how students develop socially, emotionally, and cognitively; what students are like at different ages; and how they differ from one another. In Part II, you were introduced to those pieces of the puzzle that pertain to the learning process and how different views of learning can be used to guide the type of instruction you provide. The puzzle pieces in this part deal with the importance of establishing a classroom environment that will motivate students to learn and of maintaining that positive atmosphere over time.

In this chapter, we address the question of why students strive (or don't strive) for academic achievement—that is, what motivates students? The importance of motivation was vividly pointed out by Larry Cuban, a Stanford University professor of education who returned to teach a high school class for one semester after a 16-year absence. Of this experience, he says, "If I wanted those students to be engaged intellectually, then every day—and I *do* mean *every* day—I had to figure out an angle, a way of making connections between whatever we were studying and their daily lives in school, in the community, or in the nation" (1990, pp. 480–481).

The senior author of this book remembers an instance from his days as a school psychologist that reinforces Cuban's observation. A teacher referred a ten-year-old student for testing and possible placement in a special education class (this was before the advent of inclusive classrooms) because the student's classroom performance, particularly in math, was very poor. On almost every test and homework assignment he received grades of F or D. Two pieces of evidence led to the conclusion that this student suffered more from lack of motivation than from intellectual deficits. First, his score on an individually administered intelligence test was average. Second, and most significant, he made pocket money in the evenings by keeping score for several bowling teams at the neighborhood bowling alley. Obviously, there was nothing wrong with this student's ability to learn or with his arithmetic skills!

Motivation can be defined as the selection, persistence, intensity, and direction of behavior (Fulmer & Frijters, 2009). In practical terms, motivation is simply the willingness of a person to expend a certain amount of effort to achieve a particular goal under a particular set of circumstances. Nevertheless, many teachers have at least two major misconceptions about motivation that prevent them from using this concept with maximum effectiveness. One misconception is that some students are unmotivated. Strictly speaking, that is not an accurate statement. As long as a student chooses goals and expends a certain amount of effort to achieve them, she is, by definition, motivated. What teachers really mean is that students are not motivated to behave in the way teachers would like them to behave. In other words, their motivation is negatively, rather than positively, oriented. The second misconception is that one person can directly motivate another. This view is inaccurate because motivation comes from within a person. What you *can* do, with the help of the various motivation theories discussed in this chapter, is create the circumstances that *influence* students to do what you want them to do (Martin & Dowson, 2009; Matos, Lens, Vansteenkiste, 2009).

Many factors determine whether the students in your classes will be motivated or not motivated to learn. You should not be surprised to discover that no single theoretical interpretation of motivation explains all aspects of student interest or lack of it. Different theoretical interpretations do, however, shed light on why some students in a given learning situation are more likely to want to learn than others (Pressley, Gaskins, Solic, & Collins, 2006). Furthermore, each theoretical interpretation can help you develop techniques for motivating students in the classroom.

Revealing Assumptions

pause & reflect

Have you ever heard a teacher or professor say something similar to "I taught it, but students didn't learn it"? Such comments require us to view teaching as independent of learning. Are you willing to accept that proposition? Now consider the comment, "teachers can't motivate some students." The comment reveals an assumption that aspiring teachers sometimes make: teachers are the most important source of student motivation. How do you see your role with regard to student motivation? How do you think about the relationship between teaching and learning? What role does motivation play in that relationship?

Teaching . . . Learning . . . Motivation

"I was in the teachers' lounge," says Antonio, "and there were several teachers discussing the eighth graders. They were frustrated by the performance of the kids, especially in comparison to the group they had last year. After a while one of the teachers said something that has stuck in my head for the last 3 weeks. She said, 'I taught that unit extremely well, but the students just didn't learn it. Those kids are just not motivated.'"

"I heard something like that the other day," Celeste says. "We were having a discussion in class about instructional planning. One of the students described a history class she observed. She said the teacher was really outstanding and that she had never heard a better explanation of how years of legal strategy and political organizing resulted in the unanimous Supreme Court decision to desegregate schools. And then she said, 'This guy was doing some great teaching but the students just weren't interested.'"

"That sounds about right," says Don. "I think there will always be some kids that we just won't be able to motivate."

Connie draws in a big breath and exhales a long "hmmm." "Let's see," she says. "If it's true that something can be taught but not learned, then it follows that teaching is unconnected to learning. And if it's also true that there will always be some students whom we, as teachers, cannot motivate, then teachers must be the source of student motivation."

The group is silent for nearly a minute before Celeste says, "There's something wrong with this picture."

THE BEHAVIORAL VIEW OF MOTIVATION

Earlier in the text we noted that some psychologists explain learning from a theoretical perspective that focuses exclusively on the effects of observable stimuli, responses, and consequences on our propensity to exhibit particular behaviors. This approach is called operant conditioning, and its application to motivation has focused on the effect of reinforcement.

The Effect of Reinforcement

In Chapter 7 on behavioral learning theory, we discussed Skinner's emphasis on the role of reinforcement in learning. After demonstrating that organisms tend to repeat actions that are reinforced and that behavior can be shaped by reinforcement, Skinner developed the technique of programmed instruction to make it possible for students to be reinforced for every correct response. Supplying the correct answer—and being informed by the program that it *is* the correct answer—motivates the student to go on to the next frame, and as the student works through the program, the desired terminal behavior is progressively shaped.

Following Skinner's lead, many behavioral learning theorists devised techniques of behavior modification. Students are motivated to complete a task by being promised a reward of some kind. Many times, the reward takes the form of praise or a

Behavioral view of motivation: reinforce desired behavior

grade. Sometimes it is a token that can be traded in for some desired object, and at other times the reward may be the privilege of engaging in a self-selected activity.

Operant conditioning interpretations of learning help reveal why some students react favorably to particular subjects and dislike others. For instance, some students may enter a required math class with a feeling of delight, whereas others may feel that they have been sentenced to prison. Skinner suggests that such differences can be traced to past experiences. He would argue that the student who loves math has been shaped to respond that way by a series of positive experiences with math. The math hater, in contrast, may have suffered a series of negative experiences.

Limitations of the Behavioral View

Although approaches to motivation based on positive reinforcement are often useful, you should be aware of the disadvantages that can come from overuse or misuse of such techniques. Most of the criticisms of the use of reinforcement as a motivational incentive stem from the fact that it represents **extrinsic motivation.** That is, the learner decides to engage in an activity (such as participate in class, do homework, study for exams) to earn a reward that is not inherently related to the activity (such as praise from the teacher, a high grade, or the privilege of doing something different). By contrast, students under the influence of **intrinsic motivation** study a subject or acquire a skill because it produces such inherently positive consequences as becoming more knowledgeable, competent, and independent.

Although extrinsic motivation is widespread in society (individuals are motivated to engage in many activities because they hope to win certificates, badges, medals, public recognition, prizes, or admiration from others), this approach has at least three potential dangers (Covington, 2009; Kaufman & Beghetto, 2009; Kohn, 1999; 2006):

1. Changes in behavior may be temporary. As soon as the extrinsic reward has been obtained, the student may revert to such earlier behaviors as studying inconsistently, turning in poor-quality homework, and disrupting class with irrelevant comments and behaviors.
2. Students may develop a materialistic attitude toward learning. They may think (or say), "What tangible reward will I get if I agree to learn this information?" If the answer is "none," they may decide to make little or no effort to learn it.
3. Giving students extrinsic rewards for completing a task may lessen whatever intrinsic motivation they may have for that activity.

This last disadvantage, which is referred to as the *undermining effect,* has been extensively investigated by researchers (Akin-Little, Eckert, Lovett, & Little, 2004; Deci, Koestner, & Ryan, 1999, 2001; Marinak & Gambrell, 2008; Wiechman & Gurland, 2009). It appears that giving students rewards may indeed decrease their intrinsic motivation for a task, but only under certain conditions. Under other conditions, external rewards may enhance intrinsic motivation. Figure 11.1 summarizes recent research on this subject. Notice, in particular, that intrinsic motivation falls when students must compete for a limited supply of rewards. In contrast, intrinsic motivation rises when the reward consists of positive verbal feedback and is available to all who meet the standard.

Making students compete against each other for limited rewards (the "grading on the curve" practice we first mentioned in our discussion of Erik Erikson's psychosocial theory of development) is particularly damaging to intrinsic motivation because of its impact on self-worth. Whether intended or not, children in our society base their sense of self-worth on their accomplishments. When we artificially limit opportunities to attain the highest level of accomplishment, intrinsic motivation declines in an effort to protect one's sense of worth (Covington, 2009; Wiechman & Gurland, 2009).

Extrinsic motivation: occurs when learner does something to earn external rewards

---

pause & reflect

What percentage of your behavior do you think stems from intrinsic motivation? From extrinsic motivation? Is it possible to change this ratio? How?

Intrinsic motivation: occurs when learner does something to experience inherently satisfying results

---

Excessive use of external rewards may lead to temporary behavior change, materialistic attitudes, decreased intrinsic motivation

---

Intrinsic motivation enhanced when reward provides positive feedback, is available to all who qualify

---

Intrinsic motivation undermined by forcing students to compete for limited supply of rewards

Figure 11.1 Conditions Determining Effect of External Rewards on Intrinsic Motivation

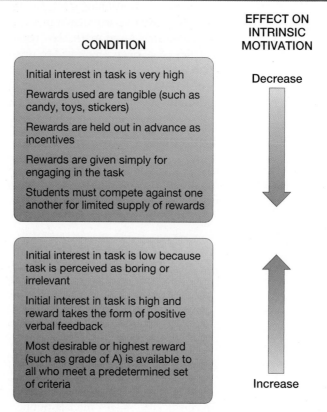

EFFECT ON
INTRINSIC
CONDITION   MOTIVATION

Initial interest in task is very high   Decrease

Rewards used are tangible (such as
candy, toys, stickers)

Rewards are held out in advance as
incentives

Rewards are given simply for
engaging in the task

Students must compete against one
another for limited supply of rewards

Initial interest in task is low because
task is perceived as boring or
irrelevant

Initial interest in task is high and
reward takes the form of positive
verbal feedback

Most desirable or highest reward
(such as grade of A) is available to
all who meet a predetermined set
of criteria   Increase

SOURCES: Cameron (2001); Cameron, Banko, & Pierce (2001); Covington (2009); Deci, Koestner, & Ryan (2001); Marinak & Gambrell (2008).

Give rewards sparingly, especially on tasks of natural interest	Taken as a whole, these results strongly suggest that teachers should avoid the indiscriminate use of rewards for influencing classroom behavior, particularly when an activity seems to be naturally interesting to students. Instead, rewards should be used to provide students with information about their level of competence on tasks they have not yet mastered and to encourage them to explore topics in which their initial interest is low.

THE SOCIAL COGNITIVE VIEW OF MOTIVATION

Social cognitive view of motivation: observe and imitate admired models; raise self-efficacy	Social cognitive theorists, such as Albert Bandura, Dale Schunk, and Barry Zimmerman, emphasize two factors that strongly influence motivation to learn: (1) the models to which people are exposed and (2) people's sense of self-efficacy, or how capable they believe they are to handle a particular task.

Power of Persuasive Models

One factor that positively affects students' self-efficacy and motivation to learn certain behaviors is the opportunity to see other people exhibiting those behaviors and to observe the consequences that occur. Social cognitive theorists refer to this as observation, imitation, and vicarious reinforcement. As we pointed out in discussing social cognitive theory in an earlier chapter, *vicarious* reinforcement means that we expect to receive the same reinforcer that we see someone else get for exhibiting a particular behavior.

A student who observes an older brother or sister reaping benefits from earning high grades may strive to do the same with the expectation of experiencing the same or similar benefits. A student who notices that a classmate receives praise from the teacher after acting in a certain way may decide to imitate such behavior to win similar rewards. A student who identifies with and admires a teacher may work hard partly to please the admired individual and partly to try becoming like that individual. Both vicarious reinforcement and direct reinforcement can raise an individual's sense of self-efficacy for a particular task, which, in turn, leads to higher levels of motivation.

The Importance of Self-Efficacy

An individual's sense of self-efficacy can affect motivation to learn through its influence on the learning goal one chooses, the outcome one expects, and the reasons (or attributions) one gives to explain successes and failures.

Choice of Learning Goal Analyses of learning goals suggest that a student may choose a task mastery goal, a performance-approach goal, a performance-avoidance goal, or a combination of task mastery and performance-approach goals (Britner & Pajares, 2006; Murayama & Elliot, 2009; Pintrich & Schunk, 2002; Urdan & Mestas, 2006; Walker & Greene, 2009; Usher & Pajares, 2008b).

- *Task mastery goals* involve doing what is necessary to learn meaningfully the information and skills that have been assigned. Students with high levels of self-efficacy choose this goal more often than do students with low levels of self-efficacy. In pursuit of task mastery goals, students with high efficacy will use a variety of encoding techniques, do more organizing of information to make it meaningful, review and practice more frequently, monitor their understanding more closely, formulate more effective learning strategies, and treat mistakes as part of learning.
- *Performance-approach goals* involve demonstrating to teachers and peers one's superior intellectual ability by outperforming most others in class. If the best way to accomplish this goal is to do assignments neatly and exactly according to directions, or to memorize large amounts of information to get a high grade

When students admire and identify with classmates who are positively reinforced for their behavior, the observing students' self-efficacy and motivation to exhibit the same behavior may be strengthened. Copyright © Bob Daemmrich/ Photo Edit

on a test without necessarily understanding the ideas or how they relate to one another, then these tactics will be used. Students who adopt performance-approach goals often do well on tests, but they are less likely than students who adopt mastery goals to develop a strong interest in various subjects. On the other hand, students who choose performance goals tend to have high levels of self-efficacy.

- *Performance-avoidance goals* involve reducing the possibility of failure so as not to appear less capable than other students. Students can reduce their chances of failure by avoiding novel and challenging tasks or by cheating. They can also engage in *self-handicapping behaviors,* such as putting off homework or projects until the last minute, studying superficially for an exam, and getting involved in many in-school and out-of-school nonacademic activities. The purpose of self-handicapping is to be able to blame poor performance on the circumstances rather than on one's ability. Students most likely to choose performance-avoidance goals are boys and those with low grades and low academic self-efficacy.

Teachers may unwittingly encourage self-handicapping behaviors, even in students whose sense of self-efficacy is at least adequate, by using a norm-referenced grading system. Because students are compared with one another to determine the top, middle, and low grades, this system encourages students to attribute their grades to a fixed ability. Students who have doubts about their ability are then more likely to engage in self-handicapping behaviors (Thrash & Hurst, 2008; Urdan, Ryan, Anderman, & Gheen, 2002).

Outcome Expectations A second way in which self-efficacy can affect motivation is in terms of the outcomes that students expect. Those with high levels of self-efficacy more often expect a positive outcome. As a result, they tend to be more willing to use the more complex and time-consuming learning skills and to persist longer in the face of difficulties. (It is possible, however, for a student to have a relatively high level of self-efficacy but expect a relatively low grade on a test because the student believes the teacher is prejudiced or grades unfairly.) Those with lower levels of self-efficacy are more likely to expect a disappointing outcome, tend to use simpler learning skills, and are likely to give up more quickly when tasks demand greater cognitive efforts (Pajares, 2007).

Attributions A third way in which self-efficacy influences motivation is through the reasons students cite to explain why they succeeded or failed at a task. Those with a high level of self-efficacy for a subject are likely to attribute failure to insufficient effort (and so vow to work harder the next time) but credit their success to a combination of ability and effort. Their peers who are lower in self-efficacy are likely to explain their failures by saying that they just don't have the ability to do well, but they will chalk their successes up to an easy task or luck. As we point out a bit further on in this chapter, this latter attribution pattern undercuts motivation (Graham & Williams, 2009).

Self-efficacy affects choice of goals, expectations of success, attributions for success and failure

OTHER COGNITIVE VIEWS OF MOTIVATION

In addition to social cognitive theorists, researchers who take other cognitive approaches to learning have done extensive studies of motivation. The views described in this section emphasize how the following five characteristics affect students' intrinsic motivation to learn: the inherent need to construct an organized and logically consistent knowledge base, one's expectations for successfully completing a task, the factors that one believes account for success and failure, one's beliefs about the nature of cognitive ability, and one's interests.

You should also be aware that intrinsic motivation for school learning is fairly well developed by about nine years of age (fourth grade) and becomes increasingly stable through late adolescence. Thus it is important to develop intrinsic motivation in students in the primary grades, as well as to identify students with low levels of academic motivation (Marinak & Gambrell, 2008).

Cognitive Development and the Need for Conceptual Organization

The cognitive development view is based on Jean Piaget's principles of equilibration, assimilation, accommodation, and schema formation, which we discussed in the chapter on stage theories of development. Piaget proposes that children possess an inherent desire to maintain a sense of organization and balance in their conception of the world (equilibration). A sense of equilibration may be experienced if a child assimilates a new experience by relating it to an existing scheme, or the child may accommodate by modifying an existing scheme if the new experience is too different.

In addition, individuals will repeatedly use new schemes because of an inherent desire to master their environment. This explains why young children can, with no loss of enthusiasm, sing the same song, tell the same story, and play the same game over and over and why they repeatedly open and shut doors to rooms and cupboards with no apparent purpose. It also explains why older children take great delight in collecting and organizing almost everything they can get their hands on and why adolescents who have begun to attain formal operational thinking will argue incessantly about all the unfairness in the world and how it can be eliminated (Stipek, 2002).

| Cognitive development view of motivation: strive for equilibration; master the environment

The Need for Achievement

Have you ever decided to take on a moderately difficult task (such as taking a course on astronomy even though you are a history major and have only a limited background in science) and then found that you had somewhat conflicting feelings about it? On the one hand, you felt eager to start the course, confident that you would be pleased with your performance. But on the other hand, you also felt a bit of anxiety because of the small possibility of failure. Now try to imagine the opposite situation. In reaction to a suggestion to take a course outside your major, you refuse because the probability of failure seems great, whereas the probability of success seems quite small.

| Need for achievement revealed by desire to attain goals that require skilled performance

In 1964, John Atkinson proposed that such differences in achievement behavior are due to differences in something called the *need for achievement*. Individuals with a high need for achievement have a stronger expectation of success than they do a fear of failure for most tasks and therefore anticipate a feeling of pride in accomplishment. When given a choice, high-need achievers seek out moderately challenging tasks because they offer an optimal balance between challenge and expected success. By contrast, individuals with a low need for achievement avoid such tasks because their fear of failure greatly outweighs their expectation of success, and they therefore anticipate feelings of shame. When faced with a choice, they typically choose either relatively easy tasks because the probability of success is high or very difficult tasks because there is no shame in failing to achieve a lofty goal. Atkinson's theory was an early version of what is currently called *expectancy-value theory* (Pekrun, Elliot, & Maier, 2009; Wigfield, Tonks, & Klauda, 2009). An individual's level of motivation for a particular task is governed by that person's expectation of success and the value placed on that success (Cole, Bergin, & Whittaker, 2008).

| High-need achievers prefer moderately challenging tasks

| Low-need achievers prefer very easy or very hard tasks

Atkinson's point about taking fear of failure into account in arranging learning experiences has been made by William Glasser in *Choice Theory in the Classroom* (2001) and *The Quality School* (1998). Glasser argues that for people to succeed at life in general, they must first experience success in one important aspect of their lives (Kerr & Grasby, 2009). For most children, that one important part should be school.

Erik Erikson made the same point by maintaining that the primary psychosocial task for school-age children is to successfully resolve the issue of industry versus inferiority.

Explanations of Success and Failure: Attribution Theory

Some interesting aspects of success and failure are revealed when students are asked to explain why they did or did not do well on some task (McCrea, 2008). The four most commonly given reasons stress ability, effort, task difficulty, and luck. To explain a low score on a math test, for example, different students might make the following statements:

"I just have a poor head for numbers." (lack of ability)
"I didn't really study for the exam." (lack of effort)
"That test was the toughest I've ever taken." (task difficulty)
"I guessed wrong about which sections of the book to study." (luck)

Unsuccessful students attribute success to luck, easy tasks; failure, to lack of ability

Because students *attribute* success or failure to the factors just listed, research of this type contributes to what is referred to as **attribution theory** (Graham & Williams, 2009). We have already touched on this topic in discussing self-efficacy.

Students with long histories of academic failure and a weak need for achievement typically attribute their success to easy questions or luck and their failures to lack of ability. Ability is a stable attribution (that is, people expect its effect on achievement to be pretty much the same from one task to another), whereas task difficulty and luck are both external attributions (in other words, people feel they have little control over their occurrence). Research has shown that stable attributions, particularly concerning ability, lead to expectations of future success or failure and that internal attributions (those under personal control) lead to pride in achievement or to shame following failure. Because low-achieving students attribute failure to low ability, they see future failure as more likely than future success. In addition, ascribing success to factors beyond one's control diminishes the possibility of taking pride in achievement and placing a high value on rewards. Consequently, satisfactory achievement and reward may have little effect on the failure-avoiding strategies that poor students have developed over the years (Elliott & Bempechat, 2002; Graham & Williams, 2009).

Successful students attribute success to effort, ability; failure, to lack of effort

Success-oriented students (high-need achievers), in contrast, typically attribute success to ability and effort and failure to insufficient effort. Consequently, failure does not diminish expectancy of success, feelings of competence, or reward attractiveness for these students. They simply resolve to work harder in the future. This attribution pattern holds even for academically gifted students who might be expected to focus on ability because they excel at most tasks and are well aware of their superior capabilities. Citing effort as a factor in their success or failure is thought to be more motivating than citing just ability because effort is a modifiable factor that allows one to feel in control of one's destiny (Graham & Williams, 2009).

The typical attribution pattern of high-achieving students highlights an important point: both effort and ability should be credited with contributing to one's success. Students who attribute their success mostly to effort may conclude that they have a low level of ability because they have to work harder to achieve the same level of performance as others (McCrea, 2008).

pause & reflect

Do you fit the pattern of most successful students, attributing success to effort and ability and failure to lack of effort? If so, how did you get this way? Is there anything you can draw from your own experiences to help students develop this pattern?

Beliefs About the Nature of Cognitive Ability

Children's motivation for learning is affected by their beliefs about the nature of ability. During the primary and elementary grades, children create and refine their conception of ability. By the time they reach middle school, most children start to think of themselves and others as belonging to particular categories in terms of ability.

Changes in Beliefs About Ability According to Carol Dweck (2002a, 2002b; see also Dweck & Master, 2009), a leading theorist and researcher on this subject, noticeable changes in children's ability conceptions occur at two points in time: between seven and eight years of age and between ten and twelve years of age. Compared with kindergarten and early primary grade children, seven- and eight-year-olds are more likely to do the following:

- Show an increased interest in the concept of ability and take greater notice of peer behaviors that are relevant to achievement comparisons.
- Distinguish ability from such other characteristics as social skills, likeability, and physical skills and believe that the same person can have different levels of ability for different academic skills (such as reading, writing, and mathematics).
- Think of ability as a more internal and less observable characteristic that is defined normatively (that is, by comparing oneself to others).
- Think of ability as a characteristic that is stable over time and can therefore be used to make predictions about future academic performance.
- Engage in self-criticism related to ability and compare their performance with that of others.

Compared with seven- and eight-year-olds, ten- to twelve-year-old children are more likely to do the following:

- Distinguish between effort and ability as factors in performance. Consequently, some are more likely to say of two students who receive the same grade on a test or assignment that the one who exerted more effort has less ability.
- Evaluate their academic ability more accurately, although more begin to underestimate their ability.
- Think of ability as being both a stable characteristic and a fixed capacity that explains the grades they currently receive and will receive in the future. It is not uncommon to hear older children and adolescents talk about peers who do or do not have "it" (Anderman & Maehr, 1994). Consequently, students who believe their ability in a particular subject is below average seek to avoid additional courses in that subject. Girls, especially high-achieving ones, are more likely than boys to adopt this view of ability, and this may partly explain their greater reluctance to take advanced science and math classes in high school.
- Value performance goals (getting the highest grade possible) over learning goals (making meaningful connections among ideas and how they relate to the world outside of school).

Why these changes occur, and why they occur in some individuals but not others, is not entirely known, but comparing the performance of a student with the performance of every other student in a class to determine who gets which grades (the practice of grading on the curve that we mentioned earlier) is suspected of playing a major role. One casualty of this belief, as we've indicated, is motivation for learning (Chen & Pajares, 2010; Lepper, Corpus, & Iyengar, 2005).

Types of Beliefs About Ability According to the work of Dweck (2002a) and others (e.g., Chen & Pajares, 2010; Dweck & Master, 2009; Quihuis, Bempechat, Jiminez, & Boulay, 2002), students can be placed into one of three categories based on their beliefs about the nature of cognitive ability:

1. *Entity theorists.* Some students subscribe solely to what is called an entity theory; they talk about intelligence as if it were a thing, or an entity, that has fixed characteristics.

2. *Incremental theorists.* Other students subscribe solely to what is called an incremental theory, believing that intelligence can be improved gradually by degrees or increments as they refine their thinking skills and acquire new ones. Entity and incremental theorists hold to their respective views for all subjects.

3. *Mixed theorists.* Students in this group subscribe to both entity and incremental theories, depending on the subject. A mixed theorist may, for example, be an entity theorist for math but an incremental theorist for science, whereas the opposite (or some other) pattern may prevail for another student.

> Students with incremental beliefs tend to have mastery goals and are motivated to learn meaningfully, improve skills

Students with incremental beliefs tend to be motivated to acquire new and more effective cognitive skills and are said to have *mastery goals*. They seek challenging tasks and do not give up easily, because they see obstacles as a natural part of the learning process. They often tell themselves what adults have told them for years: "think carefully," "pay attention," and "try to recall useful information that you learned earlier." They seem to focus on the questions, "How do you do this?" and "What can I learn from this?" Errors are seen as opportunities for useful feedback. Not surprisingly, they are more likely than entity theorists to attribute failure to insufficient effort and ineffective learning skills.

> Students with entity beliefs tend to have performance goals and are motivated to get high grades, avoid failure

Students who believe that intelligence is an unchangeable entity are primarily motivated to appear smart to others by getting high grades and praise and by avoiding low grades, criticism, and shame. Such students are said to have *performance goals*. When confronted with a new task, their initial thought is likely to be, "Am I smart enough to do this?" They may forgo opportunities to learn new ideas and skills if they think they will become confused and make mistakes, and they tend to attribute failure to low ability rather than insufficient effort.

However, among students who subscribe to the entity theory, there is a difference between those with high confidence in their ability and those with low confidence. High-confidence entity theorists are likely to demonstrate such mastery-oriented behaviors as seeking challenges and persisting in the face of difficulty. Those with low confidence, in contrast, may be more interested in avoiding failure and criticism—even after achieving initial success—than in continuing to be positively reinforced for outperforming others. Because of their anxiety over the

Students who believe that intelligence is a collection of cognitive skills that can be refined are likely to adopt mastery goals and attribute failure to insufficient effort, whereas students who believe that intelligence is an unchangeable capacity are likely to adopt performance goals and attribute failure to low ability. © Elizabeth Crews Photography

possibility of failure, these low-confidence entity theorists are less likely than students who have an incremental view of ability to exhibit subsequent motivation for a task (Cury, Da Fonseca, Zahn, Elliot, 2008; Rawsthorne & Elliot, 1999). If avoidance is not possible, they become discouraged at the first sign of difficulty. This, in turn, produces anxiety, ineffective problem solving, and withdrawal from the task (as a way to avoid concluding that one lacks ability and thereby maintain some self-esteem). According to attribution theory, entity theorists should continue this pattern, because success is not attributed to effort, but failure is attributed to low ability.

The Effect of Interest on Intrinsic Motivation

Interest can be described as a psychological state that involves focused attention, increased cognitive functioning, persistence, and emotional involvement (Ainley, Hidi, & Berndorff, 2002; Miller & Brickman, 2004; Schraw & Lehman, 2001). A person's interest in a topic can come from personal and/or situational sources:

Personal interest marked by intrinsic desire to learn that persists over time; situational interest is context dependent and short term

- *Personal interest* (also referred to as individual or topic interest) is characterized by an intrinsic desire to understand a topic, a desire that persists over time and is based on preexisting knowledge, personal experience, and emotion.
- *Situational interest* is more temporary and is based on context-specific factors, such as the unusualness of information or its personal relevance. For example, baseball teams that qualify for or win a League Championship or World Series after many years of not doing so (think Chicago Cubs or Boston Red Sox) often spark temporary interest in the players and the games among people who live in those cities. Similarly, people who buy a company's stock often become interested, albeit temporarily, in the company's activities.

The degree of personal interest a student brings to a subject or activity has been shown to affect intrinsic motivation for that task. Such students pay greater attention to the task, stay with it for a longer period of time, learn more from it, and enjoy their involvement to a greater degree (Miller & Brickman, 2004; Schraw & Lehman, 2001; Tabachnick, Miller, & Relyea, 2008).

It is possible, of course, that situational interest in a topic can grow into a personal interest. Consider, for example, a high school student who knows nothing of how information is stored in and retrieved from memory but learns about it when she has to read a chapter on memory in her psychology textbook. Fascinated with the description of various forms of encoding and retrieval cues because of her own problems with being able to recall information for tests accurately, she searches for additional books and articles on the topic and even thinks about majoring in psychology in college (Renninger & Hidi, 2002; Schraw & Lehman, 2001).

Factors That Influence Personal Interest   A long-term interest in a particular subject or activity may be influenced by one or more of the following factors (Hidi, 2001; Miller & Brickman, 2004; Schraw & Lehman, 2001; Tabachnick, Miller, & Relyea, 2008):

- *Ideas and activities that are valued by one's culture or ethnic group.* As we discussed in the chapter on cultural diversity, culture is the filter through which groups of people interpret the world and assign values to objects, ideas, and activities. Thus, inner-city male youths are likely to be strongly interested in playing basketball and following the exploits of professional basketball players, whereas a rural midwestern male of the same age is likely to be interested in fishing and hunting.
- *The emotions that are aroused by the subject or activity.* Students who experience extreme math anxiety, for example, are less likely to develop a strong interest in math-related activities than those who experience more positive emotions.

- *The degree of competence one attains in a subject or activity.* People typically spend more time pursuing activities that they are good at than activities at which they do not excel.
- *The degree to which a subject or activity is perceived to be relevant to achieving a goal.* As noted in the chapter on approaches to instruction, many students fail to perceive such relevance, partly because teachers rarely take the time to explain how a topic or lesson may affect students' lives.
- *Level of prior knowledge.* People are often more interested in topics they already know something about than in topics they know nothing about.
- *A perceived hole in a topic that the person already knows a good deal about.* A person who considers himself to be well informed about the music of Mozart would likely be highly interested in reading the score of a newly discovered composition by Mozart.

Factors That Influence Situational Interest Some of the factors that spark a spontaneous and short-term interest in a topic or activity include (Hidi, 2001; Montalvo, Mansfield, & Miller, 2007; Reeve & Halusic, 2009; Schraw & Lehman, 2001):

- *A state of cognitive conflict or disequilibrium.* Teachers can sometimes spark students' interest in a topic by showing or telling them something that is discrepant with a current belief. Consider, for example, a high school class on government. The teacher has a lesson planned on government spending and wants to avoid the usual lack of interest that this topic produces. One tactic would be to ask students if they believe that the money they contribute to social security from their part-time jobs (or the full-time jobs they will eventually have) is placed in an account with their name on it, where it remains until they become eligible for benefits in their mid-sixties. Most will probably believe something like that. The teacher could then tell them that the contributions they make today are actually used to pay the benefits of current retirees and that their social security benefits will come from the social security taxes levied on a future generation of workers.
- *Well-written reading material.* Texts and other written materials that are logically organized and engaging are rated as more interesting by students and produce higher levels of comprehension than more poorly written material.
- *The opportunity to work on a task with others.* As we saw earlier in the book, cooperative arrangements are highly motivating and produce high levels of learning.
- *The opportunity to engage in hands-on activities.*
- *The opportunity to observe influential models.*
- *The teacher's use of novel stimuli.*
- *The teacher's use of games and puzzles.*

These findings have a number of clear instructional implications. Given that some students may develop a strong interest in a topic as a result of a classroom activity or assignment and that this initial interest may grow into a personal interest and the adoption of mastery goals, a general recommendation is for teachers to do what constructivist learning theory implies: involve students in a variety of subject matters and meaningful activities (Zhu et al., 2009). If you think about it, the purpose of exposing students to a wide variety of topics during their school years is not simply to provide them with basic knowledge of all of those topics but also to increase the likelihood that students will encounter those topics in situations that engage them, perhaps to the point at which topics grow into personal interests. Many of us have "discovered" our personal interests, and indeed our careers, as a result of situational interest growing into personal interest.

TeachSource

Video Case ◄◄ ► ►►

Motivating Adolescent Learners: Curriculum Based on Real Life

Go to the Education CourseMate website and watch the Video Case, and then answer the following questions:

1. Explain the concepts of personal and situational interest. How do these concepts relate to the school store project depicted in this Video Case?

2. For the students in this Video Case, is working in the school store an extrinsic or an intrinsic motivator? Explain your answer.

Our Case in Print illustrates how a program to help children in China learn to read uses personal and situational interest to develop intrinsic motivation. The section on Suggestions for Teaching offers further recommendations.

| Flow experienced as intense engagement or absorbed concentration

Flow and Engagement The concept of "flow" has been championed for more than three decades by Mihaly Csikszentmihalyi. Flow is the mental state of high engagement in an activity. It is characterized by intense concentration, sustained interest, and enjoyment of the activity's challenge (Csikszentmihalyi, 1975, 1996, 2000, 2002; Nakamura & Csikszentmihalyi, 2009). If you have ever been engaged in an activity (e.g., playing a video game or reading a novel) that captured your interest so completely that you lost track of time and had trouble breaking away from the activity, you have experienced something like the state of flow. Factors that influence either personal or situational interest can result in students experiencing flow and developing intrinsic motivation. For example, researchers in China have seen how flow influences engagement in instant messaging (IM) behavior and the selection of the particular IM product (Lu, Zhou, & Wang, 2008).

Research has used the concept of flow as a way of investigating the effects of student engagement in classrooms (Inal & Cagiltay, 2007; Owston, Wideman, Sinitskaya, & Brown, 2009). Rathunde and Csikszentmihalyi (2005) compared the academic experiences of nearly 300 middle school students divided into two groups: those who were enrolled in a program that took advantage of the factors that influence both personal and situational interest (called a "Montessori" middle school program) and students in a traditional middle school program. The students in the two groups were matched on a number of demographic factors to help ensure that any differences between the groups were most likely due to the kind of program they attended. The study produced two major findings. First, the students in both types of middle school programs reported very similar experiences while engaged in nonacademic activities at school. Second, when engaged in academic activities, the Montessori students reported more flow experiences, more energetic engagement in the academic activities, and greater intrinsic motivation than the students in the traditional middle school.

Another study by Csikszentmihalyi and his colleagues used the concept of flow to examine how high school students spent their time in school and the conditions under which the students felt engaged. They studied a longitudinal sample of more than 500 high school students from across the United States. The high school students reported increased engagement in academic activities when both the challenge of the activity and their own skill were high, when the instruction was perceived as relevant, and when the students felt control over the learning environment. In more concrete terms, the high school students were more engaged in individual and group learning activities than in listening to lectures, watching videos, or taking exams (Shernoff, Csikszentmihalyi, Schneider, & Shernoff, 2003). The researchers concluded that a sense of flow (i.e., intense engagement) is more likely when students feel a sense of control over their own learning and when the learning activities challenge students at a level appropriate to their skills.

Limitations of Cognitive Views

Cognitive Development   Although cognitive development theory, with its emphasis on people's need for a well-organized conception of the world, can be useful as a means for motivating students, it has a major limitation: it is not always easy or even possible to induce students to experience a cognitive disequilibrium sufficient to stimulate them to seek answers (Johnson & Johnson, 2009a). This is particularly true if an answer can be found only after comparatively dull and unrewarding information and skills are mastered. (How many elementary school students, for example, might be expected to experience a self-impelled urge to learn English grammar or acquire skill in mathematics?) You are likely to gain some firsthand experience with the difficulty of arousing cognitive disequilibrium the first time you ask students to respond to what you hope will be a provocative question for class discussion. Some students may experience a feeling of intellectual curiosity and be eager to clarify their thinking, but others may stare out the window or surreptitiously do homework for another class.

> Often difficult to arouse cognitive disequilibrium

Need for Achievement   Perhaps the major problem that teachers have in using Atkinson's theory of need for achievement is the lack of efficient and objective instruments for measuring its strength. Although you could probably draw reasonably accurate conclusions about whether a student has a high or low need for achievement by watching that student's behavior over time and in a variety of situations, you may not be in a position to make extensive observations. And the problem with short-term observations is that a student's achievement orientation may be affected by more or less chance circumstances.

> Need for achievement difficult to assess on basis of short-term observations

Attribution Theory and Beliefs About Ability   The major implication of the idea that faulty attributions are at least partly responsible for sabotaging students' motivation to learn is that students must be taught to make more appropriate attributions. But this is likely to be a substantial undertaking requiring a concerted, coordinated effort. One part of the problem in working with students who attribute failure to lack of ability is that ability tends to be seen as a stable factor that is relatively impervious to change. The other part of the problem is that the same students often attribute their success to task difficulty and luck, two factors that cannot be predicted or controlled because they are external and random.

> Faulty attributions difficult to change

An additional limitation is that attribution training is not likely to be fully effective with elementary school children. For them, two individuals who learn the same amount of material are equally smart despite the fact that one person has to work twice as long to achieve that goal. Older children and adolescents, however, have a better grasp of the concept of efficiency; they see ability as something that influences the amount and effectiveness of effort (McCrea, 2008; Stipek, 2002).

Now that you are familiar with some of the approaches to motivation, it is time to consider Suggestions for Teaching that show how these ideas can be converted into classroom practice.

Case in Print

Taking an Interest in Learning

Interest can be described as a psychological state that involves focused attention, increased cognitive functioning, persistence, and emotional involvement. . . . A person's interest in a topic can come from personal and/or situational sources: Personal interest (also referred to as individual or topic interest) is characterized by an intrinsic desire to understand a topic, a desire that persists over time and is based on preexisting knowledge, personal experience, and emotion. Situational interest is more temporary and is based on context-specific factors, such as the unusualness of information or its personal relevance. . . . Factors that influence either personal or situational interest can result in students experiencing flow and developing intrinsic motivation. (p. 377–379)

Program Aims to Make Reading Easier, More Fun, for Children in China

CRAIG CHAMBERLAIN

News Bureau, University of Illinois, 10/18/2006

CHAMPAIGN, Ill.—What could an English-speaking American reading expert hope to discover from studying how Chinese learn their language? And what might he and his colleagues have to offer as a result?

For one thing: A new program to make books and reading more fun for Chinese children, and a publishing company started in order to produce the materials and train teachers how to use them.

The company is just 4 years old, but its "shared book" program already is in use with 250,000 children ages 3 to 5 in more than 8,000 kindergarten classrooms across urban China. There are about 60 million Chinese in that age group.

"Chinese is not an easy language to learn to read," says Richard Anderson, who has led a research project at the University of Illinois at Urbana-Champaign since the early 1990s on the process and psychology of learning to read Chinese. He also is the director of the U. of I. Center for the Study of Reading.

For most Chinese children, Anderson said, the process of learning to read begins in the first grade with the hard work of learning Chinese characters, largely through drill and practice. They are expected to memorize 1,200 characters by the end of the second grade and 2,500 by the end of the sixth grade.

And the Chinese don't have a strong tradition of reading to their preschool-age children or doing other activities connected with books, said Anderson, who also is a U. of I. professor of educational psychology. Their books for young children tend to be heavily moralistic and "not designed to be really exciting

fiction," he said. They are not books young children can learn to read themselves.

Anderson and his research colleagues, from both the U. of I. and Beijing Normal University, sought to design a program that would not only lay the foundation for literacy, but also would encourage young children to read more and to read for pleasure.

"We wanted them to feel it was worth the trouble. We wanted to build in them an intrinsic motivation for reading. . . . We wanted children to become really excited by reading so that they can hang in there during those tough first several years of school."

China is fertile ground for a program such as this because literacy is becoming essential for many jobs in the nation's growing economy. In addition, most couples now have only one child, the result of the country's population policies, Anderson said. "Making sure your child gets a good education is a very, very high priority."

The seeds for the research project in China were planted in the early 1980s, as the nation was opening up to the West. Anderson visited China with a group of educators. Connections made then eventually led to doctoral students and researchers from Beijing Normal coming to work with Anderson and his Illinois colleagues.

What they've found, along with other researchers in the field, are surprising similarities in the way children learn to read each language, Anderson said. "It's amazing the extent to which the fundamental processes are the same, or at least highly similar, between

Chinese and English, considering that everything is different," he said.

The shared book approach being promoted by the publishing company, which Anderson started with Chinese investors, grew out of another line of research studying Chinese schools and their approach to teaching reading. They saw some strengths in the Chinese approach, but were concerned about an over-reliance on rewards and punishments, and too much emphasis on intensive reading aimed at learning fundamentals, Anderson said.

"We discovered not much extensive reading," he said, meaning reading for pleasure and practice.

Through the shared book approach, "we want to lay a foundation for reading in an easy, natural way—one that will build children's excitement about reading," Anderson said. "In this approach, we're trying to make progress on all aspects of Chinese reading, but we're especially trying to build oral language facility, which is very important."

The program involves significant time spent reading stories with students, using large illustrated books. Children are able to learn quite a few Chinese characters simply from reading the stories again and again, he said.

In one key activity, each child is encouraged to do his or her own "book," which requires the child to create a story, do the drawings, and then explain the story to a parent (usually the mother), who writes out the story below the pictures.

In doing these activities, "we get a huge amount of parent collaboration, which is also good for the development of literacy," Anderson said.

Questions and Activities

1. According to this chapter, interest in learning is influenced by several individual and situational factors. Review the lists of these factors and then identify which factors were probably operating in the program described in this article.

2. Explain how the approach to motivation taken by the researchers in the Chinese reading project is consistent with a constructivist view of learning.

3. What insights into intrinsic and extrinsic motivation are provided by this cross-cultural glimpse into educational practices?

Suggestions for Teaching

Motivating Students to Learn

JOURNAL ENTRY
Using Behavior
Modification Techniques
to Motivate

1 **Use behavioral techniques to help students exert themselves and work toward remote goals.**

Techniques you might use for this purpose were described in Chapter 7 on behavioral and social learning theories. They include verbal praise, shaping, modeling, symbolic reinforcers (smile faces, stars, and the like), and contingency contracting.

a. Give praise as positive reinforcement, but do so effectively.

Think about the times when you've been praised for a job well done, particularly when you weren't sure about the quality of your work. In all likelihood, it had a strong, maybe even dramatic, effect on your motivation. That being the case, you might think that effective positive reinforcement in the form of verbal praise is a common occurrence in the classroom. But you would be wrong. Observation of classrooms has revealed that verbal praise is given infrequently and is often given in ways that limit its effectiveness (Brophy, 1981, 1984; Reinke, Lewis-Palmer, & Merrell,

2008). Jere Brophy and others who have followed him recommend that teachers use praise in the following ways:

- As a spontaneous expression of surprise or admiration. ("Why, Juan! This report is really excellent!")
- As compensation for criticism or as vindication of a prediction. ("After your last report, Lily, I said I knew you could do better. Well, you have done better. This is really excellent.")
- As an attempt to impress all members of a class. ("I like the way Nguyen just put his books away so promptly.")
- As a transition ritual to verify that an assignment has been completed. ("Yes, Maya, that's very good. You can work on your project now.")
- As a consolation prize or as encouragement to students who are less capable than others. ("Well, Josh, you kept at it, and you got it finished. Good for you!")

In an effort to help teachers administer praise more effectively, Brophy drew up the guidelines for effective praise listed in Table 11.1.

b. Use other forms of positive reinforcement.

In addition to verbal praise, you can make use of such other forms of positive reinforcement as modeling, symbolic reinforcers, and contingency contracts.

Table 11.1   Guidelines for Effective Praise

Effective Praise	Ineffective Praise
1. Is delivered contingently	1. Is delivered randomly or unsystematically
2. Specifies the particulars of the accomplishment	2. Is restricted to global positive reactions
3. Shows spontaneity, variety, and other signs of credibility; suggests clear attention to the student's accomplishment	3. Shows a bland uniformity, which suggests a conditional response made with minimal attention
4. Rewards attainment of specified performance criteria (which can include effort criteria, however)	4. Rewards mere participation, without consideration of performance process or outcomes
5. Provides information to students about their competence or the value of their accomplishments	5. Provides no information at all or gives students information about their status
6. Orients students toward better appreciation of their own task-related behavior and thinking about problem solving	6. Orients students toward comparing themselves with others and thinking about competing
7. Uses students' own prior accomplishments as the context for describing new accomplishments	7. Uses the accomplishments of peers as the context for describing students' present accomplishments
8. Is given in recognition of noteworthy effort or success at tasks that are difficult (for *this* student)	8. Is given without regard to the effort expended or the meaning of the accomplishment (for *this* student)
9. Attributes success to effort and ability, implying that similar successes can be expected in the future	9. Attributes success to ability alone or to external factors such as luck or easy task
10. Leads students to expend effort on the task because they enjoy the task or want to develop task-relevant skills	10. Leads students to expend effort on the task for external reasons—to please the teacher, win a competition or reward, etc.
11. Focuses students' attention on their own task-relevant behavior	11. Focuses students' attention on the teacher as an external authority figure who is manipulating them
12. Fosters appreciation of and desirable attributions about task-relevant behavior after the process is completed	12. Intrudes into the ongoing process, distracting attention from task-relevant behavior

SOURCES: Brophy (1981); Hester, Hendrickson, & Gable (2009); Reinke, Lewis-Palmer, & Merrell (2008).

EXAMPLES

- Arrange for students to observe that classmates who persevere and complete a task receive a reinforcer of some kind. (But let this occur more or less naturally. Also, don't permit students who have finished an assignment to engage in attention-getting or obviously enjoyable self-chosen activities; those who are still working on the assignment may become a bit resentful and therefore less inclined to work on the task at hand.)

- Draw happy faces on primary grade students' papers, give check marks as students complete assignments, write personal comments acknowledging good work, and assign bonus points.

- Develop an individual reward menu, or contract, with each student based on the Premack principle (Grandma's rule), which we discussed earlier in the book. After passing a spelling test at a particular level, for example, each student might be given class time to work on a self-selected project.

- When making use of such motivational techniques, you might do your best to play down overtones of manipulation and materialism. Point out that rewards are used in almost all forms of endeavor to induce people to work toward a goal. Just because someone does something to earn a reward does not mean that the activity should never be indulged in for intrinsic reasons. For example, athletes often compete to earn the reward of being members of the best team, but they still enjoy the game.

JOURNAL ENTRY
Ways to Arrange Short-Term Goals

2 **Make sure that students know what they are to do, how to proceed, and how to determine when they have achieved goals.**

Many times students do not exert themselves in the classroom because they say they don't know what they are supposed to do. Occasionally, such a statement is merely an excuse for goofing off, but it may also be a legitimate explanation for lack of effort. Recall that knowing what one is expected to do is important information in the construction of a learning strategy.

For reasons illustrated by behavioral theorists' experiments with different reinforcement schedules, students are more likely to work steadily if they are reinforced at frequent intervals. If you set goals that are too demanding or remote, lack of reinforcement during the early stages of a unit may derail students, even if they started out with good intentions. Whenever you ask students to work toward a demanding or remote goal, try to set up a series of short-term goals.

EXAMPLE

- One way to structure students' learning efforts is to follow the suggestions offered by Raymond Wlodkowski for drawing up a personal contract. He recommends that such a contract should contain four elements. A sample contract from Wlodkowski (1978, p. 57) is presented here, with a description of each element in brackets.

Date _____

1. Within the next two weeks I will learn to multiply correctly single-digit numbers ranging between 5 and 9, for example, 5×6, 6×7, 7×8, 8×9, 9×5. [What the student will learn]
2. When I feel prepared, I will ask to take a mastery test containing 50 problems from this range of multiplication facts. [How the student can demonstrate learning]
3. I will complete this contract when I can finish the mastery test with no more than three errors. [The degree of proficiency to be demonstrated]
4. My preparation and study will involve choosing work from the workbook activities, number games, and filmstrip materials. [How the student will proceed]

Signed _____

③ Encourage low-achieving students to attribute success to a combination of ability and effort and failure to insufficient effort.

Should you decide to try to alter the attributions of a student who is having difficulty with one or more subjects, here are three suggestions based on an analysis of 20 attribution training studies (Robertson, 2000):

- Make sure the student has the ability to succeed on a task before telling the student to attribute failure to insufficient effort. Students who try hard but lack the cognitive skills necessary for success are likely to become convinced not only that they lack the ability but also that they will never become capable of success on that type of task.

- Tell students that having the ability for a subject is the same as knowing how to formulate and use a learning strategy for that subject. Thus success is attributable to an appropriate strategy (which is controllable), whereas failure is attributable to insufficient effort at formulating the strategy (also controllable).

- Combine attribution training with strategy instruction for students who don't understand the relationship between strategy use and success and failure.

JOURNAL ENTRY
Ways to Promote an Incremental View of Intelligence

④ Encourage students to think of ability as a set of cognitive skills that can be added to and refined, rather than as a fixed entity that is resistant to change, by praising the processes they use to succeed.

The work that Carol Dweck (2002a, 2002b; Dweck & Master, 2009) has done on students' beliefs about ability clearly shows that those who adopt an entity view are more likely to develop a maladaptive approach to learning than are students who adopt an incremental view. One way to help students develop incremental rather than entity beliefs is to praise them for their effort and use of effective skills rather than for their ability after doing well on a task.

Many parents and teachers believe they are strengthening a student's motivation for learning by praising their ability with such comments as, "You did very well on this test; you certainly are smart" or "You're really good at this." Dweck's research shows that this type of praise encourages students to develop entity beliefs that impede their motivation. A better alternative is to offer what Dweck calls process praise. Examples of process praise are: "That's a really high score; you must have worked really hard at these problems"; "Now that you've mastered this skill, let's go on to something a bit harder that you can learn from"; and "You did a fine job on this paper because you started early and used the writing skills we practiced in class."

⑤ Encourage students to adopt appropriate learning goals.

As we noted earlier, students may adopt task mastery goals, performance-approach goals, or performance-avoidance goals. To briefly review, students who have task mastery goals are motivated to use effective learning tactics to acquire new knowledge and skills even if it means an occasional disappointing performance. Students who adopt performance-approach goals, on the other hand, are principally motivated to outscore others on exams and assignments to demonstrate their ability. Students who adopt performance-avoidance goals are principally motivated to avoid failure and appear less capable than their peers by engaging in such behaviors as self-handicapping, avoiding novel and challenging tasks, and cheating. To help students maintain high levels of motivation and achievement, you should establish conditions that encourage the adoption of mastery goals (Midgley, Middleton, Gheen, & Kumar, 2002). The problem with performance-approach goals is that they suppress intrinsic interest in tasks and encourage students to equate failure with low ability. Performance-avoidance goals have many obvious problems, including the reinforcement of low self-efficacy and stunted intellectual growth.

a. Help students develop mastery learning goals.

The following suggestions (Urdan & Midgley, 2001) were designed with middle school students in mind but are just as applicable to both lower and higher grades:

- Group students by topic, interests, or their own choice rather than by ability.
- Use a variety of assessment techniques (discussed in Chapter 14, "Assessment of Classroom Learning") rather than just one, and make the top grade potentially achievable by all students by evaluating performance according to a predetermined set of criteria.
- Provide students with feedback about their progress rather than feedback about how they scored relative to the rest of the class.
- Recognize students who demonstrate progress rather than focusing just on students who have achieved the highest grades.
- Provide students with opportunities to choose what projects they will do, what electives they will take, and for how long they wish to study a particular subject rather than having these decisions made exclusively by administrators and teachers.
- Treat mistakes as a part of learning, encourage students to take academic risks, and allow students to redo work that does not meet some minimum satisfactory standard.
- Provide students with complex and challenging tasks that require comprehension and problem solving rather than tasks that require little more than rote learning and verbatim recall.
- Use cross-age tutoring, peer tutoring, and enrichment activities rather than grade retention with students who are falling behind.
- Use cooperative-learning methods rather than competition. Because so much has been written about the use of cooperative-learning techniques and their demonstrated effectiveness in raising motivation and learning, we discuss this recommendation in more detail next.

b. Use cooperative-learning methods.

As we pointed out in previous chapters, cooperative-learning methods have proven effective in increasing self-esteem and motivation for learning, redirecting attributions for success and failure, fostering positive feelings toward classmates, and increasing performance on tests of comprehension, reasoning, and problem solving (Johnson & Johnson, 1995, 2009a, 2009b; Johnson et al., 1995; Slavin, 1995). Accordingly, you may want to try one or more of the cooperative learning techniques described by David Johnson and Roger Johnson (Johnson et al., 1994), Robert Slavin (1995), and Kath Murdoch and Jeni Wilson (2004). To familiarize you with these methods, we will briefly describe the Student Teams–Achievement Divisions (STAD) method that Slavin and his associates at Johns Hopkins University devised.

STAD is one of the simplest and most flexible of the cooperative-learning methods, having been used in grades 2 through 12 and in such diverse subject areas as math, language arts, social studies, and science. As with other cooperative-learning methods, students are assigned to four- or five-member groups, with each group mirroring the makeup of the class in terms of ability, background, and gender. Once these assignments are made, a four-step cycle is initiated:

1. *Teach.* The teaching phase begins with the presentation of material, usually in a lecture-discussion format. Students should be told what it is they are going to learn and why it is important.
2. *Team study.* During team study, group members work cooperatively with teacher-provided worksheets and answer sheets.
3. *Test.* Each student *individually* takes a quiz. Using a scoring system that ranges from 0 to 30 points and reflects degree of individual improvement over previous quiz scores, the teacher scores the papers.

4. *Recognition*. Each team receives one of three recognition awards, depending on the average number of points the team earned. For example, teams that average 15 to 19 improvement points receive a GOODTEAM certificate, teams that average 20 to 24 improvement points receive a GREATTEAM certificate, and teams that average 25 to 30 improvement points receive a SUPERTEAM certificate.

The cooperative learning method Teams-Games-Tournaments is similar to STAD except that students compete in academic tournaments instead of taking quizzes.

Another popular cooperative learning technique, Jigsaw, was created by Elliott Aronson. The class is divided into groups of about five or six, each group works on the same project, and each member of a group is solely responsible for a particular part of the project. For a project on energy consumption in the United States, for example, one student of each group may be responsible for researching and reporting to the other group members on how the price of oil is determined. Another student in each group may report on the factors that determine the size and efficiency of automobiles, still another on the status of alternative energy sources, and so on. To control for the fact that some students may not listen attentively to or may criticize the reports of others in the group because of preexisting animosities (Maria thinks Brandon is a jerk because he insulted her friend last week), they are reminded that they will be taking an exam based on the content of each person's report. So it is in Maria's interest to lay aside her dislike of Brandon because he is the only source of part of the information she will be tested on. Before reporting to the other members of their group, the students from each group with identical assignments get together to share information, discuss ideas, and rehearse their presentations. They are referred to as the "expert" group. Research on Jigsaw shows improvements in listening, interpersonal relationships, and achievement when compared with traditional instruction (Aronson, 2002; Johnson & Johnson, 2009b).

6 **Maximize factors that appeal to both personal and situational interest.**

    a. Find out what your students' interests are and design as many in-class and out-of-class assignments as possible around those interests.

    b. Try to associate subjects and assignments with pleasurable rather than painful experiences by using such techniques as cooperative learning and constructivist approaches to teaching, as well as providing students with the information-processing tools they need to master your objectives.

    c. Link new topics to information students are already likely to have or provide relevant background knowledge in creative yet understandable ways.

    d. Select reading materials that are logically organized and written in an engaging style.

7 **Try to make learning interesting by emphasizing activity, investigation, adventure, social interaction, and usefulness.**

About 40 years ago, May Seagoe suggested an approach to motivation that is based on students' interests and is consistent with many of the motivation theories and technology tools mentioned in this chapter. Among the "points of appeal that emerge from studies of specific interests," she lists the following:

> (a) the opportunity for overt bodily activity, for manipulation, for construction, even for observing the movement of animals and vehicles of various sorts; (b) the opportunity for investigation, for using mental ingenuity in solving puzzles, for working problems through, for creating designs, and the like; (c) the opportunity for adventure, for vicarious experiences in make believe, in books, and in the mass media; (d) the opportunity

for social assimilation, for contacts with others suitable to the maturity level of the child (ranging from parallel play to discussion and argument), for social events and working together, for human interest and humanitarianism, and for conformity and display; and (e) the opportunity for use of the new in real life, making the new continuous with past experience and projecting it in terms of future action. (1970, p. 25)

One approach that incorporates most or all of these features and that can be used with preschool and primary grade children is the project approach. Lillian Katz and Sylvia Chard (2000) define a project as an in-depth study of a particular topic that one or more children undertake, that extends over a period of days or weeks, and that involves children seeking answers to questions that they formulate by themselves or in consultation with the teacher. Projects may involve an initial discussion that captures the students' interest (for example, discussing how a house is built); dramatic play; drawing, painting, and writing; group discussions; field trips; construction activities; and investigation activities. As many researchers (e.g., Barab & Dede, 2007; Barab, Gresalfi et al., 2009, Gresalfi et al., 2009) have noted, class projects for all grade levels can be designed to make use of various forms of technology. Because projects are based on children's natural interests and involve a wide range of activities, they are more likely to be intrinsically motivating.

Diane Curtis (2002) describes a fifth-grade project that helped students fulfill state curriculum standards in social studies, math, writing, and technology. Building on their interest in architecture, the students completed a project on several of the major memorial buildings in Washington, D.C. (such as those honoring Presidents Washington and Jefferson, as well as the Vietnam War Memorial). They gathered information from books, the Internet, and architects about the memorials, drew computer models of them, created a timeline of construction, and researched the contributions of Jefferson and others to the writing of the U.S. Constitution. This was followed by a field trip to Washington, D.C., and a presentation of their work to community members.

One potential drawback to the use of projects is the amount of time they take. To help teachers overcome that barrier, several websites offer project-based programs that provide curriculum materials, assignments, resources, and contact with experts. See, for example: **www.jasonproject.org**, **www.learner.org/jnorth**, and **www. thinkquest.org**.

For quick links to websites mentioned here, use the web links section of the textbook's Education CourseMate website.

May Seagoe found that students respond with interest to school situations that are active, investigative, adventurous, social, and useful. Having members of a fifth-grade class play the roles of state government officials is an activity that includes almost all these features. © Richard Hutchings/Photo Edit

As you think about how you are going to organize your lesson plans for each day and each period, you might ask yourself: "Are there ways that I can incorporate activity, investigation, adventure, social interaction, and usefulness into this presentation?" "Are there projects that I can assign to students, particularly as cooperative groups, that incorporate most of these features?" Here are some examples of techniques you might use.

ACTIVITIES

JOURNAL ENTRY
Ways to Make Learning
Active

- Have several students go to the board. Give a rapid-fire series of problems to be solved by those at the board, as well as by those at their desks. After five problems, have another group of students go to the board, and so on.

- Think of ways to move out of the classroom legitimately every now and then. Teach geometry, for instance, by asking the class to take several balls of string and lay out a baseball diamond on the side lawn of the school.

INVESTIGATIONS

JOURNAL ENTRY
Ways to Promote
Investigation

- In elementary grade classrooms (and in some middle school and high school classrooms), set up a variety of learning centers with themes such as library, games, social science, cultural appreciation, and computer use and organize these with intriguing displays and materials. For example, your social science center could be stocked with maps, charts, and documents. Your computer center might include educational software such as CD-ROMs and database programs; student-created publications made with desktop publishing or word processing programs; a computer with Internet access; and lists of appropriate and interesting online sites.

- In middle school and high school classrooms, you might arrange centers that pertain to different aspects of a single subject. In a science class, for example, you might have an appreciation center stressing aesthetic aspects of science, a display center calling attention to new developments in the field, a library center consisting of attractive and provocative books, and so on.

ADVENTURES

JOURNAL ENTRY
Ways to Make Learning
Seem Adventurous

- Occasionally, use techniques that make learning entertaining and adventurous. Such techniques might be particularly useful when you introduce a new topic. You might employ devices used by advertisers and the creators of *Sesame Street,* for instance. Use intensity, size, contrast, and movement to attract attention. Make use of color, humor, exaggeration, and drama to introduce a new unit. Take students by surprise by doing something totally unexpected.

- The night before you introduce a new unit, redecorate part of the room. Then ask the class to help you finish it.

- Arrange a "Parade of Presidents" in which each student selects a president of the United States and presents a State of the Union message to the rest of the class, with the rest of the class taking the part of members of Congress.

- Hand out a duplicated sheet of 20 questions based on articles in each section of a morning newspaper. Students compete against each other to discover how many of the questions they can answer in the shortest period of time. Typical questions: "Why is the senator from Mississippi upset?" "Who scored the most points in the UCLA–Notre Dame basketball game?" "What city suffered widespread flood damage?"

SOCIAL INTERACTIONS

JOURNAL ENTRY
Ways to Make Learning
Social

- Have students pair off and ask each other questions to prepare for an exam. Do the same with difficult-to-learn material by suggesting that pairs cooperate—for example, in developing mnemonic devices or preparing flashcards—to help each other master information.

- Organize an end-of-unit extravaganza in which individuals and groups first present or display projects and then celebrate by having refreshments.

JOURNAL ENTRY
Ways to Make Learning
Useful

USEFULNESS

- Continually point out that what is being learned can be used outside class. Ask students to keep a record of how they use in real life what they learn in class.

- Develop exercises that make students aware that what they are learning has transfer value. Have students in an English class write a job application letter; have math students balance a checkbook, fill out an income tax form, or work out a yearly budget; have biology students think about ways they can apply what they have learned to avoid getting sick.

For interactive Netlabs on motivation, go to the Education CourseMate website.

THE HUMANISTIC VIEW OF MOTIVATION

Abraham Maslow earned his Ph.D. in a psychology department that supported the behaviorist position. After he graduated, however, he came into contact with Gestalt psychologists (a group of German psychologists whose work during the 1920s and 1930s laid the foundation for the cognitive theories of the 1960s and 1970s), prepared for a career as a psychoanalyst, and became interested in anthropology. As a result of these various influences, he came to the conclusion that American psychologists who endorsed the behaviorist position had become so preoccupied with overt behavior and objectivity that they were ignoring other important aspects of human existence (hence, the term *humanistic* to describe his views). When Maslow observed the behavior of especially well-adjusted persons—or *self-actualizers*, as he called them—he concluded that healthy individuals are motivated to seek fulfilling experiences.

Maslow's Theory of Growth Motivation

Maslow describes 17 propositions, discussed in Chapter 1 of *Motivation and Personality* (1987), that he believes would have to be incorporated into any sound theory of *growth motivation* (or *need gratification*). Referring to need gratification as the most important single principle underlying all development, he adds that "the single, holistic principle that binds together the multiplicity of human motives is the tendency for a new and higher need to emerge as the lower need fulfills itself by being sufficiently gratified" (1968, p. 55).

Maslow elaborates on this basic principle by proposing a five-level hierarchy of needs. *Physiological* needs are at the bottom of the hierarchy, followed in ascending order by *safety, belongingness and love, esteem,* and *self-actualization* needs (see Figure 11.2). This order reflects differences in the relative strength of each need. The lower a need is in the hierarchy, the greater is its strength, because when a lower-level need is activated (as in the case of extreme hunger or fear for one's physical safety), people will stop trying to satisfy a higher-level need (such as esteem or self-actualization) and focus on satisfying the currently active lower-level need (Maslow, 1987).

The first four needs (physiological, safety, belongingness and love, and esteem) are often referred to as **deficiency needs** because they motivate people to act only when they are unmet to some degree. Self-actualization, by contrast, is often called a **growth need** because people constantly strive to satisfy it. Basically, **self-actualization** refers to the need for self-fulfillment—the need to develop all of one's potential talents and capabilities. For example, an individual who felt she had the capability to write novels, teach, practice medicine, and raise children would not feel self-actualized until she had accomplished all of these goals to some minimal degree. Because it is at the top of the hierarchy and addresses the potential of the whole person, self-actualization is discussed more frequently than the other needs.

People are motivated to satisfy deficiency needs only when those needs are unmet

Figure 11.2 Maslow's Hierarchy of Needs

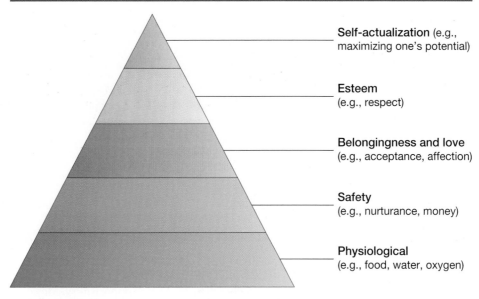

Self-actualization (e.g., maximizing one's potential)

Esteem (e.g., respect)

Belongingness and love (e.g., acceptance, affection)

Safety (e.g., nurturance, money)

Physiological (e.g., food, water, oxygen)

SOURCE: Maslow (1943).

pause & reflect

Maslow states that for individuals to be motivated to satisfy self-actualization needs, deficiency needs have to be satisfied first. Has this been true in your experience? If not, what was different?

Self-actualization depends on satisfaction of lower needs, belief in certain values

Maslow originally thought that self-actualization needs would automatically be activated as soon as esteem needs were met, but he changed his mind when he encountered individuals whose behavior did not fit this pattern. He concluded that individuals whose self-actualization needs became activated and met held in high regard such values as truth, goodness, beauty, justice, autonomy, and humor (Feist & Feist, 2001).

In addition to the five basic needs that compose the hierarchy, Maslow describes cognitive needs (such as the needs to know and to understand) and aesthetic needs (such as the needs for order, symmetry, or harmony). Although not part of the basic hierarchy, these two classes of needs play a critical role in the satisfaction of basic needs. Maslow maintains that such conditions as the freedom to investigate and learn and fairness, honesty, and orderliness in interpersonal relationships are critical because their absence makes satisfaction of the five basic needs impossible. (Imagine, for example, trying to satisfy your belongingness and love needs or your esteem needs in an atmosphere characterized by dishonesty, unfair punishment, and restrictions on freedom of speech.)

Implications of Maslow's Theory

The implications of Maslow's theory of motivation for teaching are provocative. One down-to-earth implication is that a teacher should do everything possible to see that the lower-level needs of students are satisfied so that students are more likely to function at the higher levels. Students are more likely to be primed to seek satisfaction of the esteem and self-actualization needs, for example, if they are physically comfortable, feel safe and relaxed, have a sense of belonging, and experience self-esteem. William Glasser (1998), whose ideas we mentioned earlier in this chapter, states that low-achieving students have told him they would like to get better grades but don't make more of an effort because, in their eyes, teachers don't care about them or what they do (see also Montalvo et al., 2007).

Theorists such as Abraham Maslow, who argue that deficiency needs such as belongingness and self-esteem must be satisfied before students will be motivated to learn, call attention to the importance of positive teacher-student relationships in the classroom. John Lei/ Stock Boston

> When deficiency needs not satisfied, person likely to make bad choices

Only when the need for self-actualization is activated is a person likely to choose wisely when given the opportunity. Maslow emphasizes this point by making a distinction between *bad choosers* and *good choosers*. When some people are allowed freedom to choose, they seem to make wise choices consistently. Most people, however, frequently make self-destructive choices. An insecure student, for example, may choose to attend a particular college more on the basis of how close it is to home than on the quality of its academic programs.

Growth, as Maslow sees it, is the result of a never-ending series of situations offering a free choice between the attractions and dangers of safety and those of growth. If a person is functioning at the level of growth needs, the choice will ordinarily be a progressive one. Maslow adds, however, that "the environment (parents, therapists, teachers) . . . can help by making the growth choice positively attractive and less dangerous, and by making the regressive choice less attractive and more costly" (1968, pp. 58–59). This point can be clarified by a simple diagram Maslow uses to illustrate a situation involving choice (1968, p. 47).

Enhance the dangers		Enhance the attraction
Safety	← Person →	**Growth**
Minimize the attractions		Minimize the dangers

> Encourage growth choices by enhancing attractions, minimizing dangers

This diagram emphasizes that if you set up learning situations that impress students as dangerous, threatening, or of little value, they are likely to play it safe, make little effort to respond, or even try to avoid learning. If, however, you make learning appear appealing, minimize pressure, and reduce possibilities for failure or embarrassment, your students are likely to be willing, if not eager, to do an assigned task.

Limitations of Maslow's Theory

> Teachers may be able to satisfy some deficiency needs but not others

Although Maslow's speculations are thought provoking, they are also sometimes frustrating. Quite often, you may not be able to determine precisely which of a student's needs are unsatisfied. Even if you *are* quite sure that a student lacks interest in learning because he feels unloved or insecure, you may not be able to do much about it. A girl who feels that her parents do not love her or that her peers do not accept her may not respond to your efforts. And if her needs for love, belonging, and esteem are not satisfied, she is less likely to be in the mood to learn.

Then again, there will be times when you can be quite instrumental in helping to satisfy certain deficiency needs. The development of self-esteem, for example, is closely tied to successful classroom achievement for almost all students. Although you may not be able to feed students when they are hungry or protect them from physical danger, you can always take steps to help them learn more effectively.

THE ROLE OF SELF-PERCEPTIONS IN MOTIVATION

Current interest in the effects of self-perceptions on school motivation and achievement runs high and seems to have been prompted by several developments, including the following: a better understanding of the nature of self-concept and self-esteem, Albert Bandura's introduction of the self-efficacy concept, advances in the measurement of self-perceptions, and the consistent finding of a positive relationship among self-perceptions, motivation, and school achievement (Trautwein, Ludtke, Koller, & Baumert, 2006). Much of this interest can be traced to ideas published during the 1960s and 1970s by psychologists such as Abraham Maslow, Carl Rogers, and Arthur Combs. These individuals stressed that how students see and judge themselves and others plays an important part in determining how motivated they are and how much they learn.

In the next section we focus on the relationship of academic self-concept to motivation and learning. As we noted earlier in the book, self-concept is somewhat different from self-esteem, self-efficacy, and identity. Table 11.2 offers a quick review of these terms.

> Self-esteem is global judgment we make of self; self-concept is judgment we make of self in specific domains; self-efficacy is belief in our ability to carry out a specific action

Table 11.2	Comparing Identity, Self-Esteem, Self-Concept, and Self-Efficacy	
Type of Self-Perception	**Major Characteristics**	**Examples**
Identity	• The largely nonevaluative picture people have of themselves and the groups to which they belong.	• "I am an animal-lover." • "I am female." • "I am going to be a writer."
Self-esteem (self-worth)	• The global evaluative judgments people make of themselves. • Identity describes who you are and with whom you identify; self-esteem indicates how you feel about that identity.	• "I am a good person." • "I am happy with myself the way I am." • "I feel inferior to most people."
Self-concept	• The evaluative judgments people make of their competence in specific areas or domains and their associated feelings of self-worth. • Past-oriented. • For older students, self-concepts may be hierarchically arranged. For example, academic self-concept = verbal self-concept + mathematical self-concept + science self-concept, etc.	• "I'm pretty good at sports." • "I have always done well in math." • "My academic skills are about average." • "I get tongue-tied when I have to speak in public."
Self-efficacy	• The beliefs people have about their ability to carry out a specific course of action. • Future-oriented.	• "I believe I can learn how to use a computer program." • "I don't think I'll ever figure out how to solve quadratic equations." • "I'm sure I can get at least a B in this course."

SOURCES: Bong & Skaalvik (2003); Harter (1999); Kaplan & Flum (2009); Kernis (2002); Schunk & Pajares (2002).

The Role of Academic Self-Concept in Motivation and Learning

Over the years, researchers have consistently found a moderately positive relationship (called a correlation) between measures of academic self-concept and school achievement. Students who score relatively high on measures of academic self-concept tend to have higher-than-average grades. But correlation does not imply causation. The fact that students with high academic self-concept scores tend to have high grades is not sufficient grounds for concluding that high academic self-concept causes high achievement. It is just as plausible that high achievement causes increased academic self-concept or that increases in both variables are due to the influence of a third variable: for example, the extent of ability grouping in a student's high school (Ireson & Hallam, 2009). Recent work on the relationship between academic self-concept and achievement has begun to shed some light on what causes what.

On the basis of their own research with children in grades 2, 3, and 4 and of the research of others, Frédéric Guay, Herbert Marsh, and Michel Boivin (2003) propose the causal explanation depicted in Figure 11.3. These researchers maintain that academic self-concept and achievement have what are called reciprocal effects. That is, not only does prior achievement affect children's academic self-concept, but also the current strength of a child's academic self-concept influences subsequent achievement. In addition, prior achievement has a significant positive relationship with subsequent achievement, and prior self-concept has a significant positive relationship with subsequent self-concept.

Although the role of motivation was not directly tested in this study, related research suggests that the effect of academic self-concept on subsequent achievement is likely to be influenced by motivation. So a student with a strong academic self-concept for, say, social studies is likely to be highly motivated to take additional courses in that subject and to use effective learning skills, which produce higher levels of achievement. At the same time, high levels of achievement strengthen the student's academic self-concept, which supports a high level of motivation, which supports high levels of achievement, and so on.

The instructional implication that flows from this research is fairly clear: teachers should design instructional programs that are aimed directly at improving both academic self-concept and achievement. The former can be accomplished by, for example, pointing out to students how well they have learned certain skills and bodies of knowledge, and the latter can be accomplished by teaching students the information processing and self-regulation skills we discussed in the chapters on information processing theory and social cognitive theory.

Academic self-concept and achievement can positively affect each other

Design instruction to improve both academic self-concept and achievement

Figure 11.3 Relationship Between Academic Self-Concept and Achievement

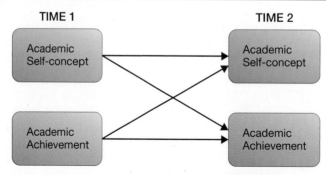

SOURCE: Adapted from Guay, Marsh, & Boivin (2003).

Increase Motivation by Maintaining High Self-Worth

There is no getting around the fact that classrooms are competitive places, largely because students know they are there to develop certain competencies and that some are better equipped to do so than others. Consequently, the decisions students make that affect their motivation to learn revolve around creating and maintaining a sense of self-worth. When a student pays attention to and imitates the behavior of high-achieving models, strives to develop high levels of self-efficacy in various subject areas, selects task mastery goals, attributes success and failure to appropriate combinations of effort and ability, believes that intellectual ability can be learned and refined, and strives to satisfy growth needs, the student is driven by the need to feel good about herself (self-esteem or self-worth).

The leading proponent of this view, Martin Covington (2009), points out that students who believe they are less capable than others (in terms of acquiring the academic competencies demanded by parents, teachers, and society at large) will be less motivated to strive for high levels of achievement because of the increased risk of failure, and they will be more motivated to engage in such self-protective behaviors as reducing effort and self-handicapping.

You can establish the conditions that lead to high levels of motivation by following the many suggestions made in this and other chapters. In particular (and we know we have raised this issue before), do not turn your classroom into a cutthroat, survival-of-the-fittest contest for a limited supply of As, Bs, awards, and praise. Instead, help students acquire the skills they need to meet the learning standards established by you, your school district, and your state. Remember, your primary role in the classroom is to teach, not to sort.

What Do You Think?

Do you agree with the argument that teachers should "teach, not sort"? How will you apply your beliefs in your classroom? To delve further into this issue, see the Take a Stand! section of the textbook's student website.

Motivation and Identity

Generally speaking, the relationship between motivation and identity is seen as the link between a person's goal-directed behavior and that person's perception of who she or he is or may become (Kaplan & Flum, 2009). Jacquelynne Eccles (2009), for example, argues that identity can be conceptualized as two sets of self-perceptions: (1) perceptions of skills, characteristics, and competencies; and (2) perceptions of personal values and goals. In combination, these two sets of self-perceptions determine a person's expectations for success and what kinds of tasks she or he views as important. Thus, identity influences behavioral actions: what one chooses to do and how one chooses to engage in what they do. Think back to our earlier discussions of self-efficacy and how efficacy perceptions are context specific: a student may feel confident in science class, but not as confident in a literature class. A student's self-efficacy perceptions can influence her or his perceptions of self and, therefore, her or his sense of identity.

K. Ann Renninger (2009) sees the connection between motivation and identity as the interaction of interest and identity. In her view, a student who is "interested" in science "identifies with" the content of science. In this view, understanding a student's motivation means understanding what kinds of content and activities attract a student. Renninger's conception is consistent with what we have examined as intrinsic motivation. The instructional implication here suggests that enhancing motivation in a particular area is a matter of creating opportunities for students to develop their interest in various academic pursuits. Interest can be "triggered" by a situation that attracts their attention. That interest can be maintained through interactions with others that help the student connect their skills and prior knowledge to the situation. Seeing their own skills and experiences as connected to the situation helps students "identify with" that situation to the point where they begin to engage and re-engage similar situations on their own. A student who sees a teacher hold a plastic bag filled with water and then pierce that bag with a sharp pencil—without bursting the bag or spilling even a drop of water (yes, it works like a charm as long as you use the right kind of plastic bag)—may re-enact the event for family and friends outside the classroom and eventually develop a personal interest in investigating the elastic properties of various substances. This view helps teachers think about the instructional events they plan for their students as opportunities for students to "identify with" those events and, thus, develop an interest that will motivate them in the future. (We will consider instructional planning in Chapter 13, "Approaches to Instruction.")

As we learned in Chapter 2, "Theories of Psychosocial and Cognitive Development," identity is a crucial issue during adolescence. Middle and high school students are consumed with many questions: "Who am I?" "What am I going to do with my life?" "How do I fit in with others in my group?" (Eccles, 2009). The perceptions that your students develop—their self-concept, self-esteem, sense of self-efficacy,

Students who have strong academic self-concepts often are more highly motivated and earn higher grades than students with weaker academic self-concepts. John Howard/Jupiter Images

and identity—are part of what they will learn in and out of school and in and out of your classroom. The learning opportunities you provide will influence not only their academic skills and knowledge, but how they come to perceive and understand themselves.

Now that you are familiar with approaches to motivation based on humanistic theories and on self-perceptions, consider the additional Suggestions for Teaching that follow.

Suggestions for Teaching

Satisfying Deficiency Needs and Strengthening Self-Perceptions

1 Make learning inviting to students.

Motivation researchers (e.g., Riggs & Gholar, 2009; Tomlinson, 2002) maintain that students care about learning when they are invited to learn. Teachers extend such invitations when they do the following:

JOURNAL ENTRY
Ways to Invite Students to Learn

- Meet Maslow's safety and belonging needs. Examples of meeting students' safety and belonging needs include never ridiculing a student for lack of knowledge or skills or letting other students do the same, praising students when they do well and inquiring about possible problems when they do not, relating lessons to students' interests, and learning students' names as quickly as possible.

- Provide opportunities for students to make meaningful contributions to their classroom. Examples here include having students help classmates master instructional objectives through short-term tutoring or cooperative learning arrangements and inviting students to use personal experiences and background as a way to broaden a lesson or class discussion. One classroom teacher created overhead transparencies of students' work for use as an instructional tool; this gave students the sense that they were a contributing part of a community (Gilness, 2003).

- Create a sense of purpose for the material students are required to learn. As we point out in Chapter 13, "Approaches to Instruction," students rarely ask "Why do I have to learn this?" (although it is uppermost in their minds), and teachers rarely offer an explanation without being prompted. One way to create purpose for a reading lesson is to engage the students in a discussion of an issue they are interested in that is at the heart of a story or novel they are about to read.

- Allow students to develop a sense of power about their learning. Students who believe that the knowledge and skills they are learning are useful to them now (using history as a tool for thinking about the present, for example), who know what constitutes good-quality work and believe themselves capable of producing it, and who know how to set goals and meet them are more likely than other students to believe they are in control of their learning.

- Create challenging tasks for students. Students who work hard, who feel they are being stretched, yet who succeed more often than not are more likely to enjoy learning and to approach future tasks with increased motivation than are students whose work is routine and consistently at a low level of difficulty.

2 **Direct learning experiences toward feelings of success in an effort to encourage an orientation toward achievement, high self-esteem, and a strong sense of self-efficacy and academic self-concept.**

To feel successful, an individual must first establish goals that are neither so low as to be unfulfilling nor so high as to be impossible and then be able to achieve them at an acceptable level.

    a. Make use of learning goals and objectives that are challenging but attainable and, when appropriate, that involve student input.

As will be discussed in Chapter 13, "Approaches to Instruction," you will have primary responsibility for choosing the learning objectives for your students. You can use this process to heighten motivation by inviting your students to participate in selecting objectives or at least in thinking along with you as you explain why the objectives are worthwhile. This will tend to shift the emphasis from extrinsic to intrinsic motivation.

    To help students suggest appropriate objectives, you may want to use the techniques recommended by Robert Mager (1997). You might assist your students in stating objectives in terms of a time limit, a minimum number of correct responses, a proportion of correct responses, or a sample of actions.

EXAMPLES

- "How many minutes do you think you will need to outline this chapter? When you finish, we'll see that film I told you about."

- "George, you got six out of ten on this spelling quiz. How many do you want to try for on the retest?"

    b. Help students master your objectives.

    As you have seen, a student's past accomplishments on a particular task influence his or her self-efficacy and academic self-concept. Consequently, you should do whatever you can to help students achieve at an acceptable level. One important recommendation for helping students become better learners was made earlier: teach them how to create and use learning strategies. Another suggestion that will help them get the most out of their strategies is to assign moderately difficult tasks and provide the minimum amount of assistance necessary to complete the task successfully (think of Vygotsky's zone of proximal development and the concept of scaffolding).

JOURNAL ENTRY
Ways to Encourage Students to Set Their Own Objectives

JOURNAL ENTRY
Ways to Help Students Master Objectives

More ideas for your journal can be found in the Reflective Journal Questions at the textbook's student website, Education CourseMate.

Many of the motivational techniques we have suggested in this chapter can be enhanced by the appropriate use of technology. To conclude the chapter, we discuss research on the link between technology and motivation, and we survey a number of kinds of technology that have been shown to be useful.

MOTIVATING STUDENTS WITH TECHNOLOGY

Extrinsic Versus Intrinsic Motivation

Previously in this chapter, we contrasted the behavioral, or extrinsic, approach to motivation with various cognitive, or intrinsic, approaches. Our goal was not to demonstrate that one approach is inherently superior to the other but to point out how and when both approaches can profitably be used to support classroom learning. A parallel situation exists with regard to the motivating effects of technology. Behavioral psychologists, for example, argue that students who work on computer-based drill-and-practice programs are motivated by the immediate feedback they receive and the steady progress they make. Cognitive psychologists argue that involving students in fantasy environments or authentic tasks that are directed to audiences besides the teacher is intrinsically motivating because such programs and tasks give students a sense of confidence, personal responsibility, and control over their own learning (Fok & Watkins, 2009; Hewitt, 2002; Moreno & Mayer, 2002, 2005).

> Technology can be used to support both extrinsic and intrinsic motivation

Despite the differences in these two approaches to motivation, they are not mutually exclusive. Some of the most innovative and effective technological aids to learning combine both approaches (Shin, 2009). Consider, for example, the Quest Atlantis project we mentioned in Chapter 10 on constructivist learning theory.

Using Technology to Increase Motivation to Learn

Computer-based technology can accommodate both extrinsic and intrinsic approaches to motivation. But does it, in fact, increase students' motivation to learn?

> Technology increases intrinsic motivation by making learning more interesting and meaningful

Critics of computer-based learning argue that any observed increases in student motivation are likely to be short term and due largely to the novelty when students engage new programs, games, or virtual environments. But several studies have demonstrated that the use of computer-based instruction increases students' intrinsic motivation and performance:

- First graders in urban schools who were at risk of failing to learn basic literacy skills engaged in computer-assisted literacy instruction. Not only did the technology engage the students in ways that enhanced their listening, reading, and writing skills, but it did so in ways that made the students less anxious about difficulties they encountered and more likely to persist when difficulties were encountered (Blachowicz et al., 2009).
- Eighth graders who were judged to be candidates to drop out of school because of academic and social problems received 2 weeks of instruction on the Bill of Rights. Those who were given a chance to create and present a computer-based multimedia project on the subject scored better on tests of both subject matter and attitudes toward learning than peers who engaged in traditional classroom projects (Woodul, Vitale, & Scott, 2000).
- High school seniors working in cooperative learning groups created PowerPoint presentations about poets of the Romantic period. Compared with previous classes, this group showed a much higher level of motivation for learning about this subject matter (Marr, 2000).
- High school students in Israel—where engineering education is part of the high school curriculum—have used technology, including creating their own computer programs, to design and build, using LEGO blocks, robots, cars, cranes, and even a system that would allow a boat to cross a waterfall in both directions (Doppelt, 2009). According to the researchers, "The laboratory became a

second home to the pupils. They came to work on their projects during breaks and free hours, and even after school" (Doppelt & Barak, 2002, p. 26).

Computer-based or augmented programs are often used to improve students' literacy skills and motivation for reading and writing. For example, a technology-enhanced summer program designed to help low-achieving inner-city middle school children improve their reading and writing skills produced noticeable improvements in motivation. Students used data gathering tools, data management tools, and presentation tools to complete inquiry projects and present the results to an audience of parents, peers, and siblings. As the students shared their efforts with one another and noticed the impact of such features as computer graphics, web pages, PowerPoint slide shows, and videotaped interviews, they quickly and eagerly revised their own projects to incorporate one or more of these features (Owens, Hester, & Teale, 2002).

TeachSource Video Case ◀◀ ▶ ▶▶

Integrating Internet Research: High School Social Studies

Go to the Education CourseMate website to watch the Video Case, and then answer the following questions:

1. Does the Civil Rights Scrapbook Project promote extrinsic motivation, intrinsic motivation, or both? What evidence can you cite based on observing the students in this Video Case?

2. If you were a student in this class, would you find this technology project motivating? Why or why not? What aspects of the lesson are especially motivating? What ideas do you have to make the lesson more motivating for students?

A survey of elementary grade teachers who published students' writing projects on a classroom website revealed a similar motivating effect. Students were more inclined to complete their projects and to do high-quality work when they knew it would be seen by a wider audience (Karchmer, 2001). According to one fourth-grade teacher:

> Before the Internet, my children did not write as much, as writing without a purpose was not fulfilling. We have a purpose now and that makes the work more interesting for the children. They are really proud to see their work on the Internet. . . . I believe the students are being more careful with their language arts skills. Their errors are pretty easy to see, and they do not seem to have any problem with changing them. In paper and pencil writing, it is very difficult to get them to change what they are writing. (Karchmer, 2001, p. 459)

E-mail and other messaging systems are often used to heighten student interest and motivation. Pen-pal projects can link students in different locales or countries. Rebecca Sipe (2000) described a project in which her preservice teacher education undergraduates corresponded with 10th-grade English students, who helped the preservice students formulate realistic classroom beliefs and practices. Carole Duff (2000) described how female high school students use e-mail to get career advice, academic guidance, and personal support from a professional woman mentor. Diane Friedlaender (2009) described how, at the onset of the Iraq War, a teacher arranged for middle school students in Oakland, California, to become pen pals with students in Iraq. The Oakland students ". . . studied the reasons given for the war, listened to and spoke with guest speakers on a weekly basis, and wrote, directed, and acted in a play about the impact of war on families. Students even marched down Market Street in San Francisco holding up pictures of their pen pals . . ." (Friedlander, 2009, p. 10). Connecting students to real people and real events provides extrinsic motivation to learn at the same time it stimulates students' intrinsic motivation.

To review this chapter, try the tutorial quizzes and other study aids on the textbook's Education CourseMate website.

Challenging Assumptions

Teaching . . . Learning . . . Motivation

"Antonio," says Connie, "you said that the comment you heard in the teachers' lounge—that something was taught, but not learned—really stayed with you. Why is that, do you think?"

"I'm not exactly sure, but it seems to me that for a teacher to say 'I taught that but the students didn't learn it' is like a salesperson saying 'I sold that but the customer didn't buy it.'"

"You know, more than 70 years ago, John Dewey said something very much like that," Connie says. "So if teaching should be examined—its quality understood—in light of the learning it facilitates, what does that mean for motivation?"

"It means we have to facilitate its development in students," says Antonio. He gazes out the window for a moment. "We can't learn for our students. They have to construct their own understandings, their own knowledge representations, but we can facilitate their construction. In terms of motivation, we can also be facilitators. We can provide opportunities for students to explore their interests and to discover new ones. In the same way we should facilitate their development of knowledge and skills in a content area such as math or English, we should facilitate their development of self-knowledge and the skills to use their own interests to help them achieve learning goals. If we can help students experience success as learners, they'll develop a sense of self-efficacy and a strong academic self-concept." He is silent for another moment. "Teaching is about facilitating student learning. I want to be a teacher who helps students learn that they can succeed as learners."

Summary

1. Motivation is the willingness to expend a certain amount of effort to achieve a particular goal under a particular set of circumstances.

2. The behavioral (operant conditioning) view of motivation is based on the desire of students to obtain a positive reinforcer for exhibiting a particular behavior or behavior pattern.

3. A potential limitation of operant conditioning theory is its emphasis on extrinsic sources of motivation. The learner is motivated to attain a goal so as to receive a reward that is not inherently related to the activity. This may produce only temporary changes in behavior, a materialistic attitude toward learning, and an undermining of whatever intrinsic motivation a student may have for a particular task.

4. Intrinsic motivation can be undermined by extrinsic reinforcement when initial interest in a task is high, the rewards are tangible, the rewards are promised in advance as an incentive to exhibit the desired behavior, the reward is given just for engaging in an activity, and students have to compete with one another for a limited supply of rewards.

5. Extrinsic rewards may enhance intrinsic motivation when initial interest in a task is low because it is seen as boring or irrelevant; when initial interest in a task is high and reward involves positive verbal feedback; and when the highest level of reward is potentially available to all who qualify.

6. The social cognitive view of motivation is based largely on giving students the opportunity to observe and imitate the behavior of models they admire and enhancing students' self-efficacy for particular tasks.

7. A student's level of self-efficacy—how capable one believes one is to perform a particular task—affects motivation by affecting the learning goals that are chosen, the outcome the student expects, and the attributions the student makes for success and failure.

8. Students may choose a task mastery goal, a performance-approach goal, a performance-avoidance goal, or a combination of the first two. Students who choose task mastery goals use meaningful learning strategies and treat mistakes as part of learning. Students who choose

performance-approach goals are motivated to demonstrate superior ability by outperforming others. Students who choose performance-avoidance goals are motivated to avoid the possibility of failure so as not to appear less capable than others; they may also engage in self-handicapping behaviors so that they have an excuse for poor performance.

9. Students with high self-efficacy generally expect a positive outcome for tasks they take on. Students with low self-efficacy are more likely than students with high self-efficacy to expect negative academic outcomes.

10. The cognitive development view holds that people are inherently motivated by a need to achieve equilibration by overcoming inconsistencies or contradictions between what they know and what they experience.

11. Atkinson proposes that people are motivated by a need for achievement, which is a general desire to attain goals that require some degree of competence. Individuals with a high need to achieve have a greater expectation of success than they do a fear of failure. They prefer moderately difficult tasks because such tasks provide an optimal balance between the possibility of failure and the expectation of success. Individuals with a low need to achieve are dominated by a fear of failure. Consequently, they prefer either very easy tasks (because success is ensured) or very difficult tasks (because there is no shame in failing to do well at them).

12. Research on attribution theory has found marked differences between high achievers and low achievers. High achievers attribute success to ability and effort, and failure to insufficient effort. Low achievers attribute success to luck or easiness of the task and failure to lack of ability.

13. Compared with younger children, seven- and eight-year-olds show greater awareness of the concept of ability, distinguish ability from other characteristics, think of ability as an internal capability that is stable over time, and are more likely to compare their performance to those of their peers.

14. Compared with seven- and eight-year-olds, ten- to twelve-year-old children are more likely to distinguish between ability and effort, to evaluate their ability accurately, to think of ability as a stable and fixed characteristic, and to be concerned with getting the highest grade.

15. Some students are less motivated than others because they subscribe to what Dweck calls an entity theory of cognitive ability. Because they believe that intelligence is a fixed capacity, they

are primarily interested in getting high grades and appearing smart to others and tend to avoid challenging tasks if uncertain of success. Students who subscribe to an incremental theory tend to pursue more meaningful learning opportunities because they think of intelligence as something that can be improved through experience and corrective feedback.

16. Level of interest in a subject is related to intrinsic motivation for that subject. In some instances, students have a preexisting interest in a subject (personal interest), but in other instances, interest grows out of involvement with the subject (situational interest). Students with a personal interest in a topic or subject are more likely to be intrinsically motivated to learn about that topic or subject.

17. Personal interest in a subject may be influenced by such factors as the student's own emotions, degree of competence attained, relevance to a goal, and level of prior knowledge.

18. Situational interest in a subject may be influenced by such factors as hands-on activities, a state of cognitive disequilibrium, well-written material, the opportunity to work with others, and observing influential models.

19. Csikszentmihalyi and other researchers concluded that a sense of flow (i.e., intense engagement) is more likely when students feel a sense of control over their own learning and when the learning activities challenge students at a level appropriate to their skills.

20. One limitation of the cognitive development view is that teachers may not always find it possible to induce a sense of disequilibrium in students.

21. A problem with need-for-achievement theory is the lack of instruments with which to measure that need and the unreliability of short-term observations.

22. A limitation of attribution theory and beliefs about ability is the difficulty of changing students' faulty attribution patterns and beliefs about the nature of cognitive ability.

23. Maslow's humanistic view of motivation is based on the idea that a person must satisfy a hierarchical sequence of deficiency needs (physiological, safety, belongingness and love, and esteem) before satisfying the growth need for self-actualization.

24. A limitation of the humanistic view is that the teacher may not always find it possible to identify a student's unmet deficiency needs or to satisfy them once they are identified.

25. The relationship between a student's academic self-concept and achievement is reciprocal. That is, not only does academic self-concept influence

motivation for learning a particular subject, which influences achievement, but also prior achievement has a positive effect on both motivation and academic self-concept.

26. Digital environments have been shown to have a beneficial effect on students' motivation to learn because they make learning interesting and meaningful.

Resources for Further Investigation

● Motivational Theory

In the *Handbook of Motivation at School* (2009), edited by Kathryn Wentzel and Allan Wigfield, all of the theories of motivation in this chapter are addressed in Section I. Section II examines how context and social influences affect motivation. Section III focuses on motivation in the context of teaching and learning.

In *Culture, Self, and, Motivation: Essays in Honor of Martin L. Maehr* (2009), edited by Avi Kaplan, Stuart Karabenick, & Elizabeth De Groot, motivational theory that focuses on the development and perceptions of self and on the context of culture are examined. The essays delve into personal motivation and sociocultural processes (recall constructivism in Chapter 10).

● Cognitive Views of Motivation

Motivation and Self-Regulated Learning (2007), edited by Dale Schunk and Barry Zimmerman, focuses on the role of motivational processes—such as goals, attributions, self-efficacy, outcome expectations, self-concept, self-esteem, social comparisons, emotions, values, and self-evaluations—in self-regulated learning.

Frank Pajares is a prolific and award-winning teacher and researcher at Emory University. In addition to his books and articles, he has developed several extraordinarily useful

and interesting websites. One of them is called "Information on Self-Efficacy: A Community of Scholars." For those interested in self-efficacy, there is no better place to start than this site: **www.des.emory.edu/mfp/self-efficacy.html**.

● Motivational Techniques for the Classroom

In the second edition of their book, *Strategies That Promote Student Engagement: Unleashing the Desire to Learn* (2009), Ernestine Riggs and Cheryl Gholar focus on designing a lesson that "invites" and engages students. Chapter 3 of the book is entitled "Where Learning Lives," an intriguing metaphor and a frame that could provide a rich source for entries in your Reflective Journal.

Basic information about motivation and ideas on how to affect student motivation can be found on the Web. The KidSource website has a page titled "Student Motivation to Learn" (accessible from **www.kidsource.com/kidsource/pages/ed.k12.html**). It discusses the factors that influence the development of motivation, the advantages of intrinsic motivation, how motivation to learn can be fostered in the school setting, and what can be done to help unmotivated students.

For ideas on how to motivate students to learn math, visit the web page titled "Mathematics and Motivation: An Annotated Bibliography" at the following site: **mathforum.com/~sarah/Discussion.Sessions/biblio.motivation.html**.

12 Classroom Management

The Education CourseMate website for this text offers many helpful resources. Go to **CengageBrain.com** to preview this chapter's Concept Maps and Chapter Themes.

KEY POINTS

These key points will help you learn the important information in this chapter. To help you study, they also appear in the margins of the pages, next to the text where they are discussed.

Authoritarian, Permissive, and Authoritative Approaches to Classroom Management

- Authoritative approach to classroom management superior to permissive and authoritarian approaches

Preventing Problems: Techniques of Classroom Management

- Ripple effect: group response to a reprimand directed at an individual
- Teachers who show they are "with it" head off discipline problems
- Being able to handle overlapping activities helps maintain classroom control
- Teachers who continually interrupt activities have discipline problems
- Keeping entire class involved and alert minimizes misbehavior
- Identify misbehavers; firmly specify constructive behavior
- Effective teachers plan how to handle classroom routines
- During first weeks, have students complete clear assignments under your direction
- Manage behavior of adolescents by making and communicating clear rules and procedures

Suggestions for Teaching: Techniques of Classroom Management

- Establish, call attention to, and explain class rules the first day
- Establish a businesslike but supportive classroom atmosphere

Techniques for Dealing with Behavior Problems

- Use supportive reactions to help students develop self-control
- Give criticism privately; then offer encouragement
- I-message: tell how you feel about an unacceptable situation
- Determine who owns a problem before deciding on course of action

Suggestions for Teaching: Handling Problem Behavior

- Be prompt, consistent, reasonable when dealing with misbehavior

Violence in American Schools

- Incidents of crime and serious violence occur relatively infrequently in public schools and have been decreasing in recent years
- Boys, girls favor different forms of bullying
- Male aggressiveness due to biological and cultural factors
- Middle school and junior high boys with low grades may feel trapped
- Misbehavior of high school students may reveal lack of positive identity
- Classroom disruptions can be significantly reduced by various approaches
- Violence less likely when schoolwide programs teach students constructive ways to handle conflicts

---

By now you have no doubt begun to realize what we pointed out at the beginning of the book: teaching is a complex enterprise. It is complex for the following reasons:

- Students vary in their physical, social, emotional, cognitive, and cultural characteristics.
- Learning occurs gradually and only with extensive and varied practice.
- Different students learn at different rates.
- Systematic preparations have to be made to ensure that students master the objectives that teachers lay out.

- Different students, or groups of students, are often working on different tasks at any point in time.
- Student behaviors are somewhat unpredictable.
- Students are motivated to learn (or not learn) by different factors.
- Learning can be measured and evaluated in a variety of ways.

If not managed properly, an endeavor as complex as teaching can easily become chaotic. When that happens, students are likely to become confused, bored, uninterested, restless, and perhaps even disruptive. But a well-managed classroom is not what many people think: students working silently at their desks (or in front of their computers), speaking only when spoken to, and providing verbatim recitations of what the teacher and textbook said. Such a classroom is incompatible with the contemporary views of learning and motivation described in the preceding chapters. If some of your goals are for students to acquire a meaningful knowledge base, become proficient problem solvers, and learn how to work productively with others, then you have to accept the idea that these goals are best met in classrooms that are characterized by a fair amount of autonomy, physical movement, and social interaction (Emmer & Stough, 2001).

To help you accomplish these goals *and* keep student behavior within manageable bounds, we describe in this chapter a general approach to classroom management that is related to an effective parenting style, various techniques that you can use to prevent behavior problems from occurring, and a set of techniques for dealing with misbehavior once it has occurred. In addition, we analyze the issue of school violence and bullying, summarize approaches to reducing its frequency, and note how technology has been used to encourage underachieving and disruptive students to stay in school.

Revealing Assumptions

Managing Classrooms and Leading Learning

From Connie's point of view, the Friday meeting has gone well. Her young colleagues have connected important constructivist principles of learning and motivation to their experiences and observations. As the meeting winds down, the group becomes reflective.

Celeste says, "I've been thinking about all of these ideas for enhancing learning and motivation. I know they are critical. But, to be honest, I'm worried that I'll never get to use them."

"What is it, exactly, that worries you?" asks Connie. "What do you think might prevent you from using what you are learning?"

Celeste thinks for a moment and says, "To be honest, I'm worried that I won't be able to control my class."

"Yeah, I'm worried about that, too," says Don. "I mean before you can teach, you have to have control over your students. If they aren't paying attention, then how can they learn? And how do you keep them working all day long, every day? How do you keep them doing what they are supposed to be doing instead of what they want to do?"

Antonio is smiling to himself, and Connie notices. She catches his eye and nods as though to say, "You know what they are saying and it's important; let them hear from you."

Antonio says, "I remember having that exact feeling and it was scary. I even wondered whether I should be a teacher. But one thing I've learned from the 'vets' on my teaching team is to view classroom management differently. By applying those ideas about learning and motivation, you engage students in learning. Engaged students don't have to be controlled. They are already busy learning: learning the content, learning about themselves, and learning to be better learners. Classroom management is not a matter of controlling students, but a matter of leading learning."

pause & reflect

Research on beliefs and attitudes shows that many aspiring teachers are anxious about classroom management. It can be daunting to contemplate how you are going to establish and maintain a classroom environment that keeps students focused on learning. Celeste and Don demonstrate those concerns. They assume that managing a classroom means controlling student behavior. How do you perceive the role of classroom manager? Is your current perception of the role closer to Celeste's and Don's or to Antonio's? Perhaps you have known teachers who managed by "controlling students" and others who managed by "leading learning." How did your experience as a student differ in those two kinds of classrooms?

AUTHORITARIAN, PERMISSIVE, AND AUTHORITATIVE APPROACHES TO CLASSROOM MANAGEMENT

You may recall from Chapter 3 on age-level characteristics that Diana Baumrind (1971, 1991a) found that parents tend to exhibit one of four styles in managing the behavior of their children: authoritarian, permissive, authoritative, or rejecting-neglecting. The first three of these styles have been applied to a teacher's actions in the classroom. We will quickly review Baumrind's categories and then take a brief look at how teachers' approaches to management can be characterized by these styles, too.

Authoritarian parents establish rules for their children's behavior and expect them to be blindly obeyed. Explanations of the reason a particular rule is necessary are almost never given. Instead, rewards and punishments are given for following or not following rules. *Permissive* parents represent the other extreme. They impose few controls. They allow their children to make many basic decisions (such as what to eat, what to wear, when to go to bed) and provide advice or assistance only when asked. *Authoritative* parents provide rules but discuss the reasons for them, teach their children how to meet them, and reward children for exhibiting self-control. Authoritative parents also cede more responsibility for self-governance to their children as the children demonstrate increased self-regulation skills. This style, more so than the other two, leads to children's internalizing the parents' norms and maintaining intrinsic motivation for following them in the future.

You can probably see the parallel between Baumrind's work and classroom management. Teachers who adopt an authoritarian style are likely to have student compliance rather than autonomy as their main goal ("Do what I say because I say so") and make heavy use of rewards and punishments to produce that compliance. Teachers who adopt a permissive style are likely to rely heavily on students' identifying with and respecting them as their main approach to classroom management ("Do what I say because you like me and respect my judgment"). Teachers who adopt an authoritative style are likely to want their students to learn to eventually regulate their own behavior. By explaining the rationale for classroom rules and adjusting those rules as students demonstrate the ability to govern themselves appropriately, authoritative teachers hope to convince students that adopting the teacher's norms for classroom behavior as their own will lead to the achievement of valued academic goals ("Do what I say because doing so will help you learn more"). The students of authoritative teachers better understand the need for classroom rules and tend to operate within them most of the time (Walker & Hoover-Dempsey, 2006).

Two studies support the extension of Baumrind's parenting styles to classroom teachers. In one, middle school students who described their teachers in terms that reflect the authoritative style (for example, the teacher sets clear rules and explains the penalty for breaking them, trusts students to carry out certain tasks independently, treats all students fairly, does not criticize students for not having the right answer, and has high expectations for academic achievement and behavior) scored higher on measures of motivation, prosocial behavior, and achievement than did students who described their teachers in more authoritarian terms (Wentzel, 2002). The other study demonstrated that a teacher's decision to either support student autonomy or be more controlling of what students do in class is very much a function of the environment in which they work. When teachers have curriculum decisions and performance standards imposed on them for which they will be held accountable and when they feel that students are not highly motivated to learn, their intrinsic motivation for teaching suffers. This lowered intrinsic motivation, in turn, leads them to be less supportive of student autonomy and more controlling (Pelletier, Séguin-Lévesque, & Legault, 2002).

The next part of this chapter will describe guidelines you might follow to establish and maintain an effective learning environment.

Authoritative approach to classroom management superior to permissive and authoritarian approaches

PREVENTING PROBLEMS: TECHNIQUES OF CLASSROOM MANAGEMENT

Kounin's Observations on Group Management

Interest in the significance of classroom management was kindled when Jacob Kounin wrote a book titled *Discipline and Group Management in Classrooms* (1970). Kounin noted that he first became interested in group management when he reprimanded a college student for blatantly reading a newspaper in class. Kounin was struck by the extent to which the entire class responded to a reprimand directed at only one person, and he subsequently dubbed this the **ripple effect.** Chances are you can recall a situation in which you were diligently working away in a classroom and the teacher suddenly became quite angry at a disruptive classmate. If you felt a bit tense after the incident (even though your behavior was blameless) and tried to give the impression that you were a paragon of student virtue, you have had personal experience with the ripple effect.

> **Ripple effect: group response to a reprimand directed at an individual**

Once his interest in classroom behavior was aroused, Kounin supervised a series of observational and experimental studies of student reactions to techniques of teacher control. In analyzing the results of these various studies, he came to the conclusion that the following classroom management techniques appear to be most effective:

pause & reflect

Would you use the ripple effect deliberately? Why or why not?

> **Teachers who show they are "with it" head off discipline problems**

1. *Show your students that you are "with it."* Kounin coined the term **withitness** to emphasize that teachers who prove to their students that they know what is going on in a classroom usually have fewer behavior problems than teachers who appear to be unaware of incipient disruptions. An expert at classroom management will nip trouble in the bud by commenting on potentially disruptive behavior before it gains momentum. An ineffective teacher may not notice such behavior until it begins to spread and then perhaps hopes that it will simply go away.

   At first glance Kounin's suggestion that you show that you are with it might seem to be in conflict with operant conditioning's prediction that nonreinforced behavior will disappear. If the teacher's reaction is the only source of reinforcement in a classroom, ignoring behavior may cause it to disappear. In many cases, however, a misbehaving student gets reinforced by the reactions of classmates. Therefore, ignoring behavior is much less likely to lead to extinction of a response in a classroom than in controlled experimental situations.

> **JOURNAL ENTRY**
> Learning to Deal with Overlapping Situations

2. *Learn to cope with overlapping situations.* When he analyzed videotapes of actual classroom interactions, Kounin found that some teachers seemed to have one-track minds. They were inclined to deal with only one thing at a time, and this way of proceeding caused frequent interruptions in classroom routine. One primary grade teacher whom Kounin observed, for example, was working with a reading group when she noticed two boys on the other side of the room poking each other. She abruptly got up, walked over to the boys, berated them at length, and then returned to the reading group. By the time she returned, however, the children in the reading group had become bored and listless and were tempted to engage in mischief of their own.

> **Being able to handle overlapping activities helps maintain classroom control**

   Kounin concluded that withitness and skill in handling overlapping activities seemed to be related. An expert classroom manager who is talking to children in a reading group, for example, might notice two boys at the far side of the room who are beginning to scuffle with each other. Such a teacher might in midsentence tell the boys to stop and make the point so adroitly that the attention of the children in the reading group does not waver.

JOURNAL ENTRY
Learning to Handle
Momentum

Teachers who continually
interrupt activities have
discipline problems

JOURNAL ENTRY
Ways to Keep the Whole
Class Involved

*ADD
TERMS*

Keeping entire class involved and
alert minimizes misbehavior

3. *Strive to maintain smoothness and momentum in class activities.* This point is related to the previous one. Kounin found that some teachers caused problems for themselves by constantly interrupting activities without thinking about what they were doing. Some teachers whose activities were recorded on videotape failed to maintain the thrust of a lesson because they seemed unaware of the rhythm of student behavior (that is, they did not take into account the degree of student inattention and restlessness but instead moved ahead in an almost mechanical way). Others flip-flopped from one activity to another. Still others would interrupt one activity (for example, a reading lesson) to comment on an unrelated aspect of classroom functioning ("Someone left a lunch bag on the floor"). There were also some who wasted time dwelling on a trivial incident (making a big fuss because a boy lost his pencil). And a few teachers delivered individual, instead of group, instruction ("All right, Charlie, you go to the board. Fine. Now, Rebecca, you go to the board"). All of these types of teacher behavior tended to interfere with the flow of learning activities.

4. *Try to keep the whole class involved, even when you are dealing with individual students.* Kounin found that some well-meaning teachers had fallen into a pattern of calling on students in a predictable order and in such a way that the rest of the class served as a passive audience. Unless you stop to think about what you are doing during group recitation periods, you might easily fall into the same trap. If you do, the "audience" is almost certain to become bored and may be tempted to engage in troublemaking activities just to keep occupied.

Some teachers, for example, call on students to recite by going around a circle, or going up and down rows, or following alphabetical order. Others call on a child first and then ask a question. Still others ask one child to recite at length (read an entire page, for example). All of these techniques tend to spotlight one child in predictable order and cause the rest of the class members to tune out until their turn comes. You are more likely to maintain interest and limit mischief caused by boredom if you use techniques such as the following:

- Ask a question, and after pausing a few seconds to let everyone think about it, pick out someone to answer it. With subsequent questions, call on students in an unpredictable order so that no one knows when he or she will be asked to recite. (If you feel that some students in a class are very

Jacob Kounin found that
teachers who were "with it"
could deal with overlapping
situations, maintained
smoothness and momentum
in class activities, used a
variety of activities, kept the
whole class involved, and
had few discipline problems.
Bob Daemmrich/Bob
Daemmrich Photography

apprehensive about being called on, even under relaxing circumstances, you can either ask them extremely easy questions or avoid calling on them at all.)

- If you single out one child to go to the board to do a problem, ask all other students to do the same problem at their desks, and then choose one or two at random to compare their work with the answers on the board.
- When dealing with lengthy or complex material, call on several students in quick succession (and in unpredictable order) and ask each to handle one section. In a primary grade reading group, for example, have one child read a sentence; then pick someone at the other side of the group to read the next sentence, and so on.
- Use props in the form of flashcards, photocopied or computer-printed sheets, or workbook pages to induce all students to respond to questions simultaneously. Then ask students to compare answers. One ingenious elementary school teacher whom Kounin observed had each student print the 10 digits on cards that could be inserted in a slotted piece of cardboard. She would ask a question such as "How much is 8 and 4?" and then pause a moment while the students arranged their answers in the slots and then say, "All show!"

5. *Introduce variety and be enthusiastic, particularly with younger students.* After viewing videotapes of different teachers, Kounin and his associates concluded that some teachers seemed to fall into a deadly routine much more readily than others. They followed the same procedure day after day and responded with the same, almost reflexive comments. At the other end of the scale were teachers who introduced variety, responded with enthusiasm and interest, and moved quickly to new activities when they sensed that students either had mastered or were satiated by a particular lesson. It seems logical to assume that students will be less inclined to sleep, daydream, or engage in disruptive activities if they are exposed to an enthusiastic teacher who varies the pace and type of classroom activities.

6. *Be aware of the ripple effect.* When criticizing student behavior, be clear and firm, focus on behavior rather than on personalities, and try to avoid angry outbursts. If you take into account the suggestions just made, you may be able to reduce the amount of student misbehavior in your classes. Even so, some behavior problems are certain to occur. When you deal with these, you can benefit from Kounin's research on the ripple effect. On the basis of observations, questionnaires, and experimental evidence, he concluded that "innocent" students in a class are more likely to be positively impressed by the way the teacher handles a misbehavior if the following conditions exist:

Identify misbehavers; firmly specify constructive behavior

- The teacher identifies the misbehaver and states what the unacceptable behavior is. ("Jorge! Don't flip that CD at Jamal.")
- The teacher specifies a more constructive behavior. ("Please put the CD back in the storage box.")
- The teacher explains why the deviant behavior should cease. ("If the CD gets broken or dirty, no one else will be able to use it, and we'll have to try to get a new one.")
- The teacher is firm and authoritative and conveys a no-nonsense attitude. ("All infractions of classroom rules will result in an appropriate punishment—no ifs, ands, or buts.")
- The teacher does not resort to anger, humiliation, or extreme punishment. Kounin concluded that extreme reactions did not seem to make children behave better. Instead, anger and severe reprimands upset them and made them feel tense and nervous. ("Roger, that was an incredibly stupid thing to do. Do it again and you'll be sorry.") Not only is this recommendation consistent with common sense, but it is also supported by research. Students who were consistently the target of verbal abuse from teachers, such as

ridicule, name-calling, shaming, yelling, and negative comparisons to other students, were more likely than students who were not treated this way to exhibit subsequent behavior problems and to achieve at lower levels (Brendgen, Wanner, Vitaro, Bukowski, & Tremblay, 2007).

- The teacher focuses on behavior, not on personality. (Say, "Ramona, staring out the window instead of reading your textbook is unacceptable behavior in my classroom" rather than "Ramona, you're the laziest student I have ever had in class.")

Contemporary Studies of Classroom Management

Stimulated by Kounin's observations, researchers have published thousands of studies over the past 40 years on various aspects of classroom management. A recent review of a sample of that research concluded that 20 classroom management practices (such as arranging the classroom environment to minimize distractions, extensive use of praise, and use of token economies) have enough support in the literature that they can be considered for classroom adoption (Simonsen, Fairbanks, Briesch, Myers, & Sugai, 2008). Suggestions for implementing many of these research-based practices can be found in many classroom management books and articles (see, for example, Emmer & Evertson, 2009; Evertson & Emmer, 2009; Ross, Bondy, Galllingane, & Hambacher, 2008; Smith & Bondy, 2007; Woolfolk Hoy & Weinstein, 2006). According to these authors, the basic keys to successful classroom management are as follows:

Effective teachers plan how to handle classroom routines

1. On the first day with a new class, very effective teachers clearly demonstrate that they have thought about classroom procedures ahead of time. They have planned first-day activities that make it possible for classroom routine to be handled with a minimum of confusion. They also make sure students understand why the procedures are necessary and how they are to be followed.
2. A short list of basic classroom rules is posted or announced (or both), and students are told about the penalties they will incur in the event of misbehavior.

During first weeks, have students complete clear assignments under your direction

3. During the first weeks with a new group of students, effective teachers have students engage in whole-group activities under teacher direction. Such activities are selected to make students feel comfortable and successful in their new classroom.
4. After the initial orientation period is over, effective teachers maintain control by using the sorts of techniques that Kounin described: they show they are with it, cope with overlapping situations, maintain smoothness and momentum, and avoid ignoring the rest of the class when dealing with individual students.
5. Effective teachers give clear directions, hold students accountable for completing assignments, and give frequent feedback without being punitive.
6. Effective teachers demonstrate that they care about students, meaning they are interested in and ready to support students in their personal and academic lives.

TeachSource Video Case ◀◀ ▶ ▶▶

Elementary Classroom Management: Basic Strategies

Go to the Education CourseMate website and watch the Video Case, and then answer the following questions:

1. Would you describe Ms. Moylan's classroom management style as authoritarian, permissive, or authoritative? Provide specific examples from the Video Case to support your answer.
2. What elements of the well-managed classroom do you see in this Video Case?

Managing the Middle, Junior High, and High School Classroom

Most of the classroom management techniques and suggestions we have discussed so far are sufficiently general that they can be used in a variety of classroom settings and with primary through secondary grade students. Nevertheless, teaching preadolescents and adolescents is sufficiently different from teaching younger students that the management of the middle school, junior high, and high school classroom requires a slightly different emphasis and a few unique practices.

Classroom management has to be approached somewhat differently in the secondary grades (and in those middle schools in which students change classes several times a day) because of the segmented nature of education for these grades. Instead of being in charge of the same 25 to 30 students all day, most junior high or high school teachers (and some middle school teachers) are responsible for as many as five different groups of 25 to 30 students for about 50 minutes each. This arrangement results in more individual differences, a greater likelihood that these teachers will see a wide range of behavior problems, and a greater concern with efficient use of class time. A survey of beginning middle school and high school teachers found persistent problems with students talking, being out of their seats without permission, using cell phones and electronic games, refusing to complete assignments, and being argumentative when confronted with violations of classroom and school rules (National Comprehensive Center for Teacher Quality & Public Agenda, 2008a).

Because of the special nature of adolescence, relatively short class times, and consecutive classes with different students, middle school, junior high, and high school teachers must concentrate their efforts on preventing misbehavior. Edmund Emmer and Carolyn Evertson (2009), in *Classroom Management for Middle and High School Teachers*, discuss how teachers can prevent misbehavior by carefully organizing the classroom environment, establishing clear rules and procedures, and delivering effective instruction.

According to Emmer and Evertson, the physical features of the classroom should be arranged to optimize teaching and learning. They suggest an environment in which (1) the arrangement of the seating, materials, and equipment is consistent with the kinds of instructional activities the teacher favors; (2) high-traffic areas, such as the teacher's desk and the pencil sharpener, are kept free of congestion; (3) the teacher can easily see all students; (4) frequently used teaching materials and student supplies are readily available; and (5) students can easily see instructional presentations and displays.

In too many instances, teachers spend a significant amount of class time dealing with misbehavior rather than with teaching and learning, either because students

Because middle school, junior high, and high school students move from one teacher to another every 50 minutes or so, it is important to establish a common set of rules that govern various activities and procedures and to clearly communicate the reasons for those rules. Copyright © Mary Kate Denny/Photo Edit

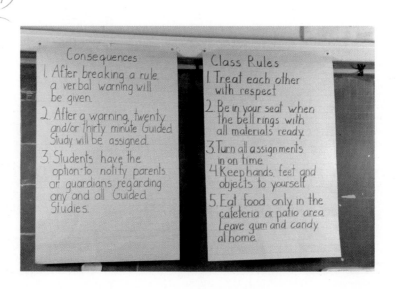

are never told what is expected of them or because rules and procedures are not communicated clearly. Accordingly, Emmer and associates suggest that classroom rules be specifically stated, discussed with students on the first day of class, and, for seventh, eighth, and ninth grades, posted in a prominent place. Sophomores, juniors, and seniors should be given a handout on which the rules are listed. A set of five to eight basic rules should be sufficient. Some examples of these basic rules follow:

Bring all needed materials to class.
Be in your seat and ready to work when the bell rings.
Respect and be polite to all people.
Do not talk or leave your desk when someone else is talking.
Respect other people's property.
Obey all school rules.

Manage behavior of adolescents by making and communicating clear rules and procedures

In addition to rules, various procedures need to be formulated and communicated. Procedures differ from rules in that they apply to a specific activity and are usually directed at completing a task rather than completing a behavior. To produce a well-run classroom, you will need to formulate efficient procedures for beginning-of-the-period tasks (such as taking attendance and allowing students to leave the classroom), use of materials and equipment (such as the computer, dictionary, and pencil sharpener), learning activities (such as discussions, seatwork, and group work), and end-of-the-period tasks (such as handing in seatwork assignments, returning materials and equipment, and making announcements).

Much of what Jacob Kounin, Carolyn Evertson, and Edmund Emmer mention in relation to the characteristics of effective instruction has been described in previous chapters. For example, they recommend that short-term (daily, weekly) and long-term (semester, annual) lesson plans be formulated and coordinated, that instructions and standards for assignments be clear and given in a timely manner, that feedback be given at regular intervals, and that the grading system be clear and fairly applied. As the next section illustrates, technology can help you carry out these tasks efficiently and effectively.

TeachSource Video Case ◄◄ ► ►►

Secondary Classroom Management: Basic Strategies

Go to the Education CourseMate website and watch the Video Case, and then answer the following questions:

1. How does Mr. Turner achieve successful classroom management with his high school students? What specific strategies from the textbook do you see in action?

2. Examine the arrangement of Mr. Turner's secondary-level classroom (e.g., arrangement of student desks, location of equipment, etc.). How do these factors influence Mr. Turner's management of the classroom?

Technology Tools for Classroom Management

The message of the first section of this chapter is that an ounce of prevention is worth a pound of cure. In other words, clear classroom rules, good classroom management practices, and effective instruction are likely to prevent more instances of classroom disruption than heavy-handed, arbitrary punishment. And as we mentioned in the chapter on operant conditioning, *an integrated learning system* may be a useful tool for helping teachers establish and maintain a well-managed classroom.

These systems, which are also referred to as curriculum courseware and management systems, provide a type of individualized instruction. They adjust the difficulty level and content of lessons to each student's pattern of progress, allow students to progress at their own rate, and provide teachers with continuous assessment reports that are keyed to state and professional organization learning standards.

In addition to keeping teachers continually updated on students' progress, these reports can be used to group students according to strengths and weaknesses for additional classroom instruction (Herr, 2000). As one fifth-grade teacher said, "Thanks to the management system, I clearly became more of a facilitator of learning, rather than the 'sage on the stage.' It did not replace my role as teacher; it simply made my job easier and expanded my role in ways I never thought possible" (Herr, 2000, p. 4).

New Classroom Roles for Teachers   The little research there is on how technology typically affects a teacher's management style suggests that teachers should become comfortable with a classroom that is more student-centered and less teacher-directed. It would not be unusual in a well-equipped classroom or computer lab for several groups of students to be using laptop computers, desktop computers, handheld calculating devices, and personal digital assistants as they worked cooperatively on various parts of an assignment. Naturally, this environment produces higher levels of student talk and physical activity than many teachers, particularly novices, may be used to or comfortable with (Bolick & Cooper, 2006). But as we point out repeatedly in this book, meaningful learning is active learning that frequently takes place in small groups. Just keep in mind what we said at the beginning of this discussion: clear classroom rules, good classroom management practices, and effective instruction will go a long way to helping you effectively manage your classroom regardless of whether you favor a teacher-directed approach or a student-centered approach.

The following Suggestions for Teaching will help you become an effective manager of student behavior in the classroom.

Suggestions for Teaching

Techniques of Classroom Management

1 Show you are confident and prepared the first day of class.

The first few minutes with any class are often crucial. Your students will be sizing you up, especially if they know you are a new teacher. If you act scared and unsure of yourself, you will probably be in for trouble. Even after years of experience, you may find that confronting a roomful of strange students for the first time is a bit intimidating. You will be the center of attention and may feel the equivalent of stage fright. To switch the focus of attention and begin identifying your students as individuals rather than as a threatening audience, you might consider using this strategy. Hand out 4-by-6-inch cards as soon as everyone is seated, and ask your students to write down their full names, the names they prefer to be called, what their hobbies and favorite activities are, and a description of the most interesting experience they have ever had. (For primary grade students who are unable to write, substitute brief oral introductions.)

As they write, you will be in a position to make a leisurely scrutiny of your students as individuals. Recognizing that you are dealing with individuals should reduce the tendency to feel threatened by a group. Perhaps you have read about singers who pick out a single sympathetic member of the audience and sing directly to that person. The sea of faces as a whole is frightening; the face of the individual is not. Even if you are not bothered by being the center of attention, you might still consider using this card technique to obtain information that you can use to learn names rapidly and to individualize instruction. Whatever you do during the first few minutes, it is important to give the impression that you know exactly what you are doing. The best way to pull that off is to be thoroughly prepared.

2 **Think ahead about how you plan to handle classroom routine, and explain basic procedures the first few minutes of the first day.**

JOURNAL ENTRY
Planning How to Handle Routines

To demonstrate that you are a confident, competent instructor, you should plan exactly how you will handle classroom routines. You will pick up at least some ideas about the details of classroom management during student teaching experiences, but it might be worth asking a friendly experienced teacher in your school for advice about tried-and-true procedures that have worked in that particular school. (You might also read one of the books on classroom management recommended at the end of this chapter in Resources for Further Investigation.)

Try to anticipate how you will handle such details as taking attendance, assigning desks, handing out books and materials, permitting students to go to the restroom, and so forth. If you don't plan ahead, you will have to come up with an improvised policy on the spur of the moment, and that policy might turn out to be highly inefficient or in conflict with school regulations.

3 **Establish class rules, call attention to them, and explain why they are necessary.**

Establish, call attention to, and explain class rules the first day

Some teachers list standard procedures on a chart or bulletin board; others simply state them the first day of class or hand out a flyer to students. Either technique saves time and trouble later because all you have to do is refer to the rule when a transgression occurs. The alternative to this approach is to interrupt the lesson and disturb the whole class while you make a hurried, unplanned effort to deal with a surprise attack. Your spur-of-the-moment reaction may turn out to be clumsy and ineffective.

When you introduce rules the first day, take a positive, nonthreatening approach. If you spit rules out as if they were a series of ultimatums, students may feel you have a chip on your shoulder, which the unwritten code of the classroom obligates them to try knocking off. Whatever your approach, encourage understanding of the reasons for the rules. You can make regulations seem desirable rather than restrictive if you discuss why they are needed. Reasonable rules are much more likely to be remembered and honored than pronouncements that seem to be the whims of a tyrant.

EXAMPLES

- "During class discussion, please don't speak out unless you raise your hand and are recognized. I want to be able to hear what each person has to say, and I won't be able to do that if more than one person is talking."

- "During work periods, I don't mind if you talk a bit to your neighbors. But if you do it too much and disturb others, I'll have to ask you to stop."

- "If you come in late, go to your desk by walking along the side and back of the room. It's disturbing—and not very polite—to walk between people who are interacting with each other."

4 **Begin class work the first day with an instructional activity that is clearly stated and can be completed quickly and successfully.**

When selecting the very first assignment to give to a new class, refer to the suggestions for preparing instructional objectives proposed by Robert Mager and Norman Gronlund (see Chapter 13, "Approaches to Instruction"), and arrange a short assignment that students can complete successfully before the end of the period. Clearly specify what is to be done, and perhaps state the conditions and criteria for determining successful completion. In addition, mention an activity (such as examining the assigned text) that students should engage in after they have completed the assignment. In the elementary grades, you might give a short assignment that helps students review material covered in the preceding grade. At the secondary level, pick out an initial assignment that is short and interesting and does not depend on technical knowledge.

EXAMPLES

- "Your teacher from last year told me that most of you were able to spell all of the words on the list I am going to read. Let's see if you can still spell those words. If you have trouble with certain ones, we can work together to come up with reminders that will help you remember the correct spelling."

- "The first chapter in our natural science text for this fall is about birds. I want you to read the first ten pages, make a list of five types of birds that are described, and prepare your own set of notes about how to recognize them. At 10:30, I am going to hold up pictures of ten birds, and I want you to see if you can correctly identify at least five of them."

- In a high school history class, ask students to write a brief description of a movie they have seen that depicted historical events. Then ask them to indicate whether they felt the film interpretation was accurate.

5 **During the first weeks with a new group of students, have them spend most of their time engaging in whole-class activities under your direction.**

The effective teachers studied by researchers followed the strategy just described, which makes sense when you stop to think about it. You can't expect students to adjust to the routine of a new teacher and classroom in just a few days. Accordingly, it would be wise to make sure students have settled down before asking them to engage in relatively unstructured activities such as cooperative learning. Furthermore, group discussions or cooperative-learning arrangements usually work out more successfully when the participants have a degree of familiarity with one another and a particular set of background factors (such as a chapter in a textbook). Thus, during the first weeks with a new class, prepare instructional objectives that ask students to complete assignments under your direction. Postpone using the other techniques just mentioned until later in the report period.

6 **Give clear instructions, hold students accountable for carrying them out, and provide frequent feedback.**

All three of these goals can be achieved by making systematic use of instructional objectives (as described in Chapter 13, "Approaches to Instruction") and by putting into practice the model of instruction described throughout this book.

7 **Continually demonstrate that you are competent, well prepared, and in charge.**

As students work to achieve instructional objectives, participate in group discussions, or engage in any other kind of learning activity, show them that you are a competent classroom manager. Arrange periods so that there will be a well-organized transition from one activity to the next, maintain smoothness and momentum, and don't waste time. Use a variety of teaching approaches so that you please most of your students at least some of the time. Show you are with it by being alert for signs of mischief or disruptive behavior, and handle such incidents quickly and confidently by using the techniques described later in this chapter.

8 Be professional but pleasant, and try to establish a businesslike but supportive classroom atmosphere.

> Establish a businesslike but supportive classroom atmosphere

Teachers who establish a businesslike and professional atmosphere, but do so in a pleasant and supportive way, have been referred to as warm demanders (Ross, Bondy, Gallingane, & Hambacher, 2008). Warm demanders insist that students meet their expectations, treat the teacher with respect, treat classmates with respect, put forth an honest effort to learn, and encourage their classmates to do the same. They do this by making sure their students understand and practice expected behaviors, providing both positive and negative examples of expected behavior, repeating a request until the student complies, reminding students of expected behaviors, reinforcing expected behaviors, and, when necessary, using negative consequences.

EXAMPLES

- "At the beginning of class you may speak quietly to your classmates, but when I start a lesson, all eyes are on me and all talking stops."

- "Jacob, please show everyone the proper way to line up to go out for recess."

- "When someone gives a wrong answer to a question, do we laugh at him or her? No! We remind ourselves that school is where we come to learn and that making mistakes is a normal part of learning."

- "Eduardo, thank you for helping Sonia finish my assignment on time. That is exactly what I mean when I say we should help one another do our best."

TECHNIQUES FOR DEALING WITH BEHAVIOR PROBLEMS

If you follow the procedures just discussed, you should be able to establish a well-managed classroom. Even if you do everything possible to prevent problems from developing, however, you are still likely to have to deal with the relatively minor disruptions of an individual student or two. This section contains some practical suggestions for keeping individual students more task-oriented. More broad-based interventions that attempt to reduce the frequency of more serious problems, such as physical and verbal violence between students, and that involve entire classrooms or the entire school, are discussed in a later section.

Influence Techniques

In *Mental Hygiene in Teaching* (1959), Fritz Redl and William Wattenberg describe a list of behavior management interventions called *influence techniques*. This list was modified by James Walker, Thomas Shea, and Anne Bauer in *Behavior Management: A Practical Approach for Educators* (2007). In the following sections and subsections, based on the ideas of both sets of individuals, we will offer specific examples, roughly reflecting a least-direct to most-direct ordering. You might use the Journal Entries to pick out or devise techniques that seem most appropriate for your grade level or that you feel comfortable about.

The value of these techniques is that they appeal to self-control and imply trust and confidence on the part of the teacher. However, they may become ineffective if they are used too often, and that is why we describe so many different techniques. The larger your repertoire is, the less frequently you will have to repeat your various gambits and ploys.

Planned Ignoring   As we pointed out in Chapter 7 on behavioral learning theory, you might be able to extinguish inappropriate attention-seeking behaviors by merely ignoring them. Such behaviors include finger snapping, body movements, book dropping, hand waving, and whistling. If you plan to use the planned-ignoring technique, make sure the student is aware that he is engaging in the inappropriate behavior. This technique should not be used if the behavior in question is interfering with other students' efforts.

Example
- Carl has recently gotten into the habit of tapping his pencil on his desk as he works on an assignment as a way to engage you in a conversation that is unrelated to the work. The next several times Carl does this, do not look at him or comment on his behavior.

Signals   In some cases, a subtle signal can put an end to budding misbehavior. The signal, if successful, will stimulate the student to control herself. (Note, however, that this technique should not be used too often and that it is effective only in the early stages of misbehavior.)

Examples
- Clear your throat.
- Stare at the offender.
- Stop what you are saying in midsentence and stare.
- Shake your head (to indicate no).
- Say, "Someone is making it hard for the rest of us to concentrate" (or the equivalent).

Proximity and Touch Control   Place yourself close to the misbehaving student. This makes a signal a bit more apparent.

Examples
- Walk over and stand near the student.
- With an elementary grade student, it sometimes helps if you place a gentle hand on a shoulder or arm.

Interest Boosting   If the student seems to be losing interest in a lesson or assignment, pay some additional attention to the student and the student's work.

Example
- Ask the student a question, preferably related to what is being discussed. (Questions such as, "Ariel, are you paying attention?" or "Don't you agree, Ariel?" invite wisecracks. *Genuine* questions are preferable.) Go over and examine some work the student is doing. It often helps if you point out something good about it and urge continued effort.

JOURNAL ENTRY
Signals to Use to Nip
Trouble in the Bud

Use supportive reactions to help
students develop self-control

Humor   Humor is an excellent all-around influence technique, especially in tense situations. However, remember that it should be *good*-humored humor—gentle and benign rather than derisive. Avoid irony and sarcasm.

Signals such as staring at a misbehaving student or putting a finger to one's lips are examples of the influence techniques suggested by Redl and Wattenberg. © Image Source/Alamy

Example

- "Shawn, for goodness sake, let that poor pencil sharpener alone. I heard it groan when you used it just now."

Perhaps you have heard someone say, "We're not laughing at you; we're laughing *with* you." Before you say this to one of your students, you might take note that one second grader who was treated to that comment unhinged the teacher by replying, "I'm not laughing."

Helping over Hurdles Some misbehavior undoubtedly occurs because students do not understand what they are to do or lack the ability to carry out an assignment.

Examples

- Try to make sure your students know what they are supposed to do.
- Arrange for students to have something to do at appropriate levels of difficulty.
- Have a variety of activities available.

Program Restructuring At the beginning of this book, we noted that teaching is an art because lessons do not always proceed as planned and must occasionally be changed in midstream. The essence of this program restructuring technique is to recognize when a lesson or activity is going poorly and to try something else.

Examples

- "Well, class, I can see that many of you are bored with this discussion of the pros and cons of congressional term limits. Let's turn it into a class debate instead, with the winning team getting 50 points toward its final grade."

JOURNAL ENTRY
Using Alternative Activities
to Keep Students on Task

- "I had hoped to complete this math unit before the Christmas break, but I can see that most of you are too excited to give it your best effort. Since today is the last day before the break, I'll postpone the lesson until school resumes in January. Let's do an art project instead."

Antiseptic Bouncing Sometimes a student will get carried away by restlessness, uncontrollable giggling, or the like. If you feel that this is nonmalicious behavior and due simply to lack of self-control, ask the student to leave the room. (You may have recognized that antiseptic bouncing is virtually identical to the *time-out* procedure described by behavior modification enthusiasts.)

Examples
- "Nancy, please go down to the principal's office and sit on that bench outside the door until you feel you have yourself under control."
- Some high schools have "quiet rooms": supervised study halls that take extra students any time during a period, no questions asked.

Physical Restraint Students who lose control of themselves to the point of endangering other members of the class may have to be physically restrained. Such restraint should be protective, not punitive; that is, don't shake or hit. This technique is most effective with younger children; such control is usually not appropriate at the secondary level.

Example
- If a boy completely loses his temper and starts to hit another child, lead him gently but firmly away from the other students, or sit him in a chair, and keep a restraining hand on his shoulder.

Direct Appeals When appropriate, point out the connection between conduct and its consequences. This technique is most effective if done concisely and infrequently.

Examples
- "We have a rule that there is to be no running in the halls. Scott forgot the rule, and now he's down in the nurse's office having his bloody nose taken care of. It's too bad Mr. Harris opened his door just as Scott went by. If Scott had been walking, he would have been able to stop in time."
- "If everyone would stop shouting, we'd be able to get this finished and go out to recess."

Criticism and Encouragement On those occasions when it is necessary to criticize a particular student, do so in private if possible. When public criticism is the only possibility, do your best to avoid ridiculing or humiliating the student. Public humiliation may cause the child to resent you or to hate school, to counterattack, or to withdraw. Because of the ripple effect, it may also have a negative impact on innocent students (although nonhumiliating public criticism has the advantage of setting an example for other students). One way to minimize the negative after-effects of criticism is to tack on some encouragement in the form of a suggestion as to how the backsliding can be replaced by more positive behavior.

Give criticism privately; then offer encouragement

Examples
- If a student doesn't take subtle hints (such as stares), you might say, "LeVar, you're disturbing the class. We all need to concentrate on this." It sometimes adds punch if you make this remark while you are writing on the board or helping some other student.

- Act completely flabbergasted, as though the misbehavior seems so inappropriate that you can't comprehend it. A kindergarten teacher used this technique to perfection. She would say, "Adam! Is that you?" (Adam has been belting Lucy with a shovel.) "I can't believe my eyes. I wonder if you would help me over here." Obviously, this gambit can't be used too often, and the language and degree of exaggeration have to be altered a bit for older students. But indicating that you expect good behavior and providing an immediate opportunity for the backslider to substitute good deeds can be very effective.

Defining Limits   In learning about rules and regulations, children go through a process of testing the limits. Two-year-olds particularly, when they have learned how to walk and talk and manipulate things, feel the urge to assert their independence. In addition, they need to find out exactly what the house rules are. (Does Mommy *really* mean it when she says, "Don't take the pots out of the cupboard"? Does Daddy *really* mean it when he says, "Don't play with that hammer"?) Older children do the same thing, especially with new teachers and in new situations. The technique of defining limits includes not only establishing rules (as noted earlier) but also enforcing them.

Examples

- Establish class rules, with or without the assistance of students, and make sure the rules are understood.
- When someone tests the rules, show that they are genuine and that there *are* limits.

Postsituational Follow-Up   Classroom discipline occasionally has to be applied in a tense, emotion-packed atmosphere. When this happens, it often helps to have a postsituational discussion—in private if an individual is involved, with the whole class if it was a groupwide situation.

Examples

- In a private conference: "Leila, I'm sorry I had to ask you to leave the room, but you were getting kind of carried away."
- "Well, everybody, things got a bit wild during those group work sessions. I want you to enjoy yourselves, but we practically had a riot going, didn't we? And that's why I had to ask you to stop. Let's try to hold it down to a dull roar tomorrow."

Marginal Use of Interpretation   Analysis of behavior can sometimes be made while it is occurring rather than afterward. The purpose here is to help students become aware of potential trouble and make efforts to control it.

Example

- To a restless and cranky prelunch class, you might say, "I know that you're getting hungry and that you're restless and tired, but let's give it all we've got for 10 minutes more. I'll give you the last 5 minutes for some free visiting time."

I-Messages

I-message: tell how you feel about an unacceptable situation

JOURNAL ENTRY
Using I-Messages

In *Teacher and Child,* Haim Ginott offers a cardinal principle of communication: "Talk to the situation, not to the personality and character" (1972, p. 84). Instead of making derogatory remarks about the personalities of two boys who have just thrown bread at each other, Ginott suggests that as a teacher you deliver an **I-message** explaining how you feel. Don't say, "You are a couple of pigs"; say, "I get angry when I see bread thrown around. This room needs cleaning." According to Ginott, guilty students who are told why a teacher is angry will realize the teacher is a real person, and this realization will cause them to strive to mend their ways.

Ginott offers several examples of this cardinal principle of communication in Chapter 4 of *Teacher and Child*. And in Chapter 6 he offers some observations on discipline:

- Seek alternatives to punishment.
- Try not to diminish a misbehaving student's self-esteem.
- Try to provide face-saving exits.

Despite the fact that Ginott's work is over 30 years old, its usefulness is demonstrated by the fact that his ideas appear regularly in recent books and articles on classroom management (Bloom, 2009; Carter & Doyle, 2006; Henley, 2006).

Problem Ownership

Determine who owns a problem before deciding on course of action

In *TET: Teacher Effectiveness Training* (1974), Thomas Gordon suggests that teachers try to determine who owns a problem before they decide how to handle that problem. If a student's misbehavior (such as disrupting the smooth flow of instruction with inappropriate comments or joking remarks) results in the teacher's feeling annoyed, frustrated, or angry at not being able to complete a planned lesson, the teacher owns the problem and must respond by doing something to stop the disruptive behavior. But if a student expresses anger or disappointment about some classroom incident (getting a low grade on an exam), that student owns the problem.

JOURNAL ENTRY
Speculating About
Problem Ownership

Gordon suggests that failure to identify problem ownership may cause teachers to intensify difficulties unwittingly, even as they make well-intended efforts to diminish them. If a student is finding it difficult to concentrate on schoolwork because her needs are not satisfied, the situation will not be ameliorated if the teacher orders, moralizes, or criticizes. According to Gordon, such responses act as roadblocks to finding solutions to student-owned problems because they tend to make the student feel resentful and misunderstood.

Some practical suggestions for handling problem behavior appear in the following Suggestions for Teaching.

pause & reflect

Ginott and Gordon both recommend that when responding to misbehavior, teachers speak about the behavior and not the character of the student. How often have you seen this done? If it strikes you as a good approach, what steps will you take to use it as often as possible with your own students?

Suggestions for Teaching

Handling Problem Behavior

1 Have a variety of influence techniques planned in advance.

You may save yourself a great deal of trouble, embarrassment, and strain if you plan ahead. When first-year teachers are asked which aspects of teaching bother them most, classroom control is almost invariably near the top of the list. Perhaps a major reason is that problems of control frequently erupt unexpectedly, and they often demand equally sudden solutions. If you lack experience, your shoot-from-the-hip reactions may be ineffective. Initial attempts at control that are ineffective tend to reinforce misbehavior, and you will find yourself trapped in a vicious circle. You can avoid this sort of trap if you devise specific techniques ahead of time. Being familiar with several of the techniques mentioned in the preceding section will prepare you for the inevitable difficulties that arise.

Teachers who excel at classroom management have at their disposal a variety of influence techniques that they consistently and immediately apply to prevent or deal with misbehavior. In each case, they use a technique that is appropriate to the severity of the misbehavior. © Ellen B. Senisi/The Image Works

If you find yourself forced to use prepared techniques too often, some self-analysis is called for. How can you prevent so many problems from developing? Frequent trouble is an indication that you need to work harder at motivating your class. Also, check on your feelings when you mete out punishment. Teachers who really like students and want them to learn consider control techniques a necessary evil and use them only when they will provide a better atmosphere for learning.

❷ Be prompt, consistent, and reasonable.

Be prompt, consistent, reasonable when dealing with misbehavior

No attempt to control behavior will be effective if it is remote from the act that provokes it. If a troublemaker is to comprehend the relationship between behavior and counterreaction, one must quickly follow the other. Don't postpone dealing with misbehaving students or make vague threats to be put into effect sometime in the future (such as not permitting the students to attend an end-of-the-year event). By that time, most students will have forgotten what they did wrong. They then feel resentful and persecuted and may conclude that you are acting out of sheer malice. However, retribution that is too immediate and applied when a student is still extremely upset may also be ineffective. At such times, it is often better to wait a bit.

Being consistent about classroom control can save a lot of time, energy, and misery. Strictness one day and leniency the next, or roughness on one student and gentleness with another, invite all students to test you every day just to see whether this is a good day or a bad day or whether they can get away with something more frequently than others do. Establishing and enforcing class rules is an excellent way to encourage yourself to be consistent.

Harshness in meting out retribution encourages, rather than discourages, more extreme forms of misbehavior. If students are going to get into a lot of trouble for even a minor offense, they will probably figure they should get their money's worth. Several hundred years ago in England, all offenses—from picking pockets to murder—were punishable by death. The petty thief quickly became a murderer; it was a lot easier (and less risky) to pick the pocket of a dead man and, because the punishment was the same, eminently more sensible. The laws were eventually changed to make punishment appropriate to the degree of the offense. Keep this in mind when you dispense justice.

JOURNAL ENTRY
Being Prompt, Consistent, and Reasonable in Controlling the Class

3 Avoid threats.

If at all possible, avoid a showdown in front of the class. In a confrontation before the whole group, you are likely to get desperate. You may start out with a "Yes, you will"– "No, I won't" sort of duel and end up making a threat on the spur of the moment. Frequently, you will not be able to make good on the threat, and you will lose face. It's far safer and better for everyone to settle extreme differences in private. When two people are upset and angry with each other, they look silly at best and completely ridiculous at worst. You lose a great deal more than a student does when this performance takes place in front of the class. In fact, a student may actually gain prestige by provoking you successfully.

4 Whenever you have to deal harshly with a student, make an effort to reestablish rapport.

JOURNAL ENTRY
Ways to Reestablish
Rapport

If you must use a drastic form of retribution, make a point of having a confidential conference with your antagonist as soon as possible. Otherwise, she is likely to remain an antagonist for the rest of the year. It's too much to expect chastised students to come to you of their own volition and apologize. You should set up the conference and then explain that the punishment has cleared the air as far as you are concerned. You shouldn't be surprised if a recalcitrant student doesn't respond with signs or words of gratitude. Perhaps some of the causes of misbehavior lie outside school, and something you did or said may have been merely the last straw. Even if you get a sullen reaction, at least indicate your willingness to meet punished students more than halfway.

At the elementary level, you can frequently make amends simply by giving the child some privilege—for example, passing out papers or being hall monitor at recess. One teacher made it a point to praise a child for some positive action shortly after a severe reprimand.

5 If you decide that a problem is owned by a student, try to help the student solve the problem by using active listening.

As we noted earlier, when a student experiences a problem (such as feeling upset about an argument with a friend or feeling anxious about an upcoming exam) that interferes with the student's classroom performance but does not interfere with the teacher's ability to instruct, the student owns the problem. Thomas Gordon (1974) believes that it is a mistake for teachers to tell such students that they must or should change their attitude and behavior, because this suggests that there is something wrong with the student and that she is at fault for having the problem. Instead, he suggests active listening, as in the following example:

STUDENT: *"It's just that I don't know what kind of a test you're going to give and I'm afraid it'll be an essay type."*
TEACHER: *"Oh, you're worried about the kind of test we are going to have."*
STUDENT: *"Yes, I don't do well on essay tests."*
TEACHER: *"I see, you feel you can do better on objective tests."*
STUDENT: *"Yeah, I always botch up essay tests."*
TEACHER: *"It'll be a multiple-choice test."*
STUDENT: *"What a relief! I'm not so worried now."* (Gordon, 1974, p. 69)

6 When you have control, ease up some.

It is extremely difficult, if not impossible, to establish a controlled atmosphere after allowing anarchy. Don't make the mistake of thinking you will be able to start out without any control and suddenly take charge. It may work, but in most cases you will have a cold war on your hands. It is far better to adopt the authoritative approach of starting out on the structured side and then easing up a bit after you have established control. On the other hand, don't make the opposite mistake of starting out by being overly controlling and punitive. In the face of a teacher who is perceived as stern, rigid, and unyielding, some students become so anxious and fearful that they are unable to perform at their best. Higher-level thinking and learning is much more likely to occur among students who trust their teacher to be accepting and fair (Mahwinney & Sagan, 2007).

7 **Follow the advice of a master teacher.**

Metzer

Margaret Metzger is a veteran high school English teacher whose sensible and practical views on modeling and clearly communicating one's goals to students were mentioned in earlier chapters. She has also written, in the form of an open letter to new teachers, an insightful and compelling distillation of her experiences in learning the art of classroom management (Metzger, 2002). Metzger's recommendations for managing the behavior of adolescents also illustrate a point we have made in previous chapters: successful teachers formulate practices that are consistent with, if not inspired by, research-based findings. Although we offer a summary of Metzger's recommendations, this is an article we urge you to read in its entirety and refer to repeatedly during your first few years of teaching.

Metzger (2002) divides her suggestions into two lists: "simple principles of survival," created during her early years of teaching, and "more complex principles," which grew out of her experiences during her middle teaching years. Here, in summary form, are both lists.

SIMPLE PRINCIPLES OF SURVIVAL

1. *Use a light touch.* Don't immediately resort to a highly aversive technique to control students' behavior. Instead, try such simpler methods as whispering instead of yelling, using humorous statements, changing locations, talking to students privately, calling students by name, smiling a lot, and ignoring some infractions.

2. *Let students save face.* Instead of describing a student's misbehavior and issuing a reprimand, which takes time and interrupts the flow of a lesson, indicate that you've noticed the misbehavior and use such quick and somewhat humorous phrases as "It's a good thing I like you," "Here's the deal: I'll pretend I didn't see that, and you never do it again," "Consider yourself scolded," "Am I driving you over the edge?" and "That's inappropriate."

3. *Insist on the right to sanity.* To avoid becoming a burnout candidate, don't try to address all misbehaviors. Instead, make a list of possible classroom infractions and rank them. Decide which behaviors have to be addressed immediately, which can wait until some later time, and which can be ignored. Margaret Metzger, for example, decided to ignore students who came late to class. She was often so busy trying to get the class under way (returning papers, talking with students about makeup work) that she wasn't always in a position to notice who arrived late.

4. *Get help.* Learn who among the school staff (administrators, guidance counselors, truant officer, other teachers) are able and willing to help you solve certain discipline problems.

5. *Get out of the limelight.* This is Metzger's way of saying that you shouldn't feel as if you have to actively lead the class all period, every period. Learn to make appropriate use of student presentations, seatwork, movies, and group work.

MORE COMPLEX PRINCIPLES

1. *Ask questions.* Teachers often assume, incorrectly, that they have all the information they need to understand why one or more students misbehaved. Rather than make this assumption, take the time to ask students for an explanation. As Metzger says, "Sometimes you feel you have already spent too much time on the disruptive students. Frankly, you don't want to talk to them. Too bad. Do it" (2002, p. 80). Administrators, other teachers, and the students' parents can also be useful sources of information.

2. *Give adult feedback.* If students are engaging in behaviors that you find disruptive or that indicate a serious underlying problem, don't mince words. Tell them directly. Here are two examples offered by Metzger:

   - "Your posture, your mumbling under your breath, and your tardiness all show disrespect. If you hate this class, you should talk to me about it. If you like this class, you should know that you are giving misleading signals." (p. 80)

   - "You have complained about everything we have done for the past two months. I now see you as a constant whiner. You probably don't want to give this impression, and it's getting on my nerves. So for the next two months, let's have a moratorium on complaining. You can start whining again in January. Does this seem fair?" (p. 80)

3. *Respect the rights of the whole class.* Try to remember that most of your students follow the rules and are just as deserving of your attention as those who do not.

4. *Ask students to do more.* This echoes a suggestion we have made several times in earlier chapters. Often the best-behaved classes are those in which the work is interesting, relevant to students' lives, and challenging.

5. *Bypass or solve perennial problems.* There will always be students who forget to bring a pencil or book to class. Rather than erupt every time this problem arises, take steps to eliminate it. For several dollars a year, you can buy a supply of pencils and allow students to borrow one for class. For students who forget to bring their books, you can keep a few extra copies on hand. To ensure that students return at the end of class what they have borrowed, you may need to require that they leave with you something that they will not leave the classroom without, such as a shoe or a watch.

Metzger (2002) also advises teachers to reflect on themselves as a factor in classroom management by asking the following questions: "Does race or gender influence my response? Does this interaction remind me of another one? What from my background is being triggered? Am I tired, grouchy, or distracted? What else is going on in my life? Who is watching? Is the problem mine or the student's? Has the student hit some raw nerve in me? Why am I threatened by the behavior? Why do I lack resilience on this matter? Am I being inflexible? Am I being authoritative or authoritarian?" (pp. 81–82).

Metzger ends her article with a copy of a 25-point memo that she gives to all students at the beginning of each semester and that reflects her philosophy of classroom management. Read it.

If you would like to compare your current understanding of classroom management against the views of a veteran middle school teacher, take the brief six-item quiz created by Kim Chase (2002) that appears in the December 2002 issue of *Phi Delta Kappan.*

JOURNAL ENTRY
Techniques for Becoming an Expert Classroom Manager

For additional ideas for your journal writing, see the Reflective Journal Questions on the Education CourseMate student website.

TeachSource Video Case ◄◄ ► ►►

Classroom Management: Best Practices

Go to the Education CourseMate website and watch the Video Case, and then answer the following questions:

1. Can you give an example of "withitness" from this Video Case?

2. In this Video Case, several teachers provide their philosophies of and approaches to classroom management. Which statements align most closely with your own philosophies of classroom management? Are there any that you disagree with? Explain your answers.

VIOLENCE IN AMERICAN SCHOOLS

How Safe Are Our Schools?

You have probably read or heard reports about the frequency of crime in the United States, particularly among juveniles. According to figures compiled by the Office of Juvenile Justice and Delinquency Prevention (Puzzanchera, 2009), 16 percent of all juveniles (any individual below the age of eighteen) were arrested in 2007 for committing violent crimes. The good news about this figure is that it represents a 14 percent decline over the previous decade.

Because the kinds of behaviors one observes in schools tend to reflect trends in society at large, it is natural that a certain amount of violent behavior occurs on school grounds and during school hours. However, schools are still relatively safe places (see Mayer & Furlong, 2010, for an excellent discussion of school violence statistics and what they mean). One basis for that claim is that the most common types of school-based conflicts fall into a few time-honored categories: verbal harassment (name calling, insults, teasing), verbal arguments, and physical fights (hitting, kicking, scratching, and pushing). Most of the fights do not involve serious injury or violations of law (Dinkes, Kemp, Baum, & Snyder, 2007). Second, a recent government report found relatively low levels of school-based violence and crime (Dinkes et al., 2007). Here are the main findings from that report:

- From July 1, 2005, through June 30, 2006, fourteen school-age students (ages five through nineteen) were murdered at school. This translates to less than one homicide per million students for that 1-year period.
- In 2005, there were 136,500 serious violent crimes (rape, sexual assault, robbery, and aggravated assault) committed against students between the ages of twelve and eighteen. This figure translates to 5 serious violent crimes per 100,000 students. Ten years earlier the corresponding figures were considerably higher (222,500 serious crimes; 9 per 100,000 students).
- In 2005, 8 percent of high school students were threatened or injured with a weapon within a 12-month period.
- Six percent of students ages twelve through eighteen reported avoiding school activities or one or more places at school because they feared for their own safety in 2005.
- The percentage of teachers threatened with injury by a student decreased from 12 percent during the 1993–1994 school year to 7 percent during the 2003–2004 school year. The percentage of teachers who were physically attacked decreased from 4 percent during 1993–1994 to 3 percent during

---

Incidents of crime and serious violence occur relatively infrequently in public schools and have been decreasing in recent years

2003–2004. The percentage of elementary grade teachers who were attacked was twice as great as the percentage of secondary grade teachers (4 percent versus 2 percent, respectively).

These findings suggest that overall crime rates in schools are decreasing, that students feel increasingly safe at school, and that most teachers and students are likely to be physically safe in their own classrooms and school buildings. Nevertheless, school violence can occur in any school and at any time. Accordingly, you should be aware of the various explanations of school violence and the steps that can be taken to reduce its frequency.

The Problem of Bullying

Although **bullying** has existed for as long as there have been schools, it is now recognized as a significant part of the school violence problem. In fact, as this chapter was being written, a particularly tragic account of bullying came to light. A 15-year-old Massachussetts girl, who was the target of several months of face-to-face verbal abuse, threatening text messages, and derogatory Facebook postings, committed suicide. Numerous studies have been conducted and scores of books have been written about various aspects of bullying. In this section, we will take a brief look at what bullying is and how often it occurs, what characterizes a bully, what effects it has on its victims, and how schools can reduce bullying and its negative effects.

What Is Bullying? Bullying can be defined as "the repeated (not just once) harming of another through words or physical attack on the school grounds or on the way to or from school" (Devine & Cohen, 2007, p. 64). A similar definition calls it "the systematic abuse of power in interpersonal relationships" (Rigby, 2008, p. 22). In essence, bullying is a situation in which one person has more power than another and repeatedly abuses that power for his or her own benefit.

Boys, girls favor different forms of bullying

Some of the findings on bullying might surprise you. Although it occurs all too frequently, it is not the runaway problem that some might think given the coverage it gets in the media. During the 2005–2006 school year, 28 percent of twelve- to eighteen-year-olds reported having been bullied at least once. More girls than boys engage in bullying when you look at all of its forms. Girls are more likely than boys to use name-calling and insults, start and repeat rumors, and destroy property. The bullying behavior of boys, on the other hand, is more likely to take such physical forms as pushing, shoving, tripping, or spitting on someone else and trying to make someone else do things they do not want to do. Another aspect of bullying that surprises many people is that it occurs more frequently in middle school than in high school, and as students move from grade to grade a decrease in the rate of bullying usually occurs (Dinkes et al., 2009).

Although bullying often involves face-to-face encounters, it does not always take that form because of the prevalence of social networking websites. This form of bullying, in which one or more students post malicious statements about another student, is referred to as **cyberbullying.** Given the different styles of bullying behavior shown by boys and girls, it will probably not surprise you to learn that more than twice as many girls as boys engage in cyberbullying (5.3 percent versus 2.0 percent for the 2006–2007 school year) (Dinkes et al., 2009).

There are some characteristics of cyberbullying that make it different from face-to-face bullying. First, it is anonymous. Those who use social networking websites such as Facebook and MySpace to bully others are known online only by their fictitious screen names. Second, because the Internet is designed to allow social exchanges among people anywhere in the world, the number of people who bully one or more others online, and the number of people who passively watch, can be quite large. It would not be unusual for virtually all students in a school to be aware of another student's embarrassing behavior and for many to tease the student about it. Third, the bullying can be constant. Threatening, insulting, or teasing e-mail messages can bombard a target student all day, every day. Unless taken down, website postings are constantly available for everyone to see (Shariff, 2008).

Characteristics of Bullies   How are students who bully different from other students? They're different in terms of internal characteristics, their relationships with teachers and classmates, and the quality of their home life.

- Students who engage in bullying behavior are more likely than their nonbullying peers to exhibit aggressive-impulsive behavior. They are often described by their teachers as being hyperactive, disruptive, likely to act without thinking of the consequences, and inclined to respond aggressively when provoked by peers (O'Brennan, Bradshaw, & Sawyer, 2008).
- Students who engage in bullying report getting less support from their classmates and teachers. That is, they are less likely than other students to feel there is someone at school, either a friend or a teacher, who they can talk to about their problems (Flaspohler, Elfstrom, Vanderzee, & Sink, 2009).
- Children who engage in bullying are more likely to have witnessed domestic violence and are less likely to have a close relationship with their mother than their peers who do not bully others (Bowes et al., 2009).

How Bullying Affects Its Victims   Being a victim of bullying can produce any one or more of the following negative effects (Beran, 2009; Devine & Cohen, 2007; O'Brennan, Bradshaw, & Sawyer, 2008; Rigby, 2008):

- staying home from school
- avoiding certain places at school
- asking to transfer to another school
- lower grades due to difficulty concentrating on schoolwork (particularly if the victim believes he or she is not being supported by parents or teachers)
- feelings of depression, anxiety, and insecurity that produce physical ailments
- social isolation

How Schools Can Address Bullying   There are two ways that educators can deal with the problem of bullying. One is to implement schoolwide programs to reduce its frequency. These can take many forms, such as teaching students who witness such incidents to immediately report them or to intervene; promoting rules that discourage discrimination; using videos, speakers, and discussions to make students aware of the feelings of bullies and their victims; and teaching those who bully more appropriate forms of social interaction (Flaspohler, Elfstrom, Vanderzee, & Sink, 2009; Hazler & Carney, 2006; Morrison, 2008).

The other approach is for individual teachers to establish a classroom atmosphere that buffers bullying victims from its negative effects. Research (e.g., Flaspohler, Elfstrom, Vanderzee, & Sink, 2009; Meyer-Adams & Conner, 2008) has shown, for example, that students who feel valued and accepted by both their classmates and their teacher are less likely to demonstrate the negative effects of bullying than peers who do not believe they have that kind of social support.

| Male aggressiveness due to biological and cultural factors |

Analyzing Reasons for Violence

Biological Factors   One of the clear-cut gender differences that has been repeatedly supported by consistent evidence is that males are more aggressive than females (Bloomquist & Schnell, 2002; Connor, 2002; Englander, 2007). Although the cause of this difference cannot be traced precisely, it is likely due in part to one or more of the following neurological, hormonal, and physiological factors: overactive behavioral activation systems and underactive behavioral inhibition systems (both of which are located in the frontal lobes of the brain), below-average levels of neurotransmitters, higher than average levels of testosterone, elevated levels of lead in the bloodstream, and a higher tolerance for pain (Bloomquist & Schnell, 2002; Connor, 2002).

Gender-Related Cultural Influences   As noted in the discussion of age-level characteristics in an earlier chapter, there is evidence that young girls in our society are encouraged to be dependent and to be eager to please adults, whereas young boys are encouraged to assert their independence (Englander, 2007; Lancey, 2002). Furthermore, it appears that boys are more likely than girls to be reinforced by aggressive and antisocial peers for assertive and illegal forms of behavior (Bloomquist & Schnell, 2002; Jimerson, Morrison, Pletcher, & Furlong, 2006). These gender-related cultural influences may partly account for the fact that boys are more likely than girls to engage in such overt aggressive behaviors as fighting, bullying, robbery, and sexual assault and, particularly in the later elementary and middle school years, such covert aggressive behaviors as stealing, lying, vandalism, and setting fires. Girls, on the other hand, are more likely than boys to engage in what is called relational aggression—the withholding or termination of friendships and other social contacts and spreading rumors to hurt another girl's feelings (Bloomquist & Schnell, 2002; Connor, 2002).

The same reasoning may well apply to disruptive behavior in the classroom. A boy who talks back to the teacher or shoves another boy in a skirmish in the cafeteria is probably more likely to draw a favorable response from peers than is a girl who exhibits the same behavior. This cultural difference adds to the physiological factors that predispose boys to express frustration and hostility in physical and assertive ways.

Academic Skills and Performance   Boys also seem more likely than girls to experience feelings of frustration and hostility in school. For a variety of reasons (more rapid maturity, desire to please adults, superiority in verbal skills), girls earn higher grades, on the average, than boys do. A low grade almost inevitably arouses feelings of resentment and anger. In fact, any kind of negative evaluation is a very direct threat to a student's self-esteem. Thus a middle school, junior high, or high school boy who has received an unbroken succession of low grades and is unlikely to graduate may experience extreme frustration and anger. Even low-achieving students are likely to be aware that their chances of getting a decent job are severely limited by the absence of a high school diploma.

Middle school and junior high boys with low grades may feel trapped

Older high school boys can escape further humiliation by dropping out of school, but middle school and junior high boys cannot legally resort to the same solution, which may partially explain why, as of 2005, the crime rate at school is slightly higher among sixth, seventh, and eighth graders than among high school students (Dinkes et al., 2007).

Interpersonal Reasoning and Problem-Solving Skills   Children who exhibit aggressive and violent behaviors do so in part because of deficiencies in how they think about social situations. One example is known as *hostile attributional bias*. Aggressive individuals are more likely than others to misinterpret another person's actions or facial expressions as hostile and to respond in kind (Guerra & Leidy, 2008). Two other deficiencies relate to the ability to formulate realistic plans to satisfy social goals and the ability to think of several possible solutions to interpersonal problems. The former skill is referred to as *means-ends thinking*, and the latter is called *alternative-solution thinking*. Students who are deficient in these two interpersonal problem-solving skills are more likely than others to show an inability to delay gratification, to have difficulty making friends, to have emotional blowups when frustrated, to show less sympathy to others in distress, and to exhibit verbal and physical aggression (Jimerson et al., 2006; Shure, 1999).

Misbehavior of high school students may reveal lack of positive identity

Psychosocial Factors   Other explanations of violent and/or aggressive behavior in school are supplied by Erik Erikson's and James Marcia's observations on identity, which we discussed in the chapter on stage theories of development. A teenager who has failed to make a clear occupational choice, who is confused about gender roles, or who does not experience acceptance "by those who count" may exhibit what Erikson called a negative identity. Instead of striving to behave in ways that parents and teachers respond to positively, teenagers with negative identities may deliberately engage in opposite forms of behavior (Lowry, Sleet, Duncan, Powell, & Kolbe, 1995).

This hypothesis has been supported by a study of 2,000 middle and high school students. Those classified as having a diffusion identity status (no serious thought given or commitment made to occupational and gender roles) were much more likely than adolescents classified as having an achievement status to exhibit behaviors characteristic of both a conduct disorder and attention-deficit/hyperactivity disorder (Adams et al., 2001).

pause & reflect

Do you agree with the argument that school violence can be caused by a nonmeaningful, unimaginative curriculum and an impersonal school environment? If so, what can you do to make the subjects you teach lively, interesting, and useful? What ideas for making your school a more welcoming and pleasant place for students can you share with colleagues and administrators?

School Environment   So far we have mentioned the role of biological, gender-related, cultural, academic, cognitive, and psychosocial factors in school violence. Each of these explanations places the responsibility for violent behavior largely or entirely on the individual. Other explanations focus instead on schools that are poorly designed and do not meet the needs of their students. Violent behavior, in this view, is seen as a natural (though unacceptable) response to schools that are too large, impersonal, and competitive; that do not enforce rules fairly or consistently; that use punitive ways of resolving conflict; and that impose an unimaginative, meaningless curriculum on students (Lowry et al., 1995; Bloomquist & Schnell, 2002; Guerra & Leidy, 2008).

Reducing School Violence, Bullying, and Misbehavior

Classroom Interventions   Because most teachers work with two dozen or more students, some of whom have disabilities, and typically have no assistance, classroom interventions that are designed to prevent misbehavior and keep small disruptions from escalating into serious problems need to be both effective and easy to implement.

One such intervention, which has been shown to work with mainstreamed students with behavior disorders as well as with regular students, is called the Good Behavior Game. It is based on the group contingency concept that we mentioned in Chapter 7 ("Behavioral Learning Theory: Operant Conditioning").

The reinforcement contingency used in the Good Behavior Game is called the interdependent group contingency because it allows all students in a group or in the entire class to receive reinforcement as long as the group's performance meets or exceeds some specified level of performance, such as an average grade on a homework assignment or not exceeding a certain number of classroom rule violations. The advantage of this system is that all students must participate and make a contribution, but the group is not automatically denied reinforcement if a small number of students do not perform as well as the others. The Good Behavior Game was designed to prevent or reduce such highly disruptive behaviors as verbal and physical aggression, but it has also been used to moderate out-of-seat behavior, excessive talking, and low levels of classroom participation (Tingstrom, Sterling-Turner, & Wilczynski, 2006).

Classroom disruptions can be significantly reduced by various approaches

Some experts on school violence argue that impersonal and punitively oriented schools produce higher-than-average levels of school violence. © Richard Hutchings/Photo Edit

Another violence reduction program that has shown positive results was devised for ethnic minority students in grades 3–6 but is applicable to all types of students. Initially called Brain Power, but later changed to Best Foot Forward when the scope of the program was expanded (Hudley, Graham, & Taylor, 2007), the program is designed to help students realize that the negative actions of others, such as when a classmate bumps into them or knocks their books off their desk, can have one of several causes. It may have been accidental, an attempt to be helpful, or, least likely, it may have been deliberately hostile. Students who are on the receiving end of the negative action are taught how to respond to these incidents in nonaggressive and appropriate ways. If, for example, they are sure the negative behavior was intentional, they are taught to report the incident to an adult. Students who initiate the incident are taught how to apologize and explain the reasons for their behavior. For example, on bumping into another student, the first student might say, "Sorry, I tripped and accidentally bumped into you." Evaluations of the program have shown that in comparison to a control group, those in the program were less likely to think that they were the deliberate target of a hostile act, became angry less often, and were less likely to respond aggressively.

There are, of course, many other effective classroom-wide approaches to managing student behavior that space limitations do not allow us to discuss. Aside from the two mentioned above, we suggest you also read about Judicious Discipline (Landau & Gathercoal, 2000), the Classroom Check-Up (Reinke, Lewis-Palmer, & Merrell, 2008), and Positive Peer Reporting (Morrison & Jones, 2007). Note the emphasis on praising desired student behavior in most of these programs. Our Case in Print describes a successful schoolwide program that also is based on the idea of rewarding students for following school and classroom rules.

Schoolwide Programs to Reduce Violence and Improve Discipline

Although classroom interventions such as the ones described in the previous section can make life less threatening and more enjoyable for individual teachers and their students, they do not address disruptive behavior elsewhere in a school, and they may conflict with other teachers' procedures. Consequently, some educators have designed violence reduction programs that can be implemented throughout an entire school. This section describes three such approaches. While each program has been proven successful in reducing aspects of school violence, they are not unusual

Case in Print

Teachers who adopt an authoritative style are likely to want their students to learn to eventually regulate their own behavior. By explaining the rationale for classroom rules and adjusting those rules as students demonstrate the ability to govern themselves appropriately, authoritative teachers hope to convince students that adopting the teacher's norms for classroom behavior as their own will lead to the achievement of valued academic goals. (p. 405)

To Teach Good Behavior, Schools Try More Carrots and Fewer Sticks

VALERIE SCHREMP HAHN

St. Louis Post-Dispatch, 12/18/2008

If you were a student at Halls Ferry Elementary School in Florissant, you'd know that when soft music comes on in the cafeteria, it's time to finish eating. If your teacher asked you to "slant," you'd know the acronym means to sit up straight and get ready to listen.

And if you were new here, and needed a primer on all the school's rules and procedures—and there are lots of them—you'd be invited to join the Newcomer's Club.

"I just think that's so good for kids, to come into an environment and know what is expected of them," said Lisa Hazel, principal of Halls Ferry, in the Ferguson-Florissant School District.

All schools have rules; just try keeping 500 children in line without them.

But schools like Halls Ferry have rules nailed down to a science. Administrators say they are using rules not just to keep order, but also to set kids up to succeed.

The schools practice PBS, or Positive Behavior Support. It's sometimes called PBIS, or Positive Behavioral Interventions and Supports.

Ask any of these schools to show you their rules and regulations binder, and you'll see procedures and lesson plans for everything.

Everything. How to line up in the cafeteria. How to use "nice hands and feet" on the bus. How to be kind to classmates.

But the program isn't about creating endless lists of rules and cracking down on violators. Instead, the focus is on setting expectations and catching students being good. In other words, schools are offering more carrots and fewer sticks.

Hazel said the approach makes her job easier—about half as many students were sent to her office last school year as the year before.

Positive Behavior Support is in schools in all 50 states. Halls Ferry was one of the first local schools to start it 10 years ago.

Hazelwood, University City, Clayton, Pattonville, Kirkwood, and Webster Groves are among area districts that have signed on more of their schools in the past few years.

The approach is not rigid; it evolves with the needs of a school. But there is consistency within individual schools.

"Everyone in the school uses the same words," says Thurma DeLoach, director of Kirkwood's special programs. "It's not like when I was in school, where in one classroom these were the expectations; in another classroom, you can get away with murder."

Teachers set up their own classroom rules and procedures, but they reflect the school's general philosophy and are similar to those in other classrooms in the same grade level.

The program is based on the theory that about three-fourths of students in the school don't have behavior issues. About a fourth of students might need some help, which could mean they get a mentor or an invitation to attend a school "social skills club." A small percentage of students have chronic issues and need more help; they're likely to be put on behavior plans.

When schools decide to adopt the program, they might start small with a problem that their school can work on, like cafeteria behavior. Teachers and staff members—from the recess aides to the janitors—agree on a way to address each issue.

At Eureka Elementary in the Rockwood district, cafeteria workers give tickets to students for every positive behavior they observe. Grade levels keep track of how many tickets they get and compete to win the week's "Golden Tray Award"—a spray-painted plastic cafeteria tray.

"It's unbelievable," Eureka Principal Brian Gentz said. "It has changed an entire lunch."

With the rules comes a common theme to make following them fun.

At Ritenour Middle School, Huskies get "paws for applause" for good behavior. At Ackerman School in Florissant, part of the Special School District, students' names are placed on a bee, which is taped next to a central beehive in a hallway. Halls Ferry students see handprints as a common theme, and they agree to follow the "high fives." There are six of them: Be safe, kind, cooperative, respectful, peaceful and responsible.

"When we do the high fives, you can earn good listening tickets and you can earn a lot of things, like lunch with a teacher," Halls Ferry second-grader Reggie Ross said.

The approach translates to good feelings all around, said Carol Fouse, principal of Hazelwood East Middle School in the Spanish Lake area. She recalled the story of a girl who visited her office at the end of last school year and asked, "Did you make up this school?"

"Yes, as far as coming up with the rules and everything," Fouse responded.

"Well, you did a good job," the girl said. "You know what? I haven't needed to fight this year. I got into fights all the time at elementary school, but I feel safe at this school."

"That," said Fouse, "was very cool."

Questions and Activities

1. Are PBS programs more consistent with Diana Baumrind's authoritarian or authoritative approaches? Why?

2. According to the article, schools that have a Positive Behavior Support program have rules and regulations for virtually every school setting and type of behavior. Despite their claimed success, do you think there are any drawbacks to having so many rules?

3. Find a nearby school that has a PBS program or something similar, observe for a day or two, and then talk to students, teachers, and administrators to see if they respond in the same way as those in the Halls Ferry Elementary School did to the author of this article.

in that regard. An analysis of research on 74 school-based violence reduction programs (Derzon, 2006) found that most produced reductions in criminal behavior, suspensions from school, and physical violence.

Unified Discipline In a program called Unified Discipline (Algozzine & White, 2002; White, Algozzine, Audette, Marr, & Ellis, 2001), teachers, administrators, and other school personnel create a uniform approach to managing disruptive behavior. The goal of Unified Discipline is to create a consensus about the following program elements:

- *Attitudes.* The school staff members agree that all students can improve their behavior, that learning to manage one's behavior is an important part of an education, that corrections for misbehavior should be administered in a professional manner, and that becoming angry with students for misbehaving undermines a teacher's instructional effectiveness.

- *Expectations.* The school staff members agree to the rules for student behavior and to use the program's correction procedures in the same way whenever a student breaks a rule.

- *Rules.* The rules that govern student behavior are typically divided into categories. One school, for example, created a three-level system. Class III rules pertained to such behaviors as physically assaulting another person, bringing a weapon to school, and selling drugs, tobacco, or alcohol. Class II rules pertained to behaviors such as fighting, ignoring adult requests, and vandalism. Class I rules pertained to behaviors such as disrupting others and using inappropriate language. The rules that govern classroom behavior have to be, of course,

Take a Stand!

Show Zero Tolerance for Zero Tolerance Policies

Zero tolerance policies mandate specific, nonnegotiable punishments, usually suspension from school, for specific offenses. These policies are typically aimed at curbing such serious offenses as fighting, sexual harassment, or bringing weapons or drugs to school. They are extremely popular, with as many as 75 percent of all schools having such policies. But, as we have pointed out many times in this book, popular ideas or practices are not always good ones. We believe that zero tolerance policies have more disadvantages than advantages and simply give the appearance that serious problems are being addressed. Here are several reasons why we believe educators should not support zero tolerance policies:

- The same punishment is handed out for violations that seem to be the same but that involve very different behaviors and motives. Under the terms of a zero tolerance antidrug policy, do we really want to expel from school both the child who shares a zinc cough drop with a classmate and the child who brings marijuana to school? In the case of a zero tolerance for weapons policy, do we really want to suspend both the kindergarten student who brings a plastic knife to school with which to cut cookies and the high school student who brings a large knife to school to threaten classmates?

- Zero tolerance policies do not teach students those behaviors that will produce positive reinforcement. This is why Skinner was adamantly opposed to the use of punishment as a means of modifying students' behavior.
- Zero tolerance policies result in more students being expelled from school than would otherwise be the case. For some students, being banished from an environment that they find aversive is positively reinforcing and encourages them to continue to exhibit those behaviors that produce suspension.
- Many research studies have failed to find a relationship between such policies and significant reductions in school violence.
- In some cases in which students were automatically expelled from school, extenuating circumstances should have led to a different decision.
- More often than not, courts will support an administrator's decision to suspend a student where the circumstances warrant, making zero tolerance policies redundant.

An analysis of the effectiveness of zero tolerance policies can be found in a report by the American Psychological Association's Zero Tolerance Task Force titled "Are Zero Tolerance Policies Effective in the Schools? An Evidentiary Review and Recommendations" (Skiba, Reynolds, Graham, et al., 2006).

What Do You Think?

What are your views of zero tolerance policies? Have you seen them applied in your community? To explore this issue further, go to the Take a Stand! section of the Education CourseMate website.

appropriate to the students' grade level. One group of kindergarten through second-grade teachers decided that students had to follow all teacher directions promptly, speak in an appropriate voice, keep body parts to themselves, and stay in their assigned places. Teachers in grades 3 through 5 decided that students had to follow all teacher directions promptly, stay on-task, be prepared for class, raise their hands to be recognized, and respect the rights and property of others.

- *Correction procedures.* As with rules, correction procedures vary somewhat by grade level. In the lower grades of one school, a first offense results in the teacher's putting a green ticket in a pocket with the student's name on it. The pocket is stapled to a poster board. A second offense results in a yellow ticket. At the third offense, the student receives a red ticket and has to sit in an exclusion area of the classroom for several minutes. For a fourth offense, the student gets a blue ticket and is sent to another room for a time-out of about 20 minutes. In the upper grades, students receive a verbal correction for a first offense, a loss of privilege for a second offense, and a time-out for a third offense. For students of all ages, teachers respond to infractions by stating the misbehavior, stating the rule that was violated, stating the consequence, and encouraging the student to follow the rule in the future.
- *Roles.* The principal's role is to support teachers when they follow the Unified Discipline procedures and, for the most serious offenses, make decisions about consequences based on a student's needs, history, and the circumstances surrounding the misbehavior (a refreshing change from the mindless uniform punishments dictated by "zero tolerance" policies). The teachers' role is to support the principal and not engage in second-guessing with other teachers, students, or parents.

In one elementary school, the Unified Discipline program resulted in a 20 percent decrease in referrals of students to the principal's office during the first year and decreases of 50 percent or more in subsequent years, fewer violations of classroom rules, and increases in the amount of time students spent on-task (Algozzine & White, 2002).

Smart and Good High Schools Despite reports in the media of such troubling behaviors among high school students as cheating, drug use, alcohol abuse, bullying, and disrespect toward teachers, some high schools are successful in helping their students develop positive character traits. Thomas Lickona and Matthew Davidson (2005) studied the operations of 24 high schools that had been identified by at least one organization (such as the Department of Education or the Coalition of Essential Schools) as being exemplary in an effort to determine how they helped students develop their characters. This collection of schools was quite diverse in terms of size (300 students on the small end and 4,300 students on the large end), type (public, private, and charter), and setting (urban, suburban, and rural).

Lickona and Davidson (2005) defined character as being composed of two main parts: *performance character* and *moral character.* Performance character includes such components as diligence, a strong work ethic, a positive attitude, and perseverance, and it contributes to successful academic performance. Moral character includes such components as integrity, respect, cooperation, and justice, and it contributes to productive, fulfilling personal relationships. High schools that help students develop these two aspects of character are, in their words, "Smart and Good High Schools" (xv).

The high schools that Lickona and Davidson identified as being Smart and Good employed a variety of devices to help students become (1) lifelong learners and critical thinkers, (2) diligent and capable performers, (3) socially and emotionally skilled, (4) more attuned to the ethical implications of their behaviors, (5) respectful and responsible, (6) self-disciplined, (7) contributors to their community, and (8) oriented toward creating a purposeful life. Whether such schools are judged to be more successful than other schools at reducing undesirable student behaviors has yet to be determined.

Resolving Conflict Creatively Program A somewhat different approach to decreasing physical violence, particularly between students, is the Resolving Conflict Creatively Program (RCCP), created by Linda Lantieri in 1985. The goal of the program is to teach students how to use nonviolent conflict resolution techniques in place of their more normal and more violent methods. Students are trained by teachers to monitor the school environment (such as the playground, the cafeteria, and the hallways) for imminent or actual physical confrontations between students. For example, picture two students who are arguing about a comment that struck one as an insult. As the accusations and counteraccusations escalate, one student threatens to hit the other. At that moment, one or two other students who are wearing T-shirts with the word *mediator* printed across the front and back intervene and ask if the two students would like help in resolving their problem. The

One approach to reducing school violence is to train students to mediate disputes between other students.
© Elizabeth Crews Photography

mediating students may suggest that they all move to a quieter area where they can talk. The mediators then establish certain ground rules, such as that each student gets a turn to talk without being interrupted and that name calling is not allowed.

RCCP was designed as a primary prevention program. This means that all students, even those not prone to violence, are taught how to prevent disagreements from becoming violent confrontations. In schools in which the program has been implemented, teachers have noted less physical violence in their classrooms, fewer insults and verbal putdowns, and greater spontaneous use of conflict resolution skills (Lantieri, 1995).

| Violence less likely when schoolwide programs teach students constructive ways to handle conflicts

Nevertheless, educators noticed that the program did not produce desirable results with all students. So during the 1997–1998 school year an intervention component was added for children who exhibit behaviors that are associated with violent behavior in later years. School counselors and RCCP-trained teachers, working with groups of 15 to 20 children, engaged the students in activities that were designed to increase a sense of social responsibility (caring and cooperative behaviors, for example) and to develop such interpersonal skills as active listening.

The capstone of this 30-week program was the social action project. The group had to decide on and implement a community service project, such as fixing dinner for a family in need of assistance, making Easter baskets for the mentally disabled residents of a nearby center, or collecting books and art materials for a children's hospital. An evaluation of this new component reported improvements in listening skills, anger management skills, ability to share with others, relationships with teachers and students, self-esteem, and attitudes toward school (Lantieri, 1999). RCCP has been adopted by 400 schools in the United States and by schools in Brazil, England, and Puerto Rico (Roerden, 2001). An evaluation of RCCP conducted in more than 350 New York City classrooms reported gains in interpersonal negotiation strategies, prosocial behavior, and mathematics achievement and decreases in aggressive behavior, but only in those classes in which teachers provided more instruction in RCCP techniques than the average teacher did (Brown, Roderick, Lantieri, & Aber, 2004).

Additional information about RCCP for the elementary and middle school grades can be found at **http://esrnational.org** by typing RCCP in the search box.

pause & reflect

If you were a primary or elementary grade teacher and had to choose between a program such as Positive Behavior Support (described in the Case in Print) and a peer mediation program such as the Resolving Conflict Creatively Program, which one would you choose? Why?

Using Technology to Keep Students in School

As we pointed out previously, students who exhibit poor academic performance and believe that their teachers don't care about them are prone to engage in disruptive and violent behavior. They are also at risk for dropping out of school. In 2006, 9.3 percent of sixteen- to twenty-four-year-olds were classified as dropouts (were out of school and had not earned a diploma or alternative credential). The percentages for White, Black, and Latino youths were 5.8 percent, 10.7 percent, and 22.1 percent, respectively (Planty, Hussar, et al., 2008). Although these dropout rates have steadily fallen over the past 25 years, some believe that creative uses of technology may cause them to fall even faster. Here are a few examples of how some schools have used technology to reduce student absenteeism and the dropout rate:

- The Hueneme School District in Hueneme, California, created a "smart classroom" to help retain students who are at risk of dropping out. Students in this program were given experience in computerized robotics, computer-aided manufacturing, desktop publishing, and aeronautics and pneumatic technology. Average daily attendance for this program was close to 100 percent (Cardon & Christensen, 1998).

- The Azusa Unified School District in Azusa, California, made extensive use of an integrated learning system to encourage student attendance and retention. Students spent four class periods each day working at their computer terminals on English, reading, social studies, mathematics, and science. By the end of the program's second year, the average daily attendance was 96 percent, and 93 percent of students remained in the program from one year to the next (Cardon & Christensen, 1998).

- Virtual schools, a growing phenomenon that is also referred to as distance education or distance learning, are courses or entire programs (particularly at the high school level) that are available on the Web and that may help students with high absentee rates—such as the children of migrant workers, students whose school districts don't offer desired courses, and students who are home-schooled—to take courses and complete their schooling (Roblyer, 2006). During the 2007–2008 school year, over 1 million public school students were enrolled in virtual classes (Davis, 2009), and almost all states offer some type of online education option (Ash, 2009). Although such programs are praised for the flexibility they offer, they are also criticized because low-income students may have limited Internet access, because computer failures result in lost time and assignments, and because the lack of face-to-face interaction makes learning more difficult for some students (Podoll & Randle, 2005; Roblyer, 2006). What little research exists suggests that, overall, students who take courses online learn about as much as students who take the same courses in actual classrooms. What is not known at this point is why some students succeed in a virtual school environment whereas others do not (Bernard et al., 2004; Rice, 2006).

To review this chapter, try the tutorial quizzes and other study aids on the textbook's Education CourseMate website.

Challenging Assumptions

Managing Classrooms and Leading Learning

"The way a teacher views classroom management makes a huge difference," says Celeste. "I observed a teacher last week who seemed to be very 'controlling.' The whole atmosphere of the class was pretty depressing. The teacher spent most of his time telling kids what to do and yelling at them when their attention wandered. Well, he didn't really yell, except for a couple of times, but he spent all of his time trying to make sure that students were . . . I don't know . . . it's like he spent his time making sure students were following orders."

Connie says, "Thinking back to our discussion about 'controlling students' versus 'leading learning,' perhaps you saw a teacher who hasn't learned that by focusing on opportunities for learning, you give students a chance to discover their interests and their intrinsic motivations. What do you think, Antonio?"

"That's a good way to put it. Thinking about classroom management as part of the teacher's leadership role is really helpful to me. I have a great teacher on my team who said two things to me. First, she said, 'It's important that you stay focused on what students are learning rather than on just what they are doing.' Second, she said, 'Remember that you are a leader, not a dictator.'"

"So," says Connie, "it becomes a question of which lens you look through. If you view through the lens of 'controlling students,' you are constantly looking at what students are doing. If you view classroom management through the lens of 'leading learning,' then your focus goes past what they are doing to what they are learning."

Antonio nods. "When she was talking about leading learning, she mentioned that there will always be misbehavior, but the way you respond to it can go a long way toward establishing an atmosphere of learning instead of battling with students for control." Antonio smiles for a second and adds, "She also said that you should never forget that leading is a two-way street. As you are leading learning in your classroom, you have to turn around every once in a while. If you look back and no one is following, then you aren't leading."

Summary

1. Just as parents adopt an authoritarian, permissive, authoritative, or rejecting-neglecting approach to raising children, teachers adopt similar approaches to managing the behavior of students. The authoritative approach, which revolves around explaining the rationale for classroom rules and adjusting those rules as students demonstrate the ability for self-governance, produces the highest level of desirable student behavior.

2. Jacob Kounin, one of the early writers on classroom management, identified several effective classroom management techniques. He emphasized cultivating withitness, coping with overlapping activities, maintaining the momentum of a lesson, keeping the whole class involved in a lesson, using a variety of instructional techniques enthusiastically, being aware that the ripple effect can be used to a teacher's advantage by focusing on the misbehavior of students rather than on their personalities, and suggesting alternative constructive behaviors.

3. Research on classroom management has found that in well-managed classrooms, students know what they are expected to do and do it successfully, are kept busy with teacher-designated activities, receive frequent but nonpunitive feedback, and believe that the teacher is interested in helping them learn. Such classrooms are marked by a work-oriented yet relaxed and pleasant atmosphere.

4. Classroom management can be made easier by using technology tools to carry out such tasks as test construction, record keeping, developing seating arrangements, analyzing space utilization, and monitoring student work. Successful use of current technology requires teachers to be comfortable with both teacher-directed and student-directed forms of instruction.

5. Fritz Redl and William Wattenberg proposed a set of behavior management methods in 1959 called influence techniques that were designed to help teachers deal with classroom misbehavior and that continue to be recommended and used today.

6. Haim Ginott suggests that teachers use I-messages when responding to misbehavior. These are statements that indicate to students how the teacher feels when misbehavior occurs. The aim is to comment on the situation rather than on the personality and character of the student.

7. Thomas Gordon recommends that teachers determine who owns a problem and use active listening when the student owns the problem.

8. Despite reports in the media about school-based crime and violence, classrooms and school buildings are relatively safe environments.

9. One aspect of school violence is bullying. This involves one or more students intentionally and repeatedly harming another student through the use of physical and/or psychological means.

10. When girls engage in bullying they are more likely than boys to use name-calling, insults, and malicious rumors. They are also more likely than boys to use social networking websites to do so, which is referred to as cyberbullying.

11. Possible explanations for misbehavior and violence, particularly among boys at the middle school, junior high, and high school levels, include biological factors, high levels of the male sex hormone testosterone, a culture that encourages male aggression and independence, feelings of resentment and frustration over low levels of achievement, lack of interpersonal problem-solving skills, and difficulty in establishing a positive identity.

12. Other explanations for school violence focus on the characteristics and atmosphere of schools that are so large that they seem impersonal, that emphasize competition, that do not enforce rules fairly or consistently, that use punishment as a primary means of resolving conflict, and that offer a curriculum perceived as unimaginative and meaningless.

13. Steps that classroom teachers can take to reduce school violence include using approaches that combine basic classroom management and behavior modification techniques, and teaching students how to monitor and regulate their behavior.

14. Schoolwide programs that may reduce violence and improve behavior include Unified Discipline, in which teachers and other school personnel adopt consistent rules and correction procedures and support one another in implementing them; the Resolving Conflict Creatively Program, in which students mediate disputes between other students to prevent physical violence; and Smart and Good High Schools that work to improve both performance character and moral character.

15. Some school districts have been able to reduce their absenteeism and dropout rates by getting students interested in using technological aids to learning.

Resources for Further Investigation

● Classroom Management

If you find Redl and Wattenberg's concept of influence techniques useful, recent textbooks that mention some of their ideas include *Elementary Classroom Management: Lessons from Research and Practice* (4th ed., 2007), by Carol Weinstein and Andrew Mignano, Jr.; *Principles of Classroom Management: A Professional Decision-Making Model* (6th ed., 2010), by James Levin and James F. Nolan; and *Managing the Adolescent Classroom* (2004), by Glenda Beamon Crawford. Each chapter of Crawford's book highlights the practices of outstanding teachers.

Other recent analyses of classroom management techniques can be found in *Classroom Management for Elementary Teachers* (8th ed., 2009), by Carolyn Evertson and Edmund Emmer, and *Classroom Management for Middle and High School Teachers* (8th ed., 2009), by Edmund Emmer and Carolyn Evertson.

An interesting book with an offbeat title is *Fires in the Bathroom: Advice for Teachers from High School Students* (2003), by Kathleen Cushman. Each of this book's 10 chapters covers a particular aspect of classroom management (for example, knowing students well; respect, liking, trust, and fairness; creating a culture of success) by including observations and advice from students in their own words. The end of each chapter includes a bullet-point list that summarizes the chapter's main points. Kathleen Cushman and Laura Rogers have written an identically structured book, *Fires in the Middle School Bathroom: Advice for Teachers from Middle Schoolers* (2008), for middle school teachers. Another book with an unusual title but a considerable amount of practical advice is *You Have to Go to School . . . You're the Teacher!* (3rd ed., 2008), by Renee Rosenblum-Lowden and Felicia Lowden Kimmel. The first author was a teacher in the New York City school system for over 25 years and the second author is a school counselor. The book contains advice about such management issues as how to prepare before the school year starts, what to do once it does start, and how to establish routines, administer consequences, and avoid showdowns.

Common-Sense Classroom Management for Elementary School Teachers (2nd ed., 2006), by Jill Lindberg and April Swick, is a brief (128 pages), readable, practical book written by a former special education teacher and a school principal. Each chapter includes one or more brief discussions about how to adapt a particular technique for students with disabilities and high school students. Jill Lindberg, Dianne Kelly, and April Swick have also written a companion volume, *Common-Sense Classroom Management for Middle and High School Teachers* (2005). Both books include chapters on working with non-English-speaking students and their families and Jacob Kounin's concept of withitness.

Online resources for classroom management include Teachnet.com (**www.teachnet.com**). Use the site's How-To area (click on Power Tools) to find information on classroom management techniques. Another online site, Teachers Helping Teachers, provides postings by teachers about particular topics, including classroom management. Many of these first-person comments are insightful and relevant to most beginning teachers. The site can be found at **www.pacificnet.net/~mandel.** Click on the Classroom Management link.

● School Violence

A comprehensive approach to school violence and safety can be found in *The Handbook of School Violence and School Safety* (2006), edited by Shane Jimerson and Michael Furlong. The chapters in Part III (Research-Based Prevention and Intervention Programs) and Part IV (Implementing Comprehensive Safe School Plans) are likely to be the most useful.

Ready-to-Use Conflict Resolution Activities for Elementary Students (2002), by Beth Teolis, is, as the title suggests, a collection of activities that elementary grade teachers can use to help students avoid conflicts and peacefully resolve those that do occur. The book is organized into four sections: Conflict-Resolution for Educators, Building the Groundwork for Conflict-Resolution, Conflict-Resolution Activities for Your Classroom, and Conflict-Resolution Activities for Your School. The activities for sections 2 through 4 specify an objective, materials needed, and directions.

If you want to learn more about the issue of bullying, take a look at *Children and Bullying: How Parents and Educators Can Reduce Bullying at School* (2008), by Ken Rigby, and *Cyber-Bullying: Issues and Solutions for the School, the Classroom, and the Home* (2008), by Shaheen Shariff.

13 Approaches to Instruction

 The Education CourseMate website for this text offers many helpful resources. Go to **CengageBrain.com** to preview this chapter's Concept Maps and Chapter Themes.

KEY POINTS

These key points will help you learn the important information in this chapter. To help you study, they also appear in the margins of the pages, next to the text where they are discussed.

Devising and Using Objectives

- Goals are broad, general statements of desired educational outcomes
- Instructional objectives specify observable, measurable student behaviors
- Taxonomy: categories arranged in hierarchical order
- Cognitive taxonomy: knowledge, comprehension, application, analysis, synthesis, evaluation
- Taxonomy of affective objectives stresses attitudes and values
- Psychomotor taxonomy outlines steps that lead to skilled performance
- Most test questions stress knowledge, ignore higher levels of cognitive taxonomy
- Mager: state specific objectives that identify act, define conditions, state criteria
- Gronlund: state general objectives, list sample of specific learning outcomes
- Objectives work best when students are aware of them

The Behavioral Approach to Teaching: Direct Instruction

- Direct instruction: focus on learning basic skills, teacher makes all decisions, keep students on-task, provide opportunities for practice, give feedback
- Direct instruction involves structured, guided, and independent practice
- Direct instruction helps students learn basic skills

The Cognitive Approach to Teaching: Facilitating Meaningful and Self-Regulated Learning

- Information-processing/social cognitive approach: design lessons around principles of meaningful learning, teach students how to learn more effectively

- Tell students what you want them to learn, why, and how they will be tested
- Present organized and meaningful lessons
- Present new information in small chunks
- Constructivist approach: help students construct meaningful knowledge schemes
- Meaningful learning aided by exposure to multiple points of view
- Technology supports a cognitive approach to instruction by helping students code, store, and retrieve information

The Humanistic Approach to Teaching: Student-Centered Instruction

- Maslow: help students develop their potential by satisfying their needs
- Rogers: establish conditions that allow self-directed learning
- Humanistic approach addresses needs, values, motives, self-perceptions
- Humanistic teachers show respect, courtesy, fairness, caring attitude

The Social Approach to Teaching: Teaching Students How to Learn from Each Other

- Competitive reward structures may decrease motivation to learn
- Cooperative learning characterized by heterogeneous groups, positive interdependence, promotive interaction, individual accountability
- Cooperative learning effects likely due to stimulation of motivation, cognitive development, meaningful learning
- Students with low and average ability in mixed-ability groups outperform peers in homogeneous groups on problem-solving tests; students with high ability in homogeneous groups score slightly higher than peers in mixed-ability groups
- Successful technology applications are embedded in an active social environment

---

This chapter is concerned with helping you answer two questions: What are my objectives? (or What do I want students to know and be able to do after I complete a unit of instruction?) and How can I help students achieve those objectives? The ordering of these two questions is not arbitrary. Instructional planning should always begin with a description of what you want students to know and be able to do some weeks, or even months, after the beginning of an instructional unit. If you decide in advance what you want your students to achieve, you can prepare lessons that logically lead to a particular result and also use evaluation techniques efficiently designed to determine what level of achievement has occurred.

Once you have a clear idea of what you are trying to accomplish with your students, you can consider how you are going to help get them there. Here is where you can use your knowledge of learning and motivation. After all, if the goal of teaching is to help students acquire and use a variety of knowledge and skills, what better way to do that than to use approaches and techniques that are consistent with what is known about how people learn and the conditions under which they learn best?

The theories that underlie the approaches to instruction described in this chapter emphasize different aspects of the learning process, and each has been supported by research. Thus no one theory is sufficiently comprehensive and powerful that you can rely exclusively on it as a guide for designing classroom instruction. To work effectively with the diversity of students you will almost certainly encounter, you will need to use a variety of instructional approaches and techniques. For some objectives and students, you may want to use a highly structured approach that is consistent with the principles of behavioral theory. For other objectives, you may want to emphasize cognitive approaches that focus on helping students develop more effective learning and problem-solving skills. You may also want students to work productively in groups and respond to you and to learning in positive ways and develop positive feelings about themselves as students. And you will probably also want to integrate computer-based technology with one or more of these approaches. This eclectic approach to instruction is, by the way, consistent with the concepts of teaching adaptively, which we mentioned in Chapter 1, and differentiated instruction, which we briefly discussed in Chapter 4.

Lest you think that our recommendation to combine theories is an interesting but untested idea, this integrated approach has been put into practice by the staff of an alternative middle school in Rhode Island called the Urban Collaborative Accelerated Program (UCAP) (**http://www.ucap.org/**). The purpose of UCAP was to work with students who had been retained in a grade one or more times and were therefore at risk of dropping out of school. The most radical and striking characteristic of UCAP is the use of 50 criteria to determine whether students should be promoted to the next grade. This approach is quite consistent with the behavioral view that complex behaviors cannot be properly learned until more basic behaviors are mastered and that students must clearly and convincingly demonstrate those behaviors. It is also consistent with an approach to instruction and classroom assessment called mastery learning (which we discuss in Chapter 14 on classroom assessment). Other techniques that were used, and the approaches they represent, included the following: having teachers play the role of coach instead of information provider through lectures (constructivist approach, humanistic approach), the use of problem- and project-based learning (constructivist approach), and small-group learning and peer tutoring (social approach) (DeBlois, 2005). As of 2004, UCAP was meeting the achievement targets called for by No Child Left Behind and was classified by the state as a moderately performing and improving school.

Revealing Assumptions

Who Plans for Whom?

"I'm not sure yet," Don says, "but I think my teaching style will be more discussion than lecture. I'm just not very good at holding students' attention when I do presentations."

Connie asks, "Why do you think that, Don?"

"Just from the experiences I've had so far, I guess. A couple of weeks ago, I was trying to explain day and night. I came in with this big, bright flashlight and turned out the lights. The kids were real excited at first but then as I was explaining why we have daytime and nighttime—and using the flashlight to show what I meant—they just lost interest. I remember thinking, 'I should dress up in a big yellow sun costume; I bet that would keep their attention.'"

Celeste says, "Show us what you did."

Don says, "It'll look a little goofy, but okay . . ." Don starts his presentation, pretending to be holding a flashlight. He talks about how in daytime the sun is

pause & reflect

As an aspiring teacher, perhaps you have felt some concern regarding what you will do in your classroom so that your students will respond to you, pay attention, do what you ask. It is common for new teachers to have such concerns. In many cases, those concerns lead to an assumption: that instructional plans focus primarily on what the teacher, rather than the students, will do in the classroom. How did Don's lesson reflect this assumption? How might the lesson have been different if Don had viewed the lesson from the students' perspective rather than his own? What is the starting point for instructional planning?

visible and how at nighttime the sun cannot be seen. He demonstrates how he walked around the room so that the kids could see the light when he was in front of them but not when he was in back of them. "It was just about at this point that I seemed to lose them."

Antonio says, "I wonder how developmentally appropriate that was for your students. Maybe they just couldn't understand that the flashlight represented the sun."

Celeste adds, "Maybe they already had some prior knowledge and were confused. I mean, it would have been more scientifically accurate for you to have stood in one place and have the kids stand up and turn circles. You know, their heads would each be the earth rotating on its axis and sometimes their eyes would be toward the sun and sometimes the back of their heads would be toward the sun. I don't know . . . maybe they were confused and that's why you couldn't keep their attention."

"Maybe," says Connie, "but before we rethink this particular plan, let's step back and rethink the planning. Were you planning for yourself or for your students?" Don looks at Connie with a furrowed brow. Connie smiles and says, "Think about it, my young colleague. For whom were you planning? When the school bell rings, for whom does it toll?"

DEVISING AND USING OBJECTIVES

Contrasting Objectives with Educational Goals

Goals are broad, general statements of desired educational outcomes

One way to help you understand the nature of instructional objectives is to contrast them with something with which they are often confused: educational goals. Goals are relatively broad statements of what political and educational leaders would like to see schools accomplish. Consider, for example, the following two goal statements:

- Students will acquire the thinking skills that will allow them to become responsible citizens, independent learners, and productive workers.
- All adults will be sufficiently literate, knowledgeable, and skilled to compete in a global economy and behave as responsible citizens.

Although they are ambitious and laudatory, statements of this sort do not provide very useful guidelines for teachers charged with the responsibility for achieving such goals. What exactly is meant by "thinking skills" or being "sufficiently literate, knowledgeable, and skilled"? And will these terms mean the same thing to every teacher? Thinking skills, for example, could be interpreted to mean everything from memorization to problem solving.

Instructional objectives specify observable, measurable student behaviors

Instructional objectives, in contrast to these broad educational goals, specify the kinds of observable and measurable student behaviors that make it possible for the underlying goals to be achieved. To give teachers both a common vocabulary and a system for writing different kinds of objectives, psychologists have created organizational schemes called taxonomies.

Taxonomies of Objectives

Awareness of the vagueness of educational goals stimulated a group of psychologists who specialized in testing to seek a better way to describe educational objectives. After experimenting with various ways to prepare lists of objectives that would be more useful to teachers than vaguely worded sets of goals, the test specialists decided to develop taxonomies of educational objectives.

A **taxonomy** is a classification scheme with categories arranged in hierarchical order. Because goals of education are extremely diverse, the decision was made to prepare taxonomies in three areas, or *domains*: cognitive, affective, and psychomotor. The taxonomy for the **cognitive domain** stresses knowledge and intellectual skills; the taxonomy for the **affective domain** concentrates on attitudes and values; and the taxonomy for the **psychomotor domain** focuses on physical abilities and skills.

Taxonomy: categories arranged in hierarchical order

Taxonomy for the Cognitive Domain The first and most widely used taxonomy for the cognitive domain was prepared by Benjamin S. Bloom, Max D. Englehart, Edward J. Furst, Walker H. Hill, and David R. Krathwohl (1956). It consists of six hierarchically ordered levels of instructional outcomes: knowledge, comprehension, application, analysis, synthesis, and evaluation. The taxonomy is described as a hierarchy because it was reasoned that comprehension relies on prior mastery of knowledge or facts, that application depends on comprehension of relevant ideas, and so on through the remaining levels. An abridged outline of the taxonomy for the cognitive domain follows:

Cognitive taxonomy: knowledge, comprehension, application, analysis, synthesis, evaluation

Taxonomy of Educational Objectives: Cognitive Domain

1.0 *Knowledge.* Remembering previously learned information, such as facts, terms, procedures, and principles.
2.0 *Comprehension.* Grasping the meaning of information by putting it into one's own words, drawing conclusions, or stating implications.
3.0 *Application.* Applying knowledge to actual situations, as in taking principles learned in math and applying them to laying out a baseball diamond or applying principles of civil liberties to current events.
4.0 *Analysis.* Breaking down objects or ideas into simpler parts and seeing how the parts relate and are organized. For example, discussing how the public and the private sectors differ or detecting logical fallacies in an argument.
5.0 *Synthesis.* Rearranging component ideas into a new whole. For example, planning a panel discussion or writing a comprehensive term paper.
6.0 *Evaluation.* Making judgments based on internal evidence or external criteria. For example, evaluating a work of art, editing a term paper, or detecting inconsistencies in the speech of a politician.

Although the cognitive domain taxonomy has served educators well for more than 50 years, research in the areas of cognitive psychology, curriculum and instruction, and assessment suggested to some that a change was in order. Two alternatives now exist.

The first alternative (Anderson et al., 2001) is organized as a two-dimensional table rather than as a cumulative hierarchy. The first dimension is called the Cognitive Process Dimension and contains mostly familiar concepts: Remember, Understand, Apply, Analyze, Evaluate, and Create. The second dimension is called the Knowledge Dimension and has four categories: Factual Knowledge, Conceptual Knowledge, Procedural Knowledge, and Metacognitive Knowledge. Each knowledge category is composed of two or more types. Procedural Knowledge, for example, is composed of "knowledge of subject-specific skills and algorithms," "knowledge of subject-specific techniques and methods," and "knowledge of criteria for determining when to use appropriate procedures."

The objectives that flow from the revised taxonomy reflect the intersection of these two dimensions. An objective that lies at the intersection of Apply and Conceptual Knowledge, for example, might be "The student will apply Vygotsky's principle of scaffolded instruction by teaching a struggling primary grade student how to multiply fractions."

The second alternative (Marzano & Kendall, 2007) to the original cognitive domain taxonomy is similar in structure to the first alternative in that it has two intersecting dimensions, but it is broader in scope. The first dimension is called Levels of Processing and contains six levels (Retrieval, Comprehension, Analysis, Knowledge Utilization, Metacognitive System, and Self-system). The second dimension is called Domains of Knowledge and is composed of Information, Mental Procedures, and Psychomotor Procedures. The broadness of this model comes from the metacognitive and self-systems, which are assumed to reflect affective processes, and psychomotor procedures.

Time will tell whether either alternative proves to be as popular and useful as the original.

Taxonomy for the Affective Domain In addition to arranging instructional experiences to help students achieve cognitive objectives, virtually all teachers are interested in encouraging the development of attitudes and values. To clarify the nature of such objectives, a taxonomy for the affective domain was prepared (Krathwohl, Bloom, & Masia, 1964). Affective objectives are more difficult to define, evaluate, or encourage than cognitive objectives because they are often demonstrated in subtle or indirect ways. Furthermore, certain aspects of value development are sometimes considered to be more the responsibility of parents than of teachers. Finally, because values and attitudes involve a significant element of personal choice, they are often expressed more clearly out of school than in the classroom. The complete taxonomy for the affective domain stresses out-of-school values as much as, if not more than, in-school values.

The following abridgment concentrates on the kinds of affective objectives you are most likely to be concerned with as a teacher. You will probably recognize, though, that there is not much you can do to influence substantially the kinds of objectives described in the higher levels of the taxonomy because they represent a crystallization of values formed by experiences over an extended period of time.

> **Taxonomy of affective objectives stresses attitudes and values**

Taxonomy of Educational Objectives: Affective Domain

1.0 *Receiving (attending).* Willingness to receive or attend.

2.0 *Responding.* Active participation indicating positive response or acceptance of an idea or policy.

3.0 *Valuing.* Expressing a belief or attitude about the value or worth of something.

Being familiar with the different taxonomies of objectives, such as the one for the cognitive domain, helps teachers plan lessons and create tests that require students to use different types of cognitive processes.
Corbis/Jupiter Images

4.0 *Organization*. Organizing various values into an internalized system.
5.0 *Characterization by a value or value complex*. The value system becomes a way of life.

Taxonomy for the Psychomotor Domain   Cognitive and affective objectives are important at all grade levels, but so are psychomotor objectives. Regardless of the grade level or subject you teach, at some point you are likely to want to help your students acquire physical skills of various kinds. In the primary grades, for example, you will want your students to learn how to print legibly. And in many subjects in middle school and high school, psychomotor skills (for example, driving a car, playing a violin, adjusting a microscope, manipulating a computer keyboard, operating a power saw, throwing a pot) may be essential. Recognition of the importance of physical skills prompted Elizabeth Simpson (1972) to prepare a taxonomy for the psychomotor domain. An abridged version of the taxonomy follows:

Psychomotor taxonomy outlines steps that lead to skilled performance

Taxonomy of Educational Objectives: Psychomotor Domain
1.0 *Perception*. Using sense organs to obtain cues needed to guide motor activity.
2.0 *Set*. Being ready to perform a particular action.
3.0 *Guided response*. Performing under the guidance of a model.
4.0 *Mechanism*. Being able to perform a task habitually with some degree of confidence and proficiency. For example, demonstrating the ability to get the first serve in the service area 70 percent of the time.
5.0 *Complex or overt response*. Performing a task with a high degree of proficiency and skill. For example, typing all kinds of business letters and forms quickly with no errors.
6.0 *Adaptation*. Using previously learned skills to perform new but related tasks. For example, using skills developed while using a word processor to do desktop publishing.
7.0 *Origination*. Creating new performances after having developed skills. For example, creating a new form of modern dance.

Why Use Taxonomies?   Using these taxonomies will help you avoid two common instructional failings: ignoring entire classes of outcomes (usually affective and psychomotor) and overemphasizing the lowest level of the cognitive domain. According to Benjamin S. Bloom, organizer and driving force of the team that prepared the first taxonomy,

Most test questions stress knowledge, ignore higher levels of cognitive taxonomy

> After the sale of over one million copies of the *Taxonomy of Educational Objectives—Cognitive Domain* [Bloom et al., 1956] and over a quarter of a century of use of this domain in preservice and in-service teacher training, it is estimated that over 90% of test questions that U.S. public school students are *now* expected to answer deal with little more than information. Our instructional material, our classroom teaching methods, and our testing methods rarely rise above the lowest category of the Taxonomy—knowledge. (1984, p. 13)

The next section describes how you can write and profitably use objectives.

Ways to State and Use Objectives

Many psychologists have offered suggestions for writing and using objectives, but the following discussion is limited to recommendations made by two of the most influential writers on the subject: Robert F. Mager and Norman E. Gronlund.

Mager's Recommendations for Use of Specific Objectives   With the publication of a provocative and unorthodox little treatise titled *Preparing Instructional Objectives* (1962, 1997), Mager sparked considerable interest in the use of objectives. Mager emphasizes the importance of objectives by pointing out that

Mager recommends that teachers use objectives that identify the behavioral act that indicates achievement, define conditions under which the behavior is to occur, and state the criterion of acceptable performance.
Bob Daemmrich/Bob Daemmrich Photography

if you don't know where you're going, the best-made maps won't help you get there… Without a way to communicate your instructional objectives to others:

- You wouldn't be able to decide which instructional content and procedures would help you to accomplish your objectives.
- You wouldn't be able to create measuring instruments (tests) that tell you whether your students had become competent enough to move on.
- And your students wouldn't be able to decide for themselves when to stop practicing. (1997, p. vi)

Mager then offers these suggestions for writing **specific objectives** of instruction:

1. Describe what you want learners to be doing when demonstrating achievement, and indicate how you will know they are doing it.
2. In your description, identify and name the behavioral act that indicates achievement, define the conditions under which the behavior is to occur, and state the criterion of acceptable performance.
3. Write a separate objective for each learning performance.

> Mager: state specific objectives that identify act, define conditions, state criteria

Here are some examples of the types of objectives Mager (1962) recommends:

- Correctly solve at least seven addition problems consisting of three two-digit numbers within a period of 3 minutes.
- Given pictures of 10 trees, correctly identify at least 8 as either deciduous or evergreen.
- Correctly spell at least 90 percent of the words on the list handed out last week.
- Given a computer and word processing program, set it up to type a business letter (according to the specifications provided) within 2 minutes.

Note that the criterion of acceptable performance can be stated as a time limit, a minimum number of correct responses, or a proportion of correct responses.

Mager's proposals were widely endorsed immediately after the publication of *Preparing Instructional Objectives*, but in time it became apparent that the very specific kinds of objectives he recommended were most useful in situations in which students were asked to acquire knowledge of factual information or to learn simple skills. Norman E. Gronlund concluded that a different type of objective was more appropriate for more complex and advanced kinds of learning.

Gronlund's Recommendations for Use of General Objectives   Gronlund (2004) has developed a two-step procedure for writing a more general type of objective:

1. Examine what is to be learned with reference to lists of objectives such as those included in the three taxonomies. Use such lists to formulate **general objectives** of instruction that describe types of behavior students should exhibit to demonstrate what they have learned.

2. Under each general instructional objective, list up to five *specific learning outcomes* that provide a representative sample of what students should be able to do when they have achieved the general objective. Each learning outcome should begin with an *action verb* (such as *explain* or *describe*) that names the particular action the student is expected to take.

pause & reflect

One criticism of objectives is that they limit the artistic side of teaching, locking teachers into a predetermined plan of instruction. Can you respond by recalling a teacher who provided objectives but was still enthusiastic, flexible, and inventive?

Gronlund: state general objectives, list sample of specific learning outcomes

To see how Gronlund's method differs from Mager's, imagine that you are teaching an educational psychology course and that you want to write objectives that reflect an understanding of the four stages of Piaget's theory of cognitive development. Figure 13.1 compares objectives you might develop using Gronlund's approach with objectives that follow Mager's method.

Gronlund gives several reasons for beginning with general objectives. First, most learning activities are too complex to be described in terms of a specific objective for every learning outcome, as Mager proposed. Second, the kind of specific objective Mager advocated may tend to cause instructors and students to concentrate on memorizing facts and mastering simple skills. As indicated earlier, these types of behaviors are at the lowest levels of the taxonomies of objectives. Third, specific objectives can restrict the flexibility of the teacher. Gronlund's objectives allow performance criteria to be kept separate from the objective so a teacher can revise performance standards as needed without having to rewrite the objective. This feature is useful if the same behavior is to be evaluated several times over the course of a unit of instruction, with successively higher levels of performance required. A fourth and final reason is that general objectives help keep you aware that the main

Figure 13.1 Types of Objectives: Gronlund's and Mager's Approaches Compared

Topic: Piaget's Theory of Cognitive Development

Gronlund's Approach	**Mager's Approach**
General objective	**Specific objectives**
The student will understand the characteristics of Piaget's four stages of cognitive development.	Given a list of Piaget's four stages of cognitive development, the student, within twenty minutes, will describe in his or her own words two problems that students at each stage should and should not be able to solve.
Specific learning outcomes, stated with action verbs	Given a videotape of kindergarteners presented with a conservation-of-volume problem, the student will predict the response of 90 percent of the students.
Describe in his or her own words the type of thinking in which students at each stage can and cannot engage.	Given a videotape of fifth-grade students presented with a class inclusion problem, the student will predict the response of 90 percent of the students.
Predict behaviors of students of different ages.	Given eight descriptions of instructional lessons, two at each of Piaget's four stages, the student will be able to explain in each case why the lesson would or would not succeed.
Explain why certain teaching techniques would or would not be successful with students of different ages.	

target of your instructional efforts is the general outcome (such as comprehension, application, or analysis).

Aligning Assessment with Objectives and Instruction

Writing clear objectives in language that students understand, and aligning those objectives with the tests you create to assess what students have learned, is the first step in what we refer to in Chapter 14 as assessment *for* learning (as opposed to assessment *of* learning) (Stiggins, 2009).

As we discuss in Chapter 14, there are several types of classroom assessment methods, each of which is most useful for measuring only *certain* outcomes. Multiple-choice, short-answer, and true-false tests are useful for measuring mastery of basic factual knowledge. For objectives that emphasize the comprehension, analysis, and synthesis levels of Bloom's taxonomy, essay questions that call for students to summarize, compare, and contrast would be more useful. For objectives that reflect a constructivist orientation, paper-and-pencil tests are likely to be much less useful than requiring students to solve a complex problem, create a product over an extended period of time, or work productively with a small group of peers on a project. (This type of testing, called *performance assessment*, is discussed in Chapter 14, "Assessment of Classroom Learning," and Chapter 15, "Understanding Standardized Assessment.")

Need guidance in preparing lesson plans that align objectives, activities, and assessment? Check the sample lesson plans and template at the textbook's Education CourseMate website.

Here's a small example of how things can go wrong if you don't align your tests with both your objectives and your instructional methods. If you tell students that you want them to organize information into logical structures, integrate ideas into broad themes, and make connections with knowledge learned elsewhere, and you teach them how to think along those lines, but you load your tests with short-answer and multiple-choice items that require rote memorization, don't be surprised when students simply memorize facts. From their perspective, the content and level of the test items are the real objectives.

One final comment about alignment. In the first paragraph of this section, we referred to the tests you *create* rather than the tests you *use*. These two terms imply a subtle but important distinction. The best way to ensure alignment of objectives, teaching approach, and assessment is for you to be the creator of the assessment. If you use a test that somebody else has designed, such as a standardized test, it is almost a certainty that some of the items will not match your objectives or instructional approach.

Evaluations of the Effectiveness of Objectives

Do students learn more when their teachers provide them with clearly written objectives? The answer is yes, but only under certain conditions. Although most of the research on the effectiveness of objectives was conducted over 30 years ago (see, for example, Faw & Waller, 1976; Klauer, 1984; Melton, 1978) the major conclusions drawn from it are as valid today as they were then:

Objectives work best when students are aware of them

1. Objectives seem to work best when students are aware of them, treat them as directions to learn specific sections of material, and feel they will aid learning.
2. Objectives seem to work best when they are clearly written and the learning task is neither too difficult nor too easy.
3. Students of average ability seem to profit more from being given objectives than do students of higher or lower ability.
4. Objectives lead to an improvement in intentional learning (what is stressed as important) but to a decline in incidental learning (not emphasized by the teacher). General objectives of the type that Gronlund recommended seem to lead to more incidental learning than do specific objectives of the type that Mager recommended.

pause & reflect

Based on this chapter and your own experience, do you agree that writing objectives and providing them to students are worthwhile uses of a teacher's time? If so, what steps will you take to make writing objectives a standard part of your professional behavior?

As we mentioned at the beginning of the chapter, once you have decided what it is you want your students to learn, you need to decide which approaches you will use to help them achieve those objectives. Our use of the term *approaches* is deliberate. To repeat what we said at the beginning of the chapter, different approaches to instruction are based on different theories of learning and motivation, and given the complexity of the learning process and the diversity of learners in most classrooms, no one theory can be used for all instructional purposes and for all students. So as you read through the next several sections, try to imagine how you might use each approach over the course of a school year.

THE BEHAVIORAL APPROACH TO TEACHING: DIRECT INSTRUCTION

For behavioral psychologists, learning means acquiring new behaviors, and new behaviors are learned because of the role that external stimuli play. Thus a behavioral approach to teaching involves arranging and implementing those conditions that make it highly likely that a desired response will occur in the presence of a particular stimulus (such as reading a sentence fluently, accurately using the correct mathematical operations when faced with a long-division problem, and giving the correct English translation of a paragraph written in Spanish). Perhaps the most popular approach to teaching that is based on behavioral theory is direct instruction.

The Nature of Direct Instruction

The underlying philosophy of **direct instruction** (sometimes called *explicit teaching*) is that if the student has not learned, the teacher has not effectively taught. This approach calls for the teacher to keep students consistently engaged in learning basic skills and knowledge through the design of effective lessons, corrective feedback, and opportunities for practice. It is most frequently used in the teaching of basic skills (for example, reading, mathematical computation, writing) and subject matter (for example, science, social studies, foreign language vocabulary) in the primary and elementary grades. It is also used to teach remedial classes at the middle school and high school levels. It is felt to be most useful for young learners, slow learners, and all learners when the material is new and difficult to grasp at first. Although there are several variations of direct instruction, the following represents a synthesis of descriptions offered by Bruce Joyce and Marsha Weil (2009), Barak Rosenshine and Carla Meister (1994b), Bruce Larson and Timothy Keiper (2007), and Jennifer Goeke (2009).

The main characteristics of direct instruction include:

1. Focusing almost all classroom activity on learning basic academic knowledge and skills. Affective and social objectives, such as improved self-esteem and learning to get along with others, are either deemphasized or ignored.
2. Having the teacher make all instructional decisions, such as how much material will be covered at one time, whether students work individually or in groups, and whether students work on mathematics during the morning and social studies during the afternoon.
3. Keeping students working productively toward learning new academic knowledge and skills (usually called being on-task) as much as possible.
4. Designing all lessons to include demonstration, practice, and corrective feedback.

Direct instruction: focus on learning basic skills, teacher makes all decisions, keep students on-task, provide opportunities for practice, give feedback

Teachers who subscribe to direct instruction emphasize efficient learning of basic skills through the use of structured lessons, positive reinforcement, and extensive practice. Corbis/Jupiter Images

5. Maintaining a positive classroom climate by emphasizing positive reinforcement and avoiding the use of aversive consequences.

The goal of direct instruction is to have students master basic skills and content before moving on to more advanced levels. Advocates of this method believe that students who mislearn information require substantially more time and effort to relearn concepts than would have been the case had they learned them correctly in the first place.

For obvious reasons, direct instruction is a highly structured approach to teaching and is often referred to as *teacher-directed* or *teacher-led instruction*.

The Components of Direct Instruction

JOURNAL ENTRY
Using a Direct Instruction Approach

Bruce Joyce and Marsha Weil (2009) identify five general components, or phases, that make up direct instruction: orientation, presentation, structured practice, guided practice, and independent practice. These components are not derived just from theory. They reflect the techniques that effective teachers at all grade levels have been observed to use.

Orientation During the orientation phase, the teacher provides an overview of the lesson, explains why students need to learn the upcoming material, relates the new subject either to material learned during earlier lessons or to their life experience, and tells students what they will need to do to learn the material and what level of performance they will be expected to exhibit.

Presentation The presentation phase initially involves explaining, illustrating, and demonstrating the new material. As with all other forms of instruction based on operant conditioning, the lesson is broken down into small, easy-to-learn steps to ensure mastery of each step in the lesson sequence. Numerous examples of new concepts and skills are provided, and, consistent with social learning theory, the teacher demonstrates the kind of response students should strive for (such as a particular pronunciation of foreign vocabulary, a reading of a poem or story, the steps in mathematical operations, or how to analyze a novel for theme, character, or setting). To assist comprehension, and where appropriate, material can be presented pictorially (as slides, videotapes, on computer) or graphically (as a concept map, a timeline, or in table form). At the first sign of difficulty, the teacher gives additional explanations.

The last step of the presentation phase is to evaluate students' understanding. This is typically done through a question-and-answer session in which the questions call for specific answers, as well as explanations of how students formulated their answers. Some sort of system is used to ensure that all students receive an equal opportunity to respond to questions. Throughout the lesson, efforts are made to stay on-task and avoid nonproductive digressions.

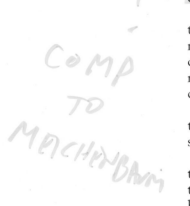

Direct instruction involves structured, guided, and independent practice

Structured, Guided, and Independent Practice   The last three phases of the direct instruction model all focus on practice, although with successively lower levels of assistance. Joyce and Weil (2009) refer to these three phases as *structured practice*, *guided practice*, and *independent practice*. Because the level of teacher assistance is gradually withdrawn, you may recognize this progression as an attempt to apply the behavioral principle of shaping. You may also recognize it as the constructivist principle of scaffolding.

Structured practice involves the greatest degree of teacher assistance. The teacher leads the entire class through each step in a problem or lesson so as to minimize incorrect responses. Visual displays, such as overhead transparencies, are commonly used during structured practice as a way to illustrate and help students recall the components of a lesson. As the students respond, the teacher reinforces correct responses and corrects errors.

During guided practice, students work at their own desks on problems of the type explained and demonstrated by the teacher. The teacher circulates among the students, checking for and correcting any errors.

When students can correctly solve at least 85 percent of the problems given to them during guided practice, they are deemed ready for independent practice. At this point, students are encouraged to practice on their own either in class or at home. Although the teacher continues to assess the accuracy of the students' work and provide feedback, it is done on a more delayed basis.

Getting the Most Out of Practice

Joyce and Weil (2009) offer the following suggestions to help make practice effective:

1. Shape student learning by systematically moving students from structured practice to guided practice to independent practice.
2. Schedule several relatively short but intense practice sessions, which typically produce more learning than fewer but longer sessions. For primary grade students, several 5- to 10-minute sessions scattered over the day are likely to produce better results than the one or two 30- to 40-minute sessions that middle school or high school students can tolerate.
3. Carefully monitor the accuracy of students' responses during structured practice to reinforce correct responses and correct unacceptable responses. The reason for this suggestion comes straight out of operant conditioning research. As you may recall from the chapter on behavioral learning theory, Skinner found that new behaviors are learned most rapidly when correct responses are immediately reinforced and incorrect responses are eliminated. When a learner makes incorrect responses that are not corrected, they become part of the learner's behavioral repertoire and impede the progress of subsequent learning.
4. To ensure the high degree of success that results in mastery of basic skills, students should not engage in independent practice until they can respond correctly to at least 85 percent of the examples presented to them during structured and guided practice.
5. Practice sessions for any lesson should be spread over several months. The habit of some teachers of not reviewing a topic once that part of the curriculum has been covered usually leads to a lower quality of learning. Once again, distributed practice produces better learning than massed practice.
6. Space practice sessions close together during structured practice but further and further apart for guided practice and independent practice.

Effectiveness of Direct Instruction

Direct instruction helps students learn basic skills

Studies of direct instruction that have been done in urban schools that enroll high percentages of minority students and students of low socioeconomic status (SES) have produced moderately positive results. For example, a version of direct instruction called the BIG Accommodation model (because instruction is organized around "big ideas") was implemented in a California middle school that served high-poverty neighborhoods. After 1 year, the percentage of seventh- and eighth-grade students who were reading at the fifth-grade level or lower declined, whereas the percentage reading at the sixth- and seventh-grade or higher levels increased. Similar results were obtained for math achievement scores. In percentage terms, the most dramatic increase occurred among English language learners. Before the program was implemented, only 10 percent scored at grade level (seventh grade or above) on reading and math tests. One year later that figure rose to about 36 percent. The largest gains in grade equivalent scores were made by White (2.1), American Indian (1.7), and Latino (1.6) students (Grossen, 2002).

Using Technology to Support Behavioral Approaches to Instruction

The computer-based approach to instruction that uses behavioral learning principles emphasizes specific performance objectives, breaking down learning into small steps, shaping student success, using immediate feedback and consistent rewards, and predefining assessment techniques. Learning is viewed much like an industrial assembly line: information is transferred efficiently from a computer program to a waiting student.

Most of the drill-and-practice computer-assisted instruction tools and integrated learning systems mentioned in the chapter on behavioral learning theory fit within this framework (Mazyck, 2002; Ysseldyke et al., 2003), as would multimedia technology if used simply to embellish a lecture with new pictures or sounds. Although this approach to the use of technology in instruction may be perceived as rote, boring, and dehumanizing, it can prove valuable if you are interested in accurate and efficient learning of basic facts and skills.

THE COGNITIVE APPROACH TO TEACHING: FACILITATING MEANINGFUL AND SELF-REGULATED LEARNING

The focus of cognitive learning theories is the mind and how it works. Hence, cognitive psychologists are primarily interested in studying those mental processes that expand our knowledge base and allow us to understand and respond to the world differently. In this section, we will lay out two approaches to instruction that are based on different forms of cognitive theory: information processing/social cognitive and constructivism. The information-processing/social cognitive approach to teaching involves implementing those conditions that help students effectively transfer information from the "outside" (a text or lecture, for example) to the "inside" (the mind), whereas the constructivist approach focuses on providing students opportunities to create their own meaningful view of reality.

The Nature and Elements of an Information-Processing/ Social Cognitive Approach

As we noted previously in the book, information-processing and social cognitive theories both focus on how human beings interpret and mentally manipulate the information they encounter. Research shows that, for information to be meaningfully learned, it must be attended to, its critical features must be noticed, it must be coded in an organized and meaningful way so as to make its retrieval more likely, and strategies must be devised that allow this process to occur for a variety of tasks and in a variety of circumstances (Joyce & Weil, 2009; Marx & Winne, 1987; Zimmerman, 2008).

The approach to teaching that flows from these theories has two main parts. First, design lessons and gear teaching behaviors to capitalize on what is known about the learning process. As you will see, this part of the information-processing/ social cognitive approach has some elements in common with the behavioral approach that we just covered. Both approaches direct you to structure the classroom environment in a certain way (and to use some of the same tactics) to improve the effectiveness and efficiency of learning. Second—and this is what makes the information-processing/social cognitive approach unique—make students aware of how they learn and how they can use those processes to improve their classroom performance. Following are several suggestions for helping students become more effective processors of classroom instruction.

Communicate Clear Goals and Objectives   The first question that students ask themselves when they take a new course, encounter a new topic, or are asked to learn a new skill is, "Why do I have to learn this?" We suspect you've asked yourself this question many times and not gotten a satisfactory answer. So, at the beginning of each lesson, tell students what you want them to accomplish, why you think it's important that they learn this knowledge or skill, and how you are going to assess their learning. If you intend to use paper-and-pencil tests, tell them what content areas will be covered, what kinds of questions you will include (in terms of whatever taxonomies you use to generate your objectives), and how many of each type of question will be on the test. Without this information, students will be unable to formulate a rational approach to learning and studying because they will be forced to guess about these features. They may, for example, take your general directive to "learn this material for the test" as a cue to memorize, when you expected them to be able to explain ideas in their own words. If you intend to use performance measures, tell students the conditions under which they will have to perform and what criteria you will use to judge their performance.

Information-processing/social cognitive approach: design lessons around principles of meaningful learning, teach students how to learn more effectively

JOURNAL ENTRY
Using an Information-Processing/Social Cognitive Approach to Instruction

Tell students what you want them to learn, why, and how they will be tested

One implication of the information-processing approach to instruction is to use attention-getting devices because information not attended to will not be learned. © Jeff Greenberg/ Photo Edit

Use Attention-Getting Devices Information-processing/social cognitive theory holds that material not attended to is not processed, and material that is not processed is not stored in memory. Consequently, you should use (but not overuse) a variety of attention-getting devices. The suggestion we just made to explain the purpose of a lesson, what students will be held accountable for learning, and how student learning will be assessed will likely capture the attention of some students. But once you are into a lesson, you may need to gain and maintain students' attention repeatedly (see our Case in Print for an illustration of how one teacher accomplishes this goal).

The first Suggestions for Teaching section ("Helping Your Students Become Efficient Information Processors") in Chapter 8, "Information-Processing Theory," mentioned a few devices for capturing students' attention. Here are several more:

- Orally emphasize certain words or phrases by raising or lowering your voice.
- Use dramatic gestures.
- Underline key words and phrases that you write on a chalkboard or whiteboard.
- When discussing the work of important people, whether in science, math, social studies, or history, dress up to look like the person and speak as you think the person might have spoken.

One approach to teaching that describes how to get students' attention by embedding lessons in unusual but meaningful contexts and that is worth examining is called *outrageous instruction* by its creator (Pogrow, 2008, 2009a).

Emphasize Organization and Meaningfulness Research studies have repeatedly found that students learn and recall more information when it is presented in an organized format and a meaningful context. Information is organized when the components that make it up are linked together in some rational way. If you teach high school physics, you can organize material according to major theories or basic principles or key discoveries, depending on your purpose. For history, you can identify main ideas and their supporting details or describe events as a chain of causes and effects. Just about any form of organization would be better than having students memorize names, dates, places, and other facts as isolated fragments of information.

| Present organized and meaningful lessons |

A popular method for organizing and spatially representing the relationships among a set of ideas is *concept mapping* (as we noted earlier in Chapter 9, "Social Cognitive Theory"). This technique involves specifying the ideas that make up a topic and indicating with lines how they relate to one another. Figure 13.2 is a particularly interesting example of both organized knowledge and a constructivist view of learning. (We will take a further look at this latter angle when we discuss constructivist approaches.)

As we pointed out in Chapters 8 and 9, meaningful learning results in richer and more stable memory representations and occurs more readily when information can be related to familiar ideas and experiences. Several techniques are known to facilitate meaningful learning:

- Using some form of overview or introduction that provides a meaningful context for new material
- Using concrete examples and analogies to illustrate otherwise abstract ideas
- Using visually based methods of representing information, such as maps, graphs, three-dimensional models
- Stressing practical applications and relationships to other subjects (You may recall from a previous chapter that this tactic is used to help adolescent girls remain interested in science.)

Present Information in Learnable Amounts and Over Realistic Time Periods When students struggle to master the information they are expected to learn, the problem sometimes arises simply from an excess of information being

Case in Print

Get Their Attention! Solving the First Challenge of Teaching

Information-processing/social cognitive theory holds that material not attended to is not processed, and material that is not processed is not stored in memory. Consequently, you should use (but not overuse) a variety of attention-getting devices. (p. 453)

Geology Teacher Finds Creative Ways to Keep Students Engaged

CHRISTINE BYERS
St. Louis Post-Dispatch, 03/23/2007

Stepping into Art Casey's earth science classroom is almost like visiting a mad scientist's laboratory, but the experiments conducted here have brought him closer to solving a mystery that teachers have struggled with for centuries: getting students to pay attention.

The black walls are covered by pictures of the estimated 8,700 students he has taught in 36 years at Fox High School—70 of whom have died, most in car accidents—along with various old inventions he has amassed in his lifetime as a self-proclaimed pack rat.

One wall has about 35 concrete blocks that enclose time vaults, which he began making with students in the 1971-1972 school year. The tradition started with students' enclosing notes to children of the future in jars to be opened in 1984 and another to be opened in 2001 to coincide with the novel *1984* and the movie "2001: A Space Odyssey."

The tradition has continued, with seniors making two vaults and opening two vaults each year. The vault opened this month came from a generation growing up 29 years ago with a fear of nuclear war. They wrote messages such as, "Civilization will be dead."

"It helps students get the concept of time," Casey said. "We talk about things in geological time, and this helps them get the feeling of the immensity of time."

Beyond the wall of vaults, a secret passage leads to the hallway, where a display case is filled with "treasure tiles," and clues on ways to find them. The tiles, which are signed by Casey's students, have been hidden in places all around the world, including the Swiss Alps and an arctic ice formation. Those who find them get cash rewards ranging from $25 to $100.

"They may think, 'I'm not going to go there,' but they're paying attention to subjects like oceanography and topography that are otherwise considered boring," he said.

Despite Casey's elaborately decorated classroom and creative traditions, students doze off in his class occasionally. But he's devised a way to combat the problem while offering a lesson at the same time: A spray bottle named Nimbus after the scientific term for rain cloud will rouse sleepy students, he said.

Beyond his unorthodox approach to teaching, Casey's oddities also have made him somewhat of a legend among parents and older siblings who relish telling incoming students about how his trademark white lab coats and black clip-on ties are stored behind a secret panel in his classroom and how administrators have approved schemes that students use to get him back at the end of the year for using "Nimbus."

"My older brother said he was crazy," said Kyle LaChance, 17, of Arnold. "He makes it interesting and everybody likes him."

He nearly foiled one attempt made by seniors equipped with water cannons by wearing an impenetrable hazardous-materials suit. Ultimately, though, one student pulled the suit away from his neck and dumped water down his back.

But perhaps one of Casey's greatest tactics for maintaining his students' attention has been keeping his personal life the ultimate secret. They listen every day in hopes he will reveal any clues as to his age, his family and where he lives.

It seems they just don't buy the Arnold water tower address and Jan. 22, 1899, birth date listed on his school identification card or the answer he gives when asked if he has children, "Yes, I have thousands of children. And they're all teenagers."

Questions and Activities

1. Teacher Art Casey uses various techniques to get students to attend to his earth science lessons. What evidence, if any, can you cite from this article that he was successful?

2. In what ways are this teacher's methods consistent with both the information-processing and constructivist approaches to teaching?

3. Would you use techniques as unorthodox as this teacher's to get your students' attention and make lessons more meaningful? Why? What, specifically, would you do?

Figure 13.2 Two Concept Maps Constructed from Identical Concepts

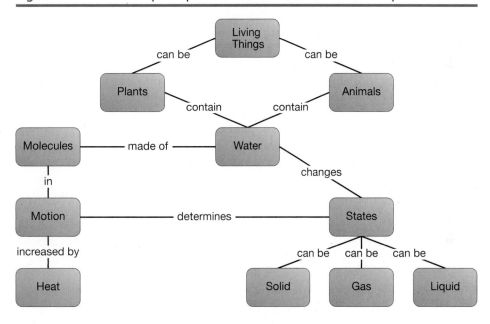

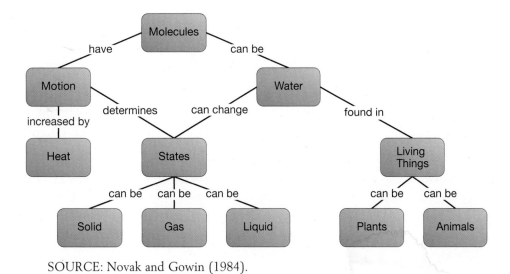

SOURCE: Novak and Gowin (1984).

presented to them at once—that is, from too great an external demand. At other times, the student's working (short-term) memory is strained because of the nature of the task itself: for instance, if the task has several components that all have to be monitored. By taking the nature of the task into consideration, you can judge how much information to expect your students to learn in a given time.

For tasks in which a set of discrete elements must be learned in a one-at-a-time fashion, such as learning foreign language vocabulary or the symbols of chemical elements, the demand on working memory and comprehension is low because the elements are independent. Learning the meaning of one word or symbol has no effect on learning any of the others. As long as the external load on working memory is kept reasonable by limiting the number of words or symbols that students have to learn at any time, learning problems should be minimal.

Other tasks make greater demands on working memory because their elements interact. Learning to produce and recognize grammatically correct utterances ("The cat climbed up the tree" versus "Tree the climbed cat up the") is a task that places a higher demand on working memory because the meaning of all the words must be considered simultaneously to determine if the sentence makes sense. For such tasks, keeping the amount of information that students are required to learn at a low level is critically important because it leaves the student with sufficient working memory to engage in schema construction (Montgomery, Magimairaj, & O'Malley, 2008; Savage, Lavers, & Pillay, 2007).

| Present new information in small chunks

One instructional recommendation that flows from this analysis is the same as one of the recommendations for direct instruction: break lessons into small, manageable parts and don't introduce new topics until you have evidence that students have learned the presented material. A second recommendation is to build into lessons opportunities for students to write about, discuss, and use the ideas they are learning. By monitoring the accuracy of their responses, you will also have the information you need to judge whether it is time to introduce new ideas. Finally, arrange for relatively short practice sessions spread over several weeks rather than one or two long practice sessions, because distributed practice leads to better learning than massed practice.

Facilitate Encoding of Information into Long-Term Memory High-quality learning rarely occurs when students adopt a relatively passive orientation. As we pointed out in Chapter 9, many students do little more than read assigned material and record ideas in verbatim form. They spend little time thinking about how ideas within topics and between topics relate to one another or to concepts they have already learned. One reason is that many students simply do not know what else to do with information. Another reason is that teachers do little to support the kind of encoding that results in more meaningful forms of learning. Recall the study we mentioned that found that teachers in primary grades through middle school provided students with suggestions for processing information less than 10 percent of the time and with explanations for the suggestions they did give less than 1 percent of the time. To help your students encode information for more effective storage in and retrieval from long-term memory, incorporate the following techniques into your classroom instruction:

- Present information through such different media as pictures, videotape, audiotape, live models, and manipulation of physical objects.
- Use lots of examples and analogies (to foster elaboration).
- Prompt students to elaborate by asking them to put ideas in their own words, relate new ideas to personal experience, and create their own analogies.

pause & reflect

In Chapter 9, on social cognitive theory, we noted that elementary grade teachers rarely give students instruction in how to process information effectively. One reason is that teacher education programs typically provide little or no coursework on this subject. Is this true of your program? What can you do when you teach to make full use of information-processing principles?

The Nature and Elements of a Constructivist Approach

In previous chapters, we noted that the essence of constructivist theory is that people learn best by creating their own understanding of reality. Using such characteristics as existing knowledge, attitudes, values, and experiences as filters, people interpret current experience in a way that seems to make sense to them at the time. As Figure 13.2 demonstrates by constructing two different concept maps from an identical set of concepts, knowledge can be organized in any number of ways, and the scheme one creates will reflect one's purpose or focal point. Thus some students understand that the Jane Austen novel *Sense and Sensibility* is as much a satire of the paternalistic class system of 1800s England as it is a love story, whereas other students see it only as a love story, and a boring one at that. The goal of constructivist-oriented teaching, then, is to provide a set of conditions that will lead students to construct a view of reality that both makes sense to them and addresses the essence of your objectives (Delgarno, 2001).

A brief description of five of the more prominent elements that help define a constructivist-oriented classroom follows. Although two of these elements reflect a social constructivist orientation, bear in mind that the goal of both cognitive and social constructivism is the same: to help students become more effective thinkers and problem solvers by helping them construct richer and more meaningful schemes. A social constructivist orientation simply gives greater weight to the role of social interaction in this process.

JOURNAL ENTRY
Using a Constructivist
Approach to Instruction

Provide Scaffolded Instruction Within the Zone of Proximal Development   As we said previously in the book, the zone of proximal development is the difference between what a learner can accomplish without assistance and what can be accomplished with assistance, and the assistance that teachers give to students as they try to master new knowledge and skills is called scaffolding.

When you introduce students to new material, one of the most straightforward ways to provide scaffolded instruction is by the time-honored technique of providing explanations. An analysis of research (Wittwer & Renkl, 2008) suggests four guidelines for creating effective instructional explanations. First, and this echoes what we said in the previous paragraph, make sure your explanations are within you students' zone of proximal development so that you make learning neither too difficult nor too easy. This guideline implies that you will need to be aware of what students know and do not know, what misconceptions they have, and what kinds of cognitive skills they posses. Second, as we do in this textbook, make your explanations meaningful by emphasizing how concepts and principles are relevant to your students' everyday lives and to what they already know. Third, give students the opportunity to use the concepts and principles that are embedded in your explanations. Finally, because of the factors mentioned in the first guideline, some students will learn best from very direct, detailed explanations whereas others will do best when left to figure things out for themselves.

The beneficial effect of a different form of scaffolding was demonstrated in a study (Hardy, Jonen, Möller, & Stern, 2006) in which third graders received either high or low levels of instructional support on a lesson about density and buoyancy (e.g., Why does a large iron ship float?). In the high-instructional-support condition, the teacher sequenced the material into consecutive units, decided when certain instructional materials and objects would be available, pointed out contradictory statements made by the students, and summarized their conclusions. In the low-instructional-support condition, students were given a variety of materials and objects and worked in small groups to conduct experiments. The teacher's major role in the low-support condition was to provide support for the process of investigation. When tested on their understanding of the concepts of density and buoyancy, both groups significantly outscored an uninstructed control group. But 1 year later, the high-support group demonstrated a better grasp of these concepts than did the low-support group.

Provide Opportunities for Learning by Discovery　By its very nature, constructivism implies the need to let students discover things for themselves. But what things? According to Jerome Bruner, whose pioneering work we mentioned in Chapter 10, on constructivist learning theory, the process of discovery should be reserved for those outcomes that allow learners to be autonomous and self-directed. These include understanding how ideas connect with one another, knowing how to analyze and frame problems, asking appropriate questions, recognizing when what we already know is relevant to what we are trying to learn, and evaluating the effectiveness of our strategies. The case we cited in Chapter 10 of the fifth-grade teacher who wanted his students to understand the relationship between the circumference of a circle and its diameter is a good example of how these outcomes can be learned by guided discovery.

Constructivist approach: help students construct meaningful knowledge schemes

Foster Multiple Viewpoints　Given the basic constructivist premise that all meaningful learning is constructed and that everyone uses a slightly different set of filters with which to build his or her view of reality, what we refer to as knowledge is actually a consensus of slightly different points of view. Thus another element of a constructivist approach to teaching is to help students understand that different views of the same phenomena exist and that they can often be reconciled to produce a broader understanding.

Meaningful learning aided by exposure to multiple points of view

The technique of **cooperative learning** is an effective way to expose students to peers who may have different views about the "right" way to do something or the "truth" of some matter and help them forge a broader understanding that is acceptable to all members of the group. In the last major section of this chapter, we describe cooperative learning in considerable detail.

Emphasize Relevant Problems and Tasks　Can you recall completing a class assignment or reading a chapter out of a textbook that had no apparent relevance to anything that concerned you? Not very interesting or exciting, was it? Unfortunately, too many students perceive too much of schooling in that light. One constructivist remedy is to create interest and relevance by posing problems or assigning tasks that are both challenging and realistic. One basic purpose of emphasizing problems and tasks that are relevant to the lives of

Adopting a constructivist approach to teaching means arranging for students to work collaboratively in small groups on relevant problems and tasks, encouraging diverse points of view, and providing scaffolded instruction. © Bob Daemmrich/The Image Works

students is to overcome the problem of inert knowledge, mentioned in Chapter 10 on constructivism. Constructivists believe that the best way to prepare students to function effectively in real-life contexts is to embed tasks in contexts that come as close as possible to those of real life (Delgarno, 2001; Jonassen, Howland, Marra, & Crismond, 2008).

Problems can be challenging either because the correct answer is not immediately apparent or because there is no correct answer. The ill-structured problems and issues that we described previously are, by their nature, challenging and realistic and do not have solutions that everyone perceives as being appropriate and useful. But if you assign students an ill-structured task to investigate, pose it in such a way that they will see its relevance. For example, instead of asking high school students to debate the general pros and cons of laws that restrict personal freedoms, have them interview their community's mayor, chief of police, business owners, and peers about the pros and cons of laws that specify curfews for individuals under a certain age and that prohibit such activities as loitering and the purchase of alcohol and tobacco. Because many adolescents consider themselves mature enough to regulate their own behavior, analyzing and debating laws that are intended to restrict certain adolescent behaviors is likely to produce a fair amount of disequilibrium.

Encourage Students to Become More Autonomous Learners According to constructivist and humanistic theory (which we discuss later in this chapter), students should, under the right circumstances, be able to work more independently of the teacher than they typically do. One important condition that paves the way for students becoming more autonomous is the way in which teachers interact with students. Students in one study (Reeve & Jang, 2006) were more likely to feel as if they were in control of their own learning when teachers engaged in such behaviors as giving students time to work on a task in their own ways, giving students the opportunity to talk, encouraging students to complete tasks, listening to students, and being responsive to students' questions. By contrast, student autonomy was more likely to be negatively related to such teacher behaviors as giving students the solutions to problems or the answers to questions, giving students commands and directions, telling students they should or should not do something, and asking students such controlling questions as, "Can you do it the way I showed you?"

If you still believe, despite the findings cited in the preceding paragraph, that school-age children simply don't have the emotional maturity and cognitive skills necessary to direct more of their own learning, a program for eighth graders in Radnor, Pennsylvania, called *Soundings* has illustrated its feasibility (Brown, 2002). The program is built around a set of questions that students have identified as being of interest and importance to them. Students then help the teacher develop the curriculum, study methods, and assessments.

In line with humanistic theory, the first goal of every school year is the development of safe and trusting relationships among students and between the students and the teacher. This goal is accomplished by having pairs of students interview each other and then introduce the other student to the class; by having students interview the teacher; and by using cooperative games. Then the teachers, who act as coordinators of the students' efforts, train students to ask meaningful and insightful questions (for example, "Why do we eat breakfast?" "Who decided which foods would be breakfast foods?" "Do people in all cultures eat the same foods for breakfast?") that flow from two general questions: "What questions and concerns do you have about yourself?" and "What questions and concerns do you have about the world?"

Working in small groups, students examine their own questions as well as those of their classmates, identify common questions that will be the subject of a large group discussion, and write their questions on large sheets that are posted on a wall and viewed by the other students in class. After viewing all the lists and discussing common themes and their importance, the students create a prioritized list of themes to study throughout the year (such as violence in our culture, medical issues affecting our lives, and surviving alien environments). Students then develop a time-line for studying the selected topics, block out time periods on the calendar, and join a small group that is interested in one of the topics.

The Challenges to Being a Constructivist Teacher

Constructivist-oriented approaches to teaching run counter to the dominant teacher-directed approach in which the teacher transmits established, accumulated knowledge to students through lecture and demonstration and students incorporate that knowledge largely through drill-and-practice exercises. Evidence that teacher-directed instruction is still the most popular approach comes from a large-scale observational study of over 2,500 first-, third-, and fifth-grade classrooms. Almost all of the instruction these students received (just over 91 percent) was in the form of either whole-class instruction or individual seatwork. Students in first and third grades received 10 times as much instruction in basic skills as in problem solving and reasoning. For fifth graders, the ratio was 5:1 (Pianta, Belsky, Houts, et al., 2007). Consequently, teachers interested in adopting a constructivist approach will have to successfully negotiate a set of challenges that Mark Windschitl (2002) describes as conceptual, pedagogical, cultural, and political.

The conceptual challenge is to fully understand the theoretical foundation on which constructivism rests and to reconcile current pedagogical beliefs with constructivist beliefs. This involves, for example, understanding the difference between cognitive and social constructivism and such concepts as cognitive apprenticeship, scaffolding, situated learning, and negotiated meaning. A solid grasp of constructivist theory will also help teachers avoid misconceptions: for instance, that direct instruction can never be used, that students must always be physically and socially active to learn, that all ideas and interpretations offered by students are equally valid, and that constructivist teaching avoids rigorous assessment practices.

The pedagogical challenge has several facets:

- Constructivist teachers need to understand how different students think, how complete each student's knowledge is about a subject, how accurate that knowledge is, and how aware students are about the state of their own knowledge.
- Teachers must know how to use a variety of methods to support understanding during problem-based activities. These methods include modeling; providing prompts, probes, and suggestions that differ in their explicitness; providing problem-solving rules of thumb; and using technology to organize and represent information.
- Teachers must guide students to choose meaningful projects or issues to investigate that are sufficiently complex, intellectually challenging, and related to the theme of the particular subject under study.
- Teachers have to teach students how to work productively in collaborative activities even though some students may be uninterested in or even opposed to working with others.
- Teachers need to have a deep enough understanding of a subject to be able to guide students who become puzzled by an observation to an explanation (as in the case of students who wonder why seedlings grow taller under weaker light than under stronger light).
- Last, constructivist teachers need to know how to use a wide range of alternative assessment devices, such as interviews, observations, student journals, peer reviews, research reports, art projects, the building of physical models, and participation in plays, debates, and dances.

The cultural challenge faced by teachers interested in adopting a constructivist approach pertains to the implicit classroom norms that govern the behavior of teachers and students. As noted, the dominant approach to instruction is a didactic one in which established facts and procedures are transmitted from an expert (the teacher) to novices (students). The classroom culture that flows from this model is one in which teachers talk most of the time while students sit, are quiet and attentive, do seatwork, and take tests. A constructivist classroom, on the other hand, is characterized by inquiry, collaboration among students, use of the teacher as a resource, explanations of points of view and solutions to problems to others, and attempts to reach consensus about answers and solutions. The major challenge for teachers is to recognize that their beliefs about what constitutes an ideal classroom are likely to have been shaped by their experiences as students in traditional classrooms.

The political challenge is to convince those who control the curriculum and influence teaching methods (school board members, administrators, other teachers, and parents) that constructivist teaching will satisfy state learning standards, is consistent with the content of high-stakes tests, and will help students meaningfully learn the key ideas that underlie various subjects. Should you run into this problem, you might cite a research study or two that supports constructivist teaching. For example, third graders in Germany whose teachers used a constructivist approach scored higher on a test of mathematical word problems and at the same level on a test of arithmetic computation problems as third graders whose teachers used the traditional direct transmission approach (Staub & Stern, 2002).

The technology section that follows presents some additional ideas for embedding learning in realistic settings.

Using Technology to Support Cognitive Approaches to Instruction

As educators begin to understand and address cognitive learning theories, the focus of technology is shifting from remediating learner skill deficiencies and rehearsing basic skills to finding ways to help the learner build, extend, and amplify new knowledge (Cennamo, Ross, & Ertmer, 2010; Jonassen, Howland, Marra, & Crismond, 2008). Your willingness and readiness to use today's technology for this purpose is likely to be partly a function of the extent to which you use computer technology to meet personal and professional goals. Fourth- and eighth-grade teachers who reported higher levels of classroom technology use and personal computer use were more likely to use constructivist teaching practices than their peers who reported lower levels of technology use (Rakes, Fields, & Cox, 2006).

| Technology supports a cognitive approach to instruction by helping students code, store, and retrieve information

Helping Students Process Information
An information-processing approach to instruction uses technology to minimize the cognitive demands of a task; to help learners form schemas, or patterns, of information; to extend or augment thinking in new directions; and to supply information overviews and memory cues. The programs for outlining and note taking mentioned in Chapter 8 on information-processing theory are consistent with this approach, as are electronic encyclopedias (for example, Grolier's *Multimedia Encyclopedia*); hypermedia databases that contain conceptual resources such as timelines, information maps, and overviews; and concept mapping software such as Inspiration that helps students organize their knowledge and ideas (Delgarno, 2001).

Discovery and Exploratory Environments
Computers are not just tools to transmit or represent information for the learner; they also provide environments that allow for discoveries and insights. In such an **exploratory environment,** students might explore ocean life or find the ideal ecosystem for a Tyrannosaurus rex dinosaur (see, for example, **www.nationalgeographic.com/xpeditions**).

Exploratory tools for learning math include Logo, the Geometric Supposer, and the Geometer's Sketchpad, all of which have been shown to help students construct meaningful knowledge networks about geometric concepts and reduce the usual rote memorizing of rules and terms (Clements, Sarama, Yelland, & Glass, 2008; Funkhouser, 2002/2003).

Another exploratory tool, GenScope, was designed to help students better understand the principles of genetics. Two studies illustrate the benefits to using this program. In the first, high school students in technical biology and general life science courses performed significantly better than did students in classes without the program on a test of genetic reasoning (Hickey, Kindfield, Horwitz, & Christie, 2003). In the second study, high school honors-biology students with little prior knowledge of the subject showed significant gains in conceptual understanding whereas students who already knew something about genetics did not (Winters & Azevedo, 2005).

Guided Learning Although students can use modeling programs and simulations to plan experiments, take measurements, analyze data, and graph findings, there is still a need for teacher scaffolding and guidance in support of the learning process (Delgarno, 2001). In these **guided learning environments**, teachers might help students set goals, ask questions, encourage discussions, and provide models of problem-solving processes. Such teachers provide a clear road map of the unit at the beginning, clear expectations and sequencing of activities, continued reinforcement and guidance, teacher modeling, opportunities for students to practice problem-solving steps, reflection on learning, and regular checking and sharing of student progress. (Note how this approach combines elements of the behavioral and social cognitive approaches.)

One guided learning environment, the Higher Order Thinking Skills program (HOTS), focuses on higher-order thinking skills among at-risk youths in grades 4 through 8 (Pogrow, 1990, 1999, 2005, 2009b). HOTS was designed around active learning, Socratic questioning, and reflection activities in using computers, and attempts to improve four key thinking processes: (1) metacognition, (2) inferential thinking, (3) transfer of learning, and (4) synthesis, or combining information from different sources into a coherent whole. Instead of the rote computer-based drills that these students would normally receive, they are prompted to reflect on their decision-making process while using computer tools. Teachers do not give away the answers but instead draw out key concepts by questioning students or telling them to go back and read the information on the computer screen. The developer of HOTS, Stanley Pogrow, calls this "controlled floundering," or leading students into frustration so that they have to reflect on the information on the screen to solve a problem. In effect, the learning dialogues and conversations between the teacher and student are the keys to learning here, not student use of the computer, as small-group discussion allows students to compare strategies and reflect on those that work. The main reason for beginning this program and this type of instruction in fourth grade is that for essentially the first time students are confronted with tasks that require them to create, synthesize, and generalize ideas. Establishing this foundation now will, Pogrow claims, lead to higher levels of achievement later without having to spend a lot of time reteaching content and engaging in test preparation (Pogrow, 2009b).

Pogrow (2005) reports that students in the HOTS program record year-to-year gains that are twice those of the national average on standardized tests of reading and math and three times those of control groups on tests of reading comprehension. These gains were still noticeable when students were tested later on other math and reading tests as well as on tests of writing, problem solving, and metacognition. Additional information on the HOTS program can be found at **www.hots.org.**

For direct links to the HOTS site and others mentioned in this chapter, go to the web links section at the textbook's website, Education CourseMate.

Problem-and Project-Based Learning Another way to implement constructivist trends in education is to use technology for **problem-based learning (PBL)**, an instructional method that requires learners to develop solutions to real-life problems.

Computer-based problem-solving programs typically provide students with story problems, laboratory problems, or investigation problems. Story problem programs are usually tutorials and are very much like the math story problems you probably encountered in school. Laboratory problems are typically simulations of laboratory science problems, such as chemistry or biology. Investigation problems are set in realistic environments (microworlds) and may involve such varied subject areas as astronomy, social studies, environmental science, and anthropology (Jonassen et al., 2008). When using PBL with technology, students can plan and organize their own research while working collaboratively with others.

Although PBL has its roots in medical and business school settings, it has been successfully adapted to the elementary, middle school, and high school grades. Problem-solving programs that are based on constructivist principles and are most likely to foster meaningful learning will do the following:

- Encourage students to be active learners, engaging in such behaviors as making observations, manipulating objects, and recording the results of their manipulations
- Encourage students to reflect on their experiences and begin to construct mental models of the world
- Provide students with complex tasks that are situated in real-world settings
- Require students to state their learning goals, the decisions they make, the strategies they use, and the answers they formulate
- Require students to work in cooperative groups in which there is a considerable amount of social interaction (Hung, 2002; Jonassen et al., 2008)

Technology is also being used to support project-based learning. Project-based learning provides structure by giving students a project or a problem, along with project goals and deadlines. A study conducted in Holland with sixteen- and seventeen-year-old high school students illustrates this approach. The students were given 5 hours to write an essay of approximately 750 words on how the behavior of Dutch youths changed during the 1950s and 1960s. Although the students worked in pairs, they did so at their own computers and interacted by means of a chat facility and a shared draft of the essay that each one could edit. They were supplied with such computer-based resources as excerpts from textbooks, interpretations of historians, photos, tables, and interviews (van Drie, van Boxtel, & van der Linden, 2006).

Situated Learning   As you may recall from Chapter 10, situated learning, or situated cognition, is the concept that knowledge is closely linked to the environment in which it is acquired. The more true to life the task is, the more meaningful the learning will be. Technology can play a key role in providing access to a wide variety of real-world learning situations. For instance, computer-based instructional technology such as CSILE (**www.knowledgeforum.com**), WISE (**http://wise.berkeley.edu**), and the GLOBE Program (**www.globe.gov**) can apprentice students into real-life learning and problem-solving settings by providing access to authentic data and the tools to manipulate the data (see, for example, Slotta & Linn, 2009, for a detailed description of the WISE science program).

One project that embodied the concept of situated learning was conducted with elementary grade students in a Northern Ireland school and a Republic of Ireland school. Called the Author-on-Line Project, students in both schools read a book called *The Cinnamon Tree* by Aubrey Flegg and wrote a book report. The students then posted their reports on a portion of the Northern Ireland Network for Education website. As new reports appeared, they were read by all of the students and discussed. At this point, the author got involved by posting his reactions to each student's report. The students discussed his comments in class and, either individually or in small groups, composed a response. At one point the author adopted the persona of the book's main character, a thirteen-year-old girl, thereby giving the students the rather unique opportunity to interact with a fictional character (Clarke & Heaney, 2003).

THE HUMANISTIC APPROACH TO TEACHING: STUDENT-CENTERED INSTRUCTION

The **humanistic approach** pays particular attention to the role of noncognitive variables in learning, specifically, students' needs, emotions, values, and self-perceptions. It assumes that students will be highly motivated to learn when the learning material is personally meaningful, when they understand the reasons for their own behavior, and when they believe that the classroom environment supports their efforts to learn, even if they struggle. Consequently, a humanistic approach to teaching strives to help students better understand themselves and to create a supportive classroom atmosphere that activates the inherent desire all human beings have to learn and fulfill their potential (Allender & Allender, 2008; Maslow, 1987; Rogers & Freiberg, 1994).

The relevance of a humanistic approach to teaching may not be immediately apparent to everyone, but it is easy to support. First, we've known for some time that learning is as much influenced by how students feel about themselves as by the cognitive skills they possess. When students conclude that the demands of a task are beyond their current level of knowledge and skill (what we referred to in a previous chapter as a low sense of self-efficacy), they are likely to experience such debilitating emotions as anxiety and fear. Once these negative self-perceptions and emotions are created, the student has to divert time and energy from the task at hand to figuring out how to deal with the negative self-perceptions and emotions. And the solutions that students formulate are not always appropriate. Some may, for instance, decide to reduce their efforts and settle for whatever passing grade they can get. Others may give up entirely by cutting class, not completing homework assignments, and not studying for tests. A considerable amount of research from the health field has shown that people are more likely to use positive methods of coping with the stress of illness and disease when they perceive their environment to be *socially supportive*. The small amount of comparable research that exists on classroom learning suggests a similar outcome (Boekarts, 1993; Ryan & Patrick, 2001).

Second, this approach has the implicit support of teachers and parents. High on their list of desired educational outcomes is for students to develop positive feelings about themselves and about learning and to perceive school as a place where they will be supported in their efforts to develop new knowledge and skills.

Pioneers of the Humanistic Approach

The humanistic approach to teaching was proposed during the 1960s principally by Abraham Maslow, Carl Rogers, and Arthur Combs.

Maslow: Let Children Grow   Abraham Maslow's approach to the study of human behavior was unique for its time (1960s). Whereas most of his colleagues studied the psychological processes of people who were having problems dealing with the demands and stresses of everyday life (as Sigmund Freud had done), Maslow decided that more could be learned by studying the behavior of especially well adjusted people, whom he referred to as *self-actualizers*. Self-actualizers, be they children, adolescents, or adults, have an inherent need for experiences that will help them fulfill their potential.

In Chapter 15 of *Toward a Psychology of Being* (1968), Maslow describes 43 basic propositions that summarize his views. Some of the most significant of these propositions are as follows:

- Each individual is born with an essential inner nature.
- This inner nature is shaped by experiences and unconscious thoughts and feelings, but it is not *dominated* by such forces. Individuals control much of their own behavior.
- Children should be allowed to make many choices about their own development.

Maslow: help students develop their potential by satisfying their needs

- Parents and teachers play a significant role in preparing children to make wise choices by satisfying their physiological, safety, love, belonging, and esteem needs, but they should do this by helping and letting children grow, not by attempting to shape or control the way they grow.

Rogers: Learner-Centered Education

Carl Rogers was a psychotherapist who pioneered a new approach to helping people cope more effectively with their problems. He called it *client-centered* (or *nondirective*) therapy, to stress the fact that the client, rather than the therapist, should be the central figure and that the therapist was not to tell the patient what was wrong and what should be done about it.

As he practiced this person-centered approach, Rogers came to the conclusion that he was most successful when he did not attempt to put up a false front of any kind; when he established a warm, positive, acceptant attitude toward his clients; and when he was able to sense their thoughts and feelings. Rogers concluded that these conditions set the stage for successful experiences with therapy because clients became more self-accepting and aware of themselves. Once individuals acquired these qualities, they were inclined and equipped to solve personal problems without seeking the aid of a therapist (Rogers, 1967).

Rogers: establish conditions that allow self-directed learning

In addition to functioning as a therapist, Rogers served as a professor. Upon analyzing his experiences as an instructor, he concluded that the person-centered approach to therapy could be applied just as successfully to teaching. He thus proposed the idea of **learner-centered education**: that teachers should try to establish the same conditions as do person-centered therapists. Rogers argues (1980) that the results of learner-centered teaching are similar to those of person-centered therapy: students become capable of educating themselves without the aid of direct instruction from teachers.

Combs: The Teacher as Facilitator

Arthur Combs assumed that "all behavior of a person is the direct result of his field of perceptions at the moment of his behaving" (1965, p. 12). From this assumption, it follows that the way a person perceives himself is of paramount importance and that a basic purpose of teaching is to help each student develop a positive self-concept. He observed, "The task of the teacher is not one of prescribing, making, molding, forcing, coercing, coaxing, or cajoling; it is one of ministering to a process already in being. The role required of the teacher is that of facilitator, encourager, helper, assister, colleague, and friend of his students" (1965, p. 16).

Combs elaborated on these points by listing six characteristics of good teachers:

1. They are well informed about their subject.
2. They are sensitive to the feelings of students and colleagues.
3. They believe that students can learn.
4. They have a positive self-concept.
5. They believe in helping all students do their best.
6. They use many different methods of instruction. (1965, pp. 20–23)

Humanistic approach addresses needs, values, motives, self-perceptions

Taken together, the observations of Maslow, Rogers, and Combs lead to a conception of education in which teachers trust pupils enough to permit them to make many choices about their own learning. At the same time, teachers should be sensitive to the social and emotional needs of students, empathize with them, and respond positively to them. Finally, teachers should be sincere, willing to show that they too have needs and experience positive feelings about themselves and what they are doing.

Teaching from a Humanistic Orientation

Teachers who adopt a humanistic orientation seek to create a classroom atmosphere in which students believe that the teacher's primary goal is to understand the student's needs, values, motives, and self-perceptions and to help the student learn.

This atmosphere is established primarily by the teacher's expressing genuine interest in and acceptance of the student and valuing the contribution each student makes to the progress of the class. The teacher avoids giving the impression that she would like the student better if only the student dressed more appropriately, had a more positive attitude toward learning, associated with a different group of peers, and so on. In this kind of setting, students will be more inclined to discuss openly their feelings about and problems with learning and related issues. The teacher is then in a position to help students figure out better approaches to their schoolwork and relationships with others. The teacher does not tell students what to do but guides them to the correct action. Because the students' perceptions and decisions are the central focus, this approach is often referred to as either *student-directed* or *nondirective* (Joyce & Weil, 2009; Tomlinson, 2002).

pause & reflect

Can you recall any teachers who practiced humanistic techniques? Did you like these teachers? Did you feel you learned as much from them as from other teachers? Would you model yourself after such teachers?

JOURNAL ENTRY
Using a Humanistic Approach to Instruction

To illustrate this approach, consider the case of a student who is unhappy about a poor grade on a test. The instinctive reaction of most teachers would be to explain how to study and prepare for the next test. The humanistically oriented teacher instead asks the student to describe his interest in the subject matter, how capable a learner the student feels himself to be, how well the student understands the subject, under what conditions the student studies, whether the student feels the teacher's instruction to be clear and well organized, and so on. To help students understand their feelings and the role they play in learning, the teacher may disclose some of her own feelings. For example, the teacher may tell this hypothetical student, "When I've had a bad day and feel as if I've let my students down, I sometimes question my ability as a teacher. Is that how you feel?" Once these self-perceptions have been raised and clarified, the teacher encourages the student to suggest a solution to the problem (Joyce & Weil, 2009).

The Humanistic Model

According to Bruce Joyce and Marsha Weil (2009), the nondirective model is made up of the following components:

1. *Defining the helping situation.* The topic that the student wants to discuss is identified, and the student is told that he or she is free to express any and all feelings that relate to the topic.
2. *Exploring the problem.* If the teacher has been able to establish the atmosphere of trust just described, it is assumed that students will be willing to describe the problem and any associated feelings. The teacher does not attempt to diagnose the student's problem but seeks to understand the situation as the student experiences it and then reflects this understanding back to the student. The teacher functions more as a resource, facilitator, and guide than as a director.
3. *Developing insight.* The student uses the information gained from exploring the problem to understand how various perceptions, emotions, beliefs, and behaviors cause various effects (such as a belief that one lacks ability, leading to incomplete homework assignments and lack of interest in the subject, or a need for affiliation that leads to more socializing than studying).
4. *Planning and decision making.* The teacher helps the student identify alternative behaviors and how they will be carried out.
5. *Integration.* The student reports on actions taken, their effects, and plans for future actions.

This approach to instruction strongly implies that students who believe their teachers care about them as people and want to help them maximize their learning

Adopting a humanistic approach to teaching means identifying and meeting students' physical, social, emotional, and intellectual needs, as well as helping students understand how their perceptions, emotions, and behaviors affect their achievement. © Cindy Charles/Photo Edit

are likely to be highly motivated. Nel Noddings (2003), an educational researcher who has written extensively about establishing a caring atmosphere in classrooms, and who we first mentioned in Chapter 2, describes this approach as one that seeks to produce happy students. She argues that happiness should be, but rarely is, an explicit and high-priority goal of educators and educational policymakers (it already is for parents—they say so in overwhelming numbers in surveys of educational goals). In her view, happy classrooms:

- satisfy the physical needs of children
- are clean and maintained, have reliable heating systems, are well lit, and are physically safe
- are those in which learning is an exciting, meaningful, and pleasurable experience
- are those in which children have an opportunity to learn through play
- avoid the use of sarcasm, humiliation, and fear
- capitalize on students' interests
- foster intellectual growth in every student
- foster the development of character
- foster interpersonal growth (learning how to get along with others)

Noddings is hardly alone in her view. Two longtime humanistic researchers, Jerome and Donna Sclarow Allender (2008), noted that the curriculum should emphasize students' interests because "opportunities for following up on where one's curiosity leads are a sure bet for initial successful learning" (p. 86). Chrystal Johnson and Adrian Thomas (2009) argue that an ideal time to establish a caring environment is the primary grades because such an environment promotes a sense of community, safety, learning-oriented values, and positive interpersonal experiences that will lead to higher levels of motivation and learning in those and later grades. And Beverly Falk (2009), author of *Teaching the Way Children Learn*, comments that "children need to be in caring communities to develop the sense of self-worth necessary to take the risks that are involved in real learning" (p. 88).

Unfortunately, classrooms that provide this type of positive emotional support appear to be exceptions rather than the rule. Observations in hundreds of primary and elementary grade classrooms (Pianta, Belsky, Houts, et al., 2007) revealed that only 17 percent of students experienced a positive emotional climate as they went from one grade to the next. There are concrete steps, however, that you can take to create a supportive climate in your own classroom. To start, you might try to observe and emulate the practices of teachers who create productive personal relationships with students. Two former school principals (Mahwinney & Sagan, 2007) found that such teachers exhibit the following characteristics:

| Humanistic teachers show respect, courtesy, fairness, caring attitude |

- They demonstrate respect, courtesy, and fairness. A veteran teacher that students rated year after year as being one of the best they ever had always said please and thank you when interacting with students, often gave students a last chance to increase their grade on a quiz or exam (we make the same recommendation in Chapter 14), insisted that students who were performing poorly see him for help, never raised his voice, and disciplined students privately.
- They demonstrate that they care about students' lives and try to put themselves in their shoes. As we note elsewhere in this and other chapters, students who believe that their teachers care about them are more likely to work harder and less likely to drop out of school.
- They use humor as a way to put students at ease and to defuse potentially disruptive situations. The veteran high school teacher whose suggestions for managing classroom behavior we summarized in Chapter 12 also suggested using a light touch at times.

Research on Aspects of Humanistic Education

As we noted previously, Maslow believed that children's academic and personal growth is enhanced when various needs are met. One of those needs, belonging, has been the subject of considerable research. Belonging, which is also referred to as relatedness and sense of community, means the desire to get support from and be accepted by teachers and classmates and to have opportunities to participate in classroom planning, goal setting, and decision making.

According to some motivational theorists (e.g., Bear, 2009), belonging is one of three basic psychological needs (autonomy and competence are the other two) essential to human growth and development. Yet the need to belong receives less attention from educators than autonomy or competence does. One possible reason for this discrepancy is the belief that students' emotional needs are best met at home and in other out-of-school groups. This attitude does a disservice to students for two reasons: teachers play an important role in helping to satisfy the need to belong (a point we elaborate on in the following paragraphs), and research has uncovered positive relationships between satisfaction of the need to belong and the following school-related outcomes (Anderman & Leake, 2007; Osterman, 2000; Patrick, Ryan, & Kaplan, 2007):

- increased intrinsic motivation to learn
- a strong sense of competence
- a heightened sense of autonomy
- a stronger sense of identity
- the willingness to conform to classroom rules and norms
- positive attitudes toward school, class work, and teachers
- higher expectations of success
- lower levels of anxiety, depression, and frustration
- supportiveness of others
- higher levels of achievement

Feelings of rejection or exclusion from the group are associated with the following negative outcomes (Anderman & Leake, 2007; Hughes & Zhang, 2007; Osterman, 2000):

- higher levels of stress, anger, and health problems
- behavior problems in school
- lower interest in school
- lower achievement
- dropping out of school

Three studies offer persuasive evidence of the positive effect that a humanistic classroom environment can have on a variety of student behaviors. The first piece of evidence comes from an unusual source: an analysis of why Japanese students outscore U.S. students after fourth grade on an internationally normed standardized test of mathematics and science (the Third International Mathematics and Science Study). After observing ten science lessons taught in five Japanese public schools, Marcia Linn, Catherine Lewis, Ineko Tsuchida, and Nancy Butler Songer (2000) attributed the difference in part to a classroom atmosphere that Abraham Maslow and Carl Rogers would have endorsed.

In addition to emphasizing cognitive development, elementary education in Japan also places a high value on children's social and ethical development. This is done by such tactics as (1) giving children various classroom responsibilities so they feel a valued part of the school, (2) emphasizing such qualities as friendliness, responsibility, and persistence, and (3) communicating to students that teachers value their presence in the classroom and the contributions they make. By fourth grade, Japanese children have been steeped in a school culture that emphasizes responsibility to the group, collaboration, and kindness. In addition, Linn and her colleagues found that almost every lesson began with an activity that was designed to spark the students' interest in the topic by connecting it to either their personal experiences or to previous lessons. The positive emotional attachment to school and the commitment to the values of hard work and cooperation that this approach produces are thought to play a strong role in how well students learn mathematics and science lessons.

The second piece of evidence that supports the positive effects of a humanistic classroom environment (Ryan & Patrick, 2001) comes from a study of eighth-grade classroom environments and their effects on students. The atmosphere created by each teacher was described along four lines:

1. Teacher support (students' perceptions of how strongly teachers valued and established personal relationships with them)
2. Promoting interaction among classmates (e.g., allowing students to share ideas, work together in small groups, give help during individual seatwork)
3. Promoting mutual respect and social harmony among classmates
4. Promoting performance goals (emphasizing competition and relative ability comparisons among classmates)

Each of these classroom environment components was related to several outcome measures, including the four listed in Figure 13.3. The figure uses plus signs and minus signs to show the significant associations that the researchers reported. Notice that the first three environmental components—the ones that humanistic educators would favor—tended to increase desirable outcomes and decrease undesirable ones. The fourth, however—stressing competition and performance goals—raised students' off-task and disruptive behavior and decreased students' confidence in being able to interact with the teacher.

Lastly, an extension of Ryan and Patrick's 2001 study on classroom environments (Patrick, Ryan, & Kaplan, 2007) found that teacher support, promoting interaction, promoting mutual respect, and student academic support (the perception that one's classmates want me to come to school every day and want me to do well) contribute

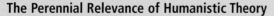

Take a Stand!

The Perennial Relevance of Humanistic Theory

As you know from reading this section, humanistic approaches to learning and teaching were formulated during the 1960s and 1970s. What you probably don't know is that they were every bit as popular at that time as, say, constructivist theories are today. But humanistic theories gradually fell from favor and eventually almost disappeared from sight. By the late 1980s, many textbooks had either drastically cut back or eliminated coverage of them, fewer papers on humanistic topics were delivered at major conferences, and fewer conceptual and research articles appeared in journals.

The reasons for the decline appeared to be threefold. First, information-processing theory, social cognitive theory, and constructivism ignited a torrent of research that promised, more than noncognitive conceptualizations, dramatic gains in achievement. Second, the humanistic theorists and researchers who came after Maslow, Rogers, and Combs were not of the same stature and did not have the same impact on the

field. Third, concerns about students' emotions, needs, and values seemed to many people to be frivolous, if not irrelevant, at a time when American students appeared to be inferior to earlier generations of students, as well as to students from other countries, in terms of standardized test scores. Teachers and students were urged to get back to basics!

In recent years, however, humanistic theory has staged something of a comeback. Current conceptualizations of classroom instruction recognize that students' needs and self-perceptions are every bit as important to understanding and improving classroom learning as the quality of their thinking. The research we have described on the effects of belongingness, teacher support, and social harmony among students exemplifies this trend. So if someone tries to convince you that humanistic theories are dead, tell them that humanistic approaches to education never die; they just hang around waiting to be acknowledged.

What Do You Think?

What are your thoughts about humanistic education? Will you use its principles in your classroom? Explore the debate about humanistic teaching at the Take a Stand! section at the Education CourseMate website.

to the adoption of mastery goals and to the strengthening of academic and social self-efficacy. These variables contributed, in turn, to task-related interactions (suggesting ideas, explaining one's reasoning, helping others), which affected self-regulation behaviors and achievement.

The findings from the above studies are supported by an analysis of 119 studies (Cornelius-White, 2007). Teachers who demonstrated empathy and warmth, encouraged thinking, and used a nondirective approach were more likely than other teachers to have students who scored significantly higher on tests of verbal skills, math skills, and critical/creative thinking skills. These students were also more likely to exhibit higher levels of class participation, score higher on measures of self-efficacy and satisfaction, and be less likely to drop out of school.

The results of research on classroom atmosphere have strong implications for teachers in urban areas whose classrooms have a high percentage of minority students. Students of color who were bused to school or were attending an urban school reported weaker feelings of belonging than students who were attending neighborhood or suburban schools (Anderman, 2002). But students of color in urban schools who said they liked going to school described their relationships with their teachers as supportive and caring (Baker, 1999). This suggests that teachers who take a humanistic approach can offset some of the negative emotions experienced by many minority students and help produce the positive outcomes we have just described.

Figure 13.3 Results of the Ryan and Patrick Study of Eighth-Grade Classrooms

Environment Created by Teacher	Outcomes			
	Self-efficacy for interacting with teacher	Self-efficacy for academic performance	Use of self-regulated learning skills	Off-task and disruptive behavior
Teacher support for students	+		+	−
Promoting interaction among classmates	+			
Promoting mutual respect and harmony		+	+	
Promoting performance goals	−			+

+ means significant increase; − means significant decrease.
Desirable outcomes indicated in **blue**, undesirable in **red**.

THE SOCIAL APPROACH TO TEACHING: TEACHING STUDENTS HOW TO LEARN FROM EACH OTHER

Classroom tasks can be structured so that students are forced to compete with one another, to work individually, or to cooperate with one another to obtain the rewards that teachers make available for successfully completing these tasks. Traditionally, competitive arrangements have been assumed to be superior to the other two in increasing motivation and learning. But several analyses of the research literature (e.g., Gillies, 2003; Ginsburg-Block, Rohrbeck, Lavigne, & Fantuzzo, 2008; Johnson & Johnson, 2009a; Slavin, Lake, & Groff, 2009) found cooperative arrangements to be far superior in producing these benefits. In this section, we will describe competitive, individual, and cooperative learning arrangements; identify the elements that make up the major approaches to cooperative learning; and examine the effect of cooperative learning on motivation, achievement, and interpersonal relationships. We would also like to point out that cooperative learning methods are fully consistent with social constructivism because they encourage inquiry, perspective sharing, and conflict resolution.

pause & reflect

Have you ever experienced a competitive reward structure in school? Were your reactions positive or negative? Why? Would you use it in your own classroom? How and when?

Types of Classroom Reward Structures

Competitive Structures   Competitive goal structures are those in which one's grade is determined by how well everyone else in the group performs (a reward structure that is typically referred to as *norm-referenced*). The traditional practice of grading on the curve predetermines the percentage of A, B, C, D, and F grades regardless of the actual distribution of test scores. Because only a small percentage of students in any group can achieve the highest rewards and because this accomplishment must come at some other students' expense, competitive goal structures are characterized by *negative interdependence*. Students try to outdo one another, view classmates' failures as an advantage, and come to believe that the winners deserve their rewards because they are inherently better (Johnson & Johnson, 1998; Johnson, Johnson, & Holubec, 2002; Johnson & Johnson, 2009a).

Some researchers have argued that competitive reward structures lead students to focus on ability as the primary basis for motivation. This orientation is reflected in the question, "Am I smart enough to accomplish this task?" When ability is the basis for motivation, competing successfully in the classroom may be seen as necessary to self-esteem (because nobody loves a loser), difficult to accomplish (because only a few can succeed), and uncertain (because success depends on how everyone else does). These perceptions may cause some students to avoid challenging subjects or tasks, give up in the face of difficulty, reward themselves only if they win a competition, and believe that their own successes are due to ability, whereas the successes of others are due to luck (Ames & Ames, 1984; Covington, 2000).

> Competitive reward structures may decrease motivation to learn

Individualistic Structures   Individualistic goal structures are characterized by students working alone and earning rewards solely on the quality of their own efforts. The success or failure of other students is irrelevant. All that matters is whether the student meets the standards for a particular task (Johnson & Johnson, 2009b; Johnson, Johnson, & Holubec, 2002) For example, 30 students working by themselves at computer terminals are functioning in an individual reward structure. According to Carole Ames and Russell Ames (1984), individual structures lead students to focus on task effort as the primary basis for motivation. This orientation is reflected in the statement, "I can do this if I try." Whether a student perceives a task as difficult depends on how successful she has been with that type of task in the past.

Cooperative Structures Cooperative goal structures are characterized by students working together to accomplish shared goals. What is beneficial for the other students in the group is beneficial for the individual and vice versa. Because students in cooperative groups can obtain a desired reward only if the other students in the group also obtain the same reward, cooperative goal structures are characterized by *positive interdependence*. Also, all groups may receive the same rewards, provided they meet the teacher's criteria for mastery. For example, a teacher might present a lesson on map reading, then give each group its own map and a question-answering exercise. Students then work with each other to ensure that all know how to interpret maps. Each student then takes a quiz on map reading. All teams whose average quiz scores meet a preset standard receive special recognition (Johnson & Johnson, 1998; Joyce & Weil, 2009; Slavin, 1995). In the Suggestions for Teaching: Motivating Students to Learn section in Chapter 11, "Motivation," we described two particular cooperative learning techniques: Student Teams–Achievement Divisions (STAD) and Jigsaw.

Cooperative structures lead students to focus on effort and cooperation as the primary basis of motivation. This orientation is reflected in the statement, "We can do this if we try hard and work together." In a cooperative atmosphere, students are motivated out of a sense of obligation: one ought to try, contribute, and help satisfy group norms (Ames & Ames, 1984). William Glasser points out that student motivation and performance tend to be highest for such activities as band, drama club, athletics, the school newspaper, and the yearbook, all of which require a team effort (Gough, 1987).

pause & reflect

Have you ever experienced a cooperative reward structure in school? Were your reactions positive or negative? Why? Would you use it in your own classroom? How and when?

Elements of Cooperative Learning

Over the past 30 years, different approaches to cooperative learning have been proposed by different individuals. The three most popular are those of David Johnson and Roger Johnson (Johnson & Johnson, 2009a), Robert Slavin (1994, 1995), and Shlomo Sharan and Yael Sharan (Sharan, 1995; Sharan & Sharan, 1999). To give you a general sense of what cooperative learning is like and to avoid limiting you to any one individual's approach, the following discussion is a synthesis of the main features of each approach.

Group Heterogeneity The size of cooperative-learning groups is relatively small and as heterogeneous as circumstances allow. The recommended size is usually four to five students. At the very least, groups should contain both males and females and students of different ability levels. If possible, different ethnic backgrounds and social classes should be represented as well.

Group Goals/Positive Interdependence A specific goal, such as a grade or a certificate of recognition, is identified for the group to attain. Students are told that they will have to support one another because the group goal can be achieved only if each member learns the material being taught (in the case of a task that culminates in an exam) or makes a specific contribution to the group's effort (in the case of a task that culminates in a presentation or a project).

Cooperative learning characterized by heterogeneous groups, positive interdependence, promotive interaction, individual accountability

Promotive Interaction This element is made necessary by the existence of positive interdependence. Students are shown how to help one another overcome problems and complete whatever task has been assigned. This may involve episodes of peer tutoring, temporary assistance, exchanges of information and material, challenging of one another's reasoning, feedback, and encouragement to keep one another highly motivated. *Promotive* means simply that students promote each other's success.

Individual Accountability   This feature stipulates that each member of a group has to make a significant contribution to achieving the group's goal. This may be satisfied by requiring the group to achieve a minimal score on a test, by having the group's test score be the sum or average of each student's quiz scores, or by having each member be responsible for a particular part of a project (such as doing the research and writing for a particular part of a history report).

Interpersonal Skills   Positive interdependence and promotive interaction are not likely to occur if students do not know how to make the most of their face-to-face interactions. And you can safely assume that the interpersonal skills most students possess are probably not highly developed. As a result, they have to be taught such basic skills as leadership, decision making, trust building, clear communication, and conflict management. The conflict that arises over differences of opinion, for example, can be constructive if it is used as a stimulus to search for more information or to rethink one's conclusions. But it can destroy group cohesion and productivity if it results in students' stubbornly clinging to a position or referring to one another as "stubborn," "dumb," or "nerdy."

Equal Opportunities for Success   Because cooperative groups are heterogeneous with respect to ability and their success depends on positive interdependence, promotive interaction, and individual accountability, it is important that steps be taken to ensure that all students have an opportunity to contribute to their team. You can do this by awarding points for degree of improvement over previous test scores, by having students compete against comparable members of other teams in a game- or tournament-like atmosphere, or by giving students learning assignments (such as math problems) that are geared to their current level of skill.

Team Competition   This may seem to be an odd entry in a list of cooperative-learning components, especially in the light of the comments we already made about the ineffectiveness of competition as a spur to motivation and learning. But we're not being contradictory. The main problem with competition is that it is rarely used appropriately. When competition occurs between well-matched teams, is done in the absence of a norm-referenced grading system, and is not used too frequently, it can be an effective way to motivate students to cooperate with each other.

Cooperative learning has been shown to produce positive cognitive, social, and affective outcomes provided its basic elements are implemented. Copyright © Bonnie Kamin/Photo Edit

Does Cooperative Learning Work?

The short answer to this question is yes. In the vast majority of studies, forms of cooperative learning have been shown to be more effective than noncooperative reward structures in raising the levels of variables that contribute to motivation, in raising achievement, and in producing positive social outcomes.

Effect on Motivation   An analysis of 15 studies that measured the effect of cooperative learning on the motivational levels of elementary grade students found moderate to strong effects in 11 of the studies. Those that had the strongest positive effects used interdependent rewards (each group member receives a reward only if the group achieves its goal) and had additional motivational components (such as individualized curriculum materials). Motivational effects were larger for minority than for nonminority students and for urban students than for suburban or rural students (Ginsburg-Block, Rohrbeck, Lavigne, & Fantuzzo, 2008).

Although most of the reported effects of cooperative learning have been positive, negative results have occasionally appeared. Eleventh-grade students whose chemistry classes used a form of cooperative learning experienced declines in motivation, whereas students in the whole-class instruction group reported slight increases. The researchers attributed this finding to students being dissatisfied with the pace and amount of learning because of an upcoming high-stakes test (Shachar & Fischer, 2004).

Effect on Achievement   The effect of cooperative learning in its various forms (such as STAD, Learning Together, Teams-Games-Tournaments, and Team-Assisted Individualization) on achievement has been extensively studied. Analyses of studies conducted during the 1970s and 1980s usually found moderate to large increases in test scores. This meant that students exposed to cooperative learning scored anywhere from 10 to 25 percentile ranks higher than students taught conventionally (Johnson, Johnson, & Smith, 1995; Slavin, 1995).

Two recent analyses of research have added to the positive results reported earlier. The first analysis (Gillies, 2003) found that students in cooperative groups who worked on problem-solving activities that required them to use all six cognitive processes represented in Bloom's taxonomy (discussed in the first section of this chapter) scored significantly higher on a subsequent achievement test than did comparable peers who also worked in groups but received no training in group interaction. The second analysis (Slavin, Lake, & Groff, 2009) found that the math scores of middle school and high school students were considerably higher when teachers used cooperative learning programs than when they used either computer-based instruction or just a textbook (and it didn't matter which textbook they used).

Effect on Social Interaction   An important part of cooperative learning programs is teaching students how to productively interact with one another, including how to ask relevant, leading questions and how to give group members cogent arguments and justifications for the explanations and help they offer. A team of researchers (Veenman, Denessen, van den Akker, & van der Rijt, 2005) examined whether pairs of students trained to interact in this way would use these skills more frequently to solve math problems than would student pairs not taught these skills. The study produced a somewhat unusual result. Although students who received training made significantly more high-level, or elaborative, responses when asking for and giving help on the math task than did the untrained students, they did so less frequently than they had before the training. Among the several explanations offered by the researchers, two appear to be particularly likely. First, the math problems that the students were given to solve were of the well-structured variety that we described in Chapter 10. This means that most students might have worked out a solution pretty much on their own, thereby reducing the need for elaborative discussions. A second possibility is that because the posttest problems were quite similar to the pretest problems, they required less effort to solve them. As one student put it: "The second time the problems were about the same as the first time; you still know how to solve them, and if you both know the answer, there is no need for an explanation" (p. 144). This finding highlights a point we have made in several previous chapters: all instructional practices and programs have their limits, and it pays to know what those limits are. The researchers also found that students who had prior experience with cooperative learning, whether or not they received specific, supplementary training in how to productively ask questions and provide assistance to a classmate, scored higher on the math task than students who had no prior exposure to cooperative learning.

Research has also shown that because average-ability students are least likely to actively participate in group discussions (high-ability students tend to take the lead), they are most in need of instruction in group interaction skills. Compared to average-ability students in untrained groups, average-ability students who have been taught how to seek and give help engage in more helping interactions and score higher on achievement tests (Saleh, Lazonder, & de Jong, 2007).

In sum, students who learn cooperatively tend to be more highly motivated to learn because of the proacademic attitudes of groupmates, appropriate attributions for success and failure, and greater on-task behavior. They also score higher on tests of achievement and problem solving and tend to get along better with classmates of different racial, ethnic, and social class backgrounds. This last outcome should be of particular interest if you expect to teach in an area marked by cultural diversity.

Why Does Cooperative Learning Work?

When researchers attempt to explain the widespread positive effects that are typically found among studies of cooperative learning, they usually cite one or more of the following explanations (Slavin, 1995).

Motivational Effect   The various features of cooperative learning, particularly positive interdependence, are highly motivating because they encourage such achievement-oriented behaviors as trying hard, attending class regularly, praising the efforts of others, and receiving help from one's groupmates. Learning is seen as an obligation and a valued activity because the group's success is based on it and one's groupmates will reward it (Ginsburg-Block, Rohrbeck, Lavigne, & Fantuzzo, 2008).

Cognitive-Developmental Effect   According to Lev Vygotsky, collaboration promotes cognitive growth because students model for each other more advanced ways of thinking than any would demonstrate individually. According to Jean Piaget, collaboration among peers hastens the decline of egocentrism and allows the development of more advanced ways of understanding and dealing with the world. Research appears to support both of these explanations depending on how the group members interact, but that is not quite the end of the story. Recent research suggests that contradictions or inconsistencies not resolved by the group stimulate later attempts by some participants to resolve the contradictions on their own (Howe, 2009).

Cooperative learning effects likely due to stimulation of motivation, cognitive development, meaningful learning

Cognitive Elaboration Effect   As we saw in the previous discussion of information-processing theory, new information that is elaborated (restructured and related to existing knowledge) is more easily retrieved from memory than is information that is not elaborated. A particularly effective means of elaboration is explaining something to someone else (Ginsburg-Block, Rohrbeck, Lavigne, & Fantuzzo, 2008).

TeachSource

Video Case ◄◄ ▶ ►►

Cooperative Learning: High School History Lesson

Go to the Education CourseMate website and watch the Video Case, and then answer the following questions:

1. How does this Video Case illustrate Vygotsky's theory of cognitive growth through collaboration?

2. Do you think the teacher's ad hoc learning groups are as effective as cooperative learning groups that are thoroughly planned in advance? Please explain your answer.

JOURNAL ENTRY
Using a Social Approach to Instruction

Teachers' Use of Cooperative Learning

As we have seen, cooperative learning produces a variety of academic benefits for most students. Consequently, you might assume that this approach is widely used in classrooms. But until a group of researchers (Antil, Jenkins, Wayne, & Vadasy, 1998) interviewed twenty-one teachers from six elementary schools to assess the extent to which they used cooperative learning methods and in what form, those remained open questions. What these researchers found was quite interesting. All of the teachers claimed they were familiar with cooperative learning through preservice learning, student teaching, graduate classes, workshops, or other teachers. Seventeen of the teachers said they used it every day in a typical week. Most reported being attracted to cooperative learning because it enabled them to address both academic and social learning goals within a single approach. But even though teachers say they use cooperative learning, they aren't necessarily using it as it was intended.

Antil et al. argued that for an instructional approach to merit the label *cooperative learning*, it must include at least the conditions of positive interdependence and individual accountability. A more stringent definition would call for the inclusion of promotive interaction, group heterogeneity, and the development of interpersonal skills. Only five of the twenty-one teachers met the two-feature criterion, and only one reported using all five features. For example, instead of creating heterogeneous groups by putting students of different ability levels together, some teachers used random assignment, allowed students to select their teammates, or allowed students who sat near one another to form groups. Similar results were obtained from a study of 216 highly rated elementary and middle school teachers. Their actual use of such critical components as individual accountability, positive interdependence, and development of interpersonal skills was significantly less than what they would have preferred (Lopata, Miller, & Miller, 2003).

Why do teachers follow the spirit but not the letter of the cooperative learning model? Antil et al. offer several possibilities:

- Perhaps teachers find the models too complicated and difficult to put into practice. For example, in Slavin's model, individual accountability involves keeping a running log of students' weekly test scores, computing individual averages and improvement scores, totaling scores for each team based on members' improvement scores, and assigning group rewards.
- Teachers don't really believe the researchers' claims that certain elements of cooperative learning are essential for improved learning, perhaps because their classroom experience has led them to believe otherwise.
- Teachers interpret the research as providing suggestions or guidelines rather than prescriptions that must be followed, leaving them free to construct personal adaptations. (Our discussion in Chapter 1 of the teacher as artist supports this behavior, provided it does not go so far that it changes cooperative learning into something else.)

- Researchers rarely explicitly state that the demonstrated benefits of cooperative learning will occur only when certain conditions are met.

Another possibility not mentioned by Antil et al. is based on studies of how teachers implement other instructional tools, such as reciprocal teaching. Sometimes, unexpected and unfavorable classroom conditions force teachers into making alterations and compromises they might not make under more favorable circumstances (Hacker & Tenent, 2002).

Do teachers' adaptations of the cooperative learning approaches advocated by researchers lead to inferior outcomes? Unfortunately, that's a question that has no definitive answer at this point, because there is little research on how effective cooperative learning is when some of its defining elements are omitted. But the following study, which looked at the effects of group heterogeneity on problem solving, suggests that you should stay as close as circumstances permit to the original features of cooperative learning.

Noreen Webb, Kariane Nemer, Alexander Chizhik, and Brenda Sugrue (1998) looked at seventh- and eighth-grade students who had been given 3 weeks of instruction on electricity concepts (such as voltage, resistance, and current) and electric circuits and who were judged as having either low ability, low-medium ability, medium-high ability, or high ability. These students were assigned to either homogeneous or heterogeneous groups and then allowed to work collaboratively to solve a hands-on physics test (create a circuit by using batteries, bulbs, wires, and resistors). Students with low and low-medium ability who worked in heterogeneous groups (that is, groups that included a student with either medium-high or high ability) outscored their peers in homogeneous groups on both the hands-on test and a subsequent paper-and-pencil test that students took individually. The difference was attributed to the active involvement of the students with lower ability in the problem-solving process. In response to the more relevant and accurate comments made by the students with high ability, the students with lower ability made and defended suggestions, asked questions, and paraphrased other students' suggestions.

A follow-up analysis of the performance of the top 25 percent of this sample was done to examine the effect of placing the students with highest ability in either homogeneous or heterogeneous groups (Webb, Nemer, & Zuniga, 2002). As in the original study, students were classified as having low, low-medium, medium-high, or high ability on the basis of preexperiment test scores. Students with high ability who worked in homogeneous groups (with just other students with high ability) earned significantly higher scores on the hands-on and paper-and-pencil tests than students with high ability who worked in groups that contained students with either medium-high or low-medium ability. But the performance of students with high ability in homogeneous groups was only slightly lower when they worked in groups that contained students with the lowest ability.

Now that you have read about the behavioral, cognitive, humanistic, and social approaches to instruction, take a few minutes to study Table 13.1. It summarizes the basic emphases of each approach and allows you to compare them for similarities and differences.

Using Technology to Support Social Approaches to Instruction

Social Constructivist Learning   Whereas the cognitive constructivist looks to find tools to help the child's mind actively construct relationships and ideas, the social constructivist looks as well for tools that help children negotiate ideas and findings in a community of peers. The social networking websites that we mentioned in Chapter 3 (YouTube, Twitter, Facebook, MySpace, and Flickr, for example), and that are collectively referred to as Web 2.0, may help teachers meet social constructivist goals. These sites allow teachers and students who share a common interest to work together on various school-related projects. In addition, there are social networking sites that are specifically designed for educators. TeacherTube

---

The Thought Questions and Reflective Journal Questions at the textbook's Education CourseMate website can help you think about the issues raised in this chapter.

Students with low and average ability in mixed-ability groups outperform peers in homogeneous groups on problem-solving tests; students with high ability in homogeneous groups score slightly higher than peers in mixed-ability groups

---

Successful technology applications are embedded in an active social environment

Table 13.1	Behavioral, Cognitive, Humanistic, and Social Approaches to Instruction
Behavioral (direct instruction)	Teacher presents information efficiently. Student accepts all information transmitted by teacher and textbook as accurate and potentially useful. Emphasis is on acquiring information in small units through clear presentations, practice, and corrective feedback and gradually synthesizing the pieces into larger bodies of knowledge.
Cognitive (information processing)	Teacher presents and helps students to process information meaningfully. Student accepts all information transmitted by teacher and textbook as accurate and potentially useful. Emphasis is on understanding relationships among ideas, relationships between ideas and prior knowledge, and on learning how to control one's cognitive processes effectively.
Cognitive (constructivist)	Teacher helps students to construct meaningful and adaptive knowledge structures by requiring them to engage in higher levels of thinking such as classification, analysis, synthesis, and evaluation; providing scaffolded instruction within the zone of proximal development; embedding tasks in realistic contexts; posing problems and tasks that cause uncertainty, doubt, and curiosity; exposing students to multiple points of view; and allowing students the time to formulate a consensus solution to a task or problem.
Humanistic	Teacher creates a classroom environment that addresses students' needs, helps students understand their attitudes toward learning, promotes a positive self-concept in students, and communicates the belief that all students have value and can learn. Goal is to activate the students' inherent desire to learn and grow.
Social	Teacher assigns students to small, heterogeneous groups and teaches them how to accomplish goals by working together. Each student is accountable for making a significant contribution to the achievement of the group goal. Because of its emphasis on peer collaboration, this approach is consistent with a social constructivist view of learning.

(www.teachertube.com), for example, contains video files, documents, audio files, photos, and blogs that teachers have posted and that other teachers can view, download, and comment on. Other sites that foster teacher collaboration are TeachAde (www.teachade.com), LearnCentral (www.learncentral.org), and We the Teachers (www.wetheteachers.com).

The claim that the quality and quantity of student learning increases when students are encouraged to be socially active, whether that be through social networking sites or some other form, is supported by a large number of studies. An analysis of the results from 122 studies found that students whose computer-based instruction took place in the context of small-group learning outscored students who worked alone at a computer by about 6 percentile ranks on individual tests of achievement. When the performance of the group as a whole was compared with that of students who worked alone, the difference increased to about 12 percentile ranks. In addition, students who worked on computer-based projects with other students exhibited more self-regulated learning behavior, greater persistence, and more positive attitudes toward group work and classmates as compared with students who worked on computers alone (Lou, Abrami, & d'Apollonia, 2001).

Cooperative and Collaborative Learning Cooperative learning is fairly well structured, with assigned roles, tasks, and procedures to help students learn material covered in a classroom setting; a related concept, **collaborative learning,** allows the students themselves to decide on their roles and use their individual areas of expertise to help investigate problems (Veermans & Cesareni, 2005). As noted throughout this book, with the emergence of the Internet and, specifically, Web 2.0 tools, there is no shortage of cooperative and collaborative learning opportunities. To cite just one example, consider the use of weblogs, or as they are more commonly known, **blogs.** A blog is basically a Web-based version of a personal journal. What makes it different from the traditional journal is that it is intended to create an almost instantaneous dialogue with others who have an interest in the author's ideas. For example, students can post examples of their latest products, such as stories or research projects, or they can describe how new ideas have caused them to change the way they think about themselves and the world in which they live. A blog post may include drawings, photos, audio files, and video. Others (friends, teachers, parents, peers from halfway around the world) are then free to comment about the post as well as comment on the comments. In this fashion, all participants are exposed to different perspectives they may not have otherwise considered (Higdon & Topaz, 2009; Rosen & Nelson, 2008; Vogel, 2009).

TeachSource V i d e o C a s e ◄◄ ▶ ►►

Using Blogs to Enhance Student Learning: An Interdisciplinary High School Unit

Go to the Education CourseMate website and watch the Video Case, and then answer the following questions:

1. The blogs created by the students are graded for both content and grammatical structure. Do you agree with this approach or do you think it might inhibit students from writing creatively and about all their thoughts on the subject of genocide?

2. The history teacher in this video contends that the use of technology—doing online research and creating a blog—will cause the students to be more engaged in the topic. Using just your own experience, do you think the teacher is correct? Why? Could this goal be accomplished just as easily without the use of an online blog?

To review this chapter, try the tutorial quizzes and other study aids on the textbook's Education CourseMate website.

Another way in which technology can be used to support cooperative and collaborative learning is through participation in virtual communities. Here are three of the many interesting opportunities that students and teachers have to enter into virtual communities with peers from other schools and countries and to share and discuss various data and ideas: ThinkQuest (**www.thinkquest.org**) is a website where teachers and students can select curriculum-relevant projects, invite students from around the world to participate, and communicate with various message tools. The WEB Project (**www.webproject.org**) allows students to interact with and receive feedback from adult experts about works in progress. Art and music students, for example, get suggestions from artists, multimedia designers, musicians, and composers (Sherry & Billig, 2002). Last, the 4Directions Project (**http://4directions.org**), which we mentioned in Chapter 5 on cultural and socioeconomic diversity, allows American Indian students in 10 states to interact with one another and with adult experts. They can, for example, discuss research ideas and career options with American Indian professionals (Allen, Resta, & Christal, 2002).

Challenging Assumptions

Who Plans for Whom?

"Okay, Don," says Connie. "Let's take another look at how you approached the planning process. Keep in mind that planning is not just something you do before you teach; planning *is* teaching. Even though it happens before you set foot in a classroom, it determines to a large extent what and how your students will learn. In the case of your 'day and night' presentation, your planning focused on you much more than on your students. Let's turn that perspective on its head and ask: What, exactly, do you expect your students to learn from the presentation? More to the point, what happens to your planning if student learning is your starting point?"

Don says, "I see what you mean. First, I have to be clear about what my students need to know and be able to do, and then decide what I can do to help them. What I do is determined by what students need to learn."

Celeste agrees. "Starting with student learning changes the way you look at teaching. And, actually, that's kind of a relief. I have been so worried about what I was going to do in my first classroom. This whole year, I have been so focused on me rather than on my kids' learning."

"That's not unusual," says Connie. "Whenever you enter a new environment, it's natural to feel uncertain about how that environment will work and how you will fit into it. Teaching is a new environment for you both. It's only natural for you to ask yourself, 'What am I going to do when I'm all alone in my own classroom?'"

"Yeah, that was a scary thought all right," says Don. "It's still scary, but at least I know where to start. It'll feel a lot better to plan for student learning rather than trying to figure out what kind of 'show' to put on."

Summary

1. Goals are broad, general statements of desired educational outcomes. Because of their general language, they mean different things to different people and cannot be precisely measured.

2. The vagueness of educational goals stimulated psychologists to specify educational outcomes as specific, clearly stated objectives and to organize objectives as taxonomies in each of three domains: cognitive, affective, and psychomotor.

3. The taxonomy for the cognitive domain that Bloom and several associates prepared is composed of six levels: knowledge, comprehension, application, analysis, synthesis, and evaluation.

4. The taxonomy for the affective domain that Krathwohl and several associates prepared is composed of five levels: receiving, responding, valuing, organization, and characterization by a value or value complex.

5. The taxonomy for the psychomotor domain that Simpson prepared is composed of seven levels: perception, set, guided response, mechanism, complex or overt response, adaptation, and origination.

6. Most teachers use test questions that measure knowledge-level objectives, largely ignoring higher-level cognitive outcomes.

7. Mager states that well-written objectives should specify what behaviors the learner will exhibit to indicate mastery, the conditions under which the behavior will be exhibited, and the criteria of acceptable performance.

8. Gronlund believes that complex and advanced kinds of learning do not lend themselves to Mager-type objectives. Complex outcomes are so broad in scope that it is impractical to ask students to demonstrate everything they have learned. Instead, Gronlund suggests that teachers first state a general objective and then specify a sample of related specific outcomes.

9. Objectives must be consistent with the instructional approach one uses and the types of tests one creates.

10. Objectives work best when students are aware of them and understand their intent, when they are clearly written, and when they are provided to average students for tasks of average difficulty.

Objectives often increase intentional learning but may decrease incidental learning.

11. Direct instruction is an approach derived from behavioral learning theory. Lessons are broken down into small steps, the teacher models the desired behavior, material is presented in a variety of formats, students are given extensive opportunities to practice, and feedback is given consistently.

12. An information-processing/social cognitive approach to teaching is based on knowledge of how information is meaningfully processed and attempts to teach students how to be self-regulated learners. Teachers should communicate their goals clearly, use attention-getting devices, present information in organized and meaningful ways, present information in relatively small chunks over realistic time periods, use instructional techniques that facilitate encoding of information in long-term memory, and model effective learning processes.

13. A constructivist approach to teaching is based on the view that meaningful learning occurs when students are encouraged and helped to create the knowledge schemes that produce a broad understanding of ideas and that lead to self-directed learning. Key elements of the constructivist approach include scaffolded instruction within a student's zone of proximal development, learning by discovery, exposure to multiple points of view, use of relevant and realistic problems and tasks, and encouraging students to become more autonomous learners.

14. Teachers who opt to use a constructivist approach will likely face conceptual, pedagogical, cultural, and political challenges.

15. A humanistic approach to teaching assumes that all students will be motivated to learn if the classroom environment satisfies their basic needs, strengthens their self-concept, provides assistance in learning new ideas and skills, and allows them to direct their learning experiences.

16. A social approach to learning focuses on teaching students how to learn from one another in a cooperative environment. For students to be able to work together successfully, the following conditions are necessary: heterogeneous groups, achievement of group goals by having students help one another to achieve individual goals, holding each student responsible for making a significant contribution to the group goal, development of interpersonal skills, giving each student an opportunity to succeed, and allowing for competition among teams.

17. Technology tools can be used to support behavioral, information-processing, learner-centered, and social approaches to instruction.

Resources for Further Investigation

• Instructional Objectives

If you would like to read Robert Mager's complete description of his recommendations for writing specific objectives, peruse his brief paperback *Preparing Instructional Objectives* (3rd ed., 1997). Norman Gronlund explains his approach to using objectives in *Writing Instructional Objectives for Teaching and Assessment* (7th ed., 2004).

• Direct Instruction

In *Explicit Direct Instruction: The Power of the Well-Crafted, Well-Taught Lesson* (2009), John Hollingsworth and Silvia Ybarra provide highly readable descriptions of how to implement the direct instruction model that we outlined earlier in this chapter.

Jennifer Goeke offers what might be thought of as a hybrid version of direct instruction in *Explicit Instruction: A Framework for Meaningful Direct Teaching* (2009). In addition to the typical direct instruction components described earlier in the chapter, Goeke's model also includes constructivist approaches to meaningful learning, self-regulated learning skills, and differentiated instruction. Appendix A offers a template for a lesson plan and Appendix B illustrates a weekly plan for teaching reading, language arts, and math.

• The Cognitive Approach to Instruction

Comprehension Instruction: Perspectives and Suggestions (2002), edited by Cathy Collins Block and Michael Pressley, contains 24 chapters that describe research-based approaches to comprehension instruction. You may want to start with Chapters 3 ("The Case for Direct Explanation of Strategies"), 12 ("Teaching Readers How to Comprehend Text Strategically"), 14 ("Preparing Young Learners for Successful Reading Comprehension: Laying the Foundation"), 16 ("Comprehension Instruction in the Primary Grades"), 22 ("Straddling Two Worlds: Self-Directed Comprehension Instruction for Middle Schoolers"), and 23 ("Improving the Reading Comprehension of At-Risk Adolescents").

Scaffolding Student Learning: Instructional Approaches and Issues (1997), edited by Kathleen Hogan and Michael Pressley, contains five chapters that describe and illustrate with actual classroom examples how to use scaffolding for a variety of instructional outcomes.

Implementing problem-based learning in kindergarten through eighth-grade classrooms is described by Ann Lambros in *Problem-Based Learning in K–8 Classrooms: A Teacher's Guide to Implementation* (2002).

The Geometric Supposer program can be purchased from the Center for Educational Technology (CET), a nonprofit organization located in Israel, or from Amazon.com. A description of the program can be found on the CET website at **www.cet.ac.il/math-international/software5.htm.** Information about the GenScope program, which you can download for free, can be found at **genscope.concord.org.**

● The Humanistic Approach to Instruction

William W. Purkey and John M. Novak describe a humanistic approach to teaching called "invitational learning" in *Inviting School Success: A Self-Concept Approach to Teaching, Learning, and Democratic Practice* (1996). Larry Holt and Marcella Kysilka describe the essence of humanistic education in Chapter 10 ("Nondirective Learning") of their book *Instructional Patterns* (2006).

● Cooperative Learning

Because cooperative learning is a small-group approach to learning, you may want to learn more about the nature of groups and the circumstances under which they work best. If so, one of the most authoritative sources is *Joining Together: Group Theory and Group Skills* (9th ed., 2006), by David W. Johnson and Frank P. Johnson.

The New Circles of Learning: Cooperation in the Classroom (5th ed., 2002), by David W. Johnson, Roger T. Johnson, and Edythe Johnson Holubec, is a readable description of the basic elements of the authors' version of cooperative learning as well as a description of how to implement and assess the effects of cooperative learning.

As the title suggests, *Cooperative Learning: Integrating Theory and Practice* (2007), by Robyn Gillies, was designed to serve a dual purpose. On the one hand, it provides an overview of the characteristics of cooperative learning and its supporting research. On the other hand, it provides practical information about how to use cooperative groups through the use of Case Study and Practical Activity features in each chapter. In this era of accountability, Chapter 6, "Assessing Small-Group Learning," is particularly valuable.

The Teacher's Sourcebook for Cooperative Learning (2002), by George Jacobs, Michael Power, and Loh Wan Inn, provides a wealth of practical suggestions for implementing cooperative learning in the classroom. Part I describes how to implement the various principles of cooperative learning, Part II answers frequently asked questions, and Part III lists print resources and websites devoted to cooperative learning.

14 Assessment of Classroom Learning

 The Education CourseMate website for this text offers many helpful resources. Go to **CengageBrain.com** to preview this chapter's Concept Maps and Chapter Themes.

KEY POINTS

These key points will help you learn the important information in this chapter. To help you study, they also appear in the margins of the pages, next to the text where they are discussed.

The Role of Assessment in Teaching

- Measurement: assigning numbers or ratings according to rules to create a ranking
- Evaluation: making judgments about the value of a measure
- Summative assessment: measure achievement; assign grades
- Formative assessment: monitor progress and plan instruction accordingly
- Summative judgments are assessments *of* learning
- Formative judgments are assessments *for* learning
- Formative assessment requires both teacher and student to learn

Ways to Measure Student Learning

- Written tests measure degree of knowledge about a subject
- Selected-response tests are objectively scored and efficient but usually measure lower levels of learning and do not reveal what students can do
- Short-answer tests easy to write but measure lower levels of learning
- Essay tests measure higher levels of learning but are hard to grade consistently
- Performance assessments measure ability to use knowledge and skills to solve realistic problems, create products
- Performance assessments may vary in degree of realism
- Rubrics increase objectivity and consistency of scoring, align instruction with assessment, communicate teachers' expectations, help students monitor progress
- Performance assessments pose several challenges for teachers
- Reliability and validity of performance assessments not yet firmly established

Ways to Evaluate Student Learning

- Norm-referenced grading: compare one student with others
- Norm-referenced grading based on absence of external criteria
- Norm-referenced grading can be used to evaluate advanced levels of learning
- Criterion-referenced grading: compare individual performance with stated criteria
- Criterion-referenced grades provide information about strengths and weaknesses
- Mastery approach: give students multiple opportunities to master goals at own pace

Improving Your Grading Methods: Assessment Practices to Avoid

- Be aware of and avoid faulty measurement and grading practices

Technology for Classroom Assessment

- Technological environments allow for a wide array of performances
- Special rubrics available to assess digital portfolios and presentations

Suggestions for Teaching: Effective Assessment Techniques

- Necessary to obtain a representative sample of behavior when testing
- Table of specifications helps ensure an adequate sample of content, behavior
- Elementary grade students tested as much for diagnostic, formative assessment purposes as for summative purposes
- Rating scales and checklists make evaluations of performance more systematic
- Item analysis tells about difficulty, discriminating power of multiple-choice items

arlier parts of this book discuss three major aspects of the teacher's role: understanding student differences and how to address them properly, understanding the learning process and how to use that knowledge to formulate effective approaches to instruction, and establishing a positive learning environment by influencing motivation to learn and creating an orderly classroom. Now we turn to assessing performance, which is an equally significant aspect of the teacher's role. Virtually everyone connected with public schools, from students to teachers and administrators to state education officials to members of the U.S. Congress, is keenly interested in knowing how much and how well students have learned.

In this and the next chapter, we describe a twofold process for assessing student learning using teacher-made measures to assess mastery of the teacher's specific objectives and using professionally prepared standardized tests to measure the extent of a student's general knowledge base and aptitudes. Although the items that make up teacher-made and standardized assessments can be very similar, if not identical, these two types of assessment differ significantly in their construction, in the conditions under which they are administered, and in the purposes for which they are used. In short, standardized tests are designed to highlight where students, classrooms, schools, and districts stand with respect to one another in terms of general levels of performance in various skills and subject areas. Period. Think of this as assessment *of* learning. Teacher-made assessments, by contrast, are designed to highlight students' strengths and weaknesses, to give students timely feedback about the effectiveness of their study habits, and to provide teachers with timely information that can help them make more effective instructional decisions. These assessments may or may not look like traditional "tests." Think of them as assessment *for* learning (Stiggins, 2007).

Revealing Assumptions

Start at the Finish Line

Celeste is a bit nervous about today's meeting. She has worked for 6 weeks on lesson plans for a biology unit on the mechanisms of cell membranes. Last week she distributed her drafts. Celeste thinks they are pretty good and is hoping for good reactions at the meeting.

Connie says, "Okay, today we are going to workshop Celeste's lesson plans." Celeste takes a deep breath, and Connie continues, "It's obvious that you have put a lot of time and effort into these plans, Celeste. There is some excellent work here." Celeste exhales with a smile.

"Let's start with your reactions to Celeste's plans," Connie says to Don and Antonio.

"I was really, really impressed," says Antonio. "I took biology in college, but I learned some new things about biology from your lesson plans. You have done a really nice job of mixing in demonstrations, discussions, and lab activities. There's a lot of variety in the instructional activities, and I think they give the kids a lot of opportunities to think. Like I said, I think they're great. There's only one thing..."

Don interrupts: "I think they're great, too. Osmosis, equilibrium, diffusion...I had no idea that plants were so talented!"

Celeste laughs, partly at Don's attempt at a joke, but mostly because she feels both relief and affirmation of her efforts.

Connie allows the smiles to fade and then asks, "What was the one thing, Antonio?"

"Well, I was thinking, now that Celeste has her lessons so well planned, there's only one thing left to

pause & reflect

As students in school, we became accustomed to a routine: first our teachers taught us, and then they tested us to see what we learned. For many people—including those who are preparing to become teachers—that routine seems to be simple common sense. Based on our experience as students, many of us assume that assessment is planned after instructional activities have been determined. What Celeste came to realize was that to plan for student learning, she must begin with the end in mind. When you began this course in educational psychology, how did you think about teaching, assessment, and evaluation? Were they separate concepts in your mind? Although they are related concepts, how is assessment distinct from evaluation?

do. And that is to plan how she is going to grade the kids."

"Hmmm, that's an interesting way to put it," says Connie, trailing off and repeating Antonio's thought: "So instruction and assessment are two different functions. First you plan your instruction and then you plan how to assess and evaluate. Is that what you're saying?"

"Yeah," Antonio says hesitantly.

"I'm just wondering if it shouldn't be the other way around," says Connie. She raises her eyebrows and glances at Celeste.

"Wait a minute!" says Celeste. "Okay, wait a minute…I see what you're getting at. I have planned what I'm going to do and what I want the students to do; I started with instructional decisions. My starting point should have been where I want them to be at the end of the unit. Is that it?"

"That's it," says Connie. "It's hard for students to know when they've completed the race if they don't know what the finish line looks like. So when it comes to planning, the finish line is a good place to start."

THE ROLE OF ASSESSMENT IN TEACHING

The role of assessment is to enhance learning. Therefore, assessment is both integral and critical to effective teaching. To help a student learn, a teacher must know what the student knows and is able to do. To determine if a lesson worked, a teacher must know if learning objectives were met. We have examined a number of theories throughout this book to see how they apply to teaching. To determine the effectiveness of how these ideas work in the classroom, however, you will need to assess student learning. Consider, for a moment, the discussion in Chapter 2 of the Vygotskian concept, the *zone of proximal development*. Suppose, as a teacher, you decide that *scaffolding*—which research has shown to be an effective teaching strategy—should be employed to help your students learn. To scaffold a student's learning, you will first need to know the student's zone of proximal development; you will need to assess the student's knowledge and understanding to determine what they know and can do on their own to determine the target of the scaffolding they need. Assessment yields information about learning. Said another way, assessment informs learning. Because teaching is an effort to enhance learning, assessment also informs teaching.

Assessing student learning is a task that many teachers dislike and few do extremely well. One reason is that many lack in-depth knowledge of assessment principles (Guskey, 2003; Stiggins, 2002; Trevisan, 2002). Another reason is that the role of assessor is seen as being inconsistent with the role of teacher, a role seen as more helper than tester. A third reason is that many teachers think of assessment as merely "grading" rather than as instruction (a misconception we will address shortly). As a consequence, high-quality assessment practices are too often not part of the culture of classrooms (Moss & Brookhart, 2009). This is unfortunate because, in fact, well-designed classroom assessment schemes contribute to student learning (Popham, 2006, 2011; Stiggins, 2002; Stiggins, Arter, Chappuis, & Chappuis, 2007).

A basic goal of this chapter is to help you understand how to use knowledge about assessment to enhance, rather than work against, your effectiveness as a teacher. Toward that end, we will begin by defining what we mean by the term *assessment* and by discussing two key elements of this process: *measurement* and *evaluation*.

What Is Assessment?

Broadly conceived, classroom assessment involves two major types of activities: first, collecting information about how much knowledge and skill students have learned (measurement), and then making judgments about the adequacy or acceptability of each student's level of learning (evaluation). Some teachers focus closely on the judgments they must make and tend to overlook the measurements that are used to make those judgments and how such information can help them teach more effectively. Those are the teachers that tend to think "grading" when they hear the word "assessment." But as we will see, both aspects of classroom assessment are critical to understanding student learning, and understanding student learning is critical to enhancing student learning.

Both measurement and evaluation activities can be accomplished in a number of ways. Teachers most commonly measure learning by having students take quizzes or exams, respond to oral questions, do homework exercises, write papers, solve problems, create products, and make oral presentations. Teachers can then evaluate the scores (i.e., the measurements taken) from those activities by comparing them either with one another or with an absolute standard (such as an A equals 90 percent correct). In this chapter, we will explain and illustrate the various ways in which you can measure and evaluate student learning with assessments that you create and administer regularly in your classroom (Airasian & Russell, 2008; Nitko & Brookhart, 2011).

Measurement: assigning numbers or ratings according to rules to create a ranking

Measurement For educational purposes, **measurement** is defined as the assignment of either numbers (such as the score from a test) or a rating (such as the designation "excellent" or "exceeds standards" from a performance assessment) to certain attributes of people according to a rule-governed system. For example, we can measure someone's level of keyboarding proficiency by counting the number of words the person accurately types per minute. For an oral presentation, we might measure the quality by using a guide called a scoring rubric (Arter & Chappuis, 2008). In a classroom or other group situation, the rules that are used to assign the numbers or provide the rating ordinarily create a ranking that reflects how much of the attribute different people possess (Airasian & Russell, 2008; Nitko & Brookhart, 2011).

Evaluation: making judgments about the value of a measure

Evaluation **Evaluation** involves using a rule-governed system to make judgments about the value or worth of a set of measures (Airasian & Russell, 2008; Nitko & Brookhart, 2011). What does it mean, for example, to say that a student answered 80 out of 100 earth science questions correctly? Depending on the rules that are used, it could mean that the student has learned that body of knowledge exceedingly well and is ready to progress to the next unit of instruction or, conversely, that the student has significant knowledge gaps and requires additional instruction.

Why Should We Assess Students' Learning?

As implied earlier, the short answer to the question of why we should assess students' learning is: To enhance student learning. Although that simple answer frames assessment as crucial to student learning—and it is—it leads to other questions about how to use assessment to enhance learning. There are two general ways in which assessment data (measurements) can be used to make judgments (evaluations). Thus, there are two kinds of evaluative judgments: summative and formative.

The distinction between summative and formative evaluation originated in the work of Michael Scriven (1967). In the years since Scriven described how assessment serves different evaluative purposes, research on classroom assessment has evolved from an emphasis on the technical aspects of assessment (called psychometric theory) to research on how assessment practice contributes to a wide range of developmental, learning, and especially motivational outcomes for students. As a consequence of this shift, the terms *summative* and *formative evaluation* have been replaced by *summative* and *formative assessment* (Brookhart, 2009a).

After briefly describing summative and formative assessment, we will compare and contrast the two uses of assessment information; our focus will be on assessment that can guide classroom teaching and learning day-to-day, hour-to-hour, or even minute-to-minute.

Summative Assessment (Assessment *of* Learning) The first, and probably most obvious, reason for assessment is to provide to all interested parties a clear, meaningful, and useful summary or accounting of how well a student has met the teacher's objectives. When testing is done for the purpose of assigning a letter or numerical grade, it is often called **summative assessment** because its primary purpose is to provide an assessment *of* learning, to sum up how well a student has performed over time and at a variety of tasks.

Summative assessment: measure achievement; assign grades

Formative Assessment (Assessment *for* Learning) A second reason for assessing students is to monitor their progress. The main things that teachers want to know from time to time are whether students are keeping up with the pace of instruction and are understanding all of the material that has been covered so far. For students whose pace of learning is either slower or faster than average or whose understanding of certain ideas is faulty, instructional accommodations may be needed (recall the techniques discussed in Chapter 6, "Accommodating Student Variability"). Because the purpose of such assessment is to facilitate, or form, learning and not to assign a grade, it is usually called **formative assessment.**

Formative assessment: monitor progress and plan instruction accordingly

Assessment of *Learning Compared with Assessment* for *Learning* A number of scholars have referred to assessment that leads to summative judgments as "assessment *of* learning" and assessment that is used to make formative judgments as "assessment *for* learning" (Moss & Brookhart, 2009; Stiggins, 2002, 2007; Tomlinson, 2007/2008).

Summative judgments are assessments *of* learning

Two of these scholars, Connie Moss and Susan Brookhart, are with the Center for Advancing the Study of Teaching and Learning (CASTL) in the School of Education at Duquesne University. They have been conducting research on how assessment practices advance teaching and learning for several years. It is important to note that their research has been conducted *with* teachers, administrators, and students in the Armstrong School District in Pennsylvania. Because they have worked closely with practicing educators, their conclusions are informed by practicing educators. Table 14.1 is based on Moss and Brookhart's work (2009): how they compare and contrast the characteristics of assessment *of* learning and assessment *for* learning.

Formative judgments are assessments *for* learning

The distinctions between summative assessment and formative assessment outlined in Table 14.1 help us see that the process of assessment—first measuring and

Table 14.1	Characteristics That Distinguish Summative and Formative Assessment
Assessment *of* Learning (Summative Assessment)	**Assessment *for* Learning (Formative Assessment)**
Purpose is to summarize and audit learning	Purpose is to improve student learning
Conducted periodically to capture what learning has occurred	Conducted continuously while learning is in progress
Focus is on products of learning	Focus is on learning in process
Often perceived as an activity that occurs after the teaching-learning process has finished	Perceived as integral to the teaching-learning process
Teacher-directed	Collaboration of teacher and student
Performance measures (e.g., scores on an exam) show where a student has arrived	Performance measures (e.g., scores on an exam) show a student's journey
Teachers use evidence to make a summary decision about success or failure (e.g., grades)	Teachers and students use evidence to make adjustments
Teachers take on the role of auditor; students are the audited	Teachers join with students as "intentional learners"

SOURCE: Adapted from Moss & Brookhart (2009).

then evaluating—is tied closely to the underlying reason or purpose for assessing. As we will see later in this chapter (and in Chapter 15 as well), summative assessment is not only legitimate, it is necessary. As a teacher, you will be required to assign grades to assignments, performances, quizzes, and tests. You will also be required to examine the grades that you have assigned to each assignment, each performance, each quiz, and each test, then issue a summary judgment: a final grade for a course or a grading period. This final grade is your summative assessment *of* learning.

Along the way to those summative assessments *of* learning, you will be engaged in helping students meet the learning goals and objectives that define successful learning in your classroom. That is where formative assessment comes into play. Formative assessments are conducted more or less continuously during an instructional unit, using both formal and informal assessment techniques. Periodic quizzes, homework assignments, in-class worksheets, oral reading, responses to teacher questions, and behavioral observations are all examples of formative assessments if the results are used to generate timely feedback about what students have learned, what the source of any problems might be, and what might be done to prevent small problems from becoming major ones later in the year. Unlike summative assessment, which is a one-time event conducted only after instruction is finished, formative evaluation has a more dynamic, ongoing, interactive relationship with teaching. The results of formative assessments affect instruction, which affects subsequent performance, and so on. Think back to our discussion of "Response to Intervention" (RTI) in Chapter 6, "Accommodating Student Variability." The RTI approach is sometimes characterized as "teach-test-teach." The teacher instructs (or intervenes to help the student learn), then student learning is measured and evaluated (to see if the intervention worked), and the teacher then modifies instruction based on the assessment. RTI can be thought of as a type of formative assessment.

Assessment* as *Learning   Moss & Brookhart (2009) define formative assessment as "an active and intentional learning process that partners the teacher and the students to continuously and systematically gather evidence of learning with the express goal of improving student achievement" (p. 6). In other words, they view "assessment *for* learning" as learning. Their claim is that unless both students and

Classroom assessments can provide both summative and formative information. The former—assessments of learning—can tell the teacher (and others) what knowledge and skills a student has acquired. The latter—assessments for learning—can tell the teacher and the student what adjustments need to be made to take the "next steps" for a student's learning. © Mary Kate Denny/Photo Edit

teachers are learning from the process, formative assessment is not occurring in the classroom. Whatever is happening might be "something like" formative assessment, but formative assessment requires that the teacher and students are learning with the intention to improve student achievement. Their argument is that assessment *for* learning is successful only when teachers and students are becoming better and better because they are learning from their assessment activities in the classroom.

> Formative assessment requires both teacher and student to learn

As we have indicated, learning about assessment is necessary to becoming an effective teacher. Mistilina Sato, Ruth Chung Wei, & Linda Darling-Hammond (2008), for example, studied how the assessment practices of math and science teachers changed as a function of pursuing National Board Certification. Teachers who are National Board candidates go through an extensive assessment procedure and, at the end of the process, a summative judgment about whether they have or have not met the standards of the National Board. One becomes a National Board Certified Teacher or one does not. When teachers who sought National Board Certification were compared with those who did not, the authors found significant differences. National Board candidates exhibited substantial changes "…in the variety of assessments used and the way assessment information was used to support student learning. National Board candidates attributed changes in practice to the National Board standards and assessment tasks" (p. 669). By being assessed themselves, the teachers learned how to improve their assessment practices with their own students. Thinking back to Moss and Brookhart's view of formative assessment, it is critical that assessment informs learning of both teachers and students.

In an essay entitled "Learning to Love Assessment," Carol Ann Tomlinson (2007/2008) reflects on her long teaching career and, in particular, what she learned about and from the practice of classroom assessment. She concludes her essay as follows:

> Lorna Earl (2003) distinguishes between assessment *of* learning, assessment *for* learning, and assessment *as* learning. In many ways, my growth as a teacher slowly and imperfectly followed that progression. I began by seeing assessment as judging performance, then as informing teaching, and finally as informing learning. In reality, all those perspectives play a role in effective teaching. The key is where we place the emphasis.
>
> Certainly a teacher and his or her students need to know who reaches (and exceeds) important learning targets—thus summative assessment, or assessment *of* learning, has a place in teaching. Robust learning generally requires robust teaching, and both diagnostic and formative assessments, or assessments *for* learning, are catalysts for better teaching. In the end, however, when assessment is seen *as* learning—for students as well as for teachers—it becomes most informative and generative for students and teachers alike. (p. 13)

Having made the argument that assessment is integral to teaching and critical for learning, we turn first to ways of measuring student learning and then to ways of evaluating student learning.

WAYS TO MEASURE STUDENT LEARNING

Just as measurement can play several roles in the classroom, teachers have several ways to measure what students have learned. Which type of measure you choose will depend, of course, on the objectives you have stated. For the purposes of this discussion, objectives can be classified in terms of two broad categories: knowing *about* something (for example, that knots are used to secure objects, that dance is a form of social expression, that microscopes are used to study things too small to be seen by the naked eye) and knowing *how to do* something (for example, tie a square knot, dance the waltz, operate a microscope). Measures that attempt to assess the range and accuracy of someone's knowledge are usually called *written tests*. And

pause & reflect

Over the past 10 to 12 years, you have taken probably hundreds of classroom tests. What types of tests best reflected what you learned? Why?

measures that attempt to assess how well somebody can do something are often referred to as *performance assessments*. Keep in mind that both types have a legitimate place in a teacher's assessment arsenal. Which type is used, and to what extent, will depend on the purpose or purposes you have for assessing students. In the next two sections, we will briefly examine the nature of both types of measures.

Written Tests

Written tests measure degree of knowledge about a subject

As we indicated at the beginning of this chapter, teachers spend a substantial part of each day assessing student learning, and much of this assessment activity involves giving and scoring some type of written test. Most written tests are composed of one or more of the following categories and item types: *selected response* (multiple-choice, true-false, and matching) and *constructed response* (short-answer and essay). In all likelihood, you have taken hundreds of these types of tests in your school career thus far.

In the next couple of pages, we will briefly describe the main features, advantages, and disadvantages of each test. As you read, bear in mind that what we said about the usefulness of both written tests and performance assessments applies here as well. No one type of written test will be equally useful for all purposes. You are more likely to draw correct inferences about students' capabilities by using a variety of selected-response and constructed-response items.

Selected-response tests are objectively scored and efficient but usually measure lower levels of learning and do not reveal what students can do

Selected-Response Tests   Selected-response tests are so named because the student reads a relatively brief opening statement (called a stem) and selects one of the provided alternatives as the correct answer. Selected-response tests are typically made up of multiple-choice, true-false, or matching items. Quite often all three item types are used in a single test. Although guidelines exist for writing selected-response items (see, for example, the 31 guidelines for writing multiple-choice items discussed by Haladyna, Downing, and Rodriguez, 2002), many of these guidelines have not been validated by research. Hence, test-item writing is currently as much an art as a science.

Characteristics   Selected-response tests are sometimes called "objective" tests because they have a simple and set scoring system. If alternative b of a multiple-choice item is keyed as the correct response and the student chooses alternative d, the student is marked wrong, and the teacher's desire for a correct response cannot change the result. Selected-response tests are typically used when the primary goal is to assess what might be called *foundational knowledge*. This knowledge comprises the basic factual information and cognitive skills that students need to do such high-level tasks as solve problems and create products (Stiggins, 2007).

Advantages   A major advantage of selected-response tests is efficiency: a teacher can ask many questions in a short period of time. Another advantage is ease and reliability of scoring. With the aid of a scoring template (such as a multiple-choice answer sheet that has holes punched out where the correct answer is located), many tests can be quickly and uniformly scored. Moreover, there is some evidence that selected-response tests, when well written, can measure higher-level cognitive skills as effectively as constructed-response tests (Nitko & Brookhart, 2011; Stiggins, 2007).

Disadvantages   Because items that reflect the lowest level of Bloom's Taxonomy (verbatim knowledge) are the easiest to write, most teacher-made tests (and many standardized tests as well) are composed almost entirely of knowledge-level items (a point we made initially in Chapter 13, "Approaches to Instruction"). As a result, students focus on verbatim memorization rather than on meaningful learning. Another disadvantage is that, although we get some indication of what students know, such tests reveal nothing about what students can do with that knowledge. A third disadvantage is that heavy or exclusive use of selected-response tests leads students to believe that learning is merely the accumulation of universally agreed upon facts (Martinez, 1999; Nitko & Brookhart, 2011).

Short-Answer Tests   As their name implies, short-answer tests require a brief written response from the student.

Characteristics   Instead of *selecting* from one or more alternatives, the student is asked to *supply* from memory a brief answer consisting of a name, word, phrase, or symbol. Like selected-response tests, short-answer tests can be scored quickly, accurately, and consistently, thereby giving them an aura of objectivity. They are primarily used for measuring foundational knowledge.

Advantages   Short-answer items are relatively easy to write, so a test, or part of one, can be constructed fairly quickly. They allow either broad or in-depth assessment of foundational knowledge because students can respond to many items within a short space of time. Because students have to supply an answer, they have to recall, rather than recognize, information.

| Short-answer tests easy to write but measure lower levels of learning

Disadvantages   Short-answer tests have the same basic disadvantages as selected-response tests. Because short-answer items ask only for short verbatim answers, students are likely to limit their processing to that level; thus these items provide no information about how well students can use what they have learned. In addition, unexpected but plausible answers may be difficult to score.

Essay Tests   Essay items require students to organize a set of ideas and write a somewhat lengthy response to a broad question.

Characteristics   The student is given a somewhat general directive to discuss one or more related ideas according to certain criteria. An example of an essay question is, "Compare operant conditioning theory and information-processing theory in terms of basic assumptions, typical research findings, and classroom applications."

Advantages   Essay tests reveal how well students can recall, organize, and clearly communicate previously learned information. When well written, essay tests call on such higher-level abilities as analysis, synthesis, and evaluation. Because of these demands, students are more likely to try to meaningfully learn the material on which they are tested (Stiggins, 2007; Nitko & Brookhart, 2011).

| Essay tests measure higher levels of learning but are hard to grade consistently

Disadvantages   Consistency of grading is likely to be a problem. Two students may have essentially similar responses yet receive different letter or numerical grades because of differences in vocabulary, grammar, and style. These test items are also very time-consuming to grade. And because it takes time for students to formulate and write responses, only a few questions at most can be given (Nitko & Brookhart, 2011; Liu, 2010). But recent developments in essay scoring by computer programs may eliminate or drastically reduce these disadvantages in the near future (Myers, 2003).

Constructing a Useful Test   Understanding the characteristics, advantages, and disadvantages of different types of written tests and knowing how to write such test items are necessary but not sufficient conditions for creating an instructionally useful test. James Popham (2006, 2011), a noted measurement scholar, maintains that a useful classroom test has the following five attributes:

- *Significance.* The test measures worthwhile skills (such as the last four levels of Bloom's Taxonomy—application, analysis, synthesis, and evaluation) and substantial bodies of important knowledge.
- *Teachability.* Effective instruction can help students acquire the skills and knowledge measured by the test.
- *Describability.* The skills and knowledge measured by the test can be described with sufficient clarity that they make instructional planning easier.
- *Reportability.* The test produces results that allow a teacher to identify areas of instruction that were probably inadequate.
- *Nonintrusiveness.* The test does not take an excessive amount of time away from instruction.

Performance Assessments

In recent years, many teachers, learning theorists, and measurement experts have argued that the typical written test should be used far less often than it is because it reveals little or nothing of the depth of students' knowledge and how students use their knowledge to work through questions, problems, and tasks. These individuals argue that because we are living in a more complex and rapidly changing world than was the case a generation ago, schools can no longer be content to hold students accountable just for how well they can learn, store, and retrieve information in more or less verbatim form. Instead, we need to teach and assess students for such capabilities as how well they can frame problems, formulate and carry out plans, generate hypotheses, find information that is relevant to the solution to a problem, and work cooperatively with others, because those are the types of skills that are necessary to cope successfully with the demands of life after school in the twenty-first century (Calfee, 2009; Cunningham, 2001; Fredrick, 2009).

For direct links to these and other websites, go to the web links section of the textbook's Education CourseMate website.

Performance assessments measure ability to use knowledge and skills to solve realistic problems, create products

In addition, the learning standards of such professional groups as the National Council of Teachers of Mathematics (**http://standards.nctm.org**), the National Council for the Social Studies (**www.socialstudies.org/standards**), the National Council of Teachers of English (**www.ncte.org/standards**), and the National Science Teachers Association (**www.nsta.org**) call for students to develop a sufficiently deep understanding of subject matter so that they can demonstrate their knowledge in socially relevant ways. One way to address these concerns is to use performance assessments.

What Are Performance Assessments?   **Performance assessments** require students to use a wide range of knowledge and skills over an extended period of time to complete a task or solve a problem under more or less realistic conditions. At the low end of the realism spectrum, students may be asked to construct a map, interpret a graph, or write an essay under highly standardized conditions. Everyone in the class completes the same task in the same amount of time and under the same conditions. At the high end of the spectrum, students may be asked to conduct a science experiment, produce a painting, or write an essay under conditions that are similar to those of real life. For example, students may be told to produce a compare-and-contrast essay on a particular topic by a certain date, but the resources students choose to use, the number of revisions they make, and when they work on the essay are left unspecified. When performance assessment is conducted under such realistic conditions, it is also called **authentic assessment** (Gronlund & Waugh, 2009; Janesick, 2001; Nitko & Brookhart, 2011).

Perhaps the clearest way to distinguish between traditional paper-and-pencil tests (such as multiple-choice tests) and performance assessments is to say that the former measure how much students know, whereas the latter measure what students can do with what they know. In the sections that follow, we will first define four different types of performance assessments and then look at their most important characteristics.

Performance assessments provide students the opportunity to demonstrate what they can do with what they know. David Young-Wolff/Getty Images

Types of Performance Assessments There are four ways in which the performance capabilities of students are typically assessed: direct writing assessments, portfolios, exhibitions, and demonstrations.

Direct Writing Assessments These tests ask students to write about a specific topic ("Describe the person whom you admire the most, and explain why you admire that person") under a standard set of conditions. Each essay is then scored by two or more people according to a set of defined criteria.

Portfolios A **portfolio** contains one or more pieces of a student's work, some of which demonstrate different stages of completion. For example, a student's writing portfolio may contain business letters; pieces of fiction; poetry; and an outline, rough draft, and final draft of a research paper. Through the inclusion of various stages of a research paper, both the process and the end product can be assessed. Portfolios can also be constructed for math and science, as well as for projects that combine two or more subject areas.

Either the student alone or the student in consultation with the teacher decides what is to be included in the portfolio. The portfolio is sometimes used as a showcase to illustrate exemplary pieces, but it also works well as a collection of pieces that represent a student's typical performances. In its best and truest sense, the portfolio functions not just as a housing for these performances but also as a means of self-expression, self-reflection, and self-analysis for an individual student (Chang, 2009; Lam & Lee, 2010).

Exhibitions Exhibitions involve just what the label suggests: a showing of such products as paintings, drawings, photographs, sculptures, videotapes, and models. As with direct writing assessments and portfolios, the products a student chooses to exhibit are evaluated according to a predetermined set of criteria.

Demonstrations In this type of performance assessment, students are required to show how well they can use previously learned knowledge or skills to solve a somewhat unique problem (such as conducting a scientific inquiry to answer a question, interpreting a graph, or diagnosing the cause of a malfunctioning engine and describing the best procedure for fixing it) or to perform a task (such as reciting

TeachSource Video Case ◄◄ ► ►►

Portfolio Assessment: Elementary Classroom

Go to the Education CourseMate website and watch the Video Case, and then answer the following questions:

1. Portfolios can be time-consuming for teachers to develop and grade. Based on the use of portfolios in this Video Case, do you think that using portfolios would be worth the extra time and effort? Explain your answer.

2. Based on this Video Case, why might some teachers find portfolios to be a more accurate representation of student abilities (as compared with other forms of assessment)?

a poem, performing a dance, or playing a piece of music). Figure 14.1 shows a performance item for graph interpretation, the partially correct response of a student, and the corrective feedback offered by two classmates.

Characteristics of Performance Assessments   Performance assessments are different from traditional written tests in that they require the student to make an active response, are more like everyday tasks, contain problems that involve many variables, are closely related to earlier instructional activities, use scoring guides that clearly specify the criteria against which responses will be evaluated, emphasize formative evaluation, and are probably more responsive to cultural diversity.

Emphasis on Active Responding   As we pointed out previously, the goal of performance assessment is to gain some insight into how competently students can carry out various tasks. Consequently, such tests focus on processes (that is, the underlying skills that go into a performance), products (an observable outcome such as a speech or a painting), or both. For example, an instrumental music teacher may want to know whether students can apply their knowledge of music technique and theory to use the correct fingering and dynamics when playing a woodwind or piano (Clark, 2002).

| Performance assessments may vary in degree of realism

Degree of Realism   Although performance assessments strive to approximate everyday tasks, not every test needs to be or can be done under the most realistic circumstances. How realistic the conditions should be depends on such factors as time, cost, availability of equipment, and the nature of the skill being measured. Imagine, for example, that you are a third-grade teacher and that one of your objectives is that students will be able to determine how much change they should receive after making a purchase in a store. If this is a relatively minor objective or if you do not have a lot of props available, you might simply demonstrate the situation with actual money and ask the students to judge whether the amount of change received was correct. If, however, you consider this to be a major objective and you have the props available, you might set up a mock store and have each student make a purchase using real money (Gronlund & Waugh, 2009).

An example of a task that is realistic in content and intellectual demands but not in its setting (it takes place in the classroom) is "Read All About It!" Playing the roles of newspaper staff writers and editorial board members, students put together a special series for their local newspaper that compares and contrasts the five major wars in which the United States was involved during the 1900s (World War I, World War II, Korean War, Vietnam War, and Persian Gulf War). Writing assignments include feature articles, opinion columns, and letters to the editor. Editorial responsibilities

Figure 14.1 Example of a Performance Assessment: Interpreting a Graph

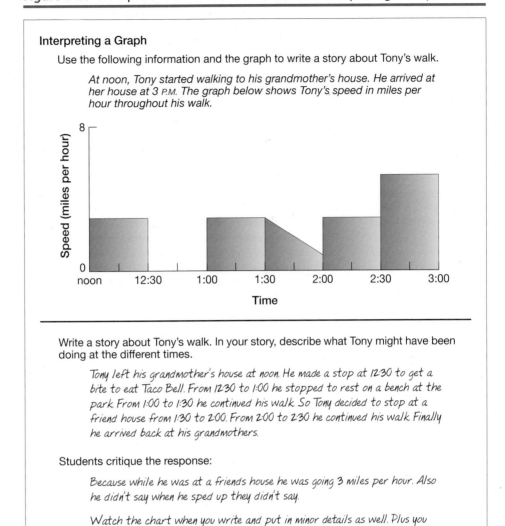

Interpreting a Graph

Use the following information and the graph to write a story about Tony's walk.

At noon, Tony started walking to his grandmother's house. He arrived at her house at 3 P.M. The graph below shows Tony's speed in miles per hour throughout his walk.

Write a story about Tony's walk. In your story, describe what Tony might have been doing at the different times.

Tony left his grandmother's house at noon. He made a stop at 12:30 to get a bite to eat Taco Bell. From 12:30 to 1:00 he stopped to rest on a bench at the park. From 1:00 to 1:30 he continued his walk. So Tony decided to stop at a friend house from 1:30 to 2:00. From 2:00 to 2:30 he continued his walk. Finally he arrived back at his grandmothers.

Students critique the response:

Because while he was at a friends house he was going 3 miles per hour. Also he didn't say when he sped up they didn't say.

Watch the chart when you write and put in minor details as well. Plus you can watch your speed.

SOURCE: Parke and Lane (1997).

include story editor, photo editor, mockup editor, layout editor, and copyeditor (Moon, 2002).

Emphasis on Complex Problems To assess how well students can use foundational knowledge and skills in a productive way, the questions and problems they are given should be sufficiently open ended and ill structured (Stiggins, 2007). The problems contained in the Quest Atlantis program that we described in earlier chapters are good examples of complex and somewhat ill-structured tasks. They have several interrelated parts, provide few cues as to how the problem might be solved, and contain some uncertainty about what constitutes an appropriate solution.

Close Relationship Between Teaching and Testing All too often students walk out of an exam in a state of high frustration (if not anger) because the content and format of the test seemed to have little in common with what was covered in class and the way in which it was taught. It's the old story of teaching for one thing and testing for something else. Performance assessment strives for a closer match between teaching and testing. Often a performance assessment can be a variation or extension of a task used during instruction. For example, the mock store assessment mentioned earlier could follow an instructional activity in which students practiced making change.

This close relationship between assessment and instruction is not automatic, however; the teacher must deliberately establish it. For example, if in giving an oral book report, a student is expected to speak loudly and clearly enough for everyone to hear, to speak in complete sentences, to stay on the topic, and to use pictures or other materials to make the presentation interesting, the student needs to be informed of these criteria, and classroom instruction should be organized around them. One proponent of performance assessment cited the old farm adage "You don't fatten the cattle by weighing them" to make this point. He then went on to note, "If we expect students to improve their performance on these new, more authentic measures, we need to engage in 'performance-based instruction' on a regular basis" (McTighe, 1996/1997, p. 7).

By the same token, the assessment of students' performances should be limited to just the criteria emphasized during instruction (Nitko and Brookhart, 2011). One reason that proponents of performance assessment push for this feature is that it has always been a standard part of successful programs in sports, the arts, and vocational education. Football coaches, for example, have long recognized that if they want their quarterback to know when during a game (the equivalent of a final exam) to attempt a pass and when not to, they must provide him with realistic opportunities to practice making this particular type of decision. Perhaps you recall our mentioning in the chapter on constructivist learning theory that realistic and varied practice are essential if students are to transfer what they learn in an instructional setting to an applied setting.

pause & reflect

Have you ever taken any kind of performance assessment as a student? Did you feel that it accurately reflected what you had learned? To what extent would you use performance measures for such academic subjects as writing, math, science, and social studies? Why?

Use of Scoring Rubrics   A **rubric** is a scoring guide that specifies the capabilities students should exhibit (also known as content standards), describes the qualitative levels or categories into which the responses will be sorted (also known as performance standards), and specifies how the responses will be scored (as separate elements or holistically). For writing tasks, which are probably the most common performance measures, some commonly used content criteria are clarity of purpose, organization, voice, word choice, grammatical usage, and spelling (Arter & Chappuis, 2008; Arter & McTighe, 2001). An example of a scoring rubric for an oral report is provided in Table 14.2.

Creating and using scoring rubrics and providing them to students at the beginning of a task is highly desirable for at least three reasons:

Rubrics increase objectivity and consistency of scoring, align instruction with assessment, communicate teachers' expectations, help students monitor progress

1. They increase the objectivity, consistency, and efficiency of scoring.
2. They help teachers match their instructional activities to the demands of the performance measure, the goal we discussed in the previous section.
3. By providing students with verbal descriptions and examples of the desired performance or product, teachers clearly communicate to students the types of behaviors that represent the range from unacceptable to exceptional performance and help students better monitor their progress and make productive changes in the quality of their work (Arter & Chappuis, 2008; Whittaker, Salend, & Duhaney, 2001). Students with learning disabilities are likely to experience the greatest benefit from being given a scoring rubric and being shown how to use it (Heacox, 2009; Jackson & Larkin, 2002).

Bear in mind, however, that scoring rubrics have their limitations. Although the rubrics used by two teachers to score writing samples may have some of the same

Table 14.2	Scoring Rubric for a Group Oral Presentation			
Level	Content	Audiovisual Components	Group Members	Audience Members
Excellent	Accurate, specific, research based, retold in own words	Are unique, add to presentation quality of materials used, are neat, present a clear message	Each member is equally involved in presentation and is well informed about the topic	Maintain eye contact with presenters, ask many questions
Good	Less detailed, lacking depth, limited number of sources used	Support topic but do not enhance presentation; some attempts at originality, clear message	Most members are active; most members are informed about the topic	Some members of the audience not attending; questions are limited or off the topic
Minimal	Limited information, general, strays from topic, not presented in own words	Inappropriate, no originality, detract from presentation, message is confusing	One or two members dominate; some members do not seem well prepared or well informed	Audience is not attending; no questions asked or questions are off the topic

SOURCE: Montgomery (2000).

content standards (such as clarity of purpose, organization, and grammar), they may differ as well (for instance, in the presence or absence of idea development, use of detail, and figurative use of language), because there are different ways to define good writing. Thus any one rubric is not likely to represent the domain of writing fully and may provide few or no opportunities for scorers to reward certain desirable writing skills (Osborn Popp, Ryan, & Thompson, 2009).

TeachSource Video Case ◀◀ ▶ ▶▶

Performance Assessment: Student Presentations in a High School English Class

Go to the Education CourseMate website and watch the Video Case, and then answer the following questions:

1. During each presentation in Laura Mosman's class, students assess their peers' performance. How do the peer assessments contribute to the learning of both the presenters and the assessors?

2. In this Video Case, Ms. Mosman claims that performance assessment allows students to demonstrate their learning in ways that tests may not. How do such demonstrations affect student learning and motivation?

Use of Formative Assessment As we pointed out earlier and as we will see in the Case in Print, tests can be used as a source of feedback to help students improve the quality of their learning efforts. Because many real-life performances and products are the result of several feedback and revision cycles, performance assessment often includes this feature as well. As anyone who has ever done any substantial amount of writing can tell you (and we are no exception), a satisfactory

Take a Stand!

Practice Assessment for Learning

The classroom assessments that teachers devise are among the most powerful influences on the quality of students' learning, largely due to their effect on self-efficacy, interest, and the types of learning strategies that students construct. Whether these assessments have positive or negative effects on students depends on how they are constructed and the purpose for which they are primarily intended.

As we have noted in this and other chapters, classroom assessments can be used both to sum up what students have learned (summative assessment) and to provide information about the effectiveness of instruction and students' specific strengths and weaknesses (formative assessment). All too often, unfortunately, formative assessment tends to be overshadowed by the summative type. Many teachers are more concerned with giving students grades than with using information gained from assessment to improve their instruction. Although both types of assessment are legitimate, we encourage you to emphasize formative assessment because of its potential to positively shape students' learning.

To help ensure that assessments serve as a positive force for learning, teachers should take the following steps:

- Make sure that you are knowledgeable about, understand, and use the basic measurement concepts and practices described in this chapter. Don't fall into the trap that so many teachers have fallen into of treating classroom assessment as a necessary evil.

- Recognize that the most accurate and useful assessments of learning are composed of multiple and varied measures. Use the full range of assessments (written tests, performance assessments, checklists, rating scales) available to you.

- Align the content of your assessments with your objectives, and fully inform students about the content and demands of your assessments.

- Finally, use the results to learn how to work even more productively with your students.

What Do You Think?

Have you been in classes in which formative evaluation was downplayed in favor of summative evaluation? What did you think of that? For more on this issue, see the Take a Stand! section of the textbook's website, Education CourseMate.

essay, story, or even personal letter is not produced in one attempt. Usually, there are critical comments from oneself and others and subsequent attempts at another draft. If we believe that the ability to write well, even among people who do it for a living, is partly defined by the ability to use feedback profitably, why should this be any different for students (Stiggins, 2001)? Some specific forms of formative assessment are dress rehearsals, reviews of writing drafts, and peer response groups (Gronlund & Waugh, 2009).

Responsiveness to Cultural Diversity

Traditional written tests have been criticized over the years for being culturally biased. That is, they are thought to underestimate the capabilities of many ethnic minority students, as well as students of low socioeconomic status, because they rely on a narrow range of item types (mainly selected response) and on content that mostly reflects the experiences of the majority culture (Johnson & Fargo, 2010; Stobart, 2005; Wang, Spalding, Odell, Klecka, & Lin, 2010). This criticism is based in large part on the constructivist view of learning: that meaningful learning occurs within a cultural context with which one is familiar and comfortable. If this is so, say the critics, then tests should be more consistent with the cultural context in which learning occurs. Performance assessments have been promoted as a way to assess more fairly and accurately the knowledge and skills of all students, and particularly minority students, because of their realism (including group problem solving) and closer relationship between instruction and assessment (Hart, 2009; Santamaria, 2009).

Performance assessments pose several challenges for teachers

Some Concerns About Performance Assessment   There is no question that alternative assessment methods have excited educators and will be used with increasing frequency. But some of the same features that make these new assessment methods attractive also create problems. One problem concerns the increased emphasis on standardized tests. Standardized tests are typically used as summative assessments (assessments *of* learning). They are given at the end of the academic year and are used solely to rank and compare students, schools, and school districts. Performance-based classroom tests, on the other hand, lend themselves to the formative assessment (assessment *for* leaning). They are given periodically to provide teachers, students, and parents with relevant information about the current level of student learning and to generate ideas about how performance might be improved. The challenge for the teachers is not to let the school district's preoccupation with high-stakes tests (those on which poor performance has significant consequences for students, teachers, and administrators) crowd out their use of performance-based tests for formative

Case in Print

How Am I Doing?

Formative assessments are conducted more or less continuously during an instructional unit, using both formal and informal assessment techniques…Unlike summative assessment, which is a one-time event conducted only after instruction is finished, formative assessment has a more dynamic, ongoing, interactive relationship with teaching. The results of formative assessments affect instruction, which affects subsequent performance, and so on. (p. 488)

Remote Tracking: Teachers Click in Quickly on Students' Performance

AMY HETZNER

Milwaukee Journal Sentinel, 4/22/2006

Hartland—When social studies teacher Maria Fricker wants to see how much her students remember about the Bosnian war or whether they know how many electoral votes are needed to elect a U.S. president, she has them take out their remote controls.

Forget asking questions and calling on the few students who raise their hands.

With a product called the Classroom Performance System, which allows students to interact with a computer program through infrared response pads, teachers such as Fricker at North Shore Middle School in Hartland can see with the press of a finger whether their students are following the lesson.

The instant feedback lets teachers know if they need to spend more time on a topic or if they're dwelling on something their students already understand and can move on.

"It shows not only the strengths and weaknesses of our kids," Fricker said, "but the strengths and weaknesses of me."

With the Classroom Performance System and other remote control-like products that have entered the educational market in recent years, technology has come to the call of schools and teachers clamoring for new ways to gauge what their students are learning.

North Shore library media specialist Sue Klopp first witnessed the Classroom Performance System at a Wisconsin Educational Media Association conference. She said she liked the instant feedback it provided and how it transfixed everyone who walked by.

Given that North Shore was looking for more ways to assess students, Klopp thought the system would be a good fit for the school's goals.

North Shore Principal Dale Fisher did, too. He authorized purchasing two systems, for about $2,000 each, for the current school year.

"The possibilities were quite endless for us to use it in the classroom," he said. "Traditional multiple-choice tests are given. The teacher can present the questions up on the board and then immediately get data on how their students understand the information…You can differentiate your instruction better. It's better time management, as I see it."

The Classroom Performance System consists of a set of response pads and a software package.

Combined with a personal computer and a projector, it allows teachers to draft a set of questions that can be beamed onto a screen and then answered by students using the pads at their desks.

The pads, shaped and run like remote controls, have only eight buttons on them so the questions generally have to be crafted for multiple-choice or yes-no answers.

Because the computer program keeps track of how many students are keying in correct answers, as well as who is getting what wrong, teachers can get immediate feedback on how their entire class is doing.

Everyone Can See It

Not far from North Shore Middle School, Merton Intermediate School acquired a set of the Classroom Response System.

The hand-held responders, which look like the clunky cell phones of yore, contain a set of keys where students can answer multiple-choice questions, a calculating device and a small screen where teachers can transmit questions.

"What I really like is the potential for it to be real-time assessment—I'm talking to you and I ask questions as the lesson's going on…I can see it, you can see it, we're getting the concept here," Merton Intermediate Principal Jon Wagner said.

A fourth-grade teacher is training herself on the system, which she plans to test with students next school year, Wagner said.

Help for Struggling Students

The Kettle Moraine School District recently purchased two sets of the responders for use with its special education students.

Carol Smiley, who teaches cognitively disabled students at Kettle Moraine High School, said the devices are beneficial because they allow her to immediately direct her attention to struggling students.

But, while students like them, they haven't been trouble-free. Any assessment given on the responders has to be limited to a single class period, she said, and the technology doesn't allow for graphics that might be more helpful for certain students.

"It's nice because it does eliminate paper-pencil kind of things," Smiley said. "And also the anonymity—not everybody can look over your shoulder and see what you're doing."

The Merton and North Shore principals say the systems meet twin goals for their schools—incorporating technology into lessons and giving teachers data to help guide their instruction.

Recently in Fricker's class at North Shore, the teacher was able to see how well her students remembered their lessons about the workings of government by giving them a sample citizenship test used by the government.

While she controlled it through a computer set up in the middle of the classroom, the screen at the front of Fricker's room moved through a series of questions from who was Martin Luther King Jr. to how many branches of government there are at the federal level.

After students had keyed in their choices from the three she offered in response to each question, she clicked a button that placed a check next to the correct selection and showed how many students answered it right.

At the same time, a computer program recorded individual scores so Fricker could check back to see how students did individually, which she promised to do on more than one question.

"Oh boy, I'm going to find out who thinks Jim Doyle is the vice president of the United States," Fricker said at one point during the quiz. "I'm going to look it up later, guys."

Lets Students Respond

In addition to giving her quick feedback on how her students are grasping the subject matter, Fricker said the anonymity of the Classroom Performance System also could come in handy in dealing with controversial areas where students otherwise might be afraid to speak their minds.

She said she could poll them on how they feel about subjects such as the death penalty and abortion, then pursue why students feel certain ways without embarrassing ones that might not want to share their beliefs.

Fricker's students are enthusiastic about the system. "I think it's better than writing, and you get to see the answers right away and whether you got it right or wrong," said Jocelyn Budzien, 13, a seventh-grader at the school.

Teachers use the systems often for pre-tests and have been creative about coming up with fun ways to use them, such as "Jeopardy!"-style quizzes, said Luke Zarling, 12.

"It's just a good way to remember certain things on the test, and it's funner," he said. "In a way, it's almost like a game. But you're learning while you play the game."

Questions and Activities

1. Formative evaluation means that teachers use assessments to make judgments about students' progress. It is also important that formative feedback be provided to students in a timely fashion. What advantages accrue to students who receive formative feedback immediately? What advantages accrue to teachers? To what extent do the advantages of the personal response system rest on a teacher's ability to formulate good questions?

2. The personal response system described in the article seems to provide useful information for students and helps teachers make instructional decisions, manage time, and maintain records of student performance. The system is also flexible in the sense that it allows teachers to tailor its use to specific lessons. But what are the disadvantages or limitations of the system described in the article? How might those disadvantages be minimized or overcome?

3. The students in the article report that using the response system is "better than writing" and "funner." Thinking back to our earlier study of motivation and social cognitive theory, how might the use of the system described in the article affect a student's sense of self-efficacy? Perhaps you or some of your friends have used a personal electronic response system in one or more of your classes. If so, reflect on your own reactions or ask your friends how they felt about their experiences with the system. To what extent did the system account for your reaction and to what extent did the questions used in the system account for your reaction?

evaluation purposes (Hargreaves, Earl, & Schmidt, 2002; Nichols & Berliner, 2007).

Reliability and validity of performance assessments not yet firmly established

There are also questions about the reliability (consistency of performance) and validity (how accurately the test measures its target) of performance measures (Bachman, 2002). Susan Brookhart (2009b) describes the "sort of" phenomenon that can occur with performance assessments: in such a case the performance "sort of taps a learning outcome but also requires extraneous skills or doesn't require all of the relevant skills" (p. 59). To illustrate, imagine a teacher who required her students to create and then perform a skit to demonstrate their understanding of a chapter in a novel the class was studying. Care would need to be taken to ensure that the assignment—and the assessment of the performance—focused on demonstrating understanding of the characters and the events in the chapter. In this situation, the teacher might be distracted by the dramatic performance and fail to assess the target of the performance.

WAYS TO EVALUATE STUDENT LEARNING

Once you have collected all the measures you intend to collect—for example, test scores, quiz scores, homework assignments, special projects, ratings of products and performances, and laboratory experiments—you will have to give the data some sort of value (the essence of evaluation). As you probably know, this is most often done by using an A-to-F grading scale. There are two general ways to approach this task. One approach is making comparisons among students. Such forms of evaluation are called norm-referenced because students are identified as average (or normal), above average, or below average. An alternative approach is called criterion-referenced because performance is interpreted in terms of defined criteria. Although both approaches can be used, we favor criterion-referenced grading for reasons we will mention shortly.

Norm-Referenced Grading

A **norm-referenced grading** system assumes that classroom achievement will naturally vary among a group of heterogeneous students because of differences in such characteristics as prior knowledge, learning skills, motivation, and aptitude (to be discussed in Chapter 15, "Understanding Standardized Assessment"). Under ideal circumstances (hundreds of scores from a diverse group of students), this variation produces a bell-shaped, or "normal," distribution of scores that ranges from low to high, has few tied scores, and has only a very few low scores and only a very few high scores. For this reason, norm-referenced grading procedures are also referred to as "grading on the curve."

Norm-referenced grading: compare one student with others

The Nature of Norm-Referenced Grading   Course grades, like standardized test scores, are determined through a comparison of each student's level of performance with the normal, or average, level of other, similar students to reflect the assumed differences in amount of learned material. The comparison may be with all other members of the student's class that year, or it may be with the average performance of several classes stretching back over several years. It is probably better for teachers to use a broad base of typical student performance made up of several classes as grounds for comparison than to rely on the current class of students. Doing so avoids two severe distorting effects: (1) when a single class contains many weak students, those with more well-developed abilities will more easily obtain the highest grades; and (2) when the class has many capable students, the relatively weaker students are virtually predestined to receive low or failing grades (Brookhart, 2009b; Gronlund & Waugh, 2009; Kubiszyn & Borich, 2010; Nitko & Brookhart, 2011).

The basic procedure for assigning grades on a norm-referenced basis involves just a few steps:

1. Determine what percentage of students will receive which grades. If, for example, you intend to award the full range of grades, you may decide to give A's to the top 15 percent, B's to the next 25 percent, C's to the middle 35 percent, D's to the next 15 percent, and F's to the bottom 10 percent.
2. Arrange the scores from highest to lowest.
3. Calculate which scores fall in which category, and assign the grades accordingly.

Many other arrangements are also possible. How large or small you decide to make the percentages for each category will depend on such factors as the nature of the students in your class, the difficulty of your exams and assignments, and your own sense of what constitutes appropriate standards. Furthermore, a norm-referenced approach does not necessarily mean that each class will have a normal distribution of grades or that anyone will automatically fail. For example, it is possible for equal numbers of students to receive A's, B's, and C's if you decide to limit your grading system to just those three categories and award equal numbers of each grade. A norm-referenced approach simply means that the grading symbols being used indicate one student's level of achievement relative to other students.

| Norm-referenced grading based on absence of external criteria

Proponents of norm-referenced grading typically point to the absence of acceptable external criteria for use as a standard for evaluating and grading student performance. In other words, there is no good way to determine externally how much learning is too little, just enough, or more than enough for some subject. And if there is no amount of knowledge or set of behaviors that all students must master, then grades may be awarded on the basis of relative performance among a group of students (Gronlund & Waugh, 2009).

Strengths and Weaknesses of Norm-Referenced Grading

There are at least two circumstances under which it may be appropriate to use norm-referenced measurement and evaluation procedures:

| Norm-referenced grading can be used to evaluate advanced levels of learning

1. *Evaluating advanced levels of learning.* You might, for example, wish to formulate a two-stage instructional plan in which the first stage involves helping all students master a basic level of knowledge and skill in a particular subject. Performance at this stage would be measured and evaluated against a predetermined standard (such as 80 percent correct on an exam). Once this has been accomplished, you could supply advanced instruction and encourage students to learn as much of the additional material as possible. Because the amount of learning during the second stage is not tied to a predetermined standard and because it will likely vary due to differences in motivation and learning skills, a norm-referenced approach to grading can be used at this stage. This situation also fits certain guidelines for the use of competitive reward structures (discussed in Chapter 13, "Approaches to Instruction") because everyone starts from the same level of basic knowledge.
2. *Selection for limited-enrollment programs.* Norm-referenced measurement and evaluation are also applicable in cases in which students with the best chances for success are selected for a limited-enrollment program from among a large pool of candidates. One example is the selection of students for honors programs who have the highest test scores and grade-point averages (Gronlund & Waugh, 2009).

The main weakness of the norm-referenced approach to grading is that there are few situations in which the typical public school teacher can appropriately use it. Either the goal is not appropriate (as in mastery of certain material and skills by all students or diagnosis of an individual student's specific strengths and weaknesses), or the basic conditions cannot be met (classes are too small or homogeneous or both). When a norm-referenced approach is used in spite of these weaknesses, communication and motivation problems are often created.

pause & reflect

Have you ever taken a class that was graded "on the curve"? Did you feel that your grade accurately reflected how much you had learned? If not, why was the grade too low or too high?

Consider the example of a group of high school sophomores having a great deal of difficulty mastering German vocabulary and grammar. The students may have been underprepared, the teacher may be doing a poor job of organizing and explaining the material, or both factors may be at work. The top student averages 48 percent correct on all of the exams, quizzes, and oral recitations administered during the term. That student and a few others with averages in the high 40s will receive the A's. Although these fortunate few may realize their knowledge and skills are incomplete, others are likely to conclude falsely that these students learned quite a bit about the German language, as a grade of A is generally taken to mean superior performance.

At the other extreme, we have the example of a social studies class in which most of the students are doing well. Because the students were well prepared by previous teachers, used effective study skills, were exposed to high-quality instruction, and were strongly motivated by the enthusiasm of their teacher, the final test averages ranged from 94 to 98 percent correct. And yet the teacher who uses a norm-referenced scheme would assign at least A's, B's, and C's to this group. Not only does this practice seriously damage the motivation of students who worked hard and performed well, but it also miscommunicates to others the performance of students who received B's and C's (Airasian & Russell, 2008).

Criterion-Referenced Grading

A **criterion-referenced grading** system permits students to benefit from mistakes and improve their level of understanding and performance. Furthermore, it establishes an individual (and sometimes cooperative) reward structure, which fosters motivation to learn to a greater extent than other systems.

Norm-referenced grading systems should rarely, if ever, be used in classrooms because few circumstances warrant their use and because they are likely to depress the motivation of all but the highest-scoring students.
Bob Daemmrich/Bob Daemmrich Photography

The Nature of Criterion-Referenced Grading Under a criterion-referenced system, grades are determined by the extent to which each student has attained a defined standard (or criterion) of achievement or performance. Whether the rest of the students in the class are successful or unsuccessful in meeting that criterion is irrelevant. Thus any distribution of grades is possible. Every student may get an A or an F, or no student may receive these grades. For reasons we will discuss shortly, very low or failing grades may occur less frequently under a criterion-referenced system.

A common version of criterion-referenced grading assigns letter grades on the basis of the percentage of test items answered correctly. For example, you may decide to award an A to anyone who correctly answers at least 85 percent of a set of test questions, a B to anyone who correctly answers 75 to 84 percent, and so on down to the lowest grade. To use this type of grading system fairly, which means specifying realistic criterion levels, you would need to have some prior knowledge of the levels at which students typically perform. You would thus be using normative information to establish absolute, or fixed, standards of performance. However, although both norm-referenced and criterion-referenced grading systems spring from a normative database (that is, from comparisons among students), only the former system uses those comparisons to directly determine grades.

Strengths and Weaknesses of Criterion-Referenced Grading Criterion-referenced grading systems (and criterion-referenced tests) have become increasingly popular in recent years primarily because of the following advantages:

- Criterion-referenced tests and grading systems provide more specific and useful information about student strengths and weaknesses than do norm-referenced

Criterion-referenced grading: compare individual performance with stated criteria

Criterion-referenced grades provide information about strengths and weaknesses

grading systems. Parents and teachers are more interested in knowing that a student received an A on an earth science test because she mastered 92 percent of the objectives for that unit than they are in knowing that she received an A on a test of the same material because she outscored 92 percent of her classmates.

- Criterion-referenced grading systems promote motivation to learn because they hold out the promise that all students who have sufficiently well-developed learning skills and receive good-quality instruction can master most of a teacher's objectives (Gronlund & Waugh, 2009). The motivating effect of criterion-referenced grading systems is likely to be particularly noticeable among students who adopt mastery goals (which we discussed in Chapter 11 on motivation) because they tend to use grades as feedback for further improvement (Moss & Brookhart, 2009; Stiggins, 2007).

One weakness of the criterion-referenced approach to grading is that the performance standards one specifies (such as a grade of A for 90 percent correct) are arbitrary and may be difficult to justify to parents and colleagues. (Why not 87 percent correct for an A? Or 92 percent?) A second weakness is that although a teacher's standards may appear to be stable from one test to another (90 percent correct for an A for all tests), they may in reality fluctuate as a result of unnoticed variation in the difficulty of each test and the quality of instruction (Gronlund & Waugh, 2009).

TeachSource **Video Case** ◀◀ ▶ ▶▶

Assessment in the Middle Grades: Measurement of Student Learning

Go to the Education CourseMate website and watch the Video Case, and then answer the following questions:

1. Evaluate the assessment practices used by Mr. Somers in this Video Case. Which ones did you find particularly effective? Support your answers using information from the textbook about effective assessment practices.

2. In this Video Case, Mr. Somers uses a written test to evaluate student understanding of course material. What are some other forms of assessment that could be used to gauge student understanding of a math unit?

Finally, we would like to alert you to a characteristic of criterion-referenced evaluation that is not a weakness but is an unfortunate fact of educational life that you may have to address. In a variety of subtle and sometimes not so subtle ways, teachers are discouraged from using a criterion-referenced approach to grading because it tends to produce higher test scores and grades than a norm-referenced approach does. The reason for the higher scores is obvious and quite justified. When test items are based solely on the specific instructional objectives that teachers write and when those objectives are clear and provided to students, students know what they need to learn and what they need to do to meet the teacher's objectives. Also, because students' grades depend only on how well they perform, not how well their classmates perform, motivation for learning tends to be higher. The result is that students tend to learn more and score higher on classroom tests. So why should this happy outcome be a cause for concern? Because individuals who are not well versed in classroom measurement and evaluation may believe that the only reason large numbers of students achieve high grades is that the teacher has lower standards than other teachers. Consequently, you may find yourself in a position of having to defend the criteria you use to assign grades. Tom Kubiszyn and Gary Borich (2010) point out that although there is a great call for excellence in education, most people are hesitant to embrace marking systems that place excellence within every student's reach.

A Mastery Approach   A particular criterion-referenced approach to grading is often referred to as a mastery approach because it allows students multiple opportunities to learn and demonstrate their mastery of instructional objectives. This approach stems in large part from the work of John Carroll (1963) and Benjamin Bloom (1968, 1976) on the concept of *mastery learning*. The basic idea behind mastery learning is that most students can master most objectives if they are given good-quality instruction and sufficient time to learn and are motivated to continue learning (Lalley & Gentile, 2008).

> Mastery approach: give students multiple opportunities to master goals at own pace

In a mastery approach, tests are used for formative as well as summative evaluation purposes. Thus students whose scores indicate deficiencies in learning are given additional instruction and a second chance to show what they have learned. Although pedagogically sound, this approach is often criticized on the grounds that life outside of school often does not give people a second chance. Surgeons and pilots, for example, are expected to do their jobs without error each and every time (Anders Ericsson, 2009; Guskey, 2003). In our view, this criticism is flawed because it is shortsighted and involves an apples-and-oranges comparison. First, even surgeons and pilots made mistakes that they were allowed to correct; surgeons made their mistakes on cadavers and pilots on flight simulators. Second, schooling is about helping students acquire the knowledge and skills they need to move from novices to experts and become self-directed learners. Life outside of school, on the other hand, frequently involves competition among individuals who are, or are expected to be, equally proficient.

If you are interested in using a mastery approach, the following suggestions can be adapted for use at any grade level and any subject area:

JOURNAL ENTRY
Trying a Mastery Approach to Grading

1. Go through a unit of study, a chapter of a text, or an outline of a lecture and pick out what you consider to be the most important points—that is, the points you wish to stress because they are most likely to have later value or are basic to later learning.

2. List these points in the form of a goal card (a list of the major concepts and skills that should be acquired by the end of an instructional unit), instructional objectives (as described by Mager, 1997, or Miller, Linn, & Gronlund, 2009), key points, or the equivalent. If appropriate, arrange the objectives in some sort of organized framework, perhaps with reference to the relevant taxonomy of educational objectives (see Chapter 13, "Approaches to Instruction").

3. Distribute the list of objectives at the beginning of a unit. Tell your students that they should concentrate on learning those points and that they will be tested on them.

4. Consider making up a study guide in which you provide specific questions relating to the objectives and a format that students can use to organize their notes.

5. Use a variety of instructional methods and materials to explain and illustrate objectives-related ideas.

6. Make up exam questions based on the objectives and the study guide questions. Try to write several questions for each objective.

7. Arrange these questions into at least two (preferably three) alternative exams for each unit of study.

8. Make up tentative criteria for grade levels for each exam and for the entire unit or report period (for example, A for not more than one question missed on any exam; B for not more than two questions missed on any exam; C for not more than four questions missed on any exam).

9. Test students either when they come to you and indicate they are ready or when you determine they have all had ample opportunity to learn the material. Announce all exam dates in advance, and remind students that the questions will be based only on the objectives you have mentioned. Indicate the criteria for different grade levels, and emphasize that any student who fails to meet a desired criterion on the first try will have a chance to take an alternate form of the exam.

10. Grade and return the exams as promptly as possible, go over questions briefly in class (particularly those that caused problems for more than a few students), and offer to go over exams individually with students. Allow for individual interpretations, and give credit for answers you judge to be logical and plausible, even if they differ from the answers you expected.

11. Schedule alternate exams, and make yourself available for consultation and tutoring the day before. (While you are giving alternative exams, you can administer the original exam to students who were absent.)

12. If students improve their score on the second exam but still fall below the desired criterion, consider a safety valve option: invite them to provide you with a completed study guide (or the equivalent) when they take an exam the second time, or give them an open-book exam on the objectives they missed to see whether they can explain them in terms other than those of a written examination. If a student fulfills either of these options satisfactorily, give credit for one extra answer on the second exam.

13. To supplement exams, assign book reports, oral reports, papers, or some other kind of individual work that will provide maximum opportunity for student choice. Establish and explain the criteria you will use to evaluate these assignments, but stress that you want to encourage freedom of choice and expression. (Some students will thrive on free choice; others are likely to feel threatened by open-ended assignments. To allow for such differences, provide specific directions for those who need them and general hints or a simple request that "original" projects be cleared in advance for the more independent thinkers.) Grade all reports Pass or Do Over, and supply constructive criticism on those you consider unsatisfactory. Announce that all Do Over papers can be reworked and resubmitted within a certain period of time. Have the reports count toward the final grade—for example, three reports for an A, two for a B, one for a C. (In addition, students should pass each exam at the designated level.) You might also invite students to prepare extra papers to earn bonus points to be added to exam totals.

This basic technique will permit you to work within a traditional A-to-F framework, but in such a way that you should be able, without lowering standards, to increase the proportion of students who do acceptable work. An example of a mastery-oriented, criterion-referenced approach to grading appears in Figure 14.2.

IMPROVING YOUR GRADING METHODS: ASSESSMENT PRACTICES TO AVOID

Be aware of and avoid faulty measurement and grading practices

Earlier in this chapter, we noted that the typical teacher has little systematic knowledge of assessment principles and as a result may engage in a variety of inappropriate testing and grading practices. We hope that the information in this chapter will help you become more proficient at these tasks. (In addition, we strongly encourage you to take a course in classroom assessment if you have not already done so.) To reinforce what you have learned here, we will describe some of the more common inappropriate testing and grading practices that teachers use. The following list is based largely on the observations of Susan Brookhart and Anthony Nitko (2008), Thomas Haladyna (1999), and Thomas Guskey (2002).

Figure 14.2 Page from a Teacher's Grade Book and Instructions to Students: A Mastery Approach

Name	1st Exam 1st Try	1st Exam 2nd Try	2nd Exam 1st Try	2nd Exam 2nd Try	3rd Exam 1st Try	3rd Exam 2nd Try	Exam Total Points	Project 1	Project 2	Project 3	Extra Project	Grade
Adams, Ann	16	18	17	18	18			P	P	P		
Baker, Charles	13	14	14	10	14			P				
Cohen, Matthew	14	16	15	16	17			P	P			
Davis, Rebecca	19	19	20					P	P	P		
Evans, Deborah	16	18	17	18	18			P	P	P		
Ford, Harold	15	16	17	15				P	P			
Grayson, Lee	10	13	12	14	12	15		P				
Hood, Barbara	16	17	15					P	P			
Ingalls, Robert	16	18	16	15				P	P			
Jones, Thomas	11	14	12	16	15			P				
Kim, David	18	19	19					P	P			
Lapine, Craig	14	16	18	16				P	P			
Moore, James	17	17	17					P	P			
Nguyen, Tuan	17	18	19	16	17			P	P	P		
Orton, John	10	10	11	9				P				
Peck, Nancy	14	15	14					P				
Quist, Ann	16	18	17	18	18			P	P			
Richards, Mary	16	17	15					P	P			
Santos, Maria	13	15	14					P				
Thomas, Eric	18	16	15	17	15			P	P			
Wong, Yvon	14	15	16					P				
Vernon, Joan	11	14	13	14	12	14		P				
Zacharias, Saul	16	18	17	18	19			P	P	P		

Instructions for Determining Your Grade in Social Studies

Your grade in social studies this report period will be based on three exams (worth 20 points each) and satisfactory completion of up to three projects.

Here are the standards for different grades:

A—Average of 18 or more on three exams, plus three projects at Pass level
B—Average of 16 or 17 on three exams, plus two projects at Pass level
C—Average of 14 or 15 on three exams, plus one project at Pass level
D—Average of 10 to 13 on three exams
F—Average of 9 or less on three exams

Another way to figure your grade is to add together points as you take exams. This may be the best procedure to follow as we get close to the end of the report period. Use this description of standards as a guide:

A—At least 54 points, plus three projects at Pass level
B—48 to 53 points, plus two projects at Pass level
C—42 to 47 points, plus one project at Pass level
D—30 to 41 points
F—29 points or less

If you are not satisfied with the score you earn on any exam, you may take a different exam on the same material in an effort to improve your score. (Some of the questions on the alternate exam will be the same as those on the original exam; some will be different.) Projects will be graded P (Pass) or DO (Do Over). If you receive a DO on a project, you may work to improve it and hand it in again. You may also submit an extra project, which may earn up to 3 points of bonus credit (and can help if your exam scores fall just below a cutoff point). As you take each exam and receive a Pass for each project, record your progress on this chart.

First Exam		Second Exam		Third Exam		Project 1	Project 2	Project 3	Extra Project	Grade
1st Try	2nd Try	1st Try	2nd Try	1st Try	2nd Try					

1. *Worshiping averages.* Some teachers mechanically average all scores and automatically assign the corresponding grade, even when they know an unusually low score was due to an extenuating circumstance. Allowances can be made for physical illness, emotional upset, and the like; a student's lowest grade can be dropped, or he can repeat the test on which he performed most poorly. Although objectivity in grading is a laudatory goal, it should not be practiced to the extent that it prevents you from altering your normal procedures when your professional judgment indicates an exception is warranted.

   Another shortcoming of this practice is that it ignores measurement error. No one can construct the perfect test, and no person's score is a true indicator of knowledge and skill. Test scores represent estimates of these characteristics. Accordingly, giving a student with an average of 74.67 a grade of D when 75 is the minimum needed for a C pretends that the test is more accurate than it really is. This is why it is so important to conduct an item analysis of your tests. If you discover several items that are unusually difficult, you may want to make allowances for students who are a point or two from the next highest grade (and modify the items if you intend to use them again). We describe a simple procedure for analyzing your test items in the next Suggestions for Teaching section.

2. *Using zeros indiscriminately.* The sole purpose of grades is to communicate to others how much of the curriculum a student has mastered. When teachers also use grades to reflect their appraisal of a student's work habits or character, the validity of the grades is lessened. This occurs most dramatically when students receive zeros for assignments that are late (but are otherwise of good quality), incomplete, or not completed according to directions and for exams on which they are suspected of cheating. This is a flawed practice for two reasons:

   - First, and to repeat what we said in point 1, there may be good reasons why projects and homework assignments are late, incomplete, or different from what was expected. You should try to uncover such circumstances and take them into account.
   - Second, zeros cause communication problems. If a student who earns grades in the low 90s for most of the grading period is given two zeros for one or more of the reasons just mentioned, that student could easily receive an overall D or F. Such a grade is not an accurate reflection of what was learned.

     If penalties are to be given for work that is late, incomplete, or not done according to directions and for which there are no extenuating circumstances, they should be clearly spelled out far in advance of the due date, and they should not seriously distort the meaning of the grade. For students suspected of cheating, for example, a different form of the exam can be given.

pause & reflect

Because students in American schools feel considerable pressure to obtain high grades, a significant number of them feel driven to cheat. What might you do to reduce your students' tendency to cheat?

3. *Providing insufficient instruction before testing.* For a variety of reasons, teachers occasionally spend more time than they had planned on certain topics. In an effort to "cover the curriculum" prior to a scheduled exam, they may significantly increase the pace of instruction or simply tell students to read the remaining material on their own. The low grades that typically result from this practice will unfortunately be read by outsiders (and this includes parents) as a deficiency in students' learning ability when in fact they more accurately indicate a deficiency in instructional quality.

4. *Teaching for one thing but testing for another.* This practice takes several forms. For instance, teachers may provide considerable supplementary material in class through lecture—thereby encouraging students to take notes and study them extensively—but base test questions almost entirely on text material. Or if teachers emphasize the text material during class discussion, they may take a significant number of questions from footnotes and less important parts of the

text. A third form of this flawed practice is to provide students with simple problems or practice questions in class that reflect the knowledge level of Bloom's Taxonomy (see Chapter 13) but to give complex problems and higher-level questions on a test. Remember what we said earlier in this book: if you want transfer, then teach for transfer.

5. *Using pop quizzes to motivate students.* If you recall our discussion of reinforcement schedules, you will recognize that surprise tests represent a variable interval schedule and that such schedules produce a consistent pattern of behavior in humans under certain circumstances. Being a student in a classroom is not one of those circumstances. Surprise tests produce an undesirable level of anxiety in many students and cause others simply to give up. If you sense that students are not sufficiently motivated to read and study more consistently, consult Chapter 11, "Motivation and Perceptions of Self," for better ideas on how to accomplish this goal.

6. *Keeping the nature and content of the test a secret.* Many teachers scrupulously avoid giving students any meaningful information about the type of questions that will be on a test or what the test items will cover. The assumption that underlies this practice is that if students have been paying attention in class, have been diligently doing their homework, and have been studying at regular intervals, they will do just fine on a test. But they usually don't—and the main reason can be seen in our description of a learning strategy (see Chapter 8, "Information-Processing Theory"). A good learning strategist first analyzes all of the available information that bears on attaining a goal. But if certain critical information about the goal is not available, the rest of the strategy (planning, implementing, monitoring, and modifying) will suffer.

7. *Keeping the criteria for assignments a secret.* This practice is closely related to the previous one. Students may be told, for example, to write an essay on what the world would be like if all diseases were eliminated and to give their imagination free rein to come up with many original ideas. But when the papers are graded, equal weight is given to spelling, punctuation, and grammatical usage. If these aspects of writing are also important to you and you intend to hold students accountable for them, make sure you clearly communicate that fact.

8. *Shifting criteria.* Teachers are sometimes disappointed in the quality of students' tests and assignments and decide to change the grading criteria as a way to shock students into more appropriate learning behaviors. For example, a teacher may have told students that mechanics will count for one third of the grade on a writing assignment. But when the teacher discovers that most of the papers contain numerous spelling, punctuation, and grammatical errors, she may decide to let mechanics determine half of the grade. As we indicated before, grades should not be used as a motivational device or as a way to make up for instructional oversights. There are far better ways to accomplish these goals.

9. *Combining apples and oranges.* Students' grades are supposed to indicate how much they have learned in different subject-matter areas. When factors such as effort and ability are combined with test scores, the meaning of a grade becomes unclear. Consequently, measurement experts routinely recommend that teachers base students' grades solely on how well they have performed on written tests and performance assessments. Assessments of effort and ability should be reported separately (Gronlund & Waugh, 2009). Nevertheless, many teachers do not follow this recommendation. A survey of just over 900 third- through fifth-grade teachers revealed that 36 percent factored a student's level of effort into a grade either quite a bit, extensively, or completely and that 47 percent used a student's ability level to help determine a grade either quite a bit, extensively, or completely. Many high school teachers engage in this practice as well (McMillan et al., 2002).

A number of technological formats and products have been developed to make the task of classroom assessment easier, more informative, and less prone to error. The next section describes several of these formats and products.

TECHNOLOGY FOR CLASSROOM ASSESSMENT

At the beginning of this chapter, we mentioned that assessment activities can account for about one third of a teacher's time. This large investment in time is partly due to the importance of assessment in both teaching and learning, but it is also related to the fact that many assessment activities involve time-consuming methods of creating, administering, and scoring tests and analyzing and recording scores. Fortunately, computer-based technology supports many of the assessment functions teachers must execute (Beatty & Gerace, 2009; Cardwell, 2000). As the number of technological tools for learning and assessment has grown, so have the expectations that aspiring teachers will demonstrate their capacity to use the technology (Yao, 2006).

Electronic Gradebooks and Grading Programs

Electronic gradebooks can store records of student test performance, compute test averages and cumulative averages, weight scores, note students with particular scores or characteristics, and print grade reports with standard as well as specific student comments. Combining digital gradebooks with grading software allows teachers to be consistent with the point-based grading systems that are used by most middle and high school teachers. These programs can scan and mark students' choices to selected-response test items (true-false, matching, multiple choice) and allow teachers to track, summarize, and present student performance in a variety of ways. But the efficiency and seeming objectivity of such programs mask a serious potential drawback: they can lead to unfair assignment of grades when used uncritically. The challenge of accurately assigning grades usually involves more than just mathematical precision.

To demonstrate the complex nature of grading and why professional judgment should supplement the use of computerized grading programs, consider the example offered by Thomas Guskey (2002) in Table 14.3.

The table represents a group of seven students, each of whom has been graded using three methods: calculating the simple average of all scores, calculating the median or middle score, and calculating the average with the lowest score deleted. Using the simple arithmetic average produces a grade of C for all students despite the differences in their grade patterns. Student 1, for example, started slowly but gradually improved. Student 2 exhibited the opposite pattern. Student 3's performance was consistently around the average. Student 4 failed the first two unit tests

Table 14.3	Summary Grades Tallied by Three Different Methods										
Student	Unit 1	Unit 2	Unit 3	Unit 4	Unit 5	Avg Score	Grade	Median Score	Grade	Delete Lowest	Grade
1	59	69	79	89	99	79	C	79	C	84	B
2	99	89	79	69	59	79	C	79	C	84	B
3	77	80	80	78	80	79	C	80	B	79.5	B
4	49	49	98	99	100	79	C	98	A	86.5	B
5	100	99	98	49	49	79	C	98	A	86.5	B
6	0	98	98	99	100	79	C	98	A	98.8	A
7	100	99	98	98	0	79	C	98	A	98.8	A

Grading Scale: 90–100% = A; 80–89% = B; 70–79% = C; 60–69% = D; 59% or lower = F.

SOURCE: Guskey (2002).

but scored near or at the top for the last three. Student 5 exhibited the opposite pattern from student 4. Student 6 had an unexcused absence for the first test and was given a score of zero but scored near or at the top for the last four tests. Student 7 had virtually perfect scores for the first four tests but was caught cheating on the last one and received a score of zero. If giving all seven students the same grade strikes you as inappropriate, note that using the median score or the average with the lowest score deleted produces grades that range from A through C, and that students 4 and 5 could receive either an A, B, or C, depending on which method is used.

Our purpose here is not to tell you which of these methods to use, as that will depend on other information that teachers typically have about student capabilities and teachers' beliefs about the appropriateness of different grading methods, but to remind you that computerized grading books should not be allowed to substitute for a teacher's professional judgment in awarding grades.

Technology-Based Performance Assessment

As you may recall from our earlier discussion, performance assessments give students the opportunity to demonstrate how well they can use the knowledge and skills that were the focus of an instructional unit to carry out realistic and meaningful tasks. Computer-based technology is an excellent vehicle for this purpose. For example, simulations are likely to be more effective than traditional paper-and-pencil tests for determining how well students understand and can carry out the process of scientific inquiry (for example, planning an investigation, collecting data, organizing and analyzing the data, forming conclusions, and communicating findings). Recent research on the development of performance assessment procedures in complex task domains such as engineering design and medical diagnosis promise even greater effectiveness of technology-based performance assessments in the future (Spector, 2006). A web-based simulation that lends itself to the assessment of scientific inquiry is the GLOBE environmental science education program (**www.globe.gov/globe_flash.html**). Students who participate in GLOBE collect environmental data at a local site and submit it to a scientific database on the Internet. About 4,000 schools from countries around the world participate in this program. Teachers could use the GLOBE database to assess how well students analyze and interpret climate data by having them use a set of climate-related criteria (such as temperature at different altitudes, amount of sunshine, and amount of snow) to determine in which of several cities the next Winter Olympics should be held (Means & Haertel, 2002). Multimedia tools with text, audio, video, and graphics components, such as the Quest Atlantis program we mentioned in previous chapters, also offer opportunities for students to demonstrate their ability to solve real-world problems in a number of content areas.

Digital Portfolios

Technological environments allow for a wide array of performances

What Is a Digital Portfolio? Digital portfolios (also called electronic portfolios) are similar in purpose to the more traditional portfolios, but they extend beyond paper versions because they can include sound effects, audio and video testimonials, voice-over explanations of a student's thinking process as a project is worked on, and photographs of such products as drawings, paintings, and musical compositions (Siegle, 2002).

The Components and Contents of Digital Portfolios Because the purposes for having students construct a digital portfolio (such as to assign grades, assess students' strengths and weaknesses, evaluate a program or curriculum) are not always the same, the portfolio structure will vary somewhat across teachers and school districts. But some components, such as those in the list that follows, are frequently recommended (for instance, Beatty & Gerace, 2009; Goldsby & Fazal, 2001; Janesick, 2001) and should always be seriously considered for inclusion:

- the goals the student was attempting to achieve
- the guidelines that were used to select the included material
- work samples
- teacher feedback
- student self-reflection
- the criteria that were used to evaluate each entry
- examples of good-quality work

Just as the general components of a digital portfolio may vary, so may the particular media that are used. Following are some specific examples of the types of media a student may use and information that would be represented by each medium (Barrett, 2000; Gatlin & Jacob, 2002; Janesick, 2001; O'Lone, 1997; Siegle, 2002):

- *Digitized pictures and scanned images:* photos of the student and/or objects he has created, artwork, models, science experiments over time, fax exchanges with scientists, spelling tests, math work, self-assessment checklists
- *Documents:* electronic copies of student writing, reflection journals, publications, copies of web pages created, and teacher notes and observations
- *Audio recordings:* persuasive speeches, poetry readings, rehearsals of foreign language vocabulary, readings of select passages, self-evaluations, interviews or voice notes regarding the rationale for work included
- *Video clips:* short videos showing the student or teams of students engaged in science experiments and explaining their steps, or showing student performances in physical education or the performing arts
- *Multimedia presentations:* QuickTime movies of interdisciplinary projects

Rubrics for Digital Portfolios and Presentations

With all the information a digital portfolio might contain, how can a classroom teacher fairly and efficiently assess student learning? First, electronic writing, just like paper-based compositions, can be assessed holistically in a general impression rating. It can also be analyzed with specific criteria such as whether the work is insightful, well organized, clear, focused, relevant, sequentially flowing, persuasive, inspirational, and original (see Arter & Chappius, 2008). There are also rubrics for analyzing the quality of a portfolio that has been posted to a website. One uses a four-point scale (exceeds requirements, meets requirements, close to meeting standards, clearly does not meet standards) to assess the design and aesthetics of the website, its usability, and the presence and clarity of the portfolio's contents (Goldsby & Fazal, 2001). The website **www.4teachers.org** contains, among other things related to technology, a tool called RubiStar that provides templates for creating rubrics for several types of digital products.

Special rubrics available to assess digital portfolios and presentations

Performance and Portfolio Assessment Problems

We would be remiss not to point out the problems often associated with technology-based performance and portfolio assessment. High-quality performance assessments require multiple assessments (for both formative and summative purposes), extensive time, electronic equipment, careful planning, and continued modification (McGrath, 2003). Electronic portfolios can become large, complex, and time-consuming to grade fairly and thus can overload teachers with work (Goodman, 2008; Pope et al., 2002).

Staff development and teacher training are additional barriers to effective use of performance assessment and digital portfolios. But with proper training, teachers may begin to find ways in which technology-based school and classroom assessment plans are practical, cost-effective, and qualitatively better than traditional assessments.

The following Suggestions for Teaching should help you properly implement the assessment concepts and research findings presented in this chapter.

Suggestions for Teaching

Effective Assessment Techniques

1 **As early as possible in a report period, decide when and how often to give tests and other assignments that will count toward a grade, and announce tests and assignments well in advance.**

If you follow the suggestions for formulating objectives presented in Chapter 13, "Approaches to Instruction," you should be able to develop a reasonably complete master plan that will permit you to devise a course outline even though you have only limited experience with teaching or with a particular text or unit of study. In doing so, you will have not only a good sense of the objectives you want your students to achieve but also the means by which achievement will be assessed.

Before the term starts is a good time to block out the number of tests you will give in that term. Recall that research cited earlier has shown that students who take six or seven tests per term (two or three per grading period) learn more than students who are tested less frequently or not at all. Don't assume, however, that if giving three tests per grading period is good, then giving five or six tests is better. A point of diminishing returns is quickly reached after the fourth test.

JOURNAL ENTRY
Announcing Exams and
Assignments

If you announce at the beginning of a report period when you intend to give exams or set due dates for assignments, you not only give students a clear idea of what they will be expected to do, but you also give yourself guidelines for arranging lesson plans and devising, administering, and scoring tests. For the most part, it is preferable to announce tests well in advance. (If you will be teaching elementary students, it will be better to announce exams and assignments for a week at a time rather than providing a long-range schedule.) When tests are announced, be sure to let students know exactly what material they will be held responsible for, what kinds of questions will be asked, and how much tests will count toward the final grade. As we noted in the Take a Stand! feature in Chapter 8 on information-processing theory, and as others have pointed out (Guskey, 2003), students need complete information about the content and nature of tests if they are to function strategically. In addition, research indicates that students who are told to expect (and who receive) an essay test or a multiple-choice test will score slightly higher on an exam than students who do not know what to expect or who are led to expect one type of test but are given another type (Lundeberg & Fox, 1991).

For term papers or other written work, list your criteria for grading the papers (for example, how much emphasis will be placed on style, spelling and punctuation, research, individuality of expression). In laboratory courses, most students prefer a list of experiments or projects and some description of how they will be evaluated (for example, 10 experiments in chemistry, 15 drawings in drafting, 5 paintings in art, judged according to posted criteria).

2 **Prepare a content outline or a table of specifications of the objectives to be covered on each exam, or otherwise take care to obtain a systematic sample of the knowledge and skill acquired by your students.**

The more precisely and completely goals are described at the beginning of a unit, the easier and more efficient assessment (and teaching) will be. The use of a clear outline will help ensure an adequate sample of the most significant kinds of behavior.

When the time comes to assess the abilities of your students, you can't possibly observe and evaluate all relevant behavior. You can't listen to more than a few pages of reading by each first grader, for example, or ask high school seniors to answer

Necessary to obtain a
representative sample of
behavior when testing

Suggestions for Teaching

For students to plan effectively how they will master your objectives, they need to know as early as possible how many tests they will have to take, when the tests will occur, what types of items each test will contain, and the content on which they will be tested.
Copyright © Bob Daemmrich/Photo Edit

Table of specifications helps ensure an adequate sample of content, behavior

---

questions on everything discussed in several chapters of a text. Because of the limitations imposed by large numbers of students and small amounts of time, your evaluation will have to be based on a sample of behavior—a 3- or 4-minute reading performance and questions covering points made in only a few sections of text material assigned for an exam. It is therefore important to try to obtain a representative, accurate sample.

Psychologists who have studied measurement and evaluation often recommend that as teachers prepare exams, they use a **table of specifications** to note the types and numbers of test items to be included so as to ensure thorough and systematic coverage. You can draw up a table of specifications by first listing along the left-hand margin of a piece of lined paper the important topics that have been covered. Then insert appropriate headings from the taxonomy of objectives for the cognitive domain (or for the affective or psychomotor domain, if appropriate) across the top of the page. An example of such a table of specifications for some of the information discussed in this chapter is provided in Figure 14.3. A computer spreadsheet program such as Microsoft Excel is an ideal tool for creating a table of specifications.

Test specialists often recommend that you insert in the boxes of a table of specifications the percentage of test items that you intend to write for each topic and each type of objective. This practice forces you to think about both the number and the relative importance of your objectives before you start teaching or writing test items. Thus, if some objectives are more important to you than others, you will have a way of ensuring that these are tested more thoroughly. If, however, a test is going to be brief and emphasize all objectives more or less equally, you may wish to put a

Figure 14.3 Example of a Table of Specifications for Material Covered in This Chapter

Topic	Objectives					
	Knows	Comprehends	Applies	Analyzes	Synthesizes	Evaluates
Nature of measurement and evaluation						
Purposes of measurement and evaluation						
Types of written tests						
Nature of performance tests						

Suggestions for Teaching

check mark in each box as you write questions. If you discover that you are overloading some boxes and that others are empty, you can take steps to remedy the situation. The important point is that by taking steps to ensure that your tests cover what you want your students to know, you will be increasing the tests' validity.

For reasons to be discussed shortly, you may choose not to list all of the categories in the taxonomy for all subjects or at all grade levels. Tables of specifications that you draw up for your own use therefore may contain fewer headings across the top of the page than the table illustrated in Figure 14.3.

JOURNAL ENTRY
Using a Table of Specifications

3 **Consider the purpose of each test or measurement exercise in the light of the developmental characteristics of the students in your classes and the nature of the curriculum for your grade level.**

In addition to considering different uses of tests and other forms of measurement when you plan assessment strategies, you should think about the developmental characteristics of the students you plan to teach and the nature of the curriculum at your grade level. As noted in the discussion of Jean Piaget's theory early in this book, there are significant differences among preoperational, concrete operational, and formal thinkers. Furthermore, because primary grade children are asked to master a curriculum that is substantially different from the curriculum upper elementary and secondary school students are expected to learn, different forms of measurement should be used at each level.

Primary grade children are asked to concentrate on learning basic skills, and their progress—or lack of it—will often be apparent even if they are not asked to take tests. A second grader who has difficulty decoding many longer unfamiliar words, for instance, will reveal that inability each time she is asked to read. Upper elementary grade and middle school students are asked to improve and perfect their mastery of skills in reading, writing, and arithmetic and also to study topics in the sciences, social studies, and other subjects. Because their success in dealing with many subjects, learning materials, and tests often depends on reading ability, you may have to create tests to diagnose weaknesses and chart improvement (a formative evaluation function), as well as to establish grades.

Elementary grade students tested as much for diagnostic, formative assessment purposes as for summative purposes

At the secondary level, testing is done largely to assign grades and to determine whether students are sufficiently prepared to take more advanced courses (as in Algebra I, Algebra II). Consequently, as you create a table of specifications for a particular instructional unit, you want to make sure that you have identified all of the important concepts and skills for that unit and that your test items cover most, if not all, of the levels of Bloom's Taxonomy.

4 **Decide whether a written test or a performance assessment is more appropriate.**

JOURNAL ENTRY
Using Different Types of
Test Items

As you think about which types of questions to use in a particular situation, consider the student characteristics and curriculum differences noted earlier. In the primary grades, you may not use any written tests in the strict sense. Instead, you might ask your students to demonstrate skills, complete exercises (some of which may be similar to completion tests), and solve simple problems (often on worksheets). In the upper elementary and middle school grades, you may need to use or make up dozens of measurement instruments, because many subjects must be graded. Accordingly, it may be necessary to make extensive use of completion, short-answer, and short-essay items that can be printed on the board or on paper. If you find it impossible or impractical to make up a table of specifications for each exam, at least refer to instructional objectives or a list of key points as you write questions. At the secondary level, you might do your best to develop some sort of table of specifications for exams not only to ensure measurement of objectives at various levels of the taxonomy but also to remind yourself to use different types of items.

In certain elementary and middle school subjects and in skill or laboratory subjects at the secondary level, performance assessments may be more appropriate than written tests. At the primary grade level, for instance, you may be required to assign a grade in oral reading. In a high school home economics class, you may grade students on how well they produce a garment or a soufflé. In a wood shop class, you may base a grade on how well students construct a piece of furniture. In such cases, you can make evaluations more systematic and accurate by using rating scales and checklists and by attempting to equate (or at least take into account) the difficulty level of the performance to be rated.

*Rating scales and checklists
make evaluations of performance
more systematic*

To evaluate a product such as a garment or a piece of furniture, you might use a checklist that you devised and handed out at the beginning of a course. Such a checklist should state the number of possible points that will be awarded for various aspects of the project—for example, accuracy of measurements and preparation of component parts, neatness of assembly, quality of finishing touches, and final appearance. To evaluate a performance, you might use the same approach, announcing beforehand how heavily you intend to weigh various aspects of execution. In music, for instance, you might note possible points to be awarded for tone, execution, accuracy, and interpretation. For both project and performance tasks, you might multiply the final score by a difficulty factor. (You have probably seen television coverage of Olympic events in which divers and gymnasts have their performance ratings multiplied by such a difficulty factor.)

5 **Make up and use a detailed answer key or rubric.**

a. Evaluate each answer by comparing it with the key or rubric.

JOURNAL ENTRY
Preparing a Detailed Key

One of the most valuable characteristics of a test is that it permits comparison of the permanently recorded answers of all students with a fixed set of criteria. A complete key or rubric not only reduces subjectivity but can also save you much time and trouble when you are grading papers or defending your evaluation of questions.

For short-answer, true-false, matching, or multiple-choice questions, you should devise your key as you write and assemble the items. With planning and ingenuity, you can prepare a key that will greatly simplify grading. For essay questions, you should also prepare answers as you write the questions. If you ask students to write answers to a small number of comprehensive essay questions, you are likely to maximize the consistency of your grading process by grading all answers to the first question at one sitting, then grading all answers to the second question, and so on. However, if a test consists of 8 or 10 short-essay items (which can usually be answered in a half-hour or so), you would have to do too much paper shuffling to follow such a procedure. One way to speed up the grading of short-essay exams (so that you can evaluate up to 30 tests in a single session of 40 minutes or so) is to use plus or minus grading. If you use a point scale to grade short-essay answers, you will spend an agonizing amount of time deciding just how much a given answer is worth. But with practice, you should be able to write short-essay questions and answers (on your key) that can be graded plus or minus.

To develop skill in writing such questions, make up a few formative quizzes that will not count toward a grade. Experiment with phrasing questions that require students to reveal that they either know or don't know the answer. Prepare your key as you write the questions. When the time comes to grade papers, simply make a yes or no decision about the correctness of each answer. With a felt-tip pen, make a bold check over each satisfactory answer on an exam, and tally the number of checks when you have read all the answers. (Counting up to 8 or 10 is obviously a lot quicker and easier than adding together various numbers of points for 8 or 10 answers.) Once you have developed skill in writing and evaluating short-essay questions that can be graded plus or minus, prepare and use summative exams. If you decide to use this type of exam, guard against the temptation to write items that measure only knowledge. Use a table of specifications, or otherwise take steps to write at least some questions that measure skills at the higher levels of the taxonomy for the cognitive domain.

b. Be willing and prepared to defend the evaluations you make.

You will probably get few complaints if you have a detailed key and can explain to the class when exams are returned how each answer was graded. To a direct challenge about a specific answer to an essay or short-essay question, you might respond by showing complainers an answer that received full credit and inviting them to compare it with their own. Perhaps the best way to provide feedback about responses to multiple-choice questions is to prepare a feedback booklet. As you write each multiple-choice question, also write a brief explanation as to why you feel the answer is correct and why the distractors are incorrect. If you follow this policy (which takes less time than you might expect), you can often improve the questions as you write your defense of the answer. If you go a step further (described in the next point), you can obtain information to use in improving questions after they have been answered. This is a good policy to follow with any exam, multiple choice or otherwise.

To maintain consistency when scoring exams, teachers should use a scoring key for selected-response and short-answer items and a rubric for essay items. © Bill Aron/ Photo Edit

JOURNAL ENTRY
Analyzing Test Items

6 **During and after the grading process, analyze questions and answers to improve future exams.**

If you prepare sufficient copies of feedback booklets for multiple-choice exams, you can supply them to all students when you hand back scored answer sheets (and copies of the question booklets). After students have checked their papers and identified and examined questions that were marked wrong, invite them to select up to three questions that they wish to challenge. Even after they read your explanation in the feedback booklet, many students are likely to feel that they selected a different answer than you did for logical and defensible reasons. Permit them to write out a description of the reasoning behind their choices. If an explanation seems plausible, give credit for the answer. If several students chose the same questions for comment, you have evidence that the item needs to be revised. (It's also possible that the information reflected in the item was not directly related to your objectives or was poorly taught.)

If you follow the procedure of supplying feedback booklets, it is almost essential to prepare at least two forms of every exam. Having two or more forms also equips you to use a mastery approach. After writing the questions, arrange them into two tests. Make perhaps half of the questions the same and half unique to each exam. (If you have enough questions, you might prepare three forms.) If you teach multiple sections, give the first form to period 1, the next form to period 2, and thereafter use the forms in random order. This procedure will reduce the possibility that some students in later classes will have advance information about most of the questions on the test.

If you find that you do not have time to prepare feedback booklets, you might invite students to select three answers to defend as they record their choices when taking multiple-choice exams. This will supply you with information about ambiguous questions, even though it will not provide feedback to students. It may also provide you with useful information about how well the items were written.

Turning back to multiple-choice questions, you may also want to use simple versions of item-analysis techniques that measurement specialists use to analyze and improve this type of item. These techniques will allow you to estimate the difficulty level and discriminating power of each item. Discriminating power is the ability of a test item to distinguish students who have learned that piece of information from students who have not. To determine the discriminating power of a test item, try the following steps:

1. Rank the test papers from highest score to lowest score.
2. If you have 50 or more, select approximately the top 30 percent, and call this the upper group. Select approximately the bottom 30 percent, and call this the lower group. Set the middle group of papers aside. If you have 30–40 students, split the scores in the middle and create upper and lower groups. If you have fewer than 30 students, you have too few to conduct an item analysis (Nitko & Brookhart, 2011).
3. For each item, record the number of students in the upper group and in the lower group who selected the correct answer and each distracter as follows (the correct answer has an asterisk next to it):

Item 1 Alternatives	A	B*	C	D	E
Upper group	0	6	3	1	0
Lower group	3	2	2	3	0

4. Estimate the item difficulty by calculating the percentage of students who answered the item correctly. The difficulty index for the preceding item is 40 percent ($8/20 \times 100$). Note that the smaller the percentage is, the more difficult the item is.
5. Estimate the item discriminating power by subtracting the number in the lower group who answered the item correctly from the number in the upper group, and divide by one-half of the total number of students included in the item analysis. For the preceding example, the discrimination index is 0.40 ($6 - 2 \div 10$). When the index is positive, as it is here, it indicates that more students in the upper group than in the lower group answered the item correctly. A negative value indicates just the opposite.

As you can see, this type of item analysis is not difficult to do, nor is it likely to be very time-consuming. It is important to remember, however, that the benefits of item analysis can quickly be lost if you ignore certain limitations. One is that you will be working with relatively small numbers of students. Therefore, the results of item analysis are likely to vary as you go from class to class or from test to test with the same class. Because of this variation, you should retain items that a measurement specialist would discard or revise. In general, you should retain multiple-choice items whose difficulty index lies between 50 and 90 percent and whose discrimination index is positive (Gronlund & Waugh, 2009). Another limitation is that you may have objectives that everyone must master. If you do an effective job of teaching these objectives, the corresponding test items are likely to be answered correctly by nearly every student. These items should be retained rather than revised to meet arbitrary criteria of difficulty and discrimination.

To review this chapter, try the tutorial quizzes and other study aids on the Education CourseMate website.

Challenging Assumptions

Start at the Finish Line

Don says, "I think it's very common for people outside of the profession to think of teaching as separate from assessment and evaluation. I was writing in my journal about the relationship between teaching and testing and so I asked some guys in one of my classes what they thought it was. They all think that teachers plan their instruction and then after they have finished instructing, they plan how they are going to test students to see what they learned. To be honest, they think a lot of professors do it exactly that way." He catches the quizzical look on Connie's face, grins broadly, and says, "They didn't mean education profs, Doc. Obviously, they were talking about, you know, other profs."

"I know, I know," says Connie. "But, seriously, think about what your friends said. They are like a lot of people who talk about teaching as if it were very simple and linear: first you tell your students something they should know and then you test to see if they know it."

"But from a learning standpoint," says Celeste, "it makes sense to determine what learning is required and then make sure you plan how that learning can best be demonstrated. Demonstrations of learning supply the data we need to evaluate not only the students but also ourselves."

Summary

1. Classroom assessment, which involves the measurement and evaluation of student learning, accounts for about one third of a teacher's class time.

2. Measurement involves ranking individuals according to how much of a particular characteristic they possess. Evaluation involves making judgments about the value or worth of a set of measures.

3. Teachers give tests and assign grades to communicate to others how well students have mastered the teacher's objectives, to find out if

students are keeping up with and understanding the learning material, to diagnose students' strengths and weaknesses, and to positively affect students' approaches to studying.

4. Research indicates that students who take four to six exams a term learn more than students who take fewer or no exams.

5. Written tests are used to measure how much knowledge people have about some topic. Test items can be classified as selected response (multiple-choice, true-false, matching), and constructed response (short-answer and essay).

6. Selected-response tests are efficient to administer and score but tend to reflect the lowest level of the cognitive domain taxonomy and provide no information about what students can do with the knowledge they have learned. They may also lead students to believe that learning is just the accumulation of factual knowledge.

7. Short-answer tests measure recall, rather than recognition, of information and allow comprehensive coverage of a topic, but they have the same disadvantages as selected-response tests.

8. Essay tests measure such high-level skills as analysis, synthesis, and evaluation but are difficult to grade consistently, are time-consuming to grade, and allow only limited coverage of material. In the near future, essay scoring by computer may reduce these disadvantages.

9. Performance assessments measure how well students use basic knowledge to perform a particular skill or produce a particular product under somewhat realistic conditions.

10. Performance assessments are characterized by active responding, realistic conditions, complex problems, a close relationship between teaching and testing, use of scoring rubrics, and use of test results for formative evaluation purposes.

11. Rubrics are beneficial for both teachers and students. They help teachers to assess student performances more objectively, consistently, and efficiently and to align instructional activities with the demands of the performance measure. They help students understand the teacher's expectations, monitor their progress, and make improvements in their work.

12. Performance assessments present such challenges to teachers as increasing time needed for assessment, explaining to parents how performance assessment scores translate to letter grades, spending more time helping students prepare for and pass tests, and not letting the summative evaluation purpose of standardized tests crowd out the formative evaluation purpose of performance assessments.

13. It has not yet been completely demonstrated that student performances and products can be measured reliably (consistently) and validly (accurately).

14. When grades are determined according to a norm-referenced system, each student's level of performance is compared with the performance of a group of similar students. A norm-referenced scheme is used by those who feel that external criteria for determining the adequacy of performance are unavailable.

15. In a criterion-referenced grading system, each student's level of performance is compared with a predetermined standard.

16. A mastery approach to criterion-referenced measurement and evaluation, which is based on the concept of mastery learning, allows students multiple opportunities to pass tests.

17. The potential benefits of measurement and evaluation activities can be undermined by any one of several inappropriate testing and grading practices.

18. Classroom assessment can be made easier through the use of such technological products and formats as electronic gradebooks, simulation programs, and digital portfolios.

19. To be sure that the number of various types of items on a test is consistent with your instructional objectives, prepare a table of specifications.

20. For primary and elementary grade students, the formative evaluation purpose of tests should be emphasized at least as much as the summative purpose.

21. Item-analysis procedures exist to determine the difficulty and discriminating power of multiple-choice items.

Resources for Further Investigation

• Suggestions for Assessment *for* Learning and Assessment *as* Learning

For a highly practical, classroom-based account of formative assessment, read *Advancing Formative Assessment in Every Classroom: A Guide for Instructional Leaders* (2009), by Connie Moss and Susan Brookhart. This book not only shows what formative assessment is, but what it is not. Many teachers believe they are formatively assessing, when in fact they are only doing "something like" formative assessment. This book shows that teachers must inquire with the clear intention to advance student achievement. Their account shows how assessment is a form of teacher learning as well as student learning. *The Handbook of Formative Assessment* (2010), edited by Heidi Andrade and Gregory Cizek, addresses the history, theory, practical implications, and challenges of formative assessment.

• Suggestions for Constructing Written and Performance Assessments

For specific suggestions on ways to write different types of items for paper-and-pencil tests of knowledge and on methods for constructing and using rating scales and checklists to measure products, performances, and procedures, consult one or more of the following books: *Assessment of Student*

Achievement (9th ed., 2009), by Norman Gronlund and C. Keith Waugh; *Classroom Assessment: What Teachers Need to Know* (6th ed., 2011), by W. James Popham; and *Educational Assessment of Students* (6th ed., 2011), by Susan Brookhart and Anthony Nitko.

● Examples of and Scoring Rubrics for Performance Assessments

The use of performance assessments in portfolios is being tested as an alternative to standardized tests by the New York Performance Standards Consortium, a coalition of successful high schools in New York (most in and around New York City). For more information on this interesting experiment and for ideas on performance-based assessments, consult the website **http://performanceassessment. org**. Another resource for useful information and examples of performance assessments is the website of the Coalition of Essential Schools (**www.essentialschools.org**).

If you use performance assessments, you will need to know how to construct and use scoring rubrics. In *Creating and Recognizing Quality Rubrics* (2008), Judith Arter and Jan Chappuis describe how to construct scoring rubrics for various performance tasks. The website of the organization Rubrician. Com (**www.rubrics.info**) contains rubrics developed by educators, organized by grade levels and content areas.

● Writing Higher-Level Questions

As Benjamin Bloom and others point out, teachers have a disappointing tendency to write test items that reflect the lowest level of the taxonomy: knowledge. To avoid this failing, carefully read Part 2 of the original taxonomy of cognitive objectives: *Taxonomy of Educational Objectives: The Classification of Educational Goals–Handbook I: Cognitive Domain* (1956), edited by Benjamin Bloom, Max Englehart, Edward Furst, Walker Hill, and David Krathwohl. Each level of the taxonomy is clearly explained and followed by several pages of illustrative test items. An updated taxonomy and how to use it to write higher-level questions can be found in *Designing and Assessing Educational Objectives: Applying the New Taxonomy* (2008), by Robert Marzano and John Kendall.

● Analyzing Test Items

Susan Brookhart and Anthony Nitko discuss item-analysis procedures for multiple-choice and performance assessments in Chapter 14 of *Educational Assessment of Students* (6th ed., 2011). For both types of tests, there are procedures for assessing both the difficulty and the discriminating power of each item. A discussion of item-analysis procedures can also be found in Chapter 11 of *Educational Testing and Measurement: Classroom Application and Practice* (9th ed., 2010), by Tom Kubiszyn and Gary Borich.

● Classroom Grading

For detailed information on how to construct an accurate and fair grading system, examine *Grading* (2nd ed., 2009), by Susan M. Brookhart; *Assessment and Grading in Classrooms* (2008), by Susan Brookhart and Anthony Nitko; and *How to Grade for Learning* (2009), by Ken O'Connor.

15 Understanding Standardized Assessment

The Education CourseMate website for this text offers many helpful resources. Go to **CengageBrain.com** to preview this chapter's Concept Maps and Chapter Themes.

KEY POINTS

These key points will help you learn the important information in this chapter. To help you study, they also appear in the margins of the pages, next to the text where they are discussed.

Standardized Tests

- Standardized tests: items presented and scored in standard fashion; results reported with reference to standards
- Basic purpose of standardized test is to obtain accurate, representative sample of some aspect of a person
- Standardized test scores are used to identify strengths and weaknesses, plan instruction, select students for programs
- Reliability: similarity between two rankings of test scores obtained from the same individual
- Validity: how accurately a test measures what users want it to measure
- Content validity: how well test items cover a body of knowledge and skill
- Predictive validity: how well a test score predicts later performance
- Construct validity: how accurately a test measures a theoretical attribute
- Meaningfulness of standardized test scores depends on representativeness of norm group
- Formal testing of young children is inappropriate because of rapid developmental changes
- Achievement tests measure how much of a subject or skill has been learned
- Diagnostic achievement tests designed to identify specific strengths and weaknesses
- Competency tests determine whether potential graduates possess basic skills
- Aptitude tests measure predisposition to develop additional capabilities in specific areas
- Norm-referenced tests compare one student with others

- Criterion-referenced tests indicate degree of mastery of objectives
- Percentile rank: percentage of scores at or below a given point
- Standard deviation: degree of deviation from the mean of a distribution
- z score: how far a raw score is from the mean in standard deviation units
- T score: raw score translated to a scale of 1–100 with a mean of 50
- Stanine score: student performance indicated with reference to a 9-point scale based on normal curve

Using Standardized Tests for Accountability Purposes: High-Stakes Testing

- High-stakes testing: using test results to hold students and educators accountable for achievement
- No Child Left Behind (NCLB) Act requires standards; annual testing in math, reading, science; annual progress for all students; public reports; accountability system
- High-stakes tests expected to improve clarity of goals, quality control, teaching methods, and student motivation
- High-stakes tests criticized because of structural limitations, misinterpretation/misuse of results, narrow view of motivation, inflexible performance standards
- High-stakes testing has so far failed to live up to its promise
- NCLB has changed how teachers teach
- No common meaning of proficiency among states

Standardized Testing and Technology

- Websites of state departments of education, private companies provide services that help prepare students for state assessments
- Computer adaptive testing: computers determine sequence and difficulty level of test items

Because standardized assessment of scholastic aptitude and achievement is such a popular practice in the United States (as well as in many other countries), this chapter will focus on the nature of standardized tests, how they are used to assess student variability, and how these test results can be employed in putting together effective instructional programs for students. As you will see, the use of standardized tests is truly a double-edged sword: it has the potential to harm students as well as help them.

Revealing Assumptions

The Right Test?

"One thing I'm worried about is meeting parents," says Don. "I was talking with a teacher at my field site and she was telling me about parent-teacher conferences. It sounds like you spend all of your time talking to parents just about their kids' standardized test scores."

"Yeah," says Celeste. "Kids in high school are really zeroed in on those test scores. They seem more concerned about standardized test scores than anything else. Every time a new topic comes up, the first thing they want to know is if it's going to be on the achievement tests or the SAT. But I guess I was the same way in high school. I mean those tests really are important."

"Same thing in middle school," says Antonio, "and it's not just parents and kids. The administration is really focused on getting our scores up on the state tests. There's a lot of pressure on teachers to make sure our students perform well on those tests. But as you guys are saying, standardized tests are so important. And, after all, they are the best measure we have."

Connie writes in her notebook as her young colleagues share their thoughts. She looks up from her notes and says, "Yes, standardized tests are important. Yes, there is a lot of emphasis placed on standardized tests. Yes, students, parents, and administrators are all very interested in test scores. Yes, a lot of time, effort, technical expertise, and money go into the construction of standardized tests. But are you sure they are the best measures of everything we need to measure?"

Connie takes a breath and continues, "To use standardized tests well, we must first understand clearly how they work; where standardized test scores come from, what the scores tell us, and—just as important—what the scores do *not* tell us. Teachers have to make decisions, and those decisions must be driven by data. Test scores can help us make judgments for our students, but we need to be clear about the judgments we are making so that we use the right data to make the right decisions."

pause & reflect

We learned in school that standardized tests are critically important to our futures. Indeed, you will likely have to pass a standardized test to earn your license to teach, even after you have earned your degree. The No Child Left Behind Act strongly emphasizes the use of testing to create a system that holds schools and school districts accountable for student progress. Because much attention is given to standardized test scores, it is commonly assumed that standardized tests are the best measures we have. But what precisely do they measure? Some standardized tests measure achievement in relation to standards. Is achievement the same thing as learning? What is the precise meaning of your SAT scores? What exactly do standardized test scores tell us about a student? A school? A district?

STANDARDIZED TESTS

Nature of Standardized Tests

The kinds of assessment instruments described in this chapter are typically referred to as **standardized tests,** although the term *published tests* is sometimes used (because they are prepared, distributed, and scored by publishing companies or independent test services). You have almost certainly taken several of these tests during your academic career, and so you are probably familiar with their appearance and general characteristics. They are called standardized tests for the following reasons:

Standardized tests: items presented and scored in standard fashion; results reported with reference to standards

- They are designed by people with specialized knowledge and training in test construction.
- Every person who takes the test responds to the same items under the same conditions.
- The answers are evaluated according to the same scoring standards.

- The scores are interpreted through comparison with the scores obtained from a group (called a norm group) that took the same test under the same conditions or (in the case of some achievement tests) through comparison with a predetermined standard.

Basic purpose of standardized test is to obtain accurate, representative sample of some aspect of a person

The basic purpose of giving a standardized test is to obtain an *accurate and representative sample* of how much of some characteristic a person possesses (such as knowledge of a particular set of mathematical concepts and operations). The benefit of getting an accurate measure from a test is obvious. When standardized tests are well designed, they are likely to be more accurate measures of a particular characteristic than nonstandardized tests. Standardized tests measure a *sample* of the characteristic, as a comprehensive measure would be too expensive, time-consuming, and cumbersome to administer (Deneen & Deneen, 2008; Koretz, 2008).

Uses of Standardized Tests

Standardized test scores are used to identify strengths and weaknesses, plan instruction, select students for programs

Historically, educators have used standardized test scores, particularly achievement tests, for a variety of instructionally related purposes. Teachers, guidance counselors, and principals have used test data to identify general strengths and weaknesses in student achievement, to inform parents of their child's general level of achievement, to plan instructional lessons, to group students for instruction, and to recommend students for placement in special programs. To cite just one example, when a child moves to a different school, it is highly desirable for those in the new school to have some idea as to what the child knows about basic subjects. Standardized achievement tests do an effective job of providing information about the mastery of general subject matter and skills and thus can be used for planning, grouping, placement, and instructional purposes.

When you read the test profiles that report how students in your classes have performed on standardized tests, you will get a general idea of some of your students' strengths and weaknesses. If certain students are weak in particular skill areas and you want to help them overcome those weaknesses, test results *may* give you *some* insights into possible ways to provide remedial instruction. If most of your students score below average in certain segments of the curriculum, you will know that you should devote more time and effort to presenting those topics and skills to the entire class. You can and should, of course, supplement what you learn from standardized test results with your own tests and observations to design potentially effective forms of remedial or advanced instruction.

pause & reflect

If you are like most people, you took a variety of standardized tests throughout your elementary and high school years. Do you think that those tests adequately reflected what you had learned and were capable of learning and therefore were always used in your best interest? What can you do to increase the chances that you will use test scores to help your students fulfill their potential?

Criteria for Evaluating Standardized Tests

Like most other things, standardized tests vary in quality. To use test scores wisely, you need to be an informed consumer—to know what characteristics distinguish well-constructed from poorly constructed tests. Four criteria are widely used to evaluate standardized tests: reliability, validity, normed excellence, and examinee appropriateness. Each of these criteria will be explained individually.

Reliability A basic assumption that psychologists make about human characteristics (such as intelligence and achievement) is that they are relatively stable, at least over short periods of time. For most people, this assumption seems to be true. Thus you should be able to count on a test's results being consistent, just as you might count on a reliable worker to do a consistent job time after time. This stability in test

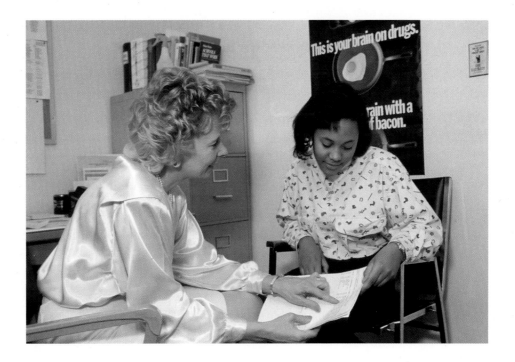

When properly used, standardized test scores can keep parents, students, and educators aware of a student's general level of achievement, and they can help teachers and administrators make decisions about placing students in special programs.
© Ilene MacDonald/Alamy

Reliability: similarity between two rankings of test scores obtained from the same individual

performance is known as **reliability.** You can think of reliability as the extent to which test scores are free of measurement errors that arise from such factors as test anxiety, motivation, correct guesses, and vaguely worded items, thereby producing a consistent performance over the course of a test or over repeated assessments of the same characteristic (Koretz, 2008). It is one of the most important characteristics of standardized tests.

To illustrate the importance of reliability, imagine that you wish to form cooperative learning groups for mathematics. Because these types of groups should be composed of five to six students who differ on a number of characteristics, including achievement, you use the students' most recent scores from a standardized mathematics test to assign two high, two medium, and two low achievers to each group. One month later, the children are retested, and you now find that many of those who scored at the top initially (and whom you thought were very knowledgeable about mathematics) now score in the middle or at the bottom. Conversely, many students who initially scored low now have average or above-average scores. What does that do to your confidence in being able to form heterogeneous groups based on scores from this test? If you want to be able to differentiate among individuals consistently, you need to use an instrument that performs consistently.

Psychologists who specialize in constructing standardized tests assess reliability in a variety of ways:

- *Split-half reliability.* Psychologists administer a single test to a group of students, create two scores by dividing the test in half, and measure the extent to which the rankings change from one half to the other. This method gauges the internal consistency of a test.
- *Test-retest reliability.* Psychologists administer the same test to the same people on two occasions and measure the extent to which the rankings change over time.
- *Alternate-form reliability.* Psychologists administer two equivalent forms of a test to the same group of students at the same time and compare the results.

Regardless of which method is used to assess reliability, the goal is to create two rankings of scores and see how similar the rankings are. This degree of consistency is expressed as a correlation coefficient (abbreviated with a lowercase *r*) that ranges from 0 to 1. Well-constructed standardized tests should have correlation coefficients of about .95 for split-half reliability, .90 for test-retest reliability, and .85 for alternate-form reliability (Kubiszyn & Borich, 2010). Bear in mind, however, that a particular test may not report all three forms of reliability and that reliabilities for subtests and for younger age groups (kindergarten through second grade) are likely to be lower than these overall figures.

Validity   A second important characteristic of a test is that it accurately measures what it claims to measure. A reading comprehension test should measure just that—nothing more, nothing less. Whenever we speak of a test's accuracy in this sense, we are referring to its **validity.**

Because most of the characteristics we are interested in knowing something about (such as arithmetic skills, spatial aptitude, intelligence, and knowledge of the American Civil War) are internal and hence not directly observable, tests are indirect measures of those attributes. Therefore, any test-based conclusions we may draw about how much of a characteristic a person possesses, or any predictions we may make about how well a person will perform in the future (on other types of tests, in a job, or in a specialized academic program, for example), are properly referred to as *inferences*. So when we inquire about the validity of a test by asking, "Does this test measure what it claims to measure?" we are really asking, "How accurate are the inferences that I wish to draw about the test taker?" (Koretz, 2008).

The degree to which these inferences can be judged accurate, or valid, depends on the type and quality of the supporting evidence that we can muster. Three kinds of evidence that underlie test-based inferences are content validity evidence, predictive validity evidence, and construct validity evidence.

Content Validity Evidence   This kind of evidence rests on a set of judgments about how well a test's items reflect the particular body of knowledge and skill (called a *domain* by measurement specialists) about which we want to draw inferences. If a test on the American Civil War, for example, contained no items on the war's causes, its great battles, or the years it encompassed, some users might be hesitant to call someone who had achieved a high score knowledgeable about this topic. Then again, other users might not be nearly so disturbed by these omissions (and the inference that would be drawn from the test score) if they considered such information to be relatively unimportant.

Predictive Validity Evidence   This evidence allows us to make probabilistic statements about how well students will behave in the future ("Based on his test scores, there is a strong likelihood that Yusef will do well in the creative writing program next year"). Many colleges, for example, require students to take the American College Testing Program (ACT) or the Scholastic Assessment Test (SAT) and then use the results (along with other information) to predict each prospective student's grade-point average at the end of the first year. All other things being equal, students with higher test scores are expected to have higher grade-point averages than students with lower test scores and thus stand a better chance of being admitted.

Construct Validity Evidence   This evidence indicates how accurately a test measures a theoretical description of some internal attribute of a person. Such attributes—for example, intelligence, creativity, motivation, and anxiety—are called *constructs* by psychologists.

To illustrate the nature of construct validity, we will use a hypothetical theory of intelligence called the Perfectly Valid theory. This theory holds that highly intelligent individuals should have higher-than-average school grades now and in the future, demonstrate superior performance on tasks that involve abstract reasoning, and be able to distinguish worthwhile from non-worthwhile goals. They may or may not, however, be popular among their peers. If the Perfectly Valid theory is accurate

---

Sidebar notes (left margin):

Validity: how accurately a test measures what users want it to measure

Content validity: how well test items cover a body of knowledge and skill

Predictive validity: how well a test score predicts later performance

Construct validity: how accurately a test measures a theoretical attribute

and if someone has done a good job of constructing an intelligence test based on this theory (the Smart Intelligence Test), people's scores on the Smart Test should vary in accordance with predictions derived from the Perfectly Valid theory. We should see, for example, a strong, positive relationship, or correlation, between intelligence quotient (IQ) scores and grade-point average but no relationship between IQ scores and measures of popularity. As more and more of this type of evidence is supplied, we can feel increasingly confident in drawing the inference that the Smart Intelligence Test is an accurate measure of the Perfectly Valid theory of intelligence.

TeachSource Video Case ⏪ ▶ ⏩

Assessment in the Elementary Grades: Formal and Informal Literacy Assessment

Go to the Education CourseMate website and watch the Video Case, and then answer the following questions:

1. In your own words, explain how the standardized test in the Video Case will benefit Myto and allow teachers to plan his instruction more effectively.

2. What factors might influence the reliability and validity of this standardized test?

Normed Excellence For a test score to have any meaning, it has to be compared with some yardstick, or measure of performance. Standardized tests use the performance of a norm group as the measure against which all other scores are compared. A **norm group** is a sample of individuals carefully chosen so as to reflect the larger population of students for whom the test is intended. In many cases, the larger population consists of all elementary school children, all middle school children, or all high school children in the United States.

> Meaningfulness of standardized test scores depends on representativeness of norm group

The norm group must closely match the larger population it represents on such major demographic variables as age, sex, race, ethnic group, region of country, family income, and occupation of head of household. These variables are considered major because they are strongly associated with differences in school performance. If, for example, the U.S. Census Bureau reports that 38 percent of all Latino males between the ages of six and thirteen live in the southwestern region of the country, a good test constructor testing in the Southwest will try to put together a norm group that contains the same percentage of six- to thirteen-year-old Latino males.

As you might suspect, problems of score interpretation arise when the major demographic characteristics of individuals who take the test are not reflected in the norm group. Suppose you were trying to interpret the score of a fourteen-year-old Black male on the EZ Test of Academic Achievement. If the oldest students in the norm group were twelve years of age and if Black children were not part of the norm group, you would have no way of knowing whether your student's score was below average, average, or above average, compared with the norm.

Examinee Appropriateness Because developing a standardized test is a substantial undertaking that requires a considerable investment of money, time, and expertise, most tests of this type are designed for nationwide use. But the curricula in school districts in different types of communities and in different sections of the country vary to a considerable extent. Therefore, it is important to estimate how appropriate a given test is for a particular group of students. When you are estimating the content validity of a test, you should pay attention not only to how well the questions measure what they are supposed to measure but also to whether they are appropriate in terms of level of difficulty and of the vocabulary and characteristics of your students.

For example, the administration of readiness tests to preschool and kindergarten children to determine whether they are ready to begin school or should be promoted to first grade has been heavily criticized on the basis of examinee appropriateness. A major problem with the use of tests for the making of admission and retention decisions in the early grades is their low reliability. Young children change physically, socially, emotionally, and intellectually so rapidly that many of them score very differently when retested 6 months later (Bjorklund, 2005).

Types of Standardized Tests

In this section we will examine two major categories of standardized tests—achievement tests and aptitude tests—each of which has several varieties. We will also examine two approaches to the interpretation of test scores: norm referenced and criterion referenced.

Achievement Tests   One type of standardized test that you probably took during your elementary school years was the **single-subject achievement test,** designed to assess how much you had learned—that is, achieved—in a particular basic school subject. The very first standardized test you took was probably designed to evaluate aspects of reading performance. Then at intervals of 2 years or so, you probably worked your way tensely and laboriously through **achievement batteries** designed to assess your performance in reading as well as math, language, and perhaps other subjects. During your high school years, you may have taken one or more achievement batteries that evaluated more sophisticated understanding of basic reading-writing-arithmetic skills, as well as course content in specific subjects.

At some point during your elementary school years, you may also have been asked to take a **diagnostic test,** a special type of single-subject achievement test intended to identify the source of a problem in basic subjects and perhaps in study skills as well.

Depending on when and where you graduated from high school, you may have been asked to take a **competency test** a few months before the end of your senior year. Competency tests came into use in the mid-1970s when it was discovered that many graduates of American high schools were unable to handle basic skills. In

Formal testing of young children is inappropriate because of rapid developmental changes

Achievement tests measure how much of a subject or skill has been learned

Diagnostic achievement tests designed to identify specific strengths and weaknesses

Competency tests determine whether potential graduates possess basic skills

Standardized achievement tests are given to assess how much of a particular subject students have learned, and aptitude tests are given to assess the level of a student's capabilities in a particular area. © Spencer Grant/ Photo Edit

many school districts, therefore, students are asked to prove that they are competent in reading, writing, and arithmetic before they are awarded diplomas.

You may have earned some of your college credits by taking the College-Level Examination Program, a **special-purpose achievement test**. Depending on the state in which you choose to teach, you may be required to take and pass another special-purpose achievement test, the Praxis II, before being granted a teaching certificate.

Aptitude Tests An aptitude is an underlying predisposition to respond to some task or situation in a particular way; it makes possible the development of more advanced capabilities (Wright, 2008). The word *aptitude* is derived from the Middle English *apte*, which meant "to grasp" or "to reach" and is related to the French *à propos*, which means "appropriate," "fitting," or "suited to a purpose."

For several decades, aptitudes have come to be identified entirely with cognitive predispositions, and **aptitude tests,** designed to indicate the level of knowledge and skill a student could acquire with effective instruction, have become increasingly common. Thus there are now a number of somewhat general tests of **scholastic aptitude** (the cognitive skills deemed most likely to predict a student's ability to cope with academic demands), such as the familiar SAT, and many specific tests of aptitude, such as tests of musical aptitude, mechanical aptitude, and spatial relations.

Some contemporary psychologists argue that we should stop trying to distinguish between aptitude (or ability) and achievement and should abandon the view that one's ability is the cause of one's achievement. Robert Sternberg (1998), for example, notes that the items that appear in various mental ability tests (such as vocabulary, reading comprehension, verbal analogies, arithmetic problem solving, and determining similarities) are often the focus of classroom instruction and are the same types of items that appear on many achievement tests. Second, he notes that achievement test scores are as good predictors of ability test scores as ability test scores are predictors of achievement test scores. Rather than thinking of such aptitudes as verbal reasoning, mathematical reasoning, spatial orientation, and musical aptitude as largely inherited capabilities that are responsible for the level of expertise one develops in a particular area, he prefers to think of aptitudes as various forms of *developing* expertise.

Norm-Referenced Tests Most of the achievement and aptitude tests just described are referred to as **norm-referenced tests** because performance is evaluated with reference to norms—the performance of others—established when the final form of the test was administered to the sample of students who made up the standardization group. After taking an achievement battery in the elementary grades, for example, you were probably told that you had performed as well on reading comprehension questions as 80 percent (or whatever) of all of the students who took the test. If you take the Graduate Record Examination (GRE), you will be told how far from the average score of 500 you are (in terms of a score to be described shortly). Thus you will learn just where you stand in a distribution of scores arranged from lowest to highest. Tests that are constructed according to norm-referenced criteria tend to cover a broad range of knowledge and skill but have relatively few items for each topic or skill tested. But an alternative approach to reporting achievement scores, the criterion-referenced method, is frequently used.

Criterion-Referenced Tests A different approach to reporting achievement test scores is used by **criterion-referenced tests.** When a test is scored in this manner, an individual's performance is not compared with the performance of others. Instead, students are evaluated according to how well they have mastered specific objectives in various well-defined skill areas. Because of this feature, you may find criterion-referenced tests more useful than norm-referenced tests in determining who needs

Aptitude tests measure predisposition to develop additional capabilities in specific areas

Norm-referenced tests compare one student with others

Criterion-referenced tests indicate degree of mastery of objectives

how much additional instruction in what areas (provided, of course, that the test's objectives closely match your own).

The criterion-referenced approach is intended to reduce overtones of competition and to emphasize mastery of objectives at a rate commensurate with students' abilities. Tests that have criterion-referenced scoring systems tend to cover less ground than norm-referenced tests but contain more items for the objectives they do assess. Because norm-referenced and criterion-referenced scoring systems provide different types of information about student achievement, many testing companies provide both types of scores.

A relatively new development in criterion-referenced testing has occurred in several states. In an attempt to counter some of the disadvantages of traditional norm-referenced standardized testing, states such as Vermont and Kentucky have begun to rely partly or entirely on performance-based measures in their statewide assessment systems. We will offer some examples from these new tests later in this chapter.

> ## pause & reflect
>
> Do you prefer norm-referenced or criterion-referenced tests? Why? Can you describe circumstances in which a norm-referenced test would be clearly preferable to a criterion-referenced test, and vice versa?

Interpreting Standardized Test Scores

Scores on the most widely used standardized tests are typically reported on student profile forms that summarize and explain the results. Although most profiles contain sufficient information to make it possible to interpret scores without additional background, you should know in advance about the kinds of scores you may encounter, particularly because you may be asked to explain scores to students as well as to their parents.

Grade Equivalent Scores   The **grade equivalent score** interprets test performance in terms of grade levels. A student who makes a grade equivalent score of 4.7 on an achievement test, for example, got the same number of items right on this test as the average fourth grader in the standardization group achieved by the seventh month of the school year.

The grade equivalent score was once widely used at the elementary level, but because it may lead to misinterpretations, it is not as popular as it once was. One problem with grade equivalent scores is the tendency to misinterpret a score above a student's actual grade level as an indication that the student is capable of consistently working at that level. This kind of assumption might lead parents or perhaps teachers themselves to consider accelerated promotion. Remember that although such scores may show that a student did somewhat better on the test than the average student a grade or two above her, they do not mean that the student tested has acquired knowledge of all the skills covered in the grade that she would miss if she skipped a grade.

| Percentile rank: percentage of scores at or below a given point |

Percentile Ranks   Probably the most widely used score for standardized tests is the **percentile rank.** This score indicates the percentage of students who are at and below a given student's score. It provides specific information about relative position.

Students earning a percentile rank of 87 did as well as or better than 87 percent of the students in the particular normative group being used. They did not get 87 percent of the questions right—unless by coincidence—and this is the point parents are most likely to misunderstand. Parents may have been brought up on the percentages grading system, in which 90 or above was A, 80 to 89 was B, and so on down the line. If you report that a son or daughter has a percentile rank of 50, some parents are horror-struck or outraged, not understanding that the child's score on this test is average, not a failure. In such cases, the best approach is to emphasize that the percentile rank tells the percentage of cases at or below the child's score. You might also talk in terms of a hypothetical group of 100; for example, a child with a percentile rank of 78 did as well as or better than 78 out of every 100 students who took the test.

Although the percentile rank gives simple and direct information on relative position, it has a major disadvantage: the difference in achievement among students clustered around the middle of the distribution is often considerably less than the difference among those at the extremes. The reason is that *most* scores are clustered around the middle of most distributions of large groups of students. The difference in raw score (number of items answered correctly) between students at percentile ranks 50 and 51 may be 1 point. But the difference in raw score between the student ranked 98 and one ranked 97 may be 10 or 15 points, because the best (and worst) students scatter toward the extremes. This quality of percentile ranks means that ranks on different tests cannot be averaged. To get around that difficulty, standard scores are often used.

Standard deviation: degree of deviation from the mean of a distribution

Standard Scores Standard scores are expressed in terms of a common unit: the **standard deviation.** This statistic indicates the degree to which scores in a group of tests (a distribution) differ from the average, or mean. (The *mean* is the arithmetical average of a distribution and is calculated by adding all scores and dividing the total by the number of scores.) The standard deviation is most valuable when it can be related to the normal probability curve. Figure 15.1 shows a normal probability curve indicating the percentage of cases to be found within three standard deviations above and below the mean. The horizontal axis indicates the score, ranging from low on the left to high on the right; the vertical axis represents the number of cases corresponding to each score. Notice, for example, that more than 68 percent of the cases fall between +1 SD (one standard deviation above the mean) and −1 SD (one standard deviation below the mean).

As you can see from the figure, the normal probability curve, or **normal curve** as it is usually known, is a mathematical concept that depicts a hypothetical bell-shaped distribution of scores. Such a perfectly symmetrical distribution rarely, if ever, occurs in real life. However, because many distributions of human characteristics and performance closely *resemble* the normal distribution, it is often assumed that such distributions are typical enough to be treated as "normal." Thus information that mathematicians derive for the hypothetical normal distribution can be applied to the approximately normal distributions that are found when human

Figure 15.1 Normal Probability Curve

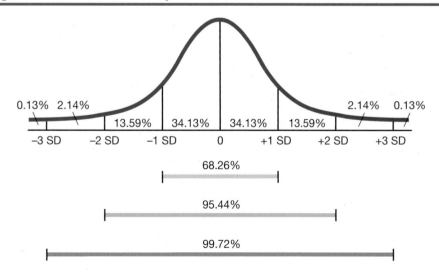

attributes are measured. When very large numbers of students are asked to take tests designed by specialists who go to great lengths to cancel out the impact of selective factors, it may be appropriate to interpret the students' scores on such tests with reference to the normal curve.

For purposes of discussion, and for purposes of acquiring familiarity with test scores, it will be sufficient for you to know about two of the standard scores that are derived from standard deviations. One, called a **z score**, tells how far a given raw score is from the mean in standard deviation units. A z score of −1.5, for example, would mean that the student was 1.5 standard deviation units below the mean. Because some z scores (such as the one in the example just given) are negative and involve decimals, **T scores** are often used instead. T scores range from 0 to 100 and use a preselected mean of 50 to get away from negative values. Most standardized tests that use T scores offer detailed explanations, either in the test booklet or on the student profile of scores, of how they should be interpreted. In fact, many test profiles adopt the form of a narrative report when explaining the meaning of all scores used.

To grasp the relationship among z scores, T scores, and percentile ranks, examine Figure 15.2. The diagram shows each scale marked off below a normal curve. It supplies information about the interrelationships of these various scores, provided that the distribution you are working with is essentially normal. In a normal distribution, for example, a z score of +1 is the same as a T score of 60 or a percentile rank of 84; a z score of −2 is the same as a T score of 30 or a percentile rank of about 2. (In addition, notice that the distance between the percentile ranks clustered around the middle is only a small fraction of the distance between the percentile ranks at the ends of the distribution.)

Stanine Scores　During World War II, U.S. Air Force psychologists developed a statistic called the **stanine score** (an abbreviation of "standard nine-point scale"). The name reflects the fact that this is a type of standard score, and it divides a population into nine groups. Each stanine is one half of a standard deviation unit, as indicated in Figure 15.3.

When stanines were introduced on test profiles reporting the performance of public school children on standardized tests, they were often used to group students. (Students in stanines 1, 2, and 3 would be placed in one class; those in

z score: how far a raw score is from the mean in standard deviation units

T score: raw score translated to a scale of 1–100 with a mean of 50

Stanine score: student performance indicated with reference to a 9-point scale based on normal curve

For help in learning the new terms introduced in this chapter, you may want to use the Glossary Flashcards on the textbook's student website, Education CourseMate.

Figure 15.2 Relationship Among z Scores, T Scores, and Percentile Ranks

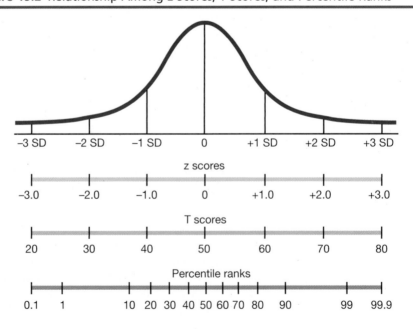

Figure 15.3 Percentage of Cases in Each Stanine (with Standard Deviation Units Indicated)

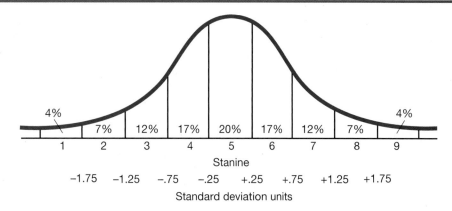

4, 5, and 6 in another class; and so on.) For the reasons given in Chapter 6, "Accommodating Student Variability," and later in this chapter, such ability grouping has become a highly controversial issue in American schools. Consequently, stanine scores are now used just to indicate relative standing. They are easier to understand than z scores or T scores, as any child or parent can understand that stanines represent a 9-point scale with 1 as the lowest, 5 as the average, and 9 as the highest. Furthermore, unlike percentile ranks, stanine scores can be averaged. When it is desirable to have more precise information about relative standing, however, percentile ranks may be more useful, even though they cannot be averaged.

Local and National Norms Percentile ranks and stanines are often used when local norms are prepared. As noted in our earlier description of how standardized tests are developed, the norms used to determine a student's level of performance are established by asking a representative sample of students to take the final form of the test. Inevitably, there will be differences between school systems (in texts used and the time during a school year or years when certain topics are covered, for instance). Accordingly, some test publishers report scores in terms of local as well as national norms. Each student's performance is thus compared not only with the performance of the members of the standardization group but also with the performance of all students in the same school system.

pause & reflect

If you had to tell parents about the results of a standardized test, which type of score could you explain most clearly: raw score, percentile rank, z score, T score, or stanine score? Which do you think would be most informative for parents? For you? If you do not understand these tests completely, what can you do about this situation?

Misconceptions About the Nature and Use of Standardized Tests

Although the concept of psychological and educational assessment is not a particularly difficult one to grasp, many members of the general public, including educators, draw incorrect inferences about what test scores mean because, for one reason or another, they have one or more of the following misconceptions (Braun & Mislevy, 2005):

1. **A test measures what its name implies.** This misconception can take a couple of forms. First, many people do not realize that a test measures a lot of things, some of which have nothing to do with its title. All test performances are influenced by, for example, familiarity with the testing situation, the type of test used, the way the test is administered, and how the test is scored. Second, a test measures

a particular attribute according to how the person who constructed the test defined that attribute. Consequently, one person's intelligence test may assess certain characteristics that another person's intelligence test chooses to ignore. A common result of holding this naïve belief is that people draw inferences from test scores that are not supported by the validity evidence for that test.

2. **All tests with the same title are the same.** Even though two tests are called seventh-grade science tests, this doesn't mean that they are interchangeable. Even if they have the same format (multiple-choice questions, for example), one may emphasize recall of factual material while the other may emphasize conceptual understanding or problem solving. The goal in assessment is to match a school district's objectives and standards with what a test measures.

3. **A test score accurately reflects what people know and can do.** No test provides a "true" score of an individual's knowledge and capabilities because all tests have built-in measurement error. Consequently, when people retake the same or an equivalent test, their scores vary. The best we can do is to say that a person's so-called true score probably lies between a lower and an upper boundary.

4. **Two tests that claim to measure the same thing can be made interchangeable.** For the reasons mentioned above in point #1, this is the exception rather than the rule. That tests are not interchangeable explains why students in some school districts score well on the reading and math tests of the National Assessment of Educational Progress (NAEP) but not as well on their state's tests of the same skills.

5. **Tests are scored by adding up the number of items people answer correctly.** Whereas this is true for unidimensional tests, or tests in which all items measure the same thing, it is not true for tests that measure different skills in different ways. A language test that measures knowledge of vocabulary and grammar, as well as reading comprehension and conversational fluency, should report separate scores for each capability.

6. **Scores of 70 percent correct, 80 percent correct, and 90 percent correct are equivalent to grades of C, B, and A, respectively.** This belief comes from the naïve assumption that all tests are basically the same. But because test items can be written at different levels of difficulty, two tests that measure the same knowledge base are likely to produce different scores when taken by the same students.

7. **Multiple-choice questions are useful only for measuring how well students can recognize and recall factual knowledge.** This belief undoubtedly stems from the fact that the vast majority of multiple-choice items that appear on tests are written at the knowledge level of Bloom's Taxonomy (first discussed in Chapter 13, "Approaches to Instruction"). But it is possible to write multiple-choice items that reflect the rest of the Taxonomy.

8. **One can tell if an item is good just by looking at it.** As with most things, the mere appearance of an item can be deceiving. Whether or not a test item is good, which is to say useful, depends largely on how well the form and cognitive demands of an item match both the instruction received by the student and the stated purpose of the test. An item for which students have not been adequately prepared or that measures factual knowledge when a test is advertised as measuring ability to apply knowledge is not a good item, at least for that particular test.

Earlier, we pointed out that standardized tests can be used in several ways to support the instructional goals of a school and a teacher. When teachers fully understand the characteristic being measured; when reliable, valid, and well-normed tests are readily available; and when teachers know how to interpret test results appropriately, this strategy for assessing individual differences can work quite well, particularly when it is supplemented with teacher observations and informal assessments. Effective remedial reading and math programs, for example, are based to a large extent on scores from diagnostic reading and math tests. But when tests are used for purposes other than those for which they were designed, misuses occur, and inappropriate decisions and controversy often result. In the next section, we'll take a look at the widespread and controversial practice of high-stakes testing: using standardized test scores to hold students, teachers, and administrators accountable for academic achievement.

USING STANDARDIZED TESTS FOR ACCOUNTABILITY PURPOSES: HIGH-STAKES TESTING

The Push for Accountability in Education

What does it mean to be held accountable for one's actions? Generally, that you must explain and justify your actions to one or more people who have a stake in what you do, and, depending on how your actions are judged, you may be either rewarded or punished. Company employees, for example, are accountable to their supervisors or managers for the decisions they make and the quality of the products they produce. Likewise, students are accountable for the quality of their learning to both their teachers and parents. What about teachers, school administrators, and entire school districts? To whom are they accountable? Historically, they have operated under a looser and less well defined accountability system. Except in cases of blatant incompetence and illegal and/or immoral behavior, teachers and administrators were not likely to be either rewarded or punished for their efforts. That situation changed in 2001, and the reasons for the change can be traced to a growing discontent during the last two decades of the twentieth century with the perceived quality of American education.

In 1983, the National Commission on Excellence in Education published a report titled *A Nation at Risk: The Imperative for Educational Reform*. The report painted a bleak picture of the quality of education in the United States. It noted, for example, that about 13 percent of all seventeen-year-olds were judged to be functionally illiterate, that standardized test scores had generally fallen below levels achieved 25 years earlier, and that many seventeen-year-olds were judged as being deficient in such higher-order thinking skills as drawing inferences from written material and writing a persuasive essay. To justify the amount of money being spent on education and to improve student outcomes, the report called for standardized tests to be used as a way of documenting students' achievement and spurring educators to focus on raising achievement in such basic areas as reading, math, and science.

Subsequent reports of students' performance on standardized tests continued to paint a bleak picture (but see Bracey, 2008a, 2008b, for alternative interpretations). Discontent with the performance of American students and the desire to improve matters resulted in a piece of landmark federal legislation in the early part of this century.

TeachSource Video Case ◀◀ ▶ ▶▶

Teacher Accountability: A Student Teacher's Perspective

Go to the Education CourseMate website and watch the Video Case, and then answer the following questions:

1. A major concern of Caitlin Hollister, the student teacher in this video, is how to deal with students' poor performance on the state exam. On the one hand, she asks how do you not get discouraged? On the other hand, she asks how do you help students learn what they did not learn initially? What advice would you offer her?

2. The principal and veteran teachers in this video all put accountability in a positive light. In what ways do they do so?

No Child Left Behind (NCLB)

In December 2001, the U.S. Congress passed legislation proposed by President George W. Bush to implement testing of students in reading and mathematics in all public schools that receive federal funds. Testing students on their knowledge of science was added in 2007. This legislation, a reauthorization of the Elementary and Secondary Education Act (ESEA), is commonly known as the No Child Left Behind (NCLB) Act. Because the scores from these tests, either by themselves or in conjunction with other data, are used to determine such rewards and punishments as whether students get promoted to the next grade or graduate from high school, whether teachers and administrators receive financial rewards or demotions, and whether school districts receive additional state funds or lose their accreditation, this practice is commonly referred to as high-stakes testing. You can read and download a copy of NCLB at the Department of Education's website (**www.ed.gov/ policy/elsec/leg/esea02/index.html**).

> High-stakes testing: using test results to hold students and educators accountable for achievement

Requirements of NCLB   The No Child Left Behind Act contains several requirements that states must meet (No Child Left Behind Act, 2001):

> NCLB requires standards; annual testing in math, reading, science; annual progress for all students; public reports; accountability system

- *Standards.* States must establish what the law calls challenging content and achievement standards in mathematics, reading or language arts, and science, but the legislation leaves it to each state to decide for itself the meaning of the word *challenging.*
- *Testing.* Annual testing of all students in grades 3 through 8 in math and reading/language arts and at least one assessment of students in grades 9 through 12 in the same two subjects. In 2007, states were required to also administer a science assessment at least once to students in grades 3 through 5, 6 through 9, and 10 through 12. Decisions about test format, length, and item type have been left to each state. Vermont's assessment program, for example, includes mathematics problem solving items, writing samples, and science performance tasks, in addition to the more familiar selected-response items (Vermont Department of Education, 2009). Kentucky's program also includes writing samples, as well as open-ended questions that require students to explain the reasoning behind their answers in reading, science, social studies, mathematics, and the humanities (Kentucky Department of Education, 2009).

To hold students accountable for learning certain subjects and skills at acceptable levels and to improve the quality of education, all states annually administer standardized achievement tests in several subject areas. These tests are linked to state learning standards.
© Bob Daemmrich/The Image Works

- *Adequate Yearly Progress (AYP).* By 2014, all students must score at least at the "proficient" level (as defined by each state) of their state assessment in reading/language arts and math. To ensure that this goal is met, states must demonstrate each year that a certain additional percentage of all students have met that goal. This feature is referred to as adequate yearly progress, or AYP. Adequate yearly progress must be demonstrated by all groups of students, including racial and ethnic minorities, students of low socioeconomic status (SES), English language learners, and students with disabilities. Schools that fail to meet the AYP requirement not only must use different instructional approaches and programs but also must choose approaches and programs that have been shown to be effective by scientific research.

- *Reporting.* States and school districts must issue report cards to parents and the general public that describe how every group of students has performed on the annual assessment.

- *Accountability System.* School districts that fail to demonstrate AYP for 2 or more consecutive years are subject to the following sanctions:

  1. Schools that fail to achieve AYP for 2 consecutive years are identified as needing improvement, and students have the option of transferring to other schools in the district.
  2. Schools that fail to achieve AYP for 3 consecutive years are subject to the actions specified in point 1, and, additionally, students must be provided with supplemental instructional services (such as tutoring) by an outside provider.
  3. Schools that fail to achieve AYP for 4 consecutive years are subject to the actions in points 1 and 2, as well as either replacement of school staff, appointment of outside experts to advise the school, extension of the school day or year, or a change in the school's organizational structure.
  4. Schools that fail to achieve AYP for 5 consecutive years are subject to the actions specified in points 1, 2, and 3, along with restructuring of the school, which can mean replacing all or most of the school staff, state takeover of school operations, or conversion to a charter school.

Schools that meet or exceed AYP for 2 or more consecutive years and that have made the greatest gains are designated "distinguished school" and may make financial awards to teachers.

Although NCLB mandates that students be tested in the areas of reading/language arts, math, and science and that they perform at a particular level, it has been left up to the states to decide which aspects of those subjects will be tested and how different levels of performance will be defined. This does not mean that states have free rein to do whatever they please; each state has an accountability plan for meeting the requirements of NCLB that has been approved by the federal government. States are free to amend these plans in the future, but changes have to be approved by the U.S. Department of Education.

Problems with Implementing NCLB The No Child Left Behind law is both complex and has high stakes attached to it. Consequently, problems with its implementation, both potential and actual, have been noted. Here are a few of them:

- When NCLB was enacted in 2002, states were allowed to specify different schedules for meeting the goal of 100 percent proficiency in math and reading/language arts by 2014. Twenty-three states opted for smaller achievement gains in the early years and larger gains as the deadline of 2014 drew closer, a schedule that is referred to as "backloading." California's goal, for example, was that 13.6 percent of students would score at the proficient or above levels in language arts for each of the first 3 years. The percentage of students scoring proficient or above would rise to 24.4 percent for each of the next 3 years. But for each year from 2007–2008 until 2013–2014, the schedule calls for increases of 11 percentage points. Because achievement gains have been harder to achieve than was anticipated, California and other states that have backloaded schedules are unlikely to meet NCLB's goal of 100 percent proficiency (Chudowsky & Chudowsky, 2008).

- Setting the cutoff score that determines whether or not a student has reached the proficiency level is based on the judgment of educators and carries significant consequences. If the score is set too low, a state's accountability plan may not pass federal muster. If it is set too high, the school may have a difficult time demonstrating AYP. This difference in defining the standard for proficiency probably accounts for a good part of the difference between low-scoring and high-scoring states (Ho, 2008).

- Some states have negotiated with the U.S. Department of Education for a larger minimum subgroup size than the law specifies (Goldberg, 2005; Popham, 2005; Sunderman, 2006), for changes in how AYP is determined, and for the ability to set different proficiency targets for different subgroups (Sunderman, 2006). The result of these changes is a lack of common accountability standards.

- The law fails to acknowledge that many minority students, students with disabilities, and English language learners have long-standing and deep-seated learning problems that make it difficult to accurately assess what they have learned (Abedi & Dietel, 2004; Thomas, 2005). For example, in some states English language learners are placed in 1-year immersion programs and are then required to take a test in English. Another problem is that because many state tests either omitted or underrepresented English language learners during the norming process, their tests may well be inaccurate measures of what these students have learned (Solórzano, 2008). Although English language learners can take state tests in their native languages, such tests are often not available (Center on Education Policy, 2005; Solórzano, 2008).

- Students who qualify for special education must, according to the Individuals with Disabilities Education Act (IDEA), have goals and objectives that match their learning levels incorporated into their individualized education programs (IEPs). But NCLB requires that these students meet the same standards as students without disabilities (Houston, 2005).

Modifications of NCLB

Because of the structural problems inherent in NCLB and the research findings that we note a bit later in this chapter, the federal government has begun to make some changes in the law's accountability system. In March of 2008 the Secretary of Education announced that the U.S. Department of Education would allow states that met certain criteria more flexibility in meeting the requirements of NCLB. Specifically, schools in which most students are meeting the AYP requirement, except for one subgroup, will not have to be labeled as needing improvement. The financial and other resources that ordinarily would have been spent on that school instead can be used to improve the test scores of the lowest-performing schools (U.S. Department of Education, 2008b).

Because of its requirements, NCLB has become a highly controversial piece of educational legislation. Since its inception in 2002, numerous arguments for and against its goals and methods have been made. What follows is a relatively brief sample of the arguments that have been made most often.

Arguments in Support of High-Stakes Testing Programs

The arguments in favor of NCLB have, admittedly, been far fewer in number than the arguments against it, and fall into one of the following four categories.

Goal Clarity A major responsibility of teachers and a contributing factor to effective teaching is the ability to clearly communicate one's educational goals. A state's content and performance standards can help teachers clarify their goals and more clearly communicate those goals to students and parents (Falk, 2002; Hamilton & Stecher, 2004).

<table>
<tr><td>High-stakes tests expected to improve clarity of goals, quality control, teaching methods, and student motivation</td></tr>
</table>

Improved Quality Control For the first time, NCLB requires educators to monitor the academic progress of such traditionally underserved groups as racial and ethnic minorities, students with disabilities, and English language learners as closely as they monitor the progress of regular students and to publicly report the progress of all groups (Cizek, 2001; Hershberg, 2005; Linn, 2003).

Beneficial Effects for Teaching The high-stakes associated with NCLB will stimulate the use of more effective instructional methods, a focus on material that directly relates to a state's content standards, and a greater degree of collaboration among teachers (Clarke, Abrams, & Madaus, 2001; Winkler, 2003).

Beneficial Effects for Students High-stakes tests may motivate students to improve their study skills and work harder to avoid the embarrassment and disruption of academic progress that comes from being retained in a grade or not being allowed to graduate from high school (Clarke et al., 2001).

Arguments Critical of High-Stakes Testing Programs

High-stakes testing programs are frequently criticized because they do not adhere to a rigorous set of assessment guidelines such as those promoted by the American Educational Research Association (2000) and because they are subject to misuse and misinterpretation. In this section we summarize these criticisms in terms of structural limitations, the way test scores are interpreted, the motivational basis on which these programs rest, and an inflexible approach to performance standards.

TeachSource Video Case ◄◄ ▶ ►►

Foundations: Aligning Instruction with Federal Legislation

Go to the Education CourseMate website and watch the Video Case, and then answer the following questions:

1. In this Video Case, various school professionals discuss the challenges of complying with NCLB. As a prospective teacher, what aspects of NCLB do you find most daunting?

2. In your opinion, has federal legislation such as NCLB improved the quality of public education? Use the material in this chapter to find information that will support your argument.

Structural Limitations High-stakes testing programs are perceived to be more of a hindrance than an aid to educators because of the nature of the components that make them up and how those parts fit together.

- NCLB contains what some claim are contradictory goals (see, for example, Linn, 2009; Rothstein, Jacobsen, & Wilder, 2009). On the one hand, NCLB requires that all students demonstrate mastery of "challenging" standards (although the definition of challenging is left up to each state). On the other hand, the law also requires all students to demonstrate proficiency in math and

English by 2014. If one accepts that students vary with respect to learning skills and motivation, that teachers vary with respect to instructional skill, and families vary with respect to how much academically related support they provide their children, then proficiency for all will never be attained regardless of how far into the future the goal is placed. One can, of course, formulate standards that most students can attain, but such standards will not challenge average and above average students and is not what the law seems to intend.

- State assessments that are narrow in scope, limited in range, and shallow in depth may not provide teachers with the type of diagnostic information they need to improve their instruction. Telling a teacher that a student's score was in the "Needs Improvement" category on a reading test does not help that teacher make the next reading lesson more effective (Cizek, 2003; Goldberg, 2005; Neill, 2003; Popham, 2008). Teachers would be better served if they were told which standards a student has or has not mastered and if the standards were described with sufficient clarity so that teachers could draw reasonably accurate inferences about how to remediate the student's weaknesses.

- A test's content, and the learning standards on which the test is based, do not necessarily reflect the knowledge and skills that the majority of people value the most and believe are most important for students to learn. For example, there have been numerous calls for students to be taught and tested for such skills as adaptive problem solving, assessing and responding to risks, managing distractions, attending to tasks, working independently, and working productively in groups (Baker, 2007; Goldberg, 2004; McKim, 2007; Sadker & Zittleman, 2004).

- States frequently adopt far more content standards than teachers can cover and students can master, and they are often worded so generally that it is difficult to be certain about the precise content or skill in question (Clarke et al., 2001; Popham, 2008).

- If you think of education in terms of inputs (teacher and student characteristics, resources, physical environment), processes (instructional and learning processes), and outputs (student knowledge and skills), the main focus of high-stakes testing programs is the output. Although NCLB requires that failing students receive remedial instruction and, if necessary, be allowed to transfer to different schools, the main thrust of the law is to drive school improvement by the imposition of output standards and accountability. High-stakes systems tend to ignore the contributions of input and process variables, or what might be called opportunity to learn. If, for example, students are not given sufficient time to learn, if the classroom and school environments are chaotic and threatening to the students' well-being, if classroom instruction is dull and unresponsive to individual differences, and if students have low levels of self-efficacy for learning and poor self-regulated learning skills, this diminished opportunity to learn is likely to result in a failing test performance (Darling-Hammond, 2009; Houston, 2007; Pianta et al., 2007).

- Schools that record consistent gains in achievement (and that would be rated "good" or "excellent" according to state standards) receive no credit for that accomplishment and are classified as "needing improvement" if the gains are too small to meet AYP requirements. This has been cited as a particularly egregious shortcoming when the gains occur among such at-risk groups as students from low-income families, English language learners, and students with disabilities (Goldberg, 2005; Houston, 2007; Linn, 2009; Mintrop & Sunderman, 2009; Nichols & Berliner, 2005).

High-stakes tests criticized because of structural limitations, misinterpretation/misuse of results, narrow view of motivation, inflexible performance standards

Misinterpretation and Misuse of Test Results   Although high-stakes testing programs do a reasonably good job of assessing mastery of certain learning standards, they do not, because they were not designed to, measure the general quality of a school or an individual teacher's effectiveness. Nevertheless, when faced with district and state report cards that rank schools, many people will draw the intuitively appealing but incorrect inference that high test scores equal good schools and teachers, that low scores equal poor-quality schools and teachers, and that rewarding or punishing schools and teachers on the basis of test scores is appropriate (Camilli, 2003; Cochran-Smith, 2003; Vogler & Kennedy, 2003).

A One-Size-Fits-All Approach to Motivation High-stakes testing programs are based on a limited and simplistic view of motivation. Whether intended or not, the use of rewards and punishments to improve educational outcomes represents a behavioral view of motivation (Houston, 2007; Nichols & Berliner, 2008; Ryan, Ryan, Arbuthnot, & Samuels, 2007). But if you go back to and quickly review Chapter 11 on motivation, you will see that many factors influence an individual's willingness and ability to master learning standards and perform well on standardized assessments. And as we pointed out in other chapters, the values students have about education (which are strongly influenced by parents and peer groups) and the sophistication of their learning skills will also affect their motivation to learn.

For some students, the prospect of gaining rewards and avoiding punishment may be sufficient incentive to work harder. But students who suffer from low self-efficacy, the adoption of avoidance goals, low levels of achievement motivation, maladaptive attributions, inappropriate beliefs about ability, an environment that does not satisfy deficiency needs, a poor academic self-concept, and poorly developed learning skills will likely see learning standards and high-stakes tests as obstacles they cannot overcome regardless of the rewards and punishments. Nevertheless, as our Case in Print illustrates, providing students with external incentives to do well on their state exam has become a prominent part of school life.

A One-Size-Fits-All Approach to Standards Using a similar line of reasoning as those who have argued that not all students will be motivated by the same rewards and punishments, Nel Noddings (2003, 2007) proposes that because students are so different in their interests, abilities, and goals, it is a mistake to hold everyone to the same set of standards. Using the teaching of mathematics as an example, she asks: "To whom shall we teach mathematics? For what ends? Mathematics of what sort? In what relation to students' expressed needs? In what relations to our primary aims?" (2003, p. 87). By raising such questions, Noddings is not necessarily arguing that mathematics should not be taught to some students (although she does believe that the question deserves serious discussion before curriculum and instructional decisions are made). Rather, she suggests that it may be more profitable for more students if they were taught different types of mathematics in different ways and held accountable for the type of mathematics taught. This argument seems particularly cogent when applied to students with disabilities. As we noted in Chapter 6, the main purpose of IDEA is to ensure a free, appropriate education to all children in the least restrictive environment in which they are capable of successfully performing. Obviously, the nature of that education and the environment in which it takes place will be different for children with different disabilities. With respect to taking high-stakes tests, Noddings (2003) says that

> some probably should be encouraged to take them, with only positive stakes attached. It is outrageous, however, to force these tests on all students in special education...If by *equity* we mean providing an appropriate education for every child, it is dead wrong to expect the same performance from each child. Having forgotten our aim, we act as though all children are academically equal and can be held to the same standard. (p. 90)

Undesirable Side Effects Critics of high-stakes testing argue that the rewards and punishments associated with high-stakes testing programs may produce one or more of the following undesirable side effects:

- Many educators fear that the press to meet the demands of NCLB and other state assessment goals will result in more time spent strengthening students' basic math and reading/language arts skills at the expense of time for such subjects as art, music, and foreign languages (Hamilton & Stecher, 2004; Nichols & Berliner, 2005).

- A similar fear has been expressed about the fate of certain forms of instruction. For example, inquiry-based science education has been praised because it emphasizes hands-on science activities as opposed to the traditional reading about science in textbooks and watching the teacher conduct an occasional experiment. But because of the pressure to have students perform well on state-mandated assessments, science educators fear that the amount of time devoted to science instruction will be reduced in favor of test preparation activities and that the instruction that does occur will emphasize drill-and-practice activities because they fit the demands of high-stakes tests (Gallagher, 2005; Nichols & Berliner, 2005).

- To avoid the negative sanctions mandated by NCLB for schools whose students continue to score poorly for several years in a row, states are likely to propose the lowest-level content and performance standards that the federal government will accept (Linn, 2003; Popham, 2005).

Research on the Effects of High-Stakes Testing

| High-stakes testing has so far failed to live up to its promise

Given all the argument about the effects of high-stakes testing, actual research on this subject is vital. But because these programs have been in existence for a relatively short time, the research on their effects is limited, the results are inconsistent, and the implications have been hotly debated. In addition, some of the evidence is merely anecdotal. Nevertheless, we will summarize for you what has been reported about the effects these programs appear to have on student achievement, student motivation, teachers' behavior, classroom instruction, the dropout rate, state standards and test quality, and the use of supplemental education services.

Effect on Achievement   A major assumption underlying NCLB is that the consequences of failing to meet its accountability standards will drive states and school districts to improve the quality of classroom instruction and the level of student achievement. This hypothesis was tested by a group of researchers (Nichols, 2007; Nichols, Glass, & Berliner, 2006) who classified 25 states in terms of how

A possible negative effect of high-stakes testing programs is that teachers may spend more time preparing students for the test and less time on topics and subjects that are not covered by the test.
© 2010 Creatas/
Jupiterimages Corporation

Case in Print

Pep Rallies for High-Stakes Tests: Does Hype Help?

Concern with rankings and the rewards and punishments attached to state assessment programs leads many teachers to provide students with intensive test preparation. Although this practice may raise scores, it often comes at the expense of meaningful learning. (p. 547)

Incentives Are All Over the MAP

VALERIE SCHREMP HAHN AND CORINNE LESTCH

St. Louis Post-Dispatch, 4/8/2009

It's that time of year when principals reward kids with Dilly Bars, pep rallies and parties, and when teachers tend to their students' needs by scrambling eggs at breakfast or assembling s'mores around a campfire.

Welcome to the season of state standardized exams.

In an era when state and federal governments are applying ever increasing pressure for all students to excel on tests, many schools in the St. Louis region are pursuing all avenues to coax better brain performance out of kids.

Tactics range from simple incentives and rewards, to elaborate themed events designed to make the drudgery of filling out test sheet bubbles seem as fun as recess.

And while critics caution about going overboard, the stakes for schools are high.

Under the federal No Child Left Behind Act, all students have to be "proficient" or better on state exams by 2014 or schools face consequences as serious as a state takeover.

This year, the window for taking the Missouri standardized test, or the Missouri Assessment Program, started March 30 and ends April 24. Illinois' two weeks of testing was last month.

Iveland Elementary School in the Ritenour district has converted classrooms into "cabins" so students equate taking a test to going to camp. They also hosted a night of activities with students, parents and teachers that included a campfire and s'mores and special camp T-shirts.

"It relieves some of the stress," said Danielle Sever, a fifth-grade teacher who spearheaded the idea of "Kamp MAP" with other faculty. "They're not taking a test, they're going to camp, and it's amazing how well my students tested this morning."

Some schools keep it low key, simply reminding parents to make sure their children get a good night's sleep and eat a good breakfast during test time.

Other schools base their test motivators on scientific research. At Hanna Woods Elementary in the Parkway district, for example, students taking the test will get goody bags from younger students that include No. 2 pencils and mints. Peppermint, according to research from the University of Cincinnati, can help increase concentration.

At Kennerly Elementary in the Lindbergh School District, the parent association encouraged parents to donate bananas, which are rich in mind-boosting potassium.

In Missouri, students in grades three to eight will be tested in math and communication arts, with students in grades five and eight also being tested in science. High school exams, meanwhile, now have a built-in incentive for students. Under a new system, schools are urged by the state to include standardized exams scores toward a student's final grade in select courses.

Keysor Elementary in Kirkwood calls the standardized testing window a "Big Show," giving students a chance to show off their intelligence.

In Pattonville, Rose Acres Elementary teachers roll out the "red carpet" (a roll of red paper) for students to walk on in the morning on their way to test.

In Brentwood, all elementary students get breakfast in the morning, not just students from low-income families. The middle school teachers even raid the school kitchen to prepare breakfast for their students, who get to carry around special MAP-testing water bottles to ensure they stay hydrated for the test.

"We encourage them, but we don't want to get them stressed out about it," said Assistant Superintendent David Faulkner.

Last week, Rapper Joka, also known as Robert McKee, visited a pep rally at Livingston Elementary in St. Louis, and performed the "MAP Rap." It says, in part: "I can be successful, I can be successful, watch me be successful, 'cause I can zap the MAP!"

Other school districts take a more temperate view on the rallies and incentives. Ladue and Clayton, for example, don't do anything particularly special to motivate students.

"While there may be snacks from parent associations during the breaks, I think the main focus is on encouraging the students to show what they know," said Kathy Reznikov, spokeswoman for Ladue schools.

Consciously or not, teachers don't want to send the message that they "teach to the test" or that the future of students relies solely within a certain testing window.

Robert Schaeffer, public education director for FairTest, a group that promotes a rethinking of standardized exams, says teachers and principals are caught between their obligation to students and policymakers who put an emphasis on standardized testing.

"Providing a good breakfast—you can't argue with that," said Schaeffer. "But some of the gimmicks, like car lotteries, go way too far. The amount of effort and money spent on getting kids ready for tests show how important a test has become. You don't do that sort of stuff for the debate society or the math team or the science fair."

David Figlio, an education and social policy professor at Northwestern University, said pretending that students are going to camp and bringing in a rapper is a way for educators to make sure students know they're responsible for their performance.

As for doling out breakfast foods and mints, Figlio said it works—but schools have to be careful of the short-term effects.

"If you carbo-load kids to do really well in March 2009, now if you're trying to make gains from there and have scores artificially inflated, what happens in 2010?" he said. "It has to be inflated even more, and you can see it kind of gets absurd."

Still, many teachers say their motivation strategies are producing surprising results.

Third-graders at Green Pines Elementary in Rockwood have capped off each morning of testing with daily rewards such as an extra recess, board game time and snacks. Teacher Kristin Kemp said one of her students missed testing time because of the flu. The girl's mother e-mailed to say how disappointed her daughter was to miss testing and class celebrations.

"I'm like, 'Excuse me?'" said Kemp, pleasantly surprised by the response.

And at Hanna Woods, Assistant Principal Nicole Evans says even the younger students who don't have to take the test get into the spirit. "We've heard them say, 'Ooh, I can't wait to take the test,'" she said.

Questions and Activities

1. The schools mentioned in this article used a variety of methods to motivate students to do well on their state's standardized test. These methods ranged from reminding parents to make sure their children get a good night's sleep and eat a balanced breakfast the morning of the test to simulating a nighttime camp experience. Which, if any, of these activities would you endorse as a teacher? Why?

2. Robert Schaeffer, the public education director of FairTest, argues against the use of extreme incentives for testing programs, partly on the grounds that schools do not do the same thing for debate societies, math teams, or science fairs. What do you think would be the first rebuttal teachers and administrators would probably make to Mr. Schaeffer's criticism?

3. High schools in Missouri are being encouraged to use students' test scores as a factor in calculating their final grade. Based on what you read in this chapter about test validity, does this strike you as a reasonable practice?

much pressure their testing programs placed on teachers and students and then examined the relationship between these various programs and performance by fourth- and eighth-grade students on the math and reading scores of the National Assessment of Educational Progress (NAEP) tests. They found no relationship between earlier pressure from high-stakes tests and later achievement.

Other analyses have reported positive but small effects. Jaekyung Lee (2008) analyzed 14 studies and concluded that the effect of high-stakes testing on NAEP reading and math scores was so modest that NCLB's goal of achieving 100 percent proficiency for all students by 2014 would not likely be attained. The Center on

Education Policy (2008a, 2009) found that between 2002 and 2008 more states reported gains in both average test scores and percentage of students scoring at the proficient level than reported declines. Gains in math were stronger than gains in reading.

Because the express purpose of NCLB is to raise the achievement of *all* students, we also need to examine the evidence pertaining to gains for minority students, low-income students, students with disabilities, and English language learners. As we noted in Chapter 5, there is a long-standing achievement gap between White students and Black and Hispanic students. The evidence to date suggests that NCLB has had, at best, a small effect on narrowing that gap. The gap between White and Black or between White and Hispanic students on NAEP reading and math scores from 2004 through 2008 has not changed (U.S. Department of Education, 2008a). On state tests, gaps between White and minority students have narrowed somewhat but still remain as large as 20 percentage points in many instances (Center on Education Policy, 2009). Similar conclusions can be drawn about the performance of low-income students, students with learning disabilities, and English language learners (Jones, 2007; Lee, 2008).

Before concluding from this limited evidence that NCLB has or has not improved students' achievement, a few important caveats need to be kept in mind. First, the gains reported by some states may be due to intensive teaching to the test, changes in the cutoff scores that define "proficiency," and the effect of school reform programs begun by some states prior to the implementation of NCLB. Second, comparing state test scores with NAEP scores should be done cautiously because NAEP tests are not as closely aligned with state standards and local curricula as are state tests (see, for example, Fuller, Gesicki, Kang, & Wright, 2006). Third, as the Center on Education Policy (2008a) points out, and as we have pointed out in earlier chapters, test scores are not the same thing as achievement because they measure learning imperfectly and incompletely.

Effect on Motivation Some evidence suggests that the presence of high stakes motivates some students to work harder. Among Massachusetts high school students who failed that state's high-stakes test the first time they took it, about two-thirds said they were now working harder and paying more attention in class, and almost 75 percent said that missing too much school was a major reason for failing the test (Cizek, 2003).

In 1996, the Chicago Public Schools instituted a high-stakes testing program that required third, sixth, and eighth graders to pass the reading and mathematics sections of the Iowa Test of Basic Skills to be promoted to the next grade. During the school year leading up to the test, students could receive extra help both before school and through an after-school program. Students who failed the test were required to attend a summer program before they could retake the test and be promoted for the fall semester. Those who failed the second test were retained.

An analysis of 102 low-achieving students (Roderick & Engel, 2001) revealed that the program affected different students in different ways. About 53 percent of the students reported greater attention to class work, increased academic expectations and support from their teachers, and greater effort both in and out of class. The students interpreted the higher expectations and support from teachers as evidence that the teachers cared about them and wanted them to succeed. A second and much smaller group (about 9 percent) also worked hard to prepare for the test but received most of their support outside of school from parents and other family members. A third group of students, about 35 percent of the sample, expressed concern about passing the test and was aware of the before- and after-school help that was available but did not take advantage of it. The fourth and smallest group of students (about 4 percent) wasn't worried about passing the test and wasn't considered by teachers to be at risk of failing.

To examine the relationship between effort and test performance, students from the first three groups were reassigned to one of the following categories: Substantial Work Effort Either in or out of School, No Substantial Work Effort, or Substantial Home or Skill Problems. Of the 53 students in the Substantial Work Effort group, 57 percent passed the test in June, 23 percent passed in August, and 20 percent were retained. Of the 28 students in the No Substantial Work Effort group, 11 percent passed in June, 25 percent passed in August, and 64 percent were retained. Of the 17 students in the Substantial Home or Skill Problems group, 12 percent passed in June, 47 percent passed in August, and 41 percent were retained.

These findings clearly show, as have other interventions mentioned in previous chapters, that no single policy or approach will work for all students because classroom learning is an extremely complex phenomenon that is only partly under the teacher's control. Although the threat of retention was sufficient to motivate some students to work harder and take advantage of the additional resources that were provided, it had a much smaller effect on students with serious learning skill deficits and/or problems at home and on students who simply declined to put forth more effort. Retaining students who fall into these latter two groups is likely to cause them to become even more disengaged and eventually drop out of school. Obviously, an alternative to retention is required to motivate these students and raise their achievement levels.

Effect on Teachers and Teaching Numerous studies have documented that high-stakes testing programs affect how teachers teach and their motivation for teaching. The effects have been mostly negative, although positive effects are occasionally noted.

NCLB changes how teachers teach

A review of research on the effects of NCLB (Au, 2007) found that teachers were focusing on small, isolated, test-size pieces of information at the expense of relating new content to other subject matter and were emphasizing lecture rather than more student-centered instructional techniques. But a few studies reported an increase in lessons that emphasized knowledge integration and the use of student-centered instruction (such as cooperative learning).

School districts have shown an increasing tendency to focus additional instructional time and resources on so-called "bubble kids." These are students who are "on the bubble," meaning they narrowly missed the proficiency cutoff score. If their scores can be raised by a relatively small amount the next time the test is given, they offer schools an easy and inexpensive way to meet their AYP requirement, but often at the expense of those who score even lower (Ho, 2008; Houston, 2007).

A 2-year study of 10 low-performing Chicago elementary schools (Finnigan & Gross, 2007) found that in response to their schools being placed on probation, a majority of teachers reported that they tried new instructional methods, increased the amount of time devoted to test preparation, grouped students by skill level, spent more time preparing lesson plans, and spent more time working with students who had failed to pass the test by a small amount (the so-called "bubble kids" referred to earlier). But these efforts were not sustained for the most part because students' subsequent test scores did not increase and administrators were not supporting teachers' efforts (many teachers complained, for example, about a lack of professional development workshops). As a result, teacher morale decreased.

Observations of and interviews with teachers in other states have reported similar findings. In response to the pressures produced by NCLB, teachers devote more time to test preparation (3 to 5 weeks by some accounts), gear lessons to the content of the test, use more teacher-directed forms of instruction (such as lecture, assigned seatwork, and asking questions that have only one brief answer), increase the pace of instruction to insure that the prescribed content for each day's lesson was covered, and spend less time devising instructional strategies aimed at helping all students understand lesson content and more time grouping and regrouping students. The only instructional benefit mentioned by teachers was that test data that was aligned with state standards could be used to identify students' weaknesses (Anderson, 2009; Center on Education Policy, 2008b; Jennings & Rentner, 2006; Thomas B. Fordham Institute, 2008; Valli & Buese, 2007).

Concern with rankings and the rewards and punishments attached to state assessment programs leads many teachers to provide students with intensive test preparation. Although this practice may raise scores, it often comes at the expense of meaningful learning (Center on Educational Policy, 2005; Goldberg, 2004; Houston, 2007; Nichols & Berliner, 2005). Consequently, there is often little transfer to other tests that purport to measure the same knowledge and skills (Linn, 2009; McGill-Franzen & Allington, 2006).

For example, in one study 83 percent of students in a Pittsburgh elementary school scored above the national norm on the reading test of the Iowa Test of Basic Skills (a standardized achievement test). But on the reading test of the state assessment, only 26 percent scored within the top two proficiency levels (Yau, 2002). The phenomenon this study highlights is sometimes referred to as WYTIWYG: what you test is what you get. In other words, high-stakes assessments lead teachers to focus on preparing students for a particular type of test, and, as a result, there is little carryover to other tests that measure the same or similar skills.

Effect on the Curriculum There is little question at this point that NCLB has caused many school districts to narrow their curricula (Au, 2007; Center on Education Policy, 2008b; Jennings & Rentner, 2006; Jones, 2007; McMurrer, 2007). A survey of 349 school districts conducted by the Center on Educational Policy (McMurrer, 2007) found that between 2001–2002 and 2006–2007 almost two thirds of these districts increased instructional time for reading and language arts by an average of 46 percent and increased math instruction by an average of 37 percent. In addition, the specific aspects of reading/language arts and math that were emphasized were those covered by their state test. Because school days are rarely lengthened, this increase had to come at the expense of other subjects and activities. As expected, almost half of the surveyed districts reported that they decreased instructional time for social studies (ironic when you think about the criticism that schools receive when students are unable to locate various countries on a map), science, art, music, physical education, lunch, and recess (recall our discussion in Chapter 3 about the value of recess). A school district in Missouri did just that when it eliminated a semester-long course on world geography to create a yearlong course on U.S. government. This change was made, despite protests from parents and some students, to align the district's curriculum with state standards and the state's assessment program (Bock, 2008).

Effect on the Dropout Rate The question of whether high-stakes exams, particularly high school exit exams, increase the dropout rate (currently about 5 percent of all high school students) is a difficult one to answer definitively. Not only is the research limited, it is also inconclusive because states define and count dropouts differently, and it is difficult for researchers to isolate the effect of a high-stakes test from other factors that may also be playing a role (Kober et al., 2006). Nevertheless, a report from the Center on Education Policy concluded that exit exams cause more students to drop out of school than would otherwise be the case (Center on Education Policy, 2006). Additional evidence in support of that claim was provided by an in-depth study of high-poverty high schools in a major urban district (McNeil, Coppola, Radigan, & Vasquez Heilig, 2008). These researchers found that the high-stakes testing system in the state of Texas contributed to high school dropout rates of approximately 45 percent for Black students and almost 50 percent for Latino students. To eliminate the arguments about calculating dropout rates that arose from different definitions and formulas, the U.S. Secretary of Education in April of 2008 announced that all states would use the same federal formula to calculate graduation and dropout rates (U.S. Department of Education, 2008b).

Effect on State Standards and Test Quality   Critics of NCLB warned that some states would be tempted to formulate weaker standards and establish lower cutoff scores for judging students proficient so as to avoid the penalties of not meeting AYP requirements. Recent research indicates that this has indeed happened. A study of 26 states by the Thomas B. Fordham Institute and the Northwest Evaluation Association (Cronin, Dahlin, Adkins, & Petrilli, 2007) found that state tests differed significantly in their difficulty, that states with the highest standards (meaning higher cutoff scores) were most likely to lower their cutoff scores than other states, that some state tests replaced more difficult items with easier items, and that tests given to eighth graders were consistently more difficult than tests given to third graders (tests for each grade level should be equally difficult for students in those grades). Because of these inconsistencies the authors of this report note, "five years into implementation of the No Child Left Behind Act, there is no common understanding of what 'proficiency' means" (p. 7). Furthermore, states that have the lowest standards for attaining proficiency happen to have larger concentrations of low-SES students and students of color. In other words, ethnic and racial minority students and students from poor homes are often held to lower standards, just the sort of discrepancy that NCLB was supposed to eliminate (Reed, 2009).

> No common meaning of proficiency among states

A major test quality issue is the breadth of testing that is done to satisfy state and federal requirements. As we noted earlier, the inferences that are drawn from test scores about what students have learned are likely to be more accurate as more and different types of tests are used. Critics of NCLB feared that states would either adopt a single commercially published standardized test whose correspondence to state standards was less than desirable, or would create relatively simple constructed-response tests for the sake of efficiency and cost. Although many states have indeed gone this route, some have opted for a broad range of assessment instruments that are likely to give teachers more diagnostically useful information. In New York, for example, a group of 28 high schools called the New York Performance Standards Consortium practices and promotes the use of alternative assessments (New York Performance Standards Consortium, 2007). These schools, which are not unlike most high schools in New York, use inquiry-based methods of learning that emphasize classroom discussion, project-based assignments, and student choice. Their assessments are performance-based, and to graduate all students must receive a passing grade on an analytic literary essay, a social studies research paper, an original science experiment, and an application of higher-level mathematics. At least one study found that 77 percent of students from these schools attended a 4-year college and earned, on average, a GPA of 2.7 (on a 1–4 scale) (Foote, 2007).

Use of Supplemental Education Services   Although NCLB requires schools that fail to meet AYP for 3 or more consecutive years to provide free tutoring to students, only 17 percent of eligible students received this service during the 2005–2006 school year (Vernez, et al., 2009). Students in small and rural school systems are less likely to receive tutoring than those in urban districts because of the lack of providers in those areas, the lack of transportation to a tutoring provider, or the lack of computers to access Internet-provided services (Goldberg, 2005; Richard, 2005). Although school districts that have failed to meet AYP goals are prohibited from providing their own tutoring services, the Department of Education in 2005 allowed the city of Chicago to do so to encourage more students to take advantage of the service. Several other large urban districts were said to be readying their own proposals for a similar exemption (Gewertz, 2005).

Recommendations for Improving High-Stakes Testing

If NCLB and state-mandated assessment programs are to fulfill their goals of improving the quality of instruction and raising achievement levels, they will have to be implemented in such a way that all stakeholders believe they are being treated fairly. On this score, NCLB appears to be off to a rocky start. A handful of school districts around the country have decided to forgo Title I money from the federal government to be free of NCLB's requirements (Hoff, 2006), and several states have sued the federal government for not providing sufficient funds to implement all of the law's provisions (Dobbs, 2005).

While political leaders complain about funding, educators argue that the goal of having all students be proficient in math and reading/language arts by 2014 is unrealistic and will bring about the demise of fundamentally sound schools (Mabry, 2008; Nichols & Berliner, 2005; Popham, 2009; Thomas, 2005). Still others (for example, Darling-Hammond, 2009; Sadker & Zittleman, 2004) argue that most accountability programs have adopted the wrong focus. A more useful accountability system is one that holds policymakers accountable for the effects of their high-stakes accountability systems. In this view, an accountability system that focuses exclusively on the test scores of students, classes, schools, and districts—ignoring wide disparities in educational opportunity because of differences in funding and facilities—is an irresponsible system.

In response to the many criticisms of high-stakes testing programs, several professional and nonprofit organizations (see, for example, Commission on Instructionally Supportive Assessment, 2002; Center on Education Policy, 2007) have made numerous recommendations for improving NCLB, including the following:

pause & reflect

Critics of high-stakes testing suggest that teachers try to persuade policymakers to change the worst aspects of such programs. They recommend steps such as these: speak out at school board meetings; organize a letter-writing campaign to the school board and legislators; assemble a delegation to visit legislators; write letters to the local newspaper; set up a workshop on the abuses of high-stakes testing. How many of these activities are you willing to engage in? Why?

1. Each state should adopt only those content standards that represent the most important knowledge and skills that students need to learn. This will help states avoid having more standards than teachers can cover, students can master, and test makers can assess. Having a more modest set of standards also allows educators, students, and parents to get feedback about performance for each standard instead of a single score summed over hundreds of standards.

2. A state's content standards should clearly describe exactly what is being assessed so teachers can create lessons that directly address those standards. Phrases such as "express and interpret information and ideas," for example, should be translated into more precise language.

3. Scores on a state assessment should be reported on a standard-by-standard basis for each student, school, and district.

4. States should provide school districts with additional assessment procedures to assess those standards that the required assessment does not cover.

5. States should monitor the curricula of school districts to ensure that instruction addresses all content standards and subjects, not just those assessed by the required state test.

6. State assessments should be designed so that all students have an equal opportunity to demonstrate which of the state's standards they have mastered. This includes providing accommodations and alternative assessments for students with disabilities and those who are limited in their English proficiency. The IEP of students with disabilities should be used to determine how they should be tested and to what standards they should be held accountable.

7. All tests should satisfy the Standards for Educational and Psychological Testing of the American Educational Research Association and similar test-quality guidelines.

8. Teachers and principals should receive professional development training that helps them use test results to optimize children's learning.

Take a Stand!

Healing the Patient: Using the Medical Model to Guide Educational Accountability

Almost everybody, including educators, accepts the contention that educators should be held accountable for their efforts. Indeed, every person should be accountable to others in some fashion. What is, and should be, vigorously debated is the way in which accountability is defined and practiced. We believe that the accountability systems of many states are less effective than they could be because their primary focus is on identifying and punishing substandard performance rather than identifying and remediating the causes of those weaknesses.

We agree with measurement expert Gregory Cizek, who argues that if high-stakes programs are to be more widely embraced by educators, students, and parents, they should mimic the assessment approach that physicians use in their practices. Medical tests tend to be diagnostic in nature because of the detailed level at which they report results. A typical analysis of a blood

sample, for example, provides information on the levels of more than 20 elements (e.g., blood sugar, sodium, potassium, calcium, protein, HDL cholesterol, LDL cholesterol, and triglyceride). Abnormal results are then followed by specific recommendations for treatment. The patient isn't accused of being inferior and charged twice the doctor's normal fee as a penalty for having "failing" test scores.

Consequently, a reasonable stand for teachers to take regarding high-stakes testing programs is that they should be constructed to provide detailed information about students' strengths and weaknesses; these results should then serve as a basis for additional instruction. In addition, professional development workshops and seminars should be provided, focusing on how teachers can help students learn the knowledge and skills that are assessed.

 What Do You Think?

Would you agree with using a medical model for high-stakes testing? What can you do in your own school to promote this view of testing? To explore this issue further, see the Take a Stand! section of the textbook's Education CourseMate website.

9. At least once every 3 years, states should be required to have their standards and assessments independently reviewed.

10. To satisfy the AYP requirement, states should have the option of substituting improvement of test scores of individual students rather than the current requirement of measuring an entire group's progress.

As this chapter was being written, the Obama administration announced that it will recommend changes to NCLB when Congress takes up the law's reauthorization. Some of the proposed changes are clearly in response to the criticisms and suggestions for improvement described earlier in this section. Here are a few of the major features the administration would like to see included in the new law. One change is that schools be graded on students' academic growth rather than on whether a certain percentage of students score at the proficient or higher levels. Second, instead of requiring that all students reach proficiency in reading and math by 2014, they will require instead that all high school graduates be prepared for college and a career. Third, schools will be judged on how well they are closing the achievement gap between poor and minority students and more affluent students. Lastly, they will propose eliminating the feature that students can transfer out of failing schools to other schools in their district or to another district. Given the myriad factors that influence the legislative process, the final form of the revised NCLB is unknowable at this point. But whatever features the new law has, you will need to be prepared to meet its demands.

STANDARDIZED TESTING AND TECHNOLOGY

Given the prevalence of standardized testing and the large amount of money that schools spend on testing programs, it is not too surprising that technology tools exist for a wide range of assessment formats, including the standard true-false, multiple-choice, and fill-in-the-blank questions, as well as alternative assessments such as essay writing, debate forums, simulations, and electronic exhibitions of student work. As we discuss in this section, technology can be used in all phases of testing, including preparing students for standardized tests, administering tests, and scoring students' responses.

Using Technology to Prepare Students for Assessments

For students to perform well on standardized tests, they need to have a clear understanding of the standards for which they will be held accountable and the types of items that will be used to assess those standards. Toward that end, many states provide web-based resources to help students become familiar with and prepare for state assessments. On the websites of state departments of education, students, teachers, and parents can read or download copies of their state's content and performance standards, study examples of the types of items that will appear on the test, and, in some cases, take practice tests. The University of Texas, for example, provides online tutorials and practice tests to that state's high school students to help them prepare for the required graduation exam (Carnevale, 2004). During the 2006–2007 school year, 112 Tennessee schools participated in the Tennessee Formative Assessment Pilot Project. Students in grades 3 through 8 took online formative assessments that were aligned with state standards to help teachers monitor which students were and were not on track to pass the end-of-year state assessment (Tennessee Department of Education, 2006).

Some states and school districts also make available the online test preparation services of private, for-profit companies. The Princeton Review, for example, has a 130,000-question test bank that school districts can use to create online practice tests that are aligned with their states' standards for grades 3 through 12. A company called Smarthinking (**www.smarthinking.com**) provides tutoring through online instructors (called "e-structors") and digital whiteboards. Students can correspond with tutors in real time or submit questions and assignments and get a response within 24 hours. The digital whiteboard is used by students to demonstrate their understanding of concepts and skills (such as English grammar or mathematical problem solving), and also by the tutor, who adds comments and corrections.

On the website of TestGEAR (**www.testu.com**), students take a diagnostic pretest and are then provided with individualized courses in various aspects of math and language arts. Teachers receive diagnostic reports that analyze students' responses to test questions. A teacher in an Orlando, Florida, school who used the TestGEAR service was convinced that it helped his students improve their scores on that state's high-stakes test, the Florida Comprehensive Assessment Test (Borja, 2003).

Using Technology to Assess Mastery of Standards

Administering standardized tests via computer (called computer-based testing, or CBT for short) is something you are likely to see more often in the coming years. One reason is that the National Assessment of Educational Progress (NAEP) is moving in that direction. The 2009 science assessment, which includes simulations, is given on computer and the 2011 writing assessment is scheduled to be given that way as well (Schneider, 2006). Another factor that may push schools in the direction of CBT is that students who take the same test either on a computer or on paper earn the same scores. This should eliminate the concern that factors like computer familiarity and anxiety will adversely affect students' scores (Wang, Jiao, Young, Brooks, & Olson, 2008). Nevertheless, you should still be aware of CBTs advantages and disadvantages. On the plus side:

- You can get scores and detailed reports at any time, from immediately after a test is completed to a few days later, and can therefore provide students with timely feedback (Chaney & Gilman, 2005; Olson, 2002; Russo, 2002).
- CBT reduces the chances of cheating by allowing you to create as many random sequences of test items as there are students taking the test (Chaney & Gilman, 2005).
- It is easier to use novel items to assess certain skills. For example, a computer screen could display the periodic table of elements with a question mark in five of the cells and the five elements that belong in those cells above the table. The student would have to drag each element to its correct location and then drop it (release the mouse button) (Zenisky & Sireci, 2002).

On the negative side:

- It is costly to buy and maintain enough computers to test large groups of students. One high school in Indiana, for example, had to close four computer labs for a month to test every student.

Websites of state departments of education, private companies provide services that help prepare students for state assessments

To explore websites mentioned in this chapter, go to the web links section of the Education CourseMate website.

- Schools need to have a plan for dealing with interruptions due to a faulty computer or a power loss (Olson, 2003).

Using Technology to Promote Mastery of Standards

Given the high stakes involved in meeting the AYP requirement of NCLB, you can expect to see school districts doing everything they can to raise test scores, including the use of technology. A case in point is a Massachusetts high school that used computer-based instruction to significantly increase the math scores of students who were at risk of failing that part of the state's standardized test, the Massachusetts Comprehensive Assessment System (MCAS). Sophomores whose eighth-grade MCAS scores were less than acceptable were required to take a daily 45-minute CBI course whose content was aligned with the math standards assessed by the MCAS. The program adopted by the school district was based on the mastery approach that we outlined in the previous chapter. Students worked independently at their own pace on relatively brief segments of material called modules. Before being allowed to progress to the next module, students had to score at least 80 percent correct on the end-of-module exam. The effect on their tenth-grade math MCAS scores was quite noticeable. Although the average scale score (a type of standardized score) of students not required to take the CBI course was higher than the average score of those who were in the CBI program (245 vs. 236, respectively), the eighth-grade scores of the CBI students (who were considered to be at-risk) were considerably lower (215 vs. 234, respectively). Thus, the CBI students experienced a greater gain from eighth-grade to tenth-grade than did the non-CBI students. The gap between these two groups in the eighth grade was 19 points (Hannafin & Foshay, 2008).

Computer Adaptive Testing

Technology has also shaped the way tests are put together and administered. Instead of subjecting every student to the same sequence of test items, **computer adaptive testing (CAT)** allows students to take tests that are geared to their own ability levels. When a student begins a test in the CAT format, the computer selects an item that matches his or her estimated ability. If the student responds correctly, the computer selects a slightly more difficult item. An incorrect response results in an easier item. After each correct or incorrect response, the computer estimates the student's

In coming years, it is likely that increasing numbers of students will take high-stakes and other standardized tests on a computer. © Michael Newman/Photo Edit

ability. The test ends when the computer determines that it has reached the limits of the student's knowledge (Olson, 2005; Wilson, 2005; Yeh, 2006).

The major advantages of CAT are tests that are only as long as they need to be for each examinee, immediate feedback on achievement growth, and information about students' strengths and weaknesses that can help teachers better target their instructional efforts (Olson, 2005). The major disadvantages are increased test anxiety and confusion for those not familiar or comfortable with taking a test on a computer and high test-taking fees because of the high cost involved in developing and implementing such a system (Latu & Chapman, 2002).

In an interesting turn of events, several states that had intended to use CAT to meet the requirements of NCLB had to change course. The reason is that NCLB requires that students be evaluated only according to the expectations for their grade level. Taking a test that contains items that are either easier or harder than what is normal for a grade level, as in the case of computer adaptive tests, is considered "out-of-level" testing and is not allowed (Trotter, 2003). One state, however, believes it has solved this problem. The Idaho Standards Achievement Test is a state assessment that contains the adaptive feature of CAT but also satisfies NCLB requirements. It does this by first presenting students with grade-level test items and then moves into the adaptive portion of the test (Olson, 2005). School districts in other states, such as South Dakota, Kentucky, and California, are using CAT either to satisfy other accountability goals or to promote the use of formative assessment (Stokes, 2005; Trotter, 2003; Wilson, 2005; see also discussion of formative assessment in Chapter 14).

In the next section we offer several Suggestions for Teaching that will help you and your students appropriately use standardized tests and interpret the scores from them.

Computer adaptive testing: computers determine sequence and difficulty level of test items

Suggestions for Teaching

Using Standardized Tests

1 **Before you give a standardized test, emphasize that students should do their best.**

For maximum usefulness, scores on standardized tests should be as accurate a representation of actual ability as possible.

Accordingly, the day before a standardized test is scheduled, tell your students that they should do their best. Emphasize that the scores will be used to help them improve their school performance and will provide useful feedback to you about the quality of your instruction. If you're thinking about ignoring this suggestion because you don't believe that students will score significantly higher on a standardized test in response to a simple pep talk, you might want to reconsider. Research has shown that students who have a positive attitude toward learning and test taking score higher on tests than do students whose attitudes are less positive or are negative (Brown & Walberg, 1993; Gulek, 2003).

JOURNAL ENTRY
Explaining Test-Taking Skills

2 **Before your students take a standardized test, give them specific suggestions for taking such tests.**

You may be able partly to reduce the anxiety and tension that are almost inevitable under formal testing conditions by giving some test-taking hints in advance. Robert

Suggestions for Teaching

Linn and M. David Miller (2005) note the following tips that might be stressed (depending on the type of test and the grade level of the student):

1. Listen to or read directions carefully.
2. Listen to or read test items carefully.
3. Set a pace that will allow time to complete the test.
4. Bypass difficult items and return to them later.
5. Make informed guesses rather than omit items.
6. Eliminate as many alternatives as possible on multiple-choice items before guessing.
7. Follow directions carefully when marking the answer sheet (for example, be sure to darken the entire space).
8. Check to be sure the item number and answer number match when marking an answer.
9. Check to be sure the appropriate response is marked on the answer sheet.
10. Go back and check the answers if time permits. (pp. 450–451)

❸ Examine the test booklet and answer sheet in advance so that you are familiar with the test.

Ideally you might take an earlier released version of the test or a publicly available practice test yourself so that you become thoroughly familiar with what your students will be doing. If there are any aspects of recording answers that are especially tricky or if the test contains unfamiliar terminology, you might mention these when you give your test-taking skills presentation or when you hand out examination booklets and answer sheets. Knowledge of test vocabulary and terminology has been found to have a significant effect on students' performance on high-stakes tests (Gulek, 2003).

JOURNAL ENTRY
Interpreting Test Scores

❹ Be cautious when interpreting scores, and always give the student the benefit of the doubt.

The profiles or reports you will receive a few weeks after a test has been administered will contain information that is potentially beneficial to you and your students. If misused or misinterpreted, however, the information is potentially harmful. Misinterpretations of scores can lead to complaints by parents. Therefore, as you examine the scores, concentrate on ways you can make positive use of the results.

For example, if a student's test scores are lower than you expected them to be, examine them to discover areas of weakness but guard against thinking, "Well, I guess he had me fooled. He's not as sharp as I thought he was. Maybe I had better lower his grades a notch on the next report card." There are many reasons a student may not do well on a test (for example, anxiety, fatigue, illness, worry about some home or school interpersonal situation), and scores may not be an accurate reflection of current capability. Thus, whenever there is a discrepancy between test scores and observed classroom performance, always assume that the more favorable impression is the one to use as an indication of general capability. Try to use indications of below-average performance in constructive ways to help students overcome inadequacies.

To spur your reflections about standardized tests, see the Thought Questions and Reflective Journal Questions on the textbook's student website, Education CourseMate.

❺ Do your best to control the impact of negative expectations.

As you peruse student test scores, do your best to resist the temptation to label or categorize students, particularly those who have a consistent pattern of low scores. Instead of succumbing to thoughts that such students are incapable of learning, you might make an effort to concentrate on the idea that they need extra encouragement and individualized attention. Use the information on test profiles to help them overcome their learning difficulties, not to justify fatalistically ignoring their problems.

6 **Be prepared to offer parents clear and accurate information about their children's test scores.**

For a variety of reasons, misconceptions about the nature of standardized tests are common. As a result, many parents do not fully understand what their children's scores mean. Parent-teacher conferences are probably the best time to correct misconceptions and provide some basic information about the meaning of standardized test scores. In an unobtrusive place on your desk, you might keep a brief list of points to cover as you converse with each parent. In one way or another, you should mention that test scores should be treated as *estimates* of whatever was measured (achievement, for example). There are two reasons for representing test scores in this fashion:

- Tests do not (indeed, they cannot) assess everything that students know or that makes up a particular capability. Standardized achievement tests, for example, tend to cover a relatively broad range of knowledge but do not assess any one topic in great depth. Therefore, students may know more than their scores suggest.

- All tests contain some degree of error because of such factors as vaguely worded items, confusing directions, and low motivation on the day the test is administered.

Remember that a student's test score reflects the extent to which the content of that test has been mastered at about the time the test was taken. A student may have strengths and weaknesses not measured by a particular test, and because of changes in such characteristics as interests, motives, and cognitive skills, test scores can change, sometimes dramatically. The younger the student is and the longer the interval is between testings (on the same test), the greater is the likelihood that a test score will change significantly.

What a test score means depends on the nature of the test. If your students took an intelligence test or a scholastic aptitude test, point out that such tests measure the current status of those cognitive skills that most closely relate to academic success. Also mention that IQ scores are judged to be below average, average, or above average on the basis of how they compare with the scores of a norm group.

If you are discussing achievement test scores, make sure you understand the differences among diagnostic tests, norm-referenced tests, and criterion-referenced tests:

- Scores from a diagnostic achievement test can be used to discuss a student's strengths and weaknesses in such skills as reading, math, and spelling.

- Scores from a norm-referenced achievement test can be used to discuss general strengths and weaknesses in one or more content areas. For achievement tests that provide multiple sets of norms, start your interpretation at the most local level (school norms, ideally), because they are likely to be the most meaningful to parents, and then move to a more broad-based interpretation (district, state, or national norms).

- Scores from a criterion-referenced achievement test can be used to discuss how well a student has mastered the objectives on which the test is based. If there is a close correspondence between the test's objectives and your own objectives as a teacher, the test score can be used as an indicator of how much the student has learned in class.

The instructional decisions you make in the classroom will be *guided* but not dictated by the test scores. Many parents fear that if their child obtains a low score on a test, she will be labeled a slow learner by the teacher and receive less attention than higher-scoring students do. This is a good opportunity to lay such a fear to rest in two ways. First, note that test scores are but *one* source of information about students. You will also take into account how well they perform on classroom tests, homework assignments, and special projects, as well as in classroom discussions. Second, emphasize that you are committed to using test scores not to classify students but to help them learn.

To review this chapter, try the tutorial quizzes and other study aids on the textbook's Education CourseMate website.

Challenging Assumptions

The Right Test?

"So, with all of these complaints about testing, is it the tests themselves or how the tests are used that's the problem?" asks Celeste.

"I have heard the complaints in my school," says Antonio. "Teachers feel a lot of pressure to make sure that kids perform well on the test so that the whole school is viewed as performing well. But I think we—and I mean teachers and administrators and even professors of education—need to make it clear that what standardized tests tell us is how students and schools and districts compare with each other in terms of general standards of skills and knowledge and aptitudes. And it's really important to remember that these tests are not perfect. There is error in measurement, even for reliable tests."

"It seems that we really are in a culture of testing," says Don, "and that means we have to be clear on what decision needs to be made and then to use the right information to make it."

"I think that's it," says Celeste. "In my mind, the technical experts who develop tests try to make sure that the tests are as reliable as possible and that they are valid.

"But it's the validity that we have to worry about. A test can show what a student has achieved in terms of instructional objectives and standards, but that doesn't mean that these tests measure everything a student is—or should be—learning. I want my students to learn to be confident, persistent, and responsible."

"So," says Connie, "even though they may be related, you all seem to be testing the notion that student achievement is synonymous with student learning. That sounds like a pretty good test to me."

Summary

1. Standardized tests are designed by people with specialized training in test construction, are given to everyone under the same conditions, are scored the same for everyone, and are interpreted with reference to either a norm group or a set of predetermined standards.

2. The purpose of giving a standardized test is to obtain an accurate and representative sample of some characteristic of a person, as it is impractical to measure that characteristic comprehensively.

3. Standardized tests are typically used to identify students' strengths and weaknesses, to inform parents of their child's general level of achievement, to plan instructional lessons, and to place students in special groups or programs.

4. One of the most important characteristics of a standardized test is its reliability—the similarity between two rankings of test scores obtained from the same individuals.

5. Another important characteristic of standardized tests is validity. A valid test accurately measures what its users intend it to measure and allows us to draw appropriate inferences about how much of some characteristic the test taker possesses. Three types of evidence that contribute to accurate inferences are content validity evidence, predictive validity evidence, and construct validity evidence.

6. A third important characteristic of a standardized test is its norm group—a sample of students specially chosen and tested so as to reflect the population of students for whom the test is intended. The norm group's performance becomes the standard against which scores are compared.

7. Standardized achievement tests measure how much has been learned about a particular subject. The major types of achievement tests are single subject, batteries, diagnostic, competency, and special purpose.

8. Diagnostic tests identify specific strengths and weaknesses in basic learning skills.

9. Competency tests measure how well high school students have acquired such basic skills as reading, writing, and computation.

10. Aptitude tests estimate an individual's predisposition to acquire additional knowledge and skill in specific areas with the aid of effective instruction.

11. Tests that use a norm-referenced scoring system compare an individual's score with the performance of a norm group.

12. Tests that use a criterion-referenced scoring system judge scores in terms of mastery of a set of objectives.

13. Percentile rank indicates the percentage of scores that are at or below a person's score.

14. A z score is a standard score that indicates how far in standard deviation units a raw score is from the mean.

15. A T score is a standard score based on a scale of 1 to 100, with a mean of 50.

16. A stanine score indicates in which of nine normal-curve segments a person's performance falls.

17. People have several misconceptions about standardized tests, including the following: (a) tests measure what their titles say they measure; (b) tests that have the same or similar titles measure the same thing; (c) test scores are highly accurate reflectors of what people know and can do; (d) two tests that claim to measure the same thing can be used interchangeably; (e) all tests are scored by simply adding up the number of items answered correctly; (f) percent-correct scores from different tests can automatically be equated to the same letter grade (such as 80 percent correct equals a grade of B); (g) multiple-choice questions are useful only for measuring the lowest level of Bloom's Taxonomy; and (h) test items can be judged as good or bad just by inspecting the item and making a subjective judgment.

18. The federal government became involved in high-stakes testing in 2001 when Congress passed the No Child Left Behind (NCLB) Act. The goal of NCLB is to have all students score at least at the proficient level in math and reading/language arts on state-administered tests by 2014.

19. The practice of using standardized test scores to determine promotion to the next grade, graduation from high school, additional state funding, job security for teachers and administrators, and school accreditation is called high-stakes testing. Although high-stakes tests are given in every state and are related to learning standards, little is known about their effects on student achievement.

20. NCLB has five main requirements. First, all states must establish challenging content and performance standards for mathematics, reading/language arts, and science. Second, the states are required to administer annual assessment tests in math, reading/language arts, and science to students in grades 3 through 8. The format of the tests, the type of items used, and the length of the tests is decided by each state. Third, states must demonstrate every year that a certain additional percentage of all students, including students in such subgroups as racial and ethnic minorities, low-income, English language learners, and special education, have scored at the proficient level or higher. This feature is known as adequate yearly progress, or AYP. Fourth, states and school districts must publish yearly reports that describe how every group of students performed on the annual assessment. Fifth, states must create an accountability system that specifies rewards and punishments for schools that do and do not meet their AYP requirement.

21. Proponents of high-stakes testing argue that it will have a number of beneficial effects: greater goal clarity, improved quality control, improvements in teaching skills and methods, and increased motivation among students.

22. Critics of high-stakes testing argue that the NCLB law will have detrimental effects because of structural limitations (such as an inherent contradiction between challenging standards and 100 percent proficiency, and assessments that are narrow in scope, limited in range, and shallow in depth), misinterpretation/misuse of test results, a narrow approach to motivation (essentially a behavioral one), inflexible standards, and undesirable side effects (such as excessive time devoted to test preparation and decreased time for nontested subjects).

23. Research on the impact of high-stakes testing has found a small number of modest positive effects and many negative effects.

24. Technology can aid in preparing students for standardized tests and in administering and scoring the tests.

● Technical and Specialized Aspects of Testing

For more information about standardized tests and how to use the information they provide appropriately, consult one or more of these books: *Measurement and Evaluation in Psychology and Education* (8th ed., 2010), by Robert M. Thorndike and Tracy Thorndike-Christ; *Measurement and Assessment in Teaching* (10th ed., 2009), by M. David Miller, Robert Linn, and Norman Gronlund; and *Measurement and Assessment in Education* (2nd ed., 2009), by Cecil Reynolds, Ronald Livingston, and Victor Wilson.

● References for Evaluating Standardized Tests

To obtain the information necessary for evaluating standardized tests, examine *The Sixteenth Mental Measurements Yearbook* (2005), edited by Robert A. Spies and Barbara Plake. You may have to check earlier editions of *Mental Measurements Yearbook* for information on a specific test, as there are far too many tests available to review in a single edition.

The American Psychological Association provides a Code of Fair Testing Practices at **www.apa.org/science/programs/testing/fair-code.aspx.**

The National Center for Fair and Open Testing (more commonly known as FairTest) is an advocacy group whose goal is the development of fair, open, and educationally sound standardized tests. Its home page can be found at **www.fairtest.org.** By following the link to "K–12 Testing," you can find additional information and publications on standardized testing, NCLB, and accountability.

● NCLB and High-Stakes Testing

Analyses of current testing issues, such as standards-based reform, NCLB, and high-stakes testing can be found in the following books: *The Nature and Limits of Standards-Based Reform and Assessment* (2008), edited by Sandra Mathison and E. Wayne Ross; *When School Reform Goes Wrong* (2007), by Nel Noddings; *No Child Left Behind: Past, Present, and Future* (2008), by William Hayes; *Test Driven: High-Stakes Accountability in Elementary Schools* (2008), by Linda Valli, Robert Croninger, Marilyn Chambliss, Anna Graeber, and Daria Buese; and *NCLB at the Crossroads: Reexamining the Federal Effort to Close the Achievement Gap* (2009), edited by Michael Rebell and Jessica Wolf.

● Computer-Based Testing

An examination of several issues that pertain to computer-based testing can be found in *Practical Considerations in Computer-Based Testing* (2002), by Cynthia Parshall, Judith Spray, John Kalohn, and Tim Davey.

Becoming a Better Teacher by Becoming a Reflective Teacher

What makes a great teacher? It is a question that every aspiring and practicing teacher *should* ask and—we believe—it is a question that every aspiring and practicing teacher who seeks to improve in her or his profession *does* ask. Amanda Ripley (2010) used this question as the title of her story in *The Atlantic Monthly* magazine. Her story opens as follows:

> On August 25, 2008, two little boys walked into public elementary schools in Southeast Washington, D.C. Both were African American fifth-graders. The previous spring, both had tested below grade level in math.

> One walked into Kimball Elementary School and climbed the stairs to Mr. William Taylor's math classroom, a tidy, powder-blue space in which neither the clocks nor most of the electrical outlets worked.

> The other walked into a very similar classroom a mile away at Plummer Elementary School. In both schools, more than 80 percent of the children received free or reduced-price lunches. At night, all the children went home to the same urban ecosystem, a ZIP code in which almost a quarter of the families lived below the poverty line and a police district in which somebody was murdered every week or so.

> At the end of the school year, both little boys took the same standardized test given at all D.C. public schools—not a perfect test of their learning, to be sure, but a relatively objective one (and, it's worth noting, not a very hard one).

> After a year in Mr. Taylor's class, the first little boy's scores went up—way up. He had started below grade level and finished above. On average, his classmates' scores rose about 13 points—which is almost 10 points more than fifth-graders with similar incoming test scores achieved in other low-income D.C. schools that year. On that first day of school, only 40 percent of Mr. Taylor's students were doing math at grade level. By the end of the year, 90 percent were at or above grade level.

> As for the other boy? Well, he ended the year the same way he'd started it—below grade level. In fact, only a quarter of the fifth-graders at Plummer finished the year at grade level in math—despite having started off at about the same level as Mr. Taylor's class down the road.

> This tale of two boys, and of the millions of kids just like them, embodies the most stunning finding to come out of education research in the past decade: more than any other variable in education—more than schools or curriculum—teachers matter. Put concretely, if Mr. Taylor's student continued to learn at the same level for a few more years, his test scores would be no different from those of his more affluent peers in Northwest D.C. And if these two boys were to keep their respective teachers for three years, their lives would likely diverge forever. By high school, the compounded effects of the strong teacher—or the weak one—would become too great.

Teachers matter. We know this to be true not only because of a story of two students, but from our own experience. Reflect for a moment on as many teachers as you can remember. How many of them were really outstanding in the sense that they established a vital, engaging learning environment, were sensitive to the needs of students, and—when you encountered difficulty—found techniques to help you learn? How many of them did an adequate job but left you bored or indifferent most of the time? How many of them made you dread entering their classrooms because they were either ineffective teachers or insensitive or even cruel in dealing with you and your classmates? Of those ineffective or vindictive teachers, how many were dissatisfied with themselves and with their jobs? How many lousy teachers are unhappy people?

At the end of this chapter is the final installment of our feature about assumptions, here combined to "Revealing and Challenging Assumptions." The final installment is a letter from Connie, the master teacher, to her young colleagues. The letter is based on the true story of a real person who, as a teacher, failed to learn *from* teaching. As you read the letter and as you recall your own ineffective teachers, recall Erikson's theory of psychosocial development from Chapter 2. The human being represented in the letter—and perhaps the dissatisfied, unhappy people who taught you—see themselves as stagnant rather than generative.

Teachers matter. And what matters most about teachers is whether they are learners. As Linda Darling-Hammond and her colleagues (2006) put it, students need "…teachers who can learn *from* teaching, as well as [learn] *for* teaching…" (p. 11, *original italics*).

Teacher learning matters. It matters to students and it matters to the teachers themselves. To become a better teacher you must learn *from* teaching. The best way to learn *from* your teaching is to become a reflective teacher. This chapter offers some suggestions.

IMPROVING YOUR REFLECTION SKILLS TO IMPROVE YOUR TEACHING

Scholars who study instructional processes (e.g., Freiberg, 2002; Yilmaz-Tuzun, 2008) often note that effective teachers know how to coordinate a diverse array of instructional elements (such as planning, lesson design, time management, classroom management, instructional methods, student motivation, and assessment techniques) and adapt them to differences in student needs, materials, and purposes. Their insights highlight the point that to be consistently effective, you will need to observe and analyze what you do in the classroom. In essence, you will be conducting formative assessment: observing and analyzing your own action with the intent to improve student outcomes. Connie Moss and Susan Brookhart (2009) state:

> Formative assessment can have a transformational effect on teachers and teaching. In a very real way, it flips a switch, shining a bright light on individual teaching decisions so that teachers can see clearly…the difference between the *intent* and the *effect* of their actions. (p. 10, *original italics*)

Thus, being reflective does not simply mean sitting back and thinking about teaching and learning; it is more active than that. Being reflective means bringing a scholarly mind-set to your work: using techniques that allow you to inquire critically into your decisions and actions as a teacher. In the sections that follow, we will explore such techniques.

As you think about the methods that can help you improve your teaching, think also about the five core propositions of the National Board for Professional Teaching Standards (NBPTS). We first encountered these propositions in Chapter 1. Consider how the techniques for reflecting and improving your teaching might contribute to the core propositions that frame the knowledge, skills, dispositions, and beliefs that characterize National Board Certified Teachers (NBCTs):

1. *Teachers are Committed to Students and Learning*
2. *Teachers Know the Subjects They Teach and How to Teach Those Subjects to Students*
3. *Teachers are Responsible for Managing and Monitoring Student Learning*
4. *Teachers Think Systematically about Their Practice and Learn from Experience*
5. *Teachers are Members of Learning Communities*

Student Evaluations and Suggestions

In many respects, students are in a better position to evaluate teachers than anyone else. They may not always be able to analyze *why* what a teacher does is effective or ineffective (even an experienced expert observer might have difficulty doing so), but they know, better than anyone else, whether they are responding and learning. Furthermore, students form their impressions after interacting with a teacher for hundreds or thousands of hours. Most principals or other adult observers may watch a teacher in action for only a few minutes at a time. It therefore makes sense to pay attention to and solicit opinions from students.

As a matter of fact, it will be virtually impossible for you to ignore student reactions. Every minute that school is in session, you will receive student feedback in the form of attentiveness (or lack of it), facial expressions, restlessness, yawns, sleeping, disruptive behavior, and the like. If a particular lesson arouses either a neutral or a negative reaction, this should signal to you that you need to seek a better way to present the same material in the future. If you find that you seem to be spending much of your time disciplining students, it will be worth your while to evaluate why and to find other methods.

In addition to informally analyzing the minute-by-minute reactions of your students, you may find it helpful to request more formal feedback. After completing a unit, you might say, "I'd like you to tell me what you liked and disliked about the way this unit was arranged and give me suggestions for improving it if I teach it again next year."

A more comprehensive and systematic approach is to distribute a questionnaire or evaluation form and ask students to record their reactions anonymously. You might use a published form or devise your own. In either case, a common format is to list a series of statements and ask students to rate them on a 5-point scale. Some of the published forms use special answer sheets that make it possible to tally the results electronically. Many rating-scale evaluation forms have some disadvantages, however:

- Responses may not be very informative unless you can compare your ratings with those of colleagues. If you get an overall rating of 3.5 on "makes the subject matter interesting," for example, you won't know whether you need to work on that aspect of your teaching until you discover that the average rating of other teachers of the same grade or subject was 4.2.
- Published evaluation forms may not be very helpful unless all other teachers use the same rating scale. Fortunately, this may be possible in school districts that use a standard scale to obtain evidence for use in making decisions about retention, tenure, and promotion.
- Many rating scales are subject to a *leniency problem*. Students tend to give most teachers somewhat above-average ratings on most traits. Although leniency may soothe a teacher's ego, wishy-washy responses do not provide the information needed to improve pedagogical effectiveness.

To get around the leniency problem and to induce students to give more informative reactions, forced-choice ratings are often used. A rating form for teachers who adopt a constructivist approach and value students' perceptions of how well constructivist learning principles are implemented in the classroom, Peter Taylor and his colleagues (Taylor & Fraser, 1998; Taylor, Fraser, & Fisher, 1997) developed the Constructivist Learning Environment Survey (CLES), which is also available on the textbook's student website.

Peer and Self-Assessment Techniques

Classroom Observation Schedules Although your students can supply quite a bit of information that can help you improve your teaching, they cannot always tell you about technical flaws in your instructional technique. This is especially true with younger students. Accordingly, you may wish to submit to a detailed analysis by a colleague of your approach to teaching.

One of the simplest classroom observation instruments to create and use is the checklist. Figure 16.1 contains a set of six relatively brief checklists that reflect many of the topics discussed in this book. You can adopt this instrument as is or modify it to suit your circumstances (such as your grade level and your state's learning standards) to help you evaluate your effectiveness in several important areas.

Another useful observation instrument was developed by Donna Sobel, Sheryl Taylor, and Ruth Anderson (2003). Called the Diversity-Responsive Teaching Observation Tool, it was created for a Colorado school district with a broad diversity of students. The instrument contains three sections and focuses on how well teachers address diversity as well as exhibit appropriate classroom instruction and classroom management behaviors. Because the form is too lengthy to reproduce here, we encourage you to consult the article in which it appears if you think you might want to have a colleague use it to evaluate your teaching.

TeachSource V i d e o C a s e ⏪ ▶ ⏩

Teaching as a Profession: Collaboration with Colleagues

Go to the Education CourseMate website and watch the Video Case, and then answer the following questions:

1. The text and this Video Case both show how colleagues play a role in improving the teaching practice of others. Which examples of peer assessment and collaboration do you think would be most helpful to you? Explain your answers.

2. In the Video Case, we see several teachers collaborating on an important issue related to their students. Briefly explain what they are trying to achieve and whether or not you think their collaborative process was successful.

Lesson Study According to Catherine Lewis, Rebecca Perry, and Shelley Friedkin (2009), "Lesson study is *a system for building and sharing practitioner knowledge* that involves teachers in learning from colleagues as they research, plan, teach, research and discuss a classroom lesson" (p. 142, *original italics*). Lesson study is focused by a cycle of inquiry conducted by a research team of, typically, three to as many as eight teachers. The team concept is critical; the cycle represented in Figure 16.2 is undertaken by a team of teacher-researchers rather than by an individual teacher.

A cycle of lesson study begins with the *study phase*. The research team studies the curriculum and formulates learning goals. In doing so, the team considers long-term learning goals for students and the professional standards that apply to the

Figure 16.1 Examples of Classroom Observation Checklists

1. Characteristics of a Good Learning Environment ____ Samples of exemplary work are displayed. ____ Criteria charts, rubrics, or expectations are visible. ____ There is evidence of students making choices. ____ Furniture arrangements allow for individual, small-group, and whole-class work. ____ Written expectations for behavior and subject matter are displayed. ____ There are a variety of materials and activities to address different learning styles. ____ There are discussions that involve many different students and points of view.	**4. Characteristics of Student Learning** ____ Students communicate ideas clearly, orally and in writing. ____ Students plan and organize their own work. ____ Students use a variety of resources. ____ Students create new products and ideas. ____ Students use prior knowledge to solve problems. ____ Students collaborate with peers and adults on projects, drafts, and investigations.
2. Characteristics of Good Teaching ____ Content and standards are being explicitly taught. ____ A variety of instructional strategies are integrated into all lessons. ____ Individual progress is monitored. ____ There are interventions for students not demonstrating mastery. ____ A variety of assessment techniques are used. ____ There is evidence of staff development impact.	**5. Questions to Ask Students Who Are On-Task** ____ What are you learning? ____ Why do you need to know this information? ____ How is this like other things you've learned? ____ What will this help you do in the future? ____ What do you do if you get stuck? ____ How do you know if your work is good enough? ____ If you want to make your work better, do you know how to improve it? ____ Do you talk about your work with your parents or other adults?
3. Patterns of Teacher Behavior ____ Gender and racial equity are observed in interactions with students. ____ There is recognition and positive reinforcement of effort as well as achievement. ____ Students are treated as individuals.	**6. Observing Individual Students Who Are Not On-Task** ____ What is the student doing while others are learning? ____ Where is the student sitting? ____ How often does the teacher make contact with the student? ____ What is the nature of the interactions? *Ask the Student:* ____ What do you think this lesson is about? ____ What would help you understand this better? ____ What would make it more interesting? ____ What do you do if you don't understand something? ____ How do you get help?

SOURCE: L. Schmidt (2003).

content being learned, and selects a topic that will be the focus for planning the lesson to be researched.

The *planning phase* of the cycle includes selecting or revising a lesson plan that focuses on the learning outcomes identified in the study phase. In some cases, a new lesson plan might be created. The lesson plan that emerges from the planning phase includes anticipating student thinking, planning data collection on student learning (for formative purposes), and providing a rationale for the activities and assessments that will be part of the lesson.

The *teaching phase* occurs when one member of the research team conducts the lesson (called the "research lesson" or the "study lesson"). Other members of the research team observe the lesson being studied and collect data.

Figure 16.2 The Lesson Study Cycle

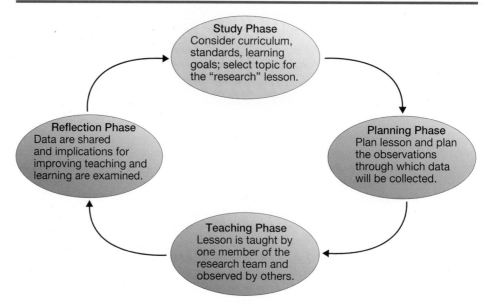

SOURCES: Adapted from Lewis, Perry, & Friedkin (2009) and Mark, Gorman, & Nikula (2009).

The *reflection phase* is again a team effort. Those who observed the research lesson share the data they collected in an effort to focus on student learning and how the teacher influenced that learning. The implications of the data collected during the lesson for broader issues of content coverage, student engagement, and lesson and unit design are also addressed.

Joanne Lieberman (2009) argues that lesson study can change the "norms of individualism" that keep many American teachers from learning with and from one another. In her case study of a math department that employed lesson study, she found that teachers became more willing to accept the uncertainty of teaching a research lesson because they wanted to discover what would happen. The norms of the teacher-researchers evolved to focus student learning more directly and to willingly design innovations that could be tested, improved, and tested again.

Lesson study, which has a long history in Japan, has only recently begun to have an impact on American teachers' efforts to learn *from* teaching (Lewis, 2009; Lewis et al., 2009; Mark, Gorman, & Nikula, 2009). But lesson study is a very promising practice, especially when considered in light of the reform effort represented by the National Board for Professional Teaching Standards. We will see more about that effort in the Case in Print; for now we examine other ideas that you might use to help you learn from teaching.

Self-Recorded Lessons If it is not possible for you to team with colleagues—or even in addition to working with a team—you might consider examining your own teaching through self-recorded lessons. Employing audio only or audio and image recording is becoming increasingly convenient with portable digital devices for audio and/or image. Once you have decided to document your teaching for further study, your first step should be to decide which classes or parts of classes you want to record, for how long, and on what day of the week. The goal should be to create a representative sample of the circumstances under which you teach. Then you should inform your students that you intend to record a sample of your lessons over a period of several weeks to study and improve your instructional methods and that you will protect their confidentiality by not allowing anyone else but you to listen to the tapes.

Soliciting comments about the effectiveness of one's teaching methods from students and colleagues and reflecting on these comments is an excellent way to become a better teacher. © Mary Kate Denny/Photo Edit

One first-year high school teacher decided after analyzing an audio recording of one of her lessons that she needed to wait longer for students to respond to high-level questions, give students more opportunities to ask questions, give students more feedback, use specific praise, review and integrate previous concepts with new lessons, and stop saying "okay" and "all right." Impressed with these insights, she continued to record and analyze her lessons, and at the end of the year was nominated for an award as the district's best new teacher (Freiberg, 2002).

Guided Reflection Protocol Analyzing self-recorded lessons, even a set of "day notes" or other written comments about the events of a lesson, can be a useful way to reflect on lessons to learn from your teaching. One analytic technique is the guided reflection protocol (McEntee et al., 2003). After choosing one or more teaching episodes that you would like to examine, try to answer as honestly as possible the following four questions:

1. *What happened?* The main requirement of this step is simply to describe the incident as fully as possible. Note, for instance, when and where the incident occurred, who was involved, and what occurred just prior to, during, and immediately after the incident. Avoid analysis and interpretation.

2. *Why did it happen?* If you've provided enough context in answering the first question, you should be able to identify the events that produced the incident.

3. *What might it mean?* Note the conditional wording of this question. Using the word *might* instead of *does* is intended to help you realize that there are usually several possible interpretations of the meaning of an incident. A teacher who reprimands a class for not finishing an assignment on time may, for example, need to examine the clarity of her objectives, the amount of time she budgets for the completion of assignments, the ability of students to use their time productively, or her ability to cope with administrative pressure to cover the curriculum in time for an upcoming high-stakes test.

4. *What are the implications for my practice?* Consider what you might do differently in a similar situation in the light of how you answered the first three questions.

Developing a Reflective Journal Seymour Sarason (1993, 2005; Glazek & Sarason, 2006), who has written extensively about schooling and school reform, points out what may seem obvious but is often missed in practice: every teacher should be an expert in both subject matter and how children learn in classrooms. The goal, and the challenge, is to figure out how to present the subject matter so that students understand it, remember it, and use it. To do that, you must constantly prepare, observe, and reflect on how closely your instructional practices relate to theory and research and produce the desired outcome (Heath, 2002). The Reflective Journal that we mentioned at the beginning of the book is intended to help you begin that process in a systematic way. Now we will give you more detailed suggestions for keeping such a journal.

We recommend that you develop a Reflective Journal for two basic purposes: (1) to serve as a repository of instructional ideas and techniques that you have either created from your own experiences or gleaned from other sources and (2) to give yourself a format for recording your observations and reflections on teaching (Lyons & Kubler LaBoskey, 2002). These two purposes can be separate from each other or, if you choose, related to each other in a cycle of reflectivity that we will describe. As you read this section, refer to Figure 16.3 for an illustration of how a journal page might look.

The form your Reflective Journal takes will probably change over the years to reflect your experiences and changing needs. But to begin, we suggest that you organize your first journal around the marginal notes in each chapter of this book that are labeled "Journal Entry." Use the Journal Entries as just what their name implies: page headings in your Reflective Journal. To allow room for both the expansion of your teaching ideas and the inclusion of your ongoing reflections, you might purchase a three-ring binder so that you can add and drop pages. Alternatively, you might want to create your Reflective Journal as computer files, which would give you unlimited capacity for interaction and expansion.

Under each heading, you can develop a two-part page or multipage entry. As illustrated in the top half of Figure 16.3, the first part should contain your own teaching ideas, custom-tailored from the Suggestions for Teaching sections of the chapters of this book and from personal experience and other sources to fit the grade level and subjects you expect to teach.

To illustrate, let's use a Journal Entry from Chapter 9, "Social Cognitive Theory"—"Ways to Teach Comprehension Tactics":

- Search your memory for techniques that your past teachers used. Did your fifth-grade teacher, for instance, have a clever way of relating new information to ideas that you had learned earlier to make the new information easier to understand? Describe the technique so you will remember to try it yourself. Did a high school teacher have an ingenious way of displaying the similarities and differences among a set of ideas? Exactly how did she or he do it?

- After you exhaust your own recollections, ask roommates or classmates if they can remember any successful ways that their teachers made understanding easier.

- Examine the examples given in the text section in which the Journal Entry "Ways to Teach Comprehension Tactics" appears. Which ones seem most appropriate for the grade level and subject you will be teaching? Jot them down. Do any of the examples suggest variations you can think of on your own? Write them down before you forget them.

- Add ideas that you pick up in methods classes or during your student-teaching experience. If you see a film in a methods class that shows how a teacher helps students understand a particular point, describe it in your journal. If your master teacher uses a successful technique to clarify difficult-to-understand material, record it.

If you follow some or all of these suggestions for using the Journal Entries, you will have a rich source of ideas to turn to when you discover that your students seem confused and anxious because of poor comprehension and you find yourself wondering if there is anything you can do about it.

Figure 16.3 Sample Page for Your Reflective Journal

Journal Entry: *Ways to Teach Comprehension Tactics*
Source: *"Information-Processing Theory"*

Ideas for Instruction

Note: All the ideas you list here will pertain to the particular journal entry/instructional goal for this journal page.

- *Customized suggestions for teaching—those points, principles, activities, and examples taken from the text and the Suggestions for Teaching that are most relevant to your own situation.*

- *Ideas generated from past experiences as a student.*

- *Ideas provided by professional colleagues.*

- *Ideas collected from student-teaching experiences.*

- *Ideas gathered from methods textbooks.*

Reflections: Questions and "Restarter" Suggestions for Instruction

Reflective Question (to focus observation of my teaching and my students' learning):
Do my students have difficulty understanding the meaning of what they read or of what I present in class?

(Record your ongoing reflections, observations, and analytic notes about your instruction and your students' learning of this topic here. If necessary, you may need to "jump-start" or reorient your instruction. One possible idea follows.)

Suggested Action: *Schedule a series of sessions on how to study. Explain the purpose of various comprehension tactics, and provide opportunities for students to practice these skills on material they have been assigned to read. Give corrective feedback.*

With this part of the journal under way, you should feel reasonably well prepared when you first take charge of a class. But given the complexity of classroom teaching, lessons or techniques that looked good on paper do not always produce the intended effect. This is the point at which you need to reflect on and analyze what you are doing and how you might bring about improvements. On the bottom half of your journal page, or on a new page, write in question form what the nature of the problem seems to be. Then try to identify the cause (or causes) of the problem and at least one possible solution. You can use this suggestion to get restarted or headed in a new direction with your teaching. If, for example, some of your students still have difficulty comprehending what they read despite the comprehension-enhancing techniques that you embedded into your lessons, you might reread Chapter 8 on information-processing theory, as well as other articles and books on information processing, and decide that your students really need systematic instruction in how to use various comprehension-directed learning tactics.

Using a Portfolio with Your Journal Middle school teacher Linda Van Wagenen used a personal portfolio along with a Reflective Journal to analyze and improve the quality of her instruction (Van Wagenen & Hibbard, 1998). She compiled a portfolio of her efforts to achieve certain teaching goals and used that to examine her effectiveness. She judged her first two efforts at analysis to be unsatisfactory because they were largely descriptive; they emphasized what she had done and ignored what effects those efforts had on her students (self-assessment), what she thought about the

Research has shown that keeping a personal journal about one's teaching activities and outcomes helps teachers improve their effectiveness because it forces them to focus on what they do, why they do it, and what kinds of results are typically obtained. © 2010 Tetra Images/Jupiterimages Corporation

quality of her own instruction (self-evaluation), or what she planned to do next (self-regulation). Her third attempt focused on ways to motivate students to improve their performance in persuasive and expository writing. She identified a set of steps that would help her understand the problem and produce improvements. Evidence of her successes and failures made up the portfolio. In addition, she kept a Reflective Journal because she thought it would help her stay focused on finding a solution to the problem and would stimulate attempts at self-evaluation and self-regulation. The result of this third attempt was judged to be much more useful than either of her first two efforts. In addition to addressing the question, "What did I do?" she also addressed the questions, "What did I learn?" and "Now what will I do?" Essentially, she engaged in "an intentional reflective process" (Lyons & Kubler LaBoskey, 2002, p. 2), which told the story of her teaching and her students' learning. Narrative accounts (i.e., telling the stories of your teaching) have been shown to be an effective form of self-study to improve teaching (Anderson-Patton & Bass, 2002). By asking and answering questions, as Linda Van Wagenen did on her third attempt, you can build a narrative account in your Reflective Journal.

In thinking about the contents of your own portfolio, you might want to start with the following list of items (Drake & McBride, 2000; Johnson, Mims-Cox, Doyle-Nichols, 2010):

1. Title page
2. A table of contents
3. A statement of your educational philosophy, which may include the reasons that you chose teaching as a career
4. A résumé
5. A statement of your teaching goals
6. Example(s) of a lesson plan, keyed to state standards
7. Examples of learning activities (especially those that contain innovative ideas)
8. Samples of students' work
9. Photographs and videotapes
10. Letters of recommendation
11. Teaching evaluations
12. Samples of college work
13. An autobiography
14. Reflections about how teaching (or student teaching) has contributed to your growth as a person and a teacher
15. Official documents (transcripts, teaching certificates, test scores)

Video Case ◄◄ ► ►►

Teaching as a Profession: What Defines Effective Teaching?

Go to the Education CourseMate website and watch the Video Case, and then answer the following questions:

1. In this Video Case, different school professionals share their thoughts on what defines an effective teacher. Of the various teacher attributes that they describe, which ones do you think are most critical (e.g., knowledge of child development, command of subject matter, being organized, knowing your students, etc.)?

2. Based on this Video Case and the content in this text, think about the concept of teacher self-reflection. In your opinion, what are some effective ways for teachers to reflect on their own practice? Which self-reflection techniques make the most sense to you?

What Makes Reflective Techniques Effective?

The answer to this question depends very much on the type of evidence one chooses to examine and the characteristics of the teachers who participated in studies on reflection. There are, for example, many positive anecdotes about the benefits of reflection on the quality of one's teaching. Research studies, on the other hand, have found generally that reflective activities produced little discernible effect on the quality of subsequent teaching behavior (Cornford, 2002).

According to Ian Cornford (2002), however, these negative outcomes are due largely to flawed research designs. Additionally, most studies of teacher effectiveness have failed to differentiate evaluative techniques according to the particular circumstances of teaching, such as subject matter and age of students (Campbell, Kyriakides, Muijs, & Robinson, 2004). There is also the issue of the research questions that were asked. For example, one could ask if a teacher engages in some kind of formal reflection and then find out if there is a difference in the behaviors of teachers who report that they reflect and those who report that they do not reflect. Or, a researcher could observe differences between teachers who, say, keep a journal and those who don't. But perhaps asking whether reflection makes a difference is the wrong question. After all, most teachers, at one point or another, reflect on their teaching. Perhaps the more important questions are: On what do they reflect? How do they reflect? Why do they reflect? What is their purpose and intention?

More recently, reflective techniques have been studied within the broader context of teacher learning directed at improving student learning. For example, the work of Connie Moss and Susan Brookhart (2009), mentioned in Chapter 14 and earlier in this chapter, looks at teacher learning through the lens of formative assessment generally. In particular, they argue for a cultural change in classrooms so the teaching process moves away from teacher-led instruction and toward a "partnership of intentional inquiry" between student and teacher. Another example of reflective practice that focuses on the critical connection between teacher inquiry (or learning *from* teaching) and student learning is Arnetha Ball's model of generative change (2009). According to Ball,

> I use the term *generativity* to refer to the teachers' ability to continually add to their understanding by connecting their personal and professional knowledge with the knowledge they gain from their students to produce or originate knowledge that is useful to them in pedagogical problem solving and in meeting the educational needs of their students. (p. 47, *original italics*)

Using data from a decade-long study of literacy teachers in the United States and in South Africa, Ball's research shows that critical analysis of one's teaching practices and beliefs—using theory and research and focused clearly on student needs and progress—is a powerful form of reflection. The teachers in her study progressed through phases of professional development that started with a sense of personal awakening via "the use of reflection through narrativization of personal experiences that motivate increased metacognitive awareness concerning the critical role of literacies in teachers' lives and in the lives of others" (p. 67). The teachers then gained a sense of agency—that they were agents for their students—which enabled them to become more effective advocates for their students. The teachers in this study emerged with a sense of efficacy: they were confident that they could help students with diverse linguistic capabilities and cultural backgrounds succeed in their classrooms. The teachers found their "voice" as they shared what they had learned; they had become generative thinkers who could solve the problems they encountered in their classrooms. As the teachers became more generative, they changed the way learning happened and so did their students.

The teachers became enthusiastic agents of generative change because they learned *from* their teaching. Their reflection was intentional and driven by a spirit of inquiry. They did not become stagnant in their practice—they did not find themselves in a rut without the imagination to find a way out—nor were they unhappy individuals who viewed themselves, as Erikson would put it, as stagnant.

USING TECHNOLOGY FOR REFLECTIVE INQUIRY

Throughout this book, we have described how you can use various technology tools to help your students become more effective learners. Now it's time to consider how you can use such technologies to reflect in ways that will help you learn from your teaching.

Digital Portals for Professional Development

Richard Elmore, in a report for the Albert Shanker Institute published in 2002, complained that schools—with increased emphasis on testing and accountability—offer "few portals" for new ideas about teaching and learning to enter into educational practice. Bill Ferriter, in his 2009 article in *Educational Leadership*, suggests that two important changes have occurred and that those changes have resulted in more portals for learning *about* teaching and learning *from* teaching.

One of those changes is the increased emphasis on professional collaboration among teachers. "Lesson study"—a way to research and thus improve teaching practice (discussed earlier in this chapter)—is one example of this emphasis on collaboration. This emerging emphasis is also exemplified in the core propositions from the NBPTS that we listed earlier in the chapter. The fifth proposition, you may recall, is: "Teachers are members of learning communities." According to the NBPTS, highly qualified teachers are collaborative in their practice. The Case in Print documents the growing number of practicing teachers who are pursuing National Board Certification.

The second change that is allowing teachers more opportunities for learning *about* teaching and learning *from* teaching, according to Ferriter (2009), is that digital tools now provide the portals that Elmore saw as lacking. In particular, Ferriter advocates for reading and writing blogs and wikis (see also, Yang, 2009). With regard to reading blogs, Ferriter states: "Some [blogs] leave me challenged. Some leave me angry. Some leave me jazzed. All leave me energized and ready to learn more" (p. 36). As to using digital tools as a forum for sharing questions and ideas in writing, Ferriter remarks: "Blogs become a forum for public articulation—and public articulation is essential for educators interested in refining and revising their thinking about teaching and learning" (p. 37). Ferriter recommends several blogging

Case in Print

Highly Qualified Teachers Are Those Who Learn from Teaching

As you think about the techniques that can help you improve your teaching, think also about the five core propositions of the National Board for Professional Teaching Standards (NBPTS). We first encountered these propositions in Chapter 1. Consider how the techniques for reflecting and improving your teaching might contribute to the core propositions that frame the knowledge, skills, dispositions, and beliefs that characterize National Board Certified Teachers (NBCTs):

1. Teachers Are Committed to Students and Learning
2. Teachers Know the Subjects They Teach and How to Teach Those Subjects to Students
3. Teachers Are Responsible for Managing and Monitoring Student Learning
4. Teachers Think Systematically about Their Practice and Learn from Experience
5. Teachers Are Members of Learning Communities *(p. 560–561)*

2009 Class of National Board Certified Teachers Advances Nation's School Reform Movement

NATIONAL BOARD FOR PROFESSIONAL TEACHING STANDARDS

ARLINGTON, VA (December 16, 2009)—The National Board for Professional Teaching Standards (NBPTS) continues its progress in advancing the National Board Certification education reform movement with *the announcement of nearly 8,900 new National Board Certified Teachers* (NBCTs). Today's announcement brings the total number of accomplished teachers and school counselors certified by NBPTS to more than 82,000.

An "extraordinary group," is how U.S. Secretary of Education Arne Duncan referred to this year's class of National Board Certified Teachers in a September interview with NBPTS. He said teachers who achieved National Board Certification have "demonstrated a commitment to taking their teaching practice and the teaching profession to a different level."

"The leadership and example they're setting for the system is phenomenal," said Duncan, former CEO of Chicago Public Schools (CPS). With more than 300 new NBCTs, CPS had more teachers achieving National Board Certification this year than any other school district in the nation.

"What if every child had a chance to be taught by a National Board Certified Teacher? I think the difference it would make in students' lives would be extraordinary," said Duncan. "As we move forward on this turnaround agenda nationally, I would love for National Board Certified Teachers to be at the forefront of that movement."

"In Chicago Public Schools we also imagined teams of National Board Certified Teachers alongside effective principals in schools that need them most," said Janet Knupp, founding president and chief executive officer, The Chicago Public Education Fund. "With our new class, we now have more than 60 Chicago public schools—traditional and charter—with 15 percent or more of their faculties National Board certified. These teachers are building cultures of excellence for everyone in their buildings, where adults as much as children aspire to the highest standards."

In many schools, districts and states across the nation, National Board Certified Teachers are assuming leadership roles—serving as mentors, facilitating professional development and leading education reform efforts in their districts and states. Several states are capitalizing on the expertise of these outstanding teacher leaders in their "Race to the Top" proposals. They are using accomplished teachers to increase effectiveness and improve school conditions to better meet the academic learning needs of students in targeted high-need schools.

"Our focus is expanding from individuals achieving National Board Certification to a systemic movement that changes the culture of classrooms, schools and districts by leveraging National Board Certified Teachers to build human capital, especially in high-need schools," said Joseph A. Aguerrebere, president and chief executive officer, NBPTS. "This announcement symbolizes what we're all about—improving the capacity of professionals in working with all students."

The latest numbers providing further evidence that the teaching quality movement is growing include:

- The number of NBCTs has more than doubled in the past five years (from more than 40,000 in 2004 to more than 82,000 in 2009).
- States with the highest number of teachers achieving National Board Certification in 2009 were: North Carolina (1,509), Washington (1,248), South Carolina (798), Illinois (732) and Florida (651).
- School districts with the highest number of teachers achieving National Board Certification in 2009 were: Chicago Public Schools, Charlotte-Mecklenburg Schools, Wake County Schools, the Los Angeles Unified School District and Miami-Dade County Public Schools.
- Fifteen states had at least a 20 percent increase in the number of 2009 NBCTs over the number of teachers who achieved certification in 2008.
- Nearly 1,700 NBCTs successfully met the standards for the "Profile of Professional Growth" to renew National Board Certification.

More than half of all NBCTs teach in Title I eligible schools as reported by the National Center for Education Statistics.

"Growing groups of National Board Certified Teachers and leveraging them to build school-based learning communities are critical components many states and districts are already using to turn around low-performing schools," said Gov. Bob Wise, chair of the NBPTS Board of Directors and former governor of West Virginia. "This whole school reform movement is creating a culture of learning we're all looking for—one that advances student engagement and achievement, retains the best teachers and improves teacher and school performance."

In a congressionally mandated report, the National Research Council (NRC) confirmed that National Board Certified Teachers advance student achievement and learning, stay in the classroom longer, support new and struggling teachers, and assume other school-based leadership roles. The NRC acknowledged that students taught by National Board Certified Teachers make higher gains on achievement tests than students taught by non-board-certified teachers. National Board Certification is recognized as a model of pay-for-performance and is supported by teachers and administrators nationwide. Many states and local school districts provide salary incentives and cover the cost for teachers who pursue and achieve this advanced teaching credential. A voluntary assessment program designed to develop, recognize and retain accomplished teachers, National Board Certification is achieved through a performance-based assessment that typically takes one to three years to complete. While state licensing systems set basic requirements to teach in each state, NBCTs have successfully demonstrated advanced teaching knowledge, skills and practices.

National Board Certification for Educational Leaders/Principals

Last week, NBPTS launched the development of National Board Certification for Principals, the first phase of an expanded program, National Board Certification for Educational Leaders, which will also lay the groundwork for a new teacher leader certification. Investments from the nation's major public, private and philanthropic sectors have contributed to the development of National Board Certification for Educational Leaders. For more information about this initiative, including the Core Propositions, visit **www.nbpts.org/principals**.

For more information about NBPTS and National Board Certification, visit **www.nbpts.org**.

Questions and Activities

1. The article describes how the education profession is changing and how the effort to certify teachers at a national level is making a difference. How do you see National Board Certification of teachers as contributing to learning *from* teaching? What kinds of assessments do you think should be used to determine if someone is a highly qualified teacher?

2. If you had the opportunity to observe National Board Certified Teachers in their classrooms, what do you think you might see? How do you think the students in those classrooms might engage with the material they are learning? With each other? With the teacher?

sites; among them is *Edublogs* (**www.edublogs.org**), a free blogging service dedicated entirely to educators.

There are numerous other websites that have been designed for K–12 teachers and contain discussion forums, chat rooms, blogs, and/or wikis. Here are five you might consider using:

- the Connect page of Active Learning Practices for Schools (ALPS), Harvard Graduate School of Education (**learnweb.harvard.edu/alps/bigideas/q5.cfm**)
- the New Teachers Online page of Teachers Network (**www.teachersnetwork.org/ntol**)
- the Interactive Forums page of the International Education and Resource Network (**www.iearn.org/index.html**)
- the Teacher2Teacher page of Teachnet.com (**www.teachnet.com/t2t**)
- the "chat center" at the teachers.net site; "chatboards" arranged by grade levels, subjects, region, and so forth (**http://teachers.net**)

Technological tools for reflection can be very helpful to teachers at any stage of their professional development. If your intention is to learn *from* teaching, the digital portals that provide access to information and the thoughts and experiences of fellow educators can help you do just that.

For direct links to these and other websites to aid your professional development, use the web links at the textbook's Education CourseMate website.

Revealing and Challenging Assumptions

Connie's Reflection

Dear Antonio, Celeste, and Don,

I write to you for three reasons. First, I write to thank all of you for the learning that you have afforded me this semester. *You helped me learn.* I hope those are words you experience often throughout your careers. Even if you do not hear the words, I hope you receive the message: maybe in the smile of a student; in the seeking of advice; in the special effort to say hello; in the return visit of a former student home from college. The words may not be spoken, but if you teach well, you will get the message many times over.

Second, I write to ask you one last question: Do you understand that teaching is a calling? Those who teach because they are called to teach find challenges and learning. Those who teach without being called find frustration that fills their teaching careers with complaints and unhappiness.

Third, I write to keep a promise I made a long time ago. I promised to tell a story to everyone I met who said that she or he wanted to be a teacher…

I had a high school teacher whom I will call Mr. B. I was in Mr. B's class my junior year. It was a class that was supposed to help kids going to college. The only thing we ever did was recite from workbook exercises. Mr. B would start the class by calling on the person sitting in the first chair of the row on either the far left of the room or the far right. The only thing that ever changed was whether he pointed to the left or to the right. Once the recitation started, it moved down each row, back to the front of the next row, down that row, until the time ran out. That's all we did for an entire semester. I hated the class and so did everyone else.

Twenty years after that class I happened to see Mr. B on a visit back to my hometown. He was sitting in a diner having a cup of coffee, and I recognized him. So I went over and sat down next to him and introduced myself. He didn't remember me, but we exchanged pleasantries for a few minutes and then he asked me what kind of work I did. I told him that I was a teacher and he smiled and nodded for a while. He asked me if I enjoyed teaching and I remember exactly what I said: "I love it. I can't imagine doing anything else."

"Then you are good at it," said Mr. B.

"I hope I am," I said. "I think I am. But you haven't seen me teach."

"It was my experience that the best teachers loved teaching. I thought I was going to be a good teacher when I started, I thought I was committed, but little by little I started to get into a rut. I stopped trying to improve and just fell into a routine. After a few years, I couldn't get myself out. I was stuck doing the same thing day in and day out. And I'll bet you know teachers right now who are stuck."

"Yeah. Now that you mention it, yes, I know some of those teachers."

"They are stuck because they are unhappy," said Mr. B. "At least that's how it happened with me." He was quiet for a moment, staring at his empty coffee cup.

"I know what students thought of me. I know that the students didn't respect me. I tried for a while, but for my last 10 or 12 years, I didn't even feel alive except in the summers and on Friday afternoons. Friday afternoons were wonderful. School would end and I would be free for the next two days. My heart would skip on the way home. Saturdays were the best. On my own and free to do whatever I wanted to do. Sunday mornings were nice. I could get up late, read the paper, just laze around. And then sometime around the middle of Sunday afternoon I would start to feel the school week coming. It was getting closer and closer. I started staying up very late on Sundays because I knew that once I went to sleep, my next waking moment would mean getting ready to go to school. I was stuck in a rut and I couldn't get out. And then the routine became my way to get through the day." He looked up at my face. "You remember the routine, don't you?"

"Yeah," I said, smiling sheepishly, "I remember."

He nodded and I decided not to say any more. He asked about my family and where I lived and some more small-talk kinds of things. And then I told him I had to go meet some old hometown friends who had, like me, come back for our 20th high school reunion.

As I stood to leave, Mr. B caught my arm and said, "Promise me something, will you? Whenever you meet someone who thinks they want to be a teacher, tell them what I just told you."

And so, my young colleagues, I have told you.

Here's what I think happened: I think Mr. B got caught in his assumptions. I don't think he ever found the opportunity to reveal and challenge them. Unless you can reflect on what you have done in the classroom and reveal the assumptions that underlie the doing, you can't evaluate your teaching. And you must find ways to evaluate your teaching.

Think of the word *evaluate*. Think of it literally: to place value. Place value on your teaching. That's what the four of us did together, we evaluated our teaching by trying to see how we thought about teaching and learning and then testing our ideas against the theory and research that is the knowledge base of our profession. As the knowledge base grows, so can you, but only if you place value on your teaching.

I have kept my promise. I trust you will realize yours.

All my best,

Connie

Summary

1. Teachers have an enormous influence on student success in school. Those teachers who bring a scholarly mind-set to their work learn from the effects of their teaching and, as a consequence, foster greater student success.

2. Becoming a better teacher through critical reflection can put a novice teacher on the path to National Board Certification.

3. Having colleagues observe and critique your teaching, using observation checklists, or implementing more formal lesson study procedures all provide rich sources of data for improving your practice.

4. Using guided reflection procedures or, better yet, engaging in systematic and rigorous self-assessment in a Reflective Journal can provide not only insight, but documentation of improvement.

5. According to Ball's model of generativity, teachers who use narrative tools to reflect *on* their teaching learn *from* their teaching. As they progress through stages of self-awakening to metacognitive awareness to self-efficacy, they emerge as change agents who generate knowledge about teaching and generate learning in their students.

6. Digital resources can provide ideas to test in the classroom, ways to connect with other teachers to gain peer feedback and support, and platforms through which to explore evidence-based information regarding effective and excellent teaching methods and techniques.

Resources for Further Investigation

● Reflective Teaching

Among the many recently published books on reflection in teaching, several are worth examining: *Teaching in K-12 Schools: A Reflective Action Approach* (5th ed., 2010), by Judy Eby, Adrienne Herrell, and Michael Jordan; *Reflective Teaching: Evidence-Informed Professional Practice* (3rd ed., 2008), by Andrew Pollard, Julie Anderson, and Mandy Maddock; *At the Heart of Teaching: A Guide to Reflective Practice* (2003), by Grace Hall McEntee, Jon Appleby, JoAnne Dowd, Jan Grant, Simon Hole, and Peggy Silva. The authors of *At the Heart of Teaching* either are or were public school teachers.

The Wisdom of Practice: Essays on Teaching, Learning, and Learning to Teach (2004), a collection of writings by Lee Shulman, one of the most influential scholars in the history of educational psychology. Shulman is president emeritus of the Carnegie Foundation for the Advancement of Teaching and Learning and was a professor of educational psychology at Michigan State University and Stanford University. The title of one of the essays in this collection was

"Those Who Understand," in response to George Bernard Shaw's infamous aphorism: "He who can does. He who cannot, teaches." Shulman ends his essay as follows: "*Those who can, do. Those who understand, teach*" (p. 212, *original italics*).

● Becoming a Better Teacher

Becoming a better teacher means learning *from* teaching. One way to learn *from* teaching and *with* other teachers is lesson study. *Lesson Study Communities: Increasing Achievement with Diverse Students* (2007), by Karin Wiburg and Susan Brown, shows not only how lesson study works, but how communities of teachers can form lesson study communities.

Becoming a better teacher also means documenting your teaching and collecting data to assess your teaching. *Developing Portfolios in Education: A Guide to Reflection, Inquiry, and Assessment* (2010), by Ruth Johnson, Sabrina Mims-Cox, and Adelaide Doyle-Nichols, provides the rationale for keeping a portfolio and guidance for developing and maintaining it as a tool to learn from your teaching.

References

Abedi, J., & Dietel, R. (2004). Challenges in the No Child Left Behind act for English-language learners. *Phi Delta Kappan, 85*(10), 782–785.

Abma, J. C., & Sonenstein, F. L. (2001). *Sexual activity and contraceptive practices among teenagers in the United States, 1988 and 1995.* Hyattsville, MD: National Center for Health Statistics. Retrieved from http://www.cdc.gov/nchs/data/series/sr_23/sr23_21.pdf.

Abrami, P. C., Lou, Y., Chambers, B., Poulsen, C., & Spence, J. C. (2000). Why should we group students within-class for learning? *Educational Research and Evaluation, 6*(2), 158–179.

Adams, G. R., & Berzonsky, M. D. (Eds.). (2006). *The Blackwell handbook of adolescence.* Malden, MA: Blackwell Publishing.

Adams, G. R., Munro, B., Doherty-Poirer, M., Munro, G., Peterson, A. R., & Edwards, J. (2001). Diffuse-avoidance, normative, and informational identity styles: Using identity theory to predict maladjustment. *Identity, 1*(4), 307–320.

Adelson, J. (1972). The political imagination of the young adolescent. In J. Kagan & R. Coles (Eds.), *Twelve to sixteen: Early adolescence.* New York: Norton.

Adelson, J. (1986). *Inventing adolescence: The political psychology of everyday schooling.* New Brunswick, NJ: Transaction Books.

Adey, P. S., Shayer, M., & Yates, C. (2001). *Thinking science* (3rd ed.). London: Nelson Thornes.

Airasian, P., & Russell, M. (2008). *Classroom assessment: Concepts and applications* (6th ed.). Boston: McGraw-Hill.

Alagic, M., & Palenz, D. (2006). Teachers explore linear and exponential growth: Spreadsheets as cognitive tools. *Journal of Technology and Teacher Education, 14*(3), 633–649.

Alasker, F. D., & Olweus, D. (2002). Stability and change in global self-esteem and self-related affect. In T. M. Brinthaupt & R. P. Lipka (Eds.), *Understanding early adolescent self and identity: Applications and interventions* (pp. 193–223). Albany, NY: State University of New York Press.

Alavi, M., & Leidner, D.E. (2001). Technology-mediated learning: A call for greater depth and breadth of research. *Information Systems Research, 12*(1), 1–10.

Alberto, P. A., & Troutman, A. C. (2009). *Applied behavior analysis for teachers* (8th ed.). Upper Saddle River, NJ: Pearson/Merrill.

Alexander, P. A., Graham, S., & Harris, K. R. (1998). A perspective on strategy research: Progress and prospects. *Educational Psychology Review, 10*(2), 129–154.

Alexander, B., & Levine, A. (2008). Storytelling: Emergence of a new genre. *EDUCAUSE Review, 43*(6), 41–56.

Alexander, P. A., & Winne, P. H. (Eds.). (2006). *Handbook of educational psychology* (2nd ed.). Mahwah, NJ: Lawrence Erlbaum Associates.

Alfassi, M. (1998). Reading for meaning: The efficacy of reciprocal teaching in fostering reading comprehension in high school students in remedial reading classes. *American Educational Research Journal, 35*(2), 309–332.

Algozzine, B., & White, R. (2002). Preventing problem behaviors using schoolwide discipline. In B. Algozzine & P. Kay (Eds.), *Preventing problem behaviors: A handbook of successful prevention strategies* (pp. 85–103). Thousand Oaks, CA: Corwin Press.

Allegreto, S. A., Corcoran, S. P., & Mishel, L. (2004). How does teacher pay compare? Economic Policy Institute: Washington, DC. Retrieved from http://www.epi.org/content.cfm/books_teacher_pay.

Allen, N., Resta, P. E., & Christal, M. (2002). Technology and tradition: The role of technology in Native American schools. *TechTrends, 46*(2), 50–55.

Allen, N., Christal, M., Perrot, D., Wilson, C., Grote, B., & Earley, M. A. (1999). Native American schools move into the new millennium. *Educational Leadership, 56*(7), 71–74.

Allender, J. S., & Allender, D. S. (2008). *The humanistic teacher: First the child, then curriculum.* Boulder, CO: Paradigm Publishers.

Allison, B. N., & Schultz, J. B. (2001). Interpersonal identity formation during early adolescence. *Adolescence, 36*(143), 509–523.

American Association of University Women. (1999). *Gender gaps: Where schools still fail our children.* New York: Marlowe & Company.

American Association on Intellectual and Developmental Disabilities. (2009). *Definition of mental retardation.* AAIDD website. Retrieved October 31, 2009, from http://www.aaidd.org/content_100.cfm?navID=21.

American Educational Research Association. (2000). *AERA position statement concerning high-stakes testing in preK-12 education.* Retrieved from http://www.aera.net/about/policy/stakes.htm.

American Educational Research Association. (2004, Summer). Teachers matter: Evidence from value-added assessments. *Research Points, 2*(2), 1–4.

American Psychiatric Association. (2000). *Diagnostic and Statistical Manual of Mental Disorders* (4th edition, Text Revision). Washington, DC: Author.

American Psychological Association. (1997). *Learner-centered psychological principles: A framework for school redesign and reform.* Retrieved from http://www.apa.org/ed/resources.html.

American Psychological Association. (2006, June 1). *Applications of psychological science to teaching and learning task force to present at 2006 AERA conference.* Retrieved from http://www.apa.org/ed/epse/interdivision.html.

Ames, C., & Ames, R. (1984). Systems of student and teacher motivation: Toward a qualitative definition. *Journal of Educational Psychology, 76*(4), 535–556.

Amiram, R., Bar-Tal, D., Alona, R., & Peleg, D. (1990). Perception of epistemic authorities by children and adolescents. *Journal of Youth and Adolescence, 19*(5), 495–510.

Anderman, L. H., & Leake, V. S. (2007). The interface of school and family in meeting the belonging needs of young adolescents. In S. B. Mertens, V. A. Anfara, Jr., & M. M. Caskey (Eds.), *The young adolescent and the middle school* (pp. 163–182.). Charlotte, NC: Information Age Publishing.

Anderman, E. M., & Midgley, C. (2004). Changes in self-reported academic cheating across the transition from middle school to high school. *Contemporary Educational Psychology, 29*(4), 499–517.

Anderman, E. M., & Murdock, T. B. (Eds.). (2007). *Psychology of academic cheating.* Boston: Elsevier Academic Press.

Anderson, L. W. (2009). Upper elementary grades bear the brunt of accountability. *Phi Delta Kappan, 90*(6), 413–418.

Anders Ericsson, K. (Ed.). (2009). *Development of professional expertise: Toward measurement of expert performance and design of optimal learning environments.* New York: Cambridge University Press.

Anderson, L. W., Krathwohl, D. R., Airasian, P. W., Cruikshank, K. A., Mayer, R. E., Pintrich, P. R., Raths, J., & Wittrock, M. C. (2001). A taxonomy for learning, teaching, and assessing: A revision of Bloom's taxonomy of educational objectives. New York: Addison Wesley Longman.

Anderson-Patton, V., & Bass, E. (2002). Using narrative teaching portfolios for self-study. In N. P. Lyons & V. Kubler LaBoskey (Eds.), *Narrative inquiry in practice: Advancing the knowledge of teaching.* New York: Teachers College Press.

Andrade, H., & Cizek, G. (Eds.). (2010). *The handbook of formative assessment.* New York: Routledge.

Andrews, K, & Marshall, K. (2000). Making learning connections through telelearning. *Educational Leadership, 58*(2), 53–56.

Angold, A., Worthman, C., & Costello, E. J. (2003). Puberty and depression. In C. Hayward (Ed.), *Gender differences at puberty* (pp. 137–164). Cambridge, England: Cambridge University Press.

Antil, L. R., Jenkins, J. R., Wayne, S. K., & Vadasy, P. F. (1998). Cooperative learning: Prevalence, conceptualizations, and the relation between research and practice. *Review of Educational Research, 35*(3), 419–454.

Applebee, A. N., Langer, J. A., Nystrand, M., & Gamoran, A. (2003). Discussion-based approaches to developing understanding: Classroom instruction and student performance in middle and high school English. *American Educational Research Journal, 40*(3), 685–730.

Appleton, N. (1983). *Cultural pluralism in education.* New York: Longman.

Armstrong, T. (1994). *Multiple intelligences in the classroom.* Alexandria, VA: Association for Supervision and Curriculum Development.

Armstrong, T. (2009). *Multiple intelligences in the classroom.* Alexandria, VA: ASCD.

Arnold, M. L. (2000). Stage, sequence, and sequels: Changing conceptions of morality, post-Kohlberg. *Educational Psychology Review, 12*(4), 365–383.

Arter, J., & Chappuis, J. (2008). *Creating and recognizing quality rubrics.* Upper Saddle River, New Jersey: Allyn & Bacon/Pearson.

Arter, J., & McTighe, J. (2001). *Scoring rubrics in the classroom.* Thousand Oaks, CA: Corwin Press.

Artiles, A. J., Klingner, J. K., & Tate, W. F. (2006). Representation of minority students in special education: Complicating traditional explanations. *Educational Researcher, 35*(6), 3–5.

Ash, C. (2000). *Voices of a new century: Students' perspectives on the achievement gap.* Chicago: North Central Regional Educational Laboratory. Retrieved from http://www.msanetwork.org.

Ash, K. (2009). Virtual approaches vary. *Education Week, 28*(26), 26–27.

Assouline, S., Nicpon, M. F., & Doobay, A. (2009). Profoundly gifted girls and autism spectrum disorder: A psychometric case study comparison. *Gifted Child Quarterly, 53*(2), 89–105.

Astington, J. W. (1998). Theory of mind goes to school. *Educational Leadership, 56*(3), 46–48.

Atkinson, R. C. (1975). Mnemotechnics in second language learning. *American Psychologist, 30*(2), 821–828.

Atkinson, R. C., & Raugh, M. R. (1975). An application of the mnemonic keyword method to the acquisition of a Russian vocabulary. *Journal of Experimental Psychology: Human Learning and Memory, 104*(2), 126–133

Atkinson, R. C., & Shiffrin, R. M. (1968). Human memory: A proposed system and its control processes. In K. W. Spence & J. T. Spence (Eds.), *The psychology of learning and motivation* (Vol. 2). New York: Academic Press.

Au, W. (2007). High-stakes testing and curricular control: A qualitative metasynthesis. *Educational Researcher, 36*(5), 258–267.

Ausubel, D. P., Novak, J. D., & Hanesian, H. (1978). *Educational psychology: A cognitive view* (2nd ed.). New York: Holt, Rinehart & Winston.

Azevedo, R. (2009). Theoretical, conceptual, methodological, and instructional issues in research on metacognition and self-regulated learning: A discussion. *Metacognition and Learning, 4*(1), 1556–1623.

Azevedo, R., Moos, D. C., Greene, J. A., Winters, F. I., & Cromley, J. G. (2008). Why is externally-facilitated regulated learning more effective than self-regulated learning with hypermedia? *Educational Technology Research and Development, 56*(1), 45–72.

Bachman, L. F. (2002). Alternative interpretations of alternative assessments: Some validity issues in educational performance assessments. *Educational Measurement: Issues and Practice, 21*(5), 5–18.

Bae, Y., Choy, S., Geddes, C., Sable, J., & Snyder, T. (2000). *Trends in educational equity of girls and women.* Washington, DC: National Center for Educational Statistics. Retrieved January 2, 2002, from http://nces.ed.gov/pubs2000/2000030.pdf.

Bailey, S. M. (1996). Shortchanging girls and boys. *Educational Leadership, 53*(8), 75–79.

Baker, E. L. (2007). The end(s) of testing. *Educational Researcher, 36*(6), 309–317.

Baker, J. A. (1999). Teacher-student interaction in urban at-risk classrooms: Differential behavior, relationship quality, and student satisfaction with school. *The Elementary School Journal, 100*(1), 57–70.

Ball, A. F. (2009). Toward a theory of generative change in culturally and linguistically complex classrooms. *American Educational Research Journal, 46*(1), 45–72.

Bandura, A. (1986). *Social foundations of thought and action: A social cognitive theory.* Englewood Cliffs, NJ: Prentice-Hall.

Bandura, A. (1997). *Self-efficacy: The exercise of control.* New York: W. H. Freeman and Company.

Bandura, A. (2001). Social cognitive theory: An agentic perspective. In S. T. Fiske, D. L. Schacter, & C. Zahn-Waxler (Eds.), *Annual Review of Psychology, 52*(1), 1–26.

Bandura, A. (2002). Social cognitive theory in cultural context. *Applied Psychology, 51*(2), 269–290.

Bandura, A., Ross, D., & Ross, S. (1961). Transmission of aggression through imitation of aggressive models. *Journal of Abnormal and Social Psychology, 63*(3), 575–582.

Bangert-Drowns, R. L., Kulik, C-L., Kulik, J. A., & Morgan, M. (1991). The instructional effect of feedback in test-like events. *Review of Educational Research, 61*(2), 213–238.

Banks, J. A. (2008). Diversity, group identity, and citizenship education in a global age. *Educational Researcher, 37*(3), 129–139.

Banks, J. A. (2009). *Teaching strategies for ethnic studies* (8th ed.). Boston: Pearson/Allyn & Bacon.

Barab, S., Dodge, T., Thomas, M., Jackson, C., & Tuzun, H. (2007). Our designs and the social agendas they carry. *The Journal of the Learning Sciences, 16*(2), 263–305.

Barab, S., Gresalfi, M., Ingram-Noble, A., Jameson, E., Hickey, D., Akram, S., & Kizer, S. (2009). Transformational play and virtual worlds: Worked examples from the Quest Atlantis project. *International Journal of Learning and Media, 1*(2). Retrieved from www.mitpressjournals.org.

Barab, S. A., & Luehmann, A. L. (2003). Building sustainable science curriculum: Acknowledging and accommodating local adaptation. *Science Education, 87*(4), 454–467.

Barab, S., Scott, B., Siyahhan, S., Goldstone, S., Ingram-Goble, A., Zuiker, S., & Warren, S. (2009). Transformational play as a curricular scaffold: Using videogames to support science education. *Journal of Science Education and Technology, 18*(4), 305–320.

Barak, M. (2005). From order to disorder: The role of computer-based electronics projects on fostering of higher-order cognitive skills. *Computers & Education, 45*(2), 231–243.

Barret, H. C. (2000). Create your own electronic portfolio. *Learning and Leading with Technology, 27*(7), 14–21.

Barros, R. M., Silver, E. J., & Stein, R. E. K. (2009). School recess and group classroom behavior. *Pediatrics, 123*(2), 431–436.

Bartlett, F. C. (1932). *Remembering.* London: Cambridge University Press.

Barton, P. E., & Coley, R. J. (2007). *The family: America's smallest school.* Princeton, NJ: Policy Evaluation and Research Center, Educational Testing Service. Retrieved from http://www.ets.org/Media/Education_Topics/pdf/5678_PERCReport_school.pdf.

Baumrind, D. (1971). Current patterns of parental authority. *Developmental Psychology Monographs, 4*(1, Pt. 2), 1–103.

Baumrind, D. (1991a). Parenting styles and adolescent development. In R. M. Lerner, A. C. Peterson, & J. Brooks-Gunn (Eds.), *Encyclopedia of adolescence.* New York: Garland Publishing.

Baumrind, D. (1991b). The influence of parenting style on adolescent competence and substance abuse. *Journal of Early Adolescence, 11*(1), 56–95.

Baumrind, D., Larzelere, R. E., & Cowan, P. A. (2002). Ordinary physical punishment: Is it harmful? Comment on Gershoff (2002). *Psychological Bulletin, 128*(4), 580–589.

Bean, T.W., & Stevens, L.P. (2002). Scaffolding reflection for preservice and inservice teachers. *Reflective Practice, 3*(2), 205–218.

Bear, G. G. (2009). The positive in positive models of discipline. In R. Gilman, E. S. Huebner, & M. J. Furlong (Eds.), *Handbook of positive psychology in schools* (pp. 305–321). New York: Routledge.

Beatty, I., & Gerace, W. (2009). Technology-enhanced formative assessment: A research-based pedagogy for teaching science with classroom response technology. *Journal of Science Education and Technology, 18*(2), 146–162.

Bee, H. L., Boyd, D. (2009). *The developing child* (12th ed.). Boston: Pearson/Allyn & Bacon.

Beilin, H., & Pufall, P. B. (Eds.). (1992). *Piaget's theory: Prospects and possibilities.* Hillsdale, NJ: Erlbaum.

Beiser, M., Erickson, D., Fleming, J. A. E., & Iacono, W. G. (1993). Establishing the onset of psychotic illness. *American Journal of Psychiatry, 150*(9), 1349–1354.

Beishuizen, J. J., & Stoutjesdijk, E. T. (1999). Study strategies in a computer assisted study environment. *Learning and Instruction, 9*(3), 281–301.

Bell, L. I. (2002/2003). Strategies that close the gap. *Educational Leadership, 60*(4), 32–34.

Bellanca, J. (2007). *A guide to graphic organizers* (2nd ed.). Thousand Oaks, CA: Corwin Press.

Bellezza, F S. (1981). Mnemonic devices: Classification, characteristics, and criteria. *Review of Educational Research, 51*(2), 247–275.

Ben-Hur, M. (1998). Mediation of cognitive competencies for students in need. *Phi Delta Kappan, 79*(9), 661–666.

Benjamin, A. (2005). *Differentiated instruction using technology: A guide for middle and high school teachers.* Larchmont, NY: Eye on Education.

Benner, A. D., & Mistry, R. S. (2007). Congruence of mother and teacher educational expectations and low-income youth's academic competence. *Journal of Educational Psychology, 99*(1), 140–153.

Bennett, C. I. (2007). *Comprehensive multicultural education: Theory and practice* (6th ed.). Boston: Pearson/Allyn & Bacon.

Bennett, L. & Pye, J. (2000). Using the internet for reflective journals in elementary teacher preparation. *Journal of Social Studies Research, 24*(2), 21–30.

Benoit, D. A., Edwards, R. P., Olmi, D. J., Wilczynski, S. M., & Mandal, R. M. (2001). Generalization of a positive treatment package for child noncompliance. *Child and Family Behavior Therapy, 23*(2), 19–32.

Beran, T. (2009). Correlates of peer victimization and achievement: An exploratory model. *Psychology in the Schools, 46*(4), 348–361.

Bergen D., & Fromberg, D. P. (2009). Play and social interaction in middle childhood. *Phi Delta Kappan, 90*(6), 426–430.

Berk, L. E. (2009). *Child development* (8th ed.). Boston: Pearson/Allyn & Bacon.

Berliner, D. C. (2002). Educational research: The hardest science of all. *Educational Researcher, 31*(8), 18–20.

Berliner, D. C. (2006). Educational psychology: Searching for essence throughout a century of influence. In P. A. Alexander & P. H. Winne (Eds.), *Handbook of educational psychology* (2nd ed., pp. 3–27). Mahwah, NJ: Lawrence Erlbaum Associates.

Berliner, D. C., & Casanova, U. (1996). *Putting research to work in your school.* Arlington Heights, IL: IRI/Skylight Training and Publishing.

Bernard, R. M., Abrami, P. C., Lou, Y., Borokhovski, E., Wade, A., Wozney, L., Wallet, P. A., Fiset, M., & Huang, B. (2004). How does distance education compare with classroom instruction? A meta-analysis of the empirical literature. *Review of Educational Research, 74*(3), 379–439.

Berry, B., Hoke, M., & Hirsch, E. (2004). The search for highly qualified teachers. *Phi Delta Kappan, 85*(9), 684–689.

Berson, I. R. (2009). Here's what we have to say! Podcasting in the early childhood classroom. *Social Studies and the Young Learner, 21*(4), 8–11.

Bielefeldt, T. (2005). Computers and student learning: Interpreting the multivariate analysis of PISA 2000. *Journal of Research on Technology in Education, 37*(4), 339–347.

Biemiller, A. (1993). Lake Woebegon revisited: On diversity and education. *Educational Researcher, 22*(9), 7–12.

Biesta, G. (2007). Why "what works" won't work: Evidence-based practice and the democratic deficit in educational research. *Educational Theory, 57*(1), 1–22.

Billig, S. H. (2000). Research on K-12 school-based service-learning: The evidence builds. *Phi Delta Kappan, 81*(9), 658–664.

Bjork, R. A. (1979). Information processing analysis of college teaching. *Educational Psychologist, 14*, 15–23.

Bjorklund, D. F. (2005). *Children's thinking: Cognitive development and individual differences* (4th ed.). Belmont, CA: Thomson/Wadsworth.

Blachowicz, C., Bates, A., Berne, J., Bridgman, T., Chaney, J., & Perney, J. (2009). Technology and at-risk young readers and their classrooms. *Reading Psychology, 30*(5), 387–411.

Black, A. C., & McCoach, D. B. (2008). Validity study of the thinking styles inventory. *Journal for the Education of the Gifted, 32*(2), 180–210.

Blanchett, W. J. (2006). Disproportionate representation of African American students in special education: Acknowledging the role of White privilege and racism. *Educational Researcher, 35*(6), 24–28.

Blanchett, W., Klingner, J., & Harry, B. (2009). The intersection of race, culture, language, and disability. *Urban Education, 44*(4), 389–409.

Block, C. C., & Pressley, M. (Eds.). (2002). *Comprehension instruction.* New York: Guilford Press.

Block, J. H., Efthim, H. E., & Burns, R. B. (1989). *Building effective mastery learning schools.* New York: Longman.

Blok, H., Oostdam, R., Otter, M. E., & Overmaat, M. (2002). Computer-assisted instruction in support of beginning reading instruction: A review. *Review of Educational Research, 72*(1), 101–130.

Bloom, B. S. (1968). Learning for mastery. *Evaluation Comment, 1*(2), 1–12.

Bloom, B. S. (1976). *Human Characteristics and school learning.* New York: McGraw-Hill.

Bloom, B. S. (1984). The two sigma problem: The search for methods of group instruction as effective as one-to-one tutoring. *Educational Researcher, 13*(6), 4–16.

Bloom, B. S., Englehart, M. B., Furst, E. J., Hill, W. H., & Krathwohl, D. R. (Eds.). (1956). *Taxonomy of educational objectives. The classification of educational goals. Handbook I: Cognitive domain.* New York: McKay.

Bloom, L. A. (2009). *Classroom management: Creating positive outcomes for all students.* Upper Saddle River, NJ: Pearson/Merrill.

Bloomquist, M. L., & Schnell, S. V. (2002). *Helping children with aggression and conduct problems: Best practices for intervention.* New York: Guilford Press.

Bocala, C., Mello, D., Reedy, K., & Lacireno-Paquet, N. (2009). *Features of state response to intervention initiatives in Northeast and Islands Region states* (Issues & Answers Report, REL 2009–No. 083). Washington, DC: U.S. Department of Education, Institute of Education Sciences, National Center for Education Evaluation and Regional Assistance, Regional Educational Laboratory Northeast and Islands. Retrieved from http://ies.ed.gov/ncee/edlabs.

Bock, J. (2008, April 14). A geography class for freshmen in the Fort Zumwalt School District could soon fall off the map. *St. Louis Post-Dispatch*, pp. C1, C8.

Boekarts, M. (1993). Being concerned with well-being and with learning. *Educational Psychologist, 28*(2), 149–167.

Bohman, J. (2009). Critical theory. *The Stanford Encyclopedia of Philosophy* (Fall, 2009 ed.), E. N. Zalta (Ed.). Retrieved from http://plato.stanford.edu/archives/fall2009/entries/critical-theory.

Bolick, C. M., & Cooper, J. M. (2006). Classroom management and technology. In C. M. Evertson & C. S. Weinstein (Eds.), *Handbook of classroom management: Research, practice, and contemporary issues* (pp. 541–558). Mahwah, NJ: Lawrence Erlbaum

Bond, C. L., Miller, M. J., & Kennon, R. W. (1987). Study skills: Who is taking the responsibility for teaching? *Performance & Instruction, 26*(7), 27–29.

Boniecki, K. A., & Moore, S. (2003). Breaking the silence: Using a token economy to reinforce classroom participation. *Teaching of Psychology, 30*(3), 224–227.

Bonk, C. J., & Reynolds, T. H. (1992). Early adolescent composing within a generative-evaluative computerized prompting framework. *Computers in Human Behavior, 8*(1), 39–62.

Borja, R. R. (2003, May 8). Prepping for the big test. *Education Week, 22*(35), 22–24, 26.

Borthick, A. F., Jones, D. R., & Wakai, S. (2003). Designing learning experiences within learners‰ zones of proximal development: Enabling collaborative learning on-site and on-line. *Journal of Information Systems, 17*(1), 107–134.

Bower, G. H., Clark, M. C., Lesgold, A. M., & Winzenz, D. (1969). Hierarchical retrieval schemes in recall of categorized word lists. *Journal of Verbal Learning and Verbal Behavior, 8*(3), 323–343.

Bowes, L., Arsenault, L., Maughan, B., Taylor, A. Caspi, A., & Moffitt, T. E. (2009). School, neighborhood, and family factors are associated with children's bullying involvement: A nationally representative longitudinal study. *Journal of the American Academy of Child and Adolescent Psychiatry, 48*(5), 545–553.

Bowman, D. H. (2002). National survey puts ADHD incidence near 7 percent. *Education Week, 21*(38), 3.

Boyer, E. L. (1983). *High school.* New York: Harper & Row.

Braaksma, M. A. H., Rijlaarsdam, G., & van den Bergh, H. (2002). Observational learning and the effects of model-observer similarity. *Journal of Educational Psychology, 94*(2), 405–415.

Bracey, G. W. (2008a). The 18th Bracey report on the condition of public education: Schools-are-awful bloc still busy in 2008. *Phi Delta Kappan, 90*(2), 103–114.

Bracey, G. W. (2008b). International comparisons: Worth the cost? In S. Mathison & E. W. Ross (Eds.), *The nature and limits of standards-based reform and assessment* (pp. 35–47). New York: Teachers College Press.

Branch, C. W., & Boothe, B. (2002). The identity status of African Americans in middle adolescence: A replication and extension of Forbes and Ashton (1998). *Adolescence, 37*(148), 815–821.

Bråten, I., & Strømsø, H. I. (2004). Epistemological beliefs and implicit theories of intelligence as predictor of achievement goals. *Contemporary Educational Psychology, 29*(4), 371–388.

Braun, H. I., & Mislevy, R. (2005). Intuitive test theory. *Phi Delta Kappan, 86*(7), 489–497.

Brendgen, M., Wanner, B., Vitaro, F., Bukowski, W. M., & Tremblay, R. E. (2007). Verbal abuse by the teacher during childhood and academic, behavioral, and emotional adjustment in young adulthood. *Journal of Educational Psychology, 99*(1), 26–38.

Brinthaupt, T. M., Lipka, R. P., & Wallace, M. (2007). Aligning student self and identity concerns with middle school practices. In S. B. Mertens, V. A. Anfara, Jr., & M. M. Caskey (Eds.), *The young adolescent and the middle school* (pp. 201–218). Charlotte, NC: Information Age Publishing.

Broekkamp, H., & Van Hout-Wolters, H. A. M. (2007). Students' adaptation of study strategies when preparing for classroom tests. *Educational Psychology Review, 19*(4), 401–428.

Broekkamp, H., van Hout-Wolters, B. H. A. M., Rijlaarsdam, G., & van den Bergh, H. (2002). Importance in instructional text: Teachers' and students' perceptions of task demands. *Journal of Educational Psychology, 94*(2), 260–271.

Brookhart, S. (2009a). Editorial. *Educational Measurement: Issues and Practice, 28*(1), 1–2.

Brookhart, S. (2009b). *Grading* (2nd ed.). Upper Saddle River, NJ: Merrill/Pearson Education.

Brookhart, S. M., & Freeman, D. J. (1992) Characteristics of entering teacher candidates. *Review of Educational Research, 62*, No. 1. pp. 37–60.

Brookhart, S., & Nitko, A. (2008). *Assessment and grading in classrooms.* Upper Saddle River, NJ: Allyn & Bacon/Pearson.

Brooks, J. G., & Brooks, M. G. (2001). *In search of understanding: The case for constructivist classrooms.* Upper Saddle River, NJ: Merrill Prentice Hall.

Brophy, J. E., & Alleman, J. (1991). Activities as instructional tools: A framework for analysis and evaluation. *Educational Researcher, 20*(4), 9–23.

Brophy, J. E., & Evertson, C. M. (1976). *Learning from teaching.* Boston: Allyn & Bacon.

Brouwer, N., & Korthagen, F. (2005). Can teacher education make a difference? *American Educational Research Journal, 42*(1), 153–224.

Brown, A. L., Campione, J. C., & Day, J. D. (1981). Learning to learn: On training students to learn from text. *Educational Researcher, 10*(2), 14–24.

Brown, D. F. (2002). Self-directed learning in an 8th grade classroom. *Phi Delta Kappan, 60*(1), 54–58.

Brown, J. L., Roderick, T., Lantieri, L., & Aber, J. L. (2004). The Resolving Conflict Creatively Program: A school-based social and emotional learning program. In J. E. Zins, R. P. Weissberg, M. C. Wang, & H. J. Walberg (Eds.), *Building academic success on social and emotional learning: What does the research say?* New York: Teachers College Press.

Brown, S. M., & Walberg, H. J. (1993). Motivational effects on test scores of elementary students. *Journal of Educational Research, 86*(3), 133–136.

Bruning, R. H., Schraw, G. J., Norby, M. M., & Ronning, R. R. (2004). *Cognitive psychology and instruction* (4th ed.). Upper Saddle River, NJ: Merrill Prentice Hall.

Brush, T., Armstrong, J., Barbrow, D., & Ulintz, L. (1999). Design and delivery of integrated learning systems: Their impact on student achievement and attitudes. *Journal of Educational Computing Research, 21*(4), 475–486.

Brush, T., & Saye, J. (2001). The use of embedded scaffolds with hypermedia-supported student-centered learning. *Journal of Educational Multimedia and Hypermedia, 10*(4), 333–356.

Bryant, D. P., Vaughn, S., Linan-Thompson, S., Ugel, N., Hamff, A., & Hougen, M. (2000). Reading outcomes for students with and without reading disabilities in general education middle-school content area classes. *Learning Disability Quarterly, 23*(4), 238–252.

Bryk, A., Bender Sebring, P., Allensworth, E., Luppescu, S., & Easton, J. (2010). *Organizing schools for improvement: Lessons from Chicago.* Chicago: University of Chicago Press.

Bryk, A., & Gomez, L. (2008). Reinventing a research and development capacity. In F. Hess (Ed.), *The future of educational entrepreneurship: Possibilities for school reform* (pp. 181–206). Cambridge, MA: Harvard Education Press.

Bucher, A. A. (1997). The influence of models in forming moral identity. *International Journal of Educational Research, 27*(7), 619–627.

Bukatko, D. (2008). *Child and adolescent development: A chronological approach.* Boston: Houghton Mifflin.

Bull, G., Hammond, T., & Ferster, B. (2008). Developing web 2.0 tools for support of historical inquiry in social studies. *Computers in the Schools, 25*(3–4), 275–287.

Bunz, U. (2009). A generational comparison of gender, computer anxiety, and computer-email-web fluency. *Studies in Media & Information Literacy Education, 9*(2), 54–69.

Burch, C. B. (1993). Teachers vs. professors: The university's side. *Educational Leadership, 51*(2), 68–76.

Burchinal, M. R., Peisner-Feinberg, E., Pianta, R., & Howes, C. (2002). The development of academic skills from preschool through second grade: Family and classroom predictors of developmental trajectories. *Journal of School Psychology, 40*(5), 415–436.

Burris, C. C., & Welner, K. G. (2005). Closing the achievement gap by detracking. *Phi Delta Kappan, 86*(8), 594–598.

Burris, C. C., Wiley, E., Welner, K., & Murphy, J. (2008). Accountability, rigor and detracking: Achievement effects of embracing a challenging curriculum as a universal good for all students. *Teachers College Record, 110*(3), 571–608.

Burtch, J. A. (1999). Technology is for everyone. *Educational Leadership, 56*(5), 33–34.

Burton, D., Lee, K., & Younie, S. (2009). Understanding learning theories and strategies. In S. Younie, S. Capel, & M. Leask (Eds), *Supporting teaching and learning in schools* (pp.82–90). New York: Routledge.

Bushrod, G., Williams, R. L., & McLaughlin, T. F. (1995). An evaluation of a simplified daily report system with two kindergarten pupils. *B.C. Journal of Special Education, 19*(1), 35–43.

Butler, R. (2005). Competence assessment, competence, and motivation between early and middle childhood. In A. J. Elliot & C. S. Dweck (Eds.), *Handbook of competence and motivation* (pp. 202–221). New York: Guilford Press.

Calderón, M. E., & Minaya-Rowe, L. (2003). *Designing and implementing two-way bilingual programs.* Thousand Oaks, CA: Corwin Press.

Calfee, R. (2009). Teacher-based assessment in the elementary and middle grades. *Perspectives on Language Learning and Education, 16*(1), 21–27.

Callahan, C. M., & McIntire, J. A. (1994). *Identifying outstanding talent in American Indian and Alaska native students.* Washington, DC: U. S. Department of Education, Office of Educational Research and Improvement.

Callahan, R. M. (2005). Tracking and high school English learners: Limiting opportunity to learn. *American Educational Research Journal, 42*(2), 305–328.

Callender, A. A., & McDaniel, M. A. (2009). The limited benefits of rereading educational texts, *Comtemporary Educational Psychology, 34*(1), 30–41.

Cambalbur, M., & Erdogan, Y. (2008). A meta-analysis on the effectiveness of computer-assisted instruction: Turkey sample. *Educational Sciences: Theory and Practice, 8*(2), 497–505.

Camilli, G. (2003). Comment on Cizek's "more unintended consequences of high-stakes testing." *Educational Measurement: Issues and Practice, 22*(1), 36–39.

Camp, C., & Stark, W. (2006). More than words on the screen [Electronic version]. Paper presented at the 2006 PEPNet conference Roots & Wings. (Proceedings available from the University of Tennessee, Postsecondary Education Consortium Web site: http://sunsite.utk.edu/cod/pec/products.html).

Campbell, J., Kyriakides, L., Muijs, D., & Robinson, W. (2004). *Assessing teacher effectiveness: Developing a differentiated model.* New York: Routledge/Falmer.

Campbell, L. (1997). How teachers interpret MI theory. *Educational Leadership, 55*(1), 14–19.

Canivez, G. L. (2008). Orthogonal higher order factor structure of the Stanford-Binet intelligence scales—fifth edition for children and adolescents. *School Psychology Quarterly, 23*(4), 533–541.

Cannamo, K., Ross, J., & Ertmer, P. (2010). Technology integration for meaningful classroom use: A standards-based approach. Belmont, CA: Wadsworth/Cengage Learning.

Cardon, P. L., & Christensen, K. W. (1998). Technology-based programs for drop-out prevention. *Journal of Technology Studies, 24*(1), 50–54.

Cardwell, K. (2000). Electronic assessment. *Learning and Leading with Technology, 27*(7), 22–26.

Carnevale, D. (2004, May 28). Online study tools help Texas students prepare for graduation exam. *The Chronicle of Higher Education, 50*(38), p. A31.

Carney, R. N., & Levin, J. R. (2002). Pictorial illustrations still improve students' learning from text. *Educational Psychology Review, 14*(1), 5–26.

Carney, R. N., Levin, J. R., & Levin, M. E. (1994). Enhancing the psychology of memory by enhancing memory of psychology. *Teaching of Psychology, 21*(3), 171–174.

Carroll, J. B. (1963). A model of school learning. *Teachers College Record, 64*(8), 723–733.

Carter, C. J. (1997). Why reciprocal teaching? *Educational Leadership, 54*(6), 64–68.

Carter, D. B. (1987). The role of peers in sex role socialization. In D. B. Carter (Ed.), *Current conceptions of sex roles and sex typing.* New York: Praeger.

Carter, K., & Doyle, W. (2006). Classroom management in early childhood and elementary classrooms. In C. M. Evertson & C. S. Weinstein (Eds.), *Handbook of classroom management: Research, practice, and contemporary issues* (pp. 373–406). Mahwah, NJ: Lawrence Erlbaum.

Case, R. (1975). Gearing the demands of instruction to the developmental capacities of the learner. *Review of Educational Research, 45*(1), 59–88.

Case, R. (1999). Conceptual development in the child and in the field: A personal view of the Piagetian legacy. In E. K. Scholnick, K. Nelson, S. A. Gelman, & P. H. Miller (Eds.), *Conceptual development: Piaget's legacy.* Mahwah, NJ: Erlbaum.

Cassady, J. C., & Smith, L. L. (2005). The impact of a structured integrated learning system of first-grade students' reading gains. *Reading & Writing Quarterly, 21*(4), 361–376.

Castagno, A. E., & Brayboy, B. M. J. (2008). Culturally indigenous youth: A review of the literature. *Review of Educational Research, 78*(4), 941–993.

Center for Applied Linguistics. (2009). *Directory of two-way bilingual immersion programs in the U.S.* Retrieved from http://www.cal.org/twi/directory.

Center for Applied Special Technology. (2008). *Universal design for learning guidelines version 1.0.* Wakefield, MA: Author. Retrieved March 11, 2009, from www.cast.org/publications/UDLguidelines/UDL_Guidelines_v1.0.doc.

Center for Effective Discipline (2009a). Discipline and the law: State laws. Retrieved from http://www.stophitting.com/index.php?page=legalinformation.

Center for Effective Discipline (2009b). Discipline at school (NCACPS): U.S.: Corporal punishment and paddling statistics by state and race. Retrieved from http://www.stophitting.com/index.php?page=statesbanning.

Centers for Disease Control and Prevention (2008, June). Youth risk behavior surveillance—United States, 2007. *MMWR, 57*(SS–4), 1–131.

Centers for Disease Control and Prevention (2009, July). Sexual and reproductive health of persons aged 10–24 years—United States, 2002–2007. *Surveillance Summaries. MMWR, 58*(SS–6),1–60.

Center on Education Policy (2005, March). *From the capital to the classroom: Year 3 of the No Child Left Behind Act.* Washington, DC: Author. Retrieved from http://www.cep-dc.org.

Center on Education Policy (2006, August). *State high school exit exams: A challenging year.* Retrieved from http://www.cep-dc.org.

Center on Education Policy. (2007, August). *Reauthorizing the elementary and secondary education act of 1965: Recommendations from the Center on Educational Policy.* Retrieved from http://www.cep-dc.org.

Center on Education Policy (2008a, June). *Has student achievement increased since 2002? State test score trends through 2006–07.* Retrieved from http://www.cep-dc.org/index.cfm?fuseaction=Page.viewPage&pageId=495&parentID=481.

Center on Education Policy. (2008b, November). *Lessons from the classroom level: Federal and state accountability in Rhode Island.* Retrieved from http://www.cep-dc.org.

Center on Education Policy (2009, October). *Are achievement gaps closing and is achievement rising for all?* Retrieved from http://www.cep-dc.org.

Cepeda, N., Coburn, N., Rohrer, D., Wixted, J., Mozer, M., & Pashler, H. (2009). Optimizing distributed practice theoretical analysis and practical implications. *Experimental Psychology, 56*(4), 236–246.

Chaney, E., & Gilman, D. A. (2005). Filling in the blanks: Using computers to test and teach. *Computers in the Schools, 22*(1/2), 157–168.

Chang, C-C. (2009). Self-evaluated effects of web-based portfolio assessment system for various student motivation levels. *Journal of Educational Computing Research. 41*(4), 391–405.

Chase, K. (2002). The brilliant inventiveness of student misbehavior: Test your classroom management skills. *Phi Delta Kappan, 84*(4), 327–328, 330.

Chance, P. (1992). The rewards of learning. *Phi Delta Kappan, 74*(3), 200–207.

Chance, P. (1993). Sticking up for rewards. *Phi Delta Kappan, 74*(10), 787–790.

Character Education Partnership. (2000). *Eleven principles of effective character education.* Retrieved from http://www.character. org.

Chen, J. A., & Pajares, F. (2010). Implicit theories of ability of Grade 6 science students: Relation to epistemological beliefs and academic motivation and achievement in science. *Contemporary Educational Psychology, 35*(1), 75–87.

Chen, J-Q., Moran, S., & Gardner, H. (Eds.). (2009). *Multiple intelligences around the world.* San Francisco: John Wiley & Sons.

Chen, M., & Bargh, J. A. (1997). Nonconscious behavioral confirmation processes: The self-fulfilling consequences of automatic stereotype activation. *Journal of Experimental Social Psychology, 33*(5), 541–560.

Choi, I., & Lee, K. (2009). Designing and implementing a case-based learning environment for enhancing ill-structured problem solving: Classroom management problems for prospective teachers. *Educational Technology Research and Development, 57*(1), 99–129.

Chudowsky, N., & Chudowsky, V. (2008, May). *Many states have taken a "back-loaded" approach to No Child Left Behind goal of all students scoring "proficient."* Retrieved from Center on Education Policy: http://www.cep-dc.org.

Cicchetti, D., & Toth, S. L. (1998). The development of depression in children and adolescents. *American Psychologist, 53*(2), 221–241.

Cizek, G. J. (2001). More unintended consequences of high-stakes testing. *Educational Measurement: Issues and Practices, 20*(4), 19–27.

Cizek, G. J. (2003). Rejoinder. *Educational Measurement: Issues and Practice, 22*(1), 40–44.

Clark, R. E., (2002). Performance assessment in the arts. *Kappa Delta Pi Record, 39*(1), 29–32.

Clark, J. M., & Paivio, A. (1991). Dual coding theory and education. *Educational Psychology Review, 3*(3), 149–210.

Clarke, L, & Heaney, P. (2003). Author On-Line: Using asynchronous computer conferencing to support literacy. *British Journal of Educational Psychology, 34*(1), 57–66.

Clarke, M., Abrams, L., & Madaus, G. (2001). The effects and implications of high-stakes achievement tests for adolescents. In T. Urdan & F. Pajares (Eds.), *Adolescence and education. Vol. 1: General issues in the education of adolescents* (pp. 201–229). Greenwich, CT: Information Age Publishing.

Clawson, M. A., & Robila, M. (2001). Relations between parenting style and children's play behavior. Issues in education. *Journal of Early Education and Family Review, 8*(3), 13–19.

Clements, D. H., Sarama, J., Yelland, N. J., & Glass, B. (2008). Learning and teaching geometry with computers in the elementary and middle school. In M. K. Heid & G. W. Blume (Eds.), *Research on technology and the teaching and learning of mathematics: Volume 1. Research syntheses* (pp. 109–154). Charlotte, NC: Information Age Publishing.

Clements, P., & Seidman, E. (2002). The ecology of middle grades schools and possible selves. In T. M. Brinthaupt & R. P. Lipka (Eds.), *Understanding early adolescent self and identity: Applications and interventions* (pp. 133–164). Albany, NY: State University of New York Press.

Cochran-Smith, M. (2003). The unforgiving complexity of teaching: Avoiding simplicity in the age of accountability. *Journal of Teacher Education, 54*(1), 3–5.

Cochran-Smith, M. (2005). The new teacher education: For better or for worse? *Educational Researcher, 34*(7), 3–17.

Colangelo, N., & Davis, G. A. (2003a). *Handbook of gifted education* (3rd ed.). Boston: Allyn & Bacon.

Colangelo, N., & Davis, G. A. (2003b) Introduction and overview. In N. Colangelo & G. A. Davis (Eds.), *Handbook of gifted education* (3rd ed., pp. 3–10). Boston: Allyn & Bacon.

Cole, J., Bergin, D., & Whittaker, T. (2008). Predicting student achievement for low stakes tests with effort and task value. *Contemporary Educational Psychology, 33*(4), 609–624.

Cole, M. (1996). *Cultural psychology: A once and future discipline.* Cambridge, MA: Harvard University Press.

Cole, M. (2005). Putting culture in the middle. In H. Daniels (Ed.), *An introduction to Vygotsky* (2nd ed.). New York: Routledge.

Cole, M., & Gajdamaschko, N. (2007). Vygotsky and culture. In H. Daniels, M. Cole, & J. Wertsch (Eds.), The Cambridge companion to Vygotsky (pp. 193–211). New York: Cambridge University Press.

Cole, J. M., & Hilliard, V. R. (2006). The effects of web-based reading curriculum on children's reading performance and motivation. *Journal of Educational Computing Research, 34*(4), 353–380.

Combs, A. W. (1965). *The professional education of teachers.* Boston: Allyn and Bacon.

Commission on Instructionally Supportive Assessment. (2002, March). *Implementing ESEA's testing provisions.* Retrieved from http://www.nea.org/accountability/ images/02eseatesting.pdf

Compton, M., Tucker, D., & Flynn, P. (2009). Preparation and perceptions of speech-language pathologists working with children with cochlear implants. *Communication Disorders Quarterly, 30*(3), 142–154.

Compton-Lilly, C. (2009). Introduction. In C. Compton-Lilly (Ed.), *Breaking the silence: Recognizing social and cultural resources students bring to the classroom* (pp.1–12). Newark, DE: International Reading Association.

Conger, J. J., & Galambos, N. L. (1997). *Adolescence and youth* (5th ed.). New York: Longman.

Connor, D. F. (2002). *Aggression and antisocial behavior in children and adolescents.* New York: Guilford Press.

Cooper, H. (2001). Homework for all—in moderation. *Educational Leadership, 58*(7), 34–38.

Cooper, H., & Dorr, N. (1995). Race comparisons on need for achievement: A meta-analytic alternative to Graham's narrative review. *Review of Educational Research, 65*(4), 438–508.

Cooper, H., Robinson, J. C., & Patall, E. A. (2006). Does homework improve academic achievement? A synthesis of research, 1987–2003. *Review of Educational Research, 76*(1), 1–62.

Corbett, C., Hill, C., & St. Rose, A. (2008). *Where the girls are: The facts about gender equity in education.* Washington, DC: American Association of University Women.

Corbett, D., & Wilson, B. (2002). What urban students say about good teaching. *Educational Leadership, 60*(1), 18–22.

Cornelius-White, J. (2007). Learner-centered teacher-students relationships are effective: A meta-analysis. *Review of Educational Research, 77*(1), 113–143.

Cornford, I. (2002). Reflective teaching: Empirical research findings and some implications for teacher education. *Journal of Vocational Education and Training, 54*(2), 219–235.

Corno, L. (2008). On teaching adaptively. *Educational Psychologist, 43*(3), 161–173.

Cornoldi, C. (2010). Metacognition, intelligence, and academic performance. In H. Salatas Waters & W. Schneider (Eds.). *Metacognition, strategy use, and instruction.* (pp. 257–280). New York: Guilford Press.

Costa, A. L., & Kallick, B. (2004). *Assessment strategies for self-directed learning.* Thousand Oaks, CA: Corwin Press.

Cothran, J. C. (2006). *A search of African-American life, achievement and culture.* Carrolltown, TX: Stardate Publishing.

Cotterall, S., & Cohen, R. (2003). Scaffolding for second language writers: Producing an academic essay. *ELT Journal, 57*(2), 158–166.

Couzijn, M. (1999). Learning to write by observation of writing and reading processes: Effects on learning and transfer. *Learning and Instruction, 9*(2), 109–142.

Covington, M. V. (2000). Goal theory, motivation, and school achievement: An integrative review. In S. T. Fiske, D. L. Schacter, & C. Zahn-Waxler (Eds.), *Annual review of psychology* (Vol. 51, pp. 171–200). Palo Alto, CA: Annual Reviews.

Covington, M. V. (2009). Self-worth theory: Retrospection and prospects. In K. Wentzel & A. Wigfield (Eds.), *Handbook of motivation at school* (pp. 141–170). New York: Routledge.

Cowan, N. (2005). *Working memory capacity.* New York: Psychology Press.

Crain, W. (2005). *Theories of development: Concepts and applications* (5th ed.). Upper Saddle River, NJ: Pearson/Prentice-Hall.

Craig, S., Chi, M., & VanLehn, K. (2009). Improving classroom learning by collaboratively observing human tutoring videos while problem solving. *Journal of Educational Psychology, 101*(4), 779–789.

Cramer, P. (2001). Identification and its relation to identity development. *Journal of Personality, 69*(5), 667–688.

Crawford, G. B. (2004). *Managing the adolescent classroom: Lessons from outstanding teachers.* Thousand Oaks, CA: Corwin Press.

Cronin, J., Dahlin, M., Adkins, D., & ingsbury, G. G. (2007, October). *The proficiency illusion.* Retrieved from Thomas B. Fordham Institute: http://www.edexcellence .net/institute/publication/publication .cfm?id=376.

Cummins, J. (1999). Alternative paradigms in bilingual education research. *Educational Researcher, 28*(7), 26–32, 41.

Cunningham, D. J. (1992). Beyond educational psychology: Steps toward an educational semiotic. *Educational Psychology Review, 4*(2), 165–194.

Cunningham, D. J. (2001, April). *Fear and loathing in the information age.* Paper presented at the annual meeting of the American Education Research Association, Seattle, WA.

Cury, F., Da Fonseca, D., Zahn, I., & Elliot, A. (2008). Implicit theories and IQ test performance: A sequential mediational analysis. *Journal of Experimental Social Psychology, 44*(3), 783–791.

Cushman, K. (2003). *Fires in the bathroom: Advice for teachers from high school students.* New York: The New Press.

Cushman, K., & Rogers, L. (2008). *Fires in the middle school bathroom: Advice for teachers from middle schoolers.* New York: The New Press.

D'Agostino, J. V., & Powers, S. J. (2009). Predicting teacher performance with test scores and grade point average: A meta-analysis. *American Educational Research Journal, 46*(1), 146–182.

Dai, D. Y., & Rinn, A. N. (2008). The big-fish-little-pond effect: What do we know and where do we go from here? *Educational Psychology Review, 20*(3), 283–317.

Daiute, C. (1985). Issues in using computers to socialize the writing process. *Educational Communication and Technology, 33*(1), 41–50.

Daly, E. (III), Martens, B., Barnett, D., Witt, J., & Olson, S. (2007). Varying intervention delivery in response to intervention: Confronting and resolving challenges with measurement, instruction, and intensity. *School Psychology Review, 36*(4), 562–581.

Daniel, D. B., & Poole, D. A. (2009). Learning for life: An ecological approach to pedagogical research. *Perspectives on Psychological Science, 4*(1), 91–96.

Dardig, J. C. (2005). The McClurg monthly magazine and 14 more practical ways to involve parents. *Teaching Exceptional Children 38*(2), 46–51.

Darling-Hammond, L. (2008). The case for university-based teacher education. In M. Cochran-Smith, S. Feiman-Nemser, D. J. McIntyre, K. E. Demers (Eds.), *Handbook of research on teacher education: Enduring questions in changing contexts* (3rd ed.) (pp. 333–346). New York: Routledge.

Darling-Hammond, L. (2009). America's commitment to equity will determine our future. *Phi Delta Kappan, 91*(4), 8–14.

Darling-Hammond, L. (with Fickel, L., Koppich, J., Macdonald, M., Merseth, K., Miller, L., Ruscoe, G., Silvernail, D., Snyder, J., Whitford, B., & Zeichner, K.) (2006). *Powerful teacher education: Lessons from exemplary programs.* San Francisco: Jossey-Bass.

Darling-Hammond, L. (with Fickel, L., Koppich, J., Macdonald, M., Merseth, K., Miller, L., Ruscoe, G., Silvernail, D., Snyder, J., Whitford, B., & Zeichner, K.) (2009). *Powerful teacher education: Lessons from exemplary programs.* San Francisco: Jossey-Bass.

Darling-Hammond, L., & Falk, B. (1997). Using standards and assessments to support student learning. *Phi Delta Kappan, 79*(3), 190–199.

Darling-Hammond, L., & Youngs, P. (2002). Defining "highly qualified teachers": What does "scientifically-based research" actually tell us? *Educational Researcher, 31*(9), 13–25.

Darling-Hammond, L., Holtzman, D. J., Gatlin, S. J., & Heilig, J. V. (2005). Does teacher preparation matter? Evidence about teacher certification, Teach for America, and teacher effectiveness. *Education Policy Analysis Archives, 13*(42), 1–51. Retrieved from http://epaa.asu.edu/epaa/v13n42.

Dasen, P., & Heron, A. (1981). Cross-cultural tests of Piaget's theory. In H. C. Triandis & A. Heron (Eds.), *Handbook of cross-cultural psychology, developmental psychology* (Vol. 4). Boston: Allyn & Bacon.

Davis, M. R. (2009). Breaking away from tradition. *Education Week, 28*(26), 8–9.

Davis, S. H. (2007). Bridging the gap between research and practice: What's good, what's bad, and how can one be sure? *Phi Delta Kappan, 88*(8), 568–578.

DeBell, M., & Chapman, C. (2003). *Computer and Internet use by children and adolescents in 2001.* Washington, DC: National Center for Educational Statistics. Retrieved January 5, 2004, from http://nces.ed.gov/pubsearch/pubsinfo.asp?pubid=2004014.

DeBlois, R. (2005). When to promote students. *Phi Delta Kappan, 87*(4), 306–310.

Delgarno, B. (2001). Interpretations of constructivism and consequences for computer assisted learning. *British Journal of Educational Technology, 32*(2), 183–194.

De Lisi, R. (2006). A developmental perspective on virtual scaffolding for learning in home and school contexts. In A. O'Donnell, C.E. Hmelo-Silver, & G. Erkens (Eds.), *Collaborative learning, reasoning, and technology.* Mahwah, NJ: Lawrence Erlbaum Associates.

Dempster, F. N. (1988). The spacing effect: A case study in the failure to apply the results of psychological research. *American Psychologist, 43*(8), 627–634.

DeNavas-Walt, C, Proctor, B. D., & Smith, J. C. (2009, September). *Income, poverty, and health insurance coverage in the United States: 2008. Current Population Reports, P60-236.* U.S. Government Printing Office, Washington, D.C. Retrieved from http://www.census.gov/prod/2009pubs/p60-236.pdf.

Denbo, S. J. (2002). Institutional practices that support African American student achievement. In S. J. Denbo & L. M. Beaulieu (Eds.), *Improving schools for African American students* (pp. 55–71). Springfield, IL: Charles C. Thomas.

Deneen, C., & Deneen, J. (2008). *Assessing student achievement: A guide for teachers and administrators.* Lanham, MD: Rowman & Littlefield Education.

DeRose, L. M., & Brooks-Gunn, J. (2009). Pubertal development in early adolescence: Implications for affective processes. In N. B. Allen & L. B. Sheeber (Eds.), *Adolescent emotional development and the emergence of depressive disorders* (pp. 56–73). Cambridge, England: Cambridge University Press.

Derry, S. J. (1996). Cognitive schema theory in the constructivist debate. *Educational Researcher, 31*(3/4), 163–174.

Derzon, J. (2006). How effective are school-based violence prevention programs in preventing and reducing violence and other antisocial behaviors? A meta-analysis. In S. R. Jimerson & M. J. Furlong (Eds.), *The handbook of school violence and school safety* (pp. 429–441). Mahwah, NJ: Lawrence Erlbaum.

Devine, J., & Cohen, J. (2007). *Making your school safe: Strategies to protect children and promote learning.* New York: Teachers College Press.

De Vries, B., Van der Meij, Boersma, K., & Pieters, J. M. (2005). Embedding e-mail in primary schools: Developing a tool for collective reflection. *Journal of Educational Computing Research, 32*(2), 167–183.

DeVries, R. (1997). Piaget's social theory. *Educational Researcher, 26*(2), 4–17.

Dijkstra, P., Kuyper, H., van der Werf, G., Buunk, A. P., & van der Zee, Y. G. (2008). Social comparisons in the classroom. *Review of Educational Research, 78*(4), 828–879.

Dill, E. M., & Boykin, A. W. (2000). The comparative influence of individual, peer tutoring, and communal learning contexts of the text recall of African American children. *Journal of Black Psychology, 26*(1), 65–78.

Dinkes, R., Kemp, J., Baum, K, & Snyder, T. D. (2009). *Indicators of school crime and safety: 2008* (NCES 2009-022/NCJ 226343). Washington, DC: U.S. Department of Education and U. S. Department of Justice. Retrieved from http:/nces.ed.gov/pubs2009/2009022.pdf.

Dobbs, M. (2005, April 21). NEA, states challenge 'No Child' program. *Washington Post*, p. A21.

Donovan, C. A., & Smolkin, L. B. (2002). Children's genre knowledge: An examination of k-5 students' performance on multiple tasks providing differing levels of scaffolding. *Reading Research Quarterly, 37*(4), 428–465.

Doppelt, Y. (2009). Assessing creative thinking in design-based learning. *International Journal of Technology and Design Education, 19*(1), 55–65.

Dornbusch, S. M., & Kaufman, J. G. (2001). The social structure of the American high school. In T. Urdan & F. Pajares (Eds.), *Adolescence and education* (Vol. 1, pp. 61–91). Greenwich, CT: Information Age Publishing.

Doty, D. E., Popplewell, S. R., & Byers, G. O. (2001). Interactive CD-ROM storybooks and young readers' reading comprehension. *Journal of Research on Computing in Education, 33*(4), 374–384.

Doyle, W. (1983). Academic work. *Review of Educational Research, 53*(2), 159–200.

Drake, F. D., & McBride, L. W. (2000). The summative teaching portfolio and the reflective practitioner of history. *The History Teacher, 34*(1), 41–60.

Drier, H. S. (2001). Conceptualization and design of Probability Explorer. *TechTrends, 45*(2), 2–24.

Drier, H. S., Dawson, K. M., & Garofalo, J. (1999). Not your typical math class. *Educational Leadership, 56*(5), 21–25.

Driscoll, M. P. (2005). *Psychology of learning for instruction* (3rd ed.). Boston: Allyn & Bacon.

Duckworth, A. L., & Seligman, E. P. (2006). Self-discipline gives girls the edge: Gender in self-discipline, grades, and achievement test scores. *Journal of Educational Psychology, 98*(1), 198–208.

Duell, O. K. (1986). Metacognitive skills. In G. D. Phye & T. Andre (Eds.), *Cognitive classroom learning.* Orlando, FL: Academic Press.

Duff, C. (2000). Online mentoring. *Educational Leadership, 58*(2), 49–52.

Duffrin, E. (2004a, May). What we know about efforts to end 'social promotion'. *Catalyst Chicago*, 8–10.

Duffrin, E. (2004b, May). Popular despite the research. *Catalyst Chicago*, 6–7.

Duffy, G. G., & Kear, K. (2007). Compliance or adaptation: What is the real message about research-based practices? *Phi Delta Kappan, 88*(5), 579–581.

Duhaney, L. M., & Duhaney, D. C. (2000). Assistive technology: Meeting the needs of learners with disabilities. *International Journal of Instructional Media, 27*(4), 393–401.

Dunlosky, J., & Bjork, R. (2008). The integrated nature of metamemory and memory. In J. Dunlosky & R. Bjork (Eds.), *Handbook of metamemory and memory* (pp. 11–28). New York: Taylor & Francis.

Dunlosky, J., & Bjork, R. (Eds.). (2008). *Handbook of metamemory and memory.* New York: Taylor & Francis.

Dupper, D. R., & Dingus, A. E. M. (2008). Corporal punishment in U.S. public schools: A continuing challenge for school social workers. *Children & Schools, 30*(4), 243–250.

Durso, F., Nickerson, R., Dumais, S., Lewandowsky, S., & Perfect, T. (Eds.). (2007). *Handbook of applied cognition* (2nd ed.). Hoboken, NJ: Wiley.

Dweck, C., & Master, A. (2009). Self-theories and motivation: Students' beliefs about intelligence. In K. Wentzel & A. Wigfield (Eds.), *Handbook of motivation at school* (pp. 55–76). New York: Routledge.

Dynarski, M., Agodini, R., Heaviside, S., Novak, T., Carey, N., Campuzano, L., Means, B., Murphy, R., Penuel, W., Javitz, H., Emery, D., & Sussex, W. (2007, March). *Effectiveness of reading and mathematics software products: Findings from the First Student Cohort.* Washington, D.C.: U.S. Department of Education, Institute of Education Sciences. Retrieved from http://ies.ed.gov/ncee/pubs/20074005.

Earl, L. (2003). *Assessment as learning: Using classroom assessment to maximize student learning.* Thousand Oaks, CA: Corwin.

Eberstadt, M. (2003). The child-fat problem. *Policy Review, 117*, 3–19.

Eby, J. W., Herrell, A., & Hicks, J. L. (2002). *Reflective planning, teaching, and evaluation: K–12.* Upper Saddle River, NJ: Merrill Prentice Hall.

Eby, J. W., Herrell, A. L., & Jordan, M. (2006). *Teaching in k–12 schools: A reflective action approach.* Upper Saddle River, NJ: Pearson Merrill Prentice Hall.

Eccles, J. (2009). Who am I and what am I doing with my life? Personal and collective identities as motivators of action. *Educational Psychologist, 44*(2), 78–89.

Eisenberger, J., Conti-D'Antonio, M., & Bertrando, R. (2005). *Self-efficacy: Raising the bar for students with learning needs* (2nd ed.). Larchmont, NY: Eye on Education.

Eisner, E. W. (2002). What can education learn from the arts about the practice of education? *Journal of Curriculum and Supervision, 18*(1), 4–16.

Elkind, D. (1968). Cognitive development in adolescence. In J. F. Adams (Ed.), *Understanding adolescence.* Boston: Allyn & Bacon.

Elkind, D. (1989). Developmentally appropriate practice: Philosophical and practical implications. *Phi Delta Kappan, 71*(2), 113–117.

Elkind, D. (2005). Response to objectivism and education. *The Educational Forum 69*(4): 328–334.

Elliott, L., Foster, S., & Stinson, M. (2002). Student study habits using notes from a speech-to-text support service. *Exceptional Children, 69*(1), 25–40.

Elliott, T., Welsh, M., Nettelbeck, T., & Mills, V. (2007). Investigating naturalistic decision making in a simulated microworld: What questions should we ask? *Behavior Research Methods, 39*(4), 901–910.

Ellis, A. K. (2001). *Teaching, learning, and assessment together: The reflective classroom.* Larchmont, NY: Eye on Education.

Elmore, R. F. (2002). *Bridging the gap between standards and achievement: The imperative for professional development in education.* Washington, DC: Albert Shanker Institute.

Emmer, E. T., & Evertson, C. M. (2009). *Classroom management for middle and high school teachers* (8th ed.). Boston: Pearson/Allyn & Bacon.

Emmer, E. T., & Stough, L. M. (2001). Classroom management: A critical part of educational psychology, with implications for teacher education. *Educational Psychologist, 36*(2), 103–112.

Engeström, Y. (1999). Activity theory and individual and social transformation. In Y. Engeström, R. Miettinen & R.-L. Punamaki (Eds.), *Perspectives on activity theory* (pp. 19–38). New York: Cambridge University Press.

Englander, E. K. (2007). *Understanding violence* (3rd ed.). Mahwah, NJ: Lawrence Erlbaum Associates.

Erben, T., Ban, R., & Castañeda, M. (2009). *Teaching English language learners through technology.* New York: Routledge.

Erdelyi, M. H., & Goldberg, B. (1979). Let's now sweep repression under the rug: Towards a cognitive psychology of repression. In J. Kihlstrom & F. Evans (Eds.), *Functional disorders of memory.* Hillsdale, NJ: Erlbaum.

Ericsson, K. A., Chase, W. G., & Faloon, S. (1980). Acquisition of a memory skill. *Science, 208*(4448), 1181–1182.

Erikson, E. H. (1963). *Childhood and society* (2d ed.). New York: Norton.

Erikson, E. H. (1968). *Identity: Youth and crisis.* New York: Norton.

Evans, G., & English, K. (2002). The environment of poverty: Multiple exposure, psychophysiological stress, and socioemotional adjustment. *Child Development, 73*(4), 1238–1249.

Evans, R. (2005). Reframing the achievement gap. *Phi Delta Kappan, 86*(8), 582–589.

Evans, R. I. (1967). *Dialogue with Erik Erikson.* New York: Harper & Row.

Evertson, C. M., & Emmer, E. T. (2009). *Classroom management for elementary teachers* (8th ed.). Boston: Pearson/Allyn & Bacon.

Fabes, R. A., Martin, C. L., & Hanish, L. D. (2003). Young children's play qualities in same-, other-, and mixed-sex peer groups. *Child Development,74*(3), 921–932.

Fadjukoff, P., Pulkkinen, L., & Kokko, K. (2005). Identity processes in adulthood: Diverging domains. *Identity, 5*(1), 1–20.

Falk, B. (2002). Standard-based reforms: Problems and possibilities. *Phi Delta Kappan, 83*(8), 612–620.

Falk, B. (2009). *Teaching the way children learn.* New York: Teachers College Press.

Faw, H. W., & Waller, T. G. (1976). Mathemagenic behaviors and efficiency in learning from prose materials. *Review of Educational Research, 46*(4), 691–720.

Fehrenbach, C. R. (1994). Cognitive styles of gifted and average readers. *Roeper Review, 16*(4), 290–292.

Feigenbaum, P. (2002). Private speech: Cornerstone of Vygotsky's theory of the development of higher psychological processes. In D. Robbins & A. Stetsenko (Eds.), *Voices within Vygotsky's non-classical psychology: Past, present, and future* (pp. 161–174). New York: Nova Science.

Feiman-Nemser, S. (2003). What new teachers need to learn. *Educational Leadership, 60*(8), 25–29.

Ferriter, W. (2009). Learning with blogs and wikis. *Educational Leadership, 66*(5), 34–38.

Feyten, C. M., Macy, M. D., Ducher, J., Yoshii, M., Park, E., Calandra, B., & Meros, J. (2002). *Teaching esl/efl with the internet.* Upper Saddle River, NJ: Merrill Prentice Hall.

Finarelli, M. G., (1998). GLOBE: A worldwide environmental science and education partnership. *Journal of Science Education and Technology, 7*(1), 77–84.

Finnigan, K. S., & Gross, B. (2007). Do accountability policy sanctions influence teacher motivation? Lessons from Chicago's low-performing school. *American Educational Research Journal, 44*(3), 594–629.

Fisher, D. (2006). Keeping adolescents 'alive and kickin' it': Addressing suicide in schools. *Phi Delta Kappan, 87*(10), 784–786.

Fitzgerald, J. (1995). English-as-a-second-language learners' cognitive reading processes: A review of the research in the United States. *Review of Educational Research, 65*(2), 145–190.

Flaspohler, P. D., Elfstrom, J. L., Vanderzee, K. L., & Sink, H. E. (2009). Stand by me: The effects of peer and teacher support in mitigating the impact of bullying on quality of life. *Psychology in the Schools, 46*(7), 636–649.

Flavell, J. H. (1976). Metacognitive aspects of problem solving. In L. B. Resnick (Ed.), *The nature of intelligence.* Hillsdale, NJ: Erlbaum.

Flavell, J. H. (1987). Speculations about the nature and development of metacognition. In F. E. Weinert & R. H. Kluwe (Eds.), *Metacognition, motivation, and understanding.* Hillsdale, NJ: Erlbaum.

Flavell, J. H., Miller, P. A., & Miller, S. A. (2002). *Cognitive development* (4th ed.). Upper Saddle River, NJ: Prentice Hall.

Fletcher, J., & Vaughn, S. (2009). Response to intervention: Preventing and remediating academic difficulties. *Child Development Perspectives, 3*(1), 30–37.

Flieller, A. (1999). Comparison of the development of formal thought in adolescent cohorts aged 10 to 15 years (1967–1996 and 1972–1993). *Developmental Psychology, 35*(4), 1048–1058.

Flinders, D. J. (1989). Does the "art of teaching" have a future? *Educational leadership, 46*(8), 16–20.

Flora, S. R. (2004). *The power of reinforcement.* Albany, NY: State University of New York Press.

Fok, A., & Watkins, D. (2009). Does a critical constructivist learning environment encourage a deeper approach to learning? *The Asia-Pacific Education Researcher, 16*(1), 1–10.

Foote, M. (2007). Keeping accountability systems accountable. *Phi Delta Kappan, 88*(5), 359–363.

Forbes, S., & Ashton, P. (1998). The identity status of African Americans in middle adolescence: A replication and extension of Watson & Protinsky (1991). *Adolescence, 33*(132), 845–849.

Foreman, P. (2009). *Education of students with an intellectual disability: Research and practice.* Charlotte, NC: Information Age Publishing.

Fosnot, C. T., & Perry, R. S. (2005). Constructivism: A psychological theory of learning. In C. T. Fosnot (Ed.), *Constructivism: Theory, perspective and practice* (2nd ed., pp. 8–38). New York: Teachers College Press.

Fox, E. (2009). The role of reader characteristics in processing and learning from informational text. *Review of Educational Research, 79*(1), 197–261.

Franzke, M., Kintsch, E., Caccamise, D., Johnson, N., & Dooley, S. (2005). Summary Street®: Computer support for comprehension and writing. *Journal of Educational Computing Research, 33*(1), 53–80.

Fredrick, T. (2009). Looking in the mirror: Helping adolescents talk more reflectively during portfolio presentations. *Teachers College Record, 111*(8), 1916–1929.

Freiberg, H. J. (2002). Essential skills for new teachers. *Educational Leadership, 59*(6), 56–60.

French, S. E., Seidman, E., Allen, L., & Aber, J. L. (2006). The development of ethnic identity during adolescence. *Developmental Psychology, 42*(1), 1–10.

Friedlaender, D. (2009). *Oakland Unified School District case study: ASCEND.* Stanford, CA: School Redesign Network at Stanford University. Retrieved 12 November 2009 from http://www.srnleads.org/resources/publications/ousd/ousd.html.

Fryer, R. G., Jr., & Torelli, P. (2005, May). *An empirical analysis of 'acting white'* (Working Paper 11334). Cambridge, MA: National Bureau of Economic Research. Retrieved from http://www.nber.org/papers/w11334.

Fuchs, D., & Fuchs, L. (2006). Introduction to response to intervention: What, why, and how valid is it? *Reading Research Quarterly, 41*(1), 93–99.

Fuchs, D., & Fuchs, L. Compton, D., Bouton, B., Caffrey, E., & Hill, L. (2007). Dynamic assessment as responsiveness to intervention: A scripted protocol to identify at-risk readers. *Teaching Exceptional Children, 39*(5), 58–63.

Fuchs, D., Fuchs, L. S., Mathes, P. G., & Simmons, D. C. (1997). Peer-assisted learning strategies: Making classrooms more responsive to diversity. *American Educational Research Journal, 34*(1), 174–206.

Fuller, B., Gesicki, K., Kang, E., & Wright, J. (2006). *Is the no child left behind act working?* (Working Paper 06-1). Berkeley, CA: University of California, Berkeley, Policy Analysis for California Education.

Fulmer, S., & Frijters, J. (2009). A review of self-report and alternative approaches in the measurement of student motivation. *Educational Psychology Review, 21*(3), 219–246.

Funkhouser, C. (2002/2003). The effects of computer-augmented geometry instruction on student performance and attitudes. *Journal of Research on Technology in Education, 35*(2), 163–175.

Furnham, A., Monsen, J., Ahmetoglu, G. (2009). Typical intellectual engagement, big five personality traits, approaches to learning and cognitive ability predictors of academic performance. *British Journal of Educational Psychology, 79*(4), 769–782.

Furth, H. G. (1970). *Piaget for teachers.* Englewood Cliffs, NJ: Prentice-Hall.

Gallagher, J. J. (2003). Issues and challenges in the education of gifted students. In N. Colangelo & G. A. Davis (Eds.), *Handbook of gifted education* (3rd ed., pp. 11–23). Boston: Allyn & Bacon.

Gallagher, W. J. (2005). The contradictory nature of professional teaching standards: Adjusting for common misunderstandings. *Phi Delta Kappan, 87*(2), 112–115.

Gallimore, R., & Tharp, R. (1990). Teaching mind in society: Teaching, schooling, and literate discourse. In L. C. Moll (Ed.), *Vygotsky and education: Instructional implications and applications of sociohistorical psychology.* Cambridge, England: Cambridge University Press.

Gantner, M. W. (1997). Lessons learned from my students in the barrio. *Educational Leadership, 54*(7), 44–45.

García, E. (2002). *Student cultural diversity: Understanding and meeting the challenge* (3rd ed.). Boston: Houghton Mifflin.

Gardner, D. (2007). Confronting the achievement gap. *Phi Delta Kappan, 88*(7), 542–546.

Gardner, H. (1999). *Intelligence reframed: Multiple intelligences for the 21st century.* New York: Basic Books.

Gardner, H., & Moran, S. (2006). The Science of multiple intelligences theory: A response to Lynn Waterhouse. *Educational Psychologist, 41*(4), 227–232.

Gatlin, L., & Jacob, S. (2002). Standards-based digital portfolios: A component of authentic assessment for preservice teachers. *Action in Teacher Education, 23*(4), 35–41.

Gee, J. P. (2007). *Good video games and good learning: Collected essays on video games, learning, and literacy.* New York: Peter Lang.

Gentile, J. R., & Lalley, J. P. (2003). *Standards and mastery learning.* Thousand Oaks, CA: Corwin Press.

Gentner D., Loewenstein J., Thompson, L., & Forbus. K. (2009). Reviving inert knowledge: Analogical abstraction supports relational retrieval of past events. *Cognitive Science, 33*(8), 1343–1382.

Gentry, M., Gable, R. K., & Rizza, M. G. (2002). Students' perceptions of classroom activities: Are there grade-level and gender differences? *Journal of Educational Psychology, 94*(3), 539–544.

Gershoff, E. T. (2002). Corporal punishment by parents and associated child behaviors and experiences: A meta-analytic and theoretical review. *Psychological Bulletin, 128*(4), 539–579.

Gersten, R. (1999). The changing face of bilingual education. *Educational Leadership, 56*(7), 41–45.

Gersten, R., & Brengelman, S. U. (1996). The quest to translate research into classroom practice: The emerging knowledge base. *Remedial and Special Education, 17*(2), 67–74.

Gersten, R., Fuchs, L. S., Williams, J. P., & Baker, S. (2001). Teaching reading comprehension strategies to students with learning disabilities: A review of research. *Review of Educational Research, 71*(2), 279–320.

Gettinger, M., & Stoiber, K. C. (2006). Functional assessment, collaboration, and evidence-based treatment: Analysis of a team approach for addressing challenging behaviors in young children. *Journal of School Psychology, 44*(3), 231–252.

Gewertz, C. (2005). Ed. dept. allows Chicago to provide NCLB tutoring. *Education Week, 25*(2), 3, 18.

Ghosh, R., Michelson, R. A., & Anyon, J. (2007). Introduction to the special issue on new perspectives on youth development and social identity in the 21st century. *Teachers College Record, 109*(2), 275–284.

Gibbons, M. (2002). *The self-directed learning handbook: Challenging adolescent students to excel.* San Francisco, CA: Jossey-Bass.

Gilberg, C. (2001). Epidemiology of early onset schizophrenia. In H. Remschmidt (Ed.), *Schizophrenia in children and adolescents* (pp. 43–59). New York: Cambridge University Press.

Gillespie, C. W., & Beisser, S. (2001). Developmentally appropriate LOGO computer programming with young children. *Information Technology in Childhood Education Annual,* 229–245.

Gillies, R. M. (2003). Structuring cooperative group work in classrooms. *International Journal of Educational Research, 39*(1–2), 35–49.

Gillies, R. M. (2007). *Cooperative learning: Integrating theory and practice.* Thousand Oaks, CA: Corwin Press.

Gilligan, C. (1979). Women's place in man's life cycle. *Harvard Educational Review, 49*(4), 431–446.

Gilligan, C. (1982). *In a different voice: Psychological theory and women's development.* Cambridge, MA: Harvard University Press.

Gilligan, C. (1988). Exit-voice dilemmas in adolescent development. In C. Gilligan, J. Ward, J. Taylor, & B. Bardige (Eds.), *Mapping the moral domain: A contribution of women's thinking to psychological theory and education.* Cambridge, MA: Harvard University Press.

Ginott, H. (1965). *Between parent and child.* New York: Macmillan.

Ginott, H. (1972). *Teacher and child.* New York: Macmillan.

Ginott, H., G., Ginott, A., & Goddard, H. W. (2003). *Between parent and child* (Revised and updated). New York: Three Rivers Press.

Ginsburg, H. P., & Opper, S. (1988). *Piaget's theory of intellectual development* (3rd ed.). Englewood Cliffs, NJ: Prentice-Hall.

Ginsburg-Block, M., Rohrbeck, C. A., & Fantuzzo, J. W. (2006). A meta-analytic review of social, self-concept, and behavioral outcomes of peer-assisted learning. *Journal of Educational Psychology, 98*(4), 732–749.

Ginsburg-Block, M., Rohrbeck, C., Lavigne, N., & Fantuzzo, J. W. (2008). Peer-assisted learning: An academic strategy for enhancing motivation among diverse students. In C. Hudley & A. E. Gottfried (Eds.), *Academic motivation and the culture of school in childhood and adolescence* (pp. 247–273). Oxford, England: Oxford University Press.

Gijbels, D., van de Watering, G., Dochy, F., & van den Bossche, P. (2006). New learning environments and constructivism: The students' perspective. *Instructional Science, 34*(3), 213–226.

Glaser, C., & Brunstein, J. C. (2007). Improving fourth-grade students' composition skills: Effects of strategy instruction and self-regulation procedures. *Journal of Educational Psychology, 99*(2), 297–310.

Glazek, S. D., & Sarason, S. B. (2006). *Productive learning: Science, art, and Einstein's relativity in educational reform.* Thousand Oaks, CA: Corwin Press.

Goeke, J. L. (2009). *Explicit instruction: A framework for meaningful direct teaching.* Upper Saddle River, NJ: Pearson Merrill.

Gold, M., & Lowe, C. (2009). The integration of assistive technology into standard classroom practices: A guide for k–12 general educators. In I. Gibson et al. (Eds.), *Proceedings of Society for Information Technology & Teacher Education International Conference 2009* (pp. 3964–3968). Chesapeake, VA: AACE. Retrieved from http://www.editlib.org/p/31275.

Goldberg, M. (2004). The test mess. *Phi Delta Kappan, 85*(5), 361–366.

Goldberg, M. (2005). Test mess 2: Are we doing better a year later? *Phi Delta Kappan, 86*(5), 389–395.

Goldsby, D., & Fazal, M. (2001). Now that your students have created web-based digital portfolios, how do you evaluate them? *Journal of Technology and Teacher Education, 9*(4), 607–616.

Gollnick, D. A., & Chinn, P. C. (2009). *Multicultural education in a pluralistic society* (8th ed.). Upper Saddle River, NJ: Pearson Merrill.

Good, J. M., & Whang, P. A. (2002). Encouraging reflection in preservice teachers through response journals. *Teacher Educator, 37*(4), 254–267.

Good, T. L., & Brophy, J. (1995). *Contemporary educational psychology* (5th ed.). New York: Longman.

Good, T. L., & Nicholls, S. L. (2001). Expectancy effects in the classroom: A special focus on improving the reading performance of minority students in first-grade classrooms. *Educational Psychologist, 36*(2), 113–126.

Goodlad, J. I. (1984). *A place called school.* New York: McGraw-Hill.

Goodman, A. (2008). Student-led, teacher-supported conferences: Improving communication across an urban district. *Middle School Journal, 39*(3), 48–54.

Goodman, G. (Ed.). (2008). *Educational psychology: An application of critical constructivism.* New York: Peter Lang Publishing.

Gordon, P. R., Rogers, A. M., Comfort, M., Gavula, N., & McGee, B. P. (2001). A taste of problem-based learning increases achievement of urban minority middle-school students. *Educational Horizons, 79*(4), 171–175.

Gordon, S., & Gilgun, J. F. (1987). Adolescent sexuality. In V B. van Hasselt & M. Hersen (Eds.), *Handbook of adolescent psychology.* New York: Pergamon Press.

Gordon, T. (1974). *TET: Teacher effectiveness training.* New York: McKay.

Gorski, P. C. (2005). *Multicultural education and the internet: Intersections and integrations* (2nd ed.). New York: McGraw-Hill.

Goswami, U. (Ed.). (2002). *Blackwell handbook of childhood cognitive development.* Malden, MA: Blackwell.

Gough, P. B. (1987). The key to improving schools: An interview with William Glasser. *Phi Delta Kappan, 69*(9), 656 662.

Gould, S. J. (1981). *The Mismeasure of Man.* New York: Norton.

Grabe, M., & Grabe, C. (2007). *Integrating technology for meaningful learning* (5th ed.). Boston: Houghton Mifflin.

Grabinger, R., Aplin, C., & Ponnappa-Brenner, G. (2008). Supporting learners with cognitive impairments in online environments. *TechTrends, 52*(1), 63–69.

Graham, S., & Hudley, C. (2005). Race and ethnicity in the study of motivation and competence. In A. J. Elliot & C. S. Dweck (Eds.), *Handbook of competence and motivation* (pp. 392–413). New York: Guilford Press.

Graham, S., & Perin, D. (2007). A meta-analysis of writing instruction for adolescent students. *Journal of Educational Psychology, 99*(3), 445–476.

Graham, S., & Taylor, A. Z. (2002). Ethnicity, gender, and the development of achievement values. In A. Wigfield & J. S. Eccles (Eds.), *Development of achievement motivation* (pp. 121–146). San Diego, CA: Academic Press.

Graham, S., & Williams, C. (2009). An attributional approach to motivation in school. In K. Wentzel & A. Wigfield (Eds.). Handbook of motivation at school (pp. 11–34). New York: Routledge.

Graue, M. E., & DiPerna, J. (2000). Redshirting and early retention: Who gets the "gift of time" and what are its outcomes? *American Educational Research Journal, 37*(2), 509–534.

Gredler, M., & Shields, C. (2004). Does no one read Vygotsky's words? Commentary on Glassman. *Educational Researcher, 33*(2), 21–25.

Green, T. D., Brown, A., & Robinson, L. (2008). *Making the Most of the Web in Your Classroom: A Teacher's Guide to Blogs, Podcasts, Wikis, Pages, and Sites.* Thousand Oaks, CA: Corwin Press.

Greene, J. A., & Azevedo, R. (2007). A theoretical review of Winne and Hadwin's model of self-regulated learning: New perspectives and directions. *Review of Educational Research, 77*(3), 334–372.

Greene, J. A., & Azevedo, R. (2009). A macro-level analysis of SRL processes and their relations to the acquisition of a sophisticated mental model of a complex system. *Contemporary Educational Psychology, 34*(1), 18–29.

Gregory, G. H. (2003). *Differentiated instructional stategies in practice.* Thousand Oaks, CA: Corwin Press.

Gregory, G. H., & Kuzmich, L. (2005). *Differentiated literacy strategies for student growth and achievement in grades 7–12.* Thousand Oaks, CA: Corwin Press.

Gresalfi, M., Barab, S., Siyahhan, S., & Christensen, T. (2009). Virtual worlds, conceptual understanding, and me: Designing for consequential engagement. *On the Horizon, 17*(1), 21–34.

Gresham, F. M., & MacMillan, D. L. (1997). Social competence and affective characteristics of students with mild disabilities. *Review of Educational Research, 67*(4), 377–415.

Griffin, H. C., Williams, S. C., Davis, M. L., & Engleman, M. (2002). Using technology to enhance cues for children with low vision. *Teaching Exceptional Children, 35*(2), 36–42.

Griffiths, A-J., VanDerHeyden, A., Skokut, M., & Lilles, E. (2009). Progress monitoring in oral reading fluency within the context of RTI. *School Psychology Quarterly, 24*(1), 13–23.

Griffiths, T. L., Steyvers, M., & Tenenbaum, J. B. (2007). Topics in semantic association. *Psychological Review, 114*(2), 211–244.

Grigorenko, E. L., Jarvin, L., & Sternberg, R. J. (2002). School-based tests of the triarchic theory of intelligence: Three settings, three samples, three syllabi. *Contemporary Educational Psychology, 27*(2), 167–208.

Gronlund, N. E. (2004). *Writing instructional objectives for teaching and assessment* (7th ed.). Upper Saddle River, NJ: Merrill Prentice Hall.

Gronlund, N., & Waugh, C. (2009). *Assessment of student achievement* (9th ed.). Boston: Allyn & Bacon.

Grossen, B. J. (2002). The BIG Accommodation model: The direct instruction model for secondary schools. *Journal of Education for Students Placed At Risk, 7*(2), 241–263.

Gruber, E., & Vonèche, J. J. (Eds.). (1977). *The essential Piaget: An interpretive reference and guide.* New York: Basic Books.

Guerra, N. G., & Leidy, M. S. (2008). Lessons learned: Recent advances in understanding and preventing childhood aggression. In R. V. Kail (Ed.), *Advances in child development and behavior* (pp. 287–330). San Diego, CA: Academic Press.

Gulek, C. (2003). Preparing for high-stakes testing. *Theory into Practice, 42*(1), 42–50.

Guskey, T. R. (2002). Computerized gradebooks and the myth of objectivity. *Phi Delta Kappan, 83*(10), 775–780.

Guskey, T. R. (2003). How classroom assessments improve learning. *Educational Leadership, 60*(5), 6–11.

Gutek, G. L. (1992). *Education and schooling in America* (3rd ed.). Boston: Allyn & Bacon.

Gutiérrez, K. D., & Rogoff, B. (2003). Cultural ways of learning: Individual traits or repertoires of practice. *Educational Researcher, 32*(5), 19–25.

Guttmacher Institute (2006, September). *Facts on American teens' sexual and reproductive health.* Retrieved from http://www.guttmacher.org/pubs/fb_ATSRH.html#n31.

Hacker, D., Dunlosky, J. & Graesser, A. (Eds.). (2009). *Handbook of metacognition in education.* New York: Routledge.

Hacker, D. J., & Tenent, A. (2002). Implementing reciprocal teaching in the classroom: Overcoming obstacles and making modifications. *Journal of Educational Psychology, 94*(4), 699–718.

Hadwin, A. F., Winne, P. H., Stockley, D. B., Nesbit, J. C., & Woszczyna, C. (2001). Context moderates students' self-reports about how they study. *Journal of Educational Psychology, 93*(3), 477–487.

Hahn, C. L., Bernard Powers, J., Crocco, M., & Woyshner, C. (2007). Social studies and gender equity research. In S. Klein (Ed.), *Handbook for achieving gender equity through education* (pp. 335–358). Mahwah, NJ: Erlbaum Publishers.

Haier, R. J. (2001). PET studies of learning and individual differences. In J. L. McClelland & R. S. Siegler (Eds.), *Mechanisms of cognitive development: Behavioral and neural perspectives* (pp. 123–145). Mahwah, NJ: Erlbaum.

Haladyna, T. (1999). *A complete guide to student grading.* Boston: Allyn & Bacon.

Haladyna, T. M., Downing, S. M., & Rodriguez, M. C. (2002). A review of multiple-choice item-writing guidelines for classroom assessment. *Applied Measurement in Education, 15*(3), 309–334.

Hallfors, D., Vevea, J. L., Iritani, B., Cho, H., Khatapoush, S., & Saxe, L. (2002). Truancy, grade point average, and sexual activity: A meta-analysis of risk indicators for youth substance abuse. *Journal of School Health, 72*(5), 205–211.

Halpern, D. F., & LaMay, M. L. (2000). The smarter sex: A critical review of sex differences in intelligence. *Educational Psychology Review, 12*(2), 229–246.

Halpern, D. F., Wai, J., & Saw, A. (2005). A psychobiosocial model: Why females are sometimes greater than and sometimes less than males in math achievement. In A. M. Gallagher & J. C. Kaufman (Eds.), *Gender differences in mathematics* (pp. 48–72). New York: Cambridge University Press.

Hamilton, L., & Stecher, B. (2004). Responding effectively to test-based accountability. *Phi Delta Kappan, 85*(8), 578–583.

Hamman, D., Berthelot, J., Saia, J., & Crowley, E. (2000). Teachers' coaching of learning and its relation to students' strategic learning. *Journal of Educational Psychology, 92*(2), 342–348.

Hamre, B. K., & Pianta, R. C. (2005). Can instructional and emotional support in the first-grade classroom make a difference for children at risk of school failure? *Child Development, 76*(5), 949–967.

Haney, J. J., & McArthur, J. (2002). Four case studies of prospective science teachers beliefs concerning constructivist teaching practices. *Science Education, 86*(6), 783–802.

Hannafin, R. D., & Foshay, W. R. (2008). Computer-based instruction's (CBI) rediscovered role in K–12: An evaluation case study of one high school's use of CBI to improve pass rates on high-stakes tests. *Education Technology Research & Development, 56*(2), 147–160.

Hansgen, R. D. (1991). Can education become a science? *Phi Delta Kappan, 72*(9), 689–694.

Hardman, M., Drew, C., & Egan, M. (2011). *Human exceptionality: School, community, and family* (10th ed.). Belmont, CA: Wadsworth/Cengage Learning.

Hardy, C. L., Bukowski, W. M., & Sippola, L. K. (2002). Stability and change in peer relationships during the transition to middle-level school. *Journal of Early Adolescence, 22*(2), 117–142.

Hardy, I., Jonen, A., Möller, K., & Stern, E. (2006). Effects of instructional support within constructivist learning environments for elementary school students' understanding of "floating and sinking." *Journal of Educational Psychology, 98*(2), 307–326.

Hargreaves, A., Earl, L., & Schmidt, M. (2002). Perspectives on alternative assessment reform. *American Educational Research Journal, 39*(1), 69–95.

Harold, R. D., Colarossi, L. G., & Mercier, L. R. (2007). *Smooth sailing or stormy waters? Family transitions through adolescence and their implications for practice and policy.* Mahwah, NJ: Lawrence Erlbaum.

Harrington, R., & Enochs, L. (2009). Accounting for preservice teachers' constructivist learning environment experiences. *Learning Environments Research, 12*(1), 45–65.

Harris, B., Plucker, J., Rapp, K., & Martínez, R. (2009). Identifying gifted and talented English language learners: A case study. *Journal for the Education of the Gifted, 32*(3), 368–393.

Harris, K. R., Alexander, P., & Graham, S. (2008). Michael Pressley's contributions to the history and future of strategies research. *Educational Psychologist, 43*(2), 89–96.

Harris, K. R., Graham, S., & Mason, L. H. (2006). Improving the writing, knowledge, and motivation of struggling young writers: Effects of self-regulated strategy development with and without peer support. *American Educational Research Journal, 43*(2), 295–340.

Harry, B., & Klingner, J. K. (2006). *Why are so many minority students in special education? Understanding race and disability in schools.* New York: Teachers College Press.

Hart, B., & Risley, T. R. (1995). *Meaningful differences in the everyday experience of young American children.* Baltimore, MD: Paul H. Brookes.

Hart, H. (2009). Strategies for culturally and linguistically diverse students with special needs. *Preventing School Failure, 53*(3), 197–208.

Harter, S. (1990). Self and identity development. In S. S. Feldman & G. R. Elliot (Eds.), *At the threshold: The developing adolescent* (pp. 352–387). Cambridge, MA: Harvard University Press.

Harter, S. (1999). *The construction of the self: A developmental perspective.* New York: Guilford.

Harter, S., Waters, P. L., & Whitesell, N. R. (1997). Lack of voice as a manifestation of false self-behavior among adolescents: The school setting as a stage upon which the drama of authenticity is enacted. *Educational Psychologist, 32*(3), 153–174.

Hartshorne, H., & May, M. A. (1929). *Studies in service and self-control.* New York: Macmillan.

Hartshorne, H., & May, M. A. (1930a). *Studies in deceit.* New York: Macmillan.

Hartshorne, H., & May, M. A. (1930b). *Studies in the organization of character.* New York: Macmillan.

Hartup, W. W. (1989). Social relationships and their developmental significance. *American Psychologist, 44*(2), 120–126.

Hatch, T. (1997). Getting specific about multiple intelligences. *Educational Leadership, 54*(6), 26–29.

Hattie, J., Biggs, J., & Purdie, N. (1996). Effects of learning skills interventions on student learning: A meta-analysis. *Review of Educational Research, 66*(2), 99–136.

Hattie, J., & Timperley, H. (2007). The power of feedback. *Review of Educational Research, 77*(1), 81–112.

Haver, J. J. (2003). *Structured English immersion: A step-by-step guide for k–6 teachers and administrators.* Thousand Oaks, CA: Corwin Press.

Hayes, W. (2008). *No child left behind: Past, present, and future.* Lanham, MD: Rowman & Littlefield Education.

Hazler, R. J., & Carney, J. V. (2006). Critical characteristics of effective bullying prevention programs. In S. R. Jimerson & M. J. Furlong (Eds.), *The handbook of school violence and school safety.* Mahwah, NJ: Lawrence Erlbaum.

Heacox, D. (2009). *Making differentiation a habit: How to ensure success in academically diverse classrooms.* Minneapolis, MN: Free Spirit Publishing.

Healy, L., & Hoyles, C. (2001). Software tools for geometrical problem solving: Potentials and pitfalls. *International Journal of Computers for Mathematical Learning, 6*(3), 235–256.

Heath, M. (2002). Electronic portfolios for reflective self-assessment. *Teacher Librarian 30*(1), 19–23.

Hecker, L., Burns, L., Elkind, J., Elkind, K., & Katz, L. (2002). Benefits of assistive reading software for students with attention disorders. *Annals of Dyslexia, 52*, 243–272.

Henderson, J. G. (Ed.). (2001). *Reflective teaching: Professional artistry through inquiry.* Upper Saddle River, NJ: Merrill Prentice Hall.

Henley, M. (2010). *Classroom management: A proactive approach* (2nd ed.). Boston: Pearson.

Henry J. Kaiser Family Foundation. (2004, September). *Children, the digital divide, and federal policy.* Retrieved from http://www.kff.org/entmedia/7090.cfm.

Herr, P. (2000). The changing role of the teacher: How management systems help facilitate teaching. *T.H.E. Journal, 28*(4), 28–34.

Hersh, R. H., Paolitto, D. P., & Reimer, J. (1979). *Promoting moral growth: From Piaget to Kohlberg.* New York: Longman.

Hester, P., Hendrickson, J., & Gable, J. (2009). Forty years later—The value of praise, ignoring, and rules for preschoolers at risk for behavior disorders. *Education and Treatment of Children, 32*(4), 513–535.

Hershberg, T. (2005). Value-added assessment and systemic reform: A response to the challenge of human capital development. *Phi Delta Kappan, 87*(4), 276–283.

Hetherington, E. M., & Parke, R. D. (1993). *Child psychology: A contemporary viewpoint* (4th ed.). New York: McGraw-Hill.

Heward, W. L. (2009). *Exceptional children: An introduction to special education* (9th ed.). Upper Saddle River, NJ: Merrill/Pearson.

Hickey, D. T., Kindfield, A. C. H., Horwitz, P., & Christie, M. T. (2003). Integrating curriculum, instruction, assessment, and evaluation in a technology-supported genetics learning environment. *American Educational Research Journal, 40*(2), 495–538.

Hiebert, J., Gallimore, R., & Stigler, J. W. (2002). A knowledge base for the teaching profession: What would it look like and how can we get one? *Educational Researcher, 31*(5), 3–15.

Higdon, J., & Topaz, C. (2009). Blogs and wikis as instructional tools: A social software adaptation of just-in-time teaching. *College Teaching, 57*(2), 105–109.

Higgins, J. W., Williams, R. L., & McLaughlin, T. F. (2001). The effects of a token economy employing instructional consequences for a third-grade student with learning disabilities: A case study. *Education and Treatment of Children, 24*(1), 99–106.

Hilbert, T., & Renkl, A. (2009). Learning how to use a computer-based concept-mapping tool: Self-explaining examples help. *Computers in Human Behavior, 25*(2), 267–274.

Hill, J. P. (1987). Research on adolescents and their families: Past and prospect. In C. E. Irwin, Jr. (Ed.), *Adolescent social behavior and health*. San Francisco: Jossey-Bass.

Hitchcock, C., & Stahl, S. (2003). Assistive technology, universal design, universal design for learning: Improved learning outcomes. *Journal of Special Education Technology, 18*(4), 45–52.

Ho, A. D. (2008). The problem with "proficiency": Limitations of statistics and policy under No Child Left Behind. *Educational Researcher, 37*(6), 351–360.

Hoegh, D. G., & Bourgeois, M. J. (2002). Prelude and postlude to the self: Correlates of achieved identity. *Youth & Society, 33*(4), 573–594.

Hoff, D. J. (2006, January 4). Colo. Town raises taxes to finance NCLB withdrawal. *Education Week, 25*(16), 3, 9.

Hoffman, B., & Schraw, G. (2009). The influence of self-efficacy and working memory capacity on problem-solving efficiency. *Learning and Individual Differences, 19*(1), 91–100.

Hoffman, M. L. (1980). Moral development in adolescence. In J. Adelson (Ed.), *Handbook of adolescent psychology*. New York: Wiley.

Hoffman, M. L. (2000). *Empathy and moral development: Implications for caring and justice*. Cambridge, England: Cambridge University Press.

Hogan, K., & Pressley, M. (Eds.). (1997). *Scaffolding student learning: Instructional approaches and issues*. Cambridge, MA: Brookline Books.

Hoge, R. D., & Renzulli, J. S. (1993). Exploring the link between giftedness and self-concept. *Review of Educational Research, 63*(4), 449–465.

Hollingsworth, J., & Ybarra, S. (2009). *Explicit direct instruction: The power of a well-crafted, well-taught lesson*. Thousand Oaks, CA: Corwin Press.

Holt, L. C., & Kysilka, M. (2006). *Instructional patterns*. Thousand Oaks, CA: SAGE.

Holzman, L. (2009). *Vygotsky at work and play*. New York: Routledge.

Hong, G., & Hong, Y. (2009). Reading instruction time and homogeneous grouping in kindergarten: An application of marginal mean weighting through stratification. *Educational Evaluation and Policy Analysis, 31*(1), 54–81.

Hong, G., & Raudenbush, S. W. (2005). Effects of kindergarten retention policy on children's cognitive growth in reading and mathematics. *Educational Evaluation and Policy Analysis, 27*(3). 205–224.

Hong, H-Y., & Sullivan, F. (2009). Towards an idea-centered, principle-based design approach to support learning as knowledge creation. *Educational Technology Research and Development, 57*(5), 613–627.

Houston, P. D. (2005). NCLB: Dreams and nightmares. *Phi Delta Kappan, 86*(6), 469–470.

Houston, P. D. (2007). The seven deadly sins of No Child Left Behind. *Phi Delta Kappan, 88*(10), 744–748.

Howard, B. C., McGee, S., Shin, N., & Shia, R. (2001). The triarchic theory of intelligence and computer-based inquiry learning. *Educational Technology Research and Development, 49*(4), 49–69.

Howe, C. (2009). Collaborative group work in middle childhood. *Human Development, 52*(4), 215–239.

Howe, N., Rinaldi, C. M., Jennings, M., & Petrakos, H. (2002). "No! the lambs can stay out because they got cozies": Constructive and destructive sibling conflict, pretend play, and social understanding. *Child Development, 73*(5), 1460–1473.

Hughes, F. P. (1999). *Children, play, and development* (3rd ed.). Boston: Allyn & Bacon.

Hughes, F. P., & Noppe, L. D. (1991). *Human development across the life span*. New York: Macmillan.

Hughes, J. N., & Zhang, D. (2007). Effects of the structure of classmates' perceptions of peers' academic abilities on children's perceived cognitive competence, peer acceptance, and engagement. *Contemporary Educational Psychology, 32*(3), 400–419.

Hung, D. (2002). Situated cognition and problem-based learning: Implications for learning and instruction with technology. *Journal of Interactive Learning Research, 13*(4), 393–414.

Hunt, N., & Marshall, K. (2006). *Exceptional children and youth* (4th ed.). Boston: Houghton Mifflin.

Hyde, J. S. (2005). The gender similarities hypothesis. *American Psychologist, 60*(6), 581–592.

Hyerle, D. (2009). *Visual tools for transforming information into knowledge* (2nd ed.). Thousand Oaks, CA: Corwin Press.

Individuals with Disabilities Education Act Amendments of 1997. (1997, June). Retrieved September 15, 2003, from http://frwebgate.access.gpo.gov/cgi-bin/useftp.cgi?IPaddress=162.140.64.21&file-name=publ17.105&directory=/diskc/wais/data/105_cong_public_laws.

Inal, Y., & Cagiltay, K. (2007). Flow experiences of children in an interactive social game environment. *British Journal of Educational Technology, 38*(3), 455–464.

Ireson, J., & Hallam, S. (2009) *Academic self-concepts in adolescence: Relations with achievement and ability grouping in schools*. Learning and Instruction, 19(3), 201–213.

Ito, M. et al. (2010). *Hanging out, messing around, and geeking out: Kids living and learning with new media*. The John D. and Katherine T. MacArthur Foundation Series on Digital Media and Learning. Cambridge, MA: MIT Press.

Ivanoff, J., Branning, P., & Marois, R. (2009). Mapping the pathways of information processing from sensation to action in four distinct sensorimotor tasks. *Human Brain Mapping, 30*(12), 4167–4186.

Jackson, A. W., & Davis, G. A. (2000). *Turning points 2000: Educating adolescents in the 21st century*. New York: Teachers College Press.

Jackson, A. W., & Larkin, M. J. (2002). Rubric: Teaching students to use grading rubrics. *Teaching Exceptional Children, 35*(1), 40–45.

Jackson, B. (2007). Homework inoculation and the limits of research. *Phi Delta Kappan, 89*(1), 55–59.

Jackson, D. B. (2003). Education reform as if student agency mattered: Academic microcultures and student identity. *Phi Delta Kappan, 84*(8), 579–585.

Jackson, J. F. (1999). What are the real risk factors for African American children? *Phi Delta Kappan, 81*(4), 308–312.

Jackson, S., Pretti-Frontczak, K., Harjusola-Webb, S., Grisham-Brown, J., & Romani, J. (2009). Response to intervention: Implications for early childhood professionals. *Language, Speech, and Hearing Services in Schools, 40*(4), 424–434.

Jacobs, G. M., Power, M. A., & Inn, L. W. (2002). *The teacher's sourcebook for cooperative learning*. Thousand Oaks, CA: Corwin Press.

Jaffee, S., Hyde, J. S., & Shibley, J. (2000). Gender differences in moral orientation: A meta-analysis, *Psychological Bulletin, 126*(5), 703–726.

Janesick, V. J. (2001). *The assessment debate: A reference handbook*. Santa Barbara, CA: ABC-CLIO.

Jean-Marie, G., Normore, A., & Brooks, J. (2009). Leadership for social justice: Preparing 21st century school leaders for a new social order. *Journal of Research on Leadership Education, 4*(1), 1–31.

Jennings, J., & Rentner, D. S. (2006). Ten big effects of the No Child Left Behind Act on public schools. *Phi Delta Kappan, 88*(2), 110–113.

Jensen, E. P. (2008). A fresh look at brain-based education. *Phi Delta Kappan, 89*(6), 409–417.

Jensen, L. A., Arnett, J. J., Feldman, S. S., & Cauffman, E. (2002). It's wrong, but everybody does it: Academic dishonesty among high school and college students. *Contemporary Educational Psychology, 27*(2), 209–228.

Jensen, L. A., Arnett, J. J., Feldman, S., & Cauffman, E. (2004). The right to do wrong: Lying to parents among adolescents and emerging adults. *Journal of Youth and Adolescence, 33*(2), 101–112.

Jeong, H., & Hmelo-Silver, C. (2010). Productive use of learning resources in an online problem-based learning environment. *Computers in Human Behavior, 26*(1), 84–99.

Jimerson, S. R. (2001). Meta-analysis of grade retention research: Implications for practice in the 21st century. *School Psychology Review, 30*(3), 420–437.

Jimerson, S. R., Anderson, G. E., & Whipple, A. D. (2002). Winning the battle and losing the war: Examining the relation between grade retention and dropping out of high school. *Psychology in the Schools, 39*(4), 441–457.

Jimerson, S. R., & Furlong, M. J. (Eds.). (2006). *The handbook of school violence and school safety.* Mahwah, NJ: Lawrence Erlbaum.

Jimerson, S. R., & Kaufman, A. M. (2003). Reading, writing, and retention: A primer on grade retention research. *The Reading Teacher, 56*(7), 622–635.

Jimerson, S. R., Morrison, G. M., Pletcher, S. W., & Furlong, M. J. (2006). Youth engaged in antisocial and aggressive behaviors: Who are they? In S. R. Jimerson & M. J. Furlong (Eds.), *The handbook of school violence and school safety* (pp. 3–19). Mahwah, NJ: Lawrence Erlbaum.

Jindal-Snape, D., & Miller, D. J. (2008). A challenge of living? Understanding the psycho-social processes of the child during primary-secondary transition through resilience and self-esteem theories. *Educational Psychology Review, 20*(3), 217–236.

Jobe, D. A. (2002/2003). Helping girls succeed. *Educational Leadership, 60*(4), 64–66.

Johnson, C. C., & Fargo, J. D. (2010). Urban school reform enabled by transformative professional development: Impact on teacher change and student learning of science. *Urban Education, 45*(1), 4–29.

Johnson, C. S., & Thomas, A. T. (2009). Caring as classroom practice. *Social Studies and the Young Learner, 22*(1), 8–11.

Johnson, D. W., & Johnson, F. P. (2006). *Joining together: Group theory and group skills* (9th ed.). Boston: Pearson/Allyn & Bacon.

Johnson, D. W., & Johnson, R. T. (1995). Cooperative learning and nonacademic outcomes of schooling: The other side of the report card. In J. E. Pedersen, & A. D. Digby (Eds.), *Secondary schools and cooperative learning* (pp. 81–150). New York: Garland Publishing.

Johnson, D. W., & Johnson, R. T. (1998). Cultural diversity and cooperative learning. In

J. W. Putnam (Ed.), *Cooperative learning and strategies for inclusion* (2nd ed.). Baltimore, MD: Brookes Publishing.

Johnson, D. W., & Johnson, R. T. (2009a). Energizing learning: The instructional power of conflict. *Educational Researcher, 38*(1), 37–51.

Johnson, D. W., & Johnson, R. T. (2009b). An educational success story: Social interdependence theory and cooperative learning. *Educational Researcher, 38*(5), 365–379.

Johnson, D. W., Johnson, R. T., & Holubec, E. J. (2002). *The new circles of learning: Cooperation in the classroom.* Edina, MN: Interaction Book Company.

Johnson, D. W., Johnson, R. T., & Smith, K. A. (1995). Cooperative learning and individual student achievement in secondary schools. In J. E. Pedersen, & A. D. Digby (Eds.), *Secondary schools and cooperative learning* (pp. 3–54). New York: Garland Publishing.

Johnson, J., Farkas, S., & Bers, A. (1997). *What American teenagers really think about their schools: A report from Public Agenda.* New York: Public Agenda.

Johnson, R. E. (1975). Meaning in complex learning. *Review of Educational Research, 45*(3), 425–460.

Johnson, R., S. Mims-Cox, J., & Doyle-Nichols, A. (2010). *Developing portfolios in education: A guide to reflection, inquiry, and assessment* (2nd ed.). Thousand Oaks, CA: SAGE.

Johnson, S. (2006). *Everything bad is good for you.* New York: Riverhead Books (Penguin Group).

Johnson, S. P. (Ed.). (2010). *Neoconstructivism: The new science of cognitive development.* New York: Oxford University Press.

Jonassen, D. H., Howland, J., Marra, R. M., & Crismond, D. (2008). *Meaningful learning with technology* (3rd ed.). Upper Saddle River, NJ: Pearson/Merrill Prentice Hall.

Jones, B. D. (2007). The unintended outcomes of high-stakes testing. *Journal of Applied School Psychology, 23*(2), 65–86.

Joo, Y-j, Bong, M., & Choi, H-j. (2000). Self-efficacy for self-regulated learning, academic self-efficacy, and internet self-efficacy in web-based instruction. *Educational Technology Research and Development, 48*(2), 5–17.

Jorgenson, O. (2003). Brain scam? Why educators should be careful about embracing "brain research." *The Educational Forum, 67*(4), 364–369.

Jovanovic, J., & King, S. S. (1998). Boys and girls in the performance-based science classroom: Who's doing the performing? *American Educational Research Journal, 35*(3), 477–496.

Joyce, B., & Weil, M. (2009). *Models of teaching* (8th ed.). Boston: Pearson/Allyn & Bacon.

Jussim, L., Eccles, J., & Madon, S. (1996). Social perception, social stereotypes, and

teacher expectations: Accuracy and the quest for the powerful self-fulfilling prophesy. In M. Zanna (Ed.), *Advances in experimental social psychology, Vol. 28.* (pp. 281–383). San Diego, CA: Academic Press.

Juvonen, J. (2000). The social functions of attributional face-saving tactics among early adolescents. *Educational Psychology Review, 12*(1), 15–32.

Juvonen, J. (2007). Reforming middle schools: Focus on continuity, social connectedness, and engagement. *Educational Psychologist, 42*(4), 197–208.

Kagan, J. (1964a). *Developmental studies of reflection and analysis.* Cambridge, MA: Harvard University Press.

Kagan, J. (1964b). Impulsive and reflective children. In J. D. Krumbolz (Ed.), *Learning and the educational process.* Chicago: Rand McNally.

Kail, R. V. (2010). *Children and their development* (5th ed.). Upper Saddle River, NJ: Pearson Prentice Hall.

Kalbaugh, P., & Haviland, J. M. (1991). Formal operational thinking and identity. In R. M. Lerner, A. C. Peterson, & J. Brooks-Gunn (Eds.), *Encyclopedia of adolescence.* New York: Garland Publishing.

Kalyuga, S. (2009). Knowledge elaboration: A cognitive load perspective. *Learning and Instruction, 19*(5), 402–410.

Kamii, C. (2000). *Young children reinvent arithmetic: Implications of Piaget's theory* (2nd ed). New York: Teachers College Press.

Kaplan, A., & Flum, H. (2009). Motivation and identity: The relations of actions and development in educational contexts—An introduction to the special issue. *Educational Psychologist, 44*(2), 73–77.

Kaplan, A., Karabenick, S., & De Groot, E. (Eds.). *Culture, self, and, motivation: essays in honor of Martin L. Maehr* (pp.161–181). Charlotte, NC: Information Age Publishing.

Kapur, M., & Kinzer, C. (2007). The effect of problem type on collaborative problem solving in a synchronous computer-mediated environment. *Educational Technology, Research and Development, 55*(5), 439–459.

Kapur, M., & Kinzer, C. (2009). Productive failure in CSCL groups. *International Journal of Computer-Supported Collaborative Learning, 4*(1), 21–46.

Karniol, R., Gabay, R., Ochion, Y., & Harari, Y. (1998). Is gender or gender-role orientation a better predictor of empathy in adolescence? *Sex Roles, 39*(1–2), 45–59.

Karpicke, J. D., Butler, A. C., & Roediger III, H. L. (2009). *Memory, 17*(4), 471–479.

Karpov, Y. V., & Bransford, J. D. (1995). L. S. Vygotsky and the doctrine of empirical and theoretical learning. *Educational Psychologist, 30*(2), 61–66.

Karpov, Y. V., & Haywood, H. C. (1998). Two ways to elaborate Vygotsky's concept of meditation. *American Psychologist, 53*(1), 27–36.

Katayama, A. D., & Robinson, D. H. (2000). Getting students "partially" involved in note-taking using graphic organizers. *The Journal of Experimental Education, 68*(2), 119–133.

Kaufman, J., & Beghetto, R. (2009). Beyond big and little: The Four C Model of Creativity. *Review of General Psychology, 13*(1), 1–12.

Kavale, K. A. (2002). Mainstreaming to full inclusion: From orthogenesis to pathogenesis of an idea. *International Journal of Disability, Development and Education, 49*(2), 201–214.

Keane, G., & Shaughnessy, M. F. (2002). An interview with Robert J. Sternberg: The current "state of the art." *Educational Psychology Review, 14*(3), 313–330.

Keengwe, J., Onchwari, G., & Wachira, P. (2008). The use of computer tools to support meaningful learning. *AACE Journal, 16*(1), 77–92.

Kehle, T. J., Bray, M. A., Theodore, L. A., Jenson, W. R., & Clark, E. (2000). A multi-component intervention designed to reduce disruptive classroom behavior. *Psychology in the Schools, 37*(5), 475–481.

Kelly, M., & Moag-Stahlberg, A. (2002). Battling the obesity epidemic. *Principal, 81*(5), 26–29.

Kelley, M. L., & Carper, L. B. (1988). Home-based reinforcement procedures. In J. C. Witt, S. N. Elliott, & F. M. Gresham (Eds.), *Handbook of behavior therapy in education.* New York: Plenum Press.

Kentucky Department of Education (2009). *2007 Kentucky core content test (kcct) released items.* Retrieved from http://www.education.ky.gov/kde/administrative+resources/testing+and+reporting+/district+support/link+to+released+items/2007+kentucky+core+content+test+(kcct)+released+items.htm.

Kerr, A., & Grasby, R. (2009). Engagement through choice: Using independent research projects to improve student interest. *Journal of Classroom Research in Literacy, 2,* 3–19.

Kerr, M. M., & Nelson, C. M. (2010). *Strategies for addressing behavior problems in the classroom* (6th Edition). Columbus, Ohio: Merrill/Prentice-Hall.

Kiewra, K. A. (2009). *Teaching how to learn.* Thousand Oaks, CA: Corwin Press.

Kim, Y., Baylor, A. L., & PALS Group. (2006). Pedagogical agents as learning companions: The role of agent competency and type of interaction. *Educational Technology Research and Development, 54*(3), 223–243.

King, A. (1992a). Comparison of self-questioning, summarizing, and notetaking-review as strategies for learning from lectures. *American Educational Research Journal, 29*(2), 303–323.

King, A. (1992b). Facilitating elaborative learning through guided student-generated questioning. *Educational Psychologist, 27*(1), 111–126.

King, A. (1994). Guiding knowledge construction in the classroom: Effects of teaching children how to question and how to explain. *American Educational Research Journal, 31*(2), 338–368.

King, A. (1998). Transactive peer tutoring: Distributing cognition and metacognition. *Educational Psychology Review, 10*(1), 57–74.

King, A. (2002). Structuring peer interaction to promote high-level cognitive processing. *Theory into Practice, 41*(1), 33–39.

King, D., Bellocchi, A., & Ritchie, S. (2008) Making connections: Learning and teaching chemistry in context. *Research in Science Education, 38*(3), pp. 365–384.

Kirk, S. A., Gallagher, J. J., & Anastasiow, N. J. (2006). *Educating exceptional children* (11th ed.). Boston: Houghton Mifflin.

Kirk, S. A., Gallagher, J. J., Coleman, M. R., & Anastasiow, N. J. (2009). *Educating exceptional children* (12th ed.). Belmont, CA: Wadsworth/Cengage Learning.

Klassen, R. (2002). Writing in early adolescence: A review of the role of self-efficacy beliefs. *Educational Psychology Review, 14*(2), 173–203.

Klauer, K. (1984). Intentional and incidental learning with instructional texts: A meta-analysis for 1970–1980. *American Educational Research Journal, 21*(2), 323–339.

Klein, S. (Ed.). (2007). *Handbook for achieving gender equity through education.* Mahwah, NJ: Erlbaum Publishers.

Kleinert, H., Browder, D., & Towles-Reeves, E. (2009). Models of cognition for students with significant cognitive disabilities: Implications for assessment. *Review of Educational Research, 79*(1), 301–326

Knapp, M. S., & Shields, P. M. (1990). Reconceiving academic instruction for the children of poverty. *Phi Delta Kappan, 71*(10), 753–758.

Knapp, M. S., Shields, P. M., & Turnbull, B. J. (1995). Academic challenge in high-poverty classrooms. *Phi Delta Kappan, 76*(10), 770–776.

Kober, N., Zabala, D., Chudowsky, N., Chudowsky, V., Gayler, K., & McMurrer, J. (2006, August). *State high school exit exams: A challenging year.* Washington, DC: Center on Education Policy. Retrieved from http://www.cep-dc.org.

Kohlberg, L. (1963). The development of children's orientations toward a moral order: 1. Sequence in the development of moral thought. *Vita Humana, 6*(1–2), 11–33.

Kohlberg, L. (1969). Stage and sequence: The cognitive-developmental approach to socialization. In D. A. Goslin (Ed.), *Handbook of socialization theory and research.* Chicago: Rand McNally.

Kohlberg, L. (1976). Moral stages and moralization: The cognitive-developmental approach. In T. Lickona (Ed.), *Moral development and behavior: Theory, research, and social issues.* New York: Holt, Rinehart & Winston.

Kohlberg, L. (1978). Revisions in the theory and practice of moral development. In W. Damon (Ed.), *New directions for child development: Moral development* (No. 2). San Francisco: Jossey-Bass.

Kohn, A. (1993). Rewards versus learning: A response to Paul Chance. *Phi Delta Kappan, 74*(10), 783–787.

Kohn, A. (2006). *The homework myth: Why our kids get too much of a bad thing.* Philadelphia: Perseus Books.

Kohn, A. (2008). Why self-discipline is overrated: The (troubling) theory and practice of control from within. *Phi Delta Kappan, 90*(3), 168–176.

Kontos, G., & Mizell, A. P. (1997). Global village classroom: The changing roles of teachers and students through technology. *TechTrends, 42*(5), 17–22.

Koohang, A., Riley, L., Smith, T., & Schreurs, J. (2009). E-learning and constructivism: From theory to application. *Interdisciplinary Journal of E-Learning and Learning Objects, 5,* 91–109.

Kordaki, M. (2009). 'MULTIPLES': A challenging learning framework for the generation of multiple perspectives within e-collaboration settings. In T. Daradoumis, S. Caballè, J. Marquès, F. Xhafa (Eds.), *Intelligent collaborative e-learning systems and applications* (pp. 37–52). Berlin: Springer-Verlag.

Kordaki, M., & Potari, D. (2002). The effect of area measurement tools on student strategies: The role of a computer microworld. *International Journal of Computers for Mathematical Learning, 7*(1), 65–100.

Koretz, D. (2008). *Measuring up: What educational testing really tells us.* Cambridge, MA: Harvard University Press.

Kornell, N., & Bjork, R. A. (2007). The promise and perils of self-regulated study. *Psychonomic Bulletin and Review, 14*(2), 219–224.

Kosunen, T., & Mikkola, A. (2002). Building a science of teaching: How objectives and reality meet in Finnish teacher education. *European Journal of Teacher Education, 25*(2/3), 135–150.

Kounin, J. S. (1970). *Discipline and group management in classrooms.* New York: Holt, Rinehart & Winston.

Kozol, J. (2007). *Letters to a young teacher.* New York: Crown.

Kozulin, A., Gindis, B., Ageyev, V., & Miller, S. (Eds.). (2003). *Vygotsky's educational theory in cultural context.* New York: Cambridge University Press.

Kozulin, A., & Presseisen, B. Z. (1995). Mediated learning experience and psychological tools: Vygotsky's and Feuerstein's perspectives in a study of student learning. *Educational Psychologist, 30*(2), 57–75.

Kramarski, B., & Zeichner, O. (2001). Using technology to enhance mathematical reasoning: Effects of feedback and self-regulation learning. *Educational Media International, 38*(2/3), 77–82.

Krathwohl, D. R., Bloom, B. S., & Masia, B. B. (1964). *Taxonomy of educational objectives. Handbook II: Affective domain.* New York: McKay.

Krätzig, G. P., & Arbuthnot, K. D. (2006). Perceptual learning style and learning proficiency. *Journal of Educational Psychology, 98*(1), 238–246.

Kroger, J. (1996). *Identity and adolescence: The balance between self and other* (2nd ed.). New York: Routledge.

Kruse, S. (2009). *Working smart: Problem-solving strategies for school leaders.* Lanham, MD: Rowman & Littlefield Education.

Kubiszyn, T., & Borich, G. (2010). *Educational testing and measurement: Classroom application and practice* (9th ed.). New York: Wiley.

Kuhn, D. (1999). A developmental model of critical thinking. *Educational Researcher, 28*(2), 16–26, 46.

Kuhn, D. (2002). What is scientific thinking and how does it develop? In U. Goswami (Ed.), *Blackwell handbook of childhood cognitive development* (pp. 371–393). Malden, MA: Blackwell Publishers.

Kulik, C-L., Kulik, J. A., & Bangert-Drowns, R. L. (1990). Effectiveness of mastery learning programs. *Review of Educational Research, 60*(2), 265–299.

Kulik, J. A. (2003a, May). *Effects of using instructional technology in elementary and secondary schools: What controlled evaluation studies say.* Arlington, VA: SRI International. Retrieved from http://www.sri.com/policy/csted/reports/sandt/it.

Kulik, J. A. (2003b). Grouping and tracking. In N. Colangelo & G. A. Davis (Eds.), *Handbook of gifted education* (3rd ed., pp. 268–281). Boston: Allyn & Bacon.

Kulik, J. A., & Kulik, C.-L. (1991). Ability grouping and gifted students. In N. Colangelo & G. A. Davis (Eds.), *Handbook of gifted education.* Boston: Allyn & Bacon.

Kusku, F., Ozbilgin, M., & Ozkale, L. (2007). Against the tide: Gendered prejudice and disadvantage in engineering. *Gender Work and Organization, 14*(2), 109–129.

Lach, C., Little, E., & Nazzaro, D. (2003). From all sides now: Weaving technology and multiple intelligences into science and art. *Learning and Leading with Technology, 30*(6), 32–35, 59.

Lacina, J. (2004/2005). Promoting language acquisitions: Technology and English language learners. *Childhood Education, 81*(2), 113–115.

Laczko-Kerr, I., & Berliner, D. C. (2003). In harm's way: How undercertified teachers hurt their students. *Educational Leadership, 60*(8), 34–39.

Ladson-Billings, G. (2002). But that's just good teaching! The case for culturally relevant pedagogy. In S. J. Denbo & L. M. Beaulieu (Eds.), *Improving schools for African American students* (pp. 95–102). Springfield, IL: Charles C. Thomas.

Lai, S.-L., Chang, T.-S., & Ye, R. (2006). Computer usage and reading in elementary schools: A cross-cultural study. *Journal of Educational Computing Research, 34*(1), 47–66.

Lalley, J., & Gentile, J. (2008). Classroom assessment and grading to assure mastery. *Theory Into Practice, 48*(1), 28–35.

Lam, R., & Lee, I. (2010). Balancing the dual functions of portfolio assessment. *ELT Journal 64*(1), 54–64.

Lambros, A. (2002). *Problem-based learning in k-8 classrooms: A teacher's guide to implementation.* Thousand Oaks, CA: Corwin Press.

Lampinen, J. M., & Odegard, T. N. (2006). Memory editing mechanisms. *Memory, 14*(6), 649–654.

Lancey, D. F. (2002). Cultural constraints on children's play. In J. L. Roopnarine (Ed.), *Conceptual, social-cognitive, and contextual issues in the fields of play* (pp. 53–60). Westport, CT: Ablex.

Landau, B. M., & Gathercoal, P. (2000). Creating peaceful classrooms: Judicious Discipline and class meetings. *Phi Delta Kappan, 81*(6), 450–452, 454.

Lantieri, L. (1995). Waging peace in our schools: Beginning with the children. *Phi Delta Kappan, 76*(5), 386–388.

Lantieri, L. (1999). Hooked on altruism: Developing social responsibility in at-risk youth. *Reclaiming Children and Youth, 8*(2), 83–87.

Larson, B. E., & Keiper, T. A. (2007). *Instructional strategies for middle and high school.* New York: Routledge.

Larson, R. W., & Sheeber, L. B. (2009). The daily emotional experience of adolescents: Are adolescents more emotional, why, and how is that related to depression? In N. B. Allen & L. B. Sheeber (Eds.), *Adolescent emotional development and the emergence of depressive disorders* (pp. 11–32). Cambridge, England: Cambridge University Press.

Latu, E., & Chapman, E. (2002). Computerised adaptive testing. *British Journal of Educational Technology, 33*(5), 619–622.

Lazear, D. G. (2003). *Eight ways of teaching: The artistry of teaching with multiple intelligences.* Thousand Oaks, CA: SAGE

Leacock, T. L., & Nesbit, J. C. (2007). A framework for evaluating the quality of multimedia learning resources. *Educational Technology & Society, 10* (2), 44–59.

Leadbeater, B. (1991). Relativistic thinking in adolescence. In R. M. Lerner, A. C. Peterson, &J. Brooks-Gunn (Eds.), *Encyclopedia of adolescence.* New York: Garland Publishing.

Lee, J. (2008). Is test-driven external accountability effective? Synthesizing the evidence from cross-state causal-comparative and correlational studies. *Review of Educational Research, 78*(3), 608–644.

Lee, J., Grigg, W., & Donahue.P. (2007). *The nation's report card: Reading 2007* (NCES 2007-496). Washington, DC: U.S. Department of Education, National Center for Education Statistics. Retrieved from http://nces.ed.gov/nationsreportcard/pubs/main2007/2007496.asp.

Lee, J-S., & Bowen, N. K. (2006). Parent involvement, cultural capital, and the achievement gap among elementary school children. *American Educational Research Journal, 43*(2), 193–218.

Leming, J. S. (1993). In search of effective character education. *Educational Leadership, 51*(3), 63–71.

Leming, J. S. (2008). Research and practice in moral and character education: Loosely coupled phenomena. In L. P. Nucci & D. Narvaez (Eds.), *Handbook of moral and character education* (pp. 134–157). New York: Routledge.

Lerner, J. W. (2003). *Learning disabilities: Theories, diagnosis, and teaching strategies* (9th ed.). Boston: Houghton Mifflin.

Lerner, J., and Johns, B. (2009). *Learning disabilities and related mild disabilities: Characteristics, teaching strategies and new directions.* Boston: Houghton Mifflin.

Lleras, C., & Rangel, C. (2009). Ability grouping practices in elementary school and African American/Hispanic achievement. *American Journal of Education, 115*(Feb), 279–304.

Lessow-Hurley, J. (2009). *The foundations of dual language instruction* (5th ed.). Boston: Pearson/Allyn & Bacon.

Levin, J., & Nolan, J. F. (2010). *Principles of classroom management: A professional decision-making model* (6th ed.). Boston: Pearson.

Levin, J. R. (1982). Pictures as prose-learning devices. In A. Flammer & W. Kintsch (Eds.), *Advances in psychology: Vol. 8. Discourse processing.* Amsterdam: North-Holland.

Levin, J. R. (1993). Mnemonic strategies and classroom learning: A 20-year report card. *Elementary School Journal, 94*(2), 235–244.

Levine, S. C., Vasilyeva, M., Lourenco, S. F., Newcombe, N. S., & Huttenlocher, J. (2005). Socioeconomic status modifies the sex difference in spatial skill. *Psychological Science, 16*(11), 841–845.

Lewandowsky, S., & Thomas, J. (2009). Expertise: Acquisition, limitations, and control. In F. Durso (Ed.), *Reviews of Human Factors and Ergonomics* (Volume 5), (pp. 140–165). Santa Monica: Human Factors and Ergonomics Society.

Lewis, T. (2005). Creativity: A framework for the design/problem solving discourse in technology education. *Journal of Technology*

Education, *17*(1). Retrieved September 16, 2006, from http://scholar.lib.vt.edu/ejournals/JTE/v17n1/lewis.html.

Lewis, C. (2009). What is the nature of knowledge development in lesson study? *Educational Action Research,* *17*(1), 95–110.

Lewis, C., Perry, R., & Friedkin, S. (2009). Lesson study as action research. In S. Noffke & B. Somekh (Eds.), *The SAGE Handbook of Educational Action Research* (pp. 142–154). Thousand Oaks, CA: SAGE.

Lewis-Moreno, B. (2007). Shared responsibility: Achieving success with English-language learners. *Phi Delta Kappan,* *88*(10), 772–775.

Ley, K., & Young, D. B. (2001). Instructional principles for self-regulation. *Educational Technology Research and Development,* *49*(2), 93–103.

Li, J. (2002). Learning models in different cultures. In J. Bempechat & J. G. Elliott (Eds.), *Learning in culture and context: Vol. 96. New directions for child and adolescent development* (pp. 45–63). San Francisco: Jossey-Bass.

Liao, Y-k. C. (2007). Effects of computer-assisted instruction on students' achievement in Taiwan: A meta-analysis. *Computers & Education,* *48*(2), 216–233.

Liben, L. S., Bigler, R. S., & Krogh, H. R. (2002). Language at work: Children's gendered interpretations of occupational titles. *Child Development,73*(3), 810–828.

Lickona, T. (1976). Research on Piaget's theory of moral development. In T. Lickona (Ed.), *Moral development and behavior: Theory, research, and social issues.* New York: Holt, Rinehart & Winston.

Lickona, T. (1998). A more complex analysis is needed. *Phi Delta Kappan,* *79*(6), 449–454.

Lickona, T., & Davidson, M. (2005). *Smart and good high schools: Integrating excellence and ethics for success in school, work, and beyond.* Cortland, NY: Center for the 4th and 5th Rs (Respect and Responsibility) / Washington, DC: Character Education Partnership. Retrieved from www.cortland.edu/character/high school.

Lieberman, J. (2009). Reinventing teacher professional norms and identities: the role of lesson study and learning communities. *Professional Development in Education,* *35*(1), 83–99.

Light, P., & Littleton, K. (1999). *Social processes in children's learning.* Cambridge, England: Cambridge University Press.

Ligorio, M. B., Talamo, A., & Pontecorvo, C. (2005). Building intersubjectivity at a distance during the collaborative writing of fairy tales. *Computers & Education,* *45*(3), 357–374.

Lim, J., Reiser, R., & Olina, Z. (2009). The effects of part-task and whole-task instructional approaches on acquisition and transfer of a complex cognitive skill. *Educational*

Technology Research and Development, *57*(1), 61–77.

Lindberg, J. A., & Swick, A. M. (2006). *Common-sense classroom management for elementary school teachers* (2nd ed.). Thousand Oaks, CA: Corwin Press.

Lindberg, J. A., Kelly, D. A., & Swick, A. M. (2005). *Common-sense classroom management for middle and high school teachers.* Thousand Oaks, CA: Corwin Press.

Linell, P. (2007). Dialogicality in languages, minds and brains: Is there a convergence between dialogism and neuro-biology? *Language Sciences 29*(5), 605–620.

Linn, M. C., & Slotta, J. D. (2000). WISE science. *Educational Leadership,* *58*(2), 29–32.

Linn, M. C., Lewis, C., Tsuchida, I., & Songer, N. B. (2000). Beyond fourth-grade science: Why do U.S. and Japanese students diverge? *Educational Researcher,* *29*(3), 4–14.

Linn, R. L. (2003). Accountability: Responsibility and reasonable expectations. *Educational Researcher,* *32*(7), 3–13.

Linn, R. L. (2009). Improving the accountability provisions of NCLB. In M. A. Rebell & J. R. Wolf (Eds.), *NCLB at the crossroads: Reexamining the federal effort to close the achievement gap* (pp. 163–184). New York: Teachers College Press.

Liu, X. (2010). *Essentials of science classroom assessment.* Thousand Oaks, CA: SAGE.

Llabo, L. D. (2002). Computers, kids, and comprehension: Instructional practices that make a difference. In C. C. Block, L. B. Gambrell, & M. Pressley (Eds.), *Improving comprehension instruction: Rethinking research, theory, and classroom practice* (pp. 275–289). San Francisco: Jossey-Bass.

Lobman, C., & Lundquist, M. (2007). *Unscripted learning: Using improv activities across the k–8 curriculum.* New York: Teachers College Press.

Lodewyk, K. R. (2007). Relations among epistemological beliefs, academic achievement, and task performance in secondary school students. *Educational Psychology,* *27*(3), 307–327.

Lodewyk, K. R., & Winne, P. H. (2005). Relations among the structure of learning tasks, achievement, and changes in self-efficacy in secondary students. *Journal of Educational Psychology,* *97*(1), 3–12.

Lopata, C., Miller, K. A., & Miller, R. H. (2003). Survey of actual and preferred use of cooperative learning among exemplar teachers. *Journal of Educational Research,* *96*(4), 232–239.

Lou, Y., Abrami, P. C., & d'Apollonia, S. (2001). Small group learning and individual learning with technology: A meta-analysis. *Review of Educational Research,* *71*(3), 499–521.

Lou, Y., Abrami, P. C., & Spence, J. C. (2000). Effects of within-class grouping on student achievement: An exploratory

model. *Journal of Educational Research,* *94*(2), 101–112.

Lowry, R., Sleet, D., Duncan, C., Powell, K, & Kolbe, L. (1995). Adolescents at risk for violence. *Educational Psychology Review,* *7*(1), 7–39.

Loyens, S., Rikers, R., & Schmidt, H. (2007). Students' conceptions of distinct constructivist assumptions. *European Journal of Psychology of Education,* *12*(2), 179–199.

Loyens, S., Rikers, R., & Schmidt, H. (2008). Relationships between students' conceptions of constructivist learning and their regulation and processing strategies. *Instructional Science,* *36*(5–6), 445–462.

Loyens, S., & Gijbels, D. (2008). Understanding the effects of constructivist learning environments: Introducing a multidirectional approach. *Instructional Science,* *36*(5–6), 351–357.

Lu, Y., Zhou, T., & Wang, B. (2008). Exploring Chinese users' acceptance of instant messaging using the theory of planned behavior, the technology acceptance model, and the flow theory. *Computers in Human Behavior,* *25*(1), 29–39.

Lundeberg, M. A., & Fox, P. W. (1991). Do laboratory findings on test expectancy generalize to classroom outcomes? *Review of Educational Research,* *61*(1), 94–106.

Lyons, N. P., & Kubler LaBoskey, V. (2002). Introduction. In N. P. Lyons & V. Kubler (Eds.), *Narrative inquiry in practice: Advancing the knowledge of teaching.* New York: Teachers College Press.

Maag, J. W. (2001). Rewarded by punishment: Reflections on the disuse of positive reinforcement in schools. *Exceptional children,* *67*(2), 173–186.

Maanum, J. L. (2009). *The general educator's guide to special education* (3rd ed.). Thousand Oaks, CA: Corwin Press.

Mabry, L. (2008). Assessment, accountability, and the impossible dream. In S. Mathison & E. W. Ross (Eds.), *The nature and limits of standards-based reform and assessment* (pp. 49–56). New York: Teachers College Press.

MacArthur, C. (1994). Peers + word processing + strategies = a powerful combination for revising student writing. *Teaching Exceptional Children,* *27*(1), 24–29.

Maccini, P., Gagnon, J. C., & Hughes, C. A. (2002). Technology-based practices for secondary students with learning disabilities. *Learning Disability Quarterly,* *25*(4), 247–261.

Macedo, D. (2000). The illiteracy of English-only literacy. *Educational Leadership,* *57*(4), 62–67.

Mackay, S., McLaughlin, T. F., Weber, K., & Derby, K. M. (2001). The use of precision requests to decrease noncompliance in the home and neighborhood: A case study. *Child and Family Behavior Therapy,* *23*(3), 43–52.

MacKinnon, J. L., & Marcia, J. E. (2002). Concurring patterns of women's identity status, attachment styles, and understanding of children's development. *International Journal of Behavioral Development, 26*(1), 70–80.

Mager, R. F. (1962). *Preparing instructional objectives.* Palo Alto, CA: Fearon.

Mager, R. F. (1997). *Preparing instructional objectives* (3d ed.). Atlanta, GA: The Center for Effective Performance.

Mahwinney, T. S., & Sagan, L. L. (2007). The power of personal relationships. *Phi Delta Kappan, 88*(6), 460–464.

Maloch, B., Fine, J., & Flint, A. S. (2002/2003). Trends in teacher certification and literacy. *Reading Teacher, 56*(4), 348–350.

Marchand, G., & Skinner, E. A. (2007). Motivational dynamics of children's academic help-seeking and concealment. *Journal of Educational Psychology, 99*(1), 65–82.

Marcia, J. E. (1966). Development and validation of ego identity status. *Journal of Personality and Social Psychology, 3*(5), 551–558.

Marcia, J. E. (1967). Ego identity status: Relationship to change in self-esteem, "general adjustment," and authoritarianism. *Journal of Personality, 35*(1), 119–133.

Marcia, J. E. (1980). Identity in adolescence. In J. Adelson (Ed.), *Handbook of adolescent psychology.* New York: Wiley.

Marcia, J. E. (1999). Representational thought in ego identity, psychotherapy, and psychosocial developmental theory. In I. E. Sigel (Ed.), *Development of mental representation: theories and application* (pp. 391–414). Mahwah, NJ: Erlbaum.

Marcia, J. E. (2001). A commentary on Seth Schwartz's review of identity theory and research. *Identity, 1*(1), 59–65.

Marcia, J. E. (2002). Identity and psychosocial development in adulthood. *Identity, 2*(1), 7–28.

Marcia, J. E. (2007). Theory and measure: The identity status interview. In M. Watzlawik & A. Born (Eds.), *Capturing identity: Quantitative and qualitative methods.* Lanham, MD: University Press of America.

Marinak, B., & Gambrell, L. (2008). Intrinsic motivation and rewards: What sustains young children's engagement with text? *Literacy Research and Instruction, 47*(1), 9–26.

Mark, J., Gorman, J., & Nikula, J. (2009). Keeping teacher learning of mathematics central in lesson study, *NCSM Journal of Mathematics Education Leadership, 11*(1), 3–11.

Marley, S. C., & Levin, J. R. (2006). Pictorial illustrations, visual imagery, and motor activity: Their instructional implications for Native American children with learning disabilities. In R. J. Morris (Ed.), *Disability research and policy: Current perspectives* (pp. 102–123). Mahwah, NJ: Erlbaum.

Marley, S. C., Levin, J. R., & Glenberg, A. M. (2007). Improving Native American children's listening comprehension through concrete representations. *Contemporary Educational Psychology, 32*(3), 537–550.

Marquis, J. G., Horner, R. H., Carr, E. G., Turnbull, A. P., Thompson, M., Behrens, G. A., Magito-McLaughlin, D., McAtee, M. L., Smith, C. E., Ryan, K. A., & Doolabh, A. (2000). A meta-analysis of positive behavior support. In R. Gersten, E. P. Schiller & S. R. Vaughn, (Eds.), *Contemporary special education research* (pp. 137–178). Mahwah, NJ: Erlbaum Associates.

Marsh, H. W., & Hattie, J. (1996). Theoretical perspectives on the structure of self-concept. In B. A. Bracken (Ed.), *Handbook of self-concept* (pp. 38–90). New York: Wiley.

Marsh, H. W., Martin, A., & Cheng, J. (2008). A multilevel perspective on gender in classroom motivation and climate: Potential benefits of male teachers for boys? *Journal of Educational Psychology, 100*(1), 78–95.

Marsh, H. W., Seaton, M., Trautwein, U., Lüdtke, O., Hau, K. T., O'Mara, A. J., & Craven, R. G. (2008). The big-fish-little-pond effect stand up to critical scrutiny: Implications for theory, methodology, and future research. *Educational Psychology Review, 20*(3), 319–350.

Martin, G., & Pear, J. (2007). *Behavior modification: What it is and how to do it* (8th ed.). Upper Saddle River, NJ: Pearson/Prentice Hall.

Martin, A., & Dowson, M. (2009). Interpersonal relationships, motivation, engagement, and achievement: Yields for theory, current issues, and educational practice. *Review of Educational Research, 79*(1), 327–365.

Martin, J. (2004). Self-regulated learning, social cognitive theory, and agency. *Educational Psychologist, 39*(2), 135–145.

Martinez, M. E. (1999). Cognition and the question of test item format. *Educational Psychologist, 34*(1), 207–218.

Marx, R. W., & Winne, P. H. (1987). The best tool teachers have—their students' thinking. In D. C. Berliner & B. V. Rosenshine (Eds.), *Talks to teachers.* New York: Random House.

Marzano, R. J. (2009). Setting the record straight on "high-yield" strategies. *Phi Delta Kappan, 91*(1), 30–37.

Marzano, R. J., & Kendall, J. S. (2007). *The new taxonomy of educational objectives* (2nd ed.). Thousand Oaks, CA: Corwin Press.

Marzano, R., & Kendall, J. (2008). *Designing & assessing educational objectives: Applying the new taxonomy.* Thousand Oaks, CA: Corwin Press.

Marzano, R. J., & Pickering, D. J. (2007). Errors and allegations about research on homework. *Phi Delta Kappan, 88*(7), 507–513.

Marzano, R. J., Pickering, D. J., & Pollock, J. E. (2005). *Classroom instruction that works: Research-based strategies for increasing student achievement.* Upper Saddle River, NJ: Pearson/Prentice Hall.

Maslow, A. H. (1968). *Toward a psychology of being* (2nd ed.). Princeton, NJ: Van Nostrand.

Maslow, A. H. (1987). *Motivation and personality* (3rd ed.). New York: Harper & Row.

Mason, L. H. (2004). Explicit self-regulated strategy development versus reciprocal questioning: Effects on expository reading comprehension among struggling readers. *Journal of Educational Psychology, 96*(2), 283–296.

Mathis, W. J. (2005). Bridging the achievement gap: A bridge too far? *Phi Delta Kappan, 86*(8), 590–593.

Mathison, S., & Ross, E. W. (Eds.). (2008). *The nature and limits of standards-based reform and assessment.* New York: Teachers College Press.

Matos, L., Lens, W., & Vansteenkiste, M. (2009). School culture matters for teachers' and students' achievement goals. In A. Kaplan, S. Karabenick, & E. De Groot (Eds.), *Culture, self, and, motivation: essays in honor of Martin L. Maehr* (pp.161–181). Charlotte, NC: Information Age Publishing.

Matthew, C., & Sternberg, R. (2009). Developing experience-based (tacit) knowledge through reflection. *Learning and Individual Differences, 19*(4), 530–540.

Matthew, K. I. (1996). The impact of CD-ROM storybooks on children's reading comprehension and reading attitude. *Journal of Educational Multimedia and Hypermedia, 5*(3/4), 379–394.

Maxim, G. (2010). *Dynamic social studies for constructivist classrooms: Inspiring tomorrow's social scientists.* Upper Saddle River, NJ: Allyn & Bacon/Pearson.

Mayer, M. J., & Furlong, M. J. (2010). How safe are our schools? *Educational Researcher, 39*(1), 16–26.

Mayer, R. E. (2008). *Learning and instruction* (2nd ed.). Upper Saddle River, NJ: Merrill Prentice Hall.

Mayer, R. E. (2009). Constructivism as a theory of learning versus constructivism as a prescription for instruction. In S. Tobias & T. Duffy (Eds.), *Constructivist instruction: Success or failure?* (pp. 184–200). New York: Routledge.

Mayer, R. E., & Moreno, R. (2003). Nine ways to reduce cognitive load in multimedia learning. *Educational Psychologist, 38*(1), 43–52.

Maynard, A. E. (2008). What we thought we knew and how we came to know it: Four decades of cross-cultural research from a Piagetian point of view. *Human Development, 51*(1), 56–65.

Mazur, J. E. (2006). *Learning and behavior* (6th ed.). Upper Saddle River, NJ: Pearson/Prentice Hall.

Mazyck, M. (2002). Integrated learning systems and students of color: Two decades of use in K–12 education. *TechTrends, 46*(2), 33–39.

McCaslin, M., & Hickey, D. T. (2001). Self-regulated learning and academic achievement: A Vygotskyian view. In B. J. Zimmerman & D. H. Schunk (Eds.), *Self-regulated learning and academic achievement: Theoretical perspectives* (pp. 227–252). Mahwah, NJ: Lawrence Erlbaum.

McCown, R., & Hopson, R. K. (2006). *Stewardship and practice: The CID ripple effect at Duquesne University*. CASTL Technical Report No. 8-06. Department of Educational Foundations and Leadership, School of Education, Duquesne University. Retrieved from http://www.castl.duq.edu.

McCrea, S. (2008). Self-handicapping, excuse making, and counterfactual thinking: Consequences for self-esteem and future motivation. *Journal of Personality and Social Psychology, 95*(2), 274–292.

McDaniel, M. A., Howard, D. C., & Einstein, G. O. (2009). The read-recite-review study strategy, *Psychological Science, 20*(4), 516–522.

McDevitt, T. M., & Ormrod, J. E. (2010). *Child development and education* (4th ed.). Upper Saddle River, NJ: Merrill.

McEntee, G. H., Appleby, J., Dowd, J., Grant, J., Hole, S., & Silva, P. (2003). *At the heart of teaching: A guide to reflective practice*. New York: Teachers College Press.

McGill-Franzen, A., & Allington, R. (2006). Contamination of current accountability systems. *Phi Delta Kappan, 87*(10), 762–766.

McGrath, D. (2003). Rubrics, portfolios, and tests, oh my! *Learning and Leading with Technology, 30*(8), 42–45.

McKenna, M. C., Cowart, E., & Watkins, J. (1997, December). *Effects of talking books on the growth of struggling readers in second grade*. Paper presented at the meeting of the National Reading Conference, Scottsdale, AZ.

McKenzie, W. (2002). *Multiple intelligences and instructional technology: A manual for every mind*. Eugene, OR: International Society for Technology in Education.

McKim, B. (2007). The road less traveled. *Phi Delta Kappan, 89*(4), 298–299.

McLoyd, V. C. (1998). Socioeconomic disadvantage and child development. *American Psychologist, 53*(2), 185–204.

McMillan, J. H., Myran, S., & Workman, D. (2002). Elementary teachers' classroom assessment and grading practices. *Journal of Educational Research, 95*(4), 203–213.

McMurrer, J. (2007, July). *Choices, change, and challenges: Curriculum and instruction in the NCLB era*. Retrieved from Center on Education Policy: http://www.cep-dc.org.

McNeil, L. M., Coppola, E., Radigan, J., & Vasquez Heilig, J. (2008). Avoidable losses: High-stakes accountability and the dropout crisis. *Education Policy Analysis Archives, 16*(3). Retrieved from http://epaa.asu.edu/epaa/v16n3.

McTighe, J. (1996/1997). What happens between assessments? *Educational Leadership, 54*(4), 6–12.

McVarish, J., & Solloway, S. (2002). Self-evaluation: Creating a classroom without unhealthy competitiveness. *Educational Forum, 66*(3), 253–260.

Means, B., & Haertel, G. (2002). Technology supports for assessing science inquiry. In National Research Council (Ed.), *Technology and assessment: Thinking ahead* (pp. 12–25). Washington, DC: National Academy Press.

Means, B., & Knapp, M. S. (1991). Introduction: Rethinking teaching for disadvantaged students. In B. Means, C. Chelemer, & M. S. Knapp (Eds.), *Teaching advanced skills to at-risk students*. San Francisco: Jossey-Bass.

Meilinger, T., Knauff, M., Butlthoff, H. (2008). Working memory in wayfinding—A dual task experiment in a virtual city. *Cognitive Science, 32*(4), 755–770.

Melton, R. F. (1978). Resolution of conflicting claims concerning the effect of behavioral objectives on student learning. *Review of Educational Research, 48*(2), 291–302.

Mendoza, J. I. (1994). On being a Mexican American. *Phi Delta Kappan, 76*(4), 293–295

Menzer, J. D., & Hampel, R. L. (2009). Lost at the last minute. *Phi Delta Kappan, 90*(9), 660–664.

Meo, G. (2008). Curriculum planning for all learners: Applying universal design for learning (UDL) to a high school reading comprehension program. *Preventing School Failure, 52*(2), 21–30.

Metzger, M. (1998). Teaching reading: Beyond the plot. *Phi Delta Kappan, 80*(3), 240–246, 256.

Metzger, M. (2002). Learning to discipline *Phi Delta Kappan, 84*(1), 77–84.

Mevarech, Z., & Susak, Z. (1993). Effects of learning with cooperative-mastery method on elementary students. *Journal of Educational Research, 86*(4), 197–205.

Meyer, M. S. (2000). The ability-achievement discrepancy: Does it contribute to our understanding of learning difficulties? *Educational Psychology Review, 12*(3), 315–337.

Meyer-Adams, N., & Conner, B. T. (2008). School violence: Bullying behaviors and the psychosocial school environment in middle schools. *Children & Schools, 30*(4), 211–221.

Midgley, C. (2001). A goal theory perspective on the current status of middle level schools. In T. Urdan & F Pajares (Eds.), *Adolescence and education: Vol. 1. General issues in the education of adolescents* (pp. 33–59). Greenwich, CT: Information Age Publishers.

Midgley, C., Middleton, M. J., Gheen, M. H., & Kumar, R. (2002). Stage-environment fit revisited: A goal theory approach to examining school transitions. In C. Midgley (Ed.), *Goals, goal structures, and patterns of adaptive learning* (pp. 109–142). Mahwah, NJ: Lawrence Erlbaum.

Miller, M. D., Linn, R. L., & Gronlund, N. E. (2009). *Measurement and assessment in teaching* (10th ed.). Upper Saddle River, NJ: Merrill/Pearson.

Miller, P., Fagley, N., & Casella, N. (2009). Effects of problem frame and gender on principals' decision making. *Social Psychology of Education, 12*(3), 397–413.

Miller, P. C., & Endo, H. (2004). Understanding and meeting the needs of ESL students. *Phi Delta Kappan, 85*(10), 786–791.

Miller, P. H. (2002). *Theories of developmental psychology* (4th ed.). New York: Worth.

Miller, R., & Brickman, S. (2004). A model of future-oriented motivation and self-regulation. *Educational Psychology Review, 16*(1), 9–33.

Miltenberger, R. G. (2008). *Behavior modification: Principles and procedures* (4th ed.). Belmont, CA: Thomson Wadsworth.

Mintrop, H., & Sunderman, G. L. (2009). Predictable failure of federal sanctions-driven accountability for school improvement—and why we may retain it anyway. *Educational Researcher, 38*(5), 353–364.

Mishel, L., & Roy, J. (2006). Accurately assessing high school graduation rates. *Phi Delta Kappan, 88*(4), 287–292.

Mistler-Jackson, M., & Songer, N. B. (2000). Student motivation and internet technology: Are students empowered to learn science? *Journal of Research in Science Teaching, 37*(5), 459–479.

Mock, D. R., & Kauffman, J. M. (2002). Preparing teachers for full inclusion: Is it possible? *The Teacher Educator, 37*(3), 202–215.

Moely, B. E., Hart, S. S., Leal, L., Santulli, K. A., Rao, N., Johnson, T., & Hamilton, L. B. (1992). The teacher's role in facilitating memory and study strategy development in the elementary school classroom. *Child Development, 63*(3), 653–672.

Molden, D. C., & Dweck, C. S. (2006). Finding "meaning" in psychology. *American Psychologist, 61*(3), 192–203.

Moll, L. C. (Ed.). (1990). *Vygotsky and education: instructional implications and applications of sociohistorical psychology*. New York: Cambridge University Press.

Montalvo, G., Mansfield, E., & Miller, R. (2007). Liking or disliking the teacher: Student motivation, engagement and achievement. *Evaluation and Research in Education, 20*(3), 144–158.

Montgomery, J. W., Magimairaj, B. M., & O'Malley, M. H. (2008). Role of working memory in typically developing children's complex sentence comprehension.

Journal of Psycholinguistics Research, 37(5), 331–354.

Montgomery, K. (2000). Classroom rubrics: Systematizing what teachers do naturally. *The Clearing House, 73*(6), 324–328.

Moon, T. R. (2002). Using performance assessment in the social studies classroom. *Gifted Child Today, 25*(3), 53–59.

Mooney, C. G. (2006). *Theories of childhood* (Special Ed.). Upper Saddle River, NJ: Merrill Prentice Hall/Pearson.

Moore, J. A., & Teagle, H. F. B. (2002). An introduction to cochlear implant technology, activation, and programming. *Language, Speech, and Hearing Services in the Schools, 33*(3), 153–161.

Moos, D. C., & Azevedo, R. (2009). Learning with computer-based learning environments: A literature review of computer self-efficacy. *Review of Educational Research, 79*(2), 576–600.

Mora, J. K., Wink, J., & Wink, D. (2001). Dueling models of dual language instruction: A critical review of the literature and program implementation guide. *Bilingual Research Journal, 25*(4), 435–460.

Morgan, H. (1997). *Cognitive styles and classroom learning.* Westport, CT: Praeger.

Morisi, T. L. (2008, February). Youth enrollment and employment during the school year. *Monthly Labor Review.* Retrieved from http://www.bls.gov/opub/mir/2008/02/art3full.pdf.

Morra, S., Gobbo, C., Marini, Z., & Sheese, R. (2008). *Cognitive development: Neo-Piagetian perspectives.* Mahwah, NJ: Lawrence Erlbaum.

Morris, P. (1977). Practical strategies for human learning and remembering. In M. J. A. Howe (Ed.), *Adult Learning.* New York: Wiley.

Morrison, C. T. (2008). "What would you do, what if it's you?" Strategies to deal with a bully. *Journal of School Health, 79*(4), 201–204.

Morrison, J. Q., & Jones, K. M. (2007). The effects of positive peer reporting as a classwide positive behavior support. *Journal of Behavioral Education, 16*(2), 111–124.

Morrison, K. (2009). Lessons of diversity learned the hard way. *Phi Delta Kappan, 90*(5), 360–362.

Moshavi, D. (2001). "Yes and . . .": Introducing improvisational theatre techniques to the management classroom. *Journal of Management Education, 25*(4), 437–449.

Moss, C. M. (2000). Professional learning on the cyber sea: What is the point of contact? *CyberPsychology and Behavior, 3*(1), 41–50.

Moss, C. M. (2001). Beyond painting the roses red: Challenging the beliefs of preservice teachers in an online community of inquiry. In K. Scanlon (Ed.), *Technology: Applications to teacher preparation. Monograph III* (pp. 32–42). The Pennsylvania Association of Colleges of Teacher Educators.

Moss, C. M., & Brookhart, S. (2009). *Advancing formative assessment in every classroom: A guide for instructional leaders.* Alexandria, VA: ASCD.

Moss, C. M., & Shank, G. (2002, May). Using qualitative processes in computer technology research on online learning: Lessons in change from "Teaching as Intentional Learning" [79 paragraphs]. *Forum Qualitative Sozialforschung / Forum: Qualitative Social Research* [On-line Journal], *3*(2). Retrieved from http://www.qualitative-research.net/fqs-texte/2-02/2-02mossshank-e.htm.

Mueller, M. (2009). The co-construction of arguments by middle school students. *The Journal of Mathematical Behavior, 28*(2–3), 138–149.

Muhlenbruck, L., Cooper, H., Nye, B., & Lindsay, J. J. (2000). Homework and achievement: Explaining the different strengths at the elementary and secondary levels. *Social Psychology in Education, 3*(4), 295–317.

Muis, K. R. (2007). The role of epistemic beliefs in self-regulated learning. *Educational Psychologist, 42*(3), 173–190.

Mullis, I. V. S., Martin, M. O., Gonzalez, E., O'Connor, K. M., Chrostowski, S. J., Gregory, K. D., Garden, R. A., & Smith, T. A. (2001). *Mathematics benchmarking report TIMSS 1999—eighth grade.* Chestnut Hill, MA: Boston College. Retrieved January 2, 2002, from www.timss.org/timss1999b/publications.html.

Murayama, K., & Elliot, A. (2009). The joint influence of personal achievement goals and classroom goal structures on achievement-relevant outcomes. *Journal of Educational Psychology, 101*(2), 432–447.

Murdock, T. B., Miller, A., & Kohlhardt, J. (2004). Effects of classroom context variables on high school students‰ judgments of the acceptability and likelihood of cheating. *Journal of Educational Psychology, 96*(4) 765–777.

Murphy, P. K., Delli, L., & Edwards, M. N. (2004). The good teacher and good teaching: Comparing beliefs of second-grade students, preservice teachers, and inservice teachers. *Journal of Experimental Education, 72*(2), 69–92.

Murphy, B. C., & Eisenberg, N. (2002). An integrative examination of peer conflict: Children's reported goals, emotions, and behavior. *Social Development, 11*(4), 534–557.

Murray, S. (2009). Telementoring: Preservice teachers and teachers partner for technology integration. In I. Gibson et al. (Eds.), *Proceedings of Society for Information Technology & Teacher Education International Conference 2009* (pp. 3493–3496). Chesapeake, VA: AACE.

Myers, M. (2003). What can computers contribute to a K–12 writing program? In M. D. Shermis & J. C. Burstein (Eds.), *Automated essay scoring* (pp. 3–20). Mahwah, NJ: Erlbaum.

Nagaoka, J., & Roderick, M. (2004, March). *Ending social promotion: The effects of retention.* Chicago, IL: Consortium on Chicago School Research. Retrieved from http://www.consortium-chicago.org/publications/p70.html.

Nagy, P., & Griffiths, A. K. (1982). Limitations of recent research relating Piaget's theory to adolescent thought. *Review of Educational Research, 52*(4), 513–556.

Nakamura, J., & Csikszentmihalyi, M. (2009). Flow theory and research. In C. Snyder & S. Lopez (Eds.), *Oxford handbook of positive psychology* (2nd ed.) (pp. 195–206). New York: Oxford University Press.

Nakkula, M. J., & Toshalis, E. (2006). *Understanding youth: Adolescent development for educators.* Cambridge, MA: Harvard Educational Press.

Narvaez, D. (2002). Does reading moral stories build character? *Educational Psychology Review, 14*(2), 155–172.

Nasir, N. S. (2008). Everyday pedagogy: Lessons from basketball, track, and dominoes. *Phi Delta Kappan, 89*(7), 529–532.

National Board for Professional Teaching Standards (2003, May 30). *What teachers should know and be able to do: The five core propositions of the national board.* Retrieved from http://www.nbpts.org/about/coreprops.cfm.

National Center for Education Statistics (2009). *The nation's report card: Mathematics 2009. National assessment of educational progress at grades 4 and 8* (NCES 2010-451). Washington, DC: U.S. Department of Education. Retrieved from http://nces/ed.gov/nationsreportcard/pdf/main2009/2010451.pdf.

National Center for Health Statistics (2007). *Health, United States, 2007 with chartbook on trends in the health of Americans.* Hyatsville, MD: U.S. Department of Health and Human Services.

National Center for Health Statistics (2008, October). *NCHS data on teenage pregnancy.* Retrieved from http://www.cdc.gov/nchs/data/infosheets/infosheet_teen_preg.htm.

National Commission on Excellence in Education. (1983). *A nation at risk: The imperative for educational reform.* Washington, DC: U.S. Department of Education.

National Comprehensive Center for Teacher Quality & Public Agenda. (2008a). *Lessons learned: New teachers talk about their jobs, challenges and long-range plans. Issue No. 1. They're no little kids anymore: The special challenges of new teachers in high schools and middle schools.* Retrieved from http://www.publicagenda.org/citizen/researchstudies/education.

National Comprehensive Center for Teacher Quality & Public Agenda. (2008b). *Lessons learned: New teachers talk about their jobs, challenges and long-range plans. Issue No. 3. Teaching in changing times.* Retrieved from http://www.publicagenda.org/citizen/researchstudies/education.

National Comprehensive Center for Teacher Quality & Public Agenda. (2008c). *Lessons learned: New teachers talk about their jobs, challenges and long-range plans. Issue No. 2. Working without a net: How new teachers from three prominent alternate route programs describe their first year on the job.* Retrieved from http://www.publicagenda.org/citizen/researchstudies/education.

National Research Council. (2000). *Inquiry and the National Science Education Standards: A guide for teaching and learning.* Washington, DC: National Academies Press.

National Research Council. (2002). *Minority students in special and gifted education* (Committee on Minority Representation in Special Education, M. S. Donovan & C. T. Cross, Eds., Division of Behavioral and Social Sciences). Washington, DC: National Academy Press.

Naughton, C. C., & McLaughlin, T. F. (1995). The use of a token economy system for students with behaviour disorders. *B.C. Journal of Special Education, 19*(2/3), 29–38.

Nebel, M., Jamison, B., & Bennett, L. (2009). Students as digital citizens on web 2.0. *Social Studies and the Young Learner, 21*(4), 5–7.

Neill, M. (2003). High stakes, high risk. *American School Board Journal, 190*(2), 18–21.

Neisser, U. (1976). *Cognition and reality.* San Francisco: Freeman.

Nesbit, J. C., & Adesope, O. O. (2006). Learning with concept and knowledge maps: A meta-analysis. *Review of Educational Research, 76*(3), 413–448.

Newman, F., & Holzman, L. (1993). *Lev Vygotsky: Revolutionary scientist.* London: Routledge.

Newman, B. M., & Newman, P. R. (2009). *Development through life: A psychosocial approach* (10th ed.). Belmont, CA: Wadsworth/Cengage Learning.

New York Performance Standards Consortium (2007, October). *The alternative to high-stakes testing.* Retrieved from http://www.performanceassessment.org.

Nichols, S. L. (2007). High-stakes testing: Does it increase achievement? *Journal of Applied School Psychology, 23*(2), 47–64.

Nichols, S. L., & Berliner, D. C. (2005, March). The inevitable corruption of indicators and educators through high-stakes testing (EPSL-0503-101-EPRU). Education Policy Studies Laboratory, Education Policy Research Unit. Retrieved from http://www.asu.edu/educ/epsl/EPRU/epru_2005_Research_Writing.htm.

Nichols, S., & Berliner, D. (2007). *Collateral damage: How high stakes testing corrupts America's schools.* Cambridge, MA: Harvard University Press.

Nichols, S. L., & Berliner, D. C. (2008). Why has high-stakes testing so easily slipped into contemporary American life? *Phi Delta Kappan, 89*(9), 672–676.

Nichols, S. L., Glass, G. V., & Berliner, D. C. (2006). High-stakes testing and student achievement: Does accountability pressure increase student learning? *Education Policy Analysis Archives, 14*(1). Retrieved from http://epaa.asu.edu/epaa/v14n1.

Nielsen, T., Kreiner, S., & Styles, I. (2007). Mental self-government: Development of the additional democratic learning style scale using Rasch measurement models. *Journal of Applied Measurement, 8*(2), 124–48.

Nieto, S. (2002/2003). Profoundly multicultural questions. *Educational Leadership, 60*(4), 6–10.

Nieto, S. (2008). *Affirming diversity: The sociopolitical context of multicultural education* (5th ed.). Boston: Pearson/Allyn & Bacon.

Nitko, A., & Brookhart, S. (2011). *Educational assessment of students* (6th ed.) Upper Saddle River, NJ: Allyn & Bacon/Pearson.

No Child Left Behind Act of 2001. (2001, January). Retrieved from http://www.ed.gov/legislation/ESEA02/107-110.pdf.

Noddings, N. (2003). *Happiness and education.* Cambridge, England: Cambridge University Press.

Noddings, N. (1984/2003). *Caring: A feminine approach to ethics and moral education* (2nd ed.). Berkeley, CA: University of California Press.

Noddings, N. (2007). *When school reform goes wrong.* New York: Teachers College Press.

Noddings, N. (2008). Caring and moral education. In L. P. Nucci & D. Narvaez (Eds.), *Handbook of moral and character education* (pp. 161–174). New York: Routledge.

Norman, D. A., & Rumelhart, D. E. (1970). A system for perception and memory. In D. A. Norman (Ed.), *Models of human memory.* New York: Academic Press.

Novak, J. D. (2009). *Learning, creating, and using knowledge: Concept maps as facilitative tools in schools and corporations.* New York: Routledge.

Novak, J. D., & Gowin, D. B. (1984). *Learning how to learn.* Cambridge, England: Cambridge University Press.

Nucci, L., & Narvaez, D. (Eds.). (2008). *Handbook of moral and character education.* New York: Routledge.

Nye, R. D. (1992). *The legacy of B. F. Skinner.* Pacific Grove, CA: Brooks/Cole.

Oakes, J. (2005). *Keeping track* (2nd ed.). New Haven, CT: Yale University Press.

Oakley, D., & Halligan, P. (2009). Hypnotic suggestion and cognitive neuroscience. *Trends in Cognitive Sciences, 13*(6), 264–270.

Obenchain, K. M., & Taylor, S. S. (2005). Behavior management: Making it work in middle and secondary schools. *The Clearing House, 79*(1), 7–11.

O'Brennan, L. M., Bradshaw, C. P., & Sawyer, A. L. (2008). Examining developmental differences in the social-emotional problems among frequent bullies, victims, and bully/victims. *Psychology in the Schools, 46*(2), 100–115.

O'Byrne, B., Securo, S., Jones, J., & Cadle, C. (2006). Making the cut: The impact of an integrated learning system on low achieving middle school students. *Journal of Computer Assisted Learning, 22*(3), 218–228.

Ochse, R., & Plug, C. (1986). Cross-cultural investigation of the validity of Erikson's theory of personality development. *Journal of Personality and Social Psychology, 50*(6), 1240–1252.

O'Connor, K. (2009). *How to grade for learning: K–12* (3rd ed.). Thousand Oaks, CA: Corwin.

O'Donnell, A. M., Dansereau, D. F., & Hall, R. H. (2002). Knowledge maps as scaffolds for cognitive processing. *Educational Psychology Review, 14*(1), 71–86.

Office of the Federal Register. (1994). *Code of Federal Regulations 34. Parts 300 to 399.* Washington, DC: Author.

Ogbu, J. U. (2003). *Black American students in an affluent suburb.* Mahwah, NJ: Erlbaum Associates.

Okagaki, L. (2001). Triarchic model of minority children's school achievement. *Educational Psychologist, 36*(1), 9–20.

Okagaki, L. (2006). Ethnicity and learning. In P. A. Alexander & P. H. Winne (Eds.), *Handbook of educational psychology* (2nd ed., pp. 615–634). Mahwah, NJ: Lawrence Erlbaum Associates.

O'Lone, D. J. (1997). Student information system software: Are you getting what you expected? *NASSP Bulletin, 81*(585), 86–93.

Olson, A. (2002). Technology solutions for testing. *The School Administrator, 59*(4), 20–23.

Olson, A. (2005). Improving schools one student at a time. *Educational Leadership, 62*(5), 37–40.

Olson, L. (2003). Legal twists, digital turns. *Education Week, 22*(41), 1, 20–21.

Orlich, D., Harder, R., Callahan, R., Trevisan, M., & Brown, A. (2010). *Teaching strategies: A guide to effective instruction.* Boston: Wadsworth/Cengage Learning.

Ornstein, A. C., Levine, D. U., & Gutek, G. (2011). *Foundations of education* (11th ed.). Belmont, CA: Wadsworth/Cengage Learning.

Osborn Popp, S., Ryan, J., & Thompson, M. (2009). The critical role of anchor paper selection in writing assessment. *Applied Measurement in Education, 22*(3), 255–271.

Osman, M. (2008). Positive transfer and negative transfer/antilearning of problem-solving skills. *Journal of Experimental Psychology: General, 137*(1), 97–115.

Osterman, K. F. (2000). Students' need for belonging in the school community. *Review of Educational Research, 70*(3), 323–367.

Owen, A. M., McMillan, K. M., Laird, A. R., & Bullmore, E. (2005). N-back working memory paradigm: A meta-analysis of normative functional neuroimaging studies. *Human Brain Mapping, 25*(1), 46–59.

Owings, W. A., & Kaplan, L. S. (2001). Standards, retention, and social promotion. *NASSP Bulletin, 85*(629), 57–66.

Owston, R., Wideman, H., Sinitskaya, N. R., & Brown, C. (2009). Computer game development as a literacy activity. *Computers and Education, 53*(3), 977–989.

Ozuru, Y., Dempsey, K., McNamara, D. (2009). Prior knowledge, reading skill, and text cohesion in the comprehension of science texts. *Learning and Instruction, 19*(3), 228–242.

Paas, F., & van Gog, T. (2009). Principles for designing effective and efficient training of complex cognitive skills. In F. Durso (Ed.), *Reviews of human factors and ergonomics* (vol. 5) (pp. 166–194). Santa Monica, CA: Human Factors and Ergonomics Society.

Pacheco, M., & Gutièrrez, K. (2009). Cultural-historical approaches to literacy teaching and learning. In C. Compton-Lilly (Ed.), *Breaking the silence: Recognizing social and cultural resources students bring to the classroom* (pp. 60–80). Newark, DE: International Reading Association.

Padilla, A. M., & Gonzalez, R. (2001). Academic performance of immigrant and U.S.-born Mexican heritage students: Effects of schooling in Mexico and bilingual/English language instruction. *American Educational Research Journal, 38*(3), 727–742.

Page, M. S. (2002). Technology-enriched classrooms: Effects on students of low socioeconomic status. *Journal of Research on Technology in Education, 34*(4), 389–409.

Pajares, F. (2007). Motivational role of self-efficacy in self-regulated learning. In B. Zimmerman & D. Schunk (Eds.), *Motivation and self-regulated learning: Theory, research, and application* (pp. 111–140). New York: Erlbaum.

Pajares, F. (2009). Toward a positive psychology of academic motivation: The role of self-efficacy beliefs. In R. Gilman, E. S. Huebner, & M. J. Furlong (Eds.), *Handbook of positive psychology in schools* (pp. 149–160). New York: Routledge.

Palincsar, A., & Brown, A. L. (1984). Reciprocal teaching of comprehension-fostering and comprehension-monitoring activities. *Cognition and Instruction, 1*(2), 117–175.

Palmer, S. B., & Wehmeyer, M. L. (2003). Promoting self-determination in early elementary school: Teaching self-regulated problem-solving and goal-setting skills. *Remedial and Special Education, 24*(2), 115–126.

Paris, S. G., & Paris, A. H. (2001). Classroom applications of research on self-regulated learning. *Educational Psychologist, 36*(2), 89–101.

Parke, C. S., & Lane, S. (1997). Learning from performance assessments in math. *Educational Leadership, 54*(6), 26–29.

Parshall, C. G., Spray, J. A., Kalohn, J. C., & Davey, T. (2002). *Practical considerations in computer-based testing.* New York: Springer-Verlag.

Patterson, B. (2002). Creating two-point perspective on the computer. *Arts & Activities, 131*(4), 52.

Patterson, G. R., DeBaryshe, B. D., & Ramsey, E. (1989). A developmental perspective on antisocial behavior. *American Psychologist, 44*(2), 329–335.

Pea, R. D. (1985). Beyond amplification: Using the computer to reorganize mental functioning. *Educational Psychologist, 21*(4), 167–182.

Pea, R. D. (2004). The social and technological dimensions of scaffolding and related theoretical concepts for learning, education, and activity. *Journal of Learning Sciences, 13*(3), 423–451.

Pedersen, S., & Liu, M. (2002). The effects of modeling expert cognitive strategies during problem-based learning. *Journal of Educational Computing Research, 26*(4), 353–380.

Pedersen, S., & Liu, M. (2002–2003). The transfer of problem-solving skills from a problem-based learning environment: The effect of modeling an expert's cognitive processes. *Journal of Research on Technology in Education, 35*(2), 303–320.

Pekrun, R., Elliot, A., & Maier, M. (2009) Achievement goals and achievement emotions: Testing a model of their joint relations with academic performance. *Journal of Educational Psychology, 101*(1), 115–135.

Pelligrini, A. D. (2009). *The role of play in human development.* Oxford, England: Oxford University Press.

Pellegrini, A. D., & Bohn, C. M. (2005). The role of recess in children's cognitive performance and school adjustment. *Educational Researcher, 34*(1), 13–19.

Pelletier, L. G., Séguin-Lévesque, C., & Legault, L. (2002). Pressure from above and pressure from below as determinants of teachers' motivation and teaching behaviors. *Journal of Educational Psychology, 94*(1), 186–196.

Peltier, G. L. (1991). Why do secondary schools continue to track students? *The Clearing House, 64*(4), 246–247.

Peña, C. M., & Alessi, S. M. (1999). Promoting a qualitative understanding of physics. *Journal of Computers in Mathematics and Science Teaching, 18*(4), 439–457.

Penfield, W. (1969). Consciousness, memory, and man's conditioned reflexes. In K. Pribram (Ed.), *On the biology of learning.* New York: Harcourt Brace Jovanovich.

Pérez, B. (2004). *Becoming biliterate: A study of two-way bilingual immersion education.* Mahwah, NJ: Erlbaum Associates.

Perkins, D. F., & Hartless, G. (2002). An ecological risk-factor examination of suicide ideation and behavior of adolescents. *Journal of Adolescent Research, 17*(1), 3–26.

Perkins, D., Tishman, S., Ritchhart, R., Donis, K., & Andrade, A. (2000). Intelligence in the wild: A dispositional view of intellectual traits. *Educational Psychology Review, 12*(3), 269–293.

Perry, N. E., VandeKamp, K. O., Mercer, L. K., & Nordby, C. J. (2002). Investigating teacher-student interactions that foster self-regulated learning. *Educational Psychologist, 37*(1), 5–15.

Peterson, A. C., Compas, B. E., Brooks-Gunn, J., Stemmler, M., Ey, S., & Grant, K. E. (1993). Depression in adolescence. *American Psychologist, 48*(2), 155–168.

Peverly, S. T., Brobst, K. E., Graham, M., & Shaw, R. (2003). College adults are not good at self-regulation: A study on the relationship of self-regulation, note taking, and test taking. *Journal of Educational Psychology, 95*(2), 335–346.

Pewewardy, C. (2002). Learning styles of American Indian/Alaska Native students: A review of the literature and implications for practice. *Journal of American Indian Education, 41*(3), 22–56.

Piaget, J. (1932). *The moral judgment of the child* (M. Gabain, Trans.). New York: Harcourt Brace.

Piaget, J. (1952a). *The language and thought of the child.* London: Routledge & Kegan Paul.

Piaget, J. (1952b). *The origins of intelligence in children.* New York: International Universities Press.

Piaget, J. (1965). *The moral judgment of the child* (M. Gabain, Trans.). Glencoe, IL: Free Press. (Original work published 1932.)

Piaget, J., & Inhelder, B. (1956). *The child's conception of space.* London: Routledge & Kegan Paul.

Piaget, J., & Inhelder, B. (1969). *The psychology of the child.* New York: Basic Books.

Pianta, R. C., Belsky, J., Houts, R., Morrison, F., & The National Institute of Child Health and Human Development Early Child Care Research Network. (2007, March 30). TEACHING: Opportunities to learn in America's Elementary Classrooms. *Science, 315*(5820), 1795–1796.

Planty, M, Hussar, W., Snyder, T., Kena, G., KewalManani, A., Kemp, J., Bianco, K. & Dinkes, R. (2009, June). *The condition of education 2009* (NCES 2009-081). Washington, DC: National Center for Educational Statistics, Institute of Education Sciences, U.S. Department of Education. Retrieved from http://nces.ed.gov/pubsearch/pubsinfo.asp?pubid=2009081.

Pleydon, A. P., Schner, J. G. (2001). Female adolescent friendships and delinquent behavior. *Adolescence, 36*(142), 189–205.

Plumm K. (2008). Technology in the classroom: Burning the bridges to the gaps in gender-biased education? *Computers and Education, 50*(3), 1052–1068.

Podoll, S., & Randle, D. (2005). Building a virtual high school . . . click by click. *T.H.E. Journal, 33*(2), 14–19.

Pogrow, S. (1990). A Socratic approach to using computers with at-risk students. *Educational Leadership, 47*(5), 61–66.

Pogrow, S. (1999). Systematically using powerful learning environments to accelerate the learning of disadvantaged students in grades 4–8. In C. M. Reigeluth (Ed.), *Instructional design theories and models, Vol. II: A new paradigm of instructional theory*. Mahwah, NJ: Erlbaum.

Pogrow, S. (2005). HOTS revisited: A thinking development approach to reducing the learning gap after grade 3. *Phi Delta Kappan, 87*(1), 64–75.

Pogrow, S. (2008). *Teaching content outrageously: How to captivate and accelerate the learning of all students in grades 4–12*. San Francisco: Jossey-Bass.

Pogrow, S. (2009a). Teaching content outrageously: Instruction in the era of on-demand entertainment. *Phi Delta Kappan, 90*(5), 379–383.

Pogrow, S. (2009b). Accelerating the learning of 4th and 5th graders born into poverty. *Phi Delta Kappan, 90*(6), 408–412.

Pollard, A., Anderson, J., & Maddock, M. (2008). *Reflective teaching: Evidence-informed professional practice* (3rd ed.). New York: Continuum.

Pomerantz, E. M. (2002). Making the grade but feeling distressed: Gender differences in academic performance and internal distress. *Journal of Educational Psychology, 94*(2), 396–404.

Pope, M., Hare, D., & Howard, E. (2002). Technology integration: Closing the gap between what preservice teachers are taught to do and what they can do. *Journal of Technology and Teacher Education, 10*(2), 191–203.

Popham, W. J. (2005). How to make use of PAP to make AYP under NCLB. *Phi Delta Kappan, 86*(10). 787–791.

Popham, W. J. (2006). *Assessment for educational leaders*. Boston: Allyn & Bacon.

Popham, W. J. (2008). Standards-based education: Two wrongs don't make a right. In S. Mathison & E. W. Ross (Eds.), *The nature and limits of standards-based reform and assessment* (pp. 15–25). New York: Teachers College Press.

Popham, W. J. (2009). Transform toxic AYP into a beneficial tool. *Phi Delta Kappan, 90*(8), 577–581.

Popham, J. (2011). *Classroom assessment: What teachers need to know*. Boston: Allyn & Bacon/Pearson.

Porter, R. P. (2000). The benefits of English immersion. *Educational Leadership, 57*(4), 52–56.

Portes, P., Dunham, R., & Del Castillo, K. (2000). Identity formation and status across

cultures: Exploring the cultural validity of Erikson's theory. In A. L. Comunian & U. Gielen (Eds.), *International perspectives on human development* (pp. 449–459). Lengerich, Germany: Pabst Science Publishers.

Posamentier, P., & Krulik, S. (2009). *Problem solving in mathematics, grades 3–6: Powerful strategies to deepen understanding*. Thousand Oaks, CA: Corwin Press.

Postholm, M. (2008). Cultural historical activity theory and Dewey's idea-based social constructivism: Consequences for educational research. *Critical Practice Studies,* (1), 37–48.

Premack, D. (1959). Toward empirical behavior laws: 1. Positive reinforcement. *Psychological Review, 66*(4), 219–233.

Pressley, M., Gaskins, I. W., Solic, K., & Collins, S. (2006). A portrait of benchmark school: How a school produces high achievement in students who previously failed. *Journal of Educational Psychology, 98*(2), 282–306.

Pressley, M., & Harris, K. R. (2006). Cognitive strategies instruction: From basic research to classroom instruction. In P. A. Alexander & P. H. Winne (Eds.), *Handbook of educational psychology* (2nd ed., pp. 265–286). Mahwah, NJ: Lawrence Erlbaum.

Pressley, M., & Hilden, K. (2006). Cognitive strategies. In D. Kuhn, & R. Siegler (Eds.), *Handbook of child psychology: Cognition, perception, and language* (Vol. 2, pp. 511–556). Hoboken, NJ: Wiley.

Provenzo, E. F., Jr., Brett, A., & McCloskey, G. N. (2005). *Computers, curriculum, and cultural change* (2nd ed.). Mahwah, NJ: Lawrence Erlbaum Associates.

Psychological Corporation. (2002). *WAIS-III WMS-III technical manual* (updated edition). San Antonio, TX: Author.

Pullin, D. L., Gitsaki, C., Baguley, M. (Eds.). (2010). *Technoliteracy, discourse and social practice: Frameworks and applications in the digital age*. Hershey, PA: IGI Global.

Purdie, N., & Hattie, J. (1996). Cultural differences in the use of strategies for self-regulated learning. *American Educational Research Journal, 33*(4), 845–871.

Purdie, N., Hattie, J., & Carroll, A. (2002). A review of the research on interventions for attention deficit hyperactivity disorder: What works best? *Review of Educational Research, 72*(1), 61–99.

Purkey, W. W., & Novak, J. M. (1996). *Inviting school success: A self-concept approach to teaching, learning, and democratic practice* (3rd ed.). Belmont, CA: Wadsworth.

Puzzanchera, C. (2009, April). Juvenile arrests 2007. *OJJDP Juvenile Justice Bulletin*. Washington, DC: U. S. Department of Justice, Office of Juvenile Justice and Delinquency Prevention. Retrieved from http://www.ncjrs.gov/pdffiles1/ojjdp/225344.pdf.

Quenneville, J. (2001). Tech tools for students with learning disabilities: Infusion

into inclusive classrooms. *Preventing School Failure, 45*(4), 167–170.

Qin, Z., Johnson, D. W., & Johnson, R. T. (1995). Cooperative versus competitive efforts and problem solving. *Review of Educational Research, 65*(2), 129–143.

Quiocho, A. L., & Ulanoff, S. H. (2009). *Differentiated literacy instruction for English language learners*. Boston: Pearson/Allyn & Bacon.

Rakes, G. C., Fields, V. S., & Cox, K. E. (2006). The influence of teachers' technology use on instructional practices. *Journal of Research on Technology in Education, 38*(4), 409–424.

Ramirez, A., & Carpenter, D. (2005). Challenging assumptions about the achievement gap. *Phi Delta Kappan, 86*(8), 599–603.

Ramirez, A., & Carpenter, D. (2009). The matter of dropouts. *Phi Delta Kappan, 90*(9), 656–659.

Ramirez-Valles, J., Zimmerman, M. A., & Juarez, L. (2002). Gender differences of neighborhood and social control processes: A study of the timing of first intercourse among low-achieving, urban, African American youth. *Youth & Society, 33*(3), 418–441.

Randi, J., & Corno, L. (2000). Teacher innovations in self-regulated learning. In M. Boekaerts, P. R. Pintrich, & M. Zeidner (Eds.), *Handbook of self-regulation* (pp. 651–685). San Diego: Academic Press.

Ratner, C. (1991). *Vygotsky's sociohistorical psychology and its contemporary applications*. New York: Plenum Press.

Raudenbush, S. W. (2009). The *Brown* legacy and the O'Connor challenge: Transforming schools in the images of children's potential. *Educational Researcher, 38*(3), 169–180.

Raugh, M. R., & Atkinson, R. C. (1975). A mnemonic method for learning a second-language vocabulary. *Journal of Educational Psychology, 67*(1), 1–16.

Ravaglia, R., Alper, T., Rozenfeld, M., & Suppes, P. (1998). Successful pedagogical applications of symbolic computation. In N. Kajler (Ed.), *Computer-human interaction in symbolic computation* (pp. 61–88). New York: Springer-Verlag.

Ravaglia, R., Sommer, R., Sanders, M., Oas, G., & DeLeone, C. (1999). Computer-based mathematics and physics for gifted remote students. *Proceedings of the International Confrence on Mathematics/Science Education and Technology* (pp. 405–410). Retrieved January 15, 2004, from http://www.epgy-stanford.edu/research/index.html?papers.

Rea, A. (2001). Telementoring: An A+ initiative. *Education Canada, 40*(4), 28–29.

Reardon, S. F. (2008, May). *Thirteen ways of looking at the black-white test score gap* (Working Paper #2008-08). Retrieved from Institute for Research on Education Policy and Practice, Stanford University: http://www.stanford.edu/group/irepp/cgi-bin/joomla/index.php?option=coom_content&task=view&id=27&ltemid=43.

Reardon, S. F., & Galindo, C. (2009). The Hispanic-White achievement gap in math and reading in the elementary grades. *Review of Educational Research, 46*(3), 853–891.

Rebell, M., & Wolf, J. (Eds.). (2009). *NCLB at the crossroads: Reexamining the federal effort to close the achievement gap.* New York: Teachers College Press.

Recesso, A., & Orrill, C. (2008). Integrating technology into Teaching: The teaching and learning continuum. Belmont, CA: Wadsworth/Cengage Learning.

Redl, F., & Wattenberg, W. W. (1959). *Mental hygiene in teaching* (2nd ed.). New York: Harcourt Brace Jovanovich.

Reed, D. S. (2009). Is there an expectations gap? Educational federalism and the demographic distribution of proficiency cut scores. *American Educational Research Journal, 46*(3), 718–742.

Reed, S. K. (2006). Cognitive architectures for multimedia learning. Educational Psychologist, 41(2), 87–98.

Reeve, J., & Halusic, M. (2009). How K–12 teachers can put self-determination theory principles into practice. *Theory and Research in Education, 7*(2), 145–154.

Reeve, J., & Jang, H. (2006). What teachers say and do to support students' autonomy during a learning activity. *Journal of Educational Psychology, 98*(1), 209–218.

Reid, C., Romanoff, B., & Algozzine, R. (2000). An evaluation of alternative screening procedures. *Journal for the Education of the Gifted, 23*(4), 378–396.

Reinke, W. M., Lewis-Palmer, T., & Merrell, K. (2008). The classroom check-up: A classwide teacher consultation model for increasing praise and decreasing disruptive behavior. *School Psychology Review, 37*(3), 315–332.

Reis, S. M., & Renzulli, J. S. (1985). *The secondary triad model.* Mansfield Center, CT: Creative Learning Press.

Reis, S., & Renzulli, J. (2009). Myth 1: The gifted and talented constitute one single homogeneous group and giftedness is a way of being that stays in the person over time and experiences. *Gifted Child Quarterly, 53*(4), 233–235.

Renkl, A., Hilbert, T., & Schworm, S. (2009). Example-based learning in heuristic domains: A cognitive load theory account. *Educational Psychology Review, 21*(1), 67–78.

Reninger, R. D. (2000). Music education in a digital world. *Teaching Music, 8*(1), 24–31.

Renninger, K.A. (2009). Interest and identity development in instruction: An inductive model. *Educational Psychologist, 44*(2), 105–118.

Renzulli, J. S. (2002). Expanding the conception of giftedness to include co-cognitive traits and promote social capital. *Phi Delta Kappan, 84*(1), 33–40, 57–58.

Renzulli, J. S., Gentry, M., & Reis, S. M. (2003). *Enrichment clusters: A practical plan for real-world, student-driven learning.* Mansfield Center, CT: Creative Learning Press.

Rest, J., Narvaez, D., Bebeau, M. J., & Thoma, S. J. (1999). *Postconventional moral thinking: A Neo-Kohlbergian Approach.* Mahwah, NJ: Erlbaum.

Reynolds, C. R., Livingston, R. B., & Wilson, V. (2009). *Measurement and assessment in education* (2nd ed.). Boston: Allyn & Bacon/Pearson.

Reynolds, T. H., & Bonk, C. J. (1996). Creating computerized writing partner and key-stroke recording tools with macro-driven prompts. *Educational Technology Research and Development, 44*(3), 83–97.

Rice, K. L. (2006). A comprehensive look at distance education in the k–12 context. *Journal of Research on Technology in Education, 38*(4), 425–448.

Richard, A. (2005, December 7). Supplemental help can be hard to find for rural students. *Education Week, 25*(14), 1, 22.

Richardson, W. (2009). *Blogs, wikis, podcasts, and other powerful web tools for classrooms* (2nd ed.). Thousand Oaks, CA: Corwin Press.

Ridgeway, V. G., Peters, C. L., & Tracy, T. S. (2002). Out of this world: Cyberspace, literacy, and learning. In C. C. Block, L. B. Gambrell, & M. Pressley (Eds.), *Improving comprehension instruction: Rethinking research, theory, and classroom practice.* San Francisco: Jossey-Bass.

Rigby, K. (2008). *Children and bullying: How parents and educators can reduce bullying at school.* Malden, MA: Blackwell Publishing.

Riggs, E., & Gholar, C. (2009). *Strategies that promote student engagement: Unleashing the desire to learn* (2nd ed.). Thousand Oaks, CA: Corwin Press.

Rikers, R., van Gog, T., & Paas, F. (2008). The effects of constructivist learning environments: a commentary. *Instructional Science, 36*(5–6), 463–467.

Ripley, A. (2010). What makes a great teacher? *The Atlantic Monthly,* (January/February). Washington DC: The Atlantic Monthly Group. Retrieved from http://www.theatlantic.com.

Robertson, A. (2001, Sept/Oct). CASE is when we learn to think. *Primary Science Review, 69,* 20–22.

Robins, K. N., Lindsey, R. B., Lindsey, D. B., & Terrell, R. D. (2006). *Culturally proficient instruction* (2nd ed.). Thousand Oaks, CA: Corwin Press.

Robinson, J. (2008). Evidence of a differential effect of ability grouping on the reading achievement growth of language-minority Hispanics. *Educational Evaluation and Policy Analysis, 30*(2), 141–180.

Robledo, M. M., & Cortez, J. D. (2002). Successful bilingual education programs: Development and dissemination of criteria to identify promising and exemplary practices in bilingual education at the national level. *Bilingual Research Journal, 26*(1), 1–21.

Roblyer, M. D. (2006). Virtually successful: Defeating the dropout problem through online school programs. *Phi Delta Kappan, 88*(1), 31–36.

Roderick, M., & Engel, M. (2001). The grasshopper and the ant: motivational responses of low-achieving students to high-stakes testing. *Educational Evaluation and Policy Analysis, 23*(3), 197–227.

Rodney, L. W., Crafter, B., Rodney, H. E., & Mupier, R. M. (1999). Variables contributing to grade retention among African American adolescent males. *Journal of Educational Research, 92*(3), 185–190.

Roerden, L. (2001). The resolving conflict creatively program. *Reclaiming Children and Youth, 10*(1), 24–28.

Roeser, R. W., & Lau, S. (2002). On academic identity formation in middle school settings during early adolescence: A motivational contextual perspective. In T. M. Brinthaupt & R. P. Lipka (Eds.), *Understanding early adolescent self and identity: Applications and interventions* (pp. 91–131). Albany, NY: State University of New York Press

Rogers, C. R. (1967). Learning to be free. In C. R. Rogers & B. Stevens (Eds.), *The problem of being human.* Lafayette, CA: Real People Press.

Rogers, C. R. (1980). *A way of being.* Boston: Houghton Mifflin.

Rogers, C. R., & Freiberg, H. J. (1994). *Freedom to learn* (3rd ed.). New York: Merrill.

Rogers, W. A., Pak, R. & Fisk, A. D. (2007). Applied cognitive psychology in the context of everyday living. In F. Durso, R. Nickerson, S. Dumais, S. Lewandowsky, & T. Perfect (Eds.), *Handbook of applied cognition* (2nd ed., pp. 3–27). Chichester: Wiley.

Rogoff, B. (1990). *Apprenticeship in thinking: Cognitive development in social context.* New York: Oxford University Press.

Rogoff, B., & Chavajay, P. (1995). What's become of research on the cultural basis of cognitive development? *American Psychologist, 50*(10), 859–877.

Rohrbeck, C. A., Ginsburg-Block, M. D., Fantuzzo, J. W., & Miller, T. R. (2003). Peer-assisted learning interventions with elementary school students: A meta-analytic review. *Journal of Educational Psychology, 95*(2), 240–257.

Roid, G. (2003). *Stanford-Binet Intelligence Scales: Fifth Edition.* Itasca, IL: Riverside Publishing.

Roller, C. M. (2002). Accomodating variability in reading instruction. *Reading & Writing Quarterly, 18*(1), 17–38.

Rolón, C. A. (2002/2003). Educating Latino students. *Educational Leadership, 60*(4), 40–43.

Romance, N. R., & Vitale, M. R. (1999). Concept mapping as a tool for learning: Broadening the framework for student-centered instruction. *College Teaching, 47*(2), 74–79.

Rop, C. (1998). Breaking the gender barrier in the physical sciences. *Educational Leadership, 55*(4), 58–60.

Roscoe, R. D., & Chi, M. T. H. (2007). Understanding tutor learning: Knowledge-building and knowledge-telling in peer tutors' explanations and questions. *Review of Educational Research, 77*(4), 534–574.

Rosen, D., & Nelson, C. (2008). Web 2.0: A new generation of learners and education. *Computers in the Schools, 25*(3–4), 211–225.

Rosen, Y. (2009). The effects of an animation-based on-line learning environment on transfer of knowledge and on motivation for science and technology learning. *Journal of Educational Computing Research, 40*(4), 451–467.

Rosenblum-Lowden, R., & Kimmel, F. L. (2008). *You have to go to school—you're the teacher!* (3rd ed.). Thousand Oaks, CA: Corwin Press.

Rosenshine, B. V., & Meister, C. (1994a). Reciprocal teaching: A review of the research. *Review of Educational Research, 64*(4), 479–530.

Rosenshine, B. V., & Meister, C. (1994b). Direct Instruction. In T. Husen & T. N. Postlewhaite (Eds.), *International encyclopedia of education* (2nd ed., Vol. 3, pp. 1524–1530). New York: Pergamon.

Rosenshine, B., Meister, C., & Chapman, S. (1996). Teaching students to generate questions: A review of the intervention studies. *Review of Educational Research, 66*(2), 181–221.

Rosenthal, R. (2002). The Pygmalion effect and its mediating mechanisms. In J. Aronson (Ed.), *Improving academic achievement* (pp. 26–36). San Diego: Academic Press.

Ross, D. D., Bondy, E., & Kyle, D. W. (1993). *Reflective teaching for student empowerment.* New York: Macmillan.

Ross, D. D., Bondy, E., Gallingane, C., & Hambacher, E. (2008). Promoting academic engagement through insistence: Being a warm demander. *Childhood Education, 84*(3), 142–146.

Ross, H. S., & Spielmacher, C. E. (2005). Social development. In B. Hopkins, R. G. Barr, G. F. Michel, & P. Rochat (Eds.), *The Cambridge encyclopedia of child development* (pp. 227–233). Cambridge, UK: Cambridge University Press.

Roth, G., Assor, A., Kanat-Maymon, Y., & Kaplan, H. (2007). Autonomous motivation for teaching: How self-determined teaching may lead to self-determined learning. *Journal of Educational Psychology, 99*(4), 761–774.

Roth, W.-M., & Lee, Y. J. (2007). Vygotsky's neglected legacy: Cultural-historical activity theory. *Review of Educational Research, 77*(2), 186–232.

Rothstein, R. (2004). A wider lens on the black-white achievement gap. *Phi Delta Kappan, 86*(2), 104–110.

Rothstein, R., Jacobsen, R., & Wilder, T. (2009). 'Proficiency for all'—An oxymoron. In M. A. Rebell & J. R. Wolf (Eds.), *NCLB at the crossroads: Reexamining the federal effort to close the achievement gap* (pp. 134–162). New York: Teachers College Press.

Rothstein-Fisch, C., Greenfield, P. M., & Trumbull, E. (1999). Bridging cultures with classroom strategies. *Educational Leadership, 56*(7), 64–67.

Rotter, K. M. (2009). Enhancing memory in your students: COMPOSE yourself. *TEACHING Exceptional Children Plus, 5*(3). Retrieved 7 November 2009 from http://escholarship.bc.edu/education/tecplus/vol5/iss3/art4.

Rowan, B. (1994). Comparing teachers' work with work in other occupations: Notes on the professional status of teaching. *Edcuational Reseracher, 23*(6), 4–17.

Rowe, S. M., & Wertsch, J. V. (2002) Vygotsky's model of cognitive development. In U. Goswami (Ed.), *Blackwell handbook of childhood cognitive development* (pp. 538–554). Oxford, England: Blackwell Publishers.

Royer, J. M., & Cable, G. W. (1975). Facilitated learning in connected discourse. *Journal of Educational Psychology, 67*(1), 116–123.

Royer, J. M., & Cable, G. W. (1976). Illustrations, analogies, and facilitative transfer in prose learning. *Journal of Educational Psychology, 68*(2), 205–209.

Royer, J. M., Tronsky, L. N., Chan, Y., Jackson, S. J., & Marchant, H., III. (1999). Math-fact retrieval as the cognitive mechanism underlying gender differences in math test performance. *Contemporary Educational Psychology, 24*(3), 181–266.

Rubin, L. J. (1985). *Artistry in teaching.* New York: Random House.

Ruggiero, V. R. (2009). *The art of thinking: A guide to critical and creative thought* (9th ed.). New York: Pearson/Longman.

Ruhland, S. K., & Bremer, C. D., (2002). Professional development needs of novice career and technical educational teachers. *Journal of Career and Technical Education, 19*(1), 18–31.

Rummel, N., Levin, J. R., & Woodward, M. M. (2003). Do pictorial mnemonic text-learning aids give students something worth writing about? *Journal of Educational Psychology, 95*(2), 327–334.

Russell, N. M. (2007). Teaching more than English: Connecting ESL students to their community through service learning. *Phi Delta Kappan, 88*(10), 770–771.

Russo, A. (2002). Mixing technology and testing. *The School Administrator, 59*(4), 6–12.

Rutledge, M. (1997). Reading the subtext on gender. *Educational Leadership, 54*(7), 71–73.

Ryan, A. M., & Patrick, H. (2001). The classroom social environment and changes in adolescents' motivation and engagement during middle school. *American Educational Research Journal, 38*(2), 437–460.

Ryan, K. E., Ryan, A. M., Arbuthnot, K., & Samuels, M. (2007). Students' motivation for standardized math exams. *Educational Researcher, 36*(1), 5–13.

Rycek, R. F., Stuhr, S. L., & McDermott, J. (1998). Adolescent egocentrism and cognitive functioning during late adolescence. *Adolescence, 33*(132), 745–749.

Sadker, D. M., & Sadker, M. P., & Zittleman, K. R. (2008). *Teachers, schools, and society* (8th ed.). Boston: McGraw-Hill.

Sadker, D., & Zittleman, K. (2004). Test anxiety: Are students failing tests—or are tests failing students? *Phi Delta Kappan, 85*(10), 740–744, 751.

Sadker, M. P., & Sadker, D. M. (1994). *Failing at fairness: How America's schools cheat girls.* New York: Charles Scribner's Sons.

Sadoski, M., Goetz, E. T., & Rodriguez, M. (2000). Engaging texts: Effects of concreteness on comprehensibility, interest, and recall in four text types. *Journal of Educational Psychology, 92*(1), 85–95.

Sadoski, M., & Paivio, A. (2007). Toward a unified theory of reading. *Scientific Studies of Reading, 11*(4), 337–356.

Saka, Y., Southerland, S., & Brooks, J. (2009). Becoming a member of a school community while working toward science education reform: Teacher induction from a cultural historical activity theory (CHAT) perspective. *Science Education, 93*(6), 996–1025.

Saleh, M., Lazonder, A. W., & De Jong, T. (2005). Effects of within-class ability grouping on social interaction, achievement, and motivation. *Instructional Science, 33*(2), 105–199.

Salmon, M., & Akaran, S. E. (2001). Enrich your kindergarten program with a cross-cultural connection. *Young Children, 56*(4), 30–32.

Salomon, G. (1988). AI in reverse: Computer tools that turn cognitive. *Journal of Educational Computing Research, 4*(2), 123–139.

Salomon, G., Globerson, T., & Guterman, E. (1989). The computer as a zone of proximal development: Internalizing reading-related metacognitions from a reading partner. *Journal of Educational Psychology, 81*(4), 620–627.

Saltzman, J. (2003, July 20). Reinstating two-way bilingual ed is hailed. *The Boston Globe* (Globe West section), p. 1.

Sameroff, A., & McDonough, S. C. (1994). Educational implications of developmental transitions: Revisiting the 5- to 7-year shift. *Phi Delta Kappan, 76*(3), 189–193.

Santamaria, L. (2009). Culturally responsive differentiated instruction: Narrowing gaps between best pedagogical practices benefiting all learners. *Teachers College Record, 111*(1), 214–247.

Sapon-Shevin, M. (2003). Inclusion: A matter of social justice. *Educational Leadership, 61*(2), 25–28.

Saracho, O. N. (2001). Cognitive style and kindergarten pupils' preferences for teachers. *Learning and Instruction, 11*(3), 195–209.

Sarason, S. B., (1993). *The case for change: Rethinking the preparation of educators.* San Francisco: Jossey-Bass.

Sarason, S. B. (2005). *Letters to a serious education president* (2nd ed.). Thousand Oaks, CA: Corwin Press.

Savage, R., Lavers, N., & Pillay, V. (2007). Working memory and reading difficulties: What we know and what we don't know about the relationship. *Educational Psychology Review, 19*(2), 185–221.

Scarr, S. Weinberg, R. A., & Levine, A. (1986), *Understanding development.* San Diego, CA: Harcourt Brace Jovanovich.

Schalock, R., Borthwick-Duffy, S., Bradley, V., Buntinx, W., Coulter, D., Craig, E., Gomez, S., Lachapelle, Y., Luckasson, R., Reeve, A., Shogren, K., Snell, M., Spreat, S., Tassé, M., Thompson, J., Verdugo-Alonso, M., Wehmeyer, M., & Yeager, M., (2010). *Intellectual disability: Definition, classification, and systems of supports* (11th edition). Washington, DC: American Association on Intellectual and Developmental Disabilities.

Scheiter, K., & Gerjets, P. (2007). Learner control in hypermedia environments. *Educational Psychology Review, 19*(3), 285–307.

Schellenberg, E. G. (2006a). Long-term positive associations between music and IQ. *Journal of Educational Psychology, 98*(2), 457–468.

Schellenberg, E. G. (2006b). Exposure to music: The truth about the consequences. In G. E. McPherson (Ed.), *The child as musician: The handbook of musical development.* Oxford, England: Oxford University Press.

Schifter, D. (1996). A constructivist perspective on teaching and learning mathematics. *Phi Delta Kappan, 77*(7), 492–499.

Schlagmüller, M., & Schneider, W. (2002). The development of organizational strategies in children: Evidence from a microgenetic longitudinal study. *Journal of Experimental Child Psychology, 81*(3), 298–319.

Schmidt, P. (2003, November 28). The label 'Hispanic' irks some, but also unites. *Chronicle of Higher Education, 50*(14), A9.

Schmitz, M. J., & Winksel, H. (2008). Towards effective partnerships in collaborative problem-solving task. *British Journal of Educational Psychology, 78*(4), 581–596.

Schneider, M. (2006, February). *Comments delivered to the American Enterprise Institute for Public Policy Research.* Retrieved from http://nces.ed.gov/whatsnew/commissioner/remarks2006/2_6_2006.asp.

Schneider, W. (2002). Memory development in childhood. In U. Goswami (Ed.), *Blackwell handbook of childhood cognitive development* (pp. 236–256). Malden, MA: Blackwell.

Schneider, W., Knopf, M., & Stefanek, J. (2002). The development of verbal memory in childhood and adolescence: Findings from the Munich longitudinal study. *Journal of Educational Psychology, 94*(4), 751–761.

Schommer-Aikins, M., Duell, O. K., & Hutter, R. (2005). Epistemological beliefs, mathematical problem-solving beliefs, and academic performance of middle school students. *The Elementary School Journal, 105*(3), 289–304.

Schreiber, J. B., & McCown, R. (2006). *Arguments for evaluating university teaching.* CASTL Technical Report No. 3-06. Department of Educational Foundations and Leadership, School of Education, Duquesne University. Retrieved from http://www.castl.duq.edu.

Schunk, D. H. (1987). Peer models and children's behavioral change. *Review of Educational Research, 57*(2), 149–174.

Schunk, D. H. (1998). Teaching elementary students to self-regulate practice of mathematical skills with modeling. In D. H. Schunk & B. J. Zimmerman (Eds.), *Self-regulated learning: From teaching to self-reflective practice* (pp. 137–159). New York: Guilford Press.

Schunk, D. H. (2001). Social cognitive theory and self-regulated learning. In B. J. Zimmerman & D. H. Schunk (Eds.), *Self-regulated learning and academic achievement: Theoretical perspectives* (pp. 125–151). Mahwah, NJ: Erlbaum.

Schunk, D. H. (2004). *Learning theories: An educational perspective* (4th ed.). Upper Saddle River, NJ: Merrill Prentice Hall.

Schunk, D. (2008). *Learning Theories: An Educational Perspective* (5th ed.). Upper Saddle River, NJ: Merrill Prentice Hall/Pearson.

Schunk, D. H., & Hanson, A. R. (1985). Peer models: Influence on children's self-efficacy and achievement. *Journal of Educational Psychology, 77*(3), 313–322.

Schunk, D. H., & Hanson, A. R. (1989). Self-modeling and children's cognitive skill learning. *Journal of Educational Psychology, 81*(2), 155–163.

Schunk, D. H., Hanson, A. R., & Cox, P. D. (1987). Peer model attributes and children's achievement behaviors. *Journal of Educational Psychology, 79*(1), 54–61.

Schunk, D. H., & Miller, S. D. (2002). Self-efficacy and adolescents' motivation. In F. Pajares & T. Urdan (Eds.), *Academic motivation of adolescents* (pp. 29–52). Greenwich, CT: Information Age Publishing.

Schunk, D. H., & Pajares, F. (2002). The development of academic self-efficacy. In A. Wigfield & J. Eccles (Eds.), *The development of achievement motivation* (pp. 16–31). San Diego: Academic Press.

Schunk, D. H., & Zimmerman, B. J. (1997). Social origins of self-regulatory competence. *Educational Psychologist, 32*(4), 195–208.

Schunk, D., & Zimmerman, B. (2007). *Motivation and self-regulated learning: Theory, research, and applications.* New York: Routledge.

Schvaneveldt, P. L., Miller, B. C., Berry, E. H., & Lee, T. R. (2001). Academic goals, achievement, and age at first sexual intercourse: Longitudinal, bidirectional influences. *Adolescence, 36*(144), 767–787.

Schwartz, D., Gorman, A. H., Nakamoto, J., & Toblin, R. L. (2005). Victimization in the peer group and children's academic functioning. *Journal of Educational Psychology, 97*(3), 425–435.

Schwartz, D., Lindgren, R., & Lewis, S. (2009). Constructivism in an age of non-constructivist assessments. In S. Tobias & T. Duffy (Eds.), *Constructivist instruction: Success or failure?* (pp. 34–61). New York: Routledge.

Schweinhart, L. J., Weikart, D. P., & Hohmann, M. (2002). The High/Scope preschool curriculum: What is it? Why use it? *Journal of At-Risk Issues, 8*(1), 13–16.

Scott, S., McGuire, J., & Shaw, S. (2003). Universal design for instruction: A new design for adult instruction in postsecondary settings. *Remedial and Special Education, 24*(6), 369–379.

Scriven, M. (1967). The methodology of evaluation. In R. Tyler, R. Gagne, & M. Scriven (Eds.), *Perspectives in curriculum evaluation.* Chicago: Rand McNally.

Seagoe, M. V. (1975). *Terman and the gifted.* Los Altos, CA: Kaufmann.

Searleman, A., & Herrmann, D. (1994). *Memory from a broader perspective.* New York: McGraw-Hill.

Seaton, M., Marsh, H. W., & Craven, R. G. (2010). Big-fish-little-pond effect: Generalizability and moderation—two sides of the same win. *American Educational Research Journal, 47*(2), 390–433.

Seddon, F. A., & O'Neill, S. A. (2006). How does formal instrumental music tuition (FIMT) impact on self- and teacher-evaluations of adolescents' computer-based compositions? *Psychology of Music, 34*(1), 27–45.

Seezink, A., Poell, R., & Kirschner, P. (2009). Teachers' individual action theories about competence-based education: The value of the cognitive apprenticeship model. *Journal of Vocational Education and Training, 61*(2), 203–215.

Selman, R. L. (1980). *The growth of interpersonal understanding: Developmental and clinical analyses.* New York: Academic Press.

Semb, G. B., & Ellis, J. A. (1994). Knowledge taught in school: What is remembered? *Review of Educational Research, 64*(2), 253–286.

Shachar, H., & Fischer, S. (2004). Cooperative learning and the achievement of motivation and perceptions of students in 11th grade chemistry classrooms. *Learning and Instruction, 14*(1), 69–87.

Shaffer, D., & Kipp, K. (2010). *Developmental psychology: Childhood and adolescence* (8th ed.). Belmont, CA: Wadsworth/Cengage Learning.

Sharan, S. (1995). Group investigation: Theoretical foundations. In J. E. Pedersen & A. D. Digby (Eds.), *Secondary schools and cooperative learning* (pp. 251–277). New York: Garland Publishing.

Sharan, Y., & Sharan, S. (1999). Group investigation in the cooperative classroom. In S. Sharan (Ed.), *Handbook of cooperative learning methods* (pp. 97–114). Westport, CT: Greenwood Press.

Shariff, S. (2008). *Cyber-bullying: Issues and solutions for the school, the classroom, and the home.* New York: Routledge.

Shayer, M. (1997). Piaget and Vygotsky: A necessary marriage for effective eductional interventions. In L. Smith, J. Dockrell, & P. Tomlinson (Eds.), *Piaget, Vygotsky, and beyond.* London: Routledge.

Shayer, M. (1999). Cognitive acceleration through science education II: Its effects and scope. *International Journal of Science Education, 21*(8), 883–902.

Shepard, R. N. (1978). Externalization of mental images and the act of creation. In B. S. Randhawa & W. E. Coffman (Eds.), *Visual learning, thinking, and communication.* New York: Academic Press.

Sherry, L., & Billig, S. H. (2002). Redefining a "virtual community of learners." *TechTrends, 46*(1), 48–51.

Shin, D. (2009). The evaluation of user experience of the virtual world in relation to extrinsic and intrinsic motivation. *International Journal of Human-Computer Interaction, 25*(6), 530–553.

Shulman, L. S. (2004). *The wisdom of practice: Essays on teaching, learning, and learning to teach.* San Francisco: Jossey-Bass.

Shure, M. B. (1999, April). Preventing violence the problem-solving way. *Juvenile Justice Bulletin.* Retrieved from http//ojjdp.ncjrs.org/pubs/violvict.html.

Siegel, D. (2002). Creating a living portfolio: Documenting student growth with electronic portfolios. *Gifted Child Today, 25*(3), 60–63.

Siegel, M. A., & Kirkley, S. E. (1998). Adventure learning as a vision of the digital learning environment. In C. J. Bonk & K. S. King (Eds.), *Electronic collaborators: Learner-centered technologies for literacy, apprenticeship, and discourse* (pp. 341–364). Mahwah, NJ: Lawrence Erlbaum.

Siegler, R. S. (1996). *Emerging minds: The process of change in children's thinking.* New York: Oxford University Press.

Siegler, R. S. (1998). *Children's thinking* (3rd ed.). Upper Saddle River, NJ: Prentice Hall.

Siegler, R. S., & Svetina, M. (2006). What leads children to adopt new strategies? A microgenetic/cross-sectional study of class inclusion. *Child Development, 77*(4), 997–1015.

Sigelman, C. K., & Shaffer, D. R. (1991). *Life-span human development.* Pacific Grove, CA: Brooks Cole.

Simon, S. (2002). The CASE approach for pupils with learning difficulties. *School Science Review, 83*(305), 73–79.

Simonsen, B., Fairbanks, S., Briesch, A., Myers, D., Sugai, G. (2008). Evidence-based practices in classroom management: Considerations for research to practice. *Education and Treatment of Children, 31*(3), 351–380.

Simpson, E. J. (1972). *The classification of educational objectives: Psychomotor domain.* Urbana, IL: University of Illinois Press.

Sinatra, G. M., & Pintrich, P. R. (Eds.). (2003). *Intentional conceptual change.* Mahwah, NJ: Lawrence Erlbaum Associates.

Singer, A. (1994). Reflections on multiculturalism. *Phi Delta Kappan, 76*(4), 284–288.

Singer, D. G., & Revenson, T. A. (1996). *A Piaget primer: How a child thinks* (rev. ed.). New York: Plume.

Singham, M. (2003). The achievement gap: Myths and reality. *Phi Delta Kappan, 84*(8), 586–591.

Sirin, S. R. (2005). Socioeconomic status and academic achievement: A meta-analytic review of research. *Review of Educational Research, 75*(3), 417–453.

Skiba, R, Reynolds, C. R., Graham, S., Sheras, P., Conoley, J. C., & Garcia-Vazquez, E. (2006, February). *Are zero tolerance policies effective in the schools? An evidentiary review and recommendations.* A Report by the American Psychological Association Zero Tolerance Task Force. Retrieved from http://www.apa.org/releases/ZTTFReport-BODRevisions5-15.pdf.

Skinner, B. F. (1948). *Walden two.* New York: Macmillan.

Skinner, B. F. (1968). *The technology of teaching.* New York: Appleton-Century-Crofts.

Skinner, B. F (1976). *Particulars of my life.* New York: Knopf.

Skinner, B. F (1979). *The shaping of a behaviorist.* New York: Knopf.

Skinner, B. F (1983). *A matter of consequences.* New York: Knopf.

Skinner, B. F (1984). The shame of American education. *American Psychologist, 39*(9), 947–954.

Slavin, R. E. (1994). Student teams-achievement divisions. In S. Sharan (Ed.), *Handbook of cooperative learning methods* (pp. 3–19). Westport, CT: Greenwood Press.

Slavin, R. E. (1995). *Cooperative learning: Theory, Research, and Practice* (2nd ed.). Boston: Allyn & Bacon.

Slavin, R. E. (2002). Evidence-based education policies: Transforming educational practice and research. *Educational Researcher, 31*(7), 15–21.

Slavin, R. E. (2008). What works? Issues in synthesizing educational program evaluations. *Educational Researcher, 37*(1), 5–14.

Slavin, R. E., & Cheung, A. (2005). A synthesis of research on language of reading instruction for English language learners. *Review of Educational Research, 75*(2), 247–284.

Slavin, R. E., Lake, C., & Groff, C. (2009). Effective programs in middle and high school mathematics: A best-evidence synthesis. *Review of Educational Research, 79*(2), 839–911.

Slavin, R. E., Madden, N. A., Chambers, B., & Haxby, B. (2009). *2 million children* (2nd ed.). Thousand Oaks, CA: Corwin Press.

Sleeter, C. E., & Grant, C. A. (2009). *Making choices for multicultural education* (6th ed.). Hoboken, NJ: John Wiley & Sons.

Slotta, J., & Linn, M. (2009). *WISE science: Web-based inquiry in the classroom.* New York: Teachers College Press.

Smith, A., & Bondy, E. (2007). "No! I Won't!" Understanding and responding to student defiance. *Childhood Education, 83*(3), 151–157.

Smith, L. (2002). Piaget's model. In U. Goswami (Ed.), *Blackwell handbook of childhood cognitive development* (pp. 515–537). Oxford, England: Blackwell Publishers.

Smith, P. K. (2005). Play. In B. Hopkins, R. G. Barr, G. F. Michel, & P. Rochat (Eds.), *The Cambridge encyclopedia of child development* (pp. 344–347). Cambridge, UK: Cambridge University Press.

Smith, D. D., & Tyler, N. C. (2010). *Introduction to special education: Making a difference* (7th ed.). Upper Saddle River, NJ: Merrill/Pearson.

Snow, R. E. (1986). Individual differences and the design of educational programs. *American Psychologist, 41*(10), 1029–1039.

Snowman, J. (1986). Learning tactics and strategies. In G. D. Phye & T. Andre (Eds.), *Cognitive classroom learning: Understanding, thinking, and problem solving.* New York: Academic Press.

Sobel, D. M., Taylor, S. V., & Anderson, R. E. (2003). Shared accountability: Encouraging diversity—responsive teaching in an inclusive classroom.

Sofronoff, K., Dalgliesh, L., & Kosky, R. (2005). *Out of options: A cognitive model of adolescent suicide and risk-taking.* Cambridge, UK: Cambridge University Press.

Soldier, L. L. (1997). Is there an 'Indian' in your classroom? Working successfully with urban Native American students. *Phi Delta Kappan, 78*(8), 650–653.

Solórzano, R. W. (2008). High stakes testing: Issues, implications, and remedies for English language learners. *Review of Educational Research, 78*(2), 260–329.

Sorell, G. T., & Montgomery, M. J. (2001). Feminist perspectives on Erikson's theory: Their relevance for contemporary identity development research. *Identity, 1*(2), 97–128.

Spear-Swerling, L., & Sternberg, R. J. (1998). Curing our "epidemic" of learning disabilities. *Phi Delta Kappan, 79*(5), 397–401.

Spector, J. M. (2006). A methodology for assessing learning in complex and ill structured task domains. *Innovations in Education and Teaching International, 43*(2), 109–120.

Spies, R. A., & Plake, B. S. (Eds.). (2005). *The sixteenth mental measurements yearbook*. Lincoln, NE: University of Nebraska Press.

Spitz, H. H. (1999). Beleaguered Pygmalion: A history of the controversy over claims that teacher expectancy raises intelligence. *Intelligence, 27*(3), 199–234.

Spörera, N., Brunstein, J., & Kieschke, U. (2009). Improving students' reading comprehension skills: Effects of strategy instruction and reciprocal teaching. *Learning and Instruction, 19*(3), 272–286.

Sprinthall, N. A., Sprinthall, R. C. (1987). *Educational psychology: A developmental approach* (4th ed.). New York: Random House.

Sprinthall, N. A., Sprinthall, R. C., & Oja, S. N. (1998). *Educational psychology: A developmental approach* (7th ed.). New York: McGraw-Hill.

Standing, L. (1973). Learning 10,000 pictures. *Quarterly Journal of Experimental Psychology, 25*(2), 207–222.

Standing, L., Conezio, J., & Haber, R. (1970). Perception and memory for pictures: Single trial learning of 2500 visual stimuli. *Psychonomic Science, 19*(2), 73–74.

Stanford, P., & Siders, J. A. (2001). E-pal writing! *Teaching Exceptional Children, 34*(2), 21–25.

Starnes, B. A. (2006). What we don't know *can* hurt them: White teachers, Indian children. *Phi Delta Kappan, 87*(5). 384–392.

Staub, F. C., & Stern, E. (2002). The nature of teachers' pedagogical content beliefs matters for students' achievement gains: Quasi-experimental evidence from elementary mathematics. *Journal of Educational Psychology, 94*(2), 344–355.

Stears, M. (2009). How social and critical constructivism can inform science curriculum design: A study from South Africa. *Educational Research, 51*(4), 397–410.

Steinberg, L. (1996). *Beyond the classroom: Why school reform has failed and what parents need to do*. New York: Simon & Schuster.

Steinberg, L. (2008). *Adolescence* (8th ed.). New York: McGraw-Hill Higher Education.

Steinberg, L., & Morris, A. S. (2001). Adolescent development. In S. T. Fiske, D. L. Schacter, & C. Zahn-Waxler (Eds.), *Annual review of psychology* (pp. 83–110). Stanford, CA: Annual Reviews.

Steinberg, L., Vandell, D. L., & Bornstein, M. H. (2011). *Development: Infancy through adolescence*. Belmont, CA: Wadsworth/Cengage Learning.

Stemler, S. E., Elliott, J. G., Grigorenko, E. L., & Sternberg, R. J. (2006). There's more to teaching than instruction: Seven strategies for dealing with the practical side of teaching. *Educational Studies, 32*(1), 101–118.

Stemler, S. E., Sternberg, R.J., Grigorenko, E. L., Jarvin, L., & Sharpes, K. (2009). Using the theory of successful intelligence as a framework for developing assessments in AP Physics. *Contemporary Educational Psychology, 34*(3), 195–209.

Stepanek, J., and Peixotto, K. (2009). *Models of response to intervention in the Northwest Region states* (Issues & Answers Report, REL 2009–No. 079). Washington, DC: U.S. Department of Education, Institute of Education Sciences, National Center for Education Evaluation and Regional Assistance, Regional Educational Laboratory Northwest. Retrieved from http://www.ies.ed.gov/ncee/edlabs.

Sternberg, R. J. (1996). Matching abilities, instruction, and assessment: Reawakening the sleeping giant of ATI. In I. Dennis & P. Tapsfield (Eds.), *Human abilities: Their nature and measurement* (pp. 167–181). Mahwah, NJ: Erlbaum.

Sternberg, R. J. (1997a). What does it mean to be smart? *Educational Leadership, 54*(6), 20–24.

Sternberg, R. J. (1997b). Technology changes intelligence: Societal implications and soaring IQ's. *Technos, 6*(2), 12–14.

Sternberg, R. J. (1998). Abilities are forms of developing expertise. *Educational Researcher, 27*(3), 11–20.

Sternberg, R. J. (2002a). Intelligence is not just inside the head: The theory of successful intelligence. In J. Aronson (Ed.), *Improving academic achievement* (pp. 227–244). San Diego, CA: Academic Press.

Sternberg, R. J. (2002b). Raising the achievement of all students: Teaching for successful intelligence. *Educational Psychology Review, 14*(4), 383–393.

Sternberg, R. J. (2003). Construct validity of the theory of successful intelligence. In R. J. Sternberg, J. Lautrey, & T. I. Lubart (Eds.), *Models of intelligence: International perspectives* (pp. 55–77). Washington, DC: American Psychological Association.

Sternberg, R. J. (2005). WICS: A model of positive educational leadership comprising wisdom, intelligence, and creativity synthesized. *Educational Psychology Review, 17*(3), 191–262.

Sternberg, R. J. (2008). The answer depends on the question: A reply to Jensen. *Phi Delta Kappan, 89*(6), 418–420.

Sternberg, R. (2009). Domain-generality versus domain-specificity of creativity. In P. Muesburger, J. Funke, & E.Wunder (Eds.), *Milieus of creativity: An interdisciplinary approach to spatiality and creativity.* (pp. 25–38). Dordrecht, Netherlands: Springer.

Sternberg, R. J., & Grigorenko, E. L. (2001). A capsule history of theory and research on styles. In R. J. Sternberg & L. Zhang (Eds.), *Perspectives on thinking, learning, and cognitive styles* (pp. 1–21). Mahwah, NJ: Erlbaum.

Sternberg, R. J., & Grigorenko, E. L. (2004). Successful intelligence in the classroom. *Theory into Practice, 43*(4), 274–280.

Sternberg, R. J., Grigorenko, E. L., & Zhang, L. (2008). Styles of learning and thinking matter in instruction and assessment. *Perspectives on Psychological Science, 3*(6), 486–506.

Sternberg, R. J., Jarvin, L., & Grigorenko, E. L. (2009). *Teaching for wisdom, intelligence, creativity, and success*. Thousand Oaks, CA: Corwin Press.

Steubing, K. K., Fletcher, J. M., LeDoux, J. M., Lyon, G. R., Shaywitz, S. E., & Shaywitz, B. A. (2002). Validity of IQ-discrepancy classifications of reading disabilities: A meta-analysis. *American Educational Research Journal, 39*(2), 469–518.

Stewart, E. B., Stewart, E. A., & Simons, R. L. (2007). The effect of neighborhood context on the college aspirations of African American adolescents. *American Educational Research Journal, 44*(4), 896–919.

Stier, H., Lewin-Epstein, N., & Braun, B. (2001). Welfare regimes, family-supportive policies, and women's employment along the life-course. *American Journal of Sociology, 106*(6), 1731–1760.

Stiggins, R. J. (2001). The unfulfilled promise of classroom assessment. *Educational Measurement: Issues and Practice, 20*(3), 5–15.

Stiggins, R. J. (2002). Assessment crisis: The absences of assessment FOR learning. *Phi Delta Kappan, 83*(10), 758–765.

Stiggins, R. J. (2007). *An introduction to student-involved assessment for learning* (5th ed.). Upper Saddle River, NJ: Merrill Prentice Hall.

Stiggins, R. (2009). Assessment FOR learning in upper elementary grades. *Phi Delta Kappan, 90*(6), 419–421.

Stiggins, R., Arter, J., Chappuis, J., & Chappuis, S. (2007). *Classroom assessment for student learning: Doing it right—using it well*. Upper Saddle River, NJ: Merrill/Pearson.

Stinson, N., Jr. (2003, August). Working toward our goal: Eliminating racial and ethnic disparities in health. *Closing the Gap*, 1-2. Retrieved from http://www.omhrc.gov/OMH/sidebar/archivedctg.htm.

Stokes, V. (2005). No longer a year behind. *Learning & Leading with Technology, 33*(2), 15–17.

Strassman, B. K., & D'Amore, M. (2002). The write technology. *Teaching Exceptional Children, 34*(6), 28–31.

Stuart, C., & Thurlow, D. (2000). Making it their own: Preservice teachers' experiences, beliefs, and classroom practices. *Journal of Teacher Education, 51*(2), 113–121.

Stull, A. T., & Mayer, R. E. (2007). Learning by doing versus learning by viewing: Three experimental comparisons of learner-generated versus author-provided graphic organizers. *Journal of Educational Psychology, 99*(4), 808–820.

Sun, K-T., Lin, Y., & Yu, C. (2008). A study on learning effect among different learning styles in a Web-based lab of science for elementary school students. *Computers & Education 50*(4), 1411–1422.

Sunderman, G. L. (2006, February). *The unraveling of No Child Left Behind: How negotiated changes transform the law.* Cambridge, MA: The Civil Rights Project at Harvard University. Retrieved from http://www.civilrightsproject.harvard.edu/research/esea/esea_gen.php.

Suomala, J., & Alajaaski, J. (2002). Pupils' problem-solving processes in a complex computerized learning environment. *Journal of Educational Computing Research, 26*(2), 155–176.

Susman, E. J. (1991). Stress and the adolescent. In R. M. Lerner, A. C. Peterson, & J. Brooks-Gunn (Eds.), *Encyclopedia of adolescence.* New York: Garland Publishing.

Swalander, L., & Taube, K. (2007). Influences of family based prerequisites, reading attitude, and self-regulation on reading ability. *Contemporary Educational Psychology, 32*(2), 206–230.

Swanson, C. B. (2004). *Who graduates? Who doesn't? A statistical portrait of public high school graduation, class of 2001.* Washington, DC: The Urban Institute. Retrieved from http://www.urban.org/url.cfm?ID=410934.

Swanson, H. L. (2006). Cross-sectional and incremental changes in working memory and mathematical problem solving. *Journal of Educational Psychology, 98*(2), 265–281.

Swanson, H. L., & Hoskyn, M. (1998). Experimental intervention research on students with learning disabilities: A meta-analysis of treatment outcomes. *Review of Educational Research, 68*(3), 277–321.

Tabachnick, S., Miller, R, & Relyea, G. (2008). The relationships among students' future-oriented goals and subgoals, perceived task instrumentality, and task-oriented self-regulation strategies in an academic environment. *Journal of Educational Psychology, 100*(3), 629–642.

Tappan, M. B. (1998). Sociocultural psychology and caring pedagogy: Exploring Vygotsky's "hidden curriculum." *Educational Psychologist, 33*(1), 23–33.

Tappan, M. (2005). Mediated moralities: Sociocultural approaches to moral development. In M. Killen & J. Smetana (Eds.), *Handbook of moral development.* Hillsdale, NJ: Lawrence Erlbaum.

Tappan, M. B. (2006). Moral functioning as mediated action. *Journal of Moral Education, 35*(1), 1–18.

Tauber, R. T., & Mester, C. S. (2006). *Acting lessons for teachers: Using performance skills in the classroom* (2nd ed.). Westport, CT: Praeger.

Taylor, A. Z., & Graham, S. (2007). An examination of the relationship between achievement values and perceptions of barriers among low-SES African American and Latino students. *Journal of Educational Psychology, 99*(1), 52–64.

Taylor, D., & Lorimer, M. (2002/2003). Helping boys succeed. *Educational Leadership, 60*(4), 68–70.

Taylor, P. (1996). Mythmaking and mythbreaking in the mathematics classroom. *Educational Studies in Mathematics, 31*(1–2), 151–173.

Taylor, P. C., & Fraser, B. J. (1998). *The constructivist learning environment survey: Mark 2.* Perth, Australia: Science and Mathematics Education Centre, Curtin University of Technology.

Taylor, P. C., Fraser, B. J., & Fisher, D. L. (1997). Monitoring constructivist classroom learning environments. *International Journal of Educational Research, 27*(4), 293–301.

Tenenbaum, H. R., & Ruck, M. D. (2007). Are teachers' expectations different for racial minority than for European American students? A meta-analysis. *Journal of Educational Psychology, 99*(2), 253–273.

Tennessee Department of Education (2006, July 20). *Schools to use technology to enhance achievement.* Retrieved from http://tennessee.gov/education/news/nr/2006/07_20_06.shtml.

Teolis, B. (2002). *Ready-to-use conflict resolution activities for elementary students.* Paramus, NJ: The Center for Applied Research in Education.

Thoma, S. J. (1986). Estimating gender differences in the comprehension and preference of moral issues. *Developmental Review, 6*(2), 165–180.

Thomas B. Fordham Institute. (2008, June). *High-achieving students in the era of NCLB.* Retrieved from http://www.edexcellence.net/detail/news.cfm?news_id=732&id=92.

Thomas, J. (2005). Calling a cab for Oregon students. *Phi Delta Kappan, 86*(5), 385–388.

Thomas, M., Barab, S., & Tuzun, H. (2009). Developing critical implementations of technology-rich innovations: A cross-case study of the implementation of Quest Atlantis. *Journal of Educational Computing Research, 41*(2), 125–153.

Thomas, V. G. (2000). Learner-centered alternatives to social promotion and retention: A talent development approach. *Journal of Negro Education, 69*(4), 323–337.

Thomas, W. P., & Collier, V. P. (1997/1998). Two languages are better than one. *Educational Leadership, 55*(4), 23–26.

Thomas, W. P., & Collier, V. P. (1999). Accelerated schooling for English language learners. *Educational Leadership, 56*(7), 46–49.

Thompson, M. S., DiCerbo, K. E., Mahoney, K., & MacSwan, J. (2002, January 25). ¿Exito en California? A validity critique of language program evaluations and analysis of English learner test scores. *Education Policy Analysis Archives, 10*(7). Retrieved from http://epaa.asu.edu/epaa/v10n7/.

Thorn, A., & Page, M. (2009). *Interactions between short-term and long-term memory in the verbal domain.* New York: Psychology Press.

Thorndike, R. M., & Thorndike-Christ, T. M. (2010). *Measurement and evaluation in psychology and education* (8th ed.). Boston: Allyn & Bacon/Pearson.

Thrash, T., & Hurst, A. (2008). Approach and avoidance motivation in the achievement domain: Integrating the achievement motive and the achievement goal traditions. In A. Elliot (Ed.), *Handbook of approach and avoidance motivation* (pp. 217–234). New York: Taylor & Francis.

Tieso, C. L. (2003). Ability grouping is not just tracking anymore. *Roeper Review, 26*(1), 29–39.

Tingstrom, D. H., Sterling-Turner, H. E., & Wilczynski, S. M. (2006). The good behavior game: 1969-2002. *Behavior Modification, 30*(2), 225–253.

Tobias, S., & Duffy, T. (2009). The success or failure of constructivist instruction: An introduction. In S. Tobias & T. Duffy (Eds.), *Constructivist instruction: Success or failure?* (pp. 3–10). New York: Routledge.

Toch, T. (2003). *High schools on a human scale.* Boston: Beacon Press.

Tomlinson, C. A. (2002). Invitations to learn. *Educational Leadership, 60*(1), 6–10.

Tomlinson, C. A. (2007/2008). Learning to love assessment. *Educational Leadership, 65*(4), 8–13.

Tomlinson, C. A., Brimijoin, K., & Narvaez, L. (2008). *The differentiated school: Making revolutionary changes in teaching and learning.* Alexandria, VA: ASCD.

Tomporowski, P. D., Davis, C. L., Miller, P. H., & Naglieri, J. A. (2008). Exercise and children's intelligence, cognition, and academic achievement. *Educational Psychology Review, 20*(2), 111–131.

Tong, F., Lara-Alecio, R., Irby, B., Mathes, P., & Kwok, O. (2008). Accelerating early academic oral English development in transitional bilingual and structured English immersion programs. *American Educational Research Journal, 45*(4), 1011–1044.

Toth, K., & King, B. (2010). Intellectual disability (mental retardation). In M. K. Dulcan (Ed.), *Textbook of child and adolescent psychiatry* (pp. 151–172). Arlington, VA: American Psychiatric Publishing.

Trautman, S. (2007). *Teach what you know.* Upper Saddle River, NJ: Prentice Hall/Pearson.

Trautwein, U., & Lüdtke, O. (2007). Epistemological beliefs, school achievement, and college major: A large-scale longitudinal study on the impact of certainty beliefs. *Contemporary Educational Psychology, 32*(6), 348–366.

Trevisan, M. S. (2002). The states' role in ensuring assessment competence. *Phi Delta Kappan, 83*(10), 766–771.

Triandis, H. C. (1986). Toward pluralism in education. In S. Modgil, G. K. Verma, K. Mallick, & C. Modgil (Eds.), *Multicultural education: The interminable debate*. London: Falmer.

Trotter, A. (2003, May 8). A question of direction. *Education Week, 22*(35), 17–18, 20–21.

Troyer, L., & Youngreen, R. (2009). Conflict and creativity in groups. *Journal of Social Issues, 65*(2), 409–427.

Trumper, R., & Gelbman, M. (2000). Investigating electromagnetic induction through a microcomputer-based laboratory. *Physics Education, 35*(2), 90–95.

Trumper, R., & Gelbman, M. (2002). Using MBL to verify Newton's second law and the impulse-momentum relationship with an arbitrary changing force. *School Science Review, 83*(305), 135–139.

Tudge, J. R. H., & Rogoff, B. (1989). Peer influences on cognitive development: Piagetian and Vygotskian perspectives. In M. H. Bornstein & J. S. Bruner (Eds.), *Interaction in human development*. Hillsdale, NJ: Lawrence Erlbaum.

Tudge, J. R. H., & Scrimsher, S. (2003). Lev S. Vygotsky on education: A cultural-historical, interpersonal, and individual approach to development. In B. J. Zimmerman & D. H. Schunk (Eds.), *Educational psychology: A century of contributions*. Mahwah, NJ: Lawrence Erlbaum.

Tudge, J. R. H., & Winterhoff, P. A. (1993). Vygotsky, Piaget, and Bandura: Perspectives on the relations between the social world and cognitive development. *Human Development, 36*(2), 61–81.

Tukey, L. (2002). Differentiation. *Phi Delta Kappan, 84*(1), 63–64, 92.

Tulving, E., & Pearlstone, Z. (1966). Availability vs. accessibility of information in memory for words. *Journal of Verbal Learning and Verbal Behavior, 5*(4), 381–391.

Turiel, E. (2008). The trouble with the ways morality is used and how they impede social equity and social justice. In C. Wainryb, J. G. Smetana, & E. Turiel (Eds.), *Social development, social inequalities, and social justice* (pp. 1–26). Mahwah, NJ: Lawrence Erlbaum.

Umar, K. B. (2003, August). Disparities persist in infant mortality: Creative approaches work to close the gap. *Closing the Gap*, 4–5. Retrieved from http://www.omhrc.gov/OMH/sidebar/archivedctg.htm.

U.S. Census Bureau. (2008a, August). *Fertility of American women: 2006*. Retrieved from http://www.census.gov/prod/2008pubs/p20-558.pdf.

U.S. Census Bureau (2008b, August). *U.S. population projections: 2008 national population projections*. Retrieved from http://www.census.gov/population/www/projections/summarytables.html.

U.S. Census Bureau. (2009). *Number in poverty and poverty rates by race and Hispanic origin using 2- and 3-year averages: 2003 to 2005*. Retrieved from http://www.census.gov/hhes/www/poverty/poverty05/table5.html.

U.S. Department of Education. (2004). *Individuals with Disabilities Education Improvement Act of 2004*. Retrieved October 17, 2006, from www.ed.gov/policy/speced/guid/idea2004.html.

U.S. Department of Education, National Center for Education Statistics (2008a). *NAEP 2008: Trends in academic progress*. Retrieved from http://nces.ed.gov/nationsreportcard/pubs/main2008/2009479.asp.

U.S. Department of Education. (2008b, March). *Differentiated accountability: A more nuanced system to better target resources*. Retrieved from http://www.ed.gov/nclb/accountability/differentiated/factsheet.pdf.

U.S. Department of Education, Office of Special Education and Rehabilitative Services, Office of Special Education Programs. (2009a). *28th Annual Report to Congress on the Implementation of the Individuals with Disabilities Education Act, 2006* (volume 1). Washington, DC: Author.

U.S. Department of Education, Office of Special Education and Rehabilitative Services, Office of Special Education Programs. (2009b). *28th Annual Report to Congress on the Implementation of the Individuals with Disabilities Education Act, 2006* (volume 2). Washington, DC: Author.

U.S. Department of Homeland Security. (2008, September). *Yearbook of immigration statistics: 2007*. Washington, D.C.: U.S. Department of Homeland Security, Office of Immigration Statistics. Retrieved from http://www.dhs.gov/xlibrary/assets/statistics/yearbook/2007/ois_2007_yearbook.pdf.

U.S. Department of Labor. (2001, October 16). *Occupational classification system manual*. Retrieved from http://www.bls.gov/ncs/ocs/ocsm/comMoga.htm.

Usher, E. L. (2009). Sources of middle school students' self-efficacy in mathematics: A qualitative investigation. *American Educational Research Journal, 46*(1), 275–314.

Usher, E. L., & Pajares, F. (2008a). Sources of self-efficacy in school: Critical review of the literature and future directions. *Review of Educational Research, 78*(4), 751–796.

Usher, E., & Pajares, F. (2008b). Self-efficacy for self-regulated learning: A validation study. *Educational and Psychological Measurement, 68*(3), 443–463.

Vallecorsa, A. L., deBettencourt, L. U., & Zigmond, N. (2000). *Students with mild disabilities in general education settings*. Upper Saddle River, NJ: Merrill Prentice Hall.

Valli, L., & Buese, D. (2007). The changing roles of teachers in an era of high-stakes accountability. *American Educational Research Journal, 44*(3), 519–558.

Valli, L., Croninger, R., Chambliss, M., Graeber, A., & Buese, D. (2008). *Test-driven: High-stakes accountability in elementary schools*. New York: Teachers College Press.

VanDerHeyden, A., Witt, J., & Gilbertson, D. (2007). A multi-year evaluation of the effects of a response to intervention (RTI) model of identification of children for special education. *Journal of School Psychology, 45*(2), 225–256.

van Drie, J., van Boxtel, C., & van der Linden, J. (2006). Historical reasoning in a computer-supported collaborative learning environment. In A. M. O' Donnell, C. E. Hmelo-Silver, & G. Erkens (Eds.), *Collaborative learning, reasoning, and technology* (pp. 265–296). Mahwah, NJ: Lawrence Erlbaum Associates.

van Laar, C. (2000). The paradox of low academic achievement but high self-esteem in African American students: An attributional account. *Educational Psychology Review, 12*(1), 33–62.

Van Overschelde, J. (2008). Metacognition: Knowing about knowing. In J. Dunlosky & R. Bjork (Eds.), *Handbook of metamemory and memory* (pp. 47–72). New York: Taylor & Francis.

Van Wagenen, L., & Hibbard, K. M. (1998). Building teacher portfolios. *Educational Leadership, 55*(5), 26–29.

Varma, S., McCandless, B. D., & Schwartz, D. L. (2008). Scientific and pragmatic challenges for bridging education and neuroscience. *Educational Researcher, 37*(3), 140–152.

Vartanian, L. R. (2000). Revisiting the imaginary audience and personal fable constructs of adolescent egocentrism: A conceptual review. *Adolescence, 35*(140), 639–661.

Vekiri, I. (2002). What is the value of graphical displays in learning? *Educational Psychology Review, 14*(3), 261–312.

Veenman, S. Denessen, E., van den Akker, A., & van der Rijt, J. (2005). Effects of a cooperative learning program on the elaborations of students during help seeking and help giving. *American Educational Research Journal, 42*(1), 115–151.

Veermans, M., & Cesareni, D. (2005). The nature of the discourse in web-based collaborative learning environments: Case studies from four different countries. *Computers & Education, 45*(3), 316–336.

Vermont Department of Education. (2009). *New England common assessment program (necap)*. Retrieved from http://education.vermont.gov/new/html/pgm_assessment/necap.html.

Vernez, G., Naftel, S., Ross, K., Le Floch, K. C., Beighley, C., & Gill, G. (2009). *State and local implementation of the No Child Left Behind Act. Volume VII—Title 1 school choice and supplemental educational services: Final report*. Washington, DC: U.S. Department of Education. Retrieved from http:www.ed.gov/rschstat/eval/choice/nclb-choice-ses-final/choice-ses-final.pdf.

Vitz, P C. (1990). The use of stories in moral development: New psychological reasons for an old educational method. *American Psychologist, 45*(6), 709–720.

Vogel, C. (2009). A call for collaboration. *Direct Administration, 25*(5), 22–25.

Vogler, K. E., & Kennedy, R. J., Jr. (2003). A view from the bottom: What happens when your school system ranks last? *Phi Delta Kappan, 84*(6), 446–448.

Vygotsky, L. S. (1986). *Thought and language* (A. Kozulin, Trans.). Cambridge, MA: MIT Press. (Original work published 1934.)

Wadsworth, B. J. (2004). *Piaget's theory of cognitive and affective development* (5th Classics ed.) Boston: Allyn and Bacon.

Wai, J., Lubinski, D., & Benbow, C. P. (2005). Creativity and occupational accomplishments among intellectually precocious youth: An age 13 to 33 longitudinal study. *Journal of Educational Psychology, 97*(3), 484–492.

Walberg, H. J. (2006). Improving educational productivity: An assessment of extant research. In R. F. Subotnik & H. F. Walberg (Eds.), *The scientific basis of educational productivity.* Greenwich, CT: Information Age.

Walker, C., & Greene, B. (2009). The relations between student motivational beliefs and cognitive engagement in high school. *Journal of Educational Research, 102*(6), 463–472.

Walker, J. E., Shea, T. M., & Bauer, A. M. (2007). *Behavior management: A practical approach for educators* (9th ed.). Upper Saddle River, NJ: Pearson/Merrill Prentice Hall.

Walker, J. M. T., & Hoover-Dempsey, K. V. (2006). Why research on parental involvement is important to classroom management. In C. M. Evertson & C. S. Weinstein (Eds.), *Handbook of classroom management: Research, practice, and contemporary issues* (pp. 665–684). Mahwah, NJ: Lawrence Erlbaum.

Wallace-Broscious, A., Serafica, F. C., & Osipow S. H. (1994). Adolescent career development: Relationships to self-concept and identity status. *Journal of Research on Adolescence, 4*(1), 127–149.

Wang, M. C., Haertel, G. D., & Walberg, H. J. (1993). Toward a knowledge base for school learning. *Review of Educational Research, 63*(3), 249–294.

Wang, J., Spalding, E., Odell, S., Klecka, C. & Lin, E. (2010). Bold ideas for improving teacher education and teaching: What we see, hear, and think. *Journal of Teacher Education, 61*(1–2), 3–15.

Wang, M. J., & Kang, M. (2006). Cybergogy for engaged learning: A framework for creating learner engagement through information and communication technology. In D. Hung & M. S. Khine (Eds.), *Engaged learning with emerging technologies* (pp. 225–253). Dordrecht, Netherlands: Springer.

Wang, S. Jiao, H., Young, M. J., Brooks, T., & Olson, J. (2008). Comparability of computer-based and paper-and-pencil testing in k-12 reading assessments. *Educational and Psychological Measurement, 68*(1), 5–24.

Wasserman, S. (1999). Shazam! you're a teacher: Facing the illusory quest for certainty in classroom practice. *Phi Delta Kappan, 80*(6), 464–468.

Wasserman, S. (2009). *Teaching for thinking today: Theory, strategy, and activities for the K–8 classroom.* New York: Teachers College Press.

Watanabe, M. (2008). Tracking in the Era of High Stakes State Accountability Reform: Case Studies of Classroom Instruction in North Carolina. *Teachers College Record, 110*(3), 489–534.

Waterhouse, L. (2006). Multiple intelligences, the Mozart effect, and emotional intelligence: A critical review. *Educational Psychologist, 41*(4), 207–225.

Waterman, A. S. (1988). Identity status theory and Erikson's theory: Communalities and differences. *Developmental Review, 8*(2), 185–208.

Waterman, A. S., & Archer, S. L. (1990). A life-span perspective on identity formation: Developments in form, function, and process. In P. B. Baltes, D. L. Featherman, & R. M. Lerner (Eds.), *Life-span development and behavior* (Vol. 10, pp. 30–57). Hillsdale, NJ: Erlbaum.

Watson, J. B. (1913). Psychology as the behaviorist views it. *Psychological Review, 20*, 158–177.

Watson, M. F., & Protinsky, H. (1991). Identity status of black adolescents: An empirical investigation. *Adolsecence, 26*(104), 963–966.

Wayne, A. J., & Youngs, P. (2003). Teacher characteristics and student achievement gains: A review. *Review of Educational Research, 73*(1), 89–122.

Webb, N. M., Nemer, K. M., Chizhik, A. W., & Sugrue, B. (1998). Equity issues in collaborative group assessment: Group composition and performance. *American Educational Research Journal, 35*(4), 607–651.

Webb, N. M., Nemer, K. M, & Zuniga, S. (2002). Short circuits or superconductors? Effects of group composition on high-achieving students' science assessment performance. *American Educational Research Journal, 39*(4), 943–989.

Wechsler, D. (1975). Intelligence defined and undefined: A relativistic appraisal. *American Psychologist, 30*(2), 135–139.

Wechsler, D. (1997). *Wechsler Adult Intelligence Scale—III.* New York: Psychological Corporation.

Wechsler, D. (2003). *Wechsler Intelligence Scale for Children—IV.* New York: Psychological Corporation.

Weichold, K., Silbereisen, R. K., & Schmitt-Rodermund, E. (2003). Short-term and long-term consequences of early versus late physical maturation in adolescents. In C. Hayward (Ed.), *Gender differences at puberty* (pp. 241–276). Cambridge, England: Cambridge University Press.

Weiler, G. (2003). Using weblogs in the classroom. *English Journal, 92*(5), 73–75.

Weinert, F. E., & Hany, E. A. (2003). The stability of individual differences in intellectual development: Empirical evidence, theoretical problems, and new research questions. In R. J. Sternberg, J. Lautrey, & T. I. Lubart (Eds.), *Models of intelligence: International perspectives* (pp. 169–181). Washington, DC: American Psychological Association.

Weinstein, C. S., & Mignano, A. J., Jr. (2007). *Elementary classroom management: Lessons from research and practice* (4th ed.). Boston: McGraw-Hill.

Weiss, R. P. (2000). Howard Gardner talks about technology. *Training & Development, 54*(9), 52–56.

Welch, O. M., Patterson, F. E., Scott, K. A., & Pollard, D. S. (2007). Gender equity for African Americans. In S. Klein (Ed.), *Handbook for achieving gender equity through education* (pp. 469–484). Mahwah, NJ: Erlbaum Publishers.

Wells, J., & Lewis, L. (2006). *Internet access in U.S. public schools and classrooms: 1994–2005* (NCES 2007-020). Washington, D.C.: National Center for Education Statistics. Retrieved from http://nces.ed.gov/pubsearch/pubsinfo.asp?pubid=2007020.

Wentzel, K. R. (2002). Are effective teachers like good parents? Teaching styles and student adjustment in early adolescence. *Child Development, 73*(1), 287–301.

Wentzel, K. R., & Wigfield, A. (2009). (Eds.). *Handbook of motivation at school.* New York: Routledge.

Wertsch, J. V. (1998). *Mind as action.* New York: Oxford University Press.

Wertsch, J. V., & Tulviste, P. (1996). L. S. Vygotsky and contemporary developmental psychology. In H. Daniels (Ed.), *An introduction to Vygotsky.* New York: Routledge.

Westerman, D. A. (1991). Expert and novice teacher decision making. *Journal of Teacher Education, 42*(4), 292–305.

Westwood, P. (2009). *What teachers need to know about students with disabilities.* Victoria, Australia: ACER Press.

Wheatley, G. H. (1991). Constructivist perspectives on science and mathematics learning. *Science Education, 75*(1), 9–21.

Wheelock, A. (1994). *Alternatives to tracking and ability grouping.* Arlington, VA: American Association of School Administrators.

White, R., Algozzine, B., Audette, R., Marr, M. B., & Ellis, E. D., Jr. (2001). Unified Discipline: A school-wide approach for managing problem behavior. *Intervention in School and Clinic, 37*(1), 3–8.

Whitehouse, P., McCloskey, E., & Ketelhut, D. J. (2010). Online pedagogy design and development: New models for 21st century online teacher professional development. In J. O. Lindberg & A. D. Olofsson (Eds.), *Online learning communities and teacher professional development: Methods for improved education delivery* (pp. 247–262). Hershey, PA: IGI Global.

Whittaker, C. R., Salend, S. J., & Duhaney, D. (2001). Creating instructional rubrics for inclusive classrooms. *Teaching Exceptional Children, 34*(2), 8–13.

Wiburg, K., & Brown, S. (2007). *Lesson study communities: increasing achievement with diverse students*. Thousand Oaks, CA: Corwin Press.

Wickens, C., Lee, J., Liu, Y., & Gordon-Becker, S. (2004). *Introduction to human factors engineering*, (2nd ed.). Upper Saddle River, New Jersey: Prentice-Hall.

Wicks-Nelson, R., & Israel, A. C. (2003). *Behavior disorders of childhood* (5th ed.). Upper Saddle River, NJ: Prentice-Hall.

Wiechman, B., & Gurland, S. (2009). What happens during the free-choice period? Evidence of a polarizing effect of extrinsic rewards on intrinsic motivation. *Journal of Research in Personality, 43*(4), 716–719.

Wigfield, A., Battle, A., Keller, L. B., & Eccles, J. S. (2002). Sex differences in motivation, self-concept, career aspiration, and career choice: Implications for cognitive development. In A. McGillicuddy-De Lisi & R. De Lisi (Eds.), *Biology, society, and behavior: The development of sex differences in cognition* (pp. 93–124). Westport, CT: Ablex.

Wigfield, A., & Eccles, J. S. (2002a). Students' motivation during the middle school years. In J. Aronson (Ed.), *Improving academic achievement* (pp. 159–184). San Diego, CA: Academic Press.

Wigfield, A., Tonks, S., & Klauda, S. L. (2009). Expectancy value theory. In K. Wentzel & A. Wigfield (Eds.), *Handbook of motivation at school* (pp. 55–76). New York: Routledge.

Wiggan, G. (2007). Race, school achievement, and educational inequality: Toward a student-based inquiry perspective. *Review of Educational Research, 77*(3), 310–333.

Wiles, J., Bondi, J., & Wiles, M. T. (2006). *The essential middle school* (4th ed.). Upper Saddle River, NJ: Pearson/Merrill Prentice Hall.

Williams, J. P., Lauer, K. D., Hall, K. M., Lord, K. M., Gugga, S. S., Bak, S-J., Jacobs, P. R., & deCani, J. S. (2002). Teaching elementary school students to identify story themes. *Journal of Educational Psychology, 94*(2), 235–248.

Willig, A. C. (1985). A meta-analysis of selected studies on the effectiveness of bilingual education. *Review of Educational Research, 55*(3), 269–318.

Willingham, D. (2008). When and how neuroscience applies to education. *Phi Delta Kappan, 89*(6), 421–423.

Willis, J. (2008). Building a bridge from neuroscience to the classroom. *Phi Delta Kappan, 89*(6), 424–427.

Willis, J. (Ed.). (2009). *Constructivist instructional design (C-ID): Foundations, models, and examples*. Charlotte, NC: Information Age Publishing.

Wilson, R. (2005). Targeted growth for every student. *Leadership, 35*(2), 8–12.

Wilson, S. M., Floden, R. E., & Ferrini-Mundy, J. (2002). Teacher preparation research: An insider's view from the outside. *Journal of Teacher Education, 53*(3), 190–204.

Windschitl, M. (2002). Framing constructivism in practice as the negotiation of dilemmas: An analysis of the conceptual, pedagogical, cultural, and political challenges facing teachers. *Review of Educational Research, 72*(2), 131–175.

Winkler, A. M. (2003). The power of the A word. *American School Board Journal, 190*(6), 22–24.

Winne, P. H. (2001). Self-regulated learning viewed from models of information processing. In B. J. Zimmerman & D. H. Schunk (Eds.), *Self-regulated learning and academic achievement: Theoretical perspectives* (2nd ed., pp. 153–189). Mahwah, NJ: Erlbaum.

Winne, P. H., & Jamieson-Noel, D. (2002). Exploring students' calibration of self reports about study tactics and achievement. *Contemporary Educational Psychology, 27*(4), 551–572.

Winne, P. H., & Jamieson-Noel, D. (2003). Self-regulating studying by objectives for learning: Students' reports compared to a model. *Contemporary Educational Psychology, 28*(3), 259–276.

Winne, P. H., & Stockley, D. B. (1998). Computing technologies as sites for developing self-regulated learning. In D. H. Schunk & B. J. Zimmerman (Eds.), *Self-regulated learning: From teaching to reflective practice* (pp. 107–136). New York: Guilford Press.

Winters, F. I., & Azevedo, R. (2005). High-school students' regulation of learning during computer-based science inquiry. *Journal of Educational Computing Research, 33*(2), 189–217.

Witkin, H. A., Moore, C. A., Goodenough, D. R., & Cox, P. W. (1977). Field-dependent and field-independent cognitive styles and their educational implications. *Review of Educational Research, 47*(1), 1–64.

Wittwer, J., & Renkl, A. (2008). Why instructional explanations often do not work: A framework for understanding the effectiveness of instructional explanations. *Educational Psychologist, 43*(1), 49–64.

Wlodkowski, R. J., & Ginsberg, M. B., (1995). A framework for culturally responsive teaching. *Educational Leadership, 53*(1), 17–21.

Wohldmann, E., Healy, A., & Bourne, L. (Jr.). (2008). Global inhibition and midcourse corrections in speeded aiming. *Memory & Cognition, 36*(7), 1228–1235.

Wong, B. Y. L. (1985). Self-questioning instructional research: A review. *Review of Educational Research, 55*(2), 227–268.

Woodhill, B. M., & Samuels, C. A. (2004). Desirable and undesirable androgyny: A prescription for the twenty-first century. *Journal of Gender Studies, 13*(1), 15–42.

Woods, P. (1996). *Researching the art of teaching: Ethnography for educational use*. New York: Routledge.

Woolfolk Hoy, A., & Weinstein, C. S. (2006). Student and teacher perspectives on classroom management. In C. M. Evertson & C. S. Weinstein (Eds.), *Handbook of classroom management: Research, practice, and contemporary issues* (pp. 181–219). Mahwah, NJ: Lawrence Erlbaum.

Wouters, P., Paas, F., & van Merriënboer, J. J. G. (2009). Observational learning from animated models: Effects of modality and reflection on transfer. *Contemporary Educational Psychology, 34*(1), 1–8.

Wright, R. J. (2008). *Educational assessment: Tests and measurements in the age of accountability*. Thousand Oaks, CA: SAGE.

Wuthrick, M. A. (1990). Blue jays win! Crows go down in defeat! *Phi Delta Kappan, 71*(7), 553–556.

Wynn, R. L., & Fletcher, C. (1987). Sex role development and early educational experiences. In D. B. Carter (Ed.), *Current conceptions of sex roles and sex typing*. New York: Praeger.

Yager, R. E. (2000). The constructivist learning model. *Science Teacher, 67*(1), 44–45.

Yamagata-Lynch, L. C., & Haudenschild, M. (2008). Teacher perception of barriers and aids of professional growth in professional development. *School-University Partnerships, 2*(2), 90–106.

Yamagata-Lynch, L. C., & Haudenschild, M. (2009). Using activity systems analysis to identify inner contradictions in teacher professional development. *Teaching and Teacher Education, 25*(3), 507–517.

Yang, S. C. (2001). Synergy of constructivism and hypermedia from three constructivist perspectives: Social, semiotic, and cognitive. *Journal of Educational Computing Research, 24*(4), 321–361.

Yang, S-H. (2009). Using blogs to enhance critical reflection and community of practice. *Educational Technology & Society, 12*(2), 11–21.

Yao, Y. (2006). Technology use as a scoring criterion. In C. Crawford, D. A. Willis, R. Carlsen, I. Gibson, K. McFerrin, J. Price, & R. Weber (Eds.), *Proceedings of the Society for Information Technology and Teacher Education International Conference 2006* (pp. 215–219). Chesapeake, VA: Association for the Advancement of Computing in Education.

Yates, F. A. (1966). *The art of memory*. London: Routledge & Kegan Paul.

Yau, R. (2002). High-achieving elementary schools with large percentages of low-income African American students: A review and critique of the current research. In S. J. Denbo & L. M. Beaulieu (Eds.), *Improving schools for African American students* (pp. 193–217). Springfield, IL: Charles C Thomas.

Yeh, S. S. (2006). Reforming federal testing policy to support teaching and learning. *Educational Policy, 20*(3), 495–524.

Yelland, N., & Masters, J. (2007). Rethinking scaffolding in the information age. *Computers & Education, 48*(3), 362–382.

Yilmaz-Tuzun, O. (2008). Preservice elementary teachers' beliefs about science teaching. *Journal of Science Teacher Education, 19*(2), 183–204.

Yoerg, K. (2002). Painting patterns with pixels. *Arts & Activities, 131*(4), 50–51.

Yonezawa, S., Wells, A. S., & Serna, I. (2002). Choosing tracks: "Freedom of choice" in detracking schools. *American Educational Research Journal, 39*(1), 37–67.

Ysseldyke, J. E., Algozzine, B., & Thurlow, M. L. (2000). *Critical issues in special education* (3rd ed.). Boston: Houghton Mifflin.

Ysseldyke, J., Kosciolek, S., Spicuzza, R., & Boys, C. (2003). Effects of a learning information system on mathematics achievement and classroom structure. *Journal of Educational Research, 96*(3), 163–173.

Zeichner, K. M., & Liston, D. P. (1996). *Reflective teaching: An introduction.* Mahwah, NJ: Erlbaum.

Zeldin, A. L., & Pajares, F. (2000). Against the odds: Self-efficacy beliefs of women in mathematical, scientific, and technological careers. *American Educational Research Journal, 37*(1), 215–246.

Zellermayer, M., Salomon, G., Globerson, T., & Givon, H. (1991). Enhancing writing-related metacognitions through a computerized writing partner. *American Educational Research Journal, 28*(2), 373–391.

Zhang, J., Scardamalia, M., Reeve, R., & Messina, R. (2009). Designs for collective cognitive responsibility in knowledge building communities. *Journal of the Learning Sciences, 18*(1), 7–44.

Zhang, L. (2005). Validating the theory of mental self-government in a non-academic setting. *Personality and Individual Differences, 38*(8), 1915–1925.

Zhang, L., & Sternberg, R. J. (2001). Thinking styles across cultures: Their relationships with student learning. In R. J. Sternberg & L.-F. Zhang (Eds.), *Perspectives on thinking, learning, and cognitive styles* (pp. 197–226). Mahwah, NJ: Erlbaum.

Zhang, L., & Sternberg, R. J. (2006). *The nature of intellectual styles.* Mahwah, NJ: Erlbaum.

Zhang, L., & Sternberg, R. J. (2009). Intellectual styles and creativity. In T. Rickards, M. Runko, & S. Moger (Eds.), *The Routledge companion to creativity* (pp. 256–266). New York: Routledge.

Zhao, Y., & Qiu, W. (2009). How good are the Asians? Refuting four myths about Asian-American academic achievement. *Phi Delta Kappan, 990*(5), 338–344.

Zhu, X., Chen, A., Ennis, C., Sun, H., Hopple, C., Bonello, M., Bae, M., & Kim, S. (2009). Situational interest, cognitive engagement, and achievement in physical education. *Contemporary Educational Psychology, 34*(3), 221–229.

Zhou, L. (2009). Revenues and expenditures for public elementary and secondary school districts: School year 2006–07 (NCES 2009-338). Washington, DC: National Center for Educational Statistics, Institute of Education Sciences, U.S. Department of Education. Retrieved from http://nces.ed.gov/pubsearch/pubsinfo.asp?pubid=2009338.

Zientek, L. R. (2007). Preparing high-quality teachers: Views from the classroom. *American Educational Research Journal, 44*(4), 959–1001.

Zimmerman, B. J. (1990). Self-regulating academic learning and achievement: The emergence of a social cognitive perspective. *Educational Psychology Review, 2*(2), 173–200.

Zimmerman, B. J. (2000). Attaining self-regulation: A social cognitive perspective. In M. Boekaerts, P. R. Pintrich, & M. Zeidner (Eds.), *Handbook of self-regulation* (pp. 13–39). San Diego: Academic Press.

Zimmerman, B. J. (2001). Theories of self-regulated learning and academic achievement: An overview and analysis. In B. J. Zimmerman & D. H. Schunk (Eds.), *Self-regulated learning and academic achievement: Theoretical perspectives* (pp. 1–37). Mahwah, NJ: Lawrence Erlbaum.

Zimmerman, B. J. (2002). Achieving self-regulation: the trial and triumph of adolescence. In F. Pajares & T. Urdan (Eds.), *Academic motivation of adolescents* (pp. 1–27). Greenwich, CT: Information Age Publishing.

Zimmerman, B. J. (2008). Investigating self-regulation and motivation: Historical background, methodological developments, and future prospects. *American Educational Research Journal, 45*(1), 166–183.

Zimmerman, B. J., & Kitsantas, A. (2002). Acquiring writing revision and self-regulatory skill through observation and emulation. *Journal of Educational Psychology, 94*(4), 660–668.

Zimmerman, B. J., & Kitsantas, A. (2005). The hidden dimension of personal competence: Self-regulated learning and practice. In A. J. Elliot and C. S. Dweck (Eds.), *Handbook of competence and motivation* (pp. 509–526). New York: Guilford Press.

Zinesky, A., & Sireci, S. G. (2002). Technological innovations in large-scale assessment. *Applied Measurement in Education, 15*(4), 337–362.

Zuo, L., & Cramond, B. (2001). An examination of Terman's gifted children from the theory of identity. *Gifted Children Quarterly, 45*(4), 251–259.

Glossary

A

accommodation The process of creating of revising a scheme to fit a new experience. (*See* **scheme**)

achievement batteries Sets of tests designed to assess performance in a broad range of subjects.

adaptation The process, described by Piaget, of creating a good fit or match between one's conception of reality and one's real-life experiences. (*See* **accommodation; assimilation**)

adolescent egocentrism The introspective, inward turning of a high school student's newly developed powers of thought, with a tendency to project one's self-analysis onto others. (*See* **egocentrism**)

adventure learning A type of learning wherein students might participate in real-life expeditions, virtual field trips, historical reenactments, and local adventures in their community, typically in structured activities with students from other schools.

affective domain taxonomy A classification of instructional outcomes that concentrates on attitudes and values.

aptitude tests Test intended to give educators some idea of the level of knowledge and skill a student could acquire with effective instruction.

assimilation The process of fitting new experience into an existing scheme. (*See* **scheme**)

assistive technology Any item, device, or piece of equipment, from low-tech equipment such as taped stories to more sophisticated technologies such as voice-recognition and speech-synthesis devices, that is used to increase, maintain, or improve the functional abilities of persons with disabilities.

attention The selective focusing on a portion of the information currently stored in the sensory register. (*See* **sensory register**)

attention-deficit/hyperactivity disorder (ADHD) A disorder that begins in childhood; is marked by abnormally high levels of impulsive behavior, distractibility, and motor activity; and leads to low levels of learning.

attribution theory A body of research into the ways that students explain their success or failure, usually in terms of ability, effort, task difficulty, and luck.

authentic assessment (*See* **performance assessments**)

authoritarian parents Parents who make demands and wield power without considering their children's point of view.

authoritative parents Parents who provide models of competence to be imitated, based on confidence in their own abilities.

B

behavior disorder (*See* **emotional disturbance**)

behavior modification The use of operant conditioning techniques to modify behavior, generally by making rewards contingent on certain action. Also called *contingency management*. (*See* **operant conditioning**)

between-class ability grouping Assigning students of similar learning ability to separate classes based on scores from standardized intelligence or achievement tests.

blogs An abbreviation of Weblogs, these are Web-based personal journals that are intended to create dialogue with others.

bullying A situation in which one person has more power than another and repeatedly abuses that power for his or her own benefit.

C

cognitive constructivism A form of constructivist learning theory that emphasizes the role of assimilation and accommodation in constructing an understanding of the world in which one lives. (*See* **accommodation; assimilation; constructivism**)

cognitive domain taxonomy A classification scheme of instructional outcomes that stresses knowledge and intellectual skills, including comprehension, application, analysis, synthesis, and evaluation. Also called *Bloom's taxonomy*.

collaborative learning Activities for which groups of learners use and combine their individual talents and areas of expertise to investigate problems, negotiate ideas, generate knowledge, and design products. (*See* **cooperative learning**)

competency test A test to determine a student's ability to handle basic subjects.

computer adaptive testing (CAT) A testing technique in which a computer program adapts the difficulty of questions to the ability level of the examinee based on her responses, thereby resulting in a reduction in test length and greater efficiency.

computer-based instruction (CBI) Teaching methods that use interactive software as an aid to learning.

concept mapping A technique for identifying and visually representing on paper the ideas that comprise a section of text and the ways in which they relate to each other.

consequential engagement Occurs when learners choose certain tools (a procedure or concept, for example) to understand and solve problems *and* when learners evaluate the effectiveness of the tools they have chosen.

conservation The recognition that certain properties stay the same despite a change in appearance or positions.

constructivism The view that meaningful learning is the active creation of knowledge structures rather than a mere transferring of objective knowledge from one person to another.

contingency contracting A behavior-strengthening technique that specifies desirable behaviors and consequent reinforcement.

cooperative learning An approach that uses small heterogeneous groups for purposes of mutual help in the mastery of specific tasks.

criterion-referenced grading A system in which grades are determined on the basis of whether each student has attained a defined standard of achievement or performance.

criterion-referenced tests Tests in which students are evaluated according to how well they have mastered specific objectives in various well-defined skill areas.

critical constructivism A form of constructivism that seeks (1) to understand why learners from some cultural and/or social groups more easily construct knowledge in school environments than others and (2) to facilitate the learning of students who experience difficulty in school environments so that all students can successfully construct knowledge.

cultural pluralism A set of tenets based on three principles: (1) every culture has its own internal coherence, integrity, and logic; (2) no culture is inherently better or worse than another; and (3) all persons are to some extent culture-bound.

culture A description of the ways a group of people perceives the world; formulates beliefs; evaluates objects, ideas, and experiences; and behaves.

cyberbullying Bullying on social networks in which one or more students post malicious statements about another student.

D

decentration The ability to think of more than one quality of an object or problem at a time. (*See* **perceptual centration**)

deficiency needs The first four levels (physiological, safety, belongingness or love, and esteem) in Maslow's hierarchy of needs, so called because these needs cause people to act only when they are unmet to some degree.

depression An emotional disorder characterized by self-deprecation, crying spells, and suicidal thoughts, afflicting between 7 and 28 percent of all adolescents.

diagnostic test A single-subject achievement test intended to identify the source of a problem in basic subjects and perhaps in study skills. (*See* **single-subject achievement test**)

direct instruction An approach to instruction that emphasizes the efficient acquisition of basic skills and subject matter through lectures and demonstrations, extensive practice, and corrective feedback.

discovery learning A teaching strategy that encourages children to seek solutions to problems either on their own or in group discussion.

discrimination A process in which individuals learn to notice the unique aspects of seemingly similar situations and thus learn different ways of responding.

distributed practice The practice of breaking up learning tasks into small, easy-to-manage pieces that are learned over several relatively brief sessions.

dual coding theory A theory of elaboration that states that concrete objects and words are remembered better than abstract information because they are coded in memory as both visual images and verbal labels, whereas abstract words are only encoded verbally.

E

early-maturing boy A boy whose early physical maturation typically draws favorable adult responses and promotes confidence and poise, thus contributing to leadership and popularity with peers. (*See* **late-maturing boy**)

early-maturing girl A girl whose early physical maturation typically makes her socially out of step with her peers. (*See* **late-maturing girl**)

educational psychology The branch of psychology that specializes in understanding how different factors affect the classroom behavior of both teachers and students.

egocentrism Difficulty in taking another person's point of view, a characteristic typical of young children.

elaborative rehearsal A process that consciously relates new information to knowledge already stored in long-term memory. Also called *elaborative encoding*. (*See* **long-term memory**)

emotional disturbance An emotional condition in which inappropriate aggressive or withdrawal behaviors are exhibited over a long period of time and to a marked degree, adversely affecting a child's educational performance.

empirical learning The use of noticeable characteristics of objects and events to form spontaneous concepts; a form of learning typical of young children.

epigenetic principle The notion that a child's personality develops as the ego progresses through a series of interrelated stages, much as the human body takes shape during its fetal development.

epistemological beliefs Refers to what learners believe about the nature of knowledge and how we come to know things.

equilibration The tendency to organize schemes to allow better understanding of experiences. (*See* **scheme**)

ethnic group A collection of people who identify with one another on the basis of such characteristics as ancestral origin, race, religion, language, values, political or economic interests, and behavior patterns.

evaluation In assessment, the use of a rule-governed system to make judgments about the value or worth of a set of measures.

exploratory environment Electronic environments that provide students with materials and resources to discover interesting phenomena and construct new insights; for example, computer simulations. Also called *discovery environments*. (*See* **discovery learning**)

extinction The weakening of a target behavior by ignoring it.

extrinsic motivation A form of incentive based on a system of rewards not inherent in a particular activity. (*See* **intrinsic motivation**)

F

far transfer The ability to use knowledge and skills learned at an earlier point in time in a particular context to help one learn new information or solve a problem in a very different context at a much later point in time.

field-dependent style A learning style in which a person's perception of and thinking about a task or problem are strongly influenced by such contextual factors as additional information and other people's behavior.

field-independent style A learning style in which a person's perception of and thinking about a task or problem are influenced more by the person's knowledge base than by the presence of additional information or other people's behavior

formative evaluation, or formative assessment A type of assessment that monitors an student's progress in order to facilitate learning rather than to assign a grade.

full inclusion The practice of eliminating pullout programs (those outside the classroom) and providing regular teachers with special training so as to keep special needs students in regular classrooms. Also called *inclusion*.

G

gender bias The tendency of teachers to respond differently to male and female students when there is no educationally sound reason for doing so.

gender roles Sets of behaviors typically identified with either males or females in a society; young children's awareness of these roles show up clearly in the different toys and activities that boys and girls prefer.

general objectives Objectives that use the three taxonomies (cognitive, affective, and psychomotor) to describe types of behavior that would demonstrate a student's learning. (*See* **affective domain taxonomy; cognitive domain taxonomy; and psychomotor domain taxonomy**)

general transfer A situation in which prior learning aids subsequent learning due to the use of similar cognitive strategies.

generalization The learned ability to respond in similar ways to similar stimuli.

gifted and talented A student who show unusual ability in any of a variety of ways and who may require services not ordinarily provided by his school

grade equivalent score A measurement that interprets test performance in terms of grade levels.

growth need A yearning for personal fulfillment that people constantly strive to satisfy. (*See* **self-actualization**)

growth spurt The rapid and uneven physical growth that besets adolescents during the middle school years.

guided learning environment Environments in which teachers, experts, or more knowledgeable peers support student inquiry by helping students set plans and goals, ask questions, discuss issues, solve problems, and reflect on strategies and solutions. Also called *guided discovery learning*. (*See* **constructivism**)

H

heuristics General approaches to solving problems, such as studying worked examples and breaking problems into parts, that can be applied to different subject areas.

high-road transfer A situation involving the conscious, controlled, somewhat effortful formulation of an "abstraction" (that is, a rule, a schema, a strategy, or an analogy) that allows a connection to be made between two tasks.

humanistic approach An approach to instruction that emphasizes the effect of student needs, values, motives, and self-perceptions on learning.

I

identity A relatively stable conception of where and how one fits into a society that is strongly influenced by the perception of one's physical appearance, the goals one established and achieves, and recognition from significant others in the environment.

identity statuses A style of approach that adolescents adopt to deal with such identity-related issues as career goal, gender-role orientation,

and religious beliefs. James Marcia identified four identity statues: identity diffusion, moratorium, foreclosure, and identity achievement.

ill-structured problems Vaguely stated problems with unclear solution procedures and vague evaluation standards. (*See* **well-structured problems**)

I-message A first-person statement by a teacher that emphasizes the teacher's feelings about a situation rather than her feeling about the students.

impulsive A learning style in which students respond relatively quickly to questions or tasks for which there is no obvious correct answer or solution.

inclusion An extension of the least restrictive environment provision of IDEA in which students with disabilities are placed in regular classrooms for the entire school day and receive some instruction and support from a special education teacher. (*See also* **full inclusion**)

individualized education program (IEP) A written statement describing an educational program designed to meet the unique needs of a child with a particular disability.

inert knowledge Information, typically memorized verbatim, that is unconnected, lacking in context, and not readily accessible for application to real-world tasks. (*See* **meaningful learning** and **situated learning**)

information-processing theory An area of study that seeks to understand how people acquire, store, and recall information and how their current knowledge guides and determines what and how they will learn.

instructional objectives Statements written by teachers that specify the knowledge and skills students should be able to exhibit after a unit of instruction.

integrated learning systems (ILS) Computer-based instructional systems that provide sequenced and self-paced learning activities to students in many different content areas as well as appropriate remediation or enrichment activities.

intellectual disability Previously referred to as mental retardation. Defined by the AAIDD as "…a disability characterized by significant limitations both in intellectual functioning and in adaptive behavior, which covers many everyday social and practical skills. This disability originates before the age of 18."

intelligence The ability of an individual to use a variety of cognitive and noncognitive capabilities to formulate goals, logically work toward achieving those goals, and adapt to the demands of the environment.

interpersonal reasoning The ability to understand the relationship between motives and behavior among a group of people.

intrinsic motivation A form of incentive inherent in a particular activity, such as the positive consequence of becoming more competent or knowledgeable. (See **extrinsic motivation**)

irreversibility The inability of a young child to mentally reverse physical or mental processes, such as pouring water from a tall, thin glass back into a short squat one.

issues Ill-structured problems that arouse strong feelings. (See **ill-structured problems**)

J

Joplin Plan An ability grouping technique that combines students of different grade levels according to their standardized test scores. (See **regrouping**)

L

late-maturing boy A boy whose delayed physical maturation typically causes inferiority feelings and leads to bossy and attention-getting behavior. (See **early-maturing boy**)

late-maturing girl A girl whose delayed physical maturation typically makes her more poised than others her age and elicits praise from elders, thus conferring leadership tendencies. (See **early-maturing girl**)

learner-centered education An educational philosophy in which the teacher helps guide students to construct knowledge meaningfully and monitor their own learning by emphasizing student choice, responsibility, challenge, intrinsic motivation, and ownership of the learning process.

learning disabilities Problems in otherwise mentally fit students who are unable to respond to certain aspects of the curriculum presented in regular classrooms because of disorders in one or more basic psychological processes.

learning strategy A general plan that a learner formulates for achieving a somewhat distant academic goal.

learning style A consistent tendency or preference to respond to a variety of intellectual tasks and problems in a particular fashion.

learning tactic A specific technique that a learner uses to accomplish an immediate learning objective.

least restrictive environment A requirement (under the 1994 Code of Federal Regulations governing the implementation of IDEA) that disabled children be provided with education in the least restrictive setting possible, usually by including them in regular classrooms. (See **mainstreaming**)

long-term memory (LTM) Storehouse of permanently recorded information in an individual's memory.

loss of voice The tendency of adolescent females to suppress their true beliefs about issues and with claims that they have no opinion or state what they think others want to hear because of socialization practices.

low-road transfer A situation in which a previously learned skill or idea is almost automatically retrieved from memory and applied to a highly similar current task. (See **high-road transfer**)

M

mainstreaming The policy of placing students with disabilities in regular classes.

maintenance rehearsal A rather mechanical process that uses mental and verbal repetition to hold information in short-term memory for some immediate purpose. Also called *rote rehearsal* or *repetition*. (See **short-term memory**)

massed practice An approach to learning that emphasizes a few long, infrequently spaced study periods.

mastery learning An approach that assumes most students can master the curriculum if certain conditions are established: (1) sufficient aptitude, (2) sufficient ability to understand instruction, (3) a willingness to persevere, (4) sufficient time, and (5) good-quality instruction.

meaningful learning Learning that occurs when new information or activities are made relevant by relating them to personal interests and prior experiences or knowledge.

measurement The assignment of numbers to certain attributes of objects, events, or people according to a rule-governed system.

melting pot A term referring to the assimilation of diverse ethnic groups into one national mainstream.

metacognition Knowledge about the operations of cognition and how to use them to achieve a learning goal.

microcomputer-based laboratories A microcomputer with attached sensors and probes that can quickly represent such data as temperature or speed in multiple ways in order to help students explore concepts, test hypotheses, and repair scientific misconceptions.

microworld A computer scenario intended to foster cognitive development and overcome misconceptions by allowing students the chance to explore relationships among variables tor concepts and build personal models of how things work.

mnemonic device A memory-directed tactic that helps a learner transform or organize information to enhance its retrievability.

morality of constraint Piaget's term for the moral thinking of children up to age ten or so, in which they hold sacred rules that permit no exceptions and make no allowance for intentions. Also called *moral realism*.

morality of cooperation Piaget's term for the moral thinking of children age eleven or older, based on flexible rules and considerations of intent. Also called *moral relativism*.

multicultural education An approach to learning and teaching that seeks to foster an understanding of and mutual respect for the values, beliefs, and practices of different cultural groups.

multidisciplinary assessment team A group of people involved in determining the nature of a child's disability, typically consisting of a school psychologist, guidance counselor, classroom teacher, school social worker, school nurse, learning disability specialist, physician, and psychiatrist.

multi-user virtual environments (MUVEs) Online virtual worlds in which several people work together to solve various types of problems, an example of which is Quest Atlantis.

near transfer The ability to use knowledge and skills learned at an earlier point in time in a particular context to help one learn new information or solve a problem in a very similar context and soon after the original learning.

negative reinforcement A way of strengthening a target behavior by removing an aversive stimulus after a particular behavior is exhibited. (*See* **positive reinforcement**)

negative transfer A situation in which one's prior learning interferes with subsequent learning. (*See* **positive transfer**)

normal curve The bell-shaped distribution of scores that tends to occur when a particular characteristic is measured in thousands of people.

norm group A sample of individuals carefully chosen to reflect the larger population of students for whom a test is intended.

norm-referenced grading A system of grading that assumes classroom achievement will vary among a group of heterogeneous students because of such differences as prior knowledge, learning skills, motivation, and aptitude, and so

compares the score of each student to the scores of other students in order to determine grades.

norm-referenced tests Tests in which individual performance is evaluated with reference to the performance of a norm group.

observational learning or modeling The part of the triadic reciprocal causation model of social cognitive theory that describes the role of observing and imitating the behavior of models in learning new capabilities.

operant conditioning The theory of behavior developed by B. F. Skinner, based on the fact that organisms respond to their environments in particular ways to obtain or avoid particular consequences.

organization The tendency to systematize and combine processes into coherent general systems.

peer tutoring An approach to learning that involves the teaching of one student by another, based on evidence that a child's cognitive growth benefits from exposure to alternative cognitive schemes.

percentile rank A score that indicates the percentage of students who are at or below a given student's achievement level, providing specific information about relative position.

perceptual centration The tendency to focus attention on only one characteristic of an object or aspect of a problem or event at a time.

performance assessments Assessment devices that attempt to gauge how well students can use basic knowledge and skill to perform complex tasks or solve problems under more or less realistic conditions. Also called *performance-based assessment* and *authentic assessment*.

permissive parents Parents who make few demands on their children and fail to discourage immature behavior, thus reflecting their own tendency to be disorganized, inconsistent, and lacking in confidence.

personal agency The idea that people rather than environmental forces are the primary cause of their own behavior.

portfolio A collection of one or more pieces of a person's work, some of which typically demonstrate different stages of completion.

positive reinforcement A way of strengthening a target behavior (increasing and maintaining the probability that a particular behavior will be repeated) by supplying a positive stimulus immediately after a desired response. (*See* **negative reinforcement**)

positive transfer A situation in which prior learning aids subsequent learning, when, for example, a new learning task calls for essentially the same response that was made to a similar earlier-learned task. (*See* **negative transfer**)

Premack principle A shaping technique that allows students to indulge in a favorite activity after completing a set of instructional objectives. Also called *Grandma's rule*. (*See* **shaping**)

problem representation or problem framing The process of finding ways to express a problem so as to recall the optimal amount of solution-relevant information from long-term memory. (*See* **long-term memory**)

problem solving The identification and application of knowledge and skills that result in goal attainment.

problem-based learning (PBL) An instructional method that requires learners to develop solutions to authentic and complex problems through problem analysis, hypothesis generation, collaboration, reflection, and extensive teacher coaching and facilitation.

psychological androgyny An acquired sense of gender that combines traditional masculine and feminine traits.

psychomotor domain taxonomy A classification of instructional outcomes that focuses on physical abilities and skills.

psychosocial moratorium A period of identity development marked by a delay of commitment, ideally a time of adventure and exploration having a positive, or at least neutral, impact on the individual and society.

punishment A method of weakening a target behavior by presenting an aversive stimulus after the behavior occurs.

R

recognition A cognitive process that involves noting key features of a stimulus and relating them to previously stored information in an interactive manner.

reflective A learning style in which students collect and analyze information before offering an answer to a question or a solution to a problem.

reflective teaching A way of teaching that blends artistic and scientific elements through thoughtful analysis of classroom activity.

regrouping A form of ability grouping that brings together students of the same age ability, and grade but from different classrooms, for instruction in a specific subject, usually reading or mathematics.

rejecting-neglecting parents Parents who make no demands on their children, provide no structure at home, and do not support their children's goals, activities, and emotional needs.

reliability Consistency in test results, related to the assumption that human characteristics are relatively stable over short periods of time.

response cost The withdrawal of previously earned positive reinforcers as a consequence of undesirable behavior, often used with a token economy. (*See* **token economy**)

Response to Intervention (RTI) A diagnostic technique that assesses how well students respond to instructional interventions in order to identify the type of instruction and special education services that students require to succeed.

ripple effect The extent to which an entire class responds to a reprimand directed at only one student.

role confusion Uncertainty as to what behaviors will elicit a favorable reaction from others.

rubric A scoring guide used in performance assessment that helps define and clarify levels of student performance from poor to exemplary.

S

scaffolding Supporting learning during its early phases through such techniques as demonstrating how tasks should be accomplished, giving hints to the correct solution to a problem or answer to a question, and providing leading questions. As students become more capable of working independently, these supports are withdrawn.

schemata Plural of *schema*, an abstract information structure by which our store of knowledge is organized in long-term memory. *Schemas* is another plural form. (*See* **long-term memory**)

scheme An organized pattern of behavior or thought that children formulate as they interact with their environment, parents, teachers, and agemates.

scholastic aptitude The cognitive skills that most directly relate to and best predict the ability to cope with academic demands. Often used as a synonym for *intelligence*.

scientific concepts A term coined by Russian psychologist Lev Vygotsky to denote such psychological tools as language, formulas, rules, and symbols that are learned mostly with the aid of formal instruction.

self-actualization The movement toward full development of a person's potential talents and capabilities.

self-concept The evaluative judgments people make of themselves in specific areas, such as academic performance, social interactions, athletic performance, and physical appearance.

self-description The way people describe themselves to others, using statements that are largely nonevaluative.

self-efficacy The degree to which people believe they are capable or prepared to handle particular tasks.

self-esteem The overall or general evaluation people make of themselves. Also called *self-worth*.

self-image A mental self-portrait composed of a self-description, self-esteem, and self-concept. (See **self-concept; self-description; self-esteem**)

self-regulated learning The conscious and purposeful use of one's cognitive skills, feelings, and actions to maximize the learning of knowledge and skills for a given task and set of conditions.

self-reinforcement A situation in which the individual strives to meet personal standards and does not depend on or care about the reactions of others.

sensory register (SR) The primary memory store that records temporarily (for one to three seconds) an incoming flow of data from the sense receptors.

serial position effect The tendency to learn and remember words at the beginning and end of a list more easily than those in the middle.

sexually transmitted diseases (STDs) Contagious diseases, such as HIV/AIDS, gonorrhea, and herpes, that are spread by sexual contact.

shaping Promoting the learning of complex behaviors by reinforcing successive approximations to the terminal behavior.

short-term memory (STM) The second temporary memory store, which holds about seven bits of information for about twenty seconds. Also called *working memory*.

single-subject achievement test A test designed to assess learning or achievement in a particular basic school subject, such as reading or mathematics.

situated learning The idea that problem-solving skills, cognitive strategies, and knowledge are closely linked to the specific context or environment in which they are acquired; hence, the more authentic, or true to life, the task, the more meaningful the learning. Also called *situated cognition*. (See **inert knowledge**)

social class An individual's or a family's relative standing in society, determined by such factors as income, occupation, education, place of residence, types of associations, manner of dress, and material possessions.

social cognitive theory An explanation of how people learn to become self-regulated learners through the interactive effects of their personal characteristics, behaviors, and social reinforcement. (*See* **triadic reciprocal causation**)

social constructivism A form of constructivist learning theory that emphasizes how people use such cultural tools as language, mathematics, and approaches to problem solving in social settings to construct a common or shared understanding of the world in which they live. (*See* **constructivism**)

socioeconomic status (SES) A quantifiable level of social standing, determined by the federal government on the basis of a person's income, occupation, and eduction. (*See* **social class**)

special-purpose achievement test A test to determine specific qualifications, such as the College-Level Examination Program or the National Teacher Examination.

specific objectives Objectives that specify the behavior to be learned, the conditions under which it will be exhibited, and the criterion for acceptable performance.

specific transfer A situation in which prior learning aids subsequent learning because of specific similarities between two tasks.

spontaneous concepts A term coined by Russian psychologist Lev Vygotsky to denote the facts, concepts, and rules that young children acquire as a natural consequence of engaging in everyday activities.

spontaneous recovery The reappearance of a seemingly extinguished behavior. (*See* **extinction**)

standard deviation A statistic that indicates the degree to which scores in a group of tests differ from the average or mean.

standardized tests Assessment tools designed by people with specialized knowledge and applied to all students under the same conditions.

stanine score A statistic reflecting a division of a score distribution into nine groups, with each stanine being one-half of a standard deviation unit.

styles of mental self-government A theory of learning style formulated by Robert Sternberg that is based on the different functions and forms of civil government. The theory describes thirteen styles that can vary in terms of function, form, level, scope, and learning.

summative assessment Testing done for the purpose of assigning a letter or numerical grade to sum up a student's performance at a variety of tasks over time.

T

table of specifications A table used in exam preparation that notes types of numbers of included test items, ensuring systematic coverage of the subject matter.

taxonomy A classification scheme with categories arranged in hierarchical order.

teacher expectancy effect The tendency of students to behave in ways they think the teacher expects them to behave. Also called *self-fulfilling prophecy; Pygmalion effect.*

teaching as an art A way of teaching that involves intangibles such as emotions, values, and flexibility.

teaching as a science A way of teaching based on scientific methods such as sampling, control, objectivity, publication, and replication.

technology-enhanced instruction Teaching methods that use interactive software as an aid to learning. Also known as *computer-based instruction.*

telementoring The use of networking technologies by experts, mentors, instructors, and peers to demonstrate ideas, pose questions, offer insights, and provide relevant information that can help learners build new knowledge and effectively participate in a learning community.

theoretical learning Learning how to use psychological tools across a range of settings and problem types to acquire new knowledge and skills.

theory of identical elements The theory that a similarity between the stimulus and response elements in two different tasks accounts for transfer of learning from one task to the other. (*See* **transfer of learning**)

theory of mind The ability, typically developed by children around the age of four, to be aware of the difference between thinking about something and experiencing that same thing and to predict the thoughts of others.

theory of multiple intelligences A theory formulated by Howard Gardner that describes intelligence as being composed of eight, mostly independent capabilities.

time-out A procedure that weakens a target behavior by temporarily removing the opportunity for the behavior to be rewarded.

token economy A behavior-strengthening technique that uses items of no inherent value to "purchase" other items perceived to be valuable.

transfer of learning A student's ability to apply knowledge and problem-solving skills learned in school to similar but new situations.

triadic reciprocal causation The conceptual foundation of social cognitive theory, which specifies that learned capabilities are the product of interactions among an individual's personal characteristics, behaviors, and social environment. (*See* **social cognitive theory**)

triadic theory of intelligence A theory formulated by Robert Sternberg that describes intelligence as being composed of practical, creative, and analytical components.

T score A standardized test score that ranges from 0 to 100 and uses a preselected mean of 50 to avoid negative values. (*See* **z score**)

twice exceptional Students who are exceptional because they are both gifted and talented and challenged in some physical, social, emotional, or cognitive way.

two-way bilingual (TWB) education An approach to bilingual education in which instruction is provided to all students in both the minority language and the majority language. Also called *bilingual immersion* or *dual language*.

universal design for learning An approach to classroom instruction that seeks to eliminate the barriers to learning for all students no matter what challenges they bring with them to school.

validity The extent to which a test measures what it claims to measure.

vicarious reinforcement A situation in which the observer anticipates receiving a reward for behaving in a given way because someone else has been so rewarded.

Web 2.0 Social networking websites such as Facebook, Twitter, Flickr, and LinkedIn that include such tools as blogs, podcasts, and videos.

well-structured problems Clearly formulated problems with known solution procedures and known evaluation standards. (*See* **ill-structured problems**)

within-class ability grouping A form of ability grouping that involves the division of a single class of students into two or three groups for reading and math instruction.

withitness An attribute of teachers who prove to their students that they know what is going on in a classroom and as a result have fewer discipline problems than teachers who lack this characteristic.

zero transfer A situation in which prior learning has no effect on new learning.

zone of proximal development (ZPD) Vygotsky's term for the difference between what a child can do on his or her own and what can be accomplished with some assistance.

z score A standardized test score that tells how far a given raw score differs from the mean in standard deviation units. (*See* **T score**)

Credits

This page constitutes an extension of the copyright page. We have made every effort to trace the ownership of all copyrighted material and to secure permission from copyright holders. In the event of any question arising as to the use of any material, we will be pleased to make the necessary corrections in future printings. Thanks are due to the following authors, publishers, and agents for permission to use the material indicated.

Chapter 1. 13: Matthew Kay, "Teaching without a Script" from *The New York Times*, September 14, 2008. Copyright © 2008 The New York Times Co. Reprinted by permission.

Chapter 2. 64: Carolyn Bower, "Reading, Writing and Character Education" from *St. Louis Post Dispatch*, November 28, 2003. Reprinted by permission of St. Louis Post-Dispatch.

Chapter 3. 96: Carolyn Bower, "Middle Ground" from *St. Louis Post-Dispatch*, May 29, 2002. Reprinted by permission of St. Louis Post-Dispatch.

Chapter 4. 134: Associated Press, "Gender still hinders women scientists" as appeared in *The Washington Post*, September 18, 2006. Reprinted by permission of Associated Press.

Chapter 5. 145: Theresa Tighe, "Melting Pot seems to be working fine at this school" from *St. Louis Post-Dispatch*, October 20, 2006. Reprinted by permission of St. Louis Post-Dispatch.

Chapter 6. 194: Linda Perlstein, "Study Finds Special Ed Disparities" from *The Washington Post*, December 18, 2003. Copyright © 2003 The Washington Post. Reprinted by permission.

Chapter 7. 238: "Attendance Prize: schools offer kids big rewards just to get them to show up" Associated Press, December 1, 2006. Reprinted by permission of Associated Press.

Chapter 8. 268: Andrew Chung, "This is harder than we thought: Using our imagination can be pleasant and produce great things. It's just not that easy to do" from *Toronto Star*, April 23, 2006. Reprinted with permission-Torstar Syndication Services.

Chapter 9. 281: The Triadic Reciprocal Causation Model, from A. Bandura, *Self-Efficacy: The exercise of control* (New York: W.H. Freeman, 1997). Reprinted by permission. **296:** From King, A. (1992b). Facilitating elaborative learning through guided student-generated questioning, *Educational Psychologist*, 27(1), 111–126. Reprinted by permission of Taylor & Francis. **301:** Fredreka Schouten, "Students Unprepared for Rigors of College" from *USA Today*, October 30, 2003. Reprinted by permission of USA Today.

Chapter 10. 336: Steve Lohr, "At School, Technology Starts to Turn a Corner" from *The New York Times* (nytimes.com), August 17, 2008. Copyright © 2008 The New York Times Co. Reprinted by permission. **352:** Excerpts and diagrams in this section are from "Solution Using Venn Diagram," adapted from A. Whimbey and J. Lochhead, *Problem Solving and Comprehension*, Sixth Edition (Mahwah, NJ: Lawrence Erlbaum Associates, Inc., Publishers), pp. 104, 128. © 1999, reprinted by permission of Taylor & Francis.

Chapter 11. 381: Craig Chamberlain, "Program Aims to Make Reading Easier, More Fun, for Children in China." News Bureau, University of Illinois, 10/18/06. Reprinted by permission. **394:** 1 figure from "Relationship Between Academic Self-Concept and Achievement" adapted from F. Guay, H. Marsh, and Bovin, "Academic self-concept and academic achievement: Developmental perspectives on their causal ordering" in *Journal of Educational Psychology*, 95(1), pp. 124–136. Used by permission of American Psychological Association.

Chapter 12. 431: Valerie Schremp Hahn, "To Teach Good Behavior, Schools Try More Carrots and Fewer Sticks" from *St. Louis Post-Dispatch*, December 18, 2008. Reprinted by permission of St. Louis Post-Dispatch.

Chapter 13. 454: Christine Byers, "Geology Teacher Finds Creative Ways to Keep Students Engaged" from *St. Louis Post-Dispatch*, March 23, 2007. Reprinted by permission of St. Louis Post-Dispatch.

Chapter 14. 487: Moss, C. & Brookhart, S. (2009). *Advancing formative assessment in every classroom: A guide for instructional leaders*. Alexandria, VA: ASCD. **497:** Scoring Rubric for a Group Oral Presentation from K. Montgomery, "Classroom Rubrics: Systematizing what teachers do naturally," *The Clearing House*, 73(6), 2000, pp. 324–328. Reprinted by permission of Taylor & Francis. **499:** Amy Hetzner, "Remote Tracking: Teachers Click in Quickly on Students' Performance" from *Milwaukee Journal Sentinel*, April 22, 2006. Copyright © 2006. Reprinted by permission. **510:** From "Computerized Gradebooks and the Myth of Objectivity" by Thomas R. Guskey, *Phi Delta Kappan*, 83(10), 2002, pp. 775–780. Reprinted with permission of the author.

Chapter 15. 543: Valerie Schremp Hahn and Corinne Lestch, "Incentives Are All Over the MAP" from *St. Louis Post-Dispatch*, April 8, 2009. Reprinted by permission of St. Louis Post-Dispatch.

Chapter 16. 563: "Examples of Classroom Observation Checklists" from L.Schmidt, "Getting smarter about supervising instruction," *Principal*, 82(4), 2003, pp. 24–28. Reprinted with permission. Copyright 2003 National Association of Elementary School Principals. All rights reserved. **571:** 2009 Class of National Board Certified Teachers Advances Nation's School Reform Movement National Board for Professional Teaching Standards Arlington, VA—December 16, 2009. Reprinted with permission from the National Board for Professional Teaching Standards, www.nbpts.org. All rights reserved.

A

Abedi, J., 538
Aber, J. L., 34, 435
Abma, J. C., 99
Abrami, P. C., 186, 436, 478
Abrams, L., 539, 540
Adams, G. R., 4289
Adelson, J., 104
Adesope, O. O., 297
Adey, P. S., 44
Adkins, D., 548
Ageyev, Vladimir, 71
Ahmetoglu, G., 112
Airasian, E., 486, 503
Airasian, P. W., 442
Akaran, S. E., 169
Akram, S., 55, 360, 388
Alagic, M., 273
Alajaaski, J., 123
Alasker, F. D., 87
Alavi, M., 55
Alberto, P. A., 235, 239, 245, 248
Alessi, S. M., 54
Alexander, B., 105
Alexander, P., 290, 311
Alexander, P. A., 298
Alfassi, M., 310
Algozzine, B., 189, 432, 433
Algozzine, R., 212
Allegreto, S. A., 3
Alleman, Janet, 16
Allen, L., 34
Allen, N., 169, 479
Allender, D. S., 464
Allender, J. S., 464
Allensworth, E., 332
Allington, R., 547
Allison, B. N., 32
Alona, R., 103
Alper, T., 220
American Association of University
   Women, 130
American Association on Intellectual and
   Developmental Disabilities, 198
American Educational Research
   Association, 6, 539
American Psychiatric Association, 101, 205
American Psychological Association (APA),
   2, 4
Ames, C., 471, 472
Ames, R., 471, 472
Amiram, R., 103
Anastasiow, N. J., 191, 200, 213, 223
Anderman, E. M., 63
Anderman, L. H., 468, 469
Anderson, G. E., 7
Anderson, Julie, 24, 575
Anderson, L. W., 442, 547
Anderson, R. E., 562
Anderson-Patton, V., 568
Andrade, A., 114
Andrade, Heidi, 520
Angold, A., 101
Antil, L. R., 476
Anyon, J., 34
Aplin, C., 218
Applebee, A. N., 186, 339
Appleby, J., 15, 575
Appleton, N., 172, 173
Arbuthnot, K., 127, 541
Archer, S. L., 31
Armstrong, J., 234
Armstrong, T., 120, 121, 137
Arnett, J. J., 63
Arnold, M. L., 60
Arsenault, L., 427

Arter, J., 485, 496
Artiles, A. J., 191
Ash, C., 436
Ash, K., 156
Ashton, P., 34
Assor, A., 11
Assouline, S., 214
Astington, J. W., 77, 78
Atkinson, R. C., 251, 294
Au, W., 546, 547
Audette, R., 432
Ausubel, D. P., 256, 330, 351
Azevedo, R., 270, 287, 290, 312, 316, 318,
   321, 330, 359, 462

B

Bachman, L. F., 501
Baddeley, Alan, 277
Bae, M., 378
Bae, Y., 131, 132
Baguley, M., 54
Bailey, S. M., 133, 137
Bak, S.-J., 67
Baker, E. L., 540
Baker, J. A., 470
Baker, S., 204
Ball, A. F., 18, 569
Ban, Ruth, 180
Bandura, A., 97, 279, 280, 282, 283, 303,
   324, 370
Bangert-Drowns, R. L., 167, 245
Banks, J. A., 142, 149, 163, 168, 171, 180
Barab, S., 55, 56, 274, 360, 361, 362, 388
Barbrow, D., 234
Bardige, Betty, 71
Bargh, J. A., 158
Barnett, D., 192
Barret, H. C., 512
Barros, R. M., 80
Bar-Tal, D., 103
Bartlet, Sir Frederick, 261
Barton, P. E., 154, 155
Bass, E., 568
Bates, A., 398
Battle, A., 128, 131, 132
Bauer, A. M., 415
Baum, K., 425, 426, 428
Baumrind, D., 79, 100, 240
Baylor, A. L., 267, 310
Bean, T. W., 18
Bear, G. G., 468
Beatty, I., 510, 512
Bebeau, M. J., 60, 71
Bee, H. L., 108
Beghetto, R., 369
Beighley, C., 548
Beilin, Harry, 71
Beirne-Smith, Mary, 223
Beiser, M., 101
Beishuizen, J. J., 299
Beisser, S., 123
Bell, L. I., 153
Bellanca, James, 325
Bellezza, F. S., 293, 294
Bellocchi, A., 357
Belsky, J., 460, 468, 540
Benbow, C. P., 214
Bender, William, 223
Bender Sebring, P., 332
Ben-Hur, M., 155
Benjamin, A., 111, 141, 215
Benner, A. D., 158
Bennett, C. I., 149, 150, 163, 167, 189
Bennett, L., 18, 105
Benoit, D. A., 236
Beran, T., 427

Bergen, D., 75, 85
Bergin, D., 373
Berk, L. E., 74, 75, 84, 85
Berliner, D. C., 2, 3, 6, 8, 23, 38, 330, 501,
   540, 541, 542, 547, 549
Bernard, R. M., 436
Bernard Powers, J., 135
Berne, J., 398
Berry, B., 6
Berry, E. H., 99
Bers, A., 35
Berson, I. R., 105
Berthelot, J., 291
Bertrando, Robert, 325
Bianco, K., 7, 155, 173, 435
Bielefeldt, T., 233
Biemiller, A., 111
Biesta, Gert, 15
Biggs, J., 310
Bigler, R. S., 76
Billig, S. H., 173, 479
Binet, Alfred, 112, 113
Bjork, R. A., 254, 264, 277, 290
Bjorklund, D. F., 108, 528
Blachowicz, C., 398
Black, A. C., 125
Blanchett, W. J., 190, 192, 194
Block, J. H., 167
Blok, H., 233
Bloom, B. S., 314, 421, 442, 443, 444,
   505
Bloom, L. A., 420
Bloomquist, M. L., 205, 427, 428, 429
Bocala, C., 192
Bock, J., 547
Boekaerts, M., 324
Boekarts, M., 464
Boersma, K., 105
Bohman, J., 333
Bohn, C. M., 80
Bolick, C. M., 412
Bond, C. L., 271, 290
Bondi, J., 94, 108
Bondy, E., 17, 409, 415
Bonello, M., 378
Bong, M., 321
Boniecki, K. A., 236
Bonk, C. J., 55
Boothe, B., 34
Borich, G., 190, 197, 501, 505, 521, 526
Borja, R. R., 551
Bornstein, M. H., 89, 90, 100
Borokhovski, E., 436
Borthick, A. F., 55
Borthwick-Duffy, S., 199
Bourgeois, M. J, 33, 34
Bourne, L., Jr., 355
Bowen, N. K., 153, 155
Bower, Carolyn, 96
Bower, G. H., 255, 256, 265
Bowes, L., 427
Bowman, D. H., 205
Boyd, D., 108
Boyer, E. L., 181
Boykin, A. W., 167
Boys, C., 451
Braaksma, M. A. H., 309
Bradley, V., 199
Bradshaw, C. P., 427
Branch, C. W., 34
Branning, P., 251
Bransford, J. D., 51
Bråten, I., 306
Braun, B., 34
Braun, H. I., 533
Bray, M. A., 237

Brayboy, B. M. J., 149, 150, 155, 163, 164,
   167, 168, 173
Bremer, C. D., 5
Brendgen, M., 409
Brengelman, S. U., 19
Brickman, S., 345, 376, 377
Bridgman, T., 398
Briesch, A., 409
Briesch, S., 3, 409
Brimijoin, K., 111, 188, 215
Brinthaupt, T. M., 94
Brobst, K. E., 271, 290
Broekkamp, H., 291, 297, 299
Brookhart, S. M., 18, 485, 486, 488, 501,
   504, 506, 520, 521, 560, 569
Brooks, J. G., 8, 38, 332
Brooks, M. G., 8, 38
Brooks, T., 551
Brooks-Gunn, J., 89, 101, 102
Brophy, J. E., 16, 44, 161
Brouwer, N., 5
Browder, D., 191
Brown, A. L., 108, 271, 310, 333, 341
Brown, C., 379
Brown, D. F., 459
Brown, J. L., 435
Brown, Raymond, 343
Brown, S. M., 553, 575
Bruner, Jerome, 351
Bruning, R. H., 261, 277
Brunstein, J. C., 267, 308
Brush, T., 234, 320
Bryant, D. P., 204
Bryk, A., 332
Bucher, A. A., 303
Buese, D., 547, 558
Bukatko, D., 76, 84
Bukowski, W. M., 100, 409
Bull, G., 105
Bullmore, E., 251
Buntinx, W., 199
Bunz, U., 135, 136
Burch, C. B., 2
Burchinal, M. R., 79
Burns, L., 220
Burns, R. B., 167
Burris, C. C., 157, 188
Burtch, J. A., 105
Burton, D., 331
Bushrod, G., 239
Butler, A. C., 290
Butler, R., 78, 79
Butlthoff, H., 258
Buunk, A. P., 288
Byers, Christine, 454
Byers, G. O., 272

C

Cable, G. W., 265
Caccamise, D., 319
Cadle, C., 234
Cagiltay, K., 379
Caine, Geoffrey, 342
Caine, Renate Nummela, 342
Calandra, B., 178
Calderón, M. E., 174
Calfee, R., 492
Callahan, C. M., 213
Callahan, R. M., 186, 341
Callender, A. A., 290, 292
Camilli, G., 541
Camp, C., 218
Campbell, J., 569
Campbell, L., 121
Campione, J. C., 271
Canivez, G. L., 114

Cardon, P. L., 435, 436
Cardwell, K., 510
Carnevale, D., 550
Carney, J. V., 427
Carney, R. N., 293, 294
Carnine, Douglas, 223
Carpenter, D., 7, 148, 153
Carper, L. B., 236
Carroll, A., 205
Carroll, J. B., 505
Carter, C. J., 310
Carter, D. B., 76
Carter, K., 420
Casanova, Ursula, 3, 23
Case, R., 44, 45
Casella, N., 346
Caspi, A., 427
Cassady, J. C., 234
Castagno, A. E., 149, 150, 155, 163, 164,
    167, 168, 173
Castañeda, Martha, 180
Cauffman, E., 63
Cennamo, Katherine, 24
Center for Applied Linguistics, 175
Center for Applied Special Technology,
    218
Center for Effective Discipline, 241
Center on Education Policy, 538, 545,
    547, 549
Centers for Disease Control and
    Prevention, 98, 99, 101, 102
Cepeda, N., 264
Cesareni, D., 479
Chamberlain, Craig, 381
Chambers, B., 185, 186
Chan, Y., 128
Chance, P., 242, 243
Chaney, E., 551
Chaney, J., 398
Chang, C.-C., 493
Chang, T.-S., 272
Chapman, C., 135
Chapman, E., 552
Chapman, S., 295
Chappuis, J., 485, 496
Chappuis, S., 485
Chase, K., 424
Chase, W. G., 264
Chavajay, P., 45, 46
Chen, A., 378
Chen, J. A., 375
Chen, J.-Q., 119, 120
Chen, M., 158
Cheng, J., 130
Cheung, A., 177
Chi, M. T. H., 167, 354
Chinn, P. C., 142, 149, 162, 163
Chizhik, Alexander, 477
Cho, H., 99
Choate, Joyce S., 223
Choi, H.-J., 321
Choi, I., 344
Choy, S., 131, 132
Christal, M., 169, 479
Christensen, K. W., 435, 436
Christensen, T., 56, 360, 362
Christie, M. T., 462
Chrostowski, S. J., 129
Chudowsky, N., 538, 547
Chudowsky, V., 538, 547
Chung, Andrew, 268–269
Cicchetti, D., 102
Cizek, G. J., 520, 539, 540, 545
Clark, E., 237
Clark, J. M., 258
Clark, M. C., 255, 256, 265
Clark, R. E., 494
Clarke, L., 463
Clarke, M., 539, 540
Clawson, M. A., 79
Clements, D. H., 462
Clements, P., 94
Coburn, N., 264

Cochran-Smith, M., 3, 4, 541
Cohen, J., 426, 427
Cohen, R., 55
Colangelo, N., 212, 223
Colarossi, L. G., 90, 92, 103, 109
Cole, J. M., 170, 373
Cole, J. M.,
Cole, M., 49, 332
Coleman, M. R., 200, 213, 223
Coley, R. J., 154, 155
Collier, V. P., 174
Collins, Cathy, 481
Collins, S., 311, 367
Comfort, M., 161
Commission on Instructionally Supportive
    Assessment, 549
Compas, B. E., 101, 102
Compton, M., 218
Compton-Lilly, C., 127
Conezio, J., 260
Conger, J. J., 101
Conner, B. T., 427
Connor, D. F., 205, 427, 428
Conti-D'Antonio, Marcia, 325
Cooper, H., 156, 161
Cooper, J. M., 412
Coppola, E., 547
Corbett, C., 130, 131, 132
Corcoran, Allegreto, 3
Corcoran, S. P., 3
Cornelius-White, J., 470
Cornford, I., 569
Corno, L., 9, 312, 316
Cornoldi, C., 355, 356
Cortez, J. D., 174
Costa, Arthur, 324
Costello, E. J., 101
Cothran, J. C., 258
Cotterall, S., 55
Coulter, D., 199
Couzijn, M., 309
Covington, M. V., 369, 370, 471
Cowan, N., 255
Cowan, Philip, 240
Cowan, Thaddeus, 277
Cowart, E., 272
Cox, K. E., 461
Cox, P. D., 307
Cox, P. W., 124, 125
Crafter, B., 7
Craig, E., 199
Craig, S., 354
Crain, W., 44, 51
Cramer, P., 33
Cramond, B., 213
Craven, R. G., 87, 215
Crawford, Glenda Beamon, 438
Crismond, D., 359, 365, 459, 461, 463
Crocco, M., 135
Cronin, J., 548
Crowley, E., 291
Cruikshank, K. A., 442
Cummins, J., 177
Cunningham, D. J., 329, 492
Cury, F., 376
Cushman, Kathleen, 438

D
Da Fonseca, D., 376
D'Agostino, J. V., 6
Dahlin, M., 548
Dai, D. Y., 87
Daiute, C., 55
Dalgliesh, L., 103
Daly, E., III, 192
Damon, William, 71
D'Amore, M., 272
Daniel, D. B., 8
Dansereau, D. F., 297
d'Apollonia, S., 186, 478
Dardig, J. C., 189
Darling-Hammond, L., 6, 7, 540, 549, 560
Dasen, P., 45

Davey, Tim, 558
Davidson, M., 434
Davis, C. L., 80
Davis, G. A., 186, 212
Davis, Gary, 223
Davis, M. L., 219
Davis, M. R., 436
Davis, S. H., 8
Davison, Janet E., 223
Dawson, K. M., 273
Day, J. D., 271
DeBaryshe, B. D., 87
DeBell, M., 135
deBettencourt, L. U., 183
DeBlois, R., 440
deCani, J. S., 67
De Groot, Elizabeth, 402
De Jong, T., 186, 475
Del Castillo, K., 34
DeLeone, C., 220
Delgarno, B., 457, 459, 461, 462
De Lisi, R., 55, 141
Delli, L., 18
Dempsey, K., 329
Dempster, Frank, 264
DeNavas-Walt, C., 152
Deneen, C., 524
Deneen, J., 524
Denessen, E., 474
Denbo, S. J., 153, 157
Derby, K. M., 102, 236
DeRose, L. M., 89
Derry, S. J., 261
Derzon, J., 432
Devine, J., 426, 427
De Vries, B., 105
DeVries, R., 40
DiCerbo, K. E., 174, 176, 177
Dietel, R., 538
Dijkstra, P., 288
Dill, E. M., 167
Dingus, A. E. M., 240
Dinkes, R., 7, 155, 173, 425, 426, 428,
    435
DiPerna, J., 7
Dobbs, M., 549
Dochy, F., 329
Dodge, T., 361
Doherty-Poirer, M., 429
Donahue, P., 153
Donis, K., 114
Donovan, C. A., 55
Doobay, A., 214
Dooley, S., 319
Doppelt, Y., 123, 398
Dornbusch, S. M., 184
Dorr, N., 156
Doty, D. E., 272
Dowd, J., 15, 24, 565, 575
Downing, S. M., 490
Dowson, M., 367
Doyle, W., 253, 420
Doyle-Nichols, A., 568, 575
Drake, F. D., 568
Drew, C., 213
Drew, Clifford, 200
Drier, H. S., 54, 273
Driscoll, M. P., 50, 253, 257, 331
Ducher, J., 178
Duckworth, Angela, 130
Duell, O. K., 270, 306
Duff, C., 56
Duffrin, E., 7
Duffy, G. G., 12
Duffy, T., 329
Duhaney, D. C., 219, 220, 496
Duhaney, L. M., 219, 220
Duncan, C., 429
Dunham, R., 34
Dunlosky, J., 254, 277
Dupper, D. R., 240
Durso, Frank, 277
Dweck, C. S., 95, 313, 375, 385

E
Earl, L., 489, 501
Earley, M. A., 169
Easton, J., 332
Eberstadt, M., 85
Eby, J. W., 15, 17
Eby, Judy, 23, 575
Eccles, J. S., 94, 128, 158, 395
Edwards, M. N., 18
Edwards, R. P., 236
Efthim, H. E., 167
Egan, M., 200, 213
Einstein, G. O., 290, 298
Eisenberg, N., 82
Eisenberger, Joane, 325
Eisner, E. W., 10
Elfstrom, J. L., 427
Elkind, D., 38, 43, 46
Elkind, J., 220
Elkind, K., 220
Elliot, A., 371, 373, 376
Elliott, J. G., 120
Elliott, T., 54
Ellis, E. D., Jr., 432
Ellis, E. K., 15
Ellis, John, 262
Elmore, R. F., 570
Emmer, E. T., 235, 248, 404, 409, 410,
    438
Endo, H., 172
Engel, M., 545
Engeström, Y., 332
Englander, E. K., 427, 428
Englehart, M. B., 314, 442, 444, 521
Engleman, M., 219
English, K., 150
Ennis, C., 378
Enochs, L., 333
Erben, Tony, 180
Erdelyi, M. H., 260
Erickson, D., 101
Ericsson, K. A., 264
Ertmer, Peggy, 24
Evans, G., 150
Evans, R., 71, 154
Evertson, C. M., 161, 235, 247, 409,
    410, 438
Ey, S., 101, 102

F
Fabes, R. A., 776
Fadjukoff, P., 28, 32
Fagley, N., 346
Fairbanks, S., 3, 409
Falk, B., 7, 467, 539
Faloon, S., 264
Fantuzzo, J. W., 166, 471, 474, 475
Fargo, J. D., 498
Farkas, S., 35
Faw, H. W., 447
Fazal, M., 512
Fehrenbach, C. R., 125
Feigenbaum, P., 84
Feiman-Nemser, Sharon, 12
Feldman, S., 63
Ferrini-Mundy, J., 6
Ferriter, W., 570
Ferster, B., 105
Feynman, Richard, 346
Feyten, C. M., 178
Fickel, L., 560
Fields, V. S., 461
Finarelli, M. G., 56
Fine, J., 5
Finnigan, K. S., 546
Fischer, S., 474
Fiset, M., 436
Fisher, D., 103
Fisk, A. D., 259
Fitzgerald, J., 177
Flanagan, Dawn, 140
Flaspohler, P. D., 427
Flavell, J. H., 108, 266, 267

Flegg, Aubrey, 463
Fleming, J. A. E., 101
Fletcher, C., 76
Fletcher, J. M., 192, 203
Flieller, A., 45
Flinders, D. J., 10, 12
Flint, A. S., 5
Floden, R. E., 6
Flora, S. R., 242, 247
Flum, H., 393, 395
Flynn, P., 218
Fok, A., 332, 339, 398
Foote, M., 548
Forbes, S., 34
Forbus, K., 334
Foreman, Phil, 223
Foshay, W. R., 552
Fosnot, C. T., 331
Fox, E., 280
Fox, P. W., 513
Franzke, M., 319
Fraser, B. J., 562
Fredrick, T., 492
Freeman, D. J., 18
Freiberg, H. J., 464, 560, 565
French, S. E., 34
Friedkin, S., 562, 564
Friedlaender, D., 399
Frieman, Jerome, 277
Frijters, J., 367
Fromberg, D. P., 75, 85
Fryer, R. G., 156
Fuchs, D., 189, 192, 197, 207
Fuchs, L. S., 189, 192, 197, 204, 207
Fuller, B., 545
Fulmer, S., 367
Funkhouser, C., 462
Furlong, M. J., 425, 428, 438
Furnham, A., 112
Furst, E. J., 314, 442, 444, 521
Furth, Hans, 71

G
Gabay, R., 36
Gable, R. K., 94
Gagnon, J. C., 220
Gajdamaschko, N., 332
Galambos, N. L., 101
Galindo, C., 153
Gallagher, J. J., 191, 200, 212, 213, 215, 223
Gallagher, Patricia, 223
Gallagher, W. J., 542
Gallimore, R., 12, 15, 53
Gallingane, C., 409, 415
Gambrell, L., 369, 370
Gamoran, A., 186, 339
Gantner, Myrna, 162
García, E., 147, 149, 163, 164
Garden, R. A., 129
Gardner, D., 153, 157, 160
Gardner, H., 117, 118, 119, 120, 122, 130
Garofalo, J., 273
Gaskins, I. W., 311, 367
Gathercoal, P., 430
Gatlin, L., 512
Gatlin, S. J., 6
Gavula, N., 161
Gayler, K., 547
Geddes, C., 131, 132
Gee, J. P., 122, 360
Gelbman, M., 54
Gentile, J. R., 167, 505
Gentner, D., 334
Gentry, M., 94, 215
Gerace, W., 510, 512
Gerjets, P., 321
Gershoff, E. T., 240, 241
Gersten, R., 19, 174, 204
Gesicki, K., 545
Gewertz, C., 548
Gheen, M. H., 94, 385
Gholar, C., 396, 402

Ghosh, R., 34
Gibbons, Maurice, 324
Gijbels, D., 329, 333
Gilberg, C., 101
Gilbertson, D., 192
Gilgun, J. F., 99
Gill, G., 548
Gillespie, C. W., 123
Gillies, R. M., 471, 474, 482
Gilligan, C., 34, 35, 60, 71, 132
Gilman, D. A., 551
Gindis, Boris, 71
Ginott, A., 76
Ginott, H. G., 76, 219
Ginsberg, M. B., 166
Ginsburg, H. P., 47, 71
Ginsburg-Block, M., 166, 471, 474, 475
Gitsaki, C., 54
Givon, H., 55
Glaser, C., 308
Glass, B., 462
Glass, G. V., 542
Glasser, William, 373, 472
Glenberg, A. M., 150
Globerson, T., 55
Gobbo, C., 52
Goddard, H. W., 76
Goeke, Jennifer, 448, 481
Goetz, E. T., 258
Gold, M., 219
Goldberg, B., 260
Goldberg, M., 538, 540, 547, 548
Goldsby, D., 512
Goldstone, S., 274
Gollnick, D. A., 142, 149, 162, 163
Gomez, L., 332
Gomez, S., 199
Gonzalez, E., 129
Gonzalez, R., 177
Good, J. M., 18
Good, T. L., 44, 158, 159
Goodenough, D. R., 124, 125
Goodlad, John, 243
Goodman, A., 333
Goodman, G., 512
Gordon, P. R., 161
Gordon, S., 99
Gordon, T., 420, 422
Gordon-Becker, S., 252
Gorman, A. H., 82
Gorman, J., 564
Gorski, Paul, 180
Goswami, U., 108
Gould, S. J., 113
Grabe, C., 232, 274
Grabe, M., 232, 274
Grabinger, R., 218
Graeber, Anna, 558
Graesser, Arthur, 277
Graham, M., 271, 290
Graham, S., 156, 159, 271, 290, 298, 308, 311, 372, 374
Grant, C. A., 144, 150
Grant, J., 15, 24, 565, 575
Grant, K. E., 101, 102
Grasby, R., 373
Graue, M. F., 7
Gredler, M., 49
Green, T. D., 108
Greene, B., 371
Greene, J. A., 287, 290, 312, 316
Greenfield, P. M., 172
Gregory, G. H., 215
Gregory, K. D., 129
Gresalfi, M., 55, 56, 360, 362, 388
Gresham, F. M., 203
Griffin, H. C., 219
Griffiths, A. K., 44
Griffiths, A.-J., 192
Griffiths, T. L., 261
Grigg, W., 153
Grigorenko, E. L., 114, 115, 116, 117, 120, 121, 122, 123, 127, 136, 140, 346

Grisham-Brown, J., 192
Groff, C., 210, 471, 474
Groninger, Marilyn Chambliss, 558
Gronlund, N. E., 444, 445, 446, 481, 492, 494, 498, 501, 502, 504, 505, 509, 519, 520, 557
Gross, B., 546
Grossen, B. J., 451
Grote, B., 169
Gruber, Howard, 71
Guerra, N. G., 428, 429
Gugga, S. S., 67
Gulek, C., 553, 554
Gurland, S., 369
Guskey, T. R., 485, 505, 506, 510, 513
Gutek, G. L., 44, 169, 181, 183, 185, 189
Guterman, E., 55
Gutiérrez, K. D., 127, 148
Guttmacher Institute, 99

H
Haber, R., 260
Hacker, D. J., 277, 317, 477
Hadwin, A. F., 290
Haertel, G. D., 14
Hahn, C. L., 135
Hahn, Valerie Schremp, 431
Haier, R. J., 251
Haladyna, T. M., 490, 506
Hall, G. Stanley, 92
Hall, K. M., 67
Hall, R. H., 297
Hallam, S., 187, 394
Hallfors, D., 99
Halligan, P., 260
Halpern, D. F., 128, 130, 141
Halusic, M., 378
Hambacher, E., 409, 415
Hamff, A., 204
Hamilton, L. B., 291, 539, 542
Hamman, D., 291
Hammond, T., 105
Hampel, R. L., 153
Hamre, B. K., 157
Hanesian, H., 256, 330
Haney, J. J., 38, 338
Hanish, L. D., 76
Hannafin, R. D., 552
Hansgen, R. D., 10
Hanson, A. R., 307
Hany, E. A., 114
Harari, Y., 36
Harder, R., 341
Hardman, M., 200, 213
Hardy, C. L., 100
Hardy, I., 338, 457
Hare, D., 512
Hargreaves, A., 501
Harjusola-Webb, S., 192
Harold, R. D., 90, 92, 103, 109
Harrington, R., 333
Harris, Anita, 141
Harris, B., 213
Harris, K. R., 290, 298, 308, 311, 325
Harrison, Patti, 140
Harry, B., 190, 191, 194
Hart, B., 155
Hart, H., 498
Hart, S. S., 291
Harter, S., 86, 133, 393
Hartless, G., 103
Hartshorne, H., 63
Hartup, W. W., 81
Hatch, T., 118, 119
Hattie, J., 86, 205, 310, 314, 317
Hattie, John, 150
Hau, K. T., 87
Haudenschild, M., 332
Haver, Johanna, 180
Haviland, J. M., 42
Haxby, B., 185
Hayes, William, 558

Haywood, H. C., 267
Hazler, R. J., 427
Healy, A., 355
Healy, L., 54
Heaney, P., 463
Heath, M., 566
Hecker, L., 220
Heilig, J. V., 6
Henderson, J. G., 15, 24
Henry J. Kaiser Family Foundation, 155
Hermann, Douglas, 277
Heron, A., 45
Herr, P., 412
Herrell, Adrienne, 15, 17, 23, 575
Herrmann, D., 250, 252
Hersh, R. H., 68
Hershberg, T., 539
Hetherington, E. M., 84, 85, 90
Hetzner, Amy, 499
Heward, W. L., 200, 208, 209
Hibbard, K. M., 567
Hickey, D. T., 55, 324, 360, 388, 462
Hicks, J. L., 17
Hiebert, J., 12, 15
Higdon, J., 479
Higgins, J. W., 236, 237
Hilbert, T., 347, 348
Hilden, K., 290, 292, 299
Hill, C., 130, 131, 132
Hill, J. P., 100
Hill, W. H., 314, 442, 444
Hill, Walker, 521
Hilliard, V. R., 170
Hirsch, E., 6
Hitchcock, C., 217
Hmelo-Silver, C., 334, 336
Ho, A. D., 538, 546
Hoegh, D. G., 33, 34
Hoff, D. J., 549
Hoffman, B., 349
Hoffman, M. L., 59, 71, 91
Hogan, Kathleen, 481
Hoge, R. D., 215
Hohmann, M., 79
Hoke, M., 6
Hole, S., 15, 24, 565, 575
Hollingsworth, John, 481
Holt, Larry, 482
Holtzman, D. J., 6
Holubec, E. J., 471
Holzman, L., 52, 71
Hong, G., 7, 185, 187
Hong, H.-Y., 362
Hong, Y., 185, 187
Hoover-Dempsey, K. V., 405
Hopple, C., 378
Hopson, R. K., 143
Horwitz, P., 462
Hoskyn, M., 206
Hougen, M., 204
Houlbec, Edythe Johnson, 482
Houston, P. D., 540, 541, 546, 547
Houts, R., 460, 468, 540
Howard, B. C., 122
Howard, D. C., 290, 298
Howard, E., 512
Howe, N., 82
Howes, C., 79
Howland, J., 359, 365, 459, 461, 463
Hoyles, C., 54
Huang, B., 436
Hudley, C., 156, 159
Hughes, C. A., 220
Hughes, F. P., 45, 108
Hughes, J. N., 469
Hung, D., 334, 335, 463
Hunt, N., 200, 204, 223
Hurst, A., 372
Hussar, W., 7, 435
Huttenlocher, J., 128
Hutter, R., 306
Hyde, J. S., 62, 130
Hyerle, David, 325

I

Iacono, W. G., 101
Ikier, Simay, 141
Inal, Y., 379
Individuals with Disabilities Education Act Amendments of 1997, 189, 190
Ingram-Goble, A., 274
Ingram-Noble, A., 55, 360, 388
Inhelder, B., 40
Inhelder, Barbel, 71
Inn, Loh Wan, 482
Irby, B., 176
Ireson, J., 187, 394
Iritani, B., 99
Israel, A. C., 209
Ivanoff, J., 251

J

Jackson, A. W., 186
Jackson, B., 161
Jackson, C., 361
Jackson, D. B., 156
Jackson, J. F., 154
Jackson, S. J., 128, 192
Jacob, S., 512
Jacobs, George, 482
Jacobs, P. R., 67
Jacobsen, R., 539
Jaffee, S., 62
Jameson, E., 55, 360, 388
Jamieson-Noel, D., 271, 290
Jamison, B., 105
Janesick, V. J., 492, 512
Jang, H., 459
Jarvin, L., 114, 115, 116, 117, 120, 121, 140, 346
Jean-Marie, G., 332
Jenkins, J. R., 476
Jennings, J., 547
Jennings, M., 82
Jensen, E. P., 10
Jensen, L. A., 63
Jenson, W. R., 237
Jeong, H., 334, 336
Jiao, H., 551
Jimerson, S. R., 7, 428, 438
Jindal-Snape, D., 93, 94
Jobe, D. A., 133
Johns, B., 203, 205, 206, 223
Johnson, C. C., 498
Johnson, Chrystal, 467
Johnson, D. W., 44, 380, 386, 471, 472, 474, 482
Johnson, David, 167
Johnson, Frank P., 482
Johnson, J., 35
Johnson, N., 319
Johnson, R. C., 568
Johnson, R. E., 256
Johnson, R. T., 44, 380, 386, 471, 472, 474, 482
Johnson, Roger, 167
Johnson, Ruth, 575
Johnson, S., 360
Johnson, S. P., 38
Johnson, T., 291
Jonassen, D. H., 359, 365, 459, 461, 463
Jonen, A., 338, 457
Jones, B. D., 547
Jones, D. R., 55
Jones, J., 234
Jones, K. M., 430
Joo, Y.-J., 321
Jordan, Michael, 15, 23, 575
Jorgenson, O., 251
Jovanovic, J., 131
Joyce, B., 448, 450, 452, 466, 472
Juarez, L., 99
Jussim, L., 158
Juvonen, J., 94

K

Kagan, Jerome, 123
Kail, R. V., 75, 88, 108, 270, 277
Kalbaugh, P., 42
Kallick, Bena, 324
Kalohn, John, 558
Kalyuga, S., 347
Kameenui, Edward, 223
Kamii, C., 45, 47
Kanat-Maymon, Y., 11
Kang, E., 545
Kang, Myunghee, 127
Kaplan, A., 393, 395, 402
Kaplan, H., 11
Kaplan, L. S., 7
Karabenick, Stuart, 402
Karniol, R., 36
Karpicke, J. D., 290
Karpov, Y. V., 52, 267
Katayama, Andrew, 296
Katz, L., 220
Kauffman, J. M., 191, 192, 223
Kaufman, A. M., 7
Kaufman, J. G., 184, 369
Kavale, K. A., 191, 192
Kay, Matthew, 13–14
Keane, G., 114
Kear, K., 12
Keengwe, J., 274
Kehle, T. J., 237
Keiper, T. A., 108, 448
Keller, L. B., 128, 131, 132
Kelley, M. L., 236
Kelly, Diane, 438
Kelly, M., 85
Kemp, J., 7, 155, 173, 425, 426, 428, 435
Kena, G., 7, 155, 173, 435
Kendall, J. S., 443
Kennedy, R. J., Jr., 541
Kennon, R. W., 271, 290
Kentucky Department of Education, 536
Kerr, A., 373
Kerr, Margaret, 223
Ketelhut, D. J., 56, 136
KewalManani, A., 7, 155, 173, 435
Khatapoush, S., 99
Kieschke, U., 267
Kiewra, Kenneth, 325
Kim, S., 223, 378
Kim, Y., 267, 310
Kimmel, Felicia Lowden, 438
Kindfield, A. C. H., 462
King, A., 295, 296, 314
King, B., 203
King, D., 357
King, S. S., 131
Kingsbury, G. G., 548
Kintsch, E., 319
Kipp, K., 34
Kirk, S. A., 191, 200, 213, 223
Kirkley, S. E., 105
Kirschner, P., 333
Kitsantas, A., 281, 285, 286, 290, 300
Kizer, S., 55, 360, 388
Klassen, R., 308
Klauda, S. L., 373
Klauer, K., 447
Klecka, C., 498
Klein, Susan, 141
Kleinert, H., 191
Klingner, J. K., 190, 191, 194
Knapp, M. S., 161, 166, 511
Knauff, M., 258
Knopf, M., 290
Kober, N., 547
Kohlberg, L., 58, 59, 62
Kohlhardt, J., 63, 112
Kohn, A., 242
Kokko, K., 28
Kolbe, L., 429
Kontos, G., 169
Koohang, A., 329
Koppich, J., 560

Kordaki, M., 54, 331
Koretz, D., 524, 525, 526
Kornell, N., 290
Korthagen, F., 5
Kosciolek, S., 451
Kosky, R., 103
Kosunen, T., 12
Kounin, Jacob, 342, 406, 410
Kozol, Jonathon, 11, 13
Kozulin, A., 71, 257
Kramarski, B., 319
Krathwohl, D. R., 314, 442, 443, 444, 521
Krätzig, G. P., 127
Kreiner, S., 125
Kroger, J., 33, 71
Krogh, H. R., 76
Kruse, S., 343, 345
Kubiszyn, T., 190, 197, 501, 505, 521, 526
Kubler LaBoskey, V., 566, 568
Kuhn, D., 83
Kulik, C.-L. C., 167, 215, 245
Kulik, J. A., 54, 167, 185, 186, 215, 232, 234, 245
Kumar, R., 94, 385
Kusku, F., 136
Kuyper, H., 288
Kuzmich, L., 215
Kwok, O., 176
Kyle, D. W., 17
Kyriakides, L., 569
Kysilka, Marcella, 482

L

Lach, C., 122, 274
Lachapelle, Y., 199
Lacina, J., 177
Lacireno-Paquet, N., 192
Laczko-Kerr, I., 6
Ladson-Billings, G., 153, 171
Lai, S.-L., 272
Laird, A. R., 251
Lake, C., 210, 471, 474
Lalley, J. P., 167, 505
Lam, R., 493
LaMay, M. L., 128
Lambros, Ann, 481
Lampinen, J. M., 261
Lancey, D. F., 76, 428
Landau, B. M., 430
Langer, J. A., 186, 339
Lantieri, L., 434, 435
Lara-Alecio, R., 176
Larson, B. E., 108, 448
Larson, R. W., 92, 93
Larzelere, Robert, 240
Latu, E., 552
Lau, S., 94
Lauer, K. D., 67
Lavers, N., 456
Lavigne, N., 471, 475
Lazear, David, 137
Lazonder, A. W., 186, 475
Leacock, T. L., 253, 254, 274
Leadbeater, B., 45
Leake, V. S., 468, 469
Leal, L., 291
LeDoux, J. M., 203
Lee, I., 493
Lee, J., 153, 252, 544
Lee, J.-S., 153, 155
Lee, K., 331, 344
Lee, T. R., 99
Lee, Y. J., 55, 332
Le Floch, K. C., 548
Legault, L., 405
Leidner, D. E., 55
Leidy, M. S., 428, 429
Leming, J. S., 65
Lens, W., 367
Lerner, J., 203, 205, 206, 223
Lerner, J. W., 205
Lesgold, A. M., 255, 256, 265
Lessow-Hurley, Judith, 180

Levin, J. R., 150, 292, 293, 294, 438
Levin, M. E., 294
Levine, A., 33, 105
Levine, D. U., 144, 169, 185, 189
Levine, S. C., 128
Lewandowsky, S., 261
Lewin-Epstein, N., 34
Lewis, C., 469, 562, 564
Lewis, L., 170
Lewis, S., 330, 338
Lewis, T., 121
Lewis-Moreno, B., 176
Lewis-Palmer, T., 382, 383, 430
Ley, K., 312
Li, J., 150
Liao, Y.-K. C., 232
Liben, L. S., 76
Lickona, T., 58, 68, 434
Lieberman, J., 564
Light, P., 43, 50
Ligorio, M. B., 105
Lilles, E., 192
Lim, J., 358
Lin, E., 498
Lin, Y., 127
Linan-Thompson, S., 204
Lindberg, Jill, 438
Lindgren, R., 330, 338
Lindsay, J. J., 161
Lindsey, Delores B., 180
Lindsey, Randall B., 189
Linn, M., 272, 273, 463, 469
Linn, R. L., 505, 539, 553, 540, 542, 547, 557
Lipka, R. P., 94
Liston, Daniel P., 23
Little, E., 122, 274
Littleton, K., 43, 50
Liu, M., 318, 319
Liu, Y., 252
Livingston, Ronald, 557
Lixson, Thomas, 71
Lleras, C., 186, 187
Lobman, Carrie, 23
Lodewyk, K. R., 306
Loewenstein, J., 334
Lopata, C., 476
Lord, K. M., 67
Lorimer, M., 133
Lou, Y., 186, 436, 478
Lourenco, S. F., 128
Lowe, C., 219
Lowry, R., 429
Loyens, S., 329, 333
Lu, Y., 379
Lubinski, D., 214
Luckasson, R., 199
Lüdtke, O., 87, 306
Luehmann, A. L., 56, 274
Lundeberg, M. A., 513
Lundquist, Matthew, 23
Luppescu, S., 332
Luria, Alexander, 277
Lyon, G. R., 203
Lyons, N. P., 566, 568

M

Maag, J. W., 242
Maanum, J. L., 218
Mabry, L., 549
MacArthur, C., 220
Maccini, P., 220
Macdonald, M., 560
Macedo, D., 174
Mackay, S., 102, 236
MacKinnon, J. L., 33
MacMillan, D. L., 203
MacSwan, J., 174, 176, 177
Macy, M. D., 178
Madaus, G., 539, 540
Madden, N. A., 185
Maddock, Mandy, 575
Madon, S., 158

Mager, R. F., 397, 444, 445, 446, 481, 505
Magimairaj, B. M., 456
Mahadevan, Rajan, 277
Maher, Frances, 141
Mahoney, K., 174, 176, 177
Mahwinney, T. S., 423
Maier, M., 373
Maloch, B., 5
Mandal, R. M., 236
Mansfield, E., 378, 391
Marchand, G., 289
Marchant, H., III, 128
Marcia, J. E., 28, 32, 33, 34, 57
Marini, Z., 52
Mark, J., 564
Marley, S. C., 150
Marlow, Bruce, 364
Marois, R., 251
Marr, M. B., 432
Marra, R. M., 359, 365, 459, 461, 463
Marsh, H. W., 86, 87, 130, 215
Marshall, K., 204, 223
Marshall, Kathleen, 200
Martens, B., 192
Martin, A., 130, 367
Martin, C. L., 76
Martin, Garry, 248
Martin, J., 281
Martin, M. O., 129
Martinez, M. E., 491
Martinez, R., 213
Marx, R. W., 452
Marzano, R. J., 3, 23, 161, 443
Masia, B. B., 443
Maslow, A. H., 390, 464
Mason, L. H., 308, 310
Master, A., 375, 385
Masters, J., 55
Mathes, P., 176
Mathes, P. G., 176, 207
Mathison, Sandra, 558
Matos, L., 367
Matthew, C., 345
Matthew, K. I., 272
Matthews, Kay, 13–14
Maughan, B., 427
Maxim, George, 365
May, M. A., 63
Mayer, M. J., 425
Mayer, R. E., 254, 274, 297, 329, 338, 442
Maynard, A. E., 45
Mazur, James E., 247
Mazyck, M., 234, 451
McArthur, J., 38, 338
McBride, L. W., 568
McCandless, B. D., 10
McCaslin, Mary, 324
McClintic, Carol, 342
McCloskey, E., 56, 136
McCoach, D. B., 125
McCown, R., 143
McCrea, S., 374, 380
McDaniel, M. A., 290, 292, 298
McDermott, J., 43
McDevitt, T. M., 90
McDonough, S. C., 46
McEntee, G. H., 15, 24, 565, 575
McGee, B. P., 161
McGee, S., 122
McGill-Franzen, A., 547
McGillicuddy-DeLisi, Anne, 141
McGrath, D., 512
McGuire, J., 217
McIntire, J. A., 213
McKenna, M. C., 272
McKenzie, W., 122
McKim, B., 540
McLaughlin, T. F., 102, 236, 237, 239
McLoyd, V. C., 159
McMillan, J. H., 509
McMillan, K. M., 251
McMurrer, J., 547

McNamara, D., 329
McNeil, L. M., 547
McTighe, J., 496
McVarish, J., 18
Means, B., 161, 511
Meilinger, T., 258
Meister, C., 295, 310, 448
Mello, D., 192
Melton, R. F., 447
Mendoza, J. I., 169
Menzer, J. D., 153
Mercer, Ann R., 223
Mercer, Cecil D., 223
Mercer, L. K., 315
Mercier, L. R., 90, 92, 103, 109
Meros, J., 178
Merrell, K., 382, 383, 430
Merseth, K., 560
Messina, R., 360
Mester, Cathy Sargent, 12, 23
Mestre, Jose, 365
Metzger, M., 313, 423, 424
Mevarech, Zemira, 295
Meyer, M. S., 203
Meyer-Adams, N., 427
Michelson, R. A., 34
Middleton, M. J., 94, 385
Midgley, C., 63, 94, 97, 385
Mignano, Andrew, 438
Mikkola, A., 12
Miller, A., 63, 112
Miller, B. C., 99
Miller, D. J., 93, 94
Miller, David, 553, 557
Miller, K. A., 476
Miller, L., 277, 560
Miller, M. D., 505
Miller, M. J., 271, 290
Miller, P., 346
Miller, P. A., 108
Miller, P. C., 172
Miller, P. H., 80
Miller, Patricia, 71
Miller, R., 345, 376, 377, 378, 391
Miller, R. H., 476
Miller, S. A., 108
Miller, S. D., 317
Miller, Suzanne, 71
Miller, T. R., 166
Mills, V., 54
Miltenberger, R. G., 235, 239, 240
Mims-Cox, J., 568
Mims-Cox, Sabrina, 575
Minaya-Rowe, L., 174
Mintrop, H., 540
Mishel, L., 3, 153
Mislevy, R., 533
Mistler-Jackson, M., 56
Mistry, R. S., 158
Mizell, A. P., 169
Moag-Stahlberg, A., 85
Mock, D. R., 191, 192
Moely, B. E., 291
Moffitt, T. E., 427
Molden, D. C., 313
Moll, Luis, 71
Möller, K., 338, 457
Monsen, J., 112
Montalvo, G., 378, 391
Montgomery, J. W., 456
Montgomery, M. J., 34, 35
Moon, T. R., 495
Mooney, Carol Garhart, 71
Moore, C. A., 124, 125
Moore, J. A., 218
Moore, S., 236
Moos, D. C., 318, 321, 359
Mora, J. K., 174
Moran, S., 119, 120
Moreno, R., 254, 274
Morgan, H., 124, 125
Morgan, M., 245
Morisi, T. L., 100

Morra, S., 52
Morris, A. S., 34, 93, 100
Morris, P., 203
Morrison, C. T., 427
Morrison, F., 460, 468, 540
Morrison, G. M., 428
Morrison, J. Q., 430
Morrison, K., 149, 150
Moshavi, D., 12
Moss, C. M., 18, 485, 487, 488, 504, 520, 560, 569
Mueller, M., 349
Muhlenbruck, L., 161
Muijs, D., 569
Muis, K. R., 285, 287
Mullis, I. V. S., 129
Munro, B., 429
Munro, G., 429
Mupier, R. M., 7
Murayama, K., 371
Murdoch, Kath, 386
Murdock, T. B., 63
Murphy, B. C., 82
Murphy, J., 188
Murphy, P. K., 18, 112
Murray, S., 56, 136
Myers, D., 3, 409
Myers, M., 491
Myran, S., 509

N
Naftel, S., 548
Nagaoka, J., 7
Naglieri, J. A., 80
Nagy, P., 44
Nakamoto, J., 82
Nakkula, M. J., 109
Narvaez, D., 60, 66, 71
Narvaez, L., 111, 188, 215
Nasir, N. S., 157
National Board Certified Teachers (NBCTs), 571
National Board for Professional Teaching Standards, 3, 560, 571
National Center for Education Statistics, 99, 153
National Center for Health Statistics, 85
National Comprehensive Center for Teacher Quality & Public Agenda, 5, 6, 19, 410
National Research Council, 40, 191
Naughton, C. C., 237
Nazzaro, D., 122, 274
NBCTs. See National Board Certified Teachers (NBCTs)
Nebel, M., 105
Neill, M., 540
Nelson, C., 105, 223, 479
Nemer, Kariane, 477
Nesbit, J. C., 253, 254, 274, 290, 296–297
Nettelbeck, T., 54
Newcombe, N. S., 128
Newman, B. M., 28
Newman, Fred, 71
Newman, P. R., 28
New York Performance Standards Consortium, 548
Nicholls, S. L., 158, 159
Nichols, S. L., 330, 338, 501, 540, 541, 542, 547, 549
Nicpon, M. F., 214
Nielsen, T., 125
Nieto, S., 153, 159, 167, 171
Nikula, J., 564
Nitko, A., 506, 521
No Child Left Behind Act of 2001, 536
Noddings, N., 62, 71, 467, 541, 558
Nolan, James F., 438
Noppe, L. D., 45
Norby, M. M., 261, 277
Nordby, C. J., 315
Norman, D. A., 251
Normore, A., 332

Novak, J. D., 256, 297, 330
Novak, John M., 482
Nucci, Larry, 71
Nye, B., 161
Nye, Robert, 247
Nystrand, M., 186, 339

O
Oakes, J., 183, 192
Oakley, D., 260
Oas, G., 220
Obenchain, K. M., 239
O'Brennan, L. M., 427
O'Byrne, B., 234
Ochion, Y., 36
Ochse, R., 35, 61
O'Connor, K. M., 129, 521
Odegard, T. N., 261
Odell, S., 498
O'Donnell, A. M., 297
Office of the Federal Register, 208
Ogbu, J. U., 153, 156
Oja, S. N., 44
Okagaki, L., 148, 150, 155, 156
Olina, Z., 358
Olmi, D. J., 236
O'Lone, D. J., 512
Olson, A., 551, 552, 553
Olson, J., 551
Olson, S., 192
Olweus, D., 87
O'Malley, M. H., 456
O'Mara, A. J., 87
Onchwari, G., 274
O'Neill, S. A., 274
Oostdam, R., 233
Opper, S., 47, 71
Orlich, D., 341
Ormrod, J. E., 90
Ornstein, A. C., 144, 169, 185, 189
Orrill, Chandra, 24
Osborn Popp, S., 497
Osipow, S. H., 32
Osman, M., 355
Osterman, K. F., 468, 469
Otter, M. E., 233
Overmaat, M., 233
Owen, A. M., 251
Owings, W. A., 7
Owston, R., 379
Ozbilgin, M., 136
Ozkale, L., 136
Ozuru, Y., 329

P
Paas, F., 319, 329, 348
Pacheco, M., 127
Padilla, A. M., 177
Page, M. S., 170, 254, 257, 364
Paivio, A., 258
Pajares, F., 132, 279, 281, 282, 283, 285, 305, 307, 317, 324, 371, 372, 375, 393, 402
Pak, R., 259
Palenz, D., 273
Palincsar, A., 310, 333
Palmer, S. B., 253
PALS Group, 267, 310
Paolitto, D. P., 68
Paris, A. H., 290
Paris, S. G., 290
Park, E., 178
Parke, R. D., 84, 85, 90
Parshall, Cynthia, 558
Patall, E. A., 161
Paterson, Annette Hatcher, 141
Patrick, H., 464, 469
Patterson, B., 274
Patterson, G. R., 87
Patton, James, 223
Pea, R. D., 55
Pear, Joseph, 248
Pearlstone, Z., 259

Pedersen, S., 318, 319
Peisner-Feinberg, E., 79
Peixotto, K., 192
Pekrun, R., 373
Peleg, D., 103
Pelligrini, A. D., 80, 83, 108
Peltier, G. L., 183
Peltier, L. G., 405
Peña, C. M., 54
Penfield, Wilder, 259
Pérez, B., 174, 177
Perin, D., 271, 308
Perkins, D. F., 103, 114
Perlstein, Linda, 194
Perney, J., 398
Perrot, D., 169
Perry, N. E., 315
Perry, R. S., 331, 562, 564
Peters, C. L., 220
Peterson, A. C., 101, 102
Peterson, A. R., 429
Petrakos, H., 82
Peverly, S. T., 271, 290
Pewewardy, C., 149
Piaget, J., 40, 58, 71
Pianta, R. C., 79, 157, 460, 468, 540
Pickering, D. J., 3, 23, 161
Pieters, J. M., 105
Pillay, V., 456
Pintrich, P. R., 290, 324, 442
Plake, Barbara, 557
Planty, M., 7, 155, 173, 435
Pletcher, S. W., 428
Pleydon, A. P., 100
Plucker, J., 213
Plug, C., 35, 61
Plumm, K., 131
Podoll, S., 436
Poell, R., 333
Pogrow, S., 157, 453, 462
Pollard, Andrew, 24, 575
Pollock, J. E., 3, 161
Pomerantz, E. M., 129
Ponnappa-Brenner, G., 218
Pontecorvo, C., 105
Poole, D. A., 8
Pope, M., 512
Popham, James, 491
Popham, W. J., 485, 520, 538, 540, 542,
   549
Popplewell, S. R., 272
Porter, R. P., 174
Portes, P., 34
Postholm, M., 332
Potari, D., 54
Poulsen, C., 186
Powell, K., 429
Power, Michael, 482
Powers, S. J., 6
Premack, D., 236
Presseisen, B. Z., 257
Pressley, M., 290, 292, 299, 311, 367, 481
Pretti-Frontczak, K., 192
Proctor, B. D., 152
Protinsky, H., 34
Psychological Corporation, 113
Pufall, Peter, 71
Pulkkinen, L., 28, 32
Pullin, D. L., 54
Purdie, N., 150, 205, 310
Purkey, William W., 482
Puzzanchera, C., 425
Pye, J., 18

Q

Qin, Z., 44
Qiu, Wei, 159
Quenneville, J., 123
Quiocho, Alice, 180

R

Radigan, J., 547
Rakes, G. C., 461

Ramirez, A., 7, 148, 153
Ramirez-Valles, J., 99
Ramsey, E., 87
Randi, J., 312, 316
Randle, D., 436
Rangel, C., 186, 187
Rao, N., 291
Rapp, K., 213
Raths, J., 442
Ratner, C., 53, 71
Raudenbush, S. W., 7, 154, 155
Raugh, M. R., 294
Ravaglia, R., 220
Rea, A., 56
Reardon, S. F., 153
Rebell, Michael, 558
Recesso, Arthur, 24
Redl, F., 415
Reed, D. S., 254, 548
Reed, S. K., 274
Reedy, K., 192
Reeve, A., 199
Reeve, J., 378, 459
Reeve, R., 360
Reid, C., 212
Reimer, J., 68
Reinke, W. M., 382, 383, 430
Reis, S. M., 213, 215
Reiser, R., 358
Relyea, G., 377
Reninger, R. D., 274
Renkl, A., 347, 348, 457
Renninger, K. A., 395
Renshaw, Peter, 343
Rentner, D. S., 547
Renzulli, J., 213, 215
Renzulli, J. S., 212, 215
Rest, J., 60, 71
Resta, P. E., 479
Revenson, T. A., 47
Reynolds, Cecil, 557
Reynolds, T. H., 55
Riccio, David, 277
Rice, K. L., 436
Richard, A., 548
Richardson, W., 108
Ridgeway, V. G., 220
Rigby, K., 426, 427, 438
Riggs, E., 396
Riggs, Ernestine, 402
Rijlaarsdam, G., 299, 309
Rikers, R., 329
Riley, L., 329
Rinaldi, C. M., 82
Rinn, A. N., 87
Ripley, A., 559
Risley, T. R., 155
Ritchhart, R., 114
Ritchie, S., 357
Rizza, M. G., 94
Robertson, A., 44
Robila, M., 79
Robins, Kikanza Nuri, 180
Robinson, Daniel, 297
Robinson, J., 186, 190
Robinson, J. C., 161
Robinson, L., 108
Robinson, W., 569
Robledo, M. M., 174
Roblyer, M. D., 436
Roderick, M., 7, 545
Roderick, T., 435
Rodney, H. F., 7
Rodney, L. W., 7
Rodriguez, M. C., 258, 490
Roediger, H. L., III, 290
Roerden, L., 435
Roeser, R. W., 94
Rogers, A. M., 161
Rogers, C. R., 464, 465
Rogers, Laura, 438
Rogers, W. A., 259
Rogoff, B., 44, 45, 46, 51, 82, 127, 148

Rohrbeck, C. A., 166, 471, 474, 475
Rohrer, D., 264
Roid, G., 113
Rolón, C. A., 171
Romance, N. R., 297
Romani, J., 192
Romanoff, B., 212
Ronning, R. R., 261, 277
Rop, C., 138
Roscoe, R. D., 167
Rosen, D., 105, 479
Rosen, Y., 356, 359
Rosenblum-Lowden, Renee, 438
Rosenshine, B. V., 295, 310, 448
Rosenthal, R., 158
Ross, D. D., 17, 303, 409, 415
Ross, H. S., 81, 85
Ross, John, 24
Ross, K., 548
Ross, S., 303
Roth, G., 11
Roth, W.-M., 55, 332
Rothstein, R., 153, 539
Rothstein-Fisch, C., 172
Rotter, K. M., 206
Rowan, B., 3
Rowe, S. M., 49
Roy, J., 153
Royer, J. M., 128, 265
Rozenfeld, M., 220
Rubin, L. J., 10, 23, 188
Ruck, Martin, 159
Ruggiero, V. R., 344, 345, 350, 353, 354,
   365
Ruhland, S. K., 5
Rumelhart, D. E., 251
Rummel, N., 293
Ruscoe, G., 560
Russell, M., 486, 503
Russell, Natalie, 173
Russo, A., 551
Rutledge, M., 138
Ryan, A. M., 464, 469, 541
Ryan, J., 497
Ryan, K. E., 541
Rycek, R. F., 43

S

Sable, J., 131, 132
Sadker, D. M., 128, 143, 540, 549
Sadker, M. P., 128, 143
Sadoski, M., 258
Sagan, L. L., 423
Saia, J., 291
Saka, Y., 332
Saleh, M., 186, 475
Salend, S. J., 496
Salmon, M., 169
Salomon, G., 55
Saltzman, J., 176
Sameroff, A., 46
Samuels, C. A., 36
Samuels, M., 541
Sanders, M., 220
Santamaria, L., 498
Santulli, K. A., 291
Sapon-Shevin, M., 191, 192
Saracho, O. N., 125
Sarama, J., 462
Sarason, S. B., 566
Savage, R., 456
Saw, A., 128, 130
Sawyer, A. L., 427
Saxe, L., 99
Saye, J., 320
Scardamalia, M., 360
Scarr, S., 33
Schalock, R., 199
Scheiter, K., 321
Schellenberg, E. G., 120, 121
Schifter, D., 8
Schlagmüller, M., 292
Schmidt, H., 329

Schmidt, M., 501
Schmidt, P., 148, 563
Schmitt-Rodermund, E., 90
Schmitz, M. J., 53
Schneider, M., 551
Schneider, W., 83, 88, 290, 292
Schnell, S. V., 205, 427, 428, 429
Schner, J. G., 100
Schommer-Aikins, M., 306
Schraw, G. J., 261, 277, 349
Schreurs, J., 329
Schultz, J. B., 32
Schunk, D. H., 191, 259, 261, 277, 279,
   281, 287, 288, 289, 290, 303, 305, 307,
   312, 315, 317, 324, 370, 393, 402
Schvaneveldt, P. L., 99
Schwartz, D., 82, 330, 338
Schwartz, D. L., 10
Schweinhart, L. J., 79
Schworm, S., 347
Scott, B., 274
Scott, S., 217
Scrimsher, S., 50, 52
Scriven, Michael, 486
Seagoe, M. V., 112
Searleman, A., 250, 252, 277
Seaton, M., 87
Securo, S., 234
Seddon, F. A., 274
Seezink, A., 333
Séguin-Lévesque, C., 405
Seidman, E., 34, 94
Seligman, Martin, 130
Selman, R. L., 91
Semb, George, 262
Serafica, F. C., 32
Serna, I., 186, 187
Shachar, H., 474
Shaffer, D., 34
Shaffer, D. R., 44
Shank, G., 18
Sharan, S., 472
Sharan, Y., 472
Sharpes, K., 115, 117, 346
Shaughnessy, M. F., 114
Shaw, R., 271, 290
Shaw, S., 217
Shayer, M., 44, 45
Shaywitz, B. A., 203
Shaywitz, S. E., 203
Shea, T. M., 415
Sheeber, L. B., 92, 93
Sheese, R., 52
Shepard, R. N., 258
Sherry, L., 479
Shia, R., 122
Shibley, J., 62
Shields, C., 49
Shields, P. M., 161, 166
Shiffrin, R. M., 251
Shin, D., 398
Shin, N., 122
Shogren, K., 199
Shulman, Lee, 575
Siders, J. A., 220
Siegel, D., 511, 512
Siegel, M. A., 105
Siegler, R. S., 39, 45
Sigelman, C. K., 44
Silbereisen, R. K., 90
Silva, P., 15, 24, 565, 575
Silver, E. J., 80
Silvernail, D., 560
Simmons, D. C., 207
Simon, S., 44
Simons, R. L., 154
Simonsen, B., 3, 409
Simpson, Elizabeth, 444
Sinatra, G. M., 290
Singer, A., 163
Singer, D. G., 47
Singham, M., 153
Sinitskaya, N. R., 379

Sink, H. E., 427
Sippola, L. K., 100
Sirin, S. R., 153
Siyahhan, S., 56, 274, 360, 362
Skinner, B. F., 226, 231, 247
Skinner, E. A., 289
Skokut, M., 192
Slavin, R. E., 12, 44, 82, 167, 177, 185, 210, 386, 471, 472, 474, 475
Sleet, D., 429
Sleeter, C. E., 144, 150
Slotta, J., 273, 463
Smith, A., 409
Smith, D. D., 191, 200
Smith, J. C., 152
Smith, K. A., 474
Smith, L., 36
Smith, L. L., 234
Smith, P. K., 76
Smith, T., 329
Smith, T. A., 129
Smolkin, L. B., 55
Smutny, Joan, 223
Snell, M., 199
Snowman, J., 293
Snyder, J., 560
Snyder, T., 7, 131, 132, 155, 173, 435
Snyder, T. D., 425, 426, 428
Sobel, D. M., 562
Sofronoff, K., 103
Soldier, L. L., 150, 173
Solic, K., 311, 367
Solloway, S., 18
Solórzano, R. W., 538
Sommer, R., 220
Sonenstein, F. L., 99
Songer, N. B., 56, 469
Sorell, G. T., 34, 35
Southerland, S., 332
Spalding, E., 498
Spear, Norman, 277
Spearman, Charles, 113
Spear-Swerling, L., 203
Spector, J. M., 511
Spence, J. C., 186
Spicuzza, R., 451
Spielmacher, C. E., 81, 85
Spies, Robert A., 557
Spitz, H. H., 158
Spörera, N., 267
Spray, Judith Sprat, 558
Spreat, S., 199
Sprinthall, N. A., 44, 45
Sprinthall, R. C., 44, 45
St. Rose, A., 130, 131, 132
Stahl, S., 217
Standing, L., 260
Stanford, P., 220
Stark, W., 218
Starnes, B. A., 148, 150
Staub, F. C., 461
Stears, M., 332
Stecher, B., 539, 542
Stefanakis, Evangeline, 140
Stefanek, J., 290
Stein, R. E. K., 80
Steinberg, L., 34, 35, 36, 48, 71, 89, 90, 93, 100, 108
Stemler, S. E., 115, 117, 120, 346
Stemmler, M., 101, 102
Stepanek, J., 192
Sterling-Turner, H. E., 429
Stern, E., 338, 457, 461
Sternberg, R. J., 10, 114, 115, 116, 117, 120, 121, 122, 123, 125, 126, 127, 130, 136, 140, 141, 203, 214, 223, 277, 345, 346, 529
Steubing, K. K., 203
Stevens, L. P., 18
Stewart, E. A., 154
Stewart, E. B., 154
Steyvers, M., 261
Stier, H., 34

Stiggins, R. J., 447, 484, 485, 487, 490, 491, 495, 498, 504
Stigler, J. W., 12, 15
Stinson, N., Jr., 154
Stockley, D. B., 290
Stokes, V., 553
Stough, L. M., 404
Stoutjesdijk, E. T., 299
Strassman, B. K., 272
Strømsø, H. I., 306
Stuart, C., 18
Stuhr, S. L., 43
Stull, A. T., 297
Styles, I., 125
Subotnik, Rena, 23
Sugai, G., 3, 409
Sugrue, Brenda, 477
Sullivan, F., 362
Sun, H., 378
Sun, K.-T., 127
Sunderman, G. L., 538, 540
Suomala, J., 123
Suppes, P., 220
Susak, Ziva, 295
Susman, E. J., 92
Svetina, M., 45
Swalander, L., 305
Swanson, C. B., 153
Swanson, H. L., 206, 270
Swick, April, 438

T

Tabachnick, S., 377
Talamo, A., 105
Tappan, M., 50, 52, 63
Tassé, M., 199
Tate, W. F., 191
Taube, K., 305
Tauber, Robert, 12, 23
Taylor, A., 427
Taylor, A. Z., 156
Taylor, D., 133
Taylor, Jill, 71
Taylor, P., 333
Taylor, P. C., 562
Taylor, S. S., 239
Taylor, S. V., 562
Teagle, H. F. B., 218
Tenenbaum, J. B., 261
Tenent, A., 317, 477
Tenenbaum, Harriet, 159
Tennessee Department of Education, 550
Terman, Lewis, 112
Terrell, Raymond D., 180
Tharp, R., 53
The National Institute of Child Health and Human Development Early Child Care Research Network, 460, 468, 540
Theodore, L. A., 237
Thoma, S. J., 60, 61, 71
Thomas, Adrian, 467
Thomas, J., 261, 538, 549
Thomsø, M., 274, 361
Thomas, V. G., 7
Thomas, W. P., 174
Thomas B. Fordham Institute, 547, 548
Thompson, Charles, 277
Thompson, J., 199
Thompson, L., 334
Thompson, M., 497
Thompson, M. S., 174, 176, 177
Thorn, A., 254, 257
Thorndike-Christ, Tracy, 557
Thrash, T., 372
Thurlow, D., 18
Thurlow, M. L., 189
Tieso, C. L., 188
Tighe, Theresa, 145
Timperley, H., 314, 317
Tingstrom, D. H., 429
Tishman, S., 114
Tobias, S., 329
Toblin, R. L., 82

Toch, T., 35, 220
Tomlinson, C. A., 111, 141, 188, 215, 396, 466, 487, 489
Tomporowski, P. D., 80
Tong, F., 176
Tonks, S., 373
Topaz, C., 479
Torelli, P., 156
Toshalis, E., 109
Toth, K., 203
Toth, S. L., 102
Towles-Reeves, E., 191
Tracy, T. S., 220
Trautman, Steve, 365
Trautwein, U., 87, 306, 393
Tremblay, R. E., 409
Trevisan, M. S., 341, 485
Triandis, H. C., 168
Tronsky, L. N., 128
Trotter, A., 553
Troutman, A. C., 235, 239, 245, 248
Troyer, L., 344
Trumbull, E., 172
Trumper, R., 54
Tsuchida, Ineko, 469
Tucker, D., 218
Tudge, J. R. H., 44, 50, 52, 82
Tukey, Lori, 138
Tulving, E., 259
Tulviste, P., 49, 50
Turnbull, B. J., 161, 166
Tuzun, H., 274, 361
Tyler, N. C., 191, 200

U

Ugel, N., 204
Ulanoff, Sharon, 180
Ulintz, L., 234
Umar, K. B., 154
U.S. Census Bureau, 146, 147, 152
U.S. Department of Education, 192, 193, 196, 202, 538, 545, 547
U.S. Department of Labor, 3
U.S. Office of Homeland Security, 146
Usher, E., 371
Usher, E. L., 305, 307, 317

V

Vadasy, P. F., 476
Vallecorsa, A. L., 183
Valli, L., 547, 558
van Boxtel, C., 463
VandeKamp, K. O., 315
Vandell, D. L., 89, 90, 100
van den Akker, A., 474
van den Bergh, H., 299, 309
van den Bossche, P., 329
VanDerHeyden, A., 192
van der Linden, J., 463
Van der Meij, 105
van der Rijt, J., 474
van der Werf, G., 288
Vanderzee, K. L., 427
van der Zee, Y. G., 288
van de Watering, G., 329
van Drie, J., 463
van Gog, T., 329, 348
Van Hout-Wolters, H. A. M., 291, 297, 299
van Laar, C., 156
VanLehn, K., 354
van Merriënboer, J. J. G., 319
Van Overschelde, J., 266
Vansteenkiste, M., 367
Van Wagenen, L., 567
Varma, S., 10
Vartanian, L. R., 43
Vasilyeva, M., 128
Vasquez Heilig, J., 547
Vaughn, S., 192, 204
Veenman, S., 474
Veermans, M., 479
Vekiri, I., 266

Verdugo-Alonso, M., 199
Vermont Department of Education, 536
Vernez, G., 548
Vevea, J. L., 99
Vitale, M. R., 297
Vitaro, F., 409
Vitz, P. C., 60
Vogel, C., 479
Vogler, K. E., 541
Vonèche, Jacques, 71
Vygotsky, L. S., 52, 71

W

Wachira, P., 274
Wade, A., 436
Wadsworth, B. J., 42, 47
Wai, J., 128, 130, 214
Wakai, S., 55
Walberg, H. J., 553
Walberg, Herbert, 3, 14, 23
Walker, C., 371
Walker, J. E., 415
Walker, J. M. T., 405
Wallace, M., 94
Wallace-Broscious, A., 32
Waller, T. G., 447
Wallet, P. A., 436
Wang, B., 379
Wang, J., 498
Wang, M. C., 14
Wang, Minjuan, 127
Wang, S., 551
Wanner, B., 409
Ward, Janie Victoria, 71, 141
Warren, S., 274
Wasserman, Selma, 10–11, 140
Watanabe, M., 188
Waterhouse, L., 119
Waterman, A. S., 31
Waters, P. L., 133
Watkins, D., 332, 339, 398
Watkins, J., 272
Watson, John, 225
Watson, M. F., 34
Wattenberg, W. W., 415
Waugh, C., 492, 494, 498, 501, 502, 504, 509, 519, 521
Wayne, A. J., 6
Wayne, S. K., 476
Wayne Ross, E., 558
Webb, Noreen, 477
Weber, K., 102, 236
Wechsler, D., 113
Wehmeyer, M. L., 199, 253
Weichold, K., 90
Weikart, D. P., 79
Weil, M., 448, 449, 450, 452, 466, 472
Weiler, J., 272
Weinberg, R. A., 33
Weinert, F. E., 114
Weinstein, C. S., 409, 438
Weiss, R. P., 122
Welch, Olga, 141
Wells, A. S., 186, 187
Wells, J., 170
Welner, K. G., 157, 188
Welsh, M., 54
Wentzel, K. R., 402, 405
Wertsch, J. V., 49, 50
Westerman, D. A., 12
Westwood, P., 219, 220
Whang, P. A., 18
Wheatley, G. H., 8
Wheelock, A., 183
Whipple, A. D., 7
White, R., 432, 433
Whitehouse, P., 56, 136
Whitesell, N. R., 133
Whitford, B., 560
Whittaker, C. R., 496
Whittaker, T., 373
Wiburg, Karin, 575
Wickens, C., 252

Wicks-Nelson, R., 209
Wideman, H., 379
Wiechman, B., 369
Wigfield, A., 94, 128, 131, 132, 373, 402
Wiggan, G., 150, 153
Wilczynski, S. M., 236, 429
Wilder, T., 539
Wiles, J., 94, 108
Wiles, M. T., 94, 108
Wiley, E., 188
Williams, C., 372, 374
Williams, J. P., 67, 204
Williams, R. L., 236, 237, 239
Williams, S. C., 219
Willig, A. C., 177
Willingham, D., 10
Willis, J., 20, 364
Wilson, C., 169
Wilson, Jeni, 386
Wilson, R., 552, 553
Wilson, S. M., 6
Wilson, Victor, 557
Windschitl, M., 331, 332, 333
Windschitl, Mark, 460
Wink, D., 174
Wink, J., 174
Winkler, A. M., 539

Winksel, H., 53
Winne, P. H., 251, 252, 271, 290, 306, 452
Winterhoff, P. A., 44, 50
Winters, F. I., 462
Winzenz, D., 255, 256, 265
Witkin, H. A., 124, 125
Witt, J., 192
Wittrock, M. C., 442
Wittwer, J., 457
Wlodkowski, R. J., 166, 384
Wohldmann, E., 355
Wolf, Jessica, 558
Wong, Bernice, 295
Woodhill, B. M., 36
Woods, Peter, 23
Woodsworth, Barry, 71
Woodward, M. M., 293
Woolfolk Hoy, A., 409
Workman, D., 509
Worthman, C., 101
Woszczyna, C., 290
Wouters, P., 319
Woyshner, C., 135
Wozney, L., 436
Wright, J., 545
Wright, R. J., 529

Wuthrick, M. A., 159
Wynn, R. L., 76

Y

Yager, R. E., 38
Yamagata-Lynch, L. C., 332
Yang, S.-H., 570
Yates, C., 44
Yau, R., 547
Ybarra, Silivia, 481
Ye, R., 272
Yeager, M., 199
Yeh, S. S., 552
Yelland, N. J., 55, 462
Yilmaz-Tuzun, O., 560
Yoerg, K., 274
Yonezawa, S., 186, 187
Yoshii, M., 178
Young, D. B., 312
Young, M. J., 551
Youngreen, R., 344
Youngs, P., 6
Youngs, Wayne, 6
Younie, S., 331
Ysseldyke, J. E., 189, 451
Yu, C., 127

Z

Zabala, D., 547
Zahn, I., 376
Zangwill, Israel, 144
Zeichner, K., 560
Zeichner, Kenneth M., 23
Zeichner, O., 319
Zeidner, Moshe, 324
Zeldin, Amy, 132
Zellermayer, M., 55
Zhang, D., 469
Zhang, J., 360
Zhang, L., 122, 123, 125, 126, 127, 136, 140, 141
Zhao, Yong, 159
Zhou, T., 379
Zhu, X., 378
Zientek, L. R., 137
Zigmond, N., 183
Zimmerman, B., 402
Zimmerman, B. J., 279, 280, 281, 282, 285, 286, 290, 300, 307, 324, 370, 452
Zimmerman, M. A., 99
Zittleman, K. R., 143, 540, 549
Zuiker, S., 274
Zuniga, S., 477
Zuo, L., 213

Subject Index

Page numbers followed by f indicate figure
Page numbers followed by t indicate table

A

AAIDD. *See* American Association on Intellectual and Developmental Disabilities (AAIDD)

AAMR. *See* American Association of Mental Retardation (AAMR)

Ability: analytical, 115, 115f, 116, 122; attribution and, 374; changes in beliefs about, 375; practical, 115, 115f, 116, 122; types of beliefs about, 375–377; visual-spatial, 128

Ability-grouped classrooms, 183

Ability grouping, 157, 181; assumptions underlying, 185; between class, 184–185, 186, 187; evaluations of, 186–187; to group or not to group, 187–188; Joplin plan, 185, 186; regrouping, 185; resources on, 223; within-class, 185, 186

Abstractions, fifth and sixth graders and, 46

Academic skills, 7

Accelerated instruction, 214–215

Accident rates, third grade and, 81

Accommodation, 37, 331

Accountability, 535–542, 545–550

Accountability, individual, 473

Accountability system, 537

Achievement: effect of cooperative learning on, 474; effects of modeling on, 307–309; epistemological beliefs and, 305–306; higher, 14; identity, 33t; levels of, graduation rates and, 152–153; need for, 155, 373–374, 380; outcome of, 8; self-efficacy and, 305–306; self-regulation processes and, 305–306

Achievement batteries, 528

Achievement gap, 142, 153

Achievement tests, 528–529

Acquired immunodeficiency syndrome (AIDS), 99

Acronyms, 294t

Acrostics, 294t

ACT. *See* American College Testing Program (ACT)

Acting Lessons for Teachers: Using Performance Skills in the Classroom (Tauber and Mester), 12, 23

Acting skills, 12

Active responding, 494

Activity: of preschool and kindergarten children, 74, 75, 76; of primary grade children, 80; sexual, high school students and, 98, 98t, 99

ADAAA. *See* American with Disabilities Act Amendments Act of 2008 (ADAAA)

Adaptation, defined, 37

Adaptive inferences, 288

Adaptive teaching, 9

Adderall, for ADHD, 205

Adequate Yearly Progress (AYP), 537, 538, 557

ADHD. *See* Attention-deficit/hyperactivity disorder (ADHD)

Adolescence/adolescents: adolescent egocentrism, 25, 43, 94; after school employment, 100; characteristics of, 90t; classroom climate for, 94–95; classroom management and, 410; concept of efficiency and, 380; constructivist approach to teaching, 387; early adolescence, 89, 92–93, 94; emerging, 89, 92, 93; emotional disorder during, 101–102; emotional turmoil, 92; Erikson's theory and, 28, 29; HIV/AIDS prevalence, 99; identity statuses, 31–34, 36; motivating learners, 379; overestimating capabilities of, 45; Piaget's theory and, 39; rehearsal and, 292; resources on characteristics of, 108–109; as series of transitions, 89; social and emotional development, 103. *See also* High school age-level characteristics; Middle school age-level characteristics

Adolescence (Steinberg), 108

Adult Library Services Association (YALSA), 272

Adults: characteristics of, 90t; emotions of adolescents *vs.*, 93; intimacy *vs.* isolation in, 29

Advancing Formative Assessment in Every Classroom: A Guide for Instructional Leaders (Moss and Brookhart), 520

Adventure learning programs, 105–106

Aesthetic needs, 391

Affective domain, 442

Affective (emotional) outcomes, 8

Affective processes, 285

Affton High School, 145–146

African Americans. *See* Blacks

Age: interpretation of rules and, 56–57; trends in metacognition, 270–271

Age-graded classrooms, growth of, 183

Aggressive behavior, 241

AIDS. *See* Acquired immunodeficiency syndrome (AIDS)

Alaska Native Knowledge Network, 169

Albert Shanker Institute, 570

Algorithm, 343

Alien Rescue, 318

ALPS. *See* Connect page of Active Learning Practices for Schools (ALPS)

Alternate-form reliability, 525

Alternative-solution thinking, 428

American Association of Mental Retardation (AAMR), 198

American Association of University Women, 130

American Association on Intellectual and Developmental Disabilities (AAIDD), 198

American College Testing Program (ACT), 526

American culture, 149

American Educational Research Association, 6

American Indians. *See* Native Americans

American Journal on Intellectual and Developmental Disabilities, 198

American Journal on Mental Retardation, 198

American Management Association, 327

American Printing House for the Blind, 219

American Psychiatric Association, 205

American Psychological Association (APA), 2, 4, 557

Americans with Disabilities Act Amendments Act of 2008 (ADAAA), 198

Analogous problem, 349

Analysis, 285, 290, 314, 315

Analytical ability, 115, 115f, 116, 122

Anarchic style, 126t

Angelou, Maya, 355

Annual Review of Psychology (2001), 324

Anorexia nervosa, 101

Antiseptic bouncing, 418

Anxiety, 96, 101, 102, 280, 526

APA's Board of Educational Affairs, 2

Apple Computer, 219

Applications of Psychological Science to Teaching and Learning Task Force, 4

Applied Behavior Analysis for Teachers (Alberto and Troutman), 248

Aptitude tests, 529

Argumentative passes, 309

Armstrong School District in Pennsylvania, 487

Arnetha Ball's model of generative change, 569

Aronson, Elliott, 387

"Arranging Consequences That Decrease Behavior" (Alberto and Troutman), 248

Artistry in Teaching (Rubin), 23

Art of Thinking, The (Ruggiero), 365

Arts: teaching as, 10–12, 14–15; technology tools for, 273–274

Asian culture, 149

Asians: achievement expectations for, 159; family environment and, 155; motivation/beliefs/attitudes and, 156; multicultural education and, 163t; nonverbal communication and, 149; percentage of school-age children, 147t; population of, 146; poverty and, 152f; special education and, 194; standardized achievement tests, 46; support for academic achievement, 155

Asperger syndrome, 214

Assessment and Grading in Classrooms (Brookhart and Nitko), 521

Assessment for learning. *See* Formative assessment

Assessment of learning. *See* Summative assessment

Assessment of Student Achievement (Gronlund and Waugh), 520–521

Assessment(s): aligning with objectives, 447; authentic, 492; defined, 485–486; formative, 17, 497–498, 560; of intelligence, 115; as learning, 488–489; of learning *vs.* assessment for learning, 487–488, 489; role in teaching, 485–489; as teacher responsibility, 196–197; techniques, 513–519; technology-based performance, 511. *See also* Evaluations; Performance assessment

Assessment Strategies for Self-Directed Learning (Costa and Kallick), 324

Assignment criteria, 509

Assimilation, 37

Assistive technology, 218

Astronomy Village (computer simulation program), 122

Asuza Unified School District in Asuza, California, 436

Atkinson, John, 373

"At School, Technology Starts to Turn a Corner" (Lohr), 336

"Attaining Self-Regulation: A Social Cognitive Perspective" (Zimmerman), 324

"Attendance Prize: Schools Offer Kids Big Rewards Just to Get Them to Show Up" (Cruver), 238

Attention, 200, 252, 252f, 253–254, 263, 264

Attention-deficit/hyperactivity disorder (ADHD), 205–207, 220

Attention focusing, 287

At the Heart of Teaching: A Guide to Reflective Practice (McEntee, Appleby, Dowd, Grant, Hole, and Silva), 24, 575

Attitudes: moral, 61; students', 155–156; unified discipline and, 432

Attributional bias, 428

Attributions, 372

Attribution theory: beliefs about ability and, 380; explanations of success and failure, 374–377

Augmented programs, 399

Authentic assessments, 492

Authentic problems, 331

Authoritarian parents, 79, 405

Authoritative parents, 79, 405

Author-on-Line Project, 463

Autism, 193, 196t

Autism spectrum disorder, 214

Autonomous learners, 459–460. *See also* Self-regulated learners

Autonomy *vs.* shame and doubt (Two to three years; preschool), 29

Aversion, 156

Aversive stimulus, 227

AYP. *See* Adequate Yearly Progress (AYP)

B

Backloading, 537–538

Backward fading, 349

"Be Aware," "Be Creative," "Be Critical," "Communicate Your Ideas" (Ruggiero), 365

Beginning teachers: focus of, 12; preparation programs and, 5–6; training and, 5

Behavior: delinquent, 87; emotionally disturbed students and, 211; intellectual, 97; patterns of, 280, 281f; planful, 39; self-efficacy and, 284–285; social, 97. *See also* Behavior and thought processes; Behavior modification; Behavior problems

Behavioral approach to instruction, 451, 478t

Behavioral approach to teaching, 448–451

Behavioral learning theory. *See* Operant conditioning

Behavioral view of motivation: effect of reinforcement on, 368–369; limitations of, 369–370

Behavior and thought processes: new findings mean revised ideas, 1, 10–11; research and, 8; selection and interpretation of data, 9; teaching and learning and, 8–9

Behavior disorder, 208

Behavior Management: A Practical Approach for Educators (Walker, Shea, Bauer), 415

Behavior modification: contingency contracting, 237, 239; extinction, time-out, and response cost, 239–241; resources on, 247–248; shaping, 235–236; token economies, 236–237; use of, 241–242. *See also* Behavior

Behavior Modification: What It Is and How to Do It (Martin and Pear), 248

Behavior problems: bullying, 426–430; handling, 420, 424; influence techniques and, 415–420; problem ownership, 420; techniques for dealing with, 415–420

Beliefs: ability and changes in, 376; about nature of cognitive ability, 374–375; students', 155–156; types of, 375–377

Belongingness, 391t

Benchmark School in Media, Pennsylvania, 311

Best Foot Forward program, 430

Between-class ability grouping, 184–185, 186, 187

Between Parent and Child (Ginott, Ginott, and Goddard), 76

BIG Accommodation Model, 451

Big-fish-little-pond effect, 87

Bilingual education, 173–177, 180

Bilingual immersion. *See* Two-way bilingual (TWB) education

Bilingual programs, two-way, 174–175

Biological factors, violence and, 427–428

Biology, Society, and Behavior: The Development of Sex Differences in Cognition (Mcgillicuddy-DeLisi and De Lisi), 141

Blacks: achievement expectations for, 159; classroom environment and, 157; cooperative learning and, 151, 167; cultural diversity and, 144; drop-out of, 153; emotional disorders and, 101; family environment and, 154, 155; high school graduation and, 152–153; instructional formats and, 150; lead and, 154; motivation, beliefs, attitudes and, 156; multicultural education and, 169; need for achievement and, 156; percentage of school-age children and, 147f; poverty and, 152, 152f; self-esteem and, 153, 156; social class and, 152, 153, 158; special education and, 191–192, 194; suicide attempts and, 101; support for academic achievement, 155; testing and, 153

Blackwell Handbook of Childhood Cognitive Development (Goswami), 108

Blogs, 272, 479

Blogs, Wikis, Podcasts, and Other Powerful Web Tools for Classrooms (Richardson), 108

Bloom's taxonomy, 474, 490, 492, 534

Bodily-kinesthetic intelligence, 117, 118t

Body animation, 12

Book reviews, 217

Books, electronic grade, 510–511

Boyle's law, 137

Braille 'n Speak, 219

Brain-based approaches to education, 10

Brain Power program, 430

Brown v. Board of Education (1954), 189, 191, 192

Bubble kids, 546

Bulimia nervosa, 101

Bullying: characteristics of bullies, 427; cyberbullying, 426; defined, 426; reducing, 429–430; resources on, 438; schools and, 427; victims and, 427

C

C. A. R. M. E. *See* Conservation of Area and Its Measurement, The (C. A. R. M. E)

Career choice and selection, gender bias and, 131–132

Care Theory, Noddings's, 61–62

Caring: A Feminine Approach to Ethics and Moral Education (Nodding), 61, 62, 71

Caring orientation: Gilligan's, 71; to moral development, 79–83; Nodding's, 71

Carnegie Corporation, 4, 186

CASE (Cognitive Acceleration through Science Education), 44

"Case for Direct Explanation of Strategies, The" (Block and Pressley), 481

Case in Print: on authoritative teachers, 431; on behavior modification, 238; on constructivism, 336; on cultural diversity, 145; described, 20; on formative assessment, 499; on gender bias, 134; on imagination/metacognition, 268; on Information-processing/social cognitive theory, 454; on mainstreaming, 194; on middle school age-level, 96; on moral values, 64; on reflective teaching, 571; on self-regulated learners, 301; on taking an interest in learning, 381; on teacher-artist, 13; on technology and constructing knowledge, 336; on thinking about what we think about, 268; on violence, 268

CAST. *See* Center for Applied Special Technology (CAST)

CASTL. *See* Center for Advancing the Study of Teaching and Learning (CASTL)

Casual attributions, 288

CAT. *See* Computer adaptive testing (CAT)

Catcher in the Rye (Salinger), 353

Categories, 39

Causal attributions, 288

"Causes, Correlates, and Caveats: Understanding the Development of Sex Differences in Cognition" (Halpern and Ikier), 141

CBI. *See* Computer-based instruction (CBI)

CBT. *See* Computer-based testing (CBT)

Center for Advancing the Study of Teaching and Learning (CASTL), 487

Center for Applied Linguistics, 180

Center for Applied Special Technology (CAST), 218

Center for Educational Technology (CET), 481–482

Center for Multicultural Education, 180

Center on Education Policy, 538, 545, 547

Centers for Disease Control and Prevention, 99, 101

CEP. *See* Character Education Partnership (CEP)

Challenging assumptions: on bilingual education, 178; on classroom assessment, 519; on classroom management, 436; described, 18–19; on desirable stimulus, 246; on groupthink, 139; on high school age-levels, 106; on information/meaning, 275; on multiculturalism, 178; on operant conditioning, 246; on planning, 480; on problem solving, 363; on reflective teaching, 573–574; on standardized tests, 556; on taking learning personally, 322; on teachers, 139; on teaching, learning, and motivation, 400; on teaching in service learning, 221; on theories of development, 106; on what/how students know, 69

Character, 434

Character Education Partnership (CEP), 71

Character Education Programs, 64; research on, 65–67; resources on, 71

Characteristics of Emotional and Behavioral Disorders of Children and Youth (Kauffman), 223

CHAT. *See* Cultural-historical activity theory (CHAT)

Chicago Public Schools, 571

Childhood and Society (Erikson), 71

Children: applying Piaget's theory of cognitive development to, 46–48; Piaget's analysis of moral judgment of, 56–57; resources on development of, 109; resources on play behavior, 108; standard achievement tests of, 46; understanding capabilities of, 44–45

Children, Play, and Development (Hughes), 108

Children and Bullying: How Parents and Educators Can Reduce Bullying at School (Rigby), 438

Children and Their Development (Kail), 108

Children's Thinking: Cognitive Development and Individual Differences (Bjorklund), 108

Choice Theory in the Classroom (Glasser), 373

Chunking information, 264

Classifying process, 46

Class inclusion, concept of, 46

Class participation, gender bias and, 132–133

Classroom: ability-grouped, 183; achievement, students and, 160–162; age-graded, growth of, 183; applying social cognitive theory in, 312–318; assessment, technology for, 510–512; constructivist, characteristics of, 335t; eighth-grade, study on, 470t; environment of, 157, 211; gender equity in, 133, 135; instruction, resources on, 140; interventions, 429–430; reward structures, 471–472; space of, 12. *See also* Classroom management

Classroom 2.0, 252, 272

Classroom Assessment: What Teachers Need to Know (Popham), 521

Classroom Check-Up (Reinke, Lewis-Palmer, & Merrell), 430

Classroom Instruction That Works: Research-Based Strategies for Increasing Student Achievement (Marzano, Pickering, and Pollock), 23

Classroom learning assessment, role in teaching, 485–489

Classroom management: authoritarian/ permissive/authoritative approach to, 405; behavior problems and, 454–462; contemporary studies of, 409; on handling problem behavior, 420–424; of middle, junior high, and high school classroom, 409–412; resources on, 438; techniques of, 406–415; technology tools for, 411–412. *See also* Violence

Classroom Management for Elementary Teachers (Evertson and Emmer), 247–248, 438

Classroom Management for Middle and High School Teachers (Emmer and Evertson), 248, 410, 438

Classroom observation checklists, 563f

Classroom Performance System, 499

Class rules, establishing, 413

CLES. *See* Constructivist Learning Environment Survey (CLES)

Client-centered therapy, 465

Clinical depression, 101

CLT. *See* Cognitive load theory (CLT)

Coalition for Psychology, 42

Code of Fair Testing Practices (APA), 558

Code of Federal Regulations, 190

Cognitive ability, beliefs about, 374–375

Cognitive Acceleration through Science Education (CASE), 44

Cognitive apprenticeship, 333–334

Cognitive approach to teaching/instruction, 478t; constructivist theory and, 457; information-processing theory and, 254, 259, 260, 451–453, 456–460; resources on, 481; technology and, 461–463, 477–478

Cognitive characteristics: of children with intellectual disability, 199–200; elementary grades age-level and, 88; high school age-level and, 103–104; middle school age-level, 94–95; preschool/kindergarten age-level, 77–80; primary grades age-level, 82–84

Cognitive constructivism, 331, 333

Cognitive development: accommodating student variability and, 200; background of, 26; culture and, 45–46, 49–50; effect of technology on, 105–106; high school age-level and, 98t; instruction and, 43–44, 50–53; limitations of theory, 380; middle-school age-level and, 89t; need for conceptual organization and, 373; preschool and kindergarten age-level and, 75t; primary grade age-level and, 81t; resources on, 108; social interaction and, 50; technology and, 54–56. *See also* Piaget's theory of cognitive development; Vygotsky's theory of cognitive development

Cognitive-developmental effect, cooperative learning and, 475

Cognitive Development (Flavell, Miller, and Miller), 108

Cognitive domain, 442

Cognitive elaboration effect, cooperative learning and, 475

Cognitive feedback, 319

Cognitive immaturity hypothesis, 80

Cognitive load theory (CLT), 254

Cognitive Process Dimension, 442

Cognitive processes, 285

Cognitive Psychology and Instruction (Bruning, Schraw, Norby, and Ronning), 277

"Cognitive Strategies Instruction: From Basic Research to Classroom Instruction" (Alexander, Winne, Pressley, and Harris), 325

Cognitive theory. *See* Piaget's theory of cognitive development; Vygotsky's theory of cognitive development

Cognitive (thinking) outcomes, 8

Cognitive views of motivation, 372–380

Collaborative learning, 479

Collaborative standard, 288

Collaborative strategic reading, 204–205

Collectivism, 172

College entrance, gender and, 128

Commission on Instructionally Supportive Assessment, 549

Commitment, psychosocial moratorium and, 31

Common-Sense Classroom Management for Elementary School Teachers (Lindberg and Swick), 438

Common-Sense Classroom Management for Middle and High School Teachers (Lindberg, Kelly and Swick), 438

Community of practice, 56

Community service activities, 175

Comorbidity, 205

Competence, 79; coursework and, 5–6; degree of, 378; encouraging, 79

Competency test, 528–529

Competitive goal structures, 471

Comprehension-directed tactics, 292, 314

Comprehension Instruction: Perspectives and Suggestions (Block and Pressley), 481

"Comprehension Instruction in the Primary Grades" (Block and Pressley), 481

Comprehension tactics, self-regulated learners and, 313

Comprehensive Multicultural Education: Theory and Practice (Bennett), 180

Computer adaptive testing (CAT), 552–553

Computer-based instructional technology, 463

Computer-based instruction (CBI), 231–235; effect of self-efficacy on, 321–322; effect of self-regulated learning skills on, 320–321; evaluation of, 234–235; research on the effects of, 231–233; types of programs, 232t

Computer-based programs, 399

Computer-based testing (CBT), 551–552, 558

Computers: computer technology as information processing tool, 271–275; hearing-impaired students and, 218; Piaget's cognitive theory and, 54; software programs for drills/tutorials/simulations/games 243, 248; visually-impaired students and, 219; Vygtosky's theory of cognitive development and, 55. *See also* Computer-based instruction (CBI)

Computer-supported intentional learning environments (CSILE), 359–360, 463

Conceptions of Giftedness (Sternberg and Davison), 223

Concept mapping, 292, 296–297, 453, 455f

Concepts, 39, 49

Conceptual organization, cognitive development and need for, 373

Concrete operational stage, in cognitive development, 39t, 41, 46

Conduct disorder, 205

Connect page of Active Learning Practices for Schools (ALPS), 573

Consequential engagement, 362

Conservation, concept of, 46

Conservation of Area and Its Measurement, The (C. A. R. M. E), 54

Conservation problems, 40

Conservative style, 126t

Constructed response, 490

Constructivism, 9, 38; Case in Print on, 336–337; challenges of constructivist teacher, 460–461; classroom management and, 404; cognitive, 331, 333; cognitive approach to teaching and, 457; conditions fostering, 333–334; constructivist learning principles, 95; critical, 332–333; defined, 328; discovery learning and, 328–329, 458; ethnocentrism and, 148; information processing and, 250, 251; motivation and, 387; multicultural education and, 164; putting constructivism in perspective, 338–339; reflective teaching and, 562; resources on, 364–365; social, 331–332, 347; suggestions for teaching, 339–343; today, 329–335; Web-based Inquiry Science Environment (WISE) and, 272–273

Constructivist Instructional Design: Foundations, Models, and Examples (Willis), 364

Constructivist Learning Environment Survey (CLES), 562

Constructs, 526

Construct validity evidence, 526–527

Contemporary Intellectual Assessment (Flanagan and Harrison), 140

Content standards, 496

Content validity evidence, 526

Contingency contracting, 237

Continuous reinforcement schedule, 230

Contributions approach, in multicultural education programs, 163

Control, 7

Controlled floundering, 462

Control processes: defined, 252; model of information processes, 252f; of short-term memory, teaching and, 259t; short-term memory and, 254

Conventional morality, 59, 59t

Cooperative goals structures, 472

Cooperative learning: defined, 167, 458, 479; effect on achievement, 474; effects of social interaction on, 474–475; effects on motivation, 474, 475; in elementary grades, 255; elements of, 472–473; learning disability and, 207; resources on, 482; teachers' use of, 476–477; using methods of, 386–387

Cooperative Learning: Integrating Theory and Practice (Gillies), 482

Cooperative Learning: Theory, Research, and Practice (Slavin), 82, 210

Corporal punishment, 240, 241

Correction procedures, 433

Coursework and competence, 5–6

Creating and Recognizing Quality Rubrics (Arter and Chappuis), 521

Creating and Sustaining the Constructivist Classroom (Marlow and Page), 364

Creativity, 526

Criterion-referenced grading: nature of, 503; strengths and weakness of, 503–505

Criterion-referenced tests, 529–530, 555

Critical constructivism, 332–333

Criticisms: encouragement and, 418–419; of Erikson's theory, 34–35; of Kohlberg's theory, 59–60; of Piaget's theory, 44–46; primary grades age-level and, 82

Cross-age tutoring, 166

Crossroads: Reexamining the Federal Effort to Close the Achievement Gap (Rebell and Wolf), 558

CSILE. *See* Computer-supported intentional learning environments (CSILE)

Cultural diversity, 144, 145

Cultural-historical activity theory (CHAT), 332

Culturally Proficient Instruction (Robins, Lindsey, Lindsey, and Terrell), 180

Culturally relevant teaching, 143

Culturally responsive pedagogy, 171

Culturally responsive schooling, 143

Culturally responsive teaching, 165, 166

Cultural norms, 143

Cultural pluralism, 144, 145, 498

Culture: American, 149; Asian, 149; cognitive development and, 45–46, 49–50; defined, 142–143; identity status and, 33–34; Piaget's cognitive theory and, 45–56

Culture, Self, and, Motivation: Essays in Honor of Martin L. Maehr (Kaplan, Karabenick, and De Groot), 402

Cumulative rehearsal, 292

Curriculum: high-stakes testing and, 547; narrowing, 547

Curve grading, 30

Cyberbullying, 426

Cyber-Bullying: Issues and Solutions for the School, the Classroom, and the Home (Shariff), 438

Cybergogy, 127

Cylert, for ADHD, 205

D

David Wechsler's Global Capacity view, 114–115

Deaf-blindness, 193, 196t

Debate forums, 550

Debates, 13

Decatur Central High School, 337

Decentration, 40

Decision-making and social action approach, in multicultural education program, 164

Decision Point! database, 320

Deduction, 259

Deferred imitation, 39

Deficiency needs, 390, 396–398

Defining Issues Test (DIT), 61

Degree of realism, 494–495

Delinquent behavior, 87

Demonstrations, 493–494

Depression, 101–102

Depressive syndrome, 101

Designing and Assessing Educational Objectives: Applying the New Taxonomy (Marzano and Kendall), 521

Designing and Developing Programs for Gifted Students (Smutny), 223

Detracking practice, 188

Developing Child, The (Bee and Boydl), 108

Developing Portfolios in Education: A Guide to Reflection, Inquiry, and Assessment (Johnson, Mims-Cox, and Doyle-Nichols), 575

Developmental theories. *See* Psychosocial development

"Development of Academic Self-Efficacy, The" (Schunk and Pjares), 324

Development of Achievement Motivation, The (Wigfield and Eccles), 324, 3224

Development of Memory in Children, The (Kail), 277

Dexedrine, for ADHD, 205

Diagnostic test, 528, 555

Dialogue problems, 317

Dialogue with Erik Erikson (Evans), 71

Differentiated instruction, 111, 138, 188, 215–216

Differentiated Instruction: A Guide for Middle and High School Teachers (Benjamin), 141

Differentiated Instruction Using Technology: A Guide for Middle and High School Teachers (Benjamin), 141

Differentiated Literacy Instruction for English Language Learners (Quiocho and Ulanoff), 180

Differentiated School: Making Revolutionary Changes in Teaching and Learning, The (Brimijoin and Narvaex), 141

Differentiating Instruction for Students with Learning Disabilities (Bender), 223

Diffusion identity status, 429

Digital divide, 135–136

Digital portals for professional development, 570, 573

Digital portfolios, 511–512

Digitized pictures, 512

Direct appeals, 418

Direct instruction: components of, 449–450; effectiveness of, 451; nature of, 448–449; resources on, 481. *See also* Instruction

Direct learning, 257

Direct writing assessments, 493

Discipline and Group Management in Classrooms (Kounin), 406

Discovery and exploratory environments, 461–462

Discovery learning, 328–329, 458

Discrimination, 229

Disequilibrium, 37, 363, 378, 380

Disinhibition, 303

Distributed position effect, 264

Distributed practice, 264

DIT. *See* Defining Issues Test (DIT)

Diversity, student identity and, 34

Diversity Responsive Teaching Observation Tool, 562

Doctrine of formal discipline, 255

Domain, 526

Domains of Knowledge, 443

Double helix, 349

Drill and practice program, 232t, 248

Dropout rates, 542; high-stakes testing programs and, 547; percentages of, 435

Dual coding theory, 258–259, 265

Dual language, Two–way bilingual (TWB) education

Dynamic Social Studies for Constructivist Classrooms: Inspiring Tomorrow's Social Scientists (Maxim), 365

E

Eagle Has Landed: The Flight of Apollo 11, The, 216

Early-maturing boys, 89, 90t

Early-maturing girls, 89–90, 90t

Edublogs, 573

Educating Exceptional Children (Kirk, Gallagher, Coleman, and Anastasiow), 223

Education: bilingual, 173–177; caring orientation to moral development and, 60–62; multicultural, 143. *See also* Special education

Educational Assessment of Students (Brookhart and Nitko), 521

Educational Leadership, 570

Educational psychology: benefits of learning about, 1, 2; coursework and competence, 5; defined, 1, 2; factors in behavior and thought processes, 7–10; nature and values of science, 6–7; reflective teaching, 15–18; research on, 3–4; teaching as art and science, 10–12; Teaching Without a Script, 13–14

Educational Psychology: A Cognitive View (Ausubel), 330

Educational Researcher, 141

Educational Software Directory, 207

Educational Testing and Measurement: Classroom Application and Practice (Kubiszyn and Borich), 521

Educational Testing Service (ETS), 22

Education for All Handicapped Children Act of 1975, 189

Education of exceptional children, resources on, 223

Education of Students with Intellectual Disability: Research and Practice (Foreman), 223

Education Program for Gifted Youth (EPGY), 220

Education World, 272

Effective praise, guidelines for, 383t

Effective teaching, 16–17

Effective Teaching Strategies That Accommodate Diverse Learners (Kameenui and Carnine), 223

Efficiency, adolescents and, 380

Egocentric level, in interpersonal reasoning, 91t

Egocentrism, 40; adolescent, 43; technology and, 104–105

Elaborative encoding. *See* Elaborative rehearsal

Elaborative rehearsal, 252, 252f, 254–255

Electronic exhibitions, 550

Electronic grade books, 510–511

Electronic portfolios. *See* Digital portfolios

Electronic Read Around, 272

Elementary and Secondary Education Act (ESEA), 536

Elementary Classroom Management: Lessons from Research and Practice (Weinstein and Mignano, Jr.), 438

Elementary school age-level characteristics: cognitive characteristics, 88; emotional characteristics, 86–87; physical characteristics, 84–85; social characteristics, 85–86

Elementary schools, 72; applying Piaget's theory and, 47–48; applying theories of development and, 84t; classroom management of, 409; concrete operational stage in, 41; cooperative learning and, 255; industry *vs.* inferiority in, 29

Elementary students, multicultural lesson for, 165

Elementary to Early Middle School, concrete operational stage in, 40

ELLs. *See* English-language learners (ELLs)

E-mail messaging systems, motivation and, 399

Emerging adolescents, 89, 92, 93

Emotional and behavior disorders, resources on, 223

Emotional arousal, 283f, 284

Emotional characteristics: elementary grades age-level, 86–87; high school age-level and, 100–103; middle school age-level, 92–94; preschool/kindergarten age-level, 76–77; primary grades age-level, 82–84

Emotional disorders, 101–102

Emotional disturbance: characteristics of, 209; as defined in IDEA, 195, 208–209; suggestions for teaching students with, 210–211

Empathy and Moral Development (Hoffman), 71

Empirical and theoretical approaches, in Vygotsky's theory, 52

Empirical learning, 51

Employment, high school students and, 100

Emulation, 300t, 303–304

Encouragement, 418–419

End Physical Punishment of Children, 240

Engagement, concept of, 379–380

English-as-a-second language (ESL), 174, 177

English immersion program, 176

English-language learners (ELLs), 176, 177

Enrichment instruction, 215–216

Entity theorists, 375, 377

Environment: classroom, 157, 211; discovery and exploratory, website of, 461–462; exploratory, 461; family, 154–155; guided learning, 462; learning, 563t; least restrictive, 190; multiple-user virtual environment, 122; school, 429; virtual, 274; visual, 274–275

Environmental factors, 280, 281f

e-pal program, 220

ePals, 106

EPGY. *See* Education Program for Gifted Youth (EPGY)

Epigenetic principle, 28

Epistemological beliefs, 286, 287, 305–306

Equilibration, 37

Erikson, Erik. *See* Erikson's theory of psychosocial development

Erikson's theory of psychosocial development, 25, 28; on adolescent identity statuses, 31–34; applying, 35–36; criticism of, 34–35; description of development, 71; epigenetic principle, 28; helping student develop sense of industry, 30–31; helping students formulate an identity, 31; intrinsic motivation and, 369–370; psychosocial crisis, 28; resources on description of development, 71; stages of psychosocial development, 29–30; suggestions for teaching, 35–36; taking a psychosocial moratorium, 31; view of identity development, 60–61; violence and, 429

ESEA. *See* Elementary and Secondary Education Act (ESEA)

ESL. *See* English-as-a-second language (ESL)

Essay tests, 491

Essay writing, 550

Essential Middle School, The (Wiles, Bondi, and Wiles), 108

Essential Piaget: An Interpretive Reference and Guide, The (Gruber and Vonèche), 71

Essentials of Human Memory (Baddeley), 277

Esteem, 390, 391, 391t

e-structors, 551

Ethnic additive approach, in multicultural education program, 163

Ethnically and culturally diverse students, 5

Ethnic group, 148

Ethnic identity, 34

Ethnicity: adequate yearly progress (AYP) and, 537; identity statuses and, 33–34; No Child Left Behind Act and, 539, 548; percentage of school-age

children and, 147f; sexual activity among high school students and, 99; social class and, 148–151, 158–159, 161–162; standardized testing and, 539; teachers expectations and, 158. *See also* Multicultural education; Multiculturalism, rise of

Ethnicity and social class, 148–160

Ethnocentrism, 147

ETS. *See* Educational Testing Service (ETS)

Europe, standard achievement tests of children in, 46

Evaluation: of ability grouping, 186–187; cognitive domain taxonomy and, 442–443; of computer-based instruction, 234–235; direct instruction and, 451; of the effectiveness of objectives, 447–448; formative, 17, 486, 487, 487t; Individuals with Disabilities Education Act, 189–190; of Kohlberg's theory, 59–60; problem solving and, 349–350; replacement, in IDEA, 189–190; of student learning, 501–506; teaching the skill of, 354. *See also* Assessment; Reflective teaching; Self-evaluation; Summative evaluation

Evaluative judgments, 486

Everything Bad Is Good for You (Johnson), 360

Examinee appropriateness, 527–528

Exceptional Children and Youth (Hunt and Marshall), 223

Exceptional students, technology and, 217–220

Executive style, 126t

Exhibitions, 493, 550

Expectancy-value theory, 373

Expectations, 432

Explicit Direct Instruction: The Power of the Well-Crafted, Well-Taught Lesson (Hollingsworth and Ybarra), 481

Explicit Instruction: A Framework for Meaningful Direct Teaching (Geeke), 481

Explicit teaching. *See* Direct instruction

Exploratory environment, 461

Externalizing students, 209

External style, 126t

Extinction, 226, 228, 229f, 239–240

Extrinsic motivation, 369, 398–399

F

Facilitation, 304

Failure, in attribution theory, 374–377

FairTest. *See* National Center for Fair and Open Testing (FairTest)

Family environment, 154–155

Far transfer, 356–357

Feedback: booklets, 517, 518; classroom management, 409, 411, 414, 424; cognitive, 319; cognitive and metacognitive, 319; direct instruction and, 478; motivation and, 366, 369, 386, 398; reinforcement and, 244–245; self-regulated learning and, 313

Females, anorexia nervosa and, 101

Field dependence/field independence, 124–125

Fill-in-the-blank questions, 550

FIMT. *See* Formal instrumental music tuition (FIMT)

Fires in the Bathroom: Advice for Teachers from High School Students (Cushman), 438

Fires in the Middle School Bathroom: Advice for Teachers from Middle Schoolers (Cushman and Rogers), 438

FI schedule. *See* Fixed interval (FI) schedule

Fixed interval (FI) schedule, 230

Fixed ratio (FR) schedule, 230–231

Flexibility, teachers and importance of, 11–12

Florida Comprehensive Assessment, 551

Flow, concept of, 379–380

Foreclosure, 33, 33t

Forethought phase, in self-regulatory system, 285, 286–287, 286f

Forethought processes, 285, 286–287

Formal instrumental music tuition (FIMT), 274

Formal operational stage: in cognitive development, 39t, 47; in Piaget's theory, 41–43, 47

Formative assessment, 17, 486, 487, 487t, 497–498, 560

Foundational knowledge, 490

Foundations of Dual Language Instruction, The (Lessow-Hurley), 180

4Directions Project, 169, 479

4 teachers, 512

Friendships: elementary grades age-level and, 85; high school age-level and, 100; middle school age-level and, 89; preschool/kindergarten age-level and, 75; primary grades age-level and, 81

Frog (Scholastic), 248

FR schedule. *See* Fixed ratio (FR) schedule

Full inclusion, 190, 191

Future Girl: Young Women in the 21st Century (Harris and Hatcher), 141

G

Games software, 248

Gannett News Service, 301

Gardner's Multiple Intelligences Theory, 120–121, 213

Gender: bias, 110, 128–133, 134, 135–136, 138; differences in cognition and achievement, 128–130; elementary-school age-level and, 76, 85; high-school age-level and, 98t; identity status and, 33–34; middle-school age-level and, 89t; moral development and, 61; preschool/kindergarten age-level and, 74, 76; resources on gender bias, 141; self-efficacy and, 321; social cognitive theory research and, 306; teacher expectancy and, 159; toy preferences difference in, 76; violence and, 428

Gender and Teaching (Maher and Ward), 141

Gender roles, 76

Gender Still Hinders Women Scientist, 134

Generalization, 229

General objectives, 446

General transfer, 355–356

GenScope program, 462, 482

"Geology Teacher Finds Creative Ways to Keep Students Engaged" (Byers), 454

Geometric Supposer program, 481

Gifted and talented students/learners: characteristics of, 213–214; classes and schools for, 215–216; defined, 212; enrichment and differentiated instruction, 215–216; identification of, 212–213; instructional options, 214–216; resources on teaching, 223; suggestions for teaching, 216–217; technology for, 220

Gilligan, Carol, 26; resources on caring orientation, 71; view of identity and moral development, 60–61

Global Learning and Observations to Benefit the Environment program (Barab and Luehmann), 56

Global style, 126t

GLOBE program, 463, 511

Goals, 280; approaches to, 174–176; group, 472; high-stakes testing and, 539; intelligence and personal, 115; learning, 371–372; learning, adopting, 385–386; long-range, importance of, 16; mastery, 285, 376; motivation and, 405; performance, 376; performance-approach, 371–372, 385; performance-avoidance,

372, 385; self-regulated learning and, 286; task mastery, 371

Good Behavior Game, 429

Good boy-nice girl orientation, 59

Good Video Games and Good Learning (Gee), 360

GPA. *See* Grade point average (GPA)

Grade equivalent scores, 530

Grade point average (GPA), 156

Grade retention, 6–7

Grades: criterion-referenced grading, 501, 503–505; electronic grading/grading programs, 510–511; essay tests and, 491; improving grading methods, 506–509; mastery approach, 505–506; norm-referenced (grading on curve), 501–503; resources on, 521

Grading (Brookhart), 521

Grading classroom, resources on, 521

Grading on the curve, 30, 94, 501

Grading programs, 510–511

Grandma's rule, 236

Graduation rates, achievement levels and, 152–153

Great Solar System Rescue (Scholastic), 248

Gronlund's recommendations for use of general objectives, 446–447, 446t

Group contingency-management techniques, 211

Group goals, 472

Group heterogeneity, 472

Group management, Kounin's observations on, 406–412

Growth motivation, theory of. *See* Maslow's theory of growth motivation

Growth need, 390

Growth spurt, 89

Guide for Elementary School Teachers, A (Benjamin), 141

Guide to Graphic Organizers, A (Bellanca), 325

Guided learning, 462

Guided learning environments, 462

Guided practice, as component of direct instruction, 450

Guided reflection protocol, 565

Guinness Book of World Records, 277

H

Habits, 38

Handbook for Achieving Gender Equity Through Education (Klein), 141

Handbook of Applied Cognition, The (Durso and associates), 277

Handbook of Educational Psychology (Alexander, Winne, Pressley, and Harris), 325

Handbook of Formative Assessment, The (Andrade and Cizek), 520

Handbook of Gifted Education (Colangelo and Davis), 223

Handbook of Metacognition in Education (Hacker, Dunlosky, and Sternberg), 277

Handbook of Metamemory and Memory (Dunlosky and Bjork), 277

Handbook of Moral and Character Education (Nucci and Narvaez), 71

Handbook of Motivation at School (Wentzel and Wigfield), 402

Handbook of School Violence and School Safety, The (Jimerson and Furlong), 438

Handbook of Self-Regulation (Boekaerts, Pintrich, and Zeidner), 324

Handicapped Children's Protection Act (PL 99-457), 189

Hanging Out, Messing Around, and Geeking Out: Kids Living and Learning with New Media (Ito and colleagues), 365

Hanna Woods Elementary, 543, 544

Harmony, needs for, 391

Harvard Graduate School of Education, 573

Hearing impairment: defined, 193, 196t; special education and, 196t; technology for students with, 218–219
Help Center (discussion forum), 178
Hierarchic style, 126t
Higher Order Thinking Skills (HOTS) program, 462
High-road transfer, 357–358
High school age-level characteristics: cognitive characteristics, 103–104; emotional characteristics, 100–103; intelligence and, 115; physical characteristics, 97–99; social characteristics, 100
High schools, 72; applying theories of development on, 98t; classroom management of, 409–410; cognitive development and, 103–104; formal operational stage in, 41; graduation rate and achievement levels, 152–154; smart and good, 433–434; trends in sexual activity among students in, 98t
High-stakes testing: accountability in education and, 535, 537; arguments critical of, 539–542; arguments in support of, 538–539; defined, 536; recommendations for improving, 549–550; research on effects of, 542, 545–550; resources on, 558. See also No Child Left Behind Act (NCLB)
Hispanics: cultural differences and, 148; motivations/beliefs, and attitudes, 156; percentage of school-age children and, 147f; poverty and, 152f; special education and, 194. See also Latinos; Mexican Americans
HIV, 99
Hostile attributional bias, 428
HOTS program. See Higher Order Thinking Skills (HOTS) program
Howard Gardner's Multiple Intelligences Theory. See Gardner's Multiple Intelligences Theory
How to Grade for Learning (O'Connor), 521
Hueneme School District in Hueneme, California, 435
Hugh Hartshorne and Mark May studies, 63
Humanistic approach to instruction, 478t
Humanistic approach to teaching: Combs and, 465; humanistic approach role, 464; humanistic model, 466–468; Maslow and, 464–465; research on, 468–470; resources on, 482; Rogers and, 465; teaching from humanistic orientation, 465–466
Humanistic theory, 459
Humor, 416–417
Hypermedia, 274; cognitive approach to teaching and, 384, 0; performance assessment and, 502, 0; problem solving and, 359; tools, 274

I

Idaho Standards Achievement Test, 553
IDEA. See Individuals with Disabilities Education Act (IDEA)
Ideas, 8
Ideas and activities, 377
Identical elements, theory of, 355
Identity: defined, 31; Erikson's theory and, 31; formulation, students and, 31–34; Gilligan's view of, 60–62; motivation and, 395; negative, 429; self-esteem, self-concept, and self-efficacy vs., 393t. See also Identity achievement; Identity status
Identity: Youth and Crisis (Erikson), 71
Identity achievement, 33, 33t
Identity diffusion, 33t
Identity in Adolescence: The Balance Between Self and Other (Kroger and Steinberg), 71

Identity status: adolescents and, 31–34, 36; cultural, ethnic, and gender factors in, 33–34; diffusion, 429; formulating, 31; James Marcia's, 33t, 34
Identity vs. role confusion (twelve to eighteen years; middle through high school), 29
IEP. See Individualized Education Program (IEP)
I Know Why the Caged Bird Sings (Angelou), 355
Ill-structured problems, 344, 350
ILS. See Integrated learning systems (ILS)
Images, scanned, 512
Imagination Express (software tool), 123
I-messages, 419–420
Imitation, 303, 370
Immigrants: ability grouping and, 183; bilingual education and, 177; growth of public education and, 183; legal, United States and, 147; multiculturalism and, 144; number of, by decade, 144t, 173; number of immigrant children in US, 183
"Improving the Reading Comprehension of At-Risk Adolescents"(Block and Pressley), 481
Improvisation, 12
Impulsivity, 123–124
In a Different Voice: Psychological Theory and Women's Development (Gilligan), 71
In Between Parent and Child (Ginott, Ginott, and Goddard), 76
"Incentives Are All Over the MAP" (Hahn and Lestch), 543–544
Inclusion: debate about, 191–192; defined, 191; policy of, 190–191; resources on, 223
Incremental theorists, 376
Independent practice, as component of direct instruction, 450
Individual accountability, 473
Individualistic goal structures, 471
Individualized Education Program (IEP), 190, 197–198, 197f, 538
Individuals with Disabilities Education Act (IDEA), 184, 189, 538; assistive technology definition in, 218; classroom teacher's responsibilities under, 195–198; disabling conditions under, 193; Individualized Education Program under, 197–198, 197f; major provisions of, 189–190; policy of inclusion and, 190–191; regular classroom teachers and, 192–193
Industry vs. inferiority (six to eleven years; elementary to middle school), 29
Inert knowledge, 334, 346
Infants, sensorimotor stage in, 39
Inferences, 526
Influence techniques, 415–421
"Information on Self-Efficacy: A Community of Scholars" (Pajares), 402
Information-processing/social cognitive approach to instruction, 452
Information-processing theory, 279; information-processing view of learning, 250–266; introduction to, 249–250; metacognition, 266–267, 270–271; model of information processing, 251–252, 252f; resources on, 277; social cognitive theory and, 279; technology and, 271–275
Information-processing tools, technology as, 271–276
Inhibition, 303
Initiative vs. guilt (four to five years; preschool to kindergarten), 29
Inspiration (software tool), 122
Institute of Education Sciences, 4
Instruction: accelerated, 214–215; aligning assessment with, 447; aligning with federal legislation, 193; awareness of

learning styles and, 126–127; cognitive development and, 43–44, 50–53; computer-based, 231–233; effect on self-regulated learning skills, 309–311; of gifted and talented students, 214–217; resources on humanistic approach to, 482; teacher-directed, 449; teacher-led, 449; technology-enhanced, 231; views of intelligence and, 119–123; Vygotskian perspective on, 257; the zone of proximal development and, 52–53. See also Cognitive approach to teaching/instruction; Direct instruction; Instruction, approaches to
Instruction, approaches to: behavioral approach to teaching, 448–451; challenges of constructivist teacher, 460–461; devising/using objectives, 441–448; humanistic approach to teaching, 464–470. See also Cognitive approach to teaching; Social approach to teaching
Instruction, differentiated, resources on, 141
Instructional goals, 165–166
Instructional methods, 167
Instructional objectives, 441, 481
Instructional Patterns (Holt and Kysilka), 482
Instructional Strategies for Middle and High School (Larson and Keiper), 108
Instruction formats/learning processes, 150–151
Instrumental relativist orientation, 59
INTASC. See Interstate New Teacher Assessment and Support Consortium (INTASC)
Integrated learning systems (ILS), 234, 411
Integrating Technology into Teaching: The Teaching and Learning Continuum (Recesso and Orrill), 24
Integration, in humanistic model, 466
Integrity vs. despair, in old age, 30
Intellectual behavior, 97
Intellectual disability: characteristics of children with, 199–200; defined, 193, 198–199; resources on teaching students with, 223; suggestions for teaching students with, 200–202
Intellectual Disability: Definition, Classification, and Systems of Supports (Schalock and others), 199
Intelligence, 526; assessment of, 115; contemporary views of, 114–115; defined, 114; instruction and new views of, 119–123; resources on new views of, 140; testing, 112–114
Intelligence quotient (IQ), 112, 114, 185, 188, 527
Intentional learning. See Self-regulated learning (SRL)
Interactive Forums, 573
Interdependent group contingency, 429
Interest, effect on intrinsic motivation, 377–380
Interest boosting, 416
Internalizing students, 209
Internal learning. See Self-regulated learning (SRL)
Internal style, 126t
International Education and Resource Network, 573
International Society for Augmentative and Alternative Communication, 219
International Telementor Program, 56
Internet, as tool for writing, 272
Interpersonal intelligence, 117, 118t
Interpersonal reasoning, 91, 91t; problem-solving skills and, 428; using technology to develop, 104–105
Interpersonal skills, 473
Interpretation, marginal use of, 419
Interstate New Teacher Assessment and Support Consortium (INTASC), 22

Intervention, response to, 192
Intimacy vs. isolation (young adulthood), 29
Intrapersonal intelligence, 117, 118t
Intrinsic interest, 286
Intrinsic motivation, 369, 372; effect of external rewards on, 370f; effect of interest on, 377–380; extrinsic motivation vs., 398–399
Introspective orientation, 17
Invariant functions, 38
Inviting School Success: A Self-Concept Approach to Teaching, Learning, and Democratic Practice (Holt and Kysilka), 482
Inviting School Success: A Self-Concept Approach to Teaching, Learning, and Democratic Practice (Purkey and Novak), 482
Iowa Test of Basic Skills, 547
Irreversibility, 40
Issues: ill structured problems, 344–345
Item analysis, 521
Iveland Elementary School, 543

J

James, William, 351
Jealousy, 77
Jean Piaget Society database, 71
Joining Together: Group Theory and Group Skills (Johnson and Johnson), 482
Joplin plan, 185, 186, 188
Journal entries: on analyzing test items, 516, 517; on arranging short-term goals, 384; behavior problems, 416, 417, 420; on capturing and maintaining attention, 263; on causes of behavior, 242; on classroom assessment, 416, 513, 515, 517; on classroom management, 424; on constructivism, 339, 340, 341, 342, 343; on constructivist approach to instruction, 457; on cooperation, 210; on cultural conflicts, 172; on dealing with overlapping situations, 406; described, 21; on direct instruction, 449; for elementary school age-level characteristics, 85, 87; on emotional disturbance, 210, 211; on encouraging competence, 79; on encouraging moral development, 67; on encouraging perseverance, 245; on encouraging students set own objectives, 397; on Erikson's theory of psychosocial development, 35; on gender bias, 138; on gifted and talented students, 216, 217; on handling momentum, 407; on handling routines, 413; on helping students master objectives, 397; for high school age-level, 102; on immediate feedback, 245; on information-processing/social cognitive approach to instruction, 452; on initiating interaction with withdrawn children, 211; on intellectual disability, 200, 201, 202; on intelligence, 137; on inviting students to learn, 396; on keeping the whole class involved, 407; on learning disabilities, 200, 201, 202, 206; on mastery approach to grading, 505; on memory tactics, 314; on minimizing ethnocentric tendencies, 147; on minimizing subjectivity, 162; on motivation, 382, 389, 390; on multicultural education, 171, 172; on organizing information into categories, 265; on Piaget's cognitive development theory, 47, 48; for preschool/kindergarten age-level characteristics, 74, 76, 77; on presenting information correctly, 265; for primary grade age-level characteristics, 80–81, 82, 83; on productive techniques of teaching, 161; on promoting incremental view of intelligence, 385; on promoting social sensitivity, 90, 91;

on reinforcement, 243; on self-efficacy, 316; on self-regulated learning, 312, 314, 315, 316; on social approach to instruction, 476–477; on standardized tests, 553, 554; on taking notes, 314; on use of chunking to facilitate learning, 264; on using humanistic approach to instruction, 466

Journal of Teacher Education, 3

Journal problems, classroom management and, 421, 424

Judicial style, 126t

Judicious Discipline (Landau & Gathercoal), 430

Junior high school, classroom management of, 409–410

Justice, 259

K

Keeping Track (Oakes), 223

Kennerly Elementary School, 543

Kentucky Department of Education, 536

Keysor Elementary in Kirkwood, 543

Keywords, 294t

Kidlink organization, 105

Kids as Global Scientists project (Mistler-Jackson and Songer), 56

Kindergarten: children, languages and, 78; self-regulated learning in, 315

Kindergarten/preschool/age-level characteristics: cognitive characteristics, 77–80; emotional characteristics, 76–77; physical characteristics, 74; social characteristics, 75–76

Knowledge: constructing, 38; domains of, 443; foundational, 490; inert, 334, 346; moral, 63; technology tools for construction of, 359–362

Knowledge-building, 166

Knowledge Dimension, 442

Knowledge Forum. *See* Computer-supported intentional learning environments (CSILE)

Knowledge-of-person variables, 267

Knowledge-of-strategy variables, 267

Knowledge-of-task variables, 267

Kohlberg, Lawrence, 26; criticisms and evaluations of moral theory, 59–60; description of moral development, 57–58; resources on stages of moral development, 71; stages of moral reasoning, 58–59, 59t; use of moral dilemmas, 57–58. *See also* Moral development

Kurzweil Reader, 219

L

Laboratory experiments, 16

Ladue Middle School, 96

Language: kindergarten children and, 78; use by children, 46; use of, gender and, 129

Language and Thought of the Child, The (Piaget), 71

Language arts, teaching from triarchic perspective, 121t

Languages, kindergarten and, 78

Late-maturing boys, 89, 90t

Late-maturing girls, 90, 90t

Latinos: achievement expectations for, 159; classroom environment and, 157; collectivism and, 172; cooperative learning and, 148, 167; cultural differences and, 148; direct instruction and, 451; dropout rates and, 153; emotional disorders and, 101; family environment and, 155; high school graduation and, 152–153; motivations/beliefs/attitudes and, 156; multicultural education and, 169; nonverbal communication and, 149; population and, 146; social class and, 152; suicidal attempts, 102; support for academic achievement, 155; testing and, 153, 169; time orientation and, 149; verbal communication and, 149. *See also* Hispanics

LD. *See* Learning disabilities (LD)

LearnCentral, 478

Learner-centered education, 465

Learner-centered psychological principles, 2

Learning: adventure, 105; behavior and thought processes and, 8–9; collaborative, 479; complexity of teaching and, 8–9; computer-based technology on, 231; cooperation, resources on, 482; cooperative, 458, 479; direct, 257; effect of social class on, 151–152; effects of ethnicity on, 148–149; empirical, 51; equilibration, disequilibration, and, 37; guided, 462; information-processing view of, 250–266; integrated systems, 234; meaningful, 458; measuring, 489–498, 501; mediated, 257; norm-referenced grading, 501–503; of primary grades age-level and, 83; problem-and project-based, 462–463; project-based, 462–463; resources on, 24; self-regulated, 289–290; situated, 334, 463; social constructivist, 477–478; theoretical, 51–52; transfer of, 354–358; virtual, 54. *See also* Learning disabilities; Learning styles; Transfer of learning

Learning and Behavior (Mazur), 247

Learning Disabilities: Characteristics, Identification, and Teaching Strategies (Bender), 223

Learning Disabilities and Related Mild Disabilities: characteristics, Teaching Strategies, and New Directions (Lerner and Johns), 223

Learning disabilities (LD): characteristics of students with, 202–203; identifying students with, 203; problems with psychological processes, 204–205; resources on teaching students with, 223; suggestions for teaching students with, 206–207; technology for students with, 219–220

Learning environment, 563f

Learning from teaching, 569

Learning goals, 371–372

Learning skills, 9

Learning strategy, 291, 297

Learning styles, 110, 123–128; resources on, 140; using awareness to guide instruction, 126–127

Learning tactics, 291, 297, 325

Learning Theories: An Educational Perspective (Schunk), 277

Learning Together, Teams-Games-Tournaments, and Team-Assisted Individualization, 474

"Learning to Love Assessment" (Tominson), 489

Least restrictive environment, 190

Legacy of B. F. Skinner, The (Nye), 247

Legislative style, 126t

LEGO/LOGO, 123

Leniency problem, 561

Lessons, self-recorded, 564–565

Lesson study: cycle, 465; defined, 562; planning phase in, 563, 564f; reflection phase in, 564, 564f; study phase in, 562–563, 564f; in teaching phase, 563, 564f

Lesson Study Communities: Increasing Achievement with Diverse Students (Wiburg and Brown), 575

Letters to a Young Teacher (Kozol), 11, 13

Level of voice, 132

Levels of Processing, 443

Liberal style, 126t

Limits, defining, 419

Linguistic intelligence, 117, 118t

Living and Learning with New Media: Summary of Findings from the Digital Youth Project, 360, 361

Livingston Elementary, 543

Local and national norms, 533

Local style, 126t

Loci method, 294t

Logical-mathematical intelligence, 117, 118t

Long-term memory (LTM): about, 259–260; organization of information in, 260–262

Love, 390, 391t

Low-road transfer, 357, 358

Low-socioeconomic-status (SES), 117

LTM. *See* Long-term memory (LTM)

M

MacArthur Foundation, 274, 360, 365

Mager's recommendations for use of specific objectives, 444–445, 446t

Magnetic resonance imaging (MRI), 251

Mainstreaming, 190, 194, 223

Maintenance programs, 174

Maintenance rehearsal, 252, 252f, 254

Making the Most of the Web in Your Classroom (Green, Brown, and Robinson), 108

Management for Elementary Teachers (Evertson and Emmer), 438

Managing the Adolescent Classroom (Crawford), 438

Mapping the Moral Domain: A Contribution of Women's Thinking to Psychological Theory and Education (Gilligan, Ward, Taylor, and Bardige), 71

Maslow's theory of growth motivation, 390–391; hierarchy of needs, 391t; implications of, 391–392; limitations of, 392

Massachusetts Comprehensive Assessment System (MCAS), 552

Massed practice, 264

Mastery approach to grading, 505–506

Mastery criterion, 288

Mastery goals, 376, 385

Mastery learning, 167–168, 505

Mathematical problem-solving skills, improving students', 307

Mathematical reasoning, 128

Mathematics: teaching from triarchic perspective, 121t; technology tools for, 272–273

Matter of Consequences, A (Skinner), 247

Maturation, early and late, 90t

MCAS. *See* Massachusetts Comprehensive Assessment System (MCAS)

Meaningful learning, 458; cognitive constructivism and, 331; within constructivist framework, 328–335; defined, 256–257; information-processing theory and, 274; problem-solving learning and, 359; situated learning and, 334; stored knowledge and, 256; using constructivist approach to, 339–343

Meaningful Learning with Technology (Jonassen, Howland, Marra, and Crismond), 365

Meaningfulness, 256–258, 453, 456–460

Means-end thinking, 428

Measurement, 486

Measurement and Assessment in Education (Reynolds, Livingston, and Wilson), 558

Measurement and Assessment in Teaching (Miller, Linn, and Gronlund), 558

Measurement and Evaluation in Psychology and Education (Thorndike and Thorndike-Christ), 558

Mediated learning, 257

Mediation process, 50

Melting Pot, The (Zangwill), 144

Melting pot phenomenon, 144

"Melting Pot Seems to Be Working Fine at This School" (Tighe), 145–146

Memory, 128–129; elementary grade age-level and, 88; information-processing theory and 377-378, 254–262; intelligence and, 112, 113, 120; learning disabilities and, 201–202, 203, 207; learning tactics and, 270, 271; long-term, 259–262; memorization techniques, 270; mental retardation and, 201, 202; resources on individual differences in, 277; resources on memory structures and processes, 277; resources on structures and processes, 277; self-regulated learners and, 313; sensory register and, 253; short-term, 254–259; single memory system, 252; skills, 88; student differences and designing lessons/test for, 136–138; test and gender, 128–129; verbal, 251. *See also* Long-term memory (LTM)

Memory: Phenomena and Principles (Spear and Riccio), 277

Memory-directed tactics, 292

Memory from a Broader Perspective (Searleman and Herrmann), 277

Memory Observed: Remembering in Natural Contexts (Neisser and Hyman, Jr.), 277

Memory Search by a Memorist (Thompson, Cowan, and Frieman), 277

Memory stores, 251

Mental Hygiene in Teaching (Redly and Wattenberg), 415

Mental Measurements Yearbook, 558

Mental retardation. *See* Intellectual disability

Mental Retardation: An Introduction to Intellectual Disability (Beirne-Smith, Patton, and Kim), 223

Mental self-government styles, 125, 126t

Metacognition: age trends in, 270–271; children and, 199; nature and importance of, 266–267, 268; resources on, 277

Metacognitive feedback, 319

Mexican Americans, 159, 168; competition and individual accomplishments, 143; cooperative learning and, 150; ESL/bilingual education of, 177; lead levels and, 154. *See also* Hispanics

Mexico, baby-sitting responsibilities in, 46

Microcomputer-based laboratories, 54

Micromoral issues, 60

Microworlds, 54

Middle age, generativity *vs.* stagnation in, 30

"Middle Ground" (Bower), 96–97

Middle school age-level characteristics: cognitive characteristics, 94–95, 97; emotional characteristics, 92–94; physical characteristics, 89–90; social characteristics, 91–92

Middle schools, 72; anxieties in, 96; applying Piaget's theory on, 47–48; applying theories of development on, 89; classroom management of, 409–410; early, concrete operational stage in, 41; formal operational stage in, 41; industry *vs.* inferiority, 29; meeting intellectual needs of students in, 95; resources on teaching, 108

Middle through high school, identity *vs.* role confusion, 29

MiddleWeb, 108

MIDI. *See* Musical instrument digital interface (MIDI)

Milwaukee Journal Sentinel, 499

Mind, theory of, 77

Mindfulness, 298

Mind of a Mnemonist: A Little Book About a Vast Memory, The (Luria), 277

Mindtools, 359

Minority Student Achievement Network, 156

Misbehavior, reducing, 429–430

Missouri Assessment Program, 543
MI theory. See Multiple intelligences theory (MI)
Mixed theorists, 376
Mnemonic devices, 201, 292–293, 294t, 295
Models/modeling, 300, 304, 318–319; Arnetha Ball's model of generative change model, 569; BIG Accommodation model, 451; effect on achievement, 307–309; effects on self-efficacy, 307–309; Humanistic model, 466–468; of infor-mation processing, 251–262, 270–271, 305; observing weak and strong, 309; self modeling, effect of, 307; self-regulated learning and, 300, 300t, 303–305, 318–322; Slavin, 476; for strategy development, 308; vs. practice, 309–311; WICS model, 120
Monarchic style, 126t
Moral attitude, 61, 62
Moral behavior, moral thinking and, 63
Moral character, 434
Moral development: caring orientation to education and, 60–62; elementary school age-level and, 26, 84t; encouraging, 67–68; Hartshorne and May Studies, 63; high school age-level and, 98t; middle-school age-level and, 89t; Piaget's analysis of, 56–57; preschool and kindergarten age-level and, 75t; primary grade age-level and, 81t. See also Gilligan, Carol; Kohlberg, Lawrence; Noddings, Nel
Moral Development and Behavior: Theory, Research, and Social Issues (Lickona), 71
Moral education programs. See Character Education Programs
Morality of constraint (moral realism): defined, 57; vs. morality of cooperation, 58t; vs. moral relativism, 57
Morality of cooperation (moral relativism): defined, 57; morality of constraint vs., 58t; moral realism vs., 57
Moral Judgment of the Child, The (Lickona), 71
Moral realism. See Morality of constraint (moral realism)
Moral relativism. See Morality of cooperation (moral relativism)
Moral thinking, moral behavior and, 63
Moral values, 66–67
Moratorium, 33t
Mothers Against Drunk Driving, 345
Motivation, 526; behavioral view of, 368–370; behavior modification and, 245; Case in Print on, 381; competitive reward structures and 384, 471; defined, 367; effect of cooperative learning on, 474; e-mail messaging systems and, 399; gifted/talented students and, 213; on high-stakes testing, 541, 545; high-stakes testing and, 545–546; humanistic view of, 390–392; identity and, 395; information-processing theory and, 267; mental retardation and, 199; multicultural education and, 168; norm-referenced grading and, 501, 502; objectives and, 397; other cognitive views of, 372–380; parenting styles/classroom management and, 405; reinforcement and 222, 239, 368–369; resources on, 402; rewards and, 225; role of self-perceptions in, 393–396; self-efficacy and, 285, 370–372; self-regulated learning and, 299; social cognitive view of, 370–372; suggestions for teaching, 382–390; technology and, 398–399
Motivational processes, 285

Motivation and Self-Regulated Learning (Schunk and Zimmerman), 402
MRI. See Magnetic resonance imaging (MRI)
Multicultural education, 143; rationale for, 168–170; resources on, 180; suggestions for teaching, 171–173. See also Multicultural education programs
Multicultural Education and the Internet: Intersections and Integrations (Gorski), 180
Multicultural education programs, 162–173; assumptions and goals, 163, 163t; basic approaches, 163–164
Multiculturalism, rise of, 144
Multicultural teachers, characteristics of, 164–165
Multidisciplinary assessment team, 197
Multimedia: computer-based instruction and, 274; digital portfolios and, 512; learning disability and, 207; performance assessment and, 511, 512; tools, 274
Multimedia presentations, 512
Multimodal programs, 205
Multiple-choice questions, 534
Multiple disabilities, 193, 196t
Multiple Intelligences and Portfolios (Stefanakis), 140
Multiple intelligences theory (MI), 117–119, 118t, 120–121
Multiple perspectives, constructivism and, 333–334
Multiple role taking, in interpersonal reasoning, 91t
Multiple-user virtual environments (MUVEs), 55, 122, 274
Multi-store model, 251–252
Music, technology tools for, 273–274
Musical instrument digital interface (MIDI), 274
Musical intelligence, 117, 118t
Musical Savants: Exceptional Skill in the Mentally Retarded (Miller), 277
MUVEs. See Multiple user virtual environments (MUVEs)
My Reading Coach (MindPlay Educational Software), 248

N
NAEP. See National Assessment of Educational Progress (NAEP)
NASA, 274
National Assessment of Educational Progress (NAEP), 153, 534, 545, 551
National Association for Multicultural Education, 180
National Board Certification, 489, 570, 571, 572
National Board Certification for educational leaders/principals, 572–573
National Board Certified Teachers (NBCTs), 561, 570, 571, 572
National Board for Professional Teaching Standards (NBPTS), 3, 19, 22, 560, 564, 570, 571
National Center for Fair and Open Testing (FairTest), 558
National Center for Health Statistics, 273
National Coalition to Abolish Corporal Punishment in Schools, 240
National Commission on Excellence in Education, 535
National Comprehensive Center for Teacher Quality & Public Agenda, 6
National Council for Social Studies, 492
National Council of Teachers of English, 492
National Council of Teachers of Mathematics, 492
National Educational Technology Standards for students, 20
National Federation of the Blind, 219

National Forum to Accelerate Middle-Grades Reform, 108
National Geophysical Data Center, 273
National Middle School Association, 96
National Oceanic and Atmospheric Administration, 273
National Research Center on the Gifted and Talented, 223
National Research Council, 41, 191, 572
National Science Foundation, 274
National Science Teachers Association, 492
Nation at Risk: The Imperative for Educational Reform (National Commission on Excellence in Education), 535
Native Americans: competition and individual accomplishments, 143; cooperative learning and, 167; cultural differences and, 148; culture, 149; direct instruction and, 451; 4Directions Project and, 169; gifted/talented students and, 213; high school graduation and, 152; instructional formats and, 150; nonverbal communication and, 149; poverty and, 152f; social class and, 152; technology and, 169; tests and, 153; time orientation and, 149; verbal communication and, 149
Native Son (Wright), 355
Naturalist intelligence, 117, 118t
Nature, of science, 6–7
Nature and Limits of Standards-Based Reform and Assessment, The (Mathison and Ross), 558
Nature of Intellectual Styles, The (Zhang and Sternberg), 140
NBCTs. See National Board Certified Teachers (NBCTs)
NBPTS. See National Board for Professional Teaching Standards (NBPTS)
NCLB. See No Child Left Behind Act (NCLB)
NCLB at the Crossroads: Reexamining the Federal Effort to Close the Achievement Gap (Rebell and Wolf), 558
Near transfer, 356–357
Need for achievement, 155–156, 373–374, 380
Need gratification, theory of, 390
Negative identity, 429
Negative interdependence, 471
Negative reinforcement, 227
Negative transfer, 355
Negotiated meaning, 332
Negotiation of understanding, 330
Neuroscience research, 10
New Circles of Learning: Cooperation in the Classroom, The (Johnson, Johnson, and Holubec), 482
New Directions for Child Development: Moral Development (Damon), 71
News Bureau, University of Illinois, 381
New Teachers Online page of Teachers Network, 573
New Teachers Project, 6
New York Performance Standards Consortium, 548
New York Times, 13, 336
No Child Left Behind: Past, Present, and Future (Hayes), 558
No Child Left Behind Act (NCLB) of 2001, 4, 160, 194, 330, 541–542, 548; contradictory goals, 539; effects of, 545, 546; modifications of, 538; problems with implementing, 537–538; proficiency in state exams, 543; requirements of, 536–537, 540
Noddings, Nel, 60; care theory, 61–62; resources on caring orientation, 71
"Nondirective Learning" (Holt and Kysilka), 482
Nondirective therapy, 465, 466

Nonverbal communication, 149
Normal probability curve, 531f
Normative standard, 288
Normed excellence, 527
Norm group, 527
Norm-referenced, 471
Norm-referenced grading: defined, 501; nature of, 501–502; strengths and weaknesses of, 502–503
Norm-referenced tests, 529, 555
Norms, local and national, 533
Northern Ireland school, 463
Northwest Evaluation Association, 548
Note taking, 292, 295–296
Number, use by children, 46

O
Obesity: elementary school children and, 84–85; high school students and, 98
Objectives: assessment and, 447; communicating goals and, 452; evaluations of effectiveness of, 447–448; general, 446, 446f; instructional, 441; motivation and, 397; specific, 444–445, 446f
Objectivity, 7
Object permanence, as cognitive development milestone, 39
Observation, 300t, 370; information-processing theory and, 253; reflective teaching and 552, 562–564; scientific, 7; unsystematic, 6–7
Observational learning, 300
Office of Juvenile Justice and Delinquency Prevention, 462
Office of the Federal Register, 208
Oligarchic style, 126t
One size fits all approach to motivation, 541
One size fits all approach to standards, 541
Operant conditioning: basics of, 226–231; educational applications of, 231–237; motivation and, 369; resources on, 247; social cognitive theory and, 278–279; suggestions for teaching, 242–246
Operation, defined, 40
Operation Frog (Scholastic), 248
Optimal representation, 345–346
Order, needs for, 391
Ordering process, 46
Oregon Trail program (The Learning Company), 248
Organization, 37, 207, 255–256, 265, 453
Orientation, as component of direct instruction, 449
Origins of Intelligence in Children, The (Piaget), 71
Orthopedic impairments, 193, 196t, 219
Overestimating capabilities of, 45
Overlapping situations, dealing with, 406

P
Paivio's dual coding theory, 258–259, 265
Parents: authoritarian, 79, 405; authoritative, 79, 405; of competent children, 79; lying to, 63; of minority students, working with, 173; permissive, 79; rejecting-neglecting, 79–80
Parkway Northeast Middle School, 96
Particulars of My Life (Skinner), 247
Partner reading, 204
PAT. See Psychology Applied to Teaching (PAT)
Patterns of Teacher behavior, characteristics of, 563f
Pause and reflect: on ability grouping, 185; on accommodating student variability, 182; on achievement tests score, 46; on assumptions, 27; on balancing art and science of teaching, 15; on behavior modification, 240; on classroom learning assessment, 484;

on classroom management, 404, 420, 422; on competitive reward structure, 471; on constructivism, 38, 148, 338; on cooperative reward structures, 472; on decentration of children, 57; described, 20; on effective learners, 279–280; on elementary school age-level characteristics, 87; on emulation, 303; on ethnic/racial minority groups, 158; on ethnocentrism, 147; on fads, 10; on gender bias, 131; on gifted and talented programs, 216; on grading, 503, 508; on groups, 112; on high-stakes testing, 549; on IDEA, 198; on identity problems, 31; on Individuals with Disabilities Act (ADAAA), 198; on industry vs. inferiority, 30; on information/meaning, 250; on information-processing principles, 456; on instructional objectives, 446; on instructional planning, 441; on intelligence, 112, 114, 119; on intrinsic motivation, 369; on learning strategies/tactics, 310; on learning styles, 127; on memory, 251; on minority students dropping out of school, 153; on moral development, 67; on moral dilemmas, 60; on motivation 407, 408, 391; on multicultural education, 164; on multiple intelligence, 119; on objectives, 446, 448; on operant conditioning, 226, 234; on peer groups and rules, 92; on performance assessment, 496; on Piaget's cognitive development theory and early formal schooling, 46; on Piaget's concrete operational stage, 41; on preschool/kindergarten age-level cognitive characteristics, 79; on problem solving, 328, 350; on punishment, 240; on reducing students drop out, 152; on reducing students' tendency to cheat, 508; on reflective teaching, 18; on resolving moral dilemmas, 60; on retention, 7; on reward for accomplishments, 225; on "right answers", 73–74; on ripple effect, 406; on self-efficacy, 284; on self-regulated learning, 282, 291; on setting aside time about teaching activities, 18; on sex education, 99; on standard achievement tests of children, 46; on standardized tests, 523, 524, 530, 533; on student retention, 7; on teachers as artists, 12; on tests, 490; on transfer of learning, 362; on values in evaluation, 143; on violence, 429, 435

PBL. See Problem-based learning (PBL)
Peer and self-assessment techniques, 562–568
Peer assisted learning, 166
Peer groups: elementary school age-level and, 84t, 85, 87; high school age-level and, 98t, 99, 100, 101, 103; middle school age-level and, 89, 89t, 90, 90t, 91, 92, 93; preschool/kindergarten age-level and, 75, 76, 78; primary grades age-level and, 80, 82
Peer models, effect of, 307
Peer-questioning, 295
Peer tutoring, 166–167
Percentile ranks, 530–531, 532f
Perceptual centration, 40
Perfectly Valid theory, 526, 527
Performance accomplishments, 283, 284
Performance-approach goals, 371–372, 385
Performance assessment, 447, 490; characteristics of, 494–498; concerns about, 498, 501; problems of, 512; requirements of, 492; technology-based, 511; traditional paper-and-pencil vs., 492–493; types of, 493–494
Performance-avoidance goals, 372, 385
Performance-based classroom tests, 498

Performance-based measures, 530
Performance character, 434
Performance goals, 376
Performance phase, in self-regulatory system, 285, 287–288
Performance processes, 285
Performance standards, 496, 540, 542, 551
Permissive parents, 79
Personal agency, 281
Personal characteristics, 280, 281f
Personal interest, 377–378, 387
Personality development, 28
Persuasive models, power of, 370–371
PET. See Positron emission tomography (PET)
Phi Delta Kappan, 424
Physical characteristics: elementary school age-level and, 84–85; high school age-level and, 97–99; middle-school age-level and, 89–90; preschool/kindergarten age-level and, 74; primary grades age-level and, 80–81
Physical restraint, 418
Physiological needs, 390, 391t
Piaget, Jean, 49, 50, 104; analysis of moral judgment of the child, 56–57. See also Piaget's theory of cognitive development
Piaget for Teachers (Furth), 71
Piaget's Theory: Prospects and Possibilities (Beilin and Pufall), 71
Piaget's Theory of Cognitive and Affective Development (Wadsworth), 71
Piaget's theory of cognitive development, 26; applying, 46–48; basic principles of, 36–38; concrete operational stage, 39t, 41; criticisms of, 44–46; formal operational stage, 39t, 41–43; preoperational stage, 39t, 40; resources on description of moral development, 71; resources on theory of cognitive development, 71; role of social interaction and instruction, 43–44; sensorimotor stage, 39, 39t; stages of, 38–43, 39t; technology applied to, 54
Piaget's Theory of Intellectual Development (Ginsburg and Opper), 71
Planful behavior, 39
Planning phase, in lesson study, 563f
Play activities, benefits of, 85–86
Plessy v. Ferguson, 137
Pop quizzes, 509
Portfolio assessment problems, 512
Portfolios, 493, 511–512
Positive interdependence, 472
Positive Peer Reporting (Morrison & Jones), 430
Positive reinforcement,226–227, 241
Positive reinforcer, 226
Positive transfer, 355
Positron emission tomography (PET), 251
Postconventional morality, 59, 59t
Postconventional Moral Thinking: A Neo-Kohlbergian Approach (Rest, Narvaez, Bebeau, and Thoma), 71
Postsituational follow-up, 419
Power of Reinforcement, The (Flora), 247
Practical ability, 115, 115f, 116, 122
Practical Considerations in Computer-Based Testing (Parshall, Sprat, Kalohn, and Davey), 558
Praxis II, psychology applied to teaching and, 22
Preconventional morality, 59, 59t
Predictive validity evidence, 526
Preferences, 123
Premack principle, 236
Preoperational, 45
Preoperational stage, in cognitive development, 39t, 40, 46
Preparing Instructional Objectives (Mager), 444, 445, 481
"Preparing Young Learners for Successful Reading Comprehension: Laying the Foundation" (Block and Pressley), 481

Preschool grade, preoperational stage in, 40
Preschool/kindergarten age-level, 72; applying Piaget's theory on, 47–48; autonomy vs. shame and doubt, 29; cognitive characteristics, 77–80; cognitive development, 75t; emotional characteristics, 76–77; general factors, 75t; initiative vs. guilt, 29; moral development, 75t; physical characteristics of, 74; preoperational stage in, 40; psychosocial development, 75t; social characteristics of, 75–76
Prescribed stimulant medication, 205
Presentation, 449–450, 512
Presentation punishment, 227
Primary grades: preoperational stage in, 40; self-regulated learning in, 315
Primary grades age-level characteristics, 72; cognitive characteristics, 82–84; emotional characteristics, 82–84; physical characteristics, 80–81; preoperational stage in, 40; self-regulated learning and, 315–316; social characteristics, 81–82
Principles of Classroom Management: A Professional Decision-Making Model (Levin and Nolan), 438
Prior knowledge, level of, 378
Private speech phenomenon, 84
Problem-Based Learning in K–8 Classrooms: A Teacher's Guide to Implementation (Lambros), 481
Problem-based learning (PBL), 106, 336, 462–463
Problem finding. See Problem recognition
Problem framing. See Problem representation
Problem recognition, 345
Problem representation, 346
Problem solving: defined, 343; resources on, 365; students and, 345–350; suggestions for teaching, 350–354; technology for, 359–362; types of problems, 343–350
Problem Solving in Mathematics (Posamentier and Krulik), 365
Problem-solving processes, resources on, 365
Problem-solving programs, 232t
Problem-solving skills, 16; interpersonal reasoning and, 428–429; teaching, 327
"Program Aims to Make Reading Easier, More Fun, for Children in China" (Chamberlain), 381–382
Program restructuring, 417
Project-based learning, 462–463
Promotive interaction, 472
Proximal development. See Zone of proximal development (ZPD)
Psychiatric disorders, 100–101
Psychological androgyny, 36
Psychological Development of Girls and Women: Rethinking Change in Time, The (Greene), 141
Psychological processes, problem with, 204–205
Psychological tools, cognitive development and, 49–50
Psychological tools, Vygotsky and, 49–50
Psychology Applied to Teaching (PAT): INTASC and, 22; Praxis II and, 22
"Psychology as the Behaviorist Views It" (Watson), 225
Psychology of the Child, The (Piaget & Inhalder), 71
Psychometric theory, 486
Psychomotor domain, 442
Psychosocial crisis, in Erikson's theory, 28
Psychosocial development: background on, 26; elementary school age-level and, 84t; high school age-level and, 98t; middle-school age-level and, 89t; preschool and kindergarten age

level, 75t; primary grade age-level and, 81t. See also Erikson's theory of psychosocial development
Psychosocial factors, violence and, 429
Psychosocial moratorium, 31, 36
Psychostimulants, 205
Pubertal development, 90
Publication, 7
Public education: growth of, 183; in Individuals with Disabilities Education Act (IDEA), 189
Published tests. See Standardized tests
Punishment: conditions defining, 226, 227–228, 229f; corporal, 240, 241; positive reinforcement vs., 241; states that ban, 241
Punishment-obedience orientation, 59
Putting Research to Work in Your School (Berliner and Casanova), 23

Q
Quality control, 539
Quality School, The (Glasser), 373
Quarrels, primary grades age-level and, 82
Quest Atlantis, 55, 56, 274–275, 360–362, 365, 495, 511
Questions: to ask students who are on-task, 563f; higher-level, resources on writing, 521
Quest Page of San Diego State University, 220
QuickTime movies, 512
Quizzes, pop, 509

R
RCCP. See Resolving Conflict Creatively Program (RCCP)
Reading: gifted and talented students and, 217; technology tools for, 272
"Reading, Writing, and Character Education" (Bower), 64
Reading Assistant from Scientific learning, 178
Reading Assistant-Scientific Learning, 178
Reading Upgrade program, 170
Ready-to-Use Conflict Resolution Activities for Elementary Students (Teolis), 438
Realism, degree of, 494–495
Reciprocal questioning (RQ), 311
Reciprocal teaching (RT), 310, 317
Recognition, 252, 252f, 253, 387
Record-keeping techniques, students with intellectual disability and, 202
Referrals, 195
Reflection phase, in lesson study, 564, 564f
Reflective Journal: developing, 566–567, 567f; using portfolio with, 567–568
Reflective teaching, 16–17; Case in Print on, 571; effectiveness of reflective techniques, 569–570; peer/self assessment techniques and, 562–568; process of, 1, 15–18; resources on, 23–24, 575; revealing/challenging assumptions on, 573–574; students evaluations/suggestions and, 561–562; technology and, 570, 573
Reflective Teaching: An Introduction (Zeichner and Liston), 23
Reflective Teaching: Evidence-Informed Professional Practice (Pollard, Anderson, and Maddock), 575
Reflective Teaching: Evidence-Informed Professional Practice (Pollard and Anderson), 23–24
Reflective Teaching: Professional Artistry Through Inquiry (Henderson), 24
Reflectivity, 123–124
Reflexes, 38
Regrouping, 185, 186
Rehearsal, 254, 264, 280, 287, 292
Reinforcement: conditions defining, 229f; effect of, 368–369; negative, 227; positive, 226–227; preference list, 245;

schedules of, 230–231, 244; using, 243–244
Rejecting-neglecting parents, 79–80
Reliability, 524–526
"Remote Tracking: Teachers Click in Quickly on Students' Performance" (Hetzner), 499–500
Repetition. *See* Maintenance rehearsal
Replication, 7
Republic of Ireland School, 463
Rereading, as form of rehearsal, 292
Research, 2, 12, 15; on aspects of humanistic education, 468–470; on behavior and thought processes, 8; on bilingual education, 176–177; on character education programs, 65–67; on complexity of teaching and learning, 8–9; educational psychology, usefulness of, 3–4; on the effects of computer-based instruction, 231–233; on the effects of teachers' expectancies, 158–159; limited focus of, 8; neuroscience, 10; on retention, 7; selection and interpretation of data in, 9
Research and character education programs, 65–67
Research evidence, 15
Researching the Art of Teaching: Ethnography for Educational Use (Woods), 23
Resolving Conflict Creatively Program (RCCP), 434–435
Resources for further investigation: on ability grouping, 223; on art/science of teaching, 23; on basic principles of operant conditioning, 247; on behavior modification, 247–248; on bilingual education, 180; on characteristics of adolescence, 108–109; on children's play behavior, 108; on classroom management, 438; on cognitive approach to instruction, 481; on cognitive development, 108; on cognitive views of motivation, 402; on computer-based testing, 558; on constructivism, 364–365; on cooperative learning, 482; described, 21; on differentiated instruction, 141; on direct instruction, 481; on education of exceptional children, 223; on Erikson's description of development, 71; on how children develop, 108; on humanistic approach to instruction, 482; on impact of gender bias on students, 141; on instructional objectives, 481; on learning styles and classroom instruction, 140; on learning tactics and strategies, 325; on mainstreaming and inclusion, 223; on motivational techniques for the classroom, 402; on motivational theory, 402; on multicultural education theory and practice, 280; on nature of information-processing theory, 277; on NCLB and high-stakes testing, 558; on new views of intelligence, 140; on Piaget's theory of cognitive development, 71; on problem-solving processes, 365; on reflective teaching, 23, 575; on school violence, 438; on social cognitive theory, 324–325; on teaching gifted and talented learners, 223; on teaching middle school grades, 108; on teaching students with emotional and behavior disorders, 223; on teaching students with intellectual disability, 223; on teaching students with learning disabilities, 223; on technology, teaching, and learning, 24; on technology tools, 365; on transfer of learning, 365
Response cost, 239–240
Response to Intervention (RTI), 189, 192, 197, 488

Results feedback, 319
Retention. *See* Grade retention
Revealing assumptions: on classroom assessment, 484–485; on classroom management, 404; described, 18–19; on group differences, 108–109; on group think, 111; on information/meaning, 250; on instructional planning, 440–441; on motivation, 368; on problem solving, 327–328; on reflective teaching, 573–574; on rewards, 225, 246; on "right answers," 73–74; on standardized test, 523; on taking learning personally, 279–280; on teaching in service of learning, 182; on values in evaluation, 143; on what/how students know, 27, 69
Reversing, concept of, 46
Revolutionary Scientist (Newman and Holzman), 71
Rhyme, 294t
Ridgewood Middle School in Arnold, 64
Ripple effect, 406, 408
Ritalin, for ADHD, 205
Robert Sternberg's triarchic theory of successful intelligence, 120
Role of Play in Human Development, The (Pellegrini), 108
Rose Acres Elementary, 543
Rote rehearsal. *See* Maintenance rehearsal
RQ. *See* Reciprocal questioning (RQ)
RT. *See* Reciprocal teaching (RT)
RTI. *See* Response to Intervention (RTI)
Rubrics, 496, 512, 521
Rule(s): class, establishing, 413; governing student behavior, 432–433; Grandma's, 236

S

Safety, 390, 391t
Sampling, 7
SAT. *See* Scholastic Assessment Test (SAT)
SAT Reasoning Test, 128
Scaffolded instruction, 443; providing, 319–320; zone of proximal development and, 457–458
Scaffolding, 162, 300, 362; effect of, 457; instruction, 319–320; optimizing the effects of, 53; problems of, 317; as teaching strategy, 485; technique of, 52–53
Scaffolding Student Learning: Instructional Approaches and Issues (Hogan and Pressley), 481
Scaffolding technique, 52–53
Scaffolds, Vygotsky's theory of cognitive development and, 319–320
Schemata, 260–261
Schemes, 37, 39
Schizophrenia, 101
Scholastic aptitude, 529
Scholastic Assessment Test (SAT), 526
School-based psychological/educational programs, 205
Schools: environment, 429; virtual, 436
Science: nature and value of, 6–7; teaching as, 10–12, 14–15; teaching from triarchic perspective, 121t; technology tools for, 272–273; using information-processing strategies, 261
Science Fair Assistant, 178
Science Leadership Academy, 13
Scientific Basis of Educational Productivity, The (Subotnik and Walberg), 23
Scientific concepts, 51
Scientific information: on behavior and mental processes, 10; interpretation of, 10
Scientific learning, 178
Scientific methods, 7
Scientific observation: strengths of, 7; unsystematic, 6–7
Scoring rubrics, 486, 496–497, 497t

Section 504 of Vocational rehabilitation Act of 1973, 198
Selected response tests, 490
Selection processes, 284
Self-actualization
Self-actualization needs, 390, 391, 391t
Self-actualizers, 464
Self-assessed competence, 78
Self-beliefs, 285
Self-concept, 86, 393t
Self-control, 281, 286f, 287, 300t, 304
Self-control processes, 287
Self-description, 86
Self-directed learners. *See* Self-regulated learners
Self-Directed Learning Handbook: Challenging Adolescent Students to Excel, The (Gibbons), 324
Self-discipline. *See* Self-control
Self-efficacy, 97, 131; behaviors affected by, 284–285; cognitive processes and, 285; defined, 280; effect on computer-based instruction, 321–322; effects of modeling on, 307–309; epistemological beliefs, self-regulation processes, achievement and, 305–306; factors affecting, 283–284; identity, self-esteem, and self-concept *vs.*, 393t; importance of, 371–372; resources on, 324–325; role in self-regulation, 282–283, 283f; types of behavior affected by, 284–285
Self-Efficacy: Raising the Bar for Students with Learning Needs (Eisenberger, Conti-D'Antonio, and Berttrando), 325
Self-esteem, 86, 282; ability grouping and, 186; identity, self-concept, and self-efficacy *vs.*, 393t; impact of early/late maturation and, 90, 90t; intellectual disability and, 200–201; learning disabilities and, 207; mental retardation and, 199; multicultural education and, 153, 156, 163t, 165
Self-evaluation, 288
Self-experimentation, 287, 288
Self-fulfillment, need for, 390
Self-handicapping behaviors, 372
Self-image, 86–87
Self-instruction, 286, 287
Self-judgment, 286f, 288
Self-modeling, effect of, 307
Self-monitoring. *See* Self-observation processes
Self-motivational beliefs, 286, 313
Self-observation, 286f, 287, 313
Self-observation processes, 287
Self-perceptions: role in motivation, 393–396; suggestions of teaching, 396–398
Self-questioning, 292, 295, 296t
Self-reaction, 286f, 288
Self-recorded lessons, 564–565
Self-recording, 287
Self-reflection phase, in self-regulatory system, 285, 286, 288–289
Self-reflection processes, 285
Self-regulated learners, 290; Case in Print on, 301; helping students become, 289–290. *See also* Self-regulated learning (SRL)
"Self-Regulated Learning and Academic Achievement: A Vygotskyian View" (McCaslin and Hickey), 324
Self-Regulated Learning and Academic Achievement: Theoretical Perspectives (Zimmerman and Schunk), 324
Self-regulated learning (SRL), 289–300; applied in classroom, 312–317; Case in Print on, 301; components of self-regulatory system, 285–289; defined, 289–290; effect on computer-based instruction, 320–321; effects of instruction on, 309–311; how prepared are students for, 290–291; learning

tactics/strategies and, 291–297; modeling and, 300, 303–305; resources on, 324; social cognitive model of, 300t; using technology/computers for, 318–322. *See also* Self-regulated learners
Self-regulated strategy development (SRSD), 308
Self-regulation, 281–282, 304–305, 330; effects of modeling on, 307–309; phases and categories of, 286f; role of self-efficacy in, 282–283; self-efficacy, epistemological beliefs, achievement and, 305–306; social cognitive model of, 300t
Self-regulatory processes, 286
Self-reinforcement, 288
Self-satisfaction, 288
Self-worth. *See* Self-esteem
Sense of industry: children and development of, 28; helping students develop, 30
Sensorimotor stage, in cognitive development, 39, 39t
Sensory register (SR), 252–253, 252f
Serial position effect, 264
Seriation, concept of, 46
SES. *See* Low-socioeconomic-status (LES); Socioeconomic status (SES)
Sex: among high school students, 98, 98t, 99; curiosity and interest about, 90
Sexually transmitted diseases (STDs), 99
Shaping, 230, 235–236
Shaping of a Behaviorist, The (Skinner), 247
Short-answer tests, 491
Short-term memory (STM), 254–259
Signals, 416
Simulation programs, 16, 232, 232t, 233, 234, 248, 551
Single-subject achievement test, 528
Situated learning, 334, 463
Situational interest, 377, 378–379, 387
Sixteenth Mental Measurements Yearbook, The (Spies and Plake), 558
Six to eleven years, industry *vs.* inferiority in, 29
Skills: academic, 7; acting, 12
Skinner's theory of operant conditioning, 226–231
Slavin model, 476
Smarthinking, 551
Smart Intelligence Test, 527
Smooth Sailing or Stormy Waters: Family Transitions Through Adolescence and Their Implications for Practice and Policy (Harold, Colarossi, and Mercier), 109
Social and conventional system, 91t
Social approach to teaching/instruction, 478t; cooperative learning and, 472–477; reward structures and, 471–472; technology and, 477–479
Social behavior, 97
Social characteristics: elementary school age-level, 85–86; high school age-level and, 100; preschool and kindergarten age-level, 75–76; primary grade age-level, 81–82
Social class: effect on learning, 151–152; ethnicity and, 158–159, 161–162
Social Cognitive theory: described, 279; motivation and, 370–380, 383–390; observational learning and, 300; research on, 305–311; resources on, 324–325; suggestions for teaching, 312–322; triadic model and, 278, 281. *See also* Self-efficacy; Self-regulated learning (SRL)
"Social Cognitive Theory: An Agentic Perspective" (Bandura), 324
Social cognitive view of motivation, 370–372
Social constructivism, 331–332, 333

Social constructivist learning, 477–478
Social contract orientation, 59
Social information role taking, in interpersonal reasoning, 91t
Social interaction, 330; cognitive development and, 43–44, 50–51; effect of cooperative learning on, 474–475; emotionally disturbed students and, 210
Social interactions, 389–390
Socialization skills, 6
Socially maladjusted, 208
Socially supportive environment, 464
Social studies: integrating Internet research in, 151; teaching from triarchic perspective, 121t
Social values two, 149–150
Sociocultural theory. *See* Vygotsky's theory of cognitive development
Socioeconomic status (SES), 151, 181, 451, 537
Software: on drills, tutorials, stimulations, and games, 248; games, 248; idea generation and prewriting, 122–123; Inspiration, 303; programs, 248; Reading Partner and Writing Partner, 55
Soundings, 459
Space, concept of, 46
Spanking children, 241
Spatial intelligence, 117, 118t
Special education, 183–184, 194–195, 196t
Special needs students, 5
Special-purpose achievement test, 529
Specific learning disability, 195
Specific transfer, 355–356
Speech, private, 84
Speech or language impairment, 195, 196t, 219
Split-half reliability, 525
Spontaneous concepts, 50–51
Spontaneous recovery, 228–229
SR. *See* Sensory register (SR)
SRL. *See* Self-regulated learning (SRL)
SRSD. *See* Self-regulated strategy development (SRSD)
St. Louis Post-Dispatch, 64, 431–432, 454
STAD. *See* Student-Achievement Divisions (STAD)
Standard deviation, 531
Standardized tests, 498, 522; accountability purposes and, 535–542, 545–550; achievement tests, 528–529; Aptitude tests, 529; criteria for evaluating, 524–525; criterion-referenced tests, 529–530; grade equivalent scores, 530; local and national norms, 533; misconceptions about, 533–535; nature of, 523–524; norm-referenced tests, 529; percentile ranks, 530–531; resources on, 558; standard scores, 531–533; suggestions for teaching, 553–555; technology and, 550–553; use of, 524
Standard nine-point scale, 532–533
Stanford-Binet Intelligence Scales-Fifth Edition (SB-5), 113
Stanford-Binet intelligence test, 120
Stanine score, 532–533, 533f
State standards, high-stakes testing and, 548
STDs. *See* Sexually transmitted diseases (STDs)
Sternberg's Mental Self-Government Styles, 126t
Sternberg's Triarchic Theory of Successful Intelligence, 115–117, 115f, 120, 121f, 199
STM. *See* Short-term memory (STM)
"Straddling Two Worlds: Self-Directed Comprehension Instruction for Middle Schoolers" (Block and Pressley), 481
Strategic behavior, 39
Strategic learners. *See* Self-regulated learners

Strategies for Addressing Behavior Problems in the Classroom (Kerr and Nelson), 223
Strategies That Promote Student Engagement: Unleashing the Desire to Learn (Riggs and Gholar), 402
Strategy development, modeling for, 308
Strategy-training program, 310, 317
Strategy use problems, 317
Structured English Immersion: A Step-by-Step Guide for K–6 Teachers and Administrators (Haver), 180
Structured practice, as component of direct instruction, 450
Structured problems, 345–349
Student-Achievement Divisions (STAD), 472
Student-directed approach, 466
Student learning, characteristics of, 563f
Students: assessing learning of, 486–488; certified teachers, 6; evaluating learning, 501–506; formulating identity, 31; helping develop sense of industry, 30; measuring learning of, 489–498, 501; not on-task, observing, 563f; sense of industry, 30–31. *See also* Special needs students
Students' strategy, 297–299
"Students Unprepared for Rigors of College" (Schouten), 301–302
Study Finds Special Ed Disparities (Perlstein), 194–195
Study phase, in lesson study, 563f
Study skills, 8
"Stuff for Students," 178
"Styles of Thinking as a Basis of Differentiated Instruction" (Sternberg and Zhang), 141
Substance abuse, 101
Success: in attribution theory, 374–377; equal opportunities for, 473
Successful Inclusive Teaching: Proven Ways to Detect and Correct Special Needs (Choate), 223
Successful intelligence, theory of. *See* Robert Sternberg's triarchic theory of successful intelligence
Suggestions for Teaching: on assessment techniques, 513–516, 513–519; on classroom achievement, 160–162, 171–173; on classroom management, 412–415; on constructivism, 339–343; on cultural differences, 147–148; described, 19; on emotional disturbance, 210–212; on Erikson's theory of psychosocial development, 35–36; on gifted and talented students, 216–217; on information processing, 263–266; on intellectual disability, 200–206; on learning disabilities and ADHD, 206–209; on moral development, 67–68; on motivation, 382–390; on needs and self-perceptions, 396–398; on operant conditions in the classroom, 242–246; on Piaget's theory of cognitive development, 46–48; on problem behavior, 420–424; on problem-solving techniques, 350–354; on social cognitive theory in the classroom, 312–318; standardized tests, 553–555; on student differences, 136–138
Suicide, 101
Summary Street (program), 319
Summative assessment, 486, 487, 487t
Sunbuddy Writer (software tool), 122
Supplemental Education Services, high-stakes testing and, 548–550
Symmetry, needs for, 391

T

Tactics (task strategies), 286, 287
Take a Stand: on ability grouping, 188; on accountability, 550; on assessment for learning, 498; on bilingual education,

177; described, 19–20; on educational accountability, 550; on gender bias, 133; on humanistic approach to teaching, 470; on middle school age-level, 95; on motivation, 395; on positive reinforcement *vs.* punishment, 241; on promoting industry, 31; on self-regulated learners, 299; on students as learners, not just performers, 262; on transfer of learning, 358; on zero tolerance, 433
Talks to Teachers (James), 351
Task analysis, 285, 286, 286f
Task mastery goals, 371
Taxonomies, 117; for affective domain, 443–444; for cognitive domain, 442–443; defined, 442; of objectives, 442–444; organizing ideas in, 49; for psychomotor domain, 444; reason for using, 444. *See also* Bloom's taxonomy
Taxonomy of Educational Objectives: The Classification of Educational Goals–Handbook I: Cognitive Domain (Bloom, Englehart, Furst, Hill, and Krathwohl), 521
Taxonomy of Educational Objectives-Cognitive Domain (Bloom et al.), 314, 444
Teach adaptively, 9
TeachAde, 478
Teacher and Child (Ginott), 76, 419
Teacher-directed instruction, 449
Teacher expectancy effect, 158
Teacher-led instruction, 449
Teachers: as artistic scholar, 15; certified, 6; coursework and competence, 5; educational psychology and, 1, 2; as facilitators, 465; high-stakes testing programs and, 546; learning about educational psychology and, 2; multicultural, 164–175; new classroom roles for, 412; responsibilities under IDEA, 195–198; traditionally trained, 6; use of cooperative learning, 476–477. *See also* Beginning teachers; Teaching
Teachers' expectancies, 158–159
Teachers for a New Era program, 4
Teachers.net, 573
Teachers Network, 573
Teacher's Sourcebook for Cooperative Learning, The (Jacobs, Power, and Wan Inn), 482
Teacher2Teacher, 573
Teacher training, satisfaction with, 9–10
TeacherTube, 477–478
Teach for America program, 6
Teaching: adaptive, 9; as an art, 10–12; behavior and thought processes, 8–9; characteristics of, 563f; as complex enterprise, 3; complexity of learning and, 8–9; control processes of short-term memory and, 259t; decision-making process, 10; effective, 16–17; high-stakes testing programs and, 539, 546; from humanistic orientation, 465–466; joy of being teacher-artist, 13; in lesson study, 563; resources on, 24; role of assessment in, 485–489; as science, 12, 14–15; successful, 12; testing and, 495–496. *See also* Cognitive approach to teaching; Reflective teaching; Social approach to teaching/instruction; Teachers
Teaching English Language Learners Through Technology (Erben, Ban, and Castäneda), 180
Teaching for Thinking Today (Wasserman), 140
Teaching for Wisdom, Intelligence, Creativity, and Success (Sternberg, Jarvin, and Grigorenko), 140

Teaching How to Learn (Kiewra), 325
Teaching in K-12 Schools: A Reflective Action Approach (Eby, Herrell, and Jordan), 23, 575
"Teaching Readers How to Comprehend Text Strategically" (Block and Pressley), 481
Teaching Strategies for Ethnic Studies (Banks), 180
"Teaching Students to Manage Their Own Behavior" (Alberto and Troutman), 248
Teaching Students with Behavior Disorders: Techniques and Activities for Classroom Instruction (Gallagher), 223
Teaching Students with Learning Problems (Mercer and Mercer), 223
Teaching the Way Children Learn (Falk), 467
Teaching without a script (Kay), 13–14
Teachnet.com, 573
TeachSource video cases, 20
Teach What You Know (Trautman), 365
Team competition, 473
Technology: age-levels and, 104–105; applied to Piaget, 54; applied to Vygotsky, 55–56; assistive, 218; behavioral approaches to instruction and, 451; bilingual education and, 177–178; bridging the cultural and SES gap with, 169–170; for classroom assessment, 510–512; cognitive development and, 26, 35, 54–56; exceptional children and, 217–221; gender difference and, 135–136; gifted and talented students and, 220; hearing impairments students and, 218–219; as information-processing tool, 271–276; intelligence and, 121–123; learning disabilities students and, 219–220; learning styles and, 127–128; motivating student with, 398–399; multicultural education and, 169–170; orthopedic impaired students and, 219; reflective teaching and, 570, 573; resources on, 24; role in learning and instruction, 20; for self-regulated learning, 318–322; social approach to teaching and, 477–479; standardized testing and, 550–553; violence and, 435–436; visual impairments students and, 219. *See also* Technology tools
Technology Access Program, 218
Technology-based performance assessment, 511
Technology-enhanced instruction, 231
Technology Integration for Meaningful Classroom Use: A Standards-Based Approach (Cennamo, Ross, and Ertmer), 24
Technology of Teaching, The (Skinner), 247
Technology tools: for arts and music, 273–274; for classroom management, 411–412; for knowledge construction and problem solving, 359363; for reading, 272; resources on, 365; for Science and math, 272–273; for writing, 271–272. *See also* Technology
Telementoring program, 56, 216
Tennessee Formative Assessment Pilot Project, 511
Terminal behavior, 230
Test Driven: High-Stakes Accountability in Elementary Schools (Valli, Croninger, Chambliss, Graeber, and Buese), 558
TestGEAR, 551
Testing, teaching and, 495–496
Test-retest reliability, 525
Test(s): aptitude, 529; constructing useful, 491–492; diagnostic, 528, 555; essay, 491; quality, high-stakes testing and, 548; score, 534, 554; selected response, 490–491; short-answer, 491
TET: Teacher Effectiveness Training (Gordon), 420

The American Psychological Association, 4
The Associated Press, 238
Theoretical learning, 51–52
Theories of Childhood (Mooney), 71
Theories of development: elementary grade age-level and, 84t; high school age-level and, 98t; middle-school age-level and, 89t; preschool and kindergarten age-level and, 75t; primary grade age-level and, 81t
Theories of Developmental Psychology (Miller), 71
"Theories of Self-Regulated Learning and Academic Achievement: An Overview and Analysis" (Zimmerman), 324
Theory, defined, 259
Thinking: alternative-solution, 428; elementary grade age-level and, 88; learning disability and, 207; mental imagery and, 258
Thinking Styles (Sternberg), 140
ThinkQuest, 479
"This Is Harder than We Thought: Using Our Imagination Can Be Pleasant and Produce Great Things; It's Just Not That Easy to Do" (Chung), 268
Thomas B. Fordham Institute, 548
Threats, avoiding, 422
Time, concept of, 46
Time orientation, 149
Time-out, 228, 239–240
Toddlers, sensorimotor stage in, 39
Token economies, 236–237
Tom Sawyer (Twain), 355
"To Teach Good Behavior, Schools Try More Carrots and Fewer Sticks" (Hahn), 431–432
Toward a Psychology of Being (Maslow), 464
Tracking, 184–185, 186
Training, classroom challenges and, 5
Transfer of learning: defined, 354; high-road transfer, 357–358; low-road transfer, 357, 358; near and far transfer, 356–357; negative transfer, 355; positive transfer, 355; resources on, 365; specific and general transfer, 355–356; theory of identical elements, 355; zero transfer, 355. *See also* Learning
Transfer of Learning from a Modern Multidisciplinary Perspective (Mestre), 365
Transformative approach, in multicultural education program, 163
Transition programs, 174
Traumatic brain injury, 195, 196t
Triadic reciprocal causation (triadic model), 279, 280–281, 281f
Triad Middle School, 96
Triarchic Theory of Successful Intelligence. *See* Robert Sternberg's Triarchic Theory of Successful Intelligence
Troops to Teachers program, 6
True-false questions, 550
Trust *vs.* mistrust (birth to one year), 29
T scores, 532, 532f
Tutorial program, 232t
Tutoring, 166–167
Tutors, gifted and talented students as, 217
TWA strategy, 311
Twelve to eighteen years, identity *vs.* role confusion in, 29
Twice exceptional, 214
Two-factor theory of intelligence, 113
2009 Class of National Board Certified teachers Advances Nation's School Reform Movement (National Board for Professional Teaching Standards), 571–572
Two to three years, autonomy *vs.* shame and doubt in, 29
Two-way bilingual programs. *See* Two-way bilingual (TWB) education

Two-way bilingual (TWB) education, 175–176
Two-way immersion. *See* Two-way bilingual (TWB) education
Type I punishment, 227
Type II punishment, 228

U

UCAP. *See* Urban Collaborative Accelerated Program (UCAP)
UDL. *See* Universal design for learning (UDL)
Undermining effect, 369
Understanding Youth: Adolescent Development for Educators (Nakkula and Toshalis), 109
Unified Discipline program, 432
United States: baby-sitting responsibilities in, 46; changing face of, 146–147; number of immigrants, by decade, 144t
Universal design for learning (UDL), 217–218
Universal ethical principle orientation, 59
Unscripted Learning: Using Improv Activities Across the K-8 Curriculum (Lobman and Lundquist), 23
Unsystematic observation, limitations of, 6–7
Urban Collaborative Accelerated Program (UCAP), 440
U.S. Department of Education, 189, 192, 199, 202, 538, 545, 548

V

Validity, 526
Values: in evaluation, 143; moral, 66–67; of science, 6–7
Variable interval (VI) schedule, 231
Variable ratio (VR) schedule, 231
Verbal communication, 149
Verbal persuasion, 283, 283f
Verbal reasoning problems, 352
Vermont Department of Education, 536
Vicarious experience, 283, 284
Vicarious reinforcement, 303, 370–371
Video Cases: on aligning instruction with federal legislation, 539; on assessment in elementary grades, 527; on assessment in the middle grades, 504; on bilingual education, 176; on blogs, 479; on classroom management, 240, 425; on computer-based simulation, 233; on constructivism, 338, 347; on cooperative learning, 476; on cooperative learning in elementary grades, 255; on definition of literacy, 21; on differentiated instruction, 216; on effective teaching, 16; on elementary classroom management, 409; on elementary school language, 329; on gender equity in the classroom, 135; on grouping strategies, 188; on IDEA, 193; on influence of peer groups, 92; on information processing, 257; on Integrating Internet research, 399; on integrating Internet research in social studies, 151; on integrating technology, 56, 233; on metacognition, 297; on motivation 417, 437, 379; on multicultural lesson for elementary students, 165; on multiple intelligences, 119; on No Child Left Behind Act, 539; on peer groups influence, 92; on performance assessment, 289, 497; on portfolio assessment, 483, 494; on reflective teaching, 562, 569; on secondary school management, 411; on social and emotional development in adolescents, 103; on social cognitive theory, 305–306; on teacher accountability, 535; on using information-processing

strategies, 261; on Vygotsky's zone of proximal development, 53
Violence: analyzing reasons for, 427–428; reducing, 429–430, 432–535; resources on, 438; safety in schools and, 425–426; technology and, 435–436
Virtual environments, 274–275
Virtual learning, 54
Virtual schools, 436
VI schedule. *See* Variable interval (VI) schedule
Visual argument hypothesis theory, 265–266
Visual Assistive Technology Center, 219
Visual forms, for problem solving, 350–351
Visual imagery encoding, 258–259
Visual impairments: blindness and, 195; special education services and, 196t; technology for students with, 219
Visual-spatial ability, 128
Visual Tools for Transforming Information Into Knowledge (Hyerle), 325
Vocational Rehabilitation Act of 1973, 198
Voice: level of, 132; loss of, 133
Voice animation, 12
VR schedule. *See* Variable ratio (VR) schedule
Vygotsky and Education: Instructional Implications and Applications of Sociohistorical Psychology (Moll), 71
Vygotsky's Educational Theory in Cultural Context (Kozulin, Gindis, Ageyev, and Miller): 71
Vygotsky's Sociohistorical Psychology and Its Contemporary Application (Ratner and Vygotsky), 71
Vygotsky's theory of cognitive development: culture and cognitive development, 49–50; instruction and cognitive development, 50–53; on metacognitive knowledge, 267; psychological tools, 49–50; resources on, 71; social interaction and cognitive development, 50; technology applied to, 55–56; theory of cognitive development, 48–49, 71

W

Walden Two (Skinner), 247
Warm demanders, 415
Washington Post, 134, 194
WBI. *See* Web-based instruction (WBI)
Web 2.0, 105, 127, 272, 477, 478
Web-based Inquiry Science Environment (WISE) Project, 272–273, 463
Web-based instruction (WBI), 321
Weblogs, 272
WEB Project, 479
Web Quest Page of San Diego State University, 220
Website(s): Alaska Native Knowledge Network, 169; American Printing House for the Blind, 219; APA on learner-centered psychological principles, 2; APA's Board of Educational Affairs, 2; Apple Computer, 219; on bilingual education, 178; Center for Applied Linguistics, 180; Center for Educational Technology (CET), 481–482; Center for Educational Technology's Geometric Supposer program, 481–482; Center for Multicultural Education, 180; Character Education Partnership, 71; Classroom 2.0, 272; on classroom management, 438; for Code of Fair Testing Practices, 558; computer-based instructional technology, 463; Computer-supported intentional learning environments (CSILE), 463; Corporation for National and Community Service, 173; on digital storytelling classroom project, 105; 4Directions Project, 169, 479; of discovery and exploratory environments,

461–462; Educational Software Directory, 207; Educational Testing Service, 22; Education Program for Gifted Youth, 220; Education World, 272; 4teachers, 512; Global Online Adventure Learning, 106; GLOBE program, 463, 511; Information on Self-Efficacy: A Community of Scholars, 402; Institute of Education Sciences, 4; International Society for Augmentative and Alternative Communication, 219; International Society for Technology in Education, 20; International Telementor Program, 56; Jean Piaget Society database, 71; Kidlink Project/organization, 105, 272; LearnCentral, 479; MiddleWeb, 108; on motivation to learn math, 402; of the multicultural Pavilion, 180; National Association for Multicultural Education, 180; National Board Certification for Educational leaders/principals, 572–573; National Board for Professional Teaching Standards, 3; National Campaign to Prevent Teen and Unplanned Pregnancy, 99; National Center for Fair and Open Testing, 558; National Center for Health Statistics, 273; National Federation of the Blind, 219; National Forum to Accelerate Middle-Grades Reform, 108; National Geographic, 461; National Geophysical Data Center, 273; National Oceanic and Atmospheric Administration, 273; National Research Center on the Gifted and Talented, 223; NCLB at department of education, 536; of the organization Rubrician, 521; on performance assessment, 492; performance-based assessment, 521; Podcasts from students in New Zealand school, 105; Praxis II Educational testing Service, 22; Quest Atlantis, 274, 362, 365; Quest Page of San Diego State University, 220; of Resolving Conflict Creatively Program, 435; on self-efficacy, 402; Smarthinking, 551; on speech and language impairments computer programs, 219; on student motivation, 402; TeachAde, 478; *Teacher Tap*, 365; TeacherTube, 477–478; Technology Access Program, 218; telementoring programs, 216; TestGear, 551; ThinkQuest, 106, 479; Urban Collaborative Accelerated Program, 440; Visual Assistive Technology Center, 219; Web-based Inquiry Science Environment (WISE) Project, 272–273, 463; WEB Project, 479; Web Quest page of San Diego State University, 220; on Web 2.0 technologies in education, 272; We the Teachers, 478; What Works Clearinghouse, 4
Wechsler Adult Intelligence Scale-III, 1
Wechsler Intelligence Scale for Children-IV, 113, 120
Well-structured assignments, 305–306
Well-structured problems, 343–344, 346
Well-written reading material, 378
We the Teachers, 478
What Works Clearinghouse, 4
When School Reform Goes Wrong (Noddings), 558
Where in the World Is Carmen Sandiego? (The Learning Company), 248
White (Non Hispanics): achievement expectations for, 159; direct instruction and, 451; disciplinary action and, 159; drop-out of, 153; emotional disorders and, 101; motivation, beliefs, attitudes and, 156; percentage of school-age children and, 147f, self-esteem and, 156; suicidal attempts and, 101; support for academic achievement, 155

Whole-class instruction, 94, 186, 317
WICS model (wisdom, intelligence, creativity, and success), 120
Wisconsin Educational Media Association, 499
Wisdom of Practice: Essays on Teaching, Learning, and Learning to Teach, The (Shulman), 575
WISE Project. *See* Web-based Inquiry Science Environment (WISE) Project
Within-class ability grouping, 185, 186

Withitness, 406
Word identification, 204
Words, recall of, 256f
Writing: gifted and talented students and, 217; technology tools for, 271–272
Writing Instructional Objectives for Teaching and Assessment (Gronlund), 481
Writing skills, improving, 308
Written problems, 346
Written tests, 489, 490, 491

WYTIWYG (what you test is what you get), 547

Y

YALSA. *See* Adult Library Services Association (YALSA); Young Adult Library Services Association (YALSA)
You Have to Go to School . . . You're the Teacher! (Rosenblum-Lowden and Kimmel), 438

Young Adult Library Services Association (YALSA), 272

Z

Zero transfer, 355
Zone of proximal development (ZPD), 485; instruction and, 52–53, 56; scaffolded instruction and, 457–458
ZPD. *See* Zone of proximal development (ZPD)
Z score, 532, 532f

Correlation Chart for INTASC Principles and Standards

INTASC: The following chart compares the content of *Psychology Applied to Teaching* with the ten principles and related standards published by the Interstate New Teacher Assessment and Support Consortium (INTASC). See Chapter 1 of the text for a discussion of INTASC. For the most up-to-date INTASC Standards and a more detailed version of this chart, please visit this text's Education CourseMate website at **CengageBrain.com.**

INTASC Principles and Standards	Psychology Applied to Teaching
1. Subject Matter Expertise The teacher understands the central concepts, tools of inquiry, and structures of the discipline(s) he or she teaches and can create learning experiences that make these aspects of subject matter meaningful for students.	Chapter 1: The Nature and Values of Science, pp. 6–10 Chapter 8: Meaningfulness, pp. 256–259; How Information Is Organized in Long-Term Memory, pp. 260–261; Suggestions for Teaching 4 and 5, p. 265 Chapter 10: Constructivism Today, pp.329–333
2. Learning and Development The teacher understands how children learn and develop and can provide learning opportunities that support their intellectual, social, and personal development.	Chapter 2, entire chapter, pp. 25–71 Chapter 3, entire chapter, pp. 72–109 Chapter 7, entire chapter, pp. 224–248 Chapter 8, entire chapter, pp. 249–277 Chapter 9, entire chapter, pp. 278–325 Chapter 10, entire chapter, pp. 326–365 Chapter 13, entire chapter, pp. 439–482
3. Diverse Learners The teacher understands how students differ in their approaches to learning and creates instructional opportunities that are adapted to diverse learners.	Chapter 4, entire chapter, pp. 110–141 Chapter 5, entire chapter, pp. 142–180 Chapter 6, entire chapter, pp. 181–223
4. Instructional Strategies The teacher understands and uses a variety of instructional strategies to encourage students' development of critical thinking, problem solving, and performance skills.	Chapter 7, entire chapter, pp. 224–248 Chapter 8, entire chapter, pp. 249–277 Chapter 9, entire chapter, pp. 278–325 Chapter 10, entire chapter, pp. 326–365 Chapter 13, entire chapter, pp. 439–482
5. Motivation and Classroom Management The teacher uses an understanding of individual and group motivation and behavior to create a learning environment that encourages positive social interaction, active engagement in learning, and self-motivation.	Chapter 11, entire chapter, pp. 366–402 Chapter 12, entire chapter, pp. 403–438 Chapter 13, entire chapter, pp. 439–482